# Development and Causality

Gerald Young

# Development and Causality

## Neo-Piagetian Perspectives

Springer

Gerald Young
Glendon College
York University
2275 Bayview Avenue
Toronto, Ontario
Canada M4N 3M6
gyoung@glendon.youku.ca

ISBN 978-1-4419-9421-9 e-ISBN 978-1-4419-9422-6
DOI 10.1007/978-1-4419-9422-6
Springer New York Dordrecht Heidelberg London

Library of Congress Control Number: 2011923228



Printed on acid-free paper

Springer is part of Springer Science+Business Media (www.springer.com)

# Foreword

## Introduction

The reader will find that this book has been written at multiple levels and for multiple audiences. It is based on the work of Piaget and Neo-Piagetians, but also it covers other major models in development. It has elements that make it attractive as a teaching text, but it is especially research-focused. It has clinical applications. It presents many new ideas and models consistent with the past literature, which is reviewed extensively. Students, researchers, and practitioners should find it useful.

The models presented in the present work build on models that I introduced in prior publications (e.g., Young, 1990a, 1990b, 1997). My first publication on Piaget dates to 1977. In my other branch of research, on the topic of psychological injury and law, I have applied Piagetian and developmental concepts to the stages in the development of chronic pain (e.g., Young, 2008). At the same time, that area of research has given me a broader perspective on causality (e.g., Young, 2010) that I have applied to the current work in terms of development.

## Teaching

The present work is a teaching text as well as a research one. At the teaching level, it introduces the student to basic concepts and theories in child and lifespan development. These theories are powerful ones that hold prominent positions in many areas of psychology, and often are highlighted in introductory psychology texts. The student will learn about Piaget, Freud, Erikson, Vygotsky, Bandura, Bowlby, Maslow, and Darwin, as well as the great theories that they spawned (e.g., structural cognitive, psychodynamic, psychosocial, sociocultural, social learning, attachment, self-actualization, ethology). Also, the student will be informed of contemporary work that is rapidly transforming the field, such as information processing, ecological theory, the biopsychosocial model, epigenetics, nonlinear dynamical systems theory, evolutionary psychology, and multilevel selection theory. At the same time, the student will learn about some of the historical antecedents to these theories, especially the work of James and Baldwin.

At times in the book, I give basic tutorials so that the foundational models on which the present work is based, as well as its chain of logic, are more evident. In addition, I provide some focused literature reviews on fascinating areas of research, such as emotional development, theory of mind/social cognition, self-regulation, developmental neuroscience, storytelling or narrative development, and manual and hemispheric specialization.

By learning this backdrop of basic theories in the field of psychology, in general, and development, in particular, the student will be equipped to follow better the critical thinking process that has led to the synthetic model presented in the book. The model stems from a question I posed to myself as an undergraduate when I first learned of stage theories. I had wondered how Freud could have proposed a five-step model at the affective level and Piaget could have proposed a four-step model at the cognitive level, and why the two domains of study were often considered distinct. This led to my quest to create a superordinate model that integrates contemporary Piagetian and Freudian (or Eriksonian) models. In other words, the question that I had asked myself as an undergraduate lives in and animates the answer to it that I provide in the present book. The student entering the university years has the power to enter new levels of critical thought and have them keep growing throughout the adult years. My lifelong intellectual (and affective) quest in critical thinking on the present topic illustrates the meta-trajectory that students could experience.

## Research

In terms of the research level of the present work, it is especially theoretical. I review the basic theoretical models in the field, and especially concentrate on Piaget and the Neo-Piagetians. The book critically compares the work of Fischer and Case, and builds a model that integrates them and other Neo-Piagetians. I do not describe empirical studies undertaken personally in support of the model. Rather, I review in depth multiple models and analyze in depth some main areas of research related to them. Through this procedure, I created a superordinate model that is carefully crafted to include the prior models and the outcome of their critical comparison that I had undertaken. As well, the superordinate model integrates the reviews of contemporary research that I had undertaken, including ones not typically undertaken by proponents of the others.

It is important to note that I illustrate how the superordinate model that I have developed can inform the prior theoretical and empirical work, offering new avenues in their conceptualization and empirical study. In this regard, I maintain that the present work constitutes a sophisticated scholarly effort to integrate multiple areas of theoretical modeling and empirical work. Therefore, it could contribute in a widespread fashion to the growth and application of the field of child development, in particular, and other areas of psychology and beyond, in general, such as education and mental health therapy.

The book is a massive one, and in the first chapter, I offer summary tables of its major contributions. On the one hand, this risks confusing the reader, because complex ideas are presented right away. On the other hand, I have adopted this course in order to provide a concise, visual framework of the material to which the reader can refer at any point in reading the book. Moreover, for similar reasons, the book includes much tabular and graphic material to help the reader, and often I provide rich tabular notes and figure captions to explain them. In the end, the book is about describing the "what" of development over the lifespan, and also "how" it happens, or the "why" of development. It might seem disparate in models broached, research described, and topics examined, but it coalescences around one model aimed at understanding the contents and causation of development. For purposes of using a concise way of referring to the present model and other similar ones in the index, please check "cognitive affective models" (e.g., cognitive affective models – Young).

## Practice

Practitioners might find the book important because it gives a better basis for understanding development. Aside from helping practitioners by describing lifespan normative development through the stages and substages described, and how the proposed model can accommodate individual differences in development, the present work describes the concept of the cognitive (mis)perception of the other, which could help understand the cognitive-affective filters that patients could use in governing their behavior. Moreover, I have extended the model to applied areas, such as progressive changes in therapy and regressive ones in chronic pain. As well, I refer to transition therapy because of the lifespan component of the model and to activation–inhibition coordination in therapy.

## References

Young, G. (1990a). Early neuropsychological development: Lateralization of functions – hemispheric specialization. In C. A. Hauert (Ed.), *Developmental psychology: Cognitive, perceptuomotor and neuropsychological perspectives* (pp. 113–181). Amsterdam: North Holland.

Young, G. (1990b). The development of hemispheric and manual specialization. In G. E. Hammond (Ed.), *Cerebral control of speech and limb movements* (pp. 79–139). Amsterdam: North Holland.

Young, G. (1997). *Adult development, therapy, and culture: A postmodern synthesis*. New York: Plenum.

Young, G. (2008). Psychological injury: Systems, change processes, development. *Psychological Injury and Law, 1*, 243–254.

Young, G. (2010). Causes in the construction of causal law: A psycho-ecological model. *International Journal of Law and Psychiatry, 33*, 73–83.

# Preface

## Introduction

In the preface, I present the goals of the book, its parts and sections, and the distinction between product and process, in development (the "what" and the "why"). The reader will find that I present a synthetic model that integrates both product and process in a unified conception from a relational metaframe.

## Goal

The present work bears the title of *Development and Causality: Neo-Piagetian Perspectives*, but in many ways it deals with child development, in general. Piaget is one of the major theoreticians in the field, and his models and empirical methods are continually evolving through the work of contemporary Piagetians and Neo-Piagetians. The former scholars adhere to his basic model, for example, by keeping the classic four-stage sequence that he described from infancy to adolescence, and by emphasizing his concepts on transition processes, such as equilibration and adaptation. The latter scholars modify his model, for example, by altering the stage sequence that he had proposed and by suggesting more differentiated approaches to understanding the process underlying stage transitions. In this work, I review: the classic approach of Piaget, how Piagetians are changing it, and how Neo-Piagetians are suggesting major modifications.

A major goal of the present work is to compare recent Neo-Piagetian models in terms of their cognitive and affective components and correspondences and, in this regard, I examine closely the models of Case and Fischer, as well as my own (Young, 1997). In the present work, I emphasize the value and validity of the present model of stages and substages in development. It consists of five stages having five cyclically recurring substages, a developmental lifespan pattern that yields a 25-step developmental sequence stretching from the prenatal period right to the last phases of life. It proposes parallel socioaffective acquisitions according to a Neo-Eriksonian model, in particular. There are other socioaffective parallels proposed, as well.

## Relational Metaframe

**Table P.1** Relational metatheory and associated frames

| Relational metaframe | Definition |
|---|---|
| A relational metatheory | Predicated on a postmodern philosophical perspective that transcends Cartesian dualism, developmental systems theories are framed by a relational metatheory for human development. There is, then, a rejection of all splits between components of the ecology of human development (e.g., between nature-and nurture-based variables), and between continuity and discontinuity and between stability and instability, systemic syntheses or integrations replace dichotomizations, or other reductionist partitions of the developmental system |
| The integration of levels of organization | Relational thinking and the rejection of Cartesian splits is associated with the idea that all levels of organization within the ecology of human development are integrated, or fused. These levels range from the biological and physiological through the cultural and historical |
| Developmental regulation across ontogeny involves mutually influential individual ←→ context relations | As a consequence of the integration of levels, the regulation of development occurs through mutually influential connections among all levels of the developmental system, ranging from genes and cell physiology through individual mental and behavioral functioning to society, culture, and the designed and natural ecology and, ultimately, history. These mutually influential relations may be represented generically as Level 1 ←→ Level 2 (e.g., family ←→ context) – they constitute the fundamental unit of analysis in the study of the basic process of human development |
| Integrated actions, individual ←→ context relations, are the basic unit of analysis within human development | The character of developmental regulation means that the integration of actions – of the individual on the context and of the multiple levels of the context on the individual (individual ←→ context) – constitute the fundamental unit of analysis in the study of the basic process of human development |
| Temporality and plasticity in human development | As a consequence of fusion of the historical level of analysis – and therefore temporality – in the levels of organization comprising the ecology of human development, the developmental system is characterized by the potential for systematic change, by plasticity. Observed trajectories of intraindividual change may vary across time and place as a consequence of such plasticity |
| Relative plasticity | Developmental regulation may both facilitate and constrain opportunities for change. Thus, change in individual ←→ context relations is not limitless, and the magnitude of plasticity (the probability of change in a developmental trajectory occurring in relation to variation in contextual conditions) may vary across the life span and history. Nevertheless, the potential for plasticity at both individual and contextual levels constitutes a fundamental strength of all human development |

(continued)

**Table P.1** (continued)

| Relational metaframe | Definition |
|---|---|
| Intraindividual change, interindividual differences in intraindividual change, and the fundamental substantive significance of diversity | The combinations of variables across the integrated levels of organization within the developmental system that provide the basis of the developmental process will vary at least in part across individuals and groups. This diversity is systematic and lawfully produced by idiographic, group differential, and generic (nomothetic) phenomena. The range of interindividual differences in intraindividual change observed at any point in time is evidence of the plasticity of the developmental system, and makes the study of diversity of fundamental substantive significance for the description, explanation, and optimization of human development |
| Optimism, the application of developmental science, and the promotion of positive human development | The potential for and instantiations of plasticity legitimate an optimistic and proactive search for characteristics of individuals and of their ecologies that, together, can be arrayed to promote positive human development across life. Through the application of developmental science in planned attempts (interventions) to enhance (e.g., through social policies or community-based programs) the characters of humans' developmental trajectories, the promotion of positive human development many be achieved by aligning the strengths (operationalized as the potentials for positive change) of individuals and contexts |
| Multidisciplinary and the need for change-sensitive methodologies | The integrated levels of organization comprising the developmental system require collaborative analyses by scholars from multiple disciplines. Multidisciplinary knowledge is sought. The temporal embeddedness and resulting plasticity of the developmental system requires that research designs, methods of observation and measurement, and procedures for data analysis be change-sensitive and able to integrate trajectories of change at multiple levels of analysis |



The reader should keep in mind that science functions from dominant paradigms and metatheories, and the present work is firmly ensconced in the relational metatheory metaframe, and adopts a systems perspective (see Table P.1, Lerner, 2006; Overton, 2006). Piaget is associated with his stage model of development, but covered these aspects in his work. Previously, I had labeled the present model as postmodern (in Young, 1997), given its initial Vygotskian emphasis. Although the present book fits in that perspective, I take a larger metaview this time. A relational metaframe views antimonies as coordinates not to be split, and reality as neither out there or internal to the sensori-perceptual-cognitive apparatus of the organism, but as constituted in the interactive, superordinate, grounded, participatory relations of the individual in context, especially the social one. All related divisions, such as mind-body, nature-nurture, continuity–discontinuity, and stability–instability, are artificially imposed heuristics with limited advantages and limiting disadvantages. (If I do lapse at times into dualistic language, it is more due to inadvertence than insistence).

## Summary of Major Developmental Models

**Table P.2** Determinant factors in first-generation developmental approaches

| | Factor | | |
|---|---|---|---|
| Approach | Environmental | Biological | Personal |
| Freud | Superego (parental strictures) | Id (libidinal investment; stages) | Ego (self component) |
| Behaviorism | Conditioning | | |
| Ethology | | Imprinting | |
| Piaget | | | Construction |

Freud elaborated a developmental model that includes environmental (e.g., superego), biological (e.g., id), and personal (e.g., ego) factors. For Freud, the person is considered a passive recipient of developmental influences, despite the inclusion of the concept of the ego in the model. Models that developed in the first wave after his psychodynamic model articulated better theoretical understanding of each of the three influences that he conceived as important in development (environment – behaviorism; biology – ethology; personal – Piaget)

**Table P.3** Determinant change in first-generation developmental approaches

| Approach | Elicitor(s) → | Determinant factor(s) → | Developmental outcome |
|---|---|---|---|
| Psycho-dynamism | Invested objects | Personality structure (unconscious, id, ego, etc.) | Psychosexual stage |
| Behaviorism | Stimuli | External reinforcement | Behavioral response |
| Ethology | Releaser (sign) stimuli | Innate releasing mechanism | Fixed action pattern |
| Piaget | Unassimilable object | Equilibration | Schematic accommodation |

One way of describing the developmental models is in terms of their understanding of elicitors of behavior, mediating factors, and outcome responses. In this table, I show how the first wave of developmental theorists align in this way

**Table P.4** Determinant change in second-generation developmental approaches

| Approach | Elicitor(s) → | Determinant factor(s) → | Developmental outcome |
|---|---|---|---|
| Erikson | Invested objects | Personality structure is more social, ego-related, lifespan | Psychosexual stage |
| Social learning | Stimulus | Cognitive mediators (beliefs, expectations, sense of self-efficacy, observational imitation) | Behavioral response |
| Attachment | Caregiver sensitivity | Internal working model (secure, insecure related) | Attachment quality |
| Neo-Piagetian | Domain problems | Regulatory mechanisms, transformations, etc. | Skills, central conceptual structures, etc. |

After the first wave of developmental models, the four that were involved differentiated (e.g., Freud → Erikson). The concept of elicitor-mediator-outcome relations was altered in these revised versions of the models

**Table P.5** Determinant change in some recent developmental approaches

| Approach | Elicitor(s) → | Determinant factor(s) → | Developmental outcome |
|---|---|---|---|
| Information processing | Input | Information processing mechanisms (e.g., storage, working memory, programs, rules) | Output |
| Systems theory | Information, initial conditions | Homeostasis, self-organization, feedback, controlling parameters, etc. | State, pattern, attractor, chaos, complexity, etc. |
| Vygotsky | Sociocultural material | Internalization, guidance in the zone of proximal development | Higher mental function |
| Ecological model | Social | Layer of environment (concentrically organized influences) | Relational |

In a second wave of developmental models, new ones distinct from the original series evolved, or came to the fore. They considered elicitor-outcome connections in different ways compared to prior models, and had different determinant factors.

Tables P.2–P.5 provide a concise summary of the major theories in developmental psychology, while illustrating their historical origins. The initial encompassing theory is the Freudian one, and this perspective led to the development of three other models aimed at better explaining its primary components (behaviorism, ethology, Piaget's). These four basic models led to more advanced models. Erikson, social learning theory, attachment theory, and Neo-Piagetians, respectively, developed more refined theories. Other important models that emerged included the Vygotskian, ecological, information processing, and systems views. In the tables, the models are compared in terms of how they elicitors to developmental outcomes by way of determinants. Overall, I show how the different models differ in terms of their approach to the biological, social, and personal factors that influence development.

Throughout the book, as needed, I refer to and elaborate these various models highlighted in the tables. However, the book serves to show how each of them has contributed to our understanding of development and the factors that they might emphasize as more important in development interact in a multifactorial way.

## Summary of Prior Work in Young (1997)

The present work is based on the previously presented 25-step model (5 stages × 5 substages) of cognitive-affective correspondences in development (Young, 1997). In that work, I had summarized the scope of the book in three tables, which listed its contributions in terms of structure, transition, processes, and other areas (see Tables P.6–P.8). By including these tables of the prior book in the present one, they help set the stage for presentation of summary tables of the key contributions being made in the present work. The prior book had focused on Vygotskian theory, although it took a multitheoretical approach. The present work concentrates especially on the Neo-Piagetian enterprise, which had been only introduced in the prior book.

**Table P.6** Summary of key contributions of Young (1997): structure

| Area | Contribution |
|---|---|
| Levels | 5 stages (reflexive, sensorimotor, perioperational, abstract, collective intelligence) × 5 substages (coordination, hierarchization, systematization, multiplication, integration; and perhaps × 5 steps) = 25 substages and up to 125 steps in development |
| Applied to | In particular, the stages describe developmental progressions in cognition and language (e.g., storytelling), on the one hand, and socioemotions, on the other hand. The socioemotional parallel refers to the 25 socioemotional systems structured around three dimensions of appraisal related to goal compatibility (positive, negative), activity-reactivity, and context (figure-ground) (author note: last application promised for inclusion in and delivered in present work). But the parallels range across diverse domains, e.g., self, family, parenting strategies, couples, personality, the unconscious, institutions, censorship. For example, 5 stages in the evolution of adult relationships are seen to develop as reflections of the five general developmental stages; they are attraction, attachment, commitment, growth, and mutuality |
| Stage | The fifth stage of collective intelligence is defined as involving a cognitive-emotional symbiotic fusion, where the individual contributes to and takes from communal interaction, e.g., in brainstorming, especially in terms of forming superordinate, metasystemic principles. It is seen as a postmodern intelligence |
| Underpinnings | Each substage has neurological and phylogenetic bases. Moreover, each stage is shown to have evolved through a particular evolutionary pressure. These pressures also were seen to be associated with specific parenting styles; Reflexive stage = style of physical parenting, early reptilian in origin, due to natural selection; Sensorimotor stage = attachment – promotion parenting, early mammalian, due to evolutionary pressure of kin selection; Perioperational stage = educational parenting, early ape, group for individual level of pressure; Abstract stage = parenting to promote immediate community linkage, *Homo sapiens*, due to reciprocal altruism; Collective intelligence stage = parenting to promote wider community linkage, contemporary humans, due to group selection |
| Individual differences | The model of development permits individual differences on the universal scaffold provided by the 25 steps in the model |
| Scale | Two scales derived from the 25-step model of development created for discourse contexts. One examines the degree of cognitive complexity of texts, whereas the other looks at the degree of social support that is offered by others in producing texts (e.g., mothers of children) (two studies are described which support the empirical value of the scales and the validity of the theory) |

**Table P.7** Summary of key contributions Young (1997): transition processes

| Area | Contribution |
|---|---|
| Neo-Piagetian | *Cognitive control units*: mechanisms such as schemata, schemes, operations. One per substage=25 in all |
| Neo-Eriksonian | *Psychosocial affectivity*: Erikson's 8 stages are embedded in the 25-step sequence of socioemotional system that develops in parallel with the cognitive substages. All the 25 systems are marked by Eriksonian crises-challenges that influence cognitive development |
| Neo-Bowlbian | *Social self-working schemata*: internal working models, with social embeddedness emphasized. Also, 25 levels of them. They carry attachment experiences into the developing individual's cognition (author note: this concept was promised for and is in present work) |
| Neo-Banduran | *Self-efficacy in levels*: a sense of self-competence also develops in concert with the 25 steps, and influences cognitive development |
| Neo-systemic | *Fractalization*: the five cyclic substages show a parallel with the five stages in which they recur. This self-similarity across different levels might mark development and psychology, in general |
| | *Complexity*: transitions across substages and levels may be frequent (up to 125), because they function as self-organizing attractors that reach controlling parameter thresholds, e.g., at the "edge of chaos," or system balance of disorder and order |
| Neo-Vygotskian | *Coappropriation*: in a process that includes sociocultural buffers in a potentially negative or hostile world, the developing individual internalizes sociocultural material through the equilibration of mutually derived coschemes |
| Activation–inhibition coordination | Underlying both of the structure and transition mechanisms in development might be a metric where activation and inhibition processes coordinate in dynamic interplay |



**Table P.8** Summary of key contributions of Young (1997): other areas

| Area | Contribution |
|---|---|
| Cognitive (mis) perception of the other | Each child is perceived as being capable of developing at best to one or the other of the 25 substages in development, depending on the affective lens that parents use to filter the world, which usually is based on their own parenting experiences, in a process of intergenerational transmission. Each level of (mis)perception elicits a particular reaction in the child (e.g., being raised with a misperception of being capable of functioning at the perioperational stage at best, and so open to manipulation, can lead to resistance). Adults might be perceived by their partners or their cultures in the same way (e.g., reflexive at best in a despotic regime) and manifest reactions similar to that of the child (e.g., revolt in this case) |
| Therapy | A type of activation–inhibition coordination therapy that I use is outlined in terms of internalization of agency and externalization of the problem (after Michael White). The therapy is narrative, coconstructive, and postmodern. It is labeled *transition therapy* because of its integration of present developmental model and its emphasis on the continual change function in human growth. Graphic representations are employed. The 25 dangers – crises – challenges in the 25 steps in development can be used in this therapy, when needed. Thus, for example, externalizations in therapy are presented in terms of story themes reflective of the particular 25 developmental levels of the present model. The five-stage model of couple development that I have developed is used in marital counseling |

(continued)

**Table P.8** (continued)

| Area | Contribution |
|---|---|
| Attachment | A model of different qualities of care giving and consequent attachment types is presented. Links to the substages in development are discussed. (author note: this concept was promised for and is in present work) |
| Emotions | A model of emotional development is included among the 25 socioemotional systems. It argues that there are at least 48 basic emotional families organized along four dimensions, including one involving the six cognitive substages in the first 2 years of life (author note: this concept was promised for and is in present work) |
| Epistemology | A synthetic model of six different constructivist, postmodern schools is presented |
| Universe | The adult mind develops into a collective symbiotic thought process. Postmodernism leads to a sensitive empathy for the others. It is grounded in relational mutuality, as is the Vygotskian approach. Lévinas speaks of a responsibility for all others. Systems theory implies the presence of a supersystem of the individual in the cosmos. Fractals transmit patterns from one laminar structure of substance organization to the next. Quantum theory speaks of correlated states even when particles move at the speed of light in opposite directions. Gaia refers to a self-correcting planet Earth that ensures life. I describe supraindividual Relational Meaning Worlds with constituent co-memes (e.g., on cultural identity, the IWEMEUS) that vibrate with living attributes and mediate human development as much as we mediate their development. The human task of becoming being in the world is world work and world love. Development is transformation toward facilitating universal developing transformation |
| Overall | A comprehensive, multidomain integration based upon a 25-stage theory of human development is described. It is a rigorous, empirically grounded theory based on the theory and work of other researchers. It has been tested in some studies, and leads to testable, falsifiable predictions in areas where I have yet to study it |

Reprinted with the permission of Springer Science+Business Media: Young, G. (1997). [Table 1.3, Page. 30]

## Outline of the Book

The first part of the book deals with the cognitive portion of the present Neo-Piagetian model and other related models by Neo-Piagetians, as well as the affective correspondences from stage to stage described in them. It begins with an overview of the book, and then examines a variation of the biopsychosocial model that I call the bio-personal-social model. In the third chapter, I present the foundational model of Piaget. Next, I describe in depth the present Neo-Piagetian model of 25 steps in cognitive development and their socioaffective correspondences. I end the subsection with a comparative presentation of the models of Fischer, Case, and myself in terms of stages, substages, and cognitive/socioaffective correspondences. This analysis establishes the validity of the present model.

The next portion of the book extends the present model. First, I review and extend work from Young (1997) on the development of the self and the role of the cognitive (mis)perception of the other in development. Next, I examine the topics of theory of mind and self-regulation. Both areas are in flux, and even these terms are not established (e.g., social cognition is also used for the former, emotion regulation is also used for the latter). Then, I focus on cognitive extensions of the present work which are: (a) based on the concepts of hypercognition and multiple intelligences, and (b) by extending Commons' and colleagues work on postformal intelligence.

Next, the book examines the development of personality, emotions, and attachment. For each topic, I show how the present cognitive model can be applied to develop further cognitive-affective correspondences. For example, I review the present Neo-Eriksonian model (Young, 1997), and extend the model by refining Maslow's classic model in its light. Next, I present a model for the development of basic emotions in the first 2 years of life consistent with Piagetian theory. Also, I present a model of internal working representations in attachment theory that consists of 25 steps derived from the 25 steps of the present model. By presenting these extensions, the value of the present model becomes better established.

The third part of the book looks farther afield. The book shifts focus, dealing with factors involved in transition mechanisms, specifically, and causality, generally. I present my work on hemispheric and manual specialization, relating it to the developmental steps in the present model. I emphasize a model on activation–inhibition coordination. The book examines nonlinear dynamical systems theory, and I develop a model of transition processes based on steps involving attractors and complex adaptive systems. Next, I examine evolutionary mechanisms and epigenesis, in particular. I emphasize that there are multifactorial and interactive factors involved in development.

To conclude the book, I speculate on evolutionary forces underlying the stages of the present model. For example, I engage in speculation about the proposed five-step stage model being representative of, or an exemplar of, generic change processes in living and nonliving systems. Also there might be a different evolutionary pressure associated with each of the stages, including ones related to group processes. The subsection on narrative development reviews the literature on narrative, text, discourse analysis, and storytelling in development. It presents comprehensive coding schemes for analyzing cohesion and coherence, in particular. The work in this area is arduous to undertake. For example, the classic model of Halliday and Hasan (1976) has not been developed extensively for use in developmental psychology. The two chapters on narrative development should help in this regard. This could help in the study of narrative development in relation to Neo-Piagetian models, reviewed previously. Conclusions of the book return to the topic of causality. I end the book by presenting the concept of "re-responsibilities." By exploring these issues in the book, its potential scope is highlighted.

In this way, the book deals with the two fundamental questions found in the study of development, in general, and in the work of Piaget and those who followed him, in particular – the what and the why, or the content and the mechanism of development, which I refer to as product and process, respectively. In the following, I elaborate further on product and process in development.

## Product and Process

In terms of product, the major contribution of the present work lies in an integrated model of stages and substages in development based on the work of Case, Fischer, and Young. In previous publications introducing the model, I had indicated how I borrowed from the work of Case and Fischer, in particular, in constructing the present model (Young, 1990a, 1990b, 1997). The superordinate, integrated model newly described in the present work points out how the three models can work together. Nevertheless, the present model serves as the axis for the other two in the proposed combined model. Moreover, our models exist only because of the work of Piaget and the chain that preceded him (philosophers and psychologists who had worked in understanding development), as well as the many who followed him.

In terms of process, the major contribution of the present work relates to an underpinning nonlinear dynamical systems model. It describes how steps in the proposed developmental sequence are buttressed by a parallel five-step transitional sequence involving attractors and complex systems. I describe how attractors evolve into complex adaptive systems, which in turn become superordinate in character. An important concept presented in the present work concerns activation–inhibition coordination, which can serve as a "binding" or translational mechanism to help explain in similar terms different levels of the developmental "manifold" (Gottlieb, 1991, 2007), from genes to brain and neuronal processes to behavior, including at the social level.

About the integrative, combined model, it indicates how the proposed 25-step model of cognitive-affective parallels in development can serve as an umbrella model for the Neo-Piagetian models of Case and Fischer, as well those of Commons on four steps in the postformal period and Feldman on two phases within each stage of cognitive development. In effect, the present book serves to justify all major Neo-Piagetian models, and that our endeavors are making important contributions to psychology.

## Conclusions

In addition, the book has applied implications, for example, through its concept of the cognitive (mis)perception of the other and application of its stage model to regressive changes, such as in chronic pain. Moreover, I suggest that psychotherapy involves helping clients move through stages equivalent to those in development and optimizing activation–inhibition coordination dynamics.

I conclude the book with the concept that humans develop increasingly towards understanding the importance of and committing to undertaking our nexus of "re-responsibilities." The philosopher Lévinas had emphasized the importance of responsibility in becoming and being, and I have extended the concept to encompass "re-responsibilities." It refers to the need for each of us to engage in continual rededication to each of our multiple responsibilities in daily life – from family, to work or study, to the wider society. In the book, this aspect of our cognitive-affective growth is also presented from the perspective of the present stage and substage model.

These concepts point to the potential wide-ranging nomological network of approaches covered in the present work. The tighter the links that the present model maintains with other approaches and the more far-ranging they are, the greater is its theoretical, empirical, and practical appeal. At the same time, the model is one that lends itself to further theoretical refinement and to empirical confirmation and further investigation. For example, about research study, I offer scales related to parenting-families and narrative development and analysis that are consistent with the model.

The reader interested in other recent books from the Piagetian/ Neo-Piagetian perspective should consult Ferrari and Vuletic (2010), Morra, Gobbo, Marini, and Sheese (2008), and Müller, Carpendale, and Smith (2009). They complement the present book, but they do not consider with the same depth and critical focus the comparison of the models of Fischer and Case that has been undertaken in the present work. Moreover, they do not consider transition mechanisms in the same way of the present work. For example, I have included six chapters on hemispheric specialization, systems theory, and epigenesis, topics that are not considered much in the other books mentioned.

## References

Ferrari, M., & Vuletic L. (Eds.). (2010). *Developmental relations among mind, brain and education.* New York: Springer.

Gottlieb, G. (1991). Experiential canalization of behavioral development: Theory. *Developmental Psychology, 27*, 4–13.

Gottlieb, G. (2007). Probabilistic epigenesis. *Developmental Science, 10*, 1–11.

Lerner, R. M. (2006). Developmental science, developmental systems, and contemporary theories of human development. In W. Damon & R. M. Lerner (Eds.), *Handbook of child psychology: Vol. 1. Theoretical models of human development* (6th ed., pp. 1–14). Hoboken: Wiley.

Morra, S., Gobbo, C., Marini, Z., & Sheese, R. (2008). *Cognitive development: Neo-Piagetian perspectives.* New York: Erlbaum.

Müller, U., Carpendale, J. I. M., & Smith, L. (Eds.). (2009). *The Cambridge companion to Piaget.* New York: Cambridge University Press.

Overton, W. F. (2006). Developmental psychology: Philosophy, concepts, methodology. In W. Damon, & R. M. Lerner (Eds.), *Handbook of child psychology: Vol. 1. Theoretical models of human development* (6th ed., pp. 18–80). Hoboken: Wiley.

Young, G. (1990a). Early neuropsychological development: Lateralization of functions – hemispheric specialization. In C. A. Hauert (Ed.), *Developmental psychology: Cognitive, perceptuo-motor and neuropsychological perspectives* (pp. 113–181). Amsterdam: North Holland.

Young, G. (1990b). The development of hemispheric and manual specialization. In G. E. Hammond (Ed.), *Cerebral control of speech and limb movements* (pp. 79–139). Amsterdam: North Holland.

Young, G. (1997). *Adult development, therapy, and culture: A postmodern synthesis.* New York: Plenum.

# Acknowledgments

My teachers and mentors have provided much support throughout my career, and I thank them. In particular, the Piagetians Thérèse Gouin Décarie and Peter Wolff have both inspired and educated me. My family have been the best supporters (grandchildren giggling lead the way), along with my students and clients. My department chair, Timothy Moore, and the faculty dean (principal), Ken McRoberts, have provided constant support. My clinical office staff workers deserve special thanks for their dedicated work towards the development of the book – Joyce Chan, Jessica Chan, and Michelle Wong, in particular, as well as Leena Anand, Rahul Vinod, and Laura Scrivener. Most important, Sharon Panulla at Springer has provided unstinting support for this book and all my projects with Springer in the area of psychological injury and law (see http://www.asapil.org). Sylvana Ruggirello has offered her expert assistance for which I am grateful. Felix Portnoy shepherded the book through production, and deserves many thanks. The team that he headed (Ravi Amina, Mishra Manoranjan) did a remarkable job, and the reader should thank them as much as me.

# Contents

**1 Overview of the Present Work** 1
Introduction 1
Summary of the Present Work 1
Piaget and the Neo-Piagetians 2
Introduction by Morra, Gobbo, Marini, and Sheese (2008) 2
Two Piagets 11
Logical 12
Dialectical 12
Interim Summary 15
Product: The "What" of Development 15
Stages Exist and Provide Critical Scaffolds 15
Transtheoretical Neo-Piagetian Model 16
Process: The How or Why of Development 16
The Biopsychosocial Model 16
Systems Theory 21
Activation–Inhibition Coordination in Development 23
Summary 24
References 24

**2 The Biopsychosocial and Bio-Personal-Social Models** 27
Introduction 27
The Biopsychosocial Model and Medical Model 27
The Biopsychosocial Model 27
The Medical Model 29
Piaget on the Social, Relational 30
Piaget and the Social 30
Piaget and the Relational 31
Piaget and the Biological, Psychological, and Social 31
Piaget's Bio, Psycho, Social Legacy 32
The Biological, Psychological, Social Embodiment Model 32
The Bio-Personal-Social Model 33

Understanding Major Developmental Models in Terms of the Biopsychosocial Model ..... 35
Introduction ..... 35
Biological ..... 35
Social ..... 37
Psychological ..... 40
Conclusions ..... 42
Summary ..... 44
References ..... 44

**3 Piaget and Development** ..... 47
Introduction ..... 47
Representations and Concepts in Development ..... 47
Introduction ..... 47
Representations ..... 48
Concepts ..... 49
Conclusion ..... 50
Comment ..... 50
Piaget ..... 50
Introduction ..... 50
Piaget's Model ..... 51
Interim Summary ..... 57
Further Piaget ..... 57
Piaget on Cognitive Socioaffective Parallels ..... 57
Interim Summary ..... 62
Adult Thought in the Piagetian View ..... 63
Piaget ..... 63
Piagetians ..... 63
On Piaget ..... 64
Comment ..... 64
Piagetians Expanding ..... 64
Introduction ..... 64
Stages and Substages ..... 65
Transition Mechanisms ..... 68
Summary and Conclusions ..... 69
References ..... 70

**4 The Present Cognitive-Affective Stage Model: I Cognition** ..... 73
Introduction ..... 73
Neo-Piagetians ..... 73
The Models ..... 73
Comment ..... 77
Overview of the Present Neo-Piagetian Model ..... 78
Introduction ..... 78
Formulation ..... 81
Stages ..... 81

Substages ... 82
Substages: Details ... 84
Sensorimotor Substages in Chimpanzees ... 85
Ages ... 86
Cognitive Control Units ... 86
Summary ... 88
References ... 88

**5 The Present Model: II Postformal Stage, Neo-Eriksonian Parallels, Systems** ... 91
Introduction ... 91
Postformal Stage ... 91
Neo-Piagetians ... 92
The Present Model of Postformal Intelligence ... 97
Interim Summary ... 100
Neo-Eriksonian Model ... 100
The Steps ... 100
Conclusion ... 104
Other Socioaffective Modeling ... 105
Developmental Process in the Current Work ... 105
Nonlinear Dynamical Systems Theory ... 105
Fractals ... 106
Concepts ... 107
Summary and Conclusions ... 110
References ... 110

**6 Substages in the Neo-Piagetian Models of Case, Fischer, and Young** ... 113
Introduction ... 113
The Major Neo-Piagetian Stage-Substage Models ... 113
Case's Neo-Piagetian Model: Cognition ... 116
Cognitive Stages ... 116
Cognitive Substages ... 118
Fischer's Neo-Piagetian Model: Cognition ... 119
The Cognitive Model ... 119
Early Fischer ... 121
Interim Summary ... 124
Introducing the Comparison of Fischer, Case, and Young ... 124
Comparison with Case and Fischer on Substages ... 125
Similarities and Differences ... 125
The Missing Stages and Substages in Case and in Fischer ... 126
Possible Logic in the Construction of Case's and Fischer's Models ... 130
Steps in the Development of Egocentrism ... 133
Introduction ... 133
Piaget ... 134
Kesselring and Müller ... 134

Cognition and Affect .... 135
Comment .... 135
Summary and Conclusions .... 135
References .... 136

**7 Parallels in Cognitive Substages and Socioaffectivity in Case** .... 139
Introduction .... 139
Case's Neo-Piagetian Model: Socioaffective Correspondences .... 139
Earlier Case .... 139
Later Case .... 150
Steps in Self-Development in Case .... 153
Introduction .... 153
Summary and Conclusions .... 156
References .... 156

**8 Parallels in Cognitive Substages and Socioaffectivity in Fischer** .... 159
Introduction .... 159
Parallels in Socioaffective Development in Fischer .... 159
Oedipus .... 159
Social Roles .... 161
Emotional Correspondences .... 161
Conclusions on Fischer .... 166
Self-Development from a Fischerian Perspective (Harter) .... 167
The Model .... 167
Age Periods .... 168
Comment .... 172
Summary and Conclusions .... 173
References .... 174

**9 Case and Fischer on Language and the Brain** .... 177
Introduction .... 177
Case and Fischer on Language Development .... 177
Case .... 177
Fischer .... 185
Children's Narrative Development .... 185
Case .... 185
Fischer .... 187
Comparison .... 188
Present Model .... 189
Interim Summary .... 189
Case and Fischer on Transition Mechanisms .... 191
Models .... 191
Comments .... 196
Corresponding Cortical Reorganization .... 198
Case .... 198

Fischer ..... 200
Conclusion ..... 202
Summary and Conclusions ..... 203
References ..... 204

**10 Recent Case and Colleagues** ..... 207
Introduction ..... 207
Central Conceptual, Number, Narrative, and Social Structures ..... 207
Introduction ..... 207
Research ..... 208
Conclusions ..... 209
Interim Summary ..... 209
Case's Colleagues ..... 210
Infant Development ..... 210
Narrative Structure from a Casian Perspective ..... 214
Cognition and Emotion ..... 218
Development of Cognition–Emotion Relationships ..... 221
Emotion-Cognitive Self-Regulation ..... 222
Hypercognition and Domains ..... 225
Summary and Conclusions ..... 230
References ..... 230

**11 Further Fischer: Comprehensive Summary, Adult Development** ..... 235
Introduction ..... 235
Comprehensive Summary of Fischer ..... 235
Cognition and Construction ..... 235
Web ..... 236
Interim Summary ..... 245
Adult Development ..... 246
Reflective Thinking ..... 246
Erikson ..... 250
Other Fischerian Models ..... 254
Summary and Conclusions ..... 258
References ..... 258

**12 Recent Fischer: Emotional Development** ..... 261
Introduction ..... 261
An Integrated, Lifespan Perspective ..... 261
Introduction ..... 261
Architecture ..... 263
Components ..... 263
Brain ..... 263
Skills ..... 264
Web ..... 264
Inter-Subjectivity ..... 265

Emotional Development .... 265
Preview .... 265
Mascolo and Fischer (2007) .... 266
Mascolo and Fischer (1995) .... 275
Summary and Conclusions .... 286
References .... 286

**13 Self-Development** .... 289
Introduction .... 289
Steps in Self-Development in Sroufe, Selman, and Loevinger .... 290
Sroufe's Theory .... 290
Selman's Theory of Self-Development in Children and Adolescents .... 292
Loevinger's Theory of Self-Development in Adolescents and Adults .... 294
The Present Model of Self-Development .... 296
Model .... 296
Comment .... 301
Environmental Support .... 301
Model .... 301
Comment .... 306
Summary .... 306
References .... 309

**14 Cognitive (Mis)Perception of the Self and Other** .... 311
Introduction .... 311
The Cognitive (Mis)Perception of the Other .... 311
Model .... 311
Scales of the Cognitive (Mis)Perception of the Other .... 317
The Cognitive (Mis)Perception of Self and Other .... 323
Other Self Topics .... 326
Self-Efficacy .... 326
Themes in Self Stories .... 326
Summary and Conclusions .... 329
References .... 329

**15 Social Cognition/Theory of Mind** .... 331
Introduction .... 331
The Development of Social Understanding .... 332
Introduction .... 332
Comment .... 333
Developmental Issues .... 333
Infants .... 333
Children .... 334
Development in Theory of Mind .... 335
Infants .... 335
Children .... 338

Embodiment and Communities ........ 339
Embodiment ........ 339
Comment ........ 339
Theories ........ 341
Modular ........ 341
General ........ 342
Conclusion ........ 342
Human vs. Animal Intelligence ........ 342
Theories ........ 342
Reinterpreting Human Uniqueness in Light of the Present Model ........ 343
Learning ........ 345
Human Uniqueness ........ 345
Skills ........ 345
Intentionality ........ 346
Human Uniqueness ........ 346
Trajectories ........ 347
Education ........ 347
Human Uniqueness ........ 347
Comment ........ 347
Conclusions ........ 348
Environment ........ 349
Vygotsky ........ 349
Coappropriation ........ 351
Reinterpretations in Preschooler Theory of Mind ........ 353
Reinterpreting the 3–4 Transition in Light of the Present Model ........ 353
Reinterpreting Other Theories in Light of the Present Model ........ 355
Conclusion ........ 356
Summary and Conclusions ........ 356
References ........ 357

**16 Self-Definition and Relatedness/Self-Regulation in Development** ........ 361
Introduction ........ 361
Self-Regulation ........ 361
Introduction ........ 361
The Development of Executive Function ........ 362
Psychobiology/Neurobiology ........ 364
Conclusion ........ 366
Modeling ........ 367
Specific Models ........ 367
General Models ........ 369
Self-Regulation According to Piaget ........ 373
The Present Model of Self-Regulation ........ 374
Stages in the Model ........ 374
Conclusion ........ 378

Relatedness and Self-Definition in Development ..... 378
Model ..... 378
Related Models ..... 378
Development ..... 379
Comment ..... 379
Learning ..... 382
Summary and Conclusion ..... 386
References ..... 386

**17 Cognitive/Socioaffective Complexes and Multiple Intelligences** ..... 391
Introduction ..... 391
The Cognitive/Socioaffective Complex ..... 391
Piagetian Work ..... 391
Multiple Processing Modes ..... 392
Multiple Components ..... 394
Adaptation ..... 394
Memory ..... 395
Multiple and Parallel Cognition ..... 396
Development of Intelligence ..... 397
An Integrating Cognition ..... 398
Development of the Cognitive/Socioaffective Complex ..... 399
The Complex ..... 399
The Stages ..... 400
Comments ..... 402
Multiple Intelligences ..... 403
Models of Multiple Intelligences ..... 403
Present Model ..... 405
Individual Differences ..... 408
Summary and Conclusions ..... 410
References ..... 411

**18 Postformal Thought: Commons' Model** ..... 413
Introduction ..... 413
Commons' Model ..... 413
The Model ..... 413
Post-Postformal Stage: The Present Model ..... 419
Domains of Development ..... 420
Evolution and Empathy ..... 421
Management ..... 426
Management Styles: The Present Model ..... 427
Other Topics in Commons ..... 430
Transition Mechanisms ..... 432
Summary and Conclusions ..... 435
References ..... 435

**19 Development of Personality and Motivational Needs** ........ 439
Introduction ........ 439
Reviews of the Literature ........ 439
Caspi and Shiner ........ 439
Mervielde et al. ........ 441
Comment ........ 442
Development, Stages, Personality, Disorder, Relationships ........ 443
Introduction ........ 443
Present Stage Model in Relation to the Five Factor Model ........ 443
Temperament and Personality Over the Life Span ........ 445
Narrative Identity ........ 445
Model ........ 445
Development ........ 446
Comment ........ 447
Interim Summary ........ 447
Revising Maslow's Model of Motivational Needs ........ 447
Renovating Maslow ........ 447
Commentaries ........ 452
Present Model ........ 453
Comment ........ 456
The Revised Needs Model and Romantic Relations ........ 457
Introduction ........ 457
Model ........ 458
Summary and Conclusion ........ 458
Summary ........ 458
Conclusion ........ 459
References ........ 460

**20 Socioemotional Systems and Neo-Eriksonian Dangers** ........ 463
Introduction ........ 463
Socioemotional Systems ........ 463
Introduction ........ 463
The Systems ........ 466
Summary and Conclusions ........ 475
Neo-Eriksonian Steps ........ 475
References ........ 479

**21 Approaches to Emotions** ........ 481
Introduction ........ 481
The Reality and Relevance of Emotions ........ 481
Introduction ........ 481
Emotion–Cognition Relations ........ 482
Comment ........ 488
Reductionism ........ 488

Major Approaches in Emotions ... 489
Biology ... 492
Cognition ... 493
Functions ... 493
Culture ... 494
Dimensions ... 495
Dynamical Approach ... 498
Summary and Conclusions ... 500
References ... 500

**22 Emotional Development in Infancy** ... 505
Introduction ... 505
Trends in Emotional Development ... 505
Introduction ... 505
Developmental Patterns ... 506
Comment ... 511
Recent Research ... 512
A Dimensional Model of Basic Emotions ... 513
The Model ... 513
The Dimensional Model ... 514
Development ... 516
Comment ... 519
Summary ... 519
Summary and Conclusion ... 520
References ... 521

**23 Attachment Basics** ... 523
Introduction ... 523
Attachment ... 524
Introduction ... 524
Phases ... 525
Biology ... 525
Evolution ... 526
Attachment Category Classification ... 528
Standard Model ... 528
Crittenden ... 532
Parenting and Attachment ... 534
Bowlby ... 534
Precursors ... 534
The Caregiving System ... 536
Outcome ... 538
Childhood ... 538
The Adult Attachment Interview ... 539
Attachment Types: Cross-Age Model ... 540
Attachment Types in Adults ... 540

Model of Attachment Types for Children and Adults ... 541
Summary and Conclusions ... 544
References ... 544

**24 Internal Working Models and Social Self Working Schemata** ... 549
Introduction ... 549
Internal Working Models ... 549
Early Work ... 549
Later Work ... 554
Attachment Phases ... 559
Present Model ... 560
Social Self Working Schemata ... 564
Summary and Conclusions ... 568
References ... 568

**25 Development of Hemispheric Specialization** ... 573
Introduction ... 573
Manual and Inhibition Development ... 574
Activation–Inhibition Coordination ... 574
Evidence ... 577
Comment ... 583
Invariant Lateralization ... 584
Models ... 584
Summary ... 586
References ... 587

**26 Lateralization and Developing Cognition** ... 593
Introduction ... 593
Early Lateralization and Developing Cognition ... 593
Evidence ... 593
Present Model ... 596
Relations Between Ontogenesis and Phylogenesis ... 603
Evolution ... 603
Evolutionary Progression ... 604
Evolution of Mind ... 605
Toward the Theoretic Mind ... 605
Toward the Extended Mind ... 605
Towards the Postformal Mind ... 606
Summary and Conclusions ... 609
References ... 609

**27 Systems and Development** ... 613
Introduction ... 613
Development and Systems ... 613
Development ... 613

Systems 615
Change 615
Causality 616
Comment 617
System Dynamics 617
Systems 617
Components 618
Patterns 620
Living Systems 621
Causality and Prediction 622
States 623
Resource Flow 624
Energy 625
Hierarchies 626
Stability 627
Iteration and Feedback 628
Change 628
Perturbations 629
Self-Organization 629
Emergence 630
Dynamical Approach to Emotional Development 630
Summary 633
References 633

**28 Attractors, Complexity** 637
Introduction 637
Attractors 637
Introduction 637
Latent Attractors 639
Attractor Types 640
Chaotic Change 642
Bifurcation 643
Fractals 643
Complexity 644
Introduction 644
Steps in the Evolution of Complexity 645
Controlling Parameters 649
Development 650
Chaos and Complexity 650
Circular Causality and Emergence 651
Summary and Discussion 653
Appendix 653
References 654

**29 Causes and Determinants of Behavior** 657
Introduction 657

Four Causes, Four Questions, and, Four Forces ........ 658
Aristotle ........ 658
Tinbergen ........ 659
Conclusion ........ 660
Evolution ........ 661
Genes × Environment ........ 664
Introduction ........ 664
Probabilistic Epigenesis ........ 665
Neuroconstructivism ........ 666
Gene-Environment Correlation ........ 667
Other Models ........ 668
Epigenesis ........ 669
Introduction ........ 669
Mechanisms in Epigenesis ........ 672
Epigenesis in Rodents ........ 673
Gene-Environment Interactions and the Development of Risk ........ 674
G × E Interactions ........ 674
Psychological Disorders and Life Stress ........ 674
Additional Research ........ 675
Summary ........ 676
References ........ 676

**30 Gene–Environment Interactions: Other Topics** ........ 681
Introduction ........ 681
Interaction of Genes and Environment in Early Plasticity and Susceptibility ........ 681
*DRD4* ........ 682
*MAOA* ........ 682
*5-HTTLPR* ........ 683
Conclusion ........ 684
Links Between Genes, Behavior, Brain, and the Environment ........ 685
Frontal Lobe Left-Right Asymmetry, Temperament, and the *DRD4* Gene ........ 685
Maternal Social Support, Temperament, and the *5-HTTLPR* Gene ........ 686
Developmental Pathways ........ 686
Mirror Neurons ........ 688
Hebbian Learning ........ 688
Therapy ........ 690
Other Topics ........ 691
Epigenesis and the *BDNF* Gene ........ 691
Epistasis ........ 692
Environment ........ 692
Brain ........ 692
Intervention ........ 692
Atypical Epigenesis ........ 693
Attention Genes ........ 693

Attachment ... 694
Social Genomics ... 694
Generalist Genes ... 695
Generalist Stress ... 695
Summary and Comments on Recent Literature ... 696
Epigenetics ... 696
Causality ... 700
Evolution ... 700
Free Will ... 702
Causality Map or Landscape ... 703
References ... 704

**31 Stages and Change in Development and Other Systems** ... 709
Introduction ... 709
Caveats ... 710
Generic Change ... 711
Introduction ... 711
Five Steps in Change ... 712
Comment ... 712
Complexity Theory in Human Organization ... 714
Model ... 714
Comment ... 717
History of Major Schools of Thought in Developmental Psychology ... 717
Introduction ... 717
Stages ... 718
Closer Look at the Generic Step Model ... 724
Development ... 724
Pain and Therapy ... 725
Psychological Injury and Law ... 728
Summary and Conclusions ... 729
References ... 729

**32 Collective Intelligence and Multilevel Selection** ... 733
Introduction ... 733
Evolution ... 734
Multilevel Selection and Psychological Acquisitions ... 734
Multilevel Selection and Evolution ... 735
Human Applications ... 737
Multilevel Selection and Bioeconomic Organization ... 737
Evolutionary Dynamic Model of Cooperation ... 738
Cultural Evolutionary Theory ... 740
Evolution of Multilevel Selection ... 741
Introduction ... 741
Cognitive Applications ... 743

Young's Stage Model of Cognitive Development and Multilevel Selection ........ 745
Review ........ 745
Steps ........ 746
Gene Co-opting ........ 748
Introduction ........ 748
Qualifications ........ 748
Model ........ 749
Steps ........ 752
Related Topics ........ 754
Co-Memes and Co-Genes ........ 754
Social Selection and Society ........ 755
Dynamic Darwinism and Coevolutionary Cofractalization ........ 756
Summary and Conclusions ........ 756
References ........ 757

**33 Narrative Discourse Coding: Cohesion in Children's Narratives** ........ 759
Introduction ........ 759
Narrative Development in Children ........ 759
Narrative and Cognition ........ 759
Narrative and Cohesion–Coherence ........ 760
Comment ........ 760
Discourse and Narratives ........ 761
Introduction ........ 761
Cohesion ........ 763
Cohesion in Discourse: Toward a Coding Scheme ........ 769
Preamble ........ 769
Subcategories ........ 770
Cohesion Quality ........ 778
Summary and Conclusions ........ 780
References ........ 780

**34 Narrative Discourse Coding: Syntactic Complexity-Errors and Coherence** ........ 785
Introduction ........ 785
Syntactic Complexity ........ 785
Two Prior Schemes ........ 785
Combining the Two Prior Schemes ........ 789
Syntactic Problems ........ 792
Coherence ........ 794
Introduction ........ 794
Research ........ 794
Positive Text Coherence ........ 795
Negative Text Coherence ........ 800
Nonverbal Level ........ 803

Introduction ........ 803
Measure ........ 804
Comment ........ 804
Summary and Conclusions ........ 805
References ........ 806

**35 Book Conclusions** ........ 807
Introduction ........ 807
Causality Upfront ........ 808
Philosophy ........ 808
Other Disciplines ........ 808
Comment ........ 809
Epistemology ........ 810
The Unconscious and Free Will ........ 811
Lévinas and the Philosophy of Responsibility ........ 812
Lévinas ........ 812
Present Model ........ 812
A Philosophy of Re-responsibilities and of Freedom from Will ........ 813
Model ........ 813
Re-responsibilities ........ 815
Relational Meaning Worlds ........ 816
Development as Complexity and Development as Causality ........ 816
Back to Causality ........ 821
Introduction ........ 821
Model ........ 821
Legal Philosophy ........ 823
Other Disciplines ........ 826
Activation–Inhibition Coordination Processes in Generic Change ........ 826
Activation–Inhibition in Development, Therapy ........ 826
Steps in Activation–Inhibition Coordination ........ 828
Book Conclusion ........ 830
Development ........ 830
Psychology as Ways of Living ........ 831
Therapy ........ 832
Book Ends ........ 834
References ........ 836

**Index** ........ 839

# Chapter 1
# Overview of the Present Work

## Introduction

This chapter sets the stage by summarizing in a tabular format the major contributions of this work. Next, it describes the present Neo-Piagetian stage model, which helps understand the "what" of development, and my conception of the transition mechanisms involved in their growth, which helps understand the "how" or the "why" of development. The summary tables provide a map of the book, as well. The "what" and "why" questions about development are common to the field, and the book emphasizes the value of stage conceptions and the interactive complexity of causal factors underlying their transition. The particular Neo-Piagetian stage model presented consists of 25 steps (5 stages × 5 substages), and it describes parallel cognitive and socioaffective acquisitions. The stages are referred to as reflexive, sensorimotor, perioperational (representational; preoperational and concrete operational), abstract, and collective intelligence. The substages are referred to as coordination, hierarchization, systematization, multiplication, and integration.

The model builds on the work of Fischer and Case, in particular, and I chart how the different theories are different yet compatible, with my own serving as an axis. As for the transition mechanisms, I innovate here as well by describing that underpinning the development through the stage sequence lays down a sequence of changes in attractors and complex adaptive systems, which are related to nonlinear dynamical system modeling. Moreover, I relate the changes in the stages to the construct of activation–inhibition coordination, which seem to underlie different levels of the neurodevelopmental axis. The summary tables describe multiple concepts and models that I have developed from these fundamental starting points of the present work.

## Summary of the Present Work

In the present work, I show how the 25-step-model Neo-Piagetian model that I had presented in Young (1997) differs from but builds on and integrates other Neo-Piagetian models (those of Fischer, Case, in particular). In addition, I describe

G. Young, *Development and Causality: Neo-Piagetian Perspectives*,
DOI 10.1007/978-1-4419-9422-6_1, © Springer Science+Business Media, LLC 2011

in depth cognitive–affective correspondences in the prior theories and my own. Also, the present work provides an elaborate description of transition mechanisms that promote passage through the stages of the model in terms of nonlinear dynamical systems theory, the concept of activation–inhibition coordination, and epigenetics.

It took eight tables to summarize the key contributions of the present work. They illustrate the range and depth of the critical analysis and conceptualization found in the present work. There are many more examples that I could have included in the tables, but they would have become unwieldy. They provide a map of the major points that have been raised in the book. They are provided at the beginning of the book to facilitate reading. In essence, they constitute the book's conclusions and could have been placed at the book's end so that their justification and detailed elaboration in the text would have preceded them. However, by placing them at the beginning, the reader can refer to them, as needed, as the reading proceeds. The risk in presenting them right away is that the reader feels overwhelmed by the range and depth of the critical analysis and new conceptualizations, but the advantage is that the map facilitates the reading and understanding of the book and offers a guide to where it is heading. In other words, the summaries of the present work show how the basis for the present model created in the 1997 book has been greatly elaborated and expanded.

The eight summary tables of the present book are organized around its key contributions related to its 25-step stage model (5 stages × 5 substages) and how it can help understand multiple areas of development. To give one example that should capture the imagination of the reader, I have reworked Maslow's concept of a hierarchy of needs in terms of the present model. Maslow's model consists of five levels, and I show how they can be reworked to relate to the five developmental stages of the present model. Another example that should provoke interest relates to a reworking of the concept of internal working models in attachment theory in terms of their development through the steps of the present model. Finally, among other features of the present book, I reworked the concept of theory of mind, or social cognition, and that of multiple intelligences as well, in terms of the steps of the present model (Tables 1.1–1.8).

## Piaget and the Neo-Piagetians

### *Introduction by Morra, Gobbo, Marini, and Sheese (2008)*

Morra et al. (2008) described cognitive development from a Neo-Piagetian perspective. They described Piaget in depth and then moved on to the first Neo-Piagetians, Pascual-Leone (1970) and Halford (1978). They also focused on contemporary Neo-Piagetians, such as Demetriou (Demetriou et al., 2005), the "French connection" (e.g., de Ribaupierre, 2001; Lautrey, 1990; Rieben, de Ribaupierre, & Lautrey, 1990), and Fischer and Case. They included in their book other cognitive workers, such as Siegler (2006) and Karmiloff-Smith (1992), who speak of Neo-Piagetian

**Table 1.1** Summary of key contributions of the author's model carried forward from Young (1997)

| Area | Contribution |
|---|---|
| 25 steps in development over Neo-Piagetian and Neo-Eriksonian stages and substages | The present work is based on a Neo-Piagetian model of 25 steps in development, consisting of five stages having a cyclic recursion of five substages. Parallel to the cognitive steps, 25 Neo-Eriksonian steps are described. The cognitive steps include the five stages of reflexes, sensorimotor acquisitions, perioperations (preoperations and concrete operations), abstract thought (formal), and collective intelligence (postformal). The substages involve coordination, hierarchization, systematization, multiplication, and integration. The 25 Neo-Eriksonian steps are presented as poles involving acts comparable to Erikson's original sequence of eight stages. The stages and substages provide a scaffold for the development of individual differences. This is the only lifespan model of cognitive development that stretches from the prenatal to the end-of-life periods. Moreover, its description of the adult postformal period as one of collective intelligence is novel (and is based on the work of Labouvie-Vief, in part) |
| Socioaffective correspondences | Aside from the Neo-Piagetian–Neo-Eriksonian parallels in development, the present work posits that major socioaffective acquisitions develop in correspondence with the stages and substages. These include the development of phases in attachment, in working schemata in attachment, in basic emotions, in socioemotional systems, in factors in personality, in the marital cycle, and in the cognitive (mis)perception of the other. It is noted that the cognitive and socioaffective form an integrated system in development (e.g., cognitive-affective structures), but they are separated at times in the present work for heuristic reasons |
| Other correspondences | The present stage–substage model was shown to apply to other cognitive-related areas, such the development of storytelling, themes in personal narratives, and the self |
| Role of the environment | The present work adopts a Neo-Vygotskian point of view, for example, involving the concepts of coappropriation and co-memes. The environment provides buffers to facilitate development right from birth |
| Role of biology | Each substage of the present 25-step model was associated with a step in the development of manual skill and/or hemispheric specialization, based on an activation/inhibition model. Possible phylogenetic-evolutionary origins were explored |
| Systems view | The transition mechanisms posited in development were considered especially systemic, rather than purely biological or environmental, with the individual's developing self involved in the process. Difficulties in development arise from multiple interacting factors |

matters but who are not Neo-Piagetians themselves. They branched out into workers in the Neo-Piagetian tradition who deal with emotions, such as Lewis and Mascolo, who are colleagues of Case and Fischer, respectively. They also considered models related to Neo-Piagetians, such as connectionism. In addition, they dealt with areas related to cognition that are involved in Neo-Piagetian work, but not originally in Piaget, such as the topics of working memory and executive control.

**Table 1.2** Summary of key contributions of the present work related to its overall perspective

| Area | Contribution |
|---|---|
| | The present Neo-Piagetian model provides a unique theoretical perspective of a 25-step sequence in development. This sequence has far more steps than any of the other Neo-Piagetian models. It was developed through a network of logic and careful analysis of other similar models. Given its comprehensive 25-step sequence, (a) it constitutes the only Neo-Piagetian cognitive model that fully covers the life span, (b) it is the only model that includes corresponding socioaffective Neo-Eriksonian steps, (c) it is the only one that does not have inconsistent age gaps between substages at any point over the full life span, and (d) it is the only model that can serve as an umbrella one for the others. (e) Also, it is the model that respects most Piaget's work as a starting point to its formulation, taking care to keep his best-established components. (f) In addition, by way of the present work, it is the only model that carefully compares and contrasts all the models, pointing out their inconsistencies and proposing modifications to make them more consistent. (g) Finally, it is the model that expands most its applications to other areas of human development and even to systems in development that are not about individuals in development (e.g., chronic pain, societies, nonliving systems) |
| Synthetic model | Aside from its critical comparison of the Neo-Piagetian models of Fischer, Case, and Young, which has led to the development of a transtheoretical Neo-Piagetian model of cognitive development and parallel socioaffective acquisitions in development, the full scope of the present model suggests a synthetic model of development |
| Bio-personal-social model | The biopsychosocial model relates biological, psychological, and social factors in the study of health and illness. However, the term is a misnomer because it separates psychological factors as distinct from biological and social ones in its very term, despite integrating them in the concept itself. Moreover, the term is applied to developmental mental disturbances and diseases, in particular, and, for the most part, not to normal development. In these regards, I suggest that a generic term that covers both normal and abnormal development and that fully includes biological, personal, and sociocultural factors within a psychological term is the "bio-personal-social" model |
| Dynamical systems theory | The nonlinear dynamical systems approach is transdisciplinary, and in the present work, I have applied it to help understand the organization, development, and causality of behavior |
| Paradigm shift | The present work does not constitute a paradigm shift. It is constituted by careful description of existing theory and empirical research in developmental psychology, and builds its models and innovations from that basis. It covers all major theories in developmental psychology and incorporates each of them into its framework. It ranges over multiple topics in developmental psychology, but all with the aim of creating a scientifically informed integration. There is much room for testing the models that have been presented and for elaborating them in the collective process that is science |
| | The reader might be taxed by the multiple theoretical innovations and research suggestions. At the same time, they all derive from an analytic and synthetic process that is standard in science. In enumerating gaps and inconsistencies in the prior work, I do not minimize that work. To the contrary, they deserve kudos for their contributions, and the gaps and inconsistencies pointed to proposed solutions in the wave in science to which I hope to have contributed |

**Table 1.3** Summary of key contributions of present work related to the comparison of Neo-Piagetian models (especially of Fischer, Case, and Young)

| Area | Contribution |
|---|---|
| Parallels in cognitive-affective development and other areas in other Neo-Piagetian models having stages and substages | I describe in detail the developmental cognitive models of Kurt Fischer and Robbie Case, in particular, upon whose work the present Neo-Piagetian model is constructed. They both have formulated a model of cyclic recursion of three substages over major stages in development (although the models are based on developing skills, domains, etc., and are called tiers and levels or the like, aside from stages and substages). Also, I describe in depth the social and emotional correspondences that they posited to take place at each substage. I examine the most recent work by Fischer and Case or their colleagues; the work covers a broad range of developmental areas. (Case passed away prematurely a decade ago, but his colleagues continue to publish. Marc Lewis is a leading colleague of Case, and Michael Mascolo of Fischer.) As I reviewed some of these areas, I developed new innovations in the present model (e.g., stages and substages in emotional regulation, or self-regulation) |
| Critique of the models of other Neo-Piagetians and comparison with the present model | Both for the cognitive and affective sequences presented by Case and Fischer, I indicate difficulties in conceptualization or application that seem to arise. In particular, I indicate where their models seem lacking with respect to the stages described, the substages included, and the socioemotional correspondences given. The major difficulties related to the models of Case and Fischer include (a) an absence of a complete stage–substage sequence that covers the life span, (b) missing substages relative to my own model and what should be present, and (c) presenting models of development in some domains that reveal inconsistencies because of these lacunae. I also scrutinize Common's model of hierarchical complexity. For all the models, I point out instances where my own model can account for better the data and examples provided. In addition, I point out how their models can be modified or improved |
| Integrated model of Young, Case, Fischer, Commons, and Feldman | I recognize the positive contributions of each of the major Neo-Piagetian models analyzed, and build one combined model that accommodates all of them, yet with my own model as the major axis. The combined model keeps the 25-step progression that is in my model but at times adds to the labels of the stages to fit the contributions of Case, Fischer, and Commons, in particular. It adds Feldman's notion of two phases in each stage. It groups the five substages of the present model by putting three in the first phase and two in the second |
| Applications to other developmental phenomena | The combined model can accommodate the various socioaffective parallels described in the present model. New innovations in the present work relative to those in Young (1997) include description of new parallels with the cognitive steps of the present model, elaborations of a model of attachment types, and a nonlinear dynamical systems model of transitioning from step to step, including the concept of superordinate complex adaptive systems |

To introduce their work, Morra et al. (2008) discussed the basic distinction in development research that relates to macro- and microdevelopment. Macrodevelopment concerns the development of broad cognitive structures, such as substages and stages. Microdevelopment refers to developmental change processes on a short

**Table 1.4** Summary of key contributions in the present work related to the 25-step model of development

| Area | Contribution |
|---|---|
| Cognitive/ socioaffective complex | Demetriou is a Neo-Piagetian who made several notable contributions, although not at the level of specifying a model of stages and substages in cognitive development. He specified well the cognitive architecture that is involved in cognitive structure building. Aside from core capacities such as processing speed, the cognitive system involves a hypercognitive mechanism that integrates online lower-order structures as the developing person deals with adaptive needs. Demetriou and colleagues also specified that domains are important, as the hypercognitive mechanisms are applied to major fields, and in doing so cross-task conceptual structures form, as per Case, and the developing person passes through cognitive stages, as per Case. I expanded the notion of a hypercognitive system, in particular, to indicate that cognitive-affective structures form, in that cognition and socioaffective acquisitions are integrated |
| Multiple intelligences | Gardner described up to nine intelligences, but these appear to be domains more than anything else. According to the present work, multiple intelligences are akin to the different cognitive capacities that develop in each stage (and substage). I review literature that indicates that with growth sensorimotor intelligence is never lost and even expands, for example. Also, different intelligences associated with the various stages and substages can be coupled or yoked, increasing the extent of individual differences that can form as intelligence is deployed |
| Self-(cognitive-emotional) regulation | I describe a model of self (cognitive-emotional)-regulation that includes the cognitive/socioaffective complex, and that develops over the stages and substages of the present model. The labels given to the steps in the model are based on the labels of the stages in Baldwin's model of cognitive development, which Piaget had elaborated into his classic model. Therefore, I present and expand the sequence of Baldwin (e.g., prelogical, quasi-logical, logical, hyperlogical), and use it as I describe several areas in development |
| Stages in other areas | The present stage model provides a generic sequence that can be applied to multiple domains that lend themselves to influence if not direct underpinning by cognitive complexity and its development through stages and substages. For example, the construct of theory of mind is considered to develop through the 25 steps in development, although I developed the concept of the "construction of the cognitive-emotion-body of the other" to render the term applicable across the life span and to include multiple aspects of perspective-taking of the other. I have reworked Maslow's hierarchical model of five motivational needs to correspond to the five cognitive stages of the present model. I reworked the previous model of steps in the marital lifecycle that I had developed (Young, 1997) to incorporate my Neo-Maslovian perspective (e.g., I referred to couples as having "co-needs"). In terms of the five factor model of personality, I apply the present model to the development of personality and its precursors. Also, I show how the model can be applied to management styles, and I describe five styles that derive from the five stages of the present model. Further, the model can be applied to quality and complexity of storytelling construction and other narrative construction in discourse |

**Table 1.5** Summary of other contributions of the present work amenable to elaboration according to the 25-step developmental model

| Area | Contribution |
|---|---|
| Attachment types | After reviewing the work on basic classifications of attachment types, including some revised models, I present a model of attachment types based on the axes of parental warmth and control (after Baumrind). In each of the four quadrants created by the intersection of these two dimensions, I placed an insecure attachment type (avoidant, ambivalent, disoriented/disorganized, and clingy/dependent and their equivalents at the level of the adult, e.g., preoccupied, dismissive). The clingy/dependent category is not typically included in models of attachment types, but it is consistent with the parental dimension model provided. Research needs to elaborate how the different attachment types evolve according to the present 25-step model |
| Self-definitional self/relatedness self | The classic distinction in describing the self involves the "I" self and the "Me" self (James). Blatt described the basic polarity in experience in terms of self-definition and interpersonal relatedness. These experiences dynamically interact and integrate in development. Based on this concept, I elaborated a model of the self that comprises a self-definitional self and a relatedness self. These components are considered to develop dynamically and integratively. Research could establish how the two proposed selves change in the course of development according to the present stage–substage model, and therefore further leading to understanding the proposed duality of a personal self and a self in context |
| The cognitive (mis)perception of the self and other by the self and perceived in the other | In constructed a multimodal model of the self based on the concept of the cognitive (mis)perception of the other and the distinction between the self-definitional self and the relatedness self. As originally defined, the cognitive mis(perception) of the other was not considered a component of the self, and it was not applied to self-perception. In the present expansion of the concept, individuals are understood to not only cognitively (mis)perceive the other but also the self. Moreover, the (mis)perception could be not only about how the self (mis)perceives the self and other but also how the self perceives others (mis)perceiving the person or others. This fourfold model of (mis)perception in self, when coupled with the two types of selves, leads to a model of self components in terms of cognitive (mis)perception comprised of eight components. Research could be undertaken to determine how the self components being proposed are elaborated as development proceeds through the various stages and substages of the present model |
| Cohesion and coherence in narratives | Language development peaks with pragmatic, conversational, and story telling skills in narrative construction. Storytelling follows a grammar of its own in terms of plot/subplot and start, middle, and end-point conventions. Children create stories that make sense by learning to use cohesive devices over and within phrases/sentences and by creating story integrity or coherence. I present a coding scheme for the different types of cohesion developed in the functionalist approach of Halliday and Hasan. It provides a structure integrating many items, potentially simplifying empirical analyses. Also, I describe a coding scheme that I developed for coherence in stories and story grammar. Research could be undertaken to show how passage through the various steps of the present model alters cohesion and coherence in discourse |

(continued)

**Table 1.5** (continued)

| Area | Contribution |
|---|---|
| A philosophy of re-responsibilities and of freedom of will | This constitutes the penultimate contribution of the present work because it combines philosophy with the pragmatisms of every day self and relational life. In terms of philosophy, I expand Lévinas's concept of responsibility for the other to show how the sense of responsibility might grow as the developing individual passes through the developmental steps proposed in the present model. For the adult phase, I refer to re-responsibilities, and the constant imperative to rededicate ourselves at each moment to our multiple responsibilities. In terms of freedom of will, I show how it could involve a similar passage through the steps of the present model toward a psychological, mature, wise, and continually present stage in which free will is a constantly lived experience in the daily participation in life, that is, where the individual is genuinely free |

**Table 1.6** Summary of other key contributions of the author's model related to stages

| Area | Contribution |
|---|---|
| Stages apply to micro- and to macro-developmental change | The present cognitive stage and substage model of 25 steps can be applied to micro- as well as macrodevelopmental processes. It is a generic model that can apply to different developmental levels, stretching from moment-to-moment ones to life span ones and stretching from isolated, local acquisitions to global, cross-task/domain ones |
| Stages apply to progressive and to regressive change | Development is not always in a progressive direction, but can stall, go awry, or be regressive, too. I review briefly my work in rehabilitation, where chronic pain can appears be described in terms of regression according to the present substage model. Similarly, progress in therapy can be described in terms of growth through the substages |
| Stages apply to groupings beyond the individual | The 25-step model is phrased in generic terms, especially for its substage sequence. Therefore, it is potentially applicable to help describe and understand change processes nor only in the developing individual but also in any psychological entity beyond the individual person. One research suggestion would be to explore further the change in group or family dynamics according to the model |
| Stages apply to multiple areas of study | The change model presented is generic enough to apply changes in systems over history, changes in societies and in politics, evolution of behavior, and even changes in nonliving systems. I describe how the field of developmental psychology seems to have evolved through the substages of the present model |
| Stages apply to therapy | I present a simplified version of my stage model at the end of the book, and indicate it can be used to help clients in transition in therapy. Psychology is considered as the study of ways of living and therapy as a developmental process that can help foster optimal transitions to rejoining joy |

timescale (Granott & Parziale, 2002a, 2002b). Early Piagetians had considered microdevelopmental analyses, but now it is much more widespread (Siegler, 2006).

Morra et al. (2008) also discussed the distinction between continuity and discontinuity in development. Developmental continuity refers to gradual increments in cognitive and related capacity, rather than sudden shifts or spurts in qualitatively distinct acquisitions. Discontinuity refers not only to stage models of development

**Table 1.7** Summary of key contributions of the present work related to causality

| Area | Contribution |
|---|---|
| Developmental biopsychosocial | The causes and determinants of behavior are considered multifactorial. The author espouses a biopsychosocial model that is developmental and dynamic in orientation. For example, for the development of somatization, I have proposed a comprehensive, 100-factor biopsychosocial model. I note, as well, that a truly biopsychosocial model is also developmental, evolutionary, and personal, in the sense that the developing organism is a seat of active influence on developmental change. Another term for biopsychosocial might be bio-personal-social, to indicate that psychological processes include all three components and psychology is not separate from and interactive with the others but essentially defined by all of them equally and integrally |
| Legal | I have worked on understanding causality in the area of psychological injury and law. First, I have developed a synthetic model of product and process in legal causality. Second, I have proposed a combined biopsychosocial and forensic model of causality for use in dealing with the injured person. These ideas are presented briefly. There are similarities in the study of causality across disciplines |
| Gene co-opting/ Epigenetics | For the biological component of the causes and determinants of behavior, I describe some work in epigenetics. In particular, I present a model of epigenetic reaction range. In terms of evolutionary underpinnings to the five stages of the model, I present speculations concerning gene co-opting. Brain–behavior relationships are treated throughout the book |
| Nonlinear dynamical system transition mechanisms | Nonlinear dynamical systems theory provides the integrating framework needed to grasp the multiple components of causality and how they interact. I provide a comprehensive tutorial on the terms in the model, such as states, butterfly effects, attractors, and complexity. I propose a sequence of nonlinear dynamical transitional mechanisms that are seen to underlie the changes through the substages of the present model. They concern an evolution of increasingly complex attractors to complex adaptive systems and superordinate complex adaptive systems |
| Fractals | Fractals provide a universal, cross-level metric unifying diverse phenomena in development, and relating development to other change processes in different systems, including nonliving ones. For example, I proposed that development is a codevelopment, cofractal process involving core givers as activation–inhibition coordination fractalization buffers and evolution is a process of dynamic coevolutionary cofractalization Darwinism |
| Circular emergence | The concepts of circular causality and emergence in systems can be combined into one concept to help explain how change can spread within and through different levels of a system. The proposed combined concept of circular emergence is applicable to simpler systems right up to more complex adaptive ones. As a nonlinear dynamical systems transition mechanism, it itself can be explained in terms of the most basic of mechanisms proposed to account change in systems, that of activation–inhibition coordination. The latter concept has been proposed as one basic to the functioning and transformation of systems |

(continued)

**Table 1.7** (continued)

| Area | Contribution |
|---|---|
| Environment | I emphasize the relational, coconstructive, coparticipatory, transactional nature of person-context interaction in development. This includes understanding cognition as developing coschemes and co-operations in coappropriation and coeducational processes that speak to what is considered unique in our species – enhanced learning and enhanced instruction/teaching/education. However, the environment might provide a hostile, nonbuffering relational frame in which negative as opposed to positive learning could develop |

**Table 1.8** Summary of overall contributions of the present work to developmental psychology and the study of causality

| Area | Contribution |
|---|---|
| Neo-Piagetians on the value/validity of stages/substages | Different Neo-Piagetians have different models of the stages and substages in cognitive development, or their equivalents, e.g., with respect to skill development, domains. Aside from reviewing the major models in the field, I point out how they differ, the difficulties that they present, how the present model can help resolve them, and how some data and examples that they provide supports the present model even more than their own. However, these comments and critiques should not be taken as directed toward the value of the Neo-Piagetian enterprise. The concept of stages and substages might differ from one theorist to another, but we all agree that some form of a model having qualitatively different steps in development is fundamental to its understanding |
| Cognition/socio-emotional integration over multiple areas in development | Throughout the present work, I highlight the combined nature of cognition and socioaffectivity. For example, Piaget had described the development of cognitive structures, in particular. However, others have described the coordinated nature of cognition and emotions in structures that develop. In the present work, I highlight the parallels in Neo-Piagetian and Neo-Eriksonian development through the 25 steps of the present model, which cover the life span. For the hypercognitive mechanism thought to integrate lower-order structures in adapting to the environment, solving tasks, etc., I refer to them as cognitive/socioaffective complexes. I describe a model of the development of basic emotions that is tied to the development of the cognitive substages in the sensorimotor period of infancy. For attachment, I indicate that the internal working representations that develop are socioaffective in nature. I describe a model of the self that includes self-definitional and relational components, and misperceptions in these regards. For self-regulation, I describe an integrated cognitive-emotional product and process |
| Causality, product, and process in development | To understand any area of development and change, we need to understand the "what" and the "why," or the product and process. The present work addresses both aspects of development and change. A good understanding of causality requires good models in both areas. Causality is not only about transition mechanisms, genes, environment, and so on, but also is about what develops and changes. Good models of causality are synthetic in integrating understanding of product and process. The present work has aimed toward this goal. In addition, I develop the concept of "hot" and "cold" causality concerning whether individuals perceive that they have a sense of free will |

(continued)

**Table 1.8** (continued)

| Area | Contribution |
|---|---|
| Piaget and collective intelligence | Piaget has been marginalized in the study of development in many ways. First, many researchers in the field have put aside the idea of stages and substages in development. Second, Neo-Piagetians have altered his model at times to the point that his contributions are misunderstood or inappropriately diluted at these junctures. For example, he did consider the relationship between cognition and emotions, despite giving the latter secondary importance. This being said, the Neo-Piagetians have kept his work as a major focus in the field and those working more directly in the Piagetian tradition are still active. Researchers of both persuasions work together, and they expand their collective efforts into areas such as underlying areas of the brain that are involved in cognitive development and related socioaffective development. They apply contemporary models in nonlinear dynamical systems theory to the cognitive models that they develop. Piaget's *oeuvre* is continually expanding and is continually integrating other approaches, such as the Vygotskian and Eriksonian. The collective research and modeling efforts reflect the type of collective intelligence and brainstorming that I describe as taking place in the postformal period. We are on the cusp of a paradigm shift where Neo-Piagetians and Piagetians are helping lead the way in understanding development |
| Activation–inhibition coordination | A particular concept that I propose as having widespread value in both developmental psychology and other fields of psychology is activation–inhibition coordination. I have shown its ubiquity in the manual activity, hemispheric specialization, therapy, etc., and argued that it is widespread in behavior and in developmental processes, including in neuronal activity and brain processes. In addition, I have shown how it is found in genetic activity, in particular, epigenesis. Indeed, activation–inhibition coordination might be the essential binding mechanism in fractalization and its ubiquity in nature |

but also to changes in more local domains. Neo-Piagetian theorists have particularly concentrated on describing these qualitative shifts for local or specific skills, or at the microdevelopmental level. Morra et al. (2008) indicated that workers are modeling discontinuous changes in terms of nonlinear mathematical models (e.g., van der Maas & Molenaar, 1992, for general stage transitions; van der Maas & Jansen, 2003, for the specific task "balance scale problem").

## *Two Piagets*

### Introduction

Morra et al. (2008) described that there are two Piagets, the "logical" and the "dialectical." The "logical" Piaget viewed cognitive development as a sequence of stages that are defined in terms of "logical competence." The "dialectical" Piaget was concerned with the developmental transition processes that help generate new cognitive stages. The authors maintained that the "logical" Piaget has been "superseded some time ago." In contrast, the "dialectical" Piaget still "has great currency."

### Comment

It should be noted that the approach of the present work is that the "logical" Piaget still has "great currency" and has not been "superseded," but only supplemented and modified. Moreover, the approach of the present work is that the "dialectical" Piaget does not have "great currency" and has been "superseded." I exaggerate to some extent as a rhetorical device, but nevertheless, my argument is that Piaget's stage model is still fundamental in the sense that it is still at the heart of current Neo-Piagetian stage models. However, his "dialectical" model has been quite supplanted, or at least complemented, by nonlinear dynamical systems theory and related models in understanding the developmental process, and they can be referred to without reference to Piaget, per se.

## *Logical*

Morra et al. (2008) described how the 1940s constituted the period in which Piaget was most productive. In that time frame, he formulated his stage model that cognitive development takes place over four stages – sensorimotor, perioperational, concrete operational, and formal operational. For Piaget, each of the stages was viewed as characterized by "logical capabilities of growing generality and complexity." In particular, for operations that develop at the psychological level, Piaget considered them as internalized and reversible, having a logical basis. For example, Piaget (1972) wrote, "a psychologically equilibrated structure is, at the same time, a logically formalizable structure…. Logic is the axiomatics of the operational structures…" (p. 15; quote in Morra et al., 2008, p. 8).

## *Dialectical*

In terms of the "dialectical" Piaget, Morra et al. (2008) pointed out how Piaget had grappled with the transition mechanisms in development throughout his work. In 1975/1985, Piaget addressed the transition processes in development in terms of – equilibrium, multiple disequilibria, and reequilibration. He maintained that a cognitive system attains a state of equilibrium when it can assimilate objects in external reality to its schemes, or when it can accommodate easily these schemes to objects in reality. Systems are conservative and tend toward maintaining their equilibrium so that movement into a state of disequilibrium constitutes the first step in developmental progress. Reequilibrium is not a return to an anterior equilibrium, but the assembly of a new state of equilibrium.

Disequilibrium is set in motion by two types of disturbances or perturbations. First, objects offer resistances to the accommodation of schemes. Errors result from failure to accommodate, which leads to negative feedback. Second, assimilations might be insufficient and thereby provoke search for new information, leading to a process of positive feedback. Regulation results because the developing individual seeks to avoid a state of incoherence. The new equilibrium is short-lived, as it leads to new perturbations and disturbances, and the process recycles.

Piaget described three ways in which the developing person could react to disturbances and perturbations. First, the person might ignore the disturbance. This would deform the lack of fit of the object to the existing scheme. The compensation that would result would be only partially successful, and the equilibrium would be unstable. Second, the developing person could try to modify the cognitive structure, as described. Third, the developing individual could adopt an advanced reaction and anticipate possible variations in the problem at hand. Indeed, in this sense, perturbations and disturbances become variations with which to work rather than unsettling events. The manner in which the developing person can move to anticipations is by a "series of interactions between 'observables' and 'coordinations' or 'inferences'..." In reequilibrating, the developing person arrives at a state where there can be new observables and coordinations.

## Authors' Commentary

### Logical Piaget

In terms of the "logical" Piaget, Morra et al. (2008) stated that currently it is "widely recognized" that the logical basis that Piaget had understood as underpinning cognitive development through its various stages is inadequate as a developmental model. Indeed, Piaget (1974/1980) himself had recognized that his operational theory "is too strongly" related to models in classical logic, which can lead to "paradoxes" at the psychological level. Toward the end of his life, he was developing instead concepts related to a "logic of meanings" (Piaget, 1974/1980). Piaget and Garcia (1989) were attempting to develop a "psycho-logic" of meaning and related concepts, but they still were tying this new approach to concepts in his logical model.

### Dialectical Piaget

Morra et al. (2008) concluded that the nature of the regulation process in Piaget "remains rather indeterminate." They asked how repercussions come about. If there are gaps or lacunae in the child's application of existing schemes that produce errors in the assimilation process, how is it possible that the child can build new schemes? How does the concept of feedback help explain the construction of new schemes?

For Morra et al., Piaget provided an unsatisfactory answer to the question. First, the developing child cannot deal with everything at once so that he or she can only handle certain characteristics or elements. This creates negative pressure or "contradictions or incompatibilities," which lead to elements being omitted or repressed. These elements are the ones that lead to feedback. Therefore, perturbation or disturbance results from the "tendency for an element initially 'repressed' to penetrate the field of observables" (p. 116, Piaget, 1975/1985). The process of creation of a new structure takes place through a dialectical integration, where the whole goes beyond the elements involved.

Morra et al. (2008) asked the trenchant question, "Yet, what is it that confers on the 'initially repressed' elements the power 'to penetrate the field of observables,' to cause new coordinations and inferences, to expand the field of attention, to introduce new relations in the cognitive system and finally to provide a new, more stable equilibrium?" (p. 13). They concluded that the Neo-Piagetian program has shed necessary light on the causal mechanisms and development.

## Conclusions

In the conclusions of their work, Morra et al. (2008) examined the relationship between Piaget's original ideas and how they have evolved in the work of various Neo-Piagetians. On the one hand, I note that the evolution in the work of the Neo-Piagetians respected highly his contributions but; on the other hand, there is much variation in the approach of contemporary Neo-Piagetians in their modifications and elaborations of Piaget. Some of the issues on which they differ concern the generality and specificity in stage development, the continuity and discontinuity in stage development, the variability in development, individual differences in development, the place of working memory and capacity and speed in development, and the manner of interaction of maturation and the environment in development. Nevertheless, for Morra et al., the Neo-Piagetians agree that children possess cognitive structures and that they pass through developmental stages by way of equilibrations that are "minimally dialectic" in the Piagetian sense.

Morra et al. (2008) wrote an excellent review of Neo-Piagetian modeling and empirical research. They focused not only on the work of Fischer and Case but also of others not dealt with in the present book (e.g., Halford, 1978; Pascual-Leone, 1970). For Case and Fischer (and their colleagues), they devoted one chapter to each of them on their cognitive models. For their work on affect, they included it in another chapter. However, the Morra et al. book did not attempt to compare critically the work of Fischer and Case and their colleagues in terms of their models of stages and substages, which is the prime focus of the present work. For example, in comparing the theories in this regard they only mention that Fischer's model covers the childhood period in one stage but for Case there are two (p. 363). Morra et al. compared extensively many other aspects of the work of Case and Fischer, along with other Neo-Piagetians, and this book should be considered complementary to the present one. Another important, recent book on Piaget is by Müller, Carpendale, and Smith (2009), which is a "companion" work to his oeuvre.

### Interim Summary

Morra et al. (2008) described the work of Piaget in terms of the logical and the dialectical to represent his efforts in generating a stage model of development and the transition mechanisms that underlie their growth. The present work is dedicated to exploring the two Piagets, the one who created a stage model and the one who examined transition mechanisms in their development.

Another more general way of describing the stages and the mechanisms in development is to describe the products and processes of development, or the "what" and the "why." The two Piagets can be construed as attempting to specify the product and process in development, respectively. In the following section, I explore further the product what and the process why of development as I discuss the stages and causes in development. For the stages, I present an integrated transtheoretical model, in particular. For the causes, I present the biopsychosocial, dynamical systems, and activation–inhibition models.

## Product: The "What" of Development

### Stages Exist and Provide Critical Scaffolds

There is an ongoing debate in developmental psychology about the validity of stage models. Stages are discontinuous, abruptly appearing, qualitatively distinct steps in development that exhibit a degree of coherence and global organization over different domains in development. Alternative conceptions of development consider that development is quantitative, continuous, gradual, and modular so that it can be understood without recourse to stage models. The present work is avowedly stage-oriented and builds on the two basic stage models in development, that of Piaget for cognition and of Erikson for affective acquisitions [Erikson having modified the classic model of Freud].

Nevertheless, there is legitimacy in the criticisms leveled at stage models, and there are advantages of quantitative (nonstage) models. First, classic conceptions of stage models, at least in the cognitive tradition, cast them as too abrupt in appearance and monolithic in organization, with little room for individual difference. However, contemporary versions, such as in the Neo-Piagetian tradition, have created more flexible stage models that allow for – series of modular acquisitions in particular skills and also less general and less abruptly appearing forms. Moreover,

Neo-Piagetian models have been constructed to permit individual differences in cognitive development. The stages in these models are considered to provide scaffolds on which individual differences can emerge, based on the particulars of personal experience, participatory relationships, and contexts encountered.

### *Transtheoretical Neo-Piagetian Model*

The present model of 25 steps in development has been constructed based on the work of the Neo-Piagetians Fischer and Case, in particular. The tables in this section (see Tables 1.9 and 1.10) illustrate how the present model can accommodate their models and those of two other Neo-Piagetian workers, Commons and Feldman. Nevertheless, the present model is considered the axis that integrates the others, and furthermore, it can stand by itself. The transtheoretical model that integrates mine with the others also shows how the others are not as inclusive of the full scope of stages, substages, and ages included in my model.

## Process: The How or Why of Development

### *The Biopsychosocial Model*

#### Introduction

In contrast to the behavioral and medical models, contemporary psychological models of development and of mental problems or illness are broader in scope. For development, they consider causality in terms of multifactorial or multicausal systemic models. For health, they are referred to as biopsychosocial to reflect the multidimensional origins of the conditions involved (e.g., Johnson, 2007; Olson & Sameroff, 2009; Sperry, 2009). That is, in both cases, behavior is seen as an outcome of multiple influences, interacting synergistically, where it is difficult to single out one source or the other.

#### Biology

According to the biopsychosocial model, in the determination of behavior, especially where health problems are involved, there are always biological influences of one sort or another. In particular, this might involve genetically based factors or conditions, such as found in several types of intellectual deficiency in which genetic defects are primary factors. Other ways biology influences behavior and disease are less evident, but there are genes implicated in (a) schizophrenia and other major mental disorders or psychopathological conditions, (b) various personality

**Table 1.9** Transtheoretical Neo-Piagetian and Neo-Eriksonian model of development: stages, phases, substages, ages

| Young's 5 stages and 10 phases (2/stage) (Piaget indicated in parentheses) | Substages (5/stage) in phases ($N=25$) (and substage start ages[a]) | Combined 5 stages and 10 phases model (Young, Case, Fischer, Commons, Feldman) | Erikson's 8 stages[b] and 17 others added |
|---|---|---|---|
| Reflexive | | Reflexive | |
| Primary construction | Coordination (–9) | Primary | Distance |
| | Hierarchization (–4) | Reflexive | Nursing |
| | Systematization (–7) | | Outcome |
| Secondary extension/ elaboration | Multiplication (–) | Reflexive/orienting | Caregiving |
| | Integration (0) | | Emotional |
| Sensorimotor | | Sensorimotor | |
| Primary | Coordination (1) | Primary | Dyadic |
| | Hierarchization (4) | Sensorimotor | Trust[b] |
| | Systematization (8) | | Sociability |
| Secondary | Multiplication (12) | Sensorimotor/ representational | Autonomy[b] |
| | Integration (18) | | Interdigitation |
| Perioperational | | Perioperational/ representational | |
| Primary | Coordination (2) | Interrelational/ representational | Superordinate |
| | Hierarchization (3½) | | Initiative[b] |
| | Systematization (5) | | Identification |
| Secondary (concrete operational) | Multiplication (7) | Concrete operational/ dimensional | Industry[b] |
| | Integration (9) | | Role |
| Abstract (formal) | | Abstract | |
| Primary | Coordination (11) | Primary abstract/ vectorial | Consciousness |
| | Hierarchization (13) | | Identity[b] |
| | Systematization (16) | | Nurturing |
| Secondary | Multiplication (19) | Consolidated formal | Intimacy[b] |
| | Integration (22) | | Universal |
| Collective intelligence | | Collective intelligence/ principles | |
| Primary | Coordination (25) | Perisystematic collective principles | Postmetaphysical |
| | Hierachization (28) | | Generativity[b] |
| | Systematization (39) | | Catalytic |
| Secondary | Multiplication (50) | Periparadigmatic collective principles | Ego integrity[b] |
| | Integration (61+) | | Cathartic |

The combined, transtheoretical model presented in the table provides a coherent developmental framework in several senses. (a) First, it describes a 25-step model of development based on Young (1997) that is both Neo-Piagetian and Neo-Eriksonian. The 25 steps derive from a 5 stage × 5 substage structure. (b) In addition, I added to my model two phases within each stage in which the substages can be grouped (of the five involved, the first three are considered primary, the next two secondary). This procedure allows a more precise parallel with Piaget and also allows a clearer comparison with other Neo-Piagetian models. (c) The combined model is still built on my own, but the names of the stages and substages have been altered to make it more inclusive of the other Neo-Piagetians (Case, Fischer, Commons) and the phases reflect the work of Feldman. For example, for

(continued)

**Table 1.9** (continued)

Fischer, the terminology that he used has been adapted for three stages (first, third, fifth). For Case, in the combined model, he contributed to six phases (from the second reflexive one to the first abstract one). For Commons, both phases in the collective phase reflect his model

[a]The negative start ages indicate prematurity; the – age indicates birth; all age periods approximate

[b]The table presents only the first part of the two poles of each of Erikson's eight stages. The 17 others that I have formulated to complete the Neo-Eriksonian model are based on the corresponding cognitive substages involved and the interpolation needed to present a coherent scheme in the development of 25 steps in this portion of the model

**Table 1.10** Transtheoretical Neo-Piagetian model of cognitive development: integrating Young, Case, Fischer, Commons, Feldman

| Young's cognitive stage model | Substage phases (3 in phase 1; 2 in phase 2) | Combined cognitive stage model |
|---|---|---|
| Reflexive | | Reflexive |
| | Primary (construction) | Primary reflexive |
| | Secondary (extension/ elaboration) | Reflexive/orienting |
| Sensorimotor | | Sensorimotor |
| | Primary | Primary sensorimotor |
| | Secondary | Sensorimotor/representational |
| Perioperational | | Perioperational/representational |
| Preoperational | Primary | Interrelational/representational |
| Concrete operational | Secondary | Concrete operational/dimensional |
| Abstract (formal) | | Abstract |
| | Primary | Primary abstract/vectorial |
| | Secondary | Consolidated formal |
| Collective intelligence | | Collective intelligence/principles |
| | Primary | Perisystematic collective principles |
| | Secondary | Periparadigmatic collective principles |

Contributors

The basic structure of the transtheoretical model is based on the 25-step Neo-Piagetian model that I have developed in the present work. Neo-Piagetian models of stages and substages in development are based on Piaget

(a) All the models used to develop the transtheoretical one list in their models Piaget's sensorimotor stage

(b) Also, most use the term abstract for the formal stage described by Piaget

(c) In constructing the transtheoretical model, I found that each major Neo-Piagetian had something to offer. Case contributed the terms orienting for the stage before the sensorimotor stage. Also, he contributed the terms interrelational (preoperational), dimensional (concrete operational), and vectorial (abstract) for the stages after it

(d) Fischer contributed the term reflexive for the stage before the sensorimotor one. Also, he contributed the terms representational (preoperational and concrete operational) and principles (postformal)

(e) For the postformal period, Commons contributed the terms systematic and paradigmatic among the terms used for the four postformal stages of his model. Therefore, I grouped them and I used

(continued)

**Table 1.10** (continued)

the label "peri" for them, just as I did for the combined term that I created for the preoperational and concrete operational stages of Piaget

(f) As for Feldman, he divided each of Piaget's four classic stages into two phases: active construction and active extension and elaboration. I applied the idea to the present sequence of five cyclically recurring substages in development

Extrapolating from his work, I considered that the last two substages of multiplication and integration in the present model are especially extension/elaboration ones, compared to the first three, so I grouped them together into one phase. The first three substages involve coordination, hierarchization, and systematization, which can be considered substages of active construction (that prepare the way for the extension/elaboration that follows)

In the present conceptualization, there is not a one-to-one fit of Feldman's sequence with the present one; for example, for each of the preoperational and concrete operational phases, he proposed the presence of a construction and an extension/elaboration phase. However, in the present model I have collapsed preoperations and concrete operations into one stage, so could not adapt fully the work of Feldman. However, I do have construction and extension/elaboration phases for the combined perioperational stage

Construction

*Introduction.* In constructing the labels for the combined stage model, I modified two from my original model based on Fischer's model. For the perioperational stage of my model, I added his concept of it being representational. This fits with Piaget, as well, who also called the combined preoperational and concrete operational stages as representational. In terms of the postformal stage that I refer to as collective intelligence, Fischer refers to it as a stage involving principles, so that this term was added to the combined name for the stage

*Phases.* (a) In constructing the labels for the various two-step phases of each stage, I considered the model of Case for the reflexive stage in my model. Recall that Case referred to the initial stage of his model as orienting. I did not call the combined stage that I had formulated as reflexive/orienting, because the orienting component of Case's model appears to apply best to the secondary phase of the combined model, which relates to the period at and after birth in the first month of life. It made sense to label the first phase of the combined model as primary reflexive to underscore its quite basic reflexive nature, given its prenatal origin, and relative to the second more advanced phase

(b) For the sensorimotor stage in the combined model, I labeled the first phase, which covers the remainder of the first year of life after the reflexive stage, as the primary sensorimotor one. Both Case and Fischer had curtailed the scope of the sensorimotor stage as conceived by Piaget. In my model, I had resisted this, and kept intact the sensorimotor series of substages that he had described, except that I had placed the first one after birth as part of the presensorimotor reflexive stage. By dividing the sensorimotor stage into two phases, an opening has been created to arrive at a common solution that should satisfy all theorists involved. On the one hand, the first phase becomes the main focus of basic sensorimotor acquisitions. On the other hand, in the second phase advances are being made toward the development of representations in the next stage of cognitive development that begins at 2 years of age. Nevertheless, I still maintain that these sensorimotor representations, if I may call them that at this age, are grounded in perceptual-action sequencing, as Piaget had described, and they are not quite purely representational

(c) In naming the two phases in the combined perioperational/representational stage of the transtheoretical model, which starts at about 2 years of age, I considered together the work of Piaget, Case, and Fischer. For the first phase, I used the label interrelational/representational, which is consistent with the terms used by Case and Fischer, respectively, for this age period. For the second phase, I used the original stage name of Piaget, concrete operational, and I added Case's label of dimensional. Fischer does not have a separate step for this age period, as he included it under the rubric of his representational stage

(d) As for the procedure followed in constructing the terms for the two phases of the combined abstract stage of the present transtheoretical model, I used Case's term of vectorial to accompany the term for the first phase. I reverted to Piaget's terminology for the second, calling it consolidated formal. This is in keeping with my use of Piaget's terms in each of the second phases of the

(continued)

**Table 1.10** (continued)

prior two stages. In addition, Piaget had used the term of consolidation in describing how his sequence of stages can pass through transitions

(e) Finally, the process followed in creating the names for the first and second phases in the combined, postformal transtheoretical stage is especially based on the work of Commons. He described four postformal stages. Previously, I had shown that his work can be mapped onto my own by referring to them as substages, and by adding a substage between the first and second ones. In the present reworking of his model, I apply it directly to the combined postformal stage, as he is the sole theorist among the others who has elaborated a postformal model with steps

*Conclusion*. Each of the theorists cited have contributed through their models to the transtheoretical model that I have developed. This integrated model provides an axis to integrate their theoretical and empirical work. The present combined model remains the only one that can serve this umbrella function. It can serve this function because of its lifespan perspective of five stages, its five-substage recursive model, its tight organization in terms of age ranges, either using Piaget's original ones or splitting them, and its incorporation of parallel Neo-Eriksonian stages, among other socioaffective correspondences

Despite the value of the combined model, I do not refer to it after its initial presentation. It stands more as a model to explore given that the present work is based mostly on a careful analysis of the separate models of Fischer, Case, and Young

predispositions or disorders, such as neuroticism or instability in relations, (c) learning disability and other neuropsychological conditions, and (d) predispositions to anxiety, depression, and so on. In the biopsychosocial model, biological influences are seen to vary on a continuum from quite high risk to no or little risk, depending on the individual.

## Psychology

The psychological part of the biopsychosocial model refers to the personal resources that individuals possess, from their thinking processes to their personality, emotional, and social skills. What are peoples' long-lasting, enduring, and stable personality traits, dispositions, temperaments, and so on? How does personality and related variables influence health and behavior? How well can individuals socialize, recruit social support to help cope with stress, relate to people, solve problems, and so on? Do social skills moderate and mediate health and behavior? Stress is a constant in peoples' lives, but the manner in which they handle it varies from one person to the other, depending on their personal and social resources, their appraisal and coping capacities, etc. One finds individual differences in the degree of psychological skills in dealing with stress or, in inverse terms, the degree of risk to the effects of stress that individuals confront. Similarly, how much of a role does motivation play in health and behavior? We are not simply passive receptacles of biological and environmental influences on ourselves. Rather, in facing stress, we can be either more active or passive, with good self-confidence or less so, and determined to sufficient degree or not. Individuals vary in terms of what they bring to the stress equation along all these lines.

### Social

The social component of the biopsychosocial model refers to the influence of the wider environment on behavior. We are raised in families, go to school, work, socialize, get partners, raise children in our turn, participate in institutional life from the military to the religious, live in neighborhoods, receive messages from the media, live in a political society, and are imbued in general with cultural values, constraints, and directives. The environment is not monolithic, but is variegated and layered, in an ecological network. We transact with all these levels at all times and need to become aware of these influences. Once more, individuals are considered to vary.

### Comment

I have refrained from describing in depth all of the multiple influences on behavior in each of the three areas of biology, psychology, and sociology. In Young (2008), for the area of somatization, I listed 100 factors to consider in these three areas. These factors are summarized in tables in the last chapter of the book.

## *Systems Theory*

### Systems

In systems theory, the adage is that the whole is considered greater than the sum of its parts. For example, the sum total of the characteristics of the elements composing a system cannot explain the characteristics of the whole pattern to which they contribute. Also, any change in one area of a system influences change in others. System components interact with and reciprocally influence each other over time; that is, they interact with each other transactionally. Given the multiple elements involved in any system, they engage in a multiple, simultaneous interactions. The lower levels and higher levels of systems mutually influence each other, in a coordinated "top-down" and "bottom-up" process.

For systems theory, development is an emergent process constructed through the interaction of multiple parameters in a dynamical net. Moreover, development is seen to take place both at the moment-to-moment, microdevelopmental, local, task specific level and at the more global, macrodevelopment, cross-task, and over-age (stage) level. The former changes accumulate and come to mark the individual's cognitive development with time. They take on system-wide attributes not anticipated by the characteristics of the cumulative changes that develop in the stage at issue. Also, they might modify through the action of various control parameter components and begin the process of emergence into unique forms.

The pattern emanating out of the whole in a system precipitates out of its ongoing state structure in a self-organized manner, without external forces involved. The most economical, graceful, or adaptive alignment of the parts of a system builds as ongoing form. Therefore, abrupt changes to the state of the system might materialize due to self-organizational solutions to the perturbations, or system-disorganizing inputs, impinging on the extant pattern of the system at any one time. Novel, emergent, unpredictable solutions might obtain due to these self-organizational tendencies.

## Nonlinear Dynamical Systems

Systems theory includes traditional and more recent dynamic conceptions. The former includes homeostasis, feedback, and part-whole relations, whereas the latter includes sensitivity to initial conditions, the butterfly effect (where a small change in one part of the system can lead to major, abrupt changes in the system), catastrophic change, chaos, attractors, controlling parameters, far-from-equilibrium dynamics, circular causality, and complexity. Chaos in system theory language does not refer to the impossibility of change because things are so chaotic, but to the local unpredictability of system outcome despite global predictability because things are so complex to the point that anything can happen. For example, one positive component of the self, such as underlying self-esteem or optimism, might be improved only somewhat, but the result could be a major improvement in psychological outcomes such as more optimism about success, greater happiness, and increased empathy, beyond any level that could have been predicted by the one change. Therefore, systems both constrain how the parts are stitched together, but at times, even a minimal change in a part could be sufficient to cast the system into a new organizational frame.

## Development

The present work takes a multimodal perspective on factors involved in the transition processes in development. Piaget's concept of equilibration (assimilation, accommodation) presaged some of these perspectives, but in retrospect, it was clearly incomplete. Contemporary understanding of causality of behavior and transition mechanisms includes nonlinear dynamical systems theory, the specific concepts of which Piaget had not considered, such as attractors and complex adaptive systems. Moreover, contemporary science is elucidating groundbreaking understanding of how genes and environment interact in development (epigenetics), and these concepts were not available to Piaget.

What is the relationship between these two more recent models of causation and determination of behavior – nonlinear dynamical systems theory and epigenesis? Thelen and Smith (2006) indicated that earlier conceptions of epigenesis anticipated major themes in dynamic systems theory. However, they did not describe the particular gene–environment interactions now being described in the field. Nor did they describe aspects of complexity theory, such as complex adaptive systems. Nevertheless, my understanding of nonlinear dynamical systems theory indicates that its proponents would argue that although epigenesis specifies the biological and genetic–environmental interactions in development, a superordinate model is needed that encapsulates and explains the whole of the developmental process, with genetic–environment interaction being one of the constituents involved in the system. Therefore, given the characteristics of the nonlinear dynamical systems model, I maintain that the epigenetic model helps specify components of it, and the two are complementary, although the dynamical one is the superordinate one of the two models. In this regard, it is the one that is considered transdisciplinary.

## *Activation–Inhibition Coordination in Development*

In the present work, I also give prominence to the concept of activation–inhibition coordination, which appears to be involved in transitioning in development (Young, 1990a, 1990b, 1997; Young et al., 1983). In my research on manual lateralization with newborns and infants (e.g., Young & Gagnon, 1990), I appreciated that in reaching behavior the very young infant is already coordinating activation with inhibition to produce the exquisitely synchronized movements involved. The infant must somehow use nascent motor skills to direct toward the target, open the hand, and then grasp and manipulate. Inhibition stood out for me as the crucial controlling parameter involved in the sequence because there are so many possible interfering movements that could dysregulate the directed activity. Therefore, given the early manual specialization for the right hand that I found, I posited that the left hemisphere is specialized for activation–inhibition coordination over subtle sequences. The concept applies to left hemisphere specialization for language, as well, given the complexities in the coordination of activation and inhibition needed in producing speech. In addition, the concept of activation–inhibition coordination seemed one that could apply over multiple levels of behavior, brain, and mind, so I viewed it as a common metric that could govern different levels of the neurodevelopmental axis (Young, 1997). It also applies to the ebb and flow of complex social interactions, whether at the dyadic or group level.

In these regards, in the present work, I adopt the stand that activation–inhibition coordination is involved in the transition from stage to stage and substage to substage. I have posited that a nonlinear dynamical systems model underlies the emergence of stages and substages in the present model. At the same time, the metric that might serve as the common control parameter in the emergence of new steps in development could relate to this type of coordination, given that it describes a fundamental, common characteristic in the behavior, brain, and mind of the developing person and one's social relations in context.

## Summary

This first chapter of the book gives an overview of its major contributions. It presents the specifics of my Neo-Piagetian stage model and my approach to transition mechanisms. In particular, the latter relate to the biopsychosocial model, as well as to types of attractors, complex adaptive systems, and activation–inhibition coordination. All of these models and concepts are explained in depth in the chapters that follow. However, before beginning that process, in the next chapter I describe in detail the biopsychosocial model, which can serve as an umbrella model for understanding the developing person in context. Moreover, it allows me to introduce other major developmental models. The present work focuses on the developmental theories of Piaget and the Neo-Piagetians, in particular, along with that of Erikson. However, for the broader understanding that is needed to obtain a full grasp of development and where the various theories that I emphasize fit in, it helps to describe briefly other major developmental theories.

## References

de Ribaupierre, A. (2001). Working memory and attentional processes across the lifespan. In P. Graf & N. Otha (Eds.), *Lifespan development of human memory* (pp. 59–80). Cambridge: MIT Press.

Demetriou, A., Kui, Z. X., Spanoudis, G., Christou, C., Kyriakides, L., & Plastidou, M. (2005). The architecture, dynamics, and development of mental processing: Greek, Chinese, or universal? *Intelligence, 33*, 109–141.

Granott, N., & Parziale, J. (2002a). Micro-development: A process-oriented perspective for studying development and learning. In N. Granott & J. Parziale (Eds.), *Microdevelopment: Transition processes in development and learning* (pp. 1–28). Cambridge: Cambridge University Press.

Granott, N., & Parziale, J. (Eds.). (2002b). *Microdevelopment: Transition processes in development and learning*. New York: Cambridge University Press.

Halford, G. S. (1978). Toward a working model of Piaget's stages. In J. A. Keats, K. F. Collis, & G. S. Halford (Eds.), *Cognitive development: Research based on a neo-Piagetian approach* (pp. 169–220). London: Wiley.

Johnson, N. F. (2007). *Simply complexity: A clear guide to complexity theory*. New York: Oxford University Press.

Karmiloff-Smith, A. (1992). *Beyond modularity: A developmental perspective on cognitive science*. Cambridge: MIT Press/Bradford Books.

Lautrey, J. (1990). Unicité ou pluralité dans le développement cognitive: les relations entre image mentale, action et perception [Unicity and plurality in cognitive development: Relations between mental images, actions, and perception]. In G. Netchine-Grynberg (Ed.), *Développement et fonctionnement cognitive chez l'enfant [Development and cognitive functioning in the child]* (pp. 71–89). Paris: Presses Universitaires de France.

Morra, S., Gobbo, C., Marini, Z., & Sheese, R. (2008). *Cognitive development: Neo-Piagetian perspectives*. New York: Erlbaum.

Müller, U., Carpendale, J. I. M., & Smith, L. (Eds.). (2009). *The Cambridge companion to Piaget*. New York: Cambridge University Press.

Olson, S. L., & Sameroff, A. J. (2009). *Biopsychosocial regulatory processes in the development of childhood behavioral problems*. New York: Cambridge University Press.

Pascual-Leone, J. (1970). A mathematical model for the transitional rule in Piaget's developmental stages. *Acta Psychologica, 63*, 301–345.

Piaget, J. (1972). Intellectual evolution from adolescence to adulthood. *Human Development, 15*, 1–12.

Piaget, J. (1974/1980). *Adaptation and intelligence: Organic selection and phenocopy*. Chicago: University of Chicago Press. (Original work published 1974).

Piaget, J. (1975/1985). *The equilibration of cognitive structures: The central problem in intellectual development* (T. Brown & K. J. Thampy, Trans.). Chicago: University of Chicago Press. (Original work published in 1975).

Piaget, J., & Garcia, R. (1989). *Psychogenesis and the history of science*. New York: Columbia University Press.

Rieben, L., de Ribaupierre, A., & Lautrey, J. (1990). Structural invariants and individual modes of processing: On the necessity of a minimally structuralist approach of development for education. *Archives de Psychologie, 58*, 29–53.

Siegler, R. S. (2006). Microgenetic analyses of learning. In W. Damon, R. M. Lerner, D. Kuhn, & R. S. Siegler (Eds.), *Handbook of child psychology: Vol. 2. Cognition, perception, and language* (6th ed., pp. 464–510). Hoboken: Wiley.

Sperry, L. (2009). *Treatment of chronic medical conditions: Cognitive-behavioral therapy strategies and integrative treatment protocols*. Washington: American Psychological Association.

Thelen, E., & Smith, L. B. (2006). Dynamic systems theories. In W. Damon & R. M. Lerner (Eds.), *Handbook of child psychology: Vol. 1. Theoretical models of human development* (6th ed., pp. 258–312). Hoboken: Wiley.

van der Maas, H. L., & Jansen, B. R. (2003). What response times tell of children's behavior on the balance scale task. *Journal of Experimental Child Psychology, 58*, 141–177.

van der Maas, H. L., & Molenaar, P. C. (1992). Stagewise cognitive development: An application of catastrophe theory. *Psychological Review, 99*, 395–417.

Young, G. (1990a). Early neuropsychological development: Lateralization of functions – hemispheric specialization. In C. A. Hauert (Ed.), *Developmental psychology: Cognitive, perceptuo-motor and neuropsychological perspectives* (pp. 113–181). Amsterdam: North Holland.

Young, G. (1990b). The development of hemispheric and manual specialization. In G. E. Hammond (Ed.), *Cerebral control of speech and limb movements* (pp. 79–139). Amsterdam: North Holland.

Young, G. (1997). *Adult development, therapy, and culture: A postmodern synthesis*. New York: Plenum.

Young, G. (2008). Somatization, and medically unexplained symptoms in psychological injury: Diagnoses and dynamics. *Psychological Injury and Law, 1*, 224–242.

Young, G., Bowman, J. G., Methot, C., Finlayson, M., Quintal, J., & Boissonneault, P. (1983). Hemispheric specialization development: What (inhibition) and how (parents). In G. Young, S. J. Segalowitz, C. M. Carter, & S. E. Trehub (Eds.), *Manual specialization and the developing brain* (pp. 119–140). New York: Academic Press.

Young, G., & Gagnon, M. (1990). Neonatal laterality, birth stress, familial sinistrality, and left brain inhibition. *Developmental Neuropsychology, 6*, 127–150.

# Chapter 2
# The Biopsychosocial and Bio-Personal-Social Models

## Introduction

The present work emphasizes the Piagetian model and the work of Neo-Piagetians. In the present chapter, I try to place this work in the context of a metatheoretical frame and in relation to other major schools of thought in developmental psychology. I develop a model based on the biopsychosocial formulation, termed the bio-personal-social model. Surprisingly, I discovered that Piaget had written about a similar conceptualization.

## The Biopsychosocial Model and Medical Model

### *The Biopsychosocial Model*

#### Introduction

Models that reduce human behavior to especially one variable or a set of variables are called reductionist or mechanistic. First, they ascribe causality, determination, or origin of behavior to one prominent factor or variable (set). Second, they do so in a manner such that cause is considered linear or direct and also proportional to the intensity or other quantitative aspect of the factor(s) involved. Moreover, models such as this are considered dualistic, or divisive of the essential unity in the system of mind and behavior (as well as brain and sociality) that constitutes human behavior. Behaviorism is an example of a reductionist, mechanical model on the environmental side. The medical model is an example of a mechanistic one on the biological side. Both models consider the individual as passive before internal and external causal forces.

In the health field, psychologists adhere to integrated models of behavior and how it can become disturbed. Stress plays an important role in psychological models of health, chronic disease, somatization, and illness behavior or unexplained symptoms (Johnson, 2008; Martz & Livneh, 2007; Sperry, 2009; Woolfolk & Allen, 2007;

G. Young, *Development and Causality: Neo-Piagetian Perspectives*,
DOI 10.1007/978-1-4419-9422-6_2, © Springer Science+Business Media, LLC 2011

Young, 2007, 2008a). Others have been applying the biopsychosocial model to the developmental context (Olson & Sameroff, 2009).

## Mind–Body

In general, the mind and body always interact and represent a unity out of which behavior manifests. This is especially evident when problems arise with our health, for psychological factors might either retard recovery or accelerate it. (a) For example, recovery from physical injury could be influenced by degree of optimism, by coping skills, and by spiritual factors. Recovery might also be influenced by the ability to express emotions, which, in turn, is influenced by personality style, unconscious influences, and so on (Johnson, 2008; Sperry, 2009; Young, 2008b). (b) Anger facilitates cardiovascular disease, especially when it becomes dispositional in a hostile attitude, is coupled with time pressures, and so on (Kendall-Tackett, 2010a). Depression has been found to be even more of a risk factor for coronary heart disease than hostility (Frasure-Smith & Lespérance, 2005). Depression, along with stress, is involved in a complex synergism of mind, brain, and environment, including at the social level, in eliciting body inflammation and poorer health outcomes (Robles, Glaser, & Kiecolt-Glaser, 2005). (c) To some extent, the brain is plastic or modifiable after a traumatic brain injury, especially when a therapeutic regime is followed (Hart, 2010; Ricker, 2010). This is even truer for children. (d) Stress is capable of influencing health and chronic disease, as evidenced in the new field of psychoneuroimmunology (Kendall-Tackett, 2010b). For example, something as simple as a head cold might be affected by social parameters, such as social support, through explicit effects on immune system components (Cohen, Doyle, Turner, Alper, & Skoner, 2003). Also, wound healing is delayed in situations of stress (Kiecolt-Glaser et al., 2005).

## Illness and Therapy

For Sperry (2006, 2009), the best manner to treat chronic illness is by using the biopsychosocial approach. The mental health practitioner needs to understand the psychosocial components of the illness in question, as well as the state of disease progression, the level of impairment, the symptoms and their triggers, the client's perception of the illness, or its meaning, causal attributions about the illness, and so on. These biological factors cannot be separated from psychosocial ones because the factors form a web of systemic interactions. In treatment, all components of the illness need to be treated together for the client to make progress.

Sperry used rheumatoid arthritis (RA) as an example of a chronic illness that could be explained better by the biopsychosocial model compared to the biomedical or psychosocial models alone. RA is multifactorial in origin, and there are genetic predispositions, environmental factors, and personal factors involved. The medical model adheres to a dose–response relationship across pathophysiology, disease progression, and resultant disability. However, this linear conceptualization does not account for factors such as stress, personality, appraisal, coping, affect, and psychosocial functioning.

In the biopsychosocial approach to chronic illness presented by Sperry, coping capacity stands as the mediator between the effects of stress on the neuroendocrine system of the individual and disease exacerbation (Folkman & Greer, 2000; Lazarus & Folkman, 1984). If the appraisal of the individual is that a diagnosis of a disease cannot lead to improvement and that control of events lies outside the self, and so on, feelings of helplessness will persist and deployment of advantageous coping mechanisms will be minimized. Personality can affect appraisal for better or for worse. Examples of differing appraisals in people include differing degrees of optimism, neuroticism, and a sense of hardiness. Minor stressors that are chronically present could exact effects on the person with RA to the point that it facilitates negative progression of the disease (Walker, Jackson, & Littlejohn, 2004). This happens through cycles and feedback loops in a complex, dynamic, nonlinear process over time. Similarly, Johnson (2008) described a biopsychosocial approach to medically unexplained symptoms, an approach that integrates psychological treatment with medical care.

To conclude, behavior is a result of multiple factors that interact, and it is impossible to absolutely single out whether one factor, such as biology, is more important in understanding how individuals cope with stress, illness, injury, and pain. The biopsychosocial model affords an interactional perspective, placing the crux of understanding behavior and how it can go awry at the intersection of biology, psychology, and sociology.

Despite this knowledge that the body and mind interact, the predominant model of disease remains the medical one, where physical factors are considered primary in disease onset and maintenance. The medical model is a reductionist one that explains health and disease in a linear, mechanistic way, without considering the interactive effects of psychological and social factors.

## *The Medical Model*

Models of human behavior that attempt to separate mind and body are called dualistic and stem from the French philosopher Descartes. This tradition has led to the medical model where disease is reduced to (a) somatic, physical bodily processes and to (b) etiological mechanisms that can derange them, such as microbial pathogens and agents of injury. In the medical model, physical problems are thought to vary with the severity of the causal impetus, in a one-to-one correspondence, or in a dose–response relationship. Medical practitioners arrive at diagnoses of their patients' medical problems according to standard categories of diagnoses of disease. Moreover, for any one diagnosis, usually there are specified causes and, most often, there is only one cause or a small number of causes for any one diagnosis. The specific treatment(s) recommended for any one medical condition hinges on the specified cause(s). Psychology has little role to play in this model, and medical techniques, such as surgery and prescribing medications, are the treatments of choice.

The medical model of psychiatric illness or psychopathology follows the general medical model of disease, and it seeks physiological or biological explanations for the problems at hand. As well, it seeks physiological or biological solutions, such as through psychopharmacological treatment. It is a linear model where causal sources such as genetic defects or biochemical imbalances are thought to create psychological abnormalities.

**Interim Summary**

The medical model is a linear simplified explanation of health difficulties that excludes a role for psychosocial factors in health. The biopsychosocial model was developed to account for the multiple influences on health. In the area of development, multifactorial models are also prominent. Piaget is noted for his developmental stage model of development, but he also broached the topic of transition mechanisms and causality from many different angles. In the following, I show that he considered all the main factors in the biopsychosocial model. After considering his work and that of Overton (2004, 2006), this leads to the development of my own model, labeled the "bio-personal-social model."

## Piaget on the Social, Relational

### *Piaget and the Social*

Carpendale and Müller (2004) examined the social interactional frame in Piaget's theory. They distinguished between individualistic and collectivist approaches and pointed out that Piaget (1965/1995) elaborated a solution to the question of the relationship between individual and society. His model emphasized neither the individual nor the collective. He referred to it as "relational structuralism" (Piaget, 1970b/1973, p. 22). In this model, relations between elements of structure are primary, and they involve systems of interactions or their transformations. Therefore, he proposed that the collective is a "system of interactions which modify the very structure of individuals" (Piaget, 1965/1995, p. 42).

For Piaget, because of their relational origins, social and cognitive structures are continuously reconstructed. The child does not submit passively to social pressuring. Rather, the child "actively selects among available possibilities." Then, the child "reconstructs them and assimilates them in his [/her] own manner" (Piaget, 1965/1995, p. 33, 36). The child is constantly reworking his or her collections of ideas through his or her own activity and logical thought. Therefore, knowledge and meaning both derive from the child's constructive activity. Identical structuration processes are involved in the coordination of the developing person's actions and the coordination of actions of the individual with other people. Therefore, although individuals construct knowledge and meaning, they do so through cooperative interactions, which include the developing person achieving an understanding of the other's point of view. In sum, for Piaget: "rationality is essentially social in nature" (Carpendale & Müller, 2004, p. 15). Or as Piaget had noted: "social life is a necessary condition for the development of logic" (Piaget, 1965/1995, p. 210).

Kitchener (2004) noted that Piaget formulated a concept of "sociological relativism" as an intermediate point of view between individualistic and collectivist sociological concepts. This illustrates that the widely held view that Piaget ignored or underestimated the importance of social factors is a misconception. Kitchener (2004) noted that for Piaget, "the social is an essential factor in the development of knowledge" (p. 62). In this regard, Piaget wrote, "[S]ocial life is a necessary condition for the development of logic" (1965/1995, p. 210).

## *Piaget and the Relational*

Overton (2004, 2006) examined further the relational perspective on developing cognition. He argued that in conceptions in behavior, it is inappropriate to split related elements of a unity, such as self and other and mind and body. He termed his approach a relational metatheory one, and he opposed it to a split metatheoretical approach. Piaget was clearly committed to the "relational" approach. For example, he wrote, "Wholeness is a defining mark of structures" (1970, pp. 6–7). He also wrote in Piaget (1936/1952/1963, p. 10), "Every totality is a system of relationships just as every relationship is a segment of totality." For Overton (2004), Piaget described a dialectic of opposites that are indissociable coequals. For example, he wrote, "Knowledge, therefore, is neither S nor O but the interaction" (Piaget, 1977, p. 31; S = Subject, and O = Object).

## *Piaget and the Biological, Psychological, and Social*

Overton (2004) continued that synthesis develops out of opposites. Piaget (1995) argued for a broad synthesis of contributing factors to development. *Piaget wrote*, "everything in the individual is always at once biological, psychological, and social" (Piaget, 1995, p. 216). He maintained that psychology should not be assimilated to either the biological or the social. He also wrote, "[T]his does not mean that the psychological factor is negligible, however, because the existence of a *synthesizing factor* cannot be denied" (Piaget, 1995, p. 294, italics added by Overton, 2004, p. 31). Piaget offered that his theory is "person-centered."

Overton (2006) added that Piaget adopted an epigenetic explanation for the biological × psychological × environmental interaction (Piaget, 1967/1971, 1974/1980).

He conceived of the genotype–phenotype relationship in terms of the concept of the "phenocopy." In this model, phenotypic adaptations in the individual impact indirectly the genotype so that behavioral changes that result could be transmitted intergenerationally. Influences could be bottom-up or top-down over levels in the total system and concepts in nonlinear dynamical systems theory can help explain how this happens. In addition, the concept of equilibration, along with those of disequilibrium and reequilibrium, includes factors that work to affect intergenerational transmission.

## Piaget's Bio, Psycho, Social Legacy

### *The Biological, Psychological, Social Embodiment Model*

Overton (2004, 2006) elaborated these arguments by Piaget to create a synthetic model of biological, person, and cultural embodiment (see Fig. 2.1). For Overton, embodiment involves psychological processes being contextualized by the activity of persons with particular bodies. Our bodies precondition our psychological behaviors, experiences, and meanings. For Overton, embodiment is a relational concept. Pertaining to biological embodiment, Overton (2004) quoted Damasio (1994), who wrote, "Mind is probably not conceivable without some sort of embodiment" (p. 234). For sociocultural embodiment, Overton (2004) presented Boesch's (1991) notion of "The I and the body," which relates to cultural constructions. For psychological embodiment, Overton (2004) referred to the "person" as

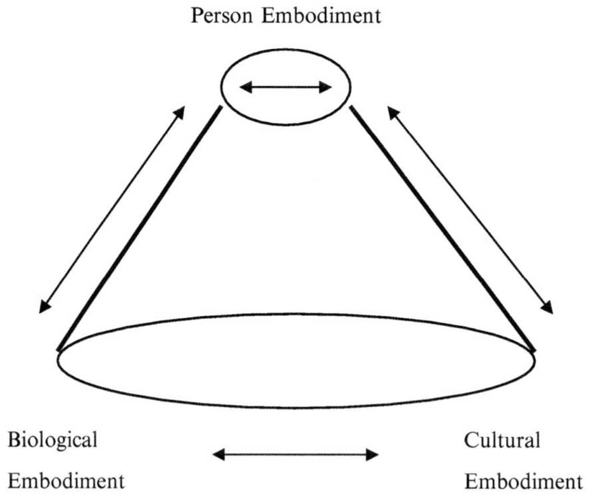


**Fig. 2.1** Embodied person, biology, and culture. The figure presents an embodied view of the person as acting with the physical form of the body in sociocultural context with her or his individual difference. Reprinted with the permission of John Wiley & Sons, Inc. Overton, W. F. (2006). Copyright © 2006 and John Wiley & Sons, Inc. [Figure 2.7, Page. 48]

an active agent having psychological components, such as executive function. He referred to Piaget (1970), who pointed out that the person is different from the agent, "Structures ... do not belong to the subject's consciousness but to ... his [/her] operational behavior, which is something quite different" (p. 68).

Overton (2004) concluded that the person and agent form a nucleus for mind, which, therefore, becomes a person-centered concept that emerges from "a relational biocultural activity matrix" (Overton, 2004, p. 37). Overton (2004) continued that, "mind bridges naturally to both the biological and sociocultural" (pp. 37–38). Overton (2006) added that as a relational concept, embodiment involves more than physical structures of the body. In addition, it includes the body as a form of lived experiences, which is actively engaged in the world of social, cultural, and material objects. I would add that the body is actively engaged in the world of psychological objects, as well. Overton (2006) maintained that the body as physical form refers to biological embodiment, the body as lived experiences refers to psychological embodiment, and the body as actively engaged in the world refers to sociocultural embodiment.

### Comment

I note that in the present model, mind does not emerge from a biocultural matrix, nor does it bridge the biological and the sociocultural. Rather, it is a coequal constituent as part of the person behaving with a certain biology in a certain context. I explain the integrated, interactive nature of the components of the present model in the following.

## *The Bio-Personal-Social Model*

### The Model

It seems logical to propose that the biopsychosocial model should be applied to normal development as well as disturbed development. The field of developmental psychopathology is based on the concept of a seamless relationship between normal and abnormal development rather than their separation based on the medical model (Cicchetti & Toth, 1995).

In this regard, there have been changes in terminology related to integrating the three components of the term biopsychosocial in describing normal development. As mentioned, Overton (2004) described the need for a relational developmental model integrating biological, personal, and cultural "embodiment." Recently, the biopsychosocial model has taken the form of a new interdisciplinary field, entitled "developmental social neuroscience" (de Haan & Gunnar, 2009).

In Young (2007), I described that Christopher (2004) had modified the term for the biopsychosocial model, referring to the "bio-psycho-sociocultural evolutionary perspective." This label includes in the term the ecological aspect of the person's environment as well as the evolutionary history of our species. For the model to address the cascading physical and psychological effects, it also should be described as dynamic. In order to be complete, any revised label of the term "biopsychosocial" should consider the developmental history of the person. Taking into account all these suggestions, while avoiding the creation of a too complex and clumsy term, I suggest that a better term for the term biopsychosocial might be the "*bio-personal-social* model." This term embraces the person as the active source of integration of the influencing variables derived from himself or herself, biology, and environment.

In the following section, I justify referring to the term "bio-personal-social" to refer to the biopsychosocial model in the normal context. It has the advantage of integrating normal and abnormal development under one umbrella term, and it serves to remove from the term biopsychosocial the very separation of psychology from biology and sociology that it tried to avoid.

## Advantages

An advantage of the term "bio-personal-social" to represent a critical, integrative model in psychology is that it removes the phrase "psycho" from the term. The presence of the term "psycho" in the term "biopsychosocial" creates a disjoint for the goal of the model to find an inclusive term to represent the various psychological and other influences in the expression of behavior. By using the term biopsychosocial, it might lend to lapsing into a Cartesian separation of mind and body, with one's psychology removed from the biological and the social. If the psychological portion of a psychological model is distinguished from the biological and sociocultural portions, conceptual inconsistencies arise because one might be led to believe that biological and sociocultural factors can stand apart from purely psychological ones. By using the term "bio-personal-social" instead of the term biopsychosocial to represent the influences on behavioral expression, the person himself or herself (and all his or her strengths, weaknesses, and individual psychology) is considered a critical component in the expression of behavior and how it develops. The term bio-personal-social emphasizes the agency of the person as actor in contributing to her or his own developmental trajectory in the context of the influences of endogenous and exogenous factors.

Despite the advantages of the term of bio-personal-social that I am recommending, the term "biopsychosocial" has gained widespread currency and is used in the present work for heuristic purposes in applied areas. However, when referring to development, in general, the term bio-personal-social is recommended.

## Interim Summary

I have traced the evolution of the medical model to the biopsychosocial one and proposed a generalization of the latter to the normal developmental context in terms of a revised bio-personal-social model. In the following, I examine the major schools of thought in developmental psychology from the perspective of how they situate with respect to the biopsychosocial, or bio-personal-social model. This serves to place the Piagetian model within the frame of the dominant theories in the field. Also, the exercise prepares the way for describing the history of the development of the theories from the perspective of the present stage model of development, which I describe toward the end of the book.

## Understanding Major Developmental Models in Terms of the Biopsychosocial Model

### *Introduction*

The three components of the biopsychosocial model – the biological, the psychological, and the social – are variously emphasized as the most powerful in the determination of human behavior. Generally, developmental theories are aligned more with one of the factors than the others. In the following section, I examine various models that putatively emphasize one or the other component and show that, in effect, there is always an interactive synergy described in them. Another goal of the section of the chapter is to list the major types of influences on behavior. The section included ten figures that provide an array of factors and how they are emphasized as primary as influences on behavior. The tenth figure in the series indicates how influences on behavior are multiple. From the biological and unconscious to the sociocultural and politicohistorical, and back to the individual who is active in her or his own development, wide-ranging and interactive forces sculpt and shape us as we grow, and in an ever-changing and dynamic manner.

### *Biological*

*Behavior genetics*. Adherents of the view that biology serves the predominant role in the development of behavior might undertake behavior genetic studies, with twins (for a recent special issue on behavior genetics, see Kremen & Jacobson, 2010). They examine the concordance in twins in a trait being studied, such as a particular temperament. To simplify, concordance refers to when both members of a twin pair express a trait, or when they both do not express a trait. Discordance refers to when the twins differ in the presence or absence of a trait. A role for genes in the determination of behavior is espoused when, in a study, concordance for monozygotic or identical twins is greater than concordance for dizygotic or fraternal twins because identical twins share the same genes, whereas fraternal twins share 50% of the same genes on the average, much like any pair of siblings.

However, concordance for behavioral traits in identical twins is never 100%, unlike the possibility to reach this level for physical traits such as eye color. Therefore, even for behavior with the highest concordance rates in identical twins, twin studies never support a purely genetic basis for genes in the determination of behavioral differences. Therefore, they do support an interactive concept between genes and environment in the determination of behavior.

*Evolution.* The most powerful biological model is the Darwinian one of natural selection (Cartwright, 2008). Natural selection involves the concept of "survival of the fittest." Fitness refers to the evolution of traits in species, whether the traits are physical or behavioral, because of the adaptive fit of the traits in the environmental niche in which individual members of the species possessing the traits find themselves. That is, some individual members of species possess physical or behavioral traits governed by underlying genes that help the individual members (phenotypes) survive and reproduce better than others in the species. The genes that are the focus of natural selection are passed on to the next generation and come to characterize the species over time, as other individuals do not pass on, at all or as much, their genes given their associated, less adaptive traits.

Therefore, individual species' members that possess underlying genes (genotypes) that help in fitness are passed on to the next generation, and they help offspring survive better and reproduce better. In terms of the present argument, we see that these traits that are passed on for their fitness possess adaptive characteristics for survival and reproduction in the *environmental* niche in which the individuals inhabit. Further, new species arise partly from this constant change in species' characteristics due to constant adaptation to changes in environmental niche over generations (although other factors are involved in speciation, such as geographic isolation of species' members so that they are freer to change without as much competition).

Because of the concept of environmental niche in understanding how natural selection works, we might ask whether biology is the most powerful influence in the process of Darwinian evolution, through factors such as gene action. Or could it be that the most powerful influence in the process of Darwinian evolution is the environment, or the niche, in which individual species' members attempt to adapt? As the environmental niche changes for individuals and species, different genes, which had been less widespread because they had been associated with less adaptive traits, become newly selected or favored. It would appear that in this evolutionary model of behavior, although, ostensibly, it is a biological theory, in reality, it is an interactive one, involving both genes and environment in the determination of behavior.

In another example, in the *ethologists*' concept of imprinting, a biologically governed rapid learning takes place during a critical period in the first hours of life in birds such as ducks. They learn to follow around the appropriate parental figure, ensuring survival, and eventual reproduction with conspecifics of the imprinted figure. The point is that neither biology nor learning is primary in the development of imprinting – both are involved even though ethology is typically considered a biological and evolutionary model (Fig. 2.2).

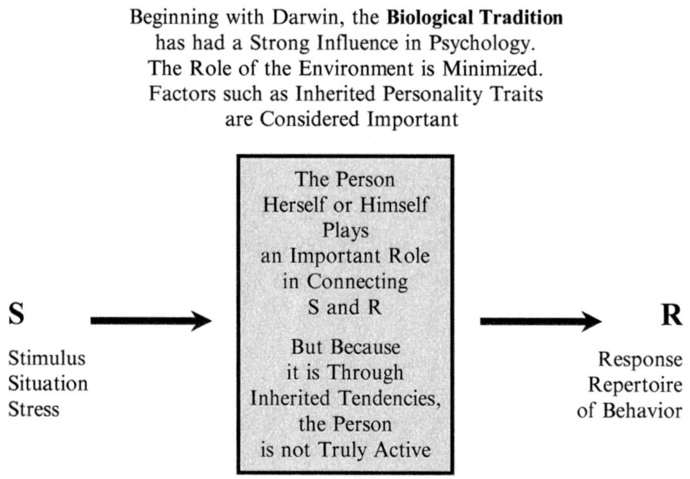


**Fig. 2.2** Nature (biology) influences. Psychologists generally maintain that behavior is quite influenced by heredity, genes, chromosomes, biology, physiology, and so on. In this view, even though there is little control of the person through the environment, the person is still controlled but by biological factors

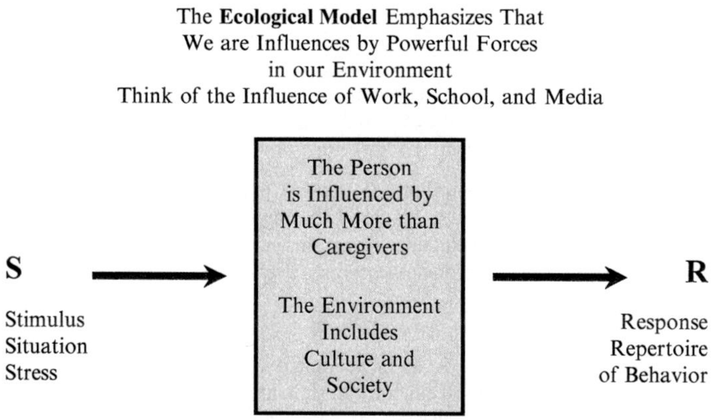


**Fig. 2.3** Ecology influences. Psychologists examine wider influences on the person, including social, cultural, vocational, political, and historical factors, such as work environment, discrimination, poverty, and government policy

## *Social*

*Ecological.* Next, I turn to the social component of the biopsychosocial model, and also query whether there is an interactive component involved in social models in psychology. The ecological model is a prominent psychological model emphasizing social factors in development (Bronfenbrenner & Morris, 2006; see Fig. 2.3). It describes how there are different layers in the environment, from the family, to school and work, to the wider sociocultural world. At the same time, it indicates that at the core of development we find a biological being that interacts with the environment at these various levels. Once more, a model more aligned with one factor in the biopsychosocial grid is revealed to have several factors at work.

*Social learning*. In another example, social learning theory, with its emphasis on imitation as a social learning mechanism (Bandura, 1997; see Fig. 2.4), evolved from behaviorism, which had denied any role for factors such as the mental (see Fig. 2.5). However, imitation takes place especially when the observer is attentive

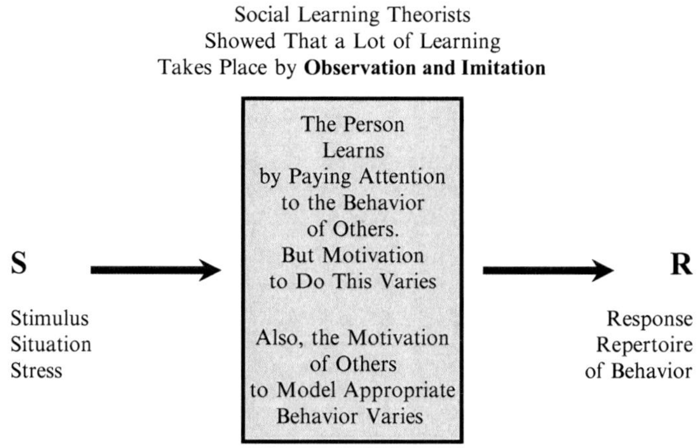


**Fig. 2.4** Social life influences. An influential view in psychology is that much behavior is acquired by imitating others who serve as models. Learning takes place not just by reinforcement or instruction. In imitating, learning is facilitated, and this creates self-confidence, a belief in one's ability to learn and, therefore, more efficient learning

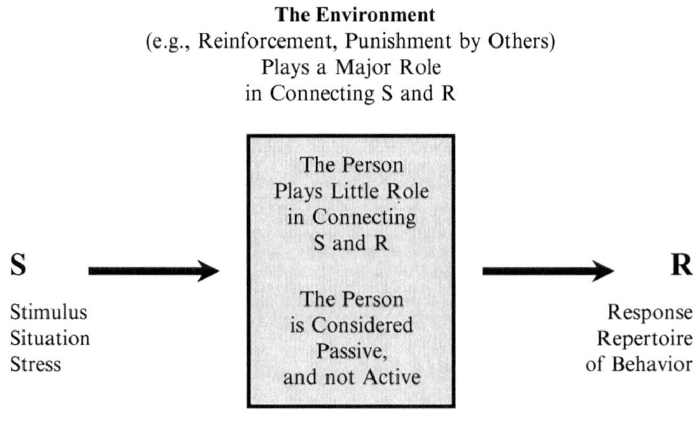


**Fig. 2.5** Environmental influences. Behaviorists maintain that behavior is the product of stimulus–response connections and how the environment modifies them. The person plays little role in this process. The environment controls the person

and motivated so that mental processes are involved. Thus, social learning theory might give the impression of being strictly environmental, but it recognizes the mental and personal, as well.

*Erikson.* In an additional example, Freudian theory has evolved from Freud's initial psychosexual theory to the psychosocial one of Erikson. Freud had emphasized unconscious and biological influences on behavior (see Fig. 2.6), whereas Erikson added that behavior is also a result of social mutuality. In addition, there are challenges involving social issues that materialize at each stage (e.g., the adolescent's quest for identity) (Blatt, 2008; see Fig. 2.7). Therefore, for Erikson, development is highly interactive in psychosexual and psychosocial factors.

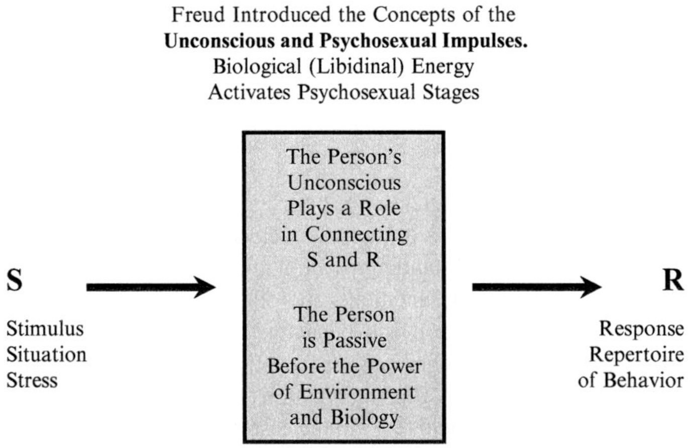


**Fig. 2.6** Unconscious emotional influences. Freudian-oriented psychologists believe that the unconscious plays a major role in determining behavior. However, the unconscious is still developed by what happens in the environment and is influenced by biological impulses. The person, again, has little control of herself/himself

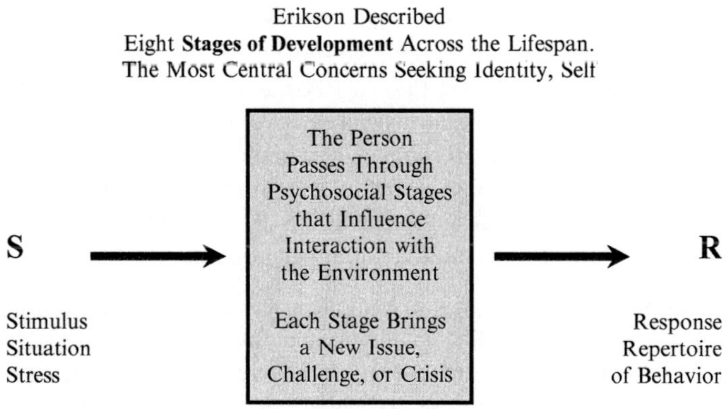


**Fig. 2.7** Self, identity influences. Some psychologists support stage models of development. In Erikson's theory, each stage brings a new challenge or crisis. For example, the first one concerns trust vs. mistrust. Piaget has developed a cognitive stage developmental model

*Vygotsky.* Another important psychological theory is the sociocultural one of Vygotsky (1987, 1993; included in Fig. 2.3). Children are viewed as learning from experts, such as parents and teachers. However, Vygotsky recognized that children learn on two planes or levels; first, they learn from the instruction of experts, and second, they learn from what they actually incorporate or internalize from that instruction. Also, children vary in terms of how much they can profit from expert instruction. Thus, in several ways, we see that the individual psychological structure of the child influences what can be learned. Once more, we see that a school of thought in contemporary psychology is intrinsically interactive in approach, no matter what ostensibly appears to be its primary emphasis.

## *Psychological*

### Cognitive and Related

*Cognitive therapy.* In this section, I describe both cognitive and socioaffective models that illustrate the interactive effects of multiple factors in development. At the cognitive level, a major way of understanding psychological influences is in terms of the cognitive schemas, models, representations, and other thinking filters that are interposed between sensory registration and behavior. Does the individual possess an equilibrated range of adequate cognitions, or have they been distorted, are maladaptive, or have otherwise gone awry? Can interventions that examine underlying thought processes and promote options help (e.g., in the case of depression can pessimism be controlled, and in the case of the injured person can catastrophizing be better managed; Young, Rygh, Weinberger, & Beck, 2008; Young, 2008a,b, respectively)?

*Piaget.* Another prominent way of examining the psychological processes that govern individuals is in terms of the unfolding or maturation of these cognitive structures through stages in development (Piaget, 1983). For example, Piaget formulated a theory of cognitive development that emphasized stages, and in these stages, Piaget conceptualized that cognitive schemas or structures change as they pass through the various stages (see Fig. 2.8). Aside from his maturational perspective, Piaget viewed the child as intrinsically active, curious, and constructive of cognitive structures. In addition, for Piaget, children can learn very well for certain problems when they try to resolve problems in communication among themselves (and without much guidance from teachers). As the present book demonstrates, Neo-Piagetians continue in this multifactorial perspective.

*Information processing.* Other cognitive models are also interactive. For example, the information-processing model maintains that we function like computers in analyzing input to prepare the output of an adaptive response (Siegler, Deloache, & Eisenberg, 2010). We have cognitive skills that we use, and rely on memory processes, including that of working memory that pulls out of storage what is needed to solve problems. However, at the same time, individuals vary in their motivation,

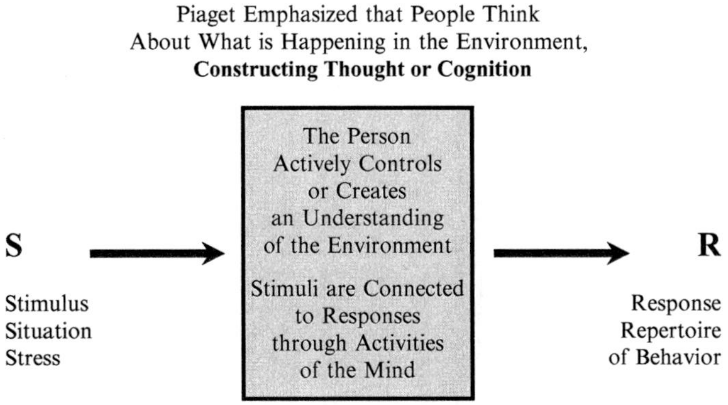


**Fig. 2.8** Thinking (mind) influences. Cognitive psychologists believe that we create thoughts, ideas, concepts, representations, abstract notions, schemata, models, and so on, which influence how we perceive and interpret the world and influence our response to it

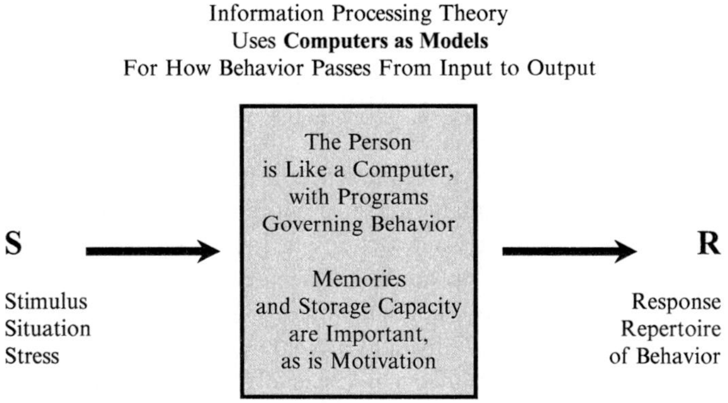


**Fig. 2.9** Machine, memory, motivation influences. Information processing models affirm that we can learn how people think through the analogy of computer hardware and software. It adds that people may be motivated to pay attention and to learn in differing degrees

attentional, and memory capacities, the quality of their "computer programs," and so on (see Fig. 2.9). This illustrates that there are multiple influences that affect behavior in this model, from "computer hardware" to personal factors, such as motivation, and to quality of instruction.

## Socioaffective

*Attachment.* As for socioaffective development, attachment theory proposes that we have an innate ability due to our biology to form internal working models of the self and of the other and that they govern our attachments to other people

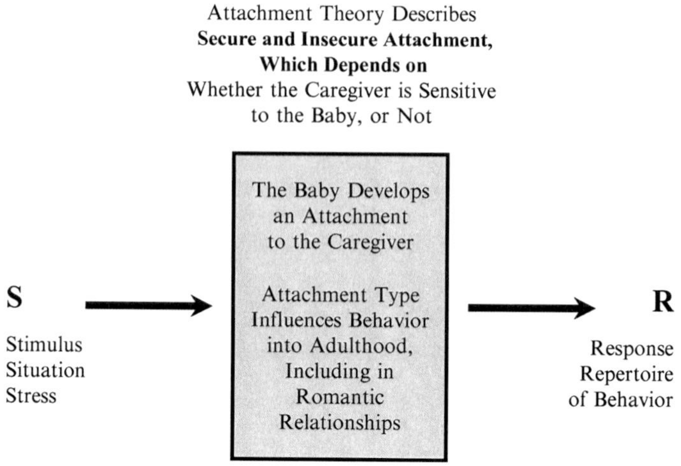


**Fig. 2.10** Nurture, care influences. Psychologists in the attachment tradition look for patterns in relating to romantic partners that are based on early experiences that individuals have had with their caregivers. Attachments can be secure or insecure

(Cassidy & Shaver, 2008; see Fig. 2.10). The theory posits a biological origin to attachment, lying in our evolutionary need to be close or in contact to our caregivers when we are young. However, at the same time, the theory indicates that the quality of attachment varies with the quality of sensitivity in early caregiving that infants receive. Experience in our early interactions in life molds whether the internal working models that we develop are of the secure or insecure kind. Moreover, generally we carry forward these internal working models into our adult life, and they influence how we interact with adults around us, especially with our romantic partners. Therefore, attachment theory is especially interactive in its conceptualization of human behavior.

## *Conclusions*

This brief tour of the separate biological, psychological, and social components of the biopsychosocial model has emphasized that no matter how every component is conceived or how much they are considered primary, they relate in an interactive way to the other components. Behavior and its change are always genuine multiplicative composites of all three components. The systems model (e.g., Thelen & Smith, 2006), presented in the prior chapter, perhaps best captures this complexity in human behavior, for it does not place a limit on the number of elements and layers that interact to produce behavior, and presents a refined view of how behavior can emerge out of systems in context, including influences from the past.

To conclude, there are psychological models, such as the systems and biopsychosocial models, which are intrinsically integrative. They view all the various

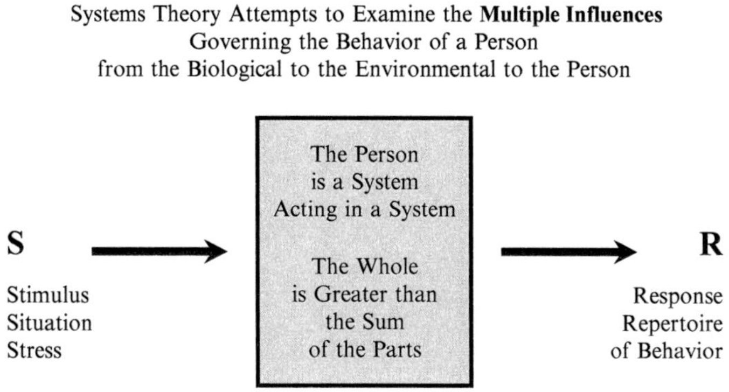


**Fig. 2.11** Multiple influences. A growing perspective seeks the dynamic changes in behavior that result from the multiple influences on behavior. New patterns of behavior can emerge that cannot be predicted by past behavior or from the sum of the parts or influences involved

factors involved in development as mutually interacting and influential (see Fig. 2.11). They realize that one cannot really divorce the biological and the social from the psychological.

Because of their fundamental similarities, the biopsychosocial model, systems theory, and the multicausal approach to behavior are all especially valuable in understanding individual differences in developing behavior. At any one moment in time, there are multiple factors that coalesce to produce ongoing behavior to contextual demands. Behavior emerges out of the ensemble of elements impinging on the person, whether vestigial from the past, in the present, or anticipatory toward the future, whether biological, psychological, or social, and whether interior, or exterior, either immediately contextual or from the wider ecological context. There are so many elements converging on and constituting the person that innumerable individual differences develop in our life course, behavioral history, psychological difficulties, and outcome. Models that diminish the multiple nature of the factors comprising the person and the origins of their psychological difficulties underestimate the complexity of human behavior, how it can get disturbed, and how it can recover in therapy.

The role of psychological factors in creating individual differences is important to psychologists. The role of the person in the biopsychosocial or bio-personal-social models of behavior should not underestimate the role that we play in our own development, the agency we constitute in ourselves, or the "active" as opposed to "passive" role that we have in our development (Piaget). What particular personality, temperament, character, style, attribute, thought process, coping mechanism, way of thinking, or cognitive filter does the individual bring into her or his own growth beyond the effects of biology and environment? Does the self contribute to its own growth beyond the powerful influences of biology and environment? Can individuals self-regulate the various external impacts and stresses on themselves, and control the effects of these on their bodily functions? To answer questions such as these, we need a developmental perspective. The book is aimed at providing answers to these types of questions from a Neo-Piagetian perspective, in particular.

We need to keep in mind that what biology allows, environment constructs. Moreover, as we grow, we can alter what has been constructed. *Biology may predispose, environments may dispose, but it is we who compose.*

## Summary

This chapter has surveyed the major approaches to developmental psychology from two perspectives. First, can a metatheory be described that encapsulates the various modes of influence on development? In this regard, I present the bio-personal-social model, which is a variant of the biopsychosocial model that is important in health psychology. In addition, Piaget had developed concepts similar to it. In the following chapter, I present in depth Piaget's model of stages in development. The second way major approaches to developmental psychology were considered in the present chapter related to describing the major schools in the area. They were related to their positioning in terms of the biopsychosocial model. The emphasis in the present work given to the theories of Piaget and Neo-Piagetians should not mask that all the major schools of thought in the area contribute to understanding the developing person.

## References


Bandura, A. (1997). *Self-efficacy: The exercise of control*. New York: Freeman.

Blatt, S. J. (2008). *Polarities of experience: Relatedness and self-definition in personality development, psychopathology, and the therapeutic process*. Washington: American Psychological Association.

Boesch, E. E. (1991). *Symbolic action theory and cultural psychology*. Berlin: Springer.

Bronfenbrenner, U., & Morris, P. A. (2006). The bioecological model of human development. In W. Damon & R. M. Lerner (Eds.), *Handbook of child psychology: Vol. 1. Theoretical models of human development* (6th ed., pp. 793–828). Hoboken: Wiley.

Carpendale, J. I. M., & Müller, U. (2004). Social interaction and the development of rationality and morality: An introduction. In J. I. M. Carpendale & U. Müller (Eds.), *Social interaction and the development of knowledge* (pp. 1–18). Mahwah: Erlbaum.

Cartwright, J. (2008). *Evolution and human behavior: Darwinian perspectives on human nature* (2nd ed.). Cambridge, MA: MIT Press.

Cassidy, J., & Shaver, P. R. (2008). *Handbook of attachment: Theory, research, and clinical applications* (2nd ed.). New York: Guilford Press.

Christopher, M. (2004). A broader view of trauma: A biopsychosocial-evolutionary view of the role of the traumatic stress response in the emergence of pathology and/or growth. *Clinical Psychology Review, 24*, 75–98.

Cicchetti, D., & Toth, S. L. (1995). A developmental psychopathology perspective on child abuse and neglect. *Journal of American Academy of Child & Adolescent Psychiatry, 34*, 541–565.

Cohen, S., Doyle, W. J., Turner, R., Alper, C. M., & Skoner, D. P. (2003). Sociability and susceptibility to the common cold. *Psychosomatic Medicine, 14*, 389–395.

Damasio, A. R. (1994). *Descartes' error: Emotion, reason, and the human brain*. New York: Avon.

de Haan, M., & Gunnar, M. R. (Eds.). (2009). *Handbook of developmental social neuroscience*. New York: Guilford Press.

Folkman, S., & Greer, S. (2000). Promoting psychological well-being in the face of serious illness: When theory, research, and practice inform each other. *Psycho-Oncology, 9*, 11–19.

Frasure-Smith, N., & Lespérance, F. (2005). Depression and coronary heart disease: Complex synergism of mind, body, and environment. *Current Directions in Psychological Science, 14*, 39–43.

Hart, T. (2010). Cognitive rehabilitation. In R. G. Frank, M. Rosenthal, & B. Caplan (Eds.), *Handbook of rehabilitation psychology* (pp. 285–300). Washington: American Psychological Association.

Johnson, S. K. (2008). *Medically unexplained illness: Gender and biopsychosocial implications*. Washington: American Psychological Association.

Kendall-Tackett, K. (2010a). Depression, hostility, posttraumatic stress disorder, and inflammation: The corrosive health effects of negative mental states. In K. Kendall-Tackett (Ed.), *The psychoneuroimmunology of chronic disease: Exploring the links between inflammation, stress, and illness* (pp. 113–132). Washington: American Psychological Association.

Kendall-Tackett, K. (2010b). *The psychoneuroimmunology of chronic disease: Exploring the links between inflammation, stress, and illness*. Washington: American Psychological Association.

Kiecolt-Glaser, J. K., Loving, T. J., Stowell, J. R., Malarkey, W. B., Lemeshow, S., Dickinson, S. L., et al. (2005). Hostile martial interactions, proinflammatory cytokine production, and wound healing. *Archives of General Psychiatry, 62*, 1377–1384.

Kitchener, R. F. (2004). Piaget's social epistemology. In J. I. M. Carpendale & U. Müller (Eds.), *Social interaction and the development of knowledge* (pp. 45–66). Mahwah: Erlbaum.

Kremen, W. S., & Jacobson, K. C. (2010). Introduction to the special issue: Pathways between genes, brain, and behavior. *Behavior Genetics, 40*, 111–113.

Lazarus, R. S., & Folkman, S. (1984). *Stress, appraisal, and coping*. New York: Springer.

Martz, E., & Livneh, H. (2007). *Coping with chronic illness and disability: Theoretical, empirical, and clinical aspects*. New York: Springer.

Olson, S. L., & Sameroff, A. J. (2009). *Biopsychosocial regulatory processes in the development of childhood behavioral problems*. New York: Cambridge University Press.

Overton, W. F. (2004). A relational and embodied perspective on resolving psychology's antinomies. In J. I. M. Carpendale & U. Müller (Eds.), *Social interaction and the development of knowledge* (pp. 19–44). Mahwah: Erlbaum.

Overton, W. F. (2006). Developmental psychology: Philosophy, concepts, methodology. In W. Damon & R. M. Lerner (Eds.), *Handbook of child psychology: Vol. 1. Theoretical models of human development* (6th ed., pp. 18–80). Hoboken: Wiley.

Piaget, J. (1936/1952/1963). *The origins of intelligence in children.* New York: International Universities Press and Norton. (Original work published in 1936).

Piaget, J. (1970a). *Structuralism.* New York: Basic Books.

Piaget, J. (1970b/1973). *Main trends in interdisciplinary research.* London: George Allen & Unwin. (Original work published 1970).

Piaget, J. (1974/1980). *Adaptation and intelligence: Organic selection and phenocopy*. Chicago: University of Chicago Press. (Original work published 1974).

Piaget, J. (1977). The role of action in the development of thinking. In W. F. Overton & J. M. Gallagher (Eds.), *Knowledge and development* (pp. 17–42). New York: Plenum.

Piaget, J. (1983). Piaget's theory. In W. Kessen (Ed.), *History, theory, and methods* (pp. 103–126). New York: Wiley.

Piaget, J. (1995). *Sociological studies*. (T. Brown, R. Campbell, N. Emler, M. Ferrari, M. Gribetz, R. Kitchener, W. Mays, A. Notari, C. Sherrard, & L. Smith, Trans.). London: Routledge. (Original work published 1965).

Ricker, J. H. (2010). Traumatic brain injury in adults. In R. G. Frank, M. Rosenthal, & B. Caplan (Eds.), *Handbook of rehabilitation psychology* (pp. 43–62). Washington: American Psychological Association.

Robles, T. F., Glaser, R., & Kiecolt-Glaser, J. K. (2005). Out of balance: A new look at chronic stress, depression, and immunity. *Current Directions in Psychological Science, 14*, 111–115.

Siegler, R. S., Deloache, J., & Eisenberg, N. (2010). *How children develop* (3rd ed.). New York: Worth.

Sperry, L. (2006). *Psychological treatment of chronic illness: The biopsychosocial therapy approach*. Washington: American Psychological Association.

Sperry, L. (2009). *Treatment of chronic medical conditions: Cognitive-behavioral therapy strategies and integrative treatment protocols*. Washington: American Psychological Association.

Thelen, E., & Smith, L. B. (2006). Dynamic systems theories. In W. Damon & R. M. Lerner (Eds.), *Handbook of child psychology: Vol. 1. Theoretical models of human development* (6th ed., pp. 258–312). Hoboken: Wiley.

Vygotsky, L. S. (1987). The collected works of L. S. Vygotsky. In R. W. Rieber & A. S. Carton (Eds.), & N. Minick (Trans.), *The collected works of L. S. Vygotsky: Vol. 1. Problems of general psychology including the volume thinking and speech*. New York: Plenum.

Vygotsky, L. S. (1993). The collected works of L. S. Vygotsky. In R. W. Rieber & A. S. Aaron (Eds. & Trans.), *The collected works of L. S. Vygotsky: Vol. 2. Fundamentals of defectology (Abnormal psychology and learning disabilities)*. New York: Plenum.

Walker, J., Jackson, H., & Littlejohn, G. (2004). Models of adjustment to chronic illness: Using the example of rheumatoid arthritis. *Clinical Psychology Review, 24*, 461–488.

Woolfolk, R. L., & Allen, L. A. (2007). *Treating somatization: A cognitive-behavioral approach*. New York: Guilford Press.

Young, G. (2007). Multicausal perspectives on psychological injury III: Conclusions. In G. Young, A.W. Kane, & K. Nicholson, *Causality of psychological injury: Presenting evidence in court* (pp. 187–196). New York: Springer Science+Business Media.

Young, G. (2008a). Psychological injury: Systems, change processes, development. *Psychological Injury and Law, 1*, 243–254.

Young, G. (2008b). Somatization, and medically unexplained symptoms in psychological injury: Diagnoses and dynamics. *Psychological Injury and Law, 1*, 224–242.

Young, J. E., Rygh, J. L., Weinberger, A. D., & Beck, A. T. (2008). Cognitive therapy for depression. In D. H. Barlow (Ed.), *Clinical handbook of psychological disorders: A step-by-step treatment manual* (4th ed., pp. 250–305). New York: Guilford Press.

# Chapter 3
# Piaget and Development

## Introduction

This chapter presents the grand developmental theory of Piaget, in terms of both its stage models and their transition mechanisms. It reviews his work on socio-affectivity in cognitive development. It considers the work of Piagetians who elaborated his work. They have shown the validity of his substage model in the infant sensorimotor period, for example, and its applicability to animal cognition.

## Representations and Concepts in Development

### *Introduction*

Müller and Racine (2010) explicated the constructs of (a) representations and (b) concepts, as understood in the field of developmental psychology. They explained that there are neither simple definitions nor a consensus on the nature of these terms, and in fact, there are opposing approaches that reflect opposite perspectives on the study of mind.

About representations, Müller and Racine indicated that there are various meanings for the term, but that they can be divided into two major frameworks. Representations can refer to either (a) presentational, perceptual, and direct varieties or (b) re-presentational and mediated varieties. By re-presentational content, the authors refer to content that had been given directly by perception but now denotes a standing-in-for relation and a reproduction by acts of thought. Therefore, the reference to the object that is denoted is mediated by some entity, such as a language symbol.

Müller and Racine (2010) noted that their approach to representation differs from those of others, such as that of Bialystok and Craik (2010). In the latter work, representation connotes a sense of mapping, and is equated with information and

G. Young, *Development and Causality: Neo-Piagetian Perspectives*,
DOI 10.1007/978-1-4419-9422-6_3, 

the storage of knowledge. For Müller and Racine (2010), representation involves a higher-order construct, in that it refers to intentional use of a stand-in referring to something other than itself. That is, for them, information and storage knowledge are not representational.

Given the intentional nature of the construction of representation, the authors underlined that the construction of representation involves human agency and is particular to the person undertaking it. That is, they adopt an active view of mind rather than a passive view. A contemporary passive perspective on mind is labeled the representational theory of mind (Heil, 2004). The views of Müller and Racine are more consistent with the active-mind conception of Kant rather than the passive-mind approach of other philosophers, such as Locke.

## *Representations*

### Piaget

Müller and Racine (2010) indicated that in Piaget (1936/1952/1963) two very different definitions of representation are evident. The first applies to infancy. Piaget referred to "nonsymbolic meanings," which are similar to the first type of representation mentioned above – that is, infant representations are more perceptual and direct in their representation. The infant creates meaning in an active way, but only by applying schemes to the world rather than by using symbols. Next, the child develops the capacity to represent in the sense of re-presentation and creation of symbolic meanings. This involves the capacity to use symbols and signs to represent an object that is not present. According to Piaget (1936/1952/1963), as children think symbolically, they are integrating schemes and symbolic representations.

For Piaget, symbolic representational thought requires "signifiers" and "signifieds." The former refers to representational items that convey meaning and the latter refers to the meaning carried by what stands as the signifier. Signifiers and signifieds are differentiated from their referents. For signifiers that form a system, Piaget used the term "semiotic function" to characterize it (Piaget & Inhelder, 1966/1969). The semiotic function subsumes both symbols and signs. He considered symbols (e.g., mental images) as "motivated signifiers" and signs (e.g., words) as "arbitrary and conventional signifiers." For Piaget, thinking involves the manipulation of symbols and signs.

In Piaget's approach, the signifiers and signs in the infant sensorimotor stage are not differentiated from to what they refer. Therefore, he used the label "indications" to refer to "undifferentiated signifiers." As for signifieds, in the sensorimotor stage, they refer to schemes that confer meaning. About symbolic representations, Piaget indicated that they develop in the second year of life by way of mental images. As the child develops, the symbolic representations take the form of deferred imitation, pretend play, and understanding invisible displacements in object permanence tasks.

### Baillargeon

Baillargeon (2004a, 2004b) has undertaken contemporary research on the development of early infant representation. Her methodology involves studying the looking behavior of infants, for example, in tasks having a violation of expectancy or impossible events. However, Müller and Racine (2010) indicated that this is not how the term of representation is used normally. They recalled that the term of representation normally is used to indicate a standing-in-for relation. They added that Baillargeon's concept of representation is consistent with the passive model of mind. In her paradigm, there is no intentionality or agent. Her model is neonativist and empiricist, such that the relationship between the infant and the world is extrinsic. By contrast, in Piaget's theory, the mind is considered active and the relationship that the infant establishes with the world is considered intrinsic.

## *Concepts*

### Models

As far as concepts are concerned, the classical view of concepts considers them as definitionally related (Müller and Racine 2010). In this view, features that are both necessary and jointly sufficient define concepts. The ecological view maintains that concepts are prototypes, in which categories are represented by whole summary descriptions. Prototypes include family resemblances and graded memberships. The naïve theory approach underscores that concepts are embedded in commonsense theories. This approach includes the concepts of "natural kinds" and essentialism. The naïve theory approach (e.g., Gelman, 2009) is the dominant one in contemporary study of conceptual development. However, Müller and Racine (2010) maintained that it reflects a passive conception of mind.

### Piaget

According to Müller and Racine (2010), the Piagetian approach (e.g., Piaget, 1945/1962) to understanding concepts in the study of development combines the best features of the other approaches. Piaget distinguished between practical concepts in the sensorimotor stage, which he referred to as action schemes, and prototypes at higher-order stages. For Piaget, the active child interacting in the world grounds concepts in activity. Concepts are considered as rooted in embodied sensorimotor activity (Mounoud, Duscherer, Moy, & Perraudin, 2007).

## *Conclusion*

Müller and Racine (2010) concluded their review of representations and concepts in development by pointing to three areas: distancing, social interaction, and differentiation/integration. For distancing, they noted that the child is able to develop symbolic representation because of the capacity to create distance between subject and object. Piaget (1937/1954) noted that distancing obtains from the twin processes of differentiation and integration – first, of action schemes in infancy and, then, of conceptual schemes in childhood. For Piaget (1936/1952/1963), as schemes are applied to objects in the sensorimotor period, they lose their ties to the objects and become more flexible, which allows for their coordination with other schemes. As for early symbolic representations, they develop out of pragmatic, communicative activities. About social interaction, Müller and Racine (2010) supported Carpendale and Lewis' (2010) relational approach. In that approach, the distinction between individualistic and social approaches to understanding mind is nullified in a combined model. About differentiation and integration, development proceeds from a relative lack of differentiation to increasing differentiation and integration. The authors concluded that representations and concepts should not be treated as if they had a life of their own, but should be analyzed for their functional patterns in development.

## *Comment*

Müller and Racine (2010) have disentangled a difficult area about the fundamental units in cognition, representations, and concepts. They have placed Piaget's work at the center of the field, consistent with the present model. For example, they indicated how his developmental model can accommodate both practical and symbolic representations and how his understanding of the child as active reflects the grounded, embodied nature of cognition. In the following, the work of Piaget is introduced in depth.

# Piaget

## *Introduction*

In the next part of the chapter, I examine more closely Piaget's basic approach to describing stages in development and their transition mechanisms. First, I provide the general approach that characterizes Piaget's account of stages in development (Tables 3.1–3.3).

**Table 3.1** Piaget's stages

| Stage (and age in year) | Represents (or has schemata for) | Knowledge constructed |
|---|---|---|
| Sensorimotor (0–2) | Current, available sensorimotor experiences e.g., represents smell, taste, touch, sound of sensory and motor acts | Physical knowledge e.g., suckables, lookables e.g., animate-inanimate distinction |
| Preoperations (2–6) | Concrete objects and events e.g., represents names and attributes of objects and events | Perceptual knowledge e.g., big-little; heavy-light; red-blue e.g., self-other distinction |
| Concrete operations (6–11) | Relationship between objects and events e.g., represents transformations; how objects and events are organized in series, classes, and dimensions | Logical (concrete) knowledge e.g., dimensions of number, time, and space e.g., conservation; class inclusion e.g., inner-outer worlds distinction |
| Formal operations (11–18) | Relationships between concepts e.g., represents variables, dimensions; how concepts, classes of events are organized | Logical (abstract) knowledge e.g., categories, systems e.g., analogies e.g., control of variables e.g., personality types distinction |


This contemporary presentation of Piaget's stages of cognitive development is noteworthy in several regards. First, despite variations in the number of stages in Piaget's model, even when he described it, it gives the predominant view that there are four stages. Second, the age periods provided are not always those of Piaget, for example, he typically divided the concrete operational period from the sensorimotor one at age 7. Third, the sensorimotor stage is described in terms of having representational capacities, but note that in this period these are tied to sensorimotor acts. Similarly in this regard, the columnar heading of representations is inclusive of schemata. Note that some of the terms are used in ways different from contemporary psychology, for example, "perception" is used to describe the representations acquired in the preoperational period

## *Piaget's Model*

### Approach

Piaget's theory is (a) constructivist, (b) structural, and (c) genetic or developmental (e.g., Ferrari & Vuletic, 2010; Morra, Gobbo, Marini, & Sheese, 2008; Müller, Carpendale, & Smith, 2009; Piaget, 1983). That is, the child is considered to actively construct the cognitive structures used, and they develop. This happens both in terms of local schemes or operations, but also in terms of their overall organization into stages.

In terms of constructivism, Piaget maintained that children construe actively their understanding of the world. Knowledge is not given, passively received, or a direct copy of reality, but is constructed by a probing interior mind, which increasingly develops a grasp of knowledge in keeping with external reality.

**Table 3.2** Different order of the stages in cognitive development in Piaget's works

| Stage | Substage | Ages |
|---|---|---|
| Piaget (1964/1968; cited as 1940 because first article in book dated as 1940) | | |
| Hereditary actions | | 0 |
| First motor habits | | <1 mo |
| Sensorimotor | | 1 yr |
| Intuitive | | 2 |
| Concrete | | 7 |
| Formal | | 11 |
| Piaget (1947/1960) | | |
| Sensorimotor | | 0 |
| Preoperational | Conceptual | 2 |
| | Intuitive | |
| Concrete | | 7 |
| Formal | | 11 |
| Piaget and Inhelder (1966) | | |
| Sensorimotor | | 0 |
| Concrete | Preoperational | 2 |
| | Concrete | 7 |
| Formal | | 11 |
| Piaget (1967/1971) | | |
| Sensorimotor | | 0 |
| Concrete | Preoperational | 2 |
| | Concrete | 7 |
| Formal | | – |
| Piaget (1970) | | |
| Sensorimotor | | 0 |
| Preoperational | 1 | 2 |
| | 2 | |
| Concrete | 1 | 7 |
| | 2 | |
| Formal | | 11 |

With material taken from Droz, R., & Rahmy, M. (1974). [Table 3, Page. 59]

Piaget first presented his cognitive developmental model in the 1920s (Droz & Rahmy, 1974). However, it is still very influential today, especially through the work of Neo-Piagetians, such as Case (e.g., 1985, 1992a–d), Fischer (e.g., 1980, Fischer & Bidell, 2006), and their colleagues. Piaget presented a model of four stages in development, but (a) he varied in the labels he gave them; (b) he was inconsistent whether there were four stages involved in development, or a different number; and (c) he was not consistent whether substages were evident in development, nor their number, as shown in this table

Piaget considered himself a genetic epistemologist rather than a psychologist, and his academic roots began in biology. He was more interested in how knowledge acquisition unfolds, and he borrowed biological concepts such as adaptation

This led him to describe that cognitive schemes are applied by the child to the problem at hand, and either assimilation results, whereby the scheme involved is not altered, or accommodation takes place, in which the scheme adjusts and changes to fit the task, and develops into a different structure. Cumulative changes take place in schemes through this process of alternating application of schemes and then change. However, shifts to new stages take place by additional mechanisms, such as maturation and reflective abstraction, which is a cognitive activity

Note that Piaget did not believe that the environment could have much of a role in cognitive development, except perhaps at transition periods. He thought that the cognitive conflict engendered in peer problem solving was a more effective means of encouraging cognitive acquisitions than formal instruction

**Table 3.3** Six substages in Piaget's sensorimotor stage in infancy

| Substage | Age (mo) | Activity |
|---|---|---|
| Reflex exercise | 0–1 | Sucking, looking, grasping, etc. |
| Primary circular reactions | 1–4 | Repetitive actions re body discovered accidentally (e.g., suck thumb) |
| Secondary circular reactions | 4–8 | Repetitive actions re objects discovered accidentally (e.g., shake rattle); seeks partially hidden object |
| Coordination of secondary schemes | 8–12 | Use one schema in coordination with another, e.g., means-ends; seek fully hidden object (but not if it is moved or displaced behind second screen) |
| Tertiary circular reactions | 12–18 | Lots of trial and error, e.g., altering means ends relationships accidentally, seeks hidden object behind second screen if sees displacement to it from first one |
| Inventing new means by mental combination | 18–24 | Plans in behavior in anticipate ends to means, but still with action component, seeks hidden object behind second screen even if displacement not visible |



Piaget described substages in the infant sensorimotor period that were quite detailed and that were based on sound observations of his own children. They illustrate the cognitive developmental structural approach, in which steps develop in a universal order, without skipping steps, and with each new step integrating prior ones

The sensorimotor substages are described as generalized structures, but with different specific domains, such as object permanence, causality, and means–end relationships. The ages given in the table are the typical periods of development of the substages for middle class children

Even though the first substage involves reflexes, they do not involve only spinal cord-mediated nonflexible varieties. That is, they involve exercise and modification of habits, such as sucking, looking, and grasping. Even though the last substage involves mental combination, this does not mean that the infant is in the representational stage, where action can be totally divorced from action. The substages involve an increasing complexity in behavior that witnesses the development of purpose from the start of a behavior, which indicates Piaget's emphasis that the child constructs the cognitive schemata that govern sensorimotor activity

As for structuralism, Piaget stated that the mental structures that filter, decipher, and form reality constitute integrated totalities of relations, called stages of cognitive development. It is well known that Piaget proposed that cognitive development comprises four major stages in development. They possess characteristics such as emerging in one sequence and without skipping of a step being possible. In addition, each stage integrates the stage that had preceded it.

In terms of genetic epistemology, these stages that Piaget described were considered to change with growth. First, they are comprised of simpler reflex-based schemes, and then they shift to become symbolic and logic-based structures. In arriving at a new cognitive (sub)stage, children do not undergo a total transformation, for there is a gradual spreading of the new ability throughout the child's cognitive repertoire. Often, within any one stage, a child can manifest several developmental sequences, each having its own time course, reflecting the different ways that different abilities develop. Piaget developed special terminology for both types of these time-based developmental regularities. Those that take place within a stage are called *horizontal décalages*. Similarities from one stage to the next are called *vertical décalages* (e.g., the infant's sensorimotor object concept bears resemblance to the concrete operational child's concept of conservation).

Note that Piaget considered himself a genetic epistemologist rather than a developmental psychologist. He focused on how knowledge is acquired through the cognitive structures that he described. He was less interested in individual differences, and described cognitive stages that he considered as universal, or similar in developmental progression across peoples, although rates of acquisition could vary. The environment had a role to play, for example, in training during transition periods, and in having children attempt problem resolutions together in order to provoke cognitive change. However, for Piaget, much of the stage sequencing that unfolded took place through maturational processes.

## Schemes and Schemata

*Schemes/schemata.* Piaget distinguished between schema and schemes (Cowan, 1978). In infancy, the latter are general, organized action systems that are iteratively put to use. For example, the infant possesses a grasping scheme that concerns more than one isolated grasp response. However, it is applied operatively, leading to combinations of movements without attempts to adjust it to the situation; that is, it is essentially assimilative, but changes or accommodations do occur. By contrast, schemata are more specific, accommodative, and figurative (matched to an external configuration, not operative). For the most part in the current work, when discussing the Piagetian school, I refer to both schemes and schemata without distinguishing them. Note that the Piagetian conception of schemata differs from the way information processing theorists approach the concept. In the latter view, schemata are generic representations that actively guide memory, cognition, etc. They can become conscious, unlike its conceptualization in the case for Genevan schemata. Moreover, they differ from the latter especially by their generalized attributes (Howes, 1990).

*Comment.* Note that the concept of schemes and schemata applies especially to the infancy period. These cognitive structures eventually transform into symbolic thought and logical operations. Also note that the infancy period is a particular one in that it is the only one for which Piaget had developed a comprehensive model of substages (six of them; see below).

In the Neo-Piagetian perspective, cognitive schemes are procedures or knowledge structures aimed at problem solving (Case, 1991). No longer are they defined uniquely in terms of sensorimotor programs or symbolic logic, and as part of stages or totalities cutting across all cognitive domains. Rather, they are viewed as local, specific structures defined by their form, complexity, and levels of hierarchic integration, with each capable of its own development.

Thinking and affect are not simply products of fixed mental or central generators, because each is dynamically constructed moment-to-moment in context. They are constructed in changing cognitive-affective structures, such as schemes and operations – from momentary, local ones to more integrated cross-structure ones, to substages and stages. In this regard, in Young (1997) I referred to cognitive schemes as co-schemes. Presently, I would add that cognitive operations should be referred to as "co-operations."

## Stages

*Structure.* Piaget described four major stages of cognitive development, with the second and third often grouped together, for example, as Representations. (a) In the sensorimotor period from birth to 2 years, infants derive knowledge of the environment by relating perception and direct action. At first, basic reflexes are used. These reflexes undergo metamorphosis into voluntary, organized patterns of behavior (schemes). (b) Next, 2- to 7-year-olds in the preoperational stage represent objects and events in the world by using symbols, words, images, and gestures. Mental processes become increasingly structured, but still lack complete fluidity. For example, there is egocentric perspective-taking and there is an absence of reversal in thought pathways. (c) Then, older children come to think logically in the physical situations confronting them by using "concrete" mental operations. These are interiorized action patterns that allow nonegocentric perspective-taking and reversibility in thought. (d) Finally, adolescents embark on abstract, experimental hypothesis-testing in their imagination, for example, when faced with abstract problems to solve, dealing with the possible, the future, etc. Piaget did not consistently use this model of four stages in cognitive development, but it is the one traditionally associated with him.

*Method.* Piaget maintained that by understanding errors of children's thinking strategies, a mirror is provided into their underlying cognitive structures. The preoperational child, for example, would fixate on one of the two dimensions in a conservation problem. In this type of problem, transformations take place at the physical level, and in order for the child to appreciate that the variable of interest has remained the same despite the transformation, the child must consider both dimensions involved instead of centering on one only (e.g., after an equivalence is established between two containers of water of equal shape and height of the water, the water is poured from one container to another of a different shape [lower but wider]; the child is asked if the water is still the same). Or, if the child is in the middle of a transition to the next stage of concrete operations, in answering questions about conservation problems, one and then the other of the two dimensions involved would be of focus, but not both simultaneously.

Piaget determined children's thinking strategies on these tasks by asking specific questions, in what he termed the clinical method. In this manner, he ascertained that conserving children not only understood that (a) the dimensions in conservation tasks involve a relationship of compensation, but they also could provide other types of logical justifications. For example, they might indicate that (b) the objects or items in the tasks remain the same despite the transformations (identity), (c) nothing was added or taken away (addition/subtraction), or (d) the actions can be reversed (negation; e.g., the water can be poured back into the original container).

*Comment*. Piaget considered all four logical justifications on conservation tasks equally probable, because they reflect an underlying structural logic and form a system; when one appears the others must also appear, reflective of the logical structure with which they are associated. However, Piaget did place special emphasis on the reversing or negation explanation, because he considered reversibility in thought as supreme evidence of logical thought in conservation testing, as well as on other concrete operational tasks, such as classification. Note that Young and Gouin Décarie (1977) studied the frequency of use of the four justifications in various conservation tasks, and found that the justification of negation was used the least frequently, even with clinical probing. This raises the question of individual differences in Piagetian cognitive development, as well as the value of conceiving stages in terms of having underlying logic-related structures with uniform properties.

Cognitive development is based on the gradual transformation of local schemes and schemata to the point that a critical mass is reached and a qualitatively distinct ensemble forms at the global level, ushering in a new stage. The so-called learning paradox is how this qualitative transformation to a new global stage arises out of local cognitive adjustments and advances (Boom, 2004). This leads to the question of Piaget's conception of transition mechanisms.

As for the concept of stages in cognitive development in the Neo-Piagetian perspective, there is no one universally accepted definition (Case, 1987). Current conceptions of stages in cognitive development might be in flux, but they do emphasize that stages are not extensive, all-encompassing entities; rather, they are more limited families of semi-independent structures liable to individual differences (Young, 1990; Young & Gouin Décarie, 1977).

## Transitions

*Equilibration*. According to Piaget, development progresses especially because of accommodatory adaptation of schemes, symbols, or operations after they fail in their assimilatory attempts on actions on environmental stimuli. The twin functions of accommodation and assimilation together constitute the major transition mechanism in development, that of equilibration. These functions take place simultaneously in any one cognitive act, buy usually they are represented as circular, reciprocal functions with each leading to the other (e.g., ACCOMMODATION <==> ASSIMILATION). However, cognitive development is spurred by factors other than equilibration, as well, such as maturation, as mentioned, and a process called reflective abstraction, which involves self-organization through meta-cognitive activity. Piaget espoused the fundamental proposition that the child is active in the construction of schemes through an inherent curiosity, energy, fuel, will, etc.

Morra et al. (2008) further described Piaget's conception of equilibration. For Piaget (1975/1985), disequilibrium benefits the child by creating the conditions for re-equilibration at a higher developmental level. Perturbations arise in two major ways. First, attempts at assimilation do not succeed. There is insufficient assimilation of reality by schemes. This leads to search for new information. Elements of the field that had been subject to assimilation are at first omitted or "repressed" if they do not fit the solution. However, they might emerge from the background (in Piaget's words: "penetrate the field of observables"). Second, attempts at accommodation do not succeed. Objects present resistances that result in failure or error. However, incoherence is avoided by the development of new forms as equilibrium is constructed.

*Comment.* How do new coordinations, inferences, cognitive relations or integrations into something new, and equilibrium form? Piaget never answered well this question. Even in his last writings on the topic (Piaget, 1983), he tried to describe a logic of "meanings" to help elucidate the quality of cognitive structures, but he tied his effort to the logical structures that he thought underpinned developing cognition. Note that Neo-Piagetians have rejected Piaget's emphasis on the logico-structural aspect of his stages for its lack of dynamic understanding of the child's cognitive construction skills.

### *Interim Summary*

Piaget had developed his model over decades, and it underwent numerous revisions, in terms of both his model of stages and his conception of transition mechanisms. These changes do not detract from his work; rather, they indicate an active and productive intellectual curiosity that produced the basis for the work of other Piagetians and of Neo-Piagetian project.

In addition to his focus on cognitive development, Piaget did consider the socio-affective side of development, although he gave it much less of his intellectual energy and time. This being said, careful examination of his contributions in this area indicates that they were not mere afterthoughts.

## Further Piaget

### *Piaget on Cognitive Socioaffective Parallels*

#### Affective Parallels

*Gouin Décarie.* Piagetians have been expanding their horizons, for example, by including emotions and culture in their work (Suizzo, 2000). In this regard, Gouin Décarie (1978) described Piaget's clearest statement on the relationship between the development of intelligence and affectivity (Piaget, 1954b).

According to Gouin Décarie (1978), Piaget held that cognition and affect are indissociable or inseparable domains, always present simultaneously and irreducible one to the other. Neither appears first in the unfolding of behavior. Affect provides the energy needed for behavior. Also, Piaget maintained that cognition and affect reflect a functional parallelism. This concept is exceedingly important for the present work, and I quote Piaget (in Gouin Décarie, p. 185):

> If our previous hypotheses are correct, we shall be able to parallel, stage by stage, the intellectual structures and the levels of emotional development. Since no structure exists without dynamic and since, respectively, a new form of energizing regulation must correspond to any new structure, a certain type of cognitive structure must correspond to each new level of emotional behavior (Piaget, 1954b, p. 10).

Gouin Décarie opined that the personality theorist Erikson is the theorist who should be used to show cognitive-affective correspondences, a notion entirely consistent with the approach taken present work. She presented a table from Piaget (1954b) that is acknowledged as difficult to get through (see Table 3.4), but inspection of it confirms that Piaget not only addressed parallels with emotions in cognitive development but also mentioned personality in this regard. In fact, the sentence that Piaget had used is quite like the approach of Erikson: Piaget had argued that the individual expresses "a role and goals in society."

A major principle in relating cognition and affectivity in Piaget (1954b) concerned the role of social interaction. Curiously, Piaget denied the importance of such interaction in infancy. Emotional contacts specifically do not "affect the intellect," in Piaget's understanding. The present work provides a model of the relationship between developmental steps in Piaget and Erikson, but also it indicates how basic emotions emerge in the first 2 years of life in parallel with the Piagetian substages in this period. Piaget did not deny a correspondence between cognition and emotions, and Table 3.4, which summarized his ideas on the relationship between cognition and affect, even refers to early reflexive emotions and later adult ideological ones. Therefore, what Piaget appeared to be arguing is that although emotions develop throughout the lifespan and provide the fuel for cognition, they do not help in its construction.

*Sokol and Hammond.* Sokol and Hammond (2009) explored further Piaget's notion on the relationship between cognition and affectivity. They referred to the 1954b Sorbonne lectures mentioned by Gouin Décarie (1978), where Piaget acknowledged that there is a correspondence in development between intellectual and affective structures, although the parallel cannot be "pushed too far." For example, Piaget also wrote in the same lecture that affectivity can alter the speed of intellectual growth, but not modify its structure. Moreover, he argued that affect is necessary for the "constitution" of the development of intelligence but not sufficient. The authors concluded that Piaget seemed to be saying that affective structures can develop "alongside" intellectual ones.

*Comment.* The present work takes a different stance in that it agrees with Piaget's initial principle on how cognition and emotions relate – that of indissociability. In this regard, throughout the present work I introduce concepts related to combined cognitive-affective or cognitive-social structures. Moreover, throughout the present

**Table 3.4** Parallel tables of the stages of intellectual and affective developments (Piaget)

| Infancy | |
|---|---|
| Sensorimotor intelligence (=nonsocialized) | Intra-individual feelings (accompanying every action of the subject) |
| I. *Hereditary baggage* | *Hereditary baggage* |
| Reflexes | Instinctive tendencies |
| Instincts (collections of reflexes) | Emotions |
| II. *First acquisitions* as a function of experience during first stages of sensorimotor intelligence | *Perceptual emotions* |
| First habits | Pleasure and pain tied to perceptions |
| Differentiated perceptions | Feelings of well-being and of uneasiness |
| III. *Sensorimotor intelligence* | *Elementary regulations* |
| (From 6 to 8 months until language acquisition in the second year) | (As defined by Janet): activation, braking, reactions of termination, with feelings of success or failure |
| **Childhood and adolescence** | |
| Verbal intelligence (conceptual = social) | Interindividual feelings (affective exchanges among people) |
| IV. *Preoperational representations* | *Intuitive emotions* |
| (Interiorization of actions in the form of thoughts that are not yet reversible) | (Elementary social feelings, appearance of first moral feelings) |
| V. *Concrete operations* (7–8 to 10–11 years) | *Interiorized social emotions* |
| (Elementary operations of classification and relationships = nonformal thought) | Appearance of autonomous moral feelings with the intervention of the will (the just and the injust no longer depend on obedience to a rule) |
| VI. *Formal operations* | *"Ideological" feelings* |
| (Beginning at 11–12 years, to be fully attained at 14–15 years): logic of propositions freed from content | Interindividual feelings combine with other feelings whose aims are collective ideals |
| | Parallel elaboration of the personality: the individual assigns himself a role and goals in society |

Reprinted with the permission of Springer Science+Business Media. Gouin Décarie, T. (1978). [Table I, Page. 136]

Piaget dealt rarely with the links between cognitive and affective development. He explored the topic in 1954 (Gouin Décarie, 1978), in a manuscript he did not even deign to publish. He considered affect the province of others, such as Freud. In his 1954 work, from which the table is taken, one can see that his understanding of emotions included that they reflect the corresponding cognitive stages with which they are associated. That is, emotions evolve from perceptual, to intuitive, to interiorized, to ideological; and in parallel with the development of the stages of sensorimotor, preoperational, concrete operational, and formal operations

Therèse Gouin Décarie (1962) and Peter Wolff (1960) were the first to write books on tying Piaget's understanding of cognitive development to affect. Neither questioned the series of stages that Piaget had proposed, unlike the case for the Neo-Piagetians. Gouin Décarie branched out to study affect more directly (Young & Gouin Décarie, 1977), and Wolff gravitated to study laterality and manual development (Young & Wolff, 1976; described in Young, Segalowitz, Misek, Alp, & Boulet, 1983). I carry on their comparative task in the present work, and incorporate their post-Piagetian research work I point out that each cognitive substage is associated with corresponding development of Eriksonian-type personality. Although I limited my model of the correspondences in cognitive and emotional development to the first 2 years of life, further work should be able to differentiate whether new emotions emerge at each cognitive substage. This process might take place throughout the lifespan, as Piaget himself seems to have surmised in 1954.

*Labouvie-Vief.* Labouvie-Vief, Grühn, and Studer (2010) pointed out that Piaget (1954a/1981) was one of the first developmental psychologists who rejected the division of cognition and affect. He reasoned that they are "entirely intertwined" in a unified system. Therefore, emotional development also involves the evolution of complex representations from simpler structures. In this regard, emotional development as much as cognitive development consists of a series of stages. The authors referred to development as elaborating "cognitive-emotional schemas" in which emotional structures and emotional representations are simultaneously cognitive and emotional. As they stabilize, these structures become crystallized, and these authors referred to the resultant structures as, "crystallized cognitive-emotional structures."

Labouvie-Vief et al. (2010) indicated how emotions evolve in the Piagetian stage model. In the sensorimotor period, feelings and emotion become linked to extensions of self and the other in time and space, so that they are less characterized by the here and now. The infant increasingly explores and engages in the world, becoming more intentional. According to Labouvie-Vief et al., in his theory for the infancy period, Piaget seems to be proposing the presence of primary emotional schemas. However, despite this emphasis, for the authors, Piaget (1954a/1981) seems to have minimized the interpersonal and intersubjective context relative to his work on cognition in this age period.

In the preoperational period, children are developing representative skills, such as language. These skills permit creation and storage of feelings and related structures in memory and in imagination. They lead to better perspective-taking of the other and to the development of a beginning morality. Piaget (1954a/1981) referred to these feelings as "semi-normative" because of their lack of stability.

In the next stage of concrete operations, feelings become more intentional and children use more "will." They can engage in social comparison, create social orders, and understand justice compared to injustice.

In the formal stage, adolescents develop abstract thought and they become highly interested in feelings and group relations. They develop ethics and ideals, as well as social and interpersonal standards. "Similar to Erikson, Piaget saw this period as pivotal in the 'formation of personality'" (Labouvie-Vief et al., 2010, p. 91).

As for the postformal stage, Labouvie-Vief et al. (2010) cited Labouvie-Vief's own research (e.g., 1984). She has proposed that some people come to develop unified ways of thinking about reason, emotions, morality, and life.

*Comment.* From Labouvie-Vief's work, we learn that Piaget had described specific emotional advances that corresponded to each stage of development. Her work emphasizes the indissociable nature of cognition and affect in structural formation in development, which is a view quite consistent with Piaget's.

In the following, the chapter switches gears to examine Piaget's thought on the relationship of cognition and sociality. Once more, Piaget is shown to be more than a cognitive theorist.

## Social Parallels

Kitchener (2009) examined the role of social interaction in the development of cognition, as described in Piaget's work. He maintained that the primary position held by Piaget was that the social plays a "crucial epistemic role." A recent exchange in the literature helps qualify the nature of Piaget's thought on the role of the social in cognitive development.

*Psaltis, Duveen, and Perret-Clermont* (2009). Psaltis et al. argued that the Piagetian approach is being expanded successfully to include a sociocultural framework. In their work, they underscored that the cognitive development of children needs to be situated in its social relational context. Children develop cognitively through "operativity-in-context" or the elaboration of cognitive operations in specific social situations.

The authors contrasted Piaget's distinction between internalization and interiorization, as described by Furth (1969). Interiorization refers to the creation of a general form of knowledge and, compared to internalization, it is the more important mechanism in cognitive development. Operatory structures develop primarily through reflecting abstraction – the child reflects on his or own activity and not just on the problem or task at hand. The child acquires operative knowing through this process as opposed to a simpler, figurative knowledge, which is associated with internalization. The child engages in a "circle of knowing" (Furth) through the cycle of assimilation and accommodation, leading to operative change.

The intellectual advance suggested by Psaltis et al. in this process concerns a role for symbolic resources being brought into play as the child engages in reflexivity. Societal institutions and contextualization become importance influences in the child's cognitive development. For example, they allow a broad set of social representations to develop. Development is not just about the child alone, but also about the child as a social psychological subject.

*Nicolopoulou and Weintraub* (2009). Nicolopoulou and Weintraub argued that Psaltis et al. (2009) have raised important issues, but have not gone far enough. They agreed that Piaget was an interactional reductionist and that development takes place in a sociocultural context, which Piaget did not acknowledge sufficiently. However, they argued that a proper conception of sociocultural influence should adopt the Vygotskian perspective. That is, the developing person should be considered as drawing out or pulling out cognitive resources from the social and cultural surround by an active process of appropriation. This process is not a passive one that is reducible to imitation or other social processes that lead to internalization. Rather, culture acts constitutively and collectively on the developing person, becoming embodied in the person by providing crucial conceptual and symbolic frameworks, models, and resources. In developing cognitively, the individual does not simply draw bits and pieces of information, tools of communication, or understanding of appropriate social roles and identities. Rather, the developing person organizes, evaluates, and reworks the symbolic representations in culture into the ongoing, evolving social representations in cognitive structure. The cultural representations become elaborated forms in the developing mind that are essential for human action and thought.

Piaget referred to social representations as "collective representations" that permeate the life of individuals and societies. They form systems, as do the social relationships of individuals. Nicolopoulou and Weintraub (2009) concluded that Psaltis et al. (2009) could expand their conceptualization of sociocultural influences on the developing person by expanding their conception of social representations and how they function.

*Comment.* It should be noted that in Young (1997), I developed an elaborate Vygotskian model of the appropriation process, and referred to it as "co-appropriation" because of its co-participatory and collective nature. In this regard, I am entirely sympathetic with the argument of Nicolopoulou and Weintraub (see Fig. 15.1, where the present model is presented in detail).

## *Interim Summary*

This brief literature review indicates that Piaget examined the development of cognition, in particular, but did consider the development of parallels in affectivity, and the social origins of cognition. Other Piagetians have expanded his work. Moreover, in the comparison of the Neo-Piagetians that I have undertaken in this book, we see that they all have considered the socioaffective ground out of which cognition develops. For example, I have developed a one-to-one correspondence across stages or substages in cognitive development and the corresponding optimal social stance needed to foster the child's cognitive/socioaffective, and related development (e.g., the self). In Chap. 13, I have offered guidelines related to the ideal scaffolding that the supportive environment could provide the developing child according to the present model of 25 steps in cognitive development.

In the next part of the chapter, I consider Piaget's ideas on whether the quality of thinking in the adult differs from that of the adolescent. Piaget had denied the need to describe a postformal stage. However, Neo-Piagetians have developed several different but complementary models of postformal thought. This work constitutes a major reworking of Piaget's stage model. The concept that I espouse is that the adult develops the postformal stage of collective intelligence.

## Adult Thought in the Piagetian View

### Piaget

*Piaget (1972).* In 1972, Piaget wrote an article discussing the development of intellectual thinking in adolescence and adulthood (Piaget). He maintained that the formal operations that develop in adolescence are also used in the adult period. He considered formal operations as represented by philosophical/mathematical combinatorial systems and the Bourbaki four-groups. Perhaps this limited his ability to conceptualize a separate stage of intellectual development in the adult, because his conception of development was not based on psychological underpinnings, in particular, but on logical structures derived from the study of logic and related areas. For example, he wrote that adolescent logic "...constitutes the essence of the logic of cultured adults and even provides the basis for elementary forms of scientific thought..." (p. 6). In reference to culture, he pointed out that apprentices in trades could reason hypothetically in their areas of specialization and so think in a formal abstract sense even if they could not resolve the experimental tasks set up in his laboratory.

*Comment.* In this quote above, we see two implied notions. First, formal operations are sufficient to provide a basis for the beginnings of scientific thought, but this leaves the question of how more elaborate conceptualizations arise. Second, we see that different environments can support the abstract logic involved in formal thought so that it is not strictly scientific. In my own model, I have adopted this grounded and participatory approach to understanding adult thought, because the postformal period that I describe has characteristics such that it is not limited to trained scientific and professional thinkers.

### Piagetians

*Marchand (2001).* Marchand reflected on whether postformal thought has been demonstrated in the theories and research to date. She maintained that Piaget argued that formal thought could be extended or "integrated into more extensive systems" (Piaget, 1955, p. 121). Marchand (2001) maintained that at best the hypotheses on the nature of postformal thought in the literature reflect either developments parallel to formal thought or its extensions. She indicated that there is no evidence to date of a "hard" or even "soft" stage in the adult period. She did see some promise in the work of Commons (e.g., Commons, Trudeau, Stein, Richards, & Kraus, 1998).

*Comment.* In the present work, I have incorporated the work of Commons into my own model of postformal thought. Moreover, I consider the postformal stage a "soft" one because it does not appear universally; rather, its development depends on cognitive skill, experience, and so on. However, unlike Commons, I maintain that postformal thinking is more prevalent than rare and the major reason is that it appears in daily life in many guises in the adult, such as those that Piaget described with apprentices in trades. Intellectual development is not tied uniquely to logical tasks presented in the laboratory but it is evidenced also by the work products of daily life, by the moral dilemmas and social situations confronted in daily life, and so on. We need better measures to get at these areas of study; but nevertheless the argument is that, theoretically, the development of postformal thought probably can take place for many people.

### *On Piaget*

Vidal (1994) republished two poems written by Piaget (1918a), when he was about 20 years of age. These works were preceded by one that Piaget wrote in 1915, where the task of the poet was described as an attempt to approach in verbal echoes the transcendent and ineffable "Idea" or vision of "All" resonating within the self. Because of the "unseizable" nature of these ephemeral entities, Piaget argued that the poet expresses them poorly and only in fragments. In another work published in 1918 (Piaget, 1918b), Piaget was more optimistic about the capacity of poets to gain proximity to supreme realities. He wrote of the "joy of systematizing" speculations "into a superior harmony" and "the divine joy of creating." Moreover, these joys were seen as not limited to poets (and musicians), for scholars and philosophers also could experience them.

### *Comment*

In my opinion, these different poetics in the young Piaget illustrate his personal transition from the stage of adolescent formal abstract thought to the adult postformal stage of collective intelligence, where "superior harmonies" or overarching perspectives across systems in thought are sought through a symbiotic sharing with the community. If I am correct, it is ironic that Piaget seemed to have touched this developmental cognitive unfolding in the adult period in his poetics but not in his science, where he did not see a new stage emerging after the formal period, unlike the case for contemporary Neo-Piagetians, including me.

## Piagetians Expanding

### *Introduction*

Piagetians continue to ponder the major questions posed by Piaget, such as on stages and transition mechanisms. They distinguish themselves from Neo-Piagetians by not proposing radical transformation of his theory.

## Stages and Substages

### Infants

*Cognition.* Desrochers (2008) described post-Piagetian research that supports the traditional Piagetian model. In particular, he examined the child's understanding of number and physical causality. It is beyond the scope of the present work to provide details of the research; however, it is important to emphasize that Piagetians are finding empirical data in support of Piaget's model. In this regard, for research in the sensorimotor period, Desrochers, Ricard, and Gouin Décarie (1995) created a series of tasks for the domain of causality that correspond to the six Piagetian substages of sensorimotor intelligence. They used the series of tasks in a longitudinal study of 25 infants observed at the ages of 6, 9, 12, 15, and 18 months of age. The results supported Piaget's description of sensorimotor causality as involving the substages that he described (Piaget, 1937/1954; see Table 3.5).

*Affect.* In research outside the Piagetian school, Lewis, Koroshegyi, Douglas, and Kampe (1997) undertook a longitudinal study of infants in the sensorimotor stage. They examined infants between 2 and 13 months of age on a series of tasks that were based on Case's (1985) model of the sensorimotor stage. The 4-month tasks involved grasping and looking, adjusting reach, a revolving object, and reaching and grasping. The 8-month tasks involved a hidden object, drumming, cloth pulling, and reaching for a third object. The 13-month tasks involved fill and dump, a tube with balls, a push and go task to get a desired action, and block building. The authors also gave a series of care giver separation distress tasks. They found that especially at 6 and 10 months, separation distress corresponded to higher sensorimotor scores. They concluded that cognitive performance and emotional responsivity might be related to individual differences in attentional engagement and self-regulation, with development as a moderating factor.

For our purposes, Lewis et al. found that infants passed the tasks appropriate to a given age or stage more than half the time (at 4, 8, and 13 months). The three age periods in Case's (1985) model for this time frame are consistent with Piaget's description of the sensorimotor period, and therefore offer support for his model. Second, Lewis et al. found that cognitive development and their measure of emotions were related in the sensorimotor period, which is consistent with the present argument that the two types of development are related and form coherent structures right from the beginning of life.

### Animals

Piaget's work has also been applied to comparative animal cognition. Pepperberg (2002) argued that the Piagetian framework could be applied adequately to diverse range of species, from parrots to primates. Doré and Dumas (1987) examined data in a range of animals on sensorimotor intelligence, preoperational performance,

**Table 3.5** Causality scale: procedure, stage, and criterion responses for each of the eight tasks

| Task | Procedure | Stage | Criterion responses(s) |
|---|---|---|---|
| 1 | A bell is fastened to a wooden board, or a rattle is presented to S within reach | III | Hits the object systematically<br>or<br>Performs a repetitive motor act during the pause following presentation |
| 2 | An object, which produces an interesting show, is activated by E in front of S, and kept out of reach. Once the object stops, E puts his/her hand within S's reach | IV | Touches E's hand lightly during the pause and waits |
| 3 | E drums on the table or snaps fingers, and stops abruptly, leaving his/her hand within S's reach | IV | Touches E's hand lightly during the pause and waits |
| 4 | E moves his/her fingers along S's body to amuse S, and stops abruptly, leaving his/her hand within S's reach | IV | Touches E's hand lightly during the pause and waits |
| 5 | A small mechanical T.V. toy is turned "On" and "Off" by pushing a button in front of S, out of reach. After 2–3 demonstrations, the object is given to S | V | Demands the toy by pointing to it between demonstrations<br>or<br>Takes the T.V. and gives it back to E or to mother<br>or<br>Attempts to activate or succeeds in activating the toy |
| 6 | A roly-poly toy in the form of a Mickey Mouse is set in motion by a gentle push. This task is presented in the same way as in task 5 | V | Demands the toy by pointing to it between demonstrations<br>or<br>Takes the object and gives it back to E or to mother when it is given to S |
| 7 | Four little wooden chickens are fastened to a board and set in motion by pulling a string. This task is presented in the same way as in task 5 | V | Demands the toy by pointing to it between demonstrations<br>or<br>Acts directly on the string while looking at the toy when it is presented to S |

| | | | |
|---|---|---|---|
| 8 | From a position behind S, E throws a ball, which rolls close to S | VI | Turns head and looks for E<br>or<br>Picks up the ball and gives it to E |

With material taken from Centre de Recherche en Neurosciences Cognitives and ADRSC-Assoc Diffusion Recherches Sciences Cognitives. Desrochers, S., Richard, M., & Gouin Décarie, T. (1995)

*Note*. Table 3.5 gives a short description of the procedure used in the eight tasks along with the Piagetian stage of causality that each one was meant to assess and the criterion response(s) that demonstrate that this stage was reached by the infant

*S* subject; *E* experimenter

Object permanence is taken as the marker of sensorimotor achievement. The infant comes to recognize that when an interesting object is hidden, it still exists and can be sought, for example, by knocking away what is hiding it. However, object permanence develops through the substages of the sensorimotor period, as do all the sensorimotor acquisitions. Another one relates to causality, and Desrochers et al. (1995) demonstrated both the steps involved and how they can be studied through a series of tasks with the baby. For Piaget, in both object permanence and causality in the infant, the acquisition does not develop until the third sensorimotor substage. Moreover, they do not develop exactly in tandem. According to Piaget, each stage or substage should manifest a "structure d'ensemble," or strict synchrony in development of its different domains, within the constraints of a horizontal "décalage," which are cross-domain variations in timing of emergence due to contextual and other factors

However, usually, the different tasks that should give similar results in Piagetian series are not as coordinated as Piaget would have predicted (e.g., Uzgiris & Hunt, 1975). Nevertheless, Case (1988) developed the concept of central conceptual structures to accommodate these types of data, thereby, in my opinion, preserving the critical components of Piaget's concept. Note that in their study, Desrocher et al. derived their sequence in the development of causality directly from Piaget's theory. Moreover, the data that they obtained demonstrated the integrity of the steps in the substages that Piaget described for the development of causality in the sensorimotor period. Note that for the sensorimotor "substages" described by Piaget, authors often refer to them as "stages," a tradition I have avoided and concrete operational tasks, where it was clear to them that the sensorimotor period of intelligence offers a fruitful avenue for understanding the intelligence of a wide range of species. There has been less research using preoperational and concrete operational tasks. Because of methodological limitations and inconsistencies in the data, they questioned whether primates are capable of concrete operational performance, in contrast to what some have maintained. The latter view is consistent with my own, as presented in Chaps. 15, 18, 26, and 32.

### Comment

Piagetians are expanding the type and range of data being gathered in support of Piaget's stage model. In the research with human infants and animals, the value of Piaget's original description of the substages in infancy has been underscored. Neo-Piagetians have not appreciated the integrity of this substage sequence, in general, although my own model is heavily based on it.

## *Transition Mechanisms*

### Piagetian Blueprints

Kesselring (2009) developed a model of cognitive structures within the Piagetian tradition that differs from Piaget's logico-structural approach. He emphasized that the child and adolescent create blueprints, patterns, or schemes in their cognitive interactions with the world and do not function from strict abstract logical structures that are all encompassing within a stage. A blueprint is a program for constructing or building something; it is not static or fixed but organic and evolvable. Blueprints function repetitively or iteratively by way of activity. Blueprints are auto-regulated and also they regulate cognitive construction processes. Blueprints change when the child or adolescent learns, so that each one is not a structured object or a product. Therefore, blueprints change gradually and increase in complexity. It is blueprints that develop, and not the structures; but they regulate the development of the structures. *There could even be blueprints regulating blueprints.*

With this modified Piagetian position, Kesselring (2009) maintained that there is no longer a need to pose the question of whether the logical and algebraic structures in Piaget's theory really exist in the developing person's mind. When we understand that structural systems are by-products of construction programs or blueprints, there is no need to adopt a logico-structural perspective on the development of mind. This being said, Kesselring cautioned that blueprints are not preestablished in the person's mind.

The author concluded that although structures are built up by activities regulated by blueprints, the construction in development of higher-order levels, stages, and substages requires more than blueprint construction and application. Nevertheless, stages are comprised of cognitive structures resulting from blueprint operation that form a unity. Within a particular level, blueprints do not coexist atomistically without being related to each other. Structural patterns emanate from blueprints.

But this does not mean that all of a blueprint's component structures are used all the time or even in the same way. Each blueprint is applied to different tasks in different ways. This means that a child will not succeed in the same way on two similar tasks. There are individual differences in this regard.

The set of blueprints changes over time and new patterns in the set develop and replace prior patterns. Therefore, a child or adolescent who moves into a new level of development is demonstrating discontinuity in that way in cognitive development; however, there is simultaneously continuity in the patterns of blueprints that are carried forward. That is, blueprints, their constructions, and integrating stages and substages might be related in development, but they are not isomorphic and universal, moving together in discontinuous shifting across all individuals. Furthermore, Kesselring argued that structures that had developed in one stage do not lose their significance later on, such as structures in sensorimotor intelligence.

### Comment

Kesserling's (2009) model of the development of cognitive blueprints speaks to the present concept of cognitive/socioaffective complexes, discussed in Chap. 17, that are seen to mediate cognitive acquisitions. They also remind of Demetriou's concept of hypercognition (e.g., Demetriou, Mouyi, & Spanoudis, 2010; Demetriou, Spanoudis, & Mouyi, 2010). The concept of blueprints could be complemented by addition of nonlinear dynamical modeling, which I have done in the present work for the concept of socioaffective complexes, as shall be shown. Note that Kesserling's theme that past-developed structures are not lost but can continue to influence cognition, even if they are sensorimotor in origin, echoes the work of Thelen (2008).

## Summary and Conclusions

Throughout the chapter on Piaget's theory, I have described current thought on his ideas, and offered my own. His stage model has been extensively revised by Neo-Piagetians, but the chapter indicates that his work on the sensorimotor substages should be preserved in their efforts. As far as I know, my Neo-Piagetian model is the one that respects that sequence the most. In addition, Piaget's conception of the transition process in development is based on the concept of equilibration, in particular. Piagetians and Neo-Piagetians have worked extensively on revising Piaget's ideas on this topic. The present work does so, as well. In terms of his ideas on the description of the relationship between cognition and socioaffectivity, Piaget had not given this aspect of development much prominence. However, in this area, his ideas were pointing in the right direction and my own model builds on them.

## References

Baillargeon, R. (2004a). Infants' reasoning about hidden objects: Evidence for event-general and event-specific expectation. *Development Science, 7*, 391–414.
Baillargeon, R. (2004b). Can 12 large clowns fit in a Mini Cooper? Or when are beliefs and reasoning explicit and conscious? *Development Science, 7*, 422–424.
Bialystok, E., & Craik, F. I. M. (2010). Cognitive and linguistic processing in the bilingual mind. *Current Directions in Psychological Science, 19*, 19–23.
Boom, J. (2004). Individualism and collectivism: A dynamic systems interpretation of Piaget's interactionism. In J. I. M. Carpendale & U. Müller (Eds.), *Social interaction and the development of knowledge* (pp. 67–85). Mahwah: Erlbaum.
Carpendale, J. I. M., & Lewis, C. (2010). The development of social understanding: A relational perspective. In R. M. Lerner & W. F. Overton (Eds.), *Handbook of life-span development: Vol. 1. Cognition, biology, and methods* (pp. 584–627). Hoboken: Wiley.
Case, R. (1985). *Intellectual development: Birth to adulthood*. Orlando: Academic Press.
Case, R. (1987). Neo-Piagetian theory: Retrospect and prospect. *International Journal of Psychology, 22*, 773–791.
Case, R. (1988). The whole child: Toward an integrated view of young children's cognitive, social, and emotional development. In A. D. Pellegrini (Ed.), *Psychological bases for early education* (pp. 155–184). New York: Wiley.
Case, R. (1991). *The role of primitive defenses in the regulation and representation of early attachment relations*. Paper presented at the biennial meeting of the Society for Research in Child Development. Seattle, Washington.
Case, R. (1992a). The role of the frontal lobes in the regulation of cognitive development. *Brain and Cognition, 20*, 51–73.
Case, R. (1992b). Neo-Piagetian theories of child development. In R. J. Sternberg & C. A. Berg (Eds.), *Intellectual development* (pp. 161–196). New York: Cambridge University Press.
Case, R. (1992c). Neo-Piagetian theories of intellectual development. In H. Beilin & P. B. Pufall (Eds.), *Piaget's theory: Prospects and possibilities* (pp. 61–104). Hillsdale: Erlbaum.
Case, R. (1992d). *The mind's staircase: Exploring the conceptual underpinnings of children's thought and knowledge*. Hillsdale: Erlbaum.
Commons, M., Trudeau, E. J., Stein, S. A., Richards, F. A., & Krause, S. R. (1998). Hierarchical complexity of tasks shows the existence of developmental stages. *Developmental Review, 18*, 237–278.
Cowan, P. A. (1978). *Piaget with feeling: Cognitive, social, and emotional dimensions*. New York: Holt, Rhinehart, & Winston.
DeHart, G., Sroufe, L. A., & Cooper, R. (2004). *Child development: Its nature and course* (5th ed.). New York: McGraw-Hill.
Demetriou, A., Mouyi, A., & Spanoudis, G. (2010). The development of mental processing. In R. M. Lerner & W. F. Overton (Eds.), *The handbook of life-span development: Vol. 1. Cognition, biology, and methods* (pp. 36–55). Hoboken: Wiley.
Demetriou, A., Spanoudis, G., & Mouyi, A. (2010). A three-level model of the developing mind: Functional and neuronal substantiation and educational implications. In M. Ferrari & L. Vuletic (Eds.), *The developmental relations between mind, brain and education* (pp. 9–48). New York: Springer.
Desrochers, S. (2008). From Piaget to specific Genevan developmental models. *Child Development Perspectives, 2*, 7–12.
Desrochers, S., Richard, M., & Gouin Décarie, T. (1995). Understanding causality in infancy: A reassessment of Piaget's theory. *Cahiers de Psychologie Cognitive, 14*, 255–268.
Doré, F. Y., & Dumas, C. (1987). Psychology of animal cognition: Piagetian studies. *Psychological Bulletin, 102*, 219–233.
Droz, R., & Rahmy, M. (1974). *Reading Piaget* (2nd ed.). New York: International Universities Press [*Lire Piaget*].

Ferrari, M., & Vuletic, L. (Eds.). (2010). *Developmental relations among mind, brain and education*. New York: Springer Science + Business Media.

Fischer, K. W. (1980). A theory of cognitive development: The control and construction of hierarchies of skills. *Psychological Review, 87*, 477–531.

Fischer, K. W., & Bidell, T. R. (2006). Dynamic development of action and thought. In W. Damon & R. M. Lerner (Eds.), *Handbook of child psychology: Vol. 1. Theoretical models of human development* (pp. 313–399) New York: Wiley.

Furth, H. (1969). *Piaget and knowledge*. Upper Saddle River: Prentice-Hall.

Gelman, S. A. (2009). Learning from others: Children's construction of concepts. *Annual Review of Psychology, 60*, 115–140.

Gouin Décarie, T. (1962). *Intelligence et affectivité chez le jeune enfant [Intelligence and affect in the young child]*. Neuchâtel: Delachaux et Niestlé.

Gouin Décarie, T. (1978). Affect development and cognition in a Piagetian context. In M. Lewis & L. A. Rosenblum (Eds.), *The development of affect* (pp. 183–204). New York: Plenum.

Griffin, S. (2004). Contributions of central conceptual structure theory to education. In A. Demetriou & A. Raftopoulos (Eds.), *Cognitive development change: Theories, models and measurement* (pp. 264–295). New York: Cambridge University Press.

Heil, J. (2004). *Philosophy of mind: A contemporary introduction* (2nd ed.). New York: Routledge.

Howes, M. B. (1990). *The psychology of human cognition: Mainstream and Genevan traditions*. New York: Pergamon.

Kesselring, T. (2009). The mind's staircase revised. In U. Müller, J. I. M. Carpendale, & L. Smith (Eds.), *The Cambridge companion to Piaget* (pp. 372–399). New York: Cambridge University Press.

Kitchener, R. F. (2009). On the concept(s) of the social in Piaget. In U. Müller, J. I. M. Carpendale, & L. Smith (Eds.), *The Cambridge companion to Piaget* (pp. 110–131). New York: Cambridge University Press.

Labouvie-Vief, G., Grühn, D., & Studer, J. (2010). Dynamic integration of emotion and cognition: Equilibrium regulation in development and aging. In R. M. Lerner, M. E. Lamb, & A. M. Freund (Eds.), *The handbook of life-span development: Vol. 2. Social and emotional development* (pp. 79–115). New York: Wiley.

Lewis, M. D., Koroshegyi, C., Douglas, L., & Kampe, K. (1997). Age-specific associations between emotional responses to separation and cognitive performance in infancy. *Developmental Psychology, 33*, 32–42.

Marchand, H. (2001). Some reflections on post formal thought. *The Genetic Epistemologist, 29*(3), 2–9.

Morra, S., Gobbo, C., Marini, Z., & Sheese, R. (2008). *Cognitive development: Neo-Piagetian perspectives*. New York: Erlbaum.

Mounoud, P., Duscherer, K., Moy, G., & Perraudin, S. (2007). The influence of action perception on object recognition: A developmental study. *Developmental Science, 10*, 836–852.

Müller, U., Carpendale, J. I. M., & Smith, L. (Eds.). (2009). *The Cambridge companion to Piaget*. New York: Cambridge University Press.

Müller, U., & Racine, T. (2010). The development of representation and concepts. In R. Lerner & W. Overton (Eds.), *Handbook of lifespan human development: Vol. 1. Cognition, biology, and methods*. Hoboken: Wiley.

Nicolopoulou, A., & Weintraub, J. (2009). Why operativity-in-context is not quite a sociocultural model: Commentary on Psaltis, Duveen, and Perret-Clermont. *Human Development, 52*, 320–328.

Pepperberg, I. M. (2002). The value of the Piagetian framework for comparative cognitive studies. *Animal Cognition, 5*, 177–182.

Piaget, J. (1918a). "Première neige"; and "Je voudrais" [sonnets]. *L'aube, 2*(10), 155.

Piaget, J. (1918b). *Recherche*. Lausanne: La Concorde.

Piaget, J. (1936/1952/1963). *The origins of intelligence in children.* New York: International Universities Press and Norton. (Original work published in 1936).

Piaget, J. (1937/1954). *The construction of reality in the child.* New York: Basic Books. (Original work published 1937).

Piaget, J. (1945/1962). *Play, dreams and imitation in childhood.* New York: Norton. (Original work published 1945).

Piaget, J. (1947/1960). *The psychology of intelligence.* Totawa, NJ: Littlefield Adams. (Original work published in 1947; La psychologie de l'intelligence. Paris: Colin).

Piaget, J. (1954a/1981). *Intelligence and affectivity: Their relationship during child development* (T. Brown & C. Kaegi, Trans. and Eds.). Palo Alto: Annual Reviews Monograph. (Original work published in 1954).

Piaget, J. (1954b). Les relations entre l'affectivité et l'intelligence dans le développement mental de l'enfant. Paris: C. D. U.

Piaget, J. (1955). *The child's construction of reality.* London: Routledge and Kegan Paul.

Piaget, J. (1964/1968). *Six psychological studies* (A. Tenzer, Trans.). New York: Random House. (Original work published in 1964).

Piaget, J. (1967/1971). *Biology and knowledge.* Chicago: University of Chicago Press. (Original work published 1967).

Piaget, J. (1972). Intellectual evolution from adolescence to adulthood. *Human Development, 15*, 1–12.

Piaget, J. (1975/1985). *The equilibration of cognitive structures: The central problem in intellectual development* (T. Brown & K. J. Thampy, Trans.). Chicago: University of Chicago Press. (Original work published in 1975).

Piaget, J. (1983). Piaget's theory. In W. Kessen (Ed.), *History, theory, and methods* (pp. 103–126). New York: Wiley.

Piaget, J., & Inhelder, B. (1966/1969). *The psychology of the child.* New York: Basic Books. (Original work published 1966).

Psaltis, C., Duveen, G., & Perret-Clermont, A.-N. (2009). The social and the psychological: Structure and context in intellectual development. *Human Development, 52*, 219–312.

Sokol, B. W., & Hammond, S. I. (2009). Piaget and affectivity. In U. Müller, J. I. M. Carpendale, & L. Smith (Eds.), *The Cambridge companion to Piaget* (pp. 309–323). New York: Cambridge University Press.

Suizzo, M. A. (2000). The social-emotional and cultural contexts of cognitive development: Neo-Piagetian perspectives. *Child Development, 71*, 846–849.

Thelen, E. (2008). Grounded in the world: Developmental origins of the embodied mind. In W. F. Overton, U. Müller, & J. L. Newman (Eds.), *Development perspectives on embodiment and consciousness* (pp. 99–129). New York: Erlbaum.

Uzgiris, I. E., & Hunt, J. Mc V. (1975). *Assessment in infancy: Ordinal scales of psychologic development.* Urbana: University of Illinois Press.

Vidal, F. (1994). Piaget poète. Avec deux sonnets oubliés de 1918 [Piaget the poet. With two forgotten sonnets in 1918]. *Archives de Psychologies, 64*, 3–7.

Wolff, P. H. (1960). The developmental psychologies of Jean Piaget and psychoanalysis. *Psychological Issues, 2*, 181.

Young, G. (1990). Early neuropsychological development: Lateralization of functions – hemispheric specialization. In C. A. Hauert (Ed.), *Developmental psychology: Cognitive, perceptuo-motor and neuropsychological perspectives* (pp. 113–181). North Holland: Elsevier.

Young, G. (1997). *Adult development, therapy, and culture: A postmodern synthesis.* New York: Plenum.

Young, G., & Gouin Décarie, T. (1977). An ethology-based catalogue of facial/vocal behavior in infancy. *Animal Behavior, 25*, 95–107.

Young, G., Segalowitz, S. J., Misek, P., Alp, I. E., & Boulet, R. (1983). Is early reading left-handed? Review of manual specialization research. In G. Young, S. J. Segalowitz, C. M. Corter, & S. E. Trehub (Eds.), *Manual specialization and the developing brain* (pp. 13–32). New York: Academic Press.

Young, G., & Wolff, P. (1976). *Lateralization of manual behavior in 15-weeks-olds.* Unpublished manuscript.

# Chapter 4
# The Present Cognitive-Affective Stage Model: I Cognition

## Introduction

This chapter compares and contrasts the stages, substages, and age ranges of the Neo-Piagetian models of Fischer, Case, and Young, in particular. It includes mention of the work of Mounoud, Commons, and Feldman. Then, I describe in depth the present model in terms of its stages, substages, and age ranges. I point out how I based the present model on the work of Piaget, in particular, also borrowed stages from Fischer, substages from Mounoud, and age ranges from Case. Elsewhere in the book, I indicate the role played by Commons and Feldman in the formulation of the present model. The comparison undertaken across the models of Fischer, Case, and myself reveal their relative advantages and disadvantages. The present model has several major advantages relative to the others, such as being the only one that includes substages within stages that traverse the full lifespan from the fetal period to the elderly period. Moreover, I point out some inconsistencies in the models of Fischer and Case relative to my own. An integrated model would include the best of all the models mentioned in this chapter.

## Neo-Piagetians

### *The Models*

Table 4.1 presents the major models of Neo-Piagetian development that I used in Young (1997) in the construction of the present Neo-Piagetian model (Case, Fischer, Mounoud). These are other powerful Neo-Piagetian models (e.g., Case, 1978, 1985; Fischer, 1980; Immordino-Yang & Fischer, 2007; Mounoud, 1976, 1986; see Young, 1997) that have served in the formulation of the present substage model. However, the five-step substage sequence that I elaborated has as much to do with Piaget than Neo-Piagetians. In general, the work of Piaget remains at the heart of the present model. Nevertheless, Table 4.1 indicates that I borrowed from all of the other models either at the stage, substage, or age range levels.

G. Young, *Development and Causality: Neo-Piagetian Perspectives*,
DOI 10.1007/978-1-4419-9422-6_4, © Springer Science+Business Media, LLC 2011

**Table 4.1** Some contemporary Neo-Piagetian models of cognitive development

| Fischer (1980 on) | | | Case (1985 on) | | | Mounoud (e.g., 1986) | | |
|---|---|---|---|---|---|---|---|---|
| Stage | Substage | Age | Stage | Substage | Age | Stage | Substage | Age |
| Reflex | Set | 1 mo– | | | | | | |
| | Map | 2– | | | | | | |
| | System | 3– | | | | | | |
| Sensorimotor | Set | 4– | Sensorimotor | Precoord[a] | 0 mo | Perceptual | Global[b] | 0 mo |
| | Map | 8– | | Unifocal | 4 | | Applic | 1 |
| | System | 12– | | Bifocal | 8 | | Related | 4 |
| | | | | Elabor | 12 | | Analysis | 8 |
| | | | | | | | Synthesis | 12 |
| Representational | Set | 2 yr– | Interrelational | Unifocal | 18 | Conceptual | Global[b] | 18 |
| | Map | 5– | | Bifocal | 2 yr | | Applic | 3 yr |
| | System | 7– | | Elabor | 3.5 | | Related | 5 |
| | | | | | | | Analysis | 7 |
| | | | | | | | Synthesis | 9 |
| | | | Dimensional | Unifocal | 5 | | | |
| | | | | Bifocal | 7 | | | |
| | | | | Elabor | 9 | | | |
| Abstract | Set | 12– | Abstract | Unifocal | 11 | Semiotic | Global | 10 |
| Formal | Map | 16– | | Bifocal | 13 | | Applic | 11 |
| Operational | System | 20– | | Elabor | 16–19 | | Related | 13 |
| | System of systems | 26+ | | | | | Analysis | 15 |
| | | | | | | | Synthesis | 16–18 |

Adapted from Young (1990a)

In Young (1990a), I presented this table that served as the basis for the formulation of the present model. By juxtaposing the three main Neo-Piagetian theorists at that time (Fischer, Case, Mounoud), the comparative advantages of each became evident, as well as their differences, gaps, and inconsistencies

At that time, Case had not added his orienting period before the sensorimotor one, so Fischer's innovation in having an initial reflexive period stood out. His idea of referring to the combined preoperational and concrete operational periods as representational seemed acceptable, because Piaget had done the same thing. He had added a postformal period, but had yet to refer to it in terms of the acquisition of principles

Case had kept the traditional four-step Piagetian sequence of sensorimotor, preoperational, concrete operational, and formal operational intelligence, but he modified the labels. Many theorists refer to the formal stage as abstract, as he did. Also, his use of the terms of interrelations, dimensions, and vectors for the last three of Piaget's stages, respectively, is consistent with his conceptions. However, I refrained from using these labels, partly because of their ambiguities and limitations. For example, the concept of interrelations is too general, and can apply socially at any age as well as cognitively. For the concrete operational period, although there is an increase in dimensional thought, the child is acquiring reversibility in thought, in particular, at this age, according to Piaget. Moreover, dimensional thought is just one of the four major types of logical justifications on conservation tasks that Piaget described for this period. Piaget termed this type of thought as compensatory. The others concerned reversibility (negation) and identity, in particular (see Young & Gouin Décarie, 1977)

As for Mounoud, I did not use his description of the child's preoperational and concrete operational stages, which he referred to as "conceptual," given that infants could be understood to be forming concepts, too. Similarly, he described the formal period as a semiotic one, but the semiotic function is used differently in other fields, such as linguistics

The notes for other tables have provided comments on the substage cycles presented in the various theories. Briefly, Fischer and Case each have a three-step cyclic recursion of substages within stages, Mounoud's model has five, and my model has five, as well. I had wanted to respect the integrity of Piaget's original sensorimotor substage series, and built a five-step cyclic recursion of substages based on them by removing the first one and referring to it as a separate stage (reflexive)

As for the ages for each period, I started with the age period that Piaget had indentified for the sensorimotor period (up to 2 years). Also, in prior and subsequent cycles of the substages, I respected the age ranges provided by Piaget, as well, but added to them, as necessary, e.g., by splitting them where needed. Therefore, for any one age period, I did not abandon critical age transitions that Piaget had described

Case had adopted a similar approach to fit his cyclic recursion of substages; he either used the age points offered in Piaget, or he split them. However, Fischer did not follow the same approach. For example, in the literature available to me at that time, Fischer left a gap in his substage sequence at the 18-month period relative to Piaget, Case, and myself. That is, whereas we three described a new substage emerging in the 18–24-month period, although to some extent we disagreed on its label and contents, Fischer had bypassed this age period as a distinct one in constructing his model. Note that in later publications the gap switched to the 2 to 3½ year period, which is also problematic

[a] *Precoord* precoordination; *Elabor* elaboration

[b] *Global* global code; *Applic* code applied; *Related* codes related

**Table 4.2** Later Neo-Piagetian models of cognitive development

| Stages | Substages | Ages |
|---|---|---|
| Commons | | |
| Calculatory | One step | |
| Sensorimotor | Five steps (sensory or motor; circular sensory-motor; sensory-motor, nominal, sentential) | |
| Preoperational | Two steps (preoperational; primary) | |
| Concrete | One step | |
| Abstract | Two steps (abstract, formal) | |
| Postformal | Four steps (systematic, metasystematic, paradigmatic, cross-paradigmatic) | |
| Feldman | | |
| Sensorimotor | Active construction | 0 mo to 1 yr |
| | Active extension and elaboration | |
| Preoperational | Active construction | 2 yr to 4 |
| | Active extension and elaboration | |
| Concrete Operational | Active construction | 6–9 |
| | Active extension and elaboration | |
| Formal Operational | Active construction | 12–16 |
| | Active extension and elaboration | |

After Case, Fischer, and other earlier Neo-Piagetians had presented their models involving cyclically recurring substages over stages in cognitive development, several other models emerged in the literature. However, only Feldman's (2004) model was based on this format. Feldman used the Piagetian sequence of stages in his model. Commons did, as well, but he added a stage before the sensorimotor period and another after the formal one, similar to the approach adopted by Case, Fischer, and Young. However, he did not have a cyclically recurring substage sequence embedded in his stage sequence. Feldman did, but it was confined to a two-step cycle. Both had one extra level of steps within substages in their models, but the number varied from (sub)stage to (sub) stage

Specifically, for Commons, the stage and step sequence given in the table is abstracted from his model (see Table 18.1), but it is arranged to be consistent with the other Neo-Piagetian models. In this arrangement, most stages have several steps, but there is no cyclic recursion evident in the model either in this format or any other conceivable (they range from one step to four). Typical age ranges are not specified, given the origin of the stages in task analysis. For Feldman, he describes four stages x two substages. However, there are also steps within the substages, although not in a recursive manner. The first substage includes four steps, the last has three steps, and the remaining have two steps each

In addition, for purposes of comparison, Table 4.2 presents two other lifespan Neo-Piagetian models (Commons, 2008 ; Feldman, 2004). In general, Neo-Piagetian models express a consensus that there should be some form of stage sequence having substages or steps. This issue is independent of the question that the theorists involved might not refer to the sequences as stage-substage models, and use different terms such as tiers and levels (Fischer). Moreover, the issue that there are differences across the theories in the nature and importance of stages in development does not negate that the various theories subscribe to a stage model in one way or another. A similar proviso applies to the differences in the models in the extent that they emphasize that there are individualized skills that develop.

Despite the common foundation in the models being compared that it is important to elucidate the qualitative shifts that take place in development, not one of the models on which I based construction of my own covers the full lifespan with stages that include throughout recursive substages. In addition, some of the models are based on the traditional Piagetian stages, whereas others vary in what they consider as stages and the terminology used to describe them. Some of the models skip age periods that others consider to involve as a new step in their sequence, although some do not.

In particular, Fischer's model does not have separate substages in four age periods where the model of Case considers it important to have them. When I first compared Case and Fischer in Young (1990a, 1990b), it appeared that these gaps in substages referred to the age periods beginning at 18 months-, 3½-, 9-, 13 years-, although later renditions of the model provide different age ranges that accommodate some of these age ranges (e.g., Immordino-Yang & Fischer, 2007). This variation in age range from one version of a Neo-Piagetian model to the next illustrates that the age periods in these models are only approximations and less important than the (sub)stage sequences themselves. Nevertheless, relative to Case's model, Mounoud's, and my own, for the age ranges covered common to all the models the number of substages in Fischer's model is reduced in one way or another.

Both Fischer and Case have published extensive empirical support for their models, and the quality of the research is impressive. This being said, one possible argument about the inconsistencies across them in terms of their conception of stages and substages and the age ranges in which they appear is that the empirical research for each model is tailored toward the model's concept of its stage-substage sequence in a way that inhibits adequate comparison with other models.

The Commons model is based on empirical work in the adult period, in particular, and the remainder of the steps mentioned appears to be extrapolations of Fischer's. The Feldman model is an attempt to resurrect the traditional Piagetian approach, through theoretical modifications and with a two-step recursion in substages added, but it was presented without empirical support.

## *Comment*

In the end, the present Neo-Piagetian model provides a unique theoretical perspective that could lead to research supporting the 25-step sequence that it proposes. This sequence has far more steps than any of the others, and it was developed through a network of logic and careful analysis of other similar models. Given its comprehensive 25-step sequence, (a) it constitutes the only Neo-Piagetian cognitive model that fully covers the lifespan, (b) it is the only model that includes corresponding socioaffective Neo-Eriksonian steps, (c) it is the only one that does not have inconsistent age gaps between substages at any point over the full lifespan, and (d) it is the only model that can serve as an umbrella one for the others, (e) also, it is the model that respects most Piaget's work as a starting point to its formulation, taking care to keep his best-established components, (f) in addition, by way of the present work, it is the only model that carefully compares and contrasts all the models, pointing out their inconsistencies and proposing modifications to make them more consistent, (g) finally, it is the model that expands most its applications to other areas of human development and even to systems in development that are not about individuals in development (e.g., chronic pain, societies, nonliving systems).

## Overview of the Present Neo-Piagetian Model

### *Introduction*

The primary postulate of the present model is that there are 25 steps in Neo-Piagetian cognitive development across the lifespan, consisting of five stages with five cyclically recurring substages, and there is a corresponding 25-step sequence in affective or socioemotional development. In terms of cognition, the present model builds on the work of Case and Fischer, in particular. In terms of affect, the present model emphasizes stages in Neo-Eriksonian development and in internal working models over the lifespan, and parallels across sensorimotor substages in infancy and basic emotions. The present model of cognitive/socioaffective correspondences over steps across the lifespan provides a framework that encompasses other models (Table 4.3).

The present 25-step cognitive sequence in development provides a major anchor in the coordinated cognitive-affect unfolding in ontogenesis, but at the same time the development of affect and emotions relate to it reciprocally. That is, socio-emotional processes spur and form cognitive advances, but they are constrained by cognitive factors in their turn in, a dynamic constituting a reciprocal functional relationship.

The present model explores not only the steps in development but also the causes, determinants, or mechanisms underlying its acquisitions. The two major areas of acquisitions in development – cognitive and socioaffective – are considered to involve emergence through multifactorial, nonlinear dynamical systems processes that encompass biological, evolutionary, psychological, organismic-personal, social, and cultural (including political and historical) factors. These elements coalesce to form emergent wholes, both microdevelopmentally and macrodevelopmentally, including of the 25 steps in development proposed by the present model. The latter are the moment-to-moment acquisitions that accumulate and lead to the former. The integrative processes that lead to these qualitative shifts need specification beyond current models.

In the following, I provide a sketch of the 25 steps in development being proposed. The present cognitive developmental model builds on the stage model of Piaget, especially working from his refined description of the substages in the infancy period. Piaget described four major stages in cognitive development – the sensorimotor in infancy, the preoperational in early childhood, the concrete operational in childhood, and the formal operational or abstract in adolescence and

**Table 4.3** A model of 25 steps in Neo-Piagetian cognitive development and Neo-Eriksonian affective development

| Level | Neo-Piagetian stage | Substage | Age range | Neo-Eriksonian substage |
|---|---|---|---|---|
| 1 | Reflex | Coordination | Earlier fetal life | Distance acts vs. no acts |
| 2 | | Hierarchization | Quite premature | Nursing vs. rootless acts |
| 3 | | Systematization | Somewhat premature | Outcome vs. outcast acts |
| 4 | | Multiplication | Full-term newborn | Caregiving vs. careless giving acts |
| 5 | | Integration | 0–1 mo | Emotional vs. malemotional acts |
| 6 | Sensorimotor | Coordination | 1–4 mo | Dyadic vs. dysdyadic acts |
| 7 | | Hierarchization | 4–8 mo | Trust vs. mistrust acts |
| 8 | | Systematization | 8–12 mo | Sociability vs. unsociability acts |
| 9 | | Multiplication | 12–18 mo | Autonomy vs. doubt acts |
| 10 | | Integration | 18–24 mo | Interdigitational vs. dedigitational acts |
| 11 | Perioperational | Coordination | 2–3.5 yr | Superordinate vs. discoordinate acts |
| 12 | | Hierarchization | 3.5–5 yr | Initiative vs. guilt acts |
| 13 | | Systematization | 5–7 yr | Identification vs. problematic identification acts |
| 14 | | Multiplication | 7–9 yr | Industry vs. inferiority acts |
| 15 | | Integration | 9–11 yr | Role vs. role confusion acts |
| 16 | Abstract | Coordination | 11–13 yr | Conscious vs. contraconscious acts |
| 17 | | Hierarchization | 13–16 yr | Identity vs. identity diffusion acts |
| 18 | | Systematization | 16–19 yr | Nurturing vs. misnurturing acts |
| 19 | | Multiplication | 19–22 yr | Intimacy vs. isolation acts |
| 20 | | Integration | 22–25 yr | Universal vs. self-singular acts |
| 21 | Collective intelligence | Coordination | 25–28 yr | Metacollective vs. disillusionment acts |
| 22 | | Hierarchization | 28–39 yr | Generativity vs. self-absorption acts |
| 23 | | Systematization | 39–50 yr | Catalytic vs. midlife crisis acts |
| 24 | | Multiplication | 50–61 yr | Ego integrity vs. despair acts |
| 25 | | Integration | 61-yr | Cathartic vs. abandonment acts |

Reprinted with the permission of Springer Science+Business Media: Young, G. (1997). [Table P.1, Page. 2–7]

The table presents the essentials of the present model of Neo-Piagetian cognitive development throughout the lifespan (Young). It consists of 25 steps, comprising five stages and five cyclically recurring substages within each of them. Each substage could pass through the cyclic recursion at its level, in a fractalization process, leading to a model of 125 possible steps in development. The stage names borrow clearly from Piaget, with the perioperation one constituting a combined stage

(continued)

**Table 4.3** (continued)

of preoperations and concrete operations. The collective stage refers to the adult ability to create superordinate abstract structures, to brainstorm together, to coordinate affect in cognitive processes, etc. The substages are based on the Piagetian sensorimotor substage series, but the first one has been removed and placed as a separate stage (reflexive), having its own substages, beginning in the prenatal period, something that Piaget had not contemplated

The corresponding Neo-Eriksonian stages indicate the placement of the eight original Eriksonian stages in terms of their correspondence with the 25-step cognitive sequence. It also indicates the names of the 17 new steps that I created to complete the cognitive-affective correspondence over the 25 steps. In terms of their placement in parallel with the cognitive steps that correspond best to them from among the 25 steps of the model, the original eight Eriksonian steps appear to emerge in parallel with the second and fourth substages of each of the last four cognitive stages. I continued the Eriksonian tradition of describing them as polarities, but included the concept of acts in naming them. For the negative poles, I avoided repeating prepositions such as "mis-" or "dis-." This present model is the first lifespan model of corresponding cognitive-affective stages in development

adulthood. Piaget described six substages in the sensorimotor period of infancy, but in the stages that followed he was not as systematic about them, and, at most, he described a few in each stage. Case's and Fischer's Neo-Piagetian models posit about the same number of stages as Piaget, but they add that there is a cyclic recursion of substages over stages. In each of their models, there are three substages that are posited to repeat in each of (or most of) the stages.

The present model presents more steps (25) in Neo-Piagetian cognitive development compared to the others because it offers a model of more substages (5) that cyclically recur in each of its stages (5), leading to its sequence of 25 steps (5 stages × 5 cyclic substages). Moreover, the present model is a lifespan one, stretching from the fetal (premature) age period to the elderly age period, unlike the models of Case and Fischer, each of whom do not have stages in the adult period that have substages recurring in them throughout the adult years, and each of whom do not have a stage in the full fetal period with recurring substages.

Specifically, in the present model, I propose that in ontogenesis the developing individual passes through the Piagetian-type stages, with an extra first and last one relative to Piaget. The former is extrapolated from the initial substage of the six substages in Piaget's sensorimotor model of infancy. The latter is termed collective intelligence. Collective intelligence in the adult is considered to involve collection as several levels. (a) First, there is a fusion of cognition and emotion, which is a more difficult process for the adolescent whose thinking might not integrate these domains (a conception similar to that of Labouvie-Vief, 1992, 2006; Labouvie-Vief, Grühn, & Studer, 2010). (b) Also, there is more of a symbiotic sharing of ideas with others (e.g., brainstorming), which is consistent with views that adults aggregate into group intelligence processes (e.g., Hutchins, 1995). (c) Third, cognitively, adult abstract thinking processes lead better to overarching, metasystemic, second-order abstractions, as per the work of Commons and Richards (2002; Commons, 2008). Note that relative to Piaget, I instituted one more noticeable change in my model. When he referred together to the childhood stages of preoperations and concrete operations, he would use the term of Representations. However, I chose a more generic label that more directly encapsulates the two terms involved – that of "perioperations." With the description of these modifications that I have made to Piaget's basic stage-substage model, in the following, I present the full model that I have constructed.

## *Formulation*

I have proposed a Neo-Piagetian model of development combining cognitive and affective steps. Piaget had developed a stage model of cognitive development that included the sensorimotor, preoperational, concrete operational, and formal or abstract stages of development. The Neo-Piagetian model that I developed in Young (1990a, 1990b, 1997, 2008) consists of five similar stages: *reflexive, sensorimotor, perioperational (representational; preoperational and concrete operational), abstract, and collective intelligence.*

As for the cyclically recurring substages of the present model, they consist of the following series: *coordination, hierarchization, systematization, multiplication, and integration*. I added the initial reflex stage to the Piagetian series by splitting off and elaborating the first sensorimotor substage in Piaget as a separate initial stage of reflexes in the fetal period and the first month of life. The five-cycle substage recursion builds on the six substages that Piaget described for the sensorimotor period, but with the first reflexive substage removed in the way indicated. In this sense, to my knowledge, the present model is the only Neo-Piagetian theory that builds directly on the work of Piaget, and the only time that he described a comprehensive sequence of substages within his model of stages.

An advantage of the present model is that it integrates socioemotional growth at multiple levels. At the microlevel, it speaks of integrated cognitive and affective-like schemes. In addition, at the macrolevel I have developed a sequence of 25 steps in Neo-Eriksonian development that parallels the 25 cognitive steps of the present model, that the proposed cognitive sequence can accommodate other areas of human development, such as the Eriksonian one, which provides support for its validity. In a similar vein, I have elaborated many socioaffective parallels with the steps of the present model, for example, on early emotions and on internal working models over the lifespan.

In the following, I examine specifically how other Neo-Piagetian models have influenced the present model, in terms of its stages, substages, and their typical ages of appearance. The present model was rationally derived through the comparison with these other Neo-Piagetian models, but an important impetus was to keep as intact as possible the sensorimotor substage series that Piaget had described, given its astute observational and theoretical base.

## *Stages*

Young's Neo-Piagetian stage model consists of five cognitive stages, and it borrows from Fischer's model, in particular. In their models, both Fischer and Case have proposed an initial stage of development prior to the sensorimotor period. Fischer had called it the Reflex stage, and I used the same term. For infancy, Fischer described a sensorimotor period, like Piaget, and Case and I used the same term. Whenever Piaget described together the preoperational and concrete operational stages, he referred to the Representational period. Fischer (1980) adopted the same approach in his Neo-Piagetian model. However, in my own model, I decided to call this period the perioperational stage, because I preferred a term that encompassed both the preoperational stage and concrete operational stage, and emphasized its developing operational base. As for Case, he kept the preoperational and concrete operational stages separate, unlike Fischer's and my case, but he changed the terms related to (inter)relational and dimensional, respectively.

Other Neo-Piagetians have proposed a postformal period in the adult that follows the formal stage, the last one in the original Piagetian cognitive stage series. Piaget had rejected the ideas as he argued that adult thought is still abstract in nature, despite its increased complexity. My own work has emphasized the collective intellectual properties in adult abstract thought. I have labeled the postformal period as collective intelligence, as has been shown. Briefly, I posit that in this stage one finds higher-order abstract structures, collective brainstorming, integration of cognitive and emotional processes, and so on.

In his model, Fischer described the development of adult cognition as a system of systems, which he termed Principles (Fischer, 1980; Fischer & Bidell, 2006). However, he did not propose a separate cognitive developmental stage at this level amenable to the development of substages over the adult age span, unlike in the present model.

Therefore, to conclude, for the most part, in developing the stage component of the present Neo-Piagetian model of stages in cognitive development, I followed Fischer's model; however, I added a new stage involving the adult, that of Collective Intelligence. This addition to Fischer's approach allows for substages to develop not only up to the adult period but across the full lifespan.

## *Substages*

As for the substages that cyclically recur within stages across development, Fischer (1980) and Case (1978) had presented recursive models, in which the same three substages repeat within each stage. The present model was constructed upon a five-step substage cycle, like in Mounoud, and unlike the case for both Case and Fischer, who described a three-step cycle of recurring substages in their stage models.

Note that Fischer and Case used different terms for their conceptions of the three substages thought to recur across stages. For Fischer and Case, respectively, we find the following terms for the three substages in their sequence: first substage – single set, unifocal; second substage – mapping, bifocal; third substage – system, elaboration. In contrast, Mounoud (1976, 1986) had presented a cyclic recursion model of Neo-Piagetian substages that consisted of five recursive steps, rather than three of them.

In Table 4.1, note that I used labels to summarize Mounoud's five-step substage sequence that is consistent with their contents, instead of using the terms that he had used initially.

As I developed my own model, as mentioned, I wanted to respect the integrity of Piaget's description of the six sensorimotor substages that he described for the infancy period. In effect, I followed Fischer's by removing the first reflexive substage from the Piagetian series, and placing it as its own stage. This left a five-stage sequence of sensorimotor substages from a Piagetian point of view that constituted the core of the present model.

To my knowledge, not one of Fischer, Case, or Mounoud emphasized in their theory the sensorimotor period in infancy as a starting point for determining their version of the appropriate cyclic recursion of substages. Rather, if anything, they analyzed the behavior of preschool and/or older children, and worked backward from there to infancy (e.g., Case, 1978, p. 38; Fischer, 1980, footnote 4, p. 486; Mounoud & Bower, 1974/75, in Fischer, 1980, p. 518). This may have been one factor that led to our different understandings of the stages and their substages in cognitive development.

Once I had decided to work from Piaget's sensorimotor substage model, with the one deletion described, I examined the resultant five-step sensorimotor sequence for its superordinate properties. I sought labels for them that could be generalized to the substage sequences in the other stages of the model. Given that the present model is based on a cyclic recursion of substages, this meant that I had to choose terms for the substages that could work for any preceding and ensuing stages. Therefore, in naming the five substages in the present model, I chose generic labels that could apply to any age, as I kept in mind that substages are considered to recycle over the lifespan from the fetal to the elderly periods. In this regard, the five labels that I had to choose for the five-step substage sequence had to fit simultaneously simpler reflexive behaviors that develop earlier and more complex thoughts which emerge later in development. Moreover, it was kept in mind that the five-step recursion had to be phrased in terms general enough to incorporate a diverse array of developmental phenomena at any one level, including those concerning manual behavior, emotional behavior, attachment, and personality.

This logical procedure that I followed led to the particular substage sequence of five cyclically recurring substages described above (coordination to integration). Even though the terms of the five substages in Mounoud's model are different than the ones that I have proposed, the logical process that I followed resulted in five substages like in his model. That is, in terms of the comparison undertaken in the present work across the models of Fischer, Case, and mine, the present Neo-Piagetian model of five substages that reoccur within the stages of development is not consistent with either of the three-step ones of Fischer or Case.

Because Case and Fischer had proposed a three-step cyclic recursion of substages repeating within stages, unlike mine and Mounoud's case, they were presented with difficulties in their model construction relative to us. That is, by using a three-step recursive substage sequence over stages, which led them to truncate the sensorimotor stage in their theories to three substages. This logical process that they followed led them to undervalue one of the most powerful portions of Piaget's theory, his sensorimotor substage sequence.

Moreover, in both their models, the equivalent of the preoperational stage is considered to begin at 18 months of age (relational stage for Case; representational stage for Fischer). I recognized that there are variations in the age ranges associated with the various stages over publications in various Neo-Piagetian workers, there is no uniformity across workers at any rate, and the that age range question is relatively minor compared to the validity of the different sequences proposed themselves. Nevertheless, Piaget had maintained that the preoperational stage begins at 24 months, not 18 months. This difference in age onset for the preoperational stage in the various Neo-Piagetian models being compared is not simply a minor issue, given that it reflects the constraints of the models of Case and Fischer that derive from their use of a reduced three-step substage sequence over stages, unlike the case in my own model, where I use five of them.

## Substages: Details

*Coordination.* In the present model, coordination refers to an interrelation of two different cognitive control units (acquired in the previous substage for the most part). However, the interrelation does not specify which of the units has ascendancy in terms of either a temporal order or a dominant–subordinate relationship. The units exist in a reciprocal balance (pairing, addition, juxtaposition, opposition, etc.) of a back and forth nature. If hierarchies are established, they are tentative, tenuous structures.

*Hierarchization.* With development of the substage of hierarchization, the deficiencies in the just described coordinations are countered. Paired cognitive control units evidence a strengthened dominant–subservient relation and/or a fixed sequence in time.

*Systematization.* Systematization is marked by both an expansion and simplification of hierarchized control units. On the one hand, component units add (recruit) refinements (feedback, extra adaptive behaviors) that permit better on-target adjustment at the onset of the behavior, at its end-point, etc. On the other hand, the new structure meshes into a smoothly operating, more unified whole through a less fixed, hierarchical and more complementary coordination of the component units.

*Multiplication.* Multiplication refers to the spreading of newly-acquired system structures in the prior substage through the full system. Or, it refers to the combination of systems (even more than two at a time). This is accomplished both by chaining them over time (either repetitively, but more important, by using different ones in each slot), and/or by embedding, where primary systems are subserved by secondary ones (less elaborate than the primary ones). This produces an element of reversibility in behavior, but not as clearly as in the next substage of integration.

*Integration.* The last substage of integration in the current model of cognitive substage recursion finds multiple cognitive units more precisely differentiated in flexible branching as they are applied. This produces linear sequences or chains comprised of strings of component systems different from each other, with some embedded in others. An embedded component system may be just as elaborate as any constituent system of the main string. Moreover, it might unfold in parallel with movements or behaviors of the main string, i.e., it and the main string might unfold simultaneously. In short, the reversibility evident in the organization of this substage is a mature, efficient one. To use Fischer's language, elements of subsets can be paired without compromising the integrity or continuity of the subsets.

## *Sensorimotor Substages in Chimpanzees*

Matsuzawa (1994) analyzed the development of tool use for nut-cracking in wild chimpanzees, and found a five-step progression that corresponds to the current proposed five-substage sequence for human infants. To study tool use in chimpanzees, Matsuzawa created an informal outdoor laboratory in the home range of a West African troop. He would leave a variety of stones and palm nuts in the area.

By 1 year of age, infant chimps employed the strategy of "single object manipulation," which involved activities such as rummage for, pick-up, and perhaps mouth. The analogy with the first sensorimotor stage of the current theory, sensorimotor coordination, is clear.

Next, young chimps of about 2 years would engage in "object association manipulation," e.g., push nut on stone, or vice versa, hit nut with hand. The hierarchical relationship in these activities fits the current expectation of what should develop after a coordination substage in development.

Then, in the next stage of "relationship of object association sets," evident in 3-year-old chimps, multiple actions were performed collaboratively. For example, a nut would be placed on a larger stone, called the anvil stone, and it would be hit with a hand. The systemic behavior that one would expect from the present model, because the third developmental cognitive substage concerns systems, appears borne out in the chimpanzee's tool use.

In the next acquisition, older chimps began "coordinating multiple actions." For example, a chimp would hold in one hand one smaller stone as a hammer, and use the same hand for placing a nut on the anvil stone. Then it would engage in striking it and picking up the edible kernel exposed by the blow. Once more, one finds a marked similarity between the present model and the chimpanzee data to the point that the term "multiple" is the key root word in both cases.

Finally, 9- to 10-year-old adult chimpanzees manifested bimanual coordination within a larger action, for they took the hammer in one hand, placed the nut on the anvil with the other, and proceeded to strike the nut with the first hand (with the hand used in the gathering of the resultant morsels unspecified). Once more, a clear isomorphism with the human series is evident, for the behavior involved forms an integrated system, as I would predict.

Cognitive tasks, per se, were not administered to the chimpanzees so that there is no way of confirming exactly a correspondence with the sensorimotor series being proposed. Moreover, the age spanned in the chimpanzees was relatively large, so that the 10-year-olds tested might have developed to some extent beyond the sensorimotor stage. Nevertheless, for the particular situation in question, that of skill development in nut-cracking in chimpanzees, an approximation of the human sensorimotor substages as defined in the present model seems to have been found, which speaks to its validity.

## Ages

In terms of the ages that correspond to the proposed 25 steps in development presented in Young (1997), the work of Case (1978, 1985) provided the best fit. Case is the theorist who best respected the original age ranges corresponding to Piaget's stages and substages in development. His particular substage sequence usually provided age periods that were consistent with my model, even if the organization of the stages and substages was different in his model compared to mine. That is, of the various Neo-Piagetian models, Case had been the most diligent about keeping critical ages that served to divide stages or substages from each other in Piaget's theory. Or, he divided these periods as he developed his model without sacrificing the original age ranges involved. That is, Case added new substages to Piaget's developmental cognitive model mostly by splitting Piaget's stages and their respective age ranges. Perhaps this is why in Case's model, after the age of 1 month, there is an orderly increase in the age range of successive levels (one to several levels involving 1/3, 1/2, 1½, 2, and 3 years, in turn). In this regard, at several points Fischer's age range sequence did not fit well into the particular stage-substage sequence that I had proposed in my model. In addition, Fischer has varied at times over his publications the actual ages in the age ranges associated with the substages of his model (see Table 4.4).

## Cognitive Control Units

Piaget emphasized the way the scheme, in particular, is gradually transformed into operations in the course of passing through cognitive stages in ontogenesis. However, Case (1987) documented the way the various Neo-Piagetians have differing perspectives on what are the basic cognitive control units [fundamental (mental) structures that organize specific behaviors or thoughts], and the way they differentiate with development. In the present model, I adopted a novel perspective on the nature of development of cognitive control units. That is, I suggest that at each one of the 25 posited levels in development a new cognitive control unit emerges. Each new substage is seen to bring with it a qualitatively different mode of thought. These are described in great detail elsewhere (see Tables 26.1–26.10 in Chap. 26) In effect, these detailed tables in Chap. 26 provide the fine-grained detail needed to complement the current general description of the present model.

**Table 4.4** Developmental cycles of tiers and levels of skills presented in a timeline of material in Fischer

| | Estimate age[a] | | | | | |
|---|---|---|---|---|---|---|
| Stage/ substage (tier/level) | Fischer and Hogan (1989) | Fischer and Pruyne (2003) | Fischer, Yan, and Stewart (2003) | Fischer and Bidell (2006) | Fischer (2009) Optimal | Fischer (2009) Functional[b] |
| Reflexes | | | | | | |
| Single | 3–4 wk | 3–4 wk | – | – | – | – |
| Mappings | 7–8 wk | 7–8 wk | – | – | – | – |
| Systems | 10–11 wk | 10–11 wk | – | – | – | – |
| Sensorimotor actions | | | | | | |
| Single | 15–17 wk | 3–4 mo | – | 3–4 mo | – | – |
| Mappings | 7–8 mo | 7–8 mo | – | 7–8 mo | – | – |
| Systems | 11–13 mo | 11–13 mo | – | 11–30 mo | – | – |
| Representations | | | | | | |
| Single | 18–24 mo | 2 | 18–24 mo | 2 | 2 | 2–5 |
| Mappings | 3½–4½ | 3½–4½ | 3½–4½ | 3½–4½ | 4 | 4–8 |
| Systems | – | 6–7 | 6–7 | 6–7 | 6 | 7–12 |
| Abstractions | | | | | | |
| Single | – | 10–12 | 10–12 | 10–12 | 10 | 12–20 |
| Mappings | – | 14–16 | 14–16 | 14–16 | 15 | 17–30 |
| Systems | – | 18–20 | 19–20 | 18–20 | 20 | 23–40 yr or never for many domains |
| Principles | – | 23–25 | 24–25 | 23–25 | 25 | 30–45 yr or never for many domains |

Adapted from Fischer (2009), Fischer and Bidell (2006), Fischer and Hogan (1989), Fischer and Pruyne (2003), Fischer et al. (2003)

When I first presented Fischer's model in a table in Young (1990a), the age periods specified for each stage and substage of his model were the ones indicated in Table 4.1. Since that time, there have been slight variations in the ages associated with some developmental periods in his model The largest discrepancy in terms of when substages typically start relates to the substage of single representations, which varies between 18 months and 2 years. In Piaget's model of stages and substages in development, the 18-month period is associated with the last sensorimotor substage in his series and the 2-year mark indicates the onset of the new stage of preoperations. In Fischer's model, one finds only one (sub)stage corresponding to this age period, unlike Piaget who presented two of them. I also noted that for Fischer's representational mapping substage, which had first included the 5-year age, later renditions typically mentioned 3½ to 4½ age period

In addition, Fischer has introduced the concept of variation in age period associated with a particular substage, depending on degree of support for a developing person. The age for any one (sub) stage can vary according to whether the environment is providing optimal support or less support (see the functional column of the table). Fischer rightly points out that especially in the adult period, support offered can delay or even inhibit the development of the substages involved. However, the question becomes whether the environment can influence the age of acquisition of a skill to the degree indicated by Fischer. Are the acquisitions firmly entrenched, or are they so ephemeral as to have no durability or generalizability?

[a]In yr, unless indicated as wk or mo

[b]Ages for functional levels vary widely and are coarse estimates, based on research. Levels are highly related to education

## Summary

The present chapter is part of a pair of chapters that present in depth the present model of the development of 25 steps in cognitive-affective parallels across the lifespan. It builds on Piaget's model of stages, and the present substage sequence over all the stages of the lifespan is especially tied to that of Piaget. In this sense, although I have borrowed from the work of the Neo-Piagetians, especially Fischer and Case, the present model is more Piagetian-based than theirs in terms of its stages and substages.

In the next chapter, I review other dimensions of the present model. First, I examine in depth the postformal collective stage. Then, I present the details of the Neo-Eriksonian model proposed to exhibit correspondences with the 25 steps of the present model. Finally, I switch to discussing the process of development rather than the contents or product. In particular, I describe critical components of nonlinear dynamical systems theory.

## References


Case, R. (1978). Intellectual development from birth to adulthood: A neo-piagetian interpretation. In R. Siegler (Ed.), *Children's thinking: What develops?* (pp. 109–150). Hillsdale: Erlbaum.

Case, R. (1985). *Intellectual development: Birth to adulthood*. Orlando: Academic Press.

Case, R. (1987). Neo-Piagetian theory: Retrospect and prospect. *International Journal of Psychology, 22*, 773–791.

Commons, M. L. (2008). Introduction to the model of hierarchical complexity and its relationship to postformal action. *World Futures, 64*, 305–320.

Commons, M. L., & Richards, F. A. (2002). Organizing components in combinations: How stage transition works. *Journal of Adult Development, 9*, 159–177.

Feldman, D. H. (2004). Piaget's stages: The unfinished symphony of cognitive development. *New Ideas in Psychology, 22*, 175–231.

Fischer, K. W. (1980). A theory of cognitive development: The control and construction of hierarchies of skills. *Psychological Review, 87*, 477–531.

Fischer, K. W. (2009). Mind, brain, and education: Building a scientific groundwork for learning and teaching. *Mind, Brain, and Education, 3*, 3–16.

Fischer, K. W., & Bidell, T. R. (2006). Dynamic development of action and thought. In W. Damon & R. M. Lerner (Eds.), *Handbook of child psychology: Vol. 1. Theoretical models of human development* (pp. 313–399). New York: Wiley.

Fischer, K. W., & Hogan, A. E. (1989). The big picture for infant development: Levels and variations. In J. Lockman & N. Hazen (Eds.), *Action in social context: Perspectives on early development* (pp. 275–305). New York: Plenum.

Fischer, K. W., & Pruyne, E. (2003). Reflective thinking in adulthood: Emergence, development, and variation. In J. Demick & C. Andreoletti (Eds.), *Handbook of adult development* (pp. 169–198). New York: Kluwer Academic/Plenum.

Fischer, K. W., Yan, Z., & Stewart, J. (2003). Adult cognitive development: Dynamics in the developmental web. In J. Valsiner & K. J. Connolly (Eds.), *Handbook of developmental psychology* (pp. 493–516). London: Sage.

Hutchins, E. (1995). *Cognition in the wild*. Cambridge: MIT Press.

Immordino-Yang, M. H., & Fischer, K. W. (2007). Dynamic development of hemispheric biases in three cases: Cognitive/hemispheric cycles, music, and hemispherectomy. In D. Coch, K. W. Fischer, & G. Dawson (Eds.), *Human behavior, learning, and the developing brain: Typical development* (pp. 74–111). New York: Guilford Press.

Labouvie-Vief, G. (1992). A neo-Piagetian perspective on adult cognitive development. In R. J. Sternberg & C. A. Berg (Eds.), *Intellectual development* (pp. 197–228). Cambridge: Cambridge University Press.

Labouvie-Vief, G. (2006). Emerging structures of adult thought. In J. J. Arnett & J. L. Tanner (Eds.), *Emerging adults in America: Coming of age in the 21st century* (pp. 59–84). Washington: American Psychological Association.

Labouvie-Vief, G., Grühn, D., & Studer, J. (2010). Dynamic integration of emotion and cognition: Equilibrium regulation in development and aging. In R. M. Lerner, M. E. Lamb, & A. M. Freund (Eds.), *The handbook of life-span development: Vol. 2. Social and emotional development* (pp. 79–115). New York: Wiley.

Matsuzawa, T. (1994). Field experiments on use of stone tools by chimpanzees in the wild. In R. W. Wrangham, W. C. McGrew, F. B. M. de Waal, & P. G. Heltne (Eds.), *Chimpanzee cultures* (pp. 351–370). Cambridge: Harvard University Press and the Chicago Academy of Sciences.

Mounoud, P. (1976). Les revolutions psychologiques de l'enfant [Psychological revolutions in the child]. *Archives de Psychologie, 44*, 103–114.

Mounoud, P. (1986). Similarities between developmental sequences at different age periods. In I. Levin (Ed.), *Stage and structure: Reopening the debate* (pp. 40–58). Norwood: Ablex.

Mounoud, P., & Bower, T. (1974-1975). Conservation of weight in infants. *Cognition, 3*, 29–40.

Young, G. (1990a). Early neuropsychological development: Lateralization of functions - hemispheric specialization. In C. A. Hauert (Ed.), *Developmental psychology: Cognitive, perceptuo-motor and neuropsychological perspectives* (pp. 113–181). Amsterdam: North Holland.

Young, G. (1990b). The development of hemispheric and manual specialization. In G. E. Hammond (Ed.), *Cerebral control of speech and limb movements* (pp. 79–139). Amsterdam: North Holland.

Young, G. (1997). *Adult development, therapy, and culture: A postmodern synthesis*. New York: Plenum.

Young, G. (2008). Psychological injury: Systems, change processes, development. *Psychological Injury and Law, 1*, 243–254.

Young, G., & Gouin Décarie, T. (1977). An ethology-based catalogue of facial/vocal behavior in infancy. *Animal Behavior, 25*, 95–107.

# Chapter 5
# The Present Model: II Postformal Stage, Neo-Eriksonian Parallels, Systems

## Introduction

The present chapter is the second of two chapters introducing the primary concepts in the present work. In the previous chapter, I present the cognitive model, in general. In this chapter, I examine in depth one aspect of it, that of the postformal stage of collective intelligence that I have proposed. In addition, I examine the Neo-Eriksonian model that has been posited to develop in parallel with the Neo-Piagetian one. Finally, I switch to the other main aspect of any developmental modeling, that of transition mechanisms.

## Postformal Stage

Piaget maintained that there is no postformal stage in cognitive development after the formal one emerges in adolescence. Labouvie-Vief (1992; Labouvie-Vief, Grühn, & Studer, 2010) reminded us that the concept of the collective was important to Piaget, who wrote that adolescents feel for "collective ideals" and assign themselves goals and roles "in social life." However, this attitude was derived from their new formal operational potentials, and Piaget did not treat a collective style of cognition.

By contrast, the present model includes a postformal stage of collective intelligence. However, other Neo-Piagetians had proposed postformal steps in development before my work. In the following sections, I describe this other work, show how I have built on them, and indicate how the concept of collective intelligence captures well the essence of adult postformal thought.

G. Young, *Development and Causality: Neo-Piagetian Perspectives*,
DOI 10.1007/978-1-4419-9422-6_5, 

## *Neo-Piagetians*

### Labouvie-Vief

For Labouvie-Vief, postformal thought is characterized in part by a genuine interaction between individual and community, or self and other. Truth does not reside in any sphere alone but is constructed cooperatively in an interpersonal social process among (partially) self-organized (autonomous) beings. She also described this stage as one where there is an interaction or a fusion involving cognition and emotion.

Labouvie-Vief (2009; Labouvie-Vief et al., 2010 described results from her earlier studies that are consistent with a transition in adult thought to increase in cognitive-emotional complexity (Labouvie-Vief, Chiodo, Goguen, Diehl, & Orwoll, 1995; Labouvie-Vief, DeVoe, & Bulka, 1989). She and her coworkers (1989) defined high cognitive-emotional complexity in terms of the use of language that is complex, nonstereotypical, and nondualistic. It tolerates intraindividual and interindividual conflict. It appreciates the uniqueness of individual experience. In their study, they coded respondents' understanding of emotions, as well as their self-description and their description of others. The results indicated that with increasing age from adolescence to adulthood, the richness of emotional expressiveness increased "dramatically." For example, the participants expressed more complex historical perspectives – indicating a better differentiating of self and other. They could better integrate the tensions between negative and positive emotions involving self and other. The results were replicated in longitudinal research (Helson & Soto, 2005; Labouvie-Vief, Diehl, Jain, & Zhang, 2007) (Table 5.1, Fig. 5.1).

### Sinott

Sinnott (2002, 2009) has developed a model of postformal thought that he labeled Complex Postformal Thought. In this regard, Galupo, Cartwright, and Savage (2010) indicated that postformal thinking is marked by the capacity to evaluate and coordinate multiple systems of logic in thought and to integrate the subjective and objective in reasoning. They emphasized that social contexts are important in moving cognition toward the postformal stage. For example, Sinnott (1998) wrote that relationships likely serve as "fertile grounds" for emerging logical conflicts that could promote the development of postformal thinking.

Cartwright, Galupo, Tyree, and Jennings (2009) established the reliability and validity of the Complex Postformal Thought Questionnaire. It consisted of three major components – Multiple Elements, Subjective Choice, and Underlying Comp-lexities. Based on their data, Cartwright et al. (2009) suggested that a developmental progression takes place in postformal thought from underlying complexities to multiple elements and then subjective choice. This illustrates the cognitive–affective linkage that has been described for postformal thought.

**Table 5.1** Levels of self-representation in Labouvie-Vief

| Level | Description | Example |
|---|---|---|
| 0 (Concrete/presystemic) | The language used is simple and concrete. Characteristics and physical traits are seen as global. Events are detailed in simple seriation. Action-oriented behaviors describe activities. No references to goals or psychological processes occur | I am an engineer<br>I am physically robust, strong, (6 ft., 280 lbs)<br>I am tall<br>I am nice<br>I am pretty<br>I have two sisters |
| 1 (Interpersonal/protosystemic) | Simple evaluations are made that reflect the values of the immediate social group. Traits described are nondifferentiated. Individuals are described in terms of relationships (simple descriptors) and social networks. Emphasis is on features of the self or others that make for in-group acceptance | I like to fool around and make my friends laughs<br>I am outgoing and friendly<br>I love my family<br>I am fun to be with<br>I have lots of friends<br>I am involved in many clubs at school |
| 2 (Institutional/intrasystemic) | Interpersonal descriptors indicate a clearer sense of the individual within the social group. Traits at this level indicate a more self-directed and goal-directed individual whose evaluations are guided by achievement-oriented and conventional goals, values, and roles. Achievement of these goals and values is a frequent theme | I am family-oriented and active in my community<br>I am effective as a mother<br>I am empathic and a committed friend<br>I have not been successful in my life<br>I work hard to support my children and really love them<br>I have tried, with some success, to develop the patience of my father and devotion of my mother |
| 3 (Contextual/intersystemic) | Descriptions are critical of convention, involve an awareness of how traits change, and give a sense of individuals with their own value system. Institutional goals are reexamined and put into historical or psychological perspective<br>Descriptions involve references to processes and contrasts over time | I am a singer, an actress, and a writer and want to use those talents more creatively than I do now<br>I get along well with all people but need to develop more insights as to what motivates other people<br>I am relearning who I am<br>I am adding new dimensions to my life in as many ways as possible |

(continued)

**Table 5.1** (continued)

| Level | Description | Example |
|---|---|---|
| 4 (Dynamic/intersubjective) | Roles and traits are described at a complex psychological level and reflect awareness of underlying, often-unconscious motivation and reciprocal interaction. Activities and goals are seen as subject to continual revision as one gains knowledge of oneself and others. Reference is to multiple dimensions of life history and an emphasis on process, becoming, and emergence | I struggle with the concept of who I am; and have been identified as all-giving mother, self-sufficient, religious; and I think, feeling the need to be a more individualized woman with specific needs and desires<br>I work for profit rather than for satisfaction, partly because of my (guilty) need to continue to support my family<br>At this point in my life and my parents' lives, they are becoming dependent, and I find myself reliving the tensions of struggling to remain my adult self but getting pulled back to my younger self as I have spent more time with them |

Reprinted with the permission of American Psychological Association. Labouvie-Vief, G., Chiodo, L. M., Goguen, L. A., Diehl, M., & Orwoll, L. (1995). Copyright © 1995. [Table 1, Page. 407]

Narratives were transcribed and coded by the authors into four levels of adult emotional and self-development. The first level reflects Piagetian concrete operational thinking, and the next four formal and postformal thinking

At level 1, individuals describe the self in terms of the values of the immediate social group, such as their relationships, and the immediate social network. They emphasize features of the self and other that make for immediate group acceptance (e.g., "I am outgoing and friendly")

At level 2, one finds self-descriptions that reflect a more individualized, differentiated, and inner sense of self. For example, the self is described in terms of fairly self-directed values and goals, often related to achievement and institutionalized social roles. However, the individual accepts these roles rather than reflects on them (e.g., "I am family-oriented and active in my community")

By contrast, individuals at level 3 have a more contextual view of the self. Their descriptions often are critical of conventions, as institutional goals are reexamined and placed in historical perspective, including reflections of how they have shaped the self. One finds more dynamic self-descriptions that emphasize the role of historical and psychological factors, with many references to processes and contrasts over time (e.g., "I am relearning who I am")

Finally, at level 4 these descriptions are even more multifaceted, as individuals describe themselves in the most complex way in terms of underlying, unconscious motivations and reciprocal interactions. The view of the self is truly dynamic, in that individuals realize that activities and goals are subject to continual revision as one gains knowledge of self and others. Overall, the sense of self that is conveyed is one of process, becoming, and emergence. Thus, identity is viewed as transforming over time as a result of an inner psychological reorganization

The Labouvie-Vief model stands as an important postformal model because of the integration in cognitive and emotional components of the self and because of the integration of self and other perspectives implicit in it. The last stage's title reflects this evolution, because it is called dynamic and intersubjective, moving it away from the systems labels of the prior steps

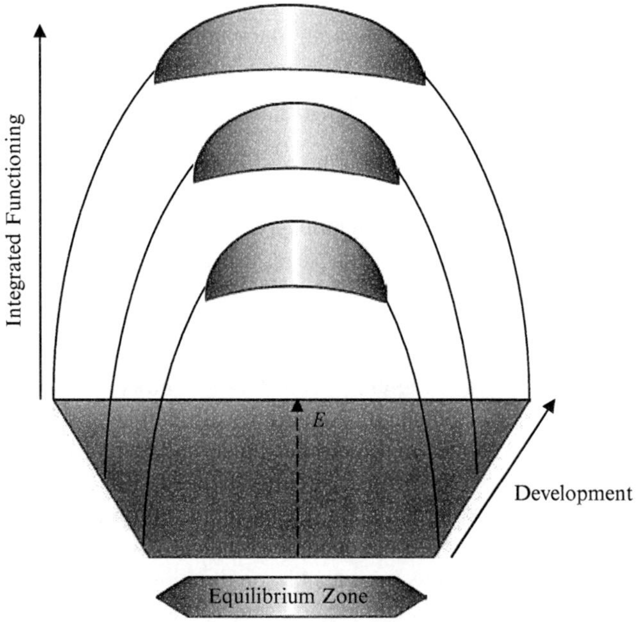


**Fig. 5.1** A complex equilibrium model indicating broadening of equilibrium zones and elevation of tension thresholds at low, moderate, and high levels of complexity of cognitive-emotional structures. Labouvie-Vief and colleagues described simple equilibrium models as involving a relationship between integrated functioning and transitioning from an equilibrium zone to areas of increasing stress and breakdown. In their complex equilibrium model, the equilibrium zone broadens with development or with higher levels of complexity of cognitive-emotional structures, allowing increased tension thresholds at the boundaries of the equilibrium zones. Piaget (1976, 1980) had developed similar concepts in terms of assimilative stability alternating with accommodative change that moves the cognitive system toward increasing complexity in schemes, operations, and stages. The child engages in automatic assimilative practices, but inconsistencies/discrepancies/incoherences appear in their application and are amplified. For Piaget, this leads to a "grasp of consciousness" and accommodatory changes, while assimilatory attempts are inhibited. The system does not run off in continued amplification because of continued negative feedback to stabilize the changes. For Piaget, the controlled process of change means that the changes involve "intelligible" change involving reintegration. After each gain, a new cycle of differentiation/disequilibrium/accommodation results, with another integration/equilibration/assimilation at a higher level. Traditionally, equilibrium zones are conceptualized in terms of correcting responses to increasing tension or deviation from ideal end states, such as in Cannon's work. Newer conceptualizations allow for tension amplification via feed-forward mechanisms that enlarges the range of system growth and stability (Lewis, 2005). In development, this takes place equally for cognition and emotion, e.g., in terms of increasingly complex representations and better automated emotion regulation, respectively. Skills in these domains automate and crystallize with development, allowing adaptation to loss of fluidity in aging. Labouvie-Vief referred to cognitive–affective structures because, according to her, Piaget (1954/1981) had proposed a common developmental trajectory for cognition and emotions. Cognitive structures are always associated with affective energetics. However, the integration of cognition and affect changes with developmental period. From adolescence to middle-age in adults, emotional understanding increases greatly. For example, the latter age group could integrate tensions better between negative and positive emotions both in the self and in the other and in relating past and present (Labouvie-Vief et al., 2007). Reprinted with the permission of IOS Press. Reprinted from Restoration Neurology and Neuroscience, Volume 27(5), Labouvie-Vief, G. (2009). Copyright 2009, with permission from IOS Press. [Figure 3, Page. 558]

Indeed, Sinnott and Berlanstein (2006) referred to "felt connection" as being part of adult cognitive development. He listed three types of "feeling connected:" connecting the sides of the self, connecting with others, and connecting with the transcendent.

Sinnott (1994) had written earlier on the postformal stage of cognitive development. It includes a subjective, self-referential meta-awareness that the world is filtered through our emotions and cognitions, an awareness that is honed in the ever-changing interpersonal realm. This leads to the ability to operate with or orchestrate different abstract systems while seeking a superordinate, unitative one, to form abstract metasystems. Also, postformal thought involves the ability to choose or commit to, through self-referential, pragmatic, and relativistic thought processes, one abstract system among many (contradictory) ones, and to know and accept that one is performing at this sometimes difficult level. The social implication here is that one realizes that the other must make equally part-subjective reality choices so that system-fitting to reality is needed in cooperative group (or collective) cognition, exploration, consensus, and solution-making.

Sinnott (2002, 2009) indicated the operations indicative of postformal thought. In metatheory shifts, individuals are capable of thinking in at least two logical systems, in that they shift between an idealized interpretation of the problem and a practical one associated with solving the problem. In process–product shifting, individuals alternate between (a) a more general process approach of adapting a logical system that would work in many cases similar to the one being considered and (b) a product approach, which is a concrete solution in context. In parameter setting, having two logics about the problem is indicated by individuals limiting or organizing the problem space. In pragmatism, a commitment is made to one of the options in logic available in problem solving. By definition, having multiple goals, methods, solutions, and causal understandings indicates postformal thought. Paradox contains within it an implicit double logic, and qualifies, as well. Finally, self-referential thought indicates postformal thought for Sinott because individuals are aware that they must be the ultimate judges of which logic to commit.

## Others

Armon's model (e.g., Armon, 1995; Armon & Dawson, 2002) emphasized individuality, autonomy, as well as community in adult thinking. Blanchard-Fields (1989) is another researcher on postformal reasoning who related its development to the socioemotional context. In this age period, adults recognize that the thinking process is influenced by subjective and interpersonal factors. At the penultimate level, the self is understood as an interpreter, and in addition, interpretive discrepancies are resolved by relating them to the self and to the other. For her, higher levels in cognition include emotions in the reasoning process.

At the structural level, the Neo-Piagetian program of Case and Fischer has described the cyclic recursion of substages in development over stages, but only Fischer has included a postformal stage (Fischer's system of systems, which develops after the abstract period). This postformal stage in cognitive development refers to the adult being able to construct a system of abstract truths and being able to work with it (compare, contrast, relate, etc.) so that the developing person realizes that there is not one primary or universal abstract truth. However, the concept of the postformal stage is not well developed in Fischer, especially in terms of including in it several stages or substages.

Commons and Richards (2002) referred to their postformal stage in adult thinking as involving orders of hierarchical complexity (Commons & Richards, 1984a, 1984b). For the tasks used, in the first stage of systematic operations, ideal completers "discriminate" from within an integrated systemic approach the frameworks for relationships between variables. Multivariate causes could be sought. Matrix representations or tables could be constructed. Multidimensionality could be evident in orderings, priorities, and preferences. Systems could be created with a unifying theme, while others would be rejected.

Next, the postformal adult moves into the stage of metasystematic order. In this stage, ideal task completers can act on the systems that had been created. Metasystematic actions function to compare and contrast systems, and to transform and synthesize them. Metasystematic actions could create meta- or supersystems. The focus is on similarities, differences, causal relationships, and the role of actors.

In the paradigmatic order stage that follows, ideal completers create new fields from multiple metasystems. New paradigms could result, where relationships between quite large and seemingly unrelated disparate bodies of knowledge are determined.

In cross-paradigmatic thought, paradigms are integrated, creating new scholarly fields, or profoundly altering old ones (think Darwin, Einstein). Note that the work of Commons is described in depth in Chap. 18.

Others have described a "group" intelligence, based on socially shared or distributed, collective processes, where communal cognition is greater than and/or qualitatively different from the individual, part cognitions involved (e.g., Wertsch, Tulviste, & Hagstrom, 1993; Williams & Sternberg, 1988; Woolley, Chabris, Pentland, Hashmi, & Malone, 2010). Also, see Halford, Wilson, and Phillips (2010) on relational knowledge and Couzin (2009) on collective cognition in animal groups. Price, Caldwell, and Whiten (2010) argued that the distinguishing feature of humans compared to other species involves the capacity for significant cumulative culture. For example, individuals joining a group working in a task in process need only see the product of the task to date to improve the product. All these conceptualizations are quite consistent with the present one that the postformal stage should be called one of collective intelligence.

## *The Present Model of Postformal Intelligence*

### Collective Intelligence

*Introduction*. Based on the work of others on the stage of postformal thought, the present approach underscores that in the postformal period, collective abstract thought is taking place. It is considered qualitatively distinct from the abstract thought of the adolescent.

This stage involves a symbiotic sharing process in abstract intelligence across individuals, permitting constitutive elaborations in intelligence and in cognitive-emotion fusion that are superordinate or overarching. That is, according to the present model, the postformal stage of intelligence ultimately involves the search for cross-abstraction abstractions and other second-order formal thought syntheses (e.g., cross-principle, cross-model, cross-domain integrations). Cognitive and affective giving and taking become cofunctions in being, as abstract meta-systems, second-order abstractions, and the like are constructed.

In addition, in the collective intelligence mode of thought, intelligent adults can expand their intellectual limits by symbiotically sharing with and contributing to collective knowledge. They work within a collective tradition even when working alone or realize the limits of their individual cognition and seek a collective solution.

In their collective intelligence, intelligent adults seek a meta-integration of abstract ideas that might be local or disparate, but also they seek an integration of the certain and uncertain, the absolute and relative, the personal and shared, the self and other, the mental and emotional, and so on, in the communal crucible. These structures are not static but are dynamic and evolve, and they are not simply a concatenation of separate parts but form integrated wholes that emerge out of the interaction of the parts, both cognitive and affective-social.

Thus, collective intelligence is more than relativistic or about multiple, locally constructed truths; for its logic is to take truths such as this and determine their pattern, even if it is only to say that the pattern involved is contextual, variable, perspectivist, etc. In this sense, a mature postformal intelligence would pursue in an active manner second-order abstract integrations without using a contextual generalities, i.e., necessarily, these would contain within them contextual qualifications.

*Qualities*. Beyond its description in communal terms, collective intelligence needs to be understood for what it is compared to what it is not. These qualifications both constrain and expand our understanding of it.

(a) Cognition needs to be conceived in terms beyond the individual, for it is a cooperative, multiperson system that surpasses the contributions of its parts; brainstorming provides the classic example of how abstract structures can be elaborated in groups.
(b) Collective thought may concern complex practical, artistic, or oral folk skills, and the like, as much as scientific and scholarly endeavors; it is not limited to the few who can arrive at superior abstract abilities or who create penultimate abstract works. It is best to conceive of abstract thought in the adolescent as limited to local, focused abstract notions, perhaps with several components or layers at best. However, the adult, especially when working with others, can construct more intricate models that cohere abstract structures such as derived at the adolescent level of thought into more integrated or refined structures. Moreover, the topics could be quite practical and mechanical, and not scientific or scholarly. Think of complex work manuals developed by individuals or groups at work.

(c) Collective intelligence thought processes need not involve group or public acts but simply may be (re)organizational ones at the level of the individual, or private ones not expressed to others. That is, although they are still considered outcomes of collective intelligence, much of the products of this process take place within individuals alone rather than in groups, for example, when an individual reads the work of others and integrates it. The process is still collective even if the thinking takes place by an individual.

(d) Collective intelligence refers to the superordinate abstract structures that are formed by individuals or groups. They do not reside in stationary products of thinking, nor necessarily correct ones. In the brainstorming process, collective ideas are formulated in the intellectual repartee and are continually improved. They might start at local and isolated levels, but eventually they cohere into superordinate abstract structures. These are continually subject to exchange and change processes that alter their contents and organization. Of course, they might be ill-conceived plans or incorrect abstract ideas, but they still possess the properties of being superordinate and cohering across local abstract domains.

    Moreover, the brainstorming might take place within an individual rather than in a group. The individual might oppose two intellectual traditions or abstract notions toward building an emergent one based on them or a new one that is outrightly different. Or the repartee could be between the dynamic constructions being framed as the person reads or otherwise learns about a topic and the revisions in it that take place through further learning and reflection.

(e) Collective intelligence not only refers to how we collect abstract ideas into superordinate abstract structures, it also refers to the integration of cognitive and affective processes in the structures. Adolescents can reflect on abstract situations removed from themselves but have more difficulty with personal ones relative to adults. Moreover, cognition and affect form a unified whole, but adults experience less difficulty in joining these different aspects of the whole into coordinated cognitive–affective structures. For example, androgyny concerns the integration of female and male gender models, and adults demonstrate improvement in the ability to express and combine their masculine and feminine parts. The stage of collective intelligence concerns symbiotically constructed transabstract intelligence complexes with socioemotional correspondences. The socioemotional systems that correspond to this stage of development are especially other-oriented (e.g., Erikson's stage of generativity).

## Comments

Together, these arguments suggest that this penultimate stage of collective intelligence in cognitive development might be more widespread in humans than some would imagine. Collective intelligence is not an esoteric acquisition but part of our group thinking process. Moreover, it functional, and impregnates many aspects of our daily lives. We need to learn to recognize it more. When we focus too much on individual cognition, we might miss the forest among the trees.

Note that signs of collective thought might be evident in earlier stages of cognitive development, but they are without the fundamental characteristics of suprasystemic conjecture and cognitive-emotional fusion so are not equivalent to the mature adult thought that is being described. The concept of collective intelligence has even been applied to the activity of the social insects (Sulis, 2009) so that it is used in different ways in different disciplines, but social ants hardly use abstract thought in their collective intelligence.

To conclude, the substages of coordination/hierarchization, systematization, and multiplication/integration in the collective intelligence stage of cognitive development might concern something as advanced as subdiscipline, discipline, and interdisciplinary levels of collective intellectual activity. However, as the examples of brainstorming indicate, the products of the process might be simpler, although no less superordinate and collectively abstract. It would be a question of degree.

### *Interim Summary*

In the previous section on adult postformal thought, I described the ultimate cognitive capacities of the developing human in terms of a Neo-Piagetian stage model. I referred to this stage in the adult as collective intelligence, and its label illustrates the mutuality of cognition and socioaffective processes. As for the socioaffective stages and substages parallel to the cognitive stages and substages of the present model, they also concern mutuality, in that they are Neo-Eriksonian in origin, and Erikson emphasized this process in development. It will be interesting for the reader to see how I characterized the steps I added to the present model, given that Erikson proposed an eight-step sequence over the lifes pan and I have a 25-step one in which his stages are inserted. For example, in terms of the prior section, what are the equivalent Neo-Eriksonian steps after Erikson's last one of ego integrity that I added to the present model to complete its formulation as a one-to-one correspondence of Neo-Piagetian and Eriksonian stages and steps in development? Of course, there is a basic distinction related to the cognitive and affective sides of the steps in development because a cognitive advance is no guarantee that its equivalent socioaffective one will emerge. In a later portion of the present work, in this regard, I refer to the concept of the cognitive (mis)perception of the other, and show how it relates to the 25 steps of the present model.

## Neo-Eriksonian Model

### *The Steps*

*Introduction*. The 25 specific Neo-Eriksonian stages considered to develop in parallel with the 25 cognitive steps of the present model include 17 stages that I constructed specifically for the present model, given that Erikson described eight stages across the life span and I sought a one-to-one correspondence across the cognitive and affective domains. In constructing the new steps in the present Neo-Eriksonian model of development, I followed his concept of opposing a positive and negative pole for each step. However, I refer to the oppositions as "acts." This relates to the notion that they are more than tendencies, but are ways of relating to the world based on grounded, participatory relational experiences reflective of an embodied psychology. Also, the oppositions involved are presented as a dialectic of competing acts to highlight their external social contextual aspect compared to their internal psychodynamic one. This approach to naming the steps involved was applied even to the traditional Eriksonian stages in the sequence (e.g., I labeled Erikson's first stage as trust vs. mistrust acts) (Table 5.2, Fig. 5.2).

Also, the particular labels that Erikson used to indicate the oppositions concern emergent characteristics that develop either optimally or nonoptimally in a variety of ways. However, the particular adjectives that he chose for the nonoptimal conditions seem too specific (e.g., problems in trust need not concern only mistrust). I have tried to accommodate to this concern in the descriptions of the oppositions created for the new steps in the revised model. Also, in choosing the labels for the negative poles, I avoided repetition of a common prefix, such as "mis" or "dys," preferring to find a different prefix for each stage.

*Steps*. By applying this logical procedure to a revised Neo-Eriksonian model of socioaffective development, I constructed the 25-step Neo-Eriksonian sequence presented in Table 4.3 (Young, 1997) (see Table 4.3, in Chap. 4). To see the challenges/dangers for each of the 25 Neo-Eriksonian stages, refer to Chap. 20. It is interesting to note that Erikson's model of stages in personality development has been modified much less in the literature (cf. Blasi & Glodis, 1995; Blatt, 2008) than Piaget's model of stages in cognitive development. Indeed, to my knowledge, to date there has not been a model proposed as a Neo-Eriksonian model of stages in development.

Because the initial stage in the Neo-Piagetian model concerns reflexive behavior beginning even before birth and up to 1 month of age, I created five Neo-Eriksonian stages to match the substages of this cognitive reflexive stage. Then, I constructed 12 more stages for the four remaining stages from infancy across the life span, adding three steps in each of the four stages, as the original eight Eriksonian stages appeared to correspond to two substages within each of these last four stages of the current model.

Specifically in terms of correspondence with the present Neo-Piagetian model, the original eight Eriksonian stages are hypothesized to appear in the last four of the five stages in development proposed in the model, with two of them emerging in each of these four stages. In particular, they appear to emerge during the even-numbered substages (2, 4) so that they are sandwiched by other Neo-Eriksonian acquisitions (in substages 1, 3, 5). Because the eight Eriksonian stages have been placed at the juncture of the second and fourth substages of each of the last four stages of the current model, it is as if specific personality-related acquisitions in the odd-numbered substages within each of the stages prepare the groundwork for spurts in classic Eriksonian personality development during the even-numbered substages. For example, Erikson's initial infant stage of trust vs. mistrust is considered

**Table 5.2** The issues-crises in Erikson's psychosocial developmental stages

| Stage (and normative age) | Issue-crisis |
|---|---|
| 1 Trust vs. mistrust (0–1) | First year devoted to acquiring sentiment of trust in self and environment. Mothers, in particular, satisfy infants' basic needs creating this feeling of positive self worth. Inconsistent, discontinuous, or rejecting care may result in a sense of loss, perception of world as dangerous, and view of the world as unreliable |
| 2 Autonomy vs. shame/ doubt (1–3) | In the following years, toddlers and young children learn the tasks of self-sufficiency such as feeding, dressing, cleaning self. They separate from the parents and learn the rules of their culture. Problems in attaining a sense of independence may produce self-doubt in capacities, expectation of defeat in a struggle involving will, and feelings of shame |
| 3 Initiative vs. guilt (3–6) | Preschoolers' energy and imagination lead not only to communication, curiosity, pretend play, acceptance of responsibility, trying to act grown-up, but also intrusive activities, consuming fantasies. The latter happenings can lead to conflicts with family members and also guilt. Excessive guilt can dampen initiative, so a balance of initiative and respect of others' requirements is needed. Children's conscience emerges here |
| 4 Industry vs. inferiority (6–12) | The school-age period before puberty sees children mater complex social and academic skills. Comparisons with peers are made. The reward for accepting instruction is praise for success, producing a sense of efficacy and self-assurance. The potential crisis is that a sense of personal inadequacy can develop if these skills escape children in their life at school or at home, causing them to avoid new activities |
| 5 Identity vs. identity diffusion (12–18) | Adolescents integrate childhood identification to create a self-identity concerning their pubertal drives, skills, social roles, and potential work roles. They choose whom to become from among the multiple possible selves available. They may want to try out many selves, but must be moderate. Confusion at these levels is temporarily unavoidable, and the risk is of role ambiguity, diffusion, or negativity (oppositional behavior against peers', parents' wishes) |
| 6 Intimacy vs. isolation (20s) | Young adults secure in their identity can establish a feeling of intimacy with the (20s) inner self and the outer world (friends, love partner). They can share all aspects of oneself with others without fearing the loss of identity. A deep sentiment of loneliness may be incurred if individuals cannot fully enter into an intimate relationship due to a fear of losing their identity |
| 7 Generativity vs. self-absorption (20s +) | In middle adulthood, mature individuals strive to establish and guide the following generation. Responsibilities concern family, work, the role of mentor, and whatever standards the culture defines. Problems here yield self-centered, self-absorbed behavior and a feeling of interpersonal emptiness |

(continued)

**Table 5.2** (continued)

| Stage (and normative age) | Issue-crisis |
|---|---|
| 8 Ego integrity vs. despair (50s +) | With intimacy and acceptance of one's efforts at generativity, elder persons can look back at their lives as meaningful, productive, satisfying, happy. They actively reminisce about the past, enthusiastically anticipate the future, and seemingly possess wisdom. At issue is whether the dominant mood will be one of contentment or disappointment with unfulfilled goals, leading to sadness, displeasure, disgust |



Erikson wrote his major works in the 1950s and 1960s (Erikson). He ameliorated the classical Freudian view of psychosexual stages in several important ways. First, he referred to the stages as psychosocial instead of psychosexual, acknowledging their contextual and mutual influences. The developing person is not just the seat of libidinal impulses and the battles to control both them and the psychodynamic conflicts that they engender. The ego has a role to play in the person's psychic apparatus, and mediates with the surround. Therefore, each stage is marked by a polarity of a new developmental challenge, crisis, issue, or danger, and the developing person negotiates each one in context

The stages stretch into adulthood; Erikson realized that development is lifelong and the psychosexual stage of the adolescent and adult period is not the last one to develop; the genital investment that it involves modifies with new psychosocial polarities at major life junctures. As an undergraduate, I asked myself how Piaget could have developed a model of four stages in cognitive development and Freud and Erikson a model having five or more in affective development. Other workers have reworked Erikson's stage model (Blatt, 2008; Young, 1997; see the Fig. 5.2)

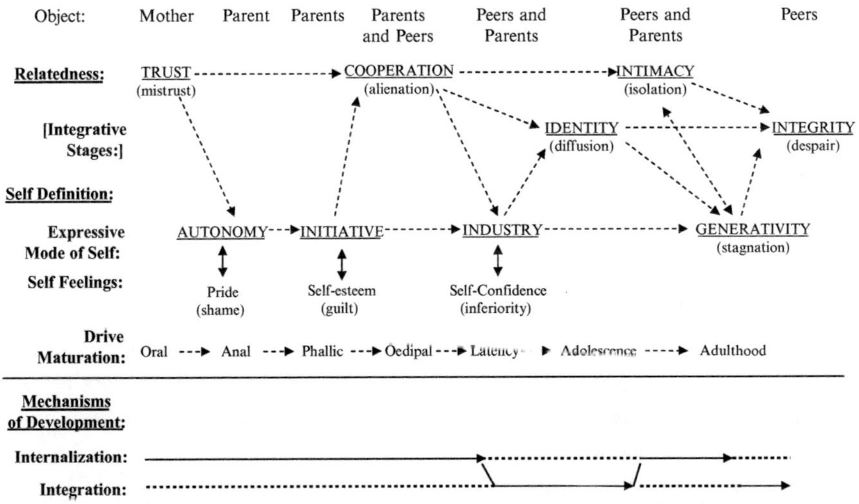


**Fig. 5.2** Eriksonian model of the process of psychological development. The figure presents Erikson's model of stages in personality development but adds in an extra stage labeled Cooperation vs. Alienation. Blatt (2008) explained the development of the stages in terms relatedness, self-definition, and internalization-integration. For the present purposes, the addition of the stage of cooperation indicates that contemporary workers are attempting revision's of Erikson's model, like in the present work. Reprinted with the permission of Lawrence Erlbaum Associates, Inc. Blatt, S. J., & Blass, R. B. (1996). Copyright 2011. [Figure 12.2, Page. 324]

to reach its apex at around the middle of the first year, and it is seen to be preceded by a system of dyadic acts (e.g., modeling, shaping) and followed by a system of sociability acts (e.g., play, seek lead). As another example, the stage involving Eriksonian adolescent identity is considered to be embedded in a sequence with conscious acts before it and nurturing acts after it (e.g., esteem for self, other; love, let love romantic partner, respectively).

Note that the Eriksonian socioemotional systems have not been transplanted without any change into the present model. The major change has been to reduce the age range to which they apply, at least for some of them. This facilitated their insertion into the present model and, in effect, permitted their expansion by showing the way they can be complemented by the intermediate systems that develop between them.

## *Conclusion*

If there are eight Eriksonian psychosocial stages in development, exactly how did I arrive at the model of how they fit into the present model of 25 Neo-Eriksonian stages? To place them in the larger sequence, I analyzed carefully their characteristics in relation to the characteristics of the cognitive stages that corresponded to them, as determined by the age ranges involved in the two sequences. Once I had established the Neo-Piagetian/Eriksonian step correspondence, I examined the 17 Neo-Piagetian cognitive steps that lacked a corresponding Eriksonian stage in terms of their nature. That is, I developed the labels and properties of the 17 new Eriksonian stages by examining the characteristics of the cognitive steps to which they had to correspond as well as the steps preceding and following them. Therefore, the properties of the all of the 25 Neo-Eriksonian steps proposed in the present are consistent with the properties of their corresponding cognitive steps. This approach that I followed highlights the fundamental assumption of the present model that Neo-Eriksonian acquisitions should develop at the indicated developmental periods because of the properties of the cognitive advances that emerge in their corresponding cognitive steps.

I was surprised by the fit of the original eight Erikson stages with the equivalent ones of my cognitive model in terms of the age periods involved. Moreover, for each of the eight cognitive steps that corresponded to the eight Erikson stages, they seemed to have characteristics equivalent to the ones of the particular Erikson stage that corresponded to them.

In keeping with Erikson's approach, challenges/dangers/issues/crises are used to present the 25 Neo-Eriksonian developmental steps in the present model. Therefore, each cognitive substage of the present model is associated with positive and negative affective poles or acts (See Chap. 20).

Given the proposed relationship between corresponding cognitive and socioaffective acquisitions over 25 steps in development, it is worthwhile to note that affective acquisitions fuel as well as feed on the corresponding cognitive ones.

Both sides are part of a unified developing cognitive–affective psychological synergy. The challenges/crises inherent at the onset of each of Erikson's eight stages must play on the psychocognitive as well as the psychosocial substrate. For example, a challenge/crisis in initiative in the young child will have cognitive as well as socioemotional underpinnings and sequelae. Thus, any model that proposes dissociation of the socioemotional and the cognitive side of the developmental equation would be erroneous, for they are intimately and intrinsically linked over the life span; challenges/crises in one inevitably become challenges/crises in the other.

Finally, note that I did not try to fit the eight Erikson stages in a series of eight cognitive steps in my cognitive model, thereby avoiding anomalous parallels. This type of logic should dictate, in general, the placement of correspondences across cognitive development and related acquisitions. When the fit is not good, the models involved should be revised.

## Other Socioaffective Modeling

Other work related to socioaffectivity in the present model, in particular, I address the issue of the basic emotions that develop in the first 2 years of life (see Chap. 22). In contrast to typical models of basic emotions that normally list ten or fewer emotions, I present a model of at least 48 basic emotional families. Each is seen to reflect an intersection of basic cognitive appraisal dimensions that are socially grounded. I examine the relation of this model of basic emotions in infancy to the six Piagetian sensorimotor substages. In other work in the book on socioaffectivity, I relate the present cognitive model to corresponding developments in attachment (Chap. 24).

Only because I had developed a broader model of Neo-Piagetian cognitive development of 25 steps over stages and substages across the life span, and realized that there were parallels between stages and substages at the cognitive and affective levels, could I develop this 25-step Neo-Eriksonian model that added 17 steps to Erikson's original eight steps. This is an example of the theoretical integration that the present model permits and fosters.

## Developmental Process in the Current Work

### *Nonlinear Dynamical Systems Theory*

*Model.* Transition mechanisms underlying development across its various stages and substages as proposed in the present model are discussed in terms of the cross-disciplinary model of systems theory. Systems theory helps understand not only the contents of development, through examination of how components of wholes cohere, but also its change mechanisms. In this regard, work in the areas of nonlinear dynamical systems theory and complex adaptive systems are instructive (e.g., Thelen & Smith, 1994; Kauffman-Smith, 1993, respectively). In the present work, these approaches have been integrated into one model of underlying change processes that govern state or system transitions in development. Moreover, systems theory permits understanding of the dynamics of change in other systems, such as in steps of positive change in therapy and steps in negative change in chronic pain.

As systems mature, they inherently gravitate to the region in their state space that lies between randomness and regularity in order to maximize the possibility of change to more complex system reorganization or attractor states (complexity theory). In this regard, I present the concept of superordinate complex adaptive systems (see Chap. 28).

Controlling parameters, or specific, quantitative scalar variables that can reach critical thresholds preparatory to general, qualitative, discontinuous change (e.g., to different attractor basins), are considered key mechanisms of change in development. In the present model, they are not presented empirically, but examples are provided in terms of critical developmental acquisitions.

A key determinant parameter in stage transitions might concern activation/inhibition coordination. Indeed, this concept could help explain much about development. Inhibition is commonly understood as important in neurological processes and in behavioral expression. Its coordination with activation can be used to describe multiple components of both the cognitive-affective structures that develop and the change processes that spearhead their development. Indeed, both the content acquisitions that mark development across the life span and their causal dynamics could be well described in terms of an activation/inhibition model.

*Conclusion.* Psychologists are especially aware of systems when they work with families or couples. For example, a family might be in a state of constant turmoil, but a positive change in one member could produce a positive cascade effect on all members. Or a family might be on the verge of turmoil despite the apparent stability it presents to the outside world. Then, a minor crisis for one member of the family could lead to major disruptions in family life for all members due to vicious cycles that materialize. Therefore, the whole defines the outcome of system component interactions more than the additive sum of the parts. Similarly, in development, to understand stages in development, we need to analyze carefully their elements and how they interact. That is, developing behavior is always constructed in context de novo out of the matrix of internal and external elements comprising its person–environment transactions, and there are top-down processes that can influence it, as well as bottom-up ones.

## *Fractals*

So far, I have mentioned that in the present model there are 25 steps in development throughout the life span. Also, the 25 steps consist of cyclic recursions of substages within stages. Presently I expand this model of 25 steps in development in the following way.

From the point of view of the concept of fractals, I propose that within the substages, there are the same cyclic recursions that take place. The substage cycle has been described in terms of coordinations, hierarchizations, systematizations, multiplications, and integrations. Therefore, within each of them, there should be a similar five-step cyclic recursion. In this regard, the present model of steps in cognitive and affective development should be seen to follow a fractal model, where change processes repeat themselves at different levels of scale within the same system.

Given this concept of fractalization over different levels of development, the contents of the present developmental model now are considered to consist not of 25 steps in development but, rather, of at least 125 steps in development. The implication of this concept is that there are multiple discontinuous changes that take place in development. It should be kept in mind that, even in such a differentiated sequence, the steps reflect individual skills and capacities rather than cross-domain and universal acquisitions.

If there are so many discontinuous changes in development that could take place, an implication is that the distinction between local and global acquisitions might not reflect two contrasting poles of what is involved in development. With so many steps in development possible according to the present model, then at the global level development should be construed as an almost continuous movement of discontinuous transitions. Change, rather than stability and nonchange, could be the norm.

Further implications of the concept of so many steps in development is that the blurring that appears to apply to the continuous–discontinuous polarity might also apply to other antimonies in the field, such as micro- and macrodevelopment, shorter-term and longer-term changes, local and global acquisitions, domain and modular ones, stable and unstable changes, and quantitative and qualitative or emergent changes.

## *Concepts*

In the following, I provide a concise summary of the major concepts in nonlinear dynamical systems theory (see Chap. 28 for more details). I add how the present work includes a five-step transition process from attractors to complex adaptive systems that could underlie the advances in stages and substages in development. In particular, the model of five nonlinear dynamical transition steps might be the critical transition mechanisms that help stages evolve in the five-step sequence that has been proposed in the current model, and also in the repetition of the five steps in the substage sequence that recurs over the stages.

(a) *Systems and states.* A system is a network of elements expressing relationship that can change over time. The elements produce patterns, in which the whole is greater than the sum of the parts. The current configuration of the components of a system constitutes its existing state.

(b) *Dynamical systems.* Dynamical systems are capable of autonomously generating self-organizing emergent forms. In nonlinear dynamical systems, the new form of the state is discontinuous, being very different than its preceding form/state.
(c) *Butterfly effect.* Quite minor inputs to the system can elicit system change, even to the point that instability and transformation materialize. That is, sensitivities to initial conditions can produce disproportionate effects in a system.
(d) *Levels.* Systems are hierarchically arranged into interacting levels; for example, they might have subsystems that interact. Lower-level interactions in systems constitute "bottom-up" processes, and higher-level interactions are considered "top-down" processes.
(e) *Self-organization.* Systems self-organize, but this does not happen due to preprogrammed internal instructions. Rather, self-organization proceeds in the system's moment-to-moment adaptive, contextual transitioning.
(f) *Emergence.* System self-organization could elicit emergence of a new pattern in system state. The news state would not be predictable uniquely from knowing the preexisting state of the system in its context. Nevertheless, a system might be constrained by its constituent elements and its context in the nature of the emergent state(s) that could assemble.
(g) *Perturbations.* Systems might change abruptly when inputs release state-shift phase transitions or bifurcations. Perturbations that move systems to change state might be minor in systems that are far from equilibrium, or in systems in which there is sensitivity to initial conditions. System transitions are facilitated by the system reaching critical thresholds of its controlling parameters, such as when water reaches zero centigrade, or just below.
(h) *Energy.* Systems are considered "open" when energy can enter and potentially perturb them. Normally, systems find equilibrium related to incoming and outgoing energy, adjusting to the changes. In human systems, information could function as an equivalent of energy.
(i) *Far from equilibrium.* Systems can maintain equilibrium even when incoming energy (or information) pushes a state of a system far from equilibrium. However, although systems might resist change to perturbations, they might be more vulnerable to change at this point. Indeed, systems might gravitate to this juncture to facilitate adaptive change.
(j) *Feedback.* In positive feedback, system interactions amplify variation and the possibility of change. In negative feedback, change is damped through interactions in existing organization. Systems that are stable in equilibrium might destabilize when the balance of feedbacks lead to inability to maintain equilibrium.
(k) *Attractors.* When the movement of a system repeatedly ends at the same place or places in the system's mathematically possible, multiple state spaces, the system states are considered attractors. Attractors are viewed as system trajectories that gravitate repeatedly to the same attractor basins, or fixed values, despite their initial values or ongoing perturbations.
(l) *Attractor types.* There are different kinds of attractors. (1) After perturbation, point or fixed attractors gravitate to a steady state or a constant value. (2) Cyclical or periodic attractors oscillate over two different locations in state

space. (3) Torus attractors integrate two oscillatory attractors. (4) "Chaotic" or "strange" attractors are orderly or antichaotic, rather than being chaotic in the common meaning of the term. At the global level of their dynamics, chaotic attractors are usually stable. However, they express instability in terms of their individual, local trajectories, which are characterized by unpredictability, in that they never exactly repeat themselves. Indeed, because of the butterfly effect, they might change unexpectedly in reaction to seemingly minor perturbations. Therefore, chaotic systems are really just quasi-stable, and although they seek to deamplify perturbations, they could become governed by destabilizing forces.

(m) *Bifurcation*. In systems, bifurcation points stand at the juncture of instability and stability. The system might split in form at these junctures, emerging with two new forms, for example.

(n) *Fractals*. In fractals, one finds that a system is self-similar across different levels. For example, a bay might have a shape equivalent to the pattern of wavelets at the shore, due to self-similar fractal forces. Fractal organization facilitates multiple-level system change toward complexity.

(o) *Complexity*. Complex systems reside at the interface of periodic, cyclic, and chaotic attractors (Kauffman-Smith, 1993). When complex multiattractor assemblies coalesce to form integrated systems, they are considered "complex adaptive systems." To use the language of nonlinear dynamical systems theory, living systems are composed of multiple attractors, and they gravitate to complex adaptive systems, either singly or in combination.

(p) *Cusp of change*. Systems might stand at or seek the "cusp of change." This region of state space facilitates movement toward increasing complexity, which helps maximize adaptation.

(q) *Steps in the evolution of complexity*. In the right circumstances, there appears to be a constant pattern that evolves in creation of complex adaptive systems out of system attractors (Young, 2008; Young & Chapman, 2006, 2007). In forming complex adaptive systems, systems appear to pass through the stages of (1) cyclic attractors, (2) chaotic attractors, (3) gravitating to the region between order and disorder, or the cusp of change, and (4) complex adaptive system organization. This four-step process might involve the insertion of a torus attractor before the chaotic one, and/or dual/multiple, but not yet integrated attractors after it.

(r) *A new step*. After the evolution of systems toward complex adaptive systems, an ensuing fifth step might be involved. In nonlinear dynamical systems evolution, complex adaptive systems themselves could evolve because of dynamical processes. In particular, complex adaptive systems might reach critical points where they self-organize into more emergently complex multiples that are superordinate to them. A good term to use for this type of system organization and phase of a nonlinear dynamical system's evolution would be "superordinate complex adaptive systems."

Superordinate complex adaptive systems would involve complex adaptive systems functioning in coordination as they work toward an integrated superordinate structure. In keeping with the present model of substages, once the coordination manifests, the system would then pass into the next phases where the coordinated structures hierarchize, systematize, and multiply, before integrating.

## Summary and Conclusions

In the space provided, it is difficult to present the full scope of the model, and how it has advantages relative to other Neo-Piagetian models. However, it is emphasized that it is not simply a reworking or relabeling of these models, but stands apart in the ways indicated. Granted, there will be theoretical inconsistencies and errors that can be found in the present model, but relative to the grand map of the stages and substages in development that the model presents, and the description of the processes that undergird their unfolding, the present model should be contributory to understanding of development and other change phenomena. Most important, among the Neo-Piagetian models, because of its comprehensive 25-step sequence, it is the only model to fully cover the life span. Moreover, it does not have inconsistent age gaps between substages, unlike some other models. However, the present model attempts to circumvent these issues by showing parallels with prior Neo-Piagetian models, and building on them. The present model of stages and their transitions provides a scaffold approach that can incorporate the notions of universal stages and individual differences. By integrating the 25-step model of the product of change with a nonlinear dynamical model related to change processes, the model attains a broad-ranging theoretical scope that merits further scrutiny.

## References

Armon, C. (1995). Moral judgement and self-reported moral events in adulthood. *Journal of Adult Development, 2*, 49–62.

Armon, C., & Dawson, T. L. (2002). The good life: A longitudinal study of adult value reasoning. In J. Demick & C. Andreoletti (Eds.), *Handbook of adult development*. New York: Plenum.

Blanchard-Fields, F. (1989). Postformal reasoning in a socioemotional context. In M. L. Commons, J. D. Sinnott, F. A. Richards, & C. Armon (Eds.), *Adult development: Vol. 1. Comparisons and applications of developmental models* (pp. 73–93). New York: Praeger.

Blasi, A., & Glodis, K. (1995). The development of identity: A critical analysis from the perspective of the self as subject. *Developmental Review, 15*, 404–433.

Blatt, S. J. (2008). *Polarities of experience: Relatedness and self-definition in personality development, psychopathology, and the therapeutic process*. Washington: American Psychological Association.

Blatt, S. J., & Blass, R. B. (1996). Relatedness and self-definition: A dialectic model of personality development. In G. G. Noam & K. W. Fischer (Eds.), *Development and vulnerability in close relationships* (pp. 309–338). Mahwah: Erlbaum.

Cartwright, K. B., Galupo, M. P., Tyree, S. D., & Jennings, J. G. (2009). Reliability and validity of the complex postformal thought questionnaire: Assessing adults' cognitive development. *Journal of Adult Development, 16*, 183–189.

Commons, M. L., & Richards, F. A. (1984a). A general model of stage theory. In M. L. Commons, F. A. Richards, & C. Armon (Eds.), *Beyond formal operations. Vol. 1: Late adolescent and adult cognitive development* (pp. 120–140). New York: Praeger.

Commons, M. L., & Richards, F. A. (1984b). Applying the general stage model. In M. L. Commons, F. A. Richards, & C. Armon (Eds.), *Beyond formal operations: Late adolescent and adult cognitive development* (pp. 141–157). New York: Praeger.

Commons, M. L., & Richards, F. A. (2002). Organizing components in combinations: How stage transition works. *Journal of Adult Development, 9*, 159–177.

Couzin, I. D. (2009). Collective cognition in animal groups. *Trends in Cognition Sciences, 13*, 36–43.

Erikson, E. H. (1980). *Identity and the life cycle*. New York: Norton.

Galupo, M. P., Cartwright, K. B., & Savage, L. S. (2010). Cross-category friendships and postformal thought among college students. *Journal of Adult Development, 14*, 497–505.

Halford, G. S., Wilson, W. H., & Phillips, S. (2010). Relational knowledge: The foundation of higher cognition. *Trends in Cognitive Sciences*.

Helson, R., & Soto, C. J. (2005). Up and down in middle age: Monotonic and nonmonotonic changes in roles, status, and personality. *Journal of Personality and Social Psychology, 89*, 194–204.

Kauffman-Smith, A. (1993). *The origins of order: Self-organization and selection in evolution*. New York: Oxford University Press.

Labouvie-Vief, G. (1992). A neo-Piagetian perspective on adult cognitive development. In R. J. Sternberg & C. A. Berg (Eds.), *Intellectual development* (pp. 197–228). Cambridge: Cambridge University Press.

Labouvie-Vief, G. (2009). Cognition and equilibrium regulation in development and aging. *Restoration Neurology and Neuroscience, 27*, 551–565.

Labouvie-Vief, G., Chiodo, L. M., Goguen, L. A., Diehl, M., & Orwoll, L. (1995). Representations of self across the life span. *Psychology and Aging, 10*, 404–415.

Labouvie-Vief, G., DeVoe, M., & Bulka, D. (1989). Speaking about feelings: Conception of emotion across the life span. *Psychology and Aging, 4*, 425–437.

Labouvie-Vief, G., Diehl, M., Jain, E., & Zhang, F. (2007). Six-year change in affect optimization and affect complexity across the adult life span: A further examination. *Psychology and Aging, 22*, 738–751.

Labouvie-Vief, G., Grühn, D., & Studer, J. (2010). Dynamic integration of emotion and cognition: Equilibrium regulation in development and aging. In R. M. Lerner, M. E. Lamb, & A. M. Freund (Eds.), *The handbook of life-span development: Vol. 2. Social and emotional development* (pp. 79–115). New York: Wiley.

Lewis, M. D. (2005). Bridging emotion theory and neurobiology through dynamic systems modeling. *Behavioral and Brain Sciences, 28*, 169–194.

Piaget, J. (1954/1981). *Intelligence and affectivity: Their relationship during child development* (T. Brown & C. Kaegi, Trans. and Eds.). Palo Alto: Annual Reviews Monograph. (Original work published in 1954).

Piaget, J. (1976). *The grasp of consciousness: Action and concept in the young child*. Cambridge: Harvard University Press.

Piaget, J. (1980). *Experiments in contradiction*. Chicago: University of Chicago Press.

Price, E. E., Caldwell, C. A., & Whiten, A. (2010). Comparative cultural cognition. *Interdisciplinary Reviews Cognitive Science, 1*, 23–31.

Sinnot, J. D. (2002). Postformal thought and adult development: Living in balance. In J. Demick & C. Andreoletti (Eds.), *Handbook of adult development* (pp. 221–237). New York: Plenum.

Sinnott, J. D. (1994). Development and yearning: Cognitive aspects of spiritual development. *Journal of Adult Development, 2*, 91–99.

Sinnott, J. D. (1998). *The development of logic in adulthood: Postformal thought and its applications*. New York: Plenum.

Sinnott, J. D. (2009). Cognitive development as the dance of adaptive transformation: Neo-Piagetian perspectives on adult cognitive development. In M. C. Smith & N. DeFrates-Densch (Eds.), *Handbook of research on adult learning and development* (pp. 103–134). New York: Routledge Taylor & Francis.

Sinnott, J. D., & Berlanstein, D. (2006). The importance of feeling whole: Learning to "feel connected", community, and adult development. In C. H. Hoare (Ed.), *Oxford handbook of adult development and learning* (pp. 381–406). New York: Oxford University Press.

Sulis, W. (2009). Collective intelligence: Observation and models. In S. J. Guastello, M. Koopmans, & D. Pincus (Eds.), *Chaos and complexity in psychology: The theory of nonlinear dynamical systems* (pp. 41–66). New York: Cambridge University Press.

Thelen, E., & Smith, L. B. (1994). *A dynamic systems approach to the development of cognition and action*. Cambridge: MIT Press.
Wertsch, J. V., Tulviste, P., & Hagstrom, F. (1993). A sociocultural approach to agency. In E. A. Forman, N. Minick, & C. A. Stone (Eds.), *Contexts for learning: Sociocultural dynamics in children's development* (pp. 336–356). New York: Oxford University Press.
Williams, W. M., & Sternberg, R. J. (1988). Group intelligence: Why some groups are better than others. *Intelligence, 12*, 351–377.
Woolley, A. W., Chabris, C. F., Pentland, A., Hashmi, N., & Malone, T. W. (2010). Evidence for a collective intelligence factor in the performance of human groups. *Science, 330*, 686–688.
Young, G. (1997). *Adult development, therapy, and culture: A postmodern synthesis*. New York: Plenum.
Young, G. (2008). Psychological injury: Systems, change processes, development. *Psychological Injury and Law, 1*, 243–254.
Young, G., & Chapman, C. R. (2006). Chronic pain and affect as a nonlinear dynamical system. In G. Young, A. W. Kane, & K. Nicholson (Eds.), *Psychological knowledge in court: PTSD, pain, and TBI* (pp. 181–192). New York: Springer Science + Business Media.
Young, G., & Chapman, C. R. (2007). Pain, affect, nonlinear dynamical systems, and chronic pain: Bringing order to disorder. In G. Young, A. W. Kane, & K. Nicholson, *Causality of psychological injury: Presenting evidence in court* (pp. 197–241). New York: Springer Science + Business Media.

# Chapter 6
# Substages in the Neo-Piagetian Models of Case, Fischer, and Young

## Introduction

The sixth chapter gives the foundational comparison of the present work, that of describing and comparing the Neo-Piagetian concepts of Fischer, Case, and myself, at the level of the cyclic recursion of substages within stages, in particular. The chapters that follow this one deal with the specific socioaffective correspondences that each of the theories describe. In this chapter, first, I review the models of Case and Fischer, in particular. Then, I compare the three models. I examine the logical procedures that seem to have been followed in theory construction in Fischer and Case. To conclude the chapter, I prepare the way for description of the cognitive/socioaffective parallels at the heart of the present work.

## The Major Neo-Piagetian Stage-Substage Models

The Neo-Piagetian theories of Case and Fischer, in particular, have inspired the current theory (in particular, their early work; Case, 1978, 1985, 1992a–c; Case & Griffin, 1990; Case, Okamoto, Henderson, & McKeough, 1993; Fischer, 1980; Fischer & Corrigan, 1981; Fischer, Knight, & Van Paris, 1993; Fischer & Rose, 1994; Fischer & Tangney, 1995). They both described cognitive development in terms of major stages with a cyclic recursion of substages that repeat within each stage. Moreover, they both extended their theory into the socioaffective realm. They both dealt with transition mechanisms, underlying memory and related functions. They both dealt with underlying brain organization. In short, both built comprehensive developmental models based on the work of Piaget. However, the primary basis in their work on which I built my own model concerned their concept of cyclically recurring substages within stages of cognitive development. (I do note that in their recursive models they refer to different concepts, such as tiers and levels instead of stages and substages.) Moreover, I considered as important their work on seeking cognitive socioaffective correspondences at each developmental step. Mounoud (1986) has a similar recursive model of substages that reoccur

G. Young, *Development and Causality: Neo-Piagetian Perspectives*,
DOI 10.1007/978-1-4419-9422-6_6, © Springer Science+Business Media, LLC 2011

within stages that also has influenced the present model. It has five steps, unlike Case and Fischer, who described three steps in their models (see Tables 6.1 and 6.2) However, Mounoud has not attempted to apply his model to developing emotion and social interaction.

Biggs and Collis (1982; also Biggs, 1992; see Tables 6.2 and 6.3) posited a five-step substage sequence consisting of prestructural, unistructural, multistructural, relational, and extended abstract levels. However, it really consists of a three-step sequence. The prestructural level in Biggs and Collis's model of substage recursions in cognitive development concerns cognitive performance below current competence level, so that it is not a substage in the sense described here. The extended abstract level refers to the acquisition of a higher stage of thought, so that it is equivalent to the unistructural level in the higher stage that follows any one stage in cognitive development. The unistructural, multistructural, and relational levels refer, respectively, to focusing on one dimension of a learning situation, then on more than one dimension, and finally to a coherent integration of dimensions. The three-step cognitive substage recursion models of Case and Fischer resemble that of Biggs and Collis, but among other advantages, they attempt to show cognitive and socioaffective parallels in development, and so are the theories chosen for focus.

**Table 6.1** Codes and representations on different levels

| Stage | Levels of representations | Type of organization |
|---|---|---|
| Birth | Sensorial representations (preformed) linked with preformed structures + new coding capacities (the perceptual code) ≥ construction of perceptual representations | Sensorimotor organization (preformed) |
| 18–24 months | Perceptual representations (constructed) + new coding capacities (the conceptual code) ≥ construction of conceptual representations | Perceptivomotor organization (constructed) |
| 9–11 years | Conceptual representations (constructed) + new coding capacities (the semiotic code) ≥ construction of semiotic representations | Conceptuomotor organization (constructed) |
| 16–18 years | Semiotic representations (constructed) | Semioticomotor organization (constructed) |



Aside from Fischer, Case, and Young, other theorists have attempted to construct revisions of Piaget's theory from the perspective of a recyclic recursion of substages. For example, Mounoud (1976, 1986) presented a model that included three stages of cognitive development (sensorimotor, conceptual, semiotic). For each of them, five substages are described to cyclically recur (see the present table and the next one, as well as Table 4.1). I have simplified the terms used to describe the five substages as; (a) global, (b) application, (c) related, (d) analysis, and (e) synthesis. They involve (a) formation of a new code, (b) juxtaposing, coordinating, and showing correspondences, (c) nondecomposable total representations, (d) partly decomposable ones, and (e) fully decomposable ones

The descriptions are not as clear as they could be in Mounoud's model. Nevertheless, his model is important because it points out there are models different than the preponderant one in the field, that of a cyclic recursion of three substages over stages in development (Fischer, Case). As mentioned, my model includes five substages that recur over stages, not three

**Table 6.2** Elaboration of new representations

| Stage 1 (month) | Stage 2 (years) | Stage 3 (years) | Steps | Process |
|---|---|---|---|---|
| 0–1 | 1½–3 | 10–11 | Initial global representations: syncretic | Sampling of object and action properties: by means of new code |
| 1–4 | 3–5 | 11–13 | New elementary representations: separated and juxtaposed | Coordination-integration of elementary representations: and establishment of correspondence with objects and situations |
| 4–8 | 5–7 | 13–15 | New total representations nondecomposable: rigid with global relationship between them | Decomposition-analysis of new total representations in their components: and establishment of correspondence with objects dimensions |
| 8–14 | 7–9 | 15–16 | New total representations partly decomposable: with partial relationship between them and their components | Composition-synthesis of the components of new total representations |
| 14–18 | 9–10 | 16–18 | New complete representations fully decomposable: with complete relationship between them and with their components | |



It is instructive to note that Mounoud is an infancy researcher, in particular, and he tried to keep intact the original Piagetian model of sensorimotor development. Since he had a model of five substages recurring in development, he was left with the dilemma of how to deal with the six-step series comprising Piaget's sensorimotor stage. His solution was to consider the last substage of sensorimotor development, as described by Piaget, as the beginning substage of the next stage of conceptual thought. Case and Fischer have adopted similar solutions, truncating the classic Piagetian sensorimotor series and placing its last substage as the first substage of the next stage in their series. However, in order to maintain a cyclic recursion of five substages over stages, I have adopted the solution of placing the first substage of reflexes in Piaget's six-step series as a separate stage and keeping intact the other five in my version of the sensorimotor period

Since I had been an infancy researcher, like Mounoud, I considered it important to emphasize the value and validity of Piaget's sensorimotor progression through the six substages that he described. In this regard, my solution respects the integrity of that series quite well, for it keeps the final substage within the sensorimotor series, and removes the first one, which is quite simple, and worthy of its own stage of reflexes. Perhaps, had Mounoud considered a presensorimotor stage, he would have arrived at the same stance as myself concerning the sensorimotor stage, and kept intact the last five of its substages, not the first five of its substages

Note that Piaget had insisted that the last stage of his sensorimotor substages is still sensorimotor in nature despite the child developing representational skills in the second year. For him, prior to the second year, although the child uses representations, these representations are still tied to their sensorimotor bases, and are not yet independently symbolic, as happens in the next stage after 2 years

I note with interest that Mounoud had described the process that is involved in the transitions from one substage to the next. He placed the description of these transition processes between the substages. Independently, I had developed a similar way of presenting the mechanisms at work in transitions (see Table 28.1)

**Table 6.3** Neo-Piagetian cognitive development (Biggs)

| Stage | Form of knowledge | Substage(s) | Onset age |
|---|---|---|---|
| Sensorimotor | Tacit | Unistructural<br>Multistructual<br>Relational | Birth |
| Ikonic | Intuitive | Unistructural<br>Multistructual<br>Relational | 1½ year |
| Concrete-symbolic | Declarative | Unistructural<br>Multistructual<br>Relational | 6 |
| Formal | Theoretical | Unistructural<br>Multistructual<br>Relational | 14 |
| Postformal | Metatheoretical | Unistructural<br>Multistructual<br>Relational | 21 |

Adapted from Biggs (1992)

Biggs (1992; Biggs & Collis, 1982) developed a Neo-Piagetian model of stages and substages in cognitive development in the context of education. Despite the use of a different label for the preoperational period, their model consists of five stages (the classic four Piagetian ones, and a postformal stage), as well as a cyclic recursion of three substages over stages. The names of the substages indicate a growing integration of cognitive abilities over their emergence, which is the same goal for all the Neo-Piagetian models (Fischer, Case, Young, Mounoud, etc.). However, to what extent is the development limited to three substages? Perhaps other models that describe five substages arrive at models that are more consistent and without gaps over the lifespan

There is no logical reason why a Neo-Piagetian model has to consist of three substages instead of another number. Somehow, the progression described needs to be consistent with the developmental data not just in one age period but in each of them, and over the lifespan, as well. This means that the cycle should even cover both the prenatal period and the elderly period. Cognitive development begins with initiating reflexes in the fetal period and terminates with the reflection of how life had been as we confront our passing. As for the substages involved, to what extent does the first substage concern a single acquisition that is then elaborated, multiplied, integrated, coordinated, related, etc. Often, these key terms appear in different places in the sequences presented by the different theorists. Perhaps, a type of coordination comes first, and then it is reworked into a tighter more global system, which then multiplies out throughout the child's psychology until it is integrated, ready for the next cycle of coordination of integrations from the prior stage? In essence, this is the approach that I have adopted in the present model

## Case's Neo-Piagetian Model: Cognition

### *Cognitive Stages*

In Case's (1985, 1992a–c) Neo-Piagetian conceptualization of the stages in cognitive development, five stages are proposed to repetitively pass through three substages (see Table 6.4). He maintained that Piaget's classic sensorimotor stage is

**Table 6.4** Case's hypothesized structure of stages and substages from birth to adolescence

| Stage | Substage(s) | Age |
|---|---|---|
| Orienting stage | Elaborated coordination | 0–4 month |
| Sensorimotor stage | Unifocal coordination | 4–8 month |
| | Bifocal coordination | 8–12 month |
| | Elaborated coordination | 12–18 month |
| (Inter) Relation stage | Unifocal coordination | 18–24 month |
| | Bifocal coordination | 2–3½ year |
| | Elaborated coordination | 3½–5 year |
| Dimensional stage | Unifocal coordination | 5–7 year |
| | Bifocal coordination | 7–9 year |
| | Elaborated coordination | 9–11 year |
| Vectorial stage | Unifocal coordination | 11–13 year |
| | Bifocal coordination | 13–15 year |
| | Elaborated coordination | 15–18 year |

Adapted from Case (1985)

Robbie Case and Kurt Fischer have been the leading Neo-Piagetians. Each has developed a model of stages in cognitive development that have recurring substages (although they might use different terminology for them, such as tiers and levels). For Case, he kept intact the integrity of the four major Piagetian stages, and added an earlier orienting one (like in the present model), although he changed the names involved for the stages in the way indicated in a prior table note. He described a three-substage cyclic recursion of substages, as did Fischer. For both of them, there is an initial acquisition or coordination that develops a doubling structure, which then systematizes or elaborates. The age periods described by Case keep the integrity of the ones suggested by Piaget, similar to myself, except that he differentiates the later stages in this regard, to fit the substages involved. Fischer's model has gaps at this level – for example, critical age periods are collapsed into one substage. Moreover, in the work of Fischer, the particular ages for the age periods involved at certain steps in his model sometimes change over publications, unlike the case for Case. Neither model has a cyclic recursion of substages in an adult postformal period, unlike in the present model, although Fischer does describe a postformal period

Note that the concept of stages in the Neo-Piagetians Fischer and Case differs from that of Piaget. Between them, more than had been the case for Piaget, they describe: (a) individual differences; (b) the effect of environment and support; (c) more than one step possible at each substage; (d) separate domain development that can become coordinated; and (e) close links with affective development. They refer to particular developmental acquisitions as "skills." They perform micro-analytic studies that demonstrate the validity of their stages and substages, as well as their order in unfolding. At the same time, neither theorist has critically examined the other one for the discrepancies, inconsistencies, and gaps across their different conceptions of the specific stages and substages posited to develop

preceded by a preliminary one of orienting responses, thought to emerge prenatally 3 months before birth. Piaget's sensorimotor period in infancy is truncated in Case's version (e.g., Piaget's last sensorimotor substage is placed at the beginning of Case's postsensorimotor stage). Piaget's preoperational, concrete operational, and formal operational stages are included in the model; however, the terms describing them are replaced with the terms: (inter) relational, dimensional, and vectorial, respectively (he used the terms interrelational and relational in referring to the preoperational child). As for the substages, they are labeled unifocal (or operational), bifocal, and elaborated coordination. The latter is considered an operational consolidation period preparatory to an ensuing unifocal coordination substage.

Case (1985) viewed the (inter) relational preoperational stage as one where children are acquiring an understanding of second-order relations of primary relations, or bipolar patterns of organization among actions, objects, people, or events in the environment. In his balance scale task, preoperational children grasp the relation between the difference in weight between two objects and the effect of this difference on the relative position of the arms of the scale. They understand that in using the scale, the heavier the objects' difference in weight, the more the heavier object lowers on the scale and the more the lighter one rises.

Case described the dimensional stage, or the one of concrete operations, in terms of skills in using dimensions during thought. Dimensions are continuous qualities that characterize the world, such as height and width. For Piaget, the hallmark of concrete operations is found in children's mastery of conservation problems, in which they realize that physical transformations do not alter objects (e.g., in pouring water from one container to another). Case emphasized the way children who conserve compare dimensions (e.g., of changing height and width) in achieving understanding that objects in conservation problems have not been altered in the course of transformation. Piaget referred to the process of compensation in this regard.

## *Cognitive Substages*

### The Model

In Case's model, the unifocal substage is characterized by an assemblage of a superordinate structure from a pair of qualitatively distinct structures already available but with functions different from their new one. The components subtly differentiate or are altered (e.g., into figurative, guiding and operative, executing constituents). This leads them to manifest a hierarchical, mapping, or dominant-subordinate (means-end) relationship. The result is a cognitive ability qualitatively different from the one prior to it (except, of course, in the case of the very first substage in development).

In the bifocal substage, the growing individual can focus in sequence on two unifocal structures coordinated in the prior period, but without their complete simultaneous comparison or integration. Subgoals are added and strategies are more refined in problem solving, but there is no reversibility as in the third and last substage.

In elaborated coordination, the effects of one structure can reverse, trade off, or compensate for the effects of another. In short, a new structure is unified out of disparate ones, and is ready for future coordinations, whether in terms of sensorimotor structures, relational symbols, dimensional concrete principles, or vectorial abstractions. Thus, this substage is considered transitional, and is seen to function in a consolidation mode as well as an elaboration one. In consequence, it is described at times in a unitary way and at times in a way indicative of coordination.

Lewis and Ash (1992) found evidence for spurt-like substages in infant cognitive development consistent with Case's theory. In a longitudinal study, they examined 31 infants weekly from the start of 2.5–3.5 months of age on six sensorimotor tasks concerning unifocal coordinated actions (grasp-and-look, swinging object, adjusted-reach, crossing-objects, reach-and-grasp, revolving-object). A pass rate of 50% was observed more or less within the same timeframe for all tasks (at 3.7–4.6 months). Moreover, task onset age within subjects revealed intraindividual synchronies in the development of new abilities, indicative of a discontinuous passage from a reflexive orienting mode to Case's first type of sensorimotor actions – unifocal coordinations.

**Comment**

On the surface, the cyclic substage progression hypothesized by Case seems logical, for a more complex restructuring seems to take place at each level. However, there is room for ambiguity. (a) An assemblage of elements takes place both at the unifocal and bifocal levels, so it may be difficult to distinguish them. Even the elaboration substage is primarily one of coordination. For example, Young (1990b) analyzed Case's description of language development, and found it difficult to discern whether several examples that were offered belonged at the substage suggested by Case, or at one substage earlier. (b) None of the substages speaks to more complex structures of three or more components. (c) The last substage is at once a coordinated dual structure, a unified whole, and at times a reversible system, allowing a wide margin of possible examples within its confines. (d) The bifocal substage sometimes is presented as one manifesting exemplary balancing of structures, sometimes not (e.g., Case & Griffin, 1990, p. 220, on describing emotions [see below]; vs. p. 207, on quantitative problems, respectively).

## Fischer's Neo-Piagetian Model: Cognition

### *The Cognitive Model*

Fischer (1980; Fischer et al., 1993; Lamborn, Fischer, & Pipp, 1994) has constructed a theory of cognitive development similar to Case's (see Table 6.5). As has been shown, it is comprised of four stages, each with three substages; also, there is one extra substage equivalent to a new stage that develops at the end of the last stage. Like Case, Fischer has partitioned Piaget's sensorimotor stage. In Case's model, the substages in Piaget's sensorimotor substage sequence begin as a reflexive stage, then continue as a sensorimotor one and, finally, commence a third stage, that of representations. For the most part, the representational stage parallels Piaget's preoperational and concrete operational periods. Finally, for Fischer, the abstract stage corresponds to Piaget's formal operational period.

**Table 6.5** Levels of cognitive development in infancy and early childhood in Fischer and Hogan (1989)

| Level | Estimated age of emergence | Examples skills |
|---|---|---|
| Rf1: single reflexes | 3–4 weeks | Single, simple species-specific action components: with fixed posture-infant looks at ball moving in front of face. Infant grasps cloth placed in hand |
| Rf2: reflex mappings | 7–8 weeks | Simple relations of a few action components: hearing voice leads to looking at eyes, infant extends arm toward seen ball |
| Rf3: reflex systems | 10–11 weeks | Complex relations of subsets of action components: looking at face and hearing voice evokes |
| | | Coordinated smiling, cooing, and nooding of head (greeting response). Infant opens hand while extending arm toward ball |
| Rf4/S1: system of reflex systems (single sensorimotor actions) | 15–17 weeks | Relations of reflex systems to produce a single, flexible sensorimotor action: infant looks at ball as it moves through a complex trajectory. Infant opens hand while extending arm toward seen ball and in middle of reach sometimes adjusts hand to changes in trajectory of ball, but coordination is still unstable |
| S2: sensorimotor mappings | 7–8 months | Simple relations of a few sensorimotor actions: infant grasps a ball in order to bring it in front of face to look at it. Infant uses looking at ball to finely guide reach for it |
| S3: sensorimotor systems | 11–13 months | Complex relations of subsets of sensorimotor actions: infant moves a rattle in different ways to see different parts of it. Infant imitates pronunciation of many single words |
| S4/Rp1: systems of sensorimotor systems (single representations) | 18–24 months | Coordination of action systems to produce concrete representations of objects, people or events: child pretends that a doll is walking. Child says "Doll walk" |
| Rp2: representational mappings | 3½–4½ years | Simple relations of a concrete representation: child pretends that two dolls are Mom and Dad interacting appropriately in terms of parental roles |
| | | Child understands that self knows a secret and Dad does not know it |

*Note*. Modal ages for middle class Western children

Reprinted with the permission of Springer Science+Business Media. Fischer, K. W., & Hogan, A. E. (1989). [Table 1, Page. 280–281]

Fischer's Neo-Piagetian cognitive developmental model includes an initial reflexive stage, and then stages involving sensorimotor actions, representations, abstract thoughts, and principles. The model is quite similar to my own, which differs only in the labels used in the five stages (I refer to the representational stage as involving perioperations and refer to the postformal period as involving collective intelligence). However, like Case, Fischer has a three-substage cyclic recursion, so that Fischer's model contrasts with the present model, which has five substages. Also, the present model includes substages in the last stage, making it the only one of the Neo-Piagetian models that is lifespan. Moreover, neither of the other two models describes corresponding stages in socioaffective acquisitions across the lifespan, contrary to the present model, which describes 25 parallel steps in Neo-Piagetian cognitive and Neo-Eriksonian affective stages and substages

This table describes quite well the detailed acquisitions in each of the first reflex, sensorimotor and representational substages described in Fischer's model for the first few years of life.

(continued)

**Table 6.5** (continued)

Fischer (1980) has developed a notation for describing the manner in which skills develop. The notation helped represent how skills cohere as they traverse the increasingly sophisticated substages within a stage. Case has developed an equivalent symbolic representational system for his conception of recycling substages. However, the representational diagrams in the models of Case and of Fischer differ across the models. I have not followed suit by describing a notation to represent the substages-stages of the present model

In terms of substages, Fischer describes the cyclic recursion of sets, mappings, and systems, a sequence that resembles Case's substages of unifocal, bifocal, and elaborated levels. Sets are classes or collections of skilful behavioral "actions." A mapping is a coordination of two sets, in which each group of constituents of the sets are ordered and then paired across sets. The result is that two sets are related into an overarching skill. A system is characterized as relations between subsets of divided sets. Each set splits in two and each of the subdivided sets of one set can be related to its paired subdivided set of the other set. "A person can relate two subsets of each of two sets in a simple skill" (Fischer, 1980, p. 486). This procedure leads to controlling two sources of variability in any one set. A system of systems relates two systems cohering into a superordinate skill, or single element, which is, in effect, a new set. Thus, the first step of each new cycle of substages can be described as either a compound of prior skills or a single entity ready for higher-order structuring.

Fischer's model of substage recycling in cognitive development is quite similar to Case's not only in its three-step model but also in its conception of the transition between cycles. That is, for both Case and Fischer, one of the three substages in the recursion serves as a kind of transition, functioning simultaneously as a complex integration yet a simplified unity disposed for further coordination. However, note that the particular substage that possesses this dual attribute differs in the two theories. That is, for Case, the particular substage concerned is the third and last one in each cycle and for Fischer it is the first one.

As for limitations of Fischer's model of recursive substages in cognitive development, the same type of problems inherent in Case's conceptualization seems to apply to Fischer's version. (a) In one way or another, each of the substages concern binary coordinations in behavior, which can lead to confusion about where best to classify such configurations, given that this creates a lack of differentiation of the substages. (b) Multiple chains are typically excluded. (c) As mentioned, one of the substages has an ambiguous transition status that allows it to cover a very broad range of behaviors. (d) Moreover, Fischer's substages are extremely geometric or quantitative in their progression; they have none of the qualitative attributes that Case occasionally uses to describe them (e.g., dominance-subordination, reversibility).

## *Early Fischer*

In his earliest publications, Fischer used a more standard Piagetian model, but did refer to his own, as well. In these studies, Fischer was not the first author. When he undertook research later on where he had been the first author, it was with older children. This might account for his move to a uniquely Neo-Piagetian model to one more based on Piaget.

## Watson and Fischer (1977)

Watson and Fischer examined 14-, 19-, and 24-month-old infants on two series of tasks – object permanence and agent use in pretending. Infants observed adult models as they pretended, and their use of pretending was then observed in free play. They used agents in the developmental sequence of: self as agent, use of an object as a passive agent, use of a substitute object as a passive agent, and use of an object as an active agent. The sequence is represented by the following examples: put head on pillow to pretend sleeping; put down doll to pretend it goes to sleep; put down block for same; and lie down doll as if it were carrying out the behavior itself. Fischer and colleague equated the first step in the sequence with Piaget's sensorimotor substage 6. Object permanence was measured with Uzgiris and Hunt's (1975) items 4–15 of their object permanence scale. The results of the study indicated that the pretend sequence was scalable and it correlated moderately with the object permanence sequence.

It is noteworthy that in the second year of life, the subjects of the study demonstrated a developmental sequence that passed from the equivalent of Piaget's sensorimotor substage 6 and then a representational stage, with two intermediary steps associated with the first step. This would imply that in Fischer's construction of his model of stages and substages in cognitive development, Piaget's original substage series could have been respected, and Piaget's preoperational stage could have been given the new label of single representations. Indeed, Watson and Fischer concluded that based on their findings with a classical approach to the sensorimotor stage of Piaget, developmental sequences can be predicted with great accuracy within a particular domain. However, despite the support for the type of modeling I have indicated that could have been undertaken by Fischer, the model proposed by Fischer (1980) did not correspond to this sequence.

## Bertenthal and Fischer (1978)

Bertenthal and Fischer examined 6-, 8-, 10-, 12, 18-, and 24-month-olds on self-recognition and object permanence tasks. There were five of the former tasks, representing the Piagetian sensorimotor substages 3–6, with a representational step evident in the last task of the sequence. The five tasks involved: tactual exploration (touch image in mirror); hat task (look up at or grab hat positioned above head once see it in mirror); toy task (see toy descending in view in mirror as it is lowered behind infant, and turn around to get it); rouge task (rouge dot put on child's nose; child had to touch own nose in mirror, noting verbally the difference); and name task (mother out of view and asks who is that to her child facing the mirror; the child gives own name, or says Me, etc). Object permanence was evaluated using the Uzgiris-Hunt task series. The results indicated that for self-recognition the task sequence was highly scalable, closely fitting the predicted sequence. As for the correlation between the self-recognition and object permanence sequences, it was moderately high (0.84, a result higher than the equivalent correlation of 0.62 in Watson and Fischer, 1977).

As with the prior study, the results of this study provide support for the presence of the sensorimotor substages that Piaget had described, with a representational step developing afterwards. Moreover, in both studies, the sensorimotor series appears to develop throughout the second year, as Piaget had proposed. Finally, the correlation of 0.84 across the object permanence and self-recognition tasks is noteworthy, suggesting it is possible to not only use the original formulation of six substages in the Piagetian model but also that there are commonalities in it across domains.

As will be shown, Case and colleagues (e.g., Case, 1998) had developed the concept of central conceptual structures to replace Piaget's concept of *structures d'ensembles* because they had found similar high intertask correspondences. However, Fischer (e.g., Fischer, 1980) had chosen to emphasize the isolated development of cognitive skills within domains, with not only some commonalities but also with much individual variation in across-task consistencies (note that Jackson, Campos, and Fischer (1978) did find across-task variations in 6- to 8-month-olds on object permanence and person permanence tasks).

## Watson and Fischer (1980)

Watson and Fischer undertook a study of the development of social roles from 1 to 7 years of age. They used Fischer's developmental model of stages and substages in development to develop expectations of role-playing skill. The substage of sensorimotor systems was posited to develop toward age 1 and the substage of single representations toward age 2, with other acquisitions developing beyond the first 2 years. The role-playing skills that were considered to index the two substages are of interest. First, there were four of them, they resembled those in Watson and Fischer (1977), and they were given similar names. Specifically, in the 1980 study, the substage of sensorimotor systems was indexed by the task of self as agent, and the substage of single representations was associated with the tasks of: active other agent, active substitute agent, and behavioral role, which is akin to the task in the prior study of use of object as active agent. Therefore, just as with the prior study, I expected that, in the present study, these tasks would be associated with the sensorimotor sequence proposed by Piaget, or the equivalent, and with the related correspondences.

It will be recalled that, in the 1978 study, the first step in the four-task sequence was associated with Piaget's sensorimotor substage 6, as were the two steps-tasks that followed it, and the last step-task in the series was taken to index a new representational step in development. However, in the 1980 study now being reviewed, the middle two steps were taken to indicate the onset of the representational stage. Granted the tasks are slightly different, which might account for the different classifications of their cognitive complexity, but the discrepancy over the two studies merits further explanation.

### *Interim Summary*

Before comparing the three models of Neo-Piagetian development under review, I provide a capsule summary of my own. The comparison will show how I built on the models of Fischer and Case, but also accommodated to gaps and inconsistencies found in them.

## Introducing the Comparison of Fischer, Case, and Young

The present model of stages in cognitive development resembles that of Fischer, in particular. In Fischer's model, the developing individual passes through the stages of reflexes, sensorimotor actions, representations (covering Piaget's preoperations and concrete operations), and abstract thought. The present model is similar, except that representations are called perioperations and I have added a postformal stage that has a cyclic recursion of substages, like in the proposed prior stages in development. Fischer describes a postformal stage of principles, but it does not include substages. Case's model also includes a reflexive stage, which he labeled orienting (Case, 1991). He maintained the traditional sensorimotor, preoperational, concrete operational, and formal stage sequence presented by Piaget, but referred to the last three stages as (inter) relational, dimensional, and vectorial, respectively. Case did not add a postformal stage.

It should be noted that both Case and Fischer modified their stage sequences as their thinking evolved. For example, Case added his orienting stage after the introduction of his model (note that this stage does not include a cyclic recursion of substages). Fischer did not describe his postformal stage as principles when first introduced, but as a system of abstract systems. Also, as shown below, he changed the typical ages when the various stages and substages in his model are considered to manifest.

Note that the conceptions of stage in Case and Fischer do not correspond to Piaget's strict genetic epistemological model in several senses. In this regard, these Neo-Piagetians focused on individual differences as much as universal sequences, and were sensitive to task and context. Furthermore, Fisher altered some fundamental properties of Piaget's conception of stage. He referred to tiers in development rather than stages. He even permitted intermediary steps in development beyond the standard substages, depending on the skills called for in the tasks and contexts studied.

In the following, I compare the present model of substages to those of Case and Fischer, to remind, my model consists of a five-step cyclic recursion that repeats over substages: coordination, hierarchization, systematization, multiplication, and integration. This sequence differs from those of Fischer and Case, who each proposed a substage model of three steps that reoccur within cognitive stages.

## Comparison with Case and Fischer on Substages

### *Similarities and Differences*

#### Case

The present model of the cognitive substages that cyclically recur in development strongly resembles elements of those of both Case and Fischer. With respect to Case, it appears that the current first and second substages together resemble his first one. Also, the current third and fourth substages together resemble his second one. Finally, the last ones in each version bear a one-to-one similarity to some extent.

In Case's unifocal substage, coordination takes place, but it is different in two ways from the first substage described in the present model. First, in Case's concept of coordination, the component units end up with a function different from the one that they had possessed originally when they had existed in isolation. In the current model, this type of creation of a new function in the coordination of elements does not have to occur, but it can. Second, Case's conception of coordination is characterized by a relationship of hierarchical, dominant-subordinate juxtaposition. In the present model, coordinated units might show this characteristic only in a tenuous, tentative way, if at all, because the characteristic comes to develop especially in the subsequent substage of hierarchization in its substage cycle.

In Case's bifocal substage, unifocal structures are coordinated, but not completely, nor with reversibility. Subgoals and strategies are added and refined. This substage differs from the comparable one in the present model of systematization in two ways. First, the additions and refinements of the kind described in Case's model exist in the current one only as attributes of the following substage of multiplication, in particular; that is, they are deemed to take place especially within the context of the establishment of a relationship between at least two separate cognitive units that are themselves hierarchized dual-component entities. Second, aside from the issue that multiplication seems to take place in its own substage in the present model, for Case, the multiplicative combinations are envisaged as incomplete and without clear reversibility. This might obtain, but the present model adds that multiplication could involve more than two units, unlike in Case.

In the elaborated substage of Case, structures are balanced in a unified entity with full reversibility. The comparable substage of integration in the current model also possesses these traits, but because it is built on multiplied systems, long organized sequences are predicted, an outcome that does not seem to be explicit in Case.

### Fischer

Fischer's conceptualization of substages bears a resemblance to that of Case's in that he describes a series of single sets, mappings, and systems, which approximates Case's series of unifocal, bifocal, and elaborated coordinations. However, there are slight differences between Fischer's and Case's views on cognitive substages.

Fischer's concept of sets refers to classes, and thus they seem potentially more variable in terms of number of constituent elements than the superordinate binary coordination of structures found in Case's equivalent concept of unifocal substage. At the same time, Fischer's concept of sets seems more limited than the concept of cognitive structure in Case's equivalent substage because, in Fischer's concept, clear coordination does not seem possible between elements of the classes.

Fischer's concept of mappings refers to a coordination of the elements of one set with those of another. In this sense, it parallel's Case's concept of a bifocal substage. However, it will be recalled that Case does not consider bifocal structures as complete, unlike the case for Fischer's concept of the equivalent cognitive structure.

Finally, in Fischer's systems substage, subsets are interrelated across sets. Case's comparable stage of elaborated coordination is not built on this step of splitting a whole in order to coordinate its parts.

In general, there is a greater affinity between my model of the substage series and Case's relative to Fischer's conceptualization of the series. Fischer especially does not characterize his substages in terms of more qualitative attributes, such as dominant-subordinate, reversible, etc.

## *The Missing Stages and Substages in Case and in Fischer*

The model of stages and substages in cognitive development that I have elaborated consists of 25 steps (5 stages × 5 substages), and those of Case and Fischer consist of less steps (13 for both; Case – orienting stage and then three substages in each of the sensorimotor, interrelational, dimensional, and vectorial or abstract stages; Fischer – three substages in each of the reflexive, sensorimotor, representational, and abstract stages, along with the stage of principles). In this section, I point out where are the lacunae in the models of Case and Fischer relative to my own, which consists of many more steps.

### Case

Case added an orienting stage before the sensorimotor one, but had not considered its prenatal origins, so that there are no substages described. However, one can add readily to his model such substages for the fetal period. A Casian might consider expanding the stage into three substages, using the same three substages that recur cyclically in his model. If one were to follow this suggestion, we would be adding two steps to his model.

There is another way Case's model can be expanded to make it more consistent with my own. Case had not added a postformal stage after the formal one of Piaget but, once more, his model can readily accommodate such a change. In keeping with the type of logic that he had used, I offer the conjecture that he might have called an extra stage in the adult the (abstract) "exponential" or "logarithmic" stage (his last two stages were called dimensional and vectorial). Moreover, Casians would be giving the stage the same three substages that recur cyclically in his model, thereby adding three more substages to his model of the steps in development.

By Casians adding these stages and substages consistent with Case's model, one would arrive at a Casian model of 6 stages × 3 substages. Relative to my own model, there still would be missing substages. Most of these absent steps would refer to the early orienting and later postformal stages, given that I have five substages in each of these periods. There would be few gaps otherwise in this revised Casian series relative to my own series of stages and substages in development. Other gaps relate to the abstract stage, for which I have constructed a model with five substages and Case has only three of them, as per the general pattern in his model.

## Fischer

### Gaps

*Introduction.* By adding some steps to Case's model from the perspective of my own, I have shown that the two models are not that dissimilar in the number of steps. However, it is more difficult to accommodate, relative to my model, Fischer's model in terms of its differences in the number of steps involved. This being said, there are many similarities in the two models. Fischer's model has the same amount of stages as my own (five), including a preliminary reflexive one and a final post-formal one. The reflexive one already has substages in his model, but the postformal one does not, as presented. Therefore, one can add three substages to the latter postformal period (called principles) according to his concept of a three-step cyclic recursion of substages. This would lead to a Fischerian model of 5 stages × 3 sub-stages. This logic would leave a 15-step progression of substages in cognitive development, which would leave a model still 10 steps short of my 25-step model.

Where do the ten missing steps lie in the comparison between my 25-step model and this revised 15-step Fischerian one? To answer, for each stage in the revised Fischerian model, there would be a shortfall of two substages relative to my model, given that I describe a cyclic recursion of five substages within each of the five stages involved, contrary to the repetition of three substages per stage in his model.

According to the accommodations to the models of Case and Fischer that I have made, the Casian series ends up as a progression that consists of 18 steps in cognitive development and the Fischerian series ends up with one that consists of 15 steps. In this regard, the revised Casian model gives the impression that it approximates better the revised Fischerian model to my own model. In this regard, note that I used their model construction procedures to revise the models, and in doing so Case's comes up seven steps short relative to my own, but Fischer comes up 10 steps short.

*Specifics.* The missing three stages in Fischer relative to Case in the revised versions proposed is an amount that is not trivial, because it indicates important gaps in Fischer's model relative to both my own and Case's. The missing steps in Fischer's model relative to Case's do not concern the initial orienting or the final postformal stages, which would be easier to accommodate. Rather, they concern missing steps in Fischer's model that lie in the middle of the developmental progression that he has described, which implicates important lacunae. At times, Fischer changes the typical ages ascribed to the various steps in this middle developmental period from one publication to the next, so there is some uncertainty in what is missing in this regard, and also the ages that he gives to the various age periods do not map perfectly with those steps that are equivalent in both Case's model and my own.

Nevertheless, it appears that the missing steps in cognitive development that are evident in Fischer's model relative to Case's and my own in the middle developmental period concern the age periods beginning at 2, 7, and 9 years. The first missing substage in Fischer compared to Case seems to happen at 2 years, which involves the starting age of Case's bifocal interrelational substage. However, for Fischer, after the 18–24 month period, his next substage typically is described as one that begins at about 3½ years. There is nothing mentioned that begins at 2 years in his model, unlike for the models of Case and myself. Not only is this lacunae about substages evident when comparing Fischer's to Case's and my own progression of substages in cognitive development, it also is an age that I describe as one where the onset of a new stage takes place, let alone a substage, which is consistent with Piaget who described a new stage starting in this age period, that of the preoperational stage.

There is a subsidiary issue of whether Fischer and Case have adequately described the qualitative differences in the substages in this time frame. For example, I have considered the onset of the preoperational stage to take place at 2 years, like Piaget, as the first step in the development of the perioperational stage in my model. In contrast, both Fischer and Case place the onset of their equivalent stages (representations, interrelations, respectively) in the timeframe of 18–24 months, a period in which only the last sensorimotor stage should be developing according to both myself and Piaget.

Next, I examine where else in Fischer's developmental substage series there appears to be missing steps relative to Case's model (and my own) because: (a) Fischer's description of the substage in the 6–8 year period resembles Case's equivalent substage in the 5–7 year period more than Case's substage in the 7–9 year period, and (b) Fischer's next substage in his series takes place in the age period of 10–12 years, effectively this leaves a gap of about 4 years in his series of substages in the middle developmental period that is presented without new substages that develop. This implies that the two missing substages in Fischer's progression of steps in middle development that have yet to be accounted for take place in the preteen years, because in this developmental phase for both Case and I, it appears that there is a new substage that develops every 2 years.

*Comment.* These missing substages that seem evident in Fischer's cognitive developmental model in middle development appear to parallel Case's dimensional bifocal and elaboration substages. Somehow, his model should be modified to add these substages or their equivalents, or other Neo-Piagetian models should be used to understand development in this age period.

## Concrete Operations

It should be pointed out that the three Neo-Piagetian models being compared suggest different ages when the concrete operational stage emerges in development. Piaget had traditionally associated the onset of this age period with the 7-year-old, and my model uses the same age for the onset of the substage in which concrete operations are embedded (the perioperational multiplication substage). However, it appears that, both for the models of Fischer and Case, the substage associated with the emergence of concrete operations develops earlier. I maintain that this anomaly in comparing the three models is not so much a question of the difficulty in establishing typical ages of emergence for the various normative acquisitions in cognitive development, but is due to the differing nature of the substage sequences described by both Fischer and Case relative to my own.

In my model, I collapsed the Piagetian stages of preoperations and concrete operations into one stage, that of perioperations. This is consistent with Fischer, who called the combined preoperational-concrete operational period a representational one, and with Piaget, who did the same when he referred to both of these stages simultaneously. I describe five substages in the development of perioperations, and coordinate the concrete operational period of Piaget with the fourth substage in my series, in particular, that of perioperational multiplication. Therefore, I respected Piaget's location of the development of concrete operations at about 7 years, an age at which he posited that this developmental acquisition typically appears.

However, it should be noted that simpler concrete operational tasks could be solved earlier than 7 years. Should this happen, it would appear that concrete operations are beginning to emerge in the third substage in my model, which is labeled perioperational systematization. Therefore, the earlier acquisitions of simpler concrete operational tasks that might develop would seem to take place before the perioperational multiplication substage with which I have especially associated it. Because the present model consists of five substages per stage, it has the flexibility to accommodate to the developmental trend that concrete operations might appear to develop over two substages. That concrete operations could begin to develop in the systematization substage of the perioperational stage of the present model makes sense, given the systematic nature of the substage. That it appears to especially continue its development in the next substage of perioperational multiplication in the present model makes eminent sense, too. Concrete operations in this age period express serial application to different tasks, involving horizontal décalages, to use Piagetian terminology – that is, they appear especially to spread out through the cognitive system in this age period in a multiplier effect.

To conclude, the present model allows some leeway in its placement of the onset of concrete operations, because it is not a monolithic structure, but develops in substages. However, the substage of the present model in which it seems to flourish, if not fully develop, concerns perioperational multiplication. The flexibility afforded by the present model in regard to the specific placement of the concrete operational stage of Piaget reflects that cognitive development is considered more than the acquisition of one particular cognitive product, even if it is cardinal, such as conservation in the concrete operational period.

## *Possible Logic in the Construction of Case's and Fischer's Models*

### Case

In Case's model, because he has a cyclic recursion of three substages and Piaget had considered that there are six in his model for the sensorimotor period in infancy, Case was left in a quandary. How could he accommodate to a cyclic recursion in the sensorimotor period involving three substages when Piaget had six? Given that the substages in his model were posited to cyclically recur over stages, he arrived at the partial solution of creating an initial orienting stage having three substages (although this step in his model was added over a decade after its initial formulation).

Case's logical procedure in model construction left him with a three-step recursion of substages in the sensorimotor period, but it ended at 12 months of age, whereas Piaget's equivalent series ended at 24 months of age. He respected the integrity of Piaget's sensorimotor series in terms of acknowledging that the six age periods involved in Piaget's sensorimotor series did indeed mark new cognitive acquisitions. However, he remained true to his format of having only three substages in each stage, so he persevered and truncated the sensorimotor series in his model to three substages. This led him to the decision to name the first step after the 12-month period as the start of a new stage, that of interrelations. Whereas, Piaget considered this age period as the one that corresponded to only the fifth in his six-step sensorimotor progression, it was dropped as part of the equivalent sensorimotor stage in the model of Case.

To repeat, the next step in Case's cycle of stages and substages had to start a new stage. In following this logic, he respected the Piagetian tradition by considering it preoperational in nature, but he changed the name of the stage to interrelations. This meant that the stage in Case's model equivalent to the preoperational stage of

Piaget started at 18 months and not at 2 years, as Piaget had intended and as I had supported in my own model.

Next, Case had a model in which the interrelational stage could last three substages. Case understood well that major developmental transitions in this time frame took place at 2, 3½, 5, and 7 years, and he placed substages at these age periods. This meant that for the interrelational stage, the three substages involved had to appear at 18 months, 2, and 3½ years, and end at 5 years. Therefore, for Case the equivalent in his model of Piaget's concrete operational stage, that of dimensions, inevitably had to start in the 5–7 year age period.

Moreover, workers had given children tasks that had shown that the easiest of concrete operational tasks could develop earlier than 7 years. However, Piaget had considered these findings, and still maintained that typically the stage, or most of it, appeared at 7 years. Nevertheless, Case had to ascribe the concrete operational stage to the earlier period of 5 years because of the nature of his stage-substage sequence. To repeat, because there were three substages spanning 18 months to 5 years in the stage in Case's model equivalent to the preoperational period of Piaget, this meant that the interrelational stage preceding the stage equivalent to Piaget's concrete operational period, that of dimensions, had to end at about 5 years, not 7. This led to Case's model starting the equivalent of the concrete operational period at 5 years, not 7, unlike Piaget's and myself.

As for the ensuing stage in the model of Case of vectors, or Piagetian abstract logic, it was also limited to three substages in Case's model, unlike the amount of substages in the equivalent stage in the present case (5). In this regard, according to the characteristics of the substages in my model and those of Case for this age period, I seem to add two substages after the three abstract substages in Case's model. That is, I do not think that Case had gaps in his model of the abstract substages. His unifocal, bifocal, and elaborated substages in this stage of his model appear to correspond to the substages in my model of coordination, hierarchization, and systematization, respectively. However, I appear to add supplementary substages of multiplication and integration to the abstract stage-substage sequence in the model of Case.

With this logic, I have shown where the last two missing substages in Case's model are positioned relative to my own. In the following, I apply to Fischer's model the same analytic procedure that I had adopted to Case's model in order to understand its origins and how it expresses gaps relative to my own in terms of the number of substages involved.

## Fischer

Fischer also was faced with the same conceptual difficulties as Case: in particular, how to accommodate Piaget's sensorimotor series of six substages when he was drawn to a model of a cyclic recursion of three substages over stages, and what to do with Piaget's preoperational and concrete operational stages. For the latter issue, Case had decided to keep in his model the preoperational and concrete operational stages, but renamed them. This logical procedure that had been adopted by Case lead to Case's model of two stages in cognitive development in the middle developmental period, with three substages in each one, or six substages total. However, Fischer did not separate the preoperational and concrete operational periods, and collapsed them into one stage, called representational. This meant that there were only three substages in this time frame in development, leaving him three substages short relative to Case's model in this age period.

Fischer faced the same difficulties confronted by Case for the sensorimotor stage of Piaget. The latter had a six-substage sequence in the stage, but Fischer, like Case, had a three-substage cyclic recursion over stages. To solve one problem, like Case, he formulated a presensorimotor phase of development in this case, called the reflexive period. Then, like Case, he was left with a three-step series of substages in the sensorimotor period. Like Case, he found that he came up short relative to Piaget's description of the start of the ensuing stage of preoperations at 2 years of age. Like Case, he put the first postsensorimotor substage in his sequence at 18 months of age. As mentioned, this led to a model of substages in middle development in Fischer's model that appears far short. On the one hand, it contains three substages or three less than in the model of Case, which has two three-substage stages in the same age frame. On the other hand, in my model, there is also one stage in this age period, like Fischer, but it has five substages, which is consistent with my model of five substage recursions over stages.

Whether considering the comparison of Fischer's model in middle development with that of Case or my own, Fischer's model appears too truncated, with important gaps in the required sequence of substages. In one way, his model is flexible enough to accommodate these gaps, because it allows for multiple steps in any one substage. This shall be shown later in the book in his description of steps in the development of guilt. However, the idiosyncrasies in this procedure could lead to inconsistencies. The option is to consider my model that includes more substages in the time frame being discussed.

For the abstract stage, it appears that Fischer encountered the same limitations that Case confronted, according to the logical analysis given above. That is, like Case, Fischer appears to have missed two abstract substages in his model, because it consists of a cyclic recursion of three substages, in contrast to the present case in which five substages are thought to recur. In Fischer's model, the three abstract substages are called sets, mappings, and systems, which are somewhat akin to the first three stages of my substage series of coordinations, hierarchizations, and systematizations. Moreover, there is a good correspondence in the age periods for the two models, although the ones in Fischer are a bit more spread out. This probably is due to the perceived need to not leave such a large gap before the next stage of principles. Therefore, what appear to be missing in Fischer's model relative to my own model of the abstract stage is that there appear to be two substages that develop after the three that he described for this period (and that I describe in my model for this period, which I have labeled multiplications and integrations).

Note that perhaps the last substage in both Case's and Fischer's model for the abstract stage resemble the last one in the present model, that of integration, more than the one given in the analyses above, that of systematization. Either way, the present model provides a coherent structure for understanding the evolution of the substages of abstract thought through its five substages, and the work of Case and Fischer do not map perfectly onto it, given that each of them describes three and not five substages in the same time frame.

### Interim Summary

Fischer and Case, as well as their colleagues, have been the predominant Neo-Piagetians over the last 30 years. Their models inspired my own, and it builds on theirs. Nevertheless, I have found gaps and inconsistencies in their models that I have tried to accommodate in my own model. Our work will continue in parallel, and I hope to continue to be enriched by their work. However, Case has passed away. But his work still has wide respect, and continues on through his colleagues and others he had inspired, as revealed in the following.

## Steps in the Development of Egocentrism

### *Introduction*

Kesselring and Müller (2011) presented an interesting version of a Piagetian Stage X Phase sequence in development that included cognitive and socioaffective components. They used Piaget's classic four stages as a basis for a model of the development of egocentrism (sensorimotor, preoperational, concrete operational, formal), and within each of the stages they posited a sequence of three phases, also following Piaget (α, β, γ; alpha, beta, gamma, respectively). In the sense that the concept of phases in their model, derived from Piaget, relates to the Neo-Piagetian one concept of substages that cyclically recur within stages because there are three steps posited, the steps in the cognitive developmental model of Kesselring and Müller resemble those of Case and Fischer. For the same ages, Case had proposed the development of four stages (sensorimotor, relational, dimensional, vectorial), with each having three cyclically recurring substages (unifocal, bifocal, elaborated) (the major difference between the form of Piaget's and Case's models is that Case added an orienting stage before the sensorimotor one, and that orienting stage is not applicable to the present context). Given that for the age period involved, Fischer had proposed a model consisting of three stages and not four, overall, Kesselring and Müller's model of the development of egocentrism resembles that of Case more than that of Fischer.

Kesselring and Müller (2011) developed their model in the context of proposing a revised understanding of egocentrism only one limited area in development, and how it changes over stages and phases. Perhaps this goal accounted for their use of the notion of phases instead of substages to describe the steps in the developmental sequence, although they did refer to the concept of substages in this regard, too.

## *Piaget*

At first, Piaget considered egocentrism as a phase in the preschooler between the infant and child periods, or after about 2 years of age, between the periods of "autistic" and logical thought (e.g., Piaget, 1926a). In this initial Piagetian conception, egocentrism is marked by a failure to distinguish subject from object, by egocentric speech, or collective monologue, etc. (Piaget, 1927/1930). Children see everything unconsciously from their own viewpoint due to a lack of differentiation (Piaget, 1926b/1929).

Piaget revised his concept of egocentrism when he realized that it is present not only in childhood but also in infancy (Piaget, 1936/1952/1963). Therefore, he considered that it manifests differently in successive stages, in a process of vertical décalage. As for the concept of egocentrism itself, in Piaget's revised concept it was considered to be the outcome of using new qualitatively distinct cognitive acquisitions that open new perspectives in dealing with the world, but egocentric thinking seemed limited by being considered "absolute." To move beyond this step, no matter in which stage it appears, the developing person must decenter, both cognitively and affectively. Inhelder and Piaget (1958) had proposed that egocentrism even marks the start of the formal period. However, Piaget had never related directly the concept of egocentrism to the concrete operational period.

## *Kesselring and Müller*

Piaget (1975/1985) subsumed the concepts of egocentrism and decentration within a broader theory of cognitive change related to autoregulation, equilibrium, and equilibration. In this regard, Kesselring and Müller (2011) reconstructed the concept of egocentrism as a sequence of development involving "strict" egocentrism (lack of perspective taking), broader egocentrism (lack of coordination in perspective taking), and decentration (presence of coordination in perspective taking). Given that there are different cognitive domains, decentration processes follow individual timetables.

According to Kesselring and Müller, these three phases in the development of egocentrism that takes place within the various stages of development relate to three types of reactions that manifest in the face of cognitive challenges or perturbations in the equilibration process (the already-mentioned alpha, beta, and gamma; Piaget, 1975/1985). These reactions lead the developing person, respectively; (a) to ignore, repress, or refuse the challenges or perturbations; (b) to consider elementary differences, but without coordinating them; and (c) to coordinate and integrate them, for example, through the process of reflective abstraction. The authors concluded that the development of cognition involves the development of the ability to handle relations.

## *Cognition and Affect*

Kesselring and Müller (2011) applied their model of steps in the development of egocentrism within each of Piaget's stages to both the cognitive and affective areas. For example, in the first, strict egocentric phase, in the sensorimotor period the newborn does not differentiate self and world/other. In the preoperational stage, the preschooler does not differentiate how he or she and another person feel and do things. In the concrete operational stage, the child centers on the group of friends itself, and any rules related to the group take second place. In the formal stage, adolescents begin to enter the community of adults, but without plans and with an overvaluation of the self.

By the third gamma step of resolving egocentrism, in the sensorimotor period, the infant develops an initial empathy; in the preoperational stage, the child develops an interpretive understanding of mind; and in the concrete operational stage, the child respects that moral rules are grounded in mutual expectations. Finally, in the formal stage, the adult can act with consistency across thought and action.

## *Comment*

Kesselring and Müller (2011) have proposed a model of cognitive-affective relationships tied to Piaget's model of stages in cognitive development. It is quite consistent with Case's model. In addition, it could be worthwhile to rework the stages into language directly related to coordinations and relations, as per the models of Case and myself, along with that of Fischer. This being said, the model proposed by Kesselring and Müller is noteworthy because it rejuvenates a Piagetian concept that even Piaget had put aside, and shows its applicability across the whole lifespan.

In addition, the description of their model prepares the way for the next portion of the present work, of describing, comparing, and contrasting the cognitive-affective parallels in Case and Fischer.

## Summary and Conclusions

The heart of the models presented by Case and Fischer involves a three-step cycle of substages that recur in four to five major stages of cognitive development. For Mounoud (e.g., Mounoud, 1986), a five-substage cycle is repeated in three stages. I attempted to show how the present model does not have the gaps and inconsistencies evident in the other models.

The Neo-Piagetian models of Case (e.g., Case, 1985) and Fischer (e.g., Fischer, 1980) on cognitive-socioaffective links in development are described and analyzed in depth in the next chapters of the present work. This being said, the present work also describes parallels in cognitive and affective development. For example, it will be shown that the present model can help modify Fischer's reformulation of the Oedipus conflict in the preschool period to give it a better fit to the process described in the literature.

To give an example from Case, it shall be shown that he had described up to four basic emotions that could develop in each cognitive substage of his cognitive developmental model, but at times there were fewer. Also, there was no inherent organization across these emotions (e.g., in terms of dimensions). As for Fischer in this regard, he has presented a more structured view of the basic emotions, for he relates them to superordinate and subordinate categories. However, he posits a limited number of basic emotions, and does not prescribe the way they might emerge relative to the cognitive substages of his model.

To give another example, but one unrelated to the models of Case or Fischer, the fast growing field of "theories of mind" in the preschooler, where the false belief paradigm is used, will be evaluated in light of the relevant substages of the present model. Compared to current theories on the topic, I will show that the present model accommodates better to the data in this area than competing theories.

A series of other workers have considered the relationship between cognition and affect from a Piagetian perspective (e.g., Cicchetti & Hesse, 1983; Cowan, 1978; Gouin Décarie, 1962, 1978; Sroufe, 1979; Wolff, 1960). Like Case and Fischer, they have built on Piaget's own speculations on the cognition-affect relationship. However, Case (e.g., Case, 1985, 1988) and Fischer (and colleagues, e.g., Fischer, 1980; Fischer, Shaver, & Carnochan, 1990) remain the most elaborate theorists along these lines, so that generally this other important body of thought is not analyzed in the present work, except where it sheds some light on the matter. With this prolog, the book moves on to the description of the approaches of Case and Fischer to the development of cognitive-affective parallels from a Neo-Piagetian perspective.

## References

Bertenthal, B. I., & Fischer, K. W. (1978). Development of self-recognition in the infant. *Developmental Psychology, 14*, 44–50.

Biggs, J. B. (1992). Modes of learning, forms of knowing, and ways of schooling. In A. Demetriou, M. Shayer, & A. Efklides (Eds.), *Neo-piagetian theories of cognitive development: Implications and applications for education* (pp. 31–51). London: Routledge.

Biggs, J. B., & Collis, K. F. (1982). *Evaluating the quality of learning: The SOLO taxonomy (Structured of the Observed Learning Outcome)*. New York: Academic Press.

Case, R. (1978). Intellectual development from birth to adulthood: A neo-piagetian interpretation. In R. Siegler (Ed.), *Children's thinking: What develops?* (pp. 109–150). Hillsdale: Erlbaum.

Case, R. (1985). *Intellectual development: Birth to adulthood*. Orlando: Academic Press.

Case, R. (1988). The whole child: Toward an integrated view of young children's cognitive, social, and emotional development. In A. D. Pellegrini (Ed.), *Psychological bases for early education* (pp. 155–184). New York: Wiley.

Case, R. (1991). Stages in the development of the young child's first sense of self. *Developmental Review, 11*, 210–230.

Case, R. (1992a). The role of the frontal lobes in the regulation of cognitive development. *Brain and Cognition, 20*, 51–73.

Case, R. (1992b). Neo-Piagetian theories of child development. In R. J. Sternberg & C. A. Berg (Eds.), *Intellectual development* (pp. 161–196). New York: Cambridge University Press.

Case, R. (1992c). Neo-Piagetian theories of intellectual development. In H. Beilin & P. B. Pufall (Eds.), *Piaget's theory: Prospects and possibilities* (pp. 61–104). Hillsdale: Erlbaum.

Case, R. (1998). The development of conceptual structures. In W. Damon, D. Kuhn, & R. S. Siegler (Eds.), *Handbook of child psychology: Vol. 2. Cognition, perception & language* (5th ed., pp. 745–800). New York: Wiley.

Case, R., & Griffin, S. (1990). Child cognitive development: The role of central conceptual structures in the development of scientific and social thought. In C. A. Hauert (Ed.), *Developmental psychology: Cognitive, perceptuomotor and neuropsychological perspectives* (pp. 193–230). Amsterdam: North Holland.

Case, R., Okamoto, Y., Henderson, B., & McKeough, A. (1993). Individual variability and consistency in cognitive development: New evidence for the existence of central conceptual structures. In R. Case & W. Edelstein (Eds.), *Contributions to human development: Vol. 23. The new structuralism in cognitive development: Theory and research on individual pathways* (pp. 71–100). New York: Karger.

Cicchetti, D., & Hesse, P. (1983). Affect and intelligence: Piaget's contribution to the study of infant emotional development. In R. Plutchik & H. Kellerman (Eds.), *Emotion: Theory, research and experience: Vol. 2. Emotions in early development* (pp. 115–169). New York: Academic Press.

Cowan, P. A. (1978). *Piaget with feeling: Cognitive, social, and emotional dimensions*. New York: Holt, Rhinehart, & Winston.

Fischer, K. W. (1980). A theory of cognitive development: The control and construction of hierarchies of skills. *Psychological Review, 87*, 477–531.

Fischer, K. W., & Corrigan, R. (1981). A skill approach to language development. In R. Stark (Ed.), *Language behavior in infancy and early childhood* (pp. 245–289). New York: Elsevier.

Fischer, K. W., & Hogan, A. E. (1989). The big picture for infant development: Levels and variations. In J. Lockman & N. Hazen (Eds.), *Action in social context: Perspectives on early development* (pp. 275–305). New York: Plenum.

Fischer, K. W., Knight, C. C., & Van Paris, M. (1993). Analyzing diversity in developmental pathways: Methods and concepts. In R. Case & W. Edelstein (Eds.), *The new structuralism in cognitive development: Theory and research on individual pathways* (pp. 33–56). Basel: Karger.

Fischer, K. W., & Rose, S. P. (1994). Dynamic development of coordination of components in brain and behavior: A framework for theory and research. In G. Dawson & K. W. Fischer (Eds.), *Human behavior and the developing brain* (pp. 3–66). New York: Guilford Press.

Fischer, K. W., Shaver, P. R., & Carnochan, P. (1990). How emotions develop and how they organize development. *Cognition and Emotion, 4*, 81–127.

Fischer, K. W., & Tangney, J. P. (1995). Self-conscious emotions and the affect revolution: Framework and overview. In J. P. Tangney & K. W. Fischer (Eds.), *Self-consious emotions: The psychology of shame, guilt, embarrassment, and pride* (pp. 3–22). New York: Guilford Press.

Gouin Décarie, T. (1962). *Intelligence et affectivité chez le jeune enfant [Intelligence and affect in the young child]*. Neuchâtel: Delachaux et Niestlé.

Gouin Décarie, T. (1978). Affect development and cognition in a Piagetian context. In M. Lewis & L. A. Rosenblum (Eds.), *The development of affect* (pp. 183–204). New York: Plenum.

Inhelder, B., & Piaget, J. (1958). *The growth of logical thinking from childhood to adolescence: An essay on the development of formal operational structures*. Trans. Parsons A., and Seagrim, S. New York: Basic Books. (Originally published 1955).

Jackson, E., Campos, J. J., & Fischer, K. W. (1978). The question of decalage between object permanence and person permanence. *Developmental Psychology, 14*, 1–10.

Kesselring, T., & Müller, U. (2011). The concept of egocentrism in the context of Piaget's theory. *New Ideas in Psychology*. doi: 10.1016/j.newideapsych.2010.03.008.
Lamborn, S. D., Fischer, K. W., & Pipp, S. (1994). Constructive criticism and social lies: A developmental sequence for understanding honesty and kindness in social interactions. *Developmental Psychology, 30*, 495–508.
Lewis, M. D., & Ash, A. J. (1992). Evidence for a Neo-Piagetian stage transition in early cognitive development. *International Journal of Behavioral Development, 15*, 337–358.
Mounoud, P. (1976). Les revolutions psychologiques de l'enfant [Psychological revolutions in the child]. *Archives de Psychologie, 44*, 103–114.
Mounoud, P. (1986). Similarities between developmental sequences at different age periods. In I. Levin (Ed.), *Stage and structure: Reopening the debate* (pp. 40–58). Norwood: Ablex.
Piaget, J. (1926a). *Language and thought of the child*. London: Routledge & Kegan Paul.
Piaget, J. (1926b/1929). *The child's conception of the world*. London: Kegan Paul Trench Trubner. (Original work published in 1926).
Piaget, J. (1927/1930). *The child's conception of physical causality*. Totowa/London: Kegan Paul Trench Trubner. (Original work published in 1927).
Piaget, J. (1936/1952/1963). *The origins of intelligence in children*. New York: International Universities Press and Norton. (Original work published in 1936).
Piaget, J. (1975/1985). *The equilibration of cognitive structures: The central problem in intellectual development* (T. Brown & K. J. Thampy, Trans.). Chicago: University of Chicago Press. (Original work published in 1975).
Sroufe, L. A. (1979). Socioemotional development. In J. Osofsky (Ed.), *Handbook of infant development* (pp. 462–518). New York: Wiley.
Uzgiris, I. E., & Hunt, J. Mc V. (1975). *Assessment in infancy: Ordinal scales of psychologic development*. Urbana: University of Illinois Press.
Watson, M. W., & Fischer, K. W. (1977). A developmental sequence of agent use in late infancy. *Child Development, 48*, 828–836.
Watson, M. W., & Fischer, K. W. (1980). Development of social roles in elicited and spontaneous behavior during the preschool years. *Developmental Psychology, 16*, 483–494.
Wolff, P. H. (1960). The developmental psychologies of Jean Piaget and psychoanalysis. *Psychological Issues, 2*, 181.
Young, G. (1990). The development of hemispheric and manual specialization. In G. E. Hammond (Ed.), *Cerebral control of speech and limb movements* (pp. 79–139). Amsterdam: North Holland.

# Chapter 7
# Parallels in Cognitive Substages and Socioaffectivity in Case

## Introduction

Case (Case, Hayward, Lewis, & Hurst, 1988) maintained that, as development proceeds, cognitive development and emotional development interrelate. He argued that emotion is an entity that is "real and distinct," with reciprocal feedback controls involving it, cognition, and other systems (Note that for purposes of simplicity, I refer to the work and model of Case or Fischer alone, at times, even when colleagues are involved in the publications being discussed). Tables 7.1–7.4 present the specific correspondences that Case had suggested across cognitive and socio-affective behavior (Case, 1985, 1988, 1991a, 1991b; Case et al., 1988). In the tables, I provide examples involving motor or cognitive examples, as required. In describing this table in the text that follows, first, I examine from a cognitive viewpoint Case's progression of substages, and then, the sequence is examined in terms of its suggested socioemotional correlates. Later in the chapter, I analyze Case's perspective on levels of self-development.

## Case's Neo-Piagetian Model: Socioaffective Correspondences

### *Earlier Case*

#### Introduction

Case provides precise, informative, representative examples of behavior for each of the substages in his model, especially from the time frame involving the elaboration orienting substage to the elaboration interrelation substage. It appears that although they are products of keen observation, these examples sometimes seem more complex than the maximal limits of complexity prescribed in their corresponding substage. Moreover, I shall demonstrate that these same examples seem to provide support for my own model of Neo-Piagetian cognitive development.

G. Young, *Development and Causality: Neo-Piagetian Perspectives*, 
DOI 10.1007/978-1-4419-9422-6_7, 

**Table 7.1** Parallels in cognitive and socioaffective development in the orienting stage in Case

| Level | Socioaffective development |
|---|---|
| Unifocal | Orienting responses are assembled |
| Bifocal | Newborns orient to more than one stimulus or aspects of one stimulus, orienting but in a rigid way (e.g., for locating, latching onto nipple). A new stimulus can interfere with ongoing activity. Newborns develop global representations of salient objects such as mothers' face. With orienting responses come attendant sensory expectations and motor and affective effects. At this level, these expectations concern relationships between stimuli. With nursing, there may be frustration, gastric pain, high arousal, and diffuse distress (e.g., at interruption). But with experience, these reactions become contentment and satisfaction. Thus "only two contrasting pairs of affective states can be experienced at birth, namely, contentment vs. distress, and sensory disengagement (a precursor of interest or awe) vs. sensory disengagement (a precursor of boredom or aversion)" (Case et al., 1988, p. 15) |
| Elaboration | Very young infants coordinate motor response and their reciprocals (e.g., in, out mouth). They coordinate head and eye movements in tracking. In visual scanning, they evidence part-to-part shifting (e.g., to mothers' eyes, to mouth, and back again). Different partial representations of mothers' facial and bodily characteristics created in this process are unified into coherent sensory representations of them. With each representation so integrated (e.g., fathers in one type of interaction), distinct affective color or feeling tones develop. New emotions possible at this age concern interest, pleasure/delight/joy (as in the joy of recognition), fear/wariness, and anger/rage from frustration. Prolonged dyadic interchanges with mothers include kicking, limb flailing, cooing, and smiling, all of which gives an "impression of joyful exuberance" (Case, 1985, p. 135). "The baby could goo and coo responsively … and delight at its power to keep the mother smiling and cooing in return" (Case, 1988, p. 166). Anticipation of seeing the mothers' eyes may bring with it an expectation of pleasure. Frustration in feeding or restraint of head movement brings more than the distress of the prior period, for rage can be expressed. Fear/wariness can be induced by the approach of abusive (secondary) caretakers, for the pain associated with the consolidated scheme for them leads to its anticipation when the scheme is activated by their approach. Distress, an emotion that was described specifically as emerging in the prior substage, may result when attachment figures hand the infants to other adults after having finished calming them. A cumulative affective charge or overall emotional orientation forms, and functions as the root of a sense of general trust or mistrust. The infants' initial attachments probably are formed |

Adapted from references to Case

Case has elaborated in great detail the correspondences between cognitive and socioaffective development in his model. Case is another theorist whose stages and substages respect the Piagetian tradition. Although he changed the names of the stages, the substages that he described reflect the

(continued)

**Table 7.1** (continued)

| |
|---|
| original Piagetian series, either keeping the age markers or adding to them, by splitting them, for example. For the age periods birth to age 19 years, because I had adopted the same approach as Case of preserving Piaget's age ranges, or splitting them, as required, there is a perfect correspondence between Case's sequence of substages as originally presented, and as described in Young (1990a, Table 2, p. 146), and the appearance in development of the equivalent substages of the present model |
| In Case (1991a, 1991b), Case renames the first age period, placing it as a separate orienting stage (It had been called sensorimotor precoordination). Because it came to be a stage instead of a substage, the model evolved to have the first age period to consist of three substages, in order that the pattern matches the one found across his other stages. This led to a divergence of the one-to-one correspondence of the substages appearing in his model from birth onward and those of the present model for the age period concerned (birth to 19 years) |
| Note that in his model Fischer also had created an initial stage before the sensorimotor one, and it also consisted of the typical three-substage sequence. In this regard, these models are more differentiated than mine in the first few months of life |
| However, the present model allows for steps in development that are embedded in the substages, so that each substage consists of five steps themselves. This suggests a phenomenon indicative of a fractalization process in development, because in the present model there are five stages, and they have five substages, and these in turn have five steps. In this regard, I suggest that careful analysis of development after birth might reveal that in the first months there could be many steps that are discernable. For example, in the last substage of the reflex stage, in the first month of life, there could be five steps that are discernable. The same would apply to the first sensorimotor substage after that (1–4 months). Therefore, in the first 4 months of life, the present model posits ten steps in development |
| Development is so rapid in these first 4 months that the transitions could be overlooked; in this regard, the suggestion bears further scrutiny. Others are finding data that illustrate the possibility of steps within the substages of the present model. For example, Karniol (1989) found that in the first months of life four steps in manual development are seen to take place within the time frame of each of the first two sensorimotor stages of the present model (see Young, 1990) |
| Moreover, in Fisher's model, he has added enough flexibility to it to accommodate steps and levels applicable to individual skill domains beyond the general structure of stages and substages that he described. Although there are some major differences between his model and my own, this conceptual addition is consistent with the present concept of possible steps within substages |
| Returning to the original point, because Case has developed a model of stages and substages in cognitive development that maps well onto the present model, and because he described so well the socioaffective developments that correspond to his substages, his work has been helpful to my equivalent efforts. At the same time, I point out the times when the examples that he provided better fit my model than his own. This being said, in describing Case's Neo-Piagetian model, I did not find myself in a position where I had to deal with missing substages relative to my own model or that of Piaget's, unlike the case for Fischer, as shown in ensuing tables |
| About the specifics of the table under discussion, Case has described well the socioaffective unfolding in the first months of life in the orienting stage. His descriptions are consistent with the literature published in the time period in which the model was elaborated. Therefore, given the parallels between his model and my own, his model adds to and enhances the description of my own |
| The same comment applies to the tables that follow this one in my presentation of Case's work in the area. However, note that his description of socioaffective correspondences involving his model of cognitive substages is sparser for the later stages. Moreover, the process of elucidating cognitive-affective correspondences in Case did not continue after the age of 19 years, because he did not include a postformal stage in his model, unlike for the present case, which adopted a lifespan view of development |

**Table 7.2** Parallels in cognitive and socioaffective development in the sensorimotor stage in Case

| Level | Socioaffective development |
|---|---|
| Unifocal | Infants several months of age coordinate orienting structures, creating sensorimotor representations or routines (e.g., using an activity, which had one end in prior level, as means to obtain a different end, such as in eliciting interesting social interaction or sounds and sights by arm swing). To invite motor play with their mothers, infants reach out and pull their hair. The infants perform manoeuvers such as these with intention, e.g., anticipating verbalizations and smiles instead of the ongoing distant neutrality once they use the means of loud babbling. Or they reciprocate with laughter if mothers respond with a behavior such as mock crying. Infants initiate conversations with similar behavior, e.g., vocalization with looking then monitoring. They request help by motor agitation and directed arm extension. Genuine reciprocal interactions take place. Infants can also coordinate one structure in memory while applying another, e.g., they call absent mothers while scanning the room. Derived feelings (e.g., when mothers reciprocate their part of a practiced dyadic pattern) may concern pleasure, exhilaration, interest, fascination, delight, elation, or power, but also frustration/anger/crankiness, distress/ sadness, and fear when the infants' expectations are not realized. For example, if absent mothers fail to return after calls or if attentive mothers suddenly leave, this may produce the first affective conflict and subsequent anxiety in infants (via representations of mothers that are simultaneously positive and negative). Infants "hatch" to both move away and closer to their mothers, and the first efforts to actively regulate attachments to them begin |
| Bifocal | Toward the end of the first year, infants can focus on two sensorimotor transactions in sequence or can maintain a record of one action-reaction pair of events/possibilities in working memory while they actively engage in another. Often this concerns experiences in the inanimate domain against the background of experiences in the inanimate one, permitting a shared sense of the external world (e.g., they imitate drum striking; glance at mothers and babble/smile/laugh while playing with an interesting toy; crawl back to mothers who they had just left for "emotional refueling," or call them for comforting if something frightening happens). In short, infants at this age can act on the environment to induce a parental response or cooperation, or they can act on the parent to affect the environment (and at the same time evaluate whether the parent is available) (Lewis, 1988). Thus, infants share and have augmented in intensity the affective experiences of joy, warmth, and a sense of containment/refuge/safety with the "secure base" to offset any negativity (frustration, overarousal, fatigue) in exploring. Conversely, clear anxiety/ insecurity manifests and is not moderated but heightens when infants face separation from mothers or when an ambiguous situation arises when they are off exploring (e.g., with strangers, odd toys). Here, infants tie the normal structure (of action-reaction with present, attentive mothers) to the structure of the effect of their leaving or to a different structure (e.g., with someone/something else, or to mothers as angry, resistant, flat in affect, etc.). Sadness or "displacements" (e.g., aggression) can take place, for infants can redirect attention from one threatening object to a second that is more vulnerable. Infants defensively "split off" cognition from affect, positive from negative affect, and the "bad" and "good" mother |

(continued)

**Table 7.2** (continued)

| Level | Socioaffective development |
|---|---|
| Elaboration | Year-olds interleave sensorimotor transactions with objects and with mothers (e.g., objects are used to attract their attention; mothers used as agents to get objects). Also, infants at this age activate one bifocal structure while maintaining a second in working memory, facilitating reversibility (e.g., undoing structure to see if effect undone) and complementarity (e.g., performing parallel structure). Thus, toddlers knock down a tower just built; imagine the joy of return upon leaving secure base; reciprocally imitate actions by their mothers on objects brought to them after a foray, all after having performed actions on the object and waiting for their mothers to do something similar; and imitate peers' actions on objects (e.g., drum banging). The imagined return voyage to mothers after exploration can induce a feeling of insecurity and hesitation if normally their mothers are not available enough. Or the infants may react angrily if their mothers are overprotective and intrusive. "In these cases exploration may become a tool of either escape or retribution" (Case, 1988, p. 172). Emotions experienced during exploration of the inanimate world may reflect directly the quality of maternal interactions. Normally, actions in the physical world have social worth and engender a sense of security (distinct from the security felt with the mother). Emotions in the maternal world can act to modulate (e.g., intensify, complement, overcome) emotions in the inanimate world, and vice versa. The balance of positive to negative emotions in this period concerns a sense of security vs. insecurity and doubt/isolation (which is excessive in abusive families) |

Adapted from references to Case

## The First Months

According to Case, neonates in the bifocal orienting substage are born with four emotions: contentment, distress, engagement (a precursor to interest), and disengagement (a precursor to aversion-boredom; see Table 7.1). The four emotions listed by Case in the newborn period seem to relate to an equilibrium state in one way or another, a function relevant to the cognitive substage and age period concerned.

According to Case, 1- to 4-month-olds in the orienting elaboration substage should show reversibility in their socioemotional behavior coordinations. The new emotions that develop in this period concern, in particular: pleasure, delight-joy, wariness-fear, and rage. Again, Case appears quite perceptive in the emotions that he ascribes to this age period.

Case's description of the socioaffective behavior in this period includes Erikson's concept of trust vs. mistrust and Bowlby's concept of attachment to the caregiver. In the present model, presented later in the book, the substage following this one and not the substage equivalent to this one is the one marked by the emergence of these cardinal acquisitions.

According to Bowlbian theory (see Chap. 23), attachment develops in a series of phases. Thus, in the 1- to 4-month-old period, interactive games that sharpen discrimination take place. The infant in this age period does not engage in attachment

**Table 7.3** Parallels in cognitive and socioaffective development in the interrelational stage in Case

| Level | Socioaffective development |
|---|---|
| Unifocal | For the first time children engage in object-centered behaviors that are *complementary* or *reciprocal* to those being performed by someone else (Case, 1985, p. 160) (e.g., get rake while parent cuts grass, push chair to table while motioning at peers to come). Imitations of social actions are sequenced appropriately (e.g., pick up tea cup, drink from it). There is a beginning cooperative system (e.g., sweep with broom while other gathers dirt with pan). In Case (1988), the complementary cooperative system is seen to involve the ability to focus on two culturally appropriate relationships simultaneously (e.g., pour tea so that other can drink). Children can either initiate joint activity or reciprocate after bids (e.g., push chair to table while motioning to peers to bring another one in order to play together). Similarly, children can maintain interest in one interaction while engaged in another (e.g., telling mum at distance about cat when with dad). Children are responsive to others' emotions (e.g., bring blanket to comfort peer). Play also reflects unifocal interrelational structuring (e.g., pretend action on object in parallel to other's real action on similar object; other executes bossily ordered action on object; other's stance toward object blocked by child's stance; other's already built tower used as model for own). In terms of dangers, children can coordinate a higher-order structure involving their relationship with their mothers and the mothers' relationship with others. If mothers are busy with another person or if they intend to leave children with another person, mothers are not available and fear/anger/sadness/jealousy/tantrum/clinging/whining may result. Children feel dominated, subjugated, rejected, and with no control. Similarly, they can relate to peers in a dominance struggle for power or possession of objects. Defense mechanisms such as verbal denial, displacement, denigration, and projective identification can be used |
| Bifocal | Because children can focus on two social interrelations simultaneously, they realize that their mothers' relation with them can override or mitigate their mothers' relation with others. For example, children realize that only they and not their younger siblings can achieve superior skill (as in figure drawing) in the eyes of their mothers, and that after their sibling's time with the mothers there will be a turn for them, as well. Circle games (e.g., get ball from left, give to child at right) also evidence bifocal social coordination. Social scripts involve multiple roles and actors in social cooperation. Assumed social roles reveal a complementarity of two or more members in social systems, such as in families or play groups. Thus, children realize that they are both their mothers' offspring and have siblings. Also, they realize that different family members relate to mothers in distinct yet unified *ways*. Psychological analysis entails relating others' external behavior and internal feelings/judgments |

(continued)

**Table 7.3** (continued)

| Level | Socioaffective development |
|---|---|
| Elaboration | Social scripts involving multiple roles become more complementary, reversible. Children compensate momentary dominance/exclusion (e.g., when mothers are busy with siblings) by integrating into the mother-other relationship (e.g., helping mothers by playing with a younger sibling produces admiration on their part). Children can engage in "projection," for attention can be redirected from cues indicative of conflict in oneself (e.g., anger at loved one) to a second person. Emotional threats include feelings of abandonment, exclusion, subjugation, and rejection, but these are balanced by more sharing at a distance, empathy, and role complementarity. Thus, the major challenge in this period is assertion/control vs. doubt/loss of control |

Adapted from references to Case

**Table 7.4** Parallels in cognitive and socioaffective development in the dimensional/vectorial stages in Case

| Stage | Socioaffective development |
|---|---|
| Dimensional | Social scripts differentiate into internal components and action components, with the latter mapped onto the former. This permits model building and control of children's own feelings and thoughts. Thus, there seems to be self-regulated rules for their display. The network of scripts for primary social relations is seen as related themselves in hierarchies and institutions. Children apprehend dimensions on which the self is ranked. These dimensions involve parents' and others' (e.g., peers') values and evaluations (and include gender stereotypes). Self-monitoring and the use of others as "social mirrors" result (involving the psychodynamic school's "superego"). Children's vulnerabilities at this age concern conflict in parent-peer standards, embarrassment, self depreciation, and a sense of rejection if their self-ranking is deemed low. "Rationalization" can occur in the bifocal substage, because children can redirect their focus to acceptable feelings-motives instead of unacceptable ones. Other possible defense mechanisms are suppression, projection, and introjection |
| Abstract | Adolescents' dimension evaluations are now abstract (e.g., personality, social status, achievement), so they build an abstract structure of their parents' and their own attributes to serve as reference points. An idealization period (unifocal) may be followed by ones of conflict (bifocal) and resolution (elaboration) in terms of adopting parental figures as models. Defense mechanisms may involve idealization, sublimation, and persecution |

Adapted from references to Case

behavior, per se, but only in attachment-related precursors. Next, in the 4- to 8-month period the first attachment develops, as indexed by preferential smiling to the caregiver; yet it is passive in nature in that the infant will not yet seek actively a departing caregiver. Active attachment behavior only develops in the next period of 8–12 months.

Given this backdrop of description of the phases in the development of attachment, it is evident that Case had been premature to ascribe to the 1- to 4-month period early acquisitions in attachment. By contrast, in the present model, which follows the line of the Bowlbian one, the first indication of a true attachment occurs beyond the 1- to 4-month-old period, i.e., in the 4- to 8-month-old period, but in a passive sense, and it then proceeds to elaborate in the 8- to 12-month period in an active sense.

As for Erikson's stage of trust vs. mistrust, unlike Case, I also hesitate to place it in the 1- to 4-month-old period. As has been shown in Chaps. 1, 4, 5, and 20, in Eriksonian theory, the issue of trust vs. mistrust is the central one confronting the infant throughout the first year. In terms of the need to specify where it becomes a critical focus in the first year, in my opinion, the issue of trust vs. mistrust reaches its apex in the 4- to 8-month-old period, just when the passive attachments of Bowlby are forming.

In my own cognitive developmental model, 1- to 4-month-olds can coordinate sensorimotor schemes so that it makes sense that they can focus on dyadic interchanges in this period. However, in the present model, it is only in the next period of 4–8 months of age that schemes can be hierarchically integrated. I suggest that it is this latter skill that permits infants to place their self-related and relational schemes as a dominant focus in the interchange with the caregiver, allowing both the first attachment and sense of trust to manifest. Thus, Case seems to have considered that these cardinal acquisitions emerge in development one substage earlier than appears to be the case.

## From 4 to 12 Months

In the unifocal sensorimotor phase of 4- to 8-month-olds, for Case, initial coordinations are central (e.g., in means-end; memory of mother and calling her; positive-negative representations of her; moving away/closer to her). However, there is no emphasis on the hierarchization of their components, which in my opinion is essential in explaining the pattern that they form. Thus, in failing to consider hierarchical characteristics in the second substage of his cycle, Case has provided examples with this attribute yet failed to describe them in this manner.

Once more, Case suggested that a series of emotions emerge in cognitive development with the onset of a new substage, but the only one that appears to be truly novel in the ones that he indicated for this age period compared to prior ones is "power." However, one could argue readily that power is not an emotion. The other emotions mentioned by Case as applicable to this substage seem to be only more complex variants of emotions mentioned in prior stages (e.g., interest-fascination; anger-crankiness, at goal blockage; distress-sadness). Thus, unlike with the prior and subsequent substages, in the present substage under discussion, it seems that Case has not offered a description of the emergence of any novel emotions that develop in parallel to the new cognitive advance.

Lewis (1993) tested Case's hypothesis that the onset of sensorimotor unifocal coordinations would be accompanied by a spurt in frustration at the interruption of or loss of a goal being pursued. He examined 29 infants weekly from 12 to 23 weeks of age on a battery of sensorimotor unifocal coordination tasks and in reaction to maternal separation and reunion. Distress intensity, as well as anger and joy expressions, in particular, was coded during the latter situations. Although cross-age cognitive-emotion correlations were found, the onset of unifocal coordination was not associated with a parallel change in emotional expression. Thus, Case's model of the manner in which cognition and affect relate at this substage was not supported by this study.

In Case's bifocal sensorimotor substage, infants approaching 12 months of age are viewed as engaging in active attachment regulation (e.g., crying after the caregiver departs). Similarly, they manifest anxiety when there is ambiguity (e.g., if mother is about to leave; if an odd toy is encountered). Case also described this age period as one involving emotional refueling, with the caregiver functioning as a secure base after engaging bouts of exploration. Case's understanding of the attachment behaviors at this age seems appropriate, in that it is consistent with the phase of active attachment described earlier.

In terms of his description of emotions in this substage, Case listed anxiety, emotions involving warmth, a sense of security/safety/containment, and displacement aggression. I concur that anxiety manifests at this juncture, and that emotions involving warmth, security/safety/containment, and displacement aggression emerge, as well.

## The Second Year

Piaget described 12- to 18-month-olds as explorers by trial and error. They create intricate behavioral chains. This is one reason why in my model the cognitive substage at this age period is characterized as "multiplicative." Piaget maintained that 1-year-olds' nascent symbol-forming skills have not allowed them to structure totally imagined plans of mental combination, accounting for the accidental nature of their attempts of discovery. Moreover, this limitation in thought precludes truly reversible conceptual processes, for return to starting point is found only in executed behavior. Therefore, it is instructive to examine the socioaffective correspondence that Case attributed to the infant at this age to determine whether it matches their cognitive abilities. Thus, for me, Case prematurely ascribed a capacity to young toddlers that only older ones can perform. That is, in terms of the Piagetian model, it seems that 1-year-old toddlers should engage in secure-base behavior but should be incapable of *imagining* the joy of returning to the secure base. However, Case not only attributed the former behavior to 1-year-olds, but also the latter.

Case depicted progress in emotional development in this period as involving anger at intrusion, retribution, etc. This does fit the literature, but he also argued that anger does emerge earlier as a distinct emotion.

Case mentioned the danger of doubt and isolation in this period, referring to Erikson's stage of autonomy vs. shame/doubt. My model also places Erikson's autonomy substage at this juncture. It naturally fits here, given 12- to 18-month-olds' proclivity for trial and error exploration. However, shame is not the inverse of autonomy because to feel ashamed children need to feel negatively evaluated. For me, sentiments such as these can only emerge in the next cognitive level where full-fledged symbolic structures can flower, as described by Piaget. Consequently, I argue that the dangers of Eriksonian autonomy are especially related to doubt and not shame.

For Case, 18- to 24-month-olds' social behavior is supremely complementary, cooperative, and reciprocal when it is positive, but it is even filled with jealousy and feelings of domination and rejection when it is negative. Knowing that toddlers in this period have symbol structures of the kind described by Piaget, this picture of 18- to 24-month-olds seems valid, except that others have found that jealousy might emerge at an earlier age period (see Chap. 22). Moreover, there must be other emotions that develop in this period (e.g., the negative emotion of shame, as discussed).

## Afterward

Case's perception of the bifocal interrelational substage in 2-year-olds seems quite reasonable, because in my model there is a comparable period involving coordination. No newly emergent emotions are offered in this cognitive substage.

In Case's model, the elaboration bifocal interrelational substage in 3½- to 5-year-olds witnesses adaptive strategies by children, such as converting a sense of domination/exclusion when mothers are with younger siblings to a sense of cooperation/inclusion (e.g., by helping, complementing their mothers' role). One of the dangers of this substage is that a sense of subjugation can develop. Thus, in terms of what the examples provided teach about my own model (examples involving domination, subjugation), it seems that the substage described by Case concerns especially the attribute of "hierarchization." In fact, in the present model, unlike for that of Case, the label for the period involves the concept of hierarchy (it is explicitly termed perioperational "hierarchization").

In Case's model, the crisis in this period concerns assertion/control vs. doubt/loss of control (the aforementioned subjugation). This conception parallels Erikson's psychosocial stage of initiative vs. guilt, and fits my version of this period. That is, for me, the children's "hierarchical" bent carries over into the socioemotional realm, leading to assertion, control-seeking, and dominance. This quest extends even to the fantasy of substituting for the same-sex parent (the Oedipus conflict) (to be discussed in the next chapter).

## Conclusion

Many examples that Case provided in support of his model seem to better fit my own, or support my model as well as his model. As a prelude to my review of examples to illustrate this argument, recall that in the current model a sequence of five substages (coordination, hierarchization, systematization, multiplication, and integration) is predicted to unfold at each major cognitive stage (reflexive, sensorimotor, perioperational, abstract, and collective intelligence).

(a) In Case's elaboration orienting substage from 1 to 4 months, clear examples of motor coordination are provided. These examples support my characterization of this age period as one of sensorimotor coordination.
(b) Case's unifocal sensorimotor substage in the next age period of 4–8 months describes means-end synchronization, which, when looked at from the perspective of the present model, supports it. That is, this example fits my emphasis that in this stage there is sensorimotor hierarchization.
(c) The next substage of bifocal coordination in the model of Case includes description of the mother-world/inanimate-world systematization that takes place in the 8- to 12-month-old, which supports my understanding of the nature of this phase. That is, in my model this stage concerns sensorimotor coordination, in particular.
(d) Next, Case described the 1-year-old as entering the level of sensorimotor elaboration, and a complex chain in behavior is offered as an example (concerning bringing a toy to the mother, awaiting a response, and reciprocal imitation). The example underscores my notion that multiplication in sensorimotor action is taking place at this age. Also, Case characterized the behavior in this age as showing signs of reversibility. However, to consider one example offered, it appears to me that the year-old does not knock down block towers *in order to rebuild them,* but does it due to trial-and-error exploration (Piaget). Another example speaks of *imagining the joy on returning* to the mother after exploration. However, as discussed, infants at this age might not be capable of reversible behavior such as this.
(e) In Case's next substage of unifocal interrelations at 18–24 months of age, he emphasizes complementarity and reciprocal relations in behavior. Many of the examples listed concern social roles, and a toddler may adopt one or the other when they are paired (e.g., sweep or hold pan). Thus, reversibility seems more evident in the behavior of this substage than in the prior one, fitting my notion that it concerns sensorimotor integration.
(f) Case depicted a bifocal interrelations substage from 2 to 3.5 years of age as the next one in his series, but he offered many examples concerning coordination. In the present model, I term the phase perioperational "coordination," and thus there seems no contradiction with my work.
(g) Finally, Case described a substage of elaboration interrelations from 3.5 to 5 years. My model refers to this period one of perioperational "hierarchization," and several of Case's examples contain elements of dominance-subordination, as I would predict.

In addition, Case described parallels in cognitive/socioaffective development in terms of attachment theory, Erikson's stages, and the primary emotions, especially for the first 5 years of life. I have made suggestions very similar to his at many points in my own model, and even have modified it in light of his work.

### Interim Summary

I have shown that despite the important contributions made by Case's model of cognitive-affective parallels in the stages-substages of development, Case's model of cognitive-affective links in development manifests certain limitations. These concern (a) ambiguities about the nature of the substages; (b) a lack of systematic structuring of the emotional system, in general, and adequate specification of all the emotions that emerge at each substage; (c) imprecision in establishing the exact correspondence between cognitive substages and the phases in the development of attachment; (d) the inappropriate placement of Erikson's stage of trust vs. mistrust with respect to his cognitive substages and, as shall be shown in the next section, (e) a view of self-development limited by his model and not always compatible with independent theories.

In the work that he undertook after the ones described in this section, Case revised some of his description of cognitive-affective parallels over stages and substages in development. In the following, I present these revisions and other works that he undertook on the topic

## *Later Case*

### Introduction

In his later work, Case (1996) examined the relationship between his model of cognitive development and two socioaffective acquisitions. First, he indicated correspondences between a child's developmental stage and the way it influences internal working models that are developing in attachments to the primary caregiver. In addition, he analyzed the evolution of psychological defenses in terms of his model, specifically, how they help the child adjust to different attachment experiences. Recall that in his cognitive model, the developing individual traverses the stages of orienting, sensorimotor actions, interrelations, dimensional thought, and vectorial or abstract thought. The latter three stages resemble the equivalent ones of Piaget (preoperations, concrete operations, formal operations, respectively). Within each stage, the developing individual passes through the cyclically recurring substages of unifocal, bifocal, and elaborated coordination. Also, the different categories of attachment, as measured upon caregiver reunion after a brief separation at 12 months of age, are the secure, avoidant, and ambivalent, and disorganized responses, in particular. Case focused on the sensorimotor to vectorial stages, especially the sensorimotor and interrelational ones. In addition, he analyzed the evolution of working models for the secure and avoidant child, in particular, leaving the others. With respect to defense mechanisms, he considered ones such as keeping a distance and displacement.

Case noted the differences in the Piagetian concept of cognitive structure and the concept of internal working models in attachment theory. First, cognitive structures are energized by emotions such as curiosity, whereas working models concern emotions such as love, fear, and anger. Second, early cognitive structures are not considered accurate, given the baby's nascent cognitive skills; however, working models fairly represent the quality of care received from the primary caregiver. Third, cognitive structures are related only indirectly to social behavior. By contrast, internal working models are formed directly in the light of the quality of social relationship.

## The First Year

Case proceeded to analyze the way secure attachments develop in infancy. In the elaborated orienting substage, the neonate develops an internal perceptual model of the primary caregiver that provides a coherent sensori-affective representation of her presence.

In the first sensorimotor substage of unifocal coordinations, which develops in the period from 4 to 8 months, cognitively, the infant can differentiate and coordinate two sensori-affective representations. For example, two-component representations are found when infants can initiate proto-conversations, request assistance nonverbally, and initiate or respond to play. They expect a response, and show either pleasure and delight or sadness and turning away, depending on the caregiver response. Therefore, the internal working models that develop in this stage are comprised of two components in coordination across the dyad.

In the next bifocal substage, from 8 to 12 months, infants can focus on two sequential social transactions. They can interleave representations of caregiver transactions with those of inanimate objects (toys). They develop a tentative intersubjectivity (Trevarthen, 1980). At the emotional level, they can heighten or dampen an emotion in one context due to experiences in another. Their internal working models come to include the nature of the transactions with the caregiver, with other people and objects, and the way these aspects can be interleaved. However, there are limits to the development of working models; they cannot incorporate yet the notion that primary caregivers can help buffer the dangers in their contexts. Therefore, in the reunion situation, the baby at this age does not rejoice at the caregiver coming back, because there had been no protest at her departure.

## The Second Year

In the next cognitive substage, elaborated sensorimotor activities are acquired, in the age period beginning at 12 months. At this age, the cognitive structures are more integrated and reversible, and the dual representations of relationship between child-caregiver and child-object are sufficiently developed so that the infant can move without difficulty between the two types of transactions. Therefore, prior to the reunion situation, infants deemed secure in attachment at this age do react when they realize that the caregiver might be leaving. Earlier in development, they might have manifested an exploratory curiosity balanced with wariness, but the wariness now predominates and turns into anxiety, fear, frustration, protest, crying, bodily reactions, and distress, and perhaps self-comforting. When the caregiver returns, they should show relief and joy followed, first, by residual frustration and anger once they are comforted and, then, a renewal of interest coupled with wariness, this time somewhat heightened.

Avoidant infants do not react in the normative manner manifested by the secure ones in this elaborated substage. Their working models are tinged with more anger and aggression. They express conflict, because they need more comfort and reassurance to deal with their anxiety of separation, but have been rejected in the past so that they approach the caregiver with higher negative affect and feel more anger and anxiety about possible rejection. They experience emotional overload as a result of the internal conflict, and they engage in defensive but protective behavior, which translates into looking away but trying to maintain physical proximity. They inhibit their hurt, and engage toys, giving the appearance of feeling fine, but their internal working model of the caregiver comes to include "bad" or rejecting components (Winnicott, 1960).

In the next substage of cognitive development in Case's model, the child attains the level of unifocal interrelations, at about 18 months of age. The toddler develops social scripts and they view others in terms of their socially scripted roles (Fischer, Hand, Watson, Van Parys, & Tucker, 1984). They can identify and label their internal states and those of others, and they can assign evaluative labels, such as nice and mean (Fischer & Elmendorf, 1986). In terms of working models, their exchanges are represented symbolically in social scripts, and they express protection, nurturance, care, a sense of security, and self-confidence.

However, in the case of the avoidant infants, there is less confidence, more frustration and anxiety, and more defensive behavior. The infants might turn more toward the environment in order to play, but they harbor residual bad feelings and anger. Therefore, defensively, they might displace their frustration by expressing anger and denigration toward siblings or peers, or they might exhibit denial.

In the dimensional stage, cognitively, children develop the ability to generate narratives. Their working models include a greater awareness of their own feelings and those of the caregiver. If the attachment is avoidant, the caregiver's lack of availability characterizes their narrative, but defenses such as projection might help them to protect themselves. In the next vectorial stage, in this regard, the increasing cognitive sophistication of children allows for defensive abstract rationalizations.

## Comment

In this later presentation of the relationship between Case's cognitive model and developments in attachment, Case did not repeat the inconsistencies found in his earlier writings on the topic. That is, in Case (1996), he placed the steps in attachment development at the correct age periods relative to their description in the literature.

This article is a tour de force in relating cognitive and attachment development. That being said, the present model expands this work, especially by developing a model of internal working models that covers the lifespan (see Chap. 24).

Moreover, Case's description of attachment behavior is excellent, as mentioned, but even then, the examples provided are more consistent with the present model relative to his own. For example, for the unifocal sensorimotor substage, my equivalent substage concerns sensorimotor hierarchies. In this regard, (a) Case (1996) described how the infant in this age period requests/initiates, expecting a response or subordinating the other to his or her initiatives. (b) For the 8- to 12-month-old, Case described complex interleavings, which is consistent with my description of this substage as systematic so that it appears to be a better label than the one Case uses (bifocal). (c) For the 12- to 18-month-old, I describe sensorimotor multiplications and Case describes sensorimotor elaborations; his examples in Case give clear sequencing, for example, which is expected according to my terminology. (d) As for the 18- to 24-month period, Case and I have a major difference of opinion. In my model, I maintain the Piagetian tradition of referring to this period as a sensorimotor one, unlike Case, who considers it an age period that is quite symbolic. He gives examples of scripts. However, scripts could reflect sensorimotor plans, as Piaget described for this age period. Also, Case mentioned the evaluative capacity of toddlers at this age. This is consistent with the present model (see Chap. 22), in which I refer to the emotions at this age as evaluative ones.

## Steps in Self-Development in Case

### *Introduction*

Case (1991b) has elaborated an important extension of his model of development by demonstrating the way parallels in cognitive and self-development might take place. He distinguished between the explicit "Me" self, or self as object of conscious reflection, and the implicit "I" self, or self as active subject (after James, 1890). Then, he posited that levels in self-development along these two lines might be seen as out-growths of his particular model of Neo-Piagetian cognitive substages.

However, there are major differences in Case's theory of self-development and my own. In my version, although I was cognizant of James' I-Me distinction, I dealt with levels of self-development in terms of the "I," in particular (Young, 1997). This being said, I attempted to incorporate directly at each level the work of independent theorists on self-development, such as Sroufe (1990), Selman (1980; Schultz & Selman, 1998), and Loevinger (1976, 1994, 1998) for the age periods of infancy, childhood-adolescence, and adolescence-adulthood, respectively. Also, I attempted to describe each level of self-development in terms of both its underlying cognitive substage and its associated socioaffective structures believed to emerge in parallel with each cognitive substage (e.g., Eriksonian acquisitions).

Case mentioned cognitive/socioaffective linkages throughout his presentation of the self substages in development, but because his model of socioaffective development is less elaborate than my own, it does not possess the differentiation of the socioaffective portion of the self that is found in my model. With this perspective, I examine in detail Case's model of self-development in relation to his model of steps in cognitive development.

## The First Months

According to Case, the elaboration orienting substage from 1 to 4 months witnesses nascent self-related experiences. The baby's cognitive faculty in sensory scanning allows the construction of integrated representations of mothers' perceptual landscapes. Moreover, these schemata become colored with the feeling tones that accompany them. Developments such as this seem to be the first signs of an implicit "I" self, which can act on the world, because there is agency in sensory differentiation, attention, and regulation of motor, emotional, and contextual (maternal) experience. Case pointed out that Stern (1985) had referred to a "core sense of self-with-other" emerging at this time. As for the explicit "Me" self, there does not appear to be any glimmer of self-reflection, so that the self can be characterized as "symbiotically undifferentiated" with respect to this issue (Mahler, Pine, & Bergman, 1975).

## 4–12 Months

In Case's model, in the next age period of 4–8 months, unifocal sensorimotor skills are acquired. They permit a more generalized sense of personal agency to emerge, one that is not tied uniquely to familiar familial interactions. For example, the absent neutral mother might be called by babbling, transforming the situation to a positive one, or the emotion of exuberance might manifest when inanimate objects are controlled by motor action. In short, the implicit "I" self becomes more overtly apparent at this stage. As for the explicit self-evaluating "Me" self, infants understand that general action-reaction effects are distinct from the maternal world, which allows them to see that certain parts of their own body (hands, legs) are controlling agents. Thus, their perceptual representations are of objects of a very distinct kind, i.e., they are perceptual "self objects" that comprise the kernel of an explicit "Me" self.

In Case's bifocal sensorimotor substage from 8 to 12 months, action-reaction pairs involving the mother and object worlds are interlinked (e.g., turn to mother to get a smile after creating an interesting effect due to object manipulation). Emotions experienced with mothers now moderate interactions with objects. Thus, the developing implicit "I" self as agent in the object world comes to manifest an appreciation of indirect agency (objects attract mothers, mothers get objects) and different roles (actor, object, agent). Also, the "I" self becomes colored by the general affective relation with mothers; a sense of security with them engenders feelings of the social worthiness of their actions in the inanimate world. As for infants' growing "Me" self, bifocal sensorimotor relations permit explicit self-knowledge of appearance-action mappings over body parts. If mirrors are available, infants learn that the face in the mirror is their own.

Note that according to Case these acquisitions continue in much the same way in the next cognitive substage of sensorimotor elaboration. It lasts from 12 to 18 months.

## After 18 Months

With the onset of unifocal interrelational thought, 18-month-olds exhibit in their repertoire higher-order patterns, or social scripts, such as cooperative play or role-playing. Thus, in terms of their implicit "I" self, they grasp a sense of their roles (e.g., as helper) and the way roles are networked. The explicit "Me" self now treats facial information in the mirror as a perceptual model that can guide action (e.g., touching some rouge surreptitiously placed by an experimenter on the nose). Also, the words "I" and "Me" emerge in toddlers' vocabulary in this period.

In the next interrelational substage of bifocal relations, at 2 years of age, a more systematic social behavior and understanding emerges (e.g., related to families). Thus, the implicit "I" self now reflects the idea that the self is a participant in an integrated social system based on refined communication and multiple roles. As for the explicit "Me" self, it comes to incorporate the self as a direct focus of reference to ponder, label, and discuss (e.g., "I'm de boss"; "Don't say I'm bad").

These types of advances also are found in the next cognitive substage of elaborated interrelations. It lasts up to 5 years of age.

In the dimensional stage of development, during the school years, an implicit knowledge of institutional or group rules emerges, as does understanding the place of the "I" self in networks such as this. The explicit "Me" self is built around internal models of control and evaluation.

In the abstract stage of development, nonconcrete constructs (e.g., personality, social status) become the focus in these regards. This is consistent with the adolescent period involved.

## Comment

Case has highlighted fundamental processes in self-development, and his differentiation of the implicit "I" self and explicit "Me" self in terms of the steps of his cognitive model is an important one. However, Case's model is marked by several limitations. (a) The first signs of a nascent self might be evident just after birth, and not only at 1 month (e.g., in some of the newborn's perceptual and emotional abilities). (b) The agency of the implicit "I" self in the orienting elaboration substage seems to reflect sensorimotor coordination (action-effect linkages), which is the label used in my own model for this age period. Similar comments about the way my model might better fit the examples presented can be made about other periods. (c) The generalized sense of personal agency that develops in the 4- to 8-month period should be broadened to include what Erikson would term a "trusting self." Also, other Eriksonian acquisitions should be used to examine cognitive/self-development linkages at other periods. (d) The lack of qualitative differentiation in Case's model of self-development in the 8–12 and 12–18-month periods seems anomalous. A similar problem arises for the last two substages of the interrelational stage and all three substages of the dimensional and abstract stages.

## Summary and Conclusions

The Neo-Piagetian models of Case and Fischer have been developed over 30 years, and in many ways they are similar. Both involve a series of major stages from the presensorimotor to the adolescent/adult periods. Both describe a cyclic recursion of three substages within stages. Both describe cognitive/socioaffective parallels from one step in their model to the next. Both seek underlying central contributions to the development involved, and both seek to determine the mediating and moderating variables involved. Both describe individual differences. Both branch out into language/narrative development, and so on. However, despite their leadership in the field, and the differences in their models, scholars have not critically compared and contrasted the theories, so that the present work constitutes the first in depth effort along these lines. Moreover, in analyzing the nature of their models, the manner in which my model accommodates to their gaps and inconsistencies is highlighted. Finally, in undertaking this analysis, I indicate that many of the examples that they provide to illustrate their models end up fitting what is expected in my model more so than their own.

## References

Case, R. (1985). *Intellectual development: Birth to adulthood*. Orlando: Academic Press.

Case, R. (1988). The whole child: Toward an integrated view of young children's cognitive, social, and emotional development. In A. D. Pellegrini (Ed.), *Psychological bases for early education* (pp. 155–184). New York: Wiley.

Case, R. (1991a). *The role of primitive defenses in the regulation and representation of early attachment relations*. Paper presented at the biennial meeting of the Society for Research in Child Development Seattle, Washington.

Case, R. (1991b). Stages in the development of the young child's first sense of self. *Developmental Review, 11*, 210–230.

Case, R. (1996). The role of psychological defenses in the representation and regulation of close personal relationships across the life span. In G. Noam & K. W. Fischer (Eds.), *Development and vulnerability in close relationships – The Jean Piaget Symposium Series* (pp. 59–88). Hillsdale: Erlbaum.

Case, R., Hayward, S., Lewis, M., & Hurst, P. (1988). Toward a neo-Piagetian theory of cognitive and emotional development. *Developmental Review, 8*, 1–51.

Fischer, K. W., & Elmendorf, D. M. (1986). Becoming a different person: Transformations in personality and social behavior. In M. R. Perlmutter (Ed.), *Cognitive perspectives on children's social development: The Minnesota symposia on child psychology* (pp. 137–178). Hillsdale: Erlbaum.

Fischer, K. W., Hand, H. H., Watson, M. W., Van Parys, M. M., & Tucker, S. L. (1984). Putting the child into socialization. In L. G. Katz, P. J. Wagemaker, & K. Steiner (Eds.), *Current topics in early childhood education* (Vol. 5, pp. 27–72). Norwood: Ablex.

James, W. (1890). *The principles of psychology* (Vol. 1 and 2). New York: Holt.

Karniol, R. (1989). The role of manual manipulative stages in the infant's acquisition of perceived control over objects. *Developmental Review, 9*, 205–233.

Lewis, M. D. (1988). Biography of the first year: A case study integrating psychoanalytic, cognitive-developmental and mother-infant systems perspectives. *Early Child Development and Care, 39*, 1–20.

Lewis, M. (1993). The emergence of human emotions. In M. Lewis & J. M. Haviland (Eds.), *Handbook of emotions* (pp. 223–235). New York: Guilford Press.

Loevinger, J. (1976). *Ego development: Conceptions and theories*. San Francisco: Jossey-Bass.

Loevinger, J. (1994). In search of grand theory. *Psychological Inquiry, 5*, 142–144.

Loevinger, J. (1998). Completing a life sentence. In P. M. Westenberg, A. Blasi, & L. D. Cohn (Eds.), *Personality development: Theoretical, empirical, and clinical investigations of Loevinger's conception of ego development* (pp. 347–354). London: Erlbaum.

Mahler, M., Pine, F., & Bergman, A. (1975). *The psychological birth of the human infant*. New York: Basic Books.

Schultz, L. H., & Selman, R. L. (1998). Ego development and interpersonal development in young adulthood: A between-model comparison. In P. M. Westenberg, A. Blasi, & L. D. Cohn (Eds.), *Personality development: Theoretical, empirical, and clinical investigations of Loevinger's conception of ego development* (pp. 181–202). London: Erlbaum.

Selman, R. L. (1980). *The growth of interpersonal understanding: Developmental and clinical analyses*. New York: Academic.

Sroufe, L. A. (1990). An organizational perspective on the self. In D. Cicchetti & M. Beeghly (Eds.), *The self in transition: Infancy to childhood* (pp. 281–207). Chicago: University of Chicago Press.

Stern, D. N. (1985). *The interpersonal world of the infant: A view from psychoanalysis and developmental psychology*. New York: Basic Books.

Trevarthen, C. (1980). The foundations of inter-subjectivity: Development of interpersonal and co-operative understanding in infants. In D. R. Olson (Ed.), *The social foundations of language and thought* (pp. 312–342). New York: Norton.

Winnicott, D. W. (1960). The theory of the parent-infant relationship. *International Journal of Psychoanalysis, 41*, 585–595.

Young, G. (1990). Early neuropsychological development: Lateralization of functions – hemispheric specialization. In C. A. Hauert (Ed.), *Developmental psychology: Cognitive, perceptuo-motor and neuropsychological perspectives* (pp. 113–181). Amsterdam: North Holland.

Young, G. (1997). *Adult development, therapy, and culture: A postmodern synthesis*. New York: Plenum.

# Chapter 8
# Parallels in Cognitive Substages and Socioaffectivity in Fischer

## Introduction

In this chapter, I review major cognitive/socioaffective correspondences in the work of Fischer and colleagues. First, I examine his account of the Oedipus situation. Then, I present his early work on particular correspondences between cognitive and affective development. The chapter moves to Harter's account of self-development in terms of parallels with Fischer's model.

## Parallels in Socioaffective Development in Fischer

### *Oedipus*

#### The Oedipus Situation

Fischer and colleagues have presented an ingenious account of the Freudian Oedipus conflict that emerges in preschoolers (Fischer & Watson, 1981; also Watson & Getz, 1990). According to Freud, children of this age become jealous of the same-sex parent because of a desire to obtain exclusively the affection and (incestuous) love of the opposite-sex parent. However, fearing the powers of the latter, children renounce these wants and identify with that parent. In so doing, the rule structure and values of the same-sex parent are incorporated (as the superego), which produces a conscience, ideals, and a sex role.

Fischer explained the Oedipal situation in the following way. Young children who have developed single representational sets are laying the groundwork for the crisis to come, while being constrained from experiencing it by the cognitive limits of the substage. That is, in this substage, symbol-guided thinking and emotional experiences flower, but the inability to coordinate them means that children find it impossible to relate representations of their own thoughts and their parents' actions. For example, they cannot contemplate whether their parents know their own

G. Young, *Development and Causality: Neo-Piagetian Perspectives*,
DOI 10.1007/978-1-4419-9422-6_8, 

thoughts; they simply assume that this is the case. Finally, children in this period do not grasp social roles. For example, they cannot coordinate the notion of girl and the notion of woman, and fail to understand that they themselves will evolve into adults. Also, arriving at the concepts of husband and wife are beyond their ken, for, to understand them, they must understand that they relate.

With the development of representational mappings, children come to comprehend the complementarity of roles (e.g., husband, wife) and the continuity of ages (e.g., boy, man). Thus, the children in this substage realize that they will be like their same-sex parent, performing her/his functions. This gives birth to the hope that they can replace the same-sex parent in a love-filled relationship. Then, they conclude that they can substitute for that parent and adopt their role in the present. Here is the crux of the Oedipus conflict.

Had the children been able to seize that parents do not stay the same age while they themselves age, they may have avoided their fallacious reasoning. However, they cannot treat simultaneously two dimensions of categorization of people. There are parent vs. child; or female vs. male; but not both in one coherent classificatory system. Thus, confusions can arise, as when they focus on the dimension of sex and ignore that of age, allowing the child and the same-sex parent to be placed in the same category so that one can replace the other.

Through the mappings of this period, children believe that they can arrive at a solution to the crisis. First, they fantasize that by eliminating the same-sex parent, contingently, the opposite-sex parent becomes available. But contingently again, the fear arises about what the children would do without the same-sex parent. Through mappings, the children also come to associate their thoughts with possible parental reactions, and so develop fear that their parents are capable of reading their thoughts.

## Resolution

For Fischer, the onset of the substage of representational systems brings the cognitive tools needed to resolve the Oedipus conflict that evolved in the prior period. With the development of this substage, children become capable of integrating simultaneous dimensions of a person's characterization. That is, children can now realize that they are not in the same class as their parents, for the latter are either female parents or male parents, while children are either female children or male children. Thus, they realize that a child can no longer substitute for the same-sex parent. Moreover, the multiple contingencies following the possible elimination of the same-sex parent are understood, e.g., the opposite-sex parent would be sad and the child would miss the same-sex parent. An understanding of the systematic interrelation of roles is acquired, so children realize that they can have an affectionate relationship simultaneously with both parents. Their conscience and sex-role identification can flourish, for organized rule systems take hold, facilitating comparison of the self with ideals or others.

### Comment

Fischer's analysis of the Oedipus conflict and its resolution in children is an important contribution, but one element seems to be missing in the chain of logic about children's thought processes in the crucial mapping substage. There is no rationale about why children seem driven to supplant the same-sex parent and vie for the love of the opposite-sex parent. The equivalent substage in my own model of cognitive development underscores that preschoolers in this age period are in an active phase of organizing hierarchical, dominant-subordinate relations among symbol plans. Thus, in the affective arena, there should be analogous hierarchical behavior and, in this regard, I have posited that children are in full Eriksonian initiative – and therefore exploring, testing, pushing, and power-seeking. This behavior should extend to the relationship with the parents and diverse significant others at many levels, so that one consequence might be the emergence of the Oedipus situation.

As for Fischer's suggested cognitive basis for the resolution of the Oedipus issue, I concord in full with his interpretation of the way this conflict is resolved. My cognitive model depicts a substage of symbol plan systematization at the same juncture that Fischer's representational system substage develops, the gains in which allow for the resolution described.

## *Social Roles*

Fischer (Fischer, Shaver, & Carnochan, 1990; Watson & Fischer, 1977) has investigated other avenues of cognitive and socioaffective interrelationship. For example, he examined the way children make dolls adopt mean and nice social roles and the way these roles can be fused. The observed developmental sequence in this skill followed the pattern predicted from his cognitive development theory of stages and substages. Similarly, Calverley, Fischer, and Ayoub (1994) examined the self-representation of sexually abused adolescent girls, and found that their responses on a self-representation interview could be scored according to the developmental pattern prescribed by Fischer's theory.

## *Emotional Correspondences*

### Introduction

Fischer (Fischer & Pipp, 1984; Fischer & Tangney, 1995; Fischer, Shaver, & Carnochan, 1989, 1990; Mascolo & Fischer, 1995; see also Shaver, Schwartz, Kirson, & O'Connor, 1987) has formulated a model of the way some basic emotions relate to cognitive levels as they develop. He postulated that, depending on the culture examined, there are five or six basic emotions (each with subcategories), which are generated by appraisals independent of any cognitive level and which are expressed by prototypical scripts (antecedents, responses, self-control constraint procedures). As with Case (Case, Hayward, Lewis, & Hurst, 1988), he showed the way the emotions evolve with passage through the various cognitive levels. However, like Case, Fischer did not address why the basic emotions first emerge when they do, exactly how these emotions relate to any corresponding cognitive level, and why other basic emotions important in development are excluded from discussion. Fischer suggested that the basic emotions vary according to three basic dimensions – negative or positive evaluation, activity-passivity, and engaged-disengaged, although cultural variation plays a role here, too. However, the basic emotions are qualified according to their positive or negative status but not specifically with respect to the other two dimensions.

According to Fischer and Tangney (1995), emotions are functional organizers of thought and action that are comprised of component processes. Cognitive appraisals are essential to them, for particular meanings attributed to environmental or internal changes lead to particular emotions. Appraisals relate to individual concerns, such as goal attainment and self-evaluation, as well as to coping potential. Included in emotional reactions are social scripts, which are patterns of events and reactions to them, such as cognitions, affective experiences, motivations, and behaviors (see Table 8.1). Behaviors need not manifest outright and, therefore, are referred to as action tendencies. Emotion-specific physiological reactions also are possible. Part of the appraisal process concerns self-monitoring of action tendencies and context; notable emotional changes are appraised in each human culture/language. They are represented by first-person, usually declarative sentences indicative of mental state (e.g., "I feel something bad"). Cognitive structures are formulated by a series of such statements, and thus can be considered universal as much as their components. Thus, universal facial expressions, such as smiling, might not have universal interpreted emotional labels, but do have universal underlying conceptual bases (e.g., in the case of smiling, "I think: something good is happening. I feel something good because of this."). Similarly, certain facial components in emotional expression have specific communicative meanings (e.g., brow raise = "I think: something is happening. I want to know more about it").

Fischer's model of cognitive and socioaffective development, including the way the basic emotions are interwoven as they unfold, is presented in Tables 8.2 and 8.3.

**Table 8.1** Prototypic script for anger in infancy

| Components | Description |
|---|---|
| Antecedents | Something interferes with the infant's plans or goals or threatens to harm him or her |
| Responses | The infant becomes energized to fight or attack the agent causing the anger |
| | The infant looks angry and moves in a heavy, tight, or exaggerated way |
| | The infant focuses on the anger-inducing situation and is persistent or obstinate in his or her effort to do something about it |
| Self-control procedures | By the end of the first year, the infant may try to inhibit his or her anger |

**Table 8.2** Parallels in cognitive and socioaffective development in the reflexive and sensorimotor stages in Fischer

| Stage/skill level | Socioaffective development |
|---|---|
| Reflex sets | Single actions are organized; most components of anger facial expression are present |
| Reflex mappings | Look at mothers' eyes when hear their voice |
| Reflex systems | Greeting response: listen to mothers' voice, look at face, smile, coo |
| Sensorimotor sets | Single categories or behavior clusters form; e.g., look at mothers' eyes when they are talking and scan face systematically; express anger at arm restraint or at an interference, as when cookie withdrawn before tasted; express joy at siblings; express distress at interaction interruption with mothers. Scripts or prototypical action patterns for all basic emotions are present, e.g., for anger: appropriate facial expression and most of rest (protest, resistance, intensified goal direction); for joy: coordinated excitement, laughter, smiling, positive response to play bids. Sensorimotor categories for "good" and "bad" are constructed without reference to self or other, e.g., infants nurse the good breast or try to nurse the bad one |
| Sensorimotor mappings | Resistance shows coordination, e.g., push away interfering hand, then grab withdrawn cookie; anticipate/avoid negative affect; distress at separation, then thumb suck to self-soothe; social reference mothers' behavior to evaluate ambiguous situation. "Good" and "bad" are related, but without reference to self and mother |
| Sensorimotor systems | Infants in this period pretend to be sad, angry, happy, etc.; they use words motor for key emotions. They integrate self and mother with good and bad, e.g., difficulties in nursing may be related to own sucking or to breast/bottle |

Adapted from references to Fischer

Compared to the models of Case and me, in Fischer's model there is less presentation of cognitive-affective parallels at each substage in development. However, he has done good work in elaborating a script model of emotional expressions, such as for anger in infancy (see Table 8.1). Also, he has developed a good model on the changing representations of nice and mean social interactions, especially in the representational stage, although these representations are not socioaffective in the sense being used in the present work. In addition, Fischer has developed a model of the development of emotions that includes superordinate, basic, and subordinate emotions but, generally, he did not relate these to corresponding cognitive substages. However, in terms of their dynamic structure, he did undertake this task for how some specific emotions change with the substages in his model (see Chap. 11). In addition, he does have a good model of emotion processing schemas, the architecture of human action, and adaptive and maladaptive pathways in emotional development (see Chap. 12)

This table complements his extensive description that has been presented of the Oedipus conflict in the representational mapping and system substages.

## The First Year

In Fischer's model, the reflex stage in the first few months of life ends with some complex patterning in social behavior, as in greeting behavior. In terms of emotions, most but not all facial components of anger emerge. No other emotions are described. It will be recalled that in my discussion of Case's equivalent model, both Case and I hypothesized that many more basic emotions have already developed by this age.

**Table 8.3** Parallels in cognitive and socioaffective development in the representational and abstract stages in Fischer

| Stage/skill level | Socioaffective development |
|---|---|
| Representational sets | At this age, infants can make a doll carry out single emotional actions (e.g., hug), and within a few months they cluster actions into emotional categories, e.g., make a doll act angry or mean (hit another passive recipient doll, take away its toy, and say, "I don't like you.") Doll A is made to act mean to B, while C is made to act nice to it. The infants produce prototypical scripts such as, "I give you hug." "Baby be happy." Spontaneous language in the home reflects an increase in talk about basic feelings (e.g., "Happy," "Bad," "Mommy mad"). The infants develop symbols of self and mother independent of any actions performed, but they are still cognitively egocentric, and cannot understand others' views. Because they cannot compare or integrate sets, they "affectively split" them, e.g., nice and mean behavior in self or other are organized separately. Coconsciousnesses different from the normal one may develop (e.g., in child abuse), but they cannot be coordinated. Frightening thoughts are controlled by shifting focus |
| Representational mappings | Emotional categories are coordinated into role relations (a role is relative to its reciprocal complement; each role is understood in relation to another). For example, one child may be mean to another because the other was mean first. Doll A is made to reject each of mean dolls B and C. Doll A can be made to be successively nice to nice doll B and mean to mean doll C. Two script participants can act in reciprocal relation with multiple role behaviors. Intentions of actions are considered, e.g., a child who accidentally hurts another is not judged as mean. A behavior can be seen as simultaneously manifesting two (opposite) emotional categories, e.g., mother can be nice and mean simultaneously. Behavior can reflect emotional category coordination. Insults appear, for representation of symbolic attack is related to representation of other's hurt feelings. Complex emotions such as resentment and jealousy can emerge at this level, for both involve the relation of two representations (see Fischer et al., 1989). Coconsciousnesses can be related, leading to repression of parts of one (the painful one) by the other. One representation can be used to anticipate another frightening one and prevent it (repress it) from being thought. Comparison of self with others and with ideals begins |
| Representational systems | Children in this period can integrate opposite behaviors into a script with reciprocal dyadic exchange, e.g., doll A says he would like to be friends with B while hitting B, who responds with simultaneous mean and friendly behaviors. (Behavior similar to this can be made to occur with three dolls). The children realize that two individuals at the same time can carry out two roles simultaneously. For example, two individuals can experience simultaneous conflicting emotions, such as when a child and her/his mother can be both nice and mean at same time in their interaction |

(continued)

**Table 8.3** (continued)

| Stage/skill level | Socioaffective development |
|---|---|
| Abstract sets | Two concrete social interactions involving simultaneous nice and mean actions are compared or simultaneously coordinated for their intentions, e.g., an apparently nice act with mean intentions is evaluated appropriately, and vice versa. Also, apologies, or lack of same, are integrated into evaluations. Behavior is organized in terms of concepts (about personality, morals). Anger scripts involve reaction to insults, illegality, discrimination, retaliation, and complex, socially constructed, culture-specific emotions such as resentment in the U.S. Preadolescents cannot coordinate these less tangible concepts, which remain "split," e.g., simultaneous attributions of benevolent and malevolent. Abstract-based coconsciousnesses can develop |
| Abstract mappings | Two interactions with opposite behaviors can be coordinated by relating two abstractions, such as intention and responsibility. Individuals with deceitful intent can be forgiven if they take responsibility in a way that reverses the effect of their deceit. Abstract-based coconsciousnesses can be repressed via their coordination. This occurs especially in cases of multiple personality and schizophrenia and in hypnosis |
| Abstract systems | Older adolescents realize the manner in which different types of intention imply different types of responsibility |

Adapted from references to Fischer

For Fischer, there is a relative explosion of emotions at 4–8 months of age, for infants enter the substage of sensorimotor sets, which are systems of reflex systems. Anger, distress, and joy are described in some detail in terms of typical scripts, but no detail is provided for the other hypothesized basic emotions that are thought to emerge – fear and love. For both Case and me, love (affection, warmth) cannot emerge until the next substage.

In Fischer's sensorimotor mapping substage between 8 and 12 months, socioaffective progress is realized in a variety of coordinations. The next stage of sensorimotor systems is more striking. In this age period of 12–18 months, advances in symbol-related structuring allow toddlers to pretend expressing emotions, to speak of emotions, and to distinguish self and mother in conceptualizations of good and bad.

## The Second Year Onward

For both Case and me, the period of from 1.5 to 3 years of age is divided into two separate cognitive substages, but in Fischer it is covered by only one, that of representational sets. For this period, Fischer describes more advanced symbolic structuring, as evidenced by role-play with dolls, emotional scripts, language use about affect, self-conscious emotions, and self-representation. Because there is incapacity to coordinate representational sets in this substage, there could develop affective splitting and separate coconsciousnesses (as happens in child abuse).

However, both Case and I would dispute the suggested mechanism for this possibility (i.e., the inability to coordinate sets). That is, from age 2 to 3.5 years in both theories, children are considered to be in a substage of dual balancing in one way or another (bifocal interrelation, perioperational coordination, respectively), so that there should not be an incapacity to coordinate representations. Rather, the nature of the coordinated cognitive balancing in this period might be limited (e.g., lacking hierarchical organization). Thus, if dissociation and separate conscious development take place in this age period due to abuse, it is not because cognitive coordinations are difficult to organize, as suggested by Fischer.

Fischer's substage of representational mapping in 4- to 6-year-olds is marked by relational reciprocities. In this substage, various repressions can take place, along with self-other/ideal comparisons. In all these phenomena, there is an element of hierarchization and not only mapping, fitting my model that in this age period perioperational hierarchization is thought to develop. Fischer also predicted that jealousy emerges at this juncture, in contrast to Case who hypothesizes that it emerges several years earlier.

The remaining substages presented by Fischer continue to follow the pattern set in his prior stages. Examples concern role-playing, scripts, and emotional conflicts and comparisons. Moreover, examples at the abstract stage involve principles guiding behavior.

## Conclusions on Fischer

Fischer's major contribution in helping explicate the link between cognition and affect resides in his analysis of the Oedipus situation in the representational mapping substage. Moreover, his general analysis of unconscious processes, such as affective splitting, coconsciousnesses, and repression, should be consulted. There seems to be some correspondence between the substages in his theory and those of my own between the representational mapping substage and the abstract system substage.

However, Fischer's account of socioaffective development is problematic in some areas. In particular, unlike with Case, there is no attempt to discuss developing infants' attachment to the caregiver or their psychosocial development according to Erikson. The range of basic emotions dealt with is limited, as far fewer of them are discussed relative to Case or me. Moreover, in comparing Fischer's theory of developing cognitive substages to those of Case and my own, it seems that, at the minimum, he has failed to differentiate a critical substage at the 2-year period and two more in the late childhood period before the abstract stage. Also, his conception of potentially limitless sublevels within levels, explained in more detail in the next section, leads to ambiguities. My own model is quite specific on the amount of sublevels within levels (5). In addition, Fischer's substages within the reflex stage very well might concern sublevels within one substage rather than separate substages, as he has presented them. That is, unlike Fischer, most theorists (e.g., Case, Mounoud, myself) do not divide the 1–4-month age period into several substages.

Lastly, in Fischer's description of the sequence of cognitive substages, some of the examples provided illustrate my model of the nature of the substages in cognitive development more than his own. In the analysis above of Case's model and the examples provided, the same support for my model appeared.

(a) For example, in Fischer's sensorimotor set substage at 4–8 months, means-end relations in infant behavior are described (e.g., look in order to scan), fitting the label that I use for this age period of sensorimotor hierarchization.
(b) His sensorimotor mappings at 8–12 months depict refined target behaviors, which I label sensorimotor systematizations.
(c) His sensorimotor systems at 12 months allow for multiplicative chains in behavior, fitting my terminology.
(d) His stage of representational sets lasts to 4 years, but considers single emotions developing into category clusters, supporting my view that two substages are involved in this age period (sensorimotor integration, perioperational coordination).
(e) His representational mappings include role relations and repression, both of which are inherently hierarchical, fitting my perspective (I describe perioperational hierarchization in my equivalent stage).

In conclusion, in the models of Fischer and me, there is one extensive age period where there is a clear agreement on the nature of cognitive development. That is, in the preadolescent and adolescent period, Fischer's substages of representational systems and abstract sets, mappings, and systems seem to correspond directly to my similar substages of perioperational systematization and abstract coordination, hierarchization, and systematization, respectively. Thus, in this regard, Fischer's model is consistent with my framework, and his description of these substages should be considered compatible with it.

## Self-Development from a Fischerian Perspective (Harter)

### *The Model*

Harter has reviewed extensively the development of the self (Harter, 1999, 2003, 2006). She differentiated well the various terms, such as the "I" self and the "Me" self (James, 1890, 1892), and other terms, such as self-concept and self-esteem. The I-self refers to the self as subject, agent, or knower, and some of its components include self-awareness and self-agency. The Me-self refers to the self as object, or known, and it involves aspects of self such as the social Me and the material Me. It relates to self-concept and self-esteem. For Harter, the self helps shape goals and also provides guides that aid in self-regulation. Harter focuses on self-representations, or how one consciously describes oneself in terms of attributes or characteristics. These self-schemata could be global or particular, general or specific, depending on the circumstance.

The constructive abilities of the I-self are dependent on the cognitive level of the developing person. The content and structure of the I-self's theory of the nature of the self reflect the I-self's knowing capacities. The self is a theory, and Harter relates its construction to Neo-Piagetian stages and substages (e.g., Case, 1985, 1992; Fischer, 1980).

The I-self develops its ability to construct the Me-self from one substage and stage to the next. I-self processes construct the template on which particular Me-self constructions are elaborated. For Harter, the models of Case and Fischer provide scaffolds of the normative development of these constructive self-processes. The resultant self-structures both differentiate and integrate. The constructions are as much social as cognitive. Socialization experiences produce individual differences in the content of representations of self and in its valence (i.e., more positive or more negative).

Harter has described the normative developments in self-representation during childhood and adolescence (see Tables 8.4 and 8.5). For each age period, Harter described acquisitions in the self for early, middle, and late age ranges. For each age period, she examined salient content, structure/organization, valence, accuracy, comparisons, and sensitivity to others. From a normative perspective, she argued that these six age periods involved in the development of self-representations map quite well onto Fischer's (1980) model of stages and substages in development. In describing this correspondence, she referred also to the equivalent model of Case (1985). Finally, she presented the equivalent work of Selman (1980) and of Higgins (1991) on correspondence between cognitive and self-development.

## *Age Periods*

### Childhood

*Early Childhood.* For the early childhood period, at 2–4 years of age, Fischer (1980) referred to single representations, and Case (1985) referred to elaborated interrelations. Higgins (1991) argued that toddlers are capable of placing themselves in the same gender category as parents, which permits identification with the same-sex parent. For example, the young boy asks himself whether he is matching his behavior with that of his father. Children at this age also are capable of detecting whether their behavior elicits a parental reaction, which, in turn, evokes in them a psychological reaction. Higgins (1991) concluded that despite children at this age realizing that their behavior could impact others, their developing I-self is not yet capable of evaluating their developing Me-self, as argued similarly by Selman (1980).

Harter described that Nelson (2003) proposed that the child in this age period is developing a social-cultural-linguistic self. It develops based on increasing capacity for autobiographical memory and the development of the narrative self. The concept indicates that in the child's social and linguistic exchanges, cultural messages are received that are meaningful to the child's developing self. The child has a new developing social and cognitive awareness and new capacities of mental representation that create a cultural self and a narrative or story-telling self (e.g., about self-history and imagined future).

It is clear from the examples provided that children at this age are developing the cognitive capacity to coordinate their behavior with that of their parents or caregivers. The example provided for gender refers to matching, and the example provided for awareness of caregiver reactions refers to reciprocity and elicitation.

**Table 8.4** Normative-developmental changes in self-representations during childhood

| Age period | Salient content | Structure/organization | Valence accuracy | Nature of comparisons | Sensitivity to others |
|---|---|---|---|---|---|
| Very early childhood | Concrete, observable characteristics; simple taxonomic attributes in the form of abilities, activities, possessions, preferences | Isolated representations; lack of coherence, coordination; all-or-none thinking | Unrealistically positive; inability to distinguish real from ideal selves | No direct comparisons | Anticipation of adult reactions (praise, criticism); rudimentary appreciation of whether one is meeting others' external standards |
| Early to middle childhood | Elaborated taxonomic attributes; focus on specific competencies | Rudimentary links between representations; links typically opposites; all-or-none thinking | Typically positive; inaccuracies persist | Temporal comparisons with self when younger; comparisons with age-mates to determine fairness | Recognition that others are evaluating the self; initial introjection of others' opinions; others' standards becoming self-guides in regulation of behavior |
| Middle to late childhood | Trait labels that focus on abilities and interpersonal characteristics; comparative assessments with peers; global evaluation of worth | Higher-order generalizations that subsume several behaviors; ability to integrate opposing attributes | Both positive and negative evaluations; greater accuracy | Social comparison for purpose of self-evaluation | Internalization of others' opinions and standards, which come to function as self-guides |

**Table 8.5** Normative-developmental changes in self-representations during adolescence

| Age period | Salient content | Structure/organization | Valence accuracy | Nature of comparisons | Sensitivity to others |
|---|---|---|---|---|---|
| Early adolescence | Social skills, attributes that influence interactions with others or one's social appeal; differentiation of attributes according to roles | Inter-coordination of trait labels into single abstractions; abstractions compartmentalized; all-or-none thinking; opposites; do not detect, integrate, opposing abstractions | Positive attributes at one point in time; negative attributes at another; leads to inaccurate overgeneralizations | Social comparison continues, although less overt | Compartmentalized attention to internalization of different standards and opinions of those in different relational contexts |
| Middle adolescence | Further differentiation of attributes associated with different roles and relational contexts | Initial links between single abstractions, often opposing attributes; cognitive conflict caused by seemingly contradictory characteristics; concern over which reflect one's true self | Simultaneous recognition of positive and negative attributes; instability leading to confusion and inaccuracies | Comparisons with significant others in different relational contexts; personal fable | Awareness that the differing standards and opinions of others represent conflicting self-guides, leading to confusion over self-evaluation and vacillation with regard to behavior; imaginary audience |
| Late adolescence | Normalization of different role-related attributes; reflecting personal beliefs, values, and moral standards; interest in future selves | Higher-order abstractions that meaningfully integrate single abstractions and resolve inconsistencies, conflict | More balanced, stable view of both positive and negative attributes; greater accuracy; acceptance of limitations | Social comparison diminishes as comparisons with one's own ideals increase | Selection among alternative self-guides; construction of one's own self-standards that govern personal choices; creation of one's own ideals toward which the self aspires |

Reprinted with the permission of Guilford Publications, Inc. Harter, S. (1999). Copyright 2011. [Table 3.1, Page. 61]

In these regards, for the age period involved at 2 years, it should be kept in mind that the present Neo-Piagetian cognitive developmental model refers to the substage of perioperational coordination. In this sense, the examples presented by Harter are quite consistent with the present model and not just those of Fischer and of Case. Indeed, relative to Case and Fischer, the label of coordination seems to capture better the child's developing cognitive capacities pertaining to the development of self-constructions in the I-self in this age period.

*Middle Childhood.* In the next age period of 5–7 years of age, Fischer (1980) referred to representational mappings and Case (1985) to unifocal dimensions. Harter summarized this by indicating that these theorists are referring to the child's developing capacity to inter-coordinate concepts. The latter concept is consistent with the present model, in that I refer to this age period as one involving perioperational hierarchizations. This notion of hierarchization taking place at this age adds to the notion that 5–7-year-olds are inter-coordinating concepts by including a dominant-subordinate relationship among the components being inter-coordinated. In this regard, it is instructive to examine the examples provided by Harter for this age period about the developing cognitive capacity of the I-self to determine whether there are indeed hierarchical components to the descriptions of what the 5- to 7-year-old is acquiring in terms of development of the cognitive skills of the I-self.

Higgins (1991) proposed that children in this age period are developing an appreciation of the perspective of others. They understand that others have "viewpoints" and do not have simply reactions toward them. Selman (1980) underscored that the perspective taking in this age period includes children understanding that others are actively "evaluating" the self of the child. These other evaluations are not fully internalized but, nevertheless, function as "self-guides." In addition, Harter described that in this age period children are engaging in certain types of social comparison. For example, children calculate whether they have received a fair share of available rewards. It is clear from the examples provided that children are actively hierarchizing, or relating self and other evaluations of the self, and are also comparing their social situations with those of others. These examples provide support for the present model that this age period involves hierarchizations, in particular, and not just simpler inter-coordinations in cognitive activity related to the self.

*Later Childhood.* In the 8–11-year period, Fischer's (1980) model described the child as developing representational systems, and Case (1985) described that the child is acquiring bifocal dimensions. Higgins (1991) indicated that children at this age are developing the capacity to construct more general evaluations of themselves as particular people or "persons." Harter referred to this age period as the age of developing global self-worth or global self-esteem. Selman (1980) referred to the child coming to incorporate the opinions and standards of the significant other, which allows the developing I-self of the child to evaluate directly the developing Me-self. In my own model, I refer this age period as involving perioperational systems. This emphasis on systems in this age period in the present model is consistent with the work of Case, Fischer, Higgins, Selman, and Harter.

### Adolescence

*Early Adolescence.* In the 12–14-year period, Harter noted that Case (1985) and Fischer (1980) both referred to Piaget's concept that adolescents are developing abstract cognitive abilities. In my own model, I refer to this stage as the abstract stage, as well, and it begins with the substage of coordination. Fischer (1980) referred to this first abstract substage as a single set, and Case (1992) referred to it as the substage of unifocal vectors in thought. The various models are quite similar. For example, Harter pointed out that the adolescent constructs abstract concepts of the self, such as being intelligent in one situation and not as intelligent in another, or being extroverted in certain situations and introverted in others.

*Middle Adolescence.* For the 15–16-year period, Fischer (1980) referred to abstract mappings, and Case (1985) referred to bifocal abstract thought. In my own model, I added the language of hierarchization to this substage. In this regard, it is instructive to examine some of the examples provided by Harter to see whether they add an element of hierarchization to adolescents' developing cognitive capacity of the I-self and its ability to construct the Me-self. For example, for this age period, Higgins (1991) indicated that teenagers can now compare their different developing Me-selves and that they experience confusion, uncertainty, indecision, and conflict about different role expectations of parents and peers. The adolescents in this age period are also capable of turning inward and reflecting upon their thinking and internal events. The search for a coherent self becomes self-conscious, as they ask who they are. They try to establish self-boundaries and to sort out their multiple Me's. They try to define their various identities. It is clear from the examples provided that the adolescent is trying to create hierarchical structures, as I would predict, for various Me-components that the I-self is constructing and, also, the adolescent is engaging in a critical self-analysis based on self- and social comparison, which is another hierarchical endeavor.

*Late Adolescence.* Fischer (1980) described this period as involving representational systems, and Case (1985) described it as involving elaborated vectors in thought. I describe it as involving perioperational systems. Higgins (1991) referred to this age period as involving the construction of one's own standards, or integrations of alternative self-guides that are becoming free from their social origins. Damon and Hart (1988) indicated that teenagers in the period of late adolescence are developing a self having an organized system of belief and values. All these descriptions are consistent with each other, including my own model.

## *Comment*

As presented above, the model of the development of self-representations in Harter is quite consistent with the work of Case, Fischer, Higgins, Selman, and me. In particular, in her work, the cognitive developmental model of Fischer

(1980) is used to provide and axis for understanding the six different phases in the development of the self. Indeed, there is a one-to-one correspondence in her three levels of childhood and her three levels in adolescence in the development of the self, and Fischer's corresponding three substages in the development of representational thought in the child and the three substages in the development of abstract thought in the adolescent.

However, there are major inconsistencies despite the surface appearance of consistency across the models. First, Harter attempted to show how Case's (1992) model is consistent with her's and Fischer's, in particular; however, for the age period covered from 2 years to the end of adolescent period, Case (1985) had described seven substages over the two stages involved in his model, and not six. Moreover, in this regard, in my presentation of the parallels across Harter, Fischer, and Case, in the paragraphs above, I had used Case's (1985) original terminology and not the particular way that Harter had presented Case. This procedure helps to establish that in her description of Case, Harter had not considered where Case's substage of elaborated dimensional thought fits into her sequence of steps in the development of self-representation.

Moreover, I have shown throughout the present work that careful inspection of Fischer's (1980) model indicates that he had missed two important substages that develop after the representational system substage and before the abstract single set substage. That is, in my own model, there are five substages that develop in the perioperational stage, including the ones of multiplication and integration after the systematization substage. By contrast, Fischer (1980) ends the equivalent stage of representational thought at the third substage of systems, without adding the equivalents of these two substages present in my model. In Chap. 13, I present a more differentiated perspective of the development of the self and self-representations that includes five substages in childhood and not three, consistent with the present model of a cyclic recursion of five substages over stages in development. Moreover, I show how the model integrates Selman's (1980) work and those of others who have presented models of self-development, such as Loevinger.

To conclude, Harter has undertaken a comprehensive literature review and theoretical integration that is consistent with the work of Fischer (1980), in particular. However, it needs further analysis and work to accommodate to other Neo-Piagetian models, including my own.

## Summary and Conclusions

This chapter completes the analysis of the basic work on cognitive/socioaffective parallels in the Neo-Piagetian theories of Case and Fischer and colleagues. In the prior chapters, I presented their early ideas on the topic, and included their work on self-development. In the following chapters, I examine their more recent work, especially pertaining to emotional development. But first, in the next chapter, I examine their perspectives on the correspondence between cognitive and language development and also their work on underlying brain development.

# References


Calverley, R., Fischer, K. W., & Ayoub, C. (1994). Complex splitting of self-representations in sexually abused adolescent girls. *Development and Psychopathology, 6*, 195–213.

Case, R. (1985). *Intellectual development: Birth to adulthood*. Orlando: Academic Press.

Case, R. (1992). The role of the frontal lobes in the regulation of cognitive development. *Brain and Cognition, 20*, 51–73.

Case, R., Hayward, S., Lewis, M., & Hurst, P. (1988). Toward a neo-Piagetian theory of cognitive and emotional development. *Developmental Review, 8*, 1–51.

Damon, W., & Hart, D. (1988). *Self-understanding in childhood and adolescence*. New York: Cambridge University Press.

Fischer, K. W. (1980). A theory of cognitive development: The control and construction of hierarchies of skills. *Psychological Review, 87*, 477–531.

Fischer, K. W., & Hogan, A. E. (1989). The big picture for infant development: Levels and variations. In J. Lockman & N. Hazen (Eds.), *Action in social context: Perspectives on early development* (pp. 275–305). New York: Plenum.

Fischer, K. W., & Pipp, S. L. (1984). Development of the structures of unconscious thought. In K. S. Bowers & D. Meichenbaum (Eds.), *The unconscious reconsidered* (pp. 88–148). New York: Wiley.

Fischer, K. W., Shaver, P. R., & Carnochan, P. (1989). A skill approach to emotional development: From basic to subordinate category emotions. In W. Damon (Ed.), *Child development today and tomorrow* (pp. 107–136). London: Jossey-Bass.

Fischer, K. W., Shaver, P. R., & Carnochan, P. (1990). How emotions develop and how they organize development. *Cognition and Emotion, 4*, 81–127.

Fischer, K. W., & Tangney, J. P. (1995). Self-conscious emotions and the affect revolution: Framework and overview. In J. P. Tangney & K. W. Fischer (Eds.), *Self-consious emotions: The psychology of shame, guilt, embarrassment, and pride* (pp. 3–22). New York: Guilford.

Fischer, K. W., & Watson, M. W. (1981). Explaining the Oedipus conflict. In K. W. Fischer (Ed.), *New directions for child development (No. 12). Cognitive development* (pp. 79–93). San Francisco: Jossey-Bass.

Harter, S. (1999). *The construction of the self: A developmental perspective*. New York: Guilford Press.

Harter, S. (2003). The development of self-representations during childhood and adolescence. In M. R. Leary & J. P. Tangney (Eds.), *Handbook of self and identity* (pp. 610–642). New York: Guilford Press.

Harter, S. (2006). The self. In W. Damon, & R. M. Lerner & N. Eisenberg (Eds.), *Handbook of child psychology: Vol. 3. Social, emotional and personality development* (6th ed., pp. 505–561). Hoboken: Wiley.

Higgins, E. T. (1991). Development of self-regulatory and self-evaluative processes: Cost, benefits, and tradeoffs. In M. R. Gunnar & L. A. Sroufe (Eds.), *Minnesota symposia on child development: Vol. 23. Self processes and development* (pp. 125–166). Hillsdale: Erlbaum.

James, W. (1890). *The principles of psychology* (Vol. 1 and Vol. 2). New York: Holt.

James, W. (1892). *Psychology: The briefer course*. New York: Henry Holt.

Mascolo, M. F., & Fischer, K. W. (1995). Developmental transformations in appraisals for pride, shame, and guilt. In J. P. Tangney & K. W. Fischer (Eds.), *Self-conscious emotions: The psychology of shame, guilt, embarrassment, and pride* (pp. 64–113). New York: Guilford Press.

Nelson, K. (2003). Narrative and self, myth, and memory: Emergence of a cultural self. In R. Fivush & C. A. Haden (Eds.), *Autobiographical memory and the construction of a narrative self: Developmental and cultural perspectives* (pp. 72–90). Mahwah: Erlbaum.

Selman, R. L. (1980). *The growth of interpersonal understanding: Developmental and clinical analyses*. New York: Academic Press.

Shaver, P. R., Schwartz, J., Kirson, D., & O'Connor, C. (1987). Emotion knowledge: Further exploration of a prototype approach. *Journal of Personality and Social Psychology, 52*, 1061–1086.

Watson, M. W., & Fischer, K. W. (1977). A developmental sequence of agent use in late infancy. *Child Development, 48*, 828–836.

Watson, M. W., & Getz, K. (1990). The relationship between oedipal behaviors and children's family role concepts. *Merrill Palmer Quarterly, 36*, 487–505.

# Chapter 9
# Case and Fischer on Language and the Brain

## Introduction

This chapter continues to compare the Neo-Piagetian theories of Case and Fischer, but beyond cognitive/socioaffective parallels. I concentrate especially on language development, which leads to a section on narrative development. As with the prior chapters, in reviewing their approaches, I point out where the present model either handles the examples better or deals with their gaps and inconsistencies. The chapter includes a brief discussion of transition mechanisms and then moves on to cortical organization in relation to the steps in cognitive development in their models. In other chapters, of the book, I present my perspective on the latter topic.

## Case and Fischer on Language Development

### *Case*

#### Introduction

In Young (1990b), I analyzed Case's (1985) description of language development according to his cognitive developmental model of stages and substages in development. My approach was to show how the examples that he provided were quite consistent with my own model, and at times better supported my model relative to his own. In addition, I proposed what seems to be involved in language development according to my model for the stages and substages with which Case did not deal. In the following section, I present the essentials of the comparison that had been made in Young (1990b), organizing the section according to the labels for the stages and substages of my model. In addition, I present Case, Marini, McKeough, Dennis, and Goldberg's (1986) ensuing work on storytelling. Later sections of the present work deal in greater depth with storytelling.

G. Young, *Development and Causality: Neo-Piagetian Perspectives*,
DOI 10.1007/978-1-4419-9422-6_9, 

Case (1985) presented his theory of cognitive development, which after an initial orienting stage, involves four stages (sensorimotor, interrelational or preoperational, dimensional or concrete operational, abstract or formal). Each stage passes through three substages (unifocal, bifocal, elaborated coordination). In Case (1985), he referred to the orienting stage as a precoordination or consolidation period, in that in his publications he had yet to refer to this period as the orienting stage.

The specific language-related behaviors that Case described at each cognitive substage are presented in Table 9.1. In the table, the 12–18 month period is listed in two ways (both as last sensorimotor substage and as first interrelational or preoperational one). This procedure matches the overlap found in the transition between cognitive stages in Case. The table gives all the behavior mentioned for the sensorimotor period (the left-hand column) and considers spontaneous utterances for the interrelational period (the right-hand column).

**Table 9.1** Summary of vocal–verbal development in early years in Case

| Substage | Sensorimotor period | Interrelational period |
|---|---|---|
| Precoordination/ consolidation | Intentionally coo to elicit or sustain adult behavior<br>Coo when alone to produce interest. Use vowel or coo sequences (e.g., ah-ee-ya) (up to 4 mo) | With adult, share/ relate to interesting event at distance (e.g., (see) Daddy) (12–18 mo) |
| Unifocal coordination | Babble consonant-vowed syllables loudly to call absent adult (also hand raising here). Coo when successful in making adult approach. Contribute to role exchange (e.g., make sound sequence then pause to listen) (4–8 mo) | Use two-word utterance with no referent present and with words relating to each other (e.g., Daddy hits) (18–24 mo) |
| Bifocal coordination | Babble loudly to get adult to fetch object out of reach (also point, turn) generate and imitate bisyllabic utterances (e.g., Mama) and use them to achieve goals (8–12 mo) | Subject–verb–object sentences appear. Words qualified (e.g., Dad kicked the ball in garden) (2–3.5 yr) |
| Elaborated coordination | Add to above the use of object name (specific word or idiosyncratic attempt). Imitate novel adult utterances and use them to achieve goals (12–18 mo) | Tell stories with episodes. Use sentences with embedded clauses (3.5–5 yr) |

Adapted from Case, R. (1985) and Young, G. (1990b). [Table 5, Page. 116]

An important way of demonstrating the validity of a new model is by analyzing observational and empirical data in the literature to show that they can be interpreted according to the new model being proposed, and even in a way better than had been originally proposed in the original model. In this regard, Case had conducted an integrative examination of the development of language according to his Neo-Piagetian model, but in Young (1990b), I examined how, at times, the present model relative to Case's better explains the developmental trajectory in language development that he had described. Also, Case's colleagues have undertaken much work on storytelling and narrative development that is consistent with his model. Later, I review this work in depth, and that of Fischer and colleagues, as well, on the topic, and present a comparative approach informed by the present model

For the first year of life, Case showed how there are sensorimotor cognitive and vocal–verbal correspondences involving the use of vocalization for social purposes, the assignment of meaning to words, and the expression of recognizable words. After discussing the steps involved in the sensorimotor period, I move on to the postinfancy period.

## Sensorimotor Language Levels

*Coordination.* In the present model, in the substage of sensorimotor coordination from 1 to 4 months, schemas that have developed in the newborn during the reflexive period begin to coordinate, but they do not form a fixed sequence. For example, the very young infant manifests primitive vision–movement coordination to an object target, but does not exhibit successful visually guided reaching.

This behavior resembles Case's description of vocal behavior in the substage of sensorimotor precoordination, the substage in his model equivalent to what I have termed sensorimotor coordination. That is, for Case, the infant at this age coos or performs other activity cycled with cooing to induce or maintain adult action. Also, the infant serially sequences separate vowel or sound units. In terms of the present model, these behaviors described by Case show that 1–4-month-olds already exhibit schema coordination in their vocal behavior. Thus, when Case labels infants at this age as "consolidating one operation" or as "precoordinated," he does not depict as well as the present model the young infants' vocal skills.

*Hierarchization.* In the next level in the present model of sensorimotor hierarchization, schema coordinations of the prior substage become fixed in their temporal order in certain situations or they exhibit a dominant–subordinate relationship. For example, in the prior substage, the 3-month-old might exhibit hand watching while being active before a target, but without moving toward the target. The infant might also use ballistic reaching to the target, but without visual surveillance throughout that act ensures reaching the target. However, in the present model, the 5-month-old is in the sensorimotor hierarchization substage and reveals refined visuomotor coordination in directed reaching. As the infant reaches, arm movement precedes hand opening/seizure and vision is subordinated to manual aiming.

This behavior of visually directed reaching in the young infant resembles the language-related examples in Case's substage of sensorimotor unifocal coordination, which is considered equivalent to the present substage of sensorimotor coordination. For Case, when the infant babbles loudly and raises the hand, the infant is trying to attain a specific goal, e.g., to call the absent adult. In infant–adult social exchange, the active role and the passive role are appropriately alternated in time. However, in behavior such as this, the infant is demonstrating more than Case's unifocal sensorimotor coordination, for there is the added element of appropriate order in behavior and of goal attainment. Moreover, as discussed above, a beginning coordination has already been indicated by related behaviors in the prior substage. Thus, once more, Case's label for the substage involved seems less applicable to the examples that he provides relative to the equivalent one of the present model.

*Systematization.* Sensorimotor systematization is the next substage to develop according to the present model. It witnesses refinements of each component of schema hierarchies. Thus, visually directed reaching can attain a new level of sophistication because it could manifest intention from the beginning of its action and also a subtlety in its target search via the primitive representation that characterizes the substage. Consequently, on object permanence tasks, the 10-month-old infant is capable of finding a fully hidden object.

This example parallels the verbal ones found in Case's level of sensorimotor bifocal coordination, which is the substage equivalent to the present one. For example, Case mentioned that infants in this period babble and point to induce an adult to get a hard-to-reach object. Also, they use utterances to achieve goals. In this regard, in the behaviors expressed, there is systematic organization from the outset toward a goal; this type of behavior is reflective of a primitive image or representational guidance, which is considered an important component underlying the behavior of the equivalent substage in the present model. Instead of visually directed reaching without adjustment to unattainable objects, as would happen in the prior substage of the present model, one now finds personal reaching by the infant being replaced by the infant calling the other to reach for the objects. Visuomotor coordination is refined to the point that the other is recruited to perform part of the action for the infant, through a nascent representational function and the behavior that it allows. Case's label of bifocal coordination for this substage is not the most accurate, given that behavior somewhat indicative of bifocal coordination seems to emerge in the prior substage. Moreover, in the equivalent substage of the present model, the infant appears systematically oriented to a goal from the onset of a behavior, via a primitive representational capacity, and Case's model does not seem to deal with this capacity.

*Multiplication.* The fourth sensorimotor substage of the present model involves multiplication of sensorimotor systems through embedding or combination, facilitating formulation of chained plans. For example, the 1-year-old begins to resolve embedded hidings or the infant explores new ends for previously learned means, as he or she linearly organizes complex sequences of changing sensorimotor schemas.

The language behavior described by Case for the period of sensorimotor elaborated coordination fits the description of the sensorimotor multiplication substage of the present model. Case indicated that the infant at this age repeats novel adult utterances, as well as naming objects in the context of efforts to enlist adults in seeking them. The former example illustrates well schema system multiplication by combination, whereas the latter one typifies sensorimotor multiplication by embedding (or use of subprograms in plans).

In Case's next substage of cognitive development, the infant develops interrelational operational consolidation. Case gives the example of the infant in this age using language to share and link events.

Again, Case's example for this substage is quite consistent with my model and therefore illustrates the efficacy of the present model in explaining the examples of language development that he provided, for in the example there is more than a general sensorimotor elaboration taking place in the 1-year-old. That is, the example supports the notion that at 1 year of age the infant is engaging in specific sensorimotor multiplication acts, with linkage and chaining processes apparently taking place.

*Integration.* The last sensorimotor substage in the present model involves integration, and it refers to the embedding of branched plans (not just branched subprograms) in primary plans to allow for more flexible adaptation. That is, the toddler's plans are symbolically organized, permitting reversible secondary offshoots, as in the resolution of a double embedded hiding.

Case's substage of unifocal coordination in the interrelational period provides linguistic examples consistent with this model. For example, he showed that the young child in this period uses two-word utterances that relate to each other in a variety of ways and that can be uttered without any referent in the immediate context. In the prior substage, the child could produce these utterances, but only through imitation. However, in the last sensorimotor stage of the present model (and for Piaget), symbol-mediated words are used spontaneously, with one word related to another to communicate a larger whole, fitting the child's world. Words that had been combined one way in one circumstance can be used in other two-word utterances in different circumstances, since the child evidences "productive" syntax. Careful examination of the language behavior at this age indicates that the child is exhibiting more than Case's unifocal interrelational coordination in his/her utterances. That is, the description of the utterances in this age period reflect the emphasis in the present model on reversible subprograms where embedding takes place in one circumstance only to be undone to prepare for a different circumstance.

## Perioperational Language Levels

*Coordination.* In the next stage of cognitive growth according to the present model, perioperational levels in thought emerge and they begin with the coordination of the symbol plans that had developed in the prior stage. The child can now balance these plans, permitting more appropriate dual-channel symbol activity. Thus, a 2- or 3-year-old can simultaneously sort two subsets of a group of objects or, in learning to read and write letters, the child can now translate the aural symbol into the written one (and vice versa).

In terms of Case's language examples offered for the bifocal coordination interrelational period, the child can structure two-word utterances into subject–verb–object sentences by coordinating different types of two-word utterances into large wholes (e.g., subject–verb with verb–object). (Sentence sequences or attempted stories, however, lack coordination). Case's examples fit the nature of the equivalent substage in the present model, but for this substage I emphasize that the child can perform more advanced linguistic-related functions than Case had described. That is, examination of the equivalent substage to Case's in the present model indicates that it better captures the young child's nascent letter learning skills, given its emphasis on a coordination of symbol plans.

*Hierarchization.* Finally, the last substage in language development that Case (1985) had dealt with is considered. He stated that storytelling using sequential events (based on sentences with embedded clauses) marks the language skill of the 5-year-old as he/she arrives at the elaborated coordination interrelational substage.

This type of behavior is exactly the one that would best characterize in terms of language ability the substage of perioperational symbol plan hierarchization in the present model. I have described this substage as one showing a dominant–subordinate relationship of symbol plans, so that, for example, symbolic gesturing could be used to supplement verbal utterances. Case's examples seem to correspond well to the description of the substage equivalent to his in the present model, for he shows that this age is marked by the subordination of clauses in sentences and of events in stories.

*Systematization.* Case continued his analysis of storytelling ability in the cognitive stage following the interrelational one (Case et al., 1986). He referred to this period as the dimensional or concrete operational stage, and it also manifests a "pre-," "uni-," "bi-," and "elaborated" substage sequence (at the ages of 3.5–5, 5–7, 7–9, 9–11 years, respectively). In the study described in Case et al. (1986), children were required to tell a story about a "cute little lamb," and the cognitive complexity of the stories was classified according to the four mentioned cognitive levels.

(a) The simplest story, corresponding to the first dimensional substage, consisted of one global episode of sequential events with no theme or plot. (Note that Case (1985) described storytelling in this age period as being comprised of "episodes." But I presume that the "episodes" in that context refer to the "events" in this one). (b) Next, the stories manifested clear plots with conventional themes, for two related episodes (problem, resolution) formed a coordinated higher-order unit. (c) Older children embedded a minor plot (usually involving a secondary problem) in a major plot, and resolved both the major and minor plots (one after the other). (d) In the most advanced level, resolutions of both the plot and subplot were usually more fully elaborated or unified, and took place in parallel, not sequentially.

The first level of storytelling in Case et al. (1986) has already been reinterpreted in the prior paragraphs of this section; therefore, I examine only the last three levels given. In terms of the present model, these three substages in Case correspond to the cognitive substages of perioperational systematization, multiplication, and integration, respectively. Perioperational systematization refers to the development of symbol plan systems through refinement of symbol plan hierarchies. This process takes place by adding to the components involved to better produce target behavior. Ultimately, the systematization in this substage allows the child to better hold things in mind and to use precursor logic (e.g., in simpler concrete operational problems).

By examining Case et al.'s description of storytelling in this age period, it appears that a whole in the child's target story develops for the first time, given that a major logical coordination of episodes over time emerges. Consequently, Case et al.'s description of storytelling in this age period seems quite consistent with the equivalent substage of the present model for this age period, that of perioperational systematization.

*Multiplication.* The next substage in the present model concerns perioperational multiplication. In this age period, the child acquires the capacity to succeed on most of Piaget's concrete operational tasks. Symbol plan systems can combine, chain, or sequence in intercoordinations, alternating patterns, and so on, improving logic, rules, reversals in thought, etc.

Once more, the examples provided in Case et al.'s description of the child's storytelling capacity fit the present model, for they describe embedded minor plots developing in this age period. By their nature, embedded plots reflect the multiplicative dimension of the symbol plans that characterize the equivalent substage to Case's in the present model. Moreover, the major and minor plots are resolved sequentially, fitting Piaget's description of thought reversals, where the child in this period returns to the starting on of his/her cognition before moving on.

*Integration.* The last substage in the perioperational period described in the present model involves perioperational integration, in which a limited logic in imagination begins to appear. The child differentiates optional branches or embeddings of logic in his/her thought and can deal with them simultaneously or in parallel to some extent, as the ability to hold things in mind forms a larger integral whole.

Again, Case et al.'s data on storytelling fits the description of the equivalent substage of the present model. Case et al. described for storytelling during this age period that the child engages in a parallel resolution of plot and subplot in a process of unity.

*Comments.* Case has provided detailed examples of the development of child language in support of his model of stages and substages in cognitive development. However, the analysis just undertaken illustrates that he seems to have systematically underestimated the language skills of the sensorimotor infant and early perioperational child as they pass through the various substages. For each of the these substages, I have pointed out how the present model depicts a more complex cognitive structure compared to Case's, and how it also better fits the language examples and data that he has provided. This conclusion addresses a point raised in Young (1990a), in which I described how in constructing the present model, I had respected as much as possible Piaget's original account of the sequence of sensorimotor substages because of the apparent validity of that sequence, and that I built up the remainder of the model from that starting point. Case's model of cognitive development (as well as Fischer's) was not constructed in the same way, or from the vantage point of the sensorimotor series in Piaget, for they both especially emphasized in their model construction data from the childhood period.

## Reflex Language Levels

Case has not analyzed language development in subsequent developmental stages. Therefore, I extend the present analysis of language development to other stages in the present model. Possible reflexive language levels could involve the following.

*Coordination.* Reflex coordination refers to fetal pairing of reflexes having no firing mechanisms. Moreover, temporal order is not specified. In terms of language precursors, reflex pairs such as these might control mouth movements associated with vegetative sounds in the womb.

*Hierachization.* With reflexive behavior hierarchies of the quite premature newborn, a specific order for the behavior actions of coordinated reflexes develops and specific activating mechanisms for them emerge. Thus, cooing produced by appropriate organization of vocal cord and lip/mouth movements might manifest reflexively in the very premature newborn.

*Systematization.* In reflexive systematization, evident in the somewhat premature newborn, a more patterned behavior results from primitive schemas. That is, non-reflexive components are added to the reflexive ones of the prior substage, refining their on-target orientation. In terms of vocalization in the almost mature prematurely born neonate, longer more varied coo units might be elicited in interest-provoking situations.

*Multiplication.* This process accelerates in the next phase. The full-term newborn exhibits reflex multiplication, where combined series of sounds might be triggered in the optimal state.

*Integration.* In reflex integration, in the first month of life, the very young infant exercises and differentiates reflexes and schema-guided behavior to render them more flexible. Vocalizations might come to differ in terms of intonation or sound variability in different circumstances, for example.

## Abstract Language Levels

As for language development in the formal, abstract language levels of the present model, generally speaking, the stage begins with the young adolescent engaging in coordination of logic in imagination, which allows resolution of problems involving classical Piagetian formal operations. In problem solving at this age, one variable at a time is allowed to vary because the young teenager can orchestrate his/her logical thought pathways, even when no physical evidence is available to help in finding solutions.

*Coordination.* Therefore, in terms of storytelling or writing, the young teenager should be able to readily construct complex plots that subserve abstract themes that he or she is exploring. However, the stories might do little more than present different abstract perspectives, with no effort at further analysis of contradictions, oppositions, and so on.

*Hierarchization.* Next in development, the middle adolescent progresses to the substage of abstract hierarchization; in this step, abstract approaches are explored and are compared either amongst themselves or in a more general perspective. Consequently, story construction should reflect this attribute in this age period, by placing plots and/or themes being explored in various relations, juxtapositions, etc.

*Systematization.* The late adolescent develops abstract systematization, a substage in which the approaches adopted in problem solving and their comparisons are qualified, leading to better understanding. Stories told by late adolescents could reflect this logical advance by a refinement of the plots and themes contained in them, thereby producing a more structured whole.

*Multiplication.* Next, young adults pass into the cognitive substage of dialectical, relativist abstraction, and weigh larger systems organized into coherent multiple frameworks. Stories told by young adults, then, should manifest creative, balanced combinations.

*Integration.* Finally, in the adult substage of abstract integration, an increasing empathic universality might emerge in stories, given that differentiated branching in logic can incorporate harmonization of self and others.

### *Fischer*

Fischer and colleagues (Fischer & Corrigan, 1981; Fischer & Hogan, 1989) also have presented a comparison of levels in Neo-Piagetian cognitive development and parallel acquisitions in language development, but only for three early cognitive levels. Instead of Case's (a) elaborated sensorimotor structures, (b) unifocal interrelations, and (c) bifocal interrelations beginning at 1, 1.5, and 2 years of life, respectively, Fischer described (a) sensorimotor systems, (b) representation sets, and (c) representational mapping at about the same ages in terms of language development. Moreover, the examples provided of language development corresponding to the cognitive levels of his model resemble, for the most part, those of Case (1985).

## Children's Narrative Development

### *Case*

*Model.* Stories have plot and subplot structures that reflect cognitive complexity, and are amenable to modeling according to underlying cognitive substrate. The later work of Case's colleagues has presented a model of the development of storytelling skills consistent with Case's model of stages and substages in cognitive development. I review in depth the work of McKeough and colleagues in Chap. 10. In the present chapter, I provide a brief summary of the work Case's colleagues, that of Fischer and colleagues, and of myself to expand the comparison of the three theories.

Table 9.2 presents the work of Case's colleagues on the evolution of story complexity (e.g., McKeough & Griffiths, 2010; see Table 9.2). Case himself did not develop a model of storytelling complexity into the abstract period, but McKeough's model fills this lacunae. Moreover, McKeough's model is not simply a repetition of Case's with steps added. In their model of cognitive complexity in text, they built on the work of Case by indicating for each substage the degree to which the developing person reflects upon the other's mental state. In addition, they examined the socialaffective structure of the stories, as well as the plot structure and the literary structure. Finally, they have related the development of narrative plot structure

**Table 9.2** General characteristics of each substage plus specific storytelling skills in Case

| | Specific manifestations | |
|---|---|---|
| Substage | General characteristics | Storytelling |
| 0. Operational consolidation (3.5–5 years) | System of second-order relations is consolidated; product can be treated as a single unit | Child can understand and relate sequences of events whose temporal relations culminate in a "problem." Child can also understand problems, and invent a sequence of events that will solve them |
| 1. Operational coordination (5–7 years) | Units of previous stage coordinated, often in a nested fashion; result is emergence of a new kind of unit of a higher order | Child can coordinate construction of event sequences that lead up to, and that resolve, problems. Result is emergence of simple "plot" as higher-order narrative unit |
| 2. Bifocal coordination (7–9 years) | Two higher-order units now considered and related, albeit in a somewhat global fashion | Child can create stories with simple plot and subplot (consisting of one or more additional problems and resolution attempts) |
| 3. Elaborated bifocal coordination (9–11 years) | Two higher-order units considered and related, via fully elaborated procedure or rule. Result is consolidation of third-order relational system, and readiness for next major qualitative shift | Child can now deal with major and minor problems in an integrated and preplanned fashion. Result is new coherence in stories, with plot/subplot structure |

Reprinted with the permission of ABC-CLIO INC. Case, R., Marini, Z., McKeough, A., Dennis, S., & Goldberg, J. (1986). Copyright 2011. [Table 5, Page. 36–37] and Reprinted with the permission of John Wiley & Sons, Inc. Case, R. (1988). Copyright © 1988 and John Wiley & Sons, Inc. [Figure 6.1, Page. 160–161]

complexity to linguistic cohesion, or links across utterances in discourse. Moreover, they indicated that cohesive devices also follow a developmental model (e.g., McKeough, Davis, Forgeron, Marini, & Fung, 2005).

*Comment.* The table indicates that Case's cognitive model and its derivations can help understand well the development of storytelling skills. In the McKeough model, relative to the present model, there does not appear to be gaps in the steps needed to understand narrative development. The descriptions in both models match sufficiently enough, although the names of the stages and substages in the present model are different from those in Case.

Fischer and colleague also have developed a model of narrative complexity (Mascolo & Fischer, 2010). In discussing it, I show that the sequence of substages in Fischer's model of steps in narrative development has gaps relative to the models in Case and my own. In the next section, I review the work of Fischer and Mascolo.

Finally, I present both scales of text complexity that have been constructed according to the present Neo-Piagetian model (Young, 1997; see below). In addition, in following chapters, I present scales of cohesion, text complexity, and syntax that can be used to relate the cognitive complexity of stories and the complexity of their linguistic components.

## Fischer

*Model.* Fischer and colleague (Mascolo & Fischer, 2010) have indicated how narrative structures should evolve according to Fischer's model of cognitive stages and substages in development (see Table 9.3). It is instructive to compare the approach of Fischer with that of Case and colleagues, who have elaborated a similar model, as described.

**Table 9.3** Developmental transformations in hierarchical complexity in the narrative domain

| | Narrative | |
|---|---|---|
| Transformation | Type | Detail |
| Abstract principles (25 yr +) | Principled integration of literary forms and genres | Principled articulation and integration of relations among multiple literary genre, methods, styles, etc. into a stable and consolidated style or narrative system that organizes a given narrative |
| Abstract systems (18–21 yr +) | Narratives structured by integrative relations | Complex or interweaving narratives organized by relations among multiple qualities of characters and events; integrative use of higher-order literary devices (e.g., anachrony, embedded narrative, higher-order tropes) |
| Abstract mappings (14–15 yr +) | Dialectic relations among stable characters | Complex narratives involving characters with inner states and continuity over time. Conflicts derive from relations among characters or events |
| Single abstractions (10–11 yr +) | Conflict-driven multilined narrative | Complex stories involving characters with mental states, motives, organized plots and subplots driven by conflicts and attempts to resolve conflicts |
| Representational systems (6–7 yr) | Intentional story lines | Temporal-causal plot lines involving characters with mental states and motives (e.g., "We went to the zoo, but then I got hungry so we took train to go buy some yummy hot dogs…") |
| Representational mappings (3.5–4 yr) | Causal–temporal action sequences | Child relates multiple actions/events in time or cause–effect relation (e.g., "We went to the zoo and then we got a hot dog") |
| Single representations (18–24 mo) | Global descriptions and shift of focus | Simple descriptions of individual events (e.g., "We went to the zoo") without links to other elements. Adults move narrative forward (shift focus) using questions |

Reprinted with the permission of the publisher (Taylor & Francis Group, http://www.informaworld.com). Mascolo, M. F. (2008) [Table 1, Page. 334–335]

The table provides samples from protocols of four participants in an extensive study on core life goals in adults (taken from a study by Mascolo & Fischer, 2010). The age ranges provided in the table, for the different (sub) stages involved, illustrate the delay in attaining abstract and principled thought for core life goals relative to other domains, in which the acquisition might be easier. At the same time, Neo-Piagetians, including Fischer, underscore that just because a model allows for later-developing stages, they might not develop, at all, for example, in individuals having a lack of support. Researchers should seek both optimal and functional tasks for adults that promote finding (a) earlier developing, (b) average, and (c) late or rarely developing abstract thought and postformal thought. By only using advanced or esoteric tasks, researchers risk masking typical or best achievements in optimal and functional supporting environments

First, it is notable that, compared to the work of Case and McKeough, Fischer and Mascolo have added (sub)stages in narrative development both before and after their sequence, which covered the period from 3 years to adolescence. Specifically, in addition to the levels covered by Case and colleagues, Fischer and Mascolo described the type of narratives produced in the substage applicable to the 2-year-old and in the adult stage. Moreover, in the work of Case, Fischer, and their colleagues, there are several similarities in their descriptions of the steps in narrative development, for example, in the 4-, 6-, 12-, 14-, and 18-year periods.

*Comment.* However, Case and colleague have added two substages in their sequences that are not found in Fischer and colleague's equivalent sequence. Specifically, for the 10- and 8-year periods, the Casian model includes the two substages of bifocal and elaborated intention-based narratives (using McKeough's terminology). They involve the development of simple plots and subplots and then more complex ones. In Fischer's model, the child passes from a substage in which there are plot lines to a substage in which there are organized plots and subplots with conflicts. It would appear that the Case model is correct in adding the two substages between these two levels.

## Comparison

The question is why would Fischer develop a model with such a great leap in narrative development from the child to the adult level, without the equivalent of the two intermediary steps proposed by Case. At several junctures in the present work, I have indicated that in our models both Case and myself do not appear to have missed describing essential substages that take place in development. In our models, we either kept the age periods for which Piaget had described new cognitive structures or we split them to accommodate our substage sequence. In contrast, Fischer appears to have not followed this basic logic in elaborating his model, leading to the various gaps described, such as the one presently under discussion.

Another way of establishing the validity of Fischer's model of narrative development is to examine whether his description of substages in his sequence is more consistent with his particular cognitive stage sequence or with any other. For example, perhaps some of the descriptions in his model of narrative development use terminology more consistent with the present model compared to his own. In this regard, there is much consistency in the five substages that are common to the models of Case, myself, and Fischer – we all have stages that cover the age periods revolving around the ages of 4, 6, 12, 14, and 18 years. For these five substages, Fischer refers to them as mappings and systems for the younger ages in this sequence, and then single sets, mappings, and systems for the older ages. In my model, the equivalent terms involved include hierarchization and systematization, and then coordination, hierarchization, and systematization. The concepts of mappings and hierarchizations are similar enough, as are the terms systems and systematizations. Intuitively, single sets seem quite different from coordinations, although single sets could be seen as described adequately enough to include this characteristic. Therefore, at the level of substage analysis for the substages common to the developmental models of narrative in Fischer, Case, and myself, there are only some differences that are involved.

However, this conclusion begs the question that, for other substages, the models of Case and Young seem to have more complete models. Moreover, there are other pertinent issues in the comparison of narrative models from a Neo-Piagetian perspective that need to be underscored. First, there appear to be other gaps in missing substages in the model of Fischer relative to my model – one at the 2-year mark, two after the 18-year mark, and five within the principle stage (which I refer to as collective intelligence). Also, as explained elsewhere in the present work, I have raised the issue that the substage that appears at 18–24 months should not be considered a purely representational one, as in Fischer (and Case), given its ongoing sensorimotor linkages, despite its symbolic advances, which is an argument that is consistent with Piaget.

## Present Model

*Model.* In Young (1997), I presented scales of analysis of text complexity based on the stages and substages of the present cognitive model. The two tables presenting this work (see Tables 9.4 and 9.5) concern scales of textual complexity for children and for teenagers and adults, respectively. The scales were derived from the present model of substages in cognitive development. The first one concerns the substages of the perioperational stage, in particular (in the scale points 1–5). In addition, I added as scale point to represent the last substage of the sensorimotor stage, and another is added to represent the abstract stage. In the next table, the latter stage is elaborated into its substages in terms of text complexity. The table also indicates the textual complexity expected in the stage of collective intelligence. The two text complexity scales that I have developed could be applied to any type of text, but inspection of its points underscores that the scales emphasize how story elements can be related in plots and subplots. In addition, the scales even have intermediate points to allow further precision.

*Comment.* Storytelling is a cognitive activity that has been analyzed for cognitive complexity in terms of other Neo-Piagetian models, as seen in prior tables. Table 9.6 provides a summary of the three models of stages in narrative development under discussion – those of Case, Fischer, and myself. The table illustrates that the present work is more comprehensiveness than the others, being the only one to cover the age range from 18 months to 28 years, and it does so without skipping any substage that should be included.

## Interim Summary

The present chapter has provided a direct comparison of the models of Case, Fischer, and Young in terms of their suggested correspondences for language development. In the next part of the chapter, it shifts especially into comparison of their work on transition mechanisms and the brain.

**Table 9.4** Text complexity scale for children

| Score | Definition |
|---|---|
| 0 | Monologue given without any structure and/or sequentiality of events, descriptions, that is, no "true" story evident |
| 0.5 | Structure and/or sequentiality in events, descriptions manifest(s) at times |
| 1 | True story attempted; events, descriptions are sequential, temporally linked. But they are not necessarily subordinated to overall episodic theme. Impression is not one of unity at any point in story even if local connections between sentences are made. (Unity refers to clear presentation of a problem, or its resolution, an event, a situation, a person, etc.) |
| 1.5 | Isolated moment of unity evident. At one point in story, an attempt is made to describe a full situation/event, but this does not occupy the whole story |
| 2 | Definite impression of overall subordination to unity in episode conveyed (e.g., stereotypic script with a setting, initiating event, response, and outcome). But there may be some unconnected utterances |
| 2.5 | Episode manifests glimmer of phase distinctions having an organization. There appears to be a clear target end point, with a preliminary contextual phase laying the groundwork. Usually this takes the form of problem and resolution described separately in a story plot. But it may also refer to subcomponent phases of events, situations, persons, etc., that manifest a working toward a concluding statement, comment, etc. The phases, however, are not yet joined, connected (e.g., a link between problem with plan to resolve it and problem resolution is not clear). For example, problem and resolution are in correct temporal sequence but show an *ambiguous* and not an explicit causal relation between them. This may also occur when either phase is not fully developed in the narration. (Score 2.25 when target end point/resolution is implicit) |
| 3 | Groundwork and end-point phases clearly connected |
| 3.5 | The story is comprised of two (or more) successive episodes, each with its own phases, with one major unit and (an)other secondary unit(s) such as a subplot, subepisode, intervening minor problem, or attempted solutions of the problem before resolution takes place. There are no longer units of somewhat equal complexity to the main unit. Secondary units may be embedded. The two elements composing the story lack an interweaving relatedness, for they are presented (and resolved, if this applies) in a sequential, associative manner. That is, there is no parallel nature to the story where the primary element can be left hanging several times and returned to each time while the remaining element is introduced and elaborated (resolved, etc.) in waves in its turn. (Score 3.25 when there are added utterances to story, but they do not constitute an episode or subplot) |
| 4 | Two (or more) successive elements manifest clear links, with a parallel interwoven relationship |
| 4.5 | The secondary element may include an embedded second plot (e.g., second problem to resolve), and not just be a subplot, so that both elements appear to be of somewhat equal complexity |
| 5 | Interweaving of two somewhat equal story elements may take place in oscillatory manner, as described in scale score 3.5 |
| 5.5 | Abstract themes, issues, comments, etc., sometimes interpolated, interspersed (in haphazard way) in story |
| 6 | The story is clearly abstract in nature (e.g., metaphorical, allegorical; about morals, values, personality) |

*Note*. Quarter-point values are assigned when intermediate scale point values seem appropriate. The whole-number values refer to (sub) stages of the synthetic theory. The numbers 1–5 refer to the five perioperational substages (coordination, hierarchization, systematization, multiplication, integration). The numbers 0 and 6 refer to the prior sensorimotor and ensuing abstract stages, respectively
Reprinted with the permission of Springer Science+Business Media: Young, G. (1997) [Table 6.1, Page. 139]

**Table 9.5** Text complexity scale for adolescents and adults

| Score and stage | Description |
|---|---|
| 6. Abstract coordination | The text, narrative, or story is abstract (e.g., metaphorical, coordination allegorical; concerns values, morals, personality). A duality (e.g., right vs. wrong) is explicit or implied. There is only one "appropriate" and/or correct way of interpreting the story, or there is only one legitimate path, theme, plot, or idea referred to |
| 7. Abstract hierarchization | There is some tolerance for accepting that the way in which a hierarchization theme or plot is interpreted or recounted may be incorrect or incomplete, but there is not complete acceptance of this idea. Certainty that one theme or idea is more important than the others. The other themes and ideas are devalued by attempts at logical reasoning |
| 8. Abstract systematization | Recognition and acceptance that there are several complementary, systematization-related perspectives/views/themes/elements of narrative events. Absolutes are preferred, even though uncertainty, exceptions, or conditional acceptance of different perspectives are allowed |
| 9. Abstract multiplication | Recognition that new perspectives–views–themes grow out of multiplication old ones can be embedded within them. Acknowledge that all viewpoints are legitimate and relevant |
| 10. Abstract integration | There is a weighing, evaluation, and comparison of viewpoints/plots/themes. There is evidence of simultaneous deduction and induction (reversibility) in fine-tuned, subtle logic (differentiation). Examination of relations, combinations of relevant viewpoints/plots/themes toward creation of overarching totality or morale (integration). However, there is no comparison or synthesis of different overarching principles |
| 11. Collective intelligence | Synthesis of different overarching viewpoints/principles is beginning to be evident. Recognition that different overarching viewpoints/ principles can occur simultaneously and also can be interactive with each other. Nevertheless, (incipient) commitment to one overarching viewpoint/principle may be evident. This viewpoint/principle should concern elements of self-abnegating symbiosis with communal future. It is intended to encapsulate the interaction between the individual and the community |

*Note*. In the current scale, there is only one level pertaining to the collective stage of intelligence. If necessary, five substages readily can be elaborated by following the prior pattern

Reprinted with the permission of Springer Science+Business Media: Young, G. (1997). [Table 8.1, Page. 187]

## Case and Fischer on Transition Mechanisms

### *Models*

*Case*. Case (1985) has formulated a comprehensive model of the causal determinants in development that lead to the passage from one cognitive level to the next. General regulatory processes include more structured problem solving, less structured exploration, imitation, and mutual regulation, as in cooperation and instruction. For each of these four determinants, there are four steps through which the child must pass. First, schemes are searched, and then they are evaluated, retagged for memory access, and consolidated. Working memory factors (e.g., short-term storage space, executive processing load, operational efficiency) act to constrain transitions from level to level in cognitive development. Both neuromaturational and experiential

**Table 9.6** Comparison of Neo-Piagetian models of stages and substages in narrative development from 1.5 to 25 years

| Young | | Mascolo and Fischer | | McKeough | |
|---|---|---|---|---|---|
| Stage/substage (and age) | Narrative | Stage/substage (and age) | Narrative | Stage/substage (and age) | Narrative |
| Sensorimotor integration (18 mo–) | Monologue given without any structure and/or sequentiality of events, descriptions. That is, no "true" story evident | Single representations (18–24 mo) | Global descriptions and shift of focus | | |
| Perioperational coordination (2 yr–) | True story attempted; events, descriptions are sequential, temporally linked | | | Preintentional, social (<4 yr) | |
| Perioperational hierarchization (3.5 yr–) | Definite impression of overall subordination to unity in episode conveyed (e.g., stereotypic script with a setting, initiating event, response, and outcome) | Representational mappings (3.5–4 yr) | Causal–temporal action sequences | Action elaborated (4 yr) | Does the story have a sequence of events? |
| Perioperational systematization (5 yr–) | Groundwork and end-point phases clearly connected | Representational systems (6–7 yr) | Intentional story lines | Intentional, dimensional unifocal (6 yr) | Does the story include explicit or implicit reference to the mental states? |
| Perioperational multiplication (7 yr–) | Two (or more) successive elements manifest clear links, with a parallel interwoven relationship | | | Intentional, dimensional bifocal (8 yr) | Does the story have a problem, a series of failed attempts or complications followed by a resolution? |
| Perioperational integration (9 yr–) | Interweaving of two somewhat equal story elements may take place in oscillatory manner, as described in scale score 3.5 | | | Intentional, dimensional elaborated (10 yr) | Does one impediment or a well-developed subplot have more significance than the others? |

| | | | | | |
|---|---|---|---|---|---|
| Abstract coordination (11 yr–) | The story is clearly abstract in nature (e.g., metaphorical, allegorical; about morals, values, personality) | Single abstractions (10–11 yr) | Conflict-driven multilined narrative | Interpretive, abstract (vectorial) unifocal (12 yr) | Does the focus of the story shift from the characters' mental states to *why* particular mental states are held? |
| Abstract hierarchization (13 yr–) | There is some tolerance for accepting that the way in which a hierarchization theme or plot is interpreted or recounted may be incorrect or incomplete, but there is not complete acceptance of this idea | Abstract mappings (14–15 yr) | Dialectic relations among stable characters | Interpretive, abstract (vectorial) bifocal (14 yr) | Are additional traits represented, such that a dialectic is created? |
| Abstract systematization (16 yrs–) | Recognition and acceptance that there are several complementary, systematization-related perspectives/ views/themes/elements of narrative events | | | Interpretive, abstract (vectorial) elaborated (18 yr) | Does the dialectical relation between states or traits act as an integrating device? |
| Abstract multiplication (19 yr–) | Recognition that new perspectives–views–themes grow out of multiplication old ones can be embedded within them | Abstract systems (18–21 yr) | Narratives structured by integrative relations | | |
| Abstract integration (22 yr–) | There is a weighing, evaluation, and comparison of viewpoints/plots/themes | | | | |
| Collective intelligence coordination (25 yr–) | Synthesis of different overarching viewpoints/principles is beginning to be evident | Abstract principles (25 yr+) | Principled integration of literary forms and genres | | |

(continued)

**Table 9.6** (continued)

Reprinted with the permission of Springer Science+Business Media: Young, G. (1997) [Table 6.1, Page. 139]. Adapted from the publisher (Taylor & Francis Group, http://www.informaworld.com). Mascolo, M. F. (2008). [Table 1. Page. 334–335]. Adapted from John Benjamins Publishing Company with permission. McKeough, A., Davis, L., Forgeron, N., Marini, A., & Fung, T. (2005). [Figure 2, Page. 249], and Adapted from American Psychological Association with permission. McKeough, A., & Genereux, R. (2003). [Figure 1, Page. 541]

There are two major Neo-Piagetian models of stages and substages in cognitive development that are compared and contrasted in the present work, those of Case and Fischer. Both theorists, with colleagues, have developed models of narrative development, such as in storytelling. Their models of narrative development have steps that correspond to the cognitive levels in their models. In the present work, I treat in depth the approach to the development of narrative skills by both Case and Fischer and colleagues, as well as my own approach. In the present table, I take material from tables in the present work on this topic from the three models for purposes of introduction and comparison. Narrative development is one of the central topics of the present work. The extrapolation that I undertook for steps in narrative development based on my own model, as well as other work that I present on cohesion and coherence in storytelling (see Chaps. 33 and 34), illustrate the place of narrative in the present work

For the age period indicated in the table, from 18 months to 25 years, the present model is the only one that includes substages without gaps. The work of McKeough, a colleague of Case, offers a model with a one-to-one correspondence in substages with my own model in the age period of 2 of 18 years. However, the model of Mascolo and Fischer appears to have gaps in the age period that they cover, which spans the same age period as my own in the table. Just in these senses, the present model of steps in narrative development is more comprehensive than the others. Moreover, I point out inconsistencies in their work that are accommodated in my own model

Another way in which the present work reveals a refinement that improves upon the others is in its narrative scoring system. McKeough et al. (2005) undertook a study in which they provided support for storytelling in first graders. They scored the stories in terms of the scale points corresponding to the cognitive substages in Case's model. The present model allows for a differentiated approach to scoring storytelling and narrative because it includes in its scoring system partial scores between substages (see Table 9.4)

**Table 9.7** Left-right hemisphere cortical network/growth spurt

| Stage onset (years) | Fischer representational system (one substage) | Case dimensional stage (three substages) |
|---|---|---|
| 5–6 | Left | Left |
| 7–8 | Bilateral | Bilateral |
| 9–10 | Right | Right |

Adapted from Case (1992) and Fischer (2009)

Both Case and Fischer have attempted to relate their developmental models to Thatcher's work (1991, 1994b) on the maturation of the hemispheres (cortical networking or growth spurt) according to EEG data. For example, they both abstracted out of his work a shift from left to bilateral to right hemisphere maturation in the 5–6 to 9–10 year period, as indicated in the table. However, there is a major difference in how they related the growth spurt to their models. For Case, the shifts correspond in a one-to-one fashion to three substages in his model within the dimensional stage. However, for Fischer, all the shifts are posited to take place within the one substage of representational systems

There are several concerns that can be raised about the difference in how Fischer and Case have dealt with in so different a manner the data of Thatcher. (a) Does Fischer have sufficient substages in his model? In this regard, has he inappropriately squeezed Thatcher's data into the one substage that he lists because the age ranges for his substages, in general, at times, are too broad, given that he appears to have skipped in his model a few distinct substages at certain critical times? The logic in proposing this possibility is reinforced by the difficulty he had dealing with the 18–24 month (or 2–3.5 year) age period, as documented in prior discussion (e.g., Chap. 6)

(b) Do maturational shifts in the hemispheres have the functional implications being proposed? For Case, does this mean that the best way of understanding cognitive development in middle childhood is in terms of shifts in hemispheric dominance from one substage to the next? Is that sufficient to explain the complexity in the development of the child's thought in this age period? Does the child really shift in predominant hemisphere used over 2 year periods in the way indicated? Granted, there is research that in developing early reading skills the child shifts from right to left hemisphere activity (Shaywitz & Shaywitz, 2008). However, the shift in Case's model for general cognitive development in this age period is in the opposite direction. Moreover, the areas of the brain localized in reading research are particular to language and related regions

(c) A more likely scenario is that each hemisphere begins to develop its specializations from birth, if not before, and they work collaboratively on most tasks. For a particular cognitive substage in any Neo-Piagetian model, there is more involved than maturational gradients. The latter might power some behaviors and prepare the way for functional differentiations of each hemisphere's specializations as well as their collaboration, but they are only part of the equation. Moreover, different indices might give different maturational gradients in the developing brain, and there is no reason to suspect that one or the other is predominant in determining functional activity or that a maturational gradient, per se, has to be dominant. More likely, as each hemisphere refines its skills, the neuronal circuitry involved takes charge of the behaviors involved and are only influenced but not determined by different maturational gradients

(d) I present a model of the development of the hemispheres in terms of different left-right functional specializations (see Young, 1990a; and Chap. 25 of the present work). In particular, I describe different inhibitory skills in the hemispheres. That is, the model underscores that a general function that could distinguish the hemispheres relates to their skills in activation–inhibition coordination. In this regard, cognitively at any one substage, there could be different activation–inhibition coordination patterns at the neurological and neuronal level that underlie each substage. Also, children might differ in domain development depending on the refinements in activation–inhibitory skills within each hemisphere and their coordination across the hemispheres

Note that Immordino-Yang and Fischer (2007) have developed a model of left–right differences in specialization that is not based on the work of Thatcher and is consistent with the present approach. Although this model appears in the same publication as the left-to-right shift model under review, the authors still advocate for the maturational gradient position (see Fig. 9.3) influences (myelination and culture/practice, respectively) affect this process. Individual differences arise from the myriad effects of all these diverse variables.

Critical to the understanding of transition mechanisms is specifying the level at which transitions in development take place. Are they taking place at the level of local schemes/operations applicable to particular skills or domains, or are they taking place globally at the level of whole stages or substages. In general, the Neo-Piagetian approach is to specify transitions at the local and not the global level. An intermediate position would be that transitions take place at the level of groupings or multiples of skills and domains. Case (1998) has developed a pertinent concept in this regard. He proposed that groups of similar concepts are coordinated into coherent central conceptual structures. The research evidence indicates that the correlations across closely related concepts are sufficiently high to indicate an underlying construct along the lines that he proposed. Central conceptual structures are not logically derived amalgamating structures, such as proposed by Piaget. Rather, they are formed in context because of their conceptual similarities. Case (1998) began to differentiate the concept of central conceptual structures into particular types, such as numerical, narrative, and social varieties (see Figs. 9.1 and 9.2).

Therefore, according to Case, in terms of the transitions in development, the relationship over the particular skills and domains evident in their groupings into central conceptual structures indicates that transitions take place both locally in terms of particular acquisitions and more broadly over similar acquisitions, such as in central conceptual structures. However, transitions do not take place in a discontinuous fashion over the full range of skills associated with any one particular stage or substage.

*Fischer*. Fischer (1980, 1987) also has described a range of causal influences on cognitive level transitions. On the one hand, he speaks of cross-cortical spurts in synapse formation and like processes. On the other hand, he refers to transformation rules. Among these is the intercoordination of skills, which leads to transition to higher substage level. Other simpler rules can produce sublevel but not substage shifts. These include compounding, focusing or shifting, substitution or generalization, and differentiation. Environmental supports are especially important for Fischer, for they help sustain optimal development, yet, at the same time, they are the source of wide individual differences. I develop further Fischer's concepts along these lines in another chapter (see Chap. 11).

## Comments

Although the current theory is a stage theory of cognitive development, it is not one that devalues individual differences at the expense of a universal cognitive architecture. Metaphors of branching trees (Case) and individually woven webs (Fischer) have been proffered to capture the way universal sequences and context-sensitive particularities can coexist simultaneously in development.

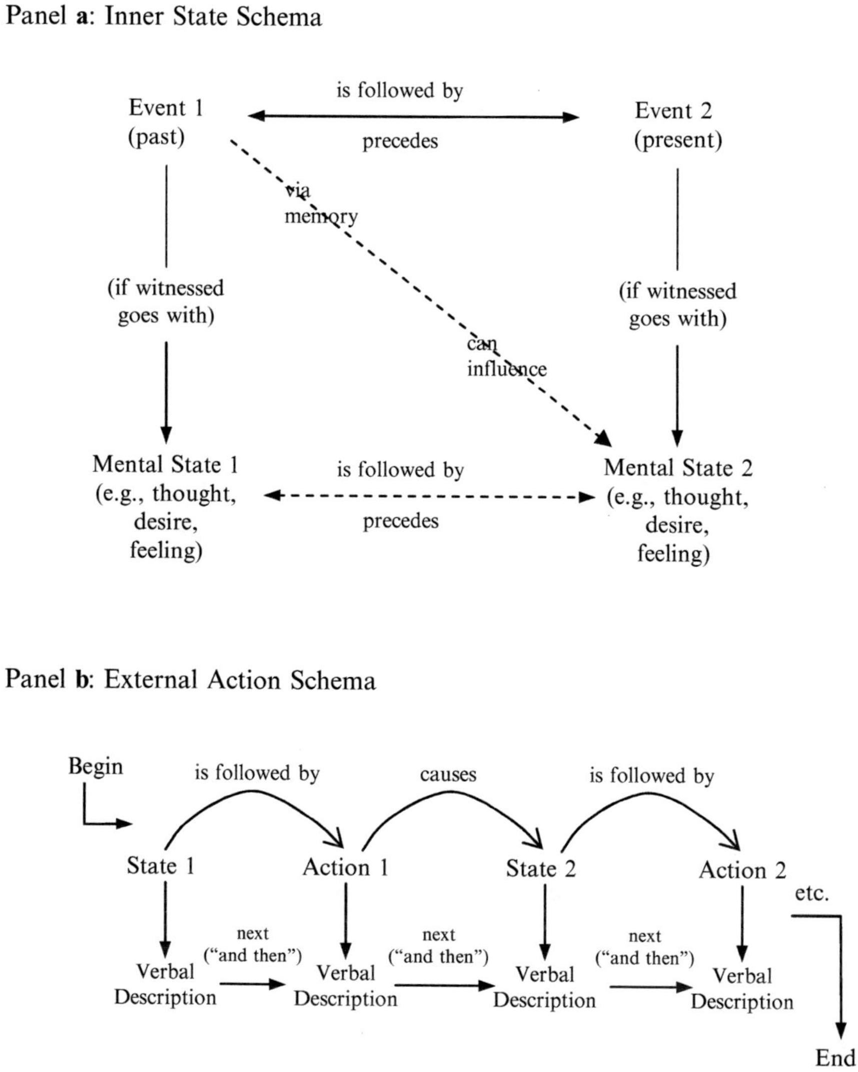


**Fig. 9.1** Central narrative structures hypothesized in preschool children. Panel (**a**) illustrates the inner state schema that permits children to infer the thoughts or feelings of others, and to solve the classic "false belief" task. Panel (**b**) illustrates the schema that permits children to verbalize the social scripts with which they are familiar and make causal statements and/or predictions about what will happen next. Reprinted with the permission of John Wiley & Sons, Inc. Case, R. (1998). Copyright © 1998 and John Wiley & Sons, Inc. [Figure 15.3, Page. 767]

Thus, for Neo-Piagetians today, a stage model of development may specify the typical sequence or common trunk that might be evident in any one cognitive domain or area, but the way development proceeds or branches on the trunk in terms of interdomain relations is individually determined. Contextual sensitivity dictates individual adaptations. Nevertheless, the axes on which the webs of individual

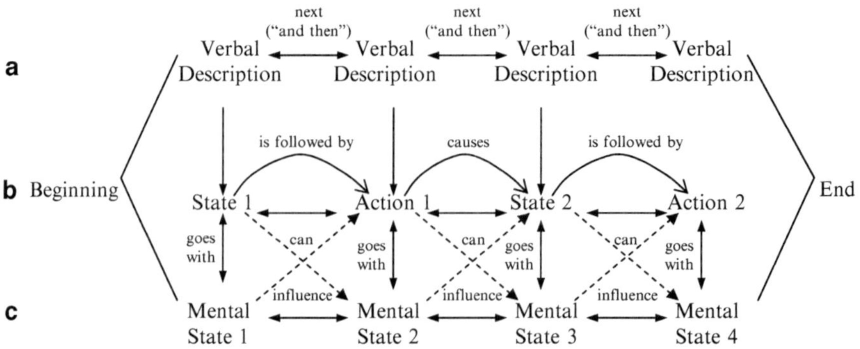


**Fig. 9.2** Central narrative structure in children. Central narrative structure (the "mental story line") hypothesized to emerge during the school years, circa 6 years of age, as a result of the elaboration and merging of the two earlier schemas show in Fig. 9.1. The three rows indicate, respectively, (**a**) knowledge of sentence forms for describing familiar events and actions, (**b**) knowledge of familiar states and actions, together with the causal or "enabling" relations that they bear to each other, and (**c**) knowledge of the role that those events play in influencing mental states and vice versa. External brackets indicate that entire structure is understood to have a characteristic beginning, middle, and end. Reprinted with the permission of John Wiley & Sons, Inc. Case, R. (1998). Copyright © 1998 and John Wiley & Sons, Inc. [Figure 15.4, Page. 767]

differences are woven provide constraints on their nature and direction and assure fundamental commonalities in their qualitative differentiation. It is as if development is simultaneously both universal and individual, both discontinuous and continuous, or both trunk and branch.

## Corresponding Cortical Reorganization

### *Case*

#### Earlier

*Model.* Case (1992) has related the cyclic recursion of unifocal, bifocal, and elaborated substages within each successive cognitive stage in his model to cyclic microcycles of cortical reorganization in development. Thatcher (1991, 1992, 1994a, 1994b) studied electroencephalogram (EEG) coherence in intrahemisphere electrode pairs from an extensive subject sample that varied in age from early to late in the life span. He obtained data during quiet, alert states. He examined the first derivative of mean EEG coherence to detect rapid changes in its mean. From these data, he could infer when growth spurts in corticocortical connections were taking place. Thatcher's data suggested a cycle of growth spurts from early infancy onward. Each cycle appears to last about 4 years, and its microcycles each last about 6–12 months. There appears to be three major microcycles in each cycle, with the first involving the left hemisphere, the second both hemispheres, and the third the right hemisphere.

In the left hemisphere spurt, intracortical connections seem to lengthen sequentially, in that longer distance accommodative connections form between the frontal lobe and the left temporal, parietal, and occipital lobes. These surplus synaptic connections are hypothesized to form through synaptogenesis, axonal sprouting, synaptic terminal expansion, and pre- and postsynaptic neurotransmitter adjustments. In the bilateral hemisphere growth spurt that follows the left hemisphere one, parallel longer distance connections in the right frontal lobe are formed, in particular. Finally, the right hemisphere growth spurt is marked by assimilative sequential contraction of intracortical connections in the right hemisphere, with shorter distance connections formed and excess connections pruned. The apparent iterative shifting from left to right hemisphere growth spurt is complicated by a parallel four-phase shift involving left lateral to left dorsal medial to right dorsal medial to right lateral cortical shift in growth spurt.

Thatcher's data revealed that the early *left, bilateral, and right* hemisphere growth spurts take place at about 1.5, 3, and 4 years of age, respectively, whereas the childhood spurts occur at about 5, 8, and 9 years, respectively. The equivalent preadolescent–adolescent spurts take place at about 10, 13, and 14 years, respectively. The correspondence in age with Case's interrelational, dimensional, and vectorial substages of unifocal, bifocal, and elaborated coordination suggested to Case that there is a common process underlying the paired recursions in cortical growth spurts and cognitive substage development. Cyclic developmental shifts, whether neurological or cognitive, might move from more integrated to differentiated functioning, for example.

*Comment.* The complementarity between Case's model of cognitive development and Thatcher's description of growth spurts in cortical reorganization is striking (Case, 1992). Nevertheless, examination of Thatcher's work indicates that there are exceptions to the parallel. For example, Thatcher's (1992) data up to the age of 7 years shows that there are two to three separate growth spurts contained within each left and right hemisphere spurt. Moreover, in the 3–5-year period, two particular growth spurts involving the right frontal lobe do not readily fit the complementary pattern described above (see p. 44).

Finally, there is no ready explanation about why growth spurts in cortical development should cycle from left to bilateral to right hemisphere involvement. Perhaps the right hemisphere growth spurt terminates a cycle because it is better at "envisioning the functioning of an overall system and differentiating it from the functioning of other systems" (Case, 1992, p. 68).

## Later

*Model.* Thatcher (2010) has presented EEG data consistent with Case's model of cognitive development. In his previous work, he documented maturational shifts from birth to age 16 within and across hemispheres according to EEG coherence data. In his most recent analysis, he has examined the same records for phase differences. He found that with development there appears to be tighter or shorter within-area or local neuronal architecture, but increasingly diffuse distal connectivity over areas. There is an increase in the number of neuronal connections locally, resulting in an increased time devoted to local processing and integration; the corollary is that there are longer phase delays between separated local domains. He interpreted this as the different sides of the same coin. With development, at once, particular areas become increasingly organized and also across areas there are decreased linkages. The results speak to an increased efficiency in long distance connections in terms of pruning activity, in particular, which helps create more precise reciprocal linkages between local and distant neurons. That there are cycles in the process of long-term connection formation reinforces Thatcher's developmental model of cortical connectivity.

*Comment.* However, it remains to be shown that there are functional correspondences to the cycle, whether in terms of the original analysis or the most recent one. To suggest that maturational shifts in regional interconnectivity can account for widespread qualitative cognitive changes in development requires empirical evidence of the cortical reorganization preceding or simultaneously developing with the hypothesized cognitive changes.

In this regard, Lewis, a colleague of Case, has undertaken important research. Lewis et al. (2008) found that 8–12-year-olds with comorbid internalizing and internalizing problems who improved in a community-based treatment program evidenced a decrease in ventral prefrontal activity, but only in the inhibitory phase of the ERP signal. The intervention appeared to have helped in the overcontrol portion of the dynamics of the children's behavioral difficulties, so that a lowering of an overinhibition factor in the ventral prefrontal cortex helped them equilibrate to some extent. This study indicates the manner in which localized regions of the brain participate in emotional regulation, but it demonstrates a role for cross-brain and behavior dynamics, such as inhibition, which is treated a great deal in the present work as an important regulatory component.

## *Fischer*

### Earlier

*Model.* Fischer (Fischer & Rose, 1994) also has developed a model of cognitive-cortical development correspondences based on the work of Thatcher. He hypothesized that as development proceeds through each of the substages of sets, mappings, and systems, Thatcher's hemisphere coherence cycle moves through a corresponding *right–left–bilateral* cycle. The entry point to the cycle has been changed to the right side in Fischer's model relative to Thatcher's left entry and to Case's adaptation of it, because a right entry "appears to fit the cognitive levels more closely" (p. 48).

*Comment.* No specific evidence is offered for the latter conjecture. Moreover, the cycle is considered to reoccur *within* each substage, and thus the model, as originally presented in Fischer and Rose, did not offer corresponding links *across* different substages, unlike the case for Case. Using these data, Fischer maintained that the three-substage cycle described in his model is accompanied by a corresponding cycle of frontal to occipitoparietal, temporal, and central spurts.

## Later

*Model.* Fischer (2009) has further specified the relationship across his developmental model of stages and substages in cognitive development and maturational growth spurts in neuronal networking (e.g., Thatcher's work on EEG coherence, 1994). According to the model, changes in the distribution of energy deriving from neural activity indicate regions of cortical growth. Moreover, the changes follow a cyclical process of neuronal rewiring in short and long distance connections and in neuronal retuning. Thatcher's results indicate that the neuronal growth process gravitates systematically around the cortex, although the spurts are relative (growth does not only happen at the leading edge of the spurts), and minor ones also take place that are not indicated. The patterns found are normative and do not deny the presence of individual and group differences (e.g., related to gender). The prefrontal cortex is involved in many of the neuronal interconnections so that many of the cortical growth spurts that emerge from the EEG data involve this region.

Fischer described the specific cycling in maturational growth spurts that appear to take place in the 6–10-year-old age range, a period when the child is expressing Fischer's representational systems substage, and transitioning to the abstract set one. At the beginning of the cycle, connections are growing front to back, or from the prefrontal cortex to the occipital cortex. In the next phase of cortical neuronal maturational growth, the cycle moves to the right hemisphere, and the spurts are, therefore, more local than distal. The spurt then shifts back to the prefrontal cortex, but locally and not distally. Then, the left hemisphere becomes involved, at first locally, and then distally, before the cycle returns to the prefrontal cortex and prefrontal–occipital connections, which starts a new cycle in the next cognitive substage that develops in Fischer's model.

As the maturational cycles repeat over substages in development, they reflect a process of growth referred to as nested networking. Fischer's Fig. 8.9 provides further details on the cortical spurts that cycle in relation to the substages of his cognitive model. They appear to involve *a right-to-left shifting*, and well as movement within the right hemisphere through the frontal, occipital, parietal, central, and temporal regions, and movement within the left hemisphere through the reverse sequence. (I could not discern the specific relationship to the three-substage cycle that takes place cyclically over the stages of his model).

In support of this type of modeling, Fischer cited the work of Bell (1998; Bell & Fox, 1996), who found that the onset of crawling in infancy is associated with elevated EEG coherence indicative of interconnectivity across frontal, occipital, and parietal cerebral regions, especially in the right hemisphere. The spurt dropped as the infants' crawling matured. It was delayed if crawling had been delayed. When one infant in the study was examined for language skill, the left rather than the right hemisphere was implicated in cortical spurting. Fischer hypothesized that right hemisphere dominance for language should lead to reverse patterning of growth spurts in the hemispheres.

*Comment.* Fischer did not cite specific evidence that reveals a statistical relationship across EEG coherence measures and steps in cognitive acquisitions. At present, the only evidence cited in support of his nested networking model involves parallel sets of data in different studies that seem to suggest a correspondence in the steps in cognitive development according to his model and independently studied spurts in EEG coherence and related data.

As for Fischer's argument that the cognitive substages might be grounded in a cortical maturation that proceeds from the anterior frontal region backward to the central one, more data are needed to confirm the sequence. Although the gradient described attributes to the frontal cortex a primary initiatory role in cortical maturation, a role consistent with its executive function, the model seems too static, and other parameters of brain development should be involved, as well.

Moreover, examination of his work presents alternative models of hemispheric specialization that are consistent with developmental phenomena and different from his Thatcherian model (see Table 9.7 and Fig. 9.3).

## *Conclusion*

Both Case and Fischer have presented models of correspondences in cognitive substage and cortical development (see Table 9.7). Although both base their work on Thatcher research, in particular, they emerge with diametrically opposite models in terms of which hemisphere starts off the maturational sequence that is posited to cycle in development. Moreover, they have different conceptions of whether the maturation involved is within, over, or both within and over substages or even stages.

Beyond these differences in their models, it is hard to imagine the way one hemisphere or the other might dominate in functional deployment for extended developmental periods, even though it may be undergoing growth spurts lasting months or longer. Different measures of cortical growth, or perhaps different means of using the EEG, might give data complementary to Thatcher's. It is more likely that the full empirical picture will reveal that the left and right hemispheres cooperate in their complementary specializations at each developmental phase and that their specializations evolve in complexity as they pass from one phase to the next.

For example, Damasio (1994) described the manner in which the brain is hierarchically organized not only into lobes but also into systems and systems of systems. It would seem to me that the different brain regions increasingly come to coordinate

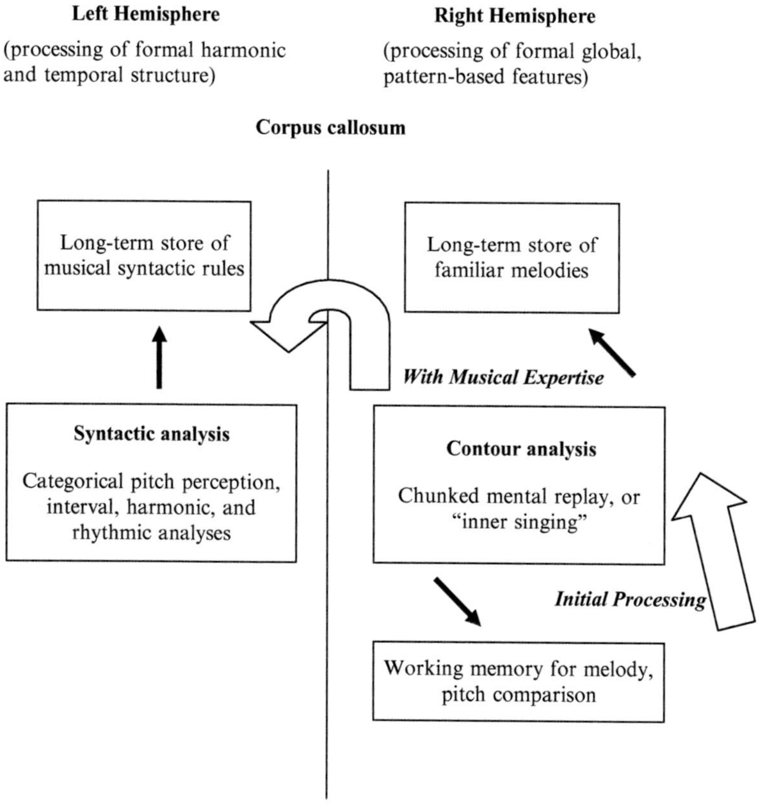


**Fig. 9.3** Right to left hemisphere shift in music processing with musical training. A schematic diagram of the neuropsychological components of music processing, illustrating a shift with musical training from mainly right-hemispheric processing to strategies associated with the left hemisphere. The boxes on the *right* hemisphere, heavily recruited regardless of expertise. The boxes on the *left* are associated with the left hemisphere and are heavily recruited in experts after initial right-hemispheric processing. Reprinted with the permission of Guilford Publications, Inc. Immordino-Yang, M. H., & Fischer, K. W. (2007). Copyright 2011. [Figure 4.5. Page. 92]

across development, and this element is missing in Case's and in Fischer's account. In my own model, this principle is of primary focus (see Chap. 26).

## Summary and Conclusions

With few exceptions, the previous chapters present the models of Case, Fischer, and colleagues without considering the extent of their most recent work. The following chapters provide a fuller picture of their models and their developmental applications. I continue to compare their models to each other and with mine. At the same time, I expand the scope of my model as I do so.

## References


Bell, M. A. (1998). The ontogeny of the EEG during infancy and childhood: Implications for cognitive development. In B. Garreau (Ed.), *Neuroimaging in child neuropsychiatric disorders* (pp. 97–111). Berlin: Springer.

Bell, M. A., & Fox, N. A. (1996). Crawling experience is related to changes in cortical organization during infancy: Evidence from EEG coherence. *Developmental Psychobiology, 29*, 551–561.

Case, R. (1985). *Intellectual development: Birth to adulthood*. Orlando: Academic Press.

Case, R. (1988). The whole child: Toward an integrated view of young children's cognitive, social, and emotional development. In A. D. Pellegrini (Ed.), *Psychological bases for early education* (pp. 155–184). New York: Wiley.

Case, R. (1992). The role of the frontal lobes in the regulation of cognitive development. *Brain and Cognition, 20*, 51–73.

Case, R. (1998). The development of conceptual structures. In W. Damon, D. Kuhn, & R. S. Siegler (Eds.), *Handbook of child psychology: Vol. 2. Cognition, perception & language* (5th ed., pp. 745–800). New York: Wiley.

Case, R., Marini, Z., McKeough, A., Dennis, S., & Goldberg, J. (1986). Horizontal structure in middle childhood: Cross-domain parallels in the course of cognitive growth. In I. Levin (Ed.), *Stage and structure* (pp. 1–38). Norwood: Ablex.

Damasio, A. R. (1994). *Descartes' error: Emotion, reason, and the human brain*. New York: Avon.

Fischer, K. W. (1980). A theory of cognitive development: The control and construction of hierarchies of skills. *Psychological Review, 87*, 477–531.

Fischer, K. W. (1987). Relations between brain and cognitive development. *Child Development, 58*, 623–632.

Fischer, K. W. (2009). Mind, brain, and education: Building a scientific groundwork for learning and teaching. *Mind, Brain, and Education, 3*, 3–16.

Fischer, K. W., & Corrigan, R. (1981). A skill approach to language development. In R. Stark (Ed.), *Language behavior in infancy and early childhood* (pp. 245–289). New York: Elsevier.

Fischer, K. W., & Hogan, A. E. (1989). The big picture for infant development: Levels and variations. In J. Lockman & N. Hazen (Eds.), *Action in social context: Perspectives on early development* (pp. 275–305). New York: Plenum.

Fischer, K. W., & Rose, S. P. (1994). Dynamic development of coordination of components in brain and behavior: A framework for theory and research. In G. Dawson & K. W. Fischer (Eds.), *Human behavior and the developing brain* (pp. 3–66). New York: Guilford Press.

Immordino-Yang, M. H., & Fischer, K. W. (2007). Dynamic development of hemispheric biases in three cases: Cognitive/hemispheric cycles, music, and hemispherectomy. In D. Coch, K. W. Fischer, & G. Dawson (Eds.), *Human behavior, learning, and the developing brain: Typical development* (pp. 74–111). New York: Guilford Press.

Lewis, M. D., Granic, I., Lamm, C., Zelazo, P. D., Stieben, J., Todd, R. M., et al. (2008). Changes in the neural bases of emotion regulation associated with clinical improvement in children with behavior problems. *Development and Psychopathology, 20*, 913–939.

Mascolo, M. F. (2008). The concept of domain in developmental analyses of hierarchical complexity. *World Futures, 64*, 330–347.

Mascolo, M. F., & Fischer, K. W. (2010). The dynamic development of thinking, feeling and acting over the lifespan. In R. M. Lerner & W. F. Overton (Eds.), *Handbook of lifespan development: Vol. 1. Cognitive, biology and methods*. Hoboken: Wiley.

McKeough, A., Davis, L., Forgeron, N., Marini, A., & Fung, T. (2005). Improving story complexity and cohesion: A developmental approach to teaching story composition. *Narrative Inquiry, 15*, 96–125.

McKeough, A., & Genereux, R. (2003). Transformation in narrative thought during adolescence: The structure and content of story compositions. *Journal of Educational Psychology, 95*, 537–552.

McKeough, A., & Griffiths, S. (2010). Adolescent narrative thought: Developmental and neurological evidence in support of a central social structures. In M. Ferrari & L. Vuletic (Eds.), *Developmental relations among mind, brain and education* (pp. 213–230). New York: Springer Science+Business Media.

Shaywitz, S. E., & Shaywitz, B. A. (2008). Paying attention to reading: The neurobiology of reading and dyslexia. *Development and Psychopathology, 20*, 1329–1349.

Thatcher, R. W. (1991). Maturation of the human frontal lobes: Physiological evidence for staging. *Developmental Neuropsychology, 7*, 397–419.

Thatcher, R. W. (1992). Cyclical cortical reorganization during early childhood. *Brain and Cognition, 20*, 24–50.

Thatcher, R. W. (1994a). Psychopathology of early frontal lobe damage: Dependence on cycles of development. *Development and Psychopathology, 6*, 565–596.

Thatcher, R. W. (1994b). Cyclic cortical reorganization: Origins of human cognitive development. In G. Dawson & K. W. Fischer (Eds.), *Human behavior and the developing brain* (pp. 232–266). New York: Guilford Press.

Thatcher, R. W. (2010). Higher-order network reworking-new findings. In M. Ferrari & L. Vuletic (Eds.), *Developmental relations among mind, brain and education* (pp. 83–104). New York: Springer Science+Business Media.

Young, G. (1990a). Early neuropsychological development: Lateralization of functions – hemispheric specialization. In C. A. Hauert (Ed.), *Developmental psychology: Cognitive, perceptuo-motor and neuropsychological perspectives* (pp. 113–181). Amsterdam: North Holland.

Young, G. (1990b). The development of hemispheric and manual specialization. In G. E. Hammond (Ed.), *Cerebral control of speech and limb movements* (pp. 79–139). Amsterdam: North Holland.

Young, G. (1997). *Adult development, therapy, and culture: A postmodern synthesis*. New York: Plenum.

# Chapter 10
# Recent Case and Colleagues

## Introduction

Robbie Case passed away prematurely in 2000. His work has had considerable influence, and his colleagues continue to build Neo-Piagetian understanding and conduct Neo-Piagetian research from his framework. The recent book edited on how Case's colleagues keep expanding his work is an example that his theory is still vibrant (Ferrari & Vuletic, 2010). In this chapter, I review in depth one of the areas that Case continued to work on before his untimely death – that of central conceptual structures. In his work, he referred to the work of Baldwin, who described stages in development that included the following: quasilogical, logical, and hyperlogical steps. Piaget built his model partly based on this work. In addition, in the present work, I built several models that included a modified version of this sequence, as I show in later chapters. After reviewing the concept of central conceptual structures, in this present chapter, I review some of the critical contributions to the field being made by Case's colleague since he passed away. In particular, I review the work of Lewis and colleagues (on infant development, cognition and emotions, regulation, and systems theory) and of Demetriou and colleagues (on hypercognition).

## Central Conceptual, Number, Narrative, and Social Structures

### *Introduction*

According to Case, Okamoto, Henderson, and McKeough (1993), Baldwin (1894) had proposed that cognitive development consists of four stages: sensorimotor, quasilogical, logical, and hyperlogical. However, Piaget (1960) reworked the theory, leading to the impact that he has had in psychology. In particular, Piaget had added to Baldwin's work the understanding that stages possess general logical structural properties, or a coherent set of cognitive rules and organization applicable

G. Young, *Development and Causality: Neo-Piagetian Perspectives*,
DOI 10.1007/978-1-4419-9422-6_10, © Springer Science+Business Media, LLC 2011 

to a broad range of developmental activity. Moreover, the logical structures at each stage of development were considered unique to it, giving each stage unique characteristics.

According to Case et al., disaffection set in about Piaget's model because it did not account for local variations, for example, across domains, modules, contexts, or tasks within domains. Stage-like growth might develop within a particular domain, but more generalized stage structures are not likely.

Despite the newer conceptualizations of development that began to dominate the field of cognitive developmental psychology, Case et al. (1993) were finding evidence of some cross-domain consistencies. They understood that they needed to bridge the general-systemic and local perspectives on the nature of stages. In order to explain their findings, they developed the concept of central conceptual structures. These are defined as systems of semantic nodes and relations that might apply to a broad range of domains due to their general properties, but they still would have domain constraints, and perhaps even neural modular ones. They are an organized set of concepts and conceptual relations, rather than a logical structure, per se. In this sense, they can vary across cultures, and they are teachable or trainable. In these various senses, the concept presented by Case et al. differed notably in its properties relative to Piaget.

## *Research*

Case et al. (1993) administered a broad range of quantitative and social tasks to 5–8-year-olds. In the numerical domain, they predicted the children would pass through the following sequence: having separate counting and addition–subtraction skills (age 4), integrating them into a more advanced number concept (age 6; e.g., permitting the understanding of quantity as a dimension from low to high magnitudes), applying the new concept recursively, thereby allowing the understanding of two properties of dimensions/scales in one context (age 8), relating two dimensions or scales that are operating in one context (age 10). Note that this sequence of acquisitions in the numerical domain is consistent with Case's description of the substages through which children pass in this age period. Case et al. referred to the development of a "mental number line" in describing the numerical gains over the sequence.

As for the social domain, Case et al. focused on tasks related to social cognition. At age 4, children have the beginnings of understanding the intentions of others (in that they develop a theory of mind of the other). Then, children at age 6 can coordinate their theory of mind of the other with an understanding of prototypic narrative scripts or action sequences involving behavioral and intentional components. The most advanced level involved explaining social interaction in terms of two intentional states. These authors did not describe narrative structures for older children, but colleagues of Case have researched them (see the review below of McKeough & Griffiths, 2010). Case et al. referred to the development of a mental story line taking place in children as they pass through the steps in this sequence.

The researchers found that intertask correlations were moderately elevated, and by contrast, relations across the numerical and social cognitive tasks were more erratic. Factor analysis gave similar results – tasks in the same domain loaded together on one factor, but not on the other.

The first set of results supports the concept of central conceptual structures. In past research that tested Piaget's notion of *structures d'ensembles*, the results had been inconsistent. However, Case had structured well the tasks in this study, facilitating finding the associations across tasks within the domains indicated. When absolute level of performance was compared across the two domains, 70% of the children were within one half of a level on the two sets of tasks. The latter result suggests that there are general structural constraints that place limits on form and content of central conceptual structures.

## Conclusions

Case et al. acknowledged that one does not find universal structures in children across tasks within a domain, just the presence of consistencies. They could have emphasized the inconsistencies but preferred to underscore the general patterns found because the typical research had been discarding Piagetian notions of coherence within stages of development. They argued that development proceeds like the growth of a tree, and there is a common trunk and branches before reaching more delicate web-like structures, as described by Fischer and colleagues (e.g., Fischer, Knight, & Van Paris, 1993).

Case (1998) elaborated the concept of central conceptual structures. For example, for a variety of numerical tasks, first children develop a mental model, then two subdimensions, and then the capacity to formulate and apply an explicit rule for modeling the relationship between the dimensions. That this happens across a broad array of numerical concepts illustrates that children acquire a general concept of number that impacts their understanding and performance on multiple tasks in a domain. However, the structure does not generalize its advances outside the domain. Aside from the research on intertask associations, Case and colleagues have demonstrated the viability of the concept by finding that the passage through the sequence of steps takes place at a common rate and that training generalizes within domains, but not across.

## Interim Summary

I consider central conceptual structures as an intermediary structure between local schemes and larger units, such as substages or stages. They concern more the content of development, the what. Later in the chapter, I describe the work of Demetriou and colleagues, who have proposed an intermediary concept concerning how cognitions are regulated and produce regulation, that of hypercognition. Case has left a conceptual legacy that colleagues have continued to elaborate and explore. Their reach has extended across the lifespan, and also has included both work on the "what" of development and the "why."

## Case's Colleagues

### *Infant Development*

#### Introduction

Lewis and Granic (2010) described the relationship between Case's cognitive developmental model in the first 3 years and their model of phases in socioemotional development (see Table 10.1). For Lewis and Granic, cognitive substages that emerge in development serve as underpinnings for parallel social–emotional acquisitions. They are cognitive tools or software that help in interpreting the world and therefore help in explaining the appearance of each of the socioemotional phases that emerge corresponding to them.

Some of the substages in the model of socioaffective development proposed by Lewis and Granic have two corresponding phases. For the authors, the pattern in the latter phases reflects alternating periods of (a) greater stability, resilience, and

**Table 10.1** Stages and substages of cognitive development as a foundation for phases of social–emotional development across the first 4–5 years of life

| Cognitive stage/substage | Socialemotional development |
|---|---|
| Sensorimotor consolidation (0–4 months) | Basic regulation |
| | Interpersonal attention |
| Unifocal (sensorimotor) coordination (4–8 months) | Interpersonal expectancy |
| | Motor initiative |
| Bifocal (sensorimotor) coordination (8–12 months) | Social referencing |
| Elaborated (sensorimotor) coordination (12–18 months) | Motor practice |
| Unifocal (interrelational) coordination (1.5–2.5 years) | Social stabilization |
| | Social negotiation |
| Bifocal (interrelational) coordination (2.5–3.5 years) | Social comparison |
| | Family membership |
| Elaborated (interrelational) coordination (3.5–5 years) | Self-consciousness |

Adapted from Springer Science+Business Media with permission. Lewis, M. D., & Granic, I. (2010). [Figure 1, Page. 183]

This table demonstrates cognitive-affective correspondences based on the work of Case for cognitive development and workers like Mahler, Sander, and Trevarthen for socioaffective development. Case's model of stages and substages served as the cognitive axis in drawing the cognitive and emotional correspondences. Like Piaget, Case described six cognitive substages in the first 2 years of life. Lewis and Granic also considered another step, for the 2–3-year-olds. The authors found that a majority of the infancy substages have two steps in corresponding socioemotional acquisitions reliance on the self and (b) greater vulnerability, dependency, and sensitivity. In terms of the relationship with Casian substages, these pairs of phases reflect the following pattern. The developmental times that are more vulnerable correspond to transitions to the substages of unifocal and bifocal coordinations, and the more stable times indicate mark the substage of elaborated coordinations.

From the viewpoint of the study of emotions, although emotions derive from cognitive activities, cognition helps in appraisals and self-regulation. Therefore, the relationship between cognition and emotion is reciprocal.

The socioemotional model of phases described by Lewis and Granic is based on the work of Mahler, Pine, and Bergman (1975), Sander (1975), Sroufe (1979, 1996), Stern (1985), Tomasello (1995), and Trevarthen and Aitken (1994), in particular. The authors relate the developments in this sphere to corresponding Casian cognitive steps in development.

## Birth

In the cognitive substage of elaborated orienting (0–4 months), babies develop the first sensorimotor schemes, and regulate their bodily reactions, states, and physiology. Sander had referred to the stage as Basic Regulation. Infants at this age build up representations coordinating actions of the self and other. They smile, manage distress, engage in face-to-face exchange, and so on, relaxing between bouts. Young infants develop internal synchronies and external ones. However, they are limited cognitively by an inability to coordinate schemes, behave with double-component actions, and express actions with the intention of having particular effects occur.

In the second socioaffective phase that develops in correspondence to the substage of elaborated orienting (at 2.5–4.5 months), the baby enters a period labeled Interpersonal Attention. The baby gives attention to the other and engages in reciprocal interaction, such as in the sequence gaze/smile/coo/delight or joy. The caregiver is fascinated, which is a source of excitement and pleasure for the baby. The baby incorporates the caregiver's behaviors into schemes that represent their shared interpersonal interactions (and the baby experiences love and a sense of intersubjectivity). However, changes in familiar interactions can lead to frustration and distress. Lewis and Granic explained this reaction by proposing that the infant in this age period can construct isolated schemes representing continued social exchange so that any abrupt change violates the scheme.

## 4 Months

Next, the 4-month-old enters into the substage of unifocal sensorimotor actions, in which the infant can coordinate two sensorimotor schemes. The coordinated schemes are accompanied by a wish for, desire, or anticipation of an outcome, indicating the presence of intentional, goal-directed actions. In coordinating an action with an outcome, the intention is to produce an effect, a change in the environment, or a new state of affairs.

In terms of socioaffective acquisitions, this new cognitive capacity translates into the development of the phase of Interpersonal Expectancy. The baby "differentiates," in Mahler's terms, developing a sense of a separate self, I, and autonomy. Interactions go back and forth, and babies are appreciative. They initiate true play. They anticipate effects with excitement. They engage in true reciprocity, by tracking both their own actions and those of the other. They participate in social sequences both willingly and consciously. Toys become highly appealing and compelling. They love the world around them and increasingly shift their attention to it. Yet, they expect the caregiver to be available for play and experience frustration if that does not happen. Separation reactions begin to develop.

In the next phase of Motor Initiative, which develops from 5.5 to 7.5 months, the young infant is completing the cognitive substage of unifocal sensorimotor coordinations. Social–emotional reactions acquire the characteristic of stability. Play becomes routinized. Reactions to loss are more muted.

## 8 Months

With development of the next cognitive substage of bifocal sensorimotor actions, which manifests at about 8 months of age, the infant enters into the phase of Social Referencing. The infant turns to the caregiver to interpret how to react to ambiguous situations by examining her or his reactions. This can be explained by the cognitive quality of the substage, in which infants develop superordinate coordinations of unifocal coordinations. The infant can behave toward a goal and recruit the caregiver to help. The infant and caregiver now can share, and in their joyful interactions, it appears that there is a dance.

Cognitively, a true social cognition develops. Infants at this age can point at desired objects and recruit the caregiver to get it for them. They can engage in joint attention, gazing together at objects pointed at. They can understand other's goals (although not their intentions). However, if the caregiver departs, the infants might react with separation distress in an effort to retrieve the hidden person. Any sign of leaving could evoke clinging, whining, and demands. If it becomes chronic, the behavior can result in anxiety, distress, and instability.

## 12 Months

In the next phase, which develops at 12 months and follows from the development of the cognitive substage of elaborated sensorimotor coordinations, the infants enter the phase of motor practice. They explore the world gleefully. Cognitively, they can use schemes to reverse their actions. Their language skills blossom, and words represent wishes, goals, or thoughts, helping to augment a sense of a shared world. They are energetic, confident, proud, optimistic, independent, and act with authority.

## 18 Months

At 1.5 years, the substage of unifocal interrelations develops, and the corresponding phase that develops is called Social Negotiation. Because of symbolic activity, the toddlers experience a vital increase in language communication, in social relationships, in understanding, in achieving joint goals and cooperation, in the development of the self, and in realizing their presence in a family. Toddlers understand that they are social in nature, sharing with others. They can compare two possible goals, but this can encourage conflict. Although they are adamant about possession and territory, they can negotiate about the degree required in compliance. This leads to insecurity to accompany their feistiness. In terms of anxiety about separations, they concern more psychological as opposed to physical separation.

The substage of unifocal interrelations witnesses the development of a second social–emotional phase, that of social stabilization. The toddler is more assured, and there is a temporary respite from the "terrible twos" that had begun at 18 months. Desires are controlled, as impulse control accelerates.

## 24 Months

In the stage of bifocal interrelations, the phases of Social Comparison (from 2 to 3 years) and Family Membership (from 3 to 3.5 years) develop in succession. Cognitively, the Social Comparison substage concerns the capacity to double coordinate symbolic units. Therefore, the child can compare one's goals and those of parents, even engaging in power relations about goals. Defiance and negativity could develop. The children can imagine consequences and could feel jealousy. The latter develops because the caregiver's ministrations usually received can be compared to those of the newcomer in the family. Of course, there are children who mellow, become content, and are cooperative. In the phase of Family Membership, children generally are calmer. They know the rules, they adjust, and they regulate better their emotions. They are quite happy to play and love toys, which provide comfort when they feel lonely or anxious.

In the last phase to develop in the first 3 years, at the age of 3.5, children enter into the cognitive substage of elaborated interrelations and the phase of Self-consciousness. They develop a theory of the mind of the other, although the authors indicate that the relationship between Case's formulation of the stage evident at this age and the parallel development of the theory of mind has not been specifically elaborated in the literature. A theory of mind refers to the child's capacity to be aware that the other has goals, feelings, internal states, cognitions, beliefs, a mind, and so on, that are independent of one's own. Therefore, children at this age become skittish about what others might be thinking of them (for example, "badly"). They might develop insecurity, the need for acceptance, lower self-confidence, irrational fears, anxiety, embarrassment, intense shame, and self-consciousness.

### Comment

Lewis and Granic (2010) have presented a description of early cognitive and affective parallels that respects the literature, builds on the work of Case, and grasps well the whole child in one narrative account. With respect to the placement of emotions in the age periods mentioned, most are consistent with Case's previous work on the topic, as shown in Chap. 7. Nevertheless, some of the emotions that Lewis and Granic ascribe to infants and children do not fit the age periods suggested according to Case's prior work or my own. For example, they mention the development of love in the 1–4-month period, and generally this affect is attributed to older infants, although they applied the term to the love of objects. For the 4–8-month period, they list several affect-related terms that usually are taken to develop in full at a later age (appreciate, wish, anticipate, will, conscious), although it is understood that precursors for them could develop earlier. For the next two age periods, the same applies to their use of the terms of desire and pride, respectively – they are listed as developing earlier than is typical for when they are deemed full blown, so it is best to speak of precursors in the age periods ascribed to them by Lewis and Granic. By contrast, they indicate that jealousy develops in the 18-month-old, and the present model considers this to be an emotion that could develop at 12 months.

Aside from these discrepancies compared to the present work, the model of Lewis and Granic on the development of cognitive–affective parallels in development complements the Casian project for the early years. In addition, Lewis and Granic mention several affective acquisitions not described in Case that deserve further scrutiny – confidence/optimism at 12 months and defiance at 2 years. They mention theory of mind in relation to the 3-year-old, and I deal with the same correspondence in the present model. However, I hypothesize an explicit link across the development of theory of mind and the cognitive substages of the present model.

## *Narrative Structure from a Casian Perspective*

### Narrative and Central Conceptual Structures

*Introduction.* McKeough and Griffiths (2010) explored further the development of narrative knowing in terms of central conceptual structures, which they describe as a central social structure for the narrative domain and for related domains (Case & Okamoto, 1996). McKeough and Griffiths (2010) provided a clear summary of the recent history in the study of narrative.

McKeough and Griffiths explained that by learning about the intention of others in stories and other narratives, children learn to better interpret intentions with appropriate meanings. Moreover, children learn to better understand event sequences that take place in their personal lives. Ways of knowing involve narrative thought and modes as much as the "paradigmatic" thought of concepts and categories (Bruner, 1986).

The central social structures that develop in children reflect narrative structure and development. They are culturally specific narratives that help make social meaning and organize social activity. They include not only storytelling structure but also structures related to understanding parental motivations, relating empathically to peers, and so on.

*Model.* As for the steps through which oral telling skills develop, according to McKeough and Griffiths (2010), they follow the Casian model. Specifically, the 4-year-old tells stories that are action-related, with one structure possible for representing mental state. Next, the 6-year-old can coordinate two different structures involving mental states. The intention of the protagonist drives the plot of the story. By age 8, children's stories have added either a failed subplot or problem, thereby requiring a second coordination of units. By age 10, narrative structures contain causal relations in external events and in internal feelings and mental states. For example, protagonists are motivated by feelings, thoughts, and desires. At the 12-year age period, adolescents can combine narrative units, such as in interpreting protagonist intentions. They create combined narratives in terms of longer-lasting attributes that are discerned based on combined experiences they have had, rather than by interpreting them based on immediate, context-related intentions and mental states. By age 14, the stories told evidence differentiated personality structure, e.g., of competing character traits. By age 18, adolescents create a dialectic over internal and external struggles and can arrive at coherent narratives.

*Research.* The sequence described by McKeough and Griffiths (2010) in the development of storytelling skill is not only derived from Case's model of stages and substages of cognitive development, but also it has been tested in studies of adolescent narratives. They administered four paper-and-pencil tasks to students in grades 5, 7, and 10 (story composition, family story interpretation, moral reasoning, social decision making). The tasks loaded substantially on a single factor, which they labeled as Narrative Knowledge. Moreover, the results confirmed the developmental sequence proposed in terms of Case's model.

The authors queried whether the central conceptual structures reflect underlying neurobiological influences. They related the acquisitions in this period to factors such as increased executive function skills and self-regulation, and metacognitive processes in the frontal lobes in adolescence (e.g., Mar, 2004).

McKeough, Davis, Forgeron, Marini, and Fung (2005) provided storytelling instructions to first graders. They demonstrated that through training children can improve in their narrative complexity and cohesion. For McKeough et al., typically, a story consists of a core narrative structure, and the child's ability to incorporate all its elements builds rapidly (Applebee, 1978; Mandler, 1984). Aside from syntactic and narrative structure, children have to learn the semantic structure of stories, such as story cohesion (Halliday & Hasan, 1976). An example of cohesion is that logical connections between events are built with certain connecting words, such as conjunctives. In their research, the authors focus on conjunctives, such as use of the words *and*, *then*, *because/so*, and *but*. These words are examples of the four types of conjunctive cohesive ties – additive, temporal, causal, and adversative.

McKeough et al. based their study of the relationship between cognitive, narrative, and cohesion development uniquely on this series of words.

Relative to a control group that received a standard, process-oriented (how to) intervention in storytelling, with the training received, the experimental group improved in story complexity and in the use of and quality in cohesion. The training was comprehensive: e.g., multimodal; pictures, graphics; oral discussion of the stories, text; introducing the "superglue" words, the conjunctives; and labeling and discussing plot structure (problem, failed attempt, resolution), story elements (setting, characters, plot), and narrative landscapes (actions, mental states). Further analyses revealed that performance was influenced by the cognitive complexity of task demands (Tables 10.2 and 10.3).

## Comment

This study is an important one for the purposes of the present book because it indicates the confluence of cognitive and narrative development, and the role that evolution through cognitive substages in the former influences the latter. Moreover, the research reported is quite consistent with the present model because in the age range considered there is quite an overlap in description of the cognitive substages posited, which are Case's, and the contents of the present cognitive stage and substage model.

**Table 10.2** Model of narrative development in McKeough

| | Plot structure | Literary structure | Socioaffective structure |
|---|---|---|---|
| Action/ event structure (leads to below) | Sequence of physical events and states (I do "A" then I do "B") | First-order event structure Script: discrete events are temporally, causally, and referentially bound (timeline reporting) | Affect limited to one event or one affect and its opposite |
| Intentional structure (leads to below) | Events and states in physical world are related to mental states (I do "A" and "B" because I feel/think "X" and "Y") | Second-order event structure Simple plot of folktale: event sequences are temporally, causally, and referentially bound (each event selected for purpose, e.g., initiating event) | Affect occurs transsituationally. One effect transforms into another via external events |
| Interpretive structure | Mental states are related to character's psychological make-up (I feel "X" and "Y" because I am a certain type of person) | Third-order event structure Complex plot of short story episode sequences are temporally, causally and referentially bound (each episode selected for a purpose, e.g., foreshadowing or flashback) | Situational affect is long terms and so defines character independently of external situation – "the long shadow of the past" is cast on the present |

**Table 10.3** Cognitive levels in narrative scoring in McKeough

| Stage | Level (and age) | Narrative plot-structure |
|---|---|---|
| Preintentional, social | 0 (<4 yr) | |
| Action | 1 (4) | Does the story have a sequence of events that are temporally, causally, or referentially related and that occur exclusively in the physical world of action and events? (Note: "happily ever after" not scored as a mental state) |
| Intentional | 2 (6) | Does the story include explicit or implicit reference to the mental states that motivate action in the physical world and is there a problem that is immediately resolved in the end? |
| | 3 (8) | Does the story have a problem, a series of failed attempts or complications followed by a resolution (not necessarily solving the problem), such that additional mental states are mentioned or implied in the context of the story? |
| | 4 (10) | Does one impediment or a well-developed subplot have more significance than the others, thereby also broadening the characters' intention/mental states? Is the impediment dealt with in the outcome, with the result that the resolution has a well-planned feeling? |
| Interpretive | 5 (12) | Does the focus of the story shift from the characters' mental states to *why* particular mental states are held? Does a constellation of mental states or constellation of social circumstances create a psychological profile or character trait that is represented across time and situations? |
| | 6 (14) | Are additional traits represented, such that a dialectic is created wherein the interaction of two states or traits lead to further psychologically oriented complications? |
| | 7 (18) | Does the dialectical relation between states or traits act as an integrating device lending a greater sense of coherence to the story? |



Finally, it prepares the way for presentation of the procedural and coding recommendations made in the present work toward relating cognitive and narrative development. In particular, I recommend that not only should similar research be undertaken using the present model of stages and substages in cognitive development, I also recommend that the research considered using the extensive scoring system on textual cohesion, coherence, and syntactic structure developed by the author (G. Young, L. Young, & Duceppe, see Chaps. 33 and 34).

Note that Halliday and Hasan have developed an extensive functional model of cohesion categories of which conjunction is but one. For example, they include other categories considered more prominent than conjunction, such as reference and lexical cohesion. However, the exemplars in these categories are difficult to discern and code relative to the simpler connectives. In general, there has been little work on the relationship between cognition and cohesion, and the complexity of Halliday and Hasan's system probably is part of the reason. Aside from the difficulties presented by its numerous categories and words, the system also is difficult to analyze because it does not lend itself to statistical analysis, especially when one word at a time is considered, such as in the work of McKeough. In this regard, I present in Chaps. 33 and 34 a coherent system of scales that can be used to measure each of the categories of cohesion as developed by Halliday and Hasan, and other researchers who have worked from their perspective, as well as scales on coherence and syntactic structure.

McKeough et al. used the cohesive category of conjunctives in their research on cognitive complexity and narrative development not only because of its relative simplicity but also because research on the use of the category by children generally has indicated a developmental progression from simpler forms to more complex forms and from less use to more frequent use. Specifically, the order of acquisition appears to be: additive, temporal, causative, and adversative (Bennett-Kastor, 1986; Bloom, Lahey, Hood, Lifter, & Fiess, 1980; Fox, 1993), with the development in frequency of use of the forms the same, except that the category of adversative conjunction is used as much as causative conjunction. The review of this literature undertaken by McKeough et al. confirms the present emphasis that within each category of cohesive devices, the exemplars can be graded on a scale of complexity or development.

## *Cognition and Emotion*

### Systems

#### Introduction

Lewis (2005a) indicated how cognition and emotions form higher-order integrated structures. Lewis argued that major approaches to the study of emotion–cognition relations include appraisal theory, functional theory, and the study of personality and clinical disorders. Appraisals concern the evaluation of a situation with respect to its personal relevance, especially in terms of goals and well-being (Lazarus, 1968). Through appraisals, the person extracts meaning from events in effort to understand the context or world. Appraisals are organized according to dimensions. In addition, they are considered antecedent to emotions, both causally and temporally. This claim has been controversial, and current appraisal theorists are undertaking moment-by-moment analyses to ascertain better the role of appraisals in emotion generation while admitting that they can influence appraisals (e.g., Scherer, 2001).

Process models of appraisal break it down into component processes. For example, Leventhal and Scherer (1987) described sensorimotor and schematic processing levels operating prior to cognitive evaluation, and others refer to rapid, preattentive, or coarse processing or preliminary appraisals (e.g., Scherer, 1999). Nevertheless, these concepts reflect psychological wholes separate from underlying neural processes.

In the functional approach, the direction of influence runs the reverse, from emotions to cognition. Emotions differentially function to direct attention to salient contextual aspects and promote corresponding action tendencies that could be implemented to changing them, depending on feasibility. In this perspective, attention is a motivated cognitive function and cognition is constrained by the nature of the emotion involved (e.g., Derryberry & Tucker, 1994).

In the personality-clinical perspective, traits are understood to condition cognitive filters used to perceive the world. For example, anxious personality type or anxious clinical disorder increases the probability of appraisals that limit the world to anxiety-generating conditions. Therefore, they can endure and increasingly color these perceptions and the action tendencies associated with them.

Lewis noted some attempts to integrate these differing perspectives, but generally they still considered cognition and emotions as separate although interacting entities. He argued that the field should consider developing more integrated concepts, such as appraisal–emotion amalgams. Concepts such as these allow construction of both momentary and more stable complexes having bidirectional causal relations across higher-order and lower-order components of the whole, including at the neural level. In appraisal–emotion amalgams, emotional interpretation passes through several phases. After a trigger phase, there is a self-amplification phase and then a self-stabilization phase, which are concepts reflective of dynamic systems.

## Nonlinear Dynamical Systems

Lewis used dynamic systems modeling as a bridge between emotion theory and neurobiology. Lewis described critical properties essential to understand nonlinear dynamical systems modeling. Nonlinear dynamical systems theory has overarching concepts, such as the following:

(a) Self-organization. A critical concept in the generative ability of nonlinear dynamical systems relates to self-organization and circular causality (Haken, 1977). In self-organization, coherent wholes can emerge and stabilize from the nonlinear interaction of constituent components of the system of which they are part. For example, newer conceptions of cognition maintain that it builds on itself, channeling its own outcomes, and also it derails deterministic predictability from one moment to the next by way of such processes. This can happen because of multiple feedback cycles that recursively and exponentially alter input through damping and amplifying processes. In these processes, output is reconfigured, perhaps even at higher levels of integration. Therefore, output is not simply a transduced, reductionist expression of the input as processed in the brain.
(b) Emergence. In emergent order, novel forms arise without inherent programming in the system, after a perturbation that upsets the equilibrium of the system; they lose degrees of freedom as they self-organize toward increasing coherence and orderliness.
(c) Positive feedback. Change in a system can lead to further changes, by amplification or autocatalysis. The new system configuration might have grown new

patterns that could be exponentially differentiating. However, the danger of positive feedback is that it runs away, and it helps break down the system's ability to handle the change.

(d) Negative feedback. Negative feedback reciprocally counters or inhibits positive feedback. It generally resists perturbations so that runaway processes are contained and stability is maintained. This takes place via negative feedback loops that keep the system in equilibrium or a continuous oscillation. Deviations are dampened and conflicts or discrepancies resolved, as the system seeks out entrainment across other system circuits and also global orderliness despite perturbations and disequilibrium pressures.

(e) Circular causality. Circular causality refers to bidirectional influences between different levels of a system. Higher-order wholes can emerge from the interaction of lower-order parts through bidirectional causal processes. The reciprocal layers of a system operate through interrelated, recursive, and multiple causal interactions. Higher-order forms can influence or "cause" lower-order couplings in system components, and these in turn can influence or "cause" higher-order forms. Examples of constraining top-down forms, or "enslaving" higher-order parameters, include appraisals, which may take nested forms of different levels.

(f) Complexity, attractors. Systems might coordinate into an increased complexity, such as when secondary appraisals complement primary ones. Systems coalesce into attractors that can move through phase transitions at bifurcation thresholds to new stabilities.

Lewis explains that neural processes do not have separate cognition and emotional centers that interact and communicate with each other. Rather, often the same centers might mediate functions that seem at once appraisal-oriented and emotion-oriented. Coherence governs behavior and its components so that it can effect accurate interpretation of context and adaptive response to it. Five mechanisms serve to cohere binding of appraisal and emotional systems: (a) nested feedback loops and self-synchronization; neuromodulation; vertical integration; action monitoring; and plasticity and learning. For example, for the first mechanism, there are three motivation-related loops that Lewis has elaborated based on contemporary neuroscience. The loops include positive and negative feedback mechanisms that interact in these integrated brain structures involved in appraisal and emotional processes (see Fig. 21.5).

## Comment

Lewis gathered much evidence in support of his model, and it is beyond the scope the present work to analyze it in detail. Suffice it to say that it is consistent with the present effort to integrate dynamic concepts into understanding emotions and their integration with cognitions. Lewis did not deal much with development, but he dismissed the commentary by Izard, Trentacosta, and King (2005) that in infancy there might be more of a cognitive-emotion separation. For example, for them, infants cannot cope well with stress. Lewis (2005b) responded that infants might look away to regulate their emotions.

Another commentary of interest to the present work is by Thayer and Lane (2005). They underscored the importance of inhibition in dynamical models related to emotion. Inhibitory processes are critical as systems move from one attractor or another, and also in each step in the sequence that Lewis described of trigger, self-amplification (through disinhibition), and self-stabilization phases. They wrote: "Inhibitory processes provide for the sculpting of neural action at all levels of the neuraxis" (p. 219). For example, they described that Constantinidis, Williams, and Goldman-Rakic (2002) found that activity in inhibitory interneurons in the prefrontal cortex of monkeys were influential at transition points in behavioral sequences. Similarly in terms of neurotransmitters, enhancement of GABA has been shown to efficiently synchronize larger populations of neurons (Fingelkurts et al., 2004). At the psychological level, perseverance in behavior might reflect a breakdown in underlying inhibition. For example, in the context of a study of conditioning, patients with generalized anxiety disorder demonstrated heart rate acceleration to threat words and a bias in explicit memory for such words, along with an associated failure to habituate to neutral words. Thayer and Lane (2005) related this to a similar study with mice showing enhanced reactivity to threat stimuli due to a reduced GABA-related receptor neuronal clustering.

The inhibitory approach espoused by Thayer and Lane (2005) and by myself in the present book is not inconsistent with a dynamical systems modeling approach. Rather, it adds to it, for example, by helping explain the different feedback mechanisms described in Lewis' (2005a) dynamical systems modeling of conjoined appraisals and emotions.

Lewis (2005c) elaborated his dynamical model developmentally in several ways. First, he indicated that as development proceeds there is a loss of degrees of freedom, or the addition cascading constraints, while trajectories take form. Also, he referred to real-time and longer-term developmental time periods functioning not only both experientially and in within- and cross-brain organization but also neuronally, revealing the synchrony of self-organization in development across multiple levels. For example, research has demonstrated that neuromodulator arousal facilitates long-term neuronal potentiation and that neuropeptide action consolidates changes at the synapse and enhances memory formation (e.g., Adamec, Kent, Anisman, Shallow, & Merali, 1998; Centonze, Picconi, Gubellini, Bernardi, & Calabresi, 2001, respectively). Synapses are elaborated (proliferate, strengthen) and pruned as they self-organize. For example, pruning of synapses in the prefrontal cortex takes place at the speed of 2,000/s (Spear, 2000), but only overtakes synaptic elaboration and proliferation in adolescence!

## *Development of Cognition–Emotion Relationships*

Lewis and Cook (2007) examined the relationship between cognition and emotion in infancy from a dynamical systems perspective. They examined 12 infants longitudinally in dyadic interaction with their mothers in 16 videotaped sessions from

12 to 55 weeks of age. They administered two sensorimotor tasks and a frustration-inducing task. From 12 to 24 weeks, a reach and grasp task and an adjusted reach task were administered. From 27 to 55 weeks, the infants were administered a hidden object task and a cloth pull task. The first two tasks involved (a) reach and palm touch and (b) adjust reach to moving object, respectively. The second set of tasks involved (a) remove object from cup and (b) pull object on cloth but out of reach, respectively. The frustration task involved a series of toy gives and takes.

The researchers coded for attention and distress and established the degree of attentional return after disengagement. They found reduced rates of re-engagement (slower return time) to the mother's face at the age periods of 4.5 and 9 months, although not if the infants were distressed, but they did not find similar results for the frustration task. The dynamic analyses undertaken through event history analyses (determining the degree to which past attentional events determine subsequent transitions) revealed the developmental shifts. The age periods involved are consistent with predictions from Case's theory of sensorimotor transitions, which parallel those of Piaget. The authors concluded that by focusing on structure or form rather than content of behavior, they could establish the normative patterns found despite the individual differences present.

## *Emotion-Cognitive Self-Regulation*

### The Neuropsychology of Self-Regulation

#### Introduction

Lewis, Todd, and Xu (2010) examined the neuropsychological underpinnings of emotion regulation. Self-regulation includes cognitive and emotional regulation, and it is the term used more frequently, so I refer to their work using this generic label. In this regard, Lewis et al. (2010) indicated that cognitive operations and emotional processes are integrated and are not differentiated in the brain. Lewis et al. (2010) related self-regulation to executive function, viewing it as a specific subclass of the function. Self-regulation could follow a cognitive act or could precede it as an anticipatory mechanism. In this perspective, cognitive operations and emotional reactions are related in a feedback process and drive each other. Cognition and emotion continuously affect each other. Emotions are not imposed on cognitive activities, but both are components of a self-organizing and self-regulating system. The system does not have a master regulator; rather, the components synchronize spontaneously.

From a developmental perspective, researchers have noted a correspondence between specific advances in cognition and change in regulatory skills. The former includes acquisitions of object permanence, specific language skills, and false-belief understanding. The latter refers to changes in the style and efficacy of self-regulation

(Carlson, Moses, & Claxton, 2004). Other research refers to the relationship between self-processes and control of emotions, impulses, and behavior, in general (e.g., Lewis, Sullivan, Stanger, & Weiss, 1989).

At the neuropsychological level, Lewis et al. (2010) indicated that self-regulation develops partly due to experience-dependent processes of synaptic shaping. This involves cortical pruning, competition, and specialization, which lead to individual differences in cortical architecture. In addition, specialized cortical regions become increasingly intercoordinated, forming extensive neural networks having increased efficiency in a variety of functions (e.g., Fair et al., 2009). In the next section, I indicate the particular cortical regions in the brain involved in this systemic development of interactions in the relationship of cognition and emotion.

## Neuropsychology

Lewis turned his attention to older children in an article with Woltering (Woltering & Lewis, 2009). They examined developmental pathways in intrinsic emotion regulation from a neuropsychological point of view. The authors described an earlier developing reactive emotional regulation and a later developing deliberate one that builds on the first one (e.g., Philips, Ladouceur, & Drevets, 2008). Reactive emotion regulation is more automatic, bodily, involuntary, fast, and stimulus-driven, having implicit evaluations of objects or events, a concept that is akin to Damasio's (1994) notion of somatic markers. Deliberative emotion regulation is slower in speed, more reflective, and more sensitive to context and open to strategy. Although it might not be conscious, it is still intentional, requiring executive control. It emerges at about 2 years of age, but there are also some earlier signs of its emergence.

In terms of developmental neuroscience, the authors argued that specific neural "hubs" or anchor points serve as central foci or epicenters in the cortical–subcortical coupling involved (e.g., in the anterior cingulate cortex and the orbitofrontal cortex; both prefrontal cortical regions). The brain appears to be organized vertically (brain stem, diencephalon, limbic system, striatum, and cortex; Tucker, Derryberry, & Luu, 2000), with emotion regulation taking place both within and between levels. Emotions are both regulated and regulatory in this process.

The two types of emotion regulation mediated by the cortex become coordinated throughout the hubs and levels of the neuroaxis. If they develop inefficiencies, a lack of coordination, or other developmental problem, the result could be the development of behaviors indicative of under- or over-control in reactive emotional regulation (e.g., aggressive regulatory style and anxious regulatory style, respectively).

Lewis and Todd (2007) elaborated that autoregulation is both emotional and cognitive. For example, at the cognitive level, executive processes participate in autoregulation. They are typically cortically controlled, voluntary, and allow for planning and intelligent action, e.g., in the development of directed attention, response inhibition, selection from among alternative courses of action, directed monitoring, adaptive responses to contingencies, dealing with challenges and conflicts, effortful control, conscious decision making, deliberative self-guidance, judgment, and goal orientation. They work top-down to influence bottom-up subcortical regulations, which are more automatic, nonvoluntary, and prepotent. They focus on response to the environment with energy, focus, direction, and accumulation of salient meanings in relevant emotion-guided activity. The two types of regulation form a reciprocal interactivity that produces the stream of behavior, and form a macrosystem with feedback circuits. As mentioned, they are centered in different neural hubs, with the anterior cingulate cortex and the limbic-hypothalamic-brain-stem systems (especially the amygdala) being the respective seats involved.

## Comments

In this article, Lewis and Todd (2007) appear to be offering a complementary perspective to the prior one of different emotional regulation neural hubs in the cortex by describing a subcortical one, too. This model is consistent with the one they offer of vertical integration in the neuroaxis. The authors also describe that different selves might be associated with each epicenter, for example, a thoughtful self might be associated with the cortical levels. This line of argument is consistent with Case's model of development of the self according to stages and substages, as well as my own model on the topic. In addition, the authors relate hemispheric specialization to their concept of epicenters, for example, the right hemisphere involves more cortico-limbic autoregulation and the left more intrafrontal system connections. This addition of hemispheric specialization to their model of regulation speaks to the present model of the development of hemispheric specialization skills and how these skills relate to the unfolding of stages and substages in cognitive development and parallel acquisitions.

Lewis and Todd elaborated that autoregulation is not necessarily self-regulation because the self is a complex concept that might not have specific corresponding brain centers. Similarly, the neat distinction between the frontal cortex and amygdala controlling more cognitive and emotional processes, respectively, is a heuristic because there is overlap. They find premature the attempt to divide executive processing into cool vs. hot varieties that reflect more cognitive relative to emotional processes. Other neural hubs have been proposed (e.g., the hippocampus as the center for intentionality in regulation; e.g., Freeman, 2000), but by adapting a vertical integration model they can incorporate other such models.

Lewis and colleagues did not explore their work on emotional regulation in terms of Neo-Piagetian cognitive stages and substages in development, but it might be worth pursuing. For example, does an aggressive style impede the cognitive coordinations, mappings, hierarchizations, and systematizations needed to organize self in relation to the other and environment in efforts to obtain an adaptive balance in control? As Thompson, Lewis, and Calkins (2008) argued, emotional regulation is not merely a reaction to emotional elicitation, but an ongoing component of emotional activation and it needs to be studied developmentally in its own right.

## *Hypercognition and Domains*

### Hypercognition

One Neo-Piagetian theorist whom I have not yet discussed is Demetriou (e.g., Demetriou, Spanoudis, & Mouyi, 2010), whose work on hypercognition deserves detailed description because of its applicability to the types of questions posed in this book. He has combined his model with Case's model of stages and substages in cognitive development, adding to its utility. In addition, he described how different domains of cognitive function develop over different age periods. The ages are consistent with Case's substage sequence and my own.

Demetriou et al. presented a Neo-Piagetian developmental model involving three components. They used Case's model of stages as one axis, adding his concept of central conceptual structures (see Fig. 10.1). They described specialized domains of thought, as well. In addition, they described processing mechanisms.

The domains refer to specialized capacity spheres, such as standard verbal, mathematical, and spatial reasoning. In their research, they added categorical,

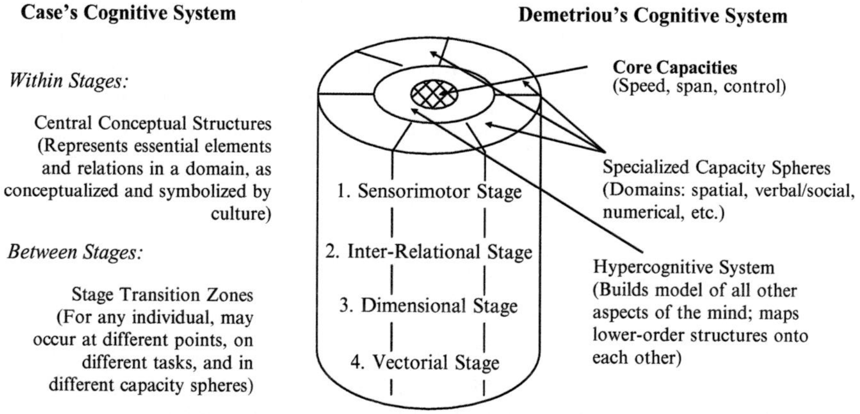


**Fig. 10.1** The general model of the architecture of the developing mind integrating concepts from the theories of Demetriou and Case. Demetriou et al. present a combined model of their work on the hypercognitive system and Case's concepts of stages in development and central conceptual structures within stages. The stages are based on Piaget, and the concept of central conceptual structures resembles Piaget's concept of *structures d'ensembles*, but it allows better for individual differences. Demetriou et al.'s concept of the hypercognitive system helps explain how individual differences are constructed in development. The hypercognitive system helps build cognitive models, supervising lower-order components of the cognitive system, and is conditioned by core capacities such as speed of processing. It applies to different domains or spheres, and is constrained by the stage in which the developing person is found. The present work presents a similar model to that of Demetriou et al., but it is constructed on the present model of five stages with five cyclically recurring substages. Also, I describe cognitive/socioaffective complexes that are posited to function like the hypercognitive system. However, through the concept of complexes, I add the socioemotional aspect thought important in underlying developing cognitive structures and mechanisms. Reprinted with the permission of Springer Science+Business Media. Demetriou, A., Spanoudis, G., & Mouyi, A. (2010). [Figure 1, Page. 10]

causal, and social reasoning. Factor analytic studies with children and adolescents yielded separate factors in the six domains. They used a large number of tasks for each domain and concluded that their interrelations in the factor structure supported Case's concept of central conceptual structures.

Demetriou et al. also posited that a hypercognitive system mediates the application of core capacities to the domains. Core capacities include processing speed, span (or representational capacity, e.g., Baddeley, 2007), and control (e.g., inhibiting a dominant but irrelevant response). The hypercognitive system builds models integrating other aspects of mind, mapping lower-order ones on higher-order ones. Hypercognition takes place both online and in the long term, where it is akin to consciousness.

Demetriou, Mouyi, and Spanoudis (2010) examined the research on mapping the developing mind and brain. First, they showed that different cognitive domains are served by different but overlapping neural networks (Galaburda, 2002). Jung and Haier (2007) developed an integrated model of networks underlying general or fluid intelligence, and referred to it as the "parietofrontal integration theory" (P-FIT) of intelligence. Demetriou, Mouyi et al. (2010) maintained that the sensory areas in the P-FIT model, in addition to other information-specific areas, seem related more to the domains of verbal, spatial, reasoning, or quantitative reasoning. The parietal area seems more related to information integration, meaning making, and inferential processes. The frontal area seems more related to working memory, attention, and executive control. Finally, the anterior cingulate seems more related to intentional planning, inhibition, and conscious selection of responses. They found that the P-FIT model was quite consistent with their hypercognitive one.

## Domains

### The Model

In general, modally, the domains develop from few less reality-oriented steps to more representations, and ones that are reciprocally constructed with the environment. Rules and principles develop that bridge more local concepts. Problem solving becomes less global and more differentiated and integrated. Development proceeds through better planning and use of alternatives and flexibility to reflection upon problem solving processes and cognition. There is an increasing self-guidance and self-awareness.

Although the ages given in their work on modal characteristics of the specific domains correspond to those age ranges associated with Case's substages in development, the authors did not take the step of relating the steps in domain development to Case's substages in development. However, in the following, I show a few interesting correspondences in this regard. Demetriou et al.'s developmental class of "single criterion classes" at 5–6 years of age seems to correspond with Case's description of the cognitive abilities in this age period as involving unifocal dimensions in thinking. Similarly, the description of the age period of 7–8 as involving logical multiplication seems to fit with Case's description of the cognitive substage in this period as involving bifocal dimensions in thinking. (Case used the label of dimensions to replace Piaget's use of the term for the stage in this period as concrete operations).

Comment

However, closer inspection of the series of classes proposed by Demetriou et al. indicates a better correspondence with my model of substages in development than Case's. For example, my equivalent stage in the 7–9 year period is called perioperational multiplication, so it uses the very same adjective of Demetriou et al. for their example. Also, note that this class is the first one in Demetriou's sequence that uses the word "logical," consistent with Piaget who had indicated that the development of logical, concrete operations develops at about 7 years. As for the prior period of 5–6 years, Demetriou et al. referred to it without the adjective of logical, which is consistent with my model in which this age period is still associated with preoperations and not concrete operations. However, for Case, the dimensional stage begins in this age period and not the one after, unlike for myself, and apparently unlike for Demetriou et al., too.

There are other examples to note in Demetriou et al.'s series of classes in domain development that are quite consistent with my model relative to Case's. For example, for the 3–4-year age period, some examples for protoclasses implicate a hierarchization, as I would predict. For the 9–10-year period, integrations seem evident, as in my model. For the 11–12 year period, the first example concerns coordination, consistent with my model. For the 13–14 year period, hierarchizations are described, as I would predict. For the 15–16 year period, I refer to systematization, and Demetriou et al. refers to networks.

Note that the model of Case provides a better correspondence to the work of Demetriou than the model of Fischer. Case's model has a substage at each age period that Demetriou et al. posit in which a class evolves (3.5–15), but Fischer's model is missing several relevant age periods in this time frame.

Demetriou has combined his model with a stage one. In this regard, he used the model of Case rather than Fischer (see Fig. 10.1). Nevertheless, the argument being made is that the present model might provide a better fit. However, it needs to be kept in mind that I have developed a combined model of my own, Case's, and Fischer's, and that my original model builds on the ones of both Fischer and Case.

## Other Considerations

Demetriou and Raftopoulous (2004) related the sequence of acquisitions in the various domains presented in Table 10.4 to their underlying representations. In the table, there are seven age periods from 3 to 15 years of age. Demetriou (2004) attributed, respectively, to these age periods the following representations; protorepresentations, dual representations, integrated representations, systems of representations, transcendent representations, foresighted representations, and implicit representations. Moreover, he added another level of principled representations.

Demetriou and Raftopoulos (1999) presented a model of the cognitive change process. They described five specific mechanisms that help bring about change, with each one being associated with a different type of change. The five mechanisms are bridging, interweaving, fusion, differentiation, and refinement. Bridging refers to the construction of a new mental scheme by establishing relations between units or

**Table 10.4** Modal characteristics of the specialized domains in development

| Age | Class | Number | Cause | Space | Verbal | Hyper |
|---|---|---|---|---|---|---|
| 3–4 | Protocategories | Protoquantitative schemes | Protocausal schemes | Global images | Primary reasoning | Differentiation between modalities (perception vs. knowing) |
| 5–6 | Single criterion classes | Coordination of protoquantitative schemes | Coordination of protocausal schemes | Single spatial dimensions or operations | Permission rules | Understanding the stream of consciousness and inner speech |
| 7–8 | Logical multiplication | Number concepts and quantitative dimensions | Experience-based prototheories | "Fluent" mental imagery | Explicit influence | Grasp of the constructive nature of thought |
| 9–10 | Logical multiplication on unfamiliar context | Construction of simple math relations (e.g., $a+5=8$) | Testable theories in action | Representation of complex realities | Logical necessity | Differentiation between cognitive functions (memory vs. attention) |
| 11–12 | Flexible logical multiplication | Proportional reasoning. Coordination of symbolic structures | Suppositions, isolation of variables | Imagination of the nonreal | Logical validity of propositions | Differentiation between clearly different domains (space vs. mathematics) |
| 13–14 | Strategic classification including relevant-irrelevant information | Algebraic reasoning based on mutually specified symbol systems | Hypothesis-driven experimentation | Originality in mental images | Grasp of formal relations | Awareness of specialized mental operations within a domain |
| 15–16 | Multilevel classes networks of classification criteria | Generalized concept of variable | Integrated theory building | Personal imaginal worlds, esthetic criteria | Reasoning on reasoning | Integrated cognitive theory |

Reprinted with the permission of Springer Science+Business Media. Demetriou, A., Spanoudis, G., & Mouyi, A. (2010). [Table 1, Page. 25]
The research of Demetriou and colleagues consistently has found six major domains, or cognitive spheres. These domains relate to the typical ones of verbal skills and mathematics, but also include other Piagetian categories, such as space and cause. Notable is that Demetriou and colleagues described how the domain acquisitions progress from age to age. The concept of domain is quite widespread in psychology, but Demetriou et al. have narrowed down their amount to six ones that are empirically supported

systems that already have been constructed. Interweaving involves an integration of unrelated mental units or systems that exist within the same organizational framework. The new construction might be preferred in cognitive activity. Fusion involves the creation of a new mental unit or system that frequently leads to the total incorporation of the units such that they are no longer available, or "disappear." Differentiation differs from the other mechanisms discussed so far because it takes an available mental unit or system and increases its accuracy, focus, or mapping. Refinement involves letting go or eliminating previously used mental units or systems because they are no longer relevant or they are redundant. The authors contrast their suggested mechanisms of change to those of Case (1985) and Fischer and Pipp (1984). For example, the concepts in Fischer and Pipp (1984) of intercoordination, compounding, and focusing are similar to the concepts presented by Demetriou and Raftopoulos of bridging, interweaving, and differentiation, respectively (Fig. 10.2).

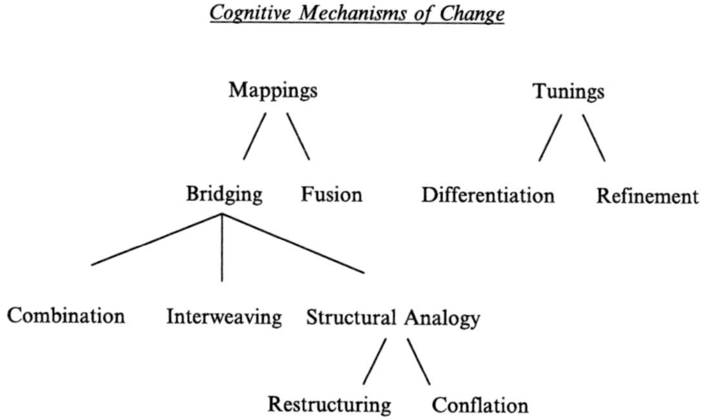


**Fig. 10.2** The taxonomy of mechanisms of change. Demetriou and Raftopoulos (1999) have posited five types of conceptual change at the cognitive level: bridging, interweaving, fusion, differentiation, and refinement. In this version of the model, bridging and fusion are considered components of mappings, and differentiation and refinement are considered components of tunings. Bridging is further broken down into components, one of which is interweaving. New components include combination, restructuring, and conflation. The model is consistent with and inclusive of cognitive mechanisms of change presented by others. The advantage of the system proposed in the present model is that the substages are described in language akin to the language of these diverse conceptual systems (the substages are labeled coordination, hierarchization, systematization, multiplication, integration). Moreover, they are taken to reflect a fractalization process so that the quality of the five stages within which the five substages recur recyclically are seen to possess the same characteristics implicit in the substage terms to which each of them corresponds. Moreover, there are steps that should be taking place within the substages corresponding to these five terms, in that the fractalization process takes place at different levels of complexity of the system. As for mechanisms of change that can boost passage through the steps at any one level, the language of nonlinear dynamical systems theory appears to provide an understanding of global mechanisms of change that are applicable to these stage, substage, and step transitions. It should be noted that when earlier versions of the model of Demetriou and colleagues was originally presented, they maintained that it reflected a developmental ordering. This fits the present model in which the equivalent of mechanisms of change (called substages, as explained, and which constitute the contents of change) pass through five substages within each stage described. Reprinted with the permission of Cambridge University Press. Raftopoulos, A., & Constantinou, C. P. (2004). Copyright © 1996 Cambridge University Press. [Figure 2.1, Page. 80]

## Summary and Conclusions

Case's colleagues keep elaborating and expanding his work, as shown in the present chapter. The work of Fischer and colleagues keeps enlarging, as well, both theoretically and empirically. The following chapters provide details on Fischer's full model. This in-depth coverage of the work of Fischer and colleagues and Case and colleagues allows for a deeper compare–contrast analysis across the two theories, and with my own. At the same time, the analysis of their collected work brings out new ideas that I have incorporated into my model.

For example, the work of Case on central conceptual structures is a welcome departure on the usual Neo-Piagetian focus on isolated acquisition of skills. There could be some of the coherence over skills that Piaget had described, although not at the level of full integration overall acquisitions in a stage. Moreover, the nature of any integration would be for individualized neuronal network and psychological reasons, and not due to any preordained and inevitable universal, cross-acquisition organization in logical structures.

That central conceptual structures differentiate into numerical, narrative, and other kinds is important to consider and speaks to the concept of modular domains. But once more, these are not considered isolated skill acquisitions, and there are just a basis few. In later chapters, I return to the concepts of central conceptual structures and domains. Another concept to which I return is the one of hypercognition. I propose a similar concept of cognitive/socioaffective complexes, which includes a hyper socioaffective side to the concept, so to speak.

In terms of the relationship between cognition and affect, Lewis has undertaken seminal work in defining appraisal–emotional amalgams, relating them to nonlinear dynamical systems theory, expanding into the area of self-regulation, and determining cognitive–affective relations in terms of neuropsychological and neurological underpinnings. In all these areas, I consider his work in developing equivalent models.

## References

Adamec, R., Kent, P., Anisman, H., Shallow, T., & Merali, Z. (1998). Neural plasticity, neuropeptides and anxiety in animals: Implications for understanding and treating affective disorder following traumatic stress in humans. *Neuroscience and Biobehavioral Reviews, 23*, 301–318.

Applebee, A. (1978). *The child's concept of story: Ages two to seventeen*. Chicago: University of Chicago Press.

Baddeley, A. D. (2007). *Working memory, thought, and action*. Oxford: Oxford University Press.

Baldwin, J. M. (1894). *The development of the child and of the race*. New York: MacMillan. (Reprinted by A. M. Kelly, 1968).

Bennett-Kastor, T. (1986). Cohesion and predication in child narrative. *Journal of Child Language, 13*, 353–370.

Bloom, W., Lahey, M., Hood, L., Lifter, K., & Fiess, K. (1980). Complex sentences: Acquisition of syntactic connectives and the semantic relations they encode. *Journal of Child Language, 7*, 235–261.

Bruner, J. (1986). *Actual minds, possible worlds*. Cambridge: Harvard University Press.

Carlson, S. M., Moses, L. J., & Claxton, L. J. (2004). Individual difference in executive functioning and theory of mind: An investigation of inhibitory control and planning ability. *Journal of Experimental Child Psychology, 87*, 299–319.

Case, R. (1985). *Intellectual development: Birth to adulthood*. Orlando: Academic Press.

Case, R. (1998). The development of conceptual structures. In W. Damon, D. Kuhn, & R. S. Siegler (Eds.), *Handbook of child psychology: Vol. 2. Cognition, perception & language* (5th ed., pp. 745–800). New York: Wiley.

Case, R., & Okamoto, Y. (1996). The role of central conceptual structures in the development of children's thought. *Monographs of the Society for Research in Child Development, 61*(1/2, Serial No. 246).

Case, R., Okamoto, Y., Henderson, B., & McKeough, A. (1993). Individual variability and consistency in cognitive development: New evidence for the existence of central conceptual structures. In R. Case & W. Edelstein (Eds.), *Contributions to human development: Vol. 23. The new structuralism in cognitive development: Theory and research on individual pathways* (pp. 71–100). New York: Karger.

Centonze, D., Picconi, B., Gubellini, P., Bernardi, G., & Calabresi, P. (2001). Dopaminergic control of synaptic plasticity in the dorsal striatum. *European Journal of Neuroscience, 13*, 1071–1077.

Constantinidis, C., Williams, G. V., & Goldman-Rakic, P. S. (2002). A role for inhibition in shaping the temporal flow of information in the prefrontal cortex. *Nature Neuroscience, 5*, 175–180.

Damasio, A. R. (1994). *Descartes' error: Emotion, reason, and the human brain*. New York: Avon.

Demetriou, A. (2004). Mind, intelligence and development: A cognitive, differential and developmental theory of intelligence. In A. Demetriou & A. Raftopoulos (Eds.), *Cognitive developmental change: Theories, models and measurement* (pp. 21–73). New York: Cambridge University Press.

Demetriou, A., Efklides, A., & Platsidou, M. (1993). The architecture and dynamics of developing mind: Experiential structuralism as a frame for unifying cognitive developmental theories. *Monographs of the Society for Research in Child Development, 58*(5/6, Serial No. 234).

Demetriou, A., Mouyi, A., & Spanoudis, G. (2010). The development of mental processing. In R. M. Lerner & W. F. Overton (Eds.), *The handbook of life-span development: Vol. 1. Cognition, biology, and methods* (pp. 36–55). Hoboken: Wiley.

Demetriou, A., & Raftopoulos, A. (1999). Modeling the developing mind: From structure to change. *Developmental Review, 19*, 319–368.

Demetriou, A., & Raftopoulos, A. (2004). *Cognitive developmental change: Theories, models and measurement*. New York: Cambridge University Press.

Demetriou, A., Spanoudis, G., & Mouyi, A. (2010). A three-level model of the developing mind: Functional and neuronal substantiation and educational implications. In M. Ferrari & L. Vuletic (Eds.), *The developmental relations between mind, brain and education* (pp. 9–48). New York: Springer Science+Business Media.

Derryberry, D., & Tucker, D. M. (1994). Motivating the focus of attention. In P. M. Niedenthal & S. Kitayama (Eds.), *The heart's eye: Emotional influences in perception and attention* (pp. 167–196). Maryland Heights: Academic Press.

Fair, D. A., Cohen, A. L., Power, J. D., Dosenbach, N. U. F., Church, J. A., Miezin, F. M., et al. (2009). Functional brain networks develop from a "local to distributed" organization. *PLoS Computational Biology, 5*, e1000381. doi: 10.1371/journal.pcbi.1000381.

Ferrari, M., & Vuletic, L. (Eds.). (2010). *Developmental relations among mind, brain and education*. New York: Springer Science+Business Media.

Fingelkurts, A. A., Fingelkurts, A. A., Kivisaari, R., Pekkonen, E., Ilmoniemi, R. J., & Kähkönen, S. (2004). Enhancement of GABA-related signalling is associated with increase of functional connectivity in human cortex. *Human Brain Mapping, 22*, 27–39.

Fischer, K. W., Knight, C. C., & Van Paris, M. (1993). Analyzing diversity in developmental pathways: Methods and concepts. In R. Case & W. Edelstein (Eds.), *The new structuralism in cognitive development: Theory and research on individual pathways* (pp. 33–56). Basel: Karger.

Fischer, K. W., & Pipp, S. L. (1984). Development of the structures of unconscious thought. In K. S. Bowers & D. Meichenbaum (Eds.), *The unconscious reconsidered* (pp. 88–148). New York: Wiley.
Fox, C. (1993). *At the very edge of the forest: The influence of literature on storytelling in children.* London: Cassell.
Freeman, W. J. (2000). Emotion is essential to all intentional behaviors. In M. D. Lewis & I. Granic (Eds.), *Emotion development and self-organization: Dynamic systems approaches to emotional development* (pp. 209–235). New York: Cambridge University Press.
Galaburda, A. M. (2002). The neuroanatomy of categories. In A. M. Galaburda, S. M. Kosslyn, & Y. Christen (Eds.), *The languages of the brain* (pp. 23–42). Cambridge: Harvard University Press.
Haken, H. (1977). *Synergetics – An introduction: Nonequilibrium phase transitions and self-organization in physics, chemistry and biology.* New York: Springer.
Halliday, M. A. K., & Hasan, R. (1976). *Cohesion in English.* New York: Longman.
Izard, C. E., Trentacosta, C. J., & King, K. A. (2005). Brain, emotions, and emotion-cognition relations. In M. D. Lewis (Ed.), *Bridging emotion theory and neurobiology through dynamic systems modeling* (pp. 208–209). New York: Cambridge University Press.
Jung, R. E., & Haier, R. J. (2007). The Parieto-frontal integration theory (P-FIT) of intelligence: Converging neuroimaging evidence. *Behavioral and Brain Sciences, 30*, 135–154.
Lazarus, R. S. (1968). Emotions and adaptation: Conceptual and empirical relations. In W. J. Arnold (Ed.), *Nebraska symposium on motivation* (Vol. 16, pp. 175–270). Lincoln: University of Nebraska Press.
Leventhal, H., & Scherer, K. (1987). The relationship of emotion to cognition: A functional approach to a semantic controversy. *Cognition and Emotion, 1*, 3–28.
Lewis, M. D. (2005a). Bridging emotion theory and neurobiology through dynamic systems modeling. *Behavioral and Brain Sciences, 28*, 169–194.
Lewis, M. D. (2005b). An emerging dialogue among social scientist and neuroscientist on the causal bases of emotion. *Behavioral and Brain Sciences, 28*, 223–234.
Lewis, M. D. (2005c). Self-organizing individual differences in brain development. *Developmental Review, 25*, 252–277.
Lewis, M. D., & Cook, M. L. (2007). Changing habits of emotion regulation at transition points in infancy: A dynamic systems analysis. *Journal of Developmental Processes, 3*, 67–89.
Lewis, M. D., & Granic, I. (2010). Phases of social-emotional development from birth to school age. In M. Ferrari & L. Vuletic (Eds.), *Developmental relations among mind, brain and education* (pp. 179–212). New York: Springer Science+Business Media.
Lewis, M., Sullivan, M., Stanger, C., & Weiss, M. (1989). Self development and self-conscious emotions. *Child Development, 60*, 146–156.
Lewis, M. D., & Todd, R. M. (2007). The self-regulating brain: Cortical-subcortical feedback and the development of intelligent action. *Cognitive Development, 22*, 406–430.
Lewis, M. D., Todd, R., & Xu, X. (2010). The development of emotion regulation: A neuropsychological perspective. In R. M. Lerner, M. E. Lamb, & A. M. Freund (Eds.), *Handbook of lifespan development: Vol. 2. Social and emotional development* (pp. 51–78). Hoboken: Wiley.
Mahler, M., Pine, F., & Bergman, A. (1975). *The psychological birth of the human infant.* New York: Basic Books.
Mandler, G. (1984). *Mind and body: Psychology of emotion and stress.* New York: Norton.
Mar, R. A. (2004). The neuropsychology of narrative: Story comprehension, story production and their interrelation. *Neuropsychologia, 42*, 1414–1434.
McKeough, A. (2000). Building on the oral tradition: How story composition and comprehension develop. In J. W. Astington (Ed.), *Minds in the making: Essays in honor of David R. Olson* (pp. 98–114). Oxford: Blackwell.
McKeough, A., Davis, L., Forgeron, N., Marini, A., & Fung, T. (2005). Improving story complexity and cohesion: A developmental approach to teaching story composition. *Narrative Inquiry, 15*, 96–125.

McKeough, A., & Genereux, R. (2003). Transformation in narrative thought during adolescence: The structure and content of story compositions. *Journal of Educational Psychology, 95*, 537–552.

McKeough, A., & Griffiths, S. (2010). Adolescent narrative thought: Developmental and neurological evidence in support of a central social structures. In M. Ferrari & L. Vuletic (Eds.), *Developmental relations among mind, brain and education* (pp. 213–230). New York: Springer Science+Business Media.

Philips, M. L., Ladouceur, C. D., & Drevets, W. C. (2008). A neural model of voluntary and automatic emotion regulation: Implications for understanding the pathophysiology and neurodevelopment of bipolar disorder. *Molecular Psychiatry, 13*, 833–857.

Piaget, J. (1960). *The psychology of intelligence*. Totawa: Littlefield Adams.

Raftopoulos, A., & Constantinou, C. P. (2004). Types of cognitive change: A dynamical, connectionist account. In A. Demetriou & A. Raftopoulos (Eds.), *Cognitive developmental change: Theories, models and measurement* (pp. 74–117). New York: Cambridge University Press.

Sander, L. W. (1975). Infant and caretaking environment: Investigation and conceptualization of adaptive behavior in a system of increasing complexity. In E. J. Anthony (Ed.), *Explorations in child psychiatry* (pp. 129–166). New York: Plenum.

Scherer, K. R. (1999). Appraisal theory. In T. Dalgleish & M. Power (Eds.), *Handbook of cognition and emotion* (pp. 637–663). Hoboken: Wiley.

Scherer, K. R. (2001). Appraisal considered as a process of multilevel sequential checking. In K. R. Scherer, A. Schorr, & T. Johnstone (Eds.), *Appraisal processes in emotion: Theory, methods, research* (pp. 92–120). Oxford: Oxford University Press.

Spear, L. P. (2000). The adolescent brain and age-related behavioral manifestations. *Neuroscience and Biobehavioral Reviews, 24*, 417–463.

Sroufe, L. A. (1979). Socioemotional development. In J. Osofsky (Ed.), *Handbook of infant development* (pp. 462–518). New York: Wiley.

Sroufe, L. A. (1996). *Emotional development: The organization of emotional life in the early years*. Cambridge: Cambridge University Press.

Stern, D. N. (1985). *The interpersonal world of the infant: A view from psychoanalysis and developmental psychology*. New York: Basic Books.

Thayer, J. F., & Lane, R. D. (2005). The importance of inhibition in dynamical systems models of emotion and neurobiology. In M. D. Lewis (Ed.), *Bridging emotion theory and neurobiology through dynamic systems modeling* (pp. 218–219). New York: Cambridge University Press.

Thompson, R. A., Lewis, M. D., & Calkins, S. D. (2008). Reassessing emotion regulation. *Child Development Perspectives, 2*, 124–131.

Tomasello, M. (1995). Joint attention as social cognition. In C. Moore & P. J. Dunham (Eds.), *Joint attention: Its origins and role in development* (pp. 103–130). Hillsdale: Erlbaum.

Trevarthen, C., & Aitken, K. J. (1994). Brain development, infant communication, and empathy disorders: Intrinsic factors in child mental health. *Development and Psychopathology, 6*, 597–633.

Tucker, D. M., Derryberry, D., & Luu, P. (2000). Anatomy and physiology of human emotion: Vertical integration of brainstem, limbic, and cortical systems. In J. C. Borod (Ed.), *The neuropsychology of emotion* (pp. 56–70). New York: Oxford University Press.

Woltering, S., & Lewis, M. D. (2009). Developmental pathways of emotion regulation in childhood: A neuropsychological perspective. *Mind, Brain, and Education, 3*, 160–169.

# Chapter 11
# Further Fischer: Comprehensive Summary, Adult Development

## Introduction

Fischer and Bidell (2006) presented a comprehensive description of Fischer's and colleagues' Neo-Piagetian model of cognitive development. In the following, I provide a thorough review of their work. In addition, I examine the work of Fischer and colleagues in adult development. As with his prior work, I indicate the strengths and scope of his work. However, I do point out where it can be improved and how my work accommodates to these exigencies.

## Comprehensive Summary of Fischer

### *Cognition and Construction*

#### Support

Fischer and Bidell (2006) began their exposition by explaining that development is dynamic and variable. For example, Fischer, Bullock, Rotenberg, and Raya (1993) showed that 7-year-old children varied the complexity of their stories depending on the degree of social support received. High social support included getting prompts about the plot by hearing a gist, or priming through modeling. These supported levels in the stories told corresponded to approximately the cognitive level of representational systems according to Fischer's cognitive model. When there was no support offered (e.g., letting the child make up a story), the level of story complexity was about one level lower in Fischer's cognitive developmental scheme (i.e., representational mappings). In terms of the effect of affect on storytelling, Ayoub and Fischer (2006) found that maltreated children would shift to negative content in stories, and the quality of their stories fell off whenever they became agitated instead of calm.

G. Young, *Development and Causality: Neo-Piagetian Perspectives*,
DOI 10.1007/978-1-4419-9422-6_11, 

## Web

Fischer and Bidell (2006) continued that Bidell and Fischer (1992) modeled variability in development as a constructive web. In different domains, the skills that developed are construed as strands of web. They are considered to vary even in order of acquisition. This happens according to the degree to which they branch out as determined by the joint interaction of the child's active construction and the support received.

For Fischer, the dynamic skills that are constructed by the child pass through the development of stages (tiers) and levels. In contrast to the approach taken by Piaget, although stages are considered clusters of discontinuities, they are not characterized by cross-domain psychological structures (modules). They are constructed in microdevelopmental contexts, leading to individual variation.

Figure 11.1 illustrates the manner in which stories of nice and mean social interactions are constructed (Ayoub & Fischer, 2006; Fischer & Ayoub, 1994). The figure presents a developmental web that develops from the representational set level to the representational system level. Children in the study (2–9-year-olds) told stories about nice, mean, and combined valence in social interaction. Development across the three valences were not necessarily developing in parallel, as represented, and they could shift toward the positive or negative pole, depending on experience and context, to the point that one or the other could develop first at each level (e.g., in abuse).

Fischer elaborated that each strand of a developmental web for a child could be represented by a nonlinear dynamic growth model. The variation within a child between low and high levels of support is termed the developmental range (similar to the concept of the zone of proximal development; Vygotsky, 1978), and the performance levels in these two support conditions are referred to as the functional and optimal levels (Fischer et al., 1993; see Tables 11.1 and 11.2). The latter optimal level can be raised even further by scaffolding, or direct coparticipation by the adult. For example, the adult acts out one of the roles of a doll in the story. With such help, the child can elevate performance to the higher steps within a particular level. (In Fischer, for any one dynamic skill, passing through any level of a tier could require several steps, depending on the task and context, and the individual).

Skills might vary greatly in range, depending on the degree of support (Fischer & Kennedy, 1997). Fischer graphed a developmental web in which some skills are more automatically ingrained. Under conditions of high stress, fatigue, or interference, a person's performance can drop to this level. Normally, without such intrusions, but also in conditions without support, the functional level manifests (good independent control of the performance). Modest support, such as in prompting and modeling, could lead to the development of optimal skill levels. With higher-level scaffolding, new steps could be constructed, but normally they would be only beginning to form.

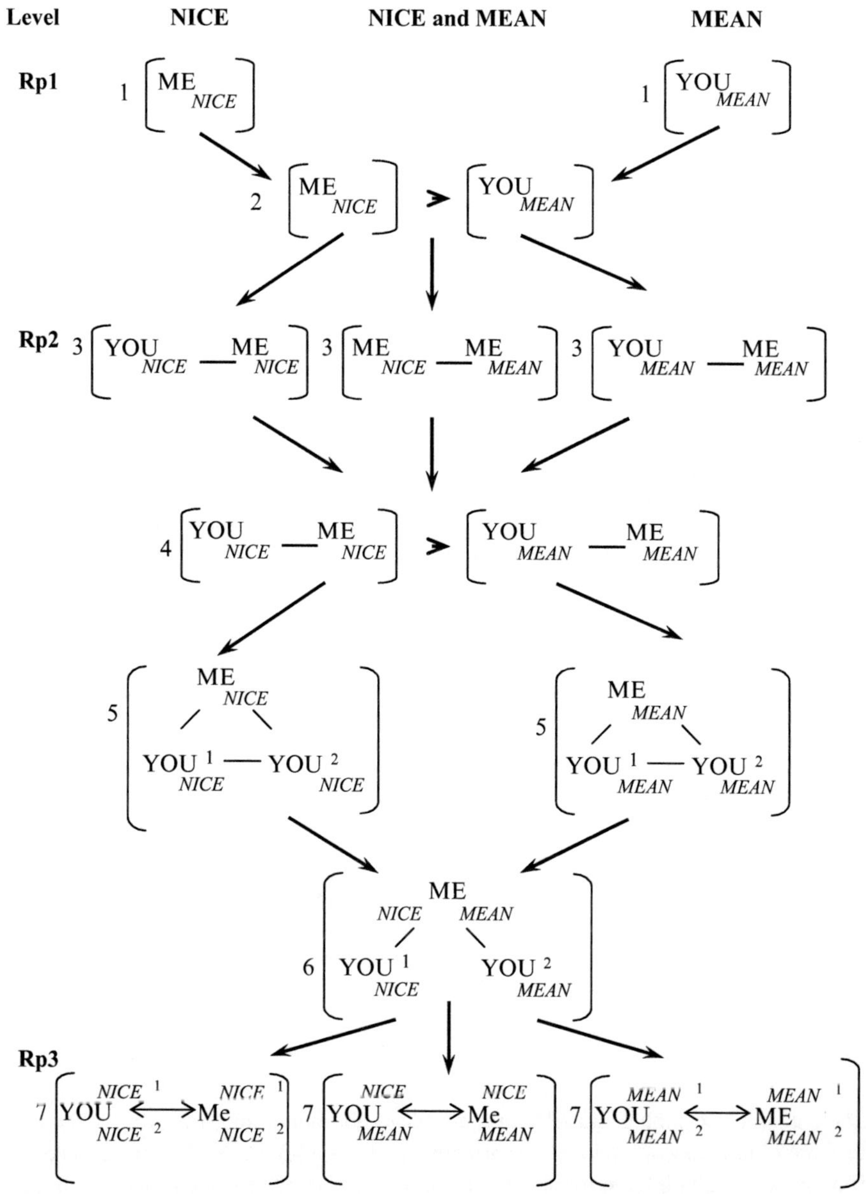


**Fig. 11.1** Developmental web for nice and mean social interactions. The numbers to the left of each set of brackets indicate the step in complexity ordering of the skill structures. The words inside each set of brackets indicate a skill structure. The *left column* designates the first step at each skill level. Reprinted with the permission of John Wiley & Sons, Inc. Fischer, K. W., & Bidell, T. R. (2006). Copyright © 2006 and John Wiley & Sons, Inc. [Figure 7.5, Page. 326]

**Table 11.1** Developmental range of a 7-year-old telling a story with varying social support

| Step | Skill level | Performance level | Social support |
|---|---|---|---|
| 1 | Rp1 | | |
| 2 | | | |
| 3 | Rp2 | Functional level | None, low |
| 4 | | | |
| 5 | | | |
| 6 | Rp3 | Optimal level | Priming through modeling, etc. |
| 7 | | | |
| 8 | Ab1 | Scaffolded level | Direct participation by adult |
| 9 | Ab2 | | |

Reprinted with the permission of Lawrence Erlbaum Associations, Inc. Fischer, K. W., Bullock, D. H., Rotenberg, E. J., & Raya, P. (1993). Copyright 2011. [Figure 4.1, Page. 98]
*Note*. Functional and optimal levels are upper limits on performance, which show stability for a task. Scaffolded level involves a range of performance indicated by the vertical line on the left, with the specific step depending on the nature of the scaffolding in combination with the 7-year-old's skill
In this table, Fischer and Biddell (2006) presented data on a single subject who received varying degrees of facilitation in story telling. Strikingly, the child varied two substages in the quality of the story told, depending on the degree of social support received. In the functional level, the child received no help, and story complexity was scored at the level of representational mapping. Moreover, the typical child obtains scores at this level (see Table 11.2, for a description of the levels). When the adult helped prime the child's story by offering models (optimal support), the quality of the story jumped a substage. When the support was even more involved (scaffolded; with direct participation by the adult), the child's story was one substage better in quality (representational systems). Note that for any one substage, there could be one to three steps in the scoring schema that had been adopted. Note that the scaffolded stories could vary in steps to be exactly at the abstract substage, the one that follows the representational one, or at one step lower or higher. In the study described in the text of the article, the scaffolding involved the adult expert acted out one of the roles of the dolls in the story. One could wonder to what degree the child's story at the advanced level of scoring indicated an ingrained, generalizable structure.
Piaget has argued that training is best accomplished when the child is ready for it, in a transition phase. Moreover, at best, the child would jump to the next level, such as the next substage or stage, depending on the series of steps involved. Therefore, for the present table, had Piaget been in a position to examine it, he might have doubted that a 7-year-old child could have jumped all the way to the abstract stage, even with support offered

## Stages

The data in these studies illustrate that stages are not monolithic structures, and when they are found, they are marked by variability at the level of skills. Therefore, generalizations across all children for all tasks about whether stages are found lead to erroneous thinking. For Fischer and Bidell (2006), "Stages both do and do not exist, depending on the dynamics of the condition and activity" (p. 332). Stages both exist and do not exist, depending on the domain, tasks, supports, individual differences, etc.

In this regard, the optimal condition appears best to facilitate growth spurts in dynamic skills. When range or zone is taken into account in terms of factors such as support, Fischer and Biddell concluded that in cognitive modeling, there is order in the variability found, and the organization of behavior does appear to develop systematically.

**Table 11.2** A developmental sequence for understanding mean and nice social interactions

| Level | Step | Skill | Examples |
|---|---|---|---|
| Rp1: Single representations | 1 | *Active agent*: A person performs at least one behavior fitting a social interaction category of mean or nice | Child pretends that one doll hits another doll ("mean") or gives another doll candy ("nice") |
| | 2 | *Behavioral category*: A person performs at least two behaviors fitting an interaction category of mean or nice | Child has one doll act nice to another doll, giving it candy and saying, "I like you." The second doll can be passive |
| Rp2: Representational mappings | 3 | *One-dimensional social interference*: The mean behaviors of one person produce reciprocal mean behaviors in a second person. The same contingency can occur for nice behaviors | Child has one doll say mean things and hit another doll, who responds by hitting and stating dislike for the first one. The second one's behavior is clearly produced by the first one's behavior |
| | 4 | *One-dimensional social influence with three characters behaving in similar ways*: Same as Step 3, but with three people interacting reciprocally in a mean way (or a nice way) | With three dolls, child has one tease the others, while a second one hits the others. The third doll rejects both of the first two because they are mean |
| | 5[a] | *One-dimensional social influence with three characters behaving in opposite ways*: The nice behaviors of one person and the mean behaviors of a second person produce reciprocal nice and mean behaviors in the third person | With three dolls, child has one act friendly to others, while a second one hits others. The third doll responds nicely to the first doll and meanly to the second |
| Rp3: Representational systems | 6 | *Two-dimensional social influence*: Two people interact in ways fitting opposite categories, such that the first one acts both nice and mean, and the second one responds with reciprocal behaviors in the same categories | Child has one doll initiate friendship with a second doll but in a mean way. The second one, confused about the discrepancy, declines the friendship because of the meanness. The first then apologizes and makes another friendly gesture, which the second one responds to accordingly |
| | 7 | *Two-dimensional social influence with three characters*: Same as Step 6 but with three people interacting reciprocally according to opposite categories | With three dolls, child has one doll act friendly to a second one, while a third initiates play in a mean way. The second doll acts friendly to the first on and rejects the third, pointing out the latter's meanness. The third then apologizes for being mean, while the first one does something new that is mean. The second doll accepts the third one's apology and rejects the first one, pointing out the change in his or her behavior |

(continued)

**Table 11.2** (continued)

| Level | Step | Skill | Examples |
|---|---|---|---|
| Rp4/A1: Single abstractions | 8 | *Single abstraction integrating opposite behaviors*: Two instances of interactions involving opposite behaviors take place as in Step 6, and the relations between the two interactions are explained in terms of some general abstraction, such as that intentions matter more actions | With three characters, child has one act friendly to a second, while a third initiates play in a mean way. The second character responds to each accordingly, but then learns that the nice one had mean intentions while the mean one had nice intentions. The second character then changes his or her behavior to each to match their intentions and explains that he or she cares more about people's intentions than their actions |
| A2: Abstract mappings | 9 | *Relation of two abstractions integrating opposite behaviors*: Two instances of interactions involving opposite behaviors are explained in terms of the relation of two abstractions, such as intention and responsibility: People who have a deceitful intention can be forgiven if they take responsibility in a way that undoes the deceit | With three dolls, child has two of them act nice on the surface to a third, both with the intention of deceiving him or her into doing their homework. When the deceit is discovered by the third character, the first one takes responsibility for the deceit by admitting the intention and reestablishing his or her honesty. But the second one does not show such responsibility. The third character forgives the first one, but not the second, because he or she cares about people taking responsibility for their deceitful intention and undoing the deceit |



[a]Step 5 is transitional between Levels Rp2 and Rp3. Apparently it can be mastered at Level Rp2, but it is much easier to do it at Level Rp3

Theorists who reject assertions that stages exist in development include Thelen and Smith (1994), but Fischer argued that these workers at one end of the spectrum of opinions on the existence of stages overlook the developmental order that can be found in the right conditions. Stages might not be gross, "hard," or wired in to manifest across the board. They might not reflect a point synchrony, resulting in a universal stage sequence having a high cross-task developmental synchrony or uniformity for all stages, tasks, conditions, and persons. At the other end of the spectrum, developmental perspectives that view psychological stages as abstract forms existing separately from the daily coparticipations in which the child is embedded will miss this kind of variability.

For example, with respect to intertask correspondences in children, the developmental data does find "interval" synchrony, in which equivalent concepts develop at about the same time. The interval is "relatively short," in general, but can be "much smaller." In this regard, Case et al. (1996) found that with a well-defined "central conceptual structure" as a starting point, different domains could be taught to children with remarkable synchrony. Similarly, Lamborn, Fischer, and Pipp (1994) found that development of the understanding of concepts such as honesty and kindness was related to the development of social but not other problem solving skills. Development is marked by generalizability only when it is specific to the original skill learned.

## Individual Differences

Continuing with this theme, Fischer and Biddell noted that there are limits in the extent to which developmental sequences demonstrate an invariant order, if at all, one that is universally present and that is relatively independent of domain. When the analysis of skill level on tasks is small-scale and detailed, individual variations can occur, as described. Nevertheless, even here, common sequences can be found, but they might differ from one type of child to the next. For example, Knight and Fischer (1992) found good and poor readers in grades one to three displayed different developmental trajectories, with poor readers not being simply delayed in their sequence relative to good readers.

This illustrates that behavior develops in specific domains that are not necessarily linked and they can vary in trajectory within domains. However, according to Fischer and Bidell, a model of domain specificity is not enough to help understand development. There are wide individual variations that characterize development, even at the stage level, and its epigenetic construction.

## Piaget

It is instructive that Fischer and Bidell cited the work on Piaget's six substages in the sensorimotor period in this regard. They noted that, for Piaget, the six-step sequence in the infant's construction of object permanence has been "confirmed" but with "some revision and clarification" by subsequent research (e.g., Uzgiris & Hunt, 1987).

For the authors, Baillargeon (1999) represents the type of researcher trying to find earlier ages for Piagetian acquisitions, and she did establish with new tasks that infants can acquire object permanence at 4–5 months, and not at 8 months, the age Piaget had highlighted using his tasks. For Fischer and Bidell, this specification of earliest age of acquisition of skills is only half of what is needed. In addition, we need to explain better the individual variations in development. Moreover, we need to do so without recourse to purely nativist arguments. Humans construct knowledge through their inherent activity and efforts at knowledge formation, and this begins with the earliest sensorimotor activities of newborns [I would add in their own way, fetuses are doing the same!]. In these regards, Fisher and Bidell share in Piaget's approach that infants actively construct their development right from birth.

## Fundamentals

Fischer and Bidell enumerated the principles of their developmental model that can help explain variations in patterns of stage development. (a) Skills are constructed hierarchically. This happens through integrations of earlier skills into more inclusive whole structures. (b) The skills that are constructed vary over multiple levels, depending on the individual, context, goals, states, supports, developmental range, and so forth. (c) Skills are constructed to help the individual adapt to specific tasks and contexts, but can they generalize to others through "specific generalizing activity" (e.g., Fischer & Immordino-Yang, 2002).

These fundamental assumptions indicate several important truths about how individuals function cognitively with respect to stage theory. (a) At any one moment, individuals do not function just at a single cognitive stage or a single level of complexity or competence. To the contrary, individuals might even function at multiple levels at the same time, even in the same situation (referring to the developmental web model, described above). (b) Developmental pathways take many different trajectory shapes, and pathways are not necessarily linear or smooth. There may be fits and starts, regressions, temporary backward steps, and so on. (c) Development is social right from birth, and often tasks are solved in collaboration. People function in social ensembles. (d) Assessments need to use multiple tasks and conditions to capture contextual variation.

## Growth

Fischer and Bidell cited van Geert (1994, 1998), in particular, on nonlinear dynamical growth models. For example, in models of growth, components are considered "growers" and they are represented by growth functions. Growers can display connectivity within a particular set of growth functions. Connections vary in strength, and the manner in which they manifest leads to different growth curves, including nonlinear ones. When growers build on each other in a hierarchical fashion, developmental stages become evident, and the data for any one individual could reveal this pattern.

Aside from hierarchical integration, other relationships are possible among growers, such as competition (e.g., relative to a prior acquired level; Fischer & Kennedy, 1997). Even minor competition can lead to major developmental perturbations, including turbulent vacillations, or "crashes and explosions." Depending on the degree of support involved, growers for different domains could be pulled to a common level (an attractor). Moreover, growers could catalyze each other so that development overshoots its carrying capacity. This is called the "Piaget effect," when an earlier speeding up of growth disturbs future levels in growth.

For Fischer and Bidell, cumulative moment-to-moment microdevelopmental changes contribute to macrodevelopmental acquisitions, but the former cannot be reduced to the latter. Similarly, macrodevelopmental processes cannot be reduced to micro ones, yet the macro ones place limits on the microdevelopmental ones. In a third level, macrodevelopmental changes are "gradually consolidated, generalized, and related," thereby creating larger, slower developmental changes. When developmental discontinuities cluster across developmental domains, "emergence zones" in development seem apparent through the consistencies present. These are not products of underlying stage structures, but of dynamical construction and constraints.

## Scalloping and Bootstrapping

In building new skills, Fischer and Bidell argued that a "scalloping" process is involved (e.g., Fischer, Yan, & Stewart, 2003). Individuals build a skill, it drops, and then it is rebuilt. The rebuildings are repeated in a wavelike pattern of construction, followed by dissolution and reconstruction. Indeed, prior to construction, individuals might even drop down a level. This facilitates rebuilding variations, and the collapses to lower level are followed by new rebuildings, leading to a more general skill over time that can be applied to variable contexts. However, the reconstruction process is fragile, and even minor change can derail the process of creating more general skill.

But how can a new form emerge from prior skills? Fischer and Bidell maintained that individuals bootstrap or bridge new constructions through directing the construction of their contents by functioning simultaneously at two levels (Case, 1992). The new level is a target, framework, pillar, or shell that works like a grasping hook, pulling activities up to its level. They are partial or fuzzy, at first, and are elaborated unconsciously (although I would add this might be different after childhood). They lead to different components of the new skill being assembled, as they are juxtaposed, shifted, and coordinated, until a new level is consolidated.

## Emotions

In the next part of their work, Fischer and Bidell turned to the study of emotions. For them, emotions are functional and are intrinsically related to cognition, operating with it rather than in opposition to it. Emotions serve ecological adaptation and are not just inner feelings. Emotions involve appraisals of notable changes in events and action tendencies, as well as resultant action, expression, physiological reactions, etc. Their expression leads to self-monitoring. Emotions help organize behavior. They reflect prototypical scripts, or a standard sequence of events shared by many individuals. Scripts include antecedents, responses, and self-control procedures (see Fig. 11.2).

There seem to be six emotion families (anger, sadness, fear, shame, love, happiness; with some subordinate items in the families considered additional categories; see Fig. 11.3). The families and categories have superior and lower-level strata in organization, and the organization varies across culture. At higher levels, categories are organized according to several dimensions forming an emotional space. Generally, research

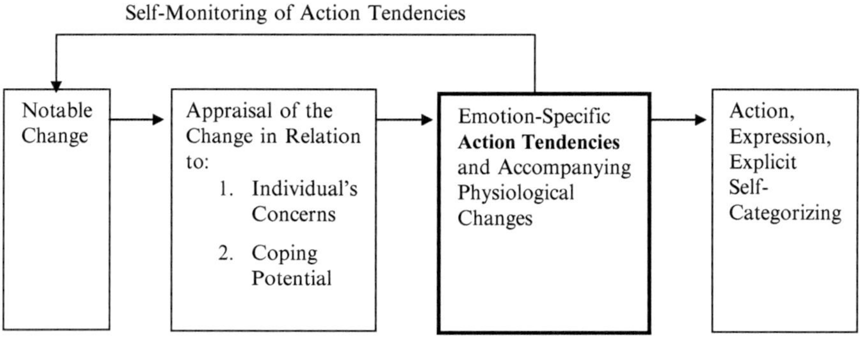


**Fig. 11.2** Emotion processing schema: from perception to appraisal to behavior and feeling. Shows how emotions unfold into action tendencies and physiological reactions after changes noticed and appraisals undertaken. Reprinted by permission of the publisher (Taylor & Francis Group, http://www.informaworld.com). Fischer, K. W., Shaver, P. R., & Carnochan, P. (1990). [Figure 1, Page. 87]

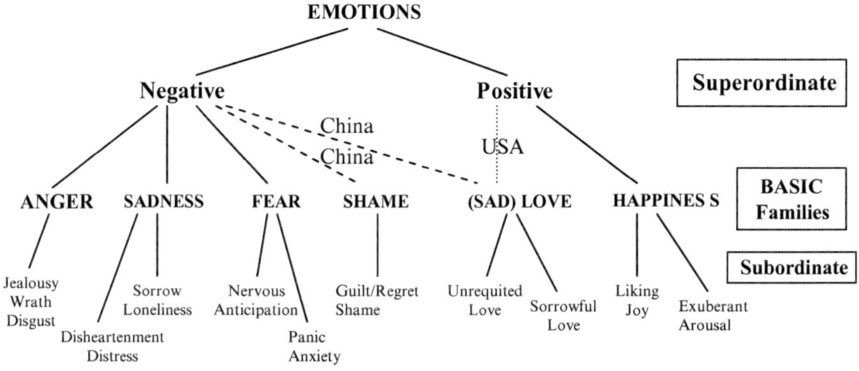


**Fig. 11.3** Cluster analysis of basic emotion families in Chinese and English. The figure presents Fischer's conception of different levels of emotions, the families within which they group, how they can differ across cultures, and how they develop. The subordinate families are from the Chinese study (Shaver, Wu, & Schwartz, 1992). Reprinted with the permission of Oxford University Press, Inc. Mascolo, M. J., Fischer, K. W., & Li, J. (2003). [Figure 20.2, Page. 382]

has found three main dimensions in emotional organization: (a) positive/negative, approach/avoidance, (b) activity, active-passive, and (c) engagement, self-other.

Fischer and Bidell terminated their discussion of emotions with applied issues, such as in the Oedipal situation, abuse, emotional splitting, and dissociation. They presented a case of a boy who developed dissociated representations in the public and private domains that differed but, nevertheless, the representations developed in sequences that accorded with their stage model at the point of the sequence of representational sets, mappings, and systems. The authors concluded that in the big picture of development, large macrodevelopmental reorganizations occur concurrently for emotions and cognition, as they work together.

### Brain

Fischer (Fischer & Rose, 1996) has developed a model of brain-behavior growth cycles based on the work of Thatcher (1994b) and van Geert (e.g., 1994). For example, for infancy, Thatcher's research and those of others found discontinuities in brain development at about 4, 8, 12, and 24 months. The prefrontal cortex, in particular, provides the resources for new developments. Fischer and Bidell reminded that their developmental model consists of tiers (stages), having levels (substages) and steps. In terms of corresponding brain development, for Fischer and Bidell, the coordinated growth cycles in brain and behavior evolve epigenetically and in coordination over the lifespan. Nevertheless, the constructive activity of the individual cannot be ignored in development: "Between nature and nurture stands the human agent whose unique integrative capacities drive the epigenesis of intelligence and organize biological and environmental contributions to the process" (Bidell & Fischer, 1996, p. 236; also see Chap. 9).

## *Interim Summary*

Fischer has not published a book on his developmental model, and this comprehensive review with Bidell stands as the work that best explains it in depth. The theory ranges from the contents of development in terms of tiers and levels, or stages, and substages, and the transition mechanisms in development, in terms of how new constructions can emerge from prior ones. As with Piaget, the child is active in the process; moreover, the developmental steps are not prespecified in a program or innately. There is much room for individual differences in development, for example through different degrees of environmental supports and the quality of support received. Skills are acquired individually, and steps could be added to the typical sequence of steps within tiers and levels. Skills that are related can cohere to some extent, but not to the degree of creating uniform, universal stages and substages in development.

Morra et al. had described Piaget as a logician or dialectician, depending on whether he was describing, respectively, cognitive structure or transition mechanism in development. The same distinction can be applied to Fischer and the other Neo-Piagetians. The question remains to what degree have they improved the original answers to the questions posed by Piaget on structure and transition mechanisms? Do their stage-substage models reflect theoretical integrity and the capacity to resolve gaps and inconsistencies? Does the best way of interpreting the examples that they provide and the data that they gather lie in their models, or are others more appropriate? Have they diluted the concept of structure to the point that it lacks theoretical coherence? Are their answers for how transition mechanisms work in development too ambiguous and they still cannot explain how qualitatively distinct cognitive structures arise? Is it sufficient to refer to brain organization systems, and epigenesis, or does one have to indicate how these different levels of causal processes interrelate? In the chapters that follow on my work, I present perspectives that approach initial answers to these types of questions, while respecting their source not only in the work of Piaget, but also in the work of Neo-Piagetians, including Fischer.

## Adult Development

### *Reflective Thinking*

#### Introduction

Fischer and Pruyne (2003) examined development of adult thinking from the perspective of Fischer's model of cognitive development. In particular, they examined the relationship between cognitive development and the development of reflective thinking in the child and adult. They found parallels across steps in the two trajectories that indicate support for Fischer's model of stages and substages in development.

Reflective thinking is an active and careful analytic evaluation process that uses evidence and reasoning, the questioning of knowledge and beliefs, and the search for justifiable conclusions. It examines conflicting viewpoints and implications, as well. Kitchener and King (1990; King & Kitchener, 1994) constructed a measure of reflective judgment, the Reflective Judgment Interview (RJI). It consists of dilemmas, such as whether chemical food additives are safe, and it provides opposing views related to them. The Prototypic Reflective Judgment Interview (PRJI; King & Kitchener, 1993) is another interview schedule on the topic, and it provides contextual support to obtain optimal performance by respondents on the instrument, unlike the case for the RJI, which addresses functional levels without support. Generally, the prompts in the questions of the PRJI raise performance levels typically obtained in the RJI by about one or two steps, which translates into a difference of anywhere between 3 and 20 years.

## Steps

Kitchener and King (1981; also see Kitchener, King, & DeLuca, 2006; Kitchener, Lynch, Fischer, & Wood, 1993) described seven steps in the development of reflective thinking (see Table 11.3). In the first three steps, the child is in a prereflective state, and adults might still be at this level of development, depending on a host of individual, educational, and cultural factors. People at this level believe that knowledge is certain and absolute. Moreover, they do not use evidence to arrive at conclusions. In the next two steps, individuals can be described as quasi-reflective. They might recognize that knowledge is relative and uncertain, but they still have difficulty in using evidence to justify beliefs, to arrive at conclusions, and so on. In the last two steps of the seven in the series on reflective judgment, the adult enters the genuine reflection period. Not only is it understood that knowledge is relative and constructed, but also the individual seeks to apply evidence to evaluate knowledge, judgments, beliefs, and arguments in context. The reflective thinker does not learn knowledge by rote, but actively reconstructs it in light of logic and evidence into new forms, including at combined and higher-order levels.

## Substages

Fischer and Pruyne (2003) posited a one-to-one correspondence across seven of the substages of Fischer's model of cognitive development and the seven steps in the development of reflective thinking. In the following, I describe the parallels that they present in Table 10.1.

In the prereflective steps in the development of reflective thinking, representational sets emerge at 2 years, and the first step in the development of reflective thinking involves maintaining that what is held as belief is true, with no justification required. In the next step, the child develops representational mappings and, in terms of reflective thinking, the child can know with certainty, perhaps because an authority had informed the child. As the child grows to about 6–7 years, representational systems develop and this translates into believing that some knowledge can be uncertain; in addition, justification does take place, but only in terms of feeling what is right at the moment.

In the quasi-reflective steps, the teenager is at the substage of single abstractions and reflective judgment takes the form of believing wholeheartedly the authorities, so that learned knowledge is considered certain. In the next substage of abstract mappings, the teenager understands that knowledge varies with context and with personal cognitive filters. Justification is involved, but limited to the context.

In the reflective steps, the student enters the stage of abstract systems, and knowledge becomes constructed by compare and contrast procedures; justification is offered for conclusions that take into account the procedures followed. Finally, the mature reflective thinker arrives at the stage of principles. The person understands that rigorous comprehensive investigation, use of evidence, argumentation

**Table 11.3** Relationships among skill levels, reflective judgment stages, and associated ages of emergence and consolidation, in relation to the development of identity in Erikson's stages

| Skill level | Reflective judgment stage | Model age (in years) of skill emergence (optimal level) | Modal educational level of reflective judgment stages (functional level) | Erikson's stages of identity: first emergence |
|---|---|---|---|---|
| Rp1<br>Single representation, concrete instances of knowing | Knowing is limited to single concrete observations: what a person observes is true | 2 | | ↕ |
| Rp2<br>Rp mapping: two concrete representations can be coordinated with each other | Two categories for knowing: right answers. Good authorities have knowledge: bad authorities lack knowledge | 3.5–4.5 | Early high school | Concrete identifications |
| Rp3<br>Rp system: Several aspects of two concrete representations can be coordinated | In some areas, knowledge is certain and authorities have that knowledge. In other areas, knowledge is temporarily uncertain. Only personal beliefs can be known | 6–7 | Late high school, early college | ↕ |
| Rp4 = Ab1<br>Two systems of Rp systems can be constructed, creating a single abstraction | Concept that knowledge is unknown in several specific cases leads to the abstract generalization that knowledge is uncertain | 10–12 | Late college | Stage 5: Identity vs. role diffusion |
| Ab2<br>Ab mapping: Abstraction can be coordinated with each other | Knowledge is uncertain and must be understood within a context, thus, justification is context specific | | Early graduate school | Stage 6: Intimacy vs. isolation |
| Ab3<br>Ab system: Several aspects of two abstractions can be coordinated | Knowledge is uncertain but constructed by comparing evidence and opinion on different sides of an issues or across contexts | 19–21 | Advanced doctoral | Stage 7: Generativity vs. stagnation |
| Ab4 = A principle: systems of Ab systems can be constructed, creating a single principle | Knowledge is the outcome of a process of reasonable inquiry. This view is equivalent to a general principle that is consistent across domains | 24–26 | Advanced doctoral | Stage 8: Ego integrity vs. despair |

Adapted from Oxford University Press with permission. Kitchener, K. S., King, P. M., & DeLuca, S. (2006). [Table 4.2, Page. 82]

*Note*. *Rp* representational; *Ab* abstract

Since most of the studies on which this table based is used traditional-age students, educational level is used here as a proxy for the age of functional level

There are several stage models that map quite well onto Fischer's model, giving it critical support. For example, the table shows that the model of stages in reflective judgment developed by Kitchener and King exhibits a one-to-one correspondence with Fischer's stages and substages in the representational, abstract, and principle stages. Both models involve seven steps in the age period of concern. Similarly, the model of self-development described by Harter maps quite well onto the representational and abstract stages of Fischer (Harter's work is described in the next table, Tables 8.4 and 8.5). Impressively, van Geert (1994) demonstrated that Fischer's cognitive developmental model and the empirical data gathered in its support could be modeled mathematically as different growers

However, the parallels in Fischer's model and those of others are not always so consistent. For example, in the table under discussion, by examining Kitchener et al. (2006) and Fischer et al. (2003), the alignment of their work and that of Erikson appears to lead to some anomalous conclusions

In terms of the functional levels of support described in this table under discussion, college students are developing their identity status. However, the extrapolations in the table suggest that, according to the models under discussion, with optimal support, even 10-year-olds might be capable of reaching identity status!

Moreover, according to the table under discussion the Eriksonian stage of generativity would appear to be capable of taking place in the 19–21-year-old!

Also, the last Eriksonian stage of ego integrity is associated with the principle stage in Fischer, which manifests in the 24–26-year-old at the optimal level. However, ego integrity is a stage in Erikson that is associated with the elderly period!

For a more nuanced comparison between the parallels in stages and substages in cognitive development and Eriksonian development in a Neo-Piagetian model, one should review the present model in Table 4.3. It is a lifespan model that has 25 steps, with substages into the postformal, adult period, and there are 25 equivalent Neo-Eriksonian steps. Since I had expanded both the Piagetian cognitive side and the Eriksonian side of the stages and substages in development in concert with each other, even the last steps in both models have a consistency, in contrast to the work of Fischer and colleagues presented in the table under discussion

In terms of the compatibility of Fischer's model with those of others related to self-reflection and self-construction, as shown in the present table and the next one, they need to consider that the models of both Case and myself include more substages than does Fischer's in the comparable age period under discussion. Moreover, both of us have presented models of steps of development of the self according to the substages of our models. In the present model, I had shown the correspondence of the work of Sroufe, Selman, and Loevinger, in particular, for the infant, child–adolescent, and adolescent–adult age periods. These workers are well-known, and the cognitive-self-development parallels that I have found based on their work might suggest possible modifications to the work of Kitchener-King and Harter

Moreover, the strategy used in the mathematical modeling undertaken by van Geert (1994) might apply to the present model, but more growers need to be taken into account, and it has to stretch over the lifespan, which is not case for the models of Fischer and for Case in contrast to my own. Note that later in the book I present a cyclically recurring model of nonlinear dynamical transition mechanisms that are considered to underlie the development of the stages and substages in the present model; the transitions are seen to move from attractor structures to complex systems. This could be the starting point for developing a more complete mathematical modeling of Neo-Piagetian cognitive development across the lifespan and justification, and defense of one's position while contradicting the alternatives together establish the validity and generalizability of one's conjectures and conclusions. Nevertheless, truth is understood as not absolute, but probabilistic or more likely than not, considering the dynamic process used to establish it.

### Comment

Fischer and Pruyne (2003) have provided a potential cognitive basis for the seven-step sequence in reflective thinking developed by Kitchener and King. However, other models of reflective thinking, or of types of thinking related to it, have more steps, such as that of Perry (1970). Moreover, Perry's model maps one-to-one to my model of stages and substages in cognitive development, except at the very end (see Tables 11.4 and 11.5). Future work in the area should consider revising the Kitchener–King model to fit the present model. It affords a differentiation of the postformal stage into five substages, and can be used to expand the last step in Kitchener and King's model, for example. In this regard, in other areas where Fischer has elucidated developmental steps consistent with his developmental model, careful reflection has indicated that his model has gaps and inconsistencies and should be expanded to fit the present model.

## *Erikson*

### Fischer's Model

Fischer et al. (2003) have expanded presentation of parallels involving Fischer's model of stages and substages in cognitive development and relevant acquisitions related to adult development (moral judgment and identity development, aside from reflective thinking). (a) For example, with respect to the development of identity (Erikson, 1968), in terms of the substage of representational systems in Fischer's model, the child is considered to create multiple concrete identities. (b) Next, in the substage of single abstractions, identities form (Erikson's stage of identity formation vs. role diffusion), but they are "globbed" together by coordinating different identifications. (c) In the next substage of abstract mappings, teenagers can relate their understanding of their identity to that of others in terms of similarities and differences. Moreover, they enter into the beginning of Erikson's stage of intimacy vs. isolation. (d) In the next substage of abstract systems, in young adults, parts of both self and other identity can be compared and contrasted. In addition, intimacy can evolve into partnerships. Erikson's stage of generativity is associated with the development of abstract systems, as well, which allows the coordination of multiple abstract identities in self and other. (e) In the ensuing stage of principles, identity takes the form of a general principle that cuts across different contexts, such as following the golden moral rule. Erikson's final stage of ego integrity is based on

**Table 11.4** Some stage theories of development from the concrete operational period onward

| Young | Kohlberg | Loevinger | Perry | Richards and Commons |
|---|---|---|---|---|
| Perioperational multiplication (7–9 yr) | Instrumental (transition stage) | Self-protective | | Concrete |
| Perioperational integration (9–11 yr) | | Rule-oriented | | |
| Abstract coordination (11–13 yr) | Mutuality | Conformist | Dualistic construction | |
| Abstract hierarchization (13–16 yr) | Logical social | Conscientious/ conformist | Multiplicity perceived, rejected | |
| Abstract systematization (16–19 yr) | Social system conscience | Conscientious | Multiplicity accepted, relegated | |
| Abstract multiplication (19–22 yr) | Transitional postconventional | Individualistic | Immersion in multiplicity | |
| Abstract integration (22–25 yr) | Prior rights and responsibilities | Autonomous | Relativism viable | Metasystematic |
| Collective coordination (25–28 yr) | Universal processes | Postautonomous | Universal relativism, commitment | Paradigmatic |
| Collective hierarchization (28–39 yr) | | | First commitments included | |
| Collective systemization (39–50 yr) | | | Commitment implications seen | Cross-paradigmatic |
| Collective multiplication (50–61 yr) | | | Restructuring, expanding commitment | |
| Collective integration (61+ yr) | Cosmic perspective | Integrated universal | | |

Adapted from Springer Science+Business Media: Young, G. (1997). [Table 3.1, Page. 71]

The next two tables are adapted from Young (1997). In the first one, I relate well-known stage theories of development from middle childhood onward to the equivalent stages in the present model of stages and substages in cognitive development. Different authors relate these well-known theories in different ways to their developmental models (e.g., Blanchard-Fields, 1989; Commons, 2008; Dawson-Tunik, 2004), depending on the details of their own models. The present model stands out by not needing to collapse several stages or substages of the other models into one of its own, because it is elaborate enough for the most part to accommodate them in a one-to-one fashion. At times, I had to leave gaps in the other models in finding the parallels with my own. At times, I filled in the gaps by taking an educated guess what the missing stages could have looked like in the original theories had they been cognizant of the needs. At times, the parallels between the present model and the others are not fully consistent, given the different origins to the other models relative to the present one. Moreover, even these classic models have changed in later publications relative to the moment the tables were constructed for my 1997 book

Note that the age periods associated with the different steps are approximate, for example, given their affective components, the increased role experience plays in their development, etc.

The second table of the two indicates a clear parallel between the steps in the present model and in Perry's model, which is more about reasoning than cognitive development, in general. The similar model of Baker-Brown et al. (1992) provides a further one-to-one parallel across the present model and one on reasoning, within the limits described

**Table 11.5** Comparison of three developmental models of reasoning for adolescents and adults

| Young | Perry (1970) | Baker-Brown et al. (1992) |
|---|---|---|
| Abstract coordination (11–13 yr) | Basic duality (right vs. wrong) | Linear reasoning:<br>One simple unidimensional rule<br>Only one way of looking at the world is legitimate |
| Abstract hierarchization (13–16 yr) | Multiplicity prelegitimate (people with other viewpoints lack enlightenment) | Still not tolerant of others' viewpoints:<br>Uncertainty is not accepted |
| Abstract systematization (16–19 yr) | Multiplicity subordinate (different views acknowledge but still adherence to absolutes) | Some tolerance or uncertainty<br>Exceptions to the rule<br>Potential or conditional acceptance of different perspectives or views |
| Abstract multiplication (19–22 yr) | Multiplicity correlate ("Everyone has the right to his or her own opinion.") | Differentiation:<br>Different viewpoints are acknowledged and there is acceptance that these viewpoints are legitimate, relevant, or valid |
| Abstract integration (22–25 yr) | Relativism correlate, Competing, or diffuse (viewpoints now compared and/or evaluated) | Tension in the weighing or evaluation of all the multiple viewpoints:<br>There is a relationship among viewpoints or alternatives<br>There is a need for further information before judgments can be made |
| Collective coordination (25–28 yr) | Commitment foreseen (all views are relativistic) | Integration:<br>Integration of viewpoints is clearly evident<br>Mutual influence<br>Different views can occur simultaneously and are also interactive<br>Synthesis of viewpoints |
| Collective hierarchization (28–39 yr) | Initial commitment | Give and take trade-offs |
| Collective systematization (39–50 yr) | Orientation in implications of commitment | Hypothesis-testing or reality testing<br>Alternatives are plans/processes/ actions that are made up of several moving parts<br>All parts effect each other in the system<br>Aware of two alternative courses of action and is able to compare their outcomes with regard to long-term implications |

(continued)

**Table 11.5** (continued)

| Young | Perry (1970) | Baker-Brown et al. (1992) |
|---|---|---|
| Collective multiplication (50–61 yr) | Developing commitment (restructuring or expanding commitments) | Several commitments accepted and all are viewed as legitimate<br>These commitments are viewed as occurring simultaneously even though some of them may be contradictory to each other |
| Collective integration (61+ yr) | Commitments consolidated (various commitments made over the lifetime solidified and integrated) | Overarching principle pertains to the nature of the relationship between alternatives<br>This principle has developed as a result of the person's simultaneous consideration of these levels<br>Realizes that one's views depends on combinations of legal, moral, and scientific judgments |

Adapted from Springer Science+Business Media: Young, G. (1997). [Table 13.1, Page. 294]
*Note*. The last stage in Perry's model and the second-to-last one in Baker-Brown et al.'s model have been extrapolated from their work by me

principles, but requires a rich life experience to bring about the grand cognitive syntheses that one could develop much later in adulthood.

## Comment

Fischer et al. (2003) have related the stages of Eriksonian development – in particular, from the identity period onwards – to Fischer's model of stages and substages in development. They took care to relate the steps in the acquisition of the former series to what seems plausible relative to the cognitive one. However, given that each substage in Fischer's cognitive sequence is related to a typical age of onset, some anomalies in their suggested cognitive-Eriksonian correspondences appear.

(a) For example, Erikson's stage of identity is placed in the cognitive substage of abstract sets of Fischer's model and this substage is associated with the 10–12 year range in Fischer's model. It could be argued that the emergence of the cognitive substage only allows for the beginnings of identity formation to take place rather than the more complex type that Fischer et al. posited to develop in this age period.
(b) Moreover, in the next cognitive stage of abstract mappings in Fischer's model, the corresponding Eriksonian stage proposed by Fischer et al. is that of intimacy. This cognitive substage is associated with the age period of 14–16 years, which is hardly the typical age associated with intimacy. Rather, the mid-adolescent period involved here would be one that is more typically associated with seeking identity, which had been ascribed by Fischer et al. to the prior early adolescent period.

(c) In another example, in Fischer's et al. model of Fischerian–Eriksonian correspondences, generativity is associated with a cognitive substage (abstract systems) that typically is found to begin in the 18-year-old. Any model that ascribes generativity to such an early age would be considered to be doing so at a premature age.
(d) Finally, Fischer et al. noted a relationship of Eriksonian ego integrity with the adult cognitive stage of principles. However, the latter begins in the mid-twenties according to Fischer's model, and ego integrity is the last Eriksonian stage, taking place at life's end. Therefore, the age difference involved in the association made by Fischer et al. of the stage of ego integrity, which takes place toward the end of life, with a cognitive stage that begins in the age period of the twenties seems too great.

### My Model

In the present work, I have attempted to relate stages and substages of cognitive development to the stages in development described by Erikson (see Chaps. 1, 4, 5, and 20). Moreover, I undertook the task for each of his eight socioaffective stages. In creating the model, I had more cognitive substages to consider, in that there are 25 steps in the present model (5 stages × 5 substages). I realized that I had to create addition steps in the Eriksonian series if the model was to make any sense. The model of Neo-Piagetian cognitive stages that I had created spanned the lifespan. I used it as a scaffold to place the eight original Erikson stages, as well as 17 others that I had to create in order to have a model of 25 parallel steps in Neo-Piagetian and Neo-Eriksonian development. By following this procedure, I ended up with a model in which there were no anomalies, such as placing the stage of ego integrity, an end of life one, in a time period that begins around 25 years of age.

## *Other Fischerian Models*

Fischer has some other research being undertaken by colleagues in support of his cognitive model. The work of Dawson-Tunik on moral reasoning supports Fischer's model (see Table 11.6, Dawson-Tunik, 2006; Dawson-Tunik, Commons, Wilson, & Fischer, 2005). Nevertheless, the gaps in Fischer's model that I have posited should be examined for similar gaps in her work.

See Table 11.7 for how Mascolo and Fischer (2010) have examined core goal structures in adulthood according to Fischer's model of the stages of abstractions and principles.

Fischer (Fischer et al. 2003) has also applied his model to analysis of the steps in the growth of Darwin's thinking about evolution. See Table 11.8 on this interesting application.

**Table 11.6** Orders of hierarchical complexity in Dawson-Tunik

| Complexity order name | Logical structure | Hierarchical order of abstraction (conceptual structure) |
|---|---|---|
| Single reflexive actions | Single reflexes | First-order reflexes |
| Reflexive mappings | Coordinates one aspect of two or more reflexes | Second-order reflexes, which coordinate first-order reflexes |
| Reflexive systems | Coordinates multiple aspects of reflexes | Third-order reflexes, which coordinate second-order reflexes |
| Single sensorimotor schemes | Abstracts single sensorimotor schemes from multiple reflexive systems | First-order sensorimotor schemes, which coordinate third-order reflexes |
| Sensorimotor mappings | Coordinates one aspect of two or more sensorimotor schemes | Second-order sensorimotor schemes, which coordinate first-order sensorimotor schemes |
| Sensorimotor systems | Coordinates multiple aspects of sensorimotor schemes | Third-order sensorimotor schemes, which coordinate second-order sensorimotor schemes |
| Single representations | Abstracts single representations from multiple sensorimotor schemes, often identifies one aspect of a single representation | First-order representations, which coordinate third-order sensorimotor schemes |
| Representational mappings | Coordinates one aspect of two or more representations | Second-order representations, which coordinate first-order representations |
| Representational systems | Coordinates multiple aspects of representations | Third-order representations, which coordinate second-order representations |
| Single abstractions | Abstracts single abstractions from multiple representational systems, often identifies one aspect of a single abstraction | First-order abstractions, which coordinate third-order representations |
| Abstract mappings | Coordinates one aspect of two or more abstractions | Second-order abstractions, which coordinate first-order abstractions |
| Abstract systems | Coordinates multiple aspects of abstractions | Third-order abstractions, which coordinate second-order abstractions |
| Single principles/ axioms | Abstracts single principles from multiple abstract systems, often identifies one aspect of a single principle | First-order principles, which coordinate third-order abstractions |



Dawson-Tunik (2006) adapted Fischer's cognitive developmental model in her work. She reinterpreted it in terms of hierarchical complexity. She added the label of axioms to Fischer's use of principles to describe the adult stage

**Table 11.7** Developmental transformation in the core goal structures in adulthood

| Step | Description |
|---|---|
| L13: Ab4/Pr1 | My faith ... underlies all other important relationships in my life. It connects me to other people and events and overlies a structure on my entire life. My faith has deepened as I have aged, and I turn over everything stressful to God. [Faith gives me the belief that] this journey is guided and is meaningful. It imbues my life with a surety, with love, and with acceptance. This has helped me to put loss in perspective, and to understand the importance of friends and families over material possessions. My faith defines my values and priorities, and allows me to demonstrate love to my family and my friends. My family is my glue! I enjoy being with them, doing things, enjoying new experiences ... I have a hierarchy of friends. Friendships are so important because they take me out of myself. I feel they support me, and I support them. These things cannot be separated. They are all guiding forces in my life, instill meaning to my life, and define who I am. My faith reinforces my belief that I am traveling on a journey of purpose, and my family and friends are my guides on that journey. This [is what] makes for a spiritual life. My faith gave me the path, my children forged it, and my friends illuminate it. I am the fortunate traveler |
| | Everyday [my friend] checks in and [we have a] power walk. We go through public gardens, past farms, we see horses, chickens, sheep – it's so rejuvenating. And we talk ... |
| | On recent cruise ... I snorkeled with my son for over 4 h and it was so beautiful! We all had so much fun together, and I love being able to have discussions with them |
| L12: Ab3 | Completing my current 2-year project, finding work and a lifestyle that will give me happiness, coming to terms with getting older. These things put together the person I want to/can become. The first two fit together chronologically; I will complete the first goal, and by that time my second goal will be completed, and who knows what will be most important to me at that time? The third – coming to terms with aging – arcs above the first two, because finding your place in life is important. Once you find your niche or pattern of being, you can be prepared to face the fact that you're getting older. While things seem to get more stable as you age, they do still change, and you have to be flexible |
| L11: Ab2 | Family is most important and it comes ahead of your career or money. However, you must reach your dreams and earn money in order to be a fulfilled person and bring joy to the family. If you are disgruntled, then you would not be an asset to your family |
| L10: Ab1 | School, work, and relationships. I think the general idea is responsibility. In school you have to be responsible and study and keep up with assignments. At work you have to be on time and be focused on what needs to be done. In relationships you have to give time and attention to the other person |



*Note*. Core goal structures of four participants at four levels of development. The lower through upper panels depict protocols from an 18–25 year-old (single abstractions, L10/Ab1); 26–35 year-old (abstract mapping, L11/Ab2); 36–45 year-old (abstract systems, L12/Ab3) and 55+ year-old (single principles, L13/Ab4/Pr1)

**Table 11.8** Development of Darwin's theory of evolution (1831–1839): a general overview

| Level | Major events | Dates |
|---|---|---|
| Ab1: single abstractions | From adolescence; musings about creation and species; separation of organic and physical worlds | Before 1831 |
| Ab2: abstract mappings | Physical world eliminates deviant organisms | |
| | People selectively breed animals and plants for desired characteristics | |
| | Voyage of Beagle; mastering Lyell's principles of geology and collecting observations | |
| | Beginning of coral-reef theory: corals vary with changes in physical world | |
| Ab3: abstract systems | Final coral-reef theory: coral reefs grow as corals adapt to changing ocean depths by growing upward to reach light | 1835–1837 |
| | Variations in Galapagos species match species characteristics with physical niche | |
| | Many species show systematic change over long time periods | |
| | Struggling with idea of multiple creations | |
| Ab4: systems of abstract systems, which are principles | Inadequate process of evolution: monad theory, branching tree | 1837 |
| | Hybridization (instead of natural selection) | |
| | Emergence of theory of evolution by natural selection (heredity, variation, natural) selection) | 1838–1839 |

Reprinted with the permission of SAGE Publications, London, Los Angeles, New Delhi and Singapore. Fischer, K. W., Yan, Z., & Stewart, J. (2003). Copyright © 2002. [Table 21.3, Page. 506]
*Note*. Skill structures in this table emphasize relations between physical and organic worlds in the various phrases of Darwin's work

Fischer has modeled the steps that Darwin had followed in arriving at the concept of evolution. He based the modeling on the substages of his model. Therefore, he described the increasing skill structures apparent in Darwin's thought process as his theory matured. Darwin appears to have passed from substages of the abstract stage into the principle one. Note that Fischer collapsed Darwin's later theoretical innovations into the last stage of his model

Since the present model consists of a postformal stage (collective intelligence) having substages, it could accommodate Darwin's later innovations into separate substages, unlike the case for the model of Fischer. For example, Darwin added a theory of within-species sexual selection to complement natural selection as processes at work in evolution. Moreover, Darwin expanded his work into precise observations of the facial expressions in children (Darwin, 1877)

The concept of natural selection could be construed as the first step of five in the development toward a complex theory of evolution. In terms of the present model, I would call this first phase of collective intelligence expressed by Darwin through construction of this concept as one of coordination, consistent with the language of substages in the present model. Recall that each stage develops through five substages in the present model: coordination, hierarchization, systematization, multiplication, and integration. In this regard, the construction of the concept of natural selection by Darwin involved coordinating the major components of the concept into a coherent theory (e.g., concerning natural variation, competition, etc.)

Darwin's two innovations after he had developed the concept of natural selection (sexual selection; human evolution) could be taken to reflect expansion of his base idea into a hierarchical structure of ideas, with the theory of evolution at the apex, as per the present model. That is, as Darwin expanded the concept of natural selection, the new models were not equivalent in emphasis and scope to natural selection, but devolved from it as part of his movement toward a more encompassing model

Darwin never arrived at a fully integrated theory of evolution, leaving the task to biologists who followed. It could be argued that the "modern synthesis," that developed in the last century

(continued)

**Table 11.8** (continued)

| |
|---|
| (it incorporated genetics) constituted the first step in that direction. That synthesis could be taken to reflect the substage of systematization in terms of the present model |
| The recent development of the "extended synthesis" could reflect the multiplication phase in the evolution of evolution, in terms of the present model (see Chaps. 18, 28, 29, and 32). Evolution now involves epigenetics, evo-devo, gene-cultural coevolution, multilevel selection, and so on |
| In this substage of elaborating Darwin's work, new ideas and discoveries keep moving the elusive target of integration nearer our grasp. Some of the ideas in the present work might help in this regard |

## Summary and Conclusions

This chapter gives a broad overview of Fischer's Neo-Piagetian model. The chapter indicates the anomalies in the parallels that Fischer has suggested for cognitive and Eriksonian development. In the next chapter, I review the work of Fischer and Mascolo on emotional development and cognitive-emotional correspondences in development. I point out where the work is fine and where it can be improved.

## References

Ayoub, C. C., & Fischer, K. W. (2006). Developmental pathways and intersections among domains of development. In K. McCartney & D. Phillips (Eds.), *Handbook of early child development* (pp. 62–82). Oxford: Blackwell.

Baillargeon, R. (1999). Young infants' expectations about hidden objects: A reply to three challenges. *Developmental Science, 2*, 115–132.

Baker-Brown, G., Ballard, E. J., Bluck, S., deVries, B., Suedfeld, P., & Tetlock, P. E. (1992). *Coding manual for conceptual/integrative complexity*. Vancouver: University of British Columbia.

Bidell, T. R., & Fischer, K. W. (1992). Beyond the stage debate: Action, structure, and variability in Piagetian theory and research. In R. J. Sternberg & C. A. Berg (Eds.), *Intellectual development* (pp. 100–140). New York: Cambridge University Press.

Bidell, T. R., & Fischer, K. W. (1996). Between nature and nurture: The role of human agency in the epigenesis of intelligence. In R. Sternberg & E. Grigorenko (Eds.), *Intelligence: Heredity and environment* (pp. 193–242). Cambridge: Cambridge University Press.

Blanchard-Fields, F. (1989). Postformal reasoning in a socioemotional context. In M. L. Commons, J. D. Sinnott, F. A. Richards, & C. Armon (Eds.), *Adult development: Vol. 1. Comparisons and applications of developmental models* (pp. 73–93). New York: Praeger.

Case, R. (1992). The role of the frontal lobes in the regulation of cognitive development. *Brain and Cognition, 20*, 51–73.

Case, R., Okamoto, Y., Griffin, S., McKeough, A., Bleiker, C., Henderson, B., et al. (1996). The role of central conceptual structures in the development of children's thought. *Monographs of the Society for Research in Child Development, 61*(5–6, Serial No. 246).

Commons, M. L. (2008). Introduction to the model of hierarchical complexity and its relationship to postformal action. *World Futures, 64*, 305–320.

Cook-Greuter, S. R. (1990). Maps of living: Ego development stages from symbiosis to conscious universal embeddedness. In M. L. Commons, C. Armon, L. Kohlberg, F. A. Richards, T. A. Grotzer, & J. D. Sinnott (Eds.), *Adult development: Vol. 2. Models and methods in the study of adolescent and adult thought* (pp. 79–104). New York: Praeger.

Darwin, C. (1877). A biographical sketch of an infant. *Mind, 2*, 286–299.

Dawson-Tunik, T. L. (2004). "A good education is …" the development of evaluation thought across the life span. *Genetic, Social, and General Psychology Monographs, 130*, 4–112.

Dawson-Tunik, T. L. (2006). The meaning and measurement of conceptual development in adulthood. In C. Hoare (Ed.), *Handbook of adult development and learning* (pp. 433–454). New York: Oxford University Press.

Dawson-Tunik, T. L., Commons, M., Wilson, M., & Fischer, K. W. (2005). The shape of development. *European Journal of Developmental Psychology, 2*, 163–195.

Erikson, E. H. (1968). *Identity: Youth and crisis*. New York: Norton.

Fischer, K. W., & Ayoub, C. (1994). Affective splitting and dissociation in normal and maltreated children: Developmental pathways for self in relationships. In D. Cicchetti & S. L. Toth (Eds.), *Disorders and dysfunctions of the self* (Vol. 5, pp. 149–222). Rochester: University of Rochester Press.

Fischer, K. W., & Bidell, T. R. (2006). Dynamic development of action and thought. In W. Damon & R. M. Lerner (Eds.), *Handbook of child psychology: Vol. 1. Theoretical models of human development* (Vol. 1, pp. 313–399). New York: Wiley.

Fischer, K. W., Bullock, D. H., Rotenberg, E. J., & Raya, P. (1993). The dynamics of competence: How context contributes directly to skill. In R. H. Wozniak & K. W. Fischer (Eds.), *Development in context: Acting and thinking in specific environments – The Jean Piaget symposium series* (pp. 93–117). Hillsdale: Erlbaum.

Fischer, K. W., & Hogan, A. E. (1989). The big picture for infant development: Levels and variations. In J. Lockman & N. Hazen (Eds.), *Action in social context: Perspectives on early development* (pp. 275–305). New York: Plenum.

Fischer, K. W., & Immordino-Yang, M. H. (2002). Cognitive development and education: From dynamic general structure to specific learning and teaching. In E. Lagemann (Ed.), *Traditions of scholarship in education*. Chicago: Spencer Foundation.

Fischer, K. W., & Kennedy, B. (1997). Tools for analyzing the many shapes of development: The case of self-in-relationships in Korea. In E. Amsel & K. A. Renninger (Eds.), *Change and development: Issues of theory, method, and application* (pp. 117–152). Mahwah: Erlbaum.

Fischer, K. W., & Pruyne, E. (2003). Reflective thinking in adulthood: Emergence, development, and variation. In J. Demick & C. Andreoletti (Eds.), *Handbook of adult development* (pp. 169–198). New York: Kluwer Academic.

Fischer, K. W., & Rose, S. P. (1996). Dynamic growth cycles of brain and cognitive development. In R. Thatcher, G. R. Lyon, J. Rumsey, & N. Krasnegor (Eds.), *Developmental neuroimaging: Mapping the development of brain and behavior* (pp. 263–279). New York: Academic Press.

Fischer, K. W., Shaver, P. R., & Carnochan, P. (1990). How emotions develop and how they organize development. *Cognition and Emotion, 4*(2), 81–127.

Fischer, K. W., Yan, Z., & Stewart, J. (2003). Adult cognitive development: Dynamics in the developmental web. In J. Valsiner & K. J. Connolly (Eds.), *Handbook of developmental psychology* (pp. 493–516). London: Sage.

King, P. M., & Kitchener, K. S. (1993). The development of reflexive thinking in the college years: The mixed results. In C. G. Schmeider & W. S. Green (Eds.), *Strengthening the college major. New directions for higher education* (Vol. 84, pp. 25–42). San Francisco: Jossey-Bass.

King, P. M., & Kitchener, K. S. (1994). *Developing reflexive judgment: Understanding and promoting intellectual growth and critical thinking in adolescents and adults*. San Francisco: Jossey-Bass.

Kitchener, K. S., & King, P. M. (1981). Reflective judgment: Concepts of justification and their relationship to age and education. *Journal of Applied Developmental Psychology, 2*, 89–116.

Kitchener, K. S., & King, P. M. (1990). The reflective judgement model: Ten years of research. In M. L. Commons, C. Armon, L. Kohlberg, F. A. Richards, T. A. Grotzer, & J. D. Sinnott (Eds.), *Adult development 3: Models and methods in the study of adolescent and adult thought* (pp. 62–78). New York: Praeger.

Kitchener, K. S., King, P. M., & DeLuca, S. (2006). Development of reflective judgment in adulthood. In C. Hoare (Ed.), *Handbook of adult development and learning* (pp. 73–98). New York: Oxford University Press.

Kitchener, K. S., Lynch, C. L., Fischer, K. W., & Wood, P. K. (1993). Developmental range of reflective judgement: The effect of contextual support and practice on developmental stage. *Developmental Psychology, 29*, 893–906.

Knight, C. C., & Fischer, K. W. (1992). Learning to read words: Individual differences in developmental sequences. *Journal of Applied Developmental Psychology, 13*, 377–404.

Kohlberg, L. (1981). *Essays on moral development: Vol. 1. The psychology of moral development.* San Francisco: Harper & Row.

Kohlberg, L. (1984). *Essays on moral development: Vol. 2. The psychology of moral development.* San Francisco: Harper & Row.

Kohlberg, L., & Ryncarz, R. A. (1990). Beyond justice reasoning: Moral development and consideration of a seventh stage. In C. N. Alexander & E. J. Langer (Eds.), *Higher stages of human development: Perspectives on adult growth* (pp. 191–207). New York: Oxford University Press.

Lamborn, S. D., Fischer, K. W., & Pipp, S. (1994). Constructive criticism and social lies: A developmental sequence for understanding honesty and kindness in social interactions. *Developmental Psychology, 30*, 495–508.

Loevinger, J. (1976). *Ego development: Conceptions and theories*. San Francisco: Jossey-Bass.

Loevinger, J. (1987). *Paradigms of personality*. San Francisco: Freeman.

Mascolo, M. F., & Fischer, K. W. (2010). The dynamic development of thinking, feeling and acting over the lifespan. In R. M. Lerner & W. F. Overton (Eds.), *Handbook of lifespan development: Vol. 1. Cognitive, biology and methods*. Hoboken: Wiley.

Mascolo, M. J., Fischer, K. W., & Li, J. (2003). Dynamic development of component systems of emotions: Pride, shame, and guilt in China and the United States. In R. J. Davidson, K. Scherer, & H. H. Goldsmith (Eds.), *Handbook of affective science* (pp. 375–408). Oxford: Oxford University Press.

Noam, G. G. (1992). Development as the aim of clinical intervention. *Development and Psychopathology, 4*, 679–696.

Perry, W. B. (1970). *Forms of intellectual and ethical development in the college years*. New York: Holt, Rinehart & Winston.

Richards, F. A., & Commons, M. L. (1990). Postformal cognitive-developmental theory and research: A review of its current status. In C. N. Alexander & E. J. Langer (Eds.), *Higher stages of human development: Perspectives on adult growth* (pp. 139–160). New York: Oxford University Press.

Shaver, P. R., Wu, S., & Schwartz, J. C. (1992). Cross-cultural similarities and differences in emotion and its representation: A prototype approach. In M. S. Clark (Ed.), *Review of personality and social psychology* (Vol. 13). Thousand Oaks: Sage.

Thatcher, R. W. (1994). Cyclic cortical reorganization: Origins of human cognitive development. In G. Dawson & K. W. Fischer (Eds.), *Human behavior and the developing brain* (pp. 232–266). New York: Guilford Press.

Thelen, E., & Smith, L. B. (1994). *A dynamic systems approach to the development of cognition and action*. Cambridge: MIT Press.

Uzgiris, I. C., & Hunt, J. M. V. (1987). *Infant performance and experience: New findings with the ordinal scales*. Urbana: University of Illinois Press.

van Geert, P. (1994). *Dynamic systems of development: Change between complexity and chaos*. New York: Harvester Wheatsheaf.

van Geert, P. (1998). A dynamic systems model of basic developmental mechanisms: Piaget, Vygotsky, and beyond. *Psychological Review, 105*, 634–677.

Vygotsky, L. S. (1978). *Mind in society: The development of higher psychological processes*. Cambridge: Harvard University Press.

Young, G. (1997). *Adult development, therapy, and culture: A postmodern synthesis*. New York: Plenum.

# Chapter 12
# Recent Fischer: Emotional Development

## Introduction

Fischer and Mascolo and colleagues have developed a comprehensive model of emotional development in relation to Fischer's model of cognitive development. They took pains to show how some basic emotions evolve through steps in their cognitive model. In the following, I describe that work, and show how it can be revised according to my model. Without their first efforts for these emotions (pride, shame, guilt, anger), the modifications described in the present work could not have been constructed.

## An Integrated, Lifespan Perspective

### *Introduction*

Mascolo and Fischer (2010) explored the implications of Fischer's cognitive developmental model for the relationship among thinking, feeling, and acting over the lifetime. First, they emphasized that thinking is not a sequence of internal cognitive processes, but is an embodied function in brain, body, action, and social context (Gallagher, 2005; Gibbs, 2006; Overton, Müller, & Newman, 2007). Cognition and emotion are not separate modules but coact as necessary components to action by the individual, who, in turn, is part of an interlocking social system. Psychological functions that appear different really develop in lock-step, codeveloping and influencing each other over the lifespan in a relational developmental system (Gottlieb, 2003; Lerner & Overton, 2008). The authors give the example of mallard ducklings responding selectively to maternal calls only if they had been exposed in utero to their own or another duck's vocalizations (Figs. 12.1 and 12.2).

G. Young, *Development and Causality: Neo-Piagetian Perspectives*,
DOI 10.1007/978-1-4419-9422-6_12, © Springer Science+Business Media, LLC 2011

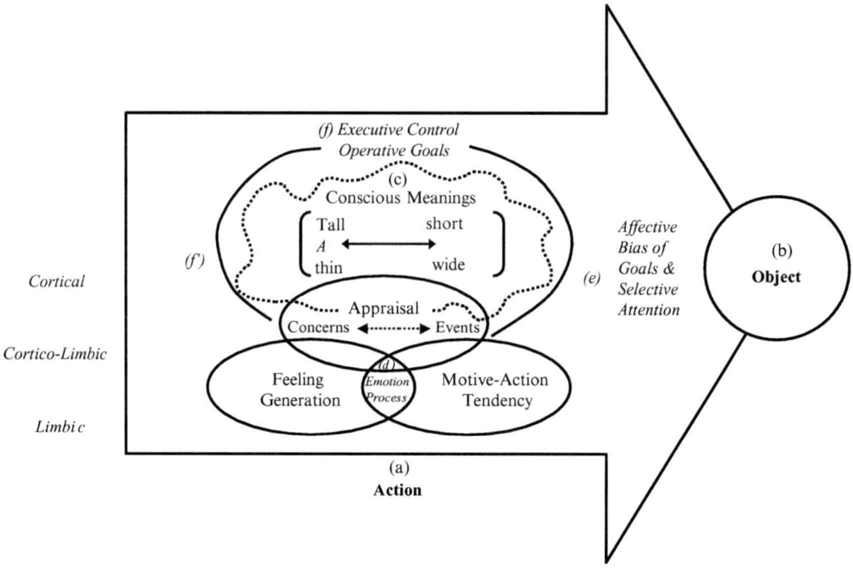


**Fig. 12.1** The architecture of human action. Psychological processes are understood as forms or components of meaning-mediated action (*a*). Psychological acts exhibit intentionality (aboutness), in the sense that they are directed toward some object, real or imagined. Psychological activity is mediated by meaning (point *c*). The structure of meaning in consciousness emerges from multiple sources. Nonconscious affect-generating processes (point *d*). Simultaneously, in any given context, higher-order executive processes (*f*) exert downward and conscious control over the construction of meaning (*f'*) and the regulation of affect (*f'*). In this way, any psychological act involves the integration of cognitive, conative, and affective processes at multiple levels of functioning. Reprinted with the permission of John Wiley & Sons, Inc. Mascolo, M. F., & Fischer, K. W. (2010). Copyright © 2010 and John Wiley & Sons, Inc. [Figure 6.1, Page. 153]

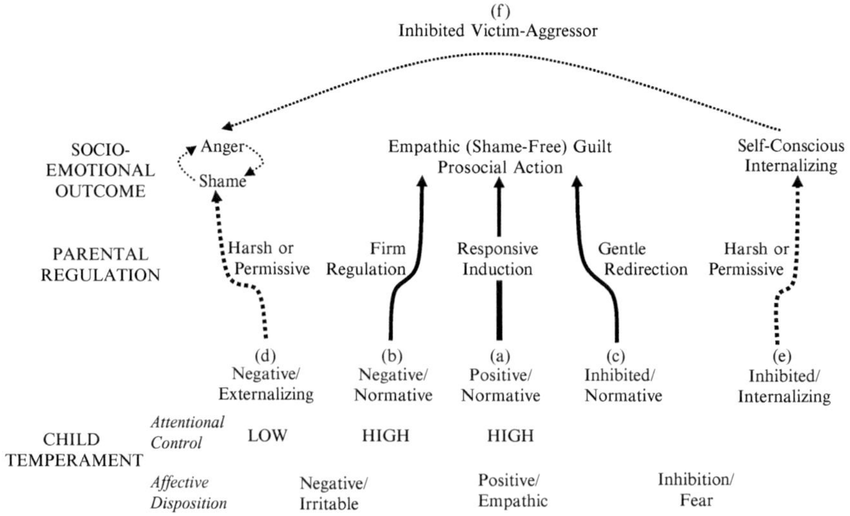


**Fig. 12.2** Diverging and converging pathways in socioemotional development. The figure shows different trajectories in socioemotional outcome in terms of different parental regulation styles and child temperament. Reprinted with the permission of John Wiley & Sons, Inc. Mascolo, M. F., & Fischer, K. W. (2010). Copyright © 2010 and John Wiley & Sons, Inc. [Figure 6.6, Page. 165]

## Architecture

Mascolo and Fischer proceeded to construct a model of the architecture of human action. It builds on MacLean's (1993) concept of a triune brain, involving the levels of limbic, cortico-limbic, and cortical structures. The authors defined psychological structure as: a basic dynamic, contextually adaptive integration or unit of motive-relevant feelings or affect, meanings which mediate them, experience, and the motor actions from which they originate. Meanings can be conscious, acts can be intentional, and goals that are operative can be involved. Cognitively, attention and selection, appraisals, and executive controls are involved. Affective processes are integral to the architecture of action, which necessarily involves an integration of the three components of cognitive, conative, and emotional processes.

## Components

For Mascolo and Fischer (2010), emotional states can be understood in terms of these latter three broad classes of components (Mascolo, Fischer, & Li, 2003). They comprise (a) motive-relevant appraisals (Lazarus, 1991; Scherer, 2004), (b) corporal or bodily experience, labeled feeling or "phenomenal" tone (Bermond, 2008; Scherer, 2004), and (c) typical motor expressions and action tendencies (Frijda 1987). Appraisals are fact-acting, nonconscious, and deliberate cognitive-motive driven activities (Barrett, Ochsner, & Gross, 2007) that increasingly involve higher-order meanings as development takes place. Just as appraisals are motive-relevant, so are action tendencies. They can be either voluntary or involuntary. They are functional in context. When expressed as a category of emotion, they involve typical patterns in the face, voice, and posture, and possibly in instrumental action, depending on context. The three components of appraisal, affect, and action regulate each other in real time, so that none are primary or first in sequence. Appraisals may generate, modulate, and modify affect and action, but affect reciprocally organizes, selects, and amplifies them.

## Brain

In terms of the neurobiological substrate of the architecture of action, Mascolo and Fischer maintained that if there are brain centers for discrete emotions in the brain, they massively interdigitate and are distributed throughout the brain (Panksepp, 1998; Thompson, 2007). Executive functions involving higher-order symbolic representations are mediated by frontal and prefrontal cortical activity (Cozolino, 2006). As sensory information is relayed from lower centers, it takes a fast-acting pathway to the amygdala, which helps in the assessment of the emotional significance of events (Labar & Ledoux, 2003). The amygdala is richly connected to the hippocampus, which is important in the consolidation of episodic memory representations. A second pathway sends the information to the prefrontal cortex, involved in the analysis of higher-order meaning and in the linking of actions to goals (Cacioppo, Visser, & Picket, 2006). The amygdala also activates the hypothalamus, involved in the hypothalamus-pituitary-adrenal (HPA) axis, and the chain of reactions in the stress response (including freezing at lower levels of activation/danger, which facilitates better assessment of the situation, and the fight or flight response at higher levels).

The findings indicate that affective processes are multiply distributed in different levels of the nervous system (Pessoa, 2008). Lower levels in the limbic and cortico-limbic systems are involved in rapid acting and nonconscious affective processing, whereas cortical functions are involved in more deliberate, higher-order activities, including executive control (Zelazo & Cunningham, 2007). Cognitive and affective processes are massively connected in the brain and are dynamically coupled in their functioning (Lewis & Todd, 2007).

## *Skills*

Psychological structures develop on this neural, cognitive, affective, and action base at the local level, and there are no all-purpose ones. They are localized skills developed in response to and applied to particular situations, and they develop according to the stages and substages (tiers and levels) of cognitive development. To review, there are five tiers (reflexes, sensorimotor actions, representations, abstractions, and principles), for which there are three levels in the first four of them (sets, mappings, systems, which cyclically recur, and in this process, systems of systems become sets for the next tier). Although dynamic skills develop in the same sequence within different domains, they vary across domains, and the typical age of acquisition is not the same for an individual across domains even if one controls context. The local skills become increasingly integrated within particular situations, but they remain bounded or encapsulated to the domain in question and do not form whole (sub)stages. The pathways are partially distinct, but higher-order levels can emerge, as previously described in discussing Fischer's concept of the developmental web.

## *Web*

The concept of the web differs in several ways from the traditional concept of a developmental ladder or staircase (Fischer, Yan, & Stewart, 2003). (a) The ladder focuses on universal acquisitions and de-emphasizes variation, whereas the web highlights local activity variations within a global order. (b) The ladder model focuses on group performance, but the web can represent developmental sequences for individuals or groups. (c) The ladder model is based on a developmental model involving functioning from one level at a time, whereas the web suggests that individuals can function at multiple levels, depending on the skills involved. (d) The ladder model indicates a single direction in development, but the web implies that multiple variations are possible, for example, in multiple domains, tasks, contexts, etc. (e) The ladder model cannot assimilate concepts of interlinked diverse developmental strands and trajectories, whereas this approach is highlighted in web models. (f) The ladder model assumes that only progress is possible along a developmental pathway [I would add, "or delay"], but a web approach acknowledges different trajectories, as well, such as backward transitions.

### *Inter-Subjectivity*

In terms of the development of early affect, Mascolo and Fischer cited the work of Trevarthen (1993), who argued that even newborns are capable of rudimentary intersubjectivity, or engaging in shared or coordinated interaction. The latter concept includes the coordination of emotional experiences (Gallagher & Hutto, 2008). Meltzoff and Moore (1989) described neonatal imitation. The discovery of "mirror" neurons (Gallese, Eagle, & Migone, 2007) that activate not only when observing behavior in others but also in undertaking the same action bolsters the possibility of such early intersubjectivity through the self-other experiential correspondences that they (or similar systems) allow (Meltzoff & Brooks, 2007). These findings have import for understanding that intersubjectivity is not a result of cognitive development but builds from it (Fogel, Garvey, Hsu, & West-Stromming, 2006). Mascolo and Fischer also dealt with emotions in adults, as they charted the change in complexity of a client's meaning structures in therapy according to their tier-level model.

## Emotional Development

### *Preview*

Mascolo and Fischer (2010) have explored the relationship between Fischer's model of stages and substages in cognitive development and the development of self-related emotions (Mascolo & Fischer, 1995, 2007; Mascolo et al., 2003). They have focused on the development of pride, shame, and guilt in the early years, in particular, but also describe parallel cognitive-emotional acquisitions into the teen years. The major contribution of this series of articles concerns the intricate demonstration of how the self-related emotions change as they pass through the various substages in cognitive development.

At the same time, in the following, I show how the details of the parallel cognitive-emotional linkages described by Fischer and colleagues offer some support of the present cognitive developmental model relative to that of Fischer's. I demonstrate how the description of the development of self-related emotions in the early years described by the authors needs to be expanded and how it is most consistent with the present Neo-Piagetian model relative to others, thereby indicating its relative value and validity.

## *Mascolo and Fischer (2007)*

### Introduction

In their most recent article in the series of articles that give the specifics of their model of the evolution of some basic emotions according to the steps of Fischer's model, Mascolo and Fischer (2007) began by documenting the impressive developments of the self, in general, in the first 2 years of life. The self integrates a cognitive, emotional, conative, and social component. The emotional components, especially those that concern self-conscious and moral aspects, are notable acquisitions early in life. The self-conscious emotions include pride, shame, and guilt. The authors also dealt with the emotion of anger, given its agentic underpinning. They argued that emotions and cognitions are intimately intertwined, for example, emotions both organize and are organized by the child's growing ability to evaluate the self in social context.

In this regard, Mascolo and Fischer (2007) referred to the codevelopment of self and sociomoral emotions in the toddler and toddlers' interactions with parents and other significant adults. They considered the self as a reflective process. For example, self-awareness develops by way of the actions and words of parents and others that channel constructive activity back onto the child's activity ("reflecting consciousness back on itself"). Therefore, socialization agents codevelop the development of internalized moral guides. As the child develops representations of self-control, they evolve into a higher-order control structures that drive social interaction.

Mascolo and Fischer (2007) added that by examining the change of self-conscious emotions over stages and substages of cognitive development, we can learn more about the development of the self. Cognitively, the toddler is developing motive-relevant appraisals as part of emotional components. These also include feeling tone and motive-action tendencies.

### Comment

#### Analysis

Figure 12.3 diagrams the series of steps in the second and third years of life in the development of anger, shame, and guilt according to Fischer's cognitive developmental model. Note that in the figure, the sequence of the stages or substages, or

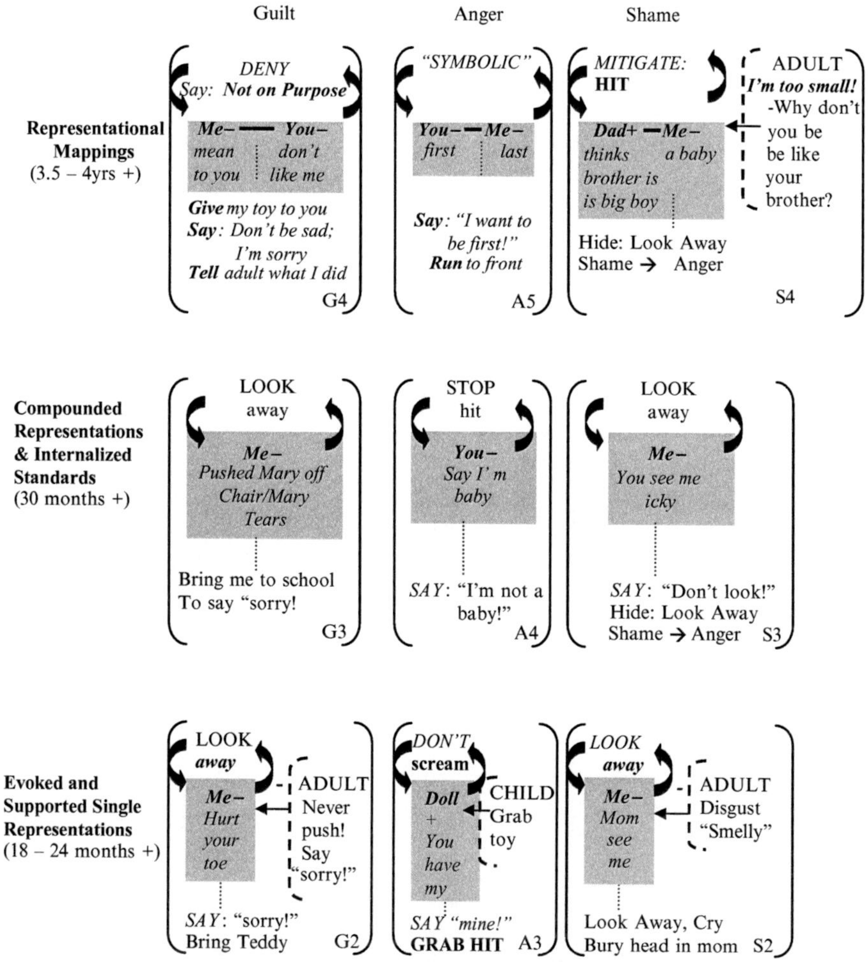


**Fig. 12.3** Developmental changes in the dynamic structure of anger, guilt, and shame. Emotional skill diagrams depicting changes in sociomoral emotions in development. The structure of the diagrams is depicted in the box in the lower right-hand corner of the figure. Using skill theory (Fischer, 1980), the shaded portion of the diagram reflects the structure of the child's appraisal activity. The lower (unshaded) portion, connected to appraisal structures with a dotted line, identifies the structure of emotion action-tendencies. The structure above the shaded portion of the diagram identifies the structure of emotional control elements. The regulation function of control elements is indicated using bidirectional, curved arrows. For some diagrams, the structure of adult action is provided to the right of the emotional skill diagram for the child. The arrow between the adult and child structures indicates the flow of action from the adult to the child. Plus and minus signs indicated the motivational valence (positive or negative) of the skill element in question. For emotions at the sensorimotor level, appraisal activity and action tendencies are represented together because, at this level, appraisal processes are embedded within sensorimotor action. The changes specified reflect changes typical of North America and Western European children. At any given age, the particular structure of emotional action varies with context, child, culture, affective state, and other important factors. Reprinted with the permission of Guilford Publications, Inc. Mascolo, M. F., & Fischer, K. W. (2007). Copyright © 2007 and Guilford Press. [Figure 3.2, Page. 74]

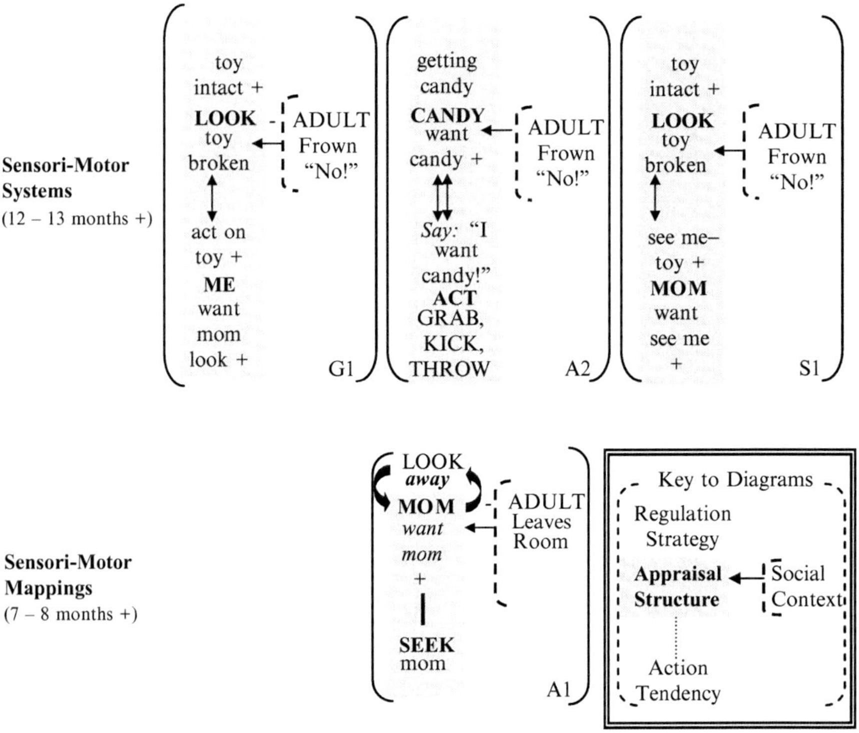


**Fig. 12.3** (continued)

tiers and levels, which Fischer typically describes in his cognitive model has been altered, where needed, by Mascolo and Fischer (2007), by including supplementary, interposed steps. This procedure is standard in the approach of Fischer because, depending on the skill being investigated, he might add steps outside the typical tier-level structure to accommodate, as needed, data or theory.

In particular, for the figure under discussion, Mascolo and Fischer (2007) added a step at 2.5 years that deals with compounded representations and internalized standards. To my knowledge, this represents the first time in all publications on Fischer's cognitive developmental model that such a step has been added to his usual sequence. Relative to the standard cognitive model in Fischer, the new step was fitted between Fischer's levels of single representations and representational mappings.

It is instructive to note that he called the substage or level that is typically included in his model for the 18–24-month period, that of single representations, as "evoked and supported," whereas he called the new substage that he added after that as "compounded and internalized." This indicates the validity of the concerns that

I have enunciated in the present work that Fischer seems to have missed in his model of cognitive development an important substage, level, or step at the 2-year period. Moreover, it supports another argument that I have made – that the single representations period at 18–24 months in his model is really a last step in the development of the sensorimotor stage. Although there are representational elements in it, it needs evoking and support to bring out the representations. In this sense, they are not pure representations, or internalized action-free symbolic systems that guide behavior, such as with sentences in language, deferred imitation, and symbolic play, as described by Piaget.

According to the adjectives used to describe the next substage of compounded representations and internalized standards, which appears at 2.5 years according to the figure, it seems clear that Fischer considered this time frame as one involving the development of truly independent representations in the Piagetian sense. The child can develop an internalized compounded representation removed from action or superordinate to it, without the conditions of being "evoked and supported."

## Further Analysis

In further analysis of the present argument, I look more carefully at the examples provided in the Fig. 12.3. First, in the single representational level, for each of guilt, anger, and shame, there seems to be some element of action necessary in both the elicitation of the emotion and in its expression and representation. For example, in the first one listed in the figure, that of guilt, the adult says, "Never push, say sorry!" and the child's action tendency is to "Say sorry" and to *bring* the teddy to the other child. By contrast, in the level of compounded representations and internalized standards, which is the substage that follows, after pushing another child off a chair and seeing the other child tearing, the child appraises that he should ask mother to "Go back to school to say sorry". There is neither an adult acting (berating the child, evoking the emotion) nor the child responding with the action of bringing a teddy bear to the other child. For the first time in Fischer's sequence being described for these emotions, the representation involved is both support- and action-free, as would be expected for the age period in question according to the present model and that of Piaget, but which is in contrast to the ascription of a representational nature of the prior step in Fischer's model.

Not only does this example indicate that there is a missing representational step in Fischer's usual model at the 2-year age period, but it also indicates that it makes sense to describe it as a coordinated one, as found in the present model (perioperational coordination). In the example given, the child coordinates the feeling of guilt in the self with the request to make amends by saying sorry. Yet, something is missing in the child's sense of guilt in this age period and, its development must wait until the next substage appears when more than coordination can be put into effect – at this point of the child's development, which is marked yet limited by the child's coordinative capacities, the feelings of the other are not part of the motivational equation for the request made by the child to the other.

I have other points about the work being analyzed that could lead to its improvement. First, the diagram to represent appraisal structures, action tendencies, regulation strategies, and social context could be improved. The manner in which it is constructed allows for an absence of social context in some of the examples. However, the social context, and usually a particular other, must always be involved in the types of emotions being discussed. Also, regulation strategies are reduced to behaviors such as look away, but many of the action tendencies described appear to be good examples of regulation strategies. Fourth, appraisals are presented as single items, but these can be more complex, especially as the child enters the 2-year period. Finally, as presented, the appraisal structures at times include both self- and other-appraisals, and these should be separated.

## Reworking of Mascolo-Fischer Model

### Introduction

Given these considerations, I have reworked Mascolo and Fischer's model of the development of guilt for the age period from 1 to 3 years (see Fig. 12.4). Moreover, by consulting their 1995 chapter, I added to this present reworking of their figure the next substage in their model. It had not been given in the 2007 publication, but did appear in that prior publication. In creating the revised model of the development of guilt, for the most part, I followed the format that they used, including using their symbolism to represent the components of appraisal structures and action tendencies [although I placed the latter in boxes rather than the former]. However, in my version of their model, I did not include the component of regulation strategy; also, for the social context, I indicated when an adult seems not directly involved, but noting this does not preclude the possibility that a general social context could be involved in some way.

This procedure that I followed in reworking Fischer and colleagues' model of the development of guilt allowed me to move those portions of the child's appraisal into the social context category when the appraisal described by them was about the other. This modification of the figure is consistent with the authors' use of the heading "You" (or other) in the appraisal box. Those specific appraisals that were about "Me" were the ones that I kept in the appraisal boxes about the self. Therefore, at each substage of the model, I presented Me-appraisals and You-appraisals that were coordinated. Note that I referred to the "You" appraisals as "Other" appraisals, a term chosen because it excludes the propositional pronoun, per se.

Finally, in the reworking of their model, I added an "Implication" step between the appraisal and action tendency steps, at least from the 2-year period onward when pure representations are considered to develop in my model of cognitive development. The concept of implications deriving from appraisals is consistent with the authors' model, and the examples provided are taken from their work for the most part. As another modification of the work of Fischer and colleagues, note that in my version of their model, I qualified the type of action tendency that

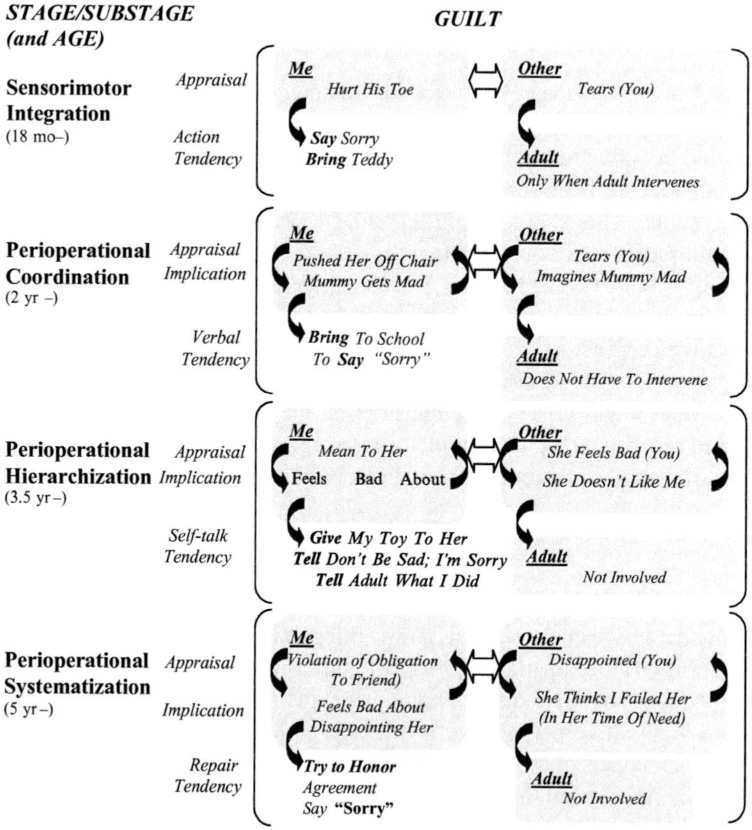


**Fig. 12.4** Appraisal structure and action tendency in the development of guilt in the early years. The figure presents a revised version of the development of guilt through the substages in cognitive development according to Fischer and colleagues. Instead of using the substages proposed in Fischer's model, I use my own. This leads to the presentation of a substage with no equivalent in Fischer's model, at 18 months of age. In terms of the structure of guilt representations in the age periods presented, I indicate the appraisals, action tendencies and, for the older periods, the implications. In terms of the self and other, the table gives the appraisals, tendencies, and implications for the developing person's understanding of the Me and the Other. For example, the 2-year-old hurts a child, sees the tears, knows mummy will be angry, and asks her to bring him to school to say Sorry. Fischer presented a model that included similar information, but in a way that is not as complete as the present version. This being said, the present model could not have been constructed without his initial contribution

seemed to be involved in each substage, because the adjective "action" might give a false impression that movement and motor tendencies must be involved. The examples provided by me indicate that the child develops an increasing sense of control and internalization of these action tendencies in passing through the various substages.

### Stages and Substages

Note that I organized the revised version of their model according to the stages provided in my model of cognitive development. In the age period involved, the child should be going through the substages of sensorimotor integrations, and then perioperational coordinations, perioperational hierarchizations, and perioperational systematizations. This should bring the child toward the next stage of perioperational multiplications in which Piaget's classic account of the development of concrete operations takes place, at 7 years. Therefore, in the revised model of the development of guilt in the early years, (a) I have shown how the child's cognitive appraisals with respect to the emotion of guilt develop in terms of the substages of the present model. (b) I describe the implications involved and the various response tendencies that might arise, while considering the child's evolving conception of the other in social context. (c) Regulatory strategies are seen to develop within the context of the appraisals, implications, tendencies, and sense of the other.

## Guilt

The figure that I have constructed as a reworking of the figure presented by Mascolo and Fischer (2007) for the development of guilt illustrates the manner in which the present model of cognitive development can explain quite well the development of guilt from a cognitive perspective in the age period of concern relative to other Neo-Piagetian models of cognitive development, such as Fischer's. In the following, I describe the figure (and model) in detail.

### Perioperational Coordination

First, I note that in the example already provided for what transpires at 2 years of age in the perioperational coordination substage, which Fischer refers to as representational compounding, the implication step of the cognitive appraisal that the index child hurt another one is that, (a) for the self, the mother of the index child will get angry, and (b) for the other, the index child can imagine the mother getting angry. The index child is coordinating not only the appraisals involved (other child is hurt, she is tearing) but also the implications involved. This analysis of guilt in this age period clearly is consistent with the present model.

Notice in the example the degree to which representations are present relative to the prior substage. The implication concerning the other is about *imagining* the mother angry. The action tendency involves a *verbal* statement ("Bring to school to say 'Sorry'"). Both of these aspects of the model of the development of guilt in this age period involve clear representations. In the prior substage of sensorimotor integrations, which Fischer refers to as representational sets but which I contend is still sensorimotor in nature, Fischer does not describe any intermediary cognitive appraisals of an implication nature that mediate the initial cognitive appraisal and the resultant action tendency. Moreover, as already discussed, the action tendency is quite sensorimotoric in nature, despite the language element.

## Perioperational Hierarchization

For the next substage of the present reworking of the Mascolo-Fischer model of the development of guilt, according to the present model, the child enters the stage of perioperational hierarchization. Fischer refers to this stage as involving representational mappings. There is not much difference in the conceptions of hierarchizations and mappings. However, the concept of a hierarchy is quite specific in the expectations that one should have about how the elements of the cognitive activity in this age period should interrelate.

By analyzing the specific examples provided by Mascolo and Fischer for the development of guilt in the 3–4-year period, I show the presence of a hierarchical structure. First, the structure has evolved relative to the one in the prior substage. Because of the changes to the schematic that I have introduced, as described above, we can see how the child is cycling across the appraisals of having been mean and the other feeling bad, leading to the implications that the index child feels bad about this and is also aware of the other not liking him because of his behavior. These cognitive notions are mapping or synchronizing with each other, as indicated by the double arrows, but they are doing more. They lead to the self-talk of involving a repair behavior. In other words, the initial perspective-taking that the child is capable of developing in this age period creates the situation in which the understanding that the other might not like oneself leads to perspective-taking as the apex of the mental mappings being constructed, which is a hierarchical structure. The result is an organization of the repair tendency for the guilt that the improper social behavior had induced. Nevertheless, for the development of guilt being described, although there is a hierarchical appearance, there is something lacking in the child's development relative to that evident in the next substage, involving systematization.

## Perioperational Systematization

In the next cognitive substage of perioperational systematization in the present model, the example provided by Mascolo and Fischer fits perfectly, and this is not surprising because they refer to this substage as one of representation systems. However, I have reworked their example, taken from Mascolo and Fischer (1995), so that it is consistent with the present schematic. In their example, the child violates an obligation to a friend and he feels guilty because the friend thinks that he failed her in a time of need. I added to the example that the implication for the self is that the child feels bad about disappointing the other and the appraisal of the other by the child is that she must feel disappointed in him. In terms of the action tendency, I referred to it as an actual repair tendency, rather than just self-talk about wanting to conduct a repair. The child at this stage will make the amends to the degree possible and try to honor the original agreement. These additions to the schematic indicate that a comprehensive systematization has taken place in the child's cognitive structuring activity at this age. The child has developed a contextually specific social rule that he applies diligently.

The next step in the child's cognitive development with respect to guilt is more advanced. The child can generalize from accumulating examples of this kind to create logical, but concrete, rules. They help guide social behavior, in general, in parallel with the cognitive development of concrete operations, as described by Piaget.

## Shame and Anger

Mascolo and Fischer (2007) graphed the development of other self-related emotions in the age period under discussion. My main concerns in reviewing them are similar to those that I had in examining their work on the development of guilt. That is, the Mascolo-Fischer description of the development of these other emotions in the early years demonstrates that there is an intermediate substage required in Fischer's general model, which typically involves in this age period transition from representational sets to mappings. Moreover, the model as presented by Mascolo and Fischer should qualify the representational set substage because it is more like a sensorimotor integration one.

For example, with respect to the emotion of anger, in the examples provided by Mascolo and Fischer, the 18-month-old is described as having a tendency to say "Mine" and to grab and hit when another child takes a toy. In my view, this is consistent with a sensorimotor nature in the emotional expression of the infant at this age. By contrast, as I would expect, the older child's anger is not described in terms of action tendencies or actions but with verbal statements. That the description just given has these properties is not notable, but that it is the first time anger is expressed representationally in the examples provided, despite the nature of the steps in the Mascolo and Fischer model that they are presumed to reflect, is notable.

Similarly, for shame, the 18-month-old is described in terms of looking away, crying, and burying the head in mother, but the older child says not to look instead of crying and burying the head. Once more, the 18-month-old is described in terms of a sensorimotor base rather than a pure representational one and the 2-year-old is the one to first manifest a representational expression in the emotion under discussion. Once more, the examples provided in Fischer's work are more consistent with the present model than his own.

Another issue about the emotions of anger and shame in the presentation of Mascolo and Fischer is whether the examples provided for the 3-year-old reflect hierarchizations more so than mappings. In this regard, for anger, the child wants to be first and runs to the front, and engages in hitting the other symbolically. However, this behavior could only take place if the child hierarchically places himself first relative to the other as second or last. Similarly, for shame, the Mascolo-Fischer example involves the father comparing negatively the child to the brother, and consequently the child feeling like a baby. I note that, in this example, the shame that results could only take place if the child hierarchically places the self as below the level of the older sibling. Therefore, for the 3-year-old period, both examples that are provided by Mascolo and Fischer end up supporting the present model more than that of Fischer.

## *Mascolo and Fischer (1995)*

### Introduction

I have already presented some of the chapter by Mascolo and Fischer (1995) in describing the cognitive-affective parallels in Fischer's work. In this section, I elaborate further on their presentation of self-related emotions (see Tables 12.1 and 12.2), and I relate their presentation to the later but somewhat reduced presentation of the same material in Mascolo et al. (2003) [In the latter publication, the authors presented the developmental sequence only for pride, and only for the American population.] (see Table 12.3).

For the development of the emotions being considered, Mascolo and Fischer (1995) started with Fischer's sensorimotor mapping substage, but in Mascolo et al. (2003), they removed this substage. In the first article, they presented two steps in the representational mapping substage, but there was only one in the later publication. This pattern is slightly different for guilt, though. For this emotion, there are three steps in the substage of representational sets, not one or two (for the age period of 18–24 months). Moreover, there is no substage in guilt that emerges at 2–3 years, unlike for the other emotions involved (pride, shame), as has been shown. Therefore, for guilt, the development of the fourth step in the sequence does not take place at 2 years, an age at which there had been steps for the other emotions; rather, it takes place at 4 years. In addition, for guilt, the numbering of the steps terminates at 7 instead of 8. Nevertheless, because of the three steps at the 18–24-month period, the same amount of steps is described in the guilt sequence as in the pride and shame sequences.

### Pride

#### Their Model

I find it instructive that in their most recent publication on the developmental sequence for pride, Fischer et al. (2003) have reduced the two representational mapping steps to one step but have not reduced the two representational sets steps to one step. This is consistent with the present argument that Fischer had originally missed an important substage at about 2 years of age in his cognitive model [and not relative to the next substage of mappings].

**Table 12.1** Development of appraisal skills for pride, shame, and guilt in Fischer (Categories)

| Stage/substage (age) | Pride skill step | Shame skill step | Guilt skill step |
|---|---|---|---|
| Sensorimotor mappings (7–8 months) | *P1: Joy* about simple action-outcome contingency | *S1: Distress* about simple action-outcome failure | *G1: Distress* about other's upset produces by simple action-outcome contingency |
| Sensorimotor systems (11–13 months) | *P2: Joy* about complex action-outcome contingency including other's evaluation | *S2: Distress* about complex action-outcome failure including other's evaluation | *G2: Distress* about other's upset produced by complex action-outcome contingency |
| Single representations (18–24 months) | *P3: Joy/Pride* about result caused by self | *S3: Distress/Shame* about result caused by self | *G3a: Distress/Guilt* about other's upset caused by self's aggressive action |
| Single representations (18–24 months) | | | *G3b: Distress/Guilt* about other's upset caused by self's negative statement |
| Single representations (18–24 months) | | | *G3c: Distress/Guilt* about other's upset caused by self's refusal to act positively |
| Single representations (2–3 years) | *P4: Pride* about result caused by self performing well | *S4: Shame* about result caused by self performing poorly | |
| Representational mappings (4–5 years) | *P5a: Pride* about comparative performance | *S5a: Shame* about comparative performance | *G4: Guilt* about failure to reciprocate |
| Representational mappings (4–5 years) | *P5b: Pride* about valued trait | *S5b: Shame* about valued trait | |
| Representational systems (6–8 years) | *P6: Pride* about comparative concrete trait | *S6: Shame* about comparative concrete trait | *G5: Guilt* about violation of obligation to friend |
| Single abstractions (10–12 years) | *P7: Pride* about general personality characteristic | *S7: Shame* about general personality characteristic | *G6: Guilt* about violation of general moral rule |
| Abstract mappings (14–17 years) | *P8: Pride* about general characteristic of other person with an identity related to one's own | *S8: Shame* about general characteristic of other person with an identity related to one's own | *G7: Guilt* about upholding moral rule less well than someone else does |

**Table 12.1** (continued)

Reprinted with the permission of Guilford Publications, Inc. Mascolo, M. F., & Fischer, K. W. (1995). Copyright 2011. [Table 3.2, Page. 74–78; Table 3.3, Page. 86–90; Table 3.4, Page. 94–100]

The table maps the development of the self-related emotions of pride, shame, and guilt according to the developmental levels in Fischer's cognitive developmental model. There is a second table that provides examples for each step in emotional development (see Table 12.2). The age range considered is from about 7 months to 17 years. The stages progress from the sensorimotor to the abstract stage, and normally there are three substages within each stage. For the age period provided, this leads to a sequence of seven steps. As for the development of the emotions, the steps are numbered and aligned with the corresponding cognitive level. Some cognitive levels are associated with more than one emotional step. The emotional steps include precursor emotions to pride, shame, and guilt, in terms of joy and distress

In the present work, I show how there are gaps in the stages and substages and the cognitive side of Fischer's model, and therefore similar gaps in the corresponding emotional steps presented. Fischer's model allows for multiple steps within any one cognitive level. However, the present model can accommodate all the extra emotional steps described through the extra cognitive levels within its sequence. In this regard, for the age range on which the present table is based, Fischer's model includes seven steps but my equivalent model includes 11 steps

In the text, and in Fig. 12.4, I elaborate the specific way Fischer's description of the development of these self emotions can be altered to fit the present model

**Table 12.2** Development of appraisal skills for pride, shame, and guilt in Fischer (examples)

| Stage/substage (age) | Pride skill step | Shame skill step | Guilt skill step |
|---|---|---|---|
| Sensorimotor mappings (7–8 months) | *P1:* An infant grasps a block and then drops it, coordinating hand movements with looking to achieve and enjoy the goal of seeing the block drop to the floor | *S1:* An infant grasps a block and then tries to drop it, coordinating hand movements with looking, but he or she fails and becomes distressed in his or her attempts to grasp and let go of the block to make it drop | *G1:* One child hits a second child on purpose, and then connects that child's crying to his or her own hitting. As a result, the first child becomes distressed |
| Sensorimotor systems (11–13 months) | *P2:* An infant throws a block, coordinating arm/hand movements to achieve and enjoy the goals of seeing the block fly through the air and seeing and hearing Dad's positive reaction | *S2:* An infant tries to throw a block, coordinating arm/hand movements with looking, but he or she fails and becomes distressed in trying to get the block to fly through the air, and also in seeing and hearing Dad's disappointed reaction | *G2:* One child hits a second child in the face on purpose to make that child stop doing something, and then connects the second child's wincing and crying to his or her own hitting. As a result, the first child becomes distressed |
| Single representations (18–24 months) | *P3:* A child throws a ball and says joyfully or pridefully to his or her pleased Mom something indicating that he or she did the throwing, such as "I throw," "Me throw," or "Robin [child's name] throw" | *S3:* A child tries to throw a ball but fails and becomes distressed or ashamed, indicating to his or her disappointed Mom that he or she failed, such as "No throw," "Me oops," or "Robin [child's name] no throw" | *G3a:* Events like those in the prior step occur, and the first child reacts with distress or guilt and indicates that he or she has caused the upset in the other child (Jason), such as "I hurt," "Hurt Jason," or "Oops Jason" |
| Single representations (18–24 months) | | | *G3b:* With two children playing blocks, one child looks at the other's block tower and says "Tower ugly," which upsets the other child. The child who spoke indicates with regret or guilt that he or she hurt the other child's feeling: "Make sad," "Hurt Jason," or "Make Jason sad" |

| | | | |
|---|---|---|---|
| Single representations (18–24 months) | | | *G3c:* With two children playing blocks, one child has many blocks, and the other requests a few to finish his or her tower. The first child refuses: "No share," which upsets the second child. The first child indicates with distress or guilt that he or she hurt the other child's feelings: "Make sad," "Hurt Jason," or "Make Jason sad" |
| Single representations (2–3 years) | *P4:* A child throws a ball, sees and hears it go far (or bounce high, or some other valued outcome), and says proudly to his or her pleased parent something indicating that he or she has thrown it well, such as "Throw ball far" or "I throw good" | *S4:* A child throws a ball, sees and hears it not go far (or not bounce, or fail to show some other valued outcome), and says shamefully to his or her disappointed parent something indicating that he or she has thrown it poorly, such as "Throw ball bad" or "I throw poor" | |
| Representational mappings (4–5 years) | *P5a:* A child throws a softball farther than another child and indicates proudly, "I can throw far and [the other child] can't," "I can throw farther than [the other child]," or something similar | *S5a:* A child throws less far than another child and indicates with shame, "I can't throw far but [the other child] can," "[The other child] can throw farther than me," or something similar | *G4:* Two children are playing, one with wooden blocks, one with Legos. When the first child asks the second for some Legos, the second shares them. But when the second asks the first for some wooden blocks, the first child refuses to share, and the second one becomes upset. The first child indicates guilt for hurting the other child's feelings by not reciprocating: "I didn't share my blocks with you when you shared yours with me" |
| Representational mappings (4–5 years) | *P5b:* A child throws well playing softball with big brother, and also throws well playing beachball with Mom. The child concludes with pride that he or she has a characteristic of being good at throwing balls | *S5b:* A child throws a softball poorly with big brother, and also throws a beachball poorly with Mom. The child concludes with shame that he or she has a characteristic of being bad at throwing balls | |

(continued)

**Table 12.2** (continued)

| Stage/substage (age) | Pride skill step | Shame skill step | Guilt skill step |
|---|---|---|---|
| Representational systems (6–8 years) | *P6:* A child performs better than some other children in both throwing and running. He or she generalizes over these acts to infer a general concrete trait (concrete generalization) that he or she is proud of: "I am good at sports, but my friend is not," or something similar | *S6:* A child performs worse than some other children in both throwing and running. He or she generalizes over these acts to infer a general concrete trait (concrete generalization) that he or she is ashamed of: "I am bad at sports, but my friend good," or something similar | *G5:* To build a Lego block structure for a school project, two children agree that the first child will bring Legos to the second child's home after school and help build the structure. However, the first child goes to play with a third child instead, and the second one becomes upset. The first child indicates guilt for hurting the other child by not honoring their agreement: "I didn't do what I said I would to help with the project" |
| Single abstractions (10–12 years) | *P7:* A youth judges himself or herself to be not only good at sports (as in the preceding step), but also smart (based on good grades in school). He or she generalizes across these two traits to attribute a general personality characteristic he or she is proud of, such as "I am a competent person," "I am more competent than my friend," Or something similar | *S7:* A youth judges himself or herself to be not only poor at sports (as in the preceding step), but also stupid (based on poor grades in school). He or she generalizes across these two traits to attribute a general personality characteristic he or she is ashamed of, such as "I am an incompetent person," "I am less competent than my friend," Or something similar | *G6:* A youth agrees to help a friend with a school project and then fails to do so. He or she also agrees to speak to a teacher about a friend's crisis and fails to do so. He or she generalizes across these incidents to attribute a moral flaw and feel guilty violating the general rule of honoring agreements with friends. He or she says, "I neglect my agreements with my friends," "I let my friends down by not doing what I say and will do," or something similar |

| | | | |
|---|---|---|---|
| Abstract mappings (14–17 years) | *P8:* A person judges someone else to be especially competent at something important, such as singing at a national event, and because of a similarity in racial/ethnic identity with that singer, the person is proud. He or she says something like, "I've never had such pride in seeing this [name of my race] woman stand up there with this great royal dignity and sing," linking her performance to his or her own identity as a person of that race, an American, or the like | *S8:* A person judges someone else to be especially incompetent at something important, such as singing at a national event, and because of a similarity in racial/ethnic identity with that singer, the person is ashamed. He or she says something like, "I've never felt such shame at seeing this [name of my race] woman stand up there and put on such a disgusting performance," linking her performance to his or her own identity as a person of that race, an American, or the like | *G7:* A person compares his or her own honoring of agreements with how friends honor their agreements, and concludes with guilt that in general the friends honor them more faithfully than he or she does, saying something like this: "My friends are more trustworthy than I am when we make agreements. They hold up their sides of our agreements in lots of situations, but I often don't hold up my side" |

**Table 12.3** Development of pride in an American sample (Fischer)

| Step and description | Developmental level and appraisal skill structure |
|---|---|
| P2: Joy over complex action-outcome contingency including other's evaluation. Child connects action(s) to a shared goal-related positive outcome (e.g., throwing a block) and is aware of parent's smile and positive vocalizations (11–13 months) | Sm3: Sensorimotor Systems<br>[ grasp let go see smile<br>ACT ↔ GOAL ↔ MOM<br>move arm see block fly hear voice ] |
| P3: Joy/proud of self as agent outcome. Child carries out action with goal-directed positive results and attributes outcome to the self. A child may throw a ball and notice the parent's smile, voice, statements and gestures (applause, "good throw!"). Child makes appraisal like "I throw!" Action tendency includes self-celebration: Child looks at others, smiles, and evaluates self positively (e.g., claps, says "I did it!") (18–24 months) | Sm4/Rp1: Single Representations<br>[ grasp let go seen<br>ACT ↔ GOAL ↔ MOM<br>move arm see ball fly heard<br>↕<br>SEE ↔ SAY ↔ HEAR<br>act "act" "act" ] ≡ [ **SELF** / *result+* ] |
| P3: Proud of self as competent agent. Child carries out action with positive goal-related results that are evaluated as special, attributes result to self, and labels it using evaluative category. For example, child may throw a ball and make an appraisal like "I throw good!" On success, parent evaluates child verbally and in gesture, smiles; praises child with exaggerated voice. Child's celebratory action tendency includes smile, social referencing, positive self-evaluation, expanding posture (2.5–3 years) | Sm4/Rp1: Single Representations<br>[ grasp let go seen<br>ACT ↔ GOAL ↔ MOM<br>move arm see ball fly heard<br>↕<br>own body "I" "I"<br>SEE ↔ SAY ↔ HEAR<br>outcome "good" "good" ] ≡ [ **SELF** / *good* ] |



In this table, with colleagues, Fischer presents the manner in which the emotion of pride develops in an American sample. Before describing that work, I point out the following

First, the age period in which joy is posited to develop (18–24 months) is consistent with the present model (see Table 22.3). Recall that I had questioned the absence of a separate substage in this age period, at times in his publications, in his model. Second, unlike in the present model, Fischer points out how emotions change in associated cognition and expression from one age period to the next. This is a definite strength of his work. Third, in the research, he examines the development of several basic emotions in the American sample, and they do not share one universal developmental pathway. This might suggest inconsistencies. Fourth, he

(continued)

**Table 12.3** (continued)

| |
|---|
| examined the development of these emotions in a different culture, the Chinese, and found different developmental patterns. Fifth, even the manner of labeling the emotions could change over cultures. In these regards, his work indicates the profound influence that a culture can have in emotional expression. Sixth, he did find that in any one substage of emotional development, there could be two steps. This speaks to a variability in his model that could be an advantage, for example, with respect to elaborating models that comprise individual differences. However, also, it could be a strategy that had developed, in part, to compensate for the absence of some substages in his model |
| In this regard, note that for the period of single representations, presented in this work as developing from 18 to 24 months, consistent with prior publications, a second step is added. This procedure of having two steps in this time frame could relate to discussion about the prior table in the present work (see Table 12.2), where variations seemed evident in the description of the substage in this time frame begin at 18 months or 2 years |
| To add to the possible ambiguities being found in Fischer's model and the age ranges associated with its substages, Fig. 12.3 of the present work illustrates that Fischer added a whole new substage in the age period at issue, called "Compounded representations and internalized standards." It was used as Fischer and Mascolo presented a model of the development of guilt, anger, and shame. The substage was positioned between the single and mapping representational substages of the general Fischer model. The age associated with it was given as 2.5 years. The substage was considered applicable to all three emotions involved |

Moreover, the present table allows for a further analysis of how the examples that Fischer and colleagues have provided for the later substages in the development of the emotions of pride, shame, and guilt are more consistent with the present cognitive model relative to their own. I elaborate the argument in the following.

For example, for Fischer's substage of single representations, the example provided by the authors concerns a child throwing a ball, or undertaking an action, toward a goal, which evokes the emotion of joy/pride and a comment such as "I throw." The example is quite consistent with my characterization of the applicable stage in this developmental period as sensorimotor integration. In this stage, according to Piaget, the child is capable of inventing new means by mental combination to get at goals, but they are still tied to sensorimotor activity, in part. In contrast to what one might expect given that the step in Fischer's model in this age period consists of single representations, the example does not give the impression of having a pure representational nature.

For the substage in Fischer's sequence called representational mappings, the example provided illustrates better the equivalent substage in the present model than Fischer's. Specifically, I refer to this stage as perioperational hierarchization, and the example provided concerns a child not only comparing his or her performance in a valued domain to that of another child [which fits Fischer's mapping concept], but also believing that his/her performance had been better than that of the other child [which goes beyond Fischer's mapping concept by adding the present emphasis on hierarchization].

## Missing Steps in Their Model

Mascolo and Fischer (1995) have provided a pertinent example for Fischer's substage of representational systems. It concerns developing pride about a comparative concrete trait. In the next substage in the sequence, the teenager develops single abstractions, and pride manifests as a general personality characteristic.

According to the present model, there should be two intermediate substages that develop between these two of Fischer. First, there should be a substage of multiplication of the system that had developed in the prior stage, and then the multiplications should become integrated into a coherent system that has spread greatly throughout the person's psychology. In the next substage after integration, a new stage can emerge because two integrations acquired in the prior substage can be coordinated, or a new acquisition in that substage can be compared and contrasted with one from the prior substage of integration.

Given this proposed generic model of substage evolution, I suggest that the examples of pride as presented by Mascolo and Fischer should indicate a lack of two developmental substages in the Fischerian sequence described. The examples that Mascolo and Fischer provided confirm my conjecture.

For the substage of representational systems, in the example provided, the pride about a comparative concrete trait involves a child judging her or his performance as better than another's in several areas. Therefore, the child generalizes and concludes that she or he has a better standing about the valued trait ("more" of it). The child creates a "concrete" generalization of which the child is proud, and it involves a comparison concerning the other not being as good as the child.

The example provided by the authors for the substage of representational systems in Fischer's model implicitly involves three phases, as predicted on the basis of the present model. According to my analysis, each should develop about 2 years apart, rather than in one age period at 6–8 years. The three phases indicated in the example of the expression of pride in the representational systems substage provided by Mascolo and Fischer are consistent with the present model for the following reasons. (a) In the first phase, the child judges positively comparative performance in a domain of interest (this behavior fits the substage of the present model of perioperational systematization). (b) In the second phase, the child judges positively comparative performance in other domains of interest (fitting the substage of the present model of perioperational multiplication). (c) Next, the child creates a cross-domain concrete generalization involving possession of a valued trait (this fits the substage of the present model of perioperational integration). [Note that this is not the first time in this section that I first wrote what I expected to find in Mascolo and Fischer's substage sequence or examples provided to illustrate them pertaining to the emotions being discussed, then looked at their text, and found that my predictions were confirmed].

### Shame

Next, I examine the development of shame in Mascolo and Fischer according to whether the examples provided are more consistent with my model relative to theirs.

The analysis corresponds to the one just undertaken for the emotion of pride, given the inverse relationship between these two emotions. For example, in Fischer's substage of single representations, the example includes clear action components (failure to throw ball elicits distress/shame), suggesting that the equivalent substage in the present model, that of sensorimotor integration, applies quite well to the example. For the substage of representational mapping, the example includes a hierarchical judgment of throwing poorer than another child, fitting the present model (its equivalent stage is perioperational hierarchization).

For Fischer's substage of representational systems, the example provided for the emotion of shame includes three phases, as had been the case for the inverse emotion of pride. Moreover, the nature of the three phases for the development of shame in this substage is consistent with the three substages of the present model for the age period involved. Specifically, in the example provided (a) the child judges negatively the comparative performance in first domain of interest (equivalent to the substage of the present model of perioperational systematization); (b) then the child judges negatively comparative performance in other domains of interest (equivalent to the substage of the present model of perioperational multiplication); and (c) then the child creates a cross-domain concrete generalization that she/he possesses a negative trait (equivalent to the substage of the present model of perioperational integration).

## Mascolo, Fischer, and Li (2003)

Mascolo et al. (2003) added to the articulation of the Fischerian model of cognitive-affective parallels in development by presenting a dynamical model of the component systems involved in emotions. Further, they showed how the emotions of pride, shame, and guilt develop differently in China and the United States. The emotion components of appraisal, affective experience, and overt action tendencies are only partially distinct, being intertwined, and they mutually regulate each other. Emotions are expressed differentially in different sociocultural contexts. Emotions self-organize over their multiple levels, and express socially sensitive and regulated assemblies or patterns that are not fixed or emotion-typical and involuntary. Nevertheless, there are a limited number of stable modal patterns, syndromes, families, or prototypes of emotions that constrain individual, group, and cultural variations in emotional expression.

The description of the Chinese cultural context for the expression of emotions presented by Mascolo et al. is fascinating in this regard. One example relates to the development of the Chinese compound emotion of shame/guilt, an emotion that is not found in the American culture.

The authors concluded that emotions could be represented as dynamically constructed attractors in which there is no one component that is privileged in the construction process and in emotional expression. Emotions are intentional and functional within the limits of the developmental levels and contexts in which they appear. They are at once biological canalizations and cultural reflections.

## Summary and Conclusions

Mascolo, Fischer, and colleagues have developed an integrated model of the development of emotions that is quite consistent with my own in many respects. For example, we have both adopted the Neo-Piagetian and the dynamical systems models in our work. The present work could not have been formulated without the critical contributions of Fischer's team of researchers and the one of Case, as well. They have informed the present model but, at the same time, the combined model that I have elaborated can inform theirs, as the current analysis of the Fischer team's work in the area of emotional development attests.

This is the last chapter in the first part of the book that presents the Neo-Piagetian models of Fischer, Case, and myself in terms of the basics on the cognitive and socioaffective sides, and the parallels across them. I have pointed out the contributions of the three models and how mine builds on the other two models. This prepares the way for further elaboration of the present model in the next part of the book. It investigates the development of self and other, theory of mind and the adult mind, personality, motivational needs, attachment, emotions, and so on. For many of these areas in development, I suggest how they evolve according to the 25 steps of the present Neo-Piagetian model. This presentation of more details of the content, product, or what side of the present model prepares the way for the last part of the book, in which the transition mechanisms, causality, process, or how and why side in the development of behavior is discussed in detail.

## References


Barrett, L. F., Ochsner, K. N., & Gross, J. J. (2007). On the automaticity of emotion. In J. Bargh (Ed.), *Social psychology and the unconscious: The automaticity of higher mental processes* (pp. 173–218). New York: Psychology Press.

Bermond, B. (2008). The emotional feeling as a combination of two qualia: A neurophilosophical-based emotion theory. *Cognition & Emotion, 22*, 897–930.

Cacioppo, J. T., Visser, P. S., & Picket, C. L. (Eds.). (2006). *Social neuroscience: People thinking about thinking people*. Cambridge, MA: MIT Press.

Cozolino, L. (2006). *The neuroscience of human relationships: Attachment and the developing social brain*. New York: Norton.

Fischer, K. W. (1980). A theory of cognitive development: The control and construction of hierarchies of skills. *Psychological Review, 87*, 477–531.

Fischer, K. W., Yan, Z., & Stewart, J. (2003). Adult cognitive development: Dynamics in the developmental web. In J. Valsiner & K. J. Connolly (Eds.), *Handbook of developmental psychology* (pp. 493–516). London: Sage.

Fogel, A., Garvey, A., Hsu, H. C., & West-Stromming, D. (2006). *Change processes in relationships: A relational-historical approach*. New York: Cambridge University Press.

Frijda, N. H. (1987). Emotion, emotion structure, and action tendency. *Cognition & Emotion, 1*, 115–143.

Gallagher, S. (2005). *How the body shapes the mind*. Oxford, UK: Oxford University Press.

Gallagher, S., & Hutto, D. D. (2008). Understanding others through primary interaction and narrative practice. In J. Zlatev, T. Racine, C. Sinha, & E. Itkonen (Eds.), *The shared mind: Perspectives on intersubjectivity*. Amsterdam: Benjamins.

Gallese, V., Eagle, M. N., & Migone, P. (2007). Intentional attunement: Mirror neurons and the neural underpinnings of interpersonal relations. *Journal of the American Psychoanalytic Association, 55*, 131–176.

Gibbs, R. W., Jr. (2006). *Embodiment and cognitive science*. New York: Cambridge University Press.

Gottlieb, G. (2003). On making behavioral genetics truly developmental. *Human Development, 46*, 337–355.

LaBar, K. S., & LeDoux, J. E. (2003). Emotional learning circuits in animals and humans. In R. J. Davidson, K. Scherer, & H. H. Goldsmith (Eds.), *Handbook of affective sciences* (pp. 52–65). New York: Oxford University Press.

Lazarus, R. S. (1991). *Emotion and adaptation*. New York: Oxford University Press.

Lerner, R. M., & Overton, W. F. (2008). Exemplifying the integrations of the relational developmental system: Synthesizing theory, research, and application to promote positive development and social justice. *Journal of Adolescent Research, 23*, 245–255.

Lewis, M. D., & Todd, R. M. (2007). The self-regulating brain: Cortical-subcortical feedback and the development of intelligent action. *Cognitive Development, 22*, 406–430.

MacLean, P. D. (1993). Perspectives on cingulate cortex in the limbic system. In B. A. Vogt & M. Gabriel (Eds.), *Neurobiology of cingulate cortex and limbic thalamus: A comprehensive handbook* (pp. 1–15). Boston: Brikhauser.

Mascolo, M. F., & Fischer, K. W. (1995). Developmental transformations in appraisals for pride, shame, and guilt. In J. P. Tangney & K. W. Fischer (Eds.), *Self-conscious emotions: The psychology of shame, guilt, embarrassment, and pride* (pp. 64–113). New York: Guilford Press.

Mascolo, M. F., & Fischer, K. W. (2007). The codevelopment of self and socialmoral emotions during the toddler years. In C. A. Brownell & C. B. Kopp (Eds.), *Socioemotional development in the toddler years: Transitions and transformations* (pp. 66–99). New York: Guilford Press.

Mascolo, M. F., & Fischer, K. W. (2010). The dynamic development of thinking, feeling and acting over the lifespan. In R. M. Lerner & W. F. Overton (Eds.), *Handbook of lifespan development: Vol. 1. Cognitive, biology and methods*. Hoboken: Wiley.

Mascolo, M. J., Fischer, K. W., & Li, J. (2003). Dynamic development of component systems of emotions: Pride, shame, and guilt in China and the United States. In R. J. Davidson, K. Scherer, & H. H. Goldsmith (Eds.), *Handbook of affective science* (pp. 375–408). Oxford, U.K.: Oxford University Press.

Meltzoff, A. N., & Brooks, R. (2007). Intersubjectivity before language: Three windows on preverbal sharing. In S. Bråten (Ed.), *On being moved: From mirror neurons to empathy* (pp. 149–174). Philadelphia: Benjamins.

Meltzoff, A. N., & Moore, M. K. (1989). Imitation in newborn infants: Exploring the range of gestures imitated and the underlying mechanisms. *Developmental Psychology, 25*, 954–962.

Overton, W. F., Müller, U., & Newman, J. L. (Eds.). (2007). *Developmental perspective on embodiment and consciousness*. Hillsdale: Erlbaum.

Panksepp, J. (1998). *Affective neuroscience: The foundations of human and animal emotions*. New York: Oxford University Press.

Pessoa, L. (2008). On the relationship between emotion and cognition. *Nature Reviews Neuroscience, 9*, 148–158.

Scherer, K. R. (2004). Feelings integrate the central representation of appraisal-driven response organization in emotion. In A. S. R. Manstead, N. H. Frijda, & A. H. Fischer (Eds.), *Feelings and emotions* (pp. 136–157). Cambridge: Cambridge University Press.

Thompson, E. (2007). *Mind in life*. Cambridge: Harvard University Press.

Trevarthen, C. (1993). The self born in intersubjectivity: The psychology of an infant communicating. In U. Neisser (Ed.), *The perceived self: Ecological and interpersonal sources of self-knowledge* (pp. 121–173). New York: Cambridge University Press.

Zelazo, P. D., & Cunningham, W. (2007). Executive function: Mechanisms underlying emotion regulation. In J. Gross (Ed.), *Handbook of emotion regulation* (pp. 135–158). New York: Guilford Press.

# Chapter 13
# Self-Development

## Introduction

The present model has been expanded to include development of the self (Young, 1997). The self consists of at least two components: the implicit, functioning I-self and the explicit, self-evaluative Me-self (Case, 1991). For the most part the I-self is treated in the present model. In particular, I have based the present model on the works of Sroufe (1990, 1996), Selman (1980), and Loevinger (1976, 1987, 1993, 1994) on infants, children-adolescents, and adolescents-adults, respectively, which suggests validity to its content. Their works are stage-oriented ones, and each maps on quite well to the steps described in the present model. The approach that I have taken differs from the ones of Case and Fischer and colleagues, whom I have shown, generally, did not follow the same procedure of basing themselves on known stage or step theorists related to self-development in constructing their models of self-development in relation to steps in cognitive development.

This chapter is the first of two chapters that reviews my approach to the development of the self and other – in terms of their perceptions and misperceptions. The end of the next chapter presents new material on the cognitive (mis)perception of the self and other, and it is based on the model of the cognitive (mis)perception of the other that had been presented in Young (1997). The elaboration of the latter concept constitutes the first of multiple conceptual innovations in the present work based on extension of the cognitive model into other domains (except that I have presented models of narrative development and of early self-conscious emotions when I presented/compared the work of Fischer and Case on the topics). I have already presented the scope of the innovations in the present work in tables summarizing its major contributions, and I have given summaries of key concepts such as on nonlinear dynamical systems theory. In addition, I have described concepts such as the bio-personal-social model. However, the material that follows on self-development and on the cognitive (mis)perception of the other is important because it prepares the way for much of what follows.

G. Young, *Development and Causality: Neo-Piagetian Perspectives*,
DOI 10.1007/978-1-4419-9422-6_13, © Springer Science+Business Media, LLC 2011

## Steps in Self-Development in Sroufe, Selman, and Loevinger

### *Sroufe's Theory*

#### Introduction

Sroufe (1990, 1996) has elaborated a six-step model of self-development in infancy that provides a one-to-one correspondence with the infancy component of the present model of 25 cognitive substages in development. The description of the relevant substages given below for the present model of self-development is strongly based on the model presented by Sroufe (1990, 1996). Sroufe's description of the steps in self-development is somewhat consistent with Piaget's six-step model of substages in sensorimotor development in infancy, although they were not formulated from that perspective. In the following, I make clearer the relationship between the models of Piaget and Sroufe, or at least do so in terms of my redescription of them.

#### The Phases

The First Year

Sroufe's (1990, 1996) model of development of the self in infancy is based on the work of Sander (1975), in particular. He emphasized the social embeddedness of the developing self early in life.

In the first phase of basic regulation, newborns are considered physiologically regulated through the interactional matrix of smooth routines provided by the caregiver. Newborns develop a preferential responsiveness to the caregiver as they turn toward the environment.

In the second phase, stating at 3 months, infants and caregivers engage in reciprocal positive exchange or coordinated dyadic sequencing that involves psychological regulation. There is much affective, vocal, and motoric play as infant tension or arousal is managed. Caregivers scaffold these interactional chains through their sensitive, cooperative adjustment, given that infants cannot represent them, and the caregivers are the only ones in the dyad that intentionally initiate interaction. Nevertheless, shared joy is derived from the repetitive, organized structures that the dyad builds.

Sroufe's third phase of self-development begins at about 6 months, and concerns "initiatory" behavior, as infants engage in directed preferred activities. In this period, infants develop purposeful action, social initiation, active participation, mastery, emotional focus on the caregiver, etc. In terms of outcome, infants acquire knowledge of goal achievement or failure. They develop a particular relationship with the caregivers as part of their inner organization, and they develop towards the establishment of an effective attachment to caregivers. In parallel, Sroufe maintained that a particular sense of self is emerging, as well. Cicchetti (1991) added that the infant's emerging inner organization relates to internalization of the history of caregiver interactions.

In the next phase of self-development, which begins at about 9 months, affective development revolves around dyadic emotional regulation in the context of specific attachment (or affective bond). Infants actively focus their increasing exploration around the secure base provided by caregivers; they come and go as they explore and return to share fears and joys. The availability and responsivity of caregivers influence the infant's appraisal of the interactions. Goals that had been organized around the caregivers might lead to alternative options in action in order to achieve goals in process if initial means at engaging caregivers are ineffective. Internal working models that represent the quality of the attachment relationship are developing as the infants and caregivers interact. The working model of the attachment relationship (which had emerged in the prior level) acquires a special saliency for infants, because images of the self as "wanted" or "unwanted" especially characterize the model of the self that is developing in this period. In this regard, the working models of infants at this age about their relationship to the world concern relationships with caregivers more than particular attributes of the individual self.

## The Second Year

In Sroufe's model of the development of the self, the fifth phase at 12 months is dominated by autonomous actions or inner aims; he referred to it as the phase of "self-assertion." Infants' initiative broadens, but there is much supervision by caregivers. Nevertheless, infants can arrive at goal success and personal gratification even independent of caregivers. Moreover, infants can pursue goals even in opposition to the wishes of caregivers. They can leave the secure base from a psychological point of view and not only a physical one; however, the search for the balance with engagement with caregivers dominates. Infants develop a sense of being independent actors. They develop inner plans that govern behavior, and awareness of the self comes to include the concept of the self as actor.

In the last phase of self-development in the first 2 years in Sroufe's model, 18-month-old toddlers acquire an awareness of self-constancy. Since they can develop appropriate symbols, toddlers realize that caregivers can be aware of their plans, especially in situations where they oppose the plans. The toddlers develop a "shared awareness," because they recognize that caregivers can be aware of what the toddlers themselves are aware. In terms of self-constancy, the toddlers are developing a self-organized center within the self. Toddlers come to view their selves as active initiators (or masters of the world) that can perturb their relationship with caregivers by purposely opposing their wishes. Moreover, the toddlers do not get overly disturbed, because they understand that there is an overriding general harmony that maintains the relationship, and the caregivers will preserve it. Toddlers coordinate their intentions with those perceived in their caregivers, which produces both the first genuine taking of perspective of the other and the roots of empathy.

### Comment

Sroufe's model of the development of the self in infancy is consistent with the work of other theorists on whom he based his work, such as Sander and Bowlby. Lewis and Granic (2010) developed a similar model of steps in emotional regulation in infancy based on these theorists. There is confluence among our efforts. I have carried the process one step further by elaborating a model of parallels in cognitive and socioaffective steps in development across multiple domains, including self-regulation and attachment (see Chaps. 16 and 24, respectively).

## *Selman's Theory of Self-Development in Children and Adolescents*

### Introduction

Selman and colleagues (Selman, 1980; Selman & Demorest, 1986; Yeates, Schultz, & Selman, 1990) described five steps in children's acquisition of self and other understanding and in coordination of social perspective taking. This model of the development of the self fits well the present model, and complements the description of the development of the self that was offered by Sroufe for infancy.

### The Phases

#### Preschoolers

In the first step in this process, Selman considered preschoolers as egocentric, or without the capacity to differentiate the other's external, physical, objective attributes (e.g., actions, appearance) from their internal, psychological, subjective ones (e.g., feelings, motives, intentions). Preschoolers cannot understand that the other may interpret a behavior differently from themselves and feel differently about it.

In the next step for Selman in the development of the self, 5-year-olds adopt a subjective, unilateral (first person) perspective. Their concept of the person manifests a clear differentiation of the physical and psychological features of people. For the 5-year-old, the other can have unique, subjective, covert feelings, and thoughts. However, in this age period, the other's psychological life is understood primarily from a one-way, unidimensional, personal perspective. For example, in 5-year-olds, the other should be content with any gift received even if it is inappropriate.

#### School Age

In Selman's next phase of self-development, school-age children (7 years) enter into the self-reflective/reciprocal phase of perspective taking. The underlying conceptual acquisition relates to the ability to adopt a second-person perspective, in which one can contemplate one's own thoughts. This leads the 7-year-old to understand that the other can perform the same feat. Thus, children at this age realize that others can deceive or act in opposition to their true purposes and feelings. Different perspectives are given differential weights. Reciprocity emerges by adopting different perspectives about both the self and the other, which helps school-age children appreciate that others might do the same. Thus, interactions come to include thoughts and feelings, and not only actions. The reciprocity that is involved in this phase is limited by a lack of mutual influence.

Older children (10 years) enter a third-person, mutual perspective taking, in which they can remove themselves from the self system. Children at this age grasp that the self and the other can be simultaneously actor and object having their perspectives coordinated or in need of such coordination. Thus, they understand that both the self and the other function in terms of effects (or behave and evaluate effects of actions on themselves). They view the coordinated perspective of self and other from a general vantage point, because one's personal perspective is understood to fit into a generalized schema of values, attitudes, and so on. For 10-year-olds, mutuality predominates in the reciprocal coordination of perspectives of self and other. They infer the way the other perceives them and their behavior, and they adopt this perspective, perceiving their self in the light of the one perceived as imagined by the other. Relationships are judged to be mutually satisfying and marked by sharing.

### High-Schoolers

In the last level that Selman describes in the self-development, the 12-year-old begins the acquisition of an in-depth/societal-symbolic perspective. They perceive others as unique psychological complexes having both conscious and unconscious motivations. At this age, and as it develops throughout the rest of the lifespan, the self is enriched and entertains commitment. The individual conceives at multiple levels relationships with others. Relative to themselves, others might share basic information, have similar values, or possess comparable abstract moral notions.

## Comment

Selman's model of self-development informs the present model; however, his sequence of four levels in self-development has been modified for the purposes of the present model. His description of the first level of self-development is consistent with the nature of the 2-year-old described in substage 11 of the present model (perioperational coordination). However, there seems to be no correspondence between any of the levels that he describes in his model of self-development and the current substage 12 (perioperational hierarchization). The next four levels in his model do correspond to the steps in the present model – they are reflected in the present substages 13–16 (perioperational systematization, perioperational multiplication, perioperational integration, and abstract coordination, respectively). Therefore, Selman's model of self-development has been fully incorporated into the present model of self-development, but with one gap in the sequence that he presents.

## *Loevinger's Theory of Self-Development in Adolescents and Adults*

### Introduction

Loevinger has developed a model of stages in ego development (Loevinger, 1976, 1987, 1993, 1994, 1998); and others who have followed her have worked with it (Cook-Greuter, 1990; Noam, 1992; Ribeiro & Hauser, 2009; Westenberg, Blasi, & Cohn, 1998). The model consists of 11 levels (stages, transition stages) of ego development over the lifespan. Ribeiro and Hauser (2009) found that ego development (Loevinger, 1976) helped moderate the relationship between psychosocial functioning and risk, and served in a protective role. Loevinger and colleagues administer an ego-related sentence completion test to respondents, and their answers are categorized according to strict criteria into the stages described.

### Earlier Steps

According to Loevinger and colleagues, the presocial-symbolic stage of self-development develops early in life, but still can apply to adults fixated at this level. It refers to adults who have no sense of self, are very dependent, and are need-oriented.

In the next impulsive stage, a nascent ego is developing, but one which is still quite dependent and need-based. Others are understood in terms of dichotomies, such as good/bad or what they give/withhold.

The third stage is a self-protective one; individuals perceive the world through their wants rather than through any insight. They act to purposefully control encounters, hoping to gain advantage.

In the next rule-oriented stage, for the most part, people learn and abide by society's rules. If they acknowledge the external world, it can lead to vacillation. For people in this stage, judgments are superficial, for example, they are based on appearance.

The next Loevingerian stage is conformist and it is characterized by an acceptance of group-sanctioned rules. If individuals in this stage break rules, they experience feelings of guilt and shame. Their interactions are action-oriented, and are aimed at promoting a sense of belonging and at projecting the image that one is nice. Feelings of individuals in this stage are clichéd. The world is viewed in terms of superficialities and stereotypes.

### Middle Steps

Most American adults perform at the conscientious-conformist level, in which there is a beginning separation of one's real and ideal selves and of personal goals and group standards. In this stage, the self can be examined as a separate object and can be assertive. Interpersonal relationships come to involve feelings as well as actions.

In addition, the relations are more reciprocal, because individuals see themselves as capable of having at least some impact on others or even on a full group. Their psychological scope expands to encompass personal adjustment, reasons for acting, analyzing problems, and choosing from among options. However, group norms still exert their influence on them, damping their individualist perspective. For example, their issues that are related to personal adjustment revolve around loneliness, self-consciousness, and other group-related sentiments.

In the next conscientious stage, the adult develops standards that are self-constructed, and one finds fissioning of the self (rational, determined, with high self-esteem) and group. The individual develops personal long-term ideals, goals, and criteria for critical thought (causes, benefits, costs). In terms of the other, they are evaluated as different from each other and as complex, and relations with them include a sense of responsibility and reciprocal sharing. In this period, individuals seek out others who have similar goals and values. Individuals evaluate themselves in terms of traits both back into the past and forward into the future. As for a general perspective on humankind, the species is conceived as perfectible, and truth is understood as discoverable.

In the individualistic stage that develops next, the self is considered as a unique entity, and is redefined independently. For the individualistic person, one's inner and outer lives become differentiated. At this stage, a wide range of individual differences is tolerated. The adult develops a concern for social problems and a sense of mutuality. In terms of cognition, relativity in the thought emerges. At this level, therefore, the adult can entertain paradoxes, accept different roles for the same person, reject the notion of absolute truth, recognize the complexity in problems, and separate means from ends, in that the latter can no longer always justify the former.

## Later Steps

In the autonomous phase of ego development, the self is marked by the other's need for individualized dependence within the context of mutual interdependence. Individuals can now seek self-fulfillment and valid commitment, and they accept the inevitability of inner conflicts (e.g., between needs and wishes) without displacing their origins in the environment. They can tolerate these conflicts and ambiguities not only within themselves but also in others. Therefore, they develop subselves that can not only remain separate, but can also be integrated.

According to Cook-Greuter (1990), postautonomous individuals, yearn to transcend their bounded ego in a web of interconnected beings as part of an infinite wholeness. Yet, they relentlessly pursue by themselves a self-determined life course. This existential paradox, as well as others, contributes to produce preoccupying inner conflicts. However, individuals in this phase accept the resultant tension and they continue their journey with commitment and positive equilibration. They judge ultimate truth as illusory, because all knowledge is understood as constructed in acts of contemplation.

In the penultimate integrated stage in Loevinger's model of ego development, people develop a universal vision and experience peace within themselves.

Inner conflicts are resolved, because they are reconciled without any confrontation. For example, in people at this phase, they merge without difficulty a sense of bonding of the self with the universe and a sense of personal uniqueness. They can adopt multiple perspectives on issues, which are navigated readily, because they feel that they are embedded in a natural global flow. For example, they apprehend simultaneously and without effort the connotative and the denotative as well as the tangible and the eternal symbolic attributes of objects. Thus, all others, whatever their characteristics, potentially can be experienced as having a unique bond, with both self and other fully accepted in a noncontrolling fashion. In this period, truth is considered immanent and accessible, but not rationally mastered.

Kohlberg has added a final seventh "soft" stage to his model of moral development (Kohlberg & Ryncarz, 1990), and it shares the approach found in the Loevingerian approach. For Kohlberg, people sense being part of a larger cosmos having a natural ultimate order. The self is moral through its transcendental, mystical, intimate experience of union or bond with the universe. Sonnert (1994) has qualified the nature of this stage, arguing that it is metadiscursive. The morally mature adult exhibits a dialogue of principles and pragmatics in which universalist, moralistic arguments are moderated by contextualist expediencies. Moreover, moral discourses are evaluated, coordinated, and examined self-referentially, rendering the moral position realistic and the realistic position moral.

#### Comment

Loevinger's model of self-development in adolescence and adulthood has been integrated into the present model in the following way. The first two stages (presocial, impulsive) have been left aside, whereas the next three stages (self-protective, rule-oriented, conformist) have informed the present substages 14–16 (perioperational multiplication, perioperational integration, abstract coordination, respectively). The next five stages (conscientious-conformist to postautonomous) have been incorporated into levels 17–21 (abstract hierarchization, abstract systematization, abstract multiplication, abstract integration, and collective intelligence coordination, respectively). Loevinger's last stage of integration has been aligned with level 25 (integrated collective intelligence), the last one of the present model.

## The Present Model of Self-Development

### *Model*

In constructing the present model of development of the self, in particular, I consulted the models described in the literature. As well, I examined the characteristics of the 25 cognitive steps of the present model, and their associated socioaffective acquisitions (e.g., Neo-Eriksonian). In the tables constructed to present the present model of self-development, where applicable, I included one- or two-sentence summaries of key portions of the prior theories. Where possible, the labels stemming from the prior theories were used to represent the 25 proposed steps in self-development. However, new labels were created when it seemed appropriate. As for the details of each level, they are presented in the Tables 13.1–13.5, in which I outline the specific correspondences that I perceive in cognitive and development of the self over the lifespan.

**Table 13.1** Substages in self-development in the reflex stage

| Substage | Self-development |
|---|---|
| 1. | *Fetal life*: Being not quite a self at this juncture, the moniker "elf" will do to describe the *nonself* |
| 2. | *Premature self I*: Motor skills unexpectedly are put to test in fragile, vulnerable prematures. Even nursing acts are problematic. We can speak of a *reflexive preself* |
| 3. | *Premature self II*: Survival being more certain, the inherent openness of babies manifests. Contact and information are sought even in the precarious circumstances of the hospital. Given the grounding of behavior in primitive control schemata, there appears to be a psychological self, which we can label the protoself. Since it is especially action- and target-oriented, it can be characterized as the *corporal protoself* |
| 4. | *Emergent self I*: Full-term newborns manifest integrating cross-modal matching abilities tied to corresponding production schemes (e.g., imitating mouth opening). This primary perceptual/representational capacity may be affiliated with perceptual learning, simple classical conditioning, and/or priming in memory. Priming is a nonconscious, facilitative effect in memory and functions to improve perceptual identification of objects. Helplessness and calling behaviors elicit care giving, making much of the intramodal world socioaffective. The emerging self seems to be a *perceptual intermodal self*. Neisser (1991) takes a similar position, for he calls the self in this period the perceptual self, and attributes to it two components- the ecological self and the interpersonal self |
| 5. | *Emergent self II*: Infants in the next weeks develop the capacity to integrate separate schemes into more unified structures, building intermodal integration skills. Usually schemes function with concomitant, most basic emotional overtones and are body-focused. We can designate this self the *primary emotional self* |



It might seem illogical to refer to the development of the self in the reflexive stage, which begins in the fetal period. However, precursors of the self are developing right from the earliest phases of the fetal period. By the time the newborn arrives, its intermodal capacities suggest that a perceptual self has developed (Neisser, 1991). Trevarthen and Aitken (2003) described a primary intersubjectivity that is present already early in life. Meltzoff and colleagues (Meltzoff & Moore 1977, 1989; Meltzoff, 2007) referred to neonatal imitation based on intermodal matching capacities. Mondloch et al. (1999) describe the early learning of the facial scheme within hours if not minutes of birth. Mirror neurons are developing even this early in life, providing one physiological basis for these acquisitions. In the first month of life, the primary emotions are developing, and add to the newborn's emerging skills an emotional color and an affective resonance and motivation

The self is defined in terms of the "I-self," or subjective sense, in particular, early in life (Harter, 2006; James, 1890; Lewis, 1991a, b, 1994). It is too early for the objective "Me-self" to develop

**Table 13.2** Substages in self-development in the sensorimotor stage

| Substage | Self-development |
|---|---|
| 6. | *Core, coordinated interaction self*: Young infants' scheme coordination skills lead to dyadic interchanges. Invariant patterns are established, but especially because of caregiver framing. This permits the infants' inherent active nature to achieve agency through participation in regulatory "games" played, connectedness of one's own actions and transactions, control of emotional reactions in the caregiver, etc. At this point, the self seems to be an *inter-coordinated incipient social self* |
| 7. | *Core initiatory self*: At midyear, we see a more hierarchical behavior (e.g., context-created, purposeful behavior, Piaget; generalized sense of personal agency; Case, 1991), which fosters social initiation, emotional focus, and particularities in relationships. A sense of trust in the surround, especially caregivers, develops when that surround facilitates successful goal-oriented behavior. Erikson's psychosocial stage of trust vs. mistrust also fits here, and suggests we call the self of this period the *end-focused trusting self* |
| 8. | *Subjective attachment self*: Given the emergence of primitive representational images, and the beginning of (hidden) object permanence, intentions come to guide behavior before its onset. Thus, mental states of self and other are better coordinated, producing more friendliness, sharing, referencing of the other (and indirect agency; Case, 1991). Attachment to the caregiver becomes active (e.g., searching when the caregiver leaves, calling/protesting her or his departure). The self at this level seems an especially *permanent intersubjective self* |
| 9. | *Verbal autonomous self*: Linear inner plans in 1-year-olds allow increased autonomous action even if in opposition to caregiver wishes. Also with planning capacities, infants can entertain leaving their caregivers' base to explore and return in a psychological and not only a physical sense. Caregivers cocreate meaning with infants through language as they toddle about exploring and returning for refueling. Thus, language facilitates the development of Erikson's autonomy through its distal and shared modalities. The conceptual awareness of self as an independent actor emerges. Thus, we can speak of an *independent autonomous self* |
| 10. | *Verbal constancy self*: In older toddlers, symbol plans, which permit mental combination, underlie behavior. Also, evaluations emerge due to these plans. Thus, social interchange becomes a complex interdigitation of plans, and a mutual awareness that the other has plans and is aware, producing the beginnings of true role taking and empathy. Toddlers develop self-constancy, whereby they realize that they can actively oppose caregivers and either reinstate their relationship or have caregivers cooperate. Thus, toddlers symbolize the self as a separate entity, seeing it as a willful agent of their symbolic plans. (Toddlers can use the words "I" and "Me" at this age). In short, the self at this age can be called an *interior implicative self*. Toddlers both implicate (evaluate) cognitively and implicate themselves (interdigitate) socially |

Reprinted with the permission of Springer Science+Business Media: Young, G. (1997). [Table 3.3, Page. 76]

The Me-Self is especially elaborated in this stage. The infant is developing rapidly many social skills and is engaging in and profiting from social interactions at both the cognitive and affective levels. The infant increasingly initiates interactions and develops a trust in the surround, which stands at the core of the self and prepares the way for active attachment to the caregiver. The attachment brings a permanency to the infant's developing sense of self, as the infant engages in intersubjective engrossment with the surround

Increasing verbal and locomotor skills create the conditions for increasing independence and distance from the caregiver, as an autonomous self develops. The infant terminates the second year with a constancy in the self that is quite interior yet socially interdigitated at the same time. The self is ready for representational elaborations in its growth

**Table 13.3** Substages in self-development in the perioperational stage

| Substage | Self-development |
|---|---|
| 11. | *Egocentric-centrated self*: Symbol plan coordination allows young children to organize cohesive, coherent wholes in behavior (e.g., in language utterances, story events, parallel tasks, and in understanding the social system of the family with its multiple roles; Case, 1991). But coordinations involving the self are egocentrically hierarchized with no or little flexibility in thought to permit decentration on the other. This cognitive egocentrism leads to a lack of differentiation of the physical and psychosocial features of the other and a lack of appreciation of their perspective. The self is an incorporating, coupling one, and so it is labeled the *coupling egocentric-centrated self* |
| 12. | *Initiative self*: Preschoolers' predilection for hierarchizing symbol plans directs them to think of themselves as dominant, or with initiative in their daily challenges. The differentiation of the other is from within the children's projected perspective. This can lead to the Oedipal situation of fantasizing about the opposite-sex parent. In summary, we can refer to a *hierarchizing initiative self* |
| 13. | *First-person perspective taking, unilateral self*: Symbol plan systems allow rule systems to be mastered and dimensions of self- and other-ranking to be apprehended. This enables identification with parental attributes and sex-appropriate gender roles. Such perspective taking is accompanied by clear differentiation of others' psychological characteristics. But a subjective, one-way understanding of the other predominates. Thus, we can speak of a *systematizing primary-perspective self* |
| 14. | *Reciprocal, second-person perspective-taking, self-reflective self*: Concrete operations permit school-age children to think more logically, facilitating the "industry" of school. This logic is also turned inward, for children to evaluate their own thoughts, and is also turned toward others, for their perspectives are evaluated. Others are understood to perform the same "other" evaluation (i.e., evaluation of the children themselves). Loevinger calls the equivalent of this stage the self-protective stage. The label *concrete operational secondary-perspective self* seems appropriate here |
| 15. | *Third-person, perspective-taking, mutual self*: Subteens' logic in imagination leads to multiple exploration. They remove themselves from the self system. A different self is imagined and mutuality in self- and other-perspective taking takes hold (third-person perspective-taking). An independence from one's own self accrues through immersion in others. Loevinger names the equivalent of this stage the rule-oriented stage. At this level there seems to be a *projecting tertiary-perspective self* |

Reprinted with the permission of Springer Science+Business Media: Young, G. (1997). [Table 3.4, Page. 78]

In this stage of cognitive development in the present model, the child is developing Piagetian preoperational and concrete operational thought and, affectively, the parallel Neo-Eriksonian stages concern, in particular, the development of initiative and "industrial" effort in life roles. According to Piaget, the child is quite egocentric at 2 years of age, for nascent representational skills help focus on the child's perspective, but not yet that of the other. As the child takes initiative, a corresponding cognitive appreciation of the other develops, in the form of a theory of the mind of the other. However, there are limits in this regard, in that the other is still considered as someone to serve the needs of the self

With increasing cognitive skills, the child can better understand the other and the social rules that govern behavior. However, the other is still not grasped objectively, so that the self remains the primary perspective. With the advent of concrete operations, a better reflection upon the other can take place, and the focus is not only upon the self. The reciprocity indicates that the self is progressing to taking secondary perspectives. In the last substage that manifests in this stage, the child can take a third-person perspective. The child can imagine different roles for the self and the other. In this regard, the self begins to remove itself from the self to explore different selves, and the same applies to the conception of the other

**Table 13.4** Substages in self-development in the abstract stage

| Substage | Self-development |
|---|---|
| 16. | *In-depth, societal-symbolic perspective-taking self*: Young adolescents can coordinate separate pathways of logic in imagination, precipitating the acquisition of formal abstract thought. Such logic enables creative conscious awareness, where adolescents have metacognitions about their cognitions and motives. Past and future are analyzed, linked, and chained, or coordinated to give a Janus-like vision in the present. Conscious esteem develops for the self, the other, and ideas. Abstract logic allows one to see the self and other as complex entities functioning simultaneously at multiple conscious and unconscious levels. If confusion sets in, excessive conformity may result. Loevinger terms the equivalent of this stage the conformist stage. At this level, the self may be described as the *abstractly aware conscious self* |
| 17. | *Conscientious-conformist self*: Adolescents can now weigh multiple variables and logically proceed to attempt to solve problems about the self, the wider world, and their relation. Accentuated by pubertal awakening, this process can lead to an evaluation of self-identity, ideology, and place in the time course. A sense of the real self, truly personal goals, concerns about personal adjustment, and options concerning the self emerge. Loevinger labels the equivalent of this stage the transitional one of the conscientious/conformist stage. One may call the self in this period the *identity-seeking self* |
| 18. | *Conscientious self*: The capacity of late adolescents for abstract systematization permits systemic understanding; personal and other perspectives can coexist in one integrated structure. Social and societal relationships are seen as components of a larger whole to which the individual must contribute. With this viewpoint come self-constructed standards, or criteria applied in critical thought. Loevinger calls the equivalent of this stage the conscientious stage. Late adolescents seem to possess a *maturing conscientious self* |
| 19. | *Individualistic self*: The dialectical, relativist thought of youth permits the self to be seen as unique yet engaged in a deep mutuality with differentiated others. Loevinger refers to the equivalent of this stage the individualistic stage. We can call this self the *mutual relativistic self*, for there is a profound nonabsolutist immersion in the self, the other, and their relation |
| 20. | *Autonomous self-sufficient self*: Adults possess abstract integration skills, which enable a universal empathy. They recognize others' need for individualized independence within a framework of reciprocal interdependence. They accept others' conflicts or ambiguities as their own. Loevinger indicates that the equivalent of this stage is the autonomous stage. This self seems an *accepting universal self* |

Reprinted with the permission of Springer Science+Business Media: Young, G. (1997). [Table 3.5, Page. 80]

The adolescent enters the stage of formal operations and develops an abstract awareness of the complexity of the self, as well as the degree to which it is embedded in a wider system of others in society. The adolescent recognizes unconscious influences in self and other expression, but could become stuck and conformist. As the adolescent grows, the process of seeking identity becomes more of a focus and, at the same time, the other is evaluated with increasing conscientiousness

As the process continues, the adolescent sees the wider picture, and might become more committed to the other. Yet, the youth of today remain focused on their self-exploration, as well. They are mutual, yet individualistic, and they are committed to the other, yet relativistic and not absolutist. As the stage ends, young adults potentially are more universalist and empathic toward all others, yet autonomous and free to think for themselves

**Table 13.5** Substages in self-development in the collective intelligence stage

| Substage | Self-development |
|---|---|
| 21. | *Postautonomous self*: Metaphysical reasoning in subdomain or generic theory-procedure coordination engenders an appreciation of the wholeness of the web of being that allows our participation in this process. Loevinger calls the equivalent of this stage the postautonomous stage. This self is termed a *holistic metaself* |
| 22. | *Generative self*: With hierarchization of the coordination in the above process, a spreading generativity (e.g., mentoring) is fostered. We can speak of an *activating generative self* |
| 23. | *Midlife self*: Domain systematization parallels the transitional midlife period. Generativity is more elaborate and systemic. It is coupled with a transformative rethinking of the self and contemplation of the end of those phases where one's potential and dream seemed to have no temporal or physical constraints. We can refer to a *catalytic midlife self* |
| 24. | *Ego integrity self*: Interdomain thought is accompanied by satisfaction and acceptance of one's life course. The self appears a *satisfied ego integrity self* |
| 25. | *Integrated self*: In the final phases of life, often there is a wider knowledge, which is accompanied by cathartic or purifying experiences. The elderly become impregnated by a holistic sense of wisdom and also feel communion or reverence with what they regard as holy. In their most meditative moments, they hope to transcend, and in consequence to be one with mystery. Loevinger gives the term for the equivalent of this stage the integrated stage. Self-development culminates in a *purified integrated self* |

Reprinted with the permission of Springer Science+Business Media: Young, G. (1997). [Table 3.6, Page. 82]
In the postformal stage, the adult moves through the productive years to looking back on those years. The stage corresponds to Eriksonian generativity and ego integrity. Loevinger refers to a Postautonomous self. Adults pass through a midlife crisis or awakening. At the end of life, when integrated, we look forward to what is looming

### *Comment*

Given that it integrates the work of multiple theorists on self-development and related work, such as on Erikson and attachment theory, the present model is comprehensive. Just as I have indicated how the present model at the cognitive level does not have age gaps or inconsistencies relative to other Neo-Piagetian models, I took care to construct in the same way the present parallel self-development model.

## Environmental Support

### *Model*

In Young (1997), by extrapolating from the present 25-step model of development and the extension from it that I had undertaken for the topic of self-development, I had described the optimal scaffolding that the family could provide the developing child (see Tables 13.6–13.10). Based on this work, I suggest in this book a model

**Table 13.6** Substages in optimal family development in the reflex stage

| Self-development | Family development |
|---|---|
| 1. Fetal life/nonself | *Nesting family*: Caregivers must psychologically, prepare themselves (and any siblings) for the new arrival. The physical setting is planned. Some ruminate on "ghosts" in the nursery, or their own psychological past, as their future as caregivers arrives |
| 2. Premature self I/reflexive preself | *Incubator family*: The family must marshal its resources to be near the endangered baby in the incubator, spending as much time as possible at the hospital |
| 3. Premature self II/corporal protoself | *Preparatory family*: With the imminent arrival of the baby in the home, whether in terms of an impending birth of a full-term newborn of the homecoming of hospitalized preterm infant, the organizational flexibility of the family is tested. Life-styles alter to accommodate to the coming offspring (e.g., childbirth courses attended, books read, room prepared, caregiving arrangements planned) |
| 4. Emergent self I/perceptual intermodal self | *Birthing family*: The style of reception and interaction with the baby in the first few days of life may set the tone for future phases. The family is concerned, present, and caring. This matches the newborn's active need for appropriate caregiving and alimentation of her or his perceptual search |
| 5. Emergent self II/primary emotional self | *Affect/rhythm family*: The very young infant's emotional world is modulated by a cherishing, doting surveillance, for basic rhythms (sleep-wake, engage-disengage, lack-satisfaction) are established. The parents are responsive, sensitive, and interested in being interesting and provoking attention |



**Table 13.7** Substages in optimal family development in the sensorimotor stage

| Self-development | Family development |
|---|---|
| 6. Core, coordinated interaction self/inter-coordinated incipient social self | *Scaffolding family*: The parents elevate their communicative level to accommodate to the growing infant's increasingly sophisticated dyadic skills. They create holding structures in which they know when to wait, when to stimulate, when to cycle with the infant's activity, when to calm the infant, etc. Framed opportunities for optimal outreach and intercourse are provided |
| 7. Core initiatory self/end-focused trusting self | *Trustworthy family*: Self-confidence is established by an honest, accepting attitude, including empathic understanding. The infant's first overt purposeful behavior is not subverted by viewing it as too imposing, and mistrust does not develop |
| 8. Subjective attachment self/permanent intersubjective self | *Interobjective family*: Responding reciprocally to the infant's intended intersubjectivity, parents give of themselves, share, encourage an active attachment, and become secure figures of attachment. They match the child's intersubjective sociality and attachment needs (serving as "objects" of attachment) |
| 9. Verbal autonomous self/independent autonomous self | *Autonomy-fostering family*: Parents match the toddler's exploratory and verbal gambits by accepting, supervising, explaining, answering, amplifying, extending, simplifying, correcting, etc. All this is undertaken with the appropriate emotional fuel necessary for the toddler. Topped up with feelings and words, the toddler accelerates into the fast lane of autonomous physical displacement toward psychological individuation |

(continued)

**Table 13.7** (continued)

| Self-development | Family development |
|---|---|
| 10. Verbal constancy self/interior implicative self | *"Exterior" family*: As the toddler advances in thinking and social skills, the family is called upon to be more flexible, reciprocal, and supportive, yet without denying limits. They must adopt a matching or complementary, even opposite role before the child (e.g., letting lead, control; confirming child's evaluation even if it is wrong in order to foster a sense of pride in self). Their "yeses" are either genuine and encourage, or qualified but do not discourage. "Nos" are firm, and explained. The psychological individual integrity of the toddler is fully respected; her/his separate self is acknowledged as exterior to other family members |



**Table 13.8** Substages in optimal family development in the perioperational stage

| Self-development | Family development |
|---|---|
| 11. Egocentric-centrated self/coupling egocentric-centrated self | *Expanding family*: The egocentric stance of the 2–3-year-old as he or she expands into the world can try the most patient parents. The family's superordinate structure is tested, and a coherent, cohesive, integrated family can accommodate to the child without stifling her or him. This process is abetted by expanding out to preschool playgroups, neighborhood play partners, grandparents, other family, etc. Also, at this point, the mother may be having, expecting, or planning an addition (expanding the family) |
| 12. Initiative self/hierarchizing initiative self | *Initiative-fostering family*: The preschooler's abundant initiative must be counterbalanced by sensible rules explicated sensitively when the situation demands such action. The preschooler's pushing forth into the world of peers and play to master and dominate is countered by realistic restraints put in place by parents |
| 13. First-person perspective taking, unilateral self/systematizing primary-perspective self | *Normative-streaming family*: Parents arrange the best schooling. Rule systems, a moral ordering, etc., are provided by the family (and the school). The family continues to model appropriate sex-role behavior, channeling identification. They correct self-ranking that depreciates self-worth, and they monitor identification, assuring equilibration |
| 14. Reciprocal, second-person perspective-taking, self-reflective self/concrete operational secondary-perspective self | *Educating family*: Parents instruct and give lessons; they help with homework and plan extracurricular activities. They protect the child from worrying too much about the opinions of others. Their forum for learning rivals that the school in some senses |
| 15. Third-person, perspective-taking, mutual self/projecting tertiary-perspective self | *Let-subteen-mirror family*: The relative status of the child and parents becomes more balanced or on equal footing, for actual adult roles are entertained or portrayed by the child. Parents are especially concerned that the subteen not only acquires independence (with peers) but also behaves responsibly with their freedom, without losing the perspective that he or she is still relatively young. They discuss realistic constraints in terms of the preadolescent's imaginings both about the self and the relation to the other and the environment. Parents act supportive. They do not feel menaced by their subteen growing toward them psychologically yet preparing distancing or independence moves. The range of the parents' reach into society (their varied activities and faces, their sense of mutuality with the surround) is mirrored in their offspring through her or his modeling function |

**Table 13.9** Substages in optimal family development in the abstract stage

| Self-development | Family development |
|---|---|
| 16. In-depth, societal-symbolic perspective-taking self/ abstractly aware conscious self | *Coconscious family*: The adolescent's free exploration of internal "distances" and external realities is not inhibited, mitigated, or compromised by a lack of same in family members, either in the present or as unresolved conflicts in the past. The teenager can perceive masks, pretense, and shells, and the well-integrated family has divested itself of such vestiges for the most part. Nevertheless, parents maintain a supervisory function; they promote their standards, and try to ensure that their offspring come to self-monitor them, while acknowledging and supporting those of their offspring |
| 17. Conscientious-conformist self/identity-seeking self | *Identity-fostering family*: The adolescent now sees the well-integrated family that has raised her or him as a vibrant, self-actualizing family, which infuses her or him with the sculpting vitality needed for the challenge of unfettered quest for identity and self-agency (which does not exclude a sense of familial communion and attachment; Gilligan, 1982). Parents help in this process by guiding, channeling, and setting limits on their adolescent's distancing efforts |
| 18. Conscientious self/maturing conscientious self | *Letting-go family*: The late adolescent's will for a harmonious integration of self-in-system is accompanied by a parental attitude allowing much more distanced freedom from the family. Parents are nonintervening and accepting, yet give counsel, negotiate consensual goals, etc. (Barnhill and Longo (1978) use the term "letting go" in conjunction with the reencountering family, level 22 in the following table. I think that it fits better here) |
| 19. Individualistic self/mutual relativistic self | *Launching family*: Parents do all they can to promote constructive, functional, preparatory activity for the tasks of adulthood. They young person feels a profound intermutuality and cooperative distancing, and the final transition to the initiation of a new family cycle is facilitated. Parents ought to be near or in the phase of Erikson's generativity at this point, so that their own transformative reappraisal of the self is matched by their offspring's final transformation into adults |
| 20. Autonomous self-sufficient self/accepting universal self | *Seconding family*: An adult is in consistent need of social–environmental support, complementing her or his sense of empathy for the social world/environment, in general. Parents serve as generative mediators, providing the needed support (advice, baby sitting, financial, etc.), but always trying to maintain a secondary role at a comfortable distance |

Reprinted with the permission of Springer Science+Business Media: Young, G. (1997). [Table 3.5, Page. 80]

**Table 13.10** Substages in optimal family development in the collective intelligence stage

| Self-development | Family development |
|---|---|
| 21. Postautonomous self/holistic metaself | *Extending family*: Parents strive to maintain strong links with all offspring and their children, and have them do the same, creating a familial web, or network. This often extends to inclusion of other relatives. That is, parents try to assure that familial distancing does not lead to neglect. Parents also encourage a more active participation in the wider community and world |
| 22. Generative self/activating generative self | *Reencountering family*: As offspring become established and their children are born and develop, empty-nest parents have more time for tasks put on hold. The second-order distance with older grandchildren becomes more equitable as they develop toward and into adolescence. This helps foster the satisfaction and acceptance of one's life course inherent in Erikson's stage of ego integrity. Also it allows their children's unfolding generativity to develop unhindered |
| 23. Midlife self/catalytic midlife self | *Transgenerational family*: As parents approach and enter retirement, they look backward and forward, e.g., integrating their children and grandchildren into their more frequent reminiscing narratives. The distance between elder parent and adult children is marked by equality. The wisdom of the older adult can act as a solder for the entire family, and a contained instigation toward growth in their midlife offspring |
| 24. Ego integrity self/satisfied ego integrity self | *Autumn family*: Many of the elderly are active, well-adjusted, and independent. Distance from family members is variable depending on need. Some may need support and care in their turn, a responsibility often undertaken dutifully even if it is difficult. Whether healthy or not, the elderly derive second-order satisfaction in seeing their offspring manifest satisfaction and acceptance of their life course. The second-order satisfaction becomes a second-order support for their offspring |
| 25. Integrated self/purified integrated self | *Rested family*: Death if seen as tranquil repose, a welcome undistancing for parents who have optimally traversed life's epochal journey. Knowledge of their children's growth to integration facilitates the passage through this process |

Reprinted with the permission of Springer Science+Business Media: Young, G. (1997). [Table 3.6, Page. 82]

of support that the environment, in general, could provide for promoting optimal development at the cognitive, self, and affective levels.

By providing support to the child that matches her or his cognitive level, or is just slightly ahead, the child's development is fostered best. The clearer the match, the better the support can be focused and successful.

In that the present model describes the critical steps in development in the preschool, school-age, and high-school age periods, it could help the educational and instructional systems concerned with children at all these ages. Other Neo-Piagetian models are not as complete in the substages given in this age range, and therefore might not have the same scope. In this regard, the model extrapolated for optimal environmental support from step to step in substage transitions appears to represent the most comprehensive model possible. Table 13.11 gives a concise summary of the cognitive support model being proposed.

## *Comment*

The types of environmental supports described in the table, generally, do not concern direct provision of educational-instructional support. Rather, the model is consistent with Piaget's contention that the child is an active constructor of the schemas and operations needed for adaptive cognitive functioning, but the environment can offer the fuel and opportunities needed for that development to take place optimally.

At the same time, this does not mean that the model supports the view that the child is a learning machine with separated mind and emotions or separated person receiving social, educational, and instructional input. Rather, in Young (1997), I supported a Neo-Vygotskian view of development that emphasized coparticipation and coappropriation in the child's developmental growth. This is consistent with the sociocultural approach to Piaget of Nicolopoulou and Weintraub (2009), as well.

## Summary

This is the first chapter in which I concentrate on the present model without comparing it to the models of Fischer and case. In the next chapters of this section of the book, I continue the process. Among other topics, I describe and discuss innovations such as: the cognitive (mis)perception of the self; a model of self-regulation that has steps that parallel the 25 steps of the present model; a type of hypercognition termed the cognitive/socioaffective complex, also seen to develop according to the steps of present model; multiple intelligences conceived in terms of the steps of the present model, as well; the developing theory of mind conceived the same way; and reworked model of Maslow's hierarchy of needs constructed in terms of these steps of the present model.

**Table 13.11** Summary of substages in cognitive self-development and corresponding optimal support

| Level | Stage | Substage | Age range | Self | Support |
|---|---|---|---|---|---|
| 1 | Reflex | Coordination | Earlier fetal life | Nonself | Nesting |
| 2 | | Hierarchization | Quite premature | Reflexive preself | Incubator |
| 3 | | Systematization | Somewhat premature | Corporal protoself | Preparatory |
| 4 | | Multiplication | Full-term newborn | Perceptual intermodal self | Birthing |
| 5 | | Integration | 0–1 months | Primary emotional self | Affect/rhythm |
| 6 | Sensorimotor | Coordination | 1–4 months | Intercoordinated incipient social self | Scaffolding |
| 7 | | Hierarchization | 4–8 months | End-focused trusting self | Trustworthy |
| 8 | | Systematization | 8–12 months | Permanent intersubjective self | Interobjective |
| 9 | | Multiplication | 12–18 months | Independent autonomous self | Autonomy fostering |
| 10 | | Integration | 18–24 months | Interior implicative self | Exterior |
| 11 | Perioperational | Coordination | 2–3.5 years | Coupling egocentric/centrated self | Expanding |
| 12 | | Hierarchization | 3.5–5 years | Hierarchizing initiative self | Initiative-fostering |
| 13 | | Systematization | 5–7 years | Systematizing primary-perspective self | Normative-streaming |
| 14 | | Multiplication | 7–9 years | Concrete operational secondary-perspective self | Educating |
| 15 | | Integration | 9–11 years | Projecting tertiary-perspective self | Let-subteen mirror |
| 16 | Abstract | Coordination | 11–13 years | Abstractly aware conscious self | Coconscious |
| 17 | | Hierarchization | 13–16 years | Identity-seeking self | Identity fostering |
| 18 | | Systematization | 16–19 years | Maturing conscientious self | Letting go |
| 19 | | Multiplication | 19–22 years | Mutual relativistic self | Launching |
| 20 | | Integration | 22–25 years | Accepting universal self | Seconding |
| 21 | Collective | Coordination | 25–28 years | Holistic metaself | Extending |
| 22 | | Hierarchization | 28–39 years | Activating generative self | Reencountering |

(continued)

**Table 13.11** (continued)

| Level | Stage | Substage | Age range | Self | Support |
|---|---|---|---|---|---|
| 23 | | Systematization | 39–50 years | Catalytic midlife self | Transgenerational |
| 24 | | Multiplication | 50–61 years | Satisfied ego integrity self | Autumn |
| 25 | | Integration | 61 + year | Purified integrated self | Rested |

Reprinted with the permission of Springer Science+Business Media: Young, G. (1997). [Table 3.7, Page. 83]

The table summarizes the present cognitive model of 25 steps in development, and gives the optimal stance that the environment can provide in order to facilitate the development. The model was conceived in Young (1997) in terms of optimal family support, but it is applicable to the wider environmental support (see Tables 13.6–13.11). The support concerns education and instruction for the school-age child, but the model especially concerns socioaffective support. The reader will notice the embedded Neo-Eriksonain model in the different levels of environmental support. This illustrates that the different steps in environmental support were generated by considering not only the cognitive but also the socioaffective steps in the growing person

The wider society can provide optimal support even in the pregnancy steps of the model through nutritional education and supplements, as needed. The origin of the present model resides in elaboration of its cognitive stages and substages, and the parallel socioaffective steps were added afterwards. Nevertheless, the optimal supports in cognitive development should be especially socioemotional, in nature. With the latter in place, the cognitive capacities of the child can attain optimal levels through educational and other cognitive-promoting systems

The model differs from equivalent ones by describing increasing support for cognitive development in terms of qualitative advances corresponding to the cognitive level of the child. Other models might generate increasing complexity in support through different degrees of prompts, involvement, encouragement of distancing and independent thinking, etc., but even these can be modeled according to the characteristics of the child so that the support remains optimal (at the child's actual level, or one step ahead, for example)

## References


Barnhill, L. H., & Longo, D. (1978). Fixation and regression in the family life cycle. *Family Process, 17*, 469–478.

Case, R. (1991). Stages in the development of the young child's first sense of self. *Developmental Review, 11*, 210–230.

Cicchetti, D. (1991). Fractures in the crystal: Developmental psychopathology and the emergence of self. *Developmental Review, 11*, 271–287.

Cook-Greuter, S. R. (1990). Maps of living: Ego development stages from symbiosis to conscious universal embeddedness. In M. L. Commons, C. Armon, L. Kohlberg, F. A. Richards, T. A. Grotzer, & J. D. Sinnott (Eds.), *Adult development: Vol. 2. Models and methods in the study of adolescent and adult thought* (pp. 79–104). New York: Praeger.

Gilligan, C. (1982). *In a different voice: Psychological theory and women's development.* Cambridge, MA: Harvard University Press.

Harter, S. (2006). The self. In W. Damon, R. M. Lerner, & N. Eisenberg (Eds.), *Handbook of child psychology, Vol. 3*, (pp. 505–570), Hoboken: Wiley.

James, W. (1890). *The principles of psychology (Vol. 1 and Vol. 2).* New York: Holt.

Kohlberg, L., & Ryncarz, R. A. (1990). Beyond justice reasoning: Moral development and consideration of a seventh stage. In C. N. Alexander & E. J. Langer (Eds.), *Higher stages of human development: Perspectives on adult growth* (pp. 191–207). New York: Oxford University Press.

Lewis, M. (1991a). Self knowledge and social influence. In M. Lewis & S. Feinman (Eds.), *Social influences and socialization in infancy* (pp. 111–134). New York: Plenum.

Lewis, M. (1991b). Ways of knowing: Objective self-awareness or consciousness. *Developmental Review, 11*, 231–243.

Lewis, M. (1994). Myself and me. In S. T. Parker, R. W. Mitchell, & M. L. Boccia (Eds.), *Self-awareness in animals and humans: Developmental perspectives* (pp. 20–34). New York: Cambridge University Press.

Lewis, M. D., & Granic, I. (2010). Phases of social-emotional development from birth to school age. In M. Ferrari & L. Vuletic (Eds.), *Developmental relations among mind, brain and education* (pp. 179–212). New York: Springer Science+Business Media.

Loevinger, J. (1976). *Ego development: Conceptions and theories*. San Francisco: Jossey-Bass.

Loevinger, J. (1987). *Paradigms of personality*. San Francisco: Freeman.

Loevinger, J. (1993). Measurement of personality: True or false. *Psychological Inquiry, 4*, 1–16.

Loevinger, J. (1994). In search of grand theory. *Psychological Inquiry, 5*, 142–144.

Loevinger, J. (1998). Completing a life sentence. In P. M. Westenberg, A. Blasi, & L. D. Cohn (Eds.), *Personality development: Theoretical, empirical, and clinical investigations of Loevinger's conception of ego development* (pp. 347–354). London: Erlbaum.

Meltzoff, A. N. (2007). 'Like me': A foundation for social cognition. *Developmental Science, 10*, 126–134.

Meltzoff, A. N., & Moore, M. K. (1977). Imitation of facial and manual gestures by human neonates. *Science, 198*, 75–78.

Meltzoff, A. N., & Moore, M. K. (1989). Imitation in newborn infants: Exploring the range of gestures imitated and the underlying mechanisms. *Developmental Psychology, 25*, 954–962.

Mondloch, C. J., Lewis, T. L., Budreau, D. R., Maurer, D., Dannemiller, J. L., Stephens, B. R., et al. (1999). Face perception during early infancy. *Psychological Science, 10*, 419–422.

Neisser, U. (1991). Two perceptually given aspects of the self and their development. *Developmental Review, 11*, 197–209.

Nicolopoulou, A., & Weintraub, J. (2009). Why operativity-in-context is not quite a sociocultural model: Commentary on Psaltis, Duveen, and Perret-Clermont. *Human Development, 52*, 320–328.

Noam, G. G. (1992). Development as the aim of clinical intervention. *Development and Psychopathology, 4*, 679–696.

Ribeiro, L. A., & Hauser, S. T. (2009). Ego development and psychosocial functioning in young adults with and without psychiatric history. *Journal of Adult Development, 16*, 263–269.

Sander, L. W. (1975). Infant and caretaking environment: Investigation and conceptualization of adaptive behavior in a system of increasing complexity. In E. J. Anthony (Ed.), *Explorations in child psychiatry* (pp. 129–166). New York: Plenum.

Selman, R. L. (1980). *The growth of interpersonal understanding: Developmental and clinical analyses*. New York: Academic Press.

Selman, R. L., & Demorest, A. P. (1986). Putting thoughts and feeling in perspective: A developmental view on how children deal with interpersonal disequilibrium. In D. J. Bearison & H. Zimiles (Eds.), *Thought and emotion: Developmental perspectives* (pp. 93–128). Hillsdale: Erlbaum.

Sonnert, G. (1994). Limits of morality: A sociological approach to higher moral stages. *Journal of Adult Development, 1*, 127–134.

Sroufe, L. A. (1990). An organizational perspective on the self. In D. Cicchetti & M. Beeghly (Eds.), *The self in transition: Infancy to childhood* (pp. 281–307). Chicago: University of Chicago Press.

Sroufe, L. A. (1996). *Emotional development: The organization of emotional life in the early years*. Cambridge, U.K.: Cambridge University Press.

Trevarthen, C., & Aitken, K. (2003). Regulation of brain development and age-related changes in infants' motives: The developmental function of regressive periods. In M. Heimann (Ed.), *Regression periods in human infancy* (pp. 107–184). London: Erlbaum.

Westenberg, P. M., Blasi, A., & Cohn, L. D. (1998). Introduction: Contributions and controversies. In P. M. Westenberg, A. Blasi, & L. D. Cohn (Eds.), *Personality development: Theoretical, empirical, and clinical investigations of Loevinger's conception of ego development* (pp. 1–9). London: Erlbaum.

Yeates, K. O., Schultz, L. H., & Selman, R. L. (1990). Bridging the gaps in child-clinical assessment: Toward the application of social-cognitive development. *Clinical Psychology Review, 10*, 567–588.

Young, G. (1997). *Adult development, therapy, and culture: A postmodern synthesis*. New York: Plenum.

# Chapter 14
# Cognitive (Mis)Perception of the Self and Other

## Introduction

In Young (1997), I had introduced the concept of the cognitive (mis)perception of the other. I had allied it to the perception of the other as person, partner, or even minority in a culture. In the present chapter, I review this concept, given its import for intersubjectivity, social relations, therapy, and group processes. In addition, I expand the concept to include the cognitive (mis)perception of the self. I relate the two concepts to Blatt's (2008) work on polarities of experience in terms of self-definition and relatedness. [Blatt is described in depth in Chap. 16.] Chapters in this section of the book provide the background for the development of this concept, and it has its roots and applications in other theories, such as Maslow's on hierarchical needs.

## The Cognitive (Mis)Perception of the Other

### *Model*

#### Stages

Table 14.1 presents the proposed model of the cognitive (mis)perception of the other. The model refers to the manner in which an individual or group is evaluated or constructed in terms of perception of permitted developmental level, and the degree to which it corresponds to potential developmental level. When environmental support is optimal, the other or others develop according to the optimal potential of their developmental program. However, for personal or societal reasons, the other or others might not be perceived optimally and, indeed, their developmental opportunities and actual developmental level might be suppressed or curtailed. Does the adult, parent, or society involved perceive the person at the optimal level attained or capable of being attained? If not, to what degree is there (mis)construal?

G. Young, *Development and Causality: Neo-Piagetian Perspectives*,
DOI 10.1007/978-1-4419-9422-6_14, © Springer Science+Business Media, LLC 2011

**Table 14.1** The cognitive (mis)perception of the other: adult/society working schema and individual/group response at each (mis)perceived cognitive stage of the other

| (Mis)perceived stage | Adult/society Schema | Behavior | Individual/group response (A vs. B) |
|---|---|---|---|
| Reflexive | Their existence inconsequential | Negate (abuse/reject/deny) | Obliteration vs. nihilism |
| Sensorimotor | They exist, so dominate | Subjugate (repress, oppose/compete, impose, manipulate) | Sterilization vs. revolution |
| Perioperational | They think, so channel | Pacify/tantalize | Assimilation vs. resistance |
| Abstract | They test, so partially disempower | Limit, partially liberate | Involution vs. evolution |
| Collective intelligence | They are wise, so empower | Humanize | Equalization vs. emancipation |

Reprinted with the permission of Springer Science+Business Media: Young, G. (1997). [Table 7.1, Page. 156]

The model of the cognitive (mis)perception of the other indicates that, at the lowest levels of (mis)perception of the other, we treat the person as an infant or young child (levels a–b of the model). Because of the devaluing nature of these levels, the person is considered as not having much equal rights, which thereby justifies any abuse or suppression undertaken. (c) As for perceiving the other only in terms of the person being akin to an older child, at best, the person engaging in the misperception treats the other as someone who could be canalized or manipulated easily, due to their perceived lack of cognitive sophistication. In the last stages of the model (d–e), the person perceives the other as a teenager or adult, or in the more mature levels of the model

On the basis of the model of the cognitive (mis)perception of the other, I developed five scales, with each involving five-points, for use in discourse situations (see Tables 14.2–14.6). The scales measure of the quality of interference, directives, or support that participants provide each other in conversations, discussions, didactic sessions, and so on (Young). The five scales were built on the basis of the five stages of the present model (reflexive to collective intelligence), and the points within them concern the coordination to integration substages. In this regard, the worst possible (mis)perception of the other concerns treating the other inhumanely (i.e., as fully reflexive). The most mature levels of perception of the other concern seeing the person as fully part of humanity (i.e., collective)

For example, could an individual be functioning at an adult level of intelligence and be living with a partner at the same level but, nevertheless, perceive the other as childlike and manipulable, if not an object of abuse? The concept of cognitive (mis)perception of the other can accommodate to this type of example both for perception of other as individual (child, partner) or group. It is considered an affectively influenced, developmentally-based cognitive filter or lens of the perception of the other or others.

The cognitive (mis)perception model addresses the levels at which we perceive others, whether children, adults, partners, minorities, or groups. Although adults typically function cognitively at the higher levels of the model, socioaffectively, they might perceive the other from the vantage point of the lower levels. For example, in abuse, whether of children or partners, others are perceived at lower levels. In addition, the same happens in societal discrimination of groups.

The levels described in the model match with the work of Clinchy, Belenky, and colleagues (e.g., Belenky, Clinchy, Goldberger, & Tartule, 1986; Clinchy, 1993, 1995). They had described five epistemological positions that developing individuals can adopt concerning truth or knowledge and the way it is acquired. Their model is incorporated into the current one as I proceed. The present model consists of five stages that are analogous to theirs, and it adds the cyclically recurring substages that are part of the present model.

## Reflexive Stage

Parents/caregivers who misperceive their child as reflexive, at best, consider the very existence of their child as inconsequential to them, so that physical or mental abuse of the child is facilitated. One could find rejection, denial, criticism, insults, incoherence, and extreme neglect in care giving. Therefore, I have termed this parental style *negation.*

In terms of couples, one adult partner might treat the other in the same way. Its equivalent at the sociopolitical level would concern despotic, tyrannical "absolutism."

Individuals conditioned to function at this level (whether child, adult partner, or member of an oppressed group) have their sense of self obliterated. They are silent, blindly obedient, with no mind, voice, or power. Or, at best, their reaction is one of nihilism. If a child tries to escape her or his parents' misperception, or if an adult tries to escape that of their partner (or a group in society tries to escape that of its oppressor), protracted (mental) anarchy or confusion could develop.

In summary, when an adult or society misperceives others such that they are not really human, or are just non-thinking and non-feeling reflexive machines, at best, even their very existence can be taken away with no remorse. The other become sterilized in self and might react with chaotic response, at best, having no other recourse until the context changes.

### Sensorimotor Stage

Parents/caregivers who misperceiving their child as functioning at the sensorimotor level, at best, might acknowledge their existence, but they might not accept that their child is capable of independent thought. These parents typically are dominated by the forces controlling them, so that they are controlling of their child in turn (e.g., subjugating the child to their own needs or desires). This leads the parents to manifest: partial negation and neglect (scant attention); repression of any incipient indices of independence; imposition of personal agendas; and a general manipulatory shaping toward self-limiting goals.

The equivalent of this style in adult relationships often would be accompanied by alcoholism or other resignations of control over the self. At the historico-political level, an example would be represented by a less absolute, self-serving form of rule, as in an enlightened authoritarian or totalitarian system.

An individual or group exposed to this regime could become sterilized in mind and behavior. External control dominates all impulses toward autonomy. There is room only for passive acceptance, a receiving of given knowledge, and conformity. Personally-derived thought is not typically possible. However, if there is sufficient base for self-assertion, a full-scale revolution and rage could take place.

To summarize, when the misconstrual is at the level where the other is perceived as having only the most basic thoughts and feelings, at best, this facilitates treating them in a dominant way, and subjugating, repressing them, etc. One's voice develops, but in a sterilized way. If there is a negative reaction, it takes the form of overt revolt.

### Perioperational Stage

When parents misperceive a child as at the perioperational level, at best, the parents are acknowledging that the child possesses basic thinking capacities, but does not possess more general, abstract logical ones. For these types of parents, a thinking child might be menacing psychologically to them, so that the child's cognitive effort must be channeled and neutralized. Thus, parents use either arguments that function to counter the child's logic, or even more radical controlling strategies. Parents might help with homework or with basic tasks. Otherwise, parents at this level function to pacify the child so that the child becomes like themselves.

Conformism might be undermining the growth of the parents. They might indoctrinate or impose rules so the child self-polices. Rewards could be used to assimilate the child to the parents' image of themselves. The child ends up developing a subjective mode of knowing (immediate intuition without logical analysis), so that, at best, reality is only partially perceived.

The spousal system might be marked by a similar relational style. Also, a society might organize itself according to similar principles.

Compared to the prior level, rejection of this mode of relating normally would entail less revolution and more resistance and disappointment. The recipient of this mode of care would have developed enough thinking skills so that the person could be(come) self-oriented to obtain more advanced ends.

To review, when the other is conceived as a limited thinking and feeling being, without consciousness, for example, it becomes easier to channel them toward personal ends without taking into consideration their views. Rewards (and punishments) can be used to guide them to the one's desired goals. As others are canalized and pacified, the receiver becomes assimilated, unless there is a more subtle resistance.

### Abstract Stage

Parents misperceiving their child or adolescent as an individual who will end up, at most, at the abstract level might attempt to inhibit her or his empathic feel. For example, an emerging, nascent belief in universal altruism could be depreciated. However, a partial freedom of mind would obtain in the adolescent. Since the parents would be undermining a global perspective in their adolescent when behaving in this manner, the behavior is labeled deglobalization.

An adult might behave similarly with a partner. Or, a society could adopt an attitude like this with its particular minorities.

The target of this approach perhaps could not combine into a coherent thinking-affective thought process by both: (a) self-focused, reasoned, analytic, judging, "cold" thought procedures and (b) selfless, connected, nonjudgmental, feeling, "warm," empathic procedures in learning and communicating.

### Collective Intelligence Stage

Parents who realize that their offspring is part of a global system empower their child as much as possible to participate constructively in it. Mature (creative, constructivist) thinkers are passionate knowers, integrating cold-analytic and warm-empathic learning procedures, self-affirmation and other confirmation, present and future, reality and imagined possibility, personal and communal, and action and morality into one whole or macrocosm. In their evolving way, many couples and societies move toward this philosophy. The human context should serve humanistic ends.

As a review, in the more advanced ways of perceiving the other, individuals are generally respected, but they might need some limits placed on them, although there can be genuine mutual respect, too. The other can arrive at evolution and emancipation, unless there is an inward turning in face of remaining barriers.

### Comment

I present a model of the cognitive (mis)perception of the other, explaining how individuals perceive the other according to their own predominant developmental level. Most likely, each developing individual simultaneously functions at all five levels of the model, either in terms of actual behavior, desired behavior, development toward mature behavior, or the hope to develop toward this end. However, most likely, the relative proportion of the five levels varies in the individual according to situation, issue, person being related to, his or her own history, and so on. The same applies to the development in couples and societies; they might also have one major way of (mis)perceiving the other, but do vary.

In terms of attachment theory, the caregiving styles of very chaotic-abusive, dismissive, and preoccupied behavior might lead to (mis)perception of the child as, at most, reflexive, sensorimotor, and peri(pre)operational in potential, respectively, leading to corresponding disorganized-disoriented, avoidant, and ambivalent-resistant attachment by the child (Main, 1991). Conjectures such as this illustrate how the present model can be applied to current topics in child development.

Next, I elaborate the model of the cognitive (mis)perception of the other according to the substages of coordination, hierarchization, systematization, multiplication, and integration. I do this for the case of the parent/caregiver. I describe the substages generically, so that they apply equally to the five stages of the present model. The same perspective could be applied to adult-partner relationships and historico-political systems. In both cases substages could manifest. After this work on substages, I present scales related to the concept that can be used in applied research.

## Substages

### Coordination

In the first substage of coordination, parents might adopt any one of the five styles just discussed in a relatively undifferentiated way. They would apply it in a similar way from one circumstance or domain to another. However, there would not be clear, articulated links across them. Moreover, secondary (more advanced) beliefs might be coupled, at times, with the primary one, and applied in particular circumstances, but with no clear organization in the parents' rule structure. Similarly, the child would be considered an undifferentiated entity, as someone that must exist as a reflection of the preponderant caregiving style. Thus, parents would be coordinating in a haphazard way their all-encompassing attitude with secondary ones, and with their child as a reflection of that attitude. In this sense, they would be acting from and perceiving their child from a coordination perspective, with no consistent hierarchy in rule structure.

### Hierarchization

When parents refine their parental style, they are better able to link their behavior in various circumstances and situations to their predominant attitude. Or, at this level of hierarchization, rules might not be applied in equal ways across all contexts because the parents may realize the need for some situational flexibility. Or, they might allow a clearer space for alternatives concerning at least some areas in raising their child. Since a primary attitude dominates their behavior, even when a secondary (more advanced) attitude applies to part(s) of their style, it would be seen through the lens of the primary style. Thus, parents who adopt this style of behavior appear to be functioning according to a hierarchical structure. In a similar vein, parents might treat their child in a more differentiated way, perceiving the child as having some independence or external existence beyond the predominant caregiving style. Thus, in this sense, as well, parental style would evidence a hierarchical structure, and serve to open up more space for alternative reactions in the child.

#### Systematization

When the primary caregiving attitude becomes more clearly differentiated in parents, and is applied with increased nuance across situations or domains, it would create a larger systematic framework with more room for secondary (more advanced) attitudes. For example, choices would reflect the predominant attitude, and as well, alternative attitudes might be offered in relevant situations. This process would serve to open even more space in the child.

#### Multiplication

In the next step, various system combinations of alternative parental styles might be created for different domains. Parents would be accentuating the process of offering options to the child.

#### Integration

Finally, parental style might become so differentiated that its primary modality might be integrated into a complex pattern, facilitating its eventual transformation into a higher-order form. Parents would behave with optimal flexibility and even reversibility with respect to the predominant attitude. They would perceive their child as having the right to the same characteristics in their behavior, within certain confines.

## *Scales of the Cognitive (Mis)Perception of the Other*

### Scale

On the basis of the model of the cognitive (mis)perception of the other, in Young (1997), I had developed five-point scales related to the stages and substages of the present model (in effect, a 25-point scale) for use in discourse or communication situations (see Tables 14.2–14.6). The scale can be used to measure the quality of

**Table 14.2** Reflexive substages of discourse quality based on the cognitive (mis)perception of the other

| Substage | Discourse quality |
|---|---|
| 1 | The child is seen as an extension of the parent's self so that he or she can negate, abuse, reject, deny, and behave absolutely, with overt insults and rejection toward the child. The intonation is abrasive, negative, and rejecting |
| 2 | The child's reasoning or position is attacked, criticized, or rejected. The parent overtly denies the possibility of the child being correct |
| 3 | The child's reasoning or position is overtly dismissed with no effort to constructively redirect or guide understanding of the other's viewpoint. The child is told that he or she is "wrong," but there is no effort to explain why |
| 4 | Only part of the child's behavior or argument is treated as indicated in the previous substage |
| 5 | Despite such behavior, part of the child's behavior or argument is acknowledged or listened to by the parent. There is a differentiation and reversibility evident in the willingness to acknowledge/listen to the child |



**Table 14.3** Sensorimotor substages of discourse quality based on the cognitive (mis)perception of the other

| Substage | Discourse quality |
|---|---|
| 6 | There is a high degree of parental control, subjugation, repression, authoritarianism, opposition, imposition, manipulation, and dominance in the conversation. It is shaped directly by the parent's ideas or agenda. The child has no independent thought, but waits for the parent to provide direction. The parent uses language to control the child's physical actions and behaviors. An order is given that directs the path in the conversation (e.g., "You don't have to say that," or "You'd better … You have to … You must …") |
| 7 | The child's reasoning-position is competed with, contradicted, countered, or opposed in an effort to subvert, manipulate, control, or undermine it |
| 8 | The child clearly is directed to speak or act in a particular way with no constructive explanation given as to why (e.g., "No," "Tell me about …," "Why don't you …") |
| 9 | Only part of the child's discourse is manipulated. Manipulative suggestions are made that flow from that part of the child's previous discourse that seems to have been judged possibly acceptable to the parent |
| 10 | Despite some signs of parental manipulation, etc., suggestions are made in a way that appears to give the child a chance to use them or not (e.g., "You know that you could get what you want if you did it this way") |

**Table 14.4** Perioperational substages of discourse quality based on the cognitive (mis)perception of the other

| Substage | Discourse quality |
| --- | --- |
| 11 | The parent channels/neutralizes/pacifies the child by disrupting/disorganizing/confusing the child (e.g., "You're not thinking right"). The parent gives "I don't know" answers to questions. The child directly attempts to keep the discussion going, but the parent does not participate or give an answer to allow the discussion to proceed. Indiscriminate rewards are used to foster a climate of compliance/assumption |
| 12 | With a younger child, passive listening without comments or encouragement is a type of pacification-channeling, because the child's thought cannot be advanced, coherent, etc., in and of itself. With an older child, a parent can pacify-channel in more indirect ways (e.g., ignore the child's thought, invalidate it; turn to own ideas after child's speaking turn without acknowledgement of listening). The parent is passive with no verbal or nonverbal expressions, direction, or guidance. The parent may acknowledge her or his listening role (e.g., "Hmm hmm"). The parent parrots or paraphrases the child's comments or requests minor restatements. Minor corrections are given by the parent (in vocabulary, pronunciation, grammar), but with no new information. The Parent may make a direct request for information, or may ask a direct question (e.g., "Say that again," "What do you think about …"). The child is rewarded if he or she follows the parent's lead or suggestions, or if the (implicit) promise of such is possible. The result is that the same comments or ideas occur during the discussion. No advances in storytelling or thought are made. An intermediary value of 12.5 is assigned when the parent asks for clarification, e.g., "Is this what you mean?" or corrects constructively, (but still with the limit that channeling, neutralizing, or pacifying is taking place) |
| 13 | The parent points out a position/option that is different from the child's own without constructive explanation (e.g., "Couldn't it be that …," or "Yes, but another way is …"). Or the parent enunciates own thought or position with some explanation |
| 14 | Despite some signs of channeling or pacification, a part of the child's discourse is acknowledged/accepted/praised on its own terms. The parent clearly acknowledges the child's answer or comment but without accepting it (e.g., "Yes, I know what you mean," or "I was just going to ask you that."). The parent shows some evidence of warmth and active interest in the child's position, although the conversation is not completely interactive |
| 15 | A glimmer of possibility is left open for the child's position or argument to emerge as being correct, but in the context of others. The parent points out relationships between the child's position and (an)other(s), their own, etc., integrating the child's view as one differentiated member of a larger perspective (e.g., "You're right, but …") |

**Table 14.5** Abstract substages of discourse quality based on the cognitive (mis)perception of the other

| Substage | Discourse quality |
| --- | --- |
| 16 | The parent indirectly encourages partially independent, novel thought of other possible dimensions to the story/reasoning/position, or the way given dimensions may interact (e.g., "Can you think of anything else"; "Why do you say that?"; "What else did he do or say?"; "How does *this* relate to *that*?"). The parent suggests that more may be possible or that there's something important missing (e.g., "Didn't you forget something?"). The parent does not provide information, but hints at a direction so the child can take the lead of the discussion. The parent listens to the child's response and continues the conversation by building on the child's responses or by asking indirect questions |
| 17 | Part of the child's reasoning is praised, reinforced by the parent directly with a constructive comment (e.g., "That's a really good idea because ..."). The parent encourages the child to continue with her on his position/idea/comment. The parent allows the child to control the pace and direction of the discussion |
| 18 | The child's whole story/reasoning/position is shown to be valid in a constructive way |
| 19 | The child is prompted to expand on the immediate/proximate implications of her or his story/reason/position |
| 20 | The child is prompted to see how her or his story/reason/position fits into a larger picture and may be harmonious with it |

Reprinted with the permission of Springer Science+Business Media: Young, G. (1997). [Table 7.5, Page. 167]

**Table 14.6** Collective intelligence substages of discourse quality based on the cognitive (mis) perception of the other

| Substage | Discourse quality |
| --- | --- |
| 21 | The child is prompted to indirectly seek or explore alternative scenarios, stories, perspectives, even ones not espoused by a parent and which may be discrepant from the parent's own point of view. The parent should be encouraging a "collective" attitude/moral/value in this line of discourse as proceed discourse (e.g., "Is there another way of seeing ...") |
| 22 | The prompts above given to the child are given in a direct manner, but only for part of, not a full, perspective. The child is encouraged to see where trade-offs, negotiations, bargaining, or give-and-take may apply to certain collective-oriented positions. However, the parent instills in the child the idea that one of them is dominant over the other(s) |
| 23 | The prompts above are direct, and are aimed at eliciting a whole new perspective. The parent encourages the child to consider alternative collective positions as being part of a larger system, and that all are considered equally valid, legitimate, and in a dynamic relationship with each other |
| 24 | The parent encourages the child to see the implications of adopting large systems and to compare them. The parent and child discuss together similarities and differences among them. The parent and child together realize that these sometimes conflicting systems can exist simultaneously |
| 25 | The parent encourages explicit attempts to put all previous systems into an overarching principle, tempered by contextual pragmatic realities, e.g., living with and growing from conflict |

*Note*. Not used by the participants in our study

Reprinted with the permission of Springer Science+Business Media: Young, G. (1997). [Table 7.6, Page. 168]

interference, directives, or support that participants provide each other in conversations, discussions, didactic sessions, and so on (see the study with teenagers where it was applied; in Young, 1997).

In terms of these scales, coordination refers to when adults treat the child in an undifferentiated, global manner, and the child must coordinate with their perspective. In hierarchization, adults especially critique the child's reasoning. In systematization, the child's reasoning is considered part of a larger system. In multiplication, the adult focuses on only part of the child's reasoning. In integration, at least part of the child's reasoning is openly listened to/acknowledged/encouraged.

In constructing the scales, the guiding logic was that they had to begin with the worst possible (mis)perception of the other (i.e., fully reflexive). They had to terminate with the most mature form (i.e., fully collective).

## Applications

### Minorities

The model of the cognitive (mis)perception of the other that I have presented provides a theoretical structure for understanding how institutions and society can forego the health needs of its clients or members. The model also provides a metric for scaling the behavior and justifications of the person or group that is (mis)-perceiving the other as they deal with the other. In this regard, in Young (1997), I presented data on political commentary published in newspapers that I analyzed for text complexity according to the scales just presented. Upon examination of the political commentary in the newspapers with the present scale of text complexity, the data showed that the surface level of statements given to the press by the government or its officials did not concord with the deep structure of what the statements were inferring between the lines, at least as far as I read them.

As an example, I provide the statement of an official in human services in Ontario that he directed toward protesters of cuts in social assistance. He communicated: "Parasitic poverty pimps, welfare cheats, the mindless mantra of community policing apologists. ... Fraud just incenses me." Also, a government minister was quoted as saying: "Let them eat dented cans of tuna." These unfortunate examples indicate the degree to which a government can (mis)perceive and mistreat a minority group in a culture.

In analyzing the first quote for surface and deep meanings according to the scale of text complexity, I noted that the official who gave the statement claimed that he was trying to help the disadvantaged, for example, by weeding out fraud. However, despite his claim that he meant to be helpful, the government instituted cuts across-the board in social assistance benefits. In terms of the text complexity scale used to score the statement, the surface level was rated as 13/25, but the deep level was rated as 1/25. Despite normative intentions, the manner in which the intentions were expressed was considered abusive.

**Table 14.7** Stages in the complexity of censorship

| Stage | Type | Description |
|---|---|---|
| Reflexive | Omnipotent censorship | Because the state deserves full power over its citizens, it has the right to censure without justifications |
| Sensorimotor | Constraining censorship | Because the state knows best, it has the right to censure in the best interest of its citizens |
| Perioperational | Enlightened censorship | State censorship should be used to contain only the worst excesses of its citizens |
| Abstract | Liberalistic censorship | State censorship should be use only when any one citizen's fundamental rights are endangered |
| Collective intelligence | Mutualistic censorship | The state and its citizen self-censor and constructively rework ideas when any one citizen's fundamental rights are endangered |

*Note*. This progression in societal censorship can be applied to other groupings such as censorship in the family or in the couple



## Censorship

In Young (1997), I presented a model of stages in the complexity of censorship that was constructed according to the model of the cognitive (mis)perception of the other (see Table 14.7). I indicated that the concept could be applied to parental, partner, and societal censorship of the other.

For the present work, I add that it could be applied to how the person self-censors or self-polices. We could learn to different degrees to inhibit our self-expression. The multivoicedness of ourselves and part-selves could be suppressed because of our environmental experiences, from family to partner to society.

Moreover, how censorship develops could be specified in terms of substages. For example, in the hierachical substage of the perioperational stage, a government policy could be oriented to some liberalization in free speech, but only as related to an overarching theme of government control. Or, in a couple, the controlling one might be functioning from the level of sensorimotor multiplication in attitude toward the other and massively inhibit freedom to talk about anything from their vantage point, as a general rule develops in this regard.

## Psychology

Note that the model presented on the cognitive (mis)perception of the other has wide-ranging applicability and could be illuminating in terms of understanding deep meaning relative to surface statement. Even in the profession of psychology, it has been alleged that leaders in the executive of the American Psychological Association had engaged in inappropriate behavior related to the torture issue bedeviling it. Many members protested existing policies and even resigned or published articles against the policies in place and the inappropriate behavior.

It would be interesting to compare the association's statements on the matter in terms of their surface structure and their deep structure, now that the information about the inappropriate behavior is coming to light. How had the psychologists being charged justify their behavior and what was their (mis)perceived view of the other? How had the upper echelon of the American Psychological Association at the time view the public, its members, and the victims? Perhaps the present scaling procedures could be applied to the surface and deep structures of the statements that have been made in these regards.

## The Cognitive (Mis)Perception of Self and Other

To review, the concept of the cognitive (mis)perception of the other refers to how we perceive others as less than implied by their actual developmental level or potential developmental level. For example, when caregivers misperceive the developing child, at best, as reflexive and without thinking capacities, this can lead to abuse of the child. Similarly, cognitive (mis)perceptions of the other can lead to abuse in by partners in couples and to discrimination and persecution of minorities by the majority culture.

Blatt's work on self-definition and relatedness as a duality in experience has led me to expand the model of the cognitive misperception of the other. In Table 14.8, I present a model with eight types of cognitive (mis)perceptions. Four of them relate to self-definition and four relate to relatedness. I refer to two components of the self – the self-definitional self and the relatedness self – and consider two other axes in the model – evaluator and target. Therefore, for each of the two self types, I describe cognitive (mis)perceptions in terms of whether the person is judging not only the other but also the self, and whether the person is referring to the self as the evaluator or the other as the evaluator.

For example, I created a sentence that corresponds best to the original concept of the cognitive misperception of the other – "I perceive the other's self as…." In the table, I have relabeled this type of cognitive misperception as the "Cognitive (mis)perception of the self of the other."

By examining the different combinations of self and other as evaluator and self and other as target of evaluation, four types of cognitive (mis)perceptions emerge for the self-definitional self and four types of cognitive (mis)perceptions emerge for the relatedness self. For example, the sentence that best characterizes what is involved in cognitive (mis)perception by the relatedness self of the other is, "I perceive the other's sense of relatedness as…."

In Chap. 13, I reviewed my work on the development of the self according to the present model of 25 steps in development. In that work, I integrated the models of Sroufe, Selman, and Loevinger. The present elaboration of the concept of cognitive (mis)perception of the self and of the other indicates that the description of the development of the self that I had formulated is being further differentiated.

**Table 14.8** A model of the self's cognitive (mis)perception of self (S) and other (O)

| Self type | Evaluator | Target | Description | Example |
|---|---|---|---|---|
| Self-definitional self | S | S | Cognitive (mis)perception of my self[a] | "I perceive my self as …" |
| | S | O | Cognitive (mis)perception of the self of the other | "I perceive the other's self as …" |
| | O | S | Cognitive (mis)perception of the other's perception of my self | "Others perceive my self as …" |
| | O | O | Cognitive (mis)perception of the other's perception of the other's self | "Others perceive their selves as …" |
| Relatedness self | S | S | Cognitive (mis)perception of the relatedness self[b] | "I perceive my sense of relatedness as …" |
| | S | O | Cognitive (mis)perception of the other's relatedness self | "I perceive the other's sense of relatedness as …" |
| | O | S | Cognitive (mis)perception of the other's perception of the relatedness self | "Others perceive my sense of relatedness as …" |
| | O | O | Cognitive (mis)perception of the other's perception of the other's relatedness self | "Others perceive their sense of relatedness as …" |

*Introduction.* James' (1890) classic distinction between the I-self and the Me-self has stood the test of time (Harter, 2006). The present work has provided two concepts related to the self. (a) First, I describe how the self develops over 25 steps in development (see Chap. 13). (b) Also, I have described the concept of the cognitive (mis)perception of the other. (a) The latter concept appears related to the I-self, in the way the person's cognitive capacity grows that permits the I-self to construct the Me-self. (b) The second concept concerns how the person perceives the self of the other

There are many refinements of the concept of the I-self and the Me-self that have been elaborated, and it is beyond the scope of the present work to investigate these in detail. However, Blatt (2008) referred to the polarities of experience along the poles of self-definition and relatedness. He reviewed a large body of literature informing this opposition, and how they integrate. He adopted an Eriksonian view of personality development (see Chap. 16)

Also, Labouvie-Vief, Grühn, and Studer (e.g., 2010) provided descriptions of dualities in self-representation, although not in a way as detailed as in Blatt's model. They did present the development of self-representations in terms of a Neo-Piagetian perspective of cognitive development (e.g., they described an integrated postformal stage)

*Dual selves.* One way of accommodating the differing conceptions of the self and related processes, and its implicit integration of dualities, is to refer them as inward-oriented and outward-oriented. In this regard, I propose that a good way of distinguishing the components of the self is to refer to them in Blatt's terms. This leads me to propose a dual model of the self, consisting of two interlinked components – the *self-definitional self* and the *relatedness self*. Blatt clearly pointed out the dynamical and integrating nature of the components of the polarities that he described, and the same applies to the current conceptualization of the two selves derived from his work

In defining these two types of self, I do not adopt a strict Blattian approach, because I incorporate elements of my own work. The self-definitional self refers to the understanding of who one is and how one is growing psychologically. For the latter aspect of the growing self, this refers to the present model of 25 steps in development. The relatedness self refers to how one functions in life contexts, both instrumental and social. The definition concerns relatedness to the task/problem/ instrumental environment and not just the social one. Moreover, it includes the mental resource

(continued)

**Table 14.8** (continued)

capacities needed to function well, as defined in the present work. Does one have the resources needed to succeed or to solve problems, such as a good functioning hypercognitive-related mechanism (the cognitive/socioaffective complex; see Chap. 17)? Does one have the social skills and supports (others or even institutions) needed to help in these regards?

The *relatedness self* appears to be a situated-situational and resource-oriented one, given its outward orientation, and is subject to positive and negative evaluations. The *self-definitional self* appears to be concerned with understanding of one's inner qualities, and is subject to positive and negative appraisals, as well

*Axes*. The model of the cognitive (mis)perception of the other that I had developed is especially about evaluation of the self-definitional self of the other, the qualities and characteristics of the other. However, the concept can be applied readily to the evaluation of one's own self-definitional self

This logical train of thought has led to a developmental model of the components of the self that is based on the *self-definitional self* and the *relatedness self*. Moreover, another pertinent distinction that I make is whether self-understanding is about the self as evaluator or about the other as evaluator. For example, in making perceptions, evaluations, or appraisals, is the evaluator of the self constructions the self or the other

Another relevant distinction in the self-other divide related to self-construction concerns whether one is addressing or orienting to perceptions, evaluations, or appraisals that are self-directed, targeted, or aimed or whether one is addressing or orienting to perceptions, evaluations, or appraisals that are other-directed, targeted, or aimed

Therefore, there seem to be four major types of self-other constructions undertaken by the self, depending on whether the evaluator is the self or the other and whether the target is the self or the other. For example, one could ask not only what is my perception of myself but also what is my understanding of the other's perception of myself? In addition, one could ask not only what is the other about but also what does the other think others are about?

Moreover, these types of questions could be asked both about the self-definitional self and relatedness self. For example, I could ask how the other defines him- or herself. Also, I could ask myself how the other thinks I am in terms of my world of relationships

*Model*. The various combinations of these: (a) two different types of self, (b) two different types of evaluators that one is constructing as actors of the constructions, and (c) two different directions, objects, or targets in construction together lead to a classification of the self in terms of eight components. In the following, I present the eight components in two sets

(1–4) These self-constructing components of the self involve self constructions: (a) by the self about the self's self-definitional self-constructions; (b) by the self about the other's self-definitional self-constructions; (c) by the other about the self's self-definitional self-constructions; and (d) by the other about the other's self-definitional self-constructions

(5–8) These same four constructions can be applied to the concept of the relational self, in addition to the self-definitional self. For example, the first type of self-construction given above becomes: by the self about the self's relatedness self-constructions

Moreover, these eight self components are not considered static. Rather, they are considered as changing dynamically both in context and over developmental time. Finally, they are presented as cognitive (mis)perceptions in order to indicate their negative and positive poles and potentials

[a] Cognitive (mis)perception of my personal self, the I-self

[b] Cognitive (mis)perception of cognitive/socioaffective complex of the self or the situated-situational resource self

In describing 25 steps in development, the cognitive model presented in the chapter on self-development helps us understand the cognitive capacities used by the I-self in constructing the Me-self. In describing different types of cognitive (mis)perceptions in development, the model of the self and the other presented in this chapter helps us understand the contents of construction in the Me-self by the increasing cognitive capacities of the I-self.

The present work can be applied to the thinking process of partners in couples and of majority and minority cultures in societies. To what degree does a partner act in a particular way because of deficiencies in the cognitive perception of the self, as per the present model? To what degree does a minority culture project its fears onto a majority culture because of perceived slights, some real, some not, leading to difficulties in cross-cultural relations? In this example, could the present model help explain the process and the degree of cognitive (mis)perception involved? Moreover, in both cases, can the models described help facilitate understanding and healing?

## Other Self Topics

In Young (1997), I had dealt with other topics related to self-development, such as the development of a sense of self-efficacy and the development of themes that one narrates about the self. Both these concepts relate to the perception that the person has of the self and other.

### *Self-Efficacy*

In Young (1997), I also examined Bandura's concept of self-efficacy from the perspective of the present model (see Table 14.9). A sense of self-efficacy resides in the developing self, and the environmental supports described in the present and last chapter would serve to optimize its development, as much as other aspects, or, inversely, could complicate it.

### *Themes in Self Stories*

Narrative development is an important theme in the present work. In Chaps. 33 and 34, I review the development of narrative ability, in general, and have done so already in the book from the perspective of the present model. In Young (1997), I described narrative therapy. In this regard, I have indicated story themes that we might tell ourselves related to the 25 steps of the present developmental model. The story themes illustrate how the self is populated by personal themes that have been co-constructed with the environment. The more supportive the environment and integrated the person, the more advanced the story complexity and theme. At the same time, as with Eriksonian challenges and dangers that accompany each developmental stage, the story themes are presented in terms of oppositions of positive and negative poles (see Table 14.10).

In a later chapter, I examine McAdams' (2010) work on narrative identity. It could be elaborated to fit the present model, for example, through these story

**Table 14.9** Steps in the development of a sense of self-efficacy

| | Self-efficacy | |
|---|---|---|
| Stage | Normally developing | Compromised |
| Reflexive | Omnipotence | Annihilation |
| | Renewal | Stagnation |
| Sensorimotor | Security | Insecurity |
| | Swagger | Stiffness |
| Perioperational | Pretension, presumption | Presumptiousness |
| | Poise | Fluster (bluster) |
| Abstract | Assurance (certitude) | Chronic uncertainty |
| | Self serenity | Chronic malaise |
| Collective intelligence | Communal confidence | Communal cynicism |
| | Integrated consciousness | Collective rejection |

Reprinted with the permission of Springer Science+Business Media: Young, G. (1997). [Table 3.8, Page. 84]

The present Neo-Piagetian cognitive developmental model consists of five cognitive stages, each having five substages that cyclically recur within them. The table indicates the manner in which the developing person develops a sense of self-efficacy as the stages and substages are traversed in lifespan development. However, in the table, only the first and last of the five substages in each stage are specified for their self-efficacy sentiments

The Me-Self should pass through the same developmental series as the I-Self (Case, 1991). In the table, it is suggested that a component of the Me-Self, one's sense of self-efficacy, as described by Bandura (1986, 1989), should develop in parallel with the cognitive steps of the present model. The table depicts the feeling about self-efficacy that should be experienced at each of the indicated steps when development is proceeding more or less normally and when it is jeopardized

(a) When the newborn is developing normally and is well cared for, he or she develops a sense of omnipotence before any task or challenge, which leads to a blind sense of renewal or rejuvenation. If this phase is not well negotiated, a sense of annihilation, at worst, or stagnation, at best, could be elicited

(b) In the next step of the series, the infant develops an appropriate sense of self-efficacy and experiences security as opposed to insecurity when participating in tasks. With increasing age, with the right support, the toddler will demonstrate a swagger as opposed to an inhibiting stiffness

(c) The perioperational child could move from an attitude of blanket pretension or presumption of success toward a preadolescent poise but, instead, might manifest presumptuous and blustery behavior

(d) The abstract adolescent is self-assured and grows toward an adult internal serenity before life's challenges. However, there might be a chronic uncertainty that culminates in a chronic malaise

(e) Finally, the maturing adult in her or his collective intelligence senses a confidence and immersion in and symbiosis with the communal surround as he or she accomplishes life's complex tasks. However, instead of an increasing opening toward an integrated awareness, there might be a cynicism toward and even a rejection of collective behavior

If the developing individual is entrained to function below her or his general developmental level, and/or have confidence in a more primitive level than the one actually achieved for a particular domain, the individual's resultant attitude might not be adaptive. That is, the adolescent or adult who carries a sensorimotor swagger or childish bluster might find that these traits are adaptive in some of their daily encounters. However, the flexibility of these levels of sense of self-efficacy compared to higher-order ones is limited. Moreover, they should be colored by various negative affective experiences, and thus hamper cognitive functioning

**Table 14.10** Positive and negative themes in stories about development

| Positive theme | Negative theme |
|---|---|
| Want to live, not hurt self | Want to die, hurt self |
| Take care of self | Not care for, ignore self |
| Be aware of, acknowledge other | Disregard, ignore other |
| Accept care from) other | Reject care from other |
| Appropriate emotion (e.g., directed, adaptive) | Inappropriate emotion (e.g., rage, fear) |
| Active dialogue, involved conversation | Monologue, one-way conversation |
| Trust, confidence in other | Mistrust, no faith in other |
| Sociability makes other secure | Not securing other |
| Independence, autonomy | Dependence, self-doubt |
| Share, give-and-take with other | Not share, give or take with other |
| Self as together, coherent | Self as not together, fragmented |
| Initiative, energy, perseverance | No initiative, inertia, guilt |
| Accept/identify with parents | Reject/not be like parents |
| Like to try best/know (e.g., at school) | Not try best feel inferior (e.g., rebellious/lazy) |
| Personality/role try out | Personality/role confusion |
| Open conscious (e.g., see past, change future) | Close, confine conscious |
| Search for identity, inner essence | Identity cut-off |
| Nurture, take care of other | Not nurture, not care for other |
| Feel mature in adult role | Feel isolated, alone |
| Empathy/genuine concern for any other, any community | Nonempathy |
| Feel integrated in society, e.g., act for community | Feel disillusioned with society, not being for community |
| Role model, demonstrate way to others | Self-absorbed, stagnate |
| Reevaluate/redefine life-course/path | Crisis/confusion in life-course/path |
| Examine/find joy in life's meaning | Despair at life's emptiness |
| Feel oneness with life, universe | Feel abandoned by life, universe |

Reprinted with the permission of Springer Science+Business Media: Young, G. (1997). [Table 10.1, Page. 234]

In the table, I discuss narrative themes and how they can be analyzed from the perspective of the present model. It presents a questionnaire based on the 25 developmental steps in the model. For each level, I chose one theme to represent it. As one descends the scale, the themes get more problematic. That is, adults who are stuck at earlier levels in their psychological growth, or who are experiencing crises related to them, will be focusing at these levels in the narratives that they create about their lives

In the following, I provide the instructions for the questionnaire. They illustrate how the story telling themes that we construct about our lives reflect the cognitive levels of the present model and their relationship to the cognitive (mis)perception of the self

Our lives are series of stories that we tell to other people and to ourselves. This questionnaire lists common themes within these stories. They go from the developmentally simple to complex. In our development, to some extent, we need both the positive and negative poles; for example, learning to become independent can only take place because of the importance of dependence in our development. Moreover, each developing individual tries to balance the positive and negative stories of each level. Also, each developing individual simultaneously lives at all levels, but with different relative proportions across them, depending on developmental history, experience, situational context, hopes, etc. Individuals might feel that they are at one developmental level for one aspect of their lives, but at another level for another aspect. Also, for any one level, individuals might feel

(continued)

**Table 14.10** (continued)

| |
|---|
| more positive than negative for one aspect of their lives but more negative than positive for another. Each person's pattern will be different, and there is no one pattern that is optimal. What is important is the person's will, acting in concert with social supports such as family and friends, to balance any dominant negative stories with positive alternate ones, and to maintain and strengthen positive ones |
| On a scale of 0–10 (e.g., 0=not applicable, 5=somewhat applicable, 10=very applicable), indicate the degree to which each of these themes is applicable to the last few months of your life, by writing beside each theme one the appropriate number. The total score for the two scores of any one line does not have to be 10. If you are not yet concerned by later particular levels, enter very low scores for them e.g., 1 and 1, 0 and 0). For the remaining relevant levels, enter the values that are right for you (e.g., if more negative than positive, 2 and 10, 3 and 7, 0 and 5; if more positive than negative, 9 and 2, 7 and 3, 5 and 0). Feel free to ask questions. If the instructions for the questionnaire apply to other than the last few months (e.g., to your hopes for next year), this will be indicated below |

themes that we coauthor about the self and other. In the end, our narrative identities are ours to author, no matter how much they have been constructed by others and life circumstances as much as ourselves.

## Summary and Conclusions

The self and other are concepts of the self generated by inter-living with the other. The cognitive-affective construct that I have proposed that mediates the relationship with the other and is co-constructed in relations with the other is called the cognitive (mis)perception of the other; a corollary one is the cognitive (mis)perception of the self. Much of psychology is about these types of perceptions, and I posit that they develop in accord with the present model of 25 steps in development.

The great developmental task is to optimize the development of these cognitive (mis)perceptions of the self and other. The great societal task is to optimize conditions that foster their optimal development.

## References

Bandura, A. (1986). *Social foundations of thought and action: A social cognitive theory*. Englewood Cliffs: Prentice Hall.

Bandura, A. (1989). Human agency in social cognitive theory. *American Psychologist, 44*, 1175–1184.

Belenky, M. F., Clinchy, B. M., Goldberger, N. R., & Tartule, J. M. (1986). *Women's ways of knowing: The development of self, voice, and mind*. New York: Basic Books.

Blatt, S. J. (2008). *Polarities of experience: Relatedness and self-definition in personality development, psychopathology, and the therapeutic process*. Washington: American Psychological Association.

Case, R. (1991). Stages in the development of the young child's first sense of self. *Developmental Review, 11*, 210–230.

Clinchy, B. M. (1993). Ways of knowing and ways of being: Epistemological and moral development in undergraduate women. In A. Garrod (Ed.), *Approaches to moral development: New research and emerging themes* (pp. 180–200). New York: Teachers College Press.

Clinchy, B. M. (1995). Commentary. *Human Development, 38*, 258–264.

Harter, S. (2006). The self. In W. Damon, R. M. Lerner, & N. Eisenberg (Eds.), *Handbook of child psychology: Vol. 3. Social, emotional and personality development* (6th ed., pp. 505–561). Hoboken: Wiley.

James, W. (1890). *The principles of psychology (Vol. 1 and 2)*. New York: Holt.

Labouvie-Vief, G., Grühn, D., & Studer, J. (2010). Dynamic integration of emotion and cognition: Equilibrium regulation in development and aging. In R. M. Lerner, M. E. Lamb, & A. M. Freund (Eds.), *The handbook of life-span development: Vol. 2. Social and emotional development* (pp. 79–115). New York: Wiley.

Main, M. (1991). Metacognitive knowledge, metacognitive monitoring, and singular coherent vs. multiple (incoherbrent) model of attachment: Findings and direction for future research. In C. M. Parkes, J. Stevenson-Hinde, & P. Morris (Eds.), *Attachment across the life cycle* (pp. 199–215). New York: Routledge.

McAdams, D. P. (2010). Narrative identity. Unpublished manuscript.

Young, G. (1997). *Adult development, therapy, and culture: A postmodern synthesis*. New York: Plenum.

# Chapter 15
# Social Cognition/Theory of Mind

## Introduction

This chapter combines two intersecting themes. First, the developing human is exquisitely social from birth and is attuned to the other in terms of fundamental concepts such as intersubjectivity, intentionality, and social understanding. Second, attributes such as these help differentiate human and animal intelligence. The chapter argues that in both cases the present model of steps in development can improve our understanding in these areas. For example, theory of mind could develop according to the steps of the present model, and the model can be used to distinguish human from animal intelligence. The model can also be used to place in context another attribute considered uniquely human – as a species, we educate and instruct our offspring to an advanced degree. Toward the end of the book, I propose how the child has evolved cognitive capacities that fit the adult capacity to educate and instruct, which in its turn had evolved to further the fitness of offspring.

The chapter is based on several recent literature reviews, in particular (Carpendale & Lewis, 2010; Caron, 2009). It emphasizes a relational perspective on social cognition and theory of mind. For infants, I review the area neonatal imitation, and I show how this area of research fits into an increased awareness of infant social cognitive skills. For children, I review the concepts of false belief and theory of mind, in particular, and show how they appear to develop in the preschooler according to the steps (substages) of the present model. I review other areas related to the topic, such as the concept of embodied practices and communities in the development of intelligence (Gibbs, 2006).

Two major areas on social cognition included in the chapter are subject to empirical and theoretical debate. The validity of neonatal imitation has been questioned. For example, it might reflect a reflexive process of opening the mouth or behaving similarly to an adult doing the same because of the saliency of oral stimuli and responses, in general. That is, it might not reflect an imitation process, per se. As for the research on theory of mind in the preschooler, controversies surround its precursors in infancy and the way it can be explained theoretically.

By presenting these topics, as well as others related to them, I provide a sufficient overview of the basics to set the stage for presenting my own model that

G. Young, *Development and Causality: Neo-Piagetian Perspectives*,
DOI 10.1007/978-1-4419-9422-6_15, © Springer Science+Business Media, LLC 2011

integrates these topics. In this chapter, I suggest that social cognition evolves through steps consistent with the present 25-step developmental model, and neonatal imitation and theory of mind are two aspects of its developmental expression.

This work in the chapter leads to an integrated hypothesis about theory of mind, labeled "construction of the cognition–emotion–body of the other." I show how this understanding of theory of mind could develop through a process of coappropriation. This train of logic leads me to develop a model of the development of the construction of the cognition–emotion–body of the other through parallel steps in coeducation, which is seen to include both informal and formal modes of learning and teaching/instruction. This model helps specify further what makes our species unique and how this develops.

## The Development of Social Understanding

### *Introduction*

Carpendale and Lewis (2010) indicated that social cognition concerns understanding social features in psychological terms, whether addressing the world, the environment, the self, or the other. For example, what are the beliefs, intentions, wishes, emotions, and desires of the other? One aspect of this domain concerns the theory of mind, which the authors refer to as social understanding, or a type of social cognition.

Carpendale and Lewis (2010) noted that the metatheoretical assumption that one adopts influences the perspective taken in a discipline (Lerner, 2006; Overton, 2006). In this regard, in child development, if one splits the relational from the individualistic, one will focus on cognition more than the social reality in the developing child.

In the relational perspective of social cognition, intersubjectivity is considered primordial, and developing cognition is considered as differentiated out of intersubjectivity by way of interpersonal interactions. The relational viewpoint perceives the child as socially engaged right from early in life so that, out of the matrix of social interactions, conceptions of self and other gradually differentiate. The infant begins life in the sensorimotor stage, according to Piaget (1936/1952/1963). Therefore, for the infant, experience is embodied in sensorimotor actions, and, as well, others are experienced as intentional agents. Action and intention go hand in hand in infancy. In this perspective, early representations of the others' beliefs, desires, and intentions are components of everyday action, rather than something to be learned about separately.

Carpendale and Lewis explained that the area of social cognition has emphasized cognitive processes but is presently taking into account interpersonal processes. The individual mind should not be considered as the primary focus in the developing person's social cognition because humans are relational beings. "From this perspective, rather than assuming individual minds as a starting point, the social process is considered primary from which minds develop" (p. 585). The authors concluded that the area of social cognition should be understood from a combined social-cognitive perspective.

## Comment

Given that the study of social cognition includes research on theory of mind, it seems critical to review the research on the development of social understanding, in general. When implications are raised for understanding theory of mind, I will highlight them. At the same time, for purposes of the present book, it needs to be kept in mind that the present 25-step model of development describes a cognitive-step model on which once can scaffold the development of social understanding, theory of mind, and social cognition, in general.

# Developmental Issues

## Infants

### Neonatal Imitation

Meltzoff and Moore (1994) maintained that human neonates can match actively in a cross-modal manner information received in one sensory channel by translating it into another one. For example, newborns have the capacity to see a model demonstrate a head movement or a mouth movement (such as opening) and, after a delay, transpose (through successive approximations) the configuration into a kinesthetic equivalent by using a supramodal representational code, thereby permitting imitation even at this early age. That is, the process of generating this internal code, called active intermodal mapping (AIM), seems to unite into one process the registration of perception with the execution of a motor plan.

With development, the deferral period before imitation lengthens. Thus, at 6 weeks of age, when infants are confronted by a passive face, they reproduce a tongue protrusion that had been imitated actively the day before. The behavior appears to be a probe or an attempt to determine by reenactment whether the adult in front of them is the same one as the day before. Infants seem to use motor imitation as a means of reidentifying with and communicating with persons before them. "Imitation is to understanding people as physical manipulation is to understanding things" (Meltzolff & Moore, 1994, p. 96).

In successive phases over infancy, the imitation becomes more socially complex, because increasingly elaborate behaviors come to be incorporated into imitative behavior. These behaviors consist of (a) social expectations at 2–3 months (routinized games such as in cooing), (b) relations to objects at 9 months (actions by others on objects), (c) intentions at 18 months (actions intended for duplication), and (d) roles at 2 years (pretending to be mommy).

Caron (2009) further specified that Meltzoff (2002) had maintained that the process of neonatal imitation involves cross-modal linkages between proprioception and exteroception based on an innate supramodal representational system. It allows the capacity to recognize conspecifics whom are "like me." This suggests that infants can readily construct shared representations for the acts of the self and of the other. Imitations and other social learning mechanisms produce sensorimotor experiences that help develop an affect neurocircuitry that is shared over perception and action.

### The Model

Meltzoff (2007) expanded on his "like me" model of social cognition. Interestingly, he noted that for Piaget infants begin life as social beings. They enter the world in a state of "solipsism" or "radical egocentrism" (Piaget, 1954). For Meltzoff, the child enters the world with self-other equivalences, in terms of the supramodal matching process previously described for neonatal imitation, that are the foundation rather than the outcome of social cognition. The actions of the self and of the other are represented simultaneously within this supramodal code, which is innately specified but experientially elaborated. Infants can use the actions of the self to understand not only the actions of the other but also their goals and psychological states. At the same time, by observing and understanding the actions and other aspects of the other, they learn about themselves and the consequences that their actions can have on others. Their supramodal capacities permit them to apprehend that the actions that they see others performing are similar to their own because the actions are ones that they can use themselves toward their own goals.

Even in the newborn period, the infant perceiving actions is given a type of recognition experience that is equivalent to "that seen event is like this felt event." The infant seems to be experiencing the equivalent of the statement: "The other acts like me and I can act like the other." Via this cross-modal knowledge, the newborn is given access to people's actions and intentions not otherwise possible. Therefore, according to Meltzoff (2007), the perception that others are "like me" is the bedrock that builds social cognition.

## *Children*

### False Belief

Children in the preschool period are tested with tasks such as the classic "Smarties" box task. In this task, target children are shown a box of Smarties candies on which there are images of candies displayed. Then, they are shown that there are items in the box such as pencils instead of candies.

When the target children are 4-year-olds, they understand that when other children are asked what is inside the box, the other children will answer that there are candies in the box, based on seeing the image of candies displayed on the box. However, when the target children are 3-year-olds, they answer that the other children believe that there are pencils in the box, bases on their personal knowledge. Of course, this is a false belief.

Caron (2009) concluded that around 4 years of age, normal children gain the capacity to attribute beliefs to themselves and to others. They conceive of the mind of the other as capable of misrepresenting situations in context.

### Theory of Mind

Piaget and Inhelder (1948/1967) undertook early research in the area of social cognition. In their three-mountain task, they studied perspective-taking or role-taking. The study of the mind of the other began with Premack and Woodruff's (1978) work with chimpanzees. The concept of theory of mind was extended to humans by Wimmer and Perner (1983), but from the metatheoretical perspective that the mind of the child is distinct and strives to understand the separate minds of others. Carpendale and Lewis (2010) referred to this approach as the standard individualistic formulation of the theory of mind.

Methodologically, Wimmer and Perner (1983) studied children's performance on false-belief tasks. Perner and Wimmer (1985) extended the paradigm to second-order false belief, or developing the understanding that it is possible to have false beliefs about the beliefs of others.

At the theoretical level, Wellman (1990) identified the child's grasp of the mind of the other as a "theory." Perner (1991) maintained that the child develops a metarepresentation of competing, yet compatible mental representations of the other/world. In reaction to this "theory" theory approach, Leslie (1991) argued that the capacity to grasp the mind of the other is innately specified in modules, and Harris (1991) argued that, rather, the child imagines or simulates the perspective of the other, but without theorizing. Russell (1992) criticized the concept of a theory in the child at this age. Bruner (1986) and Chandler (1988) considered that the concepts and methodology in this new field were too cognitive-focused, consistent with the position of Carpendale and Lewis (2010).

## Development in Theory of Mind

## *Infants*

### Infant Representation

Caron (2009) examined the infant's capacity to engage in representation. He reviewed the literature using false belief and similar tasks that are meant to tap preschoolers' development of a theory of mind. He indicated that the standard tests have been criticized as being too difficult for younger children, so that the development of theory of mind could develop earlier than indicated by research with standard tests. In this regard, he reviewed the literature on nonverbal, visual-fixation procedures and showed that the beginnings of a theory of mind develop earlier than 3 years of age.

Caron focused on how infants can engage in mental attribution earlier than had been previously understood. For example, even in the 13–15-month age period, researchers have found that infants are sensitive to false beliefs of the other and that they seem to have a representational theory of mind of the other. Earlier on, they seem to be engaging in mentalistic attribution and in construing the behavior of agents as intentional.

It should be noted that although Caron (2009) supported the notion that infants have a representational mind, this does not mean they are engaging in independent, symbolic activity, divorced from sensorimotor action. Representations can take place in infancy, but not of the pure variety of the preschooler. The arguments that Caron has made about the early skills in social understanding on infants are consistent with the work of the learning model of Meltzoff, Kuhl, Movellan, and Sejnowski (2009), who maintained that human infants are primed to learn socially and that they are tuned to the social other.

## Infant False Beliefs

Carpendale and Lewis (2010) addressed the topic of an apparent precocious understanding of false beliefs. Onishi and Baillargeon (2005) and Surian, Caldi, and Sperber (2007) have provided data indicating the 15-month-olds have an initial understanding of false belief. In Onishi and Baillargeon, the infants looked longer at an agent acting in ways unexpected from what she had been doing. The conclusion offered was that the data support the innate modular view of understanding mental state representations. According to Onishi and Baillargeon, already at 15 months the infant has a representational theory of mind. According to Surian et al., infants at this age can attribute beliefs to agents. Träuble, Marinović, and Pauen (2010) found that 15-month-olds understand different belief-inducing situations about an actor's information access in an object-transfer task in a highly flexible way. Sodian (2011) has argued that even in the first year infants have a conceptual system related to theory of mind involving attribution of motivational states, such as goals and dispositions.

## Infant Joint Attention

The related topic of joint attention in infancy (Bakeman & Adamson, 1984) has been interpreted as showing that the infant expresses social understanding. Skill in shared attention correlates with later social competence and language and cognitive development (Vaughan Van Hecke et al., 2007). Similarly, research using the still-face paradigm suggests an early social competence in maternal interaction, and one that is facilitated by general maternal contingent responsiveness (Mcquaid, Bibok, & Carpendale, 2009).

## Infant Gaze Following

In terms of the area of research on infant gaze following, Meltzoff and Brooks (2007) had suggested that it indicates the attribution of mental life to the infant, i.e., wanting to see what the other is looking at. Similarly, Meltzoff, Gopnik, and Repacholi (1999) had argued that infants could reason by analogy to obtain an understanding of the other. However, Moore (2008) argued that this interpretation by Meltzoff and colleagues is a rich rather than a more parsimonious lean interpretation. A leaner interpretation explains the behavior in terms of instrumental learning or attentional cuing, at least for younger infants. Similarly, infant pointing might not be accompanied by looking an adult to check if the adult is watching but to see if the adult will respond with a behavior. However, some research has found evidence that infant pointing does reflect some form of social understanding. Liszkowski, Albrecht, Carpenter, and Tomasello (2008) found that infants point more when the adult is watching them or when the pointing at first does not succeed in obtaining the desired outcome. For Tomasello, Carpenter, and Liszkowski (2007), joint attention and related skills demonstrate the infant's ability to understand others as intentional agents.

## Mirror Neurons

In their review of social cognition, Carpendale and Lewis (2010) dealt with the fascinating topic of mirror neurons. These neurons were found in the ventral premotor cortex of macaque monkeys. They activate not only during the performance of particular actions (e.g., nut grasp) but also when the monkey observes the same action being performed by a conspecific or human. The neurons might fire to unseen actions that can be readily predicted or to actions that are solely heard. Gallese (2007) provided indirect evidence that mirror neurons exist in humans, allowing embodied simulation of meanings and intentions of the actions of others. It has been argued that their presence solves the problem of how we understand the mind of others (Iacoboni, 2009). However, there are limits in terms of what mirror neurons can help explain about understanding the mind of the other. For example, shared experience differentiates which of multiple meanings makes the most sense in the pointing of the 12–18-month-old.

## Conclusion

Carpendale and Lewis (2010) offered a relational interpretation of the infant data instead of a cognitive-focused one. They maintained that infants at this age are learning something in a "practical, lived sense" about the social environment. The strictly Neo-Piagetian argument (Mascolo & Fischer, 2010) is that infants acquire an embodied, practical, sensorimotor form of knowledge in action and then children develop a reflective one. However, for Carpendale and Lewis, action should not be considered split from intention, and practically infants do experience others as intentional agents. For example, Reddy (2008) found that infants could engage in coyness, which indicates that they "know" minds in the sense that they are aware that they are in social exchange. The infant learns about the other through beginning relationships with caregivers. Knowledge is rooted not only through action on the physical world but also in engagement with the social one.

### Comment

The relational perspective on the early social cognition of the infant and child espoused by Carpendale and Lewis (2010) is entirely consistent with the present work. I have structured a Neo-Piagetian stage and substage model of cognitive development, and proposed Neo-Eriksonian parallels at each of the 25 steps of the model. Moreover, the model lends itself to understanding the cognitive underpinnings to a developing capacity to mentalize the other from an early age. Cognition as much about the social as the physical and the social helps develop the cognitive side of the unity formed in social cognition.

## *Children*

### Research

Wellman, Lopez-Duran, LaBounty, and Hamilton (2008) studied the longitudinal relationship between infant attention and the later development in preschoolers of a theory of mind. They found data in support of Caron's (2009) position that there are precursors to the development of a theory of mind that emerge in infancy. They studied forty-five 10–12-month-old infants in a habituation looking-time task and then tested them at 4 years of age on tasks organized according to a theory of mind progression/scale. The infant task measured social attention (the infants accorded attention to displays of intentional social actions, and decreased attention during habituation). Specifically, the authors found that the infant attention measure predicted at 4 years of age false-belief understanding. In their statistical analyses, the authors controlled for IQ, verbal competence, and executive skill. The results suggested continuity in social cognition distinct from other types of developmental continuity. Infants can understood human agents as intentional, goal-directed actors, which helps them develop their later understanding of these actors as mental beings. Therefore, an early understanding of intentional action in actors is an important facilitator of the development of theory of mind.

Miller (2009) examined the development of second-order mental states at around 5–6 years of age. These second-order mental states follow the development of first-order mental states, which are related to the classic false-belief paradigm. The tasks used for second-order false beliefs include scenarios where children are told stories and have to respond to probe questions about them and the actors' mental states. For example, a test question might be, "So John runs to look for Mary. Where do you think he has gone?" and "Why does he think that she has gone there?" (Perner & Wimmer, 1985). Other tasks that help measure second-order mental states include the Eyes Task (Baron-Cohen, Wheelright, Spong, Scahill, & Lawson, 2001), in which children are shown a series of photos of the eye region of the face and asked to identify what the target is feeling or thinking. In general, Miller's (2009) review of the literature revealed that children have an advanced mental capacity – to realize that it is possible to hold a false belief about another person's belief.

**Comment**

In conclusion, the literature reviews of Caron (2009) on the infant's representational mind and of Miller (2009) on the school-age child's second-order mental state indicate a developmental progression from infancy to childhood, with preschooler's development of a theory of mind constituting a midpoint. In this regard, I would propose that the mentalistic abilities and reasoning skills of the developing infant and child, along with relevant precursor capacities, might pass through developmental steps consistent with the present model of cognitive development (five stages each with five substages).

That is, it is possible that the infant's capacity to understand the intention of others corresponds to the limited representational skills evident in the sensorimotor stage of Piaget and the preschooler's development of a theory of mind corresponds to Piaget's representational period, which I have called the perioperational stage. Also, the older child might be developing capacities to understand second-order mental states because of a relationship with Piaget's concrete operational stage. This is not to suggest that general cognitive acquisitions determine the rate of acquisition of mentalizing and representing the other. However, it could be one factor to consider.

## Embodiment and Communities

### *Embodiment*

Gibbs (2006) described the development of theory of mind in terms of embodiment in infancy and entering a community of minds in the child. Both of these notions expand the development of the representational and mentalistic mind of an infant and child beyond the mind of the infant and child. According to Gibbs, for the infant, Gallagher (2001) maintained that understanding another person is a type of "embodied practice," and in the infant, this takes the form of sensorimotor, perceptual, emotional, and nonconceptual embodied practices. Practices such as these "constitute our primary access for understanding others and continue to do so even after we attain a theory of mind abilities" (cited on p. 235 in Gibbs, 2006).

### *Comment*

This concept of embodied practices in the development of a theory of mind is important in two ways for the present work. First, it supports the idea that sensorimotor intelligence and practices continue to have importance beyond the sensorimotor period. In this regard, von Hofsten (2007) underscored that cognitive development takes place through functional activities. For von Hofsten, "actions reflect all aspects of cognitive development." For example, action is involved in the motives of children and in problem solving.

Second, it indicates that a good model of the theory of mind should neither be only about a "theory" arrived at by the developing individual nor be only about any understanding of the other as being lodged in the "mind." That is, a good developmental model of the theory of mind should be called something like a developmental model of the "construction of the cognition–emotion–body of the other." This concept indicates that (a) the agent constructing models of the other could be developing construals that are not advanced cognitive models or theories but basic schemes, as well. (b) Moreover, the construals do not have to be just about the construals or theories of the other, but could also be about their feelings, desires, and so on. This is a standard argument in the field of theory of mind, but the label used to qualify the field seems to ignore this message. Moreover, it is artificial to separate cognition and affect anyway. Their separation is a convenient heuristic, but does not represent how the cognition–affect relationship functions, as argued at multiple points in the present work. (c) Third, use of a label such as "construction of the cognition–emotion–body of the other" includes in a concept related to theory of mind the sensorimotor, embodied notion of early intelligence and also includes in it an understanding of early mentalizations and representations about the other as being heavily corporal, action-oriented, and grounded in the physical. That is, from infancy onward, we do not create schemes and concepts just about the other as a developing mind but also about the other as a developing socioaffective person in a body.

In terms of the mechanisms of how we create these schemes and representations about the other, referring to Meltzoff's concept of supramodal matching of observed movement and kinesthetic equivalence to facilitate motor imitation, we use our bodily and sensorimotor schemes to match the bodily and sensorimotor schemes of the other. As this ability evolves into a theory of mind in the preschooler, we should not forget that the socioaffective and corporal dimensions are still involved both in the activities that we use to help us undertake our matching process and in the nature of the construals of the other that are the outcomes of the matching. The other is always more than mind, especially for an infant and young child, and the self is never just mind as we construct these construals.

Moreover, returning to the literature review by Gibbs (2006), the work of Nelson et al. (2003), on the development of a theory of mind in the 3–4-year period in terms of entering a community of minds, suggests that the infant is developing concepts such as these "construction of the cognition–emotion–body of the other" ones not only in a broader sense of the domains involved but also in a broader sense in terms of the people involved. According to Nelson et al., the child learns that people with different minds communicate for common purposes and understandings and the child learns that the community integrates into its language and talk concerns about people within the community. In this regard, Nelson et al. undertook research showing that 3–4-year-old children working on theory of mind tasks discussed their responses, participating in their community of peers, and interacting socially toward particular pragmatic ends. Both the research of Gallagher (2001) and Nelson et al. (2003) support the present model that a model of theory of mind development can be better understood according to (a) the present model of cognitive development, which runs from early infancy to childhood and beyond, (b) its emphasis on corresponding socioaffective acquisitions, and (c) the relational understanding of self and other that it embodies.

## Theories

In reviewing the theories related to the development of theory of mind, Caron (2009) divided them according to whether they are domain-general or domain-specific approaches. Domain-general approaches involve broad cognitive abilities, such as linguistic representation, working memory, and inhibitory control. Domain-specific theories include modular theories, which maintain that psychological constructions about behavior are derived directly from dedicated brain structures or modules that are innate (e.g., Baron-Cohen, 1995; Leslie, 1994). When these dedicated structures mature, they produce automatically interpretations of activity of agents with respect to intentions, desires, perceptions, and beliefs.

### *Modular*

For example, Leslie (1994) maintained that a module develops at 9 months of age that can construe human action as goal-directed. A second module develops at about 18 months of age and facilitates understanding desire and related acquisitions. Leslie (2000) indicated that a third module develops at about 3 years of age, involving inhibitory control of distracting external input.

Baillargeon, Scott, and He (2010; cited in Caron, 2009) proposed another modular approach. They maintained that an inborn computational system emerges in the early months of life. It permits infants to ascribe two types of internal states to acting agents: (a) motivational states (e.g., preferences and goals) and (b) informational states that are congruent with objective reality. For the authors, there is a second stage of the maturation of inborn computational modules for psychological reasoning. In this stage, infants can attribute to agentive actors not only reality-congruent but also reality-incongruent information, such as false belief. Given this inborn capacity, older infants can now keep in mind that there are two versions of the same scene, one indicative of objective reality (pencils are in the box) and another devoted to the actor's false belief about reality (the box contains candies). For Baillargeon, infants in the first stage are mentalizing and children in the second stage advance to representing a theory of the mind of the other even if it is a false belief.

Luo and Baillargeon (2010) have conducted research that indicates that the capacity to attribute to an agent a motivational state might appear as early as 3 months of age. Moreover, the capacity to attribute to an agent a reality-congruent informational state might appear as early as 8 months of age, if not before (which includes consideration of false belief). The authors infer that there is a system-based, mentalist model in early psychological reasoning, but that experience plays a critical role, as well, for example, through directing learning.

### General

The domain-general approaches to theory of mind hold positions against the modular view. For example, the theory-theorists (Wellman, 2002) argue that domain-general mechanisms can lead to the development of mentalist capacities.

Meltzoff (2005) has developed the most influential "like me" models in the development of theory of mind. Infants are prepared for imitation of adult facial behaviors because of an innate sensory capacity to connect internally felt movements and externally viewed movements. Woodward (2005, 2009) maintained that young infants at 5 months of age could understand actors as intentional agents because of their own personal experience of goal-directed activity. Therefore, for Caron, both Meltzoff and Woodward hold the view that infants have an inborn capacity to recognize others as like them because others behave like them; morever, for Meltzoff, this development happens right after birth.

Tomasello's (1999) model of the development of the theory of mind is also a general domain one, but he maintained that the ability develops at around 9 months of age. At this age, infants develop joint attentional skills, helping them to better understand means-ends and purposeful relationships. They can anticipate goals prior to acting toward arriving at them. This is a mentalistic stance.

### Conclusion

Caron's (2009) literature review is favorable to Baillargeon's two-stage theory that young infants start mentalizing early in the first year and then they later develop mental skills relating to theory of mind. The different theories seem to contribute in different ways to understanding the development of the infant's and the preschooler's representational and mental capacities of the other.

## Human vs. Animal Intelligence

### Theories

Penn, Holyoak, and Povinelli (2008) emphasized that humans are unique in their ability to engage in symbolic relational and higher-order systematic capabilities. They proposed a *relational reinterpretation* hypothesis in which humans are considered especially to reinterpret effectively perceptual relations in terms of higher-order, inferential, structurally systematic, role-governed relations. That is, they argued that humans are unique in their ability to engage in reasoning about higher-order structural relations in a systematic and productive way. This capacity to engage in higher-order relational reasoning leads to the construction of a "supermodule" that is a necessary but not a sufficient cognitive structure for higher-order cognitive abilities. The supermodule is "reused, shared, or called upon" in cognitive capacities, such as language. The hypothesis of Penn et al. resembles closely Karmiloff-Smith's (1992) concept of "representational redescription."

Premack (2010) considered three theories of what makes humans unique cognitively relative to animals, and maintained that the hypothesis of the Penn et al. (2008) is insufficient. For example, he maintained that chimpanzees are capable of simpler forms of analogical reasoning. Premack also dismissed another theory on human uniqueness, by Hermann, Call, Hernandez-Lloredo, Hare, and Tomasello (2007), who argued that human intelligence is *superior in the social* compared to the physical realm.

Premack (2010) favored his model that humans have developed more flexible, *domain-general abilities* rather than more limited cognitive capacities, such as domain-specific or single-goal adaptations. He maintained that humans have domain-general competence because of their capacity to flexibly interweave modular abilities. That is, humans have a generalist character in their intelligence. By contrast, and this is where the difference in human and animal intelligence lies, animals have a specialist character in their intelligence unlike our generalist one.

For example, for Premack, humans are the only species *adept in teaching*. According to Premack (2010), the examples of cats teaching kittens how to hunt and of meerkats teaching pups how to avoid being stung by scorpions are isolated examples in the animal world. By contrast, humans can teach all possible activities in a domain-general way. The activities can serve "indeterminately many goals."

Premack (2010) emphasized that humans are not only flexible in their cognitive capacity, such as in interweaving and in teaching, they are also unique in having innumerable competencies. He surmised that that is why we find the tool making in crows so intriguing. That is, putatively advanced animal cognitions and capacities happen so rarely in animals that when they do, they stand out for us. Darwin (1981) had argued, "… there is no fundamental difference between man and the higher mammals in their mental faculties" (p. 35). Premack concluded that his theory indicates otherwise and that it can even accommodate the varied individual differences found in human intelligence compared to the limited range in any particular species of animals.

## *Reinterpreting Human Uniqueness in Light of the Present Model*

### Intelligence

The three theories that have examined differences between human and animal intelligence are exploring new avenues in comparative and evolutionary psychology. At the same time, there is room for taking the best of the three models and combining them to get a better grasp of human uniqueness. For example, Penn et al. (2008) have tried to find the qualitatively distinct, higher-order skills that distinguish humans from animals. Premack's (2010) model rejects the specifics of the Penn et al. model, but the goal is a good one. He proposed a domain-general intelligence that is unique to humans. Although there is merit in this argument, it still could integrate into it some notion of a qualitatively distinct and superior cognitive capacity. As for Hermann et al. (2007), they introduced the argument that human intelligence is superiorly social.

There is room to combine a social-emotional emphasis in understanding intelligence with the typical cognitive one, and this process might enable better separation of human and animal intelligence. Finally, one could ask whether a higher-order cognitive/socioemotional intelligence in humans consists of only point of separation, or are there multiple intellectual levels that make humans distinct from animals. It could be that in seeking one primary separation point in human and animal intelligence, solutions that distinguish them on a graded, or multilevel scale has been missed, such as provided by the Neo-Piagetian perspective.

In this regard, I have proposed a Neo-Piagetian stage and substage model in the development of cognition that provides multiple cutting points to consider in the separation of human and the animal intelligence. From the Piagetian perspective, animal intelligence, at best, most probably is limited to preoperational thought and perhaps some transitional concrete operational thought. In the present model, this refers to the perioperational stage. Of course, Piaget also describes an abstract or formal stage of intelligence, and Neo-Piagetians, such as myself, have added a postformal stage, which in the present case is referred as collective intelligence. Given that there are substages proposed in the present Neo-Piagetian model, as well as in others, such as those of Case and Fischer, this suggests that there are multiple substages in the Neo-Piagetian human sequence that cannot develop in nonhuman primates.

Moreover, it is not all that clear how much animal intelligence integrates the socioemotional to the degree apparent in the human case. In this regard, for example, the present model suggests a Neo-Eriksonian sequence of steps in development that correspond on a one-to-one basis to the Neo-Piagetian steps described in the model. In conclusion, the developing theory of mind should be considered as part of the individual's growing social cognition and should be expanded to encompass a lifespan perspective.

Given that there are 25 steps in development proposed in the present model, and that the preoperational level appears to be about the upper limit of animal intelligence, the upper limit of animal intelligence appears to lie approximately in the middle of the range of the 25 steps (see Table 26.6–26.10 in Chap. 26). Moreover, the affective side of the present model of cognitive–affective parallels in development might not be as rich.

## Teaching

Premack (2010) has raised an extremely important point that part of what distinguishes human intelligence from that of animals is our capacity to teach. Animals do imitate, but this does not happen in an organized way involving explicit modeling and teaching and, moreover, humans organize institutional and other systemic ways of instructing and teaching their young. In the present model, I have argued that the perioperational stage is one where children develop cognitive and related capacities that allow them to take advantage of the instructional and educational opportunities created by adults.

Therefore, what might be unique in humans is not only our ability to teach but also our ability to develop a more generalized intelligence and ability to learn effectively what we are taught. Of course, given the social nature of instruction and teaching, this means that our social skills serve adaptive ends not only in unstructured, daily nonformal social situations but also in more structured educational and instructional ones.

## Learning

### *Human Uniqueness*

Meltzoff et al. (2009) presented a model of the foundations for a contemporary approach to learning. They argued that humans are the only species that have developed formal means to "enhance learning." The ways include the creation of schools, the development of curricula, and the use of teachers. The process of enhancing learning has developed in conjunction with the intense interest that human infants display in people, and the powerful implicit learning mechanisms related to social interactions that they possess.

The authors argued that these new forms of learning have evolved under evolutionary pressure, which had selecting them in our ancestors. In this regard, infants possess superior computational skills, permitting them to create automatically inferred models that help structure their environment according to the statistical patterns that they experience. Another principle is that learning is social. Infants do not calculate the experienced patterns by themselves in a discriminate way. People around them provide critical social cues of what to learn and when. The next principle is that the brain has been exquisitely structured to permit learning through circuits linking perception and action. These neurocognitive systems link the actions of not only self but also the other, for example, in imitative learning.

### *Skills*

Meltzoff et al. (2009) indicated that three social skills are at the foundation of human development, but they are rare in the development of animals. These skills are *imitation, shared attention, and empathic understanding*. Meltzoff and Moore (1997) found that newborns as young as 42 min of age matched gestures shown to them, including tongue protrusion and mouth opening. This happened even though they could not see their own faces, nor could they see their reflection in the mirror in their context. The mechanism proposed to account for this early imitation is that newborns already can map the behavior that they observe to equivalent acts that they can produce as a match.

For Meltzoff et al. (2009), the study of language of learning indicates that the social environment facilitates learning and that there is a neuroplasticity in the early years that facilitates its development. In a sensitive period of language acquisition in infants, neurons become committed and neural signatures are established. For example, at 6-months of age, listening to speech activates not only superior temporal areas in the brain but also parallel areas involved in speech production (Broca's area); however, listening to nonspeech sounds does not activate these centers.

Kuhl (2007) argued that speech learning is "gated" to social experience by a brain that is inherently social. For example, infants attune to the communicative intentions of others and this enhances attention to linguistic units at several levels. In this regard, research has shown that 9-month-olds exposed to a new language in a live social condition leads to the induction of "remarkable" language learning. However, infants at this age exhibit *no* learning when the language is presented by a disembodied source, such as by machines.

## Intentionality

### *Human Uniqueness*

Tomasello and Carpenter (2007) described four social-cognitive skills related to shared intentionality that are present in human 1- and 2-year-olds but not present in the behavior of chimpanzees. The skills involve *joint attention, cooperative communication, social collaboration, and instructive learning*. The authors described shared intentionality as collaborative interactions among participants sharing psychological states with each other. The concept is similar to the Vygotskian emphasis on the ability of children to learn through social interactions, collaborations, and so on.

For example, in joint attention, there is genuine intersubjective sharing. Human infants do not just follow the gaze of other people to a target and they do not just simply want other people to know that they are actively looking. Rather, they actually attempt to share attention with others (Bakeman & Adamson, 1984).

For cooperative communication, infants inform others of things in a helpful way or simply to share an experience with them. For example, they might indicate to someone else the location of a hidden object in a hiding–finding game.

As for group collaboration, children play group games and encourage adults to rejoin the game when necessary. Children will collaborate "just for the sake of collaborating," for example, in social games and in instrumental tasks. In the latter, the collaboration seems more rewarding than the instrumental goal.

For instructed learning, human infants will imitate more readily the actions of others and will do so not only to solve a problem but also to show the adult that they are "in tune" with the current situation. Moreover, human adults often teach young children things by demonstrations, or "instructed learning." However, young infants might learn more when there are demonstrations without explicit instruction. Tomasello and Carpenter (2007) concluded that human evolution transformed skills present in our ancestors toward shared intentionality in these four ways and that they represent the "cornerstones of cultural living."

### *Trajectories*

For Tomasello and Carpenter, sometime around the first year of life, two developmental trajectories emerge related to shared intentionality and each is an important evolutionary adaptation. The first development trajectory relates to a general primate or perhaps specifically great ape line of development for understanding intentional acts and perception. These skills evolved in the context of the archaic primates' competitive interactions about access to food, mates, and other important resources for survival and reproduction.

The second developmental trajectory evolved uniquely in human ancestors and concerns the *sharing of psychological states* with other people. As these two trajectories interact, they promote the development of skills and motivations for context-specific sharing of psychological states with others. Later in development, these acquisitions become skills and motivations related to social norms, collective beliefs, and cultural institutions. Tomasello and Carpenter (2007) concluded that the development of shared intentionality shows how cognitive and motivational processes work together and how biology and culture interact in development.

## Education

### *Human Uniqueness*

As for education, Meltzoff et al. (2009) emphasized that the new science of learning being elaborated is altering the approach to regular education and to intervention programs. Developmental neuroscience indicates which areas of the brain are involved in the educational process and indicates how it might work and be improved. The science of education is showing that, in formal school settings, individual face-to-face tutoring constitutes the most effective form of teaching.

In this regard, Matsuzawa (2007) examined the cognitive development of chimpanzees. He also came to the conclusion that overt teaching is a uniquely human evolutionary acquisition.

### *Comment*

In Young (1997), I have indicated how evolution has selected "Group for Individual" behavior, and I had used the example of how adults set up educational venues and learning opportunities for children. The work of Meltzoff et al. (2009) supports the validity of the concept that I presented, which is elaborated in Chap. 34.

## Conclusions

Metzoff et al. (2009) and Tomasello and Carpenter (2007) have presented somewhat similar ideas on what makes humans adept and distinct, and how early skills develop that are intrinsic to and unique to our species. They both seemed to emphasize the importance of early intersubjectivity and mentalization. They both emphasized a role for enhanced or instructed learning. To their credit, they provided clear concepts related to the terms of intersubjectivity and mentalization, such as shared or joint attention, empathic understanding, cooperative communication, and social collaboration.

One way of cohering the various attributions of human skills and uniqueness early in life is to examine them in terms of how social cognition could be seen to develop from the perspective of the present 25-step model. It lends itself to this type of modeling because it is based on the construction of parallel acquisitions at each step in cognition and socioaffectivity.

(a) In this regard, it would appear that in the neonatal period the infant develops a reflexive intersubjectivity, as in neonatal imitation that is facilitated by intramodal visual-kinesthetic processes. (b) Next, the infant in the first 2 years develops an embodied mentalization, facilitated by sensorimotor developmental processes. (c) Then, the preschooler acquires representational capacities that lead to perspective taking of the other, or the so-called theory of mind. This appears to happen in two steps – a first-order theory of mind, as revealed in the classic false-belief task, and a second-order theory of mind, for example, in the Eyes task. This two-step acquisition in theory of mind would seem to correspond to the development of Piagetian preoperational and initial concrete operational thought, respectively. (d, e) Next, the teenager develops more advanced perceptions and taking of perspective of the other, fitting the development of abstract thought (which leads to postformal equivalents in the adult).

However, the developing individual does not acquire an increasing social cognition through mental processes alone, but through relational ones involving shared experiences with the other. In Young (1997), I described the process of coappropriation in this regard (see next section). Given that, in the present chapter, a major distinction that has been posited to mark our species is that we engage in enhanced learning and in formal and informal modeling/education/instruction/teaching, it would be consistent to propose that not only is there coappropriation taking place in the child due to relational processes but there is also "coeducation" taking place in the environment in the relational processes. That is, the child is an active participant and shaper of the processes of education/instruction/teaching, and the processes are coparticipatory. As argued elsewhere in the book, coschemes and co-operations rather than schemes and operations constitute what is developing in the individual.

I have presented above an integrated conception of theory of mind that I have labeled, "construction of the cognition–emotion–body of the other." Therefore, what I have just proposed is a model of the development of the construction of the cognition–emotion–body of the other in terms of the present 25-step model. Also, I am indicating that it includes steps that accompany its series in cognitive development in terms of parallel coappropriation/coeducation processes. These would include both informal and formal modes of learning and teaching/instruction.

The five major stages in the development of the present model include: the reflexive, sensorimotor, perioperational (preoperational, concrete operational), abstract, and collective intelligence stages. The five corresponding steps in the development of construction of the cognition–emotion–body of the other include (a) reflexive intersubjectivity, (b) embodied sensorimotor intentionality, (c) theory of mind (first- and second-order, in concert with perioperational pre- and concrete operations, respectively), (d) abstract (or third-order) theory of mind, and (e) postformal theory of mind, based on collective intelligence.

Therefore, I suggest that the five corresponding coeducational steps that would accompany the developing person's coappropriation process in incorporating these modes of relational perspective-taking include the following: (a) In the reflexive stage, coeducation is constituted by scaffolded holding frames, which would include modeling to encourage reciprocal reactivity and even imitation. (b) In the sensorimotor period, the coeducation is more exploratory-promoting, within limits of safety and security. (c) In the perioperational stage, it starts as informal, instructional in the preoperational component, and includes an important co-peer component. It becomes more formally instructional toward and within the concrete operational component. (d) This latter process accelerates in the adolescent abstract stage, and includes tutoring, co-op activities, placements, etc., as it becomes more pragmatic and practical, or real-world and preparatory. (e) In the adult stage, more formal mentoring becomes involved, e.g., in the university, on the worksite. Table 15.1 provides a summary of the concept of the development of the construction of the cognition–emotion–body of the other in relation to steps in coeducation.

In terms of substages in the products and processes described in the present section, below I indicate how the present model can help explain the classic 3–4-year shift in false-belief task performance/theory of mind. This illustrates the manner in which the present model can be extended to include its complete 25 steps in the models presented in this section.

## Environment

### *Vygotsky*

Vygotsky posited that the sociocultural surround is intrinsically important to the growing child through concepts such as genetic law, genetic analysis, the zone of proximal development, mediating devices (e.g., language), and internalization, all

**Table 15.1** Stages in construction of the cognition–emotion–body of the other and in co-education

| Stage | Cognition–emotion–body of the other | Coeducation |
|---|---|---|
| Reflexive | Nascent intersubjectivity | Scaffolded holding |
| Sensorimotor | Embodied intentionality | Exploration promotion |
| Perioperation | Theory of mind | Instructional, teaching |
| Preoperational | First-order | Informal |
| Concrete operational | Second-order | Formal |
| Abstract | Third-order theory of mind | Real-world, transitional |
| Collective intelligence | Postformal theory of mind | School of life, mentoring |

The table indicates a revised model of theory of mind, and how it might develop through the stages of the present developmental model. In the table, I list the stages of the model, but it can be expanded to include the model's component of cyclically recurring substages

For several reasons, the concept that I have developed for theory of mind is referred to as "cognition–emotion–body of the other." First, perspective-taking about the other, or the development of relevant precursors in this ability, can happen at any age. Therefore, the concept of a "theory" of mind is too cognitive and limited. Similarly, the component of the term that refers to "mind" is too limited and limiting. As we develop perspective of the other, it is not only about mind, but also about affective and corporal manifestations and processes

Finally, by including all three components of the term in the term cognition–emotion–body, we acknowledge the embodied nature of theory of mind, how it can develop in the earlier more physical stages (reflexive, sensorimotor), and how it is relational, participatory, and coconstructed. It is a holistic concept and, as such, includes a contextual ground in its unfolding

In terms of the concept of coeducation, I developed it from the concept of coappropriation (Young, 1997), which itself was developed from the concept of appropriation. Developing individuals learn of and internalize the world into coschemes and co-operations in a shared, relational participation with the world. Similarly, as individuals develop, they are instructed, taught, or educated in a shared, relational participation with the world by parents, peers, and other significant adults, as well as by technological and institutional procedures. In their turn, children act on the enhanced educational contexts provided to them, thereby altering to a degree the educational contents and mechanisms received

The particular advances in the cognition–emotion–body of the other in the early stages of life refer to (a) reflexive, nascent intersubjectivity and (b) sensorimotor, embodied intentionality. The corresponding coeducational functions that can serve to buffer and optimize their development refer to a scaffolded holding frame and exploration promotion, respectively

(c) As the child enters the preschool and school-age years, an explicit theory of mind develops, as described in the literature. These acquisitions could be related, in part, to Piagetian stage acquisitions. (d, e). The teenager and adult become more differentiated in their theories of mind according to their increasing cognitive skills

For the child, coeducation takes the form of informal and formal modeling, instruction, teaching, and education. For the teenager and adult, coeducation is about preparing for and engaging in the real world, whether at school or in work

of which emphasize a mutuality in cognitive development. For example, the zone of proximal development is defined as the difference between the child's performance during independent problem solving and the child's problem solving under adult or advanced peer guidance. Others have elaborated these ideas to include the developmental range in the zone (Fischer, Bullock, Rotenberg, & Raya, 1993), distancing in the zone (Sigel, 1993), and the concept of appropriation instead of internalization (e.g., Rogoff, 1990; Saxe, 1991).

## *Coappropriation*

### Appropriation

The traditional Piagetian model of transition mechanisms in cognitive development centers on the process of equilibration, with its twin functions of adaptive accommodation and homeostatic assimilation. Vygotskians have rejected this concept because it places the source of cognitive change in the developing individual, and not a joining of the developing individual with the context. In their perspective, transition in mental function is negotiated constitutively on the intermental plane, preparatory to it being incorporated and transformed on the intramental one. Vygotsky labeled this process internalization, but to underscore its shared nature, Rogoff (1990) and Saxe (1991), for example, have labeled it appropriation. Vygotskian theory indicates that through mutuality in the development of mental function, shared mediational devices such as language are constituted through appropriation, and they possess multiple voices. Context is varied, and ranges from the parental and interpersonal to the wider cultural one and its massive agenda. The sociocultural context also varies in learning situations, going from structured, formal situations to everyday ones such as guided participation and observation (Rogoff).

### The Model

Figure 15.1 presents a recursive cycle in a proposed Neo-Vygotskian coappropriation mechanism in cognitive development, as described in Young (1997). Through their coschemes, children are considered to seek actively disequilibrating interaction with the sociocultural world. Because this world might not be supportive or might even be hostile, two trajectories in development could occur. If the context is nonsupportive, absent, deficient, or hostile, a more maladaptive, disjointed self-derived equilibration will take place. But if sociocultural buffers mediate effectively, they will moderate the disequilibrium. Environmental equilibration will result, affording the child a secure, organized world. Thus, cognitive (re)equilibration can take place in a shared, emergent process leading to coscheme (re)organization. Sociocultural buffers especially are parental for the very young, but gradually become cultural voices, such as those in school. Eventually, they develop into interior voices on the intramental plane. In order to emphasize the shared, mutually negotiated, constitutive nature of the appropriation function, I have labeled it coappropriation.

The refinements that I have instituted in this coappropriation cycle in cognitive development include (a) its foundation on the concept of shared constitutively created coschemes, (b) the insertion of a modified version of the Piagetian equilibration process into the Vygotskian model, (c) the parsing of the environment into negative and even hostile as well as positive components at the level of the cognitive

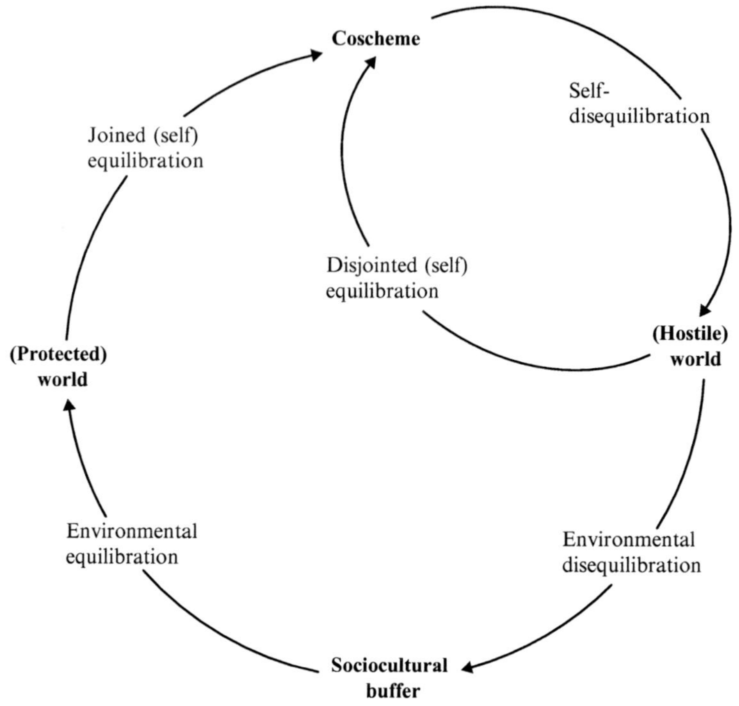


**Fig. 15.1** A Neo-Vygotskian model of coappropriation in cognitive development. The figure depicts a cyclical process Neo-Vygotskian coappropriation mechanism in cognitive development. The developing individual actively seeks catalytical disequilibration in her or his entry into the sociocultural world, via activating through coschemes. However, this world might not necessarily support the initiatives or it might even be hostile. Two pathways in development bifurcate at this juncture in the process. If the context is negative for the developing person, or if the developing person is very young and there are no supportive adults who are around, the person experiences self-equilibration. More than likely, it will be disjointed in one manner or another. However, if sociocultural buffers help mediate the person's engagement with the environment, they will modulate the disequilibration induced by the environment, especially if it is negative or hostile. Environmental equilibration results from this process, presenting the person with a cognitively protected, optimal world. In this regard, equilibration takes place in a joint, constitutive process. Therefore, I refer to the products of this developmental cycle as cognitive coschemes, and once they are developed to a different standing in the (dis) equilibration process, they are ready for the next coappropriation dynamic. The proposed coschemes in the coappropriation cycle in cognitive development are mutually, constitutively created. The coappropriation model is a modified model of Piagetian equilibration. However, unlike Piaget's model of equilibration, it accounts for the potentially negative, hostile environment at the cognitive and not only affective level. Similarly, in this regard, in terms of its original contributions, it includes the concept that sociocultural buffers can moderate poor structure or negativity in context, allowing a fuller range of individual differences in developing sociomental function. Reprinted with the permission of Springer Science+Business Media: Young, G. (1997). [Figure 8.1, Page. 186]

and not only the affective, (d) the provision for sociocultural buffers that can modulate the lack of structure or any negativity in the environment, and (e) the allowance of a role for individual differences in the sociocultural buffers and consequently in developing individuals. Thus, individual differences in mediating lenses, such as at the level of the cognitive (mis)perception of the other, affective experience (e.g., attachment history), dispositional variables, and the wider sociocultural and even historopolitical surround help determine the efficacy and nature of social buffering agents in cognitive development.

## Reinterpretations in Preschooler Theory of Mind

### *Reinterpreting the 3–4 Transition in Light of the Present Model*

#### Three-Year-Olds

*Present model.* According to the present model, during perioperational coordination, although children develop the ability to simultaneously hold in mind several symbol plans, or structured concepts, and relate these concepts to each other, they lack the ability to order them in terms of a temporal sequence, or a dominant/subordinate relationship. Instead, these concepts exist in a loose interrelationship. Hierarchies might be formed as the children coordinate symbol plans, and these hierarchies might even involve other-self relations, but they are ephemeral constructions that are easily dissolved. Thus, in children, there is no consistent ability to perceive the viewpoint of the other as primary and their own as secondary. In short, the egocentric centripetalism of perioperational coordination could permit a cognitive hierarchy of sorts, but not a full cognitive, other-centered one, for the self's needs and views are invariably fixated upon without cognitive reflection on alternatives, thereby obscuring them.

*Literature.* The false-belief evidence supports this view of 3-year-olds. They can understand others' views when value beliefs (preferences, opinions) rather than false beliefs are involved (Gopnik & Slaughter, 1991). This illustrates that, at this age, the self's and other's viewpoints can be coordinated in conceptual perspective taking, but only when task demands fit the level of skill of the age level. That is, more salient, familiar tasks could elicit basic perspective taking in these young children. However, when situations or cognitive/linguistic demands do not match the 3-year-olds' competencies, false-belief understanding is limited, fragile, and easily derailed. In this regard, Gopnick (1993) considered the cognitive capacities of 3-year-olds for these tasks as fragile and fragmented. This approach is consistent with the current view that when cognitive hierarchies are formed at this age, they are tentative and tenuous, at best.

#### Four-Year-Olds

*Present model.* According to the present model, with the onset of perioperational hierarchization, simultaneously held mental concepts can begin to be ordered, or hierarchized, in terms of temporal sequence and/or dominant/subordinate relationship.

A hallmark of the hierarchization substage in comparison to the prior coordination substage is that children can place not only their own perceptions and judgments in a dominant position but also those of others, while relegating their own to a subordinate position. Thus, 4-year-olds can form true cognitive hierarchies, for options are weighed and the self's and others' views can be prioritized.

*Literature.* Again, the false-belief data support the current theory's view of 4-year-olds. Gopnik and Slaughter (1991) underscored the capacity for relating an internal representation to the external true world as the basis for success in the false-belief task. According to them, 3-year-olds, unlike 4-year-olds, can form representations but they do not have a model of mind with coordinated representations and real world apperception. I would add to their model by suggesting that the nature of the relation between internal representation and external reality in 4-year-olds is not a simple coordination but a hierarchical one, with the true world view dominant and capable of initiating change in the subordinate representation.

That is, in perioperational hierarchization, as with the above interpretation of the traditional false-belief task, a pair of related representations is formed, and one of the pair is subservient to the other in a higher-order/lower-order relation. Thus, on the false-belief task, 4-year-olds can adopt the perspective of the protagonist (who does not know that an object location had been changed), because they can order their conceptual understanding of the self's and other's world in a hierarchical fashion, where the other's view can be primary.

## Older Children

*Literature.* As for 5-year-olds, they still have progress to make in terms of false beliefs (Strichartz & Burton, 1990). Although these children understand that the protagonist believes the falsehood (that there is candy in the bag, for example), they use factuality as the sole criterion for deciding if a statement is a "lie," regardless of the speaker's sincere belief.

*Present model.* In terms of the present approach, 5-year-olds have adopted a systematic procedure for interrelating their conceptual structures, in keeping with their cognitive level of perioperational systematization. The deficiency of this algorithm is that it cannot adapt to multiple parameters in an integrated way. The systematization that characterizes this age does not possess the flexible logic and reversibility of later substages, which are needed to avoid a unidimensional perspective on false belief. In the current view, a skill such as this develops only between 9 and 11 years of age, or in the cognitive substage of perioperational integration. Thus, it is not surprising that in the Strichartz and Burton study it is only at the age of 10 that all of the speaker's intent and belief as well as the factuality of any statement will be included together in the decision-making process. Once again, the current theory of cognitive development provides a plausible explanation of the thought processes in play in the child participating in false belief and related tasks.

## *Reinterpreting Other Theories in Light of the Present Model*

### The Theories

Wellman (1990) has a step-like view about the development of the theory of mind in children, for he charts several phases in its acquisition. In the first step according to Wellman, 2-year-olds develop simple nonrepresentational desires about real objects or states of affairs, and not more general propositions. Next, 3-year-olds come to understand the distinction between world and mind, including its hypothetical aspects and misrepresentation. However, they appear to manifest a belief-desire psychology instead of the more reality-oriented (interpretive, constructive, flexible, accurate, executive, mediating, homuncular) psychology of 4-year-olds. That is, for 3-year-olds, others can function from the perspective of their internal beliefs and imaginings, and the latter are seen as powerful enough to cause their behavior. However, 3-year-olds' belief–desire psychology lacks the interpretive, constructive characteristics of older minds, and thus is limited to an erratic "copyist" view of reality-oriented representation. When reality impacts on the individual, somehow it passively creates a direct template of itself in the mind. Beliefs are direct copies of reality so that others must function in terms of them. At best, there is only a beginning, fragile awareness of false belief (Wellman & Banerjee, 1991).

In a general sense, Wellman does relate his conceptions to Piaget's cognitive developmental theory. However, he does not try to tie the changes in young children's theory of mind to particular substages in cognitive development, unlike the case here.

The same conclusion also applies to Perner's (1991, 1992) model of theory of mind acquisition. Like Wellman (1990), Perner (1991, 1992) presented a three-step sequence of cognitive levels through which young children traverse in their growth toward a theory of mind. Primary representations develop in the first year and permit one unique model of reality. In this phase, infants develop an implicit theory of mind (e.g., following the visual regard of the caregiver; social referencing). In the next 6 months, secondary representations develop, where multiple models of the world can coexist, as in pretend play. Finally, the 4-year-old comes to develop metarepresentations, or constructed models of models, and they understand representations as distinct from their references. This permits an understanding of misrepresentation and false belief.

Leslie (1988) speaks of a shift in comprehension of the causal relationship between mind and world. Gopnik (1993) refers to the development of a truly representational perspective of representation, or the "theory theory."

### Reinterpretation

It is possible to demonstrate that the various proposed cognitive shifts from the 3 to 4 year period in the child's theory of mind all reflect a hierarchical structure, fitting the current model that this attribute is the child's predominant cognitive characteristic at this age. Wellman's suggested shift of the child coming to understand misrepresentation implies a hierarchization with veridical representation. Perner's notion of the development of a type of metarepresentation is inherently hierarchical. Leslie's referral to a new comprehension of causality also carries with it a dominant–subordinate relation. Gopnik's second-order representational "theory theory" sees a better anchoring of belief in the thought process, which speaks to hierarchization. In short, there may be compatibility between the present model and the others in explaining the development of the child's theory of mind, with all being hierarchical in one way or another.

### *Conclusion*

In conclusion, the developing theory of mind should be considered as part of the individual's growing social cognition and should be expanded to encompass a life span perspective. The present Neo-Piagetian model has been used to help explain the 3–4-year shift in theory of mind. In particular, it seems to involve movement into the substage of perioperational hierarchization. Future research could investigate the role of the different cognitive advances specified by the steps in the present model and advances in social cognition, social understanding, theory of mind, and related concepts. For example, the work of Baillargeon and colleagues presented in this chapter suggests that false belief and related concepts develop equivalent sensorimotor precursors in infancy. Moreover, these precursors also seem to undergo a coordination to hierarchization substage shift, from 3 to 8 months or so.

## Summary and Conclusions

The area of the development of social cognition is a vast one, but the relational perspective gives it coherence. I have described how the traditional concept of theory of mind could be expanded to reveal a correspondence in its development and the five major stages of the present cognitive developmental model. As with other areas discussed in the present book, this model could be expanded readily enough to include a cyclically recurring substage component. Theory of mind concerns social understanding and taking the perspective of the other so that one needs to understand the optimal social buffering that can promote it well. I have suggested how the coeducational component in the development of theory of mind includes a formal instructional/teaching component and other learning modalities, consistent with the hypothesis that the distinguishing human feature is our enhanced learning and instructional capacities. In this regard, the developmental model that I have proposed in the chapter helps specify how one concept of what distinguishes us as a species develops through the life span.

In the next chapter, I turn to the topic of self-regulation. It includes work on self-definitional and relatedness processes in development. I conclude that chapter with a model of self-regulation based on the present 25-step model of development.

## References

Baillargeon, R., Scott, R. M., & He, Z. (2010). False-belief understanding in infants. *Trends in Cognitive Sciences, 14*, 110–118.

Bakeman, R., & Adamson, L. B. (1984). Coordinating attention to people and objects in mother-infant and peer-infant interaction. *Child Development, 55*, 1278–1289.

Baron-Cohen, S. (1995). *Mindblindness: An essay on autism and theory of mind*. Cambridge: MIT Press.

Baron-Cohen, S., Wheelright, S., Spong, A., Scahill, V., & Lawson, J. (2001). Are intuitive physics and intuitive psychology independent? A test with children with Asperger syndrome. *Journal of Developmental and Learning Disorders, 5*, 47–78.

Bruner, J. (1986). *Actual minds, possible worlds*. Cambridge: Harvard University Press.

Caron, A. J. (2009). Comprehension of the representational mind in infancy. *Developmental Review, 29*, 69–95.

Carpendale, J. I. M., & Lewis, C. (2010). The development of social understanding: A relational perspective. In R. M. Lerner & W. F. Overton (Eds.), *Handbook of life-span development: Vol. 1. Cognition, biology, and methods* (pp. 584–627). Hoboken: Wiley.

Chandler, M. J. (1988). Doubt and developing theories of mind. In J. W. Astington, P. L. Harris, & D. R. Olson (Eds.), *Developing theories of mind* (pp. 387–413). New York: Cambridge University Press.

Darwin, C. (1981). *The descent of man and selection in relation to sex*. [Reprint of 1871 edition.] Princeton: Princeton University Press.

Fischer, K. W., Bullock, D. H., Rotenberg, E. J., & Raya, P. (1993). The dynamics of competence: How context contributes directly to skill. In R. H. Wozniak & K. W. Fischer (Eds.), *Development in context: Acting and thinking in specific environments – The Jean Piaget Symposium Series* (pp. 93–117). Hillsdale: Erlbaum.

Gallagher, S. (2001). The practice of mind: Theory, simulation, or primary interaction? *Journal of Consciousness Studies, 8*, 83–103.

Gallese, V. (2007). Before and below 'theory of mind': Embodied simulation and the neural correlates of social cognition. *Philosophical Transactions of the Royal Society, B, 362*, 659–669.

Gibbs, R. W., Jr. (2006). *Embodiment and cognitive science*. New York: Cambridge University Press.

Gopnik, A. (1993). How we know our minds: The illusion of first-person knowledge of intentionality. *Behavioral and Brain Sciences, 16*, 1–14.

Gopnik, A., & Slaughter, V. (1991). Young children's understanding of changes in their mental states. *Child Development, 62*, 98–110.

Harris, P. L. (1991). The work of the imagination. In A. Whiten (Ed.), *Natural theories of mind* (pp. 283–304). Oxford: Blackwell.

Hermann, E., Call, J., Hernandez-Lloredo, M. V., Hare, B., & Tomasello, M. (2007). Humans have evolved specialized skills of social cognition: The cultural intelligence hypothesis. *Science, 217*, 1360–1366.

Iacoboni, M. (2009). Imitation, empathy, and mirror neurons. *Annual Review of Psychology, 60*, 653–670.

Karmiloff-Smith, A. (1992). *Beyond modularity: A developmental perspective on cognitive science*. Cambridge: MIT Press/Bradford Books.

Kuhl, P. K. (2007). Is speech learning 'gated' by the social brain? *Developmental Science, 10*, 110–120.

Lerner, R. M. (2006). Developmental science, developmental systems, and contemporary theories of human development. In W. Damon & R. M. Lerner (Eds.), *Handbook of child psychology: Vol. 1. Theoretical models of human development* (6th ed., pp. 1–14). Hoboken: Wiley.

Leslie, A. M. (1988). Some implications of pretense for mechanisms underlying the child's theory of mind. In J. W. Astington, P. L. Harris, & D. R. Olson (Eds.), *Developing theories of mind* (pp. 19–46). New York: Cambridge University Press.

Leslie, A. M. (1991). The theory of mind impairment in autism: Evidence for a modular mechanism of development? In A. Whiten (Ed.), *Natural theories of mind* (pp. 63–78). Oxford: Blackwell.

Leslie, A. M. (1994). ToMM, ToBy, and agency: Core architecture and domain specificity in cognition and culture. In L. Hirschfeld & S. Gelman (Eds.), *Mapping the mind: Domain specificity in cognition and culture* (pp. 119–148). New York: Cambridge University Press.

Leslie, A. M. (2000). How to acquire a representation theory of mind. In D. Sperber (Ed.), *Metarepresentations: A multidisciplinary perspective* (pp. 197–224). New York: Oxford University Press.

Liszkowski, U., Albrecht, K., Carpenter, M., & Tomasello, M. (2008). Infants' visual and auditory communication when a partner is or is not visually attending. *Infant Behavior and Development, 31*, 157–167.

Luo, Y., & Baillargeon, R. (2010). Toward a mentalistic account of early psychological reasoning. *Current Directions in Psychological Science, 19*, 301–307.

Mascolo, M. F., & Fischer, K. W. (2010). The dynamic development of thinking, feeling and acting over the lifespan. In R. M. Lerner & W. F. Overton (Eds.), *Handbook of lifespan development: Vol. 1. Cognitive, biology and methods*. Hoboken: Wiley.

Matsuzawa, T. (2007). Comparative cognitive development. *Developmental Science, 10*, 97–103.

Mcquaid, N., Bibok, M., & Carpendale, J. I. M. (2009). Relationship between maternal contingent responsiveness and infant social expectation. *Infancy, 14*, 390–401.

Meltzoff, A. N. (2002). Imitation as a mechanism of social cognition: Origins of empathy, theory of mind, and the representation of action. In U. Goswami (Ed.), *Blackwell handbook of childhood cognitive development* (pp. 6–25). Malden: Blackwell.

Meltzoff, A. N. (2005). Imitation and other minds: The like-me hypothesis. In S. Hurley & N. Chater (Eds.), *Perspectives on imitation: From neuroscience to social science* (Vol. 2, pp. 55–77). Cambridge: MIT Press.

Meltzoff, A. N. (2007). 'Like me': A foundation for social cognition. *Developmental Science, 10*, 126–134.

Meltzoff, A. N., & Brooks, R. (2007). Eyes wide shut: The importance of eyes in infant gaze-following and understanding other minds. In R. Flom, K. Leem, & D. Muir (Eds.), *Gaze-following: Its development and significance* (pp. 217–241). Mahwah: Erlbaum.

Meltzoff, A. N., Gopnik, A., & Repacholi, B. M. (1999). Toddlers' understanding of intentions, desires, and emotions: Explorations of the dark ages. In P. D. Zelazo, J. W. Astington, & D. R. Olson (Eds.), *Developing theories of intention* (pp. 17–41). Mahwah: Erlbaum.

Meltzoff, A. N., Kuhl, P. K., Movellan, J., & Sejnowski, T. J. (2009). Foundations for a new science of learning. *Science, 325*, 284–288.

Meltzoff, A. N., & Moore, M. K. (1997). Explaining facial imitation: A theoretical model. *Early Development and Parenting, 6*, 179–192.

Meltzoff, A. N., & Moore, M. K. (1994). Imitation, memory, and the representation of persons. *Infant Behavior and Development, 17*, 83–99.

Miller, S. A. (2009). Children's understanding of second-order mental states. *Development of Psychology, 135*, 749–773.

Moore, C. (2008). The development of gaze following. *Child Development Perspectives, 2*, 66–70.

Nelson, K., Skwerer, D., Goldman, S., Henseler, S., Presler, N., & Walkenfeld, F. (2003). Entering a community of minds: An experientialist approach to a theory of mind. *Human Development, 46*, 24–46.

Onishi, K., & Baillargeon, R. (2005). Do 15-month-old infants understand false beliefs? *Science, 308*, 255–258.

Overton, W. F. (2006). Developmental psychology: Philosophy, concepts, methodology. In W. Damon & R. M. Lerner (Eds.), *Handbook of child psychology: Vol. 1. Theoretical models of human development* (6th ed., pp. 18–80). Hoboken: Wiley.

Penn, D. C., Holyoak, K. J., & Povinelli, D. J. (2008). Darwin's mistake: Explaining the discontinuity between human and nonhuman minds. *Behavioral and Brain Sciences, 31*, 109–178.

Perner, J. (1991). *Understanding the representational mind*. Cambridge: MIT Press.

Perner, J. (1992). Grasping the concept of representation: Its impact on 4-year-olds' theory of mind and beyond. *Human Development, 99*, 146–155.

Perner, J., & Wimmer, H. (1985). "John *thinks* that Mary *thinks* that…" Attribution of second-order beliefs by 5- to 10-year-old children. *Journal of Experimental Child Psychology, 39*, 437–471.

Piaget, J. (1936/1952/1963). *The origins of intelligence in children*. New York: International Universities Press and Norton. (Original work published in 1936).

Piaget, J. (1954/1981). *Intelligence and affectivity: Their relationship during child development* (T. Brown & C. Kaegi, Trans. and Eds.). Palo Alto: Annual Reviews Monograph. (Original work published in 1954).

Piaget, J., & Inhelder, B. (1967). *The child's conception of space*. New York: Norton. (Original work published 1948).

Premack, D. (2010). Why humans are unique: Three theories. *Perspectives on Psychological Science, 5*, 22–32.

Premack, D., & Woodruff, G. (1978). Does the chimpanzee have a theory of mind? *Behavioral and Brain Sciences, 4*, 515–526.

Reddy, V. (2008). *How infants know minds*. Cambridge: Harvard University Press.

Rogoff, B. (1990). *Apprenticeship in thinking: Cognitive development in social context*. New York: Oxford University Press.

Russell, J. A. (1992). The theory theory: So good they named it twice? *Cognitive Development, 7*, 485–519.

Saxe, G. B. (1991). *Culture and cognitive development: Studies in mathematical understanding*. Hillsdale: Erlbaum.

Sigel, I. E. (1993). The centrality of a distancing model for the development of representational competence. In R. R. Cocking & K. A. Renninger (Eds.), *The development and meaning of psychological distance* (pp. 141–158). Hillsdale: Erlbaum.

Sodian, B. (2011). Theory of mind in infancy. *Child Development Perspectives, 5*, 39–43.

Strichartz, A. F., & Burton, R. V. (1990). Lies and truth: A study of the development of the concept. *Child Development, 61*, 211–220.

Surian, L., Caldi, S., & Sperber, D. (2007). Attribution of beliefs by 13-month-old-infants. *Psychological Science, 18*, 580–586.

Tomasello, M. (1999). *The cultural origins of human cognition*. Cambridge: Harvard University Press.

Tomasello, M., & Carpenter, M. (2007). Shared intentionality. *Developmental Science, 10*, 121–125.

Tomasello, M., Carpenter, M., & Liszkowski, U. (2007). A new look at infant pointing. *Child Development, 78*, 705–722.

Träuble, B., Marinović, V., & Pauen, S. (2010). Early theory of mind competancies: Do infants understand others' beliefs? *Infancy, 15*, 434–444.

Vaughan Van Hecke, A., Mundy, P. C., Acra, C. F., Block, J. J., Delagado, C. E. F., Parlade, M. V., et al. (2007). Infant joint attention, temperament, and social competence in preschool children. *Child Development, 78*, 53–69.

von Hofsten, C. (2007). Action in development. *Developmental Science, 10*, 54–60.

Wellman, H. M. (1990). *The child's theory of mind*. Cambridge: MIT Press.

Wellman, H. M. (2002). Understanding the psychological world: Developing a theory of mind. In V. Goswami (Ed.), *Blackwell handbook of childhood cognitive development* (pp. 167–187). Malden: Blackwell.

Wellman, H. M., & Banerjee, M. (1991). Mind and emotion: Children's understanding of the emotional consequences of beliefs and desires. *British Journal of Developmental Psychology, 9*, 191–214.
Wellman, H. M., Lopez-Duran, S., LaBounty, J., & Hamilton, B. (2008). Infant attention to intentional action predicts preschool theory of mind. *Developmental Psychology, 44*, 618–623.
Wimmer, H., & Perner, J. (1983). Beliefs about beliefs: Representation and constraining function of wrong beliefs in young children's understating of deception. *Cognition, 13*, 103–128.
Woodward, A. L. (2005). The infant origins of intentional understanding. In R. V. Kail (Ed.), *Advances in child development and behavior* (Vol. 33, pp. 229–261). New York: Elsevier.
Woodward, A. L. (2009). Infants' grasp of others' intentions. *Current Directions in Psychological Science, 18*, 53–57.
Young, G. (1997). *Adult development, therapy, and culture: A postmodern synthesis*. New York: Plenum.

# Chapter 16
# Self-Definition and Relatedness/Self-Regulation in Development

## Introduction

This chapter examines several major aspects of the development of the self, including self-regulation and a model that I developed on the self-definitional and relatedness selves (after Blatt, 2008). I describe models of self-regulation from both more recent, specific perspectives (e.g., are they functional, componential?) and more general perspectives (e.g., Piaget, learning theory). In addition, I examine the role of positive and negative learning in self-development.

## Self-Regulation

### *Introduction*

Martin and Failows (2010) indicated that although there is no agreed-upon definition of executive function, generally, it is considered to involve the control of one's actions. As for the components of executive function, there is less of a consensus than for its definition, but generally the major ones listed include planning, self-monitoring, verbal self-regulation, and change of mental set.

Executive function is considered multidimensional, but there are more narrowing and broadening accounts. Often, inhibition is central to narrowing accounts. In another narrowed approach, it is considered a general capacity. As for broadening accounts, they examine multiple components related to the concept, even if they are independent, such as might be the case for inhibition and working memory. Another widening approach is to consider executive function as arising out of the distributed functioning of the components; it is located within and spread across its combined constituents. In another view, the components express unity in diversity. Miyake, Friedman, Emerson, Witzki, and Kowerter (2000) found in their empirical study that shifting, updating, and inhibition were distinguishable according to their statistical analyses, but they were not completely independent. Lehto, Juujarvi, Kooistra, and Pulkkinen (2003) found similar results for children; the same three components were "separate but interrelated."

G. Young, *Development and Causality: Neo-Piagetian Perspectives*,
DOI 10.1007/978-1-4419-9422-6_16, 

Martin and Failows (2010) pointed out that the field risks theoretical incoherence. They also pointed to the dangers of perceiving executive function as within the person and being reducible to brain and physiological processes. It resides in social relations, which is a common theme in Sokol, Müller, Carpendale, Young, and Iarocci (2010). Executive function is conceived as the activity of embodied developing individuals in their functional and sociocultural contexts.

## *The Development of Executive Function*

Zelazo, Carlson, and Kesek (2008) described some socioemotional correlates of executive function. In this regard, Carlson and Wang (2007) reported a significant association between executive function and control of emotional expressions. The study further specified a nonlinear relationship between executive function variables and emotional expression ones, in that both high and low levels of temperamental inhibition interfered with effective regulation of emotion in social context. Therefore, executive function is involved in socioemotional development and can help explain individual differences, such as in difficulty of anger control and the consequence of development of behavioral difficulties. For example, Séquin and Zelazo (2005) found that preschool-aged children having conduct problems expressed impairments in executive function.

Mischel, Shoda, and Peake (1988) found that the ability to delay gratification at 4 years of age was correlated positively with various adolescent measures, including of scholastic aptitude, and they found these results even when intelligence was controlled. Delay of gratification in preschoolers also predicted good attentional control in laboratory test at 18 years of age (Eigsti et al. 2006). Ayduk et al. (2000) found that the ability to delay gratification in preschoolers was even associated with self-regulatory and related abilities at the age of 30 years. In addition, Strayhorn (2002) found that deficiency in self-control in childhood was related to criminal behavior and to interpersonal difficulties in adulthood.

Blair and Dennis (2010) emphasized that, in development, emotions and cognitions strike an optimal balance in which they are mutually supportive. For example, children have opposite but complementary motivations to approach and withdraw, and also their behavior is regulated by intercoordination of the behavioral inhibition system (BIS) and the behavioral activation system (BAS; Carver & White, 1994; Gray, 1987).

In terms of their work on school readiness, Blair and Dennis presented their model of genetic and endophenotypic constraint. It emphasized that for school readiness (a) the context is important, (b) the child has a role to play through his or her agency and self-regulation, and (c) there are cognitive and emotional set points that act as thresholds of control of the system.

In their research, the authors worked with measures of approach–withdrawal sensitivity, using the BIS/BAS scales (Carver & White, 1994). They found that BIS/BAS sensitivity was related to physiological arousal (Blair, Peters, & Granger, 2004). In particular, the authors found that relatively higher BIS sensitivity was associated with increased cardiac vagal tone and increased salivary cortisol. The latter indicates increased reactivity of the limbic hypothalamic–pituitary–adrenal (HPA) axis. Furthermore, both BIS and HPA reactivity were correlated positively with the report of the children's teachers on their social competence and behavioral regulation, including in cognitive control (as indexed by traditional executive function measures involving ability to control interference by distractors on task performance; Blair, Granger, & Razza, 2005).

The areas of the brain involved in executive functions include the prefrontal cortex (Wolfe & Bell, 2007), which is closely associated with the BIS and HPA and which undergoes rapid development in the preschool child. The importance of executive function in understanding the child's cognition and emotional control is illustrated by the study of Blair and Razza (2007). They found that measures of executive function in young children predicted better than measures of general intelligence or cognitive ability both learning outcomes in mathematics and reading ability. The authors concluded that when there is a lack of optimal balance in BIS/BAS relations, difficulties with school readiness and behavioral difficulties could result. They added that emotional factors generally play a constructive role in cognition and school readiness.

Calkins and Marcovitch (2010) examined the development of emotional regulation and executive functioning. They maintained that emotional control skills should be considered primary in the development of the neural architecture that underlies cognitive control skills (such as attention and working memory) (Bell & Wolfe, 2004). In this regard, they cited the research of Geva and Feldman (2008), who demonstrated that pre- and perinatal brainstem functioning could affect basic arousal and attentional processes important to the expression of early emotions and their control. As early attentional processes develop, they become involved in the regulation of emotion. By contrast, the effortful control of attentional processes that contribute to cognitive activity develops afterward. The limbic system supports emotional processing and develops early, which suggests neural mechanisms for how emotional control might affect the development of and use of higher-order processes in behavioral control. The authors concluded that from both a behavioral and neuroscience point of view, the evidence supports their developmental model for the primacy of emotional control abilities over cognitive control and related abilities. However, this view does not fit the reciprocal approach to how components relate in executive function.

Jacques and Marcovitch (2010) examined executive function abilities from a developmental point of view. They defined executive function as involving higher cognitive processes that are necessary for the voluntary control of thought and action. Executive function is needed for engaging in complex, novel behavior and problem-solving when solutions are not apparent and when flexibility is needed. Lower cognitive abilities that relate to executive function include speed of processing and attentional skills. The particular components of executive function include planning, verbal fluency, sequencing, error detection and error correction, self-monitoring, attentional control, and conditional learning. However, Jacques and Marcovitch delineated three core executive function capacities – working memory, response control/inhibition, and set shifting, or cognitive flexibility.

According to the authors, false-belief tasks require much executive function deployment; furthermore, success on the tasks correlates very well with performance on executive function tasks. In the false-belief task, where a surreptitious displacement takes place seen only by target children, the children need cognitive flexibility, in particular, because they must inhibit from responding to the task on the basis of the knowledge that they possess that is unavailable to the other child or protagonist who had not seen the displacement involved.

Geldhof, Little, and Colombo (2010) described a similar concept in the area of self-regulation, the cognitive–affective processing system (after the work of Mischel; e.g., Mischel & Ayduk, 2004; Mischel & Shoda, 1995). The cognitive–affective processing system is composed of two intertwined systems, a control system and a motivational aspect. Executive function is involved in self-regulation and includes inhibitory deployment. For example, delay of gratification is evidenced in the second year of life (Vaughn, Kopp, & Krakow, 1984), and is a sign of inhibitory control. Effortful control requires inhibition and increases in the toddler period (Kochanska, Murray, & Harlan, 2000). In early childhood, switching between two rules that are incompatible is easier for the 5-year-old compared to the 3-year-old (Zelazo & Jacques, 1996). Inhibition is required in false-belief tasks and emotional control in social interaction in this age period (Carlson & Moses, 2001; Hay, Payne, & Chadwick, 2004; respectively). Inhibition predicts longitudinally noncooperative behavior up to 11 years of age (Ciairano, Visu-Petra, & Settanni, 2007).

## *Psychobiology/Neurobiology*

Bell, Greene, and Wolfe (2010) described that the executive attention capacities of the 10-month-old influences regulation of emotional reactivity. For the authors, working memory and inhibitory control are the constructs in cognitive control that are best associated with the development of attentional control (Bell & Deater-Deckard, 2007). Diamond (2002) has shown that performance on cognitive control tasks is associated with the maturation and functioning of the frontal lobes. However, infants vary in their rate of improvement in cognitive control capacities.

Bell (2011) administered to infants a task involving working memory and inhibitory control (a looking version of the classic A-not-B task). In the task, the infants must keep in mind a memory of the location of a hidden toy while controlling the impulse to search in a previous location where the object had been hidden. Bell measured electroencephalographic (EEG) coherence changes from baseline to the task activity (EEG indicates cortical involvement in task performance). The researcher divided the infants into low- and high-performing groups, and only the latter group increased their EEG coherence during task performance. These results were evident at both the frontal and posterior scalp locations. Bell et al. further developed their model that in cognitive and emotion integration one cannot "assign primacy" to either cognitive or emotional processes.

Zelazo et al. (2008) and Zelazo, Qu, and Kesek (2010) have reviewed the development of executive function in relationship to emotions. They developed a model of executive processing called the iterative reprocessing model. In the model, stimuli are processed in the thalamus and relayed to the amygdala, which leads to approach–withdrawal tendencies and additional processing of incoming stimuli by the anterior cingulate cortex and the orbitofrontal cortex (OFC). The latter two regions help initiate hypothalamic physiological responses and their representation in the insular cortex. The activity in the anterior cingulate cortex might lead to activity in the ventrolateral prefrontal cortex and the dorsolateral prefrontal cortex, in particular. The rostrolateral prefrontal cortex is involved in higher-order organization and the explicit consideration of contexts (see Fig. 16.1). (See Chap. 30 for further presentation of the work of Zelazo and Carlson.)

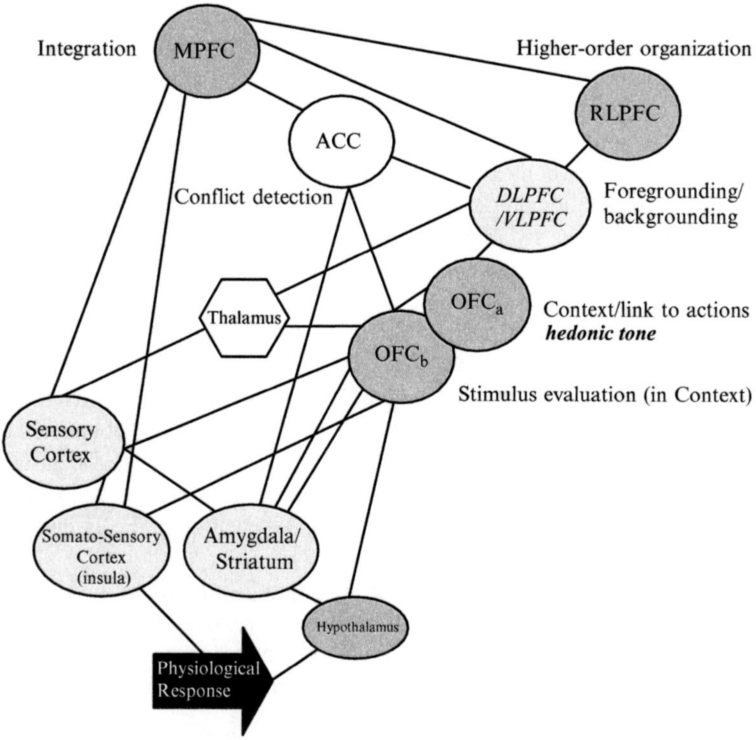


**Fig. 16.1** The iterative reprocessing model. Information about a stimulus is processed by the thalamus and projected to the amygdala, not only leading to an initial motivational tendency to approach or avoid the stimulus but also initiating further processing of the stimulus by the anterior cingulated cortex (ACC) and orbitofrontal cortex (OFC). OFC and amygdala have outputs to the hypothalamus, which then is involved in generating a physiological response. This response is cortically represented in the insular cortex, which can then serve as an input into the next stage of processing. ACC responds to the motivational significance of the situation (e.g., negative valence) and may recruit additional reprocessing of the stimulus via ventrolateral prefrontal cortex and then dorsolateral prefrontal cortex, with rostrolateral prefrontal cortex playing a transient role in the explicit consideration of contexts. Reprocessing by lateral regions of PFC corresponds to reflection, and it serves to regulate evaluative processing by amplifying or suppressing attention to certain aspects of the situation (thalamic route). Medial prefrontal cortex provides a dynamic model of the relation between reality and one's processing goals, and it influences the extent to which one engages in reprocessing. The iterative reprocessing of information requires complex, interconnected neural networks that allow for the bidirectional flow of information (all connections depicted in the figure are bidirectional). Reprinted with the permission of Elsevier. Reprinted from Trends in Cognitive Sciences, Volume 11(3), Cunningham, W. A., & Zelazo, P. D. (2007). Copyright 2007, with permission from Elsevier. [Figure 2, Page. 99]

The authors maintained that their model underscores that cognition and emotion are intrinsically related in a holistic psychological experience. Executive function might be more hot or emotional or might be more cool or reflective/cognitive, but both are involved in adaptive development. When the context is "hot," it can interfere with effective executive functioning, for example, when it elicits strong approach or avoidance tendencies that impair capacity for reflective reprocessing. This being said, a "hot" context might facilitate effective executive processing, for example, by increasing dopamine levels in the prefrontal cortex.

Lewis (2010) presented a neurobiological model of desire in relation to conceptual development. The model included feedback loops that entrain desire to goals that include appraisals and action plans. A feedback loop is involved between the desire and developing concepts. The desire is associated with dopamine production in the nucleus accumbens (NAS). Lewis emphasized that conceptual development depends on desire in the context of goal seeking. He placed desire between interest and craving on an emotional continuum.

The NAS is part of the striatum, itself a subset of the basal ganglia, and it lies at the core of the brain. It is the ventral striatal system. It has been referred to as a motivation-to-action interface (Goto & O'Donnell, 2001). The NAS activates when an individual is experiencing positive affect related to the anticipation of reward (Burgdorf & Panksepp, 2006). The NAS works in association with dorsal regions of the striatum, such as the caudate nucleus. The NAS receives input from various areas of the prefrontal cortex, especially the OFC. The NAS is also connected to the amygdala, the hippocampus, and the ventral tegmental area. The latter area supplies the NAS with dopamine and, reciprocally, the NAS acts on it, to keep going its dopamine-pumping function (Depue & Collins, 1999). Dopamine is involved in synaptic activity and influences motivation.

Lewis (2010) indicated that the motivational loop just described is one of three loops involved in reward–action circuits in the brain. Aside from the motivated action loop, there is also an object evaluation loop and a self-monitoring loop. The motivated action loop serves to keep behavior organized in a coherent direction.

## *Conclusion*

It will be recalled that Lewis, Todd, and Xu (2010) described self-regulation as a component of executive function. One of the major developmental tasks confronting the child and the child's care giving and support network relates to the development of self-regulation. Self-regulation is a component of executive function. Moreover, it is similar to emotional regulation. In addition, it consists of components such as verbal self-regulation and inhibition. The manner in which I conceive self-regulation is that it is both cognitive and affective in nature, both about the developing person and the person's relational social context and in both about developments in its higher-order and lower-order interacting levels. An important aspect about it concerns its inhibitory component as Blair and Dennis (2010) point out. Executive function requires a balance of action and inhibitory systems. As for the neurobiology of the self-regulation and its components, it does not appear to reside in one location in the brain or one neurotransmitter system; rather there are related regions, pathways, networks, and loops.

The literature appears to point out that there are two phases in the development of self-regulation. The first, is concerned with basic control of arousal and attentional processes, and the second appears to involve more effortful, deliberative, and conscious or voluntary control. Another way of describing the distinction between earlier and later self-regulation in development concerns its transfer from more external to more internal regulation, although, one must be careful to not consider these aspects as separate. A more complete developmental model would examine the development of unconscious or automatic means of self-regulation, and the cognitive underpinnings to its increasing capacity with age. In addition, the most recent research in the area is emphasizing the fine balance in emotions and cognition in executive function and self-regulation (Blair & Ursache, 2011; Perlman & Pelfrey, 2010), and the interrelationship between top-down and bottom up processes as well as development towards more advanced areas of the brain (dorsal vs. ventral). In the remainder of the chapter, I examine the literature on models in the development of self-regulation and end up describing my own model.

# Modeling

## *Specific Models*

According to Jacques and Marcovitch (2010), models of executive function can be divided in terms of whether they are representational or componential, or whether they indicate a unified executive function or more diverse models. Vygotsky (1929) had formulated a model involving representations in executive function, although it was not presented as such. Children learn in social exchanges and internalize the material. In his model, sociocultural tools, such as language, allow for increasing cognitive abilities and voluntary control of behavior. Luria (1961) added that language permits the representation of directives generated by the self or the other that allow better control of thought and behavior. Zelazo, Müller, Frye, and Marcovitch (2003) elaborated a functional model of executive function, or what it accomplishes. Other models involve consciousness, reflection, and cognitive complexity/control.

As for componential models, Diamond (2006) emphasized roles for inhibition, working memory, and cognitive flexibility. Garon, Bryson, and Smith (2008) indicated that executive function mediates conflict between different representations, between prepotent responses and representations, and between response sets that are incompatible.

Barkley (2001) formulated a functional model that integrates representational and componential themes in executive function. He emphasized the need for response inhibition and the movement from overt to covert executive skills.

First, nonverbal working memory develops to augment executive function. Then, the child develops verbal working memory, allowing self-talk. Third, the child develops self-regulation of affect/motivation/arousal. Finally, the child can use reconstitutive skills (akin to analysis/synthesis; e.g., internalization of play).

Jacques and Marcovitch (2010) considered that working memory constitutes the primary component of executive functioning, and that variability in executive functioning is partly accounted for by variability in working memory. Others who have emphasized working memory in cognitive-related skills include Case (1992), Engle and Kane (2004), and Pascual-Leone (1970). To be more precise, for Jacques and Marcovitch, "working memory is understood as the representational vehicle that permits relevant information to be kept in mind, information that is critical for one to be able to exert control over one's thoughts and behaviors, permitting cognitive flexibility on the one hand and response control on the other" (p. 448). Working memory, therefore, contributes to the other core processes (cognitive flexibility/set shifting and response control/inhibition), making it at once representational and componential. Representations are sensorimotor in nature in infancy, and they become more symbolic, conceptual, abstract, and linguistic-verbal in the preschooler (Jacques & Zelazo, 2005). More research is needed to confirm the role of sensorimotor representations in executive function in infancy, because the evidence is sparse and still essentially only that from Luria's work.

McClelland, Ponitz, Messersmith, and Tominey (2010) examined self-regulation from the perspective of a relational or holistic integration of cognition and emotion. They indicated that self-regulation is multidimensional and includes the regulation of cognition, emotion, and behavior. Specifically, they referred to the work of Barkley (2004), who defined self-regulation as "a deliberate attempt to modulate, modify, or inhibit actions and reactions" toward ends that are more adaptive.

Although their view of self-regulation is integrative, from a heuristic point of view, they referred to "hot" emotional regulation for affective and motivational components and "cool" cognitive self-regulation for the components of planning, decision-making, problem-solving, and related processes. The authors cited Lewis and Todd (2007), who found through fMRI studies that cognitive and emotional aspects do not map easily onto different areas of the brain. Nevertheless, the amygdala is more involved in "hot" stimuli and the prefrontal cortex in "cool" stimuli. This being said, regulation involves the coordination among the different brain areas. For example, Lewis and Todd found that heightened amygdala activity is followed by activity in the prefrontal cortex, which in turn serves to regulate the amygdala. Lewis and Todd also noted that the anterior cingulate cortex is involved in coordinating multiple brain regions. They concluded that adaptive regulation involves simultaneously coping with emotions while using cognitive resources in problem resolution.

For McClelland et al. (2010), self-regulation is considered a reciprocal process. For example, good ability to engage in effortful control in a child helps the child modulate the impact of caregivers who might be low in warmth or engage in negative parenting behaviors (Lengua, 2009). Similarly, children with high negative reactivity are impacted by overall parental behavior compared to children who are lower in negative reactivity (Belsky, Bakermans-Kranenburg, & van IJzendoorn, 2007). Effortful control refers to regulation of reactivity and is considered a part of early temperament (Rothbart & Bates, 2006). It is defined as the capacity to suppress dominant responses to perform less dominant ones. Self-regulation differs from effortful control by being more situation-specific rather than individual-characteristic.

As an example of how cognitive and emotion interact in self-regulation, McClelland et al. (2010) cited the work of Trentacosta and Izard (2007). They had found a relationship between academic competence in first grade and teacher ratings of emotional regulation in kindergarten. Moreover, the relationship was mediated by ratings of attention in first grade. They concluded that self-regulation is multidimensional, domain-specific, and interactional. Children with strong emotional responses who can regulate them comport better relative to children with lesser capacity to self-regulate (Rothbart & Bates, 2006).

## *General Models*

### Introduction

Bronson (2000) reviewed the literature on self-regulation in early childhood. She adopted a multiple theoretical perspective, reviewing and integrating eight models. These included the following perspectives: psychoanalytic, behavioral, social learning, social cognitive, Vygotskian, Piagetian, Neo-Piagetian, and information processing (see Table 16.1).

Bronson maintained that there is no single or simple definition of the concept of self-regulation. For example, for the young child, various terms are used for self-regulation, including impulse control, self-control, self-management, self-direction, and becoming independent. Some of these concepts relate to external control of behavior oriented toward the environment, for example, complying with requests. Other concepts concern

**Table 16.1** Sources of self-regulation and causes of development according to different psychological theories

| Theory | Source(s) of self-regulation | Cause(s) of development of self-regulation |
|---|---|---|
| Psychoanalytic | Ego deals with conflicting inner forces (id and superego), copes with the environment, and seeks "competence/efficacy" | Growth of ego strength from successful interactions with the environment and accompanying growth of self-esteem and self-confidence |
| Behavioral | Learned contingencies of reinforcement<br>Learned ability to wait for delayed reinforcement<br>Learned self-instruction strategies | Training in<br>• Experiencing delayed reinforcement<br>• Giving self-reinforcement for delaying reinforcement<br>• Giving self-instructions<br>• Giving self-reinforcement for trying and for success |

(continued)

**Table 16.1** (continued)

| Theory | Source(s) of self-regulation | Cause(s) of development of self-regulation |
|---|---|---|
| Social learning | Internalized performance standards (internalized representations of what constitutes competent or effective behavior)<br>Self-evaluation – leading to self-reward (feelings of self-efficacy) if standards are met or self-punishment (feelings of self-contempt) if standards are not met | Learning performance standards from<br>• Own performances and outcomes (reinforcement or punishment) of these<br>• Observing others and the outcomes of their behaviors<br>Experiencing and observing reinforcement for self-regulated behaviors (leading to self-efficacy evaluation for self-regulation) |
| Social cognitive | Perceived ability to control events in the environment | Experiences of control<br>Attribution of control to own actions and competence |
| Vygotskian | Innate curiosity and interest in independence | Private speech (internalized language that guides action and thought) |
| Piagetian | Equilibration – cognitive need to restore mental balance by resolving mental conflict or disequilibrium<br>Interest in exploring and creating interesting effects in the environment | Cognitive development – increasing cognitive understanding of the physical and social environment and development of logical thinking (allowing increasingly adaptive and effective thinking and interactions with people and objects in the environment) |
| Neo-Piagetian | Innate interest in problem-solving<br>Domain-specific increases in control | Development of increased information-processing capacities that support independent problem-solving and control<br>Domain-specific increases in self-regulatory skill |
| Information processing | Innate interest in problem solving and control | Development of "executive" functions, including rules, plans, and strategies that support independent thought and action |

Reprinted with the permission of Guilford Publications. Bronson, M. B. (2000). Copyright 2011. [Table 1.1, Page. 28]

Bronson's approach to describing the sources of self-regulation involved presenting them in terms of schools of thought, such as the classic psychoanalytic, behavioral, and Piagetian views, as well as presenting their theoretical offshoots and additions, such as the social learning, Neo-Piagetian, and information processing views. In terms of needs of the present work, this format is ideal, because it allows careful description of the Piagetian perspective, preparing the way for the additions of the present model. Across the theories, both the role of the individual and the role of the environment seem important (e.g., curiosity, ego, and internalization compared to learning and training, although innate factors are mentioned, as well)

In her book, Bronson described how the developing individual increases self-regulation in passing through the different Piagetian stages of cognitive development. The present work presents a model of self-regulation that builds on my Neo-Piagetian model of stages and substages in cognitive development; also, it adds other factors related to other schools described by Bronson more control of internal cognitive systems, such as focusing attention and engaging in independent learning. Bronson noted that the type of self-regulation in which the child needs to engage varies with chronological age and developmental level.

In this regard, Kopp (1982) proposed a developmental sequence in self-regulation that begins with an early "control and system organization," which one finds even in the prenatal period. Next, at about 9 months of age, the infant develops "compliance." In the second year, "impulse control" develops; and at 3 years, more sophisticated self-regulatory capacities emerge. Bronson (2000) maintained that descriptive accounts of developing self-regulation, such as this, need an explanatory theoretical framework.

## Models

### Psychoanalytic

In psychoanalytic theory, self-regulation obtains by way of the ego in dealing with inner conflicts and trying to cope with the environment. As the ego succeeds in dealing with these issues, the child develops increasing competence/efficacy, self-esteem, and self-confidence. In this tradition, White (1963) added to the model that the child develops a sense of confidence and intrinsic motivation. Erikson (1963) further added that the teenager develops a sense of identity.

### Behavioral Learning

In the behavioral approach, the sources of self-regulation concern learning contingencies and reinforcements, as well as learned strategies of self-instruction. For example, the child learns to accept delays in reinforcement and learns self-talk for having appropriate control. The child learns the value of rewards, delays in getting rewards, and controlling responses to stimuli to get the best rewards available.

The social learning perspective elaborated the behavioral approach through its concept of the child imitating modeled behavior. The child not only can imitate aggressive behavior, for example, but also can imitate control of the impulse to aggression, depending on the modeling experience. The child develops an internalized standard of performance, which leads to a sense of self-efficacy when self-control is effective. Therefore, in the social learning approach, self-regulation depends on models and events in the child's environment, the child's self-regulatory capacities, and the child's appraisal of the environment and the self.

A variant of the social learning perspective is the social cognitive one. This approach emphasizes that children are active information processors who construct coherent representational models of their social environment. For example, a child's beliefs, perceived ability, and attribution of locus of control about behavior affect the child's behavior and self-regulation.

### Sociocultural

For Vygotsky (1962, 1978), self-regulation derives from the sociocultural context and from the child's ability to incorporate the messages received, as well as to give self-instructions and follow them. The child coconstructs internalized versions of the incorporated sociocultural language that he or she hears, and the messages of other "tools." The environment functions to guide the child's participation in the learning space that is the child's zone of proximal development (Rogoff, 1990). Therefore, both the knowledge and means for the child's self-regulation are mediated socially. However, the child progresses to an internal self-control through private speech or an internalized language that guides action and thought.

### Piagetian and Neo-Piagetian

Bronson (2000) considered the work of Piaget one of the major axes in her work. For Piaget, children acquire better self-regulation as they develop through the cognitive stages of his model. This development is facilitated by the process of equilibration and is promoted by the child's inherent curiosity. In Piaget's stages, the child moves from developing sensorimotor schemes to preoperational symbolic representations. The child is still egocentric in the latter stage, without the capacity to think logically in context. Self-regulation improves in the next stage of concrete operations, in which this type of logic develops. Next, it becomes more advanced in the teenage period of abstract formal thought. In this four-step stage progression, the child's mental structures become increasingly stable, they increasingly constitute better representations of external reality, and they increasingly evidence better adaptation. Children do learn not only physical knowledge but also social knowledge, such as social rules and conventions.

For Piaget, the child can decide and behave in manners more consistent with the requirements of the environment and the problems at hand, while improving the schemes and operations being used because of the process of equilibration (that is, assimilation, disequilibrium after failed assimilation, and subsequent accommodation recreating equilibrium). According to Bronson (2000), self-regulation partly derives from the process of equilibration. It allows the incorporation of new relevant information into existing cognitive structures. Or it can lead to the modification of existing structures to adapt to new, relevant information that does not fit the structures that are being used by the child.

In the Neo-Piagetian perspective, Case (1985) and Fischer (1980) describe cognitive development in terms of accruing skills and domains rather than overall stages. In addition, they look at the underlying information processing capacities needed to develop cognitively. Therefore, in terms of self-regulation, there are domain-specific and skill-specific increases in self-control.

### Information Processing

In the information-processing view, the computer is used as a metaphor for cognitive processing. Input enters the system, it is reworked or reprocessed, and the output depends on that reworking or processing. Moreover, there are constraints in the system, such as memory capacity, encoding, software, and feedback. In terms of children, the constraints refer to attention, perception, and motivation, as well. Children develop an increasing capacity to self-regulate their behavior and thought through the development of executive functions, such as implementing rules, routines, plans, and strategies.

### Comment

In the conclusions to her book, Bronson (2000) underscored the cultural influences on developing self-regulation. In addition, she examined the role of brain development in the development of self-regulation. She suggested practical applications in teaching and promoting self-regulation in children.

In the next section of the present work, Fox and Riconscente (2008) elaborate further Piaget's cognitive developmental model with respect to self-regulation. Their work and that of Bronson function to set the stage for the present model of self-regulation.

## *Self-Regulation According to Piaget*

### Piaget

According to Fox and Riconscente (2008), in terms of conceptualizing self-regulation, Piaget differentiates himself from James (1890, 1992) and Vygotsky (1978, 1981a, 1981b, 1986) by his emphasis on the relationship of other and object. For Piaget, development involves modification of cognitive structures by way of assimilation and accommodation and their transactional equilibrium (Piaget, 1964/1968). Development requires "awareness of interaction with, and attempts to control both objects and others in the environment" (Fox & Riconscente, 2008, p. 378). Similarly, the development of self-regulation involves an equivalent process. The authors defined self-regulation as deliberate control of one's thoughts and actions.

According to the authors, in Piaget, self-regulation takes place at both the intellectual and affective levels (Piaget, 1964/1968). For the intellectual area, self-regulation involves intention, or the deliberate orientation toward specific goals of thoughts and of actions in problem-solving. As for affect, self-regulation involves will, or the control of desire and emotion. Both realms in self-regulation develop; for example, children move toward "directed socialized thought" and "directed socialized desires." Piaget (1950) wrote, "Logic is not coextensive with intelligence, but consists of the sum-total of rules of control which intelligence makes use of for its own direction. Morality plays a similar part with regard to the affective life" (p. 405).

Therefore, for Piaget, the rules of thought are governed by logic, and the rules for feeling are informed by morality. The rules are not sufficient to regulate behavior. Intention and will are the means of self-regulation that bring thought, action, emotion, and desire in accord with rules. Self-regulation of affect is especially social and requires perspective-taking about others' feelings and desires. The social includes interaction with peers who, compared to adults, provide a more equitable and cooperative social environment.

Despite the social nature of the environment in Piaget's understanding of cognitive development, the locus of the development of the child's cognition still resides in the child. Piaget (1950) wrote, "It is idle, again, to try and transform the child's mind from outside, when his own taste for active research and his desire for cooperation suffice to ensure a normal intellectual development. The adult must therefore be a collaborator and not a master, from this double point of view, moral and rational" (p. 412).

The implication for education for Piaget (1950) is that it works well when there is collaboration coupled with autonomy. James (1890, 1992) would emphasize more the individual in the educational process and Vygotsky (1978, 1981a, 1981b, 1986) more the cultural process and cultural tools. In conclusion, Fox and Riconscente (2008) considered as complementary the three perspectives of Piaget, Vygotsky, and James.

#### Comment

The description of self-regulation according to Piaget, as described by Fox and Riconscente (2008), is relevant to the present work in several ways. First, it provides a backdrop for understanding and comparing contemporary approaches to self-regulation. Second, it emphasized the integration of the cognitive and socio-affective in development and in self-regulation, which is a common theme throughout the present work. Third, coupled with Vygotsky's work on the cultural process and the use of cultural tools in education, it provides a nuanced view teaching of children. Fourth, given that it has been shown that Piaget considered important to address self-regulatory processes, extension of the present model to include steps in its development from a Neo-Piagetian perspective seems important.

## The Present Model of Self-Regulation

### *Stages in the Model*

#### Introduction

Sokol and Müller (2007) argued for a better integration of cognition and emotion in models of self-regulation. The cognitive approach to self-regulation emphasizes executive function, considered "cooler" than the "hot" affective motivational side of self-regulation. They described that Piaget understood the importance of affectivity in self-regulation, which he referred to as "will." Piaget maintained that

**Table 16.2** Stages in the development of self-regulation in parallel with Young's developmental model of cognitive stages

| Cognitive stage | Emotional regulation stage |
|---|---|
| Reflex | Nonlogical |
| Sensorimotor | Prelogical |
| Perioperational | Perilogical |
| Preoperational | Quasi-logical |
| Concrete operational | Logical |
| Abstract | Hyperlogical |
| Collective intelligence | Collective superordinate logical |

Young's model of five stages in cognitive development is presented in the left-hand column, but with the addition of the two stages of Piaget that the perioperational stage encompasses (preoperational, concrete operational). This procedure was necessitated because the right-hand column includes the names of the corresponding stages of emotional regulation that I had formulated. The latter model is partly based on Baldwin's original sequence of stages in development that Piaget had elaborated. Preparation of this model was instrumental in the creation of the combined transtheoretical model of the present work because it pointed to two phases over the five substages in the perioperational stage [there are five substages that cyclically recur in the present model], and the combined model has two phases in each stage, thereby simplifying the substage structure of the model (see Chap. 1)

"affective structures are isomorphic with intellectual structures" (1954/1981, p. 9) and that emotions complement cognition. The goal of the present model is to elucidate from a Neo-Piagetian perspective the particular manner in which this integration of cognition and emotion takes place in development.

In the present work, I have posited that there are five Neo-Piagetian stages in development, each with five substages that cyclically recur. In the following, in light of the work of Lewis and colleagues (e.g., Woltering & Lewis, 2009), I extend the model to emotional regulation (see Table 16.2). The model illustrates that for each of the five stages in the present model, one can posit the development of a corresponding, qualitatively different type of emotional regulation consistent with it. Note that I start with the sensorimotor stage and deal afterward with the reflexive one.

## Stages

### Sensorimotor Stage

In this regard, early signs of reactive emotional regulation might be present even in the early sensorimotor period, such as when the baby disengages from dyadic interaction, for example, by looking away, when fatigued, overwhelmed, and so on. For Thompson, Lewis, and Calkins (2008), the infant develops executive attentional control, and redirects attention to disengage from stimuli that are too arousing. In terms of the cognitive parallels that would accompany this stage, I note that emotion regulation requires an associated cognitive activity, even if primitive in terms of underlying structure. To say that there are signs of it in the first year means that the sensorimotor activities of the infant must be involved because emotion and cognition are intimately intertwined at all ages, in general, share the same or similar neuronal and localization platforms, etc.

Sensorimotor schemes possess the ideal properties for facilitating emotional regulation in reactive ways because they increasingly organize situation and response connections in increasingly differentiated and integrated manners. This suggests that the sensorimotor substages described in the various Neo-Piagetian models can be used to trace the development of reactive emotional regulation.

Moreover, as Piaget had suggested, the regulation activity becomes increasingly intentional, purposive, with more refined means and causal understanding as the child evolves. That is, the appearance of the more deliberative step in emotion regulation that develops after the sensorimotor one seems to be gradually prepared in a step-by-step way, in the sensorimotor substages. [I refer to a more deliberative self-regulation but appreciate that this does not make it conscious; rather, the term is used to imply only that there is a more effortful and representational basis for it].

### Perioperational Stage

That deliberative emotional regulation appears at 2 years of age makes sense from the point of view of the present model, in that the qualities that it possesses indicate that its cognitive underpinning could readily relate to the symbolic representations that characterize preoperational development, which is the first part of the stage of perioperations in the present model. For example, in deliberative emotion regulation, the child reflects, takes context into account, and formulates adaptive, flexible strategies. For Thompson et al., the child at this age uses language and internal speech, self-directed inhibition, self-distraction, reappraisal, and action monitoring, all consistent with the preoperational stage.

Nevertheless, there are constraints on deliberative emotional regulation in the young child compared to the child entering Piaget's concrete operational period, which is the second part of the present perioperational stage. In this regard, the child's deliberative emotional regulation should be lacking a logical quality that allows for the development of generalized rules that could be applied differentially to context. Therefore, from a Piagetian perspective, deliberative emotional regulation should go through two main developmental phases, which I refer to as quasi-logical and logical (after Baldwin). There should be more reflection, context-sensitivity, and adaptive or strategic planning of deliberative emotional regulation in the second phase, and one marked by underlying concrete operational cognition. For Thompson et al., the child at this age can use the increasing skills in theory of mind, emotion understanding, and appreciating sociocultural display rules. Note that a combined term that is consistent with the perioperational stage that the quasi-logical and logical types of emotional regulation appear to reflect would be "perilogical" emotional regulation.

## Abstract Stage

Continuing the analogy with Baldwin's model, the next phase in the development of emotional regulation should be labeled hyperlogical emotional regulation. It should emerge in parallel with formal or abstract logical thought, and integrate advanced and abstract planning in emotional regulation. The teenager not only should be capable of managing emotions as they emerge and control them when they are maladaptive, but also the teenager should be capable of seeing the wider picture. In this regard, the adolescent becomes cognizant of the context, where her or his education and life skills are heading, and so on, leading to a more selective approach of the contexts in which one puts oneself in and the types of problems one is willing to confront.

## Collective Intelligence Stage

There are two more stages in the present model that have not yet been considered for their possible corresponding advances in emotional regulation. First, in the present model, the postformal stage is called collective intelligence. In this sense, emotional regulation should become increasingly superordinate in abstract skills and collective in adult regulatory activities. Although adolescents are embedded in social groups at school and with friends, cognitively, they do not yet have the sophistication to undertake well the group problem-solving involved in confronting emerging problems, such as in the case of adult brainstorming at work (constructing an understanding of the problems or challenges that will help advance the functioning of the group [and therefore of themselves, too]). In this regard, the deliberative emotional regulation at this stage should be termed a "Collective superordinate logical" one.

## Reflexive Stage

Finally, the present model postulates a reflexive stage prior to the sensorimotor one. In this regard, reactive emotional regulation can be considered to have two phases, and in keeping with Baldwin, I refer to them as "nonlogical" and "prelogical." That is, the reflex stage does appear to possess some emotional regulative correspondences. For example, in the first month of life, newborns manifest self-soothing capabilities, even though most of their emotional regulation is constituted by the scaffolding and frame-holding of caregivers. However, the schemes involved lack the sensorimotor constructive abilities that are evident in the infant in the remainder of the first 2 years of life. As for the sensorimotor stage, I have already described it in terms of its apparent parallel emotional regulation capacities. To summarize, they appear to fit the notion that they constitute prelogical skills, being more advanced than nonlogical ones but not yet quasi-logical in nature.

### *Conclusion*

The model that I have presented of the development of self-regulation according to steps in Neo-Piagetian development needs further work, but it promotes the notion that there are qualitative shifts in the capacity to self-regulate. I have examined the idea in a general way, but it could be applied to the different levels of the executive function/self-regulation/componential structure involved. For example, it would be interesting to determine how verbal self-regulation develops according to the substages of the present model once it is initiated.

In the next part of the chapter, I shift to a different topic on self-development. It relates to the present model of steps in development, and prepares the way for further conceptual innovations in the chapter to follow.

## Relatedness and Self-Definition in Development

### *Model*

Blatt (2008) formulated a model of personality development, psychopathology, and the therapeutic process based on the dual polarities of experience of self-definition and relatedness. Self-definition concerns establishing and maintaining a sense of self that is coherent, realistic, differentiated, integrated, and positive. Relatedness concerns establishing and maintaining reciprocal, meaningful, and satisfying social relationships. Development takes place across the life span and involves the synergistic interaction not only of the individual with the environment, but also of the two noted fundamental dimensions in individuals' psychology. These dimensions are in constant negotiation and dynamic tension. When development leans more toward one or the other poles of the duality, problems in development could arise, including of psychological disorders. Personality might take on more of the characteristics of one pole or the other (e.g., introjective personality, or anaclitic personality).

### *Related Models*

Blatt (2008) traced some of the models and theories in the field that are consistent with his own model. For example, Bakan (1966) had proposed that agency and communion are two fundamental dimensions of personality. Agency relates to individuation and communion relates to relating with others and the world. McAdams (1985a, 1985b) referred to similar dimensions of intimacy and power as themes in personality organization. The themes of relatedness and self-definition are central to other personality theories, such as in Deci and Ryan (1992) and Ryan and Deci (2000a, 2000b). They used the terminology of an interpersonal relatedness and the need for autonomy, competence, and self-initiated action. Buber (1978) referred to the development of the "I" and "You," which are philosophical concepts that Blatt considered analogous to his distinction of self-definition and relatedness.

In terms of evolutionary theory, Blatt (2008) referred to the work of Cortina and Liotti (2007) and Tomasello (2003), who emphasized that cooperation in addition to competition is part of social organization. In his cross-cultural research, Triandis (2001) had formulated the conceptual distinction between individualism and collectivism and argued that they are expressed both at the individual level as well as the cultural level.

Erikson (1968) is one of many theorists who discussed the development of personality in terms of separation and individuation. It is well known that, for individuation, he referred to the development of identity. However, he also wrote that "True 'engagement' with others is the result and the test of firm self delineation" (p. 167). This reflects his notion that the person develops in mutuality with the social environment. Blatt (2008) organized Erikson's stages in terms of a model of whether they are more on the self-definitional pole or the relatedness pole. For example, he placed the infancy period of trust vs. mistrust on the relatedness dimension and the stage of identity vs. role diffusion on the self-definitional pole.

Blatt described other workers who had created synergistic concepts between the two polarities, consistent with the notion that they synchronize in development. For example, Sampson (1985, 1988) presented the concept of "ensembled individualism" to indicate that the different dualities of experience coalesce into an integrated construct of the self.

## *Development*

Blatt (2008) reviewed the literature on the development of precursors to self-definition and relatedness. Sander (1975, 1999) stressed that development involves an alternating interaction of experiences related to self-definition and relatedness. For the former, he referred to basic regulation, initiatory activity, and autonomous action. For the latter, he referred to coordinated interpersonal interactions and dyadic emotional regulation. Emde (1984) proposed that there are two fundamental developmental processes in the early development of the self, which he referred to as self-regulation and social "fittedness." In his developmental model, Stern (1985), referred to the "self versus other" and "self with other." In their work, Beebe et al. (2007) referred to self-regulation and interactive regulation.

## *Comment*

Blatt (2008) showed that his model of two fundamental polarities of experience has a widespread theoretical resonance and has much empirical support. He proposed that these dimensions develop through levels or steps (see Tables 16.3 and 16.4).

**Table 16.3** Blatt's dynamic structural developmental model

| Developmental level | | Behavioral indication |
|---|---|---|
| I. | Boundary constancy (2–3 months) | Smiling response, initiates engagement with others |
| II. | Recognition(libidinal) constancy (6–8 months) | Stranger anxiety, differentiation among people, emotional attachment to a specific individual |
| III. | Evocative constancy (16–18 months) | • Sense of object not immediately present in perceptual field<br>• Anticipation of invisible displacement (Piaget), initiate separation from caring agent (Mahler) |
| IV. | Self- and object constancy (30–36 months) | Stable concepts of self and other expressed in precise use of terms such as *me, mine, and I* |
| V. | Concrete operational thought (5 years) | • Capacity for coordinating several dimensions<br>• Capacity for anticipation, transformation, conservation, and reversibility of external manifest features<br>• Triadic interpersonal configurations, and the emergence of a concept of *we* |
| VI. | Formal operational thought (11–12 years) | • Transformation, reversibility, and conservation of abstract inner features, dimensions, and processes such as values and principles<br>• Recognition that one constructs meaning and a sense of reality<br>• Appreciation of personal and cultural relativism |
| VII. | Self-identity (late adolescence young adulthood) | Synthesis and integration of mature expressions of both individuality and relatedness in a capacity to be intimate with another and to contribute to a collective without losing one's individuality |
| VIII. | Integrity (mature adulthood) | Emergence of a fuller sense of *we* (i.e., "self-in-relation" [Chodorow, 1989] or "ensembled individualism" [Sampson, 1988]) |

Reprinted with the permission of University of Rochester Press. Blatt, S. J. (1995). Copyright 2011. [Table 1, Page. 8]

Blatt's (2008) dynamic structural developmental model fashions an integrated understanding of two polarities of experience, concerning self-definition and relatedness. It has been structured to help understand not only normal development, including personality development, but also developmental psychopathology, including psychotherapy. Blatt described levels of structural organization in development. The model includes the work of Kernberg (1976) on boundary articulation early in life, Mahler, Pine and Bergman (1975) on separation–individuation, Stern (1985) on the formation of the self and the sense of intersubjectivity, and the author's work on the interplay between self-definitional processes and the development of interpersonal relatedness

The first levels of the model involve constancies of object and self and how they develop. The terms are psychodynamic in origin, but also are related to the Piagetians' use of similar terms from a cognitive perspective. There are eight levels to the model, and they begin with these psychodynamic and related formulations in early infancy. Then, they pass on to a mix of Piagetian ones and psychodynamic ones in later infancy. Next, they become especially Piagetian in the preschool, school-age, and early adolescent periods. Finally, they become especially Eriksonian in the late adolescent and adult periods

The way in which different theoretical positions are intermixed from one age level to the next in Blatt's model contrasts with the approach taken toward stages in development in the present work. The present model is distinguished from Blatt's by having two parallel 25-step sequences intercoordinated in development, one Neo-Piagetian and one Neo-Eriksonian. The major stages extend the full life span, but even include prenatal and elderly development, unlike in the model presented by Blatt

**Table 16.4** Separation–individuation steps in Blatt

| Level/scale point | Description |
|---|---|
| Impairments in basic differentiation between self and others | |
| 1. Self – other boundary compromise | Basic sense of physical cohesion or the integrity of separate representations is lacking or is breached |
| 2. Self – other boundary confusion | Self and other are represented as physically intact and separate, but feelings and thoughts are amorphous, undifferentiated, or confused. Description may consist of a single global impressionistic quality or a flood of details with a sense of confusion and vagueness |
| Attempts to establish and maintain object and self-constancy | |
| 3. Self – other mirroring | Characteristics of self and other, such as physical appearance or body qualities (e.g., shape or size), are virtually identical |
| 4. Self – other idealization or denigration | Attempt to consolidate representations based on unmodulated idealization or denigration. Extreme, exaggerated, one-sided descriptions |
| 5. Semidifferentiated, tenuous consolidation of representations through splitting (polarization) or an emphasis on concrete part properties | Attempt to consolidate representations by a marked oscillation between dramatically opposite qualities, or an emphasis on manifest external features |
| Differentiated and integrated concepts of self and other (object constancy) | |
| 6. Emergent, ambivalent constancy (cohesion) of self and other, an emergent quality of interpersonal relatedness | Emerging consolidation of disparate aspects in a somewhat hesitant, equivocal, or ambivalent integration. A list of appropriate characteristics, but they lack a sense of uniqueness. Tentative movement toward a more individuated and cohesive sense of self and other |
| 7. Consolidated, constant (stable) self and other in unilateral relationships | Thoughts, feelings, needs, and fantasies are differentiated and modulated. Increasing tolerance for and integration of disparate aspects. Distinguishing qualities and unique characteristics. Sympathetic understanding of others |
| Capacity for empathic, reciprocal relationships | |
| 8. Cohesive, individuated, empathically related self and others | Cohesive, nuanced, and related sense of self and others. A definite sense of identity, an interest in interpersonal relationships, and a capacity to understand the perspective of others |
| 9. Reciprocally related integrated unfolding of self and others | Cohesive sense of self and other in reciprocal relationships that transform both the self and the other in complex, continually unfolding ways |
| 10. Creative, integrated, reflective constructions of self and other in empathic, reciprocally attuned relationships | Integrated reciprocal relations with an appreciation that one contributes to the construction of meaning in complex interpersonal relationships |



The table presents a Differentiation-Relatedness scale involving ten steps that measure the degree of articulation and stabilization of the concept of the object and interpersonal schemata. The scale also measures the degree of appreciation of mutual, empathically attuned relatedness or reciprocity

(continued)

**Table 16.4** (continued)

| |
|---|
| between the self and significant others. The higher the scale score, the greater the individual is expressing an integration or interactive consolidation of separation and relatedness aspects of representations |
| There are four sections to the scale: a lack of basic differentiation of self and other, attempts to establish, consolidate, stabilize, and maintain the constancy of the self and other as objects, emergence of object constancy, forming an integrated representation of self and other (leading to increased tolerance for ambiguity and complexity), and sustained capacity for empathic, reciprocal relationships. The last step in the latter phase, in particular, includes notions that are quite postformal in a Neo-Piagetian sense (e.g., creative, integrated reflective constructions) |
| Blatt maintained that the scale describes a developmental sequence, even though it was constructed for clinical use, but that other scale points can be added for the developmental sequence implied. I note that the scale differs in its conceptualization of development compared to the theoretical model from which it is derived. Nevertheless, the notion of representing self-other separation–individuation is a good one. However, the various Neo-Piagetian models have attempted to examine the process using more steps, stages, and substages and have integrated the separation–individuation issue into a larger framework, such as the Eriksonian |

I have used Blatt's work extensively in the present work. For example, I have developed a model of self-regulation that is partly based on his work and I have developed a model of motivational needs that borrows from his work. In addition, I have coordinated his concept of polarities of experience with my own model of the cognitive (mis)perception of the other (presented previously in Chap. 14). This had led to a model of the self's cognitive (mis)perception of the self and of the other. In addition, it needs to be kept in mind that I have developed an elaborate cognitive/socioaffective model of 25 steps of development that should be consulted in parallel with his developmental model, as presented on Tables 17.1 and 17.2.

Similarly, Greenspan (2008) proposed a developmental model that has Neo-psychoanalytic roots, and it incorporated Piagetian concepts, like in Blatt (see Table 16.5).

## Learning

The present chapter on self-regulation has not considered much what might happen when the environment is not supportive of its optimal development. In Table 16.6 presents a model of environmental support of learning that could be positive or negative. Learning could be enhanced by proper support mechanisms, or become maladaptive. The model is based on the learning approach to self-regulation described in this chapter, but it adds examples when parents or significant do not engage in enhanced support but in problematic support. The development of self-regulation and the self becomes impacted with the latter type of parenting behavior, and the type of self-definitional and relatedness components of the self might become unduly disturbed, depending on the severity, frequency, etc. of the behavior.

This model of positive and negative speaks to the model of coeducation presented in the book. Negative and deleterious learning compromises the process that society would want optimized.

**Table 16.5** Stages of functional emotional development in Greenspan

| Functional emotional developmental level | Emotional, social, and intellectual capacities |
|---|---|
| Shared attention and regulation | Affective interest in sights, sound, touch, movement, and other sensory experiences. Also, initial experiences of modulating affect (i.e., calming down) |
| Engagement and relating | Pleasurable affects characterize relationships. Growing feelings of intimacy |
| Two-way intentional, affective signaling and communication | A range of affects becomes used in back-and-forth affective signaling to convey intentions (e.g., reading and responding to affective signals) |
| Long chains of coregulated emotional signaling and the formation of a presymbolic self | Affective interactions organized into action or behavioral patterns to express wishes and needs and solve problems (showing someone what you want with a pattern of actions rather than words or pictures)<br>a. Fragmented level (little islands of intentional problem-solving behavior)<br>b. Polarized level (organized patterns of behavior expressing only one or another feeling state, e.g., organized aggression and impulsivity or organized clinging, needy, dependent behavior, or organized fearful patterns)<br>c. Integrated level (different emotional patterns – dependency, assertiveness, pleasure, etc. – organized into integrated, problem-solving affective interactions such as flirting, seeking closeness, and then getting help to find a needed object) |
| Creating representations (or ideas) | 1. Words and actions used together (ideas are acted out in action, but words are also used to signify the action)<br>2. Somatic or physical words to convey feeling state ("My muscles are exploding," "Head is aching")<br>3. Using action words instead of actions to convey intent ("Hit you!")<br>4. Conveying feelings are real rather than s signals ("I'm mad" or "Hungry" or "Need a hug" as compared with "I feel mad" or "I feel hungry" or "I feel like I need a hug"). In the first instance, the feeling state demands action and is very close to action and, in the second one, it's more a signal for something going on inside that leads to a consideration of many possible thoughts and/or actions<br>5. Global feeling states ("I feel awful," "I feel OK," etc.)<br>6. Polarized feeling states (feelings tend to be characterized as all good or all bad) |
| Building bridges between ideas: logical thinking | 1. Differentiated feelings (gradually there are more and more subtle descriptions of feeling states – loneliness, sadness, annoyance, anger, delight, happiness, etc.)<br>2. Creating connections between differentiated feeling states ("I feel angry when you are mad at me") |
| Multicause, comparative, and triangular thinking | Exploring multiple reasons for a feeling, comparing feelings, and understanding triadic interactions among feeling states ("I feel left out when Susie likes Janet better than me") |
| Emotionally differentiated gray-area thinking | Shading and gradations among differentiated feeling states (ability to describe degrees of feelings around anger, love, excitement, love, disappointment – "I feel a little annoyed") |

(continued)

**Table 16.5** (continued)

| Functional emotional developmental level | Emotional, social, and intellectual capacities |
|---|---|
| Intermittent reflective thinking, a stable sense of self, and an internal standard | Reflecting on feelings in relationship to an internalized sense of self ("it's not like me to feel so angry," or "I shouldn't feel this jealous") |
| Reflective thinking with an expanded self; the adolescent themes | Expanding reflective feeling descriptors into new realms, including sexuality, romance, closer and more intimate peer relationships, school, community, and culture, and emerging sense of identity ("I have such an intense crush on that new boy that I know it's silly. I don't even know him") |
| Reflective thinking with an expanded self; into the future | Using feelings to anticipate and judge (including probabilizing) future possibilities in light of current and past experience ("I don't think I would be able to really fall in love with him because he likes to flirt with everyone and that has always made me feel neglected and sad") |
| Reflective thinking with an expanded self; the adult years | Expanding feeling states to include reflections and anticipatory judgement with regard to new levels and types of feelings associated with the stages of adulthood, including: |
| Reflective thinking and the separation, internalization, and stabilization of the self | The ability to separate from, function independently of, and yet remain close to and internalize many of the positive features of one's nuclear family and stabilize a sense of self and internal standard |
| Reflective thinking and commitment, intimacy, and choice | Intimacy (serious long-term relationships) |
| Extending the self to incorporate family and children | The ability to nurture and empathize with one's children without over-identifying with them |
| Middle age | 1. The ability to broaden one's nurturing and empathetic capacities beyond one's family and into the larger community<br>2. The ability to experience and reflect on changing perspectives of time and space and the new feelings of intimacy, mastery, pride, competition, disappointment, and loss associated with the family, career, and intrapersonal changes of midlife |
| The aging process | The ability for true reflective thinking of an unparalleled scope or a retreat and narrowing of similar proportions. There is the possibility of true wisdom free from the self-centered and practical worries of earlier stages. It also, however, can lead to retreat into one's changing physical states, a narrowing of interests, and concrete thinking |



Greenspan (2008) presented his developmental model of emotions from a functional milestone and psychodynamic perspective. He described 15 stages in development. The model includes emotional, social, and intellectual capacities at each stage. There are four stages applicable to the infancy period, leading to the establishment of a presymbolic self. This would be akin to Piagetian sensorimotor development. In the next stage, representations are formed, as in Piaget's preoperational period. The next few stages involve logical thinking, and they transform into reflective thinking. These developments are consistent with Piaget's concrete operational and formal stages. Greenspan added other stages related to the adult, consistent with postformal elaborations of Piaget. Despite the apparent parallels with Piaget's model, Greenspan's model was not developed based on it, nor does the author present direct parallels with Piaget

**Table 16.6** Positive learning and negative learning

| Child's behavior | Parental behavior | Parental examples | |
|---|---|---|---|
| Positive (or perceived as positive; desired) | Increase positive behavior (constructive) | Additive (e.g., give praise after good behavior)<br>Neutral (e.g., be good (role) model)<br>Subtractive (e.g., withdraw a negative for a good end) | |
| | Decrease positive behavior (not constructive) | Additive (e.g., scold child after good behavior)<br>Neutral (e.g., ignore good behavior)<br>Subtractive (e.g., remove food after child good) | NEGATIVE LEARNING |
| Negative (or perceived as negative; not desired) | Increase negative behavior (not constructive) | Additive (e.g., give praise after negative behavior)<br>Neutral (e.g., model negative behavior)<br>Subtractive (e.g., stop making demand after a tantrum) | NEGATIVE LEARNING |
| | Decrease negative behavior (constructive) | Additive (e.g., scold child after he hits, keep in moderation)<br>Neutral (e.g., ignore cranky behavior)<br>Subtractive (e.g., remove dessert after a fight) | |

The table illustrates how positive and negative learning contribute to a child's development. Learning mechanisms, such as reinforcement (e.g., praise) and punishment (e.g., scolding), usually are used to promote behaviors that are positive and desired. Positive and negative behaviors in the child can be increased or decreased by parental action. For example, the strategies of giving praise and of giving good models to imitate are effective ones. Ignoring cranky behavior and limiting rewards as deterrence are other examples that might be helpful. Unfortunately, there are ways of disciplining a child that act to promote negative or undesirable behaviors. Therefore, in the table, the most important distinction being made is between positive and negative learning

When a parent's or other person's reaction is expressed after a child's behavior to increase or decrease the behavior, that adult's reaction is called a reinforcer. Positive reinforcement involves some type of reaction or reward that is presented to increase a child's behavior. Negative reinforcement involves withdrawing something, rather than offering something, to increase a child's behavior. Punishment, on the contrary, is an unpleasant response to a child's behavior to decrease it.It also could involve the removal of a pleasant stimulus to decrease it. Aside from positive and negative reinforcement and punishment, other learning mechanisms might be activated to affect a child's behavior. These techniques involve not responding after a behavior to eliminate it (extinction) or modeling or demonstrating a behavior in order that it is increased

When a parent or teacher uses these various learning mechanisms toward constructive ends, the goal is to increase positive behavior and to decrease negative behavior, in a process of positive learning. To accomplish positive learning, the parent could give praise to a positive (add), stop/remove/withdraw a negative (subtract), or perform a more neutral behavior (do or demonstrate a positive/ignore a negative)

However, when a parent or teacher uses these various learning mechanisms toward less constructive ends, and when the intervention is negative or nonconstructive, the learning is negative so that positive behavior is decreased while negative behavior is increased. Negative learning is facilitated by behavior used explicitly for negative ends, such as scolding inappropriately, ignoring a good behavior, praising a negative one, modeling a negative one, and stopping/removing a good one. For example, giving in to a tantrum is not constructive

## Summary and Conclusion

This chapter completes presentation of several chapters on work on the self and other. It culminates in a dual-component model of the self in terms of self-definition and relatedness. I use this model later in the book in presenting a revised model of Maslow's hierarchy of needs. The chapter also presents a model of self-regulation based on the present Neo-Piagetian model. Portions of the next chapter follow upon this work. In the next chapter, I discuss the development of a concept related to hypercognition, that of the cognitive/socioaffective complex. This leads to work on multiple intelligences from a Neo-Piagetian perspective.

## References

Ayduk, O., Mendoza-Denton, R., Mischel, W., Downey, G., Peake, P. K., & Rodriguez, M. (2000). Regulating the interpersonal self: Strategic self-regulation for coping with rejection sensitivity. *Journal of Personality and Social Psychology, 79*, 776–792.

Bakan, D. (1966). *The duality of human existence: An essay on psychology and religion*. Chicago: Rand McNally.

Barkley, R. A. (2001). The executive functions and self-regulation: An evolutionary neuropsychological perspective. *Neuropsychology Review, 11*, 1–29.

Barkley, R. A. (2004). Attention deficit/hyperactivity disorder and self-regulation: Taking an evolutionary perspective on executive functioning. In R. F. Baumeister & K. D. Vohs (Eds.), *Handbook of self-regulation: Research, theory, and applications* (pp. 301–323). New York: Guilford Press.

Beebe, B., Jaffe, J., Buck, K., Chen, H., Cohen, P., Blatt, S. J., et al. (2007). Six-week postpartum maternal self-criticism and dependency predict 4-month mother-infant self-and interactive regulation. *Developmental Psychology, 43*, 1360–1376.

Bell, M. A., Greene, D. R., & Wolfe, C. D. (2010). Psychobiological mechanisms of cognition-emotion integration in early development. In S. D. Calkins & M. A. Bell (Eds.), *Child development at the intersection of emotion and cognition* (pp. 115–152). Washington: American Psychological Association.

Bell, M. A. (2011). A psychobiological perspective on working memory performance at 8 months of age. *Child Development, 82*.

Bell, M. A., & Deater-Deckard, K. (2007). Biological systems and the development of self-regulation: Integrating behavior, genetics, and psychophysiology. *Journal of Developmental & Behavioral Pediatrics, 28*, 409–420.

Bell, M. A., & Wolfe, C. D. (2004). Emotion and cognition: An intricately bound developmental process. *Child Development, 75*, 366–370.

Belsky, J., Bakermans-Kranenburg, M. J., & van IJzendoorn, M. H. (2007). For better and for worse: Differential susceptibility to environmental influences. *Current Directions in Psychological Science, 16*, 300–304.

Blair, C., & Dennis, T. (2010). An optimal balance: The integration of emotion and cognition in context. In S. D. Calkins & M. A. Bell (Eds.), *Child development at the intersection of emotion and cognition* (pp. 17–35). Washington: American Psychological Association.

Blair, C., Granger, D., & Razza, R. P. (2005). Cortisol reactivity is positively related to executive function in preschool children attending Head Start. *Child Development, 76*, 554–567.

Blair, C., Peters, R., & Granger, D. (2004). Physiological and neuropsychological correlates of approach/withdrawal behavior in preschool. *Developmental Psychobiology, 45*, 113–124.

Blair, C., & Razza, R. P. (2007). Relating effortful control, executive function, and false-belief understanding to emerging math and literacy ability in kindergarten. *Child Development, 78*, 647–663.

Blair, C., & Ursache, A. (2011). Executive functions and self-regulation: A bidirectional model. In K. D. Vohs & R. F. Baumeister (Eds.), *Handbook of self-regulation: Research, theory, and applications* (2nd ed., pp. 300–320). New York: Guilford Press.

Blatt, S. J. (1995). Representational structures in psycholopathology. In D. Cicchetti & S. Toth (Eds.), *Rochester symposium on developmental psychopathology: Vol. 6. Emotion, cognition, and representation* (pp. 1–33). Rochester: University of Rochester Press.

Blatt, S. J. (2008). *Polarities of experience: Relatedness and self-definition in personality development, psychopathology, and the therapeutic process*. Washington: American Psychological Association.

Blatt, S. J., Stayner, D., Auerbach, J., & Behrends, R. S. (1996). Change in object and self-representations in long-term, intensive, inpatient treatment of seriously disturbed adolescents and young adults. *Psychiatry: Interpersonal and Biological Processes, 59*, 82–107.

Bronson, M. B. (2000). *Self-regulation in early childhood: Nature and nurture*. New York: Guilford.

Buber, M. (1978). *I and Thou* (W. Kaufman, Trans.) New York: Scribner.

Burgdorf, J., & Panksepp, J. (2006). The neurobiology of positive emotions. *Neuroscience and Biobehavioral Reviews, 30*, 173–187.

Calkins, S. D., & Marcovitch, S. (2010). Emotion regulation and executive functioning in early development: Integrated mechanisms of control supporting adaptive functioning. In S. D. Calkins & M. A. Bell (Eds.), *Child development at the intersection of emotion and cognition* (pp. 37–57). Washington: American Psychological Association.

Carlson, S. M., & Moses, L. J. (2001). Individual differences in inhibitory control and children's theory of mind. *Child Development, 72*, 1032–1053.

Carlson, S. M., & Wang, T. (2007). Inhibitory control and emotion regulation in preschool children. *Cognitive Development, 22*, 489–510.

Carver, C. S., & White, T. L. (1994). Behavioral inhibition, behavioral activation, and affective responses to impending reward and punishment: The BIS/BAS scales. *Journal of Personality and Social Psychology, 67*, 319–333.

Case, R. (1985). *Intellectual development: Birth to adulthood*. Orlando: Academic Press.

Case, R. (1992). The role of the frontal lobes in the regulation of cognitive development. *Brain and Cognition, 20*, 51–73.

Chodorow, N. (1989). *Feminism and psychoanalytic theory*. New Haven: Yale University Press.

Ciairano, S., Visu-Petra, L., & Settanni, M. (2007). Executive inhibitory control and cooperative behavior during early school years: A follow up study. *Journal of Abnormal Child Psychology, 35*, 335–345.

Cortina, M., & Liotti, G. (2007, June). *Toward a multimotivational and intersubjective model of human nature*. Paper presented at the annual meeting of Rapaport-Klein Study Group, Massachusetts.

Cunningham, W. A., & Zelazo, P. D. (2007). Attitudes and evaluation: A social cognitive neuroscience perspective. *Trends in Cognitive Sciences, 11*, 97–104.

Deci, E. L., & Ryan, R. M. (1992). The initiation and regulation of instrinsically motivated learning and achievement. In A. K. Boggiano, T. S. Pittman, & S. Thane (Eds.), *Achievement and motivation: A social-developmental perspective. Cambridge studies in social and emotional development* (pp. 9–36). New York: Cambridge University Press.

Depue, R. A., & Collins, P. F. (1999). Neurobiology of the structure of personality: Dopamine, facilitation of incentive motivation and extraversion. *Behavioral and Brain Sciences, 22*, 491–569.

Diamond, A. (2002). Normal development of the prefrontal cortex from birth to young adulthood: Cognitive functions, anatomy, and biochemistry. In D. T. Stuss & R. T. Knight (Eds.), *Principles of frontal lobe function*, (pp. 466–503). New York: Oxford University Press.

Diamond, A. (2006). The early development of executive functions. In E. Bialystok & F. Craik (Eds.), *Lifespan cognition: Mechanisms of change* (pp. 70–95). New York: Oxford University Press.

Eigsti, I. M., Zayas, V., Mischel, W., Shoda, Y., Ayduk, O., Dadlani, M. B., et al. (2006). Predictive cognitive control from preschool to late adolescence and young adulthood. *Psychological Science, 17*, 478–484.

Emde, R. N. (1984). The affective self: Continuities and transformations from infancy. In J. D. Call (Ed.), *Frontiers of infant psychiatry* (pp. 38–54). New York: Basic Books.

Engle, R. W., & Kane, M. J. (2004). Executive attention, working memory capacity, and a two-factor theory of cognitive control. In B. Ross (Ed.), *The psychology of learning and motivation* (pp. 145–199). New York: Academic Press.

Erikson, E. H. (1963). *Childhood and society*. New York: Norton.

Erikson, E. H. (1968). *Identity: Youth and crisis*. New York: Norton.

Fischer, K. W. (1980). A theory of cognitive development: The control and construction of hierarchies of skills. *Psychological Review, 87*, 477–531.

Fox, E., & Riconscente, M. (2008). Metacognition and self-regulation in James, Piaget, and Vygotsky. *Educational Psychology Review, 20*, 373–389.

Garon, N., Bryson, S. E., & Smith, I. M. (2008). Executive function in preschoolers: A review using an integrative framework. *Psychological Bulletin, 134*, 31–60.

Geldhof, G. J., Little, T. D., & Colombo, J. (2010). Self-regulation across the life span. In R. M. Lerner & W. F. Overton (Eds.), *Handbook of life-span development: Vol. 1. Cognition, biology, and methods across the lifespan*. Hoboken: Wiley.

Geva, R., & Feldman, R. (2008). A neurobiological model for the effects of early brainstem functioning on the development of behavior and emotion regulation in infants: Implications for prenatal and perinatal risk. *Journal of Child Psychology and Psychiatry, 49*, 1031–1041.

Goto, Y., & O'Donnell, P. (2001). Network synchrony in the nucleus accumbens in vivo. *Journal of Neuroscience, 21*, 4498–4504.

Gray, J. A. (1987). *The psychology of fear and stress* (2nd ed.). New York: McGraw-Hill.

Greenspan, S. I. (1997). *Developmentally based psychotherapy*. Madison: International Universities Press.

Greenspan, S. I. (2008). A dynamic developmental model of mental health and mental illness. In A. Fogel, B. J. King, & S. G. Shanker (Eds.), *Human development in the Twenty-First century: Visionary ideas from systems scientists* (pp. 157–175). Cambridge: Cambridge University Press.

Hay, D. F., Payne, A., & Chadwick, A. (2004). Peer relations in childhood. *Journal of Child Psychology and Psychiatry, 45*, 84–108.

Jacques, S., & Marcovitch, S. (2010). Development of executive function across the life span. In R. M. Lerner & W. F. Overton (Eds.), *Handbook of life-span development: Vol. 1. Cognition, biology, and methods across the lifespan*. Hoboken: Wiley.

Jacques, S., & Zelazo, P. D. (2005). Language and the development of cognitive flexibility: Implications for theory of mind. In J. W. Astington & J. A. Baird (Eds.), *Why language matters for theory of mind* (pp. 144–162). Oxford: Oxford University Press.

James, W. (1890). *The principles of psychology* (Vol. 1 and 2). New York: Holt.

James, W. (1992). *Writings 1878-1899*. New York: The Library of America.

Kernberg, O. F. (1976). *Object relations theory and clinical psychoanalysis*. New York: Aronson.

Kochanska, G., Murray, K. T., & Harlan, E. T. (2000). Effortful control in early childhood: Continuity and change, antecedents and implications for social development. *Developmental Psychology, 36*, 220–232.

Kopp, C. B. (1982). Antecedents of self-regulation: A developmental perspective. *Developmental Psychology, 18*, 199–214.

Lehto, J. E., Juujarvi, P., Kooistra, L., & Pukkinen, L. (2003). Dimensions of executive functioning: Evidence from children. *British Journal of Developmental Psychology, 21*, 59–80.

Lengua, L. J. (2009). Effortful control in the context of socioeconomic and psychosocial risk. *APA Psychological Science Agenda, 23*(1). Retrieved from http://www.apa.org/science/psa/jan09-sci-brief.html

Lewis, M. D. (2010). Desire, dopamine, and conceptual development. In S. D. Calkins & M. A. Bell (Eds.), *Child development at the intersection of emotion and cognition* (pp. 175–199). Washington: American Psychological Association.

Lewis, M. D., & Todd, R. M. (2007). The self-regulating brain: Cortical-subcortical feedback and the development of intelligent action. *Cognitive Development, 22*, 406–430.

Lewis, M. D., Todd, R., & Xu, X. (2010). The development of emotion regulation: A neuropsychological perspective. In R. M. Lerner, M. E. Lamb, & A. M. Freund (Eds.), *Handbook of lifespan development: Vol. 2. Social and emotional development* (pp. 51–78). Hoboken: Wiley.

Luria, A. R. (1961). *The role of speech in the regulation of normal and abnormal behavior* (J. Tizard, Ed.). New York: Pergamon.

Mahler, M., Pine, F., & Bergman, A. (1975). *The psychological birth of the human infant*. New York: Basic Books.

Martin, J., & Failows, L. (2010). Executive function: Theoretical concerns. In B. W. Sokol, U. Müller, J. I. M. Carpendale, A. R. Young, & G. Iarocci (Eds.), *Self and social regulation: Social interaction and the development of social understanding and executive functions* (pp. 35–55). New York: Oxford University Press.

McAdams, D. P. (1985a). *Power, intimacy, and the life story: Personological inquiries into identity*. Homewood: Dorsey.

McAdams, D. P. (1985b). Understanding personal relationships: An interdisciplinary approach. In S. Duck & S. Perlman (Eds.), *Motivation and friendship* (pp. 85–105). Thousand Oaks: Sage.

McClelland, M. M., Pointz, C. C., Messersmith, E., & Tominey, S. (2010). Self-regulation: The integration of cognition and emotion. In R. Lerner & W. Overton (Eds.), *Handbook of lifespan human development: Vol. 1. Cognition, biology, and methods*. Hoboken: Wiley.

Mischel, W., & Ayduk, O. (2004). Willpower in a cognitive-affective processing system: The dynamics of delay of gratification. In R. F. Baumeister & K. D. Vohs (Eds.), *Handbook of self-regulation: Research, theory, and applications* (pp. 99–129). New York: Guilford Press.

Mischel, W., & Shoda, Y. (1995). A cognitive-affective system theory of personality: Reconceptualizing situation, dispositions, dynamics, and invariance in personality structure. *Psychological Review, 102*, 246–268.

Mischel, W., Shoda, Y., & Peake, P. K. (1988). The nature of adolescent competencies predicted by preschool delay of gratification. *Journal of Personality and Social Psychology, 54*, 687–696.

Miyake, A., Friedman, N. P., Emerson, M. J., Witzki, A. H., & Kowerter, A. (2000). The unity and diversity of executive functions and their contributions to complex "frontal lobe" tasks: A latent variable analysis. *Cognitive Psychology, 41*, 49–100.

Pascual-Leone, J. (1970). A mathematical model for the transitional rule in Piaget's developmental stages. *Acta Psychologica, 63*, 301–345.

Perlman, S. B., & Pelphrey, K. A. (2010). Regulatory brain development: Balancing emotion and cognition. *Social Neuroscience, 5*, 533–542.

Piaget, J. (1950). *The moral judgment of the child* (M. Gabain, Trans.). Glencoe: Free Press.

Piaget, J. (1954/1981). *Intelligence and affectivity: Their relationship during child development* (T. Brown & C. Kaegi, Trans. and Eds.). Palo Alto: Annual Reviews Monograph. (Original work published in 1954).

Piaget, J. (1964/1968). *Six psychological studies* (A. Tenzer, Trans.). New York: Random House (original work published in 1964).

Rogoff, B. (1990). *Apprenticeship in thinking: Cognitive development in social context*. New York: Oxford University Press.

Rothbart, M. K., & Bates, J. E. (2006). Temperament. In N. Eisenberg, W. Damon, & R. M. Lerner (Eds.), *Handbook of child psychology: Vol. 3. Social, emotional, and personality development* (6th ed., pp. 99–166). Hoboken: Wiley.

Ryan, R. M., & Deci, E. L. (2000a). Intrinsic and extrinsic motivations: Classic definitions and new directions. *Contemporary Educational Psychology, 25*, 54–67.

Ryan, R. M., & Deci, E. L. (2000b). Self-determination theory and the facilitation of intrinsic motivation, social development, and well-being. *American Psychologist, 55*, 68–78.

Sampson, E. E. (1985). Redecentralization of identity: Toward a revised concept of personal and social order. *American Psychologist, 40*, 1203–1211.

Sampson, E. E. (1988). The debate on individualism: Indigenous psychologies of the individual and their role in personal and societal functioning. *American Psychologist, 43*, 15–22.

Sander, L. W. (1975). Infant and caretaking environment: Investigation and conceptualization of adaptive behavior in a system of increasing complexity. In E. J. Anthony (Ed.), *Explorations in child psychiatry* (pp. 129–166). New York: Plenum.

Sander, L. W. (1999). Introductory comments. *Infant Mental Health Journal, 19*, 280–287.

Séquin, J. R., & Zelazo, P. D. (2005). Executive function in early physical aggression. In R. E. Tremblay, W. W. Hartup, & J. Archer (Eds.), *Developmental origins of aggression* (pp. 307–329). New York: Guilford Press.

Sokol, B. W., & Müller, U. (2007). The development of self-regulation: Toward the integration of cognition and emotion. *Cognitive Development, 22*, 401–405.

Sokol, B. W., Müller, U., Carpendale, J. I. M., Young, A. R., & Iarocci, G. (Eds.). (2010). *Self and social regulation: Social interaction and the development of social understanding and executive functions*. New York: Oxford University Press.

Stern, D. N. (1985). *The interpersonal world of the infant: A view from psychoanalysis and developmental psychology*. New York: Basic Books.

Strayhorn, J. M., Jr. (2002). Self-control: Theory and research. *Journal of the American Academy of Child & Adolescent Psychiatry, 41*, 7–16.

Thompson, R. A., Lewis, M. D., & Calkins, S. D. (2008). Reassessing emotion regulation. *Child Development Perspectives, 2*, 124–131.

Tomasello, M. (2003). The key is social cognition. In D. Gentner & S. Goldin-Meadow (Eds.), *Language in mind: Advances in the study of language and thought* (pp. 47–57). Cambridge: MIT.

Trentacosta, C. J., & Izard, C. E. (2007). Kindergarten children's emotion competence as a predictor of their academic competence in first grade. *Emotion and Academic Competence, 7*, 77–88.

Triandis, H. C. (2001). Individualism-collectivism and personality. *Journal of Personality, 69*, 907–938.

Vaughn, B. E., Kopp, C. B., & Krakow, J. B. (1984). The emergence and consolidation of self-control from 18 to 30 months of age: Normative trends and individual differences. *Child Development, 55*, 990–1004.

Vygotsky, L. S. (1929). The problem of the cultural development of the child. *Journal of Genetic Psychology, 36*, 415–434.

Vygotsky, L. S. (1962). *Thought and language*. Cambridge: MIT.

Vygotsky, L. S. (1978). *Mind in society: The development of higher psychological processes*. Cambridge: Harvard University Press.

Vygotsky, L. S. (1981a). The genesis of higher mental functions. In J. V. Wertsch (Ed.), *The concept of activity in Soviet psychology* (pp. 144-188) (J. V. Wertsch, Trans.). Armonk: Sharpe.

Vygotsky, L. S. (1981b). The development of higher forms of attention in childhood. In J. V. Wertsch (Ed.), *The concept of activity in Soviet psychology* (pp. 189-240) (J. V. Wertsch, Trans.). Armonk: Sharpe.

Vygotsky, L. S. (1986). *Thought and language* (A. Kozulin, Trans.). Cambridge: MIT.

White, R. W. (1963). Ego and reality in psychoanalytic theory. *Psychological Issues, 3*, No. 3 (Monograph #11).

Wolfe, C. D., & Bell, M. A. (2007). The integration of cognition and emotion during infancy and early childhood: Regulatory processes associated with the development of working memory. *Brain and Cognition, 65*, 3–13.

Woltering, S., & Lewis, M. D. (2009). Developmental pathways of emotion regulation in childhood: A neuropsychological perspective. *Mind, Brain, and Education, 3*, 160–169.

Zelazo, P. D., Carlson, S. M., & Kesek, A. (2008). The development of executive function in childhood. In C. Nelson & M. Luciana (Eds.), *Handbook of developmental cognitive neuroscience* (2nd ed., pp. 553–574). Cambridge: MIT Press.

Zelazo, P. D., & Jacques, S. (1996). Children's rule use: Representation, reflection, and cognitive control. In R. Vasta (Ed.), *Annals of child development: A research annal* (Vol. 12, pp. 119–176). London: Jessica Kingsley Press.

Zelazo, P. D., Müller, U., Frye, D., & Marcovitch, S. (2003). The development of executive function in early childhood. *Monographs of the Society for Research in Child Development, 68* (3), Serial No. 274.

Zelazo, P. D., Qu, L., & Kesek, A. C. (2010). Hot executive function: Emotion and the development of cognitive control. In S. D. Calkins & M. A. Bell (Eds.), *Child development at the intersection of emotion and cognition* (pp. 97–111). Washington: American Psychological Association.

# Chapter 17
# Cognitive/Socioaffective Complexes and Multiple Intelligences

## Introduction

In this chapter, I propose two conceptual innovations related to cognition and intelligence. Both build on the work of Demetriou and colleagues, as presented in Chap. 10. In terms of their concept of hypercognition, I expand it to include other executive and cognitive processes, as well as socioaffective ones. The new concept that I developed is termed cognitive/socioaffective complexes. They also described domains of intelligence. I expand this work into a revised concept of multiple intelligences. The intelligences relate to the stages of the present model, and the concept of domains has been included in the model.

## The Cognitive/Socioaffective Complex

### *Piagetian Work*

#### Action in Piaget

For Piaget, action served as the quintessential origin of thought (Vonèche, 2008). Cognition is embodied, and is neither divorced from context nor the actions underlying them, if not expressing them directly. For example, Piaget classified his child at the sixth sensorimotor substage of inventing new means by mental combination (Piaget, 1936/1952/1963). As an example of this substage, Piaget remarked that she wished to enlarge a slit of a match box, and she mimicked, or represented, the widening of the slit by opening and shutting her mouth with an increasing opening. The representation of the wish to open the matchbox is a symbolic one, but it was achieved by a simpler motor indication rather than verbally. The mouth movement "constitutes for her the means of thinking out the situation" (p. 75). By acting out the action with her mouth movement, the representation helped the child undertake a novel action relative

G. Young, *Development and Causality: Neo-Piagetian Perspectives*,
DOI 10.1007/978-1-4419-9422-6_17, © Springer Science+Business Media, LLC 2011

to past efforts to solve the problem. Vonèche concluded that from an embodied cognitive and Piagetian perspective, the body is the "workshop" of thinking.

Thelen (2008) added that sensorimotor processes do not change or stop after the infancy period, although they become more refined, quick, flexible, and general. There is not only temporal continuity in cognitive embodiment but also continuity relating to levels. Mental events are intertwined with perceptions and actions in real-world contexts; they are separated only heuristically. Becker (2006) related neurological findings to the question that Piaget raised about the action-related origins of thought. He pointed to the research on mirror neurons in monkeys, which often selectively discharge to observations of action, in particular.

### Development of Multiple Modes and Components of Intelligence

Another tack in Piagetian research has been for Francophone scholars to support North American notions that individual variations and contextual differences are important in development as individuals pass through Piagetian stages (Larivée, Normandeau, & Parent, 2000). This work has led these Francophone workers to develop a pluralistic and multidimensional model of cognitive development. For example, it is possible for a child to use a more adaptive propositional processing mode on some harder tasks and a less adaptive analogical processing mode on others, leading to the appearance that an easier task has been skipped (Lautrey, 1990a, 1990b, 1990c). The latter processing style predominates in early development, but it can be carried forward in older years. The propositional mode is general, analytic, sequential, logical, rule-based, and context-independent, whereas the analogical mode is global, holistic, script-based, prototypic, and context-dependent. Moreover, the two modes work together, with the propositional mode providing possible solutions to problems that the analogical mode narrows down.

## *Multiple Processing Modes*

In this regard, it would appear to me that Thelen's notion that sensorimotor processes exhibit temporal continuity, or are carried forward in development in their own right, complicate the concept of propositional and analogical processing modes. For example, there could be sensorimotor processing mode, as well. Indeed, each step in development according to Neo-Piagetian models could be associated with a new processing mode. Moreover, if this were the case, there would be no reason that multiple processing modes could not be used in concert.

As the older child solves a problem, the child could be using more than two processing modes – for example, a sensorimotor, analogical, and propositional one. We are used to thinking that the child uses the form of processing associated with its highest current level of development, or at least the most advanced one that seems to be at play as it solves a problem. More likely, different strategies are being used together, perhaps simultaneously but perhaps sequentially, as needed, as the child advances in its thought processes.

Therefore, other stages comprised in the Neo-Piagetian approach to cognitive development should be associated with their own processing modes, and as the developing person moves into the teen and adult years, these can come to the forefront, as well, but still work in concert with the others. Consequently, in terms of later Neo-Piagetian stages, the last developing processing modes that should be developing according to the present hypothesis relate to the acquisition of abstract propositional processing and postformal collective (e.g., dialectical, relativistic) processing, consistent with Piaget's description of the teen years involving formal thought and present Neo-Piagetian model that the postformal stage involves collective intelligence (see Table 17.1).

The suggestion that there are five processing modes that develop, one per major developmental stage, is consistent with arguments advanced elsewhere in the book that there are five types of memory involved, as well, in cognitive development (see Chap. 24), that is, a new one evolving with each major stage in development. Working from Thelen's (2008) argument that sensorimotor processes are carried forward in development, this suggests that the developing person is not simply passing through the developing stages one by one and abandoning earlier-developed ones as they are incorporated in to more advanced ones in a sequential manner. Rather, when faced with difficulties and barriers, the developing person could resort to earlier developed cognitive schemes and modes, or use a combination or coupling of them, such as coordination of sensorimotor schemes and concrete operations, to increase cognitive skill and functioning.

**Table 17.1** Processing mode, memory, and executive skills at each stage of development

| Cognitive stage | Processing mode | Memory | Executive |
|---|---|---|---|
| Reflexive | Reflexive | Perceptual | Nonlogical |
| Sensorimotor | Sensorimotor | Procedural | Prelogical |
| Perioperational | Analogical/propositional | Semantic/episodic | Perilogical |
| Preoperational | Analogical | Semantic | Quasilogical |
| Concrete operational | Concrete propositional | Episodic | Logical |
| Abstract (formal) | Abstract propositional | Abstract | Hyperlogical |
| Collective intelligence | Collective propositional | Collective | Collective superordinate logical |

The table indicates the five cognitive stages of the present model, along with the two steps in the perioperational stage. These steps are the classic Piagetian stages of preoperations and concrete operations. This procedure gives seven steps to consider in this table and others related to it (five stages, and one with two steps). For each of these steps in cognitive development, I list the corresponding processing mode, type of memory, and executive skill. The concept of evolving processing mode derives from contemporary Piagetian work. That memory can evolve in concert with the stages derives from Piagetian work and from work in attachment. In terms of executive skills, they involve cognitive and affective components, and the labels used reflect Baldwin's (1894) original terms for the stages of cognitive development that Piaget had modified. I added some terminology to the steps in this column that are consistent with the stages of the present model

## *Multiple Components*

Aside from the concept that the cognitive stages or even substages and their associated modes are capable of forming adaptive complexes to solve problems, the same should apply to their component processes. Developing cognition is mediated by components in attention, perception, memory, learning, executive processing, regulatory and control mechanisms, as Piaget and the Neo-Piagetians have underscored. Space limitations preclude examining these acquisitions in detail. However, the present point of view is that they evolve in concert with the cognitive ones. There are implications for developing cognition that arise from this suggestion.

First, this means that cognitive components should show qualitative advances consistent with developmental advances in stages and substages in development. That is, cognitive components should shift qualitatively with each new cognitive stage or substage that develops. Second, this means that just as signs of coupled or multiple stages and substages could be evident in any one problem-solving activity or cognitive task, the same applies to the components involved. There might be several memory processes at work in a particular cognitive context, or several self-regulatory modes at work in a particular social context, depending on the stage- or substage-related resources needed for optimal adaptation.

## *Adaptation*

Fitting the dynamical theme in the present work, neither the cognitive nor the processing modes and other support mechanisms should be considered to have priority in leading, contributing to, and influencing development. Similarly, in cognitive couplings or multiple agglomerations, neither the more advanced stage/substage in evidence nor its associated components should be considered to have priority in leading, contributing to, and influencing development. No matter what seems to predominate in cognitive activity, when there are multiple levels or components at play, the relations over different levels and the relations over different components form a system.

In this regard, the whole that develops in the system in the cognitive-processing complex serves adaptive ends. Cognition is not about thinking, per se. It is about being part of an adaptive problem-solving and problem-finding process requiring the full gamut of contributing components to the activity. Cognition is not just aimed at honing logical skills to meet intellectual challenges. It is about using an integrated cognitive-emotional-processing capacity to adapt pragmatically to the subtleties of context and the immediate goals that are guiding behavior in it or that it is bringing about. At the same time, cognition is about long-term life plans and goals. Even the child possesses these types of plans, although they are partly created for her or him (e.g., get through the school year).

Finally, the context is often social, whether in terms of dyads, groups, or wider institutions and culture. Cognition is meant not merely to solve and find social problems, but to integrate in dyad and larger group mechanisms that help us function in our daily lives and with our life goals, while contributing to others in the group striving for the same, and while contributing to the group in its own collective activities, adaptation, and goals.

## Memory

In the last chapter, I have described executive functions and self-regulation. These concepts refer to organization, planning, shifting set, inhibition, self-control, goal setting, monitoring and feedback, adjusting to context as a result, etc. They are part and parcel of the support mechanisms for cognition that I have been describing. Memory is intrinsically involved here, as well. Working memory is the mental scratchpad with which we work to solve problems. It is difficult to plan effectively and monitor the progress being made toward resolution without the ability to keep in mind the problem, goal, plan, and its actual unfolding and adjustments required. Attention is especially pertinent to successful executive functioning, as well. The person functioning in context must be able to selectively attend to salient stimuli, put aside interferences, divide and combine attention, as required, keep in mind the goal of the attention, etc.

In the next part of the book, in presenting research on attachment, I discuss the development of memory in terms of five steps that parallel the five stages of the present model. These are referred to as perceptual, procedural, semantic-episodic, abstract, and collective types of memories. In that part of the present work, I also show how internal working models described in attachment pass through the stages of the present model.

Moreover, I show how they develop through the five substages of the five stages of the present model. The same modeling process should apply quite readily to the psychological capacities under consideration in the present section. That is, one can consider that each of the types of memory listed passes through five steps in its development that corresponds to the substages of the present model. For example, in the infancy period, procedural memory should reflect the evolution through the sequence of coordination, hierarchization, systematization, multiplication, and integration.

Note that the change in memory in the first 2 years that I am suggesting is not a quantitative one of increased memory space. Rather, each of the five steps posited for the development of memory in infancy involves a particular qualitative advance tied to the particular cognitive substage with which it appears to develop in parallel.

Just as processing mode and memory are being posited to change qualitatively as they pass through the five stages of the present model, while contributing to their development, the same can be said of the executive processes. Globally, they can be characterized as reflexive, sensorimotor, perioperational, abstract, and collective. In the table, though, I model the development of executive processing over developmental stages by using the terms that had been created previously in the present work for the related topic of regulation. The series that I had created involved an adaptation of the work of Baldwin, and it gave the developmental sequence of nonlogical, prelogical, quasilogical, logical, hyperlogical, and collective logical for this series. I have applied this series to executive processing in the same way in the table.

## *Multiple and Parallel Cognition*

Do these various cognitive and support mechanisms disappear as new ones emerge in the developmental sequence provided? Are they supplanted? Do they become incorporated in subsequent steps, and lost from usage? Not at all. They develop in tandem with new ones as they emerge. They keep functioning, and provide complementary perspectives to problem-solving and adaptation. We do not just function from the highest levels of cognition and support mechanisms available to us, although they function at the apex of our skills. We revert to others, as needed. This could be especially true when new levels of skill emerge or when multiple perspectives are needed in problem-solving. We begin with earlier levels and advance to an integrative use of some or all of them as needed for problem-solving and adaptive resolution.

Does this mean that we regress when we use lower-level skills? Not at all. This could happen for socioaffective reasons. Or, regressions might be initial reaction to new problems and challenges in order to get perspective and a quicker understanding of the problem or context with more automatic and well-developed skills, even if they are not as high as others in our repertoire. However, this slipping back is not regression, because it is an adaptive strategy. It is like practicing the basics in a skill, which seems like a lower-level step, but it really is part of the full organization needed to take the skill to the next level.

Does a skill developed previously at one level continue to exist at the same level as the person develops? Not at all. Think of sensorimotor schemes. They evolve into superior perceptual and motoric complexes that allow for expert athletic prowess, for example. Moreover, they do not exist apart from the other available governing modalities in behavior. They are attached to and ratcheted up to their levels. The Olympic figure skater has mastered an organizational plan through the collective participation in schooling and coaching that is quite advanced cognitively. The skater uses the embodied cognition of the sensorimotor schemes tied to the mental tools that are cognitively embodied. It is no wonder that we are learning that the cerebellum, linked to motoric action, is still developing in the adult years, a period of development that had been considered the unique province of the frontal lobes.

In this regard, it appears to me that sensorimotor skills initiated in the infancy period pass through four more stages in development, linked to the stages of the present model. In addition, the perioperational skills developed in the next period pass through three stages, and so on.

## *Development of Intelligence*

How do all the component parts related to cognition and adaptation fit together? In the present section, I argue that a comprehensive account of the development of intelligence needs to resist compartmentalizing it. The study of intelligence differs fundamentally in the psychometric and Piagetian traditions, for example. The first seeks measurements of individual differences related to skills that correlate with educational success, in particular. The second is associated with models that are more universal and not focused on obtaining quotients or scores that summarize intellectual performance. Individual differences are minimized, although they are discussed with more frequency in the Neo-Piagetian tradition.

Another distinction in the field that needs more of an integrated account concerns the one about traditional cognitive vs. emotional intelligence. In this regard, to what degree can a combined approach synthesize these differences into a framework that respects both?

Further, is intelligence really unitary and universal and can it be represented by one number or by one sequence of steps in development? Or, are there alternate trajectories, different pathways for different levels, multiple intelligences, and so on?

Are the skills that we associate with intelligence all measured on traditional tests, or does the Piagetian perspective tap different skills so that an integrated view is worthwhile considering? Perhaps the two approaches are complementary not because the former seeks continuity and stability in measurement over age, whereas the latter is qualitatively developmental and concentrates on stages of change, but because they differ fundamentally on their conceptions of the nature of intelligence and cognition.

Perhaps cognition and intelligence themselves are fundamentally different and not just variations in human behavior, belonging to the same category. What exactly is their relationship? Does intelligence serve cognition, or vice versa? It can be argued that cognition is a fundamental, core characteristic of human functioning, whereas intelligence concerns the more general notion of adaptation to the environment, which is predicated in part on what intelligence tests try to measure and their relationship to school and later vocational success. However, it also can be argued that cognition provides the epistemic understanding of knowledge and the apperception of reality needed for intelligent adaptation, so that it is primary, whereas intelligence derives from its good functioning and application.

But consider that both arguments are incorrect, because contemporary conceptions of intelligence and cognition are not complete, miss important components, artificially separate other components, etc. Perhaps cognition and intelligence are too "cold," in the sense that traditionally they do include psycho-affective components. In addition, perhaps each has missed part of the essential goals to which they are oriented. For example, cognition is now understood as quite social and intelligence as emotional, too. Although both serve and grow through the application of critical thinking and effective reasoning, it is not clear that the socioaffective matrix in which cognition is embedded is given equal weight in their conceptualizations.

What about individual, group, and sex differences? Can a combined view allow better differentiation and explanation that does not lapse into sterile, stereotyped arguments? Can it give a scaffold that helps explain any type of individual and group difference at the level of content, without lapsing into automatic thoughts about cause?

Can a combined model be constructed that represents well the increasingly important biopsychosocial view? Can it avoid the polar, limiting arguments that genetics and biology especially constitute the primary determinants of behavior, or that, in contrast, social context and culture are the primary sources?

## *An Integrating Cognition*

It appears that what is needed is a developmental account of a combined development, intelligence, cognitive, regulatory, affective, and contextualist model that asks how the developing person accomplishes adaptation as a whole both in each moment and over the lifetime. How is information processed and handled, and how can it influence executive processes and decisions taken in context? What role do cognitive functions play in the dynamics, and what factors influence their content and structure as they develop?

Neo-Piagetians ask these types of questions and try to find answers in the developmental products and processes that they study, including in real time and developmental time. They increasingly include in their work the full range of influences on cognitive development, including brain processes in real time and the effects of interactions with parents and teachers in distal time. However, there has not been a comprehensive model integrating cognitive dynamics with Neo-Piagetian models, although Case and Fischer have made good progress in these regards.

Before presenting my ideas on this matter, I consider the whole that is cognition, intelligence, processing mode, memory, attention, executive processing, self-regulation, etc. In particular, I examine to what degree their development is consistent with the present model of five stages in development. For me, they form the heart of adaptive intelligence and related processes, and they constitute a whole system of interacting parts. Adaptation refers to the evolutionary underpinnings to behavior and to the moment-to-moment adjustments in context toward the goals to which it is aimed and to the plans being implemented to achieve them. These two types of adaptation can be considered as biological and psychological, respectively, for purposes of the present discussion.

In terms of biological adaptation, behavior is not selected in isolation, but systems that guide behavior toward adaptive ends, or fitness, are selected as wider integrations. According to my understanding, in our evolutionary past, intelligence was not selected distinct from attention, motivation, curiosity, etc. In terms of psychological adaptation, behavior cannot be adaptive if it splits into incoherent components or does not integrate the intellectual-cognitive and the socioaffective/emotional sides as it adjusts to ongoing context.

If we isolate any one component term of its associated complex of components in order to represent them, we risk that the complex of which they are apart is not evident, and the problems associated with the one term relative to the contributions of the others toward understanding the complex are lost.

In terms of the present topic, that of biological and psychological adaptation of cognition, intelligence, and related dynamics, the various components of the complex include the intellectual/cognitive, socioaffective/emotional, cultural/contextual adaptive, and organismic whole. However, for simplicity I suggest that a good label for the adaptive behavioral complex under discussion is the *cognitive/socioaffective complex*. In the following, I present a model of how it might evolve through the five stages of the present model.

## Development of the Cognitive/Socioaffective Complex

### *The Complex*

The cognitive/socioaffective complex is a hypersupervisory or hyperbehavioral mechanism that coalesces out of the assembly of its component parts as behavior unfolds. It is not a preprogrammed central or neuronal pattern-generator in behavior, but an online, constructed organizing mechanism that pulls together the aspects of the diverse components needed for adaptive functioning in context. It is constructed moment-to-moment in context to facilitate the coalescing components achieving the person's goals through the plans constructed that accompany them. As each constructed complex takes on the semblance of previously constructed exemplars, more generalized complexes that might be automatically evoked are created, but they become part of the ongoing adaptation, and can be altered to fit the specifics of the context. The history of created complexes does influence the construction of present ones, but they are always reconstructed to fit the present context.

The cognitive/socioaffective complex represents an intermediate level between brain and behavior, or stimulus and response, and it is situated between core processes, such as cognition and affect, on the one hand, and action tendencies or motor activities, on the other hand. Reductionists will argue that it is merely a hypothetical construct that might help us communicate about behavior, like in the case of its constituent terms of cognition and affect, but that it has no independent reality; however, I am not reifying it in the manner in which it is being presented. It reflects the working of a different level of the person's whole behavioral system in context, and consequently is conceived of having both bottom-up influences on it and having a top-down influence on its components. However, it is not an icon in the brain, neuronal circuitry, or brain-behavior relationship, being a fixed psychological or biological entity, nor is it conceived of anything like the seat of will, motivation, consciousness, and so on.

Simply enough, the concept of cognitive/socioaffective complexes represents the working of neural maps, both local and far reaching, of its constituent components as they coordinate together to address the adaptive demands and difficulties confronting individuals. It brings a level of coherence in conceptualizing psychological activity that might be missing otherwise, and by understanding its origins as an adaptive behavioral complex, I open it to discussion that is at once biological and psychological.

With the advent of each developmental stage and substage of the present model, I posit that the complex evolves according to the characteristics of the stage. It is at the high-end of cognitive activity, integrating cognitive-intellectual and socioaffective/emotional components in context, so that it influences the characteristics of the substage with which it is associated at any one time through its repeated and ongoing construction in context.

As the complex develops through the stages and acquires an increasing complexity, sophistication, and flexibility, it moves from a fixed, reflexive processing mechanism to an increasingly logical one. In this regard, in the table, I list the types of executive processing that I have related to each of the stages in the model, as presented in Table 17.1. These executive processing types range from nonlogical and prelogical ones to hyperlogical and collective logical ones. Recall that the terms created reflect the ones proposed by Baldwin for his model of the stages of cognitive development before Piaget had reworked it.

In addition, the type of adaptation that each level of the complex can be part of is limited by the stage with which it is associated. That is, although biological and psychological adaptation are important goals of the complex, the adaptation itself evolves, contingent upon the advances being made in the development of the complex.

## *The Stages*

The adaptation that should be evident in the reflexive stage is the most basic one possible. Stimuli lead to adaptive reactions, but these are not only the spinal cord mediated type. Already in this stage, patterns of response are developing that are sensitive to contextual variations, as in sucking.

Whereas the reflexive level of the complex can be considered to organize the most basic adaptation to context, the next one associated with the sensorimotor stage in the infant becomes social, and so can be considered a co-adaptive function. The infant adapts, but in the context of an active holding frame created by caregivers.

As the child grows and enters the perioperational stage (preoperations and concrete operations), the complex takes on the character of facilitating more varied and complex social adaptation beyond the immediate caregiving environment. In this regard, I have labeled the adaptation that accompanies the complex in the perioperational stage as group adaptive. For the preoperational phase, this would refer to other-adaptive functions, such as with peers, playmates, significant others beyond caregivers. As the child enters the phase of concrete operations, I consider the complex to be an educationally adaptive one. This does not refer to the school system only, but to any type of guided participation, expert scaffolding, teacher instruction, and so on.

For the abstract complex, the type of adaptation refers to self-group dynamics, which are so important to teenagers. They move beyond the structure set up by adults at school and other settings to give importance to the groups in which they insert themselves. At the same time, the onset of their quest for a personal identity becomes salient.

For the adult who enters the stage of collective intelligence, the adaptive complex refers to more than simple passive adaptation but to creative adaptation, for example, in altering the environment, the problem, etc., to fit the individuality and extant skills of the person. The adaptation is still a self-group reciprocal one, but the role of the person takes on more import, through the accentuation of the individuation taking place at this age; moreover, the role of the group is magnified, as well, through the collective group processes that the individual permits the self to integrate into and contribute to, as in the example of brainstorming.

For each stage in the development of the cognitive/socioaffective complex, I provide an integrating label reflective of its associated cognitive stage, executive process, and adaptive function (see the last column in Table 17.2). Therefore, the first complex that develops in the reflex stage is considered a reflexive, nonlogical,

**Table 17.2** Stages in the development of the cognitive/socioaffective complex

| Cognitive stage | Executive processing | Adaptive process | Cognitive/socioaffective complex |
|---|---|---|---|
| Reflexive | Nonlogical | Adaptive | Reflexive, nonlogical adaptive |
| Sensorimotor | Prelogical | Co-adaptive | Sensorimotor, prelogical co-adaptive |
| Perioperational | Perilogical | Group adaptive | Perioperational, perilogical group adaptive |
| Preoperational | Quasilogical | Other | Preoperational, quasilogical other adaptive |
| Concrete operational | Logical | Educational adaptive | Concrete operational, logical educational adaptive |
| Abstract (formal) | Hyperlogical | Self-group adaptive | Abstract, hyperlogical self-group adaptive |
| Collective intelligence | Collective superordinate logical | Self-group creative | Collective, superordinate logical self-group creative |

Demetriou, Spanoudis, and Mouyi (2010) have described a hypercognitive system that has an integrating, building, and supervisory function in cognitive activity. The present work offers a similar model, but it includes a socioaffective aspect. It incorporates executive skills, also considered as a higher-order cognitive activity. I refer to the combined hypercognitive concept as the cognitive/socioaffective complex. I indicate how it evolves as the developing person passes through the cognitive stages and phases of the present model. The developing complex and underlying cognitive stage capacities permit adaptation to context, and the range of the adaptation is considered to increase with each stage. This helps give the sum of the major characteristics at each stage of the evolving complex adaptive one. Next, the sensorimotor infant develops a cognitive/socioaffective complex that is sensorimotor, nonlogical, and co-adaptive in nature. Third, the growing child develops a perioperational, perilogical, group adaptive complex. It is hypothesized to develop in two phases – the preoperational, quasilogical, and other-adaptive one and the concrete operational, logical, and educationally adaptive one. In the adolescent, the complex takes the form of an abstract, hyperlogical, self-group adaptation, and in the adult it is collectively intelligent and logical, permitting self-group creative adaptation.

To conclude, I have described five stages in the development of the cognitive/socioaffective complex according to the stages of the present model. They can develop according to the five substages that recur cyclically in the present model.

Presentation of this concept of the complex prepares the way for a discussion of multiple intelligences. The present hypothesis is that the type of cognitive/socioaffective complex that develops in each cognitive stage of the present model indicates the evolution of a different, more advanced type of intelligence. This implies that there are five types or modes of multiple intelligences that could appear in development, one in association with each stage of the present model.

## Comments

This conceptualization presents two points of discussion. First, how does the model move from the concept of five types of cognitive/socioaffective complexes to one of five types of intelligence? Second, how does the concept being elaborated square with current conceptions of multiple intelligences?

For the first question, in effect, I am asking how the cognitive/socioaffective complexes being described relate to a wider understanding of intelligence. In this regard, I note that the complexes are considered mediating mechanisms only, and actual functional adaptation by behavior in context defines their effectiveness. Second, because they are mediating mechanisms, they do not represent behavior, per se, but are inferred processes that coalesce in the cognitive/socioemotive organization of the developing person to help in functional adaptation and problem-solving.

Therefore, in order to derive a functional, adaptive intelligence from the present model of cognitive substages, one needs to consider the outcome of the application of the cognitive skills involved. Intelligence concerns successful application and resolution of problems, not just the possession of necessary cognitive and related skills. This means consideration of person variables, such as personality, temperament, emotion, motivation, effort, persistence, curiosity, coping abilities, speed of processing, and so on. It is beyond the scope of the present work to engage in a full-scale analysis of intelligent activity along these lines. Suffice it to say that individuals vary in the degree of their application and success in resolving problems based on factors such as these. In addition, re-conceptualization of intellectual disability by Schalock et al. (2010) is based on a tripartite model of (a) intellectual skill, (b) competencies in activities of daily living and other functional adaptations, and (c) degree of environmental support. The concept removes the intellectual disability from being inherent in the developing person and places it in the interactive product of the person's functioning in the environment and the degree of support offered by the environment.

Contemporary models of normal intellectual development should take notice of this interactive model of intelligence. If intelligence is defined in terms of successful adaptation, a comprehensive account should include right in it different degrees of environmental support. If it concerns how the individual fares in environmental adaptation, it should take into account person variables that influence outcome. By having an integrated account of intelligence in terms of these factors, the model can move beyond (but without dropping) prediction of school success as a cardinal goal to understanding actual coparticipatory success in solving problems and in understanding the environment, both animate and inanimate, as a cardinal goal. This will mean including genuine developmental models of intellectual/cognitive functioning, how the quality changes and understanding the processes behind the changes, and not just focusing on quantitative measures (although I am not suggesting that we should drop them).

In the following, I offer an integrative model of intelligence based on Neo-Piagetian, traditional, and multiple intelligence concepts. The model responds to many of the questions posed above on the nature of intelligence.

## Multiple Intelligences

### *Models of Multiple Intelligences*

What is the implication of the present model for the concept of multiple intelligences? The works of Gardner (1993, 1999) and of Demetriou, Spanoudis, and Mouyi (2010; Demetriou, Mouyi, & Spanoudis, 2010) both help toward providing an answer. I have reviewed the work of Demetriou et al. in a prior chapter (see Chap. 10). Briefly, in the present chapter I expand on their concepts of hypercognition and domains of intelligence.

Gardner developed his model of multiple intelligences to account for the limits of traditional models of intelligence. He had two major criticisms of the traditional models. First, traditional models of intelligence were limited in their understanding of intelligence. They were based too much on linguistic, verbal, mathematical, and spatial or performance abilities. He understood that intelligence also includes other types, such as musical intelligence and social intelligence (see Table 17.3). Second, he understood that the development of intelligence takes place somewhat independently in the various areas. There is not just one number that can summarize a person's intellectual capacity. Each type of intelligence develops according to the individual's strengths, weaknesses, environmental experience, and so forth. Gardner did not have an extensive empirical program to evaluate his theory, but he reviewed

**Table 17.3** Gardner's theory of multiple intelligences

| Type of intelligence | Description | Examples |
|---|---|---|
| Linguistic intelligence | Sensitivity to the meanings and sounds of words; mastery of syntax; appreciation of the ways language can be used | Poet<br>Political speaking<br>Teacher |
| Logical-mathematical intelligence | Understanding of objects and symbols, of the actions that can be performed on them, and of the relations between these actions; ability for abstraction; ability to identify problems and seek explanations | Mathematician<br>Scientist |
| Spatial intelligence | Capacity to perceive the visual world accurately, to perform transformations upon perceptions, and to recreate aspects of visual experience in the absence of physical stimuli; sensitivity to tension, balance, and composition; ability to detect similar patterns | Artist<br>Engineer<br>Chess master |
| Musical intelligence | Sensitivity to individual tones and phrases of music; an understanding of ways to combine tones and phrases into larger musical rhythms and structures; awareness of emotional aspects of music | Musician<br>Composer |
| Naturalistic intelligence | Sensitivity and understanding of plants, animals, and other aspects of nature | Biologist |
| Bodily kinesthetic intelligence | Use of one's body in highly skilled ways for expressive or goal-directed purposes; capacity to handle objects skillfully | Dancer<br>Athlete<br>Actor |
| Intrapersonal intelligence | Access to one's own feeling of life; ability to draw on one's emotions to guide and understand one's behavior | Novelist<br>Therapist<br>Patient |
| Interpersonal intelligence | Ability to notice and make distinctions among the moods, temperaments, motivations, and intentions of other people and potentially to act on this knowledge | Political leader<br>Religious leader<br>Parent<br>Teacher<br>Therapist |



Gardner (1999) had developed the concept of multiple intelligences. His approach contrasts with both the psychometric tradition, which seeks an intelligence quotient to represent intelligence, and the cognitive developmental approach, which seeks stages and substages in development. Gardner (1983) added spiritual and existential intelligences to his previously published list of multiple intelligences, as well as a limited form of moral intelligence. His original list before contained seven intelligences. He used eight criteria for determining whether a type of intelligence should be included on the list. He did not deny that other types could be added. He argued that because there are a variety of types and they are independent, each person has a unique profile of strengths and weaknesses in intelligence. He was aware of the dangers of proliferating intelligences and possible dilution of the concept the scientific literature in its support, for example, relating it to people with brain damage and, at the other extreme, prodigies early in life.

Sternberg (2000) is another theorist who developed an alternative view of intelligence. He emphasized that intelligence involves successful adaptation to the environment within one's personal capabilities and sociocultural context. People do not only adapt to the environment, they also select environments that can promote their success. In his triarchic model of intelligence, he describes three major components to intelligence. The first involves analytic abilities as measured by standard intelligence tests. However, for Sternberg, intelligence involves more than what is measured by intelligence test scores. Therefore, he argued that a second important component of intelligence involves practical or pragmatic abilities. This includes real-life reasoning about everyday problems, including social problems. In the third component of his model of intelligence, Sternberg pointed to creative abilities, for example, inventing novel techniques to tackle novel circumstances.

## *Present Model*

### Normative Development

In the Neo-Piagetian model of multiple intelligences that I have constructed, I based myself on the work of Gardner and Sternberg, but modified greatly their concepts. The point of departure of the present model is that I emphasize that as individuals develop through the Neo-Piagetian stages, they are developing qualitatively different intelligences in each stage. Given that there are five major Neo-Piagetian stages in the present model, I hypothesize that there are five major types of intelligences, as listed in Fig. 17.1. Each of the cognitive stages witnesses the development of cognitive/socioaffective complexes that help the individual understand the environment and solve the problems derived from it.

According to the present model, Gardner did not describe multiple intelligences, per se, yet his work is essential to the present model. That is, for the five major types of Neo-Piagetian intelligences that the present model describes, it can be applied to any of the nine domains described by Gardner. In effect, we can envisage a table with five multiple intelligences in the left hand column and nine kinds of domains horizontal to it in a row above the column. The scientific task would be to describe how the developing person acquires increasingly complex skills in the nine domains as they develop through the five stages and their associated type of intelligence.

The research on multiple intelligences does not generally support the concept as presented by Gardner (e.g., Sternberg, 1983; Waterhouse, 2006a, 2006b). This is consistent with the approach of the present model of not using directly Gardner's concept of multiple intelligences in defining the different types suggested by the five Neo-Piagetian stages.

Sternberg (2000) also contributed to the present model of multiple intelligences presented in Fig. 17.1. His model addresses the supplementary intellectual areas

| Intelligence/ Cognitive Stage[1] (after Young) | Cognitive/ Socio-affective Complex (Young) | Domain/ Skill (after Gardner)[2] | Adaptive Intelligence Step (after Sternberg)[3] | Degree of Speed, Effort, Motivation, Curiosity | Degree of Environmental Support (abuse to scaffolding)[4] |
|---|---|---|---|---|---|
| | | X | X | X | X |
| Reflexive | Reflexive Nonlogical Adaptive | Verbal-Linguistic | Analytic | Poor | Poor |
| Sensorimotor | Sensorimotor Prelogical Co-Adaptive | Visual-Spatial | Pragmatic | Borderline | Borderline |
| Periopera-tional | Perioperational Perilogical Group adaptive | Logico-Mathematical | Creative | Passable | Passable |
| Preopera-tional | Preoperational Quasi-logical Other adaptive | Bodily-Kinesthetic | | Very Good | Very Good |
| Concrete operational | Concrete operational Logical Educational adaptive | Musical-Rhythmic | | Excellent | Excellent |
| Abstract (Formal) | Abstract Hyperlogical Self-Group adaptive | Interpersonal | | | |
| Collective Intelligence | Collective Superordinate logical Self-Group creative | Intrapersonal | | | |
| | | Naturalistic | | | |
| | | Existential | | | |

**Fig. 17.1** Neo-Piagetian model of development of multiple intelligences: person × environment interaction. *1*, Each stage passes through five substages in the present model (coordination, hierarchization, systematization, multiplication, and integration). *2*, The nine multiple intelligences proposed by Gardner are considered domains. Each might develop through the five multiple intelligences that are proposed based on the present Neo-Piagetian cognitive developmental model (as well as through the substages). Other domains are possible, depending on skill development. *3*, The three components of Sternberg's triarchic theory correspond to steps in problem resolution. First, the developing individual tries to ascertain the problem or task at hand. Then, a pragmatic application of appropriate solution(s) is entertained. If the solution(s) do not work, perhaps the individual constructs and implements more creative solution(s). *4*, Not all possible personal or environmental factors are listed in last two columns. Three impressions are possible – average, best possible considering lowest, and best possible considering highest. Simpler or more complex scales

that are not considered in traditional accounts of intelligence, such as the pragmatic and creative ones (traditional models usually emphasize the analytic ones). However, the way I used his work to fill out the present model is in the following way. I understood that one way of understanding problem-solving is that individuals pass through three phases. First, they analyze the context, and then they apply pragmatic solutions. If these fail, they might try to find creative innovations. It is not only necessary to understand the types of the intelligence and the domains in which they could be applied. It is also necessary to understand the steps in the problem-solving process, and Sternberg has helped this way, although there are more complex models.

Do we have enough to understand the working of multiple intelligences in successful environmental adaptation? A full model of intelligence needs to consider the person and the context. The last two columns of Fig. 17.1 indicate that developing individuals apply themselves with different qualitative degrees of effort, motivation, and so on. Moreover, the figure indicates that the environment provides different degrees or qualities of support. When the latter two dimensions are optimal, the application of intellectual skills to the problems facing individuals has a better chance of success.

In the end, intelligence is about adaptation to the environment and, as Sternberg argues, selecting the appropriate environment and modifying it could be part of the process. A full developmental model of multiple intelligences needs to consider the Person × Environment interaction in concert with the different types of intelligence, the domains to which they are applied, and the problem-solving process.

**Fig. 17.1** (continued) could be constructed for these columns.
The present Neo-Piagetian model of multiple intelligences departs from traditional approaches by considering Neo-Piagetian stages as types of intelligence. These do not disappear in development, but remain functional and improve even as higher-order stages emerge. Even sensorimotor intelligence is a mode available to the adult. The traditional concept of multiple intelligences refers to Gardner's nine types, in particular. In the present model, Gardner's types refer to domains. Each domain is understood to develop through the different stages/intelligences of the model. This improves on the Gardner model by adding the understanding that each domain can develop through stages. Other factors to consider in the development of these intelligences concern the efficacy of the developing person's underlying cognitive architecture, problem-solving capacity, and environmental support. The cognitive architecture includes the cognitive/socioaffective complex, which is like Demetriou's and colleagues' hypercognitive system, but it adds a socioemotional component. This is consistent with the addition of factors such as motivation to the model and not just underlying processing speed and related factors. Needless to say, the quantity and quality of environmental support provides an important directive component to the development of the multiple intelligences and the domains to which they can be applied. The present model is consistent with that of Demetriou and colleagues. Demetriou, Spanoudis, and Mouyi (2010) described the development of cognition in various domains through stages, via factors such as hypercognition and processing speed, in addition to various environmental factors

## *Individual Differences*

In the next table (see Table 17.4), I elaborate how complex an individual's developing multiple intelligences can become, based on the present Neo-Piagetian model of stages and substages in cognitive development and how they can combine. The concept of multiple intelligences has a normative dimension but, in the end, it supports a refined model of individual differences in cognitive and related development.

**Table 17.4** Backward and forward yoking in Neo-Piagetian cognitive development: how many intelligences?

| Cognitive stage | Reflexive | Sensorimotor | Perioperational | Abstract (formal) | Collective intelligence |
|---|---|---|---|---|---|
| Reflexive | O | xx | xx | xx | xx |
| Sensorimotor | xx | O | xx | xx | xx |
| Perioperational | xx | xx | O | xx | xx |
| Abstract (formal) | xx | xx | xx | O | xx |
| Collective intelligence | xx | xx | xx | xx | O |

**Yoking**

The diagonal line represents the development of the five Neo-Piagetian stages of the present model. The stages that are paired by the intersection of the columns and rows and that are not on the diagonal represent the yoking of the paired stages. Developmental stage yoking means that the lower-order stage of any pair is still present in development even as the higher-order one to which it is connected emerges. Moreover, they do not remain in their original form, but both alter in their reciprocal organization through the yoking. For example, perioperational cognitive structures could be coupled with sensorimotor schemes

**Backward–Forward**

When the yoking involves a higher-order structure as dominant, the yoking can be qualified as backward, but when the yoking involves the lower-order stage structure as primary, the yoking is considered forward. For example, sensorimotor skills could be yoked to concrete operational ones in the perioperational phase. The stage couplings under the diagonal represent backward yoking, and those above it represent forward yoking. Ostensibly, backward yoking is the more advanced type of stage structure yoking

Because of backward and forward yoking, the developing person has more than one set of cognitive repertoires available for problem-solving. By taking into account the possibility of triplets and larger aggregates in stage structure formations, it can be shown that the amount of potential stage structure yoking is quite large

**Multiply intelligent**

This begs the question of how many types of intelligence does the individual call forth in problem-solving at a time, and how they are organized when there are multiples. It also raises the question of multiple intelligences, because there are myriad patterns of stage structure couplings that could take place in cognitive activity. Moreover, when lower-order stages are primary in yoking, does this mean that the individual is functioning at a lower level cognitively? Perhaps not, because it is the nature of the combination that must be taken into account, e.g., the secondary stage still has an impact in determining the overall level of the couplings and it does modify the activity of the lower-order stage. As development proceeds, these lower-order coupled stages continue to improve in capacity, scope, automaticity, recruitment, refinement, and extension, but without affecting the chief characteristics of the higher-order level

(continued)

**Table 17.4** (continued)

**Dual Track Stages**

The implication is that each stage in cognitive development follows two tracks. First, it lays the seeds for the development of the stage that emerges from it as the next step in the qualitatively advancing series of steps in cognitive development. Second, it continues to develop for what it is at an increasing level of complexity through the stages that follow it in development. For example, sensorimotor intelligence never leaves us, and serves us in good stead throughout our lives. However, this happens as part of the adaptive strategies that we use to accomplish daily tasks, solve daily difficulties and problems, and develop expertise in areas related to it

**Multiple Intelligences**

In terms of the concept of multiple intelligences, it appears that the present model can accommodate the concept. For example, the sequence of five stages in development could be used to represent five types of multiple intelligences. Because each stage persists even after others have developed more complexity, at any one time in development after the infancy period, the developing person can draw upon, as required, at least two of the stages

Moreover, when yoking is involved, the dual structures imply a second or combined tier of multiple intelligences. Therefore, cognitive stage structure yoking is a concept that could help explain that any of the lower level types of multiple intelligences represented by the first few of the five stages of the present model might function more or less at upper levels in cognitive activity when they are coupled with those levels

**Yoking Mechanisms**

*Hypercognitive*. How does stage-yoking take place? Does the child functioning at a more advanced stage decide to use a sensorimotor scheme as part of an overall problem-solving organizer, for example? In terms of the concept of cognitive/socioaffective complexes described in Chap. 17, the yoking or coupling of stages that might take place in development happens at an organizational level that marshals and integrates component cognitive and affective processes into a superordinate, supervisory, or hypercontrol system assembled in context

*Systems*. The system has its own intelligence, if you will, based on the nonlinear dynamical constructive processes that are inherent to systems such as the ones under discussion. Neither the system nor the child fully decides what to do, especially in a conscious and willful way. However, this does not deny that some element of volitional control is part of the child's organizational and decision-making capacities, depending on age, context, environmental support, and so on

The language of nonlinear dynamical systems theory is widespread throughout the basic and social sciences, and Piaget did begin to apply it to his work (Boom, 2009). This model affords the flexibility needed to construct the type of multimodal constructive change processes that govern stage and substage evolution in Neo-Piagetian series

*Piaget and Vygotsky*. Piaget had used concepts such as assimilation and accommodation to explain how cognitive development proceeds. Assimilation and accommodation are components of the process of equilibration. They might help explain the yoking process, in part, but they have limited utility in explaining the emergence of new stages and substages in development. For Piaget, advances to new cognitive levels are facilitated by the process of reflecting abstraction, in particular (Campbell, 2009). Abstraction refers to the parsing out of general properties of what is known and their coordinations. In the reflecting portion of the concept, for Piaget, the child first reflects or projects a structure available at a lower level onto a higher level. This process permits explicit, conscious understanding of the projected material. In the next step, the child reorganizes the structure at the higher level. Note that Vygotsky had developed a similar concept. He had argued that the child learns on two planes – first by rote and, then, by organizing the incorporated material into existing cognitive structure, which leads to its alteration as a whole

In both the case of Piaget and Vygotsky, in discussing how new, higher forms of cognition arise in development, it appears to me that too much attention is focused on the cognitive capacities of the age period involving children, compared to other ages. That is, in discussing how the child can

(continued)

**Table 17.4** (continued)

| |
|---|
| develop higher-order cognitive skills, the language lapses into concepts such as reflective abstraction and learning at two planes because the developmental processes in infants have not been considered, as well. Moreover, too much attention is given to the child's conscious, volitional activity. The change processes involved might very well include conscious awareness. However, much cognitive change takes place unconsciously and automatically in a systemic way. Moreover, just because the transitions made are out of awareness to the child and infant, both in content and mechanism, this does not mean that it is a passive process and not an active one |
| *Brain.* This being said, development to higher-orders reaches upper limits due to physical and biological constraints. For example, the brain develops its specializations and its architecture, but needs to progress through increasing superior levels of complexity in order for cognitive development to proceed to higher levels. In this regard, Pascual Leone, Johnson, and Agostino (2010) presented a fourfold model of the development of the brain that was taken to correspond to the development of the four major stages of Case's Neo-Piagetian theory. Basing their model on the work of Luria (1973) and Eccles (1980), the authors described the following four steps in the growth of the brain: primary cortical areas, secondary areas, tertiary areas, and quaternary areas. Lewis (2010) also presented a four-step model in brain development, as did Zelazo, Qu, and Kesek (2010). However, the models cover different aspects in development and are different in content |
| Nevertheless, the concept espoused by Lewis (2010) that the brain expresses a vertical integration over the four levels, contributing to the ability to create new developmental levels, in the circular causal and feedback mechanisms involved, provides a neurobiological basis for the growth in development from stage to stage. However, clearer coordination in theory on development in neural bases and observed increases in complexity and quality in functional behavior outcomes needs to be established |

## Summary and Conclusions

This chapter has presented the conceptual innovations of cognitive/socioaffective complexes and multiple intelligences from the perspective of the present Neo-Piagetian model. These concepts could help bridge the study of cognition and intelligence over Piagetian and non-Piagetian approaches. The next chapter on adult postformal thought concludes the first half of the book. I continue to explore the cognitive implications and extensions of the present model as I present the work of others. In the second half of the book, I turn to doing the same on the socioaffective side, in particular, and then devote chapters to the study of causality or transitions mechanisms, in particular. The two concepts elaborated in the present chapter address these various themes, as well. On the one hand, they include socioaffective components. On the other hand, both involve causal elements. In this regard, the study of the origins and determinants of behavior does not lie only in the study of biology/genes, environment/culture, and their interaction. By examining more closely the mediators and moderators of behavioral expression, whether in the brain itself, or whether in constructs such as the cognitive/socioaffective complex or adaptive intelligences, the topic of causality is being broached.

## References

Baldwin, J. M. (1894). *The development of the child and of the race.* New York: MacMillan. (Reprinted by Augustus M. Kelly, 1968).
Becker, J. (2006). Relation of neurological findings on decoupling of brain activity from limb movement to Piagetian ideas on the origin of though. *Cognitive Development, 21*, 194–198.
Boom, J. (2009). Piaget on equilibration. In U. Müller, J. I. M. Carpendale, & L. Smith (Eds.), *The Cambridge companion to Piaget* (pp. 132–149). New York: Cambridge University Press.
Campbell, R. L. (2009). Constructive processes: Abstraction, generalization, and dialectics. In U. Müller, J. I. M. Carpendale, & L. Smith (Eds.), *The Cambridge companion to Piaget* (pp. 150–170). New York: Cambridge University Press.
Demetriou, A., Mouyi, A., & Spanoudis, G. (2010). The development of mental processing. In R. M. Lerner & W. F. Overton (Eds.), *The handbook of life-span development* (Cognition, biology, and methods, Vol. 1, pp. 36–55). Hoboken: Wiley.
Demetriou, A., Spanoudis, G., & Mouyi, A. (2010). A three-level model of the developing mind: Functional and neuronal substantiation and educational implications. In M. Ferrari & L. Vuletic (Eds.), *The developmental relations between mind, brain and education* (pp. 9–48). New York: Springer Science+Business Media.
Eccles, J. C. (1980). *The human psyche*. Berlin: Springer.
Gardner, H. (1993). *Frames of mind: The theory of multiple intelligences*. New York: Basic Books.
Gardner, H. (1999). *Intelligence reframed: Multiple intelligences for the 21st century*. New York: Basic Books.
Larivée, S., Normandeau, S., & Parent, S. (2000). The French connection: Some contributions of French-language research in the post-Piagetian era. *Child Development, 71*, 823–839.
Lautrey, J. (1990a). Unicité ou pluralité dans le développement cognitive: les relations entre image mentale, action et perception [Unicity and plurality in cognitive development: Relations between mental images, actions, and perception]. In G. Netchine-Grynberg (Ed.), *Développement et fonctionnement cognitive chez l'enfant [Development and cognitive functioning in the child]* (pp. 71–89). Paris: Presses Universitaires de France.
Lautrey, J. (1990b). Esquisse d'un modèle pluraliste du développement cognitive [Outline of a pluralistic model of cognitive development]. In M. Reuchlin, J. Lautrey, C. Marendez, & T. Ohlman (Eds.), *Cognition: l'individuel et l'universel [The individual and the universal]* (pp. 185–216). Paris: Presses Universitaires de France.
Lautrey, J. (1990c). Des concepts unitaires aux conceptions pluralists du développement cognitive [From unitary concepts to pluralistic conceptions of cognitive development]. *Archives de Psychologie, 58*, 185–196.
Lewis, M. D. (2010). Desire, dopamine, and conceptual development. In S. D. Calkins & M. A. Bell (Eds.), *Child development at the intersection of emotion and cognition* (pp. 175–199). Washington, DC: American Psychological Association.
Luria, A. R. (1973). *The working brain*. New York: Basic Books.
Pascual-Leone, J., Johnson, J., & Agostino, A. (2010). Mental attention, multiplicative structures, and the causal problems of cognitive development. In M. Ferrari & L. Vuletic (Eds.), *The developmental relations between mind, brain and education* (pp. 49–82). New York: Springer Science+Business Media.
Piaget, J. (1936/1952/1963). *The origins of intelligence in children.* New York: International Universities Press and Norton. (Original work published in 1936).
Schalock, R. L., Borthwick-Duffy, S. A., Bradley, V. J., Buntinx, W. H. E., Coulter, D. L., Craig, E. M., et al. (2010). *Intellectual disability: Definition, classification, and systems of supports* (11th ed.). Washington, DC: AAIDD.
Sternberg, R. J. (1983). Components of human intelligence. *Cognition, 15*, 1–48.

Sternberg, R. J. (2000). The concept of intelligence. In R. J. Sternberg (Ed.), *Handbook of intelligence* (pp. 3–15). New York: Cambridge University Press.

Thelen, E. (2008). Grounded in the world: Developmental origins of the embodied mind. In W. F. Overton, U. Müller, & J. L. Newman (Eds.), *Development perspectives on embodiment and consciousness* (pp. 99–129). New York: Erlbaum.

Vonèche, J. (2008). Action as the solution to the mind-body problem in Piaget's theory. In W. F. Overton, U. Müller, & J. L. Newman (Eds.), *Development perspectives on embodiment and consciousness* (pp. 69–98). New York: Erlbaum.

Waterhouse, L. (2006a). Multiple intelligences, the Mozart effect, and emotional intelligence: A critical review. *Educational Psychologist, 41*, 207–225.

Waterhouse, L. (2006b). Inadequate evidence for multiple intelligences, Mozart effect, and emotional intelligence theories. *Educational Psychologist, 41*, 247–255.

Zelazo, P. D., Qu, L., & Kesek, A. C. (2010). Hot executive function: Emotion and the development of cognitive control. In S. D. Calkins & M. A. Bell (Eds.), *Child development at the intersection of emotion and cognition* (pp. 97–111). Washington: American Psychological Association.

# Chapter 18
# Postformal Thought: Commons' Model

## Introduction

Commons (2008a) has developed the most comprehensive model of postformal thought in the Neo-Piagetian literature. In 2008, he presented his model with colleagues in a special issue of the journal *World Futures.* The present chapter is largely based on the articles in the issue. After reviewing each article, I provide commentary. Commons (2008a) model involves four postformal stages, and mine consists of one stage with five substages. The major difference in the models is that Commons appears to have missed a step involving hierarchization after the first step in his series. In the following, I show how the descriptions that Commons provides for his four postformal steps and the examples given to elaborate them suggest that a hierarchical step is needed in his model and that it fits very well into his series. Moreover, I present several models that are comparable to those of Commons and colleagues. However, these models avoid some of the issues deriving from the Commons' model that I point out in the comparison of the two models. In particular, I describe a model of management styles derived from the present model.

## Commons' Model

### *The Model*

Commons referred to his postformal model as a "quantitative behavioral development" one, and stated that it applies universally to patterns of change not only in development but also in other domains, such as changes in societal structures, history, and even evolution. The model is labeled "Hierarchical Complexity" because it is derived from tasks and their organization arranged in an increasingly vertical manner. The model not only consists of steps in postformal thought but also presents a lifespan model. It is comprised of 15 steps, referred to as orders, which are like stages. The steps in the model are derived both from his model of stages of postformal thought and from Fischer's (1980) model of stages and substages in cognitive development from infancy to the formal abstract stage (see Tables 18.1 and 18.2).

G. Young, *Development and Causality: Neo-Piagetian Perspectives*,
DOI 10.1007/978-1-4419-9422-6_18, © Springer Science+Business Media, LLC 2011

**Table 18.1** Orders of hierarchical complexity and structure of tasks in Commons

| Order ordinal and name | General descriptions of tasks performed |
|---|---|
| 0. Calculatory | Exact without generalization<br>Task: simple machine arithmetic on 0s, 1s |
| 1. Sensory or motor | Discriminate in a rote fashion, stimuli generalization, move; move limbs, lips, eyes, head; view objects and movement<br>Discriminative and conditioned stimuli<br>Task: Either see circles, squares, etc., or instead, touch them |
| 2. Circular sensory-motor | Form open-ended classes; reach, touch, grab, shake objects, babble; Open-ended classes, phonemes<br>Task: Reach and grasp a circle or square |
| 3. Sensory-motor | Form concepts; respond to stimuli in a class successfully<br>Morphemes, concepts<br>Task: A class of open squares may be formed |
| 4. Nominal | Find relations among concepts. Use names; use names and other words as successful commands. Single words may be ejaculatory and exclamatory, and include verbs, nouns, numbers' names, letters' names<br>Task: That class may be named, "Squares" |
| 5. Sentential | Imitate and acquire sequences: follow short sequential acts; generalize match-dependent task actions; chain words together<br>Use pronouns<br>Task: The numbers, 1, 2, 3, 4, 5 may be said in order |
| 6. Preoperational | Make simple deductions; follow lists of sequential acts; tell stories. Count random events and objects; combine numbers and simple propositions. Use connectives: as, when, then, why, before; products of simple operations<br>Task: The objects in a row of 5 may be counted; last count called 5, give, cinco, etc. |
| 7. Primary | Simple logical deduction and empirical rules involving time sequence. Simple arithmetic. Can add, subtract, multiply, divide, count, prove, do series of tasks on own. Times, places, counts acts, actors, arithmetic outcome from calculation<br>Task: $1+3=4$; $5+15=20$; $5(4)=20$; $5(3)=15$ |
| 8. Concrete | Carry out full arithmetic, form cliques, plan deals. Do long division, follow complex social rules, take and coordinate perspective of other and self. Use variables of interrelations, social events, what happened among others, reasonable deals<br>Task: There are behaviors that order the simple arithmetic behaviors when multiplying a sum by a number. Such distributive behaviors require the simple arithmetic behavior as a prerequisite, not just a precursor. $5(1+3)=5(1)+5(3)=5+15=20$ |
| 9. Abstract | Discriminate variables such as stereotypes; use logical quantification; form variables out of finite classes based on an abstract feature. Make and quantify propositions; use variable time, place, act, actor, state, type; uses quantifiers (all, none, some); make categorical assertions (e.g., "We all die")<br>Task: All the forms of five in the five rows in the example are equivalent in value, $x=5$ |
| 10. Formal | Argue using empirical or logical evidence; logic is linear, one-dimensional; use Boolean logic's connectives (not, and, or, if, and only if); solve problems with one unknown using algebra, logic, and empiricism; form relationships out of variables; use terms such as if … then, thus, therefore, because; favor correct scientific solutions<br>Task: The general left hand distributive relation is $x\times(y+z)=(x\times y)+(x\times z)$ |

(continued)

**Table 18.1** (continued)

| Order ordinal and name | General descriptions of tasks performed |
|---|---|
| 11. Systematic | Construct multivariate systems and matrices, coordinate more than one variable as input; situate events and ideas in a larger context, that is, considers relationships in contexts; form or conceive systems out of relations: legal, societal, corporate, economic, national |
| | Task: The right hand distribution law is not true for numbers but is true for proportions and sets. $x+(y\times z)=(x\times y)+(x\times z)$; $x \cup (y \cap z)=(x \cap y) \cup (x \cap z)$ |
| 12. Meta systematic | Integrate systems to construct multisystems or metasystems out of disparate systems; compare systems and perspectives in a systematic way (across multiple domains); reflect on systems, that is, is metalogical, meta-analytic; name properties of systems (e.g., homomorphic, isomorphic, complete, consistent, commensurable) |
| | Task: The system of propositional logic and elementary set theory are isomorphic. $x$ & ($y$ or $z$)=($x$ & $y$) or ($x$ & $z$) Logic; $x \cap (y \cup z)=(x \cap y) \cup (x \cap z)$ Sets T(False) ⇔ ø Empty set; T(True) ⇔ Ω Universal set |
| | *Symbols*: & = and; ⇔ = equivalent to; T = Transformation of |
| 13. Paradigmatic | Discriminate how to fit, and fit, metasystems together to form new paradigms. Includes ability to show that there are no ways to fit together any set of metasystems. $\Omega_1 \circ \Omega_2 = \Psi^a$ |
| | *Symbols*: $\Omega_n$ = e.g., Algebraic Metasystems; $\Omega_n$ = e.g., Geometric Metasystems; $\Psi^a$ = Analytic Geometry as a paradigm |
| 14. Cross-paradigmatic | Fit paradigms together to form new fields. Only by crossing paradigms can the new fields be conceived and formed; it requires the coordination of multiple paradigms to form genuinely new fields |



Commons (2008a) has developed a postformal model of cognitive development that is comprised of four separate stages (systematic, metasystematic, paradigmatic, cross-paradigmatic; see the next table, Table 18.2). Careful inspection of the stages indicates that the first one can be split, given that it involves both coordinations and relations in context, which are equivalent to the substages in the present model of coordination and hierarchization. Note that other stages in Commons' full lifespan model of cognitive development presented in the table can be split, too. For example, in the concrete stage, there are indications of simpler and more advanced behavior, ones bordering on the abstract, moreover. The developmental model in the table integrates the work of Fischer into Commons' description of the stages in cognitive development. Because Common's model is task-based, it gravitates between task-type descriptions of the stages (e.g., "calculatory" for the stage before the ones related to the sensorimotor period), and more classic Piagetian-type descriptions of the stages

The examples provided show that some of the stages in Commons' model could be split, including those related to where Fischer's model had been incorporated into it, adds to the notion that Fischer's model may have gaps in it. Moreover, the examples above reveals that there may be five phases in the postformal period, not four, which is the amount posited in the present model (in the present model, the steps are called substages, not stages)

Note that Common's model appears rationally derived and empirically supported, but it did not consist of four postformal steps to begin with. The third was added after someone remarked to him that a cross-paradigmatic stage has to have a paradigmatic one before it. This illustrates that the justification for the theory as an integrated model is post-hoc. Moreover, the consistencies that Commons finds between the stages and empirical data, such as through Rasch analyses, indicate that his model is internally consistent. However, it needs further work and modifications along the lines suggested, in order to establish its external validity

Note that Dawson-Tunik (e.g., 2004) has combined the work of Commons and Fischer. She used the developmental model of Fischer, but reworked it to include the notion of orders of hierarchical complexity (see Table 11.6)

**Table 18.2** Postformal stages as described in the general model of hierarchical complexity in Commons

| Order ordinal and name | What is done | How this is done | The end results |
|---|---|---|---|
| 11. Systematic operation | Constructs multivariate systems and matrices | Coordinates more than one variable as input | Events and ideas can be situated in a larger context; systems are formed out of formal-operational relations |
| 12. Metasystematic operation | Constructs multisystems and metasystems out of disparate systems | Compares and analyzes systems in a systematic way; reflects on systems; creates metasystems of systems | Metasystems are formed out of multiple systems |
| 13. Paradigmatic operation | Fits metasystems together to form new paradigms | Synthesizes metasystems | Paradigms are formed out of multiple metasystems |
| 14. Cross-paradigmatic operation | Fits paradigms together to form new fields | Forms new fields by crossing paradigms | Fields are formed out of multiple paradigms |

Reprinted with the permission of Oxford University Press, Inc. M. L., & Bresette, L. M. (2006). [Table 12.1, Page. 259]

Commons (2008a) defined orders as ideal forms grounded in mathematical models. Stages refer to the different order levels in problem-solving or otherwise in performing according to the hierarchical complexity task sequence.

*Comment.* Note that there is some ambiguity in the distinction between orders and stages in the detailed presentation of the Commons' model (see Commons, 2008a). For example, the presensory and motor stage step is called "calculatory," a term that does not accurately reflect the nascent cognitive abilities of the newborn child. In naming stages in his adaptation of Fischer's model from infancy to the formal period, Commons did not use Fischer's labels, but his own, without giving adequate justification. Moreover, it is not clear that the model was adopted in a straight-forward manner; for example, there appears to be five sensorimotor steps between the preoperational and presensorimotor steps, but Fischer had just three (note that in the present model, I have five, like Commons). Also, the concrete and abstract steps are not as clearly demarcated in Commons' model as they could be; for example, some of the examples given for the concrete step border on the abstract. Finally, the typical age periods that are associated with steps of the developmental progression are not specified.

*Commons and Ross* (2008a). These authors estimated that in developed countries the formal operational period of Inhelder and Piaget (1958) manifests in about 30–40% of adults. In more advanced settings in these countries, such as in corporate business, service industries, and higher education, they estimate that up to 70% of the adult population engages in formal thought. They maintained that task demands of other sectors generally do not require postformal thought. In countries that are less developed, they argued that the formal stage manifests less frequently. In the article, they presented the details of postformal thought in the Commons' model.

*Systematic*. For the first postformal stage of systematic thought, people who are trying to solve problems could attempt to solve multivariate problems. This might require discriminating the frameworks of embedded relationships that form systems. The task analysis undertaken from this perspective would include establishing multivariate possible causes, building multivariate representations, and ordering multidimensional possibilities.

It is instructive to note that the latter task includes "the acts of preference and prioritization." It will be recalled that in the present model, after the initial postformal step, I had posited that there is a step of hierarchization. I have also maintained in the present work that Commons, in his developmental sequence of postformal steps, had missed a required step of hierarchization after the systematic step. Therefore, the examples that he provided of the systematic step involving "acts of preference and prioritization" are consistent with my argument that his systematic stage could be split to allow for a second hierarchization stage.

*Metasystematic*. As for the next step in his sequence, called the metasystematic stage, people compare, contrast, transform, and synthesize the systematic constructions developed in the prior stage. For Commons, this results in the development of what might be called "supersystems."

Commons' use of language like this to describe the product of a metasystematic stage is consistent with my model that the step following the hierarchization one involves systematization. That is, Commons and I seem to be working on the same wavelength for this step in postformal thought.

*Paradigmatic*. As for the next step in Commons' sequence, called the paradigmatic stage, people can create new paradigms out of the hierarchical integration of multiple metasystems or multiple supersystems. Commons defined a paradigm as a systematized set of relations among metasystems, involving a coherent set of assumptions. By definition, paradigms are great advances in a body of knowledge that stand in contrast to prior prevalent understandings in the field. Commons estimated that fewer than half of a percent of people in developed countries function at the paradigmatic stage without support.

Note that in my model, the equivalent step to Commons' paradigmatic one is called multiplication. In this step, the person takes the systems developed in the prior step and applies them throughout the cognitive repertoire. This leads to the formation of integrated totality in the last step of the sequence that follows the one of multiplication. Therefore, in my understanding of the multiplication step, a coherent integration does not form yet, in contrast to what is described in Common's step of paradigms. In my approach, one has to build toward the construction of a paradigm through multiplicative thought before integrated paradigms can be constructed.

This speaks to my concern that the Piagetian cognitive developmental model could involve the development of two stages after the formal period, not just the postformal one (Young, 1997). That is, paradigmatic thought is so complex and so rare for Commons that it might involve more than the postformal stage that has been added to Piaget's formal stage by various Neo-Piagetians. In essence, I am positing that there is a "post-postformal" stage in adult cognitive development, and in Common's paradigmatic step, he might be addressing that more than later postformal skills.

*Cross-Paradigmatic.* In the last step in Commons' description of the postformal period, he referred to the stage as cross-paradigmatic. People in this stage integrate paradigms into a new field or alter in a profound way an old field. Cross-paradigms are even more complex than those constructed in the paradigmatic stage; they could involve ideas created in interdisciplinary studies; however, just by attempting integrations of this type does not mean the constructions will be cross-paradigmatic, and therefore they are very rare. This further reinforces my notion that after the postformal stage there could be another stage that develops, and Commons is addressing this post-postformal stage more than the last step in the postformal period.

*Comment.* The estimated percentages of the adult population who engage in formal and postformal thought are striking. I have maintained that the use of postformal thought might be more widespread than Neo-Piagetians have estimated because this type of thought should not be limited mostly to esoteric scientific or advanced professional contexts. That is, even in our daily lives and in complex work environments, such as writing manuals at work, one needs to use advanced, abstract procedures, such as described in postformal thought, especially when they are undertaken in collective contexts, as with brainstorming.

In this regard, it could be that the proportion of people who are estimated to function at the formal level is underestimated. It could be that the estimates are yoked or constrained by Piaget's original conception of postformal thought. Piaget related the stage of formal thought to logical structures derived from philosophy and mathematics, such as the combinatorial 4-group, as has been shown. Rather, from a psychological point of view, it could be that the young adolescent enters the period of formal operations as soon as she or he constructs some initial abstract idea, for example, no matter how simple, in courses like mathematics, science, or literature, or in daily life involving complex social problems. Then, the adolescent can build up coordinations and interrelations over a few of these abstract ideas, thereby developing somewhat more complex systems and integrations. These might be sufficient to qualify as more advanced formal thinking, and it would be limiting to qualify these formal constructions as simpler. Because, these higher-order formal abstract concepts might be quite limited in scope, even if more integrated, and because they should be conceived as not overly taxing of mental capacities, there still would be cognitive reserve and skill available to adolescents to develop more advanced abstract ideation.

Also, consider that typical university students might be engaging in more than formal and abstract thought of a limited variety. As they use the formal ideas created in the formal stage, and even if we allow that their formal thought constructions are limited in scope, the university student could be on the way to developing initial postformal constructions both earlier and at a greater level of frequency than is typically acknowledged. That is, as they engage in their studies, write papers, participate in class discussions, and so on, university students, particularly those in senior years who apply themselves, are formulating novel integrations of several abstract notions and might be in the period of postformal thought earlier than typically described. This type of conjecture needs further elaboration; however, it is consistent with the argument that more than a small minority of adults enters the stage of postformal thought.

## *Post-Postformal Stage: The Present Model*

The final implication of this argument is that there could be a stage of cognitive development that is one order of complexity superior to postformal thought. It could be that not only does postformal thought appear more frequently than previously believed, it could be that it also proceeds to the last substages in its sequence more than would be typically believed, thereby opening the possibility of developing post-postformal thought in some people. That is, a "post-postformal" stage would be the one that is rare, esoteric, and the province of advanced intellectual and professional thinkers or those who in their daily life engage in this type of thinking.

Moreover, as medical technology increases the typical lifespan of humans, one can envisage many more people entering a postformal stage of cognitive development. This might be especially true with the computer and other technological interfacing that the future will bring. In addition, in Young (1997), the publication in which I had proposed a post-postformal stage of cognitive development, I had argued that this type of intelligence could even involve interspecies communication and creation of superordinate intelligences at that level.

Specifically, in Young (1997), I wrote,

> "In this scenario it could be that the wise elderly will spearhead genuine *communal collective intelligences*, where different species collectively contribute to and share in a symbiotically elaborated group intelligence. In the coordination and hierarchical substages, this could concern the relationship between pairs of species, in particular, either between our own and others one at a time or between two others that humans would facilitate. The systemic level would concern wider communal interspecies collective intelligences, ones that could be incorporated into multiplicative combinations, leading to a superior integrative substage. Will interspecies communication across planets be incorporated into this stage or be the basis of the one to follow?" (p. 284)

To conclude, I am suggesting that cognitive development proceeds to a stage after the postformal one, and a good label for it is Communal Collective Intelligences. It could involve interfacing with other species and different modern technologies, such as computers. Moreover, because the formal and postformal periods at present might be construed in a too complex fashion, there might be a higher percentage of people in these stages than commonly believed. Therefore, the proposed stage of communal collective intelligences could develop earlier in some people than the last period of life. The quandary, of course, is to what extent would young people interfacing with computer technology in the future arrive at the proposed stage of communal collective intelligence when they had not yet acquired the necessary experience and cognitive maturity to even enter the postformal stage? Just how much can the computer interfacing, robotics, artificial intelligence, etc., advance intelligence to the point that experience can be replaced and cognitive stages or substages can be skipped?

## *Domains of Development*

*Mascolo* (2008). Mascolo has presented the concept of domains in development. Domains refer to particular concepts, behaviors, or affects in which skills are developing. He argued that we do not advance uniformly across cognitive activities once we reach a particular step in cognitive development and that there are variations across domains. Individuals operate at a range of different levels within a stage, depending on the area of skill, the task, the context, the degree of support, and so on. He contrasted the concept domains with that of *structures d'ensembles,* or structures of the whole, that Piaget developed as part of his theory (Piaget, 1971, 1983). A *structure d'ensemble* refers to the person thinking from a single system of thought within a particular stage that applies to a broad range of tasks. It forms an integrated holistic system so that the person develops success more or less at the same time in resolving multiple tasks related to the stage. When one finds different degrees of success for different tasks associated with a stage, Piaget described the task success differences as the effect of a *horizontal décalage*.

Mascolo (2008) did not include this latter idea in his presentation on domains but, nonetheless, its absence does not modify his main argument. Mascolo contrasted the concept of *structure d'ensemble* with that of domains because domains are considered to develop relatively independently of one another. Skills develop within specific domains and refer to an individual's capacity to control aspects of acting, thinking, and feeling, within particular tasks and contexts (Fischer & Bidell, 2006). A skill is a psychological control structure and is not a general structure, that is, an all-purpose one applicable to all contexts. Therefore, skills can develop independently of each other, which means they can develop both at different rates and toward different developmental endpoints. By independence, Mascolo meant that if we have knowledge of a developmental ability in a person for one skill, it does not mean that we can predict accurately what might happen for another.

Case (1992a) described a concept similar to domains, which he referred to as central conceptual structures. Griffin (2005) described a series of central conceptual structures in number, narrative, and spatial drawing. Mascolo (2008) adapted and extended her work, as presented in Table 9.3 in Chap. 9. According to Mascolo, this type of modeling indicates that development consists of distinct conceptual domains. However, there are rarely pure conceptual domains of functioning and, moreover, they are combined in daily life. Moreover, domains reflect different levels of cognitive complexity. Both Griffin (2005) and Mascolo presented models of how domains develop through Neo-Piagetian stages (with respect to Case and Fischer, respectively).

*Comment.* In prior chapters, I have described the work of Mascolo on domains that is elaborated in this chapter. Also, in the prior chapter, I have applied the concept of domains to the development of multiple intelligences, using the model of Demetriou et al. This work by Mascolo reinforces the importance of thinking in terms of domains along these lines. However, I question the efficacy of tying the development of domains to the models of Case and Fischer for the development of stages and substages of development. For example, I have shown that Fischer's model seems to be missing several substages in its series relative to my own. With respect to Case, there are no missing substages in the age range of Griffin's and Mascolo's work on domain development, but at some points the present model provides a better description of the developing person, as shown in prior chapters.

## *Evolution and Empathy*

*Wolfsont, Ross, Miller, Commons, and Chernoff* (2008). Wolfsont et al. have made an interesting comparison between Commons' model of hierarchical complexity and each of the evolution of tool-making and the development of empathy. The former relates to an evolutionary sequence and the latter to an ontogenetic sequence. For both series, the authors indicated the stages that emerge according to the model of hierarchical complexity. The two series on the evolution of tool making and the development of empathy that have been proposed by Wolfsont et al. can be found in Table 18.3. Wolfsont et al. based their evolutionary sequence in tool-making on the work of Wynn (1981, 1993). As for empathy, they included a broader source of references, including Selman (1980).

*Comment.* It will be recalled that the Commons' model up to the postformal period is based on Fischer (1980). Also, recall that I have indicated that there are gaps of substages in that model relative to my own. In this regard, it will be interesting to examine one time period in the Wolfsont et al. work for which I indicate that there are gaps. The time frame that I look at in this regard is between the concrete and abstract steps in Commons' sequence. In addition, with respect to a gap that I perceive in the Commons' model for the postformal period, I examine the shift from systematic to metasystematic postformal operations in terms of each of the tool-making sequence and the empathy sequence. Recall that this is the developmental period for which I have indicated that Common's model is missing a hierarchical step.

**Table 18.3** Evolutionary comparison of two domains

| Order of hierarchical complexity | Stages of tool-making | Stages of empathy in humans (affect and actions) |
|---|---|---|
| 1. Sensory or motor actions | Look at stones, touch, or hold a stone. Each of these actions is done singly and not combined with other actions | Reflex reactions, e.g., lower distress, comfort with comforting stimuli, elicited smiles (Field, 1989). Reflexive imitation: stick out tongue, open mouth (Meltzoff & Moore, 1977). Emotional contagion: Cry when other infants cry (Hoffman, 1978) |
| 2. Circular sensorimotor actions | Look, reach, and grab a stone. Bang a stone by accident on another stone | Coordinate parent's emotion cues and own behavior. Adjust behavior, e.g., watch for facial expressions of a stranger (Boccia & Campos, 1989). Avoid others' aversive emotions: turn away; suppress ongoing activity, do alternative activity |
| 3. Sensorymotor | Bang a stone into another stone or other objects, both singly and in combination. Use simple concepts such as bashing a nut with a stone. Classify perceptually | Couple motor and emotional actions, match intensity of expressions when imitating. Recognize emotional disparity of different people. Console with pat, hug, or concerned look. Compare own emotional response to caretaker's; base own response to stranger upon caretaker's |
| 4. Nominal | Bash one stone on the other, coordinating the strike to hit near the immediately previous strike. Create successive modifications nonsystematically, different on any dimension. Act on named concepts seen in acts | Name and associate feelings (e.g., happy, sad) with familiar entities, events, or images. Infant respond with distressed look to adult who looks sad, then offer to adult infant's beloved doll; go to get own mother to comfort crying friend (Hoffman, 1978). React emotionally to distress, anger of family members (Zahn-Waxler, Kochanska, Radke-Yarrow & King 1979) |
| 5. Sentential | Hit one stone with the other in a constant direction of movement (each strike at the stone is done in relation to the previous one). Make Mode I tools (Wynn, 1981, 1993) requiring few bangs | Simple sequences of empathic interactions limited to egocentric helping (e.g., console crying infant). Talk about cause and effect, reflect on cause, actor, action, outcome. Relieve guilt by reparation or evasion (Kuczynski, Kochanska, Radke-Yarrow, & Girnius-Brown, 1987; Zahn-Waxler & Kochanska, 1988). Play-act, feign pretense |

(continued)

**Table 18.3** (continued)

| Order of hierarchical complexity | Stages of tool-making | Stages of empathy in humans (affect and actions) |
|---|---|---|
| 6. Preoperational | Do a sequenced set of things after another sequence to the same tool. Focus on only one aspect, e.g., to bash edges or just produce flakes | Empathize with story characters. Confuse the real and imaginary; act on mistaken beliefs. Empathy based on cultural message about context (e.g., which kind of animal may be killed). Narrate to integrate situations, context, and cues to infer what an emotion indicates |
| 7. Primary | Use beginning symmetry or constant spatial amount in early Mode II tools (Wynn, 1981, 1993). Continue the tool-making work until the task is finished | Match feelings toward the suffered to sufferer's reality, empathize with another's situation (if it is familiar or perceptible), but not coordinate the actions (feelings are more one's own than matched to other person's feelings aroused in the situation, e.g., "Me too-isms") |
| 8. Concrete | Make one part of a tool then attach it to another part (e.g., an arrowhead to a stick). Coordinate two separate reversible actions. Carry and store tools consistently | Describe feelings as inferred directly from others' expressions and linked to specific situation. Understand another's motives and feelings in terms of one's own in a similar situation. State preferences of others and values of things, acts. Coordinate how one feels now and in the same concrete (past) situation and what helped |
| 9. Abstract | Use standard unit of measure to achieve symmetry. More precisely apply constant spatial amount. Follow peer social norms (Wynn, 1993) for uniform tools. Use variables to consider effects, i.e., points, edges from dull to sharp; varying shapes | Identify degrees of feelings and suffering along a continuum as states or moods inside the person expressed externally, and understand they can be in conflict (Selman, 1980). Generalize feelings, situations without logically linking generalizations. View feeling as normative: "This is how people feel in a situation like this." Try to help in various nonsystematic ways |
| 10. Formal | Make and use specialized tools for different applications. Make instant decisions about which tool to use in which situation | Link suffering, moods, expressions, and situational variables; ask how people feel in a given situation. Aware that feelings influence immediate perspectives or perceptions. Imagine self in another's position and situation and sympathize |

(continued)

**Table 18.3** (continued)

| Order of hierarchical complexity | Stages of tool-making | Stages of empathy in humans (affect and actions) |
|---|---|---|
| 11. Systematic | Develop new tools systematically for different situations (problem finding). Adapt to available materials for best tool to function in the situation | Organize feelings and expressions into systems in each person. See self as impartial, although caring reflector of other's states and perspective. Moderate empathic responses by standing in the hierarchy of the sufferer, i.e., context influences empathic response |
| 12. Metasystematic | Compare two systems each with sets of causal relationships for making tools. Find how systematic causal relations interact | Coordinate congruent disparate emotions, know some systems of emotions conflict with other systems (e.g., personal survival, social justice). Construct and base actions on universal principles of caring, suffering |
| 13. Paradigmatic | – | See that caring, justice, and survival systems or varieties of conflicting concerns cannot be fully integrated; identify failure to find universal principles for empathy |

Reprinted with the permission of Cambridge University Press. Commons, M. L., & Miller, P. M. (2002a). © Cambridge Journals. [Table 1, Page. 405]. Reprinted with the permission of Cambridge University Press. Commons, M. L., & Miller, P. M. (2002b). © Cambridge Journals. [Table from Page. 30–31]. Reprinted by permission of the publisher (Taylor & Francis Group, http://www.informaworld.com). Wolfsont, C., Ross, S. N., Miller, P. M., Commons, M. L., & Chernoff, M. (2008). [Table 1, Page. 418–420]

This table indicates the range of reach of the Common's model of postformal adult cognitive development (hierarchical complexity). The model has been expanded to include the earliest stages of life, based on the work of Fischer. The model has been applied not only to the development of affective domains, such as empathy, but also to other series of changes over time, in the present case, to evolutionary changes in tool-making

Other presentations of the model include a stage before the sensorimotor ones and another one after the paradigmatic one. The model does not include a nesting of substages that cyclically recur in stages. However, there are five sensorimotor stages before the preoperational stage and there are four postformal stages that can be readily expanded to five stages by inclusion of a step between the systematic and metasystematic stages, as described at several points in the present work. Moreover, I have developed an inclusive model of the development of cognitive stages and substages in development that situates both the work of Commons and Fischer in a common framework, as well as two other Neo-Piagetians (Case and Feldman, see Chap. 1)

Examination of the table where the two series, related to evolution and empathy, are presented indicates that the transition from concrete to abstract thought appears to be missing two steps. Recall that I had previously demonstrated that the Fischer model on which the Commons' one is based is missing two substages relative to my own in this time frame. Therefore, present model includes the substages of multiplication and integration in the time frame between the two substages equivalent to the concrete and abstract ones of Commons. For example, for tool use, Wolfsont et al. (2008) described that at the concrete level, tool-making consists of forming one part and then attaching it to another part, such as in making an arrowhead-stick combination. In the abstract stage, the tool use involves using standard units of measure.

Given the great jump in skill in tool use from one evolutionary period to the next as described by Wolfsont et al., it would make a lot of sense to indicate that in the evolution of tool use in proto-hominids there had been two additional steps between the equivalent of the concrete and abstract steps. Moreover, it would make a lot of sense that the two missing steps in the Common's sequence on evolution involved multiplication and integration phases. For example, in the proposed multiplication period of tool use in proto-hominids, I suggest that they were learning how to make *many* tools. For the integration phase, I suggest that they were developing skills in tool use that permitted their combination, or that they constructed combined ones from other tools.

Similarly, for the development of empathy presented by Wolfsont et al. (2008), one could add after the concrete stage a series of acquisitions involving multiplications and integrations, before the developing individuals pass into the abstract stage. Specifically, for the Common's model of empathic understanding and expression, it would make sense that there is a sequence of two additional steps after the concrete step involving the spreading out of acquisitions in the system and then their consolidation into a unified structure.

As for the transition between the systematic and metasystematic postformal steps for the evolution of tool use, Wolfsont et al. described that in the systematic stage, tool use involved new tools that are different in a systematic way for different situations. They referred to this activity as problem finding. In the metasystematic step, two systems are compared in order to understand interacting causal relationships.

It could be argued that before there had been the evolution of metasystematic tool use, there was a step in evolution in which hierarchical relationships were constructed over pairs of systematic tool constructions. That is, before the species sequence concerned could pass into metasystematic tool use from the systematic stage, there had been a transition stage involving hierarchization; this step should be added to the Commons' model.

As for the steps of development of empathy, at the systematic level, Wolfsont et al. described the systematic stage as one where developing individuals organize feelings and their expressions into systems in each person, both for themselves and others. They added that the stage involves moderating empathic response to the other by "standing in the *hierarchy* of the sufferer" [italics mine]. In the metasystematic stage in the development of empathy, examples provided by Wolfsont et al. include coordinating congruent and different emotions, for example, in developing universal principles of caring and suffering.

As I predicted even before looking at the table, there had to be incorporated into their description of the systematic or metasystematic stage some form of hierarchization, because of the step missing in their model relative to my own. Prediction confirmed.

Note that Commons' effort to map his model of cognitive development onto the evolutionary sequence of tool use is important. In Young (1990a, 1990b), I presented a more comprehensive model of the evolutionary bases of the stages of my model. Moreover, in a later chapter of the present work, I present a model of the evolutionary pressures that could have acted differentially on the evolution of the stages.

*Commons and Ross* (2008b). The authors presented an interesting application of Common's hierarchical complexity model to the evolutionary sequence in animal cognition. For example, the performance of Pepperberg's (1992) African Grey parrot Alex was placed in the step preceding the preoperational step. They considered the cognitive activity of crows as high as the preoperational step. For the level after the preoperational period, they gave examples relating to rhesus monkeys and chimpanzees. For the concrete period, they gave examples for chimpanzees only. For example, one bonobo chimpanzee made simple flake tools by throwing a rock against a hard surface and then testing the flakes for sharpness (de Waal & Lanting, 1997). Another chimpanzee broke up in an impartial way conflicts among subordinate chimps (de Waal, 1996).

*Comment.* This suggestion that chimpanzees can engage in concrete operational thought should be investigated further. It is not clear from the examples provided that the chimpanzees were thinking in the logical way associated with concrete operations. In my own model, chimpanzees are limited to preoperational thought (see Chap. 26), at least from an evolutionary perspective of their ancestors. However, it could be that preoperational thought is a predominant mode of functioning for contemporary chimpanzees, but they also have evolved to use occasional concrete operational thought.

## Management

*Koplowitz* (2008). Koplowitz applied the model of hierarchical complexity to managerial hierarchies (see Table 18.4). He built on the work of Brown (1960, 1962) and Jaques (1976, 1996), who developed a model of requisite organization in managerial accountability hierarchies. Brown and Jaques developed a model of layers of complexity at work, which they labeled strata. The strata begin with taking on roles, such as bank teller at stratum 1 and being a CEO of a super-corporation at stratum VIII. It is instructive that in aligning the eight strata in Brown-Jaques with the different orders of hierarchical complexity in Commons' model, Koplowitz (2008) found it necessary to put both strata V and VI in the metasystematic stage. The examples for the stratum (IV) associated with the systematic stage involved roles such as factory manager, business unit VP, and high school principal. The level V stratum involved being a business unit president. The level VI stratum included being an external VP, and managing a portfolio of business units.

*Comment.* In terms of comparison with the present model, as has already been stated, there appears to be a step missing in Commons' model that lies between the systematic and metasystematic steps. In this regard, in Koplowitz's work, I would place the role of business unit president that had been placed in stratum V (and associated with the metasystematic stage in the Commons sequence), in a separate step labeled hierarchization. At this level of functioning, the people in this role

**Table 18.4** Parallels in Commons' model of hierarchical complexity and Jaques' model of strata in business

| Hierarchical complexity | Stratum | Sample role | Stratum mastery age range | Process | Order |
|---|---|---|---|---|---|
| – | VIII | Super corporation (IBM, GE) CEO | 50–100 years | Parallel | 4th order abstract |
| – | VII | Large bank or multinational CEO | 20–50 years | Serial | |
| 12 Metasystematic | VI | Large bank or multinational EVP (managing a portfolio of business units) | 10–20 years | Cumulative | |
| | V | Business unit president | 5–10 years | Declarative | |
| 11 Systematic | IV | Factory manager, business unit VP, secondary school principal | 2–5 years | Parallel | 3rd order (normal adult) |
| 10 Formal | III | Line manager, senior engineer, elementary school principal | 1–2 years | Serial | |
| 9 Abstract | II | Front-line manager, engineer, teacher | 3–12 months | Cumulative | |
| | I | Bank teller, machinist, sales clerk | Under 3 months | Declarative | |

Reprinted by permission of the publisher (Taylor & Francis Group, http://www.informaworld.com). Koplowitz, H. (2008). [Table 1, Page. 518]

Lining up Jaques' (1976, 1996) levels with the steps in the model of Hierarchical Complexity is tentative. Correlation of the higher strata with the cognitive model is not clear

However, it is noteworthy that, as described in the table, Jaques' series involves five steps in the stages equivalent to the postformal phases, even though in Common's model there are four postformal phases. This is consistent with the contention in the present work that the postformal stages in Commons can be expanded to five steps from four, by adding an extra step involving hierarchization after his systematic stage

should be keenly aware of the hierarchy that marks life at work, and should be taking great care to organize well their charges at the lower level, while trying to fit in and advance to the higher level.

## *Management Styles: The Present Model*

### The Model

Another application of Neo-Piagetian stage models to the managerial context would be to determine how different management styles align with the different steps in the models. The present model is quite amenable to this suggestion because I have

**Table 18.5** Five management styles according to Young's Neo-Piagetian stage model

| Management style | Description |
|---|---|
| Negate | Overlord, treat poorly, reject, deny |
| Dominate | Subjugate, repress, oppose, impose, manipulate |
| Relegate | Neutralize, channel, assimilate, pacify |
| Delegate | Offer responsibility, show concern, liberate somewhat |
| Integrate | Promote individual and collective action, creativity, thought, freedom, and awareness; empower, humanize, trust others' wisdom; facilitate emergence of constant adaptation and growth; coparticipate in process |

The table presents another way to examine the business culture, this time in terms of five management styles related to the five stages of cognitive development in the present work, in particular. In Young (1997), I had developed a model of the cognitive (mis)perception of the other based on the five stages. Although cognitively, adults function at the more advanced levels of the model, they do not necessarily perceive others at the same level. For example, management styles involving abuse or domination are potentiated when the other is perceived as reflexive or not cognitively functional, at best. In this sense, the table presents a model of five management styles that reflects the model of the five steps in the cognitive (mis)perception of the other. When a manager or a management team is functioning at the highest level of collective intelligence, and the manager or team perceives the other through this lens, better teamwork in the work environment could be promoted, for example, fitting the emphasis on brainstorming at this stage

developed a model of the cognitive (mis)perception of the other (see Chap. 14) based on the five stages and five substages of the model. Based on this work, in what follows, I extrapolate five management styles that seem to apply to functioning as a manager in a work environment (see Table 18.5). Before presenting this work, I describe briefly the cognitive (mis)perception of the other, as presented in Table 14.1 in Chap. 14.

The table illustrates that we are not only developing through stages but also perceiving others in terms of what we think are their functional developmental stage. If our own development has been limited by certain experiences in the past or by problems in the present, we might not perceive others in their full psychological breadth, in terms of either their current status or their developmental potential. I call this process of misunderstanding others "the cognitive (mis)perception of the other." In my developmental model, this cognitive (mis)perception of others can reflect the workings of any of the five stages of cognitive development of the present model. Therefore, for the adult, others can be misperceived from the perspective of the first reflexive level, the infant sensorimotor level, the child perioperational level, the adolescent abstract level, or the adult collective intelligence level.

In solving problems, we do not always think at our most advanced levels, and when we think of other people, we do not always use our most advanced thinking capacities. When this happens, we do not see their full human scope, and the more there is potential for mistreatment of the other. In general, when we misperceive the other person, we act toward them in ways that misunderstand them, or even abuse them, and inhibit their psychological development. These misconceptions would be quite destructive in the management setting, so a model that describes the different patterns that might be evident, and offers a developmental explanation for them, would seem beneficial.

## The Styles

Table 18.5 describes five different management styles associated with the five stages of the present cognitive model. The management styles are extrapolations of the five different types of cognitive (mis)perception of the other, at one per stage. The five proposed management styles range from the most bossy and overbearing approach to the most integrative and team-oriented approach.

*Negation.* The first proposed management style is marked by autocratic behavior (negation). A manager at this level acts in a rejecting fashion and functions like an overlord. The negating manager treats the worker poorly and may even abuse or harass the worker. Workers are not considered as equal human beings. The worker might submit in fear to the manager, but work performance risks becoming chaotic. This style should be avoided at all costs.

*Domination.* In the next style, the manager is less negative but, nevertheless, is quite controlling and manipulative. The manager is dominant, subverting the rights of the workers, opposing, imposing her or his will, and acting to repress. The danger of this style is that the workers simply go through the motions, work poorly, or even rebel and sabotage productivity.

*Relegation.* In the third management style, that of relegation, workers are respected more than in the prior two approaches. However, the manager still guides the workers, in an effort to lead them in the direction preferred by the manager. In effect, the workers are neutralized, assimilated, or pacified to the manager's will, creating worker automatons who will not be able to adapt well to any new demands in the work environment. Vision is limited. The manager does not see the larger picture nor do the workers. The danger of this work style is that the workers express resistance rather than revolution, but hurt productivity nonetheless.

*Delegation.* In the next management style, the manager becomes freer in feeling, thought, and behavior. The manager delegates responsibility, offering responsibilities to workers so that they are managing themselves. At the same time, the manager monitors the delegated individuals. The manager is concerned for them. Nevertheless, the larger picture might not be perceived, and optimal teamwork might be missing. The manager might worry that, one day, she or he could be replaced by one of the workers who is being empowered, so the manager partially disempowers them. The manager might delegate responsibility, but might want all the rewards. The risk here is that workers do not work to full capacity and are not fully mobilized.

*Integration.* In the most advance management style, that of integration, the manager tries to integrate the workers into a team. Individuals might work alone on their particular problems but, for larger problems, workers are organized into groups. This promotes constant back and forth, problem-solving approaches among the workers, and unleashes their collective creativity. Each worker is empowered and increasingly develops his or her skills. Success feeds on itself. The workers feel more human, wiser, and more capable of adapting to the novel circumstances that arise daily in the work world. The manager becomes part of that process; the worker and the manager may grow together as a team. This process develops to the point that, in many sense of the word, the workers might feel equal to the manager and feel free to act independently and effectively. The workers might work toward teamwork, making the manager's job much easier. In other words, in this management style, potentially, work productivity ends up effective and adaptive.

### Conclusion

To conclude, the manager needs to know when to use which style in what situation. Most probably, managing involves a combination of the various styles, and each manager displays a unique style of how they are used in combination. Although the integrated approach is ideal, pragmatic considerations might mean that other styles are deployed, as well. Effective managing can be learned, but it depends on personal factors, developmental history, company culture, worker variables, and so on. The integrated approach should be used much of the time. This strategy pays psychological dividends that, in turn, should yield financial dividends for the manager and the company.

Note that it is quite possible to describe substages in the development of each management style, consistent with Young's (1997) model. For example, the integration style might begin with a juxtaposition of it and a less advanced style. Then, the integrated style becomes hierarchically preferred over others. Next, it systematizes in one area of managing, and then spreads multiplicatively throughout the managing function. Finally, it stands as an integrated style.

## *Other Topics in Commons*

*Moral development.* In another article in the series on Commons' model, Day (2008) examined the literature on faith, religious reasoning, and so on, for consistency with respect to the stages that Commons described. He developed a reliable and valid questionnaire that allows scoring of individuals' moral language in terms of stage scores. He developed a second measure related to religious cognition.

*Comment.* Day (2008) cited the work of different stage theorists in the area of faith, such as Fowler (1981, 1996). It would be interesting to see how these different models relate to the work of the different Neo-Piagetians, including myself. In this regard, Day (2008) developed his questionnaires based on the cognitive developmental model of Fischer (1980), which has been incorporated into Commons' developmental model of steps in cognitive development. It will be recalled that I have pointed out gaps, or missing substages, in the Fischer model. Further research in the area on the development of faith, moral, and religious reasoning might profit from a more careful examination of the present model of steps in development.

*Innovation.* Commons, Bresette, and Ross (2008) described how scientific innovations proceed in the various postformal stages. For example, in the systematic stage, scientists might develop an integrated system of relationships. Scientists might build matrix representations and multidimensional ordering of possibilities, including the acts of preference and prioritization.

*Comment*. Previously in this chapter, I have indicated that preference and prioritization refer to hierarchization. As mentioned, this step of hierarchization appears to be missing in Commons' sequence, and could be added.

*Politics*. Ross and Commons (2008) suggested that the stages of political development correspond to Commons' developmental stages of hierarchical complexity. They suggested correspondences from the concrete stage to the paradigmatic stage. For example, in the systematic stage, societies coordinate systems of relations over the legal, societal, business, economic, and national domains. They develop democracies that are transparent, accountable, and so on. In the metasystematic stage, societies should, but do not necessarily, create supersystems, for example, across the legal system, international relations, environmental policies, human rights, and government.

*Comment*. Consistent with the hypothesis of the present chapter that there should be an intermediate stage between the systematic and metasystematic stages, I suggest that societies, as they develop out of the systematic stage into the metasystematic one, function according to a hierarchization level. In particular, this means that for political development, societies are taking the coordinations of the systematic stage and organizing them in primary and secondary relationships, as intermediate steps toward creating supersystems. In this regard, I would suggest that the lack evident in contemporary political societies with respect to the potential they might have for developing supersystems, as described by Ross and Commons (2008), is that they have failed to develop strategies of hierarchization among the coordinating systems. For example, for the domains mentioned, the legal system should develop to the point of encompassing what is needed to prepare for further integrations of the domains into a supersystem. This might be asking too much of nation states at their current level of development.

Note that the present concept of a post-postformal stage that has been proposed above, involving communal collective intelligences, could apply to the evolution of collections of nation states into larger unions. Hopefully, one day, there will be a morally functioning genuine union of nations.

*Societies I*. Commons and Ross (2008c) applied Commons' model of hierarchical complexity to stages in societal growth. In particular, they applied their model to the evolution of human societies from the foraging period through to the period of modernity and postmodernity. They equated the mid-modernity period to the systematic stage of Commons' model and the postmodernity stage to the metasystematic stage of Commons' model.

*Comment*. Without belaboring the point too much, I note that there should be an intermediate step involving hierarchization in this sequence of the growth of societal organization. It might be called the late-modernity period, consistent with one step in the Commons-Ross series, called the late foraging period. In the late-modernity period, human societal organization would involve adding more dominant-subordinate relations to the modernity structure. For example, historical and political study might reveal that as a society develops toward postmodernity, for one domain or another, it is taking more fluid modern concepts not having the full weight of its "-isms," and placing them as lead ideas, with paired modern ones as secondary to them.

*Societies II.* Commons and Goodheart (2008) examined the degree of cultural support that helps societies evolve through the various stages in society associated with Commons' model of hierarchical complexity. They provided a 7-point scale ranging from manipulation to helping find phenomena. In an interesting application, Commons and Goodheart (2008) argued that cultural memes might develop according to the stages of Commons' model. Dawkins (1982) defined memes as the basic unit of information that is transmitted in a culture. Memes are like viruses, because they can "infect" people. As peoples' actions develop into higher stages of development, "they are more easily infected with the most hierarchical complex memes" (p. 412). That is, memes develop in complexity according to the cognitive sophistication of the stage with which they are associated. People who create memes must educate others in the culture in order for the memes to *infect* the culture. Memes are not necessarily progressive because they can be regressive and negative. Different degrees in the quality of support for cultural memes determine the nature and quality of their radiation in cultures. Commons (2008b) reviewed evolutionary theory and learning mechanisms as they relate to his model of hierarchical complexity. He distinguished between natural selection and cultural selection, as well as genes and memes.

*Comment.* Note that in Young (1997), I described the concept of "co-memes" to indicate how cultural memes are formed in collaboration with others. I had not considered that they could evolve in complexity through the stages with which they become associated, and therefore this stands as a major contribution made by Commons and Goodheart (2008). However, they did not give a full example in this regard. Moreover, I would argue that the present model provides a better structure on which to model the evolution of cultural memes in a society. This being said, cultural ideas should initiate at more than the reflexive level, and could pass through the various stages rather quickly. Most should be modeled from the concrete period onward (the mid-region of the present cognitive developmental model). Moreover, a good account of them will need to consider the five substages of the present work, as well (see Table 18.6) for an example of how a cultural meme and associated technological innovation spread and expand in complexity according to the present stage and substage model.

In addition, in the present work I have provided an evolutionary explanation for each of the five stages of the present model and how, in the last stage, memes are involved. This especially makes sense because the last stage of the present model is called collective intelligence (see Chap. 32).

## Transition Mechanisms

*Ross* (2008). Ross argued that patterns similar to the ones in Commons' sequence should be found in all behavior because of fractal transition processes. She maintained that the Commons model of the steps in the increasing complexity of a

**Table 18.6** Five steps in the growth of the Co-meme of computer innovation according to Young's Neo-Piagetian stage model (with substages for last stage)

| Stage (and substage) | Co-Meme description | Example |
|---|---|---|
| *Stage* | | |
| Reflexive | New idea is personal, self-oriented | Work in garage |
| Sensorimotor | Demonstration to others of possible utility | Laptop marketed to company |
| Perioperational | Convince one group of its utility | One company acquires rights |
| Abstract (Formal) | Idea enshrined conceptually in group | Company sells it |
| Collective intelligence | Group contributes to its improvement | Company and innovator brainstorm to improve it |
| *Substage* | | |
| Coordination | | Ideas emerge, compared |
| Hierarchization | | Best ones chosen |
| Systematization | | Put into practice |
| Multiplication | | Products improve, expand |
| Integration | | Integrated platforms in development |

Memes refer to the cultural competition, spread, and transmission of ideas, in a process akin to natural selection involving genes (Dawkins, 1976, 1982). The differences in gene and meme survival and reproduction relate not only to biological and environmental factors but also to individual and collective factors. In this regard, I refer to memes as co-memes (Young, 1997). Because memes are ideas, they could evolve in a way that maps onto the present model of cognitive development with respect to their origins and diversification in culture. The example provided relates to computers. Note that I describe substages only for the last stage of the present model, but the substages could be applied to each of the stages

system applies to machines, cells, and animals, and not only humans. For Ross, the process of stage transitions within the model evidences a fractalization process because, at each step, at least two lower-level actions or tasks are coordinated in a nonarbitrary manner. Her examples involve cross-species similarities; for example, they include sensorimotor actions that are reflex-type, which are found not only in mollusks and newborns but also in the functioning of the switch-like mechanism in the cellular potassium channel.

Ross presented a model in which there are eight transition steps that cyclically recur within each of the 15 orders of hierarchical complexity, with eight steps possible within each of the eight transition steps. This produces a developmental sequence of 960 possible steps, which is quite unwieldy, although Ross had not presented her model with this quantification.

*Comment.* Recall that in my model there are five stages, with five substages that cyclically recur within them, and the fractalization process continues with the possibility of five levels within each of the five substages. That is, in my model there are up to 125 possible developmental steps that make sense, whereas in Ross, the amount of possible steps approaches a too complex amount. The reason for the difference is that I describe a self-similar pattern over three scales that involves only five steps. However, for Ross, the two scales in her sequence include more steps.

Also, there is a fundamental difference in our understanding of fractalization. Traditionally, fractals refer to finding the same pattern at different levels of a system, such as indicated by the wavelets at the beach creating the same pattern as the indent of the bay in the ocean. My model fits this profile of fractals, in that the same five-step structure, and the characteristics associated with each step, repeats at each of the levels of stages, substages, and levels within stages. By contrast, for Ross, fractals seem to be evident by repetition of different numbers (8, 15) at different levels.

In Ross's model, fractals are described, but not as simplified as in the classic wavelet-bay example. Her model includes repetition of a pattern, but within a level, and repetition at different levels, but not with the same pattern. That is, in both cases, Ross has described a cyclic recursion of a transition of some sort, but the examples do not include all the conditions for labeling the repetitions as genuine fractals in the sense of self-similarity at different scales of the system. By contrast, for her third example of similarities involving sub-subtasks, where the eight transition steps are repeated within subtasks, she has described a genuine fractal.

As for the particular sequence of eight steps in Ross's transition sequence, they include three steps in deconstruction dynamics of a prior thesis and then five steps in reconstruction dynamic of a new thesis, or synthesis (see Table 18.7). It is noteworthy that the construction dynamic consists of five steps, as found in my model.

**Table 18.7** Transition steps in the model of hierarchical complexity in Commons

| Step | Relation | Name | Dynamics within Step |
|---|---|---|---|
| The first three steps are deconstructive dialectics | | | |
| 1 | a = a with b | Temporary equilibrium point (thesis) | While still operating with previous stage synthesis, it does not solve all tasks<br>Deconstruction begins, an extinction process |
| 2 | b | Negation or complementation (antithesis) | Negation or complementation. Inversion, or alternate thesis. Forms a second synthesis of previous stage actions |
| 3 | a or b | Relativism (alternation of thesis and antithesis) | Relativism. Alternates between thesis and antithesis. The schemes coexist, but there is no coordination among them |
| The remaining steps are constructive dynamics | | | |
| 4 | a and b | Smash (begins synthesis) | Begins extinction of the limitations of relativism's theses |
| 5 | | Smash[1]<br>Random hits, false alarms, and misses, low correct rejections | Elements from a and b are included in a nonsystematic, uncoordinated manner<br>Incorporates various subsets of all the possible elements |
| 6 | | Smash[2]<br>More hits, excess false alarms, low misses, and correct rejections | Incorporates subsets producing hits at stage n. Basis for exclusion not sharp. Overgeneralization |
| 7 | | Smash[3]<br>Correct rejections and excess misses, low hits, and false alarms | Incorporates subsets that produce correct rejections at stage n. Produces misses. Basis for inclusion not sharp. Undergeneralization |
| 8 | a with b | New temporary equilibrium (synthesis and new thesis) | Arrives at a new, temporary equilibrium where all elements are coordinated and "settled" |

Reprinted by permission of the publisher (Taylor & Francis Group, http://www.informaworld.com). Commons, M. L. (2008a). [Table 2, Page. 313]

## Summary and Conclusions

Commons and colleagues have developed a model of postformal adult development that they have expanded it into a lifespan model. Moreover, they have applied the model to multiple areas in development and even beyond, such as to evolution and the growth of societies. In this chapter, I have pointed out that their four-step sequence of postformal steps seems to be missing a hierarchical step. By modifying their model with an inclusion of such a step, it would be more consistent with my own model, which has five postformal steps. Moreover, with this additional step, some of the inconsistencies in the application of their model would be less problematic. Finally, I have pointed out how the present model can be used in a clearer way compared to their model to understand some developmental phenomena and other systems undergoing change, such as in societies and evolution. Even their model of transition mechanisms is consistent with that of the present model.

## References


Boccia, M., & Campos, J. J. (1989). Maternal emotional signals, social referencing, and infants' reactions to strangers. *New Directions for Child Development, 44*, 25–49.

Brown, W. (1960). *Exploration in management*. London: Heinemann.

Brown, W. (1962). *Piecework abandoned: The effect of wage incentive systems on managerial authority*. Harmondsworth: Penguin.

Case, R. (1992). The role of the frontal lobes in the regulation of cognitive development. *Brain and Cognition, 20*, 51–73.

Commons, M. L. (2008a). Introduction to the model of hierarchical complexity and its relationship to postformal action. *World Futures, 64*, 305–320.

Commons, M. L. (2008b). Selectionism and stage change: The dynamics of evolution, I. *World Futures, 64*, 348–360.

Commons, M. L., & Bresette, L. M. (2006). Illuminating major creative scientific innovators with postformal stages. In C. Hoare (Ed.), *Handbook of adult development and learning* (pp. 255–280). New York: Oxford University Press.

Commons, M. L., Bresette, L. M., & Ross, S. N. (2008). The connection between postformal thought and major scientific innovations. *World Futures, 64*, 503–512.

Commons, M. L., & Goodheart, E. A. (2008). Cultural progress is the result of developmental level of support. *World Futures, 64*, 406–415.

Commons, M. L., & Miller, P. M. (2002a). A complete theory of human evolution of intelligences must consider stage changes. *Behavioral and Brain Sciences, 25*, 405.

Commons, M. L., & Miller, P. M. (2002b). A complete theory of empathy must consider stage changes. *Behavioral and Brain Sciences, 25*, 30–31.

Commons, M. L., & Ross, S. N. (2008a). What postformal thought is, and why it matters. *World Futures, 64*, 321–329.

Commons, M. L., & Ross, S. N. (2008b). Toward a cross-species measure of general intelligence. *World Futures, 64*, 383–398.

Commons, M. L., & Ross, S. N. (2008c). The hierarchical complexity view of evolution and history. *World Futures, 64*, 399–405.

Dawkins, R. (1976). *The selfish gene*. New York: Oxford University Press.

Dawkins, R. (1982). *The extended phenotype: The gene as the unit of selection*. San Francisco: Freeman.

Dawson, T. L. (2004). Assessing intellectual development: Three approaches, one sequence. *Journal of Adult Development, 11*, 71–85.
Day, J. M. (2008). Human development and the model of hierarchical complexity: Learning from research in the psychology of moral and religious development. *World Futures, 64*, 452–467.
de Waal, F. B. M. (1996). *Good natured: The origins of right and wrong in humans and other animals*. Cambridge: Harvard University Press.
de Waal, F. B. M., & Lanting, F. (1997). *Bonobo: The forgotten ape*. Berkeley, CA: University of California Press.
Field, T. (1989). Individual and maturational differences in infant expressivity. *New Directions for Child Development, 44*, 9–24.
Fischer, K. W. (1980). A theory of cognitive development: The control and construction of hierarchies of skills. *Psychological Review, 87*, 477–531.
Fischer, K. W., & Bidell, T. R. (2006). Dynamic development of action and thought. In W. Damon & R. M. Lerner (Eds.), *Handbook of child psychology* (Theoretical models of human development, Vol. 1, pp. 313–399). New York: Wiley.
Fowler, J. (1981). *Stages of faith*. San Francisco: Harper and Row.
Fowler, J. (1996). *Faithful change*. San Francisco: Harper and Row.
Griffin, S. (2005). Fostering the development of whole-number sense: Teaching mathematics in the primary grades. In M. S. Donovan & J. D. Bransford (Eds.), *How students learn: History, mathematics and science in the classroom* (pp. 257–308). Washington, DC: The National Academies Press.
Hoffman, M. L. (1978). Toward a theory of empathic arousal and development. In M. Lewis & L. A. Rosenblum (Eds.), *The development of affect* (pp. 227–256). New York: Plenum Press.
Inhelder, B., & Piaget, J. (1958). *The growth of logical thinking from childhood to adolescence: An essay on the development of formal operational structures*. (A. Parsons & S. Seagrim, Trans.). New York: Basic Books. (Originally published 1955).
Jaques, E. (1976). *A general theory of bureaucracy*. London: Heinemann.
Jaques, E. (1996). *Requisite organization: A total system for effective managerial organization and managerial leadership for the 21st century*. Arlington, VA: Cason Hall.
Koplowitz, H. (2008). In praise of top-down decision making in managerial hierarchies. *World Futures, 64*, 513–523.
Kuczynski, L., Kochanska, G., Radke-Yarrow, M., & Girnius-Brown, O. (1987). A developmental interpretation of young children's noncompliance. *Developmental Psychology, 23*, 799–806.
Mascolo, M. F. (2008). The concept of domain in developmental analyses of hierarchical complexity. *World Futures, 64*, 330–347.
Meltzoff, A. N., & Moore, M. K. (1977). Imitation of facial and manual gestures by human neonates. *Science, 198*, 75–78.
Pepperberg, I. (1992). Proficient performance of a conjunction, recursive task by an African gray parrot (Psittacus erithacus). *Journal of Comparative Psychology, 106*, 295–305.
Piaget, J. (1971). The theory of stages in cognitive development. In D. R. Green, M. P. Ford, & G. B. Flamer (Eds.), *Measurement and Piaget* (pp. 1–11). New York: McGraw Hill.
Piaget, J. (1983). Piaget's theory. In W. Kessen (Ed.), *History, theory, and methods* (pp. 103–126). New York: Wiley.
Ross, S. N. (2008). Fractal transition steps to fractal stages: The dynamics of evolution, II. *World Futures, 64*, 361–374.
Ross, S. N., & Commons, M. L. (2008). Applying hierarchical complexity to political development. *World Futures, 64*, 480–497.
Selman, R. L. (1980). *The growth of interpersonal understanding: Developmental and clinical analyses*. New York: Academic Press.
Wolfsont, C., Ross, S. N., Miller, P. M., Commons, M. L., & Chernoff, M. (2008). Domain-specific increases in stage of performance in a complete theory of the evolution of human intelligence. *World Futures, 64*, 416–429.
Wynn, T. (1981). The intelligence of Oldowan hominids. *Journal of Human Evolution, 10*, 529–541.

Wynn, T. (1993). Two developments in the mind of early Homo. *Journal of Anthropological Archaeology, 12*, 299–322.

Young, G. (1990a). Early neuropsychological development: Lateralization of functions - hemispheric specialization. In C. A. Hauert (Ed.), *Developmental psychology: Cognitive, perceptuo-motor and neuropsychological perspectives* (pp. 113–181). Amsterdam: North Holland.

Young, G. (1990b). The development of hemispheric and manual specialization. In G. E. Hammond (Ed.), *Cerebral control of speech and limb movements* (pp. 79–139). Amsterdam: North Holland.

Young, G. (1997). *Adult development, therapy, and culture: A postmodern synthesis*. New York: Plenum.

Zahn-Waxler, C., & Kochanska, G. (1988). The origins of guild. In R. A. Thompson (Ed.), *Socioemotional development: Current theory and research in motivation* (pp. 183–258). Lincoln, NB: University of Nebraska Press.

Zahn-Waxler, C., Kochanska, G., Radke-Yarrow, M., & King, R. A. (1979). Child rearing and children's prosocial initiations toward victims of distress. *Child Development, 50*, 319–330.

# Chapter 19
# Development of Personality and Motivational Needs

## Introduction

The present chapter examines three orientations to the study of personality and I show how they are consistent with the present work (Five Factor Model, narrative identity, hierarchy of needs). For the first, the five personality factors are thought to emerge in an order that is consistent with the five stages of the present model. For the second, narrative identity is construed as an acquisition that evolves with the five stages. For the third, I present a revised model of Maslow's classic five-level model and show how it is consistent with the five stages of the present model. This leads to a model of the development of romantic relationships that is consistent with the present model of stages in development and with the revision of Maslow's model.

## Reviews of the Literature

There have been two major reviews in the last few years on personality development (Caspi, Roberts, & Shiner, 2005; Caspi & Shiner, 2006; Mervielde, De Clercq, De Fruyt, & Van Leeuwen, 2005). I had reviewed these articles in Young (2008).

### *Caspi and Shiner*

#### Introduction

Caspi and Shiner (2006) indicated that, traditionally, child psychologists study temperament rather than personality, per se, but that there is much correspondence between the trait structures that are found in both. For example, Rothbart and Derryberry (2002) examined the factor structure of responses to caregivers on temperament questionnaires about their infants and toddlers, and the authors found three factors comparable to those found in older children and adults. Other research

G. Young, *Development and Causality: Neo-Piagetian Perspectives*,
DOI 10.1007/978-1-4419-9422-6_19, 

might find more factors than is evident in adults, not less, such as the factor of dependency. Overall, though, the research supports equivalence between the factors that emerge in the early years and those found in the adult, with the factors in both cases revolving around the Five Factor Model.

According to Caspi and Shiner (2006), in terms of several lines of empirical investigation, childhood personality structure appears to map onto the structure found in adults. In research on children from the age of 3 years to adolescence, questionnaires, adjective lists, and Q-sorts have been factor-analyzed, and generally they produce five factors that are akin to those in adults. The research has included measures of parental reports, teacher reports, and self-reports (e.g., Measelle, John, Ablow, Cowan, & Cowan, 2005). The temperament research with younger children has yielded a factor structure with up to four factors, and these factors are comparable to four of the Big Five factors – Surgency (Extraversion), Negative affectivity (Neuroticism), Effortful control (Conscientiousness), and Affiliativeness (Agreeableness) (with no equivalent factor for Openness to Experience). (However, according to Caspi et al. (2005), the research on early temperament reveals six traits, although not necessarily equivalent to those on the Big Five.) When behavior is analyzed in children, either on tasks or observationally, the standard five-factor structure is found.

When personality in children is studied from the perspective of personality types rather than dimensions, generally, three types are found – Resilients, Overcontrollers, and Undercontrollers. These types cannot be translated into Big Five equivalents. However, researchers are attempting to understand the variations in the Big Five dimensions that contribute to them (Mervielde et al., 2005).

Caspi and Shiner (2006) undertook a detailed literature review to justify their model of which of the lower-order traits constitute the higher-order ones in the Five Factor Model. For extraversion, they identified the lower-order traits of sociability and energy/activity level. For neuroticism, they identified those of fear, anxiety, and sadness; for conscientiousness, it was attention, self-control, achievement motivation, and orderliness; for agreeableness, they were prosocial tendencies, antagonism, and willfulness; and for openness to experience, those that emerged were intellect, creativity, curiosity. Some other lower-order traits were hypothesized to load on two rather than one of the higher-order ones (social inhibition on extraversion and neuroticism; anger/irritability and alienation/mistrust on neuroticism and agreeableness; responsibility on conscientiousness and agreeableness). (Note that Caspi et al. (2005) presented a slightly different set of lower-order factors for each higher-order factor considered developmentally in the Five Factor Model).

## Five Factors

Next, Caspi and Shiner (2006) described in depth the developmental profile of each of the five dimensions of the Five Factor Model.

For extraversion, the authors described children as varying in the degree to which they are active, surgently engaged, sociable, expressive, high-spirited, lively, socially adept, active, and energetic compared to quiet, inhibited, and lethargic. The authors related the factor of extraversion to biological underpinnings in degree to which there is present in the child behavioral approach, activation, and appetitive system implication (the Behavioral Activation System; Gray, 1987, 1990). Davidson, Pizzagalli, Nitschke, and Kalin (2003) had shown that behavioral approach might be mediated by specialized neural substrates in the left anterior cerebral cortex.

For Caspi and Shiner, neuroticism in children refers to variations in negative emotions and in general distress (in particular, in anxiety, vulnerability, tension, fright, falling part, feeling under stress, feeling guilt, moodiness, low frustration tolerance, and insecurity in social relationships). On the positive side of the pole, neuroticism refers to stability, adaptability, bouncing back, and being laid back, summarized as regulating negative emotions. Neuroticism is related to individual variation in withdrawal, inhibition, and avoidance (In this regard, the authors referred to the biologically based Behavior Inhibition System; Gray, 1987, 1990). Davidson et al. (2003) had demonstrated that behavioral withdrawal might be mediated by specialized neural substrates in the right anterior cerebral cortex.

As for conscientiousness in children, Caspi and Shiner described it in terms of self-control, especially toward completing tasks and attempting to meet standards. The more children are conscientious, the more they also demonstrate being responsible, attentive, persistent, orderly, planful, of high standards, and prone to think before acting. At the other extreme, children might be irresponsible, unreliable, careless, distractible, and give up easily. The self-regulation takes place at both the effortful voluntary and the automatic, nonvoluntary levels. Biologically, the neural substrates identified with conscientiousness include frontal regions of the brain, such as the anterior cingulate cortex.

For children, agreeableness refers to characteristics such as being warm, considerate, empathic, generous, gentle, kind, manageable, and protective of others. At the low end, it refers to being aggressive, rude, spiteful, stubborn, bossy, cynical, and manipulative. Biologically, one finds associations with substrates of the affectional system, such as endogenous opioids, oxytocin, and brain areas supporting positive emotions.

In children, openness to experience refers to eagerness to learn, cleverness, knowledge acquisition, perceptivity, imagination, curiosity, and originality. Caspi and Shiner did not describe biological associations for this trait.

## *Mervielde et al.*

### Introduction

Mervielde et al. (2005) proposed a hierarchical model of childhood personality, based on the Five Factor Model. They identified two broad bands, concerning internalizing and externalizing, and for narrow bands, they identified the five dimensions of the Big Five. In their review, they identified four basic dimensions found across different models of early temperament. These early personality precursors were identified as (Negative) Emotionality, Extraversion, Activity, and Persistence.

The Caspi and Shiner (2006) review presented above also identified four early temperament factors, but two of these factors appear different than those proposed by Mervielde et al. Therefore, it appears that further conceptualization is needed, although I do offer below a preliminary developmental model in this regard. However, it is worth noting that the early temperamental factors listed in Caspi and Shiner do correspond to Big Five factors (Surgency [Extraversion], Negative affectivity [Neuroticism], Effortful control [Conscientiousness], and Affiliativeness [Agreeableness]).

### Five Factors

Mervielde et al. (2005) reviewed the research that supported the conclusion that five broad-band factors emerge in the developmental personality literature. For example, Mervielde, Buyst, and DeFuyt (1995) examined teacher ratings of 4–12-year-olds, Mervielde and DeFuyt (2000) examined peer nominations of 9–12-year-olds, and Kohnstamm, Halverson, Mervielde, and Haville (1998) investigated parental description of child personality.

In the latter research, on the Hierarchical Personality Inventory for Children administered to parents of 9,000 Flemish children for description of personality, at each age level (5–7, 8–10, 11–13), the first five principal components reflected the factors of the Five Factor Model.

Mervielde et al. (2005) developed an instrument that examines normal personality structure, which gives findings that reveal a five-factor structure (the HiPIC; Hierarchical Personality Inventory for Children; Mervielde & DeFuyt, 2002). The factors were labeled: Extraversion, Emotional Stability, Benevolence, Conscientiousness, and Imagination.

As for the research by the authors with adolescents, De Clercq and De Fruyt (2003), and De Clercq, De Fruyt, and Van Leeuwen (2004) investigated two samples of adolescents in self-ratings of Five Factor Model inventories and personality disorder inventories. The studies used different inventories for the Five Factor Model, yet both studies emerged with patterns of results "remarkably" comparable to those in the meta-analysis on the adult research by Saulsman and Page (2004; supportive of the Five Factor Model structure).

## *Comment*

The overall conclusion to the developmental research that has been reviewed by Caspi and by Mervielde and their colleagues is that, for both the areas of early temperament and later personality development, there is enough evidence revealing a correspondence in the major personality factors found developmentally and those found in the Five Factor Model in adults. This augurs well for developing an integrated model of personality that spans the different ages. However, clearly, much more research is needed. Moreover, it appears that important developmental issues have yet to be integrated into this research, such as inclusion of the stage concept in development.

## Development, Stages, Personality, Disorder, Relationships

### *Introduction*

In order to construct a model of the relationship between the specific Five Factor Model of normal personality dimensions and that of development, in general, we need to consider several issues. First, the Five Factor Model was developed atheoretically, through factor analytic research of lexical terms. The participant population involved concerned adults, and these participants were not examined longitudinally. Therefore, at first glance, the Five Factor Model would seem to have little to offer to any developmental model, especially ones that are theoretically driven, such as stage-based ones.

However, as has been shown, (a) the Five Factor Model has been related to earlier developing temperamental and personality models in infants, children, and adolescents. (b) Neurobiological substrates for each of them have been found, except perhaps for Openness to experience. (c) The present model of development does lend itself to inclusion of a Five Factor approach to understanding developing personality.

### *Present Stage Model in Relation to the Five Factor Model*

In Young (1997), I queried the appropriate order of emergence of aspects of the Big Five personality factors in relation to their corresponding stage of development according to the present stage model of development. I had argued that the appropriate sequence of Big Five personality factors, in terms of their order of development of relevant components and precursors, consists of extraversion, agreeableness, conscientiousness, stability (neuroticism), and openness to experience. Based on the comprehensive literature reviews surveyed in the section above, I now suggest that the personality dimensions of stability and agreeableness should be switched in the proposed progression. Therefore, the present hypothesis is that in development of dimensions of temperament-personality related to the Five Factor Model and components and precursors of these traits, the order of emergence is as follows: (a) extraversion, (b) stability (neuroticism), (c) conscientiousness, (d) agreeableness, and (e) openness to experience (Table 19.1).

**Table 19.1** Correspondence between the five-factor model of personality and Young's model of developmental stages

| Personality factor | Developmental stage |
|---|---|
| Extraversion | Physical (reflexive) |
| Stability (neuroticism) | Emotional (sensorimotor) |
| Conscientiousness | Cognitive (perioperational/representational) |
| Agreeableness | Conscious (abstract) |
| Openness to experience | Spiritual (collective intelligence) |

Adapted from Young (2008)

The Five Factor Model is the predominant one in the study of normal personality. The particular polar opposites in the five dimensions and some of the facets that have been postulated for them are as follows: extraversion/introversion – gregariousness, assertiveness; agreeableness/antagonism – trust, straightforwardness; conscientiousness/lack of direction – competence, order; neuroticism/emotional stability – anxiety, angry hostility; openness to experience/closedness – ideas, fantasy

Both in the areas of early temperament in infancy and toddlers and later personality development in children and adolescents, the literature suggests a correspondence across the major temperament/personality-related factors found developmentally and the personality factors found in the Five Factor Model in adults. The present model aligns the five stages of the present model with the associated personality factors in the Five Factor Model, specifying their order of emergence in development according to the literature (see Young, 2008)

Note that according to me the neuroticism-stability factor should be renamed as the stability-neuroticism one. Of the five factors in the Five Factor Model, it is the only one that is named for the negative aspect of its underlying dimension. Should any one follow suit on this recommendation, the classic mnemonic for remembering the five factors would have to be changed from OCEAN to something like OCASE or ESCAO

For example, in the proposed sequence in the emergence of personality factors, (a) the first stage brings with it important activity components to the neonate, (b) the second emotional ones to the infant, (c) the third application of effort to the child, (d) the fourth a capacity to focus and manage to the adolescent, and (e) the fifth intellectual priority to the adult. Following, in part, Depue and Lenzenweger (2005), the extent of problems that might develop in the respective developmental stages in terms of these components of personality dimensions extend, respectively, into the following: (a) action and initial agentic components, (b) social and affiliation ones, (c) academic and self-control ones, (d) interpersonal relationship and consciousness ones, and (e) existential and spiritual ones.

On the one hand, this model might seem sufficient in representing the relationship between personality and development because it shows a possible relationship to the Big Five personality factors and the present stages of development. However, I add that the proposed order of development of the five major dimensions of personality should not materialize as clearly as presented. For example, Erikson (1968) proposed that identity is not only the critical developmental issue in the adolescent stage of development but also an issue in the stages both preceding and following the adolescent one, albeit to lesser degrees.

Similarly, I propose that components and precursors of all the five major personality dimensions surface in development right from infancy but that, one by one according to the sequence indicated, they take a prominent role in development, without denying that in each stage all five are relevant to some degree. Therefore, the components and precursors of each of the personality dimensions of the Five Factor Model are posited to develop from early in life while, at the same time, each one is hypothesized to manifest as primary in development at its presumed focal stage.

## Temperament and Personality Over the Life Span

Bates, Schermerhorn, and Goodnight (2010) addressed whether the five personality constructs in the Five Factor Model of personality develop prior to the adult period and, if so, whether there is stability in the development of these dimensions. The authors found correlates of the Big Five in childhood temperament. Also, the literature revealed that, over the life span, the five personality factors evidence continuity and stability. Some of the developmental parallels for each of the five factors that they provided in their literature review are summarized. (a) For example, for extroversion, infants are already smiling at 2 months of age. (b) For negative emotionality, 3-month-olds can be soothed and have their distress reduced. (c) For agreeableness, cooperativity is stable from infancy onward. (d) For conscientiousness, the executive attention that is part of effortful control emerges before the first birthday (Kochanska, Murray, & Harlan, 2000). (e) For openness to experience, researchers have found consistency from the age of 4 onward.

This survey does not imply that the Big Five factors all emerge in infancy but only that there are precursors to them in the first years of life. These data support the present argument that the factors emerge from beginning early in life in the sequence indicated. Moreover, the precursors for each one are evident early in life.

## Narrative Identity

### *Model*

McAdams (2010) has proposed a narrative model of self, personality, and identity. He defined narrative identity as an internalized story that provides a sense of unity, purpose, and meaning for the developing self. It includes a person's reconstruction of the past and a hoped-for future. He argued that narrative identity develops especially in the adult years and that it is constantly modified. He placed the concept of narrative identity as one level in a multilevel, integrative theory of personality and selfhood across the life span (McAdams & Cox, 2010).

McAdams (2010) indicated that Erikson (1963) set an important stage for the elaboration of the concept of identity, especially in his stage of identity formation in adolescence. Marcia (1980) has expanded Erikson's (1963) model in terms of the processes of identity exploration and commitment to identity. McAdams (2010) indicated that his work is more focused on expanding understanding of the product in identity development.

McAdams and Pals (2006) viewed the concept of narrative identity as the third layer in their model of human personality. First, they described a layer of broad dispositional traits, such as extroversion. Next, personality involves a second layer of characteristic adaptations or socially contextualized and motivational aspects, such as values and goals. Third, narrative identity adds what a person's life means to him or her and how the person relates to the surrounding world and culture over time. McAdams and Cox (2010) added that narrative identity develops in three different components related to the I-self and the Me-self – the self as actor, agent, and author. That is, the development of personality across the life span involves the person as actor (behaving), as agent (striving), and as author (narrating). For example, human infants are already social actors; next, toddlers begin to develop an actor-self; and then at 4 years of age, children develop a theory of mind. As development proceeds, the I-self becomes a goal-directed, motivated agent. In adolescence, the I-self constructs or authors for the Me-self a self-defining story or narrative. The Me-self becomes the story that the person constructs, but there are also elements of the self as actor and agent that are always present, too.

## *Development*

McAdams (2010; McAdams & Olson, 2010) indicated that by the first year of infancy, the child recognizes through both imitation and attention that the parent or primary caregiver acts with intentionality through goal-directed behaviors (Kuhlmeier, Wynn, & Bloom, 2003). The 2-year-old begins to develop the capacity to construct a Me-self through developing skills of the I-self. For example, Howe and Courage (1997) maintained that children at this age begin to encode, collect, and provide narratives of their autobiographical memories. Social context provides the ground for the development of autobiographical memories and storytelling skills. For example, according to Fivush and Nelson (2004), parents will often encourage their children to talk about their personal experiences as soon as they develop the skills that permit them to do so. By 5 years of age, children know the canonical features of a story (or story grammar; Mandler, 1984). They internalize norms and expectations about what a story involves in their culture. Their stories develop a "causal coherence," as well as a "thematic coherence" (Habermas & de Silveria, 2008), with these narrative skills increasing in the teenage years. McAdams (2010) concluded that cognitive development sets the stage for the development of narrative identity. At the same time, socioemotional and cultural factors constitute important factors in narrative identity development.

### *Comment*

McAdams has developed a model of narrative identity that emphasizes the narrative construction capacities of the developing person. Stories help define identities; storytelling skills indicate cognitive and social skills. At several levels, the present work deals with the topic of developing narrative abilities and identity. First, I have argued that the self develops according to the 25 steps of the present model, as do Eriksonian acquisitions, including of identity. Second, in a following chapter, I review the literature on the development of storytelling and narrative ability, and propose a coding system based on textual cohesion and coherence for use in discourse analysis. One could ask if there is a relationship between cognitive capacity, narrative integrity, and use of cohesive devices. Do the lower-order linguistic structures of developing narrative constructions reveal higher-order complexity in narrative story quality (see Chaps. 33 and 34)?

### *Interim Summary*

To this point in the chapter, I have focused on the Five Factor Model of personality and how it emerges in development. I have shown that it is consistent with the present model of five stages in development. I examined the concept of narrative identity, and it, too, is consistent with the present work. In the last part of the chapter, I examine another important personality theorist, and show that his work can be revised to fit the present five-step stage model.

## Revising Maslow's Model of Motivational Needs

### *Renovating Maslow*

Schaller, Neuberg, Griskevicius, and Kenrick (2010) presented a revised version of Maslow's pyramidal model of motivational needs. Maslow's (1943, 1970) classic model of hierarchy of needs consists of five levels. They involve (a) immediate physiological needs, (b) safety, (c) love (affection, belongingness), (d) esteem (respect), and (e) self-actualization (see Fig. 19.1). Maslow considered the needs innate and universal predispositions. He saw them as multiple and independent. He viewed the hierarchy as involving fundamental motivational systems in which some motives take precedence over others. For example, the motives have a sequence of cognitive priority depending on the necessities confronted by the individual. Also, they have developmental priority, in that as people mature, they move from lower to higher levels in the hierarchy. Maslow is famous for his concept of self-actualization,

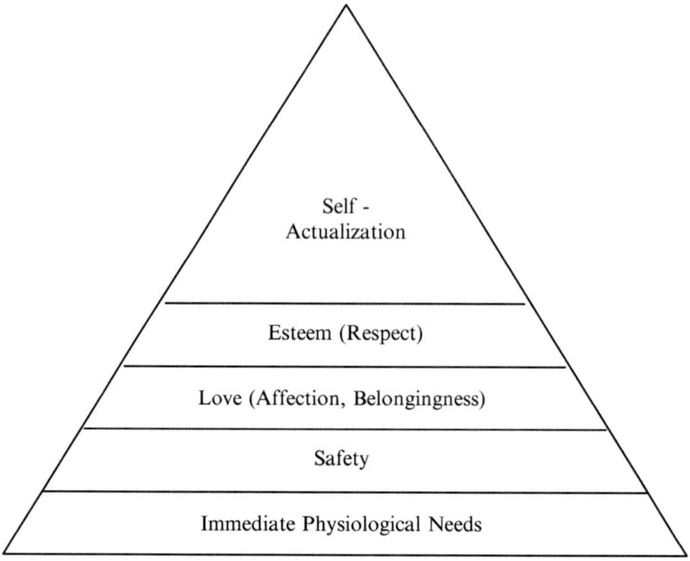


**Fig. 19.1** Maslow's classic hierarchy of needs: in his model of human motivation, Maslow (1943, 1970) distinguished between biological needs, such as hunger, sleep, and thirst, and psychological needs, such as affection, belonging, and self-esteem. Satisfaction of the biological needs ensures survival, but also one cannot develop fully as a psychological being without satisfaction of higher-order needs. Maslow created a pyramidal model of a hierarchy of needs from basic physiological needs to important psychological needs. Maslow considered as optimal motivational processes expressed when people function creatively and fulfill or actualize their potential. Reprinted with the permission of SAGE Publications. Maslow, A. H. (1943). Copyright © 1943 by Association for Psychological Science. [Figure 1, Page. 293]

which stands at the apex of his model. For Maslow, it concerns fulfilling one's creative potential. Its particular focus is determined at an individual level. It can only become a priority when other needs are satisfied. In this regard, Maslow anticipated the movement of positive psychology. I note that he maintained that cognitive and developmental priorities are not necessarily one and the same. For example, a person could be more mature developmentally on the hierarchy but face basic biological needs and revert to those as primary.

Kenrick et al. (2010) updated Maslow's model by removing self-actualization at the top of the hierarchy and replacing it with family-related functions, such as mate acquisition, mate retention, and parenting. They argued that self-actualization is not a functionally distinct human motivational need, despite its psychological importance. In terms of biological needs, the authors emphasized the inclusive fitness of motivational needs, or their Darwinian survival and reproductive value, whether directly or indirectly, through kin (e.g., Garver-Apgar, Gangestad, & Thornhill, 2008). They criticized Maslow for placing sexual desire in the same category as hunger and other essentials for survival. They argued that a more contemporary perspective would view sexual desire as part of an evolutionary strategy for Darwinian survival and reproduction, and therefore higher up on the needs hierarchy. They related self-actualization to mating motives. "Self-actualization, in this light, can provide an alternative pathway to esteem and to social status and, consequently, has indirect

**Table 19.2** Correspondence between Maslow's model of five levels of needs and Young's model of five Neo-Piagetian stages

| | Five developmental levels | |
|---|---|---|
| Age period | Neo-Piagetian stage (Young) | Level of need (Maslow) |
| Prenatal | Reflexive | Physiological |
| Newborn | Sensorimotor | Security |
| Child | Perioperational | Love (affection, belongingness) |
| Teen | Abstract | Self-esteem |
| Adult | Collective intelligence | Self-actualization |

Maslow (1943, 1970) had developed a pyramidal model of a hierarchy of motivational needs. He considered that the order of the levels approximated a developmental sequence. He was part of a movement trying to establish a third force between (a) the psychodynamic, unconscious and (b) the behaviorist, environmental-learning models. In both models, the person is considered passive, or molded, rather than active and with a self that drives behavior. In his model, Maslow structured a hierarchy of needs that included the biological, the physical, and the environmental at the lower levels, and also included the self at the upper levels. There are five levels of needs in his model, and they involve needs related to physiology, security, affection/belongingness (love), self-esteem, and self-actualization

With some modification, Maslow's model of five levels of need maps onto the present model of five stages in development. The stages of the present model refer to reflexive, sensorimotor, perioperational, abstract, and collective intelligence steps

(a) *Reflexive*. The equivalence of the reflexive and physical levels in Maslow's and the present model, respectively, is self-evident. There is debate whether this most basic level of need should include sexual needs because sex is associated with adults, and Maslow's model concerns development and not only motivational needs (Kenrick et al., 2010). I address the matter in discussion of Fig. 19.4. Suffice it to say that I relate the level of immediate physiological needs to survival and reproduction, after Darwin's evolutionary model of natural selection. Kenrick et al. do note that the needs aspect of Maslow's model does not apply developmentally in all situations, e.g., adults can regress to or continue to indulge in the most basic needs, as well

(b) *Sensorimotor*. As for the sensorimotor stage and the need of safety, their equivalence lies in the development of attachment. The sensorimotor period is one in which the infant develops attachment to the caregiver. Moreover, the infant and caregiver generally create a secure relationship. Attachment processes are considered biologically driven because of selected need to seek and maintain proximity and contact with the caregiver. Note that by expanding the notion of safety to security, I am adding a psychological component to the physical aspect in the concept of safety as a need. Strictly speaking, physical safety should be associated with the prior level of need of immediate physiological needs and not this level. The preservation of physical integrity and the avoidance of pain, for example, are immediate physical needs. That is, by expanding Maslow's concept of needs to include attachment security as well as safety, I am making the model more amenable to finding correspondences with equivalent Neo-Piagetian stages. This theme that Maslow's description of needs has to be adjusted one level to arrive at a better fit with the present cognitive model repeats as I present below other levels in Maslow's need hierarchy

(c) *Perioperational*. Maslow described the third level of motivational needs as involving love. This would seem to create a problem for the hypothesis that his model of a hierarchy of developmental needs shows parallels with the present model of developmental cognitive stages. First, love is associated with the theory of attachment that has been posited to exhibit a correspondence with the prior cognitive stage of the present model. Second, the cognitive stage with which the motivational need of love is considered as parallel is increasingly sophisticated cognitively, as it involves Piagetian preoperations and concrete operations

This conundrum led me to expand the Maslow's model in the way described in Fig. 19.4. First, I noted that there are two components to Maslow's level of love, affection, and belongingness. The latter

(continued)

**Table 19.2** (continued)

seemed more about personal needs and the former about relationship to the other. About the nature of love and affection in this period, it seems more active than passive compared to the equivalents in the attachment processes evident in the prior developmental period. Moreover, affection and belongingness could refer to a general insertion in the social niche of the child, from family to peers at school. In this regard, the need that Maslow had posited for the third level of his model could refer to a more general fit of the person in the school environment as much as anywhere else, and success at school depends on both social skills and cognitive ones. I have argued on the intimate connection between cognition and socioaffectivity throughout the present work. Therefore, I would qualify Maslow's description of the middle level of needs in his hierarchy by arguing that it refers not just to love (affection, belongingness), but more generally to adaptive social/familial/educational needs

Aside from adjusting Maslow's five-step hierarchical model of needs in the middle level to accommodate to a wider range of social influences and the targets to which they are oriented, I realized that his twofold description of love in terms of affection and belongingness could reflect that each of Maslow's five needs in his model should be elaborated in terms of a more personal and a more relational component. Elsewhere in the present work, I have elaborated a model of the self in terms of two major components, partly after the labels of the I self and the Me self described in James (1890). The two self-components in the present model were given the labels of a self-definitional self and a relatedness self, after the labels for the two polarities in experience described in Blatt (2008). With this logic, it seemed to make sense to describe a self-definitional component to each of the levels in the hierarchy of needs in Maslow's model as well as a relatedness-self component

In this regard, for the third level of love in Maslow's need hierarchy, I propose that it involves a more personal-focused self-definitional love, and place his example of an affection need in this component. As for the example of love as belongingness, I propose a more relationship-with-other focused relatedness-self love, and place his example of belongingness in this aspect of love. In addition, I added an Eriksonian focus to both sides of the love described by Maslow in his model of need, by including in the revised model the first of the two stages in Erikson's model that apply to the age period involved, that of initiative. In addition, I included the educational/instructional focus alluded to above for this age period, thereby describing the need associated with this age period as a general adaptation rather than a uniquely affective one. Finally, I used the term of affiliation for this need level, as proposed in the revision of Maslow's model by Kenrick et al. (2010)

In the end, after this train of thought, I refer to the third level of Maslow's needs in terms of two complementary components – self-definitional initiative-education/love (affection) affiliation and relatedness self initiative-education/love (belongingness) affiliation. The terms are cumbersome and, for shorthand, can be referred to as "self-definitional affiliative initiative" and "relatedness-self affiliative initiative." These terms include the connotative meaning of Maslow's term along with those of Erikson and Blatt, in particular (I used Kenrick et al.'s term that had been used to replace the too general term of Love employed by Maslow). I used the same type of procedure of finding a dual track in self- and other-related needs to come up with workable labels for the other four levels in the present model of a revised Maslovian model of hierarchical needs (see Fig. 19.4)

(d) *Abstract.* I return to the major thread of this exercise – to reveal the validity in finding parallels between the cognitive levels of the present Neo-Piagetian model with the levels of hierarchical needs in Maslow's model. For the fourth level of esteem and respect in Maslow, it needs as much reworking as Love needed in the prior age period. Self-esteem initiates especially in the childhood period compared to the adolescent period, and the fourth level of the present model concerns adolescent abstract thought. Therefore, the concept of self-esteem needs to be augmented by an addition that makes it more focused on teenagers. Once more, by turning to Erikson, and his concept of identity formation in the adolescent period, the self-process at play in the fourth period of the conjoint Neo-Piagetian-Maslow model being proposed becomes restricted enough to apply to this age period. That is, it appears that by referring to self-esteem in terms of its relationship to identity formation, in particular, it can be associated readily enough with the abstract stage of adolescence

(continued)

**Table 19.2** (continued)

| |
|---|
| (e) *Collective intelligence*. As for the final Maslow level of self-actualization in his pyramidal model of needs, once more, it appears more associated with the prior level as presently defined, that is, with an identity formation component added. Maslow defined self-actualization especially in terms of creativity and other ways of self-expression. By contrast, Erikson referred to the adult period as involving generativity, or contributing to family and society. The latter concept makes more sense as a need-type motivation for the adult period compared to the restricted nature of the concept of self-actualization in Maslow, at least as originally conceived |

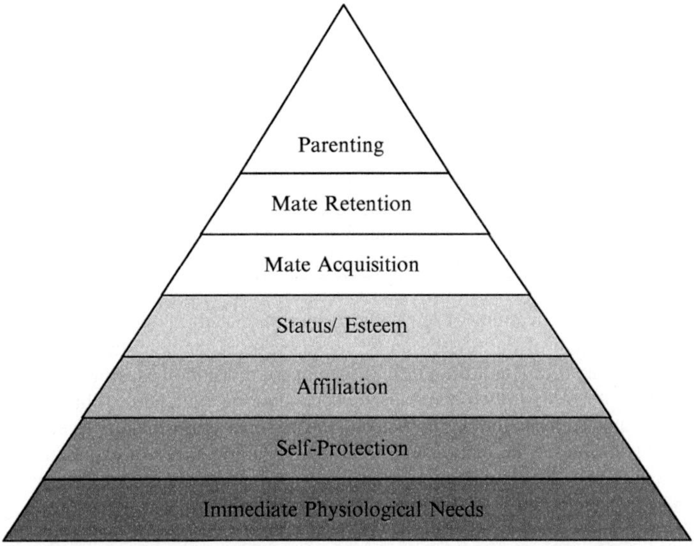


**Fig. 19.2** Revised hierarchy of needs according to Kenrick, Griskevicius, Neuberg, and Schaller (2010): an updated hierarchy of fundamental human motives. This figure integrates ideas from life-history development with Maslow's classic hierarchy. This scheme adds reproductive goals, in the order they are likely to first appear developmentally. The model also depicts the later developing goal systems as overlapping with, rather than completely replacing, earlier developing systems. Once a goal system has developed, its activation will be triggered whenever relevant environmental cues are salient. Reprinted with the permission of SAGE Publications. Kenrick, D. T., Griskevicius, V., Neuberg, S. L., & Schaller, M. (2010). Copyright © 2010 by Association for Psychological Science. [Figure 2, Page. 293]

implications for successful mating and reproductive fitness" (p. 298). In effect, they argued that natural selection has a role to play throughout development (the life history approach). For each species' life cycle, from conception to the end of life, natural selection shapes behavior to facilitate survival and reproductive success (Stearns, Allal, & Mace, 2008).

Another important contribution of Kenrick et al. (2010) was to examine more closely Maslow's category of love. First, they argued that it reflects a more general motive of social affiliation. Second, they noted that relationships differ across different social objects, such as romantic partners, family, and friends. After presenting

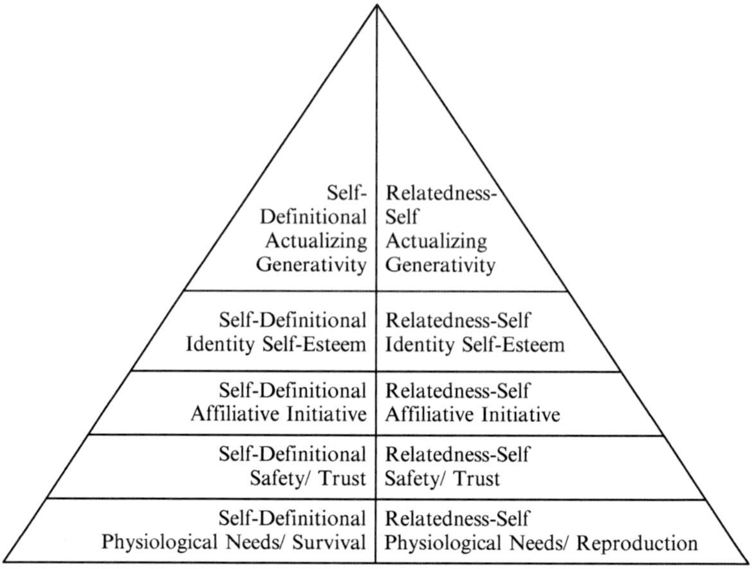


**Fig. 19.3** Neo-Piagetian hierarchy of self-definitional and relatedness self needs: the figure gives simplified terms for each of the revised motivational needs in the combined model of Maslow (1943, 1970), Erikson (1980), and Blatt (2008). The major revision of Maslow concerns dividing his different levels of needs in two components, depending on what part of the self is involved. The *left-hand* columns refer to the needs related to the personal self, while the *right hand* columns refer to the needs of the self in relationship. Blatt referred to polarities of experience in terms of self-definition and relatedness, and I borrowed these terms for this aspect of the model. As for Erikson's model of eight stages in lifespan development, there appear to be two stages in his model that correspond to each of the four more advanced needs of Maslow's model. Therefore, in deriving the labels for the present combined model, I referred to the first of the two Erikson's stages involved in each case. As for the most basic physiological level of needs, I referred to the Darwinian concept of survival and reproduction, using the latter for the personal component and the former for the relatedness component. Note that the terms used to describe the needs also refer to attachment theory for the safety level and affiliation instead of love for the middle level (after Kenrick et al., 2010)

their revised model, Kenrick et al. (2010) noted that the motivational systems are akin to the concept of "subselves." The uppermost level is more about taking care of others than the self itself and derives from higher strivings based on motivational processes that have developed much earlier, such as curiosity. They concluded that in humans, the highest motives are not only about self-gratification and self-propagation but also about selfless goals toward other people.

## *Commentaries*

Kesebir, Graham, and Oishi (2010) tried to broaden Kenrick et al. (2010) revised Maslovian model by noting that, at the psychological level, the uppermost portion of the model should include Erikson's model of generativity, and that, at the biological level, it should include the evolutionary concept of culture-gene coevolution. Aside from generativity, Kesebir et al. (2010) included achieving wisdom and acquiring meaning as important ultimate human motives. They referred to cross-cultural differences in human motivations and, therefore, argued that an evolutionary understanding of human motivation must include the concept of culture–gene evolution. The concept refers "to the process whereby cultural environments change fitness criteria for humans, leading to the selection of genes that are adapted better to those cultural environments, leading to further modification of the cultural environment and selection pressures and so on in the feedback loop" (Richerson & Boyd, 2005, p. 317).

Peterson and Park (2010) made an interesting distinction between needs that are of survival value and needs that have self-expressive value (Inglehart, 1990, 1993). These values have been used to show how societies evolve. The authors disagreed that creativity serves especially survival and reproductive needs. Instead, they proposed that creativity is expressed as part of an intrinsic motivation.

Ackerman and Bargh (2010) emphasized that the different levels of the hierarchy build upon prior levels, rather than replacing them. This is consistent with the evolutionary argument that adaptations "co-opt and extend preexisting structures."

Lyubomirsky and Boehm (2010) noted that, from an evolutionary perspective, raising children had taken place in a collective setting. Moreover, it happened earlier in the life cycle compared to today.

Schaller et al. (2010) responded to the commentaries by arguing that self-actualization and related concepts, such as self-esteem and self-enhancement, are "self-ish goals" that have developed only within contemporary, more affluent, Westernized individualistic societies. Therefore, they defended their point of view that the self-actualization should not be considered the pinnacle of motivational and developmental needs.

## *Present Model*

Kenrick et al. (2010) have undertaken a valuable revision of Maslow's pyramidal model of hierarchy of motivational and developmental needs. In particular, they have questioned the placement of self-actualization at the top of the hierarchy, the placement of sexual needs at the bottom of the hierarchy, and using the label of love in the middle of the hierarchy. Also, they added an evolutionary perspective that Maslow did not consider. Part of their solution was to take a wider perspective on sexual activity, seeing it in terms of its evolutionary value for survival and reproduction, so moving it to the top of the hierarchy in terms of seeking mates, mating, and parenting.

I agree with the general tenure of their revised perspective on Maslow. The concept of self-actualization is insufficient to understand penultimate human motivations. Moreover, an evolutionary perspective is welcome. However, for the type of difficulties that they had raised with Maslow's original model, I propose a different set of

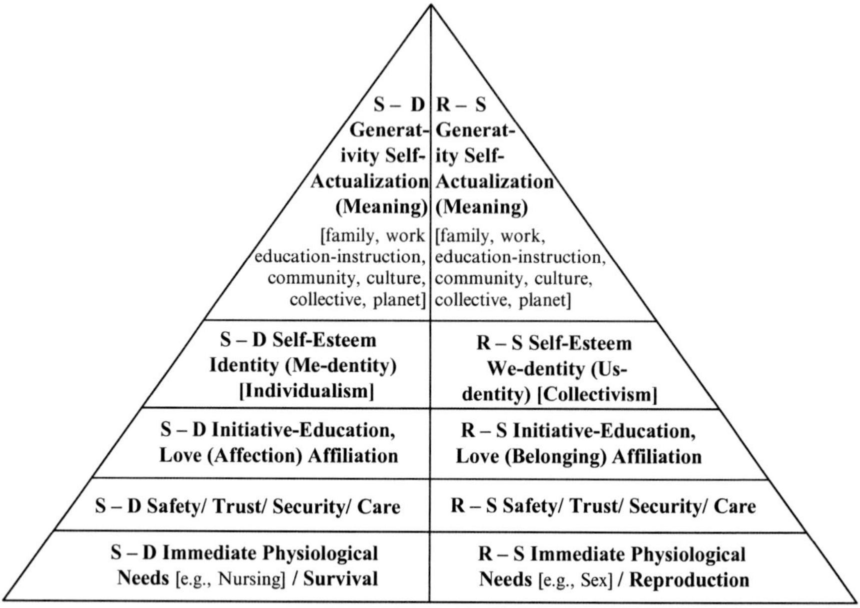


Note. S – D = Self-Definitional; R – S = Relatedness-Self

**Fig. 19.4** Combining Maslow, Erikson, and Blatt in a Neo-Piagetian model of motivational needs. The figure expands upon Fig. 19.3, presenting on a combined Maslow–Erikson–Blatt model of a hierarchy of needs in terms of developmental priorities. For each of the five levels of Maslow's model, it divides the needs into those that are self-definitional and relatedness-focused (Blatt). It includes Eriksonian language, as well, such as referring to trust in infancy and identity in adolescence. It adds elements to make it consistent with Kenrick et al. (2010). Ultimately, the revisions allow for a correspondence in the five levels of the Neo-Maslovian model and the five stages of the present Neo-Piagetian model.
(a) The lower biological levels involve Maslow's immediate physiological needs and safety needs. However, they have been expanded to include self-related components and Darwinian processes. Kenrick et al. (2010) also included evolutionary modalities in their revised model of Maslow's hierarchy of needs, but preferred to separate the sexual component to higher levels in need function due to the mate selection and parenting that could be part and parcel of sexual activity. However, in the present model, I separate sex from other basic biological needs by placing it in the component of the model about relatedness. In addition, this allows me to refer to Darwinian processes by describing basic biological processes, such as nursing, as survival-related and sexual activity as reproductive-related.
(b) The level of safety in Maslow's model of needs and motivations has been expanded to include the psychological security engendered by positive attachment experiences. The latter develops in a majority of infants but depends on the quality of care received. Attachment and Eriksonian trust develop in the first year.
(c) In the next level, Maslow's concept of love as affection and belongingness has been both split and expanded. On the one hand, affection has been placed with the self-definitional component of the model and belongingness with the one of relatedness. On the other hand, the model addresses affiliation rather than love, per se, and it includes education and instruction as part of what affiliation is about.
(d) For Maslow, esteem and respect constitute the next motivational need in the hierarchy. I have elaborated the concept to include self-definitional and relatedness components. One can argue that humans have motivations to develop their I and Me identities and their We and Us identities (e.g., the We-dentity; Becker, 2000; a concept to which I add the Me-dentity and the Us-dentity). (See below description of the concept the IWEMEUS.)

solutions compared to the ones that they have favored. First, I agree with Kesebir et al. (2010) that an Eriksonian perspective can broaden the understanding of self-actualization. Second, I agree with them that an evolutionary perspective should include culture–gene coevolution. Third, I agree with Peterson and Park (2010) that the model can be generalized to any developmental human system, such as societies.

**Fig. 19.4** (continued) (e) For the penultimate level of self-actualization in Maslow's model, Kenrick et al. (2010) modified so that it is replaced by family and related needs. However, family relates to Erikson's concept of generativity in the adult period, where the individual focuses not just on family but also work, community, and the wider collective. Adults seek meaning for their lives and their context and they try to promote for their children optimal educational and instructional experiences. Adults form formal educational institutions and other instructional opportunities in this regard, with parents contributing either directly or indirectly, thereby helping their children and other children.

It is important to note that the motivational needs hierarchy informs development, but can stand apart. For example, people slip back to basic needs when motivated. Moreover, they can have multiple, simultaneous needs. In addition, development can qualify or even override motivational needs. For the latter, for example, we learn to control our sexual impulses. For the former, they mature into from basic biological necessities to being part of deep adult relationships. As explained below, we form complexes of self and other needs, and they grow through their passage through developmental steps, for example, through the present model of Neo-Piagetian cognitive development.

The IWEMEUS: Etzioni's (1996) has developed an interesting concept of the I & WE, which can help deal with the individualism and collectivism in identity. In Young (1997), I argued that the minimum unit of identity in social organization, which the concept of I & WE addresses, must include both the subjective existential and objective evaluative side of social identity. James's (1890) I-ME distinction is aimed at the individual, and not the communal. Extrapolation to the collective from James suggests that there is an equivalent WE-US differentiation in communal identity. That is, there are numerous part selves that develop in the individual, and cultures both experience identity and reflect upon it. Therefore, I labeled the cultural identity that develops in both individuals and collectives as the IWEMEUS. Not only does it refer to the four pronouns that constitute the term but it is also an acronym for the concept of "individual-world epigenetic, mutualistic, emergent, universal (identity) stages." Below, I give a brief description of each of these components of the term. The construct of *individual-world* is consistent with the concept that self and world do not fuse but are symbiotic in their dialogue. However, it appears logical to add that adults can engage in moments of sheer union. The *epigenetic* term implies that identity development unfolds without any deterministic biological or environmental templates, but is channeled by the multiplicative conjoining of all the parameters that impinge on the developing organism, as well as by the characteristics of the developing organism itself. The term *mutualistic* refers to the relationship in which individuals and the social surround engage. The embeddedness of the other's embeddedness is grasped, and actions are undertaken that create a more harmonic field in the relationship of the other components of surround. The term *emergent* refers to the dynamical, systematic, self-organizational, and self-regulative nature of identity formation. It reflects the emphasis in the present work on nonlinear dynamical system theory. The term *universal* refers to the normative passage of the concept of social identity through the various stages of cognitive development. Everything else being equal, it should be universal, although the stages are considered scaffolds for individual differences to develop. The latter develop through the reflexive evaluation that takes place as individual and culture grow through their dialectical interaction. The term *identity stage* refers to the 25-step developmental theory that I describe in the present work. The 25-step sequence has been applied to self-development. It can be expanded readily to include a sense of cultural identity. Thus, in terms of normative development of the cultural self, just as in the case of the development of the individual self, the sequence in identity development should develop through the stages of the model, with special emphasis on the later portions of the sequence

In these regards, I have developed a revised model of Maslow's hierarchy of needs that emphasizes (a) the Eriksonian perspective, (b) the role of the other, not only the self, within the context of examining larger collective issues in society, and (c) the role of Darwinian evolutionary processes that include cultural perspectives (see Table 19.2 and Figs. 19.3 and 19.4).

In particular, I developed a model that includes for each of the five levels of Maslow's model of hierarchical needs a self-other distinction. The figure that I developed to represent the model adds to the standard five-level hierarchy, as created by Maslow, a perpendicular intersection that divides the triangle in half, one for more direct personal concerns and one for concerns more about the other. I based this conceptual innovation on the work of Blatt (2008), who described two major polarities of experience. He underscored that there are two basic self-related experiences – self-definition and relatedness (see Chap. 16). This is consistent with Kenrick et al.'s (2010) notion that Maslow's model has elements akin to "subselves."

About the inclusion of the model of Erikson in the revised model, I showed how his description of the stages in development map onto the upper four levels of Maslow's hierarchy of needs, and not just the top level of self-actualization, as had been proposed by Kesebir et al. In particular, I have proposed that, for each of the upper four levels of Maslow's hierarchy, two of Erikson's eight stages fit the levels involved.

In terms of Maslow's middle level of love, I used Kenrick et al.'s (2010) elaborated term for it (affiliation). However, I showed how Maslow's use of the example of affection in the love category fits in Blatt's (2008) concept of self-definition. Also, I showed how Maslow's example of belongingness in love fits Blatt's (2008) concept of relatedness.

Finally, in terms of evolutionary underpinnings in the model, I left Maslow's placement of sex as a basic biological need that should go at the bottom of the hierarchy. However, I separated it from hunger and related motivations by placing the latter under self-definitional motives and the former under relatedness motives.

## *Comment*

The revised model of Maslow's hierarchy of needs presented in this chapter adds several conceptual innovations that make it consistent with the present model and some crucial contemporary trends in psychology, while keeping more of its essential attributes compared to the revision presented by Kenrick et al. (2010). However, it would not have been constructed without their initial efforts. The key elements that have been added to Maslow's model for the current revision include (a) an Eriksonian component, (b) a dual model of the self, as per Blatt (2008), (c) an evolutionary perspective that involves culture–gene coevolution and keeping sexual activity as a basic physiological need, and (d) a revised understanding of self-actualization so that it is kept at the pinnacle of the hierarchy, instead of being discarded, as had been the procedure followed in Kenrick et al.

# The Revised Needs Model and Romantic Relations

## *Introduction*

In Young (1997), I had presented a model of steps in the marital cycle based on the present Neo-Piagetian model of five stages in development (see Table 19.3). In developing the Neo-Maslovian model for the present chapter, I realized the parallel with the marital model. Therefore, I examined the parallel more closely, giving the marital model a needs component.

**Table 19.3** Steps in the marital cycle

| Developmental stage | Relationship stage | Opposition |
|---|---|---|
| Reflexive | Attraction | Overpositive, realistic vs. overnegative evaluation |
| Sensorimotor | Attachment | Security fostering vs. insecurity fostering |
| Perioperational | Commitment | Cooperation, give and take vs. give or take |
| Abstract | Growth | Conscious unfolding vs. infolding |
| Collective intelligence | Mutuality | Emergent constitutiveness vs. reciprocal constraint |

*Note*. Five substages in the cycle can be described according to the typical ones in the synthetic model of development (coordination to integration)

Reprinted with the permission of Springer Science+Business Media: Young, G. (1997). [Table 4.2, Page. 91]

The model of steps in the marital cycle described in the table is based on the present model of five stages in development. In this model, generic change processes are described that can be applied to changes that take place over much shorter time frames than the lifespan time frame to which the model applies. Thus, in the present table, the marital cycle model describes a sequence of steps in marital development in which each step brings with it new potentials for the couple that are described in Eriksonian-type positive and negative poles. As the couple moves through the sequence and confront a new stage, either their relationship could lead to a working out of the oppositions in the poles toward their balance or to it could lead to conflict and crisis

(a) Specifically, fitting the initial reflexive stage in the present model, in the first step in relationships, one finds a corporal, reflexive attraction, which is accompanied by an opposition of overly positive/realistic evaluations and negative ones

(b) Second, in keeping with the next stage of infant sensorimotor development and its focus on attachment to the caregiver, in adult relationships, an emotional attachment develops. It involves the opposition of security-fostering (e.g., dialogue) and insecurity-fostering (e.g., overcontrol) behavior

(c) In the present developmental model, in the third stage the child develops perioperations, or pre-operations and concrete operations, which permit systematic representation-based thought and problem solving. Consequently, in the third phase of adult relationship development being proposed, a well-thought out emotional commitment should develop. The challenge lies in finding the balance in the opposition of cooperative give-and-take vs. asymmetric give-or-take behavior (one partner does too much taking and the other too much giving)

(d) In adolescence, abstract formal operations-logic develops, which permits hypothesis testing, experimentation, conscious awareness, visioning the future, and so on. In terms of relationships, this should lead to conscious psychological growth for each of the partners, where an unfolding process opposes an infolding one. That is, in this stage, each partner should maximize her or his growth in the reciprocal sharing and higher-order other-perspective taking permitted by formal operations

(e) Finally, in the mature adult, collective intelligence and sociality develop. In couples, this should engender transcendent mutuality, in which there is emergent constitutiveness in relationship, personality, and mind

**Table 19.4** A Neo-Maslovian model of romantic relationships

| Relationship stage | Opposition/function | Co-need (self definitional, relatedness) |
|---|---|---|
| Attraction | Evaluation | Physiological, reproduction |
| Attachment | Security | Safety, trust |
| Commitment | Cooperation | Affiliative, initiative |
| Growth | Conscious | Identity, self-esteem |
| Mutuality | Emergence | Actualizing, generativity |

The present model of the steps in the development of romantic relationships incorporates both (a) Young's (1997) model of steps in the marital life cycle and (b) the revised model of Maslow's hierarchy of needs, as described in the present work. The first two columns of the table summarize the marital model. The third column summarizes the Maslovian model. The parallels across the two five-step series are marked, as both have been developed from the present five-stage Neo-Piagetian model. For the integration being presented in the model, the psychological needs being emphasized relate to partners together and not just one or the other. In this sense, they can be described as co-needs

(a) In terms of the specific correspondences in marital stage and needs of the proposed model, the first phase of attraction in a couple corresponds quite nicely to physiological and reproductive needs. (b) The second one of attachment reflects the present emphasis of trust in the revised hierarchy. (c) The third step of commitment is quite like the need of affiliation. (d) The fourth stage of personal growth fits the equivalent need of identity/self-esteem. (e) Finally, the fifth step in the evolution in a romantic partnership involves an emerging mutuality or actualizing generativity, as described by the correspondence being suggested

### *Model*

In the revised marital model, I generalized it by referring to romantic relationships rather than only marriages, and I included the concept of co-need. Just as the needs model is considered to apply to the self-definitional and relatedness components of the individual, the co-needs model is considered to apply to both partners in a couple. By pairing the two models, for relationships and needs, the parallels between them were quite evident at the conceptual level. This illustrates the power of considering seemingly disparate developmental models from the perspective of the present Neo-Piagetian stage model (Table 19.4).

## Summary and Conclusion

### *Summary*

This chapter has examined major approaches to the study of personality (Five Factor Model, narrative identity, hierarchy of needs). I show how they are consistent with the present model. In the next chapter, I turn to the present Neo-Eriksonian model, presented at the outset of the book. It has been formulated to fit the five stages of the present model and the five substages that repeat within them. Between these two chapters, the scope of application of the present model to the study of personality development is explicated quite well. In addition, the chapter ends with a combined stage model of romantic relationships that includes the present approach and the revised approach to Maslow.

## *Conclusion*

One of the most famous models in psychology has inspired many people in self-understanding. Maslow's model of the hierarchy of human needs consists of five levels and it is shaped like a pyramid (see Fig. 19.1). Its bottom level involves immediate physiological needs and its top level concerns self-actualization. The model is developmental as well as one related to personality and motivation. The child moves through the steps of physiological needs and safety at the lower levels to love and esteem, before arriving at self-actualization.

Kenrick et al. (2010) have attempted a revision of the model and placed parenting at the top of the hierarchy, along with mate acquisition and retention, so that their version of the model consists of seven levels instead of five of them (see Fig. 19.2). The authors changed the labels slightly, for example, referring to the love step as affiliation.

In this chapter, I present a revised model of Maslow's hierarchy of needs that consists of five levels, not seven. The revised model includes relating its five levels to the five stages in development presented in the book, which are based on Piaget's stages of development. Recall that the major change from Piaget's cognitive developmental model proposed in the present model has been to add an adult stage, called collective intelligence. Adults are very good at creating complex abstract structures, such as theories, and we are very good at integrating emotions in our thoughts. Moreover, we are very good in collecting ourselves together to solve problems and to think, such as in brainstorming.

The five stages in development can be described as involving the sequence of (1) physical development in the newborn, (2) emotional development in the infant, (3) cognitive development in the child, (4) conscious development in the adolescent, and (5) spiritual development in the adult.

The present model model also incorporates Erikson's steps in psychosocial development. The major steps in Erikson's model that correspond to the ones in the present model concern the last four, and involve the sequence of: (a) trust in the infant; (b) initiative in the child; (c) identity seeking in the adolescent; and (d) generativity in the adult, which refers to being generative in family life and at work, in particular. There are other Eriksonian steps, but they are not relevant to the present discussion, as they relate to substages in the model.

In naming the five levels in my revised model of Maslow's hierarchy of needs, I integrated Erikson's steps and used Kenrick and colleagues' concept of affiliation for the third level. This led to the following sequence of steps in my model: (1) physiological needs, (2) safety/trust, (3) affiliative initiative, (4) identity self-esteem, and (5) actualizing generativity. I removed the word "self" from Maslow's concept because "actualization" should not just concern a focus on the self but how we are helping others grow, as in Erikson's concept of generativity.

In addition, I innovated by dividing the pyramid in half, and putting one type of self on the left side and another on the right side. That is, following the work of Blatt in his 2008 book, I referred to the self as having one part more focused on the personal component and another part more focused on the other person or people around us. The concept of the self involves not only how we feel about ourselves and how we present to the world but also how we feel about the people around us and how we interact socially with them.

Given the logic just described, Fig. 19.3 presents the revised version of Maslow's classic model of our hierarchy of needs. As we develop through the five stages in life, the need that corresponds to each of the stages comes into prominence. Our experience will determine how well we deal with them, and what skills that we develop to satisfy them. Of course, the better the experiences encountered by people in the earlier phases of life, the easier it is to satisfy the needs later in life.

The therapist can learn several important messages:

- First, even classic models can be revised and made more salient in psychology. In the present case, Maslow's model has been revised to integrate the important work of Piaget and Erikson, as well as of others. Scientific advances can help therapeutic practice and also patients who need help.
- Second, many people have difficulty even with the most basic level of the hierarchy of needs. We need to be especially sensitive to their difficulties. They may have experienced horrendous abuse, for example.
- Our society has needs as much as individuals in it. It grows through stages equivalent to the ones described. It needs to meet the challenges in its growth, and promote itself to the highest levels, including living with generativity, spiritually, and in actualization, and being concerned that all its members should be on the path to that level. This ideal is a very difficult one to arrive at for the individual let alone a whole society, but we need to keep it in focus.
- Lastly, therapy should focus on helping the patient acquire skills concerning both the self-defining and the relating self. The patient might be experiencing difficulties involving both personal or interior issues and those involving social interaction and societal issues. Moreover, they might not be at the same level in these two areas from among the five levels in their growth, as defined by the revised Maslovian model.
- The task of growing through life stages and resolving problems that might have arisen in doing so in childhood and adolescence might seem quite daunting. However, by understanding the model and using it, the growth of people needing professional help, or simply advice and guidance, might be facilitated.

## References

Ackerman, J. M., & Bargh, J. A. (2010). The purpose-driven life: Commentary on Kenrick et al. (2010). *Perspectives on Psychological Science, 5*, 323–326.

Bates, J. E., Schermerhorn, A. C., & Goodnight, J. A. (2010). Temperament and personality through the life span. In R. M. Lerner, M. E. Lamb, & A. M. Freund (Eds.), *The handbook of*

*life-span development: Vol. 2. Social and emotional development* (pp. 208–253). Hoboken: Wiley.
Becker, G. K. (Ed.). (2000). *The moral status of persons: Perspectives on bioethics*. Amsterdam: Editions Rodopi B.V.
Blatt, S. J. (2008). *Polarities of experience: Relatedness and self-definition in personality development, psychopathology, and the therapeutic process*. Washington: American Psychological Association.
Caspi, A., Roberts, B. W., & Shiner, R. L. (2005). Personality development: Stability and change. *Annual Review of Psychology, 56*, 453–485.
Caspi, A., & Shiner, R. L. (2006). Personality development. In W. Damon, R. Lerner, & N. Eisenberg (Eds.), *Handbook of child psychology: Vol. 3* (6th ed., pp. 300–365). New York: Wiley.
Davidson, R. J., Pizzagalli, E., Nitschke, J. B., & Kalin, N. H. (2003). Parsing the subcomponents of emotion and disorders of emotion: Perspectives from affective neuroscience. In R. J. Davidson, K. R. Scherer, & H. H. Goldsmith (Eds.), *Handbook of affective sciences* (pp. 8–24). New York: Oxford University Press.
De Clercq, B., & De Fruyt, F. (2003). Personality disorder symptoms in adolescence: A five-factor model perspective. *Journal of Personality Disorders, 17*, 269–292.
De Clercq, B., De Fruyt, F., & Van Leeuwen, K. (2004). A Little Five lexically-based perspectives on personality disorder symptoms in adolescence. *Journal of Personality Disorders, 18*, 477–496.
Depue, R. A., & Lenzenweger, M. F. (2005). A neurobehavioral dimensional model of personality disorders. In M. F. Lenzenweger & J. F. Clarkin (Eds.), *Major theories of personality disorder* (2nd ed., pp. 391–453). New York: Guilford Press.
Erikson, E. H. (1963). *Childhood and society*. New York: Norton.
Erikson, E. H. (1968). *Identity: Youth and crisis*. New York: Norton.
Erikson, E. H. (1980). *Identity and the life cycle*. New York: Norton.
Etzioni, A. (1996). A moderate communitarian proposal. *Political Theory, 24*, 155–171.
Fivush, R., & Nelson, K. (2004). Culture and language in the emergence of autobiographical memory. *Psychological Science, 15*, 573–577.
Garver-Apgar, C. E., Gangestad, S. W., & Thornhill, R. (2008). Hormonal correlates of women's mid-cycle preference for the scent of symmetry. *Evolution & Human Behavior, 29*, 223–232.
Gray, J. A. (1987). *The psychology of fear and stress* (2nd ed.). New York: McGraw-Hill.
Gray, J. A. (1990). Brain systems that mediate both emotions and cognitions. In J. A. Gray (Ed.), *Psychobiological aspects of relationships between emotion and cognition* (pp. 269–288). Hillsdale: Erlbaum.
Habermas, T., & de Silveria, C. (2008). The development of global coherence in life narratives across adolescence: Temporal, causal, and thematic aspects. *Development Psychology, 44*, 707–721.
Howe, M. L., & Courage, M. L. (1997). The emergence and early development of autobiographical memory. *Psychological Review, 104*, 499–523.
Inglehart, R. (1990). *Culture shift in advanced industrial society*. Princeton: Princeton University Press.
Inglehart, R. (1993). *Modernization and postmodernization: Cultural, economic, and political change in 43 societies*. Princeton: Princeton University Press.
James, W. (1890). *The principles of psychology* (Vol. 1 and Vol. 2). New York: Holt.
Kenrick, D. T., Griskevicius, V., Neuberg, S. L., & Schaller, M. (2010). Renovating the pyramid of needs: Contemporary extensions built upon ancient foundations. *Perspectives on Psychological Science, 5*, 292–314.
Kesebir, S., Graham, J., & Oishi, S. (2010). A theory of human needs should be human-centered, not animal-centered: Commentary on Kenrick et al. (2010). *Perspectives on Psychological Science, 5*, 315–319.
Kochanska, G., Murray, K. T., & Harlan, E. T. (2000). Effortful control in early childhood: Continuity and change, antecedents and implications for social development. *Developmental Psychology, 36*, 220–232.
Kohnstamm, G. A., Halverson, C. F., Jr., Mervielde, I., & Haville, V. (Eds.). (1998). *Parental description of child personality: Developmental antecedents of the Big Five?* Mahwah: Erlbaum.

Kuhlmeier, V., Wynn, K., & Bloom, P. (2003). Attribution of dispositional status by 12-month olds. *Psychological Science, 14*, 402–408.

Lyubomirsky, S., & Boehm, J. K. (2010). Human motives, happiness, and the puzzle of parenthood: Commentary on Kenrick et al. (2010). *Perspectives on Psychological Science, 5*, 327–334.

Mandler, J. M. (1984). *Stories, scripts, and scenes: Aspects of story schema*. Hillsdale: Erlbaum.

Marcia, J. E. (1980). Identity in adolescence. In J. Adleson (Ed.), *Handbook of adolescent psychology* (pp. 159–187). New York: Wiley.

Maslow, A. H. (1943). A theory of human motivation. *Psychological Review, 50*, 370–396.

Maslow, A. H. (1970). *Motivation and personality* (2nd ed.). New York: Harper and Row.

McAdams, D. P. (2010). Narrative identity. Unpublished manuscript.

McAdams, D. P., & Cox, K. (2010). Self and identity across the lifespan. In R. M. Lerner, M. E. Lamb, & A. M. Freund (Eds.), *The handbook of life-span development: Vol. 2. Social and emotional development* (pp. 158–207). Hoboken: Wiley.

McAdams, D. P., & Olson, B. D. (2010). Personality development: Continuity and change over the life course. *Annual Review of Psychology, 61*, 517–542.

McAdams, D. P., & Pals, J. L. (2006). A new Big Five: Fundamental principles for an integrative science of personality. *American Psychologist, 61*, 204–217.

Measelle, J., John, O. P., Ablow, J., Cowan, P. A., & Cowan, C. P. (2005). Can children provide coherent, stable, and valid self-reports on the big five dimensions? *Journal of Personality and Social Psychology, 89*, 90–106.

Mervielde, I., Buyst, V., & DeFuyt, F. (1995). The validity of the Big-5 as a model for teacher ratings of individual differences among children aged 4-12 years. *Personality and Individual Differences, 18*, 525–534.

Mervielde, I., De Clercq, B., De Fruyt, F., & Van Leeuwen, K. (2005). Temperament, personality, and developmental psychology as childhood antecedents of personality disorders. *Journal of Personality Disorders, 19*, 171–201.

Mervielde, I., & DeFuyt, F. (2000). The Big Five personality factors as a model for the structure of children's peer nominations. *European Journal of Personality, 14*, 91–106.

Mervielde, I., & DeFuyt, F. (2002). Assessing children's traits with the hierarchical personality inventory for children. In B. De Raad & M. Perugini (Eds.), *Big Five assessment* (pp. 129–146). Seattle: Hogrefe and Huber.

Peterson, C., & Park, N. (2010). What happened to self-actualization? Commentary on Kenrick et al. (2010). *Perspectives on Psychological Science, 5*, 320–322.

Richerson, P. J., & Boyd, R. (2005). *Not by genes alone: How culture transformed human evolution*. Chicago: University of Chicago Press.

Rothbart, M. K., & Derryberry, D. (2002). Temperament in children. In C. von Hofsten & L. Backman (Eds.), *Psychology at the turn of the millennium: Vol. 2. Social, developmental, and clinical perspectives* (pp. 17–35). New York: Taylor & Francis.

Saulsman, L. M., & Page, A. C. (2004). The Five-Factor Model and personality disorder empirical literature: A meta-analytic review. *Clinical Psychology Review, 23*, 1055–1085.

Schaller, M., Neuberg, S. L., Griskevicius, V., & Kenrick, D. T. (2010). Pyramid power: A reply to commentaries. *Perspectives on Psychological Science, 5*, 335–337.

Stearns, S. C., Allal, N., & Mace, R. (2008). Life history theory and human development. In C. Crawford & D. Krebs (Eds.), *Foundations of evolutionary psychology* (pp. 47–70). New York: Erlbaum.

Young, G. (1997). *Adult development, therapy, and culture: A postmodern synthesis*. New York: Plenum.

Young, G. (2008). Psychological injury: Systems, change processes, development. *Psychological Injury and Law, 1*, 243–254.

# Chapter 20
# Socioemotional Systems and Neo-Eriksonian Dangers

## Introduction

To this point, several major socioaffective acquisitions in the course of development have been discussed, especially those of the 25 steps in Neo-Eriksonian development across the lifespan and a model of the basic emotions early in life. There is no contradiction here, because just as cognitive development has global and more specific acquisitions, so does the realm of socioemotional development.

In the following, I present a general model relating stages in socioaffective development to the 25 steps in cognitive development proposed in the present model. Then, I explore further the Neo-Eriksonian model that has been previously described in terms of the challenges, issues, and dangers that appear at each stage. This prepares the way for examining emotional development as part of the socioemotional systems. This chapter completes the third of three devoted to personality. This chapter is short in text, given the scope of its tables. The next few chapters deal with other socioaffective topics, such as attachment and emotional development. Those chapters complete the second part of the book, which then turns to the topic of causality, in particular.

## Socioemotional Systems

### *Introduction*

Part of the present work on Neo-Piagetian stages in development includes a model of 25 corresponding socioemotional systems (25 in all) (see Tables 20.1–20.5; the negative sides of systems are omitted, except for the examples in outcome acts). Each of the 25 socioemotional systems being proposed is considered semi-independent of its parallel cognitive substage.

G. Young, *Development and Causality: Neo-Piagetian Perspectives*,
DOI 10.1007/978-1-4419-9422-6_20, 

**Table 20.1** Socioemotional systems (positive components) in the reflex substages

| | Dimension | | | |
|---|---|---|---|---|
| | Figure | | Ground | |
| System | Active | Reactive | Active | Reactive |
| Distance acts | Incorporate (*0 distance*) | Try to induce distance reduction | Reduce actual distance | Maintain minimum distance |
| Nursing acts | Suck, swallow | "Cycle" in hunger (*arms and legs*) | Root, mouth | Smell milk, turn |
| Outcome acts | Explore, take (*vs. aggression*) | Attract (*vs. protect*) | Approach (*vs. avoid*) | Orient (*vs. reject*) |
| Caregiving acts | Attachment (*love*) precursor | Caregiver bonds (*let*) | Imprint (*voice, smell*) | Caregiver also (*let*) |
| Emotional acts | Possesses (*pleasure*), etc. | Possessed (*contentment*), etc. | Approaching (*interest*), etc. | Approached (*delight*), etc. |

Adapted from Young (1990a)

The next series of five tables present the dimensions that organize the socioemotional systems thought to develop in parallel with the cognitive substages of the present model. They concern (a) valence: positive/negative; (b) activity: active-passive, and (c) figure-ground; figure (directly on primary focus, e.g., parent, self, object) vs. ground (context, distance, secondary other, indirectly on primary focus, etc.). The tables present the positive-valenced systems that develop in the first, third, and fifth substages of the present model, with the second and fourth being the location of the eight Eriksonian stages, at least in terms of the last four stages of the model

The dimensions are borrowed from the literature on emotions, in general. That literature also emphasizes valence and activity as dimensions, but typically engagement or self-other as a third dimension (Mascolo & Fischer, 2010). However, Stanley and Meyer (2009) found variations of the dimensions of valence and activation, in particular, as best fits to their data. Note that Carver and Harmon-Jones (2009a, 2009b) have provided evidence on the relevance of approach and withdrawal as dimensions in understanding emotions, but others have translated these into positive and negative valence. Absent consensus in the field, the third dimension in the present model was derived rationally, based on the general characteristics that seemed to cut across the differentiation made in the tables, which cover the full age range

Note that the names of the systems use the concept of acts, fitting what had been undertaken in developing the names for the Neo-Eriksonian stages that are part of the 25 systems in the series. The systems constitute the 17 Neo-Eriksonian steps newly constructed in the present model that were needed to add to the eight original ones described by Erikson. This procedure gave 25 steps in the Neo-Eriksonian series, which allowed a one-to-one correspondence with the 25 cognitive steps of the model

(a) As for the particular socioemotional systems in the first table of the series, on the reflexive stage, they cover elementary movements in the first phases of life to emotional acts in the 1-month-old
(b) For the sensorimotor substages, the systems develop from dyadic acts to other more socially implicated ones, and they include Erikson's trust and autonomy stages
(c) For the perioperational stage, the systems become representational, and the child develops initiative and industry motivations, as per Erikson, but also gender and other role acts
(d) The teenager in the abstract stage develops a consciousness that hopefully develops toward a more universalist attitude in the adult period, as well as Eriksonian identity and intimacy
(e) In the collective intelligence stage, the adult develops more principle-based and liberating sentiments, leading to catalysis and catharsis at the end of life, in addition to developing Erikson's classic generativity and ego integrity

**Table 20.2** Socioemotional systems in the odd – numbered sensorimotor substages

| | Dimension | | | |
|---|---|---|---|---|
| | Figure | | Ground | |
| System | Active | Reactive | Active | Reactive |
| Distance acts | Modeling (*eliciting imitation*) | Imitating (*built on neonatal skill*) | Classical pavlovian conditioning | Shaping, operant conditioning |
| Sociability acts | Secure with caregiver | Adapt to her departure | Seek out strangers | Adapt to their approach |
| Interdigitational acts | Join, play (*no asymmetry in relation*) | Let join, play | Lead or seek lead | Let (*seek*) lead |

Adapted from Young (1990a)

**Table 20.3** Socioemotional systems in the odd – numbered perioperational substages

| | Dimension | | | |
|---|---|---|---|---|
| | Figure | | Ground | |
| System | Active | Reactive | Active | Reactive |
| Superordinate acts | Coherence over all units | Accentuated by cohesion over related units | Syntax among neighboring units | Style (e.g., rhythm) coordinates with syntax |
| Gender acts | Same-sex identification accelerates | Complementary reaction: opposite sex | Same-sex peer identification accelerates | Complementary reaction: opposite sex |
| Role acts | In family, with friends | Even when imposed | In school, peer clubs | Observing same |

Adapted from Young (1990a)

**Table 20.4** Socioemotional systems in the odd – numbered abstract substages

| | Dimension | | | |
|---|---|---|---|---|
| | Figure | | Ground | |
| System | Active | Reactive | Active | Reactive |
| Conscious acts | Esteem for self-identity | Unrepression of unconscious | Esteem for others, ecology | Open to abstract learning |
| Nurturing acts | Love romantic partner | Let partner love | Daily responsibility, work | Listen in same |
| Universal acts | Encourage self for self | Encourage other for self | Encourage self for other | Encourage other for other |

Adapted from Young (1990a)

Primary examples of the socioemotional systems include emotions and the classic Eriksonian stages. Examples of the socioemotional systems at each of the five cognitive stages include emotional acts (e.g., pleasure, interest) in the first month of life during the substage of reflexive integration, dyadic acts (e.g., imitating) of the young

**Table 20.5** Socioemotional systems in the odd – numbered collective intelligence substages

| | Dimension | | | |
|---|---|---|---|---|
| | Figure | | Ground | |
| System | Active | Reactive | Active | Reactive |
| Metacollecting acts | Perspicacity | Awe | Relativity | Uncertainty |
| Catalytic acts | Emergent discovery | Initiative attractor | Paradigmatic shift | Catastrophic inversion |
| Cathartic acts | Wisdom | Reverence | Transcendence | Mystery |

Adapted from Young (1990b)

infant during sensorimotor coordination, gender acts (e.g., same-sex parent identification accelerates) in the child during perioperational systematization, identity acts in the adolescent during abstract hierarchization, and the issue of integrity vs. despair at the collective intelligence multiplication substage of the adult.

The 25 socioemotional systems are viewed as organized around three dimensions of appraisal – (a) compatibility/interference with ongoing goals (positive/negative), (b) activity/reactivity, and (c) context, or figure/ground. These dimensions are more fully elaborated and justified in the chapters on emotional development (Chaps. 21 and 22).

Relative to prior presentations of the socioemotional systems of the present model (Young, 1990a, 1990b), there are several slight changes in the current presentation. (a) The description of the system of nurturing acts has been modified slightly in all four cells treating it in Table 20.4. Two cells have been altered for role acts, and one partially for catalytic acts. (b) There are two new suggested systems for the reflexive period (in the second and fourth positions). (c) The previously used labels of interactional acts and metaphysical acts have been switched to the labels of interdigitational acts and metacollecting acts.

Note that the socioemotional system involving the basic emotions, which is seen to emerge in the first month of life, expands after its appearance (see Chap. 22). At each of the six substages corresponding to Piaget's sensorimotor substage series (reflexive integration plus the five sensorimotor substages of the present model), a new group of emotions appears to develop. Each group is structured around the previously mentioned dimensions of positivity/negativity and activity/reactivity. (The third socioemotional dimension of figure/ground is shown to relate to the six cognitive substages).

## *The Systems*

In Tables 20.6–20.10, I outline a more detailed summary of both the cognitive and corresponding socioaffective acquisitions that are hypothesized to develop over 25 lifespan steps in the present model. The cognitive substages are presented in the

**Table 20.6** The reflex substages and corresponding socioemotional systems

| Reflexive substage | Socioemotional system |
|---|---|
| 1. Reflexive movements pair, but not in fixed order (e.g., fingers in mid position open then flex, or vice versa, but not to any particular stimulus; also applies to arm flexion and extension) | During such behavior, distance alteration or maintenance occurs with respect to targets accidentally present. (At later levels in development, behaviors directly involve stimulus targets) |
| 2. Paired reflexes establish fixed order and firing mechanisms (hierarchy), but with second reflex on target only fortuitously (e.g., arm extends after tonic neck reflex, touching object; sounds pair by vocal cord activity and lip/mouth/tongue positioning) | Reflex pairs now manifest correct activation and order, and this leads to adept nursing behavior (e.g., suck then swallow; smell then turn) |
| 3. The two reflex pair components can more flexibly relate or associate with other movements (reflexive, other), through primitive control schemata, which help better target behavior, even if it is still brusk. This system allows the first sequence of more than two acts, even if limited (e.g., if off center, fingers adjust position slightly to facilitate ensuing grasp; target visually followed, better ensuring tonic neck reflex on appropriate side; coos variable to some extent) | With nascent schemata, more target-oriented behavior structures can manifest (e.g., explore, approach, reject), but they are still based on reflex pairs and are more functional and general than uniquely social |
| 4. Organized multiples of systematized reflex pairs controlled by patterned schemata form, with embedding possible | But unlike their paired constituents acting by themselves, these multiples are not necessarily directly to (on) target (e.g., ballistic arm movements to moving target serially performed couched in context of appropriate postural, head positioning; fingers serially extend and flex upon sheet contact with context-related turning possible, if needed; combined sound series) |
| 5. Schema-guided reflex combinations integrate or differentiate with exercise to come to incorporate (a) fully reflex-free behavior components (under independent schema control) and (b) the monitoring of movement and/or the moving target. This makes approach and target-related behavior more sustained, smooth, and flexible (e.g., reaching adjustment to swaying target), and allows an element of reversibility in the behavior (e.g., restart movement if context necessitates it), although target-related behavior is still relatively rigid (e.g., no manipulation). Also, fingers move flexibly to facilitate efficient grasping; there are situational/intonational adjustments in cooing. (For Piaget, reflex exercise brings organized patterns of behavior through generalization and differentiation of behavior schemes. Schemes vary with even slight variations in target, so that these are always "new") | The reflex-free behavior and continual monitoring of movement and/or target bring with them the first emotions, which concern arriving at relevant ends or the feelings engendered in failure to do so (e.g., quiescence, relief, distress). New emotions emerge with each succeeding cognitive substage in the sensorimotor period |

(continued)

**Table 20.6** (continued)

The next five tables present more details on the proposed 25 socioemotional systems that correspond to the 25 steps in development in the present model. These tables stand out as the ones that present the fine details of the development that takes place in the cognitive and socioaffective realms according to the present 25-step model of development. Other sets of tables have presented the cognitive levels in terms of manual examples (see Chap. 26), in particular, and they presented the socioemotional ones only in a sketchy sense. In the current five tables, in the left-hand columns, the schemes and operations at play in development are described with more generic examples, although in the first years, manual behavior necessarily is involved

Also, in these columns, I describe Piaget's equivalent model of cognitive development, in order to show how the present model is based on it, and respects its integrity while elaborating it. Based on Piaget's account, I altered the description of what is taking place in development in terms of the conceptions formulated in the present model. This procedure permitted the types of expansions of Piaget's model presented in these tables. I tried to keep the essence of his model; for example, I worked with the ages that he proposed when a new stage or substage generally appears. Therefore, in the present model, all his stages and substages have been incorporated, and others have been inserted, as appropriate, without unduly affecting the sequence that he had proposed. This has led to a lifespan model of cognitive development that is Piagetian-based, but is infused with the innovations in present-day Neo-Piagetian theory

As for the socioemotional side of the present work, which is given in the right-hand columns, they reflect the cognitive qualities of their equivalent cognitive step. They are hypothesized to possess a dimensional structure, as explained in earlier tables. In particular, they incorporate the present Neo-Eriksonian model of development. However, I provide examples outside of this structure. For example, I discuss aspects of social development in this context, although I avoid the topic of attachment at this juncture, given that, at a later point in the book, I elaborate a more detailed model of how it evolves in correspondence with the cognitive steps of the present model

The accompanying text in the book examines more recent literature from the lens of the present model. It emphasizes that there are 25 steps in development with parallel cognitive and affective acquisitions that reflect the characteristics of the Neo-Piagetian stages and substages described, which in turn condition the manner in which the corresponding socioemotional systems that accompany them manifest

In terms of the specific developments at the cognitive and socioemotional levels described in the reflex stage, I especially elaborate the last substage relative to its prior presentation in Young (1990a, 1990b). This level concerns the newborn in the first month of life, which is the stage equivalent to Piaget's first substage in his six-step progression of substages in the sensorimotor period

Note that the last reflexive substage includes mention of reversible elements to the scheme involved. For Piaget, the onset of the concrete operational period is evidenced by appearance for the first time of reversibility in thought. However, the type of reversibility described in the last reflex substage is consistent with my generic description of the substage of integration that reappears cyclically in each stage as the last step in the five-step substage sequence involved

As for the socioaffective side of the table, I elaborate descriptions of the Distance, Outcome, and Emotional acts posited to develop in the first, third, and fifth substages of the reflex stage. In addition, I add descriptions of the intermediate socioemotional systems at the second and fourth substages

The reflex period is presented as one in which there is socioemotional growth that ends up with the capacity to engage in the first social interactions after birth because of sufficient preadapted skills (subject to environment modification) that had developed fetally. Also, the reflexive period is presented as one with the capacity to express the first emotions, which are related to quiescence relief, distress, etc.

Note that these socioaffective acquisitions do not mean that congenitally the newborn is innately adapted to express critical behaviors. Rather, even fetally, there is a role for environmental input

(continued)

**Table 20.6** (continued)

in shaping behavior, and even after birth there are individual differences in energy, approach-related behavior, precursors of curiosity, etc.

In the ensuing four tables, I present the same detailed elaboration of the twin cognitive and socio-affective acquisitions in the posited steps of development. I add brief description of the eight Eriksonian stages to the latter, concentrating on the positive components of the oppositions evident at each Eriksonian stage. Later on, I present tables dealing with the negative poles of the stages, or the challenges, crises, difficulties, and dangers that are possible for development in this regard. Those tables also allow the elaboration of the 17 Neo-Eriksonian steps that I constructed in order to arrive at a full 25-step model of Neo-Eriksonian development that is consistent with the present 25 steps in cognitive development

Note that in all Piagetian models, the age periods associated with particular stages and substages are approximate. For example, typically they are elaborated for the middle-class child and teenager. Moreover, the manner in which the age period is calculated might differ across theorists, or even within them in different presentations of their work. Also, the influence of different cultures, educational experiences, degree of support, presence of deleterious experiences, or disturbed brain development and other negative factors could influence the typical age of appearance of a stage or substage. Nevertheless, the age periods indicated by Piaget have provided markers for Neo-Piagetians to follow. In another chapter, the work of Fischer is highlighted in terms of variations it allows in age of substage development of particular dynamic skills, depending on degree of environmental support, optimal conditions, etc.

**Table 20.7** The sensorimotor substages and corresponding socioemotional systems

| Sensorimotor substage | Socioemotional system |
|---|---|
| 6. Different schemata coordinate, but mostly in a parallel, back and forth way schema coordination comes to include a rather than in fixed sequence. This can occur across different sensory modalities (e.g., 3-month-olds only imitated vowel sounds matched to an adult's mouth movements, Legerstee, 1990). It allows somewhat more online behavior control after behavior onset and thus better target attainment (e.g., beginning visuomotor coordination before a target, but without visually guided reaching, i.e., watch hand while active before a target, but without forward movement to it; watch palm of hand while fingers touch target; ballistic reaching to target with some but not constant visual surveillance of movement or grasp the target without looking at it; two independent actions coordinate, e.g., foot scratch, reach; Wolff, 1987). (For Piaget, primary circular reactions concern accidentally discovered effects centered on the body that are repeated, e.g., "coordinated" schemes in sucking thumb brought to mouth. Target differentiation increases as schemes accommodate to a newly encountered object once having attempted its assimilation) | Dyadic exchange begins, because schema coordination comes to include a schema of the infant with another of the (adult) partner (Cohn & Tronick, 1988). By 3 months, infants even become upset when the dyadic flow is interrupted by mother adopting a still face (Cohn & Tronick, 1983). Not only can the infant be shaped by operant by the (adult) partner, but he/she can do the same in the "game" that is played (Watson, 1973). Similarly, not only can the infant be imitated by the partner, he/she also imitates, even in a deferred (1 day later) fashion. Neonatally acquired learning skills contribute to these social ones (e.g., see Meltzoff & Moore, 1989, 1992, 1994, for their description of neonatal cross-modally mediated facial and head movement imitation). Later in development, the shaping processes come to include parallel ones based on classical pavlovian conditioning, while the imitation ones expand to include expectations, intentions, and social roles |

(continued)

**Table 20.7** (continued)

| Sensorimotor substage | Socioemotional system |
|---|---|
| 7. Schema coordinates manifest a dominant-subordinate relationship (hierarchy) in terms of a constant temporal order and/or an interweaving toward a common end. But this is established in context only after behavior onset has produced an accidentally interesting effect, so that a goal is not evident at outset (Image schemata, or representations of analog redescriptions of basic perceptions, partake in this process (Mandler, 1992)) (e.g., target behavior with visually directed, i.e., coordinated reaching, or with closed hand reaching preceding opened hand seizure; visually guided finger manipulation of target; simple bimanual coordination with preferred hand reach then other hand grasp, or preferred hand grasps target then other hand fingers it, Rochat, 1989; one hand balances posture while other hand reaches, Rochat & Senders, 1991; self-soothing with one hand in mouth in order to use other in activities, Thelen & Fogel, 1989; babbling with hand raising to call absent adult). (For Piaget, secondary circular reactions involve accidentally discovered effects centered on the environment that are repeated [e.g., reach for and shake rattle], showing that goal schemes can be kept in mind if targets are in view and can be reached without detour [e.g., seek partially hidden, interesting object]) | A sense of "trust" develops in infants both in themselves and in the environment, for the dyadic exchanges with the caregiver in the prior substage permit a firmer relationship to consolidate. Complementary infant-caregiver schema hierarchies form in "mutual regulation" (reciprocally, each dominant in "game" played at times) |
| 8. Each constituent of schema hierarchies refines (is added to), and their coordination is more adaptive. This occurs because primitive representational images of targets permit a systematic, intentional goal from behavior onset and more subtlety in its end-point search (e.g., reach for fully hidden object even if detour needed (object permanence); exploratory, organized finger manipulation; complex bimanual coordination with preferred hand manipulation and other hand stabilization; babbling and pointing to get adult to get object; alternate gaze between mother and object being offered to her, Messinger & Fogel, 1990, in Fogel, 1991). (For Piaget, the substage of coordination of secondary schemes consists of combining schemes as means to fit new intended ends, as in object permanence tasks) | Target images facilitate highly social behavior where liked individuals and friendly strangers are sought out, engaged, and adapted to. Their departure may induce organized search and not only distress and protest |

(continued)

**Table 20.7** (continued)

| Sensorimotor substage | Socioemotional system |
|---|---|
| 9. Structured chaining of systematic schema pairs leads to the formation of linear plans. These manifest as complex combinations, but especially embeddings, or the use of subprograms in plans (e.g., resolve embedded hiding behind second screen; repeat novel adult utterance; name object to get adult to seek it. Blake and Dolgoy (1993) found that success on a means-end task (pulling a string horizontally to obtain an object) preceded the acquisition of comment gestures (e.g., point in a book) and request gestures (for adult to function as agent)). (For Piaget, tertiary circular reactions refer to deliberate trial-and-error exploration of new means for established schemes, e.g., pull blanket to get toy on it; return to starting point by reverse or alternate path) | Toddlers can begin to develop a sense of "autonomous" will, for the sociability and sense of trust of the prior substages are transformed by the current linear plans. The exploration of means-end relationships comes to include their own behavior as means in relation to an end (the "self") to be satisfied, i.e., the focus is now on the toddlers' nascent self, as much as those of others, as the appropriate self in this regard |
| 10. A primary plan integrates another plan, allowing mental detours or beginning conceptual reversibility. That is, an embedded secondary plan forms a reversible, branched sequence that can return to the primary master one (e.g., resolve double embedded or invisible hiding or resolve single one with tool; sequentially sort two subsets of a group of objects; form novel two-word utterance using words in other two-word utterances). (For Piaget, the substage of invention of new means through mental combinations occurs via symbols that represent objects/events, e.g., push carriage from side opposite handle, reversing normal procedure when situation calls for it, because symbol guides behavior) | With the advent of symbolic plans and their reversible secondary plans, toddlers can participate in a prolonged interaction either for its own sake (play) or with the seeking of control. Social interchange becomes a complex, subtle, intertwining of negotiation, stratagems, and control dynamics, at times, even in relaxed play. Rogoff (1990) describes the way children of this age begin to engage in guided participation where they actively determine the nature of their social role and the extent of their implication in social discourse |

left hand columns of the tables, and are described in more detail in terms of their cognitive, linguistic, and motoric examples than when originally presented in Young (1990a, 1990b). For the substages in the first 2 years of life, Piaget's account of sensorimotor development also is included. The socioemotional systems are presented in more detail in the right hand side of the tables.

**Table 20.8** The perioperational substages and corresponding socioemotional systems

| Perioperational substage | Socioemotional system |
|---|---|
| 11. With coordination of symbol plans, young children can regulate a series of actions in a persistent, flexible way in order to achieve a standard, conventional goal. For example, they can build a house of blocks according to a model (Bullock & Lutkenhaus, 1988). They begin to balance two symbol streams, performing dual objective tasks such as simultaneously sorting two subsets of a group of objects, although with no fixed strategy. They begin to learn to read and write individual letters, working across the auditory and visual modalities. Also, two-word utterances are coordinated, and past events are incorporated in ongoing autobiographical narratives (Howe & Courage, 1993). Piaget describes children in this period as egocentric, or incapable of decentering from their perspective. In our terms this means that symbol plan coordinations having the self's perspective as one component automatically fix that component as dominant even with the balancing that can take place: however, this dominance does not reflect a true hierarchical arrangement as in the next substage, because the dominant/subordinate relationship of the element symbol plans is not cognitively gained and flexible, capable of uncoupling in the appropriate context, but emotionally imposed and rigid or inflexible | Because there are coordinated symbol plans, whether one analyzes social peer play, pretend play, conversations, monologs, stories, etc., the beginning of superordinate structures are now evident. The target has an overall coherence to some extent, which is accentuated by cohesive relations between its parts (e.g., Halliday & Hasan, 1976). Even groups of neighboring units display more relational rules, as in the development of verbal syntax and its coordination with intonation in utterances |
| 12. Symbol plans evidence dominant/subordinate relations (hierarchies) in preschoolers. For example, in dual (multiple second) time-sharing tasks, generally language is spared relative to tapping. Speech witnesses the subordination of clauses in sentences and events in narratives. Also progress is made in recognizing and producing the written form in alphabet and in counting sequences, and in naming them. For Bialystok (1992), alphanumeric entities are formal representations where the label is affixed to the written form, or are hierarchically structured, to use our terminology. The prior period sees the beginning of the development of coordinated plans at the cognitive level | Consequently, in terms of socio-emotional systems, one sees a superordinate coherence across behaviors. Three-year-olds can come to hierarchize these superordinate coordinations. Thus, in terms of Erikson's theory, their perspective may be hierarchically positioned as dominant (in initiative) over those of others (even at the Oedipal level, if one abstracts from Freud) |
| 13. Symbol plan systems emerge from the prior hierarchies, for component symbol plans refine by adding elements and better intercoordinate in complementary ways. This produces organized rule systems by allowing children to hold things in mind, to begin to use a tentative reversibility in thought pathways about the concrete problems before them, or to return to the starting point in thought in order to select another path for comparison, and to use a precursor logic. Thus, children can begin formal schooling, and learn to read and write efficiently, all signs of organized rule system mastery. In storytelling, there are higher-order plots with related episodes involving problem and resolution. The simplest concrete operational problems of Piaget are solved | The plan systems of middle childhood enable children to increasingly relate themselves to the personalities, styles, habits, etc., of valued others. This process carries children beyond the initial phases of gender identification that begin earlier in life. In particular, identification with parents' and friends' characteristics accelerates |

(continued)

**Table 20.8** (continued)

| Perioperational substage | Socioemotional system |
|---|---|
| 14. In perioperational multiplication, children come to solve most of the problems involved in Piaget's stage of concrete operations. Symbol plan systems can combine, chain, or sequence in intercoordinations, alternating patterns, etc. This leads to improvement in logic, rules, reversals in thought, etc. Children's storytelling involves embedded minor plots which reflect the multiplicative nature of the symbol plans. Moreover, the major and minor plots are resolved sequentially, fitting Piaget's description of thought reversals, where children return to the starting point of their cognition before moving on | Children apply their concrete operational logic with its serial symbol plan systems to the "industry" of school, and its broad instruction, challenging tasks, and required production of "things" |
| 15. In perioperational integration, a limited logic in imagination comes to glimmer. Children form suppositions about the nonapparent that are amenable to further manipulation, both mental and real, even if such control of suppositions is difficult (Demetriou, Efklides, & Platsidou, 1993). They differentiate optional branches or embeddings of logic in their thought and can deal with them simultaneously or in parallel to some extent, because the ability to hold things in mind forms a larger integral whole and children accelerate in the ability to retraverse a course in thought (reversibility). Thus, in storytelling, plot and subplot resolutions are more fully elaborated and unified, and they occur in parallel, not sequentially | With the growth of logic in imagination, preadolescents come to project better their role both in the familiar social world of family and friends and in the institutions of school and peer clubs. Roles are imagined, applied, modified, and discarded, and attempts by others in doing the same are observed and assimilated |

**Table 20.9** The abstract substages and corresponding socioemotional systems

| Abstract substage | Socioemotional system |
|---|---|
| 16. With the coordination of streams of logic in imagination in young adolescence, classical Piagetian formal operational problems can be tackled, but with limited success, for the balanced synchronization of the streams is limited, not consistent. In simpler abstract problem solving, alternative hypotheses are formed and one variable at a time is allowed to vary while the other(s) are held constant, because young teenagers can orchestrate their logical thought pathways, even when no physical evidence is available to help in finding solutions | The advent of abstract logic allows higher-order conscious awareness in that young adolescents reflect on their behavior, cognitions, past, family, and future. This should lead to overt esteem for the self and others, an opening of the mind to freedom from repressed ideas, and absorption in the world of abstract ideas |
| 17. The above thought process becomes more structured in middle adolescence, for coordinated logic in imagination manifests hierarchical order across streams, permitting a spurt in formal operational thought. Abstract approaches being explored are compared either among themselves or to a more general perspective. Story construction should reflect this by placing plots and/or themes being explored in various relations, juxtapositions, etc. | Adolescents can now weigh multiple variables and logically proceed to attempt to solve problems about the self, the wider world, and their relation. This process can lead to a frontal evaluation of self-identify, ideology, and place in the time course |

(continued)

**Table 20.9** (continued)

| Abstract substage | Socioemotional system |
|---|---|
| 18. Late adolescents develop abstract systematization where the approaches examined and compared in the prior substage are qualified, or more reciprocally interrelated, leading to superordinate models. Stories could reflect this logical advance by a refinement of the plots and themes therein, producing a more structured whole | Late adolescents are permitted to undertake adult-like functions, having acquired a capacity to see themselves systemically in relation to the life course (in terms of love, advanced schooling, and perhaps work and children). Others are related to with responsibility and reciprocal sharing |
| 19. Young people pass into relativist abstraction, weighing larger systems organized into coherent multiple frameworks. Stories then should manifest creative, balanced combinations | Adult functions are vigorously adopted. Youths weigh options and usually settle into an intimate monogamous relationship and steady job/role (e.g., constant presence for offspring) |
| 20. In adults' abstract integration, an empathic universality may emerge, e.g., in values or in stories. This can take place because differentiated branching in abstract logic can come to include harmonization of self and other | If established in terms of self-knowledge, family, and daily responsibility, individuals seek the same for others, expanding their sense of harmonious integration |

**Table 20.10** The collective intelligence substages and corresponding socioemotional systems

| Collective intelligence substage | Socioemotional system |
|---|---|
| 21. Subdomain (generic, attempted collective subdomain theory/procedure; Pascual-Leone, 1990) coordination (metatheory, supra-speculation, overarching principle, second-order logical system or hypothesis, etc., building) occurs. It refers to scientific, professional, religious, moral, artistic, complex practical/technical, and other knowledge domains (even oral folk traditions). It involves personal reflection, taking place even when comprehension has not been communicated to others, or has not influenced others, if communicated | Attempted collective subdomain is accompanied by subtle coordination on principles (metaphysical abstraction reasoning), which not only engenders superior perspicacity but also a sense of awe about flux, ideas, and uncertainty |
| 22. Subdomain hierarchization can manifest, for dominant/subordinate relations established | Progress in this endeavor leads to feelings of generativity. For example, one can become a mentor of some sort to younger individuals |

(continued)

**Table 20.10** (continued)

| Collective intelligence substage | Socioemotional system |
|---|---|
| 23. Domain systematization can be attempted through mutuality in subdomain regulation. People can master (or influence) an entire domain, catalyzing its transformation. This can occur through a train of quantitative additions to the field (emergent discoveries) or by a major qualitative change in foundation (paradigmatic shift) | When these advances are radically different from the existing field's direction, we can speak of chaotic attractors and catastrophic inversions, respectively |
| 24. Interdomain efforts may be undertaken (multiplication) | Older adults who span a whole domain may experience a sense of ego integrity or satisfaction and acceptance of their life flow |
| 25. Perhaps knowledge domains are integrated. In the final phases of life, often there is a wider knowledge that is accompanied by cathartic or purifying experiences | The elderly become impregnated by a holistic sense of wisdom and also feel communion or reverence with what they regard as holy. In their most meditative moments, they hope to transcend, and feel one with mystery |

Reprinted with the permission of Springer Science+Business Media: Young, G. (1997). [Table 2.1, Page. 58]

## Summary and Conclusions

In this chapter, I have described the socioemotional systems that one considered to develop in parallel with the Neo-Piagetian ones of the present model. In particular, I provide tables that describe in depth the 25 specific cognitive and the 25 specific socioemotional steps of the present model.

## Neo-Eriksonian Steps

The Neo-Eriksonian model that has been developed incorporates the work of Erikson on the challenges/crises in development that correspond to his eight developmental stages, but adds ones that I constructed to complete the 25-step developmental model that I had developed. That is, in order to complete the 25-step Neo-Eriksonian model of stages in socioaffective development for the purpose of establishing a one-to-one correspondence with the proposed 25 steps in Neo-Piagetian development, I constructed 17 more Neo-Eriksonian stages that were inserted into the original sequence (see Chap. 5), and I used the format of listing them as oppositions or poles of challenges, issues, crises, or dangers.

Tables 20.11–20.15 present the hypothesized 25 challenges/dangers in development from a Neo-Eriksonian perspective. The proposed 25 cognitive substages in development bring with them 25 emergent personality potentials. At any one substage, if there is no supportive environment, if remnants of prior crises linger, etc., this developmental task might prove overwhelming and one could find struggle.

**Table 20.11** Dangers in development in the reflex substages

| Level | Danger and opposition in substage |
|---|---|
| 1. Distance acts vs. no stance | Distance regulation to target is irregular, too forward, or rarely "near." Without a primary base, behavior is undifferentiated |
| 2. Nursing vs. rootless acts | Basic reflexive survival mechanisms are awry, e.g., in reacting to stimuli or in nursing. Given an absence of physical alimentation, behavior is without orientation or stability |
| 3. Outcome vs. outcast acts | Target-related appetitive behavior is contextually inappropriate, over- or underenergized, too negative (e.g., avoidance, crying), etc. Because of this foundation, behavior may promote rejection |
| 4. Caregiving vs. careless giving acts | The caregiver system is not activated appropriately (e.g., newborn too passive or tests caregivers' limits, e.g., too much crying, colicky behavior). Caregivers bring their own agenda, and this may be maladaptive (e.g., indifference, postpartum depression, abuse). The will to live may be compromised by long-term, ineffective, nonoptimal, or emotionally absent caregiving due to problems with infants, caregivers, or their match |
| 5. Emotional vs. malemotional acts | Evaluations along emotion-related dimensions (e.g., whether goals being interfered with) are inaccurate. Component emotional reactions are problematic. In short, emotional scripts are not functioning normatively (e.g., too damped, too negative). For example, infants manifest distress in unpredictable ways, are not soothed in normal manner, are too fussy, and are never engaged by sensorily interesting spectacles/objects. The same extremes may be evident in other emotions as they emerge in the succeeding substages. As in prior substage (and in all subsequent substages), caregivers may contribute to these difficulties |

Reprinted with the permission of Springer Science+Business Media: Young, G. (1997). [Table P.3, Page. 11]

In the next series of tables, the negative sides or poles of the socioemotional systems are presented in detail. They involve the dangers, crises, issues, or challenges that define the present 25-step Neo-Eriksonian model of socioaffective development. In reading them, the full scope of the 17 new steps that had been constructed become more evident, as does their relationship to their corresponding cognitive steps. In addition, the value of the new steps that have been added should be evident. For example, in the sensorimotor stage, trust can develop only after some degree of social interaction, as in the proposed dyadic step hypothesized to precede the stage of trust. In the perioperational stage, it is proposed that the preschooler does not pass directly from initiative to industry, but first develops into an intermediary stage of gender acts. In the abstract stage, Erikson's famous stage of identity should be preceded by a stage involving the emergence of consciousness. In the collective stage, Eriksonian generativity has been truncated to allow for a midlife stage, involving midlife crisis when it is negative

**Table 20.12** Dangers in development in the sensorimotor substages

| Level | Danger and opposition in substage |
|---|---|
| 6. Dyadic vs. dysdyadic acts | Social dialogue is marked by poor synchrony with partner, incorrect reading of partner, misplaced actions, variable reactions, too demanding bids, excessive turning off, deficient learning skill, etc. The pleasure and joy typically inherent in a dyadic interaction with caregivers may be replaced by much frustration, gaze aversion, and disinterest instead |

(continued)

**Table 20.12** (continued)

| Level | Danger and opposition in substage |
|---|---|
| 7. Trust vs. mistrust acts | A sense of mistrust in oneself and the social world takes hold, for caregiving is unreliable, intermittent, or otherwise negative (e.g., rejecting, overintrusive smothering). Infants cannot create a normal, mutually regulated, hierarchical integration with the caregiver where at times infants are dominant and at times subordinate in a reciprocal balance of play. Emotions that emerge involve fear, sadness, crankiness, etc. |
| 8. Sociability vs. unsociability acts | A lack of sociability pervades social intercourse with the caregiver, family, and strangers. Insecurity in the attachment relationship solidifies in either an anxious avoidant or anxious ambivalent-resistant (mixed) fashion. Infants do not share with caregivers sitting as a secure base, fail to adapt to their departure, ignore them, or are ambivalent on their return, and are not optimally interactive or are negative with strangers. Thus, we see emotions such as worry, dislike, aggressive displacement, and displacement escape |
| 9. Autonomy vs. doubt acts | A sense of autonomy is stifled, for toddlers develop pervading, overly dependent behavior, doubt, hesitation, inertia, or lack of self confidence. Deliberate trial-and-error exploring becomes chaotic, trying, erroneous, imploring (dependency), flat in affect, or with exaggerated fear. Dependent behavior brings with it emotions such as jealousy, greed, and defiance |
| 10. Interdigitational vs. dedigitational acts | Mutuality in play is impossible, for young children cannot partake in prolonged, reciprocal, peaceful exchanges, have no facility in smoothly entering such social relations, and are either too overpowering/possessive or too submissive/subjugated when participating in them. Thus, give and take social behavior may be avoided. Children evaluate others with contempt, not appreciation, and evaluate themselves with the same and a sense of rejection, not pride |

Reprinted with the permission of Springer Science+Business Media: Young, G. (1997). [Table P.4, Page. 12]

**Table 20.13** Dangers in development in the perioperational substages

| Level | Danger and opposition in substage |
|---|---|
| 11. Superordinate vs. discoordinate acts | Disjointed, inappropriately juxtaposed oppositions in social behavior manifest. Children seem incoherent, fragmented, and without refined social skills. Language does not fit context, actions mismatch intentions, and emotions improperly contrast. This may be evident (in different ways) both over long stretches and neighboring behaviors. The normal egocentrism of children is inappropriate or compromised, for the "ego" is dispersed or fractionated |
| 12. Initiative vs. guilt acts | Initiative is damped by (familial) conflict deriving from too intrusive impositions or fantasies. This may even result in the Oedipus conflict (see Chap. 2). The nascent superego is saturated with guilt related to repressed wishes. Adoption of the same-sex parental identity in a nonvolatile manner is jeopardized |

(continued)

**Table 20.13** (continued)

| Level | Danger and opposition in substage |
|---|---|
| 13. Gender vs. problematic gender acts | Identification with the primary characteristics of the parents is undermined, for the process may be limited to frontal negative attributes (e.g., anger, rejection, confused signals) or dismissed, producing a frontal negativity (aggressivity, avoidance, depression). This attitude may carry over into peer- and school-related activity (e.g., disobeying parental wishes; compensatory overinclusion of negative peer models in behavior; resistance; underachievement in schooling). Self-devaluation is seeded |
| 14. Industry vs. inferiority acts | The problems above are magnified, resulting in a sense of rebelliousness, inferiority, or inadequacy. Chains of fight and/or flight become linked in children's minds, overwhelming their ego's image of itself. A propensity to overcontrol may develop as a defense mechanism, leading to exploitation, manipulation, deception, etc. |
| 15. Role vs. role confusion acts | The social roles imagined in the context of family, friends, school, and other institutions are limited and limiting. These roles are restricted ones, overreactions, compensations of lack, etc., befitting the sense of rebelliousness and/or inferiority developed previously. This emotional cauldron may produce a social (external), role-oriented individual trying to mask internal conflicts |

Reprinted with the permission of Springer Science+Business Media: Young, G. (1997). [Table P.5, Page. 13]

**Table 20.14** Dangers in development in the abstract substages

| Level | Danger and opposition in substage |
|---|---|
| 16. Conscious vs. contraconscious acts | Young adolescents can lapse into conscious self-depreciation, a closure to freeing repressed thoughts, cynical ridicule of others and their constructive efforts, and "turning off" free thinking altogether. One reaction to this confusion may be to conform excessively, and adopt the role identifications perceived as preferred by parents, peers, teachers, etc. |
| 17. Identity vs. identity diffusion acts | The search for identity can be subverted, postponed, meander, lead to back alleys, etc., as Erikson described |
| 18. Nurturing vs. misnurturing acts | Responsible adult roles cannot be envisioned. Decisions are not subjected to critical, personal standards. Social relations are more unidirectional or parallel than reciprocal. Work and school activities are not future-directed and may be demeaned. Any nurturing is superficial and considered superfluous |
| 19. Intimacy vs. isolation acts | This pattern continues, but more so, for multiple adult roles may be foisted on the individual by society. Abandonment of any such roles undertaken, or other self- and other-destructive behavior, becomes possible, yielding sentiments of loneliness, isolation, etc. Instead of a relativist, unique, yet mutual self, there is an absolute, desolate one |
| 20. Universal vs. self-singular acts | Rather than encouraging others' development, the self implodes in self-indulgent acts, or worse |

Reprinted with the permission of Springer Science+Business Media: Young, G. (1997). [Table P.6, Page. 14]

**Table 20.15** Dangers in development in the collective intelligence substages

| Level | Danger and opposition in substage |
|---|---|
| 21. Metacollecting vs. disillusionment acts | Disillusionment with society, with groups, and with constructive activity can pervade the individual, for the notion of profiting from collective symbiosis is not entertained |
| 22. Generativity vs. self-absorption acts | Generative role models with family, at work, and in the community are sacrificed for self-absorption, a sense of emptiness, and stagnation |
| 23. Catalytic vs. midlife crisis acts | Midlife crisis develops; for instead of emerging as a force in whatever collective is of concern, the adult pays the price for having skirted the collective. The confusions and changes engendered are unconscious attempts to return to prior levels through misapplied catalytic discoveries, shifts, inversions, etc., in thought |
| 24. Ego integrity vs. despair acts | Disappointment with the meaningless felt in life sets in |
| 25. Cathartic vs. abandonment acts | The elderly unwisely shut out spiritual experiences, denying any fellowship with humanity, the unknown, and the infinity |

Reprinted with the permission of Springer Science+Business Media: Young, G. (1997). [Table P.7, Page. 14]

If development goes awry, the challenges and issues become crises and dangers. Other parts of the present work deal with how this might happen, e.g., in terms of the cognitive (mis)perception of the other and the development of internal working models reflective of insecurity in attachment.

## References


Bialystok, E. (1992). Symbolic representation of letters and numbers. *Cognitive Development, 7*, 301–316.

Blake, J., & Dolgoy, S. J. (1993). Gestural development and its relation to cognition during the transition to language. *Journal of Nonverbal Behavior, 17*, 87–102.

Bullock, M., & Lutkenhaus, P. (1988). The development of volitional behavior in the toddler years. *Child Development, 59*, 664–674.

Carver, C. S., & Harmon-Jones, E. (2009a). Anger is an approach-related affect: Evidence and implications. *Psychological Bulletin, 13*, 183–204.

Carver, C. S., & Harmon-Jones, E. (2009b). Anger and approach: Reply to Watson (2009) and to Tomarken and Zald (2009). *Psychological Bulletin, 135*, 215–217.

Cohn, J. F., & Tronick, E. Z. (1983). Three-month-old infants' reaction to simulated maternal depression. *Child Development, 54*, 185–193.

Cohn, J. F., & Tronick, E. Z. (1988). Mother-infant face-to-face interaction: Influence is bidirectional and unrelated to periodic cycles in either partner's behavior. *Developmental Psychology, 24*, 386–392.

Demetriou, A., Efklides, A., & Platsidou, M. (1993). The architecture and dynamics of developing mind: Experiential structuralism as a frame for unifying cognitive developmental theories. *Monographs of the Society for Research in Child Development, 58* (5/6, Serial No. 234).

Fogel, A. (1991). *Infancy: Infant, family, and society* (2nd ed.). Saint Paul: West.

Halliday, M. A. K., & Hasan, R. (1976). *Cohesion in English*. New York: Longman.

Howe, M. L., & Courage, M. L. (1993). On resolving the enigma of infantile amnesia. *Psychological Bulletin, 113*, 305–326.

Legerstee, M. (1990). Infants use multimodel information to imitate speech sounds. *Infant Behavior and Development, 3*, 343–354.

Mandler, J. M. (1992). How to build a baby: II. Conceptual primitives. *Psychological Review, 99*, 587–604.

Mascolo, M. F., & Fischer, K. W. (2010). The dynamic development of thinking, feeling and acting over the lifespan. In R. M. Lerner & W. F. Overton (Eds.), *Handbook of lifespan development: Vol. 1. Cognitive, biology and methods*. Hoboken: Wiley.

Meltzoff, A. N., & Moore, M. K. (1989). Imitation in newborn infants: Exploring the range of gestures imitated and the underlying mechanisms. *Developmental Psychology, 25*, 954–962.

Meltzoff, A. N., & Moore, M. K. (1992). Early imitation within a functional framework: The importance of person identity, movement, and development. *Infant Behavior and Development, 15*, 479–505.

Meltzoff, A. N., & Moore, M. K. (1994). Imitation, memory, and the representation of persons. *Infant Behavior and Development, 17*, 83–99.

Messinger, D., & Fogel, A. (1990). *The role of referential gazing in object exchange*. Paper presented at the International Conference on Infant Studies, Montreal, April.

Pascual-Leone, J. (1990). Emotions, development and psychotherapy: A dialectical constructivist perspective. In J. D. Safran & L. S. Greenberg (Eds.), *Emotion, psychotherapy and change* (pp. 302–335). New York: Guilford Press.

Rochat, P. (1989). Object manipulation and exploration in 2- to 5-month-old infants. *Developmental Psychology, 25*, 871–884.

Rochat, P., & Senders, S. J. (1991). Active touch in infancy: Action systems in development. In M. J. Weiss & P. R. Zelazo (Eds.), *Newborn attention: Biological constraints and the influence of experience* (pp. 412–422). Norwood: Ablex.

Rogoff, B. (1990). *Apprenticeship in thinking: Cognitive development in social context*. New York: Oxford University Press.

Stanley, D. J., & Meyer, J. P. (2009). Two-dimensional affective space: A new approach to orienting the axes. *Emotion, 9*, 214–237.

Thelen, E., & Fogel, A. (1989). Toward an action-based theory of infant development. In J. Lockman & N. Hazen (Eds.), *Action in social context: Perspectives on early development* (pp. 23–64). New York: Plenum.

Watson, J. S. (1973). Smiling, cooing, and "the game". *Merrill Palmer Quarterly, 18*, 323–339.

Wolff, P. H. (1987). *The development of behavioral states and the expression of emotions in early infancy*. Chicago: University of Chicago Press.

Young, G. (1990a). Early neuropsychological development: Lateralization of functions – hemispheric specialization. In C. A. Hauert (Ed.), *Developmental psychology: Cognitive, perceptuo-motor and neuropsychological perspectives* (pp. 113–181). Amsterdam: North Holland.

Young, G. (1990b). The development of hemispheric and manual specialization. In G. E. Hammond (Ed.), *Cerebral control of speech and limb movements* (pp. 79–139). Amsterdam: North Holland.

Young, G. (1997). *Adult development, therapy, and culture: A postmodern synthesis*. New York: Plenum.

# Chapter 21
# Approaches to Emotions

## Introduction

In this chapter, I review major approaches to the study of emotion. These include the biological, cognitive, cultural, functional, dimensional, and dynamical approaches. First, I indicate the integrated and intercoordinated nature of cognitions and emotions. They involve brain processes but cannot be reduced to them. In the next chapter, I present my cognitive developmental model, based on the present Neo-Piagetian model of steps in development. It integrates other major approaches to the study of emotions.

## The Reality and Relevance of Emotions

### *Introduction*

Barrett (2009) began her article on the future of psychology and the connection between mind and brain by stating that "psychological states such as thoughts and feelings are real" (p. 326). Of course, no one would argue that the brain has no reality in psychology. Barrett (2009) pointed out that the problem is that psychological states and the brain are not real in the same manner. She referred to this as the "mind–brain correspondence problem."

As a solution to this mind–brain correspondence problem, Barrett maintained that emotions and cognitions are constructed categories that can be reduced to more basic psychological primitives (see Table 21.1). Moreover, they need to be described for their content and structure and explained by science in their own right. She added that cognitions and emotions are inseparable and indistinct processes in the mind that interact. They might be a product of the brain, but they do not correspond in a one-to-one fashion to organization in the brain. They are social constructions to facilitate functional language about ongoing mental activity.

Cognitions and emotions are mental contents that are redescribed at an intermediate level of psychological primitives and then at a more complex psychological level.

G. Young, *Development and Causality: Neo-Piagetian Perspectives*,

DOI 10.1007/978-1-4419-9422-6_21, 

**Table 21.1** Mind–brain correspondence

| Psychology | Example | Brain |
|---|---|---|
| Complex psychological category | Emotion (e.g., anger, sadness, fear, etc.), cognition (i.e., thoughts, memories and beliefs), the self | Neural reference space |
| Psychological primitive | Core affect, categorization, executive attention | Distributed network |
| Momentary mental state | Specific instance of anger | Neural assembly |



Barrett (2009) indicated that both thoughts-feelings and brain states are real, but not in the same way, creating the mind–brain correspondence problem. She maintained that cognitions and emotions are indeed constructed events, and they can be reduced to lower-order psychological components. However, they have reality, as well. For example, emotions can be reduced to more primitive cores and are specific expressions. The neural assemblies that shape causally higher-order components or complex categories construct instances of their expression, as in emotions

They begin as momentary mental states involving flexible neural assembly. Then, they become functional abstractions involved in distributed brain networks. They end up with a larger neural reference space, as they emerge and organize into collections of mental states, specifying the contents and structures of emotions and cognitions.

Cognitions and emotions relate closely to processes in the brain, but they are not causally related to them in a mechanical way; rather, they relate to brain processes only in a probabilistic way. Barrett specified that we should not consider emotions as causal in the following manner, "Emotion X causes Behavior X." Rather, we should argue that "Brain State A at Time 1" increases the probability of occurrence of an ensuing constructed mental state equivalent to "Brain State B at Time 2." She concluded that simple causal models, such as, "stimulus *impacts* organism, *leads to* response," are not truly explanatory compared to her approach. We should not reduce behavioral processes to brain processes because they exist at different levels and include intermediate levels involving brain states and psychological categories, which are as real as the brain activity that we can measure and the behavioral activity that we can observe.

## *Emotion–Cognition Relations*

Pessoa (2008) argued that cognition and emotions form behavioral complexes and that the brain areas that are involved in their organization and expression address both affect and cognition. They form dynamic coalitions or networks over brain regions. Moreover, certain regions express high degree of interconnectivity and, therefore, are called hubs. They serve to regulate the flow and integration of information across the regions involved in complex cognitive–emotional behavior. He concluded that there are no truly separate systems for either emotion or cognition. This perspective is nonmodular, in that elements of the circuit are only minimally decomposable.

Pessoa presented a model for the circuitry involved in executive control and emphasized that it, too, is cognitive–affective in nature (see Fig. 21.1). For example, the lateral prefrontal cortex is involved in the circuit, and according to Pessoa, it regulates inhibition at both the cognitive and affective levels. For the former, this refers to the probability that an inhibitory response is required and, for the latter, in one example given, it refers to whether negative or neutral stimuli are viewed before being required to inhibit a response.

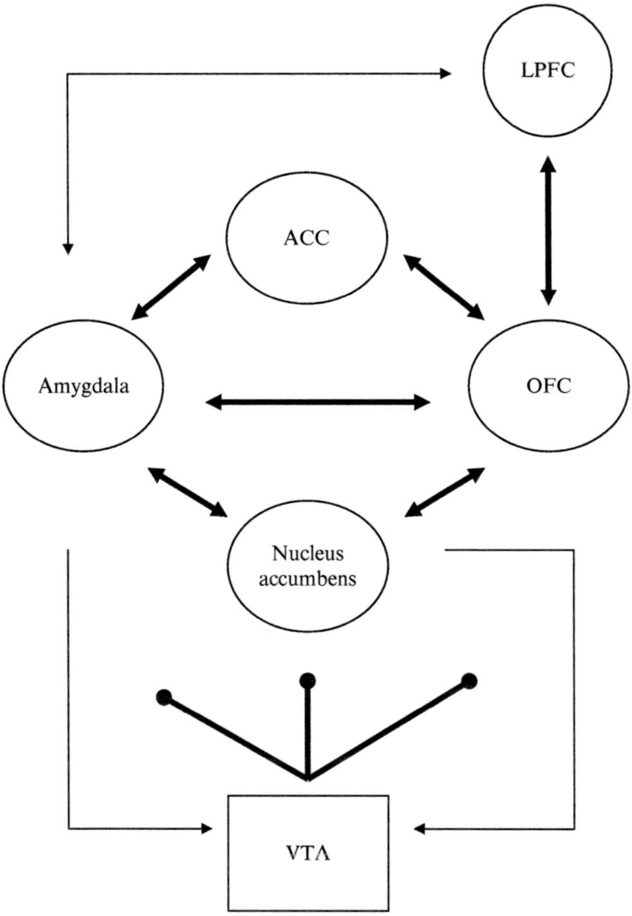


**Fig. 21.1** Circuit for executive control. This extended control circuit contains traditional control areas, such as the anterior cingulated cortex (ACC) and the lateral prefrontal cortex (LPFC), in addition to other areas commonly linked to affect to (amygdala) and motivation (nucleus accumbens). Diffuse, modulatory effects originate from dopamine-rich neurons from the ventral tegmental area (VTA). The circuit highlights the cognitive-affective nature of executive control, in contrast to more purely cognitive-control proposals. Several connections are not shown to simplify the diagram. Line thickness indicates approximate connection strength. *OFC* orbitofrontal cortex. Reprinted with the permission of Macmillan Publishers Ltd: NATURE REVIEWS NEUROSCIENCE. Pessoa, L. (2008). Copyright 2008. [Figure 3, Page. 153]

Forgas (2008) also emphasized the relationship between affect and cognition. He considered affect as adaptive and an important "adjunct" to cognition (Damasio, 1994). One evolutionary perspective views emotions as "superordinate cognitive programs" (Cosmides & Tooby, 2000). Forgas reviewed the neuroscientific research showing that social–cognitive and affective processes share overlapping neural underpinnings. He described an affect infusion model, which offered a process-based explanation of how cognition and affect are linked.

Immordino-Yang and Damasio (2007) presented an integrated model of affect and cognition, which highlighted the role of "emotional thought." It represents the platform for learning, memory, decision-making, and creativity, both in social and nonsocial contexts (see Fig. 21.2). Immordino-Yang and Damasio described that emotion-related processes help serve as "emotional rudders" to guide judgments and actions. They maintained that emotion is a basic form of decision-making and comprises cognitive processes as much as sensory processes, both of which are

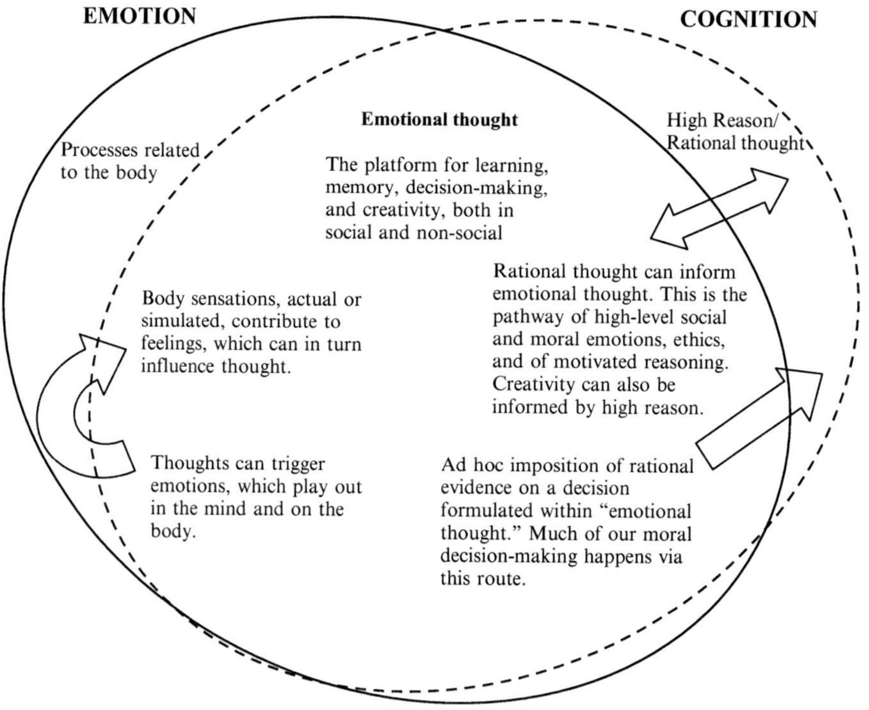


**Fig. 21.2** Emotion, cognition, and emotional thought. The evolutionary shadow cast by emotion over cognition influences the modern mind. In the diagram, the *solid ellipse* represents emotion; the *dashed ellipse* represents cognition. The extensive overlap between the two ellipses represents the domain of emotional thought. Emotional thought can be conscious or non-conscious and is the means by which bodily sensations come into our conscious awareness. High reason is a small section of the diagram and requires consciousness. Reprinted with the permission of John Wiley & Sons, Inc. Immordino-Yang, M. H., & Damasio, A. (2007). Copyright © 2007 and International Mind, Brain, and Education Society's. [Figure 1, Page. 8]

subsumed in the processes of emotion. Therefore, rational thought and logical reasoning are "hardly ever truly devoid of emotion." Moreover, "they cannot be recruited appropriately and usefully in the real world without emotion" (Immordino-Yang & Damasio, 2007, p. 8).

Note that for Lewis (2005a), cognition and emotion are linked, they organize goal-directed activity, emotions infuse mood and personality, they include neurobiological mechanisms at one level but contribute to a sense of self at another, and they can be described in terms of nonlinear dynamic systems (attractors) that can vertically integrate through circular causality. The latter mechanism indicates how emergent realities can develop out of "ingredients," to use a term from Barrett (2009), at lower levels of causality. (For further work by Lewis on cognitive–emotion interaction, see Table 21.2, and Figs. 21.3–21.5).

**Table 21.2** Three scales of emotional self-regulation, showing parallels and distinctions across scales and hypothesized psychological and neurobiological mechanisms

| | Emotional interpretation | Mood | Personality |
|---|---|---|---|
| Developmental scale | Micro | Meso | Macro |
| Duration | Seconds–minutes | Hours–days | Months–years |
| Description | Rapid convergence of cognitive interpretation with emotional state | Lasting entrainment of interpretive bias with narrow emotional range | Lasting interpretive-emotional habits specific to classes of situations |
| Dynamic systems formalism | Attractor | Temporary modification of state space | Permanent structure of state space |
| Psychological mechanism | Cognition–emotion coupling or resonance, successful goal-directed action | Cognition–emotion coupling, goal preoccupation, inhibited or unsuccessful action | Cognition–emotion complementarities that arise from and constrain coupling in emotional interpretations and moods |
| Possible neurobiological mechanism | Cortical coherence mediated by orbitofrontal organization entrained with limbic circuits | Orbitofrontal-corticolimbic entrainment, motor rehearsal and preafference, sustained neuro-hormone release | Selection and strengthening of some corticocortical and corticolimbic connections, pruning of others, loss of plasticity |
| Higher-order form in circular causality | Intention, goal | Intentional orientation | Sense of self |



According to Lewis (2000b), there are different but interrelated levels in socioaffective phenomena. The present work deals especially with the emotional one. The others concern longer lasting mood and personality dispositions. In children, one speaks of temperament rather than personality, per se

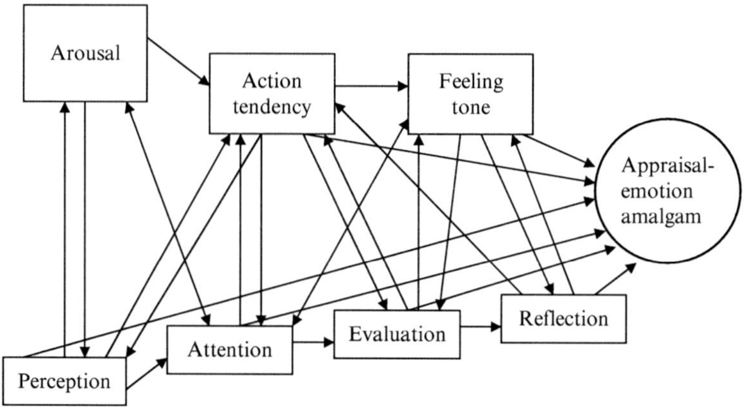


**Fig. 21.3** Appraisal-emotional amalgams. A skeletal model in which bi-directional causal relations between appraisal and emotion constituents lead to whole appraisal-emotion amalgam. This scheme captures the contribution of emotion components to whole appraisals at the psychological level of description, but the components themselves have to be re-conceptualized at the neural level. Reprinted with the permission of Cambridge University Press. Lewis, M. D. (2005a). © Cambridge Journals. [Figure 1, Page. 173]

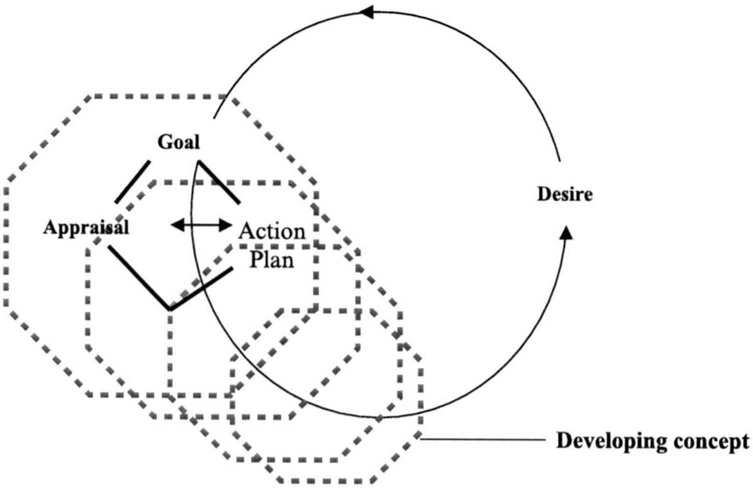


**Fig. 21.4** Desire, appraisals, goals, and plans in development. A sketch of the feedback loop that entrains desire with goals that embed cognitive events (appraisals and action plans), each augmenting the other. This feedback loop is proposed to drive conceptual development in the early years and perhaps over the life span. *Smooth lines* indicate real-time feedback cycle, and *dotted lines* indicate consolidation over development. Reprinted with the permission of American Psychological Association. Lewis, M. D. (2010). Copyright © 2009. [Figure 10.1, Page. 186]

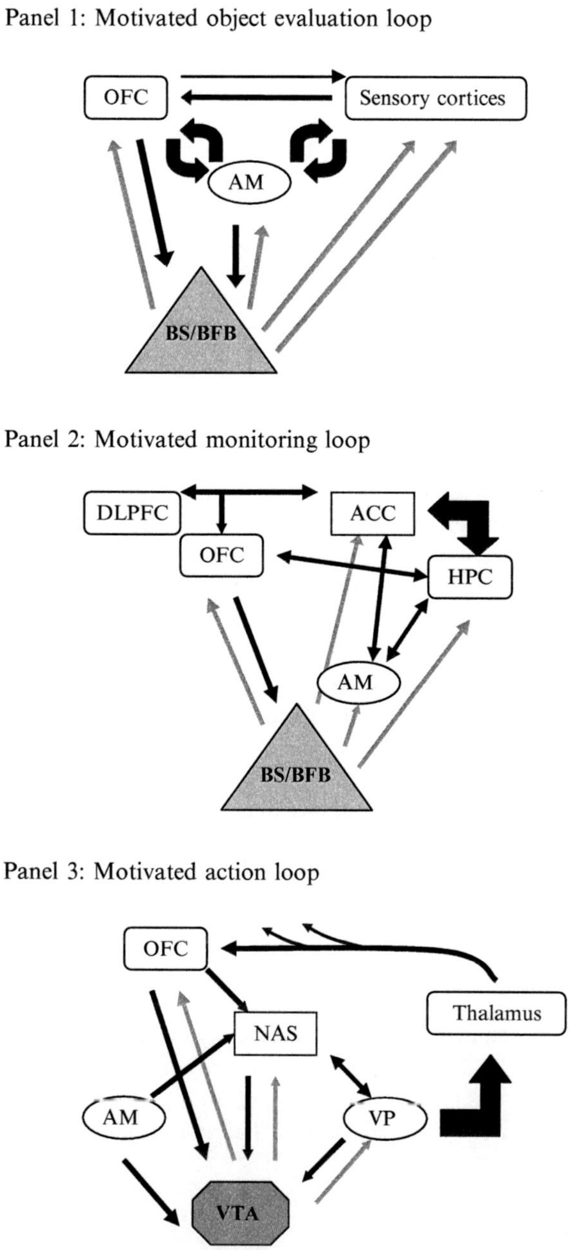


**Fig. 21.5** Motivational loops. Three higher-order loops comprised of nested feedback circuits, each integrating particular emotion and appraisal processes. *Black arrows* represent glutamatergic and GABAergic (intrinsic) synaptic pathways. *Gray arrows* represent neuromodulator (extrinsic) pathways. *ACC* anterior cingulate cortex; *AM* amygdala; *BS/BFB* brain stem/basal forebrain; *DLPFC* dorsolateral prefrontal cortex; *HPC* hippocampus; *NAS* nucleus accumbens; *OFC* orbitofrontal cortex; *VP* ventral pallidum; *VTA* ventral tegmental area. Reprinted with the permission of Cambridge University Press. Lewis, M. D. (2005a). © Cambridge Journals. [Figure 3, Page. 183]

**Table 21.3** Differentiation and integration in the CNS and brain

| Level | Brain: vertical integration | Prefrontal cortex: hierarchy (in rule representation) |
|---|---|---|
| 1 | Cortex | Orbitofrontal |
| 2 | Limbic system | Ventrolateral |
| 3 | Diencephalon | Dorsolateral |
| 4 | Brain stem | Rostrolateral |

*Note*. Adapted from SAGE Publications with permission. Bunge, S. A., & Zelazo, P. D. (2006). Copyright © 2006 by Association for Psychological Science. [Excerpt of 217 words]
In the table, two different models are given with respect to at least four levels in the development of the brain. However, the models relate to circumscribed acquisitions. The second model is complementary to the first one, as it helps differentiate its single cortical level. Therefore, between them, a more complex model could be built

## Comment

Emotions and cognition relate to each other not only behaviorally, but also centrally. The brain evidences increasing complexity as the person grows, and there has been increasing encephalization that has marked evolution. Some have attempted to relate the steps in the evolution of the brain to development, such as in MacLean's (1993) concept of the triune brain. However, the vertical or hierarchical structure of brain of humans is more complex than three levels (see Table 21.3).

Moreover, one can question to what degree any localization process is sufficient to organize development. Most likely, there might not be a specific central marker for any one cognitive or emotional acquisition, but changes in organizational variables, including through pruning, to create more efficient parallel and integrated distributed neuronal processing, both proximate and more distal.

This leaves the question of whether cognitions and emotions can be reduced to physiological processes "respected" in the brain, to use the term of Barrett (2009). If emotions have their relevance and realities, as argued, it is partly through the dynamical soft assembly involved in their online configuration in context that gives them a holistic property beyond the characteristics of their component parts. As Lewis (2005a) aptly argued, through processes of circular causality, emotion-cognition structures can emerge in the vertical organization of brain and behavior. The present model of 25 steps in cognitive development and the parallels in emotions that reflect and fuel it can be considered extensions and reworkings of this approach to the study of emotions and their link to cognition.

## Reductionism

The study of emotions needs to deal with the question of reductionism, and to what extent emotions are independent realities that can even influence behavior, or are they merely epiphenomena, at best, or otherwise without any real impact or expression in behavior? The present approach is that there are multiple reasons to consider emotions equal partners in the behavioral playing field along with other components, such as cognition and perception. Moreover, the linkage between emotion and cognition that is described in recent work reflects the important role that emotions play in cognition. Indeed, we need formulations that capture both in one concept, such as "emotional thought." (In this regard, one can equally refer to their combined or unified status as "cognitive emoting," or "emotio-cognition").

Among other factors that illustrate the reality and relevance of emotions, I list the following. Emotions are now known to:

(a) Have deep evolutionary roots
(b) Develop in concert with cognitive acquisitions, and can fuel those acquisitions
(c) Are the glue in development, in the linking of self and other
(d) Can be the leading edge or focus of developmental acquisitions (e.g., cognition serves sociality and socioaffective acquisitions, such as emotions, which are critical for adaptation)
(e) Are intrinsically related to cognitive schemes (cognitive schemes, as such, do not exist; there are only cognitive–emotional structures that develop)
(f) Provide for or influence self-regulation, coping, executive function, inhibition, and other means of self-control
(g) Are essential in communication as expressions of meaning as much as the words that accompany them
(h) Are the motivating force in our exploration and adaptation to the world, both animate and inanimate, partly defining ourselves as contributors and facilitators of our own development and psychological growth
(i) Are part of the matrix of components in the behavioral field that constitutes the person's functioning in context, equal in importance and influence to any other component in this regard, such as cognition
(j) Help promote the individual, group, gender, and sociocultural differences that make our species so interesting and complex
(k) Allow the exquisite feelings of shared realities and communal participations in life that mark the height of human activity
(l) In addition, emotions are at once not only a positive in our psychology, but also a negative, both of which need to be an important focus in parenting, in education, in relationships, and in psychotherapy

## Major Approaches in Emotions

Table 21.4 indicates the major approaches in the study of emotions. They range from the more biological to the more social and cultural. They might consider emotions as a small grouping, or they deny that they are limited to few in number. Or they deny the primacy of basic emotions and prefer to organize them according to dimensions. They examine adaptation from an evolutionary perspective, but also from an ongoing contextualist and functional one. Generally, they consider cognition as important, whether in terms of appraisals, the influence of culture, or the

**Table 21.4** Major approaches in the study of emotions

| | Emotions | | |
|---|---|---|---|
| Perspectives | Description | Function | What develops? |
| Biological (basic emotions, emotional categories) | Discrete sets of neurochemical processes–expressive behaviors–feeling states<br>Each has its own neurophysiological substrate<br>Each independent of cognition | Send social signals; foster social interaction; motivate behavior and cognitive development | Connections with other systems are established<br>Emotions themselves are largely invariant over the life span |
| Cognitive (appraisals) | Superordinate categories representing varied relations among external incentives, thoughts, and detected changes in feeling states | Direct attention; motivate thought and action; support cultural values (appraise relevant parameters) | Incentives that contribute to feeling states develop as a function of cognitive development<br>New emotions become possible |
| Structural-developmental (also Neo-Piagetian) | Subjective reactions to salient events characterized by physiological, experiential, and over behavioral change (that develop over stages and substages) | Communicate inner states; facilitate response to emergencies; promote environmental mastery; ensure (social and eventually) reproductive success | Differentiated affective systems (e.g., joy, anger, fear), undergo developmental transformation from earlier to more advance forms organized around an affective core |
| Socialcultural | Socially or culturally constructed syndromes constituted by interaction of many components related to individuals in their social and physical context | Preserve social orders and prevailing sociomoral frameworks | Syndromes change as a function of socialization, discursive practices, and enculturation |
| Functionalist (contextual) | Patterns of interaction between organism and environment in service of goal<br>Dependent on "appreciation" of relation of event to goal | Regulates flow of information, selection of response processes, and social and interpersonal behavior | Number and complexity of interaction patterns change as a function of socialization and cognitive development<br>Some "appreciations" exist at birth and are continuous over life span |

(continued)

**Table 21.4** (continued)

| Perspectives | Emotions | | What develops? |
|---|---|---|---|
| | Description | Function | |
| Dimensional | Emotions considered to organize around continua or poles, rather than existing as discrete categories | Depends on the specific continua or poles posited, such as approach–withdrawal, positive–negative, and activity–passivity | These models are not typically developmental. Young (1990a) presented a developmental model that incorporates the all the major models under discussion |
| Dynamical | Emotions coalesce out of system, without preordained structure or categories | They might include facial and vocal units with biological bases, but emotions always serve functional ends in context | They develop as underlying components develop |

Adapted from Springer Science+Business Media with permission. Griffin, S., & Mascolo, M. F. (1998). [Table 1, Page. 5]

*Note.* I added in parantheses a few inserts to this table. In addition, I added the last two major approaches to emotions listed at the bottom of the table, concerning nonlinear dynamical systems (e.g., Witherington, 2007) and dimensions

With this table, the book takes a different turn, moving from the cognitive to the emotional level. To this point, I had presented the cognitive–affective parallels in the various stages and substages of the models of Case, Fischer, and myself, but had not presented in depth the particular model of emotional development and its links to cognitive development that I had formulated in Young (1990a). Before describing the specifics of that model, first, I review the major approaches to the study of the development of emotions. Different authors have different views on what models are the most important in the study of emotions. For this table, I used the work of Griffin and Mascolo (1998), but added two other models. I indicated in the table that the model that I had developed integrates all the others mentioned in the table (also see Figs. 21.6–21.8)

Briefly, in my particular model, which is applicable to the first 2 years of life, new emotions are seen to develop with the onset of each of Piaget's six sensorimotor substages (my model is almost identical). They organize around several basic dimensions, one of which is the cognitive developmental one indicated. Given the intersection of axes of dimensions in the model along which emotions can be classified, the basic emotions take the form of families of basic emotions or categories within the intersections of the dimensions

It is worthwhile to understand the difference between a model of basic emotions tied to universals, and a model of emotions tied to ongoing dimensional appraisals related to function in context. In the former case, in the extreme form of the model, the universals are released by appraisals that elicit their activation, and their expression is governed by physiological–neurological programs that have been selected for their adaptive evolutionary fitness advantage, although culture display rules can lead to their modification in expression. In the latter case, there are no universals to begin with, but component expressions that coalesce and coact to produce rapidly changing expression in order to accomplish adaptive ongoing functional ends. Emotions serve functional ends in context, including ones conditioned within parenting families and cultures, rendering them dynamical, ongoing expressions of multiple components that do not have preformulated instructions governing their expression role of meaning. In all approaches, subjective feeling, valence or hedonic tone, or a variant, is considered important, as is physiological reactivity. The dynamical one is a newer model, and it is quite consistent with the present work.

In addition, my approach is structural developmental, in that I seek the parallels between the Neo-Piagetian cognitive substages of the present model, at least for infancy, and their corresponding basic emotions. At the same time, I organize the emotions according to dimensions and acknowledge the role of culture and function.

## *Biology*

The concept of basic emotions or categories of emotion is associated with the biological approach, which has its origins in evolutionary theory. Hess and Thibeault (2009) reviewed Darwin's (1872/1965) contribution to the study of emotions. Darwin believed that emotional expressions reflect underlying emotional states and function in communicating them. Ekman (1972) respected this argument, but added a role for the influence of culture in emotional expression. He posited that there are a handful of basic emotions that are universal and inherited from animal species. Ekman added that although basic emotions are hardwired in their prototypical facial expressions, cultural display rules influence their specific expression and social use.

According to the biological approach to emotions, the handful of basic emotions is universally present, with preprogrammed, phylogenetically derived constituents and with distinct motoric (e.g., facial) expressions, as well as neurological bases. Although researchers maintain that this approach is valid (e.g., Ekman, 1994; Izard, 1994; Panksepp, 1994; Plutchik, 1993), not all agree (e.g., Averill, 1994; Fridlund, 1994; Russell, 1994; Scherer, 1994; Shweder, 1994), and generally they adopt more of an environmental approach. For example, Fridlund's (1994) behavioral ecology view considered the purpose of emotional expressions as communicative of intentions and not of emotions. To be fair to the biological approach in this regard, as mentioned, for the approach emotions could vary in individuals and context according to learned familial and cultural display rules.

Izard (2007) distinguished between basic emotions and emotion schemata, which integrate emotion, appraisals, and higher-order cognition. He defended the point of view that there are basic or discrete emotions, and in this regard he listed: interest, joy/happiness, sadness, anger, disgust, and fear. He indicated that others have similar lists (e.g., Ekman, 1999; Panksepp, 2000; Plutchik, 1962; Tomkins, 1962), but that they vary in length (e.g., his current list is shorter than an earlier list in Izard, 1977).

As for the development of the basic emotions, for example, he found that interest was expressed as early as 2 months, if not earlier (Langsdorf, Izard, Rayias, & Hembree, 1983) and that anger was expressed at 4 months (Izard, Hembree, & Huebner, 1987). (Note that Kopp and Neufeld (2002) indicated that even newborns could express anger implicitly e.g., fussing to bodily restraint).

In terms of another prominent view of emotions, that of dimensionality, he concluded that we need both a basic emotional point view and a dimensional point of view to understand emotions. He mentioned dimensions such as positive vs. negative emotionality and approach–avoidance motivation. He argued against conceptual processes as being primary in emotional expressions indicating, instead, that cognition and affect are highly interrelated.

## *Cognition*

The cognitive approach emphasizes the appraisals or perceptions of the situations that elicit emotional expressions and, therefore, how the expressions are individualized in context, depending on particulars of the person and situation involved (Witherington & Crichton, 2007). Appraisal theories (Frijda, 1986; Scherer, 1984) include cultural norms and rules at the beginning of the appraisal process of emotion-eliciting stimuli.

Ortony and Turner (1990) maintained that emotional expression does not function by use of constrained packages of facial components constant across multiple parameters. There are no prototypical facial displays for particular emotions. Rather, separate components can be assembled in a variable way into appropriate emotional responses, fitting the individual's personality, coping strategies, particular circumstances, etc. Some of these components will be inherited configurations elicited universally when particular appraisals take place, whereas others will be less structured. Thus, for example, there may not be one kind of fear or anger found generally, but possibly two or more, with somewhat overlapping sets of components. To pursue the example, fear of a bear might induce an open mouth, tightly stretched raised eyebrows, widely opened eyes, and a stare because, in this situation, components affiliated with surprise are mixed with others associated with distress. By contrast, for the most part, fear of a possible diagnosis of cancer will yield an expression limited to distress-related reactions.

## *Functions*

The functional approach emphasizes the purpose served by emotions. The adaptive goals of the individual in context are paramount, and emotions are but one component flexibly recruited to arrive at them. According to Witherington and Crichton (2007), in the functionalist approach, emotion serves to establish, maintain, or alter the relationship of the organism to its environment (e.g., Saarni, Campos, Camras, & Witherington, 2006).

To elaborate, in the functionalist approach, emotions are considered expressions of the organism adapting in context or serving functions significant to the organism, rather than expressions of facial prototypes, neurological patterns, or other biological signatures. For example, if the organism has the goal of removing an obstacle in a forceful manner, the expression of anger is potentiated. Components of facial, vocal, and instrumental activity, along with physiological responses, are recruited flexibly to arrive at the organism's goal in a manner that adjusts to the details of the organism's context. The organism establishes what it considers as significant in its context by appraising its ongoing relationship with the environment.

Functional approaches analyze emotions such as happiness and anger in terms of their underlying meaning or goal (Barrett & Campos, 1987). The focus is upon larger emotional gestalts rather than their component units. For example, for Stein and Trabasso (1992), happiness derives from goal attainment or maintenance, sadness from failure to attain or maintain goals, anger from agents that cause such loss, and fear from anticipation of the threat of such loss. Goal plans accompany each of these emotions, i.e., respectively, goal maintenance, goal reinstatement, revenge, and avoidançe.

## *Culture*

For those adhering to the view that there are no basic emotions, the environmental and cultural components underlying emotional expression are the most powerful ones. For example, Shweder (1994) argued that emotion labels are interpretive, symbolic, re-presentational, or intentional schemes of somatic–affective feelings/experience that are culturally founded. Moreover, it is even possible that a culture has no emotions.

Gergen (1994) examined the constitution of emotions from the social constructionist perspective. They are seen to derive from or act as constitutive features of relationships, not individuals. We are relational selves before we are individuals. Relationships are neither interchanges of separate individuals nor manifestations of the societal whole. Rather, they are intersubjective interdependencies, coordinations, or coconstructed negotiations of meaning that develop through specific microsocial patterns in the relational arena. Rationality develops through local participation in social interaction, and thus is socially distributed, communal, or collaborative. It is not that individuals think, but through culturally prescribed modes of reasoning, social forms of cognition "think the individual." As another example, it is not that independent selves join in a relationship, but that self-identity is a by-product of particular relationship forms.

Similarly, for Gergen, emotions transpire within social patterns, from which their meaning derives. Emotions are performed in relationship, often through culturally determined conventions, rituals, or meanings. In this performance, they do not impact upon social life; rather, "they *constitute* social life itself." They are components of larger pragmatic interactional patterns, emotional scenarios, or narrative scripts. Thus, emotions are basic forms that are given particular shape by the network of relationships and historocultural contexts in which they are expressed. In summary, emotions are social constructions, and any attempt to describe them as basic universals will miss their contextuality.

## *Dimensions*

### Earlier Models

The dimensional view attempts to array emotional phenomena along several orthogonal dimensions, such as pleasant–unpleasant, active–passive, etc. (e.g., Frijda, 1993). The dimensions concern salient appraisals or judgments related to environmental adaptation (Lazarus, 1994). They are conceived as continuous but can be used as categorical or polar opposites (high vs. low). Thus, a point in an *N*-dimensional space (usually two- or three-dimensional) could represent any one emotional process.

Dimensions in emotional expression concern aspects such as approach–withdrawal, activation–inhibition, and positive–negative valence. For several models, dimensions relate to approach and withdrawal. These are basic behavioral processes that emerged early in phylogenesis and onto which mapped later evolving emotions. For example, anger is construed as approach as much as the infant smiling and reaching toward her mother.

Scherer (1994) presented a model of emotions having five dimensions of emotional evaluation. First, stimuli are evaluated for their novelty, or whether a novel event has occurred or is expected. Then, in intrinsic pleasantness checking, pleasant and unpleasant stimuli induce approach and avoidance tendencies, respectively. In goal/need monitoring, stimulus relevance, movement toward goals/plans, their blockage, and their realization are evaluated, producing relaxation or activation, depending on the outcome of the evaluation. In coping potential checks, the causes, control/power over, and internal adjustments to the stimulus are appraised. In norm/self compatibility verification, in particular, internal and external standards are referred to in judging potential actions taken. It seems that the middle three dimensions resemble those in various dimensional models.

Russell's (1991) review of cross-cultural research on emotions points to three major bipolar dimensions in the organization of emotions, as deduced from ratings. He termed them (a) pleasure (evaluation, valence, positivity), (b) arousal (activity, activation), and (c) dominance (potency, power, control). Thus, anger would be defined by the features of displeasure, high arousal, and dominance, as opposed to the features of pleasure, low arousal, and submissiveness. According to Russell (1991), cross-cultural research has suggested that the pleasure dimension is universal, and that usually at least one of the other two dimensions is found.

Frijda (1993) posited very similar dimensions, labeling them positive–negative, activation–engagement, and, if a third one is found, potency–dominance–aggression. According to him, it is unclear whether the dimensions are unipolar or bipolar. Fischer and Tangney (1995) referred to the dimensions of evaluation, activity, and engagement.

Workers have combined the basic emotion and dimensional approaches by describing the way basic emotions fall in the dimensional spaces that the dimensions construct (e.g., Frijda, 1993; Russell, 1991). Russell (1991), in particular, placed key basic emotions in a dimensional space elaborated by two axes, those involving pleasantness and activity. In this regard, Davidson (1992) maintained that the basic emotion and dimensional perspectives are complementary, addressing different levels of a common process. This approach is consistent with my own.

## Recent Models

Nesse and Ellsworth (2009) explained that models of basic emotions vary from two of them (positive, negative) to an infinite number. In terms of their underlying dimensions, it is quite common to find models that favor valence and intensity. The dimensional model has evolved to the point that it denies the validity of basic emotions and places emotions within multidimensional spaces without particular boundaries for them (see Fig. 21.6). In Nesse and Ellsworth's model, emotions are neither discrete basic units nor reflections of positions in a select dimensional space, but overlapping point clouds of probable central tendencies or location in an *N*-dimensional space. Moreover, emotions can be arranged according to situations that arise in goal pursuit. It is not that a specific emotion has a particular evolutionary function, but that the

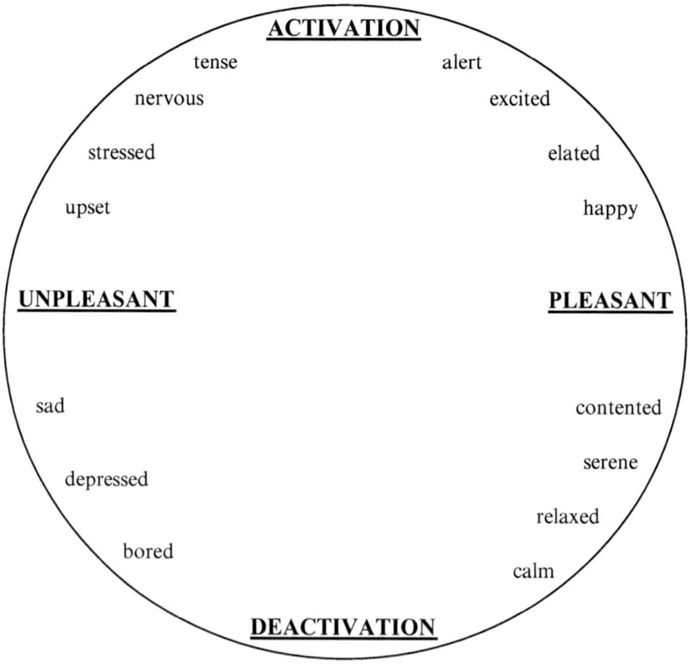


**Fig. 21.6** A circumplex model of affect. Circumplex models array basic emotions according to primary dimensions, but in a circular rather than an *n*-dimensional axis diagram. Valence and Intensity are primary dimensions in many models of emotions. Reprinted with the permission of Cambridge University Press. Posner, J., Russell, J. A., & Peterson, B. S. (2005). © Cambridge Journals. [Figure 1, Page. 716]

| | Domain | Before | Usual progress | Fast progress | Slow progress | Success | Failure |
|---|---|---|---|---|---|---|---|
| Opportunity | Physical | Desire | Engage-ment | Flow | Frustration | Pleasure | Pain |
| | Social | Excitement | Friendship | Pride | Anger Low mood | Happi-ness | Sadness |
| Threat | Physical | Fear | Coping | Confidence | Despair | Relief | Pain |
| | Social | Anxiety | Defensive Arousal | Confidence | Anger | Pride | Shame Embarrassment |

**Fig. 21.7** Emotions for situations that arise in goal pursuit. The figure indicates that emotions can be categorized according to goal pursuit, threat-opportunity, and physical-social domain. Reprinted with the permission of American Psychological Association. Nesse, R. M., & Ellsworth, P. C. (2009). Copyright © 2009. [Figure 3, Page. 133]

organism is adapting to formulating and reaching goals, and progress is expressed through a combination of emotions (see Fig. 21.7). The primary dimensions on which goal pursuit varies relate to whether there are opportunities or threat, whether the domain is physical or social, and the what is the phase of goal attainment (before, success, failure) as well as degree of progress (slow, usual, fast). The figure shows that some particular emotions are not restricted to one location in the dimensional model.

Carver and Harmon-Jones (2009) described different dimensional views of affect. Watson and Tellegen (1985) presented a model with positive and negative affect as the crucial dimensions. Cacioppo et al. (2007) prepared a similar model involving the dimensions of positivity and negativity.

Note that Vaish, Grossmann, and Woodward (2008) argued that humans express a negativity bias from early in life because of its adaptive evolutionary function. Repacholi (2009) found that the effects on the behavior of 15- and 18-month-old infants watching adults express positive, negative, or neutral affect, as they completed an action on objects, supported the negative bias perspective on emotions.

Rolls (2005) developed a model related to dimensions that involved omission/termination and delivery of rewards and punishments, and in their publication Carver and Harmon-Jones (2009) reworked this model. Carver and Harmon-Jones' (2009) own model involved approach and avoidance/withdrawal (see Fig. 21.8). The model indicates that anger is an approach-related affect. The authors referred to the evidence that anterior cortical asymmetry reflects direction of approach vs. withdrawal, rather than emotional valence (positive vs. negative), per se. They cited evidence that the even 2–3-day-old infants show greater relative left anterior cortical activation in response to sucrose compared to water (Fox & Davidson, 1986).

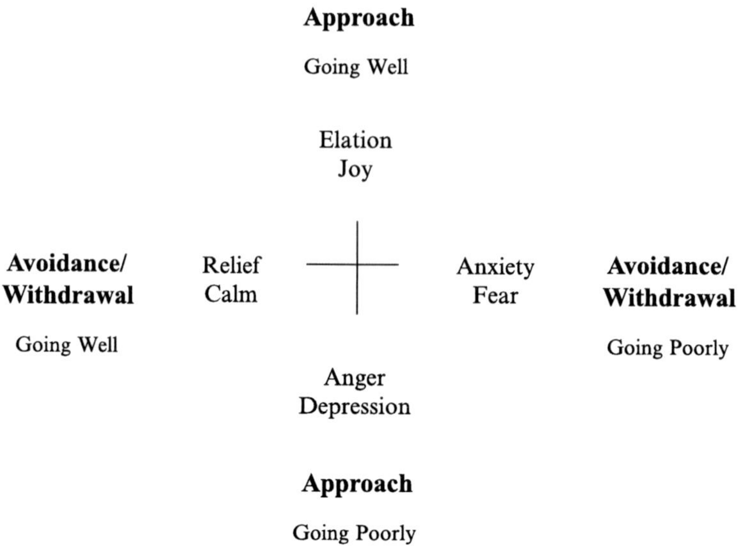


**Fig. 21.8** A two-dimensional model of basic emotions using approach-withdrawal, going well-poorly. The model indicates that anger is an approach-related emotion. Reprinted with the permission of American Psychological Association. Carver, C. S., & Harmon-Jones, E. (2009). Copyright © 2009. [Figure 1(c), Page. 194]

## *Dynamical Approach*

### Introduction

Witherington and Crichton (2007) have contrasted the functionalist and dynamic systems approaches to the understanding of emotions and their development. Both of these approaches are considered metatheoretical frameworks (Overton, 2006), rather than specific theories. The authors described that both approaches have supplanted the structuralist approach to emotions. In the structuralist approach to emotional development, behavior is considered a simple expression of internal feeling states or of programs in the central nervous system that result from maturational processes, or cognitive development processes, or both.

The dynamic system approach is complimentary to the functional approach. In the dynamic systems approach, emotions are considered self-organizing systems without internal control mechanisms or preexisting design programs (Camras & Witherington, 2005).

The dynamic approach emphasizes how emotions emerge in a self-organized manner in ongoing contexts, and how their multiple components or subsystems coalesce in emotional expression. None of the components are considered primary and the emotional expression as a whole is considered multiply determined. There is no inherent control system through a set of instructions in the organism directing emotional expression because, instead, it is context-sensitive and specific.

Some proponents of the dynamic system perspective maintain that the functional approach is inappropriately causal because in the functional approach functions serve as antecedent conditions, dictating the generation of emotional expression.

## Dynamical Emotions

Camras and Witherington (2005) provided a dynamical systems perspective on emotional development. They emphasized the self-organizational and emergent properties of systems in emotional development. They described Thelen and Smith's (1998) concept of a collective variable, which is a measure of a system that reflects its state by capturing the interrelationships among its components. Several studies have been undertaken on infant facial and vocal behavior in terms of the typical states or attractors to which it gravitates in emotional development, as revealed by collective variables.

Messinger, Fogel, and Dickson (2001) studied the temporal changes in smiling configurations and their variations in interactional contexts. They found different patterns in how components of the smile coalesced in different contexts. They concluded that qualitatively different forms of the emotion of joy are expressed in young infants (relief, positive affect sharing, readiness to play). Camras and colleagues studied the relations among infant head movements, gazing, brow raises, and mouth openings. Brow raises and mouth openings were not just associated with contexts involving surprise; the authors found that mouth openings and head/gaze raises could recruit brow raises in contexts that are familiar and not surprising. Lavelli and Fogel (2005) studied longitudinally from 1 to 14 weeks of age attention and emotion in interactions, and found a 2-month transition in their relationship. The collective variable at this age became more integrated across concentrated attention, cooing expression, and smiling in conjunction with maternal talking/smiling.

Camras, Oster, Campos, and Bakeman (2003) found that prototypical angry expressions were more prevalent than fear ones, even in fear-inducing situations, but in the latter, observers did not interpret the expressions as angry. Consistent with the dynamical model of emotional development, this study provides evidence that emotional expressions are not produced by internal programs in a one-to-one fashion and that their meanings are context-sensitive.

Michel, Camras, and Sullivan (1992) arrived at a similar conclusion in their research on brow movement configurations in 5–7-month-olds. Recruitment of co-occurring motor structures took place in situation-specific ways, suggesting a lack of control by discrete basic emotion programs (also see Wolff, 1993).

Moreover, these general emotional schemes are hypothesized to change with age in terms of both situations leading to their activation and components used to express them. Research supports this position. Lewis, Alessandri, and Sullivan (1990) found that the same emotion might be elicited for different reasons at different ages. In their study of the learning of a contingency response in 2–8-month-olds, the youngest infants reacted in anger to the violation of a learned expectancy, whereas the 4-month-olds and older infants reacted in anger in this context but also reacted in anger to a loss of a pleasant event (or control), reflective of a beginning knowledge of means-end relationships. Finally, there are age changes in the expression of emotions. Stenberg and Campos (1990) elicited a full array of facial components of anger to arm restraint in 4- and 7-month-olds, but obtained less of a response in 1-month-olds.

Camras and Shutter (2010) reviewed the evidence that infant facial expressions do not express prespecified basic or discrete emotions. They supported the alternative model that emotions function like attractors, can vary in the configuration of expression, and function according control parameters. Messinger (2007) reported data consistent with this dynamical systems theory model of emotions in his study of how gazing and smiling relate differently to each other at different ages from 1- to 10-months of age.

## Summary and Conclusions

In the next chapter, I present a model of the development of emotions that is an integrative one, as it blends the constructs of basic emotions and dimensions in emotions with my Neo-Piagetian cognitive model. Emotions are considered expressions in context deriving from the workings of dynamical systems that link cognition and emotion.

## References

Averill, J. R. (1994). In the eyes of the beholder. In P. Ekman & R. J. Davidson (Eds.), *The nature of emotion: Fundamental questions* (pp. 7–14). New York: Oxford University Press.

Barrett, L. F. (2009). The future of psychology: Connecting mind to brain. *Perspectives on Psychological Science, 4*, 326–339.

Barrett, K. C., & Campos, J. J. (1987). Perspectives on emotional development II: A functionalist approach to emotions. In J. O. Osofsky (Ed.), *Handbook of infant development* (2nd ed., pp. 555–578). New York: Wiley.

Bunge, S. A., & Zelazo, P. D. (2006). A brain-based account of the development of rule use in childhood. *Current Directions in Psychological Science, 15*, 118–121.

Cacioppo, J. T., Amaral, D. G., Blanchard, J. J., Cameron, J. L., Carter, C. S., Crews, D., et al. (2007). Social neuroscience: Progress and implications for mental health. *Perspectives on Psychological Science, 2*, 99–123.

Camras, L. A., Oster, H., Campos, J., & Bakeman, R. (2003). Emotional facial expressions in European-American, Japanese, and Chinese infants. *Annals of the New York Academy of Sciences, 1000*, 135–151.

Camras, L. A., & Shutter, J. M. (2010). Emotional facial expressions in infancy. *Emotion Review, 2*, 120–129.

Camras, L. A., & Witherington, D. C. (2005). Dynamical systems approaches to emotional development. *Developmental Review, 25*, 328–350.

Carver, C. S., & Harmon-Jones, E. (2009). Anger and approach: Reply to Watson (2009) and to Tomarken and Zald (2009). *Psychological Bulletin, 135*, 215–217.

Carver, C. S., & Scheier, M. F. (1998). *On the self-regulation of behavior*. New York: Cambridge University Press.

Carver, C. S., & Scheier, M. F. (2008). Feedback processes in the simultaneous regulation of action and affect. In J. Y. Shah & W. L. Gardner (Eds.), *Handbook of motivation science* (pp. 308–324). New York: Guilford Press.

Cosmides, L., & Tooby, J. (2000). Evolutionary psychology and the emotions. In M. Lewis & J. M. Haviland-Jones (Eds.), *Handbook of emotions* (2nd ed., pp. 91–115). New York: Guilford Press.

Damasio, A. R. (1994). *Descartes' error: Emotion, reason, and the human brain*. New York: Avon.

Darwin, C. (1965). *The expression of the emotion in man and animals*. Chicago: University of Chicago Press. (Original work published 1872).

Davidson, R. J. (1992). Prolegomenon to the structure of emotion: Gleanings from neuropsychology. *Cognition and Emotion, 6*, 245–268.

Ekman, P. (1972). Universals and cultural differences in facial expressions of emotion. In J. Cole (Ed.), *Nebraska symposium on motivation, 1971* (Vol. 19, pp. 207–283). Lincoln: University of Nebraska Press.

Ekman, P. (1994). Strong evidence for universals in facial expressions: A reply to Russell's mistaken critique. *Psychological Bulletin, 115*, 268–287.

Ekman, P. (1999). Basic emotions. In T. Dalgleish & T. Powers (Eds.), *Handbook of cognition and emotion* (pp. 45–60). New York: Wiley.

Fischer, K. W., & Tangney, J. P. (1995). Self-conscious emotions and the affect revolution: Framework and overview. In J. P. Tangney & K. W. Fischer (Eds.), *Self-conscious emotions: The psychology of shame, guilt, embarrassment, and pride* (pp. 3–22). New York: Guilford.

Forgas, J. P. (2008). Affect and cognition. *Perspectives on Psychological Science, 3*, 94–101.

Fox, N. A., & Davidson, R. J. (1986). Taste-elicited changes in facial signs of emotion and the asymmetry of brain electrical activity in human newborns. *Neuropsychologia, 24*, 417–422.

Fridlund, A. J. (1994). *Human facial expression: An evolutionary view*. San Diego: Academic.

Frijda, N. (1986). *The emotions*. Cambridge: Cambridge University Press.

Frijda, N. H. (1993). Moods, emotion episodes, and emotions. In M. Lewis & J. M. Haviland (Eds.), *Handbook of emotions* (pp. 381–403). New York: Guilford Press.

Gergen, K. J. (1994). *Realities and relationships: Soundings in social construction*. Cambridge: Harvard University Press.

Griffin, S., & Mascolo, M. F. (1998). On the nature, development, and function of emotions. In M. F. Mascolo & S. Griffin (Eds.), *What develops in emotional development* (pp. 3–27). New York: Plenum.

Hess, U., & Thibault, P. (2009). Darwin and emotion expression. *American Psychologist, 64*, 120–128.

Immordino-Yang, M. H., & Damasio, A. (2007). We feel, therefore we learn: The relevance of affective and social neuroscience to education. *Mind, Brain, and Education, 1*, 3–10.

Izard, C. E. (1977). *Human emotions*. New York: Plenum.

Izard, C. E. (1994). Innate and universal facial expressions: Evidence from developmental and cross-cultural research. *Psychological Bulletin, 115*, 288–299.

Izard, C. E. (2007). Basic emotions, natural kinds, emotion schemas, and a new paradigm. *Perspectives on Psychological Science, 2*, 260–280.

Izard, C. E., Hembree, E. A., & Huebner, R. R. (1987). Infants' emotion expressions to acute pain: Developmental change and stability of individual differences. *Developmental Psychology, 23*, 105–113.

Kopp, C. B., & Neufeld, S. J. (2002). Emotional development during infancy. In R. J. Davidson, K. R. Scherer, & H. H. Goldsmith (Eds.), *Handbook of affective sciences* (pp. 347–374). New York: Oxford University Press.

Langsdorf, P., Izard, C. E., Rayias, M., & Hembree, E. (1983). Interest expression, visual fixation, and heart rate changes in 2- to 8-month old infants. *Developmental Psychology, 19*, 375–386.

Lavelli, M., & Fogel, A. (2005). Developmental changes in the relationship between the infant's attention and emotion during early face-to-face communication: The 2-month transition. *Developmental Psychology, 41*, 265–280.

Lazarus, R. S. (1994). Universal antecedents of the emotions. In P. Ekman & R. J. Davidson (Eds.), *The nature of emotion: Fundamental questions* (pp. 163–171). New York: Oxford University Press.

Lewis, M., Alessandri, S. M., & Sullivan, M. W. (1990). Violation of expectancy, loss of control and anger expressions in young infants. *Developmental Psychology, 26*, 745–751.

Lewis, M. D. (2000b). Emotional self-organization at three time scales. In M. D. Lewis & I. Granic (Eds.), *Emotion, development, and self-organization: Dynamic systems approaches to emotional development* (pp. 37–69). Cambridge: Cambridge University Press.

Lewis, M. D. (2005a). Bridging emotion theory and neurobiology through dynamic systems modeling. *Behavioral and Brain Sciences, 28*, 169–194.

Lewis, M. D. (2010). Desire, dopamine, and conceptual development. In S. D. Calkins & M. A. Bell (Eds.), *Child development at the intersection of emotion and cognition* (pp. 175–199). Washington: American Psychological Association.

Lewis, M. D., & Todd, R. M. (2007). The self-regulating brain: Cortical-subcortical feedback and the development of intelligent action. *Cognitive Development, 22*, 406–430.

MacLean, P. D. (1993). Perspectives on cingulate cortex in the limbic system. In B. A. Vogt & M. Gabriel (Eds.), *Neurobiology of cingulate cortex and limbic thalamus: A comprehensive handbook* (pp. 1–15). Boston: Birkhauser.

Mascolo, M. F., & Griffin, S. (1998). Alternative trajectories in the development of anger-related appraisals. In M. F. Mascolo & S. Griffin (Eds.), *What develops in emotional development* (pp. 219–249). New York: Plenum.

Messinger, D. S. (2007). Emerging motivation: Modeling early interactive emotional development. Proceedings of the 7th international conference on epigenetic robotics: modeling cognitive development in robotic systems. *Lund University Cognitive Studies, 134*, 5–12.

Messinger, D. S., Fogel, A., & Dickson, K. L. (2001). All smiles are positive, but some smiles are more positive than others. *Developmental Psychology, 375*, 642–653.

Michel, G. F., Camras, L. A., & Sullivan, J. (1992). Infant interest expressions as coordinative motor structures. *Infant Behavior and Development, 15*, 347–358.

Nesse, R. M., & Ellsworth, P. C. (2009). Evolution, emotions, and emotional disorders. *American Psychologist, 64*, 129–139.

Ortony, A., & Turner, T. J. (1990). What's basic about basic emotions? *Psychological Review, 97*, 315–331.

Overton, W. F. (2006). Developmental psychology: Philosophy, concepts, methodology. In W. Damon & R. M. Lerner (Eds.), *Handbook of child psychology: Vol. 1. Theoretical models of human development* (6th ed., pp. 18–80). Hoboken: Wiley.

Panksepp, J. (1994). The basics of basic emotion. In P. Ekman & R. J. Davidson (Eds.), *The nature of emotion: Fundamental questions* (pp. 20–24). New York: Oxford University Press.

Panksepp, J. (2000). Emotions as natural kinds within the mammalian brain. In M. Lewis & J. M. Haviland-Jones (Eds.), *Handbook of emotions* (2nd ed., pp. 137–156). New York: Guilford.

Pessoa, L. (2008). On the relationship between emotion and cognition. *Nature Reviews Neuroscience, 9*, 148–158.

Plutchik, R. (1962). *The emotions: Facts, theories, and a new model*. New York: Random House.

Plutchik, R. (1993). Emotions and their vicissitudes: Emotions and psychopathology. In M. Lewis & J. M. Haviland (Eds.), *Handbook of emotions* (pp. 53–66). New York: Guilford Press.

Posner, J., Russell, J. A., & Peterson, B. S. (2005). The circumplex model of affect: An integrative approach to affective neuroscience, cognitive development, and psychopathology. *Development and Psychopathology, 17*, 715–734.

Repacholi, B. M. (2009). Linking actions and emotions: Evidence from 15- and 18-month-old infants. *British Journal of Developmental Psychology, 27*, 649–667.

Rolls, E. T. (2005). *Emotion explained*. New York: Oxford University Press.

Russell, J. A. (1991). Culture and the categorization of emotions. *Psychological Bulletin, 110*, 426–450.

Russell, J. A. (1994). Is there universal recognition of emotion from facial expression? A review of the cross-cultural studies. *Psychological Bulletin, 115*, 102–141.

Saarni, C., Campos, J. J., Camras, L. A., & Witherington, D. (2006). Emotional development: Action, communication, and understanding. In W. Damon, R. M. Lerner, & N. Eisenberg (Eds.), *Handbook of child psychology: Vol. 3. Social, emotional and personality development* (6th ed., pp. 226–299). New York: Wiley.

Scherer, K. R. (1984). On the nature and function of emotion: A component process approach. In K. R. Scherer & P. Ekman (Eds.), *Approaches to emotion* (pp. 293–317). Hillsdale: Erlbaum.

Scherer, K. R. (1994). Toward a concept of "modal emotions". In P. Ekman & R. J. Davidson (Eds.), *The nature of emotion: Fundamental questions* (pp. 25–31). New York: Oxford University Press.

Shweder, R. A. (1994). "You're not sick, you're just in love": Emotion as an interpretive system. In P. Ekman & R. J. Davidson (Eds.), *The nature of emotion: Fundamental questions* (pp. 32–44). New York: Oxford University Press.

Stein, N. L., & Trabasso, T. (1992). The organization of emotional experience: Creating links among emotion, thinking, language, and intentional action. *Cognition and Emotion, 6*, 225–244.

Stenberg, C. R., & Campos, J. J. (1990). The development of anger expressions in infancy. In N. L. Stein, B. Levanthal, & T. Trabasso (Eds.), *Psychological and biological approaches to emotion* (pp. 247–282). Hillsdale: Erlbaum.

Thelen, E., & Smith, L. B. (1998). Dynamic systems theories. In W. Damon & R. M. Lerner (Eds.), *Handbook of child psychology: Vol. 1. Theoretical models of human development* (Vol. 1, pp. 563–634). New York: Wiley.

Tomkins, S. S. (1962). *Affect, imagery, consciousness: Vol. 1. The positive affects*. New York: Springer.

Vaish, A., Grossmann, T., & Woodward, A. (2008). Not all emotions are created equal: The negativity bias in social-emotional development. *Psychological Bulletin, 134*, 383–403.

Watson, D., & Tellegen, A. (1985). Toward a consensual structure of mood. *Psychological Bulletin, 98*, 219–235.

Witherington, D. C. (2007). The dynamic systems approach as metatheory for developmental psychology. *Human Development, 50*, 127–153.

Witherington, D. C., & Crichton, J. A. (2007). Framework for understanding emotions and their development: Functionalist and dynamic systems approaches. *Emotion, 7*, 628–637.

Wolff, P. H. (1993). Behavioral and emotional states in infancy: A dynamic perspective. In L. B. Smith & E. Thelen (Eds.), *A dynamic systems approach to development: Applications* (pp. 189–208). Cambridge: MIT Press.

Young, G. (1990). Early neuropsychological development: Lateralization of functions – hemispheric specialization. In C. A. Hauert (Ed.), *Developmental psychology: Cognitive, perceptuo-motor and neuropsychological perspectives* (pp. 113–181). Amsterdam: North Holland.

# Chapter 22
# Emotional Development in Infancy

## Introduction

After a survey of research on the development of emotions and their expression, I describe the present model of emotional development in infancy. I list four major emotions that develop at each cognitive substage in infancy, which gives a list of basic emotions much longer than typically found.

Among other topics, the study of emotional development includes the study of emotional categories, the expression of emotions, receptivity to emotions, influences on their development, and their biological substrates and origins. Darwin (1877) published the first scientific study on emotional development, and the field had been dominated by a biological bent. It became more differentiated, and the concept of basic, universal emotions having phylogenetic underpinnings has fallen into disfavor. However, the present model emphasizes that emotional development needs to consider the concept of basic emotions, but especially from a cognitive and dimensional, functional perspective, although other models are involved, including the dynamical, contextual one.

## Trends in Emotional Development

### *Introduction*

Darwin's (1877) classic observations of his infant suggested a developmental progression for the emotions. For example, they seemed to the infant seemed to possess an early capability for expressing anger, and one that evolved with age. At 10 weeks of age, his son was given cold milk to drink, and Darwin noticed that "he kept a slight frown on the forehead all the time that he was sucking, so that he looked like a grown-up person made cross from being compelled to do something which he did not like. When nearly 4 months old, and perhaps much earlier … blood gushed into his whole face and scalp" (p. 287). At 7 months, the child "screamed with rage" due to a dropped

G. Young, *Development and Causality: Neo-Piagetian Perspectives*,
DOI 10.1007/978-1-4419-9422-6_22, 

lemon, and at 11 months, when he received a "wrong plaything," … "he would push it away and beat it."

The study of changes in emotional categories or expressions in infancy has taken two forms. First, how does the expression of an emotional category change with age? Second, when do new categories emerge in development? In the following section, I concentrate on the second question. For an analysis related to the first one, on the self-conscious emotions, see next.

## Developmental Patterns

*Phases.* Kopp and Neufeld (2002) indicated an important transition that takes place in the development of emotions at about 8–9 months of age and again at 12 months of age (see Fig. 22.1). For example, in the first transition, infants are developing specific fears and wariness of novelty, as well as social game playing, which leads to joint attention and social referencing. At 12-months of age, infants develop active control processes, including control of their fears and controlled action in play. The authors concluded that emotional regulation has become an important topic in the study of infant emotions.

*Stages.* Lewis (2007) presented his model of development of self-conscious emotions (see Fig. 22.2). He argued that basic emotions developed generally by 6 months of age and self-conscious emotions toward the second birthday.

Lewis's model divides emotions into primary ones (joy, fear, anger, sadness, disgust, surprise), which develop sometime in the first year of life, and secondary ones, such as self-conscious emotions, which develop in the second year.

Once infants develop the cognitive capacity to reference themselves or be self-aware at around 18 months, they can express the first set of self-conscious emotions, which include embarrassment, empathy, and envy. Lewis related the acquisition of the self-conscious emotions at about 18 months to the cognitive acquisition of the idea of "Me."

A little later, toddlers can better evaluate their actions against standards and rules, leading to a second set of self-conscious emotions, including pride, shame, and guilt. The typical thought processes associated with these emotions illustrate the self-reference involved (e.g., "I shouldn't have done it"; "I'm no good"; for the last two, respectively).

*Basic emotions.* In terms of the basic emotions, Lewis (2008) argued that newborns express general distress and pleasure/contentment. In this regard, interest develops very early in life. Trevarthen (e.g., 1984) arrived at the same conclusion, as reported in the literature review by Draghi-Lorenz, Reddy, and Costall (2001). For Lewis (2008) and Trevarthen (1984), anger develops at 2 months. For both authors, the emotion of joy develops at 3 months. Lewis (2008) noted that sadness and disgust develop in this period. However, Trevarthen (1984) considered that sadness develops in the first month. Also, Steiner, Glaser, Hawilo, and Berridge (2001) found that newborns are capable of disgust.

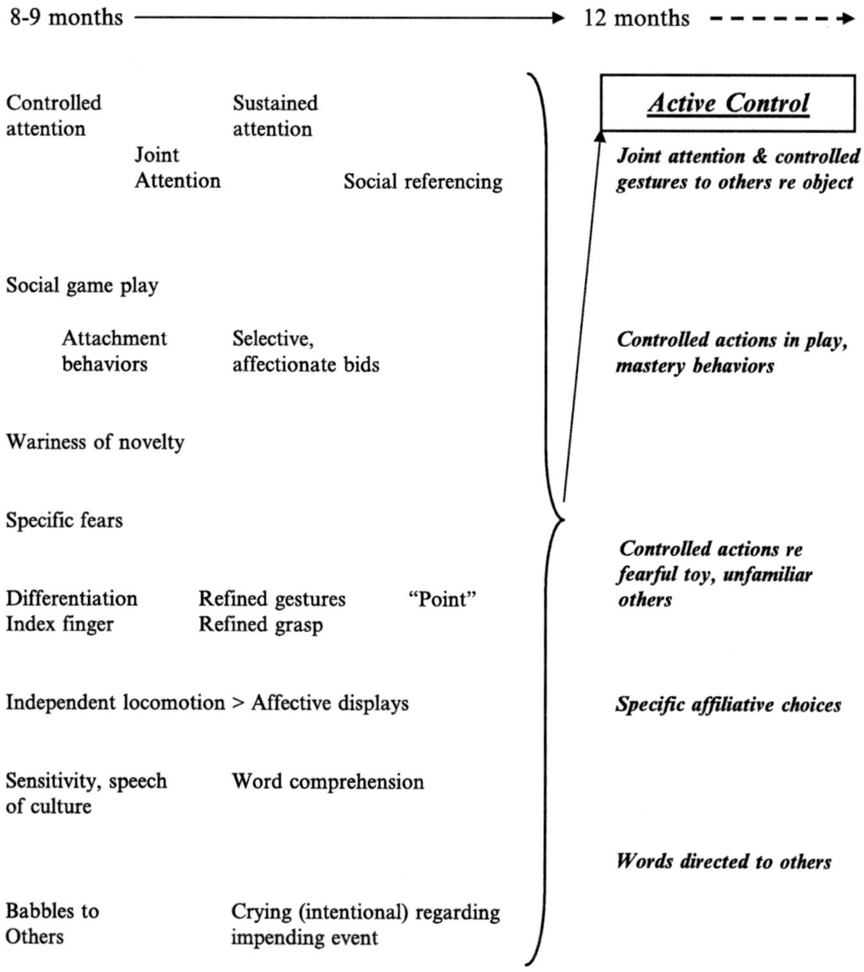


**Fig. 22.1** Developmental competencies between 8 and 12 months, and a "control" transition at 12 months. In this model, the year-old acquires increasing self-control, which is accompanied by emotional controls, as well. Reprinted with the permission of Oxford University Press, Inc. Kopp, C. B., & Neufeld, S. J. (2002). [Table 19.1, Page. 355]

For Lewis (2008), surprise develops at 6 months and fear at 7 months, although for Trevarthen (1984) fear develops at 2 months. Other research indicates that 2-month-olds express "coy" or "shy" behaviors (Reddy, 2000). Trevarthen (1984) equally referred to shyness and wariness developing at this age. He also referred to feelings of liking/friendliness, dislike, sadness, and annoyance in the first months.

Trevarthen (1984) added a variety of emotions developing from 3 to 6 months, but none are basic in the sense of the evolutionary model (e.g., laughter, humor, aggression, showing off). Unlike Lewis (2008), Trevarthen indicated that embarrassment, shame, and guilt develop at 6 months of age.

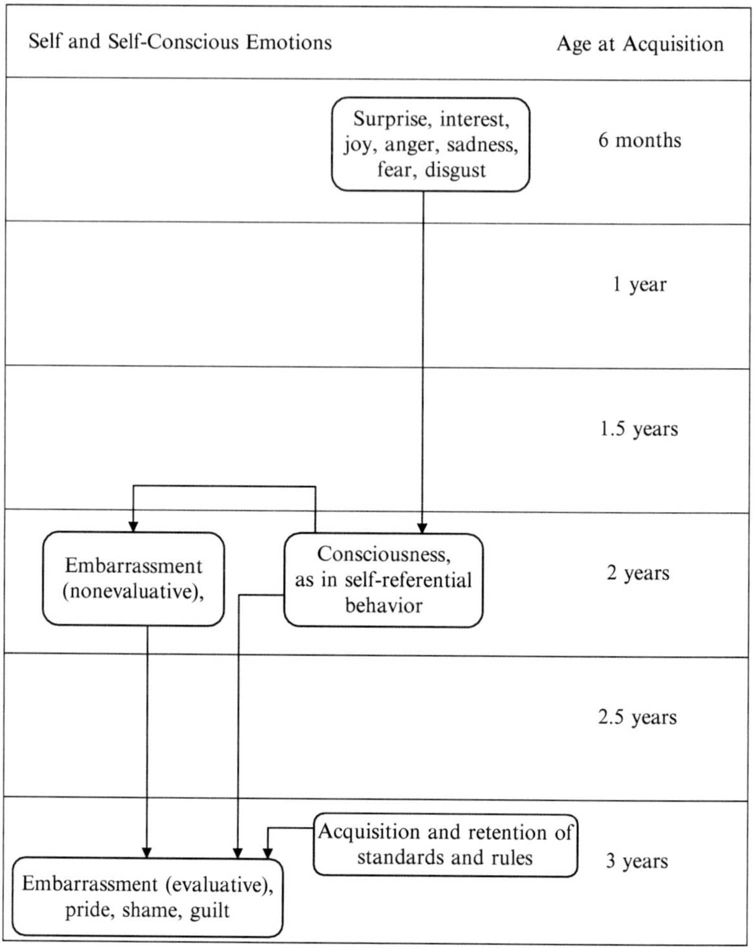


**Fig. 22.2** A model of emotional development of primary and self-related emotions. Lewis relates the development of emotions to cognitive development. In particular, infants who recognize themselves in mirrors at about 18–24 months of age enter a phase of developing self-related emotions, such as embarrassment. Reprinted with the permission of Guilford Publications, Inc. Lewis, M. (2007). Copyright 2011. [Figure 8.1, Page. 135]

Zinck and Newen (2008) presented a model of emotional development that referred to comfort and distress as the two basic reaction types in newborns (see Fig. 22.3). For them, joy emerges at 2 months, sadness at 3 months, anger at 4 months, and fear at 7 months.

*Cognitive-emotional correspondences.* The next two tables under discussion (see Tables 22.1 and 22.2) present models of cognitive and emotional correspondences in infancy (Sroufe, 1996; Trevarthen & Aitken, 2003). First, Sroufe presented the sensorimotor substage series formulated by Piaget. Then, he indicated that for each of the six substages there is a parallel socioaffective acquisition, although there is

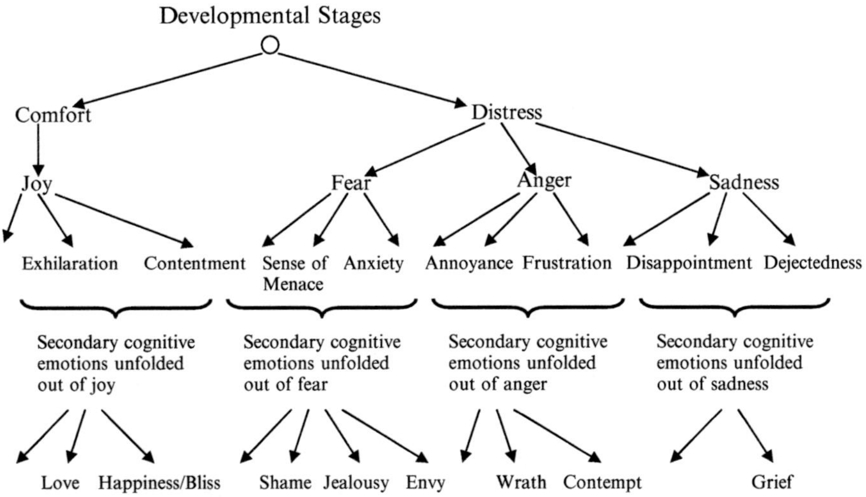


**Fig. 22.3** Development of basic emotions and their families. This is a hierarchical model of how emotions are organized at different levels in development. Reprinted with the permission of Springer Science+Business Media. With kind permission from Springer Science+Business Media: Zinck, A., & Newen, A. (2008). [Figure 1, Page. 18]

**Table 22.1** Stages of cognitive development and related changes in the affective and social domains across the first 24 months of life

| Cognitive development (Piaget) | Affective development (Sroufe) | Social development (Sander) |
|---|---|---|
| 0–1: Use of reflexes | 0–1: Absolute stimulus | 0–3: Initial regulation |
| Minimal accommodation of inborn behaviors | Barrier | Sleeping, feeding, quieting |
| | Built-in protection | Beginning preferential looking |
| 1–4: Primary circular reactions | 1–3: Turning toward orientation to external world | |
| First acquired adaptation (centered on body) | Relative vulnerability to stimulation | |
| Anticipation based on visual cues | Exogenous (social) smile | |
| Beginning coordination of schemes | | |
| 4–8: Secondary circular reactions | 3–6: Positive affect | 4–6: Reciprocal exchange |
| Behavior directed toward external world (sensorimotor "classes" and recognition) | Content-mediated affect (pleasurable assimilation, failure to assimilate, disappointment, frustration) | Mother and child coordinate feeding, caretaking activities |
| | Pleasure as an excitatory process (laughter, social responsivity) | Affective, vocal, and motor play |
| Beginning goal orientation (procedures for making interesting sights last; deferred circular reactions) | Active stimulus barrier (investment and divestment of affect) | |

(continued)

**Table 22.1** (continued)

| Cognitive development (Piaget) | Affective development (Sroufe) | Social development (Sander) |
|---|---|---|
| | 7–9: Active participation<br>Joy at being a cause (mastery, initiation of social games)<br>Failure of intended acts (experience of interruption)<br>Differentiation of emotional reactions (initial hesitancy, positive and negative social responses, and categories) | 7–9: Initiative<br>Early directed activity (infant initiates social exchange preferred activities)<br>Experience of success or interference in achieving goals |
| 8–12: Coordination of secondary schemes and application to new situations | 9–12: Attachment<br>Affectively toned schemes (specific affective bond, categorical reactions) | 10–13: Focalization<br>Mother's availability and responsivity tested (demands focused on mother)<br>Exploration from secure base<br>Reciprocity dependent on contextual information |
| 12–18: Tertiary circular reactions<br>Pursuit of novelty (active experimentation to provoke new effects)<br>Trial-and error problem solving (invention of new means)<br>Physical causality spatialized and detached from child's actions | 12–18: Practicing mother as secure base for exploration<br>Elation is mastery affect as part of context (moods, stored or delayed feelings)<br>Control of emotional expression | 14–20: Self-assertion<br>Broadened initiative<br>Success and gratification achieved apart from mother |
| 18–24: Invention of new means through mental combination<br>Symbolic representation (language, deferred imitation, symbolic play)<br>Problem solving without overt action (novel combination of schemes) | 18–24: Emergence of self-concept<br>Sense of self as active (active coping, positive self-evaluation, shame)<br>Sense of separateness (affection, ambivalence, conflict of wills, defiance) | |



not a perfect match in age periods for them, and one of the substages has two steps for the latter. He based his model on Sander's work. As for Trevarthen and Aitken, they described seven steps in the development of intersubjectivity in the first

**Table 22.2** Developments in intersubjective functions of communication and cooperative learning: first 18 months

| Steps | Transitions |
|---|---|
| Neonate | Primary intersubjectivity |
| Protoconversations | Person–person games |
| Mirror self-recognition | Person–person; object games |
| | Manipulative play |
| Self-conscious performer | Showing off; stranger fear |
| Cooperation in join tasks | |
| Protolanguage | Secondary intersubjectivity |
| Mimesis (immediate peer imitation) | First words |

Adapted from Lawrence Erlbaum with permission. Trevarthen, C., & Aitken, K. (2003). Copyright 2011. [Table 8.4, Page. 156–157]

18 months. They did not try to find correspondences with Piaget's stages, but they did emphasize the early sociality and emotionality of the infant.

In terms of particular emotions in each age period that are listed in Sroufe's model, the newborn can quiet. The 1-month-old can smile. The 4-month-old can experience joy/laughter and disappointment/frustration. The 8-month-old can develop active attachment. The 12-month-old can feel elated. The 18-month-old can experience positive self-evaluation and affection, but also shame and defiance. Trevarthen and Aitken added that showing off and stranger fear develop in the middle of infancy.

## Comment

The review of the literature indicates some consistent patterns for the ages that workers ascribe to the first emergence of basic emotions. Some of the differences are trivial, as they involve a month or two. Others might involve differences in definition, methodology, and related factors. Still others might reflect developmental differences involving different intensities of one emotion or different types of similar emotions. Overall, the literature review supports the present model described below in terms of when the basic emotions are considered to emerge for the first time.

There is one notable exception, for me; shyness is an emotion that emerges after many months but Trevarthen and Reddy have indicated it could appear in the first months. It could be a question of different levels of analysis. For example, these researchers could be focusing on shyness-related facial and head movements, and some of these might be evident early in development. However, this might not mean that shyness as an emotion fully develops so early.

I departed from the literature review in one major way. For envy, I placed it in the developmental period of 12–18 months, and not 18–24 months, as Lewis seems to be suggesting. This is because it fit the pattern of the other emotions that seem to emerge in the 12–18 month period in the present model.

Finally, one should note the number of basic emotions that has been discussed in infancy is far more than the 6–10 typically mentioned. Emotions might be limited to few in number from a phylogenetic, universally expressed way, but they might be quite large in number when a dynamical point of view of how they are expressed is considered. By coactive organization of facial, motoric, and vocalic components in context, and in individual ways for the infant, consistent patterns could be found in infants, and much more of them could be evident than in the basic emotion approach. In this regard, the present model combines a basic emotion and dimensional approach in concert with a developmental cognitive one, and as shown below, the dynamic assembly of emotional constants in this approach far surpasses the limited number of emotions in the basic emotion approach.

As for the demonstration of cognitive-emotional correspondences in infancy, the model of Sroufe (1996) is noteworthy. It has served as one inspiration for the present approach. However, the number of emotions that he describes at each Piagetian sensorimotor substage is limited. In this regard, the Neo-Piagetian model of Case, as presented in Chap. 7, stands out for the number of emotions it describes at each cognitive substage in infancy, and I have borrowed heavily from it.

## Recent Research

The most current research on the topic of emotional development that I found before submitting the manuscript for publication showed several interesting avenues of research, but not concerning the major themes under discussion. Conradt and Ablow (2010) studied 5-month-olds during maternal reunion and play. In particular, for the infants, they measured avoidance, attention-seeking, and resistance, as well as distress, with these measures embedded in structured measures. They examined the infants' physiological responses, as well, in the still-face paradigm. The infants were selected as participants because they were at risk. Maternal sensitivity predicted the infants' physiological responses and regulation, especially during the reunion episode. Other results also contributed to the author's conclusion that, already at 5 months of age in infants at risk, the behavior of caregivers influences the development of emotional regulation skills. A study by Chow, Haltigan, and Messinger (2010) also examined infants in the still-face paradigm and also emphasized the importance of the infant–parent relationship in the context of emotional expression. They examined 6-month-olds, some of whom had siblings with autism spectrum disorders. They found bidirectional affective coupling, with infant-to-parent coupling more prominent than parent-to-infant coupling. They concluded that the dyadic dynamics and coupling in the infant–parent pairs helped understand the dyads as intertwined.

Two other recent articles examined dynamic variations in emotional expression in terms of left frontal lobe electrical activity for positive emotions. Light and Coan (2009) studied 6–10-year-olds for their second-by-second lateral frontal activity in standardized tasks that elicited pleasure. The children who expressed increasing amounts of pleasure in the task that was analyzed exhibited more left lateral frontal activity. By contrast, those who expressed mild pleasure or contentment exhibited increasing right/decreasing left activity. The authors concluded that the mild pleasure in these children expressed a nonapproach-oriented form of the emotion. In general, this type of decreasing left frontal activity/increasing right frontal activity appears to reflect an internally focused, self-reflective positively valenced emotion. These results are different from but complementary to the typical ones found for left frontal activity for positive emotion and right frontal activity for negative emotion. Schmidt, Miskovic, Boyle, and Saigal (2010) found that extremely low-birth-weight newborns relative to controls were at risk to develop, as adults, greater right frontal resting electroencephalogram activity, along with internalizing behavior problems. These results are consistent with the model that the right hemisphere is associated with negative affectivity. For a detailed explanation of the frontal regional asymmetry model of emotions, see Chap. 25.

# A Dimensional Model of Basic Emotions

## *The Model*

### The Dimensions

The approach to the basic emotions adopted in the present work is somewhat similar to that of Russell (1991), for I place basic emotions within an N-dimensional space. In this model, each intersection or particular combination of poles of the dimensions is understood to correspond to a class of prototypical emotions. However, situational/individual variables can affect their expression. That is, each particular dimensional intersection is considered to induce a range of related, familial emotions or modal emotions, and these may vary in type, intensity, approach–withdrawal, situational releasers, etc.

The model sets up possible confusions because it is dimensional first and about basic emotions second. Moreover, the dimensions include appraisals or perceptions, as well as different cognitive levels, so that the placement of the basic emotions in the dimensional grid should not be considered absolute, especially because of individual differences. This creates difficulties in going one step lower and placing prototypical emotional expressions within any one point of the grid. It is hard enough to place emotional families in the grid, let alone phylogenetically fixed emotional expressions.

Thus, emotions that seem related in terminology might be placed in different loci in the three-dimensional model because they are defined by different sets of dimensional appraisals. In addition, some component emotional expressions might be present at several dimensional intersections (i.e., in several classes of emotions). Therefore, emotions might partly resemble each other in expression even if in different dimensional intersections (classes). Consequently, the prototypical emotional terms that are ascribed to each of the intersections of dimensions or classes of emotions in the present model represent general schemes of (re)action rather than specific programs fixed in expression across all situations.

The specific dimensions and emotions of the present model, first outlined in Young (1990), are now presented in detail. According to the model, emotional behavior is organized along three main axes of appraisal related to (a) socioculturally negotiated goal compatibility or incompatibility, generally leading to positive or negative hedonic tone, (b) behavioral activity/reactivity, or being led/passivity in the social context, and (c) figure (directly on primary focus, e.g., parent, self, object) vs. ground (context, distance, secondary other, indirectly on primary focus, etc.).

The first dimension speaks to the major theme in research on cognitive dimensions in emotions, that of pleasure–unpleasure; the second combines the concepts of activity, arousal, and dominance-control; and the third involves the issue of contextual focus or directionality. This dimension is mentioned rarely in the literature, but Roberts and Wedell (1994) adopted an approach similar to the current one in their study of similarity judgments of emotion words; the three dimensions that they emphasized in interpreting their results were valence (positive-negative), arousal, and context. Finally, it should be evident that a functional, social, constructivist perspective on emotions should include among its organizational dimensions of emotional processes a dimension on context.

## *The Dimensional Model*

As presented in Table 22.3, it is hypothesized that there are six types or classes of emotion that develop in parallel with the first six sensorimotor cognitive substages after the first day(s) of life. These emotion types concern: (a) arriving, (b) possessing, (c) approaching, (d) giving, (e) desiring, and (f) evaluating. The first, third, and fifth ones are considered to involve distance reduction and, thus, are labeled "ground," whereas the others seem more direct in focus and, thus, are termed "figure."

The intersection of the three dimensions (positive, negative × active, reactive × six figure-ground relations) results in a developmental model of 24 basic emotional classes, and each manifests in several exemplars. In the present version of the model, I organized the exemplars into a fourth dimension. There are at least two exemplars per class, and they represent levels of a fourth dimension of the model involving whether they appear more direct or indirect, a constructing process that yields a taxonomy of 48 basic emotions. Of the prototypical exemplars that represent each class of emotions, the ones included: (a) are not expressed in only one stereotypic way or in one modality, such as the face, (b) are not exclusive, as others could be added, and (c) do not deny other levels in the analysis of emotional expressions (e.g., component units).

It will be recalled that traditional approaches to the question of basic emotions typically have listed ten or fewer basic emotions, in contrast to the current expanded list. This current list is more elaborate than prior ones because it is not limited to specific,

**Table 22.3** Levels of emotional development in the first 2 years of life

| | | Goal compatibility/hedonic tone | |
|---|---|---|---|
| Type (age in mo) | Activity | Compatible (positive) | Not (negative) |
| Arriving (0–1) | Reactive | Relief, contentment | Distress, discontentment |
| | Active | Engagement, quiescence | Disengagement, disgust, fussiness |
| Possessing (1–4) | Reactive | Joy, delight | Wariness, aversion |
| | Active | Pleasure, interest, acceptance | Unpleasure, boredom, disappointment, rage |
| Approaching (4–8) | Reactive | Elation, surprise, exhilaration | Fear, sadness, distrust |
| | Active | Wonder, fascination | Anger, crankiness |
| Giving (8–12) | Reactive | Comfort, containment (sense of) | Anxious, worry, displacement escape |
| | Active | Affection, liking, warmth | Petulance, dislike, aggressive displacement |
| Desiring (12–18) | Reactive | Coyness, shyness, avidity | Defiance, alarm, jealousy |
| | Active | Eagerness, satisfaction | Greed, envy, retribution anger |
| Evaluating (18–24) | Reactive | Pride, selfness (sense of), approval | Shame, embarrassment, prejudice |
| | Active | Appreciation, love, empathy | Contempt, hate, guilt |

Adapted from Young, G. (1990)

*Note*. The 24 basic emotional categories over the three dimensions in the table can be split into 48 ones by the addition of a fourth dimension, i.e., one concerning direct (e.g., arrives positively) vs. indirect (e.g., gets other to arrive positively) emotions. For each of the cells in the table, the last example refers to indirect emotions and the other(s) refer to direct ones (except for disappointment and sadness)

The present model of basic emotions in infancy surpasses others in the number of emotions considered as basic. It suggests that there are at least 24 families of emotions that develop in the first 2 years. The model posits that families of emotions develop four at a time in the first 2 years, with each set emerging in concert with a corresponding substage of Piaget's six-substage sensorimotor series. Aside from the cognitive dimension of the model, there are two others, which are related to the dimensions of valence/goal compatibility and activation. The cognitive one is akin to a figure-ground dimension because the emotion types that emerge in concert with its substages vary in this regard (e.g., approach–withdrawal). The model integrates the major approaches to the study of emotions, e.g., categorical (basic), dimensional, cognitive, functional, and dynamic

innately programmed facial expressions and considers their placement according to a dimensional grid model of emotions the intersection of which involves 48 classes.

The basic emotional classes postulated to develop in the first years of life now are described in more detail. I explain the fourth dimension of the model and how it leads to 48 classes of emotions, after first presenting the model in terms of the original three dimensions and 24 classes of emotions. The model is compared to the one of Case presented in Chap. 7.

The model of emotional development presented is based on the classic Neo-Piagetian sensorimotor series, which had been transposed in the present full cognitive/socioaffective model, but reduced to a five-substage one by removing the first reflex substage and terming it an independent stage. However, for the present model related to emotional development, I refer to the first step of development in the first month of life, and do not restrict myself to the five-step sensorimotor substage series beginning at 1 month of age used in my overall model. Therefore, with this proviso, the present model of emotional development maps on perfectly to my own for the first 2 years of life, but it retains, as well, the original Piagetian approach to the sensorimotor stage.

## *Development*

### The First Months

Neonates who arrive positively at a state of acceptable equilibrium, or in ways compatible with the appropriate end point of their reflexive patterns, tend to experience quiescence (e.g., endogenous smile) or engagement. When neonates arrive actively in a negative way, leave, etc., sensory disengagement, disgust, irritable fussiness, or a comparable rejection could be manifested. Being arrived at positively (e.g., nipple given when thirsty) can induce relief or contentment. When an interfering event happens to the newborn that cannot be escaped (e.g., covering the face, physical restraint), the emotions of distress or discontentment are elicited.

Case posited that the newborn expresses four emotions. His list (contentment, distress, engagement, disengagement) is perfectly compatible with the four emotions listed in the present model, and the emotions have been incorporated in the list of possible exemplars of each of the basic emotions. Note that the placement of distress and disgust in this current version of my model compared to the version in Young (1990) has been realigned to accommodate fully Case's list of neonatal emotions. Also, the "startle" exemplar has been excluded from the 1990 list because it is not a true emotion.

The 1–4-month-old who actively explores, attends to, and/or recognizes (i.e., "possesses") an object maximizes the probability of feeling interest. If infants obtain actively something judged as compatible or acceptable, pleasure is experienced (e.g., when the caregiver smiles contingently to a social smile; mastering a new activity). Displeasure (boredom, disappointment, e.g., at a partner's poorly timed reactions in playful exchange) is induced when infants possess actively something judged incompatible, interfering, or unacceptable. Rage also is possible (e.g., at receiving an inoculation). If infants are the reactive object of possession, and they judge this as compatible or acceptable (e.g., affectionate holding by the caregiver), joy or delight is likely. Conversely, if being the reactive object of possession is incompatible or unacceptable (e.g., being held clumsily by the partner), infants should manifest aversion or wariness (with boredom/disappointment possible) and even try to avoid actively the rejected stimulus.

Once again, Case has described four new emotions for this age period (interest, boredom/rage, joy/delight, wariness/aversion), and they have been incorporated into Young's (1990) original list to create the current one because of their compatibility with the current approach. Note that the terms contentment and discontentment have been dropped from the original 1990 list of emotions for this age period because, as has just been shown, I have followed Case's example of using these two terms in the neonatal period.

## Up to 12 Months

When 4–8-month-old infants approach actively something judged compatible or acceptable, fascination or wonder is experienced (reaching for the smiling caregiver's face). Infants who express actively that something is incompatible, interfering, or unacceptable increase the likelihood that crankiness or anger is experienced (pushing away the partner's frowning face). When infants are approached and they reactively accept this as compatible, then elation, exhilaration, or perhaps surprise becomes possible (e.g., the caregiver moves forward playing a familiar game in a novel way). When infants are being approached and react by judging this incompatible, interfering, or unacceptable, they could experience distrust, soberness, fear, or sadness (e.g., the caregiver puts on a strange hat while approaching).

Once more, Case lists several emotions in this age period, and all are integrated into the current model. His terms fascination/wonder and elation/exhilaration are used instead of the ones previously used in 1990, that is, interest and delight. This is because the latter two labels have been used in the prior stage of the present model, fitting another of Case's suggestions, as has been shown.

Eight-month to year-old infants have developed the capacity to share actively and give something to partners who are judged compatible or acceptable, or to give actively something of themselves to partners judged compatible or acceptable. The emotions of affection, warmth, liking, sympathy, etc., tend to be induced in circumstances such as this (e.g., hugging an affectionate caregiver). When infants give actively in a way indicative of incompatibility or nonacceptance, or when they resist giving, probable emotions include petulance, stubbornness, disliking, and perhaps aggressive displacement or malice in hurting the partner (e.g., pouting if asked to hug a temporarily rejected caregiver). If infants react in an accepting way when being given to or receiving, indicative of compatibility, comfort or a sense of security/containment most likely is felt (e.g., reacting positively to receiving a kiss or a toy from the caregiver). Incidents indicative of incompatibility, such as having an act of giving blocked reactively or reacting negatively when being given to, tend to elicit anxious worry or displacement escape reaction (e.g., to an intrusive stranger).

As before, Case's list of emotions is highly compatible with the current one and has been integrated into it. At this age, he mentioned anxiety, warmth, displacement aggression, and security/safety/containment. The only concern that I have is with the use of the construct of anxiety to represent the infant's new fears in this age period, since it refers to a generalized state. Thus, the "worry" portion was added to the label for this emotion. It is employed instead of the previously used (in 1990) term of wariness, since this term now appears at an earlier level, following Case's model, as has been shown.

## The Second Year

Actively desiring something judged compatible or acceptable could elicit eagerness in 1-year-olds (e.g., eager anticipation of a favorite game with the caregiver or a favorite sweet that the caregiver is about to offer). Greed or anger in retribution (Case's only example at this age) is the subjective experience when infants desire actively something the present status of which is incompatible or interfering with ongoing goals (e.g., possessive of the partner or of a toy). When infants appraise that they are the object of (positive) desire, and reactively judge this as compatible or acceptable, the resultant emotion tends to be coyness or shyness (e.g., being coy or shy to an effusive visiting aunt). When infants are aware of being desired negatively or of a desire that is incompatible with ongoing goals, defiance or perhaps an extreme fear (alarm) could result (e.g., resisting an unacceptable parental command).

Note that Case views jealousy as an emotion that manifests in the 18-month-old, not the 12-month-old. However, others have judged that the 1-year-old is capable of jealousy. For example, Darwin (1877) noticed it in his infant son at 15.5 months, and suggested that it could be found even earlier. Masciuch and Kienapple (1994) confirmed this conjecture. They observed that jealousy increased in intensity and prevalence between 12 and 18 months of age in a situation where the mother cuddled another infant while ignoring her own. Thus, in the present model, jealousy is included as an emotion at this developmental period.

The state of evaluating, which manifests in 18–24-month-olds, is more advanced than the previous one of desiring. Both involve representation, but in evaluation (a) there is less of an element of action, which is found in desire, and (b) there are possibilities of considering more than the immediate environment, e.g., plans for future possibilities, could be involved.

When infants' active evaluations are compatible or acceptable, they appreciate the partner or the partner's/caregiver's behavior, and feelings such as love are experienced. If infants' evaluations are incompatible or unacceptable, hate or contempt (Case's "domination," "rejection") is likely (another child is rejected). "Willful" temper tantrums may be a sign of feelings such as these (Emde & Buchsbaum, 1989). Infants who appraise reactively that they are being evaluated as compatible or acceptable might experience pride and a sense of selfness. When the evaluation of a significant is appraised reactively as incompatible or interfering, the most likely emotion is shame, a fear about one's value, or embarrassment. For example, if children at this age attempt a relatively difficult task and partly succeed, they could experience pride or shame, depending on caregiver feedback.

The emotion of liking is no longer included among the emotions of this age period (unlike in Young, 1990), for it is placed more appropriately with the 1-year-old who expresses the similar emotions of affection and warmth, as has been shown. Moreover, an emotion with a stronger hedonic feeling (Case's love) seems to fit better here.

## Comment

In conclusion, there appears to be 24 classes of basic emotions, each with two or more distinct exemplars. The number of basic emotions seems more numerous than most have described. Part of the reason is that lists of basic emotions typically concern those with phylogenetic, neurological, and physiological bases. However, other traditions involving basic emotions envisage more of them. For example, de Rivera (1977) described a phenomenological analysis of 48 categories of basic emotions.

Because there are at least two examples of emotions in each of the 24 cells of the current model of emotional development, I have added a fourth dimension dealing with emotional expression in infancy. One dimension that seems to fit concerns whether emotions are direct or indirect. For example, de Rivera (1977) described how emotions could vary in terms of whether the person moves toward the other or the person moves the other toward her/him. Thus, in terms of the present model, emotions involving "arrives positively" could be separated for those involving "gets other to arrive positively," or the like. Similarly, emotions in the category of "given positively" could also involve ones relating to "other gets self to give positively." As for negative emotions, possesses negatively could include "difficulty in possessing," and desired negatively could involve "other gets self to desire negatively."

By referring to Table 22.3, the manner in which the basic emotions differentiate according to the dimension of direct vs. indirect emotional expression becomes clear. For each of the 24 cells of the table, the last emotion listed refers to indirect emotions, whereas the first one (or two) refers to direct ones. The only exceptions to this rule concern disappointment in level two and sadness in level three, which are more indirect.

To accommodate to this model, I had to add indirect emotions to the table that were not included either in the original model in Young (1990) or in Case's work (essentially, for all the later desiring and evaluating emotions). Lewis' (1991a, 1991b, 1993; Lewis, Sullivan, Stanger, & Weiss, 1989) model of self-conscious emotions served as a guide here (in the last line of the table), so that the current model is consistent with formulations on when the self-conscious emotions begin to develop.

## Summary

In Young (1990), I presented a model illustrating that for each of the six cognitive substages that Piaget had described in the infancy period, four emotions develop. The model reframed Piaget's six sensorimotor substages in terms of a Neo-Piagetian model but still kept its basic structure.

In the present chapter, I show how the cognitive development in six steps in infancy leads to new emotional acquisitions at each step. The original 1990 version of the present model of basic emotions consisted of 24 basic emotions, for I considered six cognitive substages in infancy, with each having four (2×2; positive/negative, active/reactive) emotions. In the present version of the model, I added at least two exemplars in each of the 24 cells of the model, expanding the range of suggested basic emotions. These exemplars seem to split into more direct and indirect ones, suggesting a fourth dimension in emotional expression, and a typology of at least 48 separate basic emotion families.

The common understanding in the field of emotion study concerning the amount of basic emotions limits them to six to ten emotions, such as happiness, sadness, interest, anger, fear, and disgust. Therefore, the present model considers the common list of basic emotions quite limited. I have proposed more basic emotions than usually encountered in the literature because I aligned them with the six cognitive substages in infancy, and considered a model of emotions having three other intersecting 2×2 dimensions at each substage.

Piaget is especially known for his model of cognitive development, but he did write on the relationship between cognitive and emotional development (Piaget, 1954). Other researchers have specified the relationship between the six cognitive substages, or their equivalents, in the sensorimotor period of infancy that Piaget described and corresponding acquisitions in emotional development (e.g., Sroufe, 1996; Trevarthen & Aitken, 2003). Theorists who have developed Neo-Piagetian models of cognitive development in infancy (Case, 1988; Fischer & Bidell, 2006) have also speculated on the relationship between the steps that they describe in cognitive development and corresponding ones in emotional development. In the present chapter, I build on the models of these workers in constructing my model. Given the specific relationships it posits across cognitive substages in infancy and corresponding emotional categories, it could lead to research that further solidifies the link between cognition and affect.

## Summary and Conclusion

This chapter reviews the literature on emotional development and presents a model of how it develops in the first 2 years of life. The model is Neo-Piagetian in nature and shows correspondences at each infant sensorimotor substage, which is considered one dimension in emotional development, with classes of emotions that revolve around three other dimensions. At the outset of the book, I describe the present goal of relating Piagetian cognitive and socioaffective development and describe, as well, Piaget's descriptions and conceptual approach to the issue. In addition, I describe the models equivalent to my own in the work of Fischer and Case. The present model builds on all their work.

The area requires fastidious observations, and I had developed a Darwinian-based observational system of infant facial expressions (Young & Gouin Décarie, 1977). Oster's (2005) coding scheme is based on the work of Ekman and has provided a sound empirical basis in the area. The work of Camras and colleagues, as described in the last chapter, on a dynamical systems approach to emotional development, in concert with a sound observational system measured in the right contexts, could help explain how the present model translates into changes in ongoing emotional expression in the infant. Careful observation of the face and other avenues of emotional expression could reveal the dynamical shifting in emotional expression taking place on a moment-to-moment basis (as undertaken by Messinger and colleagues) as the infant alters the appraisals involved in the four dimensions of the model. For example, the 18-month-old is developing evaluative emotions according to the present model and could be in the middle of expressing a positive one at this level that is active in nature, but the context and individual dynamic in the infant could shift the emotion being expressed to one at a different cognitive level, with other different dimensions involved, as well.

Finally, the present model of emotional development deals with the infancy period, in particular. It does not try to determine whether new emotions are developing after this period. The complexity that I have described in the categories of emotion in the first 2 years of life would seem to make the search for new emotions over the life span a formidable challenge. If we stick to the standard conception of basic emotions, which leads to a taxonomy of basis emotions numbering fewer than 10 for the most part, this project will lead to a few additional basic emotions to consider, if any, after the first few years of life. By contrast, by adopting modifications of the present model so that it applies over the life span, the understanding of what constitutes basic emotions broadens, and the search for them over the life span should provide a much more elaborate list.

In the next chapters, I present attachment theory and how it has been modified to fit the present model. It would be interesting to study the present model of emotions in infancy with the types of attachment qualities that have been described and how they and their underlying internal working models evolve through the substages of the present Neo-Piagetian model. The subtle dynamics in emotional expression might correspond to different attachment qualities and how they develop in infancy, and even could be diagnostic of them or the difficulties that they could lead to.

## References

Case, R. (1988). The whole child: Toward an integrated view of young children's cognitive, social, and emotional development. In A. D. Pellegrini (Ed.), *Psychological bases for early education* (pp. 155–184). New York: Wiley.

Chow, S.-M., Haltigan, J. D., & Messinger, D. S. (2010). Dynamic infant-parent affect coupling during the face-to-face/still-face. *Emotion, 10*, 101–114.

Conradt, E., & Ablow, J. (2010). Infant physiological response to the still-face paradigm: Contributions of maternal sensitivity and infants' early regulatory behavior. *Infant Behavior & Development, 33*, 251–265.

Darwin, C. (1877). A biographical sketch of an infant. *Mind, 2*, 286–299.

de Rivera, J. (1977). A structural theory of the emotions [Monograph]. *Psychological Issues* (Vol. 10). New York: International Universities Press.

Draghi-Lorenz, R., Reddy, V., & Costall, A. (2001). Rethinking the development of "nonbasic" emotions: A critical review of existing theories. *Developmental Review, 21*, 263–304.

Emde, R. N., & Buchsbaum, H. K. (1989). Toward a psychoanalytic theory of affect: II. Emotional development and signaling in infancy. In S. I. Greenspan & G. H. Pollack (Eds.), *The course of life: Vol. 1. Infancy* (pp. 193–228). Madison: International Universities Press.

Fischer, K. W., & Bidell, T. R. (2006). Dynamic development of action and thought. In W. Damon & R. M. Lerner (Eds.), *Handbook of child psychology: Vol. 1. Theoretical models of human development* (pp. 313–399). New York: Wiley.

Kopp, C. B., & Neufeld, S. J. (2002). Emotional development during infancy. In R. J. Davidson, K. R. Scherer, & H. H. Goldsmith (Eds.), *Handbook of affective sciences* (pp. 347–374). New York: Oxford University Press.

Lewis, M. (1991a). Self knowledge and social influence. In M. Lewis & S. Feinman (Eds.), *Social influences and socialization in infancy* (pp. 111–134). New York: Plenum.

Lewis, M. (1991b). Ways of knowing: Objective self-awareness or consciousness. *Developmental Review, 11*, 231–243.

Lewis, M. (1993). The emergence of human emotions. In M. Lewis & J. M. Haviland (Eds.), *Handbook of emotions* (pp. 223–235). New York: Guilford Press.

Lewis, M. (2007). Self-conscious emotional development. In J. L. Tracy, R. W. Robins, & J. P. Tangney (Eds.), *The self-conscious emotions: Theory and research* (pp. 134–149). New York: Guilford Press.

Lewis, M. (2008). The emergence of human emotions. In M. Lewis, J. M. Haviland-Jones, & L. F. Barrett (Eds.), *Handbook of emotions*. (3rd ed., pp. 304–319). New York: Guilford Press.

Lewis, M., Sullivan, M., Stanger, C., & Weiss, M. (1989). Self development and self-conscious emotions. *Child Development, 60*, 146–156.

Light, S. N., & Coan, J. A. (2009). Dynamic variation in pleasure in children predicts nonlinear change in lateral frontal brain electrical activity. *Developmental Psychology, 45*, 525–533.

Masciuch, S., & Kienapple, K. (1994). The emergence of jealousy in children 4 months to 7 years of age. *Journal of Social and Personal Relationships, 10*, 421–435.

Oster, H. (2005). The repertoire of infant facial expressions: An ontogenetic perspective. In J. Nadel & D. Muir (Eds.), *Emotional development: Recent research advances* (pp. 261–292). New York: Oxford University Press.

Piaget, J. (1936/1952/1963). *The origins of intelligence in children.* New York: International Universities Press and Norton. (Original work published in 1936).

Piaget, J. (1954). Les relations entre l'affectivité et l'intelligence dans le développement mental de l'enfant. *Affect Development and Cognition in a Piagetian Context, 6*, 183–200.

Reddy, V. (2000). Coyness in early infancy. *Developmental Science, 3*, 186–192.

Roberts, J. S., & Wedell, D. H. (1994). Context effects on similarity judgments of multidimensional stimuli: Inferring the structure of the emotion space. *Journal of Experimental Social Psychology, 30*, 1–38.

Russell, J. A. (1991). Culture and the categorization of emotions. *Psychological Bulletin, 110*, 426–450.

Sander, L. W. (1975). Infant and caretaking environment: Investigation and conceptualization of adaptive behavior in a system of increasing complexity. In E. J. Anthony (Ed.), *Explorations in child psychiatry* (pp. 129–166). New York: Plenum.

Schmidt, L. A., Miskovic, V., Boyle, M., & Saigal, S. (2010). Frontal electroencephalogram asymmetry, salivary cortisol, and internalizing behavior problems in young adults who were born at extremely low birth weight. *Child Development, 81*, 183–199.

Sroufe, L. A. (1996). *Emotional development: The organization of emotional life in the early years.* Cambridge: Cambridge University Press.

Steiner, J. E., Glaser, D., Hawilo, M. E., & Berridge, K. C. (2001). Comparative expression of hedonic impact: Affective reactions to taste by human infants and other primates. *Neuroscience and Biobehavioral Reviews, 25*, 53–74.

Trevarthen, C. (1984). Emotions in infancy. In K. R. Scherer & P. Ekman (Eds.), *Approaches to emotions* (pp. 129–157). London: Erlbaum.

Trevarthen, C., & Aitken, K. (2003). Regulation of brain development and age-related changes in infants' motives: The developmental function of regressive periods. In M. Heimann (Ed.), *Regression periods in human infancy* (pp. 107–184). London: Erlbaum.

Young, G. (1990). Early neuropsychological development: Lateralization of functions – hemispheric specialization. In C. A. Hauert (Ed.), *Developmental psychology: Cognitive, perceptuo-motor and neuropsychological perspectives* (pp. 113–181). Amsterdam: North Holland.

Young, G., & Gouin Décarie, T. (1977). An ethology-based catalogue of facial/vocal behavior in infancy. *Animal Behavior, 25*, 95–107.

Zinck, A., & Newen, A. (2008). Classifying emotion: A developmental account. *Synthèse, 161*, 1–25.

# Chapter 23
# Attachment Basics

## Introduction

Attachment theory constitutes one of the most active and far-reaching models in developmental psychology. The present chapter deals with basics concepts in the theory, and the one that follows examines the concept of internal working models. That chapter concludes with the present model of how internal working models evolve according to the steps of the present Neo-Piagetian cognitive model.

In this chapter, I work through understanding attachment as expressed behaviors and inferred systems. It is measured at 1 year in the Strange Situation (e.g., in maternal reunion after separation). I describe that the qualities or classification types that are evident in attachment vary with caregiver sensitivity, availability, etc. Secure and insecure kinds can develop, for example, depending on caregiver interactions in the first year. I continue by describing the phases in the development of attachment. In the next chapter, I present a modified view of this stage model that is consistent with the present Neo-Piagetian model in infancy.

The next part of this chapter deals with biological and evolutionary aspects of attachment. Bowlby had hypothesized that it evolved in our environment of evolutionary adaptedness. Simpson and Belsky described that each of the different qualities of attachment has its survival and reproductive advantages.

In terms of outcome, through the internal working models, early attachment experiences affect multiple areas of development, both contemporaneously with its development and years later, even into adult romantic relationships. Intergenerational research reveals how the narratives expressed in recall of one's parents in terms of attachment experiences predict eventual attachment classification of one's child. To conclude the chapter, I describe my own model of attachment types and show its relationship to the parenting dimensions of warmth and control.

G. Young, *Development and Causality: Neo-Piagetian Perspectives*,
DOI 10.1007/978-1-4419-9422-6_23, © Springer Science+Business Media, LLC 2011

# Attachment

## *Introduction*

Bowlby (1969, 1973, 1980, 1989) considered as innate in origin the contact and proximity seeking/maintaining behavior of human infants. Cassidy (2008) reviewed Bowlby's (Bowlby 1969/1982, 1973, 1980) theory of attachment in terms of the biological basis of attachment behavior and from an evolutionary perspective. For Bowlby, humans evolved in "the environment of the evolutionary adaptedness." This niche helped select proximity- and contact-seeking and promoting behavior in the infant and child for purposes of protection and survival.

Bowlby considered that attachment behaviors are organized into "an attachment behavioral system." He borrowed the concept of behavioral system from ethology. The attachment behavioral system operates in a "goal-corrected" manner. According to Bowlby, newborns are programmed congenitally to emit signals that elicit from the caregiver behaviors that assure survival and protection against harm. These behaviors modify with age and become more discriminating (infants target the preferred, consistent attachment figure). Attachment behaviors might not be observable directly (they are inferred from behavior). They are tightly linked to emotions. They manifest especially when a need arises (e.g., when frightened). The caregiver reciprocally responds with caregiving, emotional availability, and contingent sensitivity, thus forming a system with infants (Stevenson-Hinde, 1990).

A second aspect of attachment theory is related to object relations theory, a branch of psychodynamic thinking (Bretherton, 1990). Bowlby hypothesized that infants internalize in memory the nature of the caregiver–infant interaction as internal working models. These models provide a framework of interpretation of the caregiver's behavior and the way infants should respond. When the caregiver–infant relationship is characterized by a lack of reciprocity, contingency, and sensitive responding on the part of the caregiver, defensive distortions that are produced in consequence could affect the quality of infants' working models.

Kobak and Madsen (2008) explained that Bowlby (1973) refined his original definition of "set goal" in the attachment system. Bowlby had understood that it involved maintaining the caregiver's "accessibility and responsiveness" within limits comfortable to the infant/child, and that this depended on the caregiver's "availability." Kobak and Madsen further explained that Sroufe and Waters (1977) had specified that the concept of "set goal" involves an internal emotional regulation and not simply a regulation of physical distance. In this regard, they had proposed that the set goal of the attachment system involves a "felt security." Kobak and Madsen concluded that, in the attachment relationship, "intrapersonal" expectations and strategies reciprocally interact with interpersonal communication. They espoused a transactional model of attachment. In the model, the child's developing personality interacts dynamically with the quality of the ongoing attachment relationship.

## Phases

Marvin and Britner (2008) described four phases in the development of attachment in Bowlby's model. In Phase I, called "orientation and signals without discrimination of figure," newborns are responding to social stimuli and eliciting social responses from their caregivers. The caregivers organize the interactions, so Bowlby referred to them as "goal-corrected." Therefore, internal working models in this phase are primitive, for example, related to "on-again, off-again" experiences about onset and termination of specific behaviors. Marvin and Britner indicated that infants' internal working models at this age are not distinct from actual behavior in the same way that infants' sensorimotor activity should not be considered as involving separate sensory and motor components (Piaget, 1936/1952/1963).

At about 2 to 3-months of age, infants enter into Phase II of attachment, called "orientation and signals directed toward one or more discriminated figures." The attachment behavior at this age involves complex chained behavior in which infants assume more control and initiation of activity. In terms of internal working models, infants are differentiating caregivers from others, although they cannot yet conceive of them as separate objects. This is consistent with Piaget's model that infants do not yet possess object permanence.

At about 6–9 months of age, infants enter into Phase III of attachment, called "maintenance of proximity to a discriminated figure by locomotion and signals." The infants consolidate the attachment to the caregiver. This is facilitated by the development of locomotion, communication skills, exploration abilities, and new social skills. In addition, infants become more wary. In terms of working models, infants develop an internal image of the end-state or "set goal" guiding behavior. They develop a plan and monitor it as it is applied. Infants in this period have developed an internal image of the caregiver (object permanence, according to Piaget).

In Phase IV of attachment, which develops at about age three, children can enter into a "goal-corrected" partnership. This develops into the ability to take the perspective not only of the self but also of the other.

## Biology

*Temperament.* Vaughn, Bost, and van IJzendoorn (2008) reviewed studies of the relationship between developing attachment and temperament. They pointed out that attachment is a relational concept but temperament concerns reactivity and regulation of affect, attention, and motor activity governed by "set points" that are internal to the child. Vaughn and Bost (1999) reviewed the literature and found that, at best, attachment and temperament are domains that are partially related and that they rarely overlap (also see van IJzendoorn, Schuengel, and Bakermans-Kranenburg, 1999). More recent research by Burgess, Marshall, Rubin, and Fox (2003) and Marshall and Fox (2005) supported these conclusions. For example, Marshall and Fox (2005) found that emotional reactivity was not directly related to attachment security in infants but that emotional reactivity was related to subgroup classifications of attachment. Pauli-Pott, Haverkock, Pott, and Beckmann (2007) found no association between negative emotionality and attachment classifications. Vaughn et al. (2008) concluded that temperamental differences might bias an infant toward certain behavioral tendencies that could affect attachment behavior, "but the caregiving environment is what determines security (vs. insecurity)" in attachment (p. 201).

*Epigenesis.* Vaughn et al. (2008) described the research of Lakatos et al. (2000), who found that children who carried the 7-repeat allele of the dopamine D4 receptor (*DRD4*) were more likely to develop disorganized attachment. However, this finding was not replicated in six samples (Bakermans-Kranenburg & van IJzendoorn, 2007). Rather, van IJzendoorn and Bakermans-Kranenburg (2006) found an interaction effect that could explain this lack of replication. They studied 63 mothers who had experienced at least one important unresolved loss or trauma in their lives. For these mothers, their infants did express disorganization in attachment, but only when they carried the *DRD4* 7-repeat allele. Children having shorter variants of the gene did not display disorganized attachment if their mothers had experienced an unresolved loss or trauma.

*Neuroscience.* Bretherton and Munholland (2008) looked at internal working models in terms of underlying neuroscience. They described the work of Gallese (2005) on mirror neurons, and then moved to findings related to emotions and intersubjectivity. For example, Ruby and Decety (2004) found that the amygdala responded in the same way when study participants imagined their own feelings in embarrassing situations and those of their mothers. Coan (2008) reported research that internal and working models appear mediated through activity of the amygdala, nucleus accumbens, hippocampus, and prefrontal cortex. He described other research implicating subregions of the anterior cingulate cortex and the prefrontal cortex in the mediation of attachment.

## *Evolution*

### Introduction

Simpson and Belsky (2008) described the evolutionary basis for attachment theory. The modern version of the evolutionary theory underscores that much of human behavior has been selected as adaptations to overcome difficulties in facing survival and reproduction in our evolutionary history, in the sense of maximizing inclusive fitness. Life history theory (e.g., Kaplan & Gangestad, 2005) specifies that as individuals grow and survive, they invest time, effort, resources, and energy to "somatic effort" as well as reproductive effort, which includes parenting. Individuals make trade-off decisions involving somatic and reproductive effort and these are influenced by the life stage of the organism. For example, investing in traits or attributes that increase fertility and reproductive success might impact negatively the immune system and shorten survival. Also, investing in the developmental stage will retard fertility until a later age but, at the same time, in the end, serves to enhance it.

According to Simpson and Belsky (2008), Hamilton (1964) introduced the concept of kin selection. It focuses on the gene, rather than the individual, as the primary unit on which evolutionary selection operates. Hamilton (1964) proposed that an individual's total inclusive fitness, or reproductive output, depends not only on the organism's personal output but also depends on those of kin, who share some portion of the organism's genes. Therefore, individuals might behave toward facilitating the reproductive output of their biological relatives, even to the extent of self-sacrifice in certain circumstances. Inclusive fitness theory is a model that has been formulated to encompass (a) Darwin's concept of natural selection, or direct fitness due to one's own sexual reproduction, and (b) Hamilton's (1964) concept of fitness due to the reproduction by either the organism or its biological relatives, who propagate indirect descendants.

Trivers (1971) introduced the concept of reciprocal altruism. It elaborates that although individuals have so-called "selfish" genes, in the right circumstances, they still could behave cooperatively with non-kin. Trivers also proposed the theory of parental investment and sexual selection. For example, in the human case, he argued that because women typically invest more time, effort, resources, and energy in reproducing and in raising their offspring, men engage in intra-sexual competition to maximize mating with women. This has led them to develop some of the typical sex-defining characteristics in the physical, behavioral, and emotional realms that differentiate men from women. Trivers also presented in evolutionary terms the theory of parent –offspring conflict. He noted that children share half the genes of their parents and their self-interests are not necessarily the same as their parents, leading them to behave for their reproductive benefit, which inevitably will generate conflict with their parents.

## Attachment Type and Reproductive Strategy

Belsky, Steinberg, and Draper (1991) were the first to propose an evolutionary model of reproductive strategy in terms of quality of the environment. Chisholm (e.g., 1999) and Ellis (e.g., Ellis & Garber, 2000) revised the model. All these theorists proposed that father absence is an important determinant of whether individuals will adopt a quantitative or qualitative reproductive strategy or trajectory. The former strategy is associated with poorer environment, for example, it might signal low, unpredictable, or changing levels of paternal investment within families. The latter strategy is associated with environments that offer more resources for raising offspring in a successful manner, or with a "quality trajectory." Moreover, the research supports the notion that the "quantity trajectory" should be associated with more insecure and disorganized types of attachment. In this regard, the authors described an intergenerational transmission process concerning attachment. Simpson and Belsky (2008) related the difficulties in attachment to underlying nonoptimal internal working models that are carried forward.

Chisholm (1996) proposed how different attachment qualities lead to different reproductive strategies. In this regard, children with a secure attachment should optimize their long-term learning to maximize their level of developmental quality, for example, at the cognitive-perceptual and socioemotional levels. Secure attachment reflects that parents are both willing and able to invest in their offspring and that the rearing environment is nonthreatening. This leads to greater effort by parents to allocate resources towards the long-term developmental quality of their offspring, thereby enhancing their future reproductive potential.

As for avoidant and resistant children, they develop in parental environments that are marked by either unwillingness or inability to invest resources, or both, in their children. In the case of the avoidant child, the parents are unwilling to invest, no matter what their ability. For the ambivalent child, the parents are unable to invest because of a poor resource base. In terms of parental attitude, the avoidant pattern is associated with cold/rejecting caregiving, which serves to signal parental unwillingness to invest, no matter what resources are available to them. The ambivalent pattern is associated with inconsistent/unpredictable caregiving, which serves to signal parental inability to invest despite their willingness.

In response to these parental regimes and perceived availability of resources, children react differently. The avoidant child will maximize effort to obtain resources toward immediate reproduction, such as by accelerating sexual maturation and, when sexually mature, they will have shorter and unstable romantic relationships. The ambivalent child meets a willing-but-unable investment environment and reacts by attempting to extract greater investment from their parents. They try to obtain as many resources as they can but, as with the avoidant child, they funnel these resources toward earlier sexual maturation and reproduction. According to the Chisholm (1996) model, this helps explain why the ambivalent child is irritable, demanding, and hypervigilant about gaining and maintaining attention and time from their parents and, later, from their romantic partners. They might remain with their partners and children but, in their turn, would behave inconsistently and unpredictability.

Belsky, Houts, and Fearon (2010) reported data in support of the model. They found that the development of insecure attachment at 15 months of age predicted earlier initiation and completion of puberty as well as earlier menarche.

## Attachment Category Classification

### *Standard Model*

Ainsworth, Blehar, Waters, and Wall (1978) found that 1-year-old infants placed in a reunion situation with their mothers after having experienced several separations (in the so-called Strange Situation) manifested either a secure attachment to them or an insecure one (two types: avoidant or resistant-ambivalent, see Tables 23.1 and 23.2). The Strange Situation involves a series of 2-min situations in the laboratory, such as exploring a room with the mother present as a secure base, a stranger entering,

**Table 23.1** Strange Situation classification groups in 1-year-olds

| Group | Brief description |
|---|---|
| Secure (B) (Ainsworth et al., 1978) | Uses mother as secure base for exploration. Separation: signs of missing parent, especially during the second separation. Reunion: actively greets parent with smile, vocalization, or gesture. If upset, signals or seeks contact with parent. Once comforted, returns to exploration |
| Avoidant (A) (Ainsworth et al., 1978) | Explores readily, little display of affect or secure-base behavior. Separation: responds minimally, little visible distress when left alone. Reunion: looks away from, actively avoids parent; often focuses on toys. If picked up, may stiffen, lean away. Seeks distance from parent, often interested instead in toys |
| Ambivalent or resistant (C) (Ainsworth et al., 1978) | Visibly distressed upon entering room, often fretful or passive; fails to engage in exploration. Separation: unsettled, distressed. Reunion: may alternate bids for contact with signs of angry rejection, tantrums; or may appear passive or too upset to signal, make contact. Fails to find comfort in parent |
| Disorganized/disoriented (D) (Main & Solomon, 1990) | Behavior appears to lack observable goal, intention, or explanation – for example, contradictory sequences or simultaneous behavioral displays; incomplete, interrupted movement; stereotypies; freezing/stilling; direct indications of fear/apprehension of parent; confusion, disorientation. Most characteristic is lack of a coherent attachment strategy, despite the fact that the baby may reveal the underlying patterns of organized attachment (A, B, C) |



*Note*. descriptions in Groups A, B, and C are based on Ainsworth et al. (1978). Descriptions in Group D are based on Main and Solomon (1990)

Bowlby (1969/1982, 1973, 1980) developed attachment theory, and Ainsworth and colleagues (Ainsworth et al., 1978) provided empirical support by determining attachment type in the Strange Situation. The infant's reaction in the reunion situation with the caregiver, which takes place after a brief separation from her, proved the most telling in the study in establishing whether 1-year-olds were securely or insecurely attached. Secure children were glad to see the caregiver, but insecure children were either avoidant or ambivalent. Later research established a third type of insecure attachment, which is more disorganized and disoriented (Main & Solomon, 1990). Empirical research reveals associations across different qualities of secure and insecure attachment, early caregiver interaction, and later developments even into adulthood, including in romantic relationships (Cassidy & Shaver, 2008)

the mother leaving, the infant ending up alone, and the mother returning. The latter situation was referred to as the mother-reunion situation, and it is the critical one in the results that were found.

## Categories

In the traditional perspective, most infants still seem to fall into one of three attachment categories – securely attached, insecure/avoidant, and insecure/ambivalent-resistant. Main, Kaplan, and Cassidy (1985) justified the emphasis placed on this

**Table 23.2** Early childhood laboratory separation–reunion classification systems: major classification groups

| Group | Cassidy–Marvin | Crittenden | Main-Cassidy |
|---|---|---|---|
| B | *Secure*: uses parent as secure base for exploration. Reunion behavior is smooth, open, warm, positive | *Secure/balanced*: relaxed, intimate, direct expression of feelings, desires. Able to negotiate conflict or disagreement | *Secure*: reunion behavior is confident, relaxed, open. Positive, reciprocal interaction or conversation |
| A | *Avoidant*: detached, neutral nonchalance, but does not avoid interaction altogether. Avoids physical or psychological intimacy | *Defended*: acts to reduce emotional involvement or confrontation. Focuses on play and exploration at expense of interaction | Avoidant: maintains affective neutrality; subtly minimizes and limits opportunities for interaction |
| C | *Ambivalent*: protests separation strongly. Reunion characterized by strong proximity-seeking, babyish, coy behavior | *Coercive*: maximizes psychological involvement with parent; exaggerates problems and conflict. Is coercive, for example, threatening (resistant, punitive) and/or disarming (innocent, coy) | *Ambivalent*: heightened intimacy and dependency on parent. Reunion characterized by ambivalence, subtle hostility, exaggerated cute or babyish behavior |
| D | *Controlling/disorganized*: characterized by controlling behavior (punitive, caregiving) or behaviors associated with infant disorganization | | *Controlling*: signs of role reversal: punitive (rejecting, humiliating) or caregiving (cheering, reassuring, falsely positive) |
| A/C | | *Defending/coercive*: child shows both defended and coercive behaviors, appearing together or in alternation | |
| AD | | *Anxious/depressed*: sad/depressed; stares, extreme distress/panic | |
| IO or U | *Insecure/other*: mixtures of insecure indices that do not fit into any of the other groups | *Insecure/other*: acts incoherently in relation to parent | *Unclassifiable*: mixture of insecure indices that do not fit into any of the other groups including behaviors associated with infant disorganization |



*Note*. Cassidy–Marvin, Main–Cassidy: organized groups = A, B, C. Crittenden: organized groups = A, B, C, A/C

Based on Cassidy and Marvin (1992), Crittenden (1992), and Main and Cassidy (1988).

Cassidy and Marvin (1992), Crittenden (1992), and Main and Cassidy (1988) developed classification procedures for preschoolers and young children using separation and reunion laboratory situations similar to the ones developed by Ainsworth et al. for 1-year-olds. The research with older children demonstrated that the original research with infants that had specified different types of secure and insecure attachments has proved remarkably resilient and that the attachment types are stable over childhood and beyond

Crittenden added defensive–coercive and anxious depressed types to the classic four kinds (secure, and three types of insecurity) in her research with preschoolers. In the present work, I developed a model of attachment types that adds an extra insecure type, related to clinginess/dependency. Crittenden described this type for younger children (in Crittenden, e.g., 1991) small number of attachment types by arguing that attachment is a biologically based system that is canalized toward seeking/maintaining proximity/contact with primary caregivers, and thus is environmentally stable. Caregivers have a limited range of options for the tendency/intention of infants to exhibit attachment behavior. That is, caregivers could permit access to themselves, block access, or be unpredictable. These attitudes foster secure, avoidant, and ambivalent-resistant attachment, respectively.

Main and Solomon (1990) examined those infants judged unclassifiable in their previous research on attachment types, and almost all seemed to fit into a fourth attachment category, another insecure type. These infants were called "disorganized–disoriented" in attachment. Upon parental reunion, they appeared in a "daze," ceased postural movement, manifested confusion in expected sequences in behavior (e.g., avoiding then seeking), displayed simultaneously contradictory behaviors (e.g., approach and avert head), failed to complete movements, and expressed non-directed affect. At the age of six, these children were controlling or subtly caregiving themselves in their behavior upon reunion but were otherwise disorganized, depressed, etc. Many of their parents were maltreated in their own past.

## Subcategories

The traditional classification of attachment type allows for subcategories within the three major types (Ainsworth et al., 1978). Careful inspection of the subtypes indicates that some are more insecure than others, although an ordered scale is not being suggested. Secure infants (group B) consist of four subgroups that appear to manifest attachment in the following ways. Subgroup B3 infants are secure–optimal in attachment, for they consciously seek contact with the mother on reunion, attempt to maintain it, and actively resist release attempts. Subgroup B1 infants seem predominately secure–partially avoidant (or secure-avoidant), for reunion behavior is characterized by clearly positive behavior (e.g., greeting) but also some passivity and avoidance (e.g., turn away). The B2 subgroup infants appear secure–reserved because positive behavior is not as marked, but the infants do not cling or resist release. The fourth subclass of securely attached infants can be termed secure/ambivalent-resistant, for there are not only contact seeking, clinging, and release but also crying, resistance, aversion, etc.

Avoidant infants fall into two subtypes. The first are clear avoidant (A1), because the mother is ignored upon reunion, approaches are aborted, and if the infants are picked up, the infants look away and squirm to get down. Subtype A2 infants appear to manifest predominantly avoidant/partially secure (avoidant–secure) behavior, for there is much proximity avoiding intermixed with some proximity seeking. Ambivalent-resistant infants also fall into two classes, with C1 infants appearing angry-resistant/secure and C2 infants appearing passive-resistant/secure. The former are unmistakably "angry" in their resistance, even with a stranger, although proximity/contact behavior is mixed in, as well. The latter are resistant, but not angry; they signal a desire for proximity/contact instead of approaching, and they protest release instead of actively resisting.

## *Crittenden*

### Crittenden's (1992) Attachment Types

Crittenden's (1992) classificatory scheme of attachment types used terminology that permits a lifespan perspective. She added several subcategories not described before. She based her types on work with a broad range of children (e.g., lower SES, maltreated, non-Western). She expanded inferences on the processes underlying attachment behavior. In this regard, she discussed the various attachment (sub) types in terms of strategy, regulation of affect, negotiation, and so on.

Crittenden kept the classic secure (B) and two types of insecure (ambivalent-resistant (C) and avoidant (A)) attachment types in her classification system, but gave them more process-oriented labels, ones that capture the full range of behaviors involved. That is, the two insecure attachment types are viewed as coercive and defended, respectively, and these constitute the main axis of her classificatory system. Also, Crittenden noticed that some children are defensive-coercive in attachment types, alternating their insecure attachment style, either during any one day or across them. However, she did not include Main's widely cited disorganized–disoriented attachment type in her scheme because she viewed children who are manifesting this type, depending on the particular behaviors expressed, as being in transition between the previously mentioned types, in the process of constructing one of them, or better fitting one of the insecure types.

According to Crittenden, a strategy of secure children is to engage in a goal-corrected partnership with their caregivers. Defended children navigate a more difficult attachment landscape. Nevertheless, their strategy is equally adaptive compared to secure children, for it serves to maximize the probability of being protected by their caregivers and surviving to reproduce, even if accomplished by narrower means in more confined emotional fields. That is, defended children are faced with attachment figures whose anger can be aroused easily. Thus, they must attempt to maintain caregiver protection in stressful situations without provoking the caregiver's latent hostility. They accomplish this especially by not alerting the caregiver to their deep need for proximity. They become responsible for their own plans as much as possible, because their caregivers are dismissing and potentially rejecting. Thus, they end up with the physical protection that they need, but in order to maintain this protection, they end up adopting an emotional distancing between themselves and their caregiver.

Coercive children also arrive at an adaptive modus vivendi with their caregiver, one that ensures a physical proximity in moments of perceived danger. Most of the time, their caregiver is preoccupied and might even seek approval from their children. In response to this attitude of reluctant caregiving, children adopt counter means in an attempt to achieve physical availability on the part of their caregiver. Thus, they threaten or entice their attachment figure even though they feel anger and not only desire. Consequently, any sense of intimacy with their caregiver is compromised, and taking the perspective of their caregiver is avoided so as not to diminish the intensity of their own emotional needs and expression. Emotional turmoil remains unresolved to the point that the primary goal of feeling safe and secure with the caregiver could be sabotaged.

## Crittenden's (1992) Attachment Subtypes

Within the three major categories of attachment type, Crittenden described ten subcategories. She differentiated three secure, three defended, and four coercive subcategories. Secure-reserved children are more verbal than physical in their relations with their caregivers. They are verbally clear and direct in conversation and play with their caregivers, and resolve issues this way, but participate in little close proximity with them. Secure-comfortable children are the most relaxed and calm of the children. They are communicative, expressive emotionally, trusting, sharing, seek close proximity, and are adept at regulating their feelings and resolving any unease. Secure-reactive children want more closeness, reassurance, and help compared to the two other secure subtypes. They also manifest more self-doubt about their skills, proximity in play, crying when left alone, and anger. Nevertheless, the trust, openness, use of the caregiver as a resource, and so on, that characterize securely attached children, in general, also are evident in this subgroup.

Defended-inhibited children exhibit subtle means of avoidance of their caregiver. They avoid proximity, do no bid for it, make no demands, and do not signal a problem with their relationship with the caregiver. They refuse the caregiver's bids for attention, and often engage in toy play beside her/him. Sometimes, they will resist, push away, and squirm at the caregiver's attempts at physical contact. Defended/compulsive caregiving children (Bowlby, 1980) create a minimal proximity to their withdrawn caregiver by engaging in over-bright cheerfulness, rhetorical monologs, and nurturant caretaking, by keeping the attachment figure busy, and by using of other frantic behavior. They might even initiate or tolerate contact. Defended-compliant children vigilantly attend to their caregiver, over-responding in a rapid way, and exhibit a limited, guarded range of emotions, inhibiting expectable negative affect to unpleasant interference. They do not play much, tolerate extended contact, and will manifest appeasing behavior to perceived offense by their caregiver. Coercive-threatening children manipulate by angry behavior (resistance, pouting, whining, anger expressions). Coercive-disarming children "bribe" their caregiver to "rescue" them by using infantile, seductive shyness, coyness, flirting, winsome behavior, whispered entreaties, babyish intonation, "sudden glorious" smiling, the use of gifts, "lispy tenderness," etc. Coercive-punitive children openly punish, shame, or embarrass in a hostile, retaliatory manner (e.g., hard hitting, tantrum behavior, loud screeching, "impenetrable" bid rejection, affection refusal), express compliance, and use extreme immature incompetence in order to both manipulate and reproach the caregiver (e.g., freezing, babyish whimpering).

### Comment

Crittenden's (1992) account of children's adaptive responses to the range of caregiver behavior illustrates the dynamic adjustment that the developing mind undergoes in its search for proximity/contact security with the caregiver. Her attachment security subtypes describe a range of emotional reactions to different types of parental warmth. Current work in the field uses a more restricted range of attachment types and subtypes. Nevertheless, Crittenden's work contributes to understanding the psychological protective and defensive mechanisms used by children as they confront insecurity-promoting behavior on the part of the caregiver. Moreover, she elaborated a model of the attachment categories in the preschool period, presented above in Table 23.2.

# Parenting and Attachment

## *Bowlby*

Cassidy (2008) described Bowlby's perspective on the caregiving system in attachment. Bowlby considered parenting behavior "preprogrammed" to some degree. Yet, he acknowledged the influence of learning on behavior. He described an "attachment-caregiving social bond." Bowlby (1969/1982) proposed that the mother provides a "secure base" from which the infant can explore. Cassidy (2008) emphasized that parental soothing is part of the caregiving system.

Cassidy (2008) acknowledged that the infant could have multiple attachments, depending on how the caregiving system is arranged. When there are multiple caregivers, attachment figures are arranged hierarchically in the infant's attachment system. Bowlby had noted that many children end up with more than one attachment figure. Nevertheless, he maintained that evolution might have favored monotropy, or having one primary caregiver.

## *Precursors*

### Introduction

Weinfield, Sroufe, Egeland, and Carlson (2008) examined individual differences in infant-caregiver attachment. The quality of attachment will vary according to differences in the history of care given by parents and caregivers. The individual differences in attachment quality develop slowly. They are not carried by either the infant or the caregiver, but in their relationship. Infants learn to recognize their caregivers and anticipate their behavior. Infants seek comfort or reassurance, such as by approaching, crying, seeking contact, and maintaining contact. Bowlby (1969/1982) referred to these behaviors as "attachment behaviors."

The nature of the parental sensitivity and responsivity, or their availability and responsiveness (Kobak & Madsen, 2008), determines the type of attachment that develops in the infant. Weinfield et al. (2008) continued that receiving a history of unresponsive parenting or erratic parenting results in the infant not being able to direct attachment behaviors at the caregiver in moments where they are called for. This leads to a constant low-level anxiety on the part of the infant, and when there are perceived threats, the infant's anxiety is elevated. This impacts the sense of self-confidence of the infant. The infant develops insecurity, both in attachment and in dealing with the environment. Insecure attachments "compromise" the infant's exploration.

At the same time, it needs to be understood that patterns of insecure behavior are adaptations in and of themselves. For example, they might "maximize" both expressions of attachment and the infant's behavior in situations perceived as less threatening. Or, an infant might "minimize" expressions of attachment behavior when he or she perceives less threat, so as not to alienate a rejecting caregiver. Either way according to Bowlby, an infant who reacts in such a manner is responding adaptively.

Bowlby (1969/1982, 1973) proposed that attachment security develops in an infant who is confident in the caregiver's responsiveness. The infant develops positive expectations that the caregiver will respond to signs of distress or behavioral bids for proximity or contact. Bowlby also proposed that attachment experiences and expectations influence behavioral and emotional adjustment in various contexts and with different people. In addition, he proposed that as current experiences with caregivers change, the internal working models that had been generated in prior experiences could alter.

## Ainsworth

Ainsworth et al. (1978) undertook empirical investigation of the infants' attachment to the mother at 12 months of age in the Strange Situation in relation to the mother–infant interaction throughout the first year of life. To measure the mother–infant interaction at home, Ainsworth et al. used rating scales involving sensitivity to signals, cooperation–interference, acceptance–rejection, and availability–unavailability.

The researchers examined 23 dyads. They found that infants who would end up classified as insecurely attached at 12 months had been more openly angry, noncompliant, and crying in home interactions compared to infants who would be classified later on as securely attached. As for the mothers of infants classified at 12 months as insecure, when examined in dyadic interaction in the home in the course of the first year, compared to mothers of infants classified later as secure, they were rated as less sensitive, more interfering, and less responsive. For the particular category of attachment labeled "avoidant," in the home, the mothers exhibited an aversion to physical contact with their infants and expressed little emotion during the interactions.

### Replication and Causation

Weinfield et al. (2008) reported that numerous studies have replicated the relationship between insecure attachment and caregiver insensitivity (e.g., Egeland & Farber, 1984; National Institute of Child Health and Human Development (NICHD) Early Child Care Research Network, 1997). De Wolff and van IJzendoorn (1997) conducted a meta-analysis and found a significant relationship between infant attachment and caregiver sensitivity. Other research investigated whether the results could be explained by the infant's temperament, but generally the research does not support this alternative explanation (Vaughn et al., 2008).

Belsky and Fearon (2008) reviewed the literature on precursors of attachment quality. For maternal care, they listed numerous studies that replicated Ainsworth et al.'s (1978) research, that early maternal sensitivity in the first year is linked to the child's attachment security in the Strange Situation (e.g., Braungart-Rieker, Garwood, Powers, & Wang, 2001). Nevertheless, two meta-analyses have shown that the relationship between early maternal behavior and attachment security is not as strong as originally thought (Goldsmith & Alansky, 1987; De Wolff & van IJzendoorn, 1997). However, intervention studies have shown that training mothers to be more sensitive increases the probability that infants will be classified as secure (Bakermans-Kranenburg, van IJzendoorn, & Juffer, 2003; van den Boom, 1990). Belsky and Fearon (2008) concluded that there is a "truly causal" effect of maternal care on attachment security.

## *The Caregiving System*

George and Solomon (2008) described in depth their model of the caregiving system. They emphasized that in attachment theory the most important factor involved in the development of the attachment relationship is the child's experience with the caregiver. The evolutionary goal of parenting is to provide protection, comfort, and care for the child. Bowlby (1969/1982, 1973) maintained that the caregiving system and the attachment system are in reciprocal and parallel relationships.

George and Solomon (2008) expounded that caregiving behavior is guided by representational constructions. Caregiving representations comprise or reconstruct past and current experiences with the child in relation to memories of the caregiver's history of attachment. Ongoing caregiver representations create the current appraisal or thinking about the parent–child relationship (Solomon & George, 2006).

In the child, representational models organize into a "state of mind" of the caregiver. State of mind refers to how the person integrates feelings and thoughts about a relationship, as well as the processes that filter relationship-specific information concerning the individual's feeling and thinking. This concept is related to the one of the "internalized secure base." It is defined as the person's ability to draw upon internalized representations of caregivers in order to explore and integrate feelings and thoughts about attachment-related distress and possible solutions for it (George & West, 2011).

George and Solomon (2008) continued to explain the relationship between caregiving and different types of attachment. Much research describes mothers of secure children as flexible, balanced, and integrated (e.g., Steinberg & Pianta, 2006). By contrast, mothers of insecure children obtain lower scores for insight, sensitivity, reflective function, and mind-mindedness (e.g., Slade, Grienenberger, Bernbach, Levy, & Locker, 2005).

The authors (e.g., George & Solomon, 1988/1993/2005/2007; Solomon & George, 2006) have elaborated on the particular ways that mothers of insecure children develop defensive and related processes in their caregiving. For example, they refer to deactivation and cognitive disconnection as organizers of defensive exclusion, and to abdication of care in caregiving systems in the caregiver that are disabled, constricted, and impermeable. They described different types of caregiving representations for each of the different types of insecure attachment (avoidant, ambivalent, disorganized).

## Parenting Style

Baumrind (1991) organized different parenting styles according to whether they involved warmth and control, or limit setting. The different combinations of higher or lower degrees of parenting skills on these dimensions produced a model of parenting behavior involving four types: high warmth and control (authoritative); low on both (rejecting-neglecting); and high on one or the other of the dimensions (authoritarian for control and permissive for warmth). A fifth category of parenting involved one parent being more strict while the other is more nurturing, which was characterized as the traditional style.

Baumrind described the consequences that different parental styles engender in the development in children. Rejecting-neglecting parents were the least likely to promote both optimal self and optimal social competence (referring to agentic and to communal competence, respectively). Permissive parents were warm, nonpunitive, accepting, and autonomy-granting, yet made few maturity demands and rarely manifested firm control. In terms of the children's outcome, the parents expressing this style fostered little optimal competence, especially in girls, even if developmental progress when the children were young apparently had been normal. Authoritarian parents attempted to control and shape the attitudes and behavior of their children according to set external standards (e.g., religion). They limited communication because the need to listen to the word of higher authorities (e.g., parents) needs to be firmly enforced. A minority of children emerged as optimally competent under this regimen. Traditional parents adopted sex-stereotypic roles, with mothers more responsive and fathers more demanding. About half of their offspring developed optimal competence. Finally, most children of authoritative parents progressed to the optimal level of competence. These parents were rational, communicative, sharing, supportive, challenging, autonomy-fostering, and so on yet maintained firm limits and demands, when required.

## Outcome

### *Childhood*

Weinfield et al. (2008) continued that individual differences in attachment security have been shown to have long-lasting effects on later outcome. This includes results for dependency, self-reliance, and a sense of efficacy and social confidence, as well as for control of anger, anxiety, and empathy, and even for psychopathology. The authors indicated that there are various ways to explain the link between early attachment experiences and later adjustment. In particular, they emphasized that the early attachment relationship functions as a foundation for establishing emotional self-regulation. For example, Sroufe, Egeland, Carlson, and Collins (2005) maintained that secure attachment promotes flexibility in self-regulation and avoidant attachment leads to minimizing overt expressions of distress and poorer self-regulation. Also, resistant attachment leads to increased expressions of distress, but poor management of the emotions. Finally, disorganized attachment leads to unpredictable emotional regulation strategies. Generally, research supports these conjectures (NICHD Early Child Care Research Network, 2004). Weinfield et al. (2008) also indicated that the concept of internal working models could help explain how early attachment experiences are carried forward and influence later cognitive and social behavior.

Thompson (2008) continued that quality of attachment contributes to emotional regulation. For example, Gilliom, Shaw, Beck, Schonberg, and Lukon (2002) found that boys who had been evaluated as securely attached at the age of 1½ used more constructive anger management strategies at the age of 3½ (e.g., more distraction, asking questions, waiting quietly). Another study by Kochanska, Aksan, Knaack, and Rhines (2004) found that, for securely attached infants, parental responsiveness and use of gentle discipline predicted later conscience at 4 years. These and other studies in Thompson's review indicated the range of associations and outcomes related to early attachment history. Other areas of study have included theory of mind, mastery motivation, academic achievement, and cognitive and linguistic functioning, in addition to personality, social–cognitive abilities, and memory. Mediators in the relationship between early attachment history and later development especially related to caregiver sensitivity, caregiver–child interactions and conversations, caregiving/parenting strategies and child discipline practices, and internal working models. Thompson concluded that this area of study on the association between early attachment and ensuing psychological development needs to examine more incisively the mediating or intervening processes that connect them.

## *The Adult Attachment Interview*

### Security

Main and Goldwyn (1984–1998, unpublished) have performed elegant research showing the way intergenerational patterns of attachment are mediated by internal working models. First, they presented Bowlby's (1973) concept of how a growing individual might develop multiple, contradictory, incompatible models of the same aspect of the world where normally one is created. Usually one of the models predominates in influence when there are multiple, contradictory ones, but it is not accessed in consciousness, so that the result is the production of incoherent thought. Multiple models compared to coherent, organized, singular ones could develop readily in young children, because they cannot coordinate one attribute of a person with another (e.g., nice and mean) or create metarepresentations of representation (e.g., metarepresentation = "I think that I am unworthy"). Thus, caregivers who are continually behaving in preoccupied, ambivalent, conflictual, or unpredictable ways sometimes are positive with their young children, but often are not. Moreover, in recounting their caregiving skills to their children, they often distort, deny, misconstruct, or overtly deceive, thereby creating two conflicting versions of reality, one experienced by their children and one narrated to them. Without metarepresentational skills, young children cannot question the validity of what they have heard about their relations with their caregivers.

In the three-generation research performed to examine this model, Main showed that adults' discourse style in narratives during an interview about their own early attachment to their caregiver was linked to the type of their offspring's attachment to them when the latter were 1 year of age. This proved true even if the interview took place either 5 years after their infant's attachment evaluation or *before* the child was born. Moreover, the adults' own early attachment type, per se, was not predictive of their offspring's attachment type; rather, the adults' narrative coherence, integrity, or singularity revealed the association. If in their interview the adults seemed to have had a singular model of their attachment history (that is, they focused on questions, followed typical conversational pragmatics, evidenced logic in their responses, and seemed cooperative and honest), they typically had an infant who was securely attached. These caregivers also easily accessed early memories. This seemed to have been the case even for the two mothers in the sample who had manifested this interview style yet had experienced traumatic or insecure early attachment histories. Their past did not deter them from coherently understanding, communicating, and judging their early attachments. Having integrated their own difficult journey into their life story, they could escape the automatic reduplication of the attachment pattern of their early years in their life with their own children.

### Insecurity

In contrast with caregivers who manifested coherent behavior during the attachment interview, other caregiver narratives were characterized as incoherent.

The responses spoke to a history of multiple models of attachment, despite their efforts to present a singular model, and to a lack of cohesion in narrative style (contradictions, distortions, anomalies, meandering, slips of the tongue, inappropriateness, and poor memory access).

In those demonstrating incoherent narratives in recalling past attachment experiences in the adult interviews, different caregiving qualities in the adults were associated with different specific signs of incoherence. Dismissing caregivers recalled particular incidents of rejection, yet had poor memory access of their own early attachment experiences, idealized both their parents, thought that attachment relationships bore little relevance to their lives, recounted contradictory personal events, and were brief and incomplete in their interview answers. Preoccupied caregivers described a conflicting attachment relationship, yet appeared concerned by it. They described role reversals where they functioned as parent or spouse. They still were enmeshed with their parents (e.g., angry, disappointed in being unable to please), gave long responses to questions, showed contradiction in their views, responded in less relevant or direct ways, and were quite scattered in their discourse style (e.g., confusing, run-on sentences; unfinished sentences; general or nonsense terms). Chaotic caregivers generally manifested a lack of resolution of an early loss. They were more coherent in their narratives than other parents of insecurely attached infants, but manifested less plausible content. When discussing the determinants or effects of traumatic happenings, such as the death of an attachment figure, these caregivers often were quite implausible. For example, the loss might have been seen as due to some magical event or the deceased person might have been perceived as simultaneously living and dead.

In the intergenerational results of the study, a match was evident in attachment type and parenting style. Secure–autonomous mothers had securely attached infants, dismissing mothers had avoidant infants, preoccupied mothers had ambivalent-resistant infants, and disorganized–unresolved mourning mothers had infants classified as disorganized–disoriented.

## Attachment Types: Cross-Age Model

### *Attachment Types in Adults*

In terms of attachment styles in adult romantic relationships, Bartholomew (1990) had proposed a four-group model, based on Hazan and Shaver's (1987) work on infancy attachment types and the Adult Attachment Interview types (Main & Goldwyn, 1984; Main, Goldwyn, & Hesse, 2003). The attachment types proposed by Bartholomew were based on Bowlby's concept of internal working models of the self and of the other (Bowlby, 1969/1982). Bartholomew presented the working models of the self as positive (worthy of love) or negative. For the dimension of others, they were considered positive or negative in terms of their availability and sense of care (Figs. 23.1 and 23.2).

| MODEL OF OTHER (Avoidance) | MODEL OF SELF (Dependence)<br>Positive (Low) | MODEL OF SELF (Dependence)<br>Negative (High) |
|---|---|---|
| Postive (Low) | SECURE<br>Comfortable<br>with intimacy<br>and autonomy | PREOCCUPIED<br>Preoccupied (Main)<br>Ambivalent (Hazan)<br>Overly dependent |
| Negative (High) | DISMISSING<br>Denial of attachment<br>Dismissing (Main)<br>Counter-dependent | FEARFUL<br>Fear of attachment<br>Avoidant (Hazan)<br>Socially avoidant |

**Fig. 23.1** The four adult attachment styles defined by Bartholomew in terms of working models of self and others. For attachment style in adult romantic relationships, Bartholomew had proposed four types, based on the working models of the self as positive (worthy of love) or negative, and those of others as positive or negative, as well. The four attachment styles include the insecure types of dismissing, preoccupied–ambivalent, and fearful–avoidant. Reprinted with the permission of SAGE Publications. Bartholomew, K. (1990). Copyright © 1990 by International Association for Relationship Research. [Figure 1, Page. 163]

By examining the quadrants of the intersection of the self and other dimensions, four attachment styles become evident. These include the insecure types of dismissing, preoccupied–ambivalent, and fearful–avoidant.

The Mikulincer and Shaver model (e.g., Mikulincer & Shaver, 2007, 2008) on adult attachment has garnered much empirical support. It raises the perennial issue in psychology of whether behavior is organized according to types, categories, or kinds, or whether behavior reflects dimensions of high or low expression, perhaps having negative and positive poles. The Mikulincer and Shaver model incorporates both aspects.

The present work also proposes a combined model of dimensions and categories in attachment. It differs from Bartholomew's and Mikulincer and Shaver's (a) by applying to children, (b) by proposing a fourth type of insecure attachment, and (c) by using dimensions related to Baumrind's (1991) concept of dimensions in warmth and in control in parental behavior.

## *Model of Attachment Types for Children and Adults*

I have elaborated a model of attachment types that is general and can apply to both younger and older ages. Moreover, it is both categorical and dimensional (see Fig. 23.3). Finally, its structure led me to create a new type of attachment type, but it is one consistent with the literature.

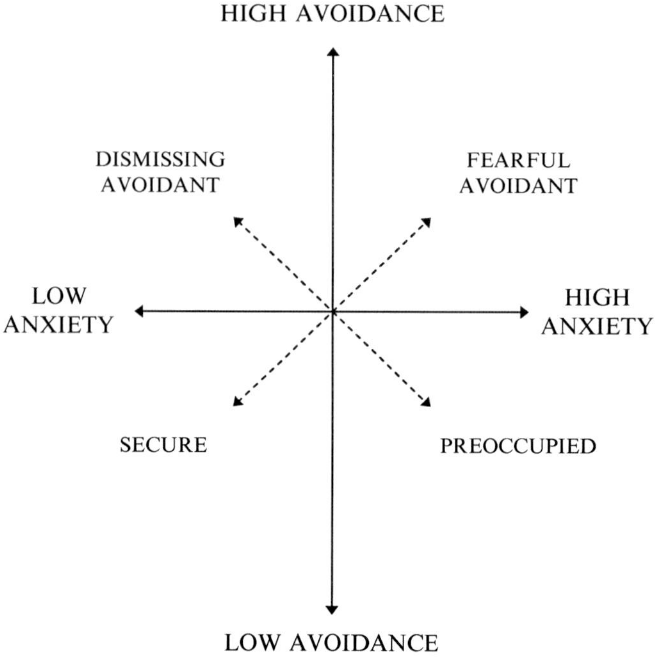


**Fig. 23.2** Diagram of the two-dimensional space defined by attachment anxiety and avoidance. Diagram of the two-dimensional space defined by attachment anxiety and avoidance, showing the names of adult attachment styles in the quadrants, as suggested by Bartholomew (1990). The Mikulincer and Shaver (2007, 2008) model has garnered much empirical support. It raises the perennial issue in psychology of whether behavior is organized according to types, categories, or kinds, or whether behavior reflects dimensions of high or low expression, perhaps having negative and positive poles. The Mikulincer and Shaver model incorporates both aspects. The present work also proposes a combined model of dimensions and categories in attachment. It differs from Bartholomew's and Mikulincer and Shaver's (2007, 2008) by applying to children, too, by proposing a fourth type of insecure attachment, and by using dimensions related to Baumrind's (1991) concept of dimensions in warmth and in control in parental behavior. Adapted from Bartholomew (1990) and Mikulincer and Shaver (2007, 2008)

In the figure, I plot the positions of secure and insecure attachment types along the dimensions of parental or caregiver control and warmth. These seem to be the fundamental dimensions along which attachment varies. To generate secure attachment, warmth should be set at a high level, but it should not become stifling or needy and, certainly, it should not be absent. Similarly, control should be balanced, and the caregiver should be neither too controlling nor too indifferent.

Therefore, in terms of the figure, for both dimensions of caregiver warmth and control, the best balance among the positive and negative possibilities lies more on the positive side. Thus, I have placed slightly away from the middle of the figure the secure attachment type.

The figure places three types of insecure attachment types according to the two axes of warmth and control – dismissing (avoidant), preoccupied (ambivalent),

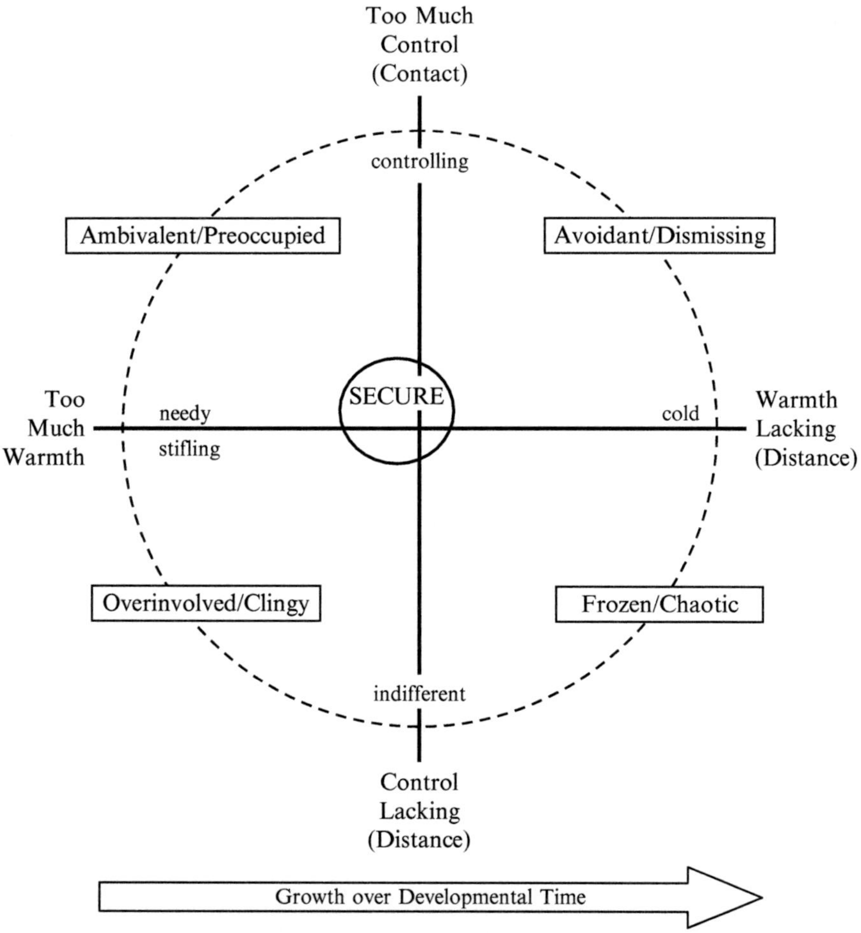


**Fig. 23.3** A model of attachment types and caregiving dimensions. Based on different conceptions of attachment types, I developed my own model. It comprises four insecure attachment classes (the three classic ones – avoidant, ambivalent, disorganized–disoriented, as well as a dependent–clingy type). The four insecure attachment categories are framed in a way that they can apply to different age ranges, including in the adult. They are organized dimensionally according to the two fundamental axes of parenting behavior proposed by Baumrind – warmth and control

and fearful (what I call "frozen" or chaotic). In terms of their axes coordinates, it appears that the avoidant/dismissing type is more controlling and cold, the preoccupied/ambivalent type is more warm and overwhelmed/overcontrolled, and the frozen/chaotic type is more indifferent and cold.

After I had performed this analysis, logic dictated that one new insecure attachment type was needed to complete the figure. The figure needed a controlling–needy/stifling type. The label of "overinvolved–clingy" could be used for this type of insecure attachment. It partially corresponds to some of the subtypes in Crittenden's scheme of types and subtypes described above, although it takes its form from the theoretical structure of the present model from which it derives more than preexisting work.

To review, caregiving involves varying degrees of warmth and control. Good balance in both facilitates secure attachment. When there is too much warmth, such as in being needy and stifling, the attachment is not secure, but is clingy or preoccupied, depending on whether control is too much or lacking. As for when there is not enough warmth, the attachment style becomes avoidant or chaotic, depending on whether control is too much or lacking.

## Summary and Conclusions

The present chapter has presented the basics in attachment theory and in so doing has shown its evolving nature. However, there has been little coordination in the work of attachment theorists with Neo-Piagetians. In my work, I consider the relationship between cognitive development and attachment, but in their work they give scant attention to stage and substage models. In this chapter, I have presented a revised model of attachment types and even have included a new category for them to consider. In the next chapter, I present two models relating Neo-Piagetian development and attachment. These models could lead to a better integration of these two evolving and related fields in developmental psychology.

## References

Ainsworth, M. D. S., Blehar, M. C., Waters, E., & Wall, S. (1978). *Patterns of attachment: A psychological study of the strange situation*. Hillsdale: Erlbaum.

Bakermans-Kranenburg, M. J., & van IJzendoorn, M. H. (2007). Research review: Genetic vulnerability or differential susceptibility in child development: The case of attachment. *Journal of Child Psychology and Psychiatry and Allied Disciplines, 48*, 1160–1173.

Bakermans-Kranenburg, M. J., van IJzendoorn, M. H., & Juffer, F. (2003). Less is more: Meta-analysis of sensitivity and attachment interventions in early childhood. *Psychological Bulletin, 129*, 195–215.

Bartholomew, K. (1990). Avoidance of intimacy: An attachment perspective. *Journal of Social and Personal Relationships, 7*, 147–178.

Baumrind, D. (1991). The influence of parenting style on adolescent competence and substance use. *Journal of Early Adolescence, 11*, 56–95.

Belsky, J., & Fearon, R. M. (2008). Precursors of attachment security. In J. Cassidy & P. R. Shaver (Eds.), *Handbook of attachment: Theory, research, and clinical applications* (pp. 295–316). New York: Guilford Press.

Belsky, J., Houts, R. M., & Fearon, R. M. (2010). Infant attachment security and the timing of puberty: Testing an evolutionary hypothesis. *Psychological Science*. Advance online publication. doi: 10.1177/0956797610379867.

Belsky, J., Steinberg, L., & Draper, P. (1991). Childhood experience, interpersonal development, and reproductive strategy: An evolutionary theory of socialization. *Child Development, 62*, 647–670.

Bowlby, J. (1969/1982). *Attachment and loss: Vol. 1. Attachment.* New York: Basic Books.

Bowlby, J. (1973). *Attachment and loss: Vol. 2. Separation: Anxiety and anger.* New York: Basic Books.

Bowlby, J. (1980). *Attachment and loss: Vol. 3. Loss: Sadness and depression.* New York: Basic Books.

Bowlby, J. (1989). The role of attachment in personality development and psychopathology. In S. I. Greenspan & G. H. Pollack (Eds.), *The course of life: Vol. 1. Infancy* (pp. 229–270). Madison: International Universities Press.

Braungart-Rieker, J. M., Garwood, M. M., Powers, B. P., & Wang, X. (2001). Parental sensitivity, infant affect, and affect regulation: Predictors of later attachment. *Child Development, 72*, 252–270.

Bretherton, I. (1990). Open communication and internal working models: Their role in the development of attachment. In R. A. Thompson (Ed.), *Nebraska symposium on motivation: Vol. 36. Socioemotional development* (pp. 57–114). Lincoln: University of Nebraska Press.

Bretherton, I., & Munholland, K. A. (2008). Internal working models in attachment relationships: Elaborating a central construct in attachment theory. In J. Cassidy & P. R. Shaver (Eds.), *Handbook of attachment: Theory, research, and clinical applications* (2nd ed., pp. 102–127). New York: Guilford press.

Burgess, K. B., Marshall, P. J., Rubin, K. H., & Fox, N. A. (2003). Infant attachment and temperament as predictors of subsequent externalizing problems and cardiac physiology. *The Journal of Child Psychology and Psychiatry and Allied Disciplines, 44*, 819–831.

Cassidy, J. (2008). The nature of the child's ties. In J. Cassidy & P. R. Shaver (Eds.), *Handbook of attachment: Theory, research, and clinical applications* (pp. 3–22). New York: Guilford.

Cassidy, J., & Marvin, R. S., with the MacArthur Attachment Working Group. (1992). *Attachment organization in preschool children: Coging guidelines* (4th ed.). Unpublished manuscript, University of Virginia.

Cassidy, J., & Shaver, P. R. (2008). *Handbook of attachment: Theory, research, and clinical applications* (2nd ed.). New York: Guilford Press.

Chisholm, J. S. (1996). The evolutionary ecology of attachment organization. *Human Nature, 7*, 1–38.

Chisholm, J. S. (1999). *Death, hope, and sex.* New York: Cambridge University Press.

Coan, J. A. (2008). Toward a neuroscience of attachment. In J. Cassidy & P. R. Shaver (Eds.), *Handbook of attachment: Theory, research, and clinical applications* (pp. 241–265). New York: Guilford Press.

Crittenden, P. M. (1991). Treatment of child abuse and neglect. *Human Systems, 2*, 161–179.

Crittenden, P. M. (1992). Quality of attachment in the preschool years. *Development and Psychopathology, 4*, 209–241.

De Wolff, M., & van IJzendoorn, M. H. (1997). Sensitivity and attachment: A meta-analysis on parental antecedents of infant attachment. *Child Development, 68*, 571–591.

Egeland, B., & Farber, E. (1984). Infant-mother attachment: Factors related to its development and changes over time. *Child Development, 55*, 753–771.

Ellis, B. J., & Garber, J. (2000). Psychosocial antecedents of variation in girls' pubertal timing. *Child Development, 71*, 485–501.

Feeney, J. A. (2008). Adult romantic attachment: Developments in the study of couple relationships. In J. Cassidy & P. R. Shaver (Eds.), *Handbook of attachment: Theory, research, and clinical applications* (2nd ed., pp. 456–481). New York: Guilford Press.

Gallese, V. (2005). Embodied simulation: From neurons to phenomenal experience. *Phenomenology and the Cognitive Sciences, 4*, 23–48.

George, C., & Solomon, J. (1988/1993/2005/2007). *The caregiving interview: Caregiving representation rating manual.* Unpublished manuscript, Mills College, Oakland.

George, C., & Solomon, J. (2008). The caregiving system: A behavioral systems approach to parenting. In J. Cassidy & P. R. Shaver (Eds.), *Handbook of attachment: Theory, research, and clinical applications* (pp. 833–856). New York: Guilford Press.

George, C., & West, M. (2011). *The Adult Attachment Projective: A new assessment of adult attachment.* New York: Guilford Press.

Gilliom, M., Shaw, D. S., Beck, J. E., Schonberg, M. A., & Lukon, J. L. (2002). Anger regulation in disadvantaged preschool boys: Strategies, antecedents, and the development of self-control. *Developmental Psychology, 38*, 222–235.

Goldsmith, H. H., & Alansky, J. A. (1987). Maternal and infant temperamental predictors of attachment: A meta-analytic review. *Journal of Consulting and Clinical Psychology, 55*, 805–816.

Hamilton, W. D. (1964). The genetical evolution of social behavior I and II. *Journal of Theoretical Biology, 7*, 1–52.

Hazan, C., & Shaver, P. R. (1987). Romantic love conceptualized as an attachment process. *Journal of Personality and Social Psychology, 52*, 511–524.

Kaplan, H. S., & Gangestad, S. W. (2005). Life history theory and evolutionary psychology. In D. M. Buss (Ed.), *The handbook of evolutionary psychology* (pp. 68–95). Hoboken: Wiley.

Kobak, R., & Madsen, S. (2008). Disruption in attachment bonds: Implications for theory, research, and clinical intervention. In J. Cassidy & P. R. Shaver (Eds.), *Handbook of attachment: Theory, research, and clinical applications* (pp. 23–47). New York: Guilford Press.

Kochanska, G., Aksan, N., Knaack, A., & Rhines, H. (2004). Maternal parenting and children's conscience: Early security as a moderator. *Child Development, 75*, 1229–1242.

Lakatos, K., Toth, I., Nemoda, Z., Ney, K., Sasvari-Szekely, M., & Gervai, J. (2000). Dopamine D4 receptor (DRD4) gene polymorphism is associated with attachment disorganization in infants. *Molecular Psychiatry, 5*, 633–637.

Main, M., & Cassidy, J. (1988). Categories of response to reunion with the parent at age 6: Predictable from infant attachment classifications and stable over a 1-month period. *Developmental Psychology, 24*, 415–426.

Main, M., & Goldwyn, R. (1984–1998). *Adult attachment scoring and classification system.* Unpublished manuscripts, University of California at Berkeley.

Main, M., & Solomon, J. (1990). Procedures for identifying infants as disorganized/disoriented during the Ainsworth Strange Situation. In M. T. Greenberg, D. Cicchetti, & E. M. Cummings (Eds.), *Attachment in the preschool years: Theory, research and intervention* (pp. 121–160). Chicago: University of Chicago Press.

Main, M., Goldwyn, R., & Hesse, E. (2003). *The Adult Attachment Interview: Scoring and classification system, Version 7.2*. Unpublished manuscript, University of California at Berkeley.

Main, M., Kaplan, N., & Cassidy, J. (1985). Security in infancy, childhood, and adulthood: A move to the level of representation. *Monographs of the Society for Research in Child Development, 50*, (1–2, Serial No. 209).

Marshall, P. J., & Fox, N. A. (2005). Relations between behavioral reactivity at 4 months and attachment classification at 14 months in a selected sample. *Infant Behavior and Development, 28*, 492–502.

Marvin, R. S., & Britner, P. A. (2008). Normative development: The ontogeny of attachment. In J. Cassidy & P. R. Shaver (Eds.), *Handbook of attachment: Theory, research, and clinical applications* (2nd ed., pp. 269–294). New York: Guilford Press.

Mikulincer, M., & Shaver, P. R. (2007). *Attachment in adulthood: Structure, dynamics, and change*. New York: Guilford Press.

Mikulincer, M., & Shaver, P. R. (2008). Adult attachment and affect regulation. In J. Cassidy & P. R. Shaver (Eds.), *Handbook of attachment: Theory, research, and clinical applications* (2nd ed., pp. 503–531). New York: Guilford Press.

National Institute of Child Health and Human Development (NICHD) Early Child Care Research Network. (1997). The effects of infant child care on mother-infant attachment security. *Child Development, 68*, 860–879.

National Institute of Child Health and Human Development (NICHD) Early Child Care Research Network. (2004). Affect dysregulation in the mother-child relationship in the toddler years: Antecedents and consequences. *Development and Psychopathology, 16*, 43–68.

Pauli-Pott, U., Haverkock, A., Pott, W., & Beckmann, D. (2007). Negative emotionality, attachment quality, and behavior problems in early childhood. *Infant Mental Health Journal, 28*, 39–53.

Piaget, J. (1936/1952/1963). *The origins of intelligence in children.* New York: International Universities Press and Norton. (Original work published in 1936).

Ruby, P., & Decety, J. (2004). How would you feel versus how do you think *she* would feel? A neuroimaging study of perspective-taking with social emotions. *Journal of Cognitive Neuroscience, 16*, 988–999.

Simpson, J. A., & Belsky, J. (2008). Attachment theory within a modern evolutionary framework. In J. Cassidy & P. R. Shaver (Eds.), *Handbook of attachment: Theory, research, and clinical applications* (pp. 131–157). New York: Guilford Press.

Slade, A., Grienenberger, J., Bernbach, E., Levy, D., & Locker, A. (2005). Maternal reflective functioning, attachment, and the transmission gap: A preliminary study. *Attachment and Human Development, 7*, 283–298.

Solomon, J., & George, C. (2006). Intergenerational transmission of dysregulated maternal caregiving: Mothers describe their upbringing and childrearing. In O. Mayseless (Ed.), *Parenting representations: Theory, research, and clinical implications* (pp. 265–295). New York: Cambridge University Press.

Solomon, J., & George, C. (2008). The measurement of attachment security and related constructs in infancy and early childhood. In J. Cassidy & P. R. Shaver (Eds.), *Handbook of attachment: Theory, research, and clinical applications* (2nd ed., pp. 383–416). New York: Guilford Press.

Sroufe, L. A., & Waters, E. (1977). Attachment as an organizational construct. *Child Development, 48*, 1184–1199.

Sroufe, L. A., Egeland, B., Carlson, E. A., & Collins, W. A. (2005). *The development of the person: The Minnesota study of risk and adaptation from birth to adulthood*. New York: Guilford Press.

Steinberg, D. R., & Pianta, R. C. (2006). Maternal representations of relationships: Assessing multiple parenting dimensions. In O. Mayseless (Ed.), *Parenting representations: Theory, research, and clinical implications* (pp. 41–78). New York: Cambridge University Press.

Stevenson-Hinde, J. (1990). Attachment within family systems: An overview. *Infant Mental Health Journal, 11*, 218–227.

Thompson, R. A. (2008). Early attachment and later development: Familiar questions, new answers. In J. Cassidy & P. R. Shaver (Eds.), *Handbook of attachment: Theory, research, and clinical applications* (pp. 348–365). New York: Guilford Press.

Trivers, R. L. (1971). The evolution of reciprocal altruism. *Quarterly Review of Biology, 46*, 35–57.

Trivers, R. L. (1972). Parental investment and sexual selection. In B. Campbell (Ed.), *Sexual selection and the descent of man, 1871–1971* (pp. 136–179). Chicago: Aldine-Atherton.

Trivers, R. L. (1974). Parent – offspring conflict. *American Zoologist, 14*, 249–264.

Van den Boom, D. (1990). Preventive intervention and the quality of mother-infant interaction and infant exploration in irritable infants. In W. Koops, H. J. G. Soppe, J. L. van der Linden, O. P. C. M. Molenaar, & J. J. F. Schroots (Eds.), *Developmental psychology behind the dikes* (pp. 249–270). Amsterdam: Eburon.

van IJzendoorn, M. H., & Bakermans-Kranenburg, M. J. (2006). DRD4 7-repeat polymorphism moderates the association between maternal unresolved loss or trauma and infant disorganization. *Attachment and Human Development, 8*, 291–307.

van IJzendoorn, M. H., Schuengel, C., & Bakermans-Kranenburg, M. J. (1999). Disorganized attachment in early childhood: Meta-analysis of precursors, concomitants, and sequelae. *Development and Psychopathology, 11*, 225–249

Vaughn, B. E., & Bost, K. K. (1999). Attachment and temperament: Redundant, independent, or interacting influences on interpersonal adaptation and personality development? In J. Cassidy & P. R. Shaver (Eds.), *Handbook of attachment: Theory, research, and clinical applications* (pp. 198–225). New York: Guilford Press.

Vaughn, B. E., Bost, K. K., & van IJzendoorn, M. H. (2008). Attachment and temperament: Additive and interactive influences on behavior, affect, and cognition during infancy and childhood. In J. Cassidy & P. R. Shaver (Eds.), *Handbook of attachment: Theory, research, and clinical applications* (pp. 192–216). New York: Guilford Press.

Weinfield, N. S., Sroufe, L. A., Egeland, B., & Carlson, E. (2008). Individual differences in infant-caregiver attachment: Conceptual and empirical aspects of security. In J. Cassidy & P. R. Shaver (Eds.), *Handbook of attachment: Theory, research, and clinical applications* (2nd ed., pp. 78–101). New York: Guilford Press.

# Chapter 24
# Internal Working Models and Social Self Working Schemata

## Introduction

In this chapter, I describe recent work on internal working models and phases in the development of attachment. The research also indicates correspondences between internal working models and theory of mind. This prepares the way for presentation of models of the development of the phases of attachment of the development of internal working models and their hierarchies over the stages and substages of the present model. To highlight their social nature, I refer to internal working models as social self working schemata.

## Internal Working Models

### *Early Work*

#### Introduction

According to Bowlby (1980), infants develop internal working models of attachment figures reflective of their quality of relations with them. Throughout the lifespan, internal working models dynamically perceive, interpret, predict, plan, and actively filter developing individuals' general interaction with attachment figures, leading to cross-generational transmission of specific types of attachment.

Main, Kaplan, and Cassidy (1985) defined internal working model as a set of conscious and/or unconscious mental representations of rules regulating attachment-related information, experiences, feelings, and thought. Cassidy (1990) emphasized that both cognitive and affective components are involved. Thus, working models (a) help construct and evaluate alternative understandings of perception, (b) help explore possible outcomes of alternative responses to those explanations, and (c) help plan coherent action sequences in attachment-related situations (Crittenden, 1992). Infants actively construct complementary internal working models of both

G. Young, *Development and Causality: Neo-Piagetian Perspectives*,
DOI 10.1007/978-1-4419-9422-6_24, 

the attachment figure and the self. These differ depending on the type of attachment (e.g., "I am worthy of love" leads to "I am loving"; or their inverse statements).

## Cognition

*Model.* Pipp (1990) distinguished internal working models in terms of simpler and more complex underpinnings in early vs. later infancy. Instead of differentiating procedural and semantic memory in this regard, she posited that there are sensorimotor-based (Piaget) and representation-based internal working models. Sensorimotor models are generalized event structures or "enactive scripts" of infant-caregiver interactions. Because they are constituted by temporally based dyadic exchanges, they reflect the vicissitudes of the ongoing relationship [even more so than representational models]. Here, she differed from Crittenden (1990), who viewed both earlier and later working models in infancy as generalized in nature. For Pipp, representational working models engender "interactional permanence," in that the infant can internally symbolize attributes of a partner or a relationship independent of their actual presence.

Pipp, Easterbrooks, and Harmon (1992) found that attachment security in 1–3-year-olds was associated with better knowledge of self and mother "featural" knowledge and agency. The featural knowledge tasks were designed to tap James' Me-self, whereas the agency tasks tapped the I-self. The results held for 2- and 3-year-old children in the former case, and for all the children in the latter case.

For Pipp et al., both sensorimotor and representational working models coexist once the latter develop, forming a dual processing mode. Verbal narratives feed the representational model (e.g., the child continually hearing, "I was such a good parent"), and these may be in opposition to the experienced sensorimotor reality.

*Comment.* Pipp's work implies that in development there are parallel steps in cognitive development and steps in internal working models (sensorimotor, then representational). The present chapter develops this concept much further, presenting a model of lifespan parallels in Neo-Piagetian cognitive development and advances in internal working models.

## Memories

*Model.* Crittenden (1992a) presented a comparable argument to Pipp's. Crittenden (1990) began by describing the different types of memory described by Tulving (1985, 1989). Bowlby (1980) had based his conception of working model on Tulving's (1972, 1979) earlier theory of episodic and semantic memory (which are declarative or descriptive), whereas Crittenden included in her scheme Tulving's later third type of memory concerning procedures. According to Tulving, procedural memory emerges in the first months of life. It consists of familiar, preconscious behavioral patterns consistently elicited by particular contexts, and thus relates to Piagetian sensorimotor schemes. For example, infants smile repeatedly to the caregiver's approach, creating a generalized pattern. Given their general nature, procedural memories are not labile or plastic, do not adjust to the unique characteristics of interactive sequences and context at hand, and they are even insensitive to contradictory information.

Semantic memory is associated with the development of representation, and consists of conscious, linguistically encoded, "impersonal, undated, world relevant facts." Thus, they permit generalizations about relationships, the parental role, etc. They are acquired both through lived experienced and told accounts. As with procedural memories, these memories are independent of the specific incidents and contexts of their acquisition, being generalized representations.

By contrast, episodic memory, which develops at about age five, is comprised of conscious, situation-specific, personal memories having particular, temporal/sequential attributes.

*Comment.* Tulving and Schacter (1990) mentioned other classificatory systems of memory, different from their own, and I wonder to what extent several other types of memory might emerge in development at key junctures in relation to the development of internal working models. For example, perceptual representation and priming memory (Tulving & Schacter, 1990) or a memory related to perceptual learning or simple classical conditioning (Squire, 1987) might be related to early (neonatal) reflexive schemes. Also, an abstract memory could be related to later (adolescent) formal thought.

Crittenden (1990) pointed out that Bowlby described early attachment and related representations in terms of semantic and/or episodic memory even early in life. However, she argued effectively that early attachment experiences are more amenable to encoding in procedural memory, especially given that they take place mostly in the first year of life. Thus, she queried to what extent initial internal working models are robust, or susceptible to accommodation based on any one individual incident, given the generalized nature of procedural memory. She argued, instead, for their stability. In this regard, I would add that the earliest attachment experiences might be more amenable to encoding in perceptual representation and priming memory, as just discussed, but still should evidence the stability that Crittenden wishes to ascribe them.

In this chapter, I end up proposing a stage model of the development of internal working models. For each stage, there should be a corresponding type of memory along the lines being discussed.

## Hierarchies

*Model.* Bretherton (1990) also has refined the concept of internal working models. She suggested that it could be conceptualized as a system of schemata organized into hierarchies consisting of a number of levels. For example, Epstein's (1980, 1994) model of self-concept is hierarchical in form, consisting of conscious and unconscious schemata (postulates) at successive levels. The base level is comprised of interactional, need-fulfilling schemata sensitive to experiential affects ("When I get hurt, mommy comes"). Next, general schemata coalesce from primary ones ("Mommy is usually there for me"). Near the summit of the hierarchy are generalized mental models subsuming a variety of ones at the level below it ("Mommy loves me"; "I'm loved").

Bretherton also underscored that internal working models form a number of hierarchies, and these are interlinked rather than being segregated, because there is feedback across them. A web of embedded, connected schema hierarchies becomes networked. These working models concern the self and other, attachment and nonattachment-related relationships, and the social and nonsocial world, i.e., the whole range of human social experience.

Next, Bretherton hypothesized that the working model organization of securely and insecurely attached individuals is different in quality of structure and in relative consistency both within and across levels. For example, the ambivalent-resistant infant might have difficulty in passing from lower-order to higher-order levels by failing to generalize from specific episodes to representative schemata (in order to create summary schemata of their attachment relationships (Bretherton, 1992b)).

Bretherton (1992b) described the dynamics of the way internal working models function. First, she noted that Bowlby viewed them as inner-world mental structures that simulate real-world action. They are composed in short-term memory, and stored in long-term memory where "procedures" can (a) locate them, (b) access specific information in them for retrieval into a temporary scratch pad in working memory, (c) operate on that information (often in light of new information, to generate revisions in information), and (d) feedback new information into the long-term structure.

Note that there seems to be evidence that schemata are derived from organizational structure at the neurological level. Damasio hypothesized that there are brain centers, which when activated, stimulate a special combination of other regions producing a type of internal representation (Damasio, 1989, 1994). These centers are "convergence zones," for they tie together specific information of the environment with stored knowledge. Supporting the hypothesis, neurons in different regions of the brain have been detected to fire in the same pattern (in terms of phase, frequency), despite their physical separation.

*Comment*. The schematic models developed by the attachment theorists (e.g., Bretherton, 1990) and the cognitive theorists (e.g., Epstein 1980, 1994) are quite similar. Both approaches emphasize the way the growing individual actively constructs schemata that serve perception and production of behavior, integrating cognitive and affective aspects in one structure. They both view schemata of the self and other as intrinsically related, although the former view these as separate but dependent whereas the latter underscore the unity of interpersonal schemata.

Both approaches depict hierarchies of levels of schemata. For Crittenden (1990), metamodels of attachment relationships are constructed across individuals, and also a person could construct them in order to generalize across varying circumstances. Bretherton (1990) viewed a web of models related to self and other, attachment and nonattachment relationships, and the social and nonsocial world. For Epstein (1980, 1994), the individual constructs generalized mental models of self that are comprised of general schemes and these, in turn, consist of more specific interactional schemes. Safran (1990a, 1990b) also viewed an interconnection of different schemata in one structure, for he described core and peripheral schemata. He presented a three-level hierarchy: first-order generalized interpersonal schemata (across attachment, nonattachment models); which integrate second-order interpersonal schemata; for which one type is attachment internal working models. These schemata, in turn, consist of more specific prototypical memories that can vary in tone from one situation to the next for the same social partner. Finally, in a related fashion, Stern (1994, 1995) described a triple-level organization in the infant's "schema-of-being-with-another," with basic formats (e.g., perception, conception, narrative entities) organized into these schemata that, in turn, form networks.

### Stern's "Schema-Of-Being-With-Another"

*Model.* Stern (1994, 1995) has elaborated his earlier model that described the nature of other-centered schemata in the infant's developing cognition. Stern positing a parallel set of schemata related to the infant's subjective experience during social intercourse. According to Stern, goal-directed motives result in a phenomenal experience of low-order modular processes, such as sensations and emotions, which he termed the "emergent moment." The emerging moment is constructed online, and so is constantly changing. It is the referent event for representation, but reflects the history of representations that had been constructed, as well. These moments are represented by at least six distinct but interrelated mid-level schematic types that form the emergent higher-order, prototypical, flexible network, which he labeled "schema-of-being-with-another". Different, simultaneous schemata might be constructed for similar experiences, and the one that is most adaptive will be selected for more activity and control in behavior. These schemata influence, in turn, lived experience and become refigured in evoked or enacted representations. Similarly, Trevarthen and Aitken (1994) referred to "self-with-other representations."

The six basic schemata are the familiar sensorimotor schemata, perceptions/images, symbols/concepts, and scripts (a represented sequential scenario of events), as well as two novel ones called "temporal feeling shapes" and "proto-narrative envelopes." The former concern the emergent, unified contour of the polyphonic feeling contours in affects/emotions, hedonics, motivations, and arousal/activations related to the phenomenal experience. The latter concern the global discursive representation of the experience that emerges to coordinate the other five schemata. Bruner (1990) argued that the narrative unit is basic for comprehending development, and because of the infant's tender age, Stern (1994) referred to the proto-plot or pre-story in this regard. He maintained that the proto-plot's axis should be built around the feeling shape, and that the former and latter merge to form the proto-narrative envelope.

*Comment.* Stern's modeling anticipated some of the themes in the present work. Self is relational as much as self-definitional. Schemata and representations include cognitive and affective components. The narrative is an inclusive representation and its development should be studied. In the present work, I elaborate a model of attachment schemata and representations that resemble Stern's "schema of being with another."

## *Later Work*

### Introduction

*Review.* Contemporary workers have been elaborating the concept of internal working models (Bretherton & Munholland, 2008; Crittenden, 1990; Main, 1991; Sroufe & Fleeson, 1988; Thompson, 2006, 2008a, 2008b). Thompson (2008a, 2000b) indicated that Bowlby's concept of internal working models is a heuristically powerful formulation of mental models of the self, caregiver figures, and the general social and relational world. They pertain to the infant's expectations about the availability and responsivity of the caregiver. Internal working models develop into broader representations in the infant and child, concerning self, the caregiver, and social relations, as well as decision rules about how to interact with people. They function as interpretive filters, which canalize interactions in relationships according to whether expectations with caregivers have been of a secure or insecure variety. In this regard, children might choose playmates whose behavior is consistent with their attachment-related expectations and who permit them to express behaviors consistent with their past history of attachment experiences.

Therefore, internal working models function as bridges between the care received from caregivers and the child's developing self-concept and related self-referential beliefs. The concept of internal working models helps explain the linkages between early attachment and later development. In this regard, internal working models constitute "crucial" bridges in another way – between early experiences of differential care giving quality and later affectively colored cognitive beliefs, expectations, and schematic filters that influence developing social relations and personality. They affect social cognition in terms of emotion understanding, social problem-solving, self-concept, emotion regulation, attribution biases, and so on.

Internal working models in infancy not only have predictive functions about the behavior of caregivers but also have interpretive functions in construing the behavior of others in ways that are congruent with the expectations contained in them. In addition, internal working models have self-regulatory functions, in that infants behave according to their contained self- and relational expectations. These different functions of internal working models illustrate their emotional side.

Internal working models influence behavior through their content and by their filtering lens. For example, as described, they affect expectations that one has of others, self-representations, and so on. Also, they bias information processing, depending on the quality of experience received in care giving and the attachment type that had developed in the person. Examples include both defensive exclusion and model-congruent selection of information.

For any one infant, there could be multiple mental working models associated with caregivers, the self, and others. Moreover, any one individual in the attachment system might have multiple mental models in the representational mind of the infant, including the self.

*Comment.* The concept of internal working models is now considered from the perspective of interpretive filters and of bridges to other facets of development.

These concepts prepare the way for relating them directly to cognitive development. Moreover, their current descriptions indicate that they are similar to cognitive/socioaffective structures described in the present work.

## Development

*Review.* Grossmann (1999) explained that Bowlby's formulation of internal working models had melded two traditions. On the one hand, the concept reflects the Freudian concept of the unconscious and the concept in object relations theory of introjection of representations of "good" and "bad" care giving experiences. On the other hand, the concept of internal working models reflects ideas in cognitive psychology, including the work of Piaget on schemas, egocentrism, and perspective-taking. Therefore, according to present understanding, internal working models are influenced by advances in cognitive development and conceptual skills and are at least partly available to consciousness.

Thompson (2008a) maintained that the concept of internal working models changes with age (Bretherton, 1991, 1993; Bretherton & Munholland, 1999; Crittenden, 1990; Main, 1991; Main et al., 1985; Sroufe & Fleeson, 1988; Thompson, 2006; Thompson, Laible, & Ontai, 2003). In early life, they take the form of rudimentary social expectations or predictions about the accessibility and responsiveness of caregivers. They develop as children incorporate understanding of the caregiver's goals, perspectives, and psychological qualities. The attachment transforms into a "goal-corrected partnership."

Thompson (2000, 2006, 2008a; Thompson et al., 2003) developed an account of internal working models as part of the child's developing representational capacities. In his integrated concept, for infancy, he included concepts such as implicit memory and social expectations and, for childhood, he included different types of memory (episodic memory, autobiographical memory). He maintained that the integrated representational capacities being developed in the child help in the development of social cognition and related social skills.

*Comment.* Thompson has elaborated further the relationship between cognitive and memory development in relationship to the growth of internal working models. He also supported the notion of their integrated and social nature.

## Concepts and Theory of Mind

*Review.* Thompson (2008a) expounded upon work relating internal working models and conceptual development. Bretherton (1991, 1993; Bretherton & Munholland, 1999) elaborated the concept of internal working models in terms of script theory, mental event representation theory, and research on constructive memory. For example, in the securely attached child, "open and fluid communication" enables emotional sharing and discussion so that potentially troubling events are rendered more coherent and accessible. For securely developing children, the constructive parent-child communication fosters a "psychological secure base" (Koren-Karie, Oppenheim, & Getzler-Yosef, 2008).

The construct of internal working models is expanding to include work on conceptual understanding (Bretherton & Munholland, 1999), event representation, and autobiographical narrative (Nelson, 2007). In this regard, preschoolers have been shown to construct and maintain representations related to attachment through conversational discourse processes involving their parents. Wellman and Lagattuta (2000) related preschoolers' developing working models to the concept of theory of mind, and proposed that internal working models could be understood as "theories of attachment."

Delius, Bovenschen, and Spangler (2008) also noted that the infant's internal working model is akin to a "theory of mind" or "theory of attachment." Thompson (2008a, 2008b) elaborated on the concept by indicating that it relates to Piaget's conception of the early childhood period involving less egocentrism and better perspective-taking. Thompson (2008a, 2008b) pointed out that perspective-taking develops even toward the end of the first year of life and in the second year. In the second and third years, children are learning to appreciate that others around them have a variety of subjective mental states that might not be the same as their own. Thompson indicated that further research is needed to relate these early social cognitions with the development of early internal working models in secure and insecure attachment.

Delius et al. (2008) continued that acquisitions in the development of the theory of mind "markedly contribute" to the development of internal working models. They specified that internal working models involve affective as well as cognitive knowledge and that they develop based on specific experiences leading to the development of event representations. They control information processing through their filters. Therefore, in all these regards, the concept of internal working models resembles the concept of theory of mind. The authors relate that internal working models concern the organization of information about a specific domain, and the theory of mind is also domain-specific. As children acquire attachment-related experiences, they develop increasingly complex theories about themselves, caregivers, and social relations. These types of theories involve aspects of emotional meanings about others and the emotional responses that they exhibit.

*Comment.* The relationship of developing cognition, social cognition, and internal working models is articulated in this section. Internal working models are construed as related to theory of mind and are considered as theories of attachment. The emphasis on the theory aspect of the models further argues for examining their development in terms of the development of Neo-Piagetian cognitive steps.

## Phases and Theory of Mind

*Review.* Delius et al. (2008) traced the development of the child's theory of attachment through the various attachment phases. First, in phases I and II, infants develop expectations of the behavior of others and understanding of their moods and emotions. They develop particular expectations of how others respond to them

(Rochat, Querido, & Striano, 1999). Therefore, in this period, infants are developing expectations about their caregivers, ways of understanding attachment-related situations, and what might happen as they are encountered.

In phase III, infants are learning to reach their goals, for example, by using social-referencing or joint attention that enable them to better guide behavior. In this age period, they differentiate their acting self from the actions of others (Flavell, Miller, & Miller, 2002). Children develop the ability to perceive the intentions and desires of others. In terms of attachment, they strive to maintain proximity and contact with the care giving figure and to understand the plans of the caregiver in order to attain their goals.

In phase IV, children reach the step of goal-corrected partnership. They realize that their caregivers have their own feelings, plans, and goals that are not necessarily equivalent to their own. They can take the perspective of the caregiver into account and negotiate plans with him or her that are shared in a goal-corrected manner.

*Comment.* This speculation is consistent with the theory of mind research that indicates that children at this age are developing representations of desires and related acquisitions. As the child develops the capacity to create better representational models of mind, the child can develop theories about belief and not just theories about desire (Perner, 1991), which enables them to better predict the behavior of other people in various situations. This enables the children to better coordinate representational plans with those of caregivers. In this regard, Meins, Fernyhough, and Wainwright (2002) have shown that the presence of attachment security predicts a better understanding of theory of mind. I would add that this type of prediction could be expanded to include different qualities of attachment and different cognitive levels or steps, and not just the phases of attachment development.

## Stability

*Review.* Broussard and Cassidy (2010) conducted a fascinating study that showed a predictive relationship between the 1-month status of infants, as perceived by their mothers, and their later adult attachment organization, as measured in the Adult Attachment Interview (AAI; George, Kaplan, & Main, 1985). The neonatal data was collected at 4–6 weeks of age. The AAI was administered 30–40 years later. The authors found that adults were classified as insecure more often when their mothers had perceived them negatively as newborns.

Broussard and Cassidy (2010) speculated that the mother's perception of her newborn affects her behavior toward the child, thereby shaping the maternal-infant interaction and relationship. More negative mothers might be less perceptive of their infants' psychological states, might have greater difficulty recognizing their infants' signals, and might be less flexible and effective in their responses to the infants. This would lead infants to have greater difficulty in regulating attention, memory function, and affect. They might end up feeling rejected and unloved. Out of this matrix, insecure attachments are more likely to develop.

Bakermans-Kranenburg and van IJzendoorn (2009) have studied the first 10,000 interviews using the AAI schedule. The interviews were conducted in over 200 studies, with different cultures, age groups, and gender of participants. In addition, the analysis included high-risk and clinical samples. The authors coded the interviews according to the system developed by Main, Goldwyn, and Hesse (2003). For the normative population, 58% were classified as secure, and 42% were classified as insecure (23% as dismissing and 19% as preoccupied). Additionally, in another analysis, 18% were classified as having unresolved loss or other trauma (most were from the insecure group). The authors found little effect on their results of gender, culture, and language. Subjects with clinical histories showed more insecure and unresolved attachment classifications. Psychological disorders that were more internalizing were associated with more preoccupied and unresolved attachments. Disorders that were more externalizing were associated with more dismissing, but also preoccupied, attachment classifications. Depression was more associated with insecure classifications. Adults with a history of abuse or posttraumatic stress disorder were associated mostly with unresolved classifications.

*Comment.* The survey of research on the AAI by Bakermans-Kranenburg and van IJzendoorn (2009) indicated that the AAI has proved its worth and research continues to deal with its coding and application. It confirms that the types of attachment found in adults generally correspond to the types in infants, and that psychological disorders are associated with more insecure types of attachment. The study illustrates the potential that developing internal working models have in relating perceived neonatal condition and long-term attachment type and mental health. I would add that the mechanism of transmission of the effect of parental and then offspring internal working models on offspring cognitive filtering, psychological integration, and social participation should be moderated by the change in the models as they evolve through cognitive developmental steps, such as described by the present Neo-Piagetian stage model.

## Memories

*Review.* How do internal working models develop? Bretherton and Munholland (2008) described that Bowlby had originally proposed that internal working models "will be stored semantically" (Bowlby, 1980, p. 62). However, in her earlier work, Bretherton (1985) had suggested that the memory underpinnings related to attachment fit the evolving concepts of scripts and event representations (e.g., Nelson & Gruendel, 1981). Nelson has added that infants first develop a nonverbal, experiential event memory that serves in model development. Moreover, in children generic event representations develop and constitute the building blocks for language-based "world" models.

Bretherton and Munholland (2008) proposed that the concept of generic event representations could be extended to encompass both intentions and affect. They considered that generic event representations are person-specific. Moreover, internal working models are constructed not in an accretion, collective fashion, but through an organized, multilayered hierarchical network or web (Bretherton, 1985, 1991). Lower levels are "near experience" scripts with particular persons, and they serve to articulate higher-order generalized nonverbal event representations.

Waters and Waters (2006) have proposed that these types of event representations with particular individuals could become embedded or nested within a "secure-base script," depending on the quality of care giving received. These generalized scripts cohere into representations of self and other, but the authors note that the typical way that they are presented (e.g., "I am loved") are verbal stand-ins for experientially formed, embodied representations.

*Comment.* These authors are relating cognitive, memory, and internal working model development. They also raise the issue of examining internal working models in terms of their hierarchies in development.

## *Attachment Phases*

### Introduction

*Review.* Another aspect of Bowlby's work concerns phases of attachment development (Bowlby, 1969). He discerned four such phases, three in the first year and a fourth in the preschool period. The phases concern (a) pre-attachment (non focused); (b) attachment-in-the-making (focused); (c) secure attachment development; and (d) corrective attachment (goal-oriented) (Ainsworth, 1973; Waters, Kondo-Ikemura, Posada, & Richters 1991).

Waters et al. (1991) revised Bowlby's model, and presented an eight-phase one. The first three phases are seen to take place in the first year (0–3, 3–5, 5–12 months, respectively), and the next phases are posited to begin at about 1, 2, 3, 4, and 6 years, respectively. These particular age ranges suggest that there has been no explicit attempt to link the phases to Piaget's six-step sensorimotor series in infancy, unlike the case here. However, it is instructive to analyze Waters et al.'s model as a starting point for the current one and it shall be shown that it is complementary to it.

In the first phase in Waters et al.'s model of attachment development, newborns are seen to continually interact with caregiver(s) who provide a familiar, predictable context for the growth of preference. Next, young infants coordinate their sensorimotor schemes [Piaget], which permits the primary caregiver to be discriminated as a separate object distinct from the self (e.g., suckable-lookable; lookable-graspable). Later in the first year, infants perceptually learn or notice their own behavior such that they infer that the self is the object of, reflection of, or point of intersection of primary caregiver schemes, a process that prepares the way for self-representation. In the next step in attachment development, 1-year-olds have mastered crawling, which facilitates the emergence of secure-base activity. Primary caregivers teach explicitly this important function of using the self as a secure base through their modeling, informing, and retrieval behavior, and accommodating their proximity and contact management behavior to the new locomotion skills of infants. In the next phase, which can occur early in the second year, protest at caregiver separation diminishes, infants acquire more experience, and their coping, toleration, and prediction skills augment. Then, preschoolers become even better at using the primary caregiver as a secure base. Next, family (and cultural) norms are socialized, partly through identification, leading to a final phase of partnership in maintaining supervision.

*Comment.* Waters et al.'s model of the phases in the development of attachment differs from the original Bowlbian conception, and it lends itself to modification to fit the current perspective that there are parallel developments cognitively and in attachment. As I proceed in describing my model in this regard, I refer to their work.

## *Present Model*

### Introduction

With this backdrop of the work of Waters et al., I describe the present model of attachment development in the first 2 years of life. Table 24.1 depicts parallel acquisitions in development of cognition, emotions and attachment in infancy, with the cognitive and emotional components based on work presented previously in the book. I list the cognitive steps that develop in infancy according to the classic Piagetian series, on which I based my own model, but indicate their equivalence to the substages in my model.

### The First Month

In the first Piagetian substage of reflex exercise, which corresponds to the substage of reflex integration in the present model, newborns in the first month of life are essentially in a phase of reflexive search where they seek to practice patterned behaviors and experience their target end-states in so doing. The implications for emotional and attachment development follow.

Thus, as described in Chap. 22, newborns manifest emotions related to arriving. In terms of attachment development, one finds the exercise of social behavior configurations when they are with the primary caregiver. Newborn behavior might be directed toward a perceived target, but the target is not a true goal. To use Piagetian terminology, there is groping in behavior, but it is objectless, or not directed to a goal object, even if the eventual targeted object in the course of discharging the behavior is perceived and ends up being an apparent goal. For example, hungry infants might manifest fussiness and groping (e.g., rooting, sucking). In response, the caregiver provides nutrients via breast or bottle, and the infants suck, thereby satisfying their thirst or hunger. However, infants are not groping for the nipple or for a return to physiological equilibrium, per se. They merely are exercising reflex-like

**Table 24.1** Parallels in cognitive, emotional, and attachment development in the first years

| Piagetian substage (age in months) | Chief characteristic | Sensorimotor (cognitive) level | Type of emotion | Phase (stage) of attachment to caregiver |
|---|---|---|---|---|
| I (0–1) | Reflexive search | Reflex exercise | Arriving | Social behavior exercise |
| II (1–4) | Directed activity | Primary circular reactions | Possessing | Attachment object engagement |
| III (4–8) | Emerging goals | Secondary circular reactions | Approaching | Passive attachment |
| IV (8–12) | Purposeful intent | Secondary schema coordination | Giving | Secure base exploration (crawling) |
| V (12–18) | Exploratory forays | Tertiary circular reactions | Desiring | Active attachment |
| VI (18–24) | Complex planning | Sensorimotor schema internalization | Evaluating | Monitoring attachment |

This table (a) reviews Piaget's six sensorimotor substages, (b) introduces the types of emotions associated with each substage, and (c) indicates the proposed stage of attachment associated with each substage. Piaget's model of infant cognitive development constitutes a major basis of the present work, and it has been reworked in the present Neo-Piagetian cognitive developmental model. In Young (1990a), I had presented the present model of six steps in emotional development that correspond to the six sensorimotor substages in Piaget's series (a sequence that is compatible with my own model in this age period). In this present table, I add that there are six stages in the development of attachment that correspond to the cognitive and emotional acquisitions in this age period. Bowlby described fewer phases in the development of attachment, but I present a more differentiated model in the growth of attachment that is consistent with the sensorimotor steps

activities that result in these end-points, and it happens only due to caregiver intervention. Thus, in terms of attachment, there is no attachment object even if there is pre-attachment behavior. As Waters et al. had explained, there is no separate, distinct primary caregiver even if there is a familiar, predictable context for the growth of preference.

## The Next Months

The second Piagetian substage of sensorimotor development in infancy in the 1-month-old is called sensorimotor coordination in the present model. It concerns repetitions of interesting, body-focused activities discovered by accident in context (e.g., thumb in, out mouth). Behavior becomes voluntary for the first time, and is directed and better target-focused once the interesting activity is discovered [thus, the current label of sensorimotor coordination].

Given these evolved target-orientation skills, emotions related to possession emerge. In terms of attachment, caregivers can be engaged reciprocally in social encounters with their infants because their focus is entrained (coordinated) in the game played.

This cognitive substage also can be examined according to object discrimination. In Piaget's terminology, the adaptive functions of assimilation and accommodation begin to differentiate. Objects are not discriminated, i.e., do not assimilate into groping schemes. Consequently, the objects induce accommodation of the schemes, and thus a more realistic discrimination via the schemes of the objects. However, progress does not proceed beyond this object differentiation to active groping for differentiated objects, because voluntary direction is initiated only in context and is not evident prior to activity. Infants cannot approach in order to possess. To be more concrete, infants smile at the recognition of having a primary caregiver enter the room, yet they do not smile to attract actively the caregiver. Thus, with respect to attachment, although infants come to better discriminate and play with the caregiver, they are not yet emotionally fixated or attached to the caregiver. In terms of Waters et al.'s model, the primary caregiver becomes a separate object (or target) of infants' sensorimotor coordinations, but the self is not yet differentiated as an object, which partially accounts for this lack of emotional attachment to the caregiver.

## Up to 12 Months

The third Piagetian sensorimotor substage of secondary circular reactions begins at 4 months of age, and corresponds to the current period of sensorimotor hierarchization. This substage witnesses the appearance of nascent goals in behavior, for interesting spectacles with objects are repeated once discovered in context. A primitive representational skill must be maturing, because partially hidden objects of interest are found quickly. In short, movement begins in a random way, and a goal becomes incorporated, but only post hoc. That is, sensory events or objects become goals only after means have been put into effect. Nevertheless, goals come to guide search behavior, with the latter subordinate to the former in a hierarchy, to use the terminology of the present Neo-Piagetian model.

With respect to emotions, infants can enter into the relation state of approaching a specific object (with interest), but only in the context of an already ongoing (social) activity. In terms of attachment, infants' affections are focused increasingly on the familiar as opposed to the unfamiliar caregiver. However, because movement lacks a goal at the outset, this attachment is passive. Infants grope for the caregiver as an object that is partially known, but this does not occur with active intention when the caregiver is not attentive or not present. Using Waters et al.'s approach, the self also is differentiating as an object as the attachment process continues [although this would seem to apply especially to the next level of the present model, which is not separated from this one in their model].

Eight- to twelve-months-olds enter into the Piagetian cognitive substage of sensorimotor secondary schema coordinations, or systems, as per the present terminology. Schemes are used as means for ends from a behavior's onset, e.g., in seeking a fully hidden, interesting toy. Infants are capable of groping or moving toward something with definite goals right from the start of a movement [Piaget]. Object groping without initial purpose, which developed previously, acquires a novel aspect, the quality of purpose with the groping's inception (i.e., behavioral organization manifests a systemic wholeness according to the present model).

For example, the emotional relation state of giving can be entered into even in the sense of giving of oneself, and giving might be construed as approaching with the explicit goal of letting a partner have something. In terms of attachment, the caregiver discriminated or attached to passively in the past now becomes both a goal object sought more actively and a secure base for crawling toward in order to share and to go off to explore again. In Waters et al.'s scheme, initial secure base activity can emerge at this level.

## The Second Year

At 1 year of age, Piaget's substage of tertiary circular reactions begins [labeled sensorimotor multiplication in the present model]. Toddlers explore deliberately and elaborately new means for known schemes, but in a haphazard way. Object groping with purpose is directed either in novel ways or toward novel objects, rather than using the first ways and objects developed in the prior substage. Consequently, in this substage, I note: (a) active discovery of new means of groping in Piaget's terms; (b) desiring in emotional terms; and (c) more active attachment from a secure base, as evidenced in behavior in the reunion after separation.

Toddlers in the second half of the second year of life arrive at the substage of Piagetian internal mental combinations, considered as sensorimotor integration in the present model. This behavioral process is characterized by complex purposeful planning without groping, because object representation now can fully guide behavior by relating thoughts.

Objects (e.g., partners in dyadic interaction) can be compared or evaluated (as in love or hate, emotions involved in this substage) because of this acquisition in symbolic thought. Thus, corrective or planned monitoring attachment to the partner eventually develops, for toddlers can keep their primary caregiver in mind while wandering, playing, etc. With toddlers' new capability to emote by loving, the attachment and emotional processes that have been developing reach their apex and become clearly fixed into one socioaffective structure.

Bowlby and Waters et al. place corrective attachment at later points in development, although in my opinion its initial onset seems to manifest in the toddlers' complex, integrated, planned activities of this period. Waters et al. emphasized a similar behavior that can blossom in this period, i.e., toleration of separation through autoregulatory processes.

## Comment

I have elaborated a model of the steps in attachment development that is consistent with Bowlby's original model, but it takes into account the literature on the topic and it structures it according to the present Neo-Piagetian model of cognitive development.

In the next section of the chapter, I apply the present model to another aspect of attachment theory, relating to the nature of internal working models that develop through the cognitive steps. I emphasize their social and hierarchical nature.

## *Social Self Working Schemata*

### The Present Model

In the following, I present a construct that integrates the prior work on schemata (see Tables 24.2–24.6). I refer to the types of schemata being discussed as "social self working schemata." The use of the descriptor "social self" (after James, 1890) accentuates both the personal "self" function of the schemata and their interpersonal social nature. The concept of "working schema" highlights the dynamic, constructive, relational nature of schema formation. Also, the term simultaneously offers a linguistic bridge between the attachment and cognitive models.

As for the different levels of the social self working schema hierarchy, I use a three (or more) level hierarchy, as in the prior research (superordinate, intermediate, subordinate). I use the adjectives "generalized" (integrating into one superordinate schema attachment and other schemata), "general" (more specific, separate, lower-level schemata, including attachment schemata), and "interactional" (e.g., particular and prototypical attachment figure sequences). Thus, the present model posits that as the developing individual enters into relationships with the sociocultural surround, these relationships are embodied by different levels of networked social self working schemata (i.e., generalized, general, interactional). Moreover, they are considered to relate to the self and other. Finally, they are posited to evolve according to the present Neo-Piagetian developmental model of stages and substages.

### Cognitive Influences

Thus, I hypothesize that with each new substage in ontogenesis, such as described by the present model, social self working schemata normally are restructured or reworked in light of the characteristics of each new step traversed. That is, the scope of the hierarchical organization of the schemata should become more elaborate with development in a way consonant with the attributes of the particular substage to which the developing individual has progressed. The nature of interplay of schemata both within and across levels should be determined in part by the characteristics of the particular cognitive substage involved (e.g., hierarchization, systematization). Moreover, as stages over the lifespan are traversed, social self working schemata might reflect a trusting self in an infant, an egocentric self in a preschooler, a self-reflective child, a conscious adolescent, a relativistic adult, or an integrated elderly person.

Pipp (1990) had adopted a similar argument relating internal working models to cognitive development. She postulated that the nature of sensorimotor internal

**Table 24.2** Positive working schemata of the self and other in each reflexive substage

| Substage | Self | Other |
|---|---|---|
| 1. | No schemata other than reflex pairings | Fetal environment is noninterfering |
| 2. | Reflex pairs coordinate and react to stimuli | Stimuli induce reactions |
| 3. | Primitive schemata form in visual, auditory, haptic, olfactory, gustatory, and kinesthetic activity/exploration; with intermodal system coordinations | Objects elicit and respond |
| 4. | Consistencies in care giving lead to the formation of bodily components-of-context associations. Patterned schemata fire mechanically | Caregivers aliment |
| 5. | Independent schemata that are not reflex controlled allow contextually adjusted, patterned behavior with emotional integrations | Caregivers respond sensitively |

An important component of attachment theory concerns "internal working models," which function as representations for secure- and insecure-attachment-promoting experiences (e.g., about the other: "The world loves me"; about the self: "I am loved"; or their inverses). These internal working models develop throughout the development of attachment, but there has been little work indicating how this might take place. The concept of internal working models has developed to include scripts, narratives, and other more advanced representations. Note that in the text I indicated why I refer to internal working models as "working schemata"

However, in this series of tables in the present work, I indicate how internal working models might evolve through the 25 steps of the present Neo-Piagetian model, thereby giving them a coherent structure to help explain how they might grow cognitively. Also, I incorporate into these developing working schemata the present developmental model of Neo-Eriksonian steps in socio-affective development. The tables present the positive or secure components to the schemata, in particular. In addition, I add to the schemata the manner in which basic emotions are fundamental to them in the infancy period

(a) The first table of the series is on the reflex stage. It indicates that working schemata in the first month include basic emotional components, and that the caregiver could already be manifesting sensitive care
(b) The next table on the sensorimotor stage presents the critical period in the first 2 years of life when working schemata are developing their secure or insecure characteristics. For the self, the schemata evolve in this stage from ones concerned with social coordination to those involved in active attachment and feeling loved, to those that are more symbolic, even if still sensorimotor. For the other, the schemata move from working models of initial social interactions, trust, and caregivers being security-promoting, to genuine interactions and constancy as object
(c) In the perioperational stage, working schemata of the self start with egocentric conceptions. They move to a better perspective-taking of the other, and to testing different roles. The other evolves from being conceived as being adjustable to having rules and modulating growth, to being capable of evaluating and of modeling roles
(d) In the abstract stage, the working model of the self develops from a conscious being to a conscientious and universalizing one. Symmetrically, the other acts to raise consciousness, conscientiousness, and universal empathy
(e) In the collective stage, the self moves toward generativity, midlife, and end of life concerns. The other is conceived in a mirror way

**Table 24.3** Positive working schemata of the self and other in each sensorimotor substage

| Substage | Self | Other |
|---|---|---|
| 1. | Working schemata become increasingly coordinative of the socializing self and the other, but only in the sense of partial components of both (e.g., the baby is contented and experiences pleasure) | Dyadic partners participate |
| 2. | As the infant develops a sense of trust, context-activated goals are added to developing schemata, which take on a hierarchical structure (e.g., components of self are interested and delighted in other) | Primary "family" encourages trust |
| 3. | Working schemata include self-defined goals, primitive representations such as images of the caregiver, and the desire for intersubjectivity and proximity and contact. The emotional side of the developing cognitive-affective structure includes feelings of affection and comfort | Attachment figures secure |
| 4. | The 1-year-old infant acts increasingly autonomous through planned exploratory behavior eagerly implemented, although this does not happen with explicit plans at the behavior's outset (it is "accidental"). The social other is integral to the working schemata being formed, but as an object of sensorimotoric-emotional activity rather than a preconceived representational goal. The primary caregiver who has been sensitive in the first year so that the infant feels "loved" is sought actively in reunion after a brief separation | Others are genuine social objects, e.g., on reunion |
| 5. | Infants at 18 months of age enact symbolically guided, planned activity, but always with a sensorimotoric and affective base. They experience appreciation and pride. Others are understood in terms of the plans, and with consistent participation in them. The infant varies plans involving them on purpose to see the effect | Others are constant objects even if absent, displaced |

working models of the attachment relationship to the caregiver in infancy shifts in complexity as the infant passes through the various sensorimotor substages from 4 to 12 months of age.

Neo-Piagetians describe the cognitive control units mediating commerce with the problems and contexts encountered by actively-constructing infants and children. In the present view, these cognitive control units are especially social, shared, co-participatory, interactional, reciprocal, bidirectional, multivoiced, self-other, and co-constructed. The product of these shared encounters are the social self working schemata formed in early attachment and other relationships, and they are carried forward to influence the multiple relationships coformed throughout life, and in turn are altered through these encounters. The types of blockages, dissociations, etc., that can develop in

**Table 24.4** Positive working schemata of the self and other in each perioperational substage

| Substage | Self | Other |
|---|---|---|
| 1. | In symbol plan coordinations, the child's plans are more focused on self egocentrically, and the other, while schematized more holistically, needs to adjust. A sense of the other as a loving one grows | Others are global and adjust |
| 2. | The child's symbol plans are more differentiated, with an initiative subordinating the other, who is still responded to with an overriding love, however | Others formulate rules |
| 3. | The "I" can take primary perspectives of the self/other through symbol plan systems and Eriksonian "industry," guided by others | Others can modulate personal growth |
| 4. | This ability grows and others are seen to evaluate the self | Others evaluate logically |
| 5. | The child's working schemata include testing of different roles, with others seen as modelers and accepting of this dynamic | Others model roles |

**Table 24.5** Positive working schemata of the self and other in each abstract substage

| Substage | Self | Other |
|---|---|---|
| 1. | Conscious "I" weighs abstractly | Others raise consciousness |
| 2. | Identity "I" tests and seeks identity | Others answer resultant questions and answer to quests |
| 3. | Conscientious "I" undertakes adult-(like) functions | Objects merit giving and responsibility |
| 4. | Relativistic "I" delves and debates | Others are intimate and multiple |
| 5. | Universal "I" harmonizes | Others universally merit empathy |

**Table 24.6** Positive working schemata of the self and other in each collective intelligence substage

| Substage | Self | Other |
|---|---|---|
| 1. | The self is collective, fused, and coordinative | Others are part of our collective thought |
| 2. | The self knows priorities, is multiply complex, and can give multiply, and not for taking | Others are our generativity's recipients |
| 3. | At midlife, the self can create and work to transform personal, social, work, and community systems | Objects differentiated into collective sense of selves |
| 4. | The elder self reviews the multiplicity of life and lives | We look back at ourselves and others widening our spheres |
| 5. | An integrated "I" is really an integrated "We" at life's end | We feel multiple, integrated self-other harmonies |

more problematic social and attachment relationships indicate an aberrant architecture of the developing schemata. These, as well, develop through the cognitive steps being described, but their contents would be less than optimal.

### Comment

Social self working schemata are considered dynamic, flexible, context-adapting engrams reflective of past and present relationships. They are considered to have three levels of organization: the generalized (superordinate), general (intermediate), and interactional (subordinate), which constitute a dynamic hierarchy of levels of representation of the self and the other formed in interpersonal transactions. As the person develops, these social self working schemata should be reorganized at each of the 25 developmental levels described in the present model according to the characteristics of the levels (i.e., coordination, hierarchization, systematization, etc.). Tables 24.2–24.6 have presented the different social self working schemata hypothesized to emerge in the course of development. The steps do not consider the contents of schemata that might form in maladaptive circumstances. Future work can verify the validity of the sequence and how they transform in both normal and problematic development.

## Summary and Conclusions

This chapter constitutes the last one of the second part of the book. In this part, I have expanded the application of the present Neo-Piagetian stage-substage model to multiple aspects of development, some considered more cognitive in nature and some considered more socioaffective in nature. However, both parts of the developing person are constituted in an integrated whole and the applications of the present model in this part of the book are complementary.

In the last part of the book, I turn to the topic of causality, determinants, and origins of developing behavior. I consider the Piagetian perspective related to this topic, but expand it greatly. Then, in the last chapters of the book, there are two chapters in narrative development and others that speculate, for example, on causality in terms of evolutionary pressures underlying the present model of stages and on the generality of stages in the change across living and nonliving systems. A concluding chapter examines topics such as free will responsibility, and activation inhibition coordination, relating them to the present model and to the topic of causality.

## References

Ainsworth, M. D. S. (1973). The development of infant-mother attachment. In B. M. Caldwell & H. N. Ricciuti (Eds.), *Review of child development research* (Child development and social policy, Vol. 3, pp. 1–94). Chicago: University of Chicago Press.

Bakermans-Kranenburg, M. J., & van IJzendoorn, M. H. (2009). The first 10, 000 adult attachment interviews: Distributions of adult attachment representations in clinical and non-clinical groups. *Attachment & Human Development, 11*, 223–263.

Bowlby, J. (1969/1982). *Attachment and loss: Vol. 1. Attachment.* New York: Basic Books.

Bowlby, J. (1980). *Attachment and loss: Vol. 3. Loss: Sadness and depression.* New York: Basic Books.

Bretherton, I. (1985). Attachment theory: Retrospect and prospect. *Monographs of the Society for Research in Child Development, 50*(1/2), 3–35.

Bretherton, I. (1990). Open communication and internal working models: Their role in the development of attachment. In R. A. Thompson (Ed.), *Nebraska symposium on motivation* (Socioemotional development, Vol. 36, pp. 57–114). Lincoln University of Nebraska Press.

Bretherton, I. (1991). Pouring new wine into old bottles: The social self as internal working model. In M. Gunnar & L. A. Sroufe (Eds.), *Minnesota symposia on child development* (Memory and affect in development, Vol. 26, pp. 237–263). Hillsdale: Erlbaum.

Bretherton, I. (1992b). Attachment and bonding. In V. B. Van Hasselt & M. Hensen (Eds.), *Handbook of social development: A lifespan perspective* (pp. 133–155). New York: Plenum.

Bretherton, I. (1993). From dialogue to internal working models: The co-construction of self in relationships. In C. A. Nelson (Ed.), *Memory and affect in development* (pp. 237–263). Hillsdale: Erlbaum.

Bretherton, I., & Munholland, K. A. (1999). Internal working models in attachment relationships: A construct revisited. In J. Cassidy & P. R. Shaver (Eds.), *Handbook of attachment: Theory, research, and clinical applications* (pp. 89–111). New York: Guilford Press.

Bretherton, I., & Munholland, K. A. (2008). Internal working models in attachment relationships: Elaborating a central construct in attachment theory. In J. Cassidy & P. R. Shaver (Eds.), *Handbook of attachment: Theory, research, and clinical applications* (2nd ed., pp. 102–127). New York: Guilford Press.

Broussard, E. R., & Cassidy, J. (2010). Maternal perception of newborns predicts attachment organization in middle adulthood. *Attachment & Human Development, 12*, 159–172.

Bruner, J. S. (1990). *Acts of meaning*. Cambridge: Harvard University Press.

Cassidy, J. (1990). Theoretical and methodological considerations in the study of attachment and the self in young children. In M. T. Greenberg, D. Ciccetti, & E. M. Cummings (Eds.), *Attachment in the preschool years: Theory, research and intervention* (pp. 87–119). Chicago: University of Chicago Press.

Crittenden, P. M. (1990). Internal representational models of attachment relationships. *Infant Mental Health Journal, 11*, 259–277.

Crittenden, P. M. (1992). Quality of attachment in the preschool years. *Development and Psychopathology, 4*, 209–241.

Damasio, A. R. (1989). The brain binds entities and events by multiregion activation from convergence zones. *Neural Computation, 1*, 123–132.

Damasio, A. R. (1994). *Descartes' error: Emotion, reason, and the human brain.* New York: Avon.

Delius, A., Bovenschen, I., & Spangler, G. (2008). The inner working model as a "theory of attachment": Development during the preschool years. *Attachment & Human Development, 10*, 395–414.

Epstein, S. (1980). A review and the proposal of an integrated theory of personality. In E. Staub (Ed.), *Personality's basic aspects and current research* (pp. 82–131). Englewood Cliffs: Prentice-Hall.

Epstein, S. (1994). Integration of the cognitive and the psychodynamic unconscious. *American Psychologist, 49*, 709–724.

Flavell, J. H., Miller, P. H., & Miller, S. A. (2002). *Cognitive development*. Upper Saddle River: Prentice Hall.

George, C., Kaplan, N., & Main, M. (1985). *Adult attachment interview protocol* (2nd ed.). Unpublished manuscript, University of California, Berkeley.

Grossmann, K. E. (1999). Old and new internal working models of attachment: The organization of feelings and language. *Attachment and Human Development, 1*, 253–269.

James, W. (1890). *The principles of psychology* (Vol. 1 and 2). New York: Holt.

Koren-Karie, N., Oppenheim, D., & Getzler-Yosef, R. (2008). Shaping children's internal working models through mother-child dialogues: The importance of resolving past maternal trauma. *Attachment & Human Development, 10*, 465–483.
Main, M. (1991). Metacognitive knowledge, metacognitive monitoring, and singular coherent vs. multiple (incoherent) model of attachment: Findings and direction for future research. In C. M. Parkes, J. Stevenson-Hinde, & P. Morris (Eds.), *Attachment across the life cycle* (pp. 199–215). New York: Routledge.
Main, M., Goldwyn, R., & Hesse, E. (2003). *The adult attachment interview: Scoring and classification system, Version 7.2*. Unpublished manuscript, University of California, Berkeley.
Main, M., Kaplan, N., & Cassidy, J. (1985). Security in infancy, childhood, and adulthood: A move to the level of representation. *Monographs of the Society for Research in Child Development, 50*, (1-2, Serial No. 209).
Meins, E., Fernyhough, C., & Wainwright, R. (2002). Maternal mind-mindedness and attachment security as predictors of theory of mind understanding. *Child Development, 73*, 1715–1726.
Nelson, K. (2007). *Young minds in social worlds*. Cambridge: Harvard University Press.
Nelson, K., & Gruendel, J. (1981). Generalized event representations: Basic building blocks of cognitive development. In M. E. Lamb & A. Brown (Eds.), *Advances in developmental psychology* (Vol. 1, pp. 131–158). Hillsdale: Erlbaum.
Perner, J. (1991). *Understanding the representational mind*. Cambridge, MA: MIT Press.
Pipp, S. (1990). Sensorimotor and representational internal working models of self, other and relationship: Mechanisms of connection and separation. In D. Cicchetti & M. Beeghly (Eds.), *The self in transition: Infancy to childhood* (pp. 243–264). Chicago: University of Chicago Press.
Pipp, S., Easterbrooks, M. A., & Harmon, R. J. (1992). The relation between attachment and knowledge of self and mother in one- to three-year-old infants. *Child Development, 63*, 738–750.
Rochat, P., Querido, J. G., & Striano, T. (1999). Emerging sensitivity to the timing and structure of protoconversation in early infancy. *Developmental Psychology, 35*, 950–957.
Safran, J. D. (1990a). Towards a refinement of cognitive therapy in light of interpersonal theory: I. Theory. *Clinical Psychology Review, 10*, 87–105.
Safran, J. D. (1990b). Towards a refinement of cognitive therapy in light of interpersonal theory: II. Practice. *Clinical Psychology Review, 10*, 107–121.
Squire, L. R. (1987). *Memory and brain*. New York: Oxford University Press.
Sroufe, L. A., & Fleeson, J. (1988). The coherence of family relationships. In R. A. Hinde & J. Stevenson-Hinde (Eds.), *Relationships within families* (pp. 27–47). Oxford: Clarendon.
Stern, D. N. (1994). One way to build a clinically relevant baby. *Infant Mental Health Journal, 15*, 9–25.
Stern, D. N. (1995). *The motherhood constellation: A unified view of parent-infant psychotherapy*. New York: Basic Books.
Thompson, R. A. (2000). The legacy of early attachments. *Child Development, 71*, 145–152.
Thompson, R. A. (2006). The development of the person: Social understanding, relationships, self, conscience. In W. Damon, R. M. Lerner, & N. Eisenberg (Eds.), *Handbook of child psychology: Vol. 3* (Social, emotional, and personality development 6th ed., pp. 24–98). New York: Wiley.
Thompson, R. A. (2008a). Attachment-related mental representations: Introduction to the special issue. *Attachment & Human Development, 10*, 347–358.
Thompson, R. A. (2008b). Early attachment and later development: Familiar questions, new answers. In J. Cassidy & P. R. Shaver (Eds.), *Handbook of attachment: Theory, research, and clinical applications* (pp. 348–365). New York: Guilford Press.
Thompson, R. A., Laible, D., & Ontai, L. (2003). Early understanding of emotion, morality, and the self: Developing a working model. In R. Kail (Ed.), *Advances in child development and behavior* (Vol. 31, pp. 137–171). San Diego: Academic Press.

Trevarthen, C., & Aitken, K. J. (1994). Brain development, infant communication, and empathy disorders: Intrinsic factors in child mental health. *Development and Psychopathology, 6*, 597–633.

Tulving, E. (1972). Episodic and semantic memory. In E. Tulving & W. Donaldson (Eds.), *Organization of memory* (pp. 381–403). New York: Academic Press.

Tulving, E. (1979). Memory research: What kind of progress? In L. G. Nilsson (Ed.), *Perspectives on memory research: Essays in honour of Uppsala University's 500th anniversary* (pp. 19–34). Hillsdale: Erlbaum.

Tulving, E. (1985). How many memory systems are there? *American Psychologist, 40*, 385–398.

Tulving, E. (1989). Remembering and knowing the past. *American Scientist, 77*, 361–367.

Tulving, E., & Schacter, D. L. (1990). Priming and human memory systems. *Science, 247*, 301–306.

Waters, E., Kondo-Ikemura, K., Posada, G., & Richters, J. (1991). Learning to love: Mechanisms and milestones. In M. Gunnar & L. A. Sroufe (Eds.), *Minnesota symposia on child psychology* (Self processes in development, Vol. 23, pp. 217–255). Hillsdale: Erlbaum.

Waters, H. S., & Waters, E. (2006). The attachment working models concept: Among other things, we build script-like representations of secure base experiences. *Attachment and Human Development, 8*, 185–197.

Wellman, H. M., & Lagattuta, K. H. (2000). Developing understandings of mind. In S. Baron-Cohen, H. Tager-Flusberg, & D. Cohen (Eds.), *Understanding other minds* (2nd ed., pp. 21–49). New York: Oxford University Press.

Young, G. (1990). Early neuropsychological development: Lateralization of functions - hemispheric specialization. In C. A. Hauert (Ed.), *Developmental psychology: Cognitive, perceptuo-motor and neuropsychological perspectives* (pp. 113–181). Amsterdam: North Holland.

# Chapter 25
# Development of Hemispheric Specialization

## Introduction

This chapter is the first of six chapters on causality, determinants, and origins of behavior. The first two parts of the book especially have dealt with the product or content of development, or the what, particularly in terms of the present Neo-Piagetian stage model and socioaffective correspondences. In these next six chapters, I deal with the process, transition mechanisms, or the how and why of development. Fitting the contemporary zeitgeist, I emphasize the interaction of biology and environment. However, I include the developing individual as the seat of the interaction and consider as cardinal to development the person's active participation in the process. Also, the biological model is not a straightforward genetic one because I consider the concept of epigenesis. Also, the environment is not considered apart from the developing person because I work from a relational metaframe.

In the present chapter and the next, I examine the brain bases of developing behavior from the perspective of the development of hemispheric specialization. My work in this area has focused on the concept of activation–inhibition coordination, which seems involved in a widespread manner in development across brain and behavior, as well as in social interaction. This work leads to a model of the evolution of behavior in terms of hemispheric specialization and related processes.

Then, in two chapters, I consider the causes and determinants of behavior in terms of nonlinear dynamical systems theory. This work leads to a model of change in development that includes shifting from attractors to complex adaptive systems. The model is considered to underpin the present Neo-Piagetian model of steps in development. I show how the concept of activation–inhibition coordination is consistent with nonlinear dynamical modeling.

The last two chapters of the book on causes and determinants in developing behavior consider epigenesis. This concept has been applied to development in terms of a probabilistic model of how it unfolds in context and in terms of how feedback from the environment can affect alleles and their manifestation in development,

G. Young, *Development and Causality: Neo-Piagetian Perspectives*,
DOI 10.1007/978-1-4419-9422-6_25, © Springer Science+Business Media, LLC 2011

with the changes transmitted to future generations. Once more, the process of activation–inhibition coordination seems to apply to the process of how this type of epigenesis works.

There are two main sections in the present chapter. First, I examine the evidence that supports the concept of hemispheric specialization for activation–inhibition coordination. The evidence ranges from manual lateralization in infancy to temperament in toddlers to depression in adults. Next, I compare the progressive and invariant models of the development of hemispheric specialization. The evidence, including my own, clearly supports the latter view. In the next chapter, I examine the relationship between lateralization and cognition. This leads to my models relating evolution, cognition, the brain, and laterality. I terminate the chapter with a discussion of the concepts of the theoretic and extended in the evolution of the human mind and also end with my own concept related to my Neo-Piagetian model.

## Manual and Inhibition Development

### *Activation–Inhibition Coordination*

*Attentional.* Case (1992d) described the way that developing executive attentional processes involve the twin processes of activating one set of components and simultaneously inhibiting potentially competing components. Logan (1995) characterized the deficiency in attention deficit hyperactivity disorder (ADHD) as a lack of inhibitory control both in an ongoing action and in the reengagement of an alternative one after inhibition.

Norman and Shallice (1986) described a model of attentional control of cognitive processes that speaks to the way that activation–inhibition coordination, in part, might take place. According to Norman and Shallice, lower-level schemata normally run off to completion when guiding more automatic behavior. However, when there is indecision or conflict, a supervisory attention system monitors situations involving novelty, feedback, and planning, or becomes involved. For example, in such circumstances, it might act to increase or inhibit the activation threshold of a specific adaptive schema. Thus, activation–inhibition coordination, in part, might reflect the play of superordinate attentive structures, and therefore, the left hemisphere (and the left frontal lobe, in particular) might excel in such attention. (Gold, Goldberg, and Weinberger (1992) have related this attentional control mechanism to the frontal lobes).

Note that the types of inhibition skills that have been described especially refer to intrahemispheric ones. It could be also that the left (and perhaps the right) hemisphere succeeds in its particular mode of inhibition specialization because it can recruit interhemispherically the contralateral hemisphere for its plans, at least marshaling its adaptive support when required, or that it has separate specializations for interhemispheric coordination or contralateral inhibition.

*Model.* In Young (1990a, 1990b; Young, 1997; Young et al., 1983; Young & Chapman, 2007; Young & Gagnon, 1990), I presented the model that the cerebral hemispheres are differentially specialized for inhibition. In the following section, I review this work and the support for it. This serves to introduce the concept of activation–inhibition coordination, considered important in the developmental process, in general, and in the passage through the proposed 25-step model of development, in particular.

In particular, the left hemisphere is considered the primary seat of inhibitory control, specializing in a sophisticated interweaving of activation and inhibitory skills. Activation–inhibition coordination especially involves the suppression of interference due to inappropriate alternative behavior, both when selecting adaptive goal-directed activity and during its (movement) transitions (see Table 25.1 and Fig. 25.1). Through this skill, the left hemisphere can control the subtle, refined sequences in both language and fine motor activities. Moreover, successful unfolding of these functions requires not only activation–inhibition intercoordination within the left hemisphere but also activation–inhibition coordination with the right one.

**Table 25.1** Different types of inhibition functions

| Type | Description |
|---|---|
| Sophisticated synchrony | Sophisticated, subtle interweaving of activation and inhibitory skills, with appropriate activations taking place because of the suppression of interference due to inappropriate alternative behavior, both when selecting adaptive goal-directed activity and during its (movement) transitions. Both subtle competing movements and gross interfering ones are countered and controlled |
| Altering synchrony | Overtly modifying/disrupting sequential activation–inhibition coordinations |
| Refining synchrony | Facilitating/refining sequential activation–inhibition coordinations |
| Long damping | Full suppression/damping activity over time |
| Short synchrony | Activation–inhibition synchrony instantaneously or for a short time period. In spatial processes, some information as figure highlighted and some as ground moderated |

The left and right hemispheres can be differentiated in terms of their underlying inhibitory skills (e.g., Young, 1990a, 1990b). Inhibition is a ubiquitous function throughout multiple levels of the behavior and brain. Because I relate the left hemisphere to more refined inhibitory functions, in particular, to activation–inhibition coordination, in this table I present various types of inhibition in terms of the degree of their complexity, demands, and refinement. Other types of inhibition could include ones without any coordinating activation, or others with less advanced skill needs, such as those short in duration. These lesser types of inhibition skills should be handled in a good enough fashion in the right hemisphere (also, see Fig. 25.1)

This should not be taken to imply that the left hemisphere handles all advanced skills and the right only left-over ones. Each hemisphere appears specialized for certain skills in a relative sense, and they collaborate to produce functionally adaptive behavior. The specialization of each hemisphere has its advantages, but it is relative, and some redundancy is built into the system, as well. Also, the different types of inhibitory skills in the right hemisphere might be conducive to its advantages, such as a more holistic spatial processing. Moreover, when damage impacts one hemisphere or the other, we learn that cortical reorganization can take place and functional recovery can also take place

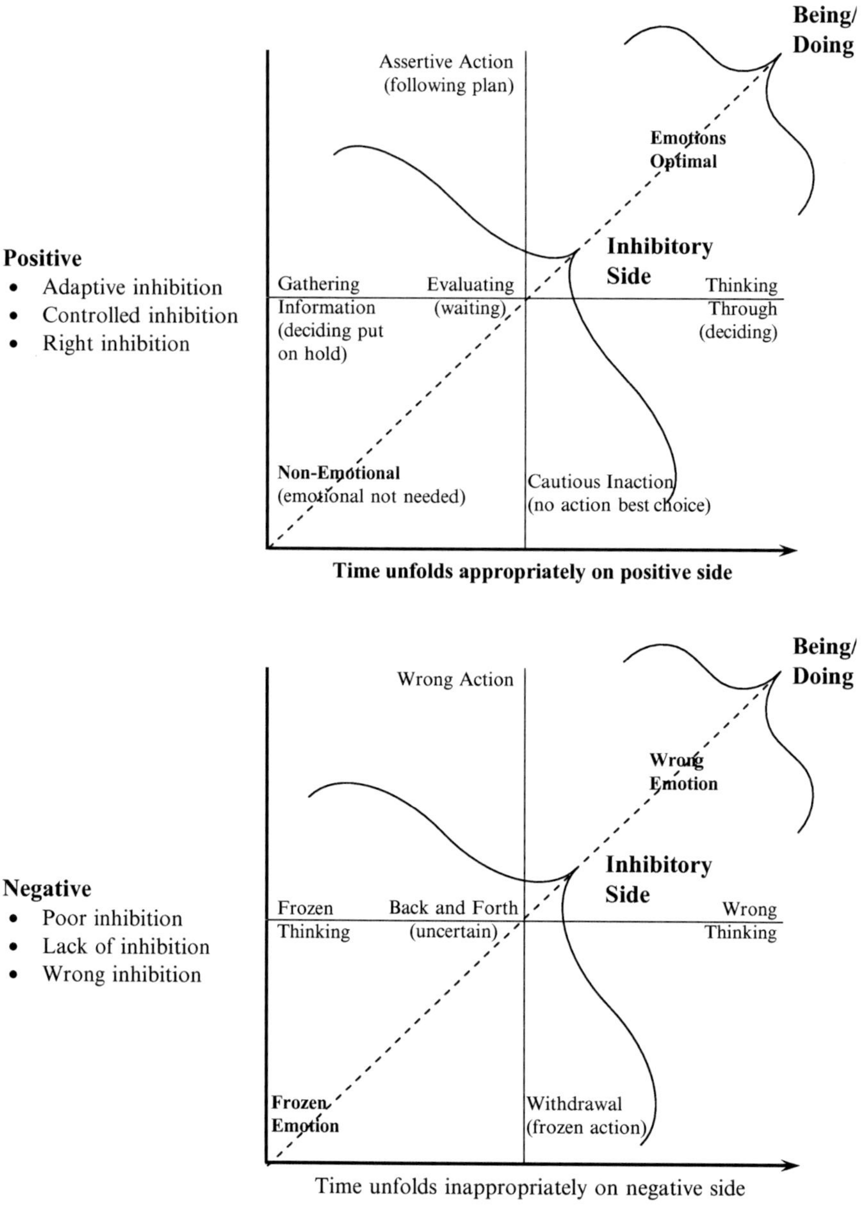


**Fig. 25.1** Activation–inhibition coordination in behavior. Behavior is not only about activation but it is also about inhibition or stopping. Inhibition can be used positively or negatively. On the positive side, stopping allows us to wait before acting, gather needed information, control inappropriate emotional reactions, plan, and then act in control. On the negative side, inhibition can freeze us, have us hesitate too much, and, in the end, lead to inappropriate feelings, thoughts, and actions

In contrast to the left hemisphere, the right hemisphere might be specialized for less dynamic inhibition, such as general damping of activity over time, or activation–inhibition coordination instantaneously or for a short time period. The latter capacity would be conducive to spatial processes because a gestalt perception needs some information as figure to be highlighted (activated) and some as ground to be moderated (inhibited).

In summary, the hemispheres seem to have complementary, cooperative specializations for inhibition. Dawson, Hessl, and Frey (1994; Dawson, Panagiotides, Klinger, & Hill, 1992; Dawson, Klinger, Panagiotides, Hill, & Spieker, 1992; Dawson, 1994a, 1994b) proposed a similar concept when they argued that the left (frontal) hemisphere's inhibition involvement includes sequential organization, such as with language, and that of the right includes disruption through novel stimulus processing.

## *Evidence*

In the following section, I examine multiple areas of research that support the model presented in Young (1990a, 1990b, 1997) that the left and right hemispheres are specialized from even the fetal period along the lines of adult. The evidence includes research on manual behavior, temperament, and emotions.

*Manual.* Developmentally, the evidence is accumulating that the left side of the brain seems specialized for more complex manual and inhibition skills. The evidence spans the early developmental period from before birth to throughout the first year.

*Neonatal.* Kooistra and Heilman (1988) found greater left-side volume of the globus pallidus both fetally and in the first years of life. This subcortical area is concerned especially with controlling the direction, amplitude, and velocity of arm movements. It is interesting to note that, for the current purposes, with limb movement or turning, the globus pallidus has its tonic neuronal firing interrupted either by bursts of activity or pauses, apparently due to inhibitory striatopallidal input. Thus, it seems that neonatal and early, directed arm movements are governed partly by inhibition of one subcortical zone by another. This latter inhibitory zone is larger on the left side of the brain even fetally, which could explain why neonatal and perhaps even fetal target-directed arm movement seems right-sided.

Young and Gagnon (1990) found that newborns turned their heads to the left more to musical compared to verbal stimuli, fitting the pattern of more left hemisphere verbal skills and more right hemisphere specialization nonverbal skills, respectively. In addition, while manifesting this turning pattern, the newborns moved their right hand away from a bar placed before them and opened the hand. These data suggest that as the right side of the brain becomes more activated, secondary manual behaviors relative to bar contact increase in frequency on the right side. A parsimonious explanation of the results is that with less left hemisphere activation, there is more interfering manual activities, fitting the current left hemisphere inhibition hypothesis.

Bertoncini et al. (1989) found a right-ear advantage for speech stimuli in newborns. Dehaene-Lambertz (2000) found that for auditory stimuli, event-related potential amplitude was larger over the left compared to the right hemisphere in 2-month-olds.

McCartney and Hepper (1999) found that between 12 and 17 weeks of gestation, fetuses exhibited more right-hand movements compared to left-hand movements. Ottaviano, Guidetti, Allemand, Spinetoli, and Seri (1989) found a right-hand preference in the spontaneous activity of full-term newborns. In this regard, Hopkins and Bard (1993) and Fagot and Bard (1995) have shown that neonate chimpanzees grasp stronger with the right compared to the left hand.

*First year.* Wentworth, Benson, and Haith (2000) looked at how infants reached for moving targets at 5.5, 8.5, and 11.5 months. Depending on the task, the children at all three ages expressed a right-hand preference. Fagard, Spelke, and von Hofsten (2009) found that 8-month-olds showed a right-hand preference in reaching for moving objects, although 6- and 10-month-olds did not.

Michel, Tyler, Ferre, and Sheu (2006) found right-side hand-use preference for apprehending objects in 7–13-month-olds. The distribution of left to right hand use was similar to that of adults. They reviewed the literature on the role of the corpus callosum in interhemispheric communication. Much of the communication concerns inhibitory functions. They noted that Netz, Ziemann, and Homberg (1995) found greater inhibitory effects in right-handers from the left to the right hemisphere than from the right to the left hemisphere.

Vauclair and Imbault (2009) found that 10–40-month-olds used their right hand for pointing even if they were left-handers or ambidextrous. A correlation between manual preference and pointing preference was strongest during the development of vocabulary spurt and the development of syntactic capacity. The results support the argument that in the left cerebral hemisphere, there are dual systems for controlling communicative gesture and language, on the one hand, and pure motor functions, such as object manipulation, on the other hand. According to the authors, the left hemisphere expresses a hypermobilization during critical periods of language acquisition because of the underlying "better facilitory/inhibitory" system in the left hemisphere. This hypothesis is quite consistent with my own about the left hemisphere's superior activation–inhibition coordination skills.

*Comment.* Morange and Bloch (1996) examined grasping and reaching in 4–7-month-olds. They found that at 4 months of age infants used the *left* hand for midline reaching and at 6 months of age they used the right hand for grasping. Reaching without contact at the midline yielded a 67% *left*-hand preference at 4 months of age and the left hand ended nearer to the object. In terms of object contact, even at this age, the right-hand succeeded 2.5 more times than the left. The right hand was opened 68% of the time during approach, and the left hand was closed 64% of the time.

The results are counter to the analysis in Young (Young 1990a, 1990b; Young et al., 1983) that even early reaching exhibits a right-hand advantage. Therefore, I examined more carefully the methods used in the study. Morange and Bloch defined reaching as extended forward movements more than 10 cm from the frontoparallel plane and tangential to the infants' body while looking at the object. Prereaching involved no contact and reaching involved contact.

Note that in my work (e.g., Young & Gagnon 1990; Young & Gouin Décarie, 1977; Young et al., 1983), I had argued that from the neonatal period the left and right hemispheres are specialized analogously to the adult and that the left hand serves a spatial function in reaching, whereas the right hand serves a directed and grasping function. I had specified that the 1-month-old uses the left hand to flail at objects in order to explore the spatial dynamics surrounding objects that they are trying to reach, but they will reach directly for objects with the right hand and also contact objects with the right hand. It would appear that Morange and Bloch's (1996) methodology was not sufficiently differentiated to capture reaching that was more like flailing than directed in nature. In this regard, it is premature to accept their conclusion that the 4-month-old reaches with the left hand in the sense of reaching in a directed manner toward the object.

Despite the difference in this one aspect of our results, we reach the same conclusions about early manual specialization. The authors concluded that the left hand is specialized for spatial calibration and the right hand for prehension.

My understanding of the study by Morange-Majoux and Bloch is supported by another study. Morange-Majoux (2010) reported that 4–6-month-olds explored with the left hand soft parts of an object using (passive) touching, whereas they pressed and tapped (active) with the right hand the hard parts.

*Temperament.* Fox and Hane (2008) reviewed the literature on electroencephalographic (EEG) asymmetry in the frontal and temporal lobes of the infant brain in emotion-producing situations. Next, I review the studies that they cite and others similar to them.

*Infants.* In their first study, Davidson and Fox (1989) found that 10-month-olds who watched videotape of an actor displaying either smiles and laughter or sadness and crying exhibited left frontal EEG asymmetry (relatively greater activation in the left frontal region). Fox and Davidson (1991) studied infants expressing positive and negative affect. They found that infants exhibited an asymmetry in the EEG favoring the left frontal region during the expression of positive affect and the right side for negative affect.

Fox and Davidson (1984) postulated that the right frontal region of the infant's brain might be specialized for withdrawal-related behavior and the left frontal region seems associated with approach-related behavior. Fox (1991, 1994) argued that the left and right frontal regions might be involved not only in behavioral expression but also in its regulation.

Other research had established that right frontal EEG asymmetry is associated with crying at maternal separation (Fox & Davidson, 1988; Fox, Bell, & Jones, 1992), and with inhibition in behavior (Calkins, Fox, & Marshall, 1996). By contrast, Shachinfar, Schmidt, and Fox (1996) found that toddlers who expressed more frequent externalizing behaviors displayed left frontal EEG asymmetry (less right frontal activation).

Hane, Fox, Henderson, and Marshall (2008) examined longitudinally infants at 4 and 9 months of age for their behavioral reactivity and frontal region electroencephalogram asymmetry. The results showed that negative reactive infants expressed more behavioral avoidance and also right frontal electroencephalogram asymmetry. In contrast, positively reactive infants expressed more approach behavior and also left frontal asymmetry. The authors concluded that an approach–withdrawal bias underlies behavioral reactivity in infants.

*Toddlers.* Davidson and colleagues (Davidson, 1991, 1992a, 1992b, 1992c; 1994; Finman, Davidson, Colton, Strauss, & Kagan, 1989) tested three groups of children assessed for their temperament in terms of their degree of inhibition. When 31 months of age, the children were separated into groups qualified as uninhibited, inhibited, or intermediate in inhibition, with the classification based on criteria related to their peer play behavior. The inhibited group seemed shy, wary, and hesitant to approach novel people and toys (e.g., robot, tunnel). The uninhibited children were quite social and outgoing.

Eight months later, the children were tested for hemispheric asymmetries in regional cortical activation using EEG procedures. Compared to the uninhibited children, the inhibited children showed more right-side frontal lobe activation, when at rest and as measured by the EEG, and the intermediate group showed results between the two others.

According to Davidson and colleagues, the inhibited children's particular deficit appears to have been a less active left frontal lobe activation, although the authors acknowledged that different types of inhibition pathways might be possible for inhibited children. All these studies provide further evidence in support of the current hypothesis that the right hemisphere is specialized for general inhibitory damping, in contrast to the more complex activation–inhibition skills of the left hemisphere.

Similarly, Fox et al. (1991; in Fox, 1992) observed the extent of behavioral inhibition in 24-month-olds placed in a variety of novel situations (tunnel, toy robot, clown, stranger). Inhibited compared to uninhibited children showed more right hemisphere activation 2 months later, according to EEG measurement taken when the infants were observed watching bubbles being blown and watching a segment of Sesame Street.

In related research, Fox et al. (1992; Bell & Fox, 1994) found that infants from 9 to 24 months of age who cried quickly in response to brief maternal separation, compared to those who did not, exhibited more right frontal activation, as measured by concurrent EEG readings. Fox et al. (1991) studied 14-month-old infants who cried at maternal separation. They examined their EEG patterns 2 months later in the two conditions mentioned above where they watched interesting events. Criers compared to noncriers manifested greater right frontal activation. Fox (1992) investigated 7–12-month-olds longitudinally in the same situations, and stable criers (on 3 or more visits out of 7) exhibited greater relative right frontal activation. Fox and Calkins (1993) reported that emotionally positive 4-month-olds exhibited left frontal activation at 9 months of age, whereas negative 4-month-olds showed the opposite pattern. Also, infants classified as ambivalent-resistant and avoidant, in terms of insecure attachment to the primary caregiver, showed the same opposition.

Fox, Calkins, and Bell (1994; Calkins et al., 1996) divided the longitudinal sample of the previous studies into three groups – right frontal in EEG asymmetry at both

9 and 24 months, left frontal in asymmetry, and a change group (one way or the other). The right group was the most behaviorally inhibited at 14 months and the least impulsive and the most compliant and tolerant of frustration at 24 months. Some interesting interaction effects also were found. To summarize, right frontal inhibited or temperamentally negative infants were the most inhibited, although some of these infants were no longer inhibited at 24 months (presumably due to transactional, supportive environmental events) [Ancillary research by Bell and Fox (1994) found that infants who succeeded on a behavioral skill task requiring the inhibition of a prepotent response (the A-not-B problem) manifested a developmental increase in left frontal activity measured in the resting state.] Finally, Fox (1994) reported that 4-year-olds who were socially inhibited in same-sex peer play in the laboratory were hypoactive in the left frontal lobe 2 weeks later, according to EEG recordings during a visual attention task, whereas sociable children were active in the left frontal lobe 2 weeks later.

*Mothers.* Dawson et al. (2000) studied attachment security in 13–15-month-old infants in relation to maternal depression and frontal region EEG asymmetry. They found that infants of mothers who were depressed and infants who were classified as insecurely attached both exhibited reduced right frontal EEG activity. Calkins and Fox (1992) found that infants who expressed right frontal EEG asymmetry were more likely to be classified as resistant in attachment. Dawson, Klinger, Panatgiotides, and Spieker (1992) found that infants classified as secure in attachment and who had depressed mothers exhibited reduced left frontal EEG activity in response to an elicitor of positive affect.

Dawson et al. (1992, 1994) found that 11–17-month-old infants of mothers with symptoms of depression compared to controls showed reduced left frontal region EEG activity during mother–infant playful interaction, and yet, an increase of activation in this region during maternal separation, a situation in which they were less behaviorally distressed than controls. Dawson, Klinger, Panagiotides, Hill, and Spieker (1992; Dawson, 1994b) noted that securely attached infants of symptomatic mothers compared to control mothers manifested less left frontal activation in peekaboo and baseline situations, whereas no difference in this regard was found for insecure infants.

Reissland, Hopkins, Helms, and Williams (2009) found that most mothers cradle infants to the left side of their body. In addition, an absence of left-sided cradling seems to be related to maternal depression. Donnot, Vauclair, and Bréjard (2008) found that newborn right-side holding was affected by depressive symptoms, but only in bottle-feeding mothers and not breastfeeding mothers. They surmised that the determination of side of infant-holding preference is multifactorial and relates to laterality factors and the mother's psychological condition.

*Happiness.* Dawson et al. (1992) reported that 21-month-olds exhibited more left frontal lobe activation during happy expressions, and right activation during sad expressions. Reilly, Stiles, Larsen, and Trauner (1995) found more left frontal activation during felt smiles in 10-month-olds, e.g., to a mother's reach, and more right frontal activation during unfelt wary smiles, e.g., to the approach of a stranger. Similarly, Ekman and Davidson (1993) reported left frontal lobe activation for genuine Duchenne smiling in undergraduates.

Dawson (1994a) also reported that in the infants that she studied anger is left-hemisphere activating. This supports the notion that there is more to hemispheric specialization than laterality of positive emotions to the left and negative emotions or stress to the right. However, whether the common factor underlying happiness and anger concern approach compared to withdrawal is open to debate. The present hypothesis that it concerns an underlying activation–inhibition coordination skill makes more sense, as discussed below.

Trevarthen and Aitken (1994) examined infant manual behaviors in different emotional contexts. They reported that during utterances elicited during happy protoconversations the right compared to the left hand was raised to a higher level and its digits made expressive movements more frequently. Also, infants who were distressed, frightened, or alone touched their mouths more with the right hand and their bodies more with the left hand. These results are consonant with those above.

*Adults.* Aron (2008) examined in adults executive functions and their relations to the frontal cortex. Using fMRI, he found relationships between certain cognitive components and localized discrete, but structurally interconnected, brain regions. For example, in laboratory tasks, he found that especially in the right hemisphere the inferior frontal cortex is critical for the behavior of stopping (Aron, 2007). In addition, Aron, Behrens, Smith, Frank, and Poldrack (2007) found that the degree of right inferior frontal cortex activation predicts the speed of stopping behavior. Aron and Poldrack (2006) found that a basal ganglia region in the subthalamic nucleus is involved in inhibitory control.

The authors built a model of wider interacting functional neuroanatomic networks in executive function. Moreover, the presupplementary motor area has been found to be relevant in this type of behavioral executive control (Nachev, Wydell, O'Neill, Husain, & Kennard, 2007). Aron (2008) proposed that Nachev et al.'s (2007) hypothesis that the presupplementary motor area is involved in "monitoring and resolving response conflict" fits his model of response control. He indicates that the three areas of the brain that have been mentioned are involved not only in canceling or stopping a response but also in breaking or slowing it. Another component of the proposed network is the dorsolateral prefrontal cortex, which is important for maintaining goals and roles (Bunge, 2004).

According to Aron (2008), a cardinal hypothesis about the role of the frontal cortex in executive control is that it functions to "inhibit and activate" representations in subcortical or posterior cortical brain regions (Miller & Cohen, 2001). Coxon, Stinear, and Byblow (2006) demonstrated that stopping takes place via an active inhibition of (potential) response tendencies and not by activation of antagonist muscle groups. These data suggest that behavioral inhibition is paralleled by neurocognitive inhibitory mechanisms that actively suppress interfering behavior. This suggests that inhibition is a valid concept both behaviorally and for the brain. As for the relevance of Aron's work for my work, it supports the notion that activation–inhibition coordination is critical to left hemisphere function, and as a corollary, other types of less complex inhibition are localized in the right hemisphere.

## Comment

Davidson (e.g., 1993) presented a model that tried to integrate these diverse findings. In it, he distinguished between hemispheric under- and overactivation as well as left and right hemisphere functioning. He maintained that left hemisphere overactivation is conducive to approach-related emotions such as mania and anger, and its underactivation facilitates depressive feelings (and I would add positive emotion-pleasure deprivation). Similarly, right hemisphere overactivation leads to withdrawal-related emotions, such as fear and disgust. Because Davidson did not discuss the fourth quadrant of the model, to complete it, I would add that right hemisphere underactivation should lead to apathy, emotional confusion, and the like.

More recent work is parsing out the lateralization of approach–withdrawal and positive and negative emotionality. For example, Balconi and Mazza (2010) examined whether the behavioral activation system (BAS) and the behavioral inhibition system (BIS) are "explicative factors" in motivational/emotional processes that are lateralized in electroencephalogram (EEG) alpha band power activity variations. They examined 19 adults who looked at a range of facial expressions. The anterior frontal sites were most active, and they exhibited a laterality effect, with increased left frontal activity for positive emotions and increased right frontal activity for negative, aversive emotions. In addition, the study examined the relationship of responses on a questionnaire on BIS and BAS and hemisphere activation for the emotional stimuli. BAS participants were more responsive to happiness in the left frontal region, and BIS participants responded more in the right region for a series of negative emotions.

It is noted that anger generated more right frontal activity, consistent with the model that the left hemisphere is specialized for positive emotions and they cannot be translated into approach-related emotions. Nevertheless, in some contexts, anger might elicit more left than right hemisphere activity, if it is translated into an activation–inhibition coordination dynamic, as explained next. In addition, anger might be more approach-related in its initial emergence in infancy (as per the research above), and then as it leads to blockages and frustrations instead of the alterations and successes sought, it could lead to more overwhelming arousal and intensity and take on more often a negative valence.

Although Davidson's model of the lateralization of emotional expression is intriguing, it cannot integrate readily more general findings in the field, such as the traditional notion that the right hemisphere is specialized for spatial skills, in particular (in what way are spatial skills equivalent to withdrawal?). Also, the model fails to consider cross-hemisphere and inhibition factors, which are underscored in the following.

(a) *Left hemisphere*. In general, it might be that a consistent inhibition or a brief coordination of inhibition with activation (e.g., in shyness, in fear, in withdrawal, in sadness, in flat negative emotion, in being raised by a mother with symptoms of depression, in avoidant, insecure attachment) are more conducive to right hemisphere function, either in the sense of right hemisphere overactivation or an underactivation of left hemisphere function because the left hemisphere is more taken with refined inhibition skills.

(b) *Right hemisphere*. The latter left-hemisphere skills would include any inter-coordination of activation and inhibition over time in order to execute subtle sequential behaviors (e.g., happy interactions, search for the missing mother, coping reactions, anger in certain contexts, ambivalence in attachment, fine motor behavior, language).

## Invariant Lateralization

### *Models*

Hämäläinen and Takio (2010) reviewed different models of the development of cerebral hemisphere asymmetry. The invariant lateralization model (e.g., Bryden, 1982; Kinsbourne & Hiscock, 1983) speaks to a congenital left-hemisphere specialization for language that remains constant across the life span. The equipotential-progressive perspective maintains that there is a bilateral symmetry in function that gradually modifies to allow for cerebral dominance for language (Lenneberg, 1967).

Several major models of progressive lateralization in the development of hemispheric specialization have been proposed which differ significantly from the standard bilateral to left shift one. There is no room to explore other models of progressive lateralization in development. The interested reader is referred to Young (1990a, b) where the progressive stage, transfer, and addition models are described in detail. Also, see Boles, Barth, and Merrill (2008) for their proposed neurodevelopmental model related to developmental limits at different ages.

In the following section, I examine data that supports an invariant lateralization model that favors the right side and other evidence in support of the left side. The data for the latter position is stronger.

#### Early Right

Portions of the right temporal lobe mature earlier than the left in the fetus (Chi, Dooling, & Gilles, 1977a, 1977b; De Schonen & Mathivet, 1989). Also, the fetal right temporal gyrus more quickly attains adult levels of choline acetyltransferase activity than its homologous region in the left hemisphere (Bracco, Tiezzi, Ginanneschi, Campanella, & Amaducci, 1984). Simonds and Scheibel (1989) found that basilar dendritic patterns in layer 5 cortical pyramids of human brains as young as 3 months revealed the right hemisphere as more prominent than the left in the first year.

At the cortical macro/gross anatomical level, the left compared to the right hemisphere language areas seem larger even in the fetal period (Simonds & Scheibel, 1989).

However, at the cortical microenvironmental level, the dendritic data indicate an early right-hemisphere maturational advantage.

Dubois et al. (2007) mapped early cortical folding in the preterm newborn brain using magnetic resonance images. They found a larger right superior temporal sulcus, suggesting an initial delay in the maturation of the gyral complexity in the left hemisphere. They argued that this is consistent with the notion that the left hemisphere relative to the right is more influenced by the in utero environment and less by genetic control.

However, the earlier right hemisphere maturation might not be long lasting (e.g., several weeks; Chi et al.). Therefore, the functional significance of any early right hemisphere maturation might be hard to determine and may be negligible.

## Multiple

Other patterns in maturation have been found. For example, Best (1988) described a three-dimensional torque twisting in hemispheric maturation. There may be multiple gradients of maturation, with no clear left or right hemisphere advantage (Greenough, 1989).

Whitaker and colleagues (Campbell & Whitaker, 1986; Satz, Strauss, & Whitaker, 1990; Whitaker, Bub, & Leventer, 1981) examined Yakovlev's (1962) data on the developing cortex in terms of its layer width, dendritic arborization, myelination, neurodensity, etc. It became clear that maturation of the areas for language in the cortical mantle is multifactorial, for it varies both spatially and temporally across the life span. Primarily, there is an anterior–posterior movement that begins in two loci, the peri-Sylvan and peri-Rolandic regions, and ends with two others, the parietal and angulus gyrus regions. According to Fig. 1 (p. 606) in Satz et al., each region is characterized by an upward, downward, and forward expansion as it matures, except for the peri-Rolandic one, which pushes posteriorly instead of anteriorly. Data in support of this progressive view of lateralization development have been obtained in research on childhood aphasia.

## Early Left

In contrast to the findings above that favor early right hemisphere maturation, an early left-side hemispheric maturational gradient has been found that is consistent with the typical finding of a left hemisphere specialization for language-related/focused, motoric skills. Witelson and Pallie (1973) and Wada, Clarke, and Hamm (1975) found that language zones, such as the planum temporale and Sylvian fissure, are larger on the left side in neonates as early as 28 weeks of gestation. Kooistra and Heilman (1988) analyzed 18 normal brains as young as 28 weeks gestational age for asymmetry in volume of the subcortical globus pallidus, which is important in arm movement control. They found that the left side was larger.

The more focal somatosensory representation in the left hemisphere (Trotman & Hammond, 1989), along with its relative lack of transcortical connections and its greater regional variability (Gur et al., 1980), might contribute to the left hemisphere's superior inhibitory specialization. Similarly, Goldberg and Costa (1981) suggest that the left hemisphere is marked by better intraregional connections (focal, dense networking).

Pena et al. (2003) played speech sounds and backward speech to newborns who were sleeping, and they found in the forward speech condition an increase in left temporal lobe blood flow, in particular. Dehaene-Lambertz, Dehaene, and Hertz-Pannier (2002) compared the effect of presenting forward and backward speech or silence to young infants. Compared to the silent condition, the speech conditions activated the left temporal lobe. As for the right hemisphere, Homae, Watanabe, Nakano, Asakawa, and Taga (2006) found right temporoparietal blood flow especially for prosody or intonation.

Liégeois, Cross, Pokey, Harness, and Vargha-Khadem (2008) examined language skills after hemispherectomy in children. Of the 30 patients examined, 19 had prenatal or perinatal pathology due to epilepsy. These patients were contrasted with those who had normal development for at least 20 months, and often more. The patients were assessed 1-year postsurgery on a variety of language tasks, in particular. The study found that children with a lone left or right hemisphere could develop well their receptive vocabularies. However, early pathology that had affected the left or the right hemisphere and postnatal damage to the left hemisphere resulted in substantial language difficulties as well as problems in short-term verbal memory, with some difficulty in verbal intelligence also present.

Dubois, Hertz-Pannier, Cachia, Mangin, Le Bihan, and Dehaene-Lambertz (2009) examined in vivo structural asymmetries in the cerebral hemispheres from 4 to 18 weeks using diffusion tensor imaging. They found early leftward-directed asymmetries in two regions studied – the arcuate fasciculus and in the corticospinal tract – with no change in degree of difference over the age period. They concluded that there is an early temporoparietofrontal connection through the left arcuate fasciculus that develops in an efficient manner. It might function to underwrite the development of speech perception and production, which the research has shown to be better organized in the left hemisphere early on. Dehaene-Lambertz, Hertz-Pannier, and Dubois (2006) indicated that strong bias for speech processing in the right side of the brain early in life has a genetic basis.

## Summary

The hand of the newborn appears to move in an erratic manner without pattern or preference. However, the behavior is more than reflexive, and it expresses specializations consistent with underlying patterns of hemispheric specialization found in the adult. Any absence of supporting evidence could reflect an absence of appropriate methodology. Further, the underlying laterality and functional significance of the behavior could reflect a left hemisphere specialization for activation–inhibition coordination with a different set of inhibition specializations in the right hemisphere. The dimension of activation–inhibition coordination appears to mark the development of behavior and the brain from early in life onward. The following chapters continue to treat its prevalence and relevance.

## References

Aron, A. R. (2007). The neural basis of inhibition in cognitive control. *Neuroscientist, 13*, 214–228.

Aron, A. R. (2008). Progress in executive-function research: From tasks to functions to regions networks. *Current Directions in Psychological Science, 17*, 124–129.

Aron, A. R., Behrens, T. E., Smith, S., Frank, M. J., & Poldrack, R. A. (2007). Converging evidence for a fronto-basal-ganglia network for inhibitory control of action and cognition. *Journal of Neuroscience, 27*, 11860–11864.

Aron, A. R., & Poldrack, R. A. (2006). Cortical and subcortical contributions to stop signal response inhibition: Role of the subthalamic nucleus. *Journal of Neuroscience, 26*, 2424–2433.

Balconi, M., & Mazza, G. (2010). Lateralisation effect in comprehension of emotional facial expression: A comparison between EEG alpha band power and behavioral inhibition (BIS) and activation (BAS) systems. *Laterality, 15*, 361–384.

Bell, M. A., & Fox, N. A. (1994). Brain development over the first year of life: Relations between electroencephalographic frequency and coherence and cognitive and affective behaviors. In G. Dawson & K. W. Fischer (Eds.), *Human behavior and the developing brain* (pp. 314–345). New York: Guilford Press.

Bertoncini, J., Morais, J., Bijeljac-Babic, R., McAdams, S., Peretz, I., & Mehler, J. (1989). Dichotic perception and laterality in neonates. *Brain and Language, 37*, 591–605.

Best, C. T. (1988). The emergence of cerebral asymmetries for perceptual and cognitive functions in infancy. In D. L. Molfese & S. J. Segalowitz (Eds.), *Brain lateralization in children: Developmental implications* (pp. 5–34). New York: Guilford Press.

Boles, D. B., Barth, J. M., & Merrill, E. C. (2008). Asymmetry and performance: Toward a neurodevelopmental theory. *Brain and Cognition, 66*, 124–139.

Bracco, L., Tiezzi, A., Ginanneschi, A., Campanella, C., & Amaducci, L. (1984). Lateralization of choline acetyltransferase (Ch. AT) activity in fetus and adult human brain. *Neurosciences Letters, 50*, 301–305.

Bryden, M. P. (1982). *Laterality: Functional asymmetry in the human brain*. New York: Academic Press.

Bunge, S. A. (2004). How we use rules to select actions: A review of evidence from cognitive neuroscience. *Cognitive, Affective, & Behavioral Neuroscience, 4*, 564–579.

Calkins, S. D., & Fox, N. A. (1992). The relations among infant temperament, security of attachment, and behavioral inhibition at twenty-four months. *Child Development, 63*, 1456–1472.

Calkins, S. D., Fox, N. A., & Marshall, T. R. (1996). Behavioral and physiological antecedents of inhibited and uninhibited behavior. *Child Development, 67*, 523–540.

Campbell, S., & Whitaker, H. A. (1986). Cortical maturation and developmental neurolinguistics. In J. E. Obrzut & G. W. Hynd (Eds.), *Child neuropsychology* (pp. 55–72). New York: Academic Press.

Case, R. (1992). The role of the frontal lobes in the regulation of cognitive development. *Brain and Cognition, 20*, 51–73.

Chi, J. G., Dooling, E. C., & Gilles, F. H. (1977a). Left-right asymmetries of the temporal speech areas of the human foetus. *Archives of Neurology, 34*, 346–348.

Chi, J. G., Dooling, E. C., & Gilles, F. H. (1977b). Gyral development of the human brain. *Annals of Neurology, 1*, 86–93.
Coxon, J. P., Stinear, C. M., & Byblow, W. D. (2006). Intracortical inhibition during volitional inhibition of prepared action. *Journal of Neurophysiology, 95*, 3371–3383.
Davidson, R. J. (1991). Cerebral asymmetry and affective disorders: A developmental approach. In D. Cicchetti & S. L. Toth (Eds.), *Internalizing and externalizing expressions of dysfunction: Rochester symposium and developmental psychopathology* (Vol. 2, pp. 123–154). Hillsdale: Erlbaum.
Davidson, R. J. (1992a). Emotions and affective style: Hemispheric substrates. *Psychological Science, 3*, 39–43.
Davidson, R. J. (1992b). Prolegomenon to the structure of emotion: Gleanings from neuropsychology. *Cognition and Emotion, 6*, 245–268.
Davidson, R. J. (1992c). Anterior cerebral asymmetry and the nature of emotion. *Brain and Cognition, 20*, 125–151.
Davidson, R. J. (1993). Cerebral asymmetry and emotion: Conceptual and methodological conundrums. *Cognition and Emotion, 7*, 115–138.
Davidson, R. J. (1994). Asymmetric brain function, affective style and psychopathology: The role of early experience and plasticity. *Development and Psychopathology, 6*, 741–758.
Davidson, R. J., & Fox, N. A. (1989). Frontal brain asymmetry predicts infants' response to maternal separation. *Journal of Abnormal Psychology, 98*, 127–131.
Dawson, G. (1994a). Frontal electrophysiological correlates of individual differences in emotional expression in infancy: A brain systems perspective on emotion. In N. A. Fox (Ed.), The development of emotion regulation: Biological and behavioral considerations. *Monograph of the Society for Research in Child Development, 59*, 135–152.
Dawson, G. (1994b). Development of emotional expression and emotion regulation in infancy: Contributions of the frontal lobe. In G. Dawson & K. Fischer (Eds.), *Human behavior and the developing brain* (pp. 346–378). New York: Guilford Press.
Dawson, G., Ashman, D. B., Hessl, D., Frey, K., Panagiotides, H., Yamada, E., et al. (2000). Infants of depressed mothers exhibit atypical frontal electrical brain activity during interactions with mother and with a familiar, non-depressed adult. *Child Development, 71*, 145–152.
Dawson, G., Hessl, D., & Frey, K. (1994). Social influences on early developing biological and behavioral systems related to risk for affective disorder. *Development and Psychopathology, 6*, 759–779.
Dawson, G., Klinger, L. G., Panagiotides, H., Hill, D., & Spieker, S. (1992). Frontal lobe activity and effective behavior of infants of mothers with depressive symptoms. *Child Development, 63*, 725–737.
Dawson, G., Panagiotides, H., Klinger, L. G., & Hill, D. (1992). The role of frontal lobe functioning in the development of infant self-regulatory behavior. *Brain and Cognition, 20*, 152–175.
de Schonen, S., & Mathivet, E. (1989). First come, first served: A scenario about the development of hemispheric specialization in face recognition during infancy. *Cahiers de Psychologie Cognitive, 9*, 3–44.
Dehaene-Lambertz, G. (2000). Cerebral specialization for speech and non-speech stimuli in infants. *Journal of Cognitive Neuroscience, 12*, 449–460.
Dehaene-Lambertz, G., Dehaene, S., & Hertz-Pannier, L. (2002). Functional neuroimaging of speech perception in infants. *Science, 298*, 2013–2016.
Dehaene-Lambertz, G., Hertz-Pannier, L., & Dubois, J. (2006). Nature and nurture in language acquisition: Anatomical and functional brain-imaging studies in infants. *Neurosciences, 29*, 367–372.
Donnot, J., Vauclair, J., & Bréjard, V. (2008). Newborn right-holding is related to depressive symptoms in bottle-feeding mothers but not in breastfeeding mothers. *Infant Behavior & Development, 31*, 352–360.
Dubois, J., Benders, M., Cachia, A., Lazeyras, F., Ha-Vinh, L. R., Sizonenko, S. V., et al. (2007). Mapping the early cortical folding process in the preterm newborn brain. *Cerebral Cortex, 18*, 1444–1454.

Dubois, J., Hertz-Pannier, L., Cachia, A., Mangin, J. F., Le Bihan, D., & Dehaene-Lambertz, G. (2009). Structural asymmetries in the infant language and sensori-motor networks. *Cerebral Cortex, 19*, 414–423.

Ekman, P., & Davidson, R. J. (1993). Voluntary smiling changes regional brain activity. *Psychological Science, 4*, 342–345.

Fagard, J., Spelke, E., & von Hofsten, C. (2009). Reaching and grasping a moving object in 6-, 8-, and 10-month-old infants: Laterality and performance. *Infant Behavior & Development, 32*, 137–146.

Fagot, J., & Bard, K. A. (1995). Asymmetric grasping response in neonate chimpanzees (Pan troglodytes). *Infant Behavior and Development, 18*, 253–255.

Finman, R., Davidson, R. J., Colton, M. B., Strauss, A. M., & Kagan, J. (1989). Psychophysiological correlates of inhibition to the unfamiliar in children. *Psychophysiology, 26*, S24.

Fox, N. A. (1991). If it's not left, it's right: Electroencephalograph asymmetry and the development of emotion. *American Psychologist, 46*, 863–872.

Fox, N. A. (1992). Frontal brain asymmetry and vulnerability to stress: Individual differences in infant temperament. In T. M. Field, P. M. McCabe, & N. Schneiderman (Eds.), *Stress and coping in infancy and childhood* (pp. 83–100). Hillsdale: Erlbaum.

Fox, N. A. (1994). Dynamic cerebral processes underlying emotion regulation. In N. A. Fox (Ed.), *The development of emotion regulation: Biological and behavioral considerations* (pp. 152–166). *Monographs of the Society for Research in Child Development, 59*, (2/3, Serial No. 240).

Fox, N. A., Bell, M. A., & Aaron, N. (1991). *The relation of frontal brain asymmetry to attachment behavior and behavioral inhibition in 14- and 24-month-old children*. Unpublished manuscript, University of Maryland, College Park, MD.

Fox, N. A., Bell, M. A., & Jones, N. A. (1992). Individual differences in response to others and cerebral asymmetry. *Developmental Neuropsychology, 8*, 161–184.

Fox, N. A., & Calkins, S. D. (1993). Pathways to aggression and social withdrawal: Interactions among temperament, attachment, and regulation. In K. H. Rubin & J. B. Asendorpf (Eds.), *Social withdrawal, inhibition, and shyness in childhood* (pp. 81–100). Hillsdale: Erlbaum.

Fox, N. A., Calkins, S. D., & Bell, M. A. (1994). Neural plasticity and development in the first two years of life: Evidence from cognitive and socioemotional domains of research. *Development and Psychopathology, 6*, 677–696.

Fox, N. A., & Davidson, R. J. (1984). Hemispheric substrates of affect: A developmental model. In N. A. Fox & R. J. Davidson (Eds.), *The psychobiology of affective development* (pp. 353–381). Hillsdale: Erlbaum.

Fox, N. A., & Davidson, R. J. (1988). Patterns of brain electrical activity during facial signs of emotion in ten month old infants. *Developmental Psychology, 24*, 230–236.

Fox, N. A., & Davidson, R. J. (1991). Hemispheric specialization and attachment behaviors: Developmental processes and individual differences in separation protest. In J. L. Gewirtz & W. M. Kurtines (Eds.), *Interactions with attachment* (pp. 147–164). Hillsdale: Erlbaum.

Fox, N. A., & Hane, A. A. (2008). Studying the biology of human attachment. In J. Cassidy & P. R. Shaver (Eds.), *Handbook of attachment: Theory, research, and clinical applications* (2nd ed., pp. 217–240). New York: Guilford Press.

Gold, J. M., Goldberg, T. E., & Weinberger, D. R. (1992). Prefrontal function and schizophrenic symptoms. *Neuropsychiatry, Neuropsychology, and Behavioral Neurology, 5*, 253–261.

Goldberg, E., & Costa, L. (1981). Hemispheric differences in the acquisition and use of descriptive systems. *Brain and Language, 14*, 144–173.

Greenough, W. T. (1989). On detecting asynchronies in brain development: Interpretations of morphological data. *Cahiers de Psychologie Cognitive, 9*, 77–79.

Gur, R., Packer, I., Hungerbuhler, J., Reivich, M., Obrist, W., Amarnek, W., et al. (1980). Differences in the distribution of gray and white matter in human cerebral hemispheres. *Science, 207*, 1226–1228.

Hämäläinen, H., & Takio, F. (2010). Integrating auditory and visual asymmetry. In K. Hugdahl & R. Westerhausen (Eds.), *The two halves of the brain: Information processing in the cerebral hemispheres* (pp. 417–437). Cambridge: MIT Press.

Hane, A. A., Fox, N. A., Henderson, H. A., & Marshall, P. J. (2008). Behavioral reactivity and approach-withdrawal bias in infancy. *Developmental Psychology, 44*, 1491–1496.

Homae, F., Watanabe, H., Nakano, T., Asakawa, K., & Taga, G. (2006). The right hemisphere of sleeping infants perceives sentential prosody. *Neuroscience Research, 54*, 276–280.

Hopkins, W. D., & Bard, K. A. (1993). Hemispheric specialization in infant chimpanzees (Pan troglodytes): Evidence for a relation with gender and arousal. *Developmental Psychobiology, 26*, 219–235.

Kinsbourne, M., & Hiscock, M. (1983). The normal and deviant development of functional lateralization of the brain. In M. Haith & M. Campos (Eds.), *Handbook of child psychology: Vol. 2* (Infancy and developmental psychobiology 4th ed., pp. 157–280). New York: Wiley.

Kooistra, C. A., & Heilman, K. M. (1988). Motor dominance and lateral asymmetry of the globus pallidus. *Neurology, 38*, 388–390.

Lenneberg, E. H. (1967). *Biological foundations of language*. New York: Wiley.

Liégeois, F., Cross, J. H., Polkey, C., Harkness, W., & Vargha-Khadem, F. (2008). Language after hemispherectomy in childhood: Contributions from memory and intelligence. *Neuropsychologia, 46*, 3101–3107.

Logan, G. D. (1995). Linguistic and conceptual control of visual spatial attention. *Cognitive Psychology, 28*, 103–174.

McCartney, G., & Hepper, P. (1999). Development of lateralized behavior in the human fetus from 12 to 17 weeks'gestation. *Developmental Medicine and Child Neurology, 41*, 83–86.

Michel, G. F., Tyler, A. N., Ferre, C., & Sheu, C. (2006). The manifestation of infant hand-use preferences when reaching for objects during the seven-to thirteen-month age period. *Developmental Psychobiology, 48*, 436–443.

Miller, E. K., & Cohen, J. D. (2001). An integrative theory of prefrontal cortex function. *Annual Review of Neuroscience, 24*, 167–202.

Morange, F., & Bloch, H. (1996). Lateralization of the approach movement and the prehension movement in infants from 4 to 7 months. *Early Development and Parenting, 5*, 81–92.

Morange-Majoux, F. (2010). Manual exploration of consistency (soft vs hard) and handedness in infants from 4 to 6 months old. *Laterality: Asymmetries of Body, Brain and Cognition, 16*, 292–312.

Nachev, P., Wydell, H., O'Neil, K., Husain, M., & Kennard, C. (2007). The role of the pre-supplementary motor area in the control of action. *Neuroimage, 36*(Suppl. 2), T155–T163.

Netz, J., Ziemann, U., & Homberg, V. (1995). Hemispheric asymmetry of transcallosal inhibition in man. *Experimental Brain Research, 104*, 527–533.

Norman, D. A., & Shallice, T. (1986). Attention to action: Willed and automatic control of behavior. In R. J. Davidson, G. E. Schwartz, & D. Shapiro (Eds.), *Consciousness and self-regulation* (Vol. 4, pp. 1–18). New York: Plenum.

Ottaviano, S., Guidetti, V., Allemand, F., Spinetoli, B., & Seri, S. (1989). Laterality of arm movement in full-term newborn. *Early Human Development, 19*, 3–7.

Pena, M., Maki, A., Kovacic, D., Dahaene-Lambertz, G., Koizumi, H., Bouquet, F., et al. (2003). Sounds and silence: An optical topography study of language recognition at birth. *Proceedings of the National Academy of Science USA, 100*, 11702–11705.

Reilly, J. S., Stiles, J., Larsen, J., & Trauner, D. (1995). Affective facial expression in infants with focal brain damage. *Neuropsychologia, 33*, 83–99.

Reissland, N., Hopkins, B., Helms, P., & Williams, B. (2009). Maternal stress and depression and the lateralisation of infant cradling. *Journal of Child Psychology and Psychiatry, 50*, 263–269.

Satz, P., Strauss, E., & Whitaker, H. (1990). The ontogeny of hemispheric specialization: Some old hypotheses revisited. *Brain and Language, 38*, 596–614.

Shahinfar, A., Schmidt, L. A., & Fox, N. A. (1996). *Right frontal EEG hypoactivation in aggressive toddlers*. Paper presented at the 36th Annual Meeting of the Society for Psychophysiological Research, Vancouver, British Columbia, Canada.

Simonds, R. J., & Scheibel, A. B. (1989). The postnatal development of the motor speech area: A preliminary study. *Brain and Language, 37*, 42–58.

Trevarthen, C., & Aitken, K. J. (1994). Brain development, infant communication, and empathy disorders: Intrinsic factors in child mental health. *Development and Psychopathology, 6*, 597–633.

Trotman, S. C. A., & Hammond, G. R. (1989). Lateral asymmetry of the scalp distribution of somatosensory evoked potential amplitude. *Brain and Cognition, 10*, 132–147.

Vauclair, J., & Imbault, J. (2009). Relationship between manual preferences for object manipulation and pointing gestures in infants and toddlers. *Developmental Science, 12*, 1060–1069.

Wada, J., Clarke, R., & Hamm, A. (1975). Cerebral hemispheric asymmetry in humans. *Archives of Neurology, 32*, 239–246.

Wentworth, N., Benson, J. B., & Haith, M. M. (2000). The development of infants' reaches for stationary and moving targets. *Child Development, 71*, 576–601.

Whitaker, H. A., Bub, D., & Leventer, S. (1981). Neurolinguistic aspects of language acquisition and bilingualism. In H. Winitz (Ed.), *Native language and foreign language acquisition* (pp. 59–74). New York: New York Academy of Sciences.

Witelson, S. F., & Pallie, W. (1973). Left hemisphere specialization for language in the newborn: Neuroanatomical evidence of asymmetry. *Brain, 96*, 641–646.

Yakovlev, P. I. (1962). Morphological criteria of growth and maturation of the nervous system in man. *Research Publications – Association for Research in Nervous and Mental Disease, 39*, 3–46.

Young, G. (1990a). Early neuropsychological development: Lateralization of functions - hemispheric specialization. In C. A. Hauert (Ed.), *Developmental psychology: Cognitive, perceptuo-motor and neuropsychological perspectives* (pp. 113–181). Amsterdam: North Holland.

Young, G. (1990b). The development of hemispheric and manual specialization. In G. E. Hammond (Ed.), *Cerebral control of speech and limb movements* (pp. 79–139). Amsterdam: North Holland.

Young, G. (1997). *Adult development, therapy, and culture: A postmodern synthesis*. New York: Plenum.

Young, G., Bowman, J. G., Methot, C., Finlayson, M., Quintal, J., & Boissonneault, P. (1983). Hemispheric specialization development: What (inhibition) and how (parents). In G. Young, S. J. Segalowitz, C. M. Carter, & S. E. Trehub (Eds.), *Manual specialization and the developing brain* (pp. 119–140). New York: Academic Press.

Young, G., & Chapman, C. R. (2007). Pain, affect, nonlinear dynamical systems, and chronic pain: Bringing order to disorder. In G. Young, A. W. Kane, & K. Nicholson, *Causality of psychological injury: Presenting evidence in court* (pp. 197–241). New York: Springer Science, Business Media.

Young, G., & Gagnon, M. (1990). Neonatal laterality, birth stress, familial sinistrality, and left brain inhibition. *Developmental Neuropsychology, 6*, 127–150.

# Chapter 26
# Lateralization and Developing Cognition

## Introduction

In this chapter, I describe evidence relating early lateralization and developing cognition. Then, I present my model on the topic. It involves the present Neo-Piagetian model and the concept of activation–inhibition coordination in left hemisphere specialization. I apply the model to relations between ontogenesis and phylogenesis, and speculate on the evolutionary sequences that have led to contemporary peoples.

## Early Lateralization and Developing Cognition

### *Evidence*

#### Children

According to Crow (2010), Annett and Kilshaw (1984) proposed the concept that lateralization is an important determinant of cognitive ability. Crow reported two cohort studies in support of the concept. Crow, Crow, Done, and Leask (1998) studied 11-year-olds. A measure of relative hand skill predicted verbal and nonverbal cognitive ability, as well as reading and mathematical skills. Peters, Reimers, and Manning (2006) studied an Internet survey in which participants filled in a self-report measure of handedness and completed simple tests of verbal and spatial ability. Right-handers had an advantage in verbal ability.

To what extent can any model of neurological development help in understanding Neo-Piagetian cognitive development? That is, are there data that suggest a correspondence across the two domains? There is increasing evidence that cognitive advance from the Piagetian perspective is partially related to underlying neurological maturation. For example, Stauder, Molenaar, and van der Mole (1993; van der Mole & Molenaar, 1994) investigated the relationship between event-related brain potentials (ERPs) on an anologue Piagetian task and the presence or absence of Piagetian

G. Young, *Development and Causality: Neo-Piagetian Perspectives*,
DOI 10.1007/978-1-4419-9422-6_26, © Springer Science+Business Media, LLC 2011

conservation in 5–7-year-old girls. Conservers compared to nonconservers, but not older versus younger girls, showed a broad ERP positivity in the centroparietal scalp distribution. Moreover, conservers showed more lateral ERP sources during the later portions of information processing, unlike the nonconservers.

## Infants

In a neuroimaging study, Raz et al. (1994) found that left- and right-side unilateral perinatal cerebral insult in prematures with intracranial hemorrhage was associated in the predicted direction with cognitive asymmetries at 5 years of age (i.e., verbal and nonverbal deficits, respectively). The work of Immordino-Yang (2007, 2008) supports the notion that each hemisphere is specialized for different language functions from early in life. She studied two hemispherectomized boys for their compensation strategies on tasks that normally related to their missing hemisphere. Nico is missing the right cerebral hemisphere, but in prosodic processing, quite difficult for adults with his condition or related ones, he succeeded more than expected by using the residual linguistic categorization skills of his intact left hemisphere. By contrast, Brooke had had his left hemisphere removed and was expected to perform worse on a task of understanding a sarcastic tone of voice in naturalistic vignettes. However, he performed even better than control children, as taken from descriptions of results in the literature. He used a heavily emotional strategy, which helped on this prosodic task, but not on others where emotions were not involved. Despite the compensations expressed by boys to the hemispherectomies, the fundamental specializations in the hemispheres were lost and affected performance in a language-related skill.

## University Students

Virtue and Czarlinski (2010) reported that Virtue and van den Broek (2005) had found that the left hemisphere appears better than the right hemisphere in inhibiting irrelevant or inconsistent information during language tasks. Virtue and Czarlinski (2010) indicated that findings about left hemisphere inhibitory skills include that it better suppresses semantic information when readers have to resolve local inconsistencies in a text (Long & Bayness, 2002). By contrast, the right hemisphere is activated when readers have to resolve global inconsistencies in text (Ferstl, Rinck, & von Cramon, 2005). They also indicated that the left dorsolateral prefrontal cortex (DLPFC) appears to exert inhibitory control over other areas of the brain involved in the selection of attention (Hoenig & Scheef, 2009). Therefore, the DLPFC might be involved in the inhibition of information related to goals during text reading.

Virtue and Czarlinski (2010) studied right-handed university students on a task of reading texts. The texts included characters having original goals and new goals, as well as unrelated information. The study participants performed a lexical decision task about the goals, with the words presented either to the left visual field-right hemisphere or the right visual field-left hemisphere.

The underlying premise of the research was that readers integrate incoming information from a text into the ongoing mental representations being constructed of the text. Further, the degree of relevance of the incoming information will determine whether it is suppressed or enhanced. Moreover, a literature review revealed that the right hemisphere seems to be involved in processing more distantly related concepts. Therefore, the left hemisphere should be more involved in suppressing irrelevant goal-related information, since it deals with more closely related semantic associations.

As for the results, when a new goal was introduced in the task, the left hemisphere expressed decreased facilitation for information about the original goal. By contrast, when the original goal was repeated, the right hemisphere exhibited a greater facilitation. The authors concluded that as the study participants processed goals during narrative text comprehension, the left hemisphere was involved in a suppression function, and in a separate mechanism, the right hemisphere was involved in an enhancement function.

In their discussion of the article, the authors indicated that the hemispheres work together in reading comprehension, with the left hemisphere involved more in the suppression or inhibition function and the right hemisphere in the activation function. I would add that the results are consistent with the present model that the left hemisphere is involved in more complex inhibitory functions, such as activation–inhibition coordination, and the right hemisphere is involved in simpler inhibitory activities.

## Adults

Joliot et al. (2009) studied cognitive inhibition of number/length interference in a Piaget-type numerical task, using a combined electrophysiological marker of event-related potentials and magnetoencephalography. On the task, the heuristic of length equaling number had to be inhibited, and Piaget (1941/1952) would have described the process needed in terms of reversibility and related executive and inhibitory processes. Early and late latencies were analyzed in the combined ERP-MEG recordings. Inhibitory processes were evident on the late components of the electromagnetic brain recordings. In terms of the results in particular for the present purposes, a right frontal orbital region activation in the P2 latency reflected the change of strategy indicative of inhibitory processes at work. The neural networks involved in task completion appear to involve other regions, as well, but in terms inhibition, the right frontal region stood out.

I would add that the type of inhibition involved in the Joliot et al. study concerned the control of interference, so that the results are consistent with the present hypothesis that the left hemisphere specializes in activation–inhibition coordination. Moreover, the Joliot et al. results confirm that lateralization processes have import for cognitive functioning, including on Piagetian-type tasks.

### Interim Summary

There is not much direct research relating Piagetian development and hemispheric specialization. In the present section, I referred to research not only on Piagetian tasks in this regard but also on other cognitive tasks and on language tasks, such as related to text. I described studies with normal children and brain-damaged ones, and covered the age range from infancy to adulthood. Where I could, I related the findings to the concept of activation–inhibition coordination. For me, it is not important to show that the left hemisphere is better for cognitive skills than the right. Rather, I try to show how the hemispheres have their specialized skills, they work together, and they relate to different inhibition functions. In the following, I apply these ideas to the evolution of behavior and the hemispheres, including at the cognitive level.

## *Present Model*

### Introduction

Hopkins and Cantalupo (2008) documented evidence in multiple species of left-hemisphere asymmetries in the processing of species-specific signaling, from frogs and birds to mammals and nonhuman primates. In addition, for the chimpanzee, Cantalupo, Pilcher, and Hopkins (2003) found leftward asymmetries in both the planum temporal and inferior frontal gyrus. Hopkins (2006) found that chimpanzees express a 2:1 ratio in right- to left-handedness on a variety of behavioral measures. They indicated that the archaeological record has found evidence of right-handedness in our ancestors that dates back to at least 2 million years.

Hopkins and Cantalupo (2008) referred to the research of Ghirlanda and Vallortigara (2004), who argued that the evolutionary origins of hemispheric specialization and related lateral asymmetries relate to avoidance strategies in populations being chased by predators. Normally in these situations, a majority of the group escapes in the same turning direction. Corballis (2010) pointed out that the laterality differences in nonhuman species generally are not as marked as in humans and are relatively easily "canceled or reversed."

Although the turning hypothesis is interesting and covers much of the comparative data, there is little reason to suspect that human laterality and hemispheric specializations in all its guises reflect turning tendencies. Nevertheless, evidence does exist for head turning lateralities and their relationship to handedness (Kinsbourne, 2009). In the previous chapter, I present evidence in support of my hypothesis that the hemispheres differ in their inhibitory functions, such that the left hemisphere is specialized for the more refined skill of coordinating activation and inhibition. This model could serve as a one that links the comparative and human research.

Inhibitory skills are essential for survival, development, self-regulation, and adaptive behavior, cognition, language, and related processes. In terms of coordination of turning tendencies to escape predators, individuals in the group must demonstrate an exquisite coordination of activation and inhibition coordination not only in their own muscle activation and interference control but also in their synchronization with others so that they are not on the outside of the group and constitute an easier target.

The model is consistent with the general principal on the topic that I have enunciated; in this regard, I wrote:

> The aesthetic simplicity of the inhibition hypothesis ... should not escape our attention. The concept of inhibition applies fluidly across many levels of psychological analysis.... There are biochemical mediators of inhibition. Inhibition is a central characteristic of neuronal network and central nervous system function. Importance is attached to inhibition in overt behavior at multiple levels: motoric, cognitive, social, personality, etc. Even environmental influences ... can be conceived in these terms (Young, 1990a, p. 119).

## Model

The particular model of developing lateralization proposed in the current theory (Young, 1990a, 1990b) does not refer to specific cerebral regions. A more general organizational pattern was sought in the current work, based on the idea that with development there is a growing neurological base for inhibitory functions within the left hemisphere. As lateralization proceeds through its phases, it is argued that the deployment of an activation–inhibition coordination or balancing helps integrate newly matured zones with previously functional ones. On the one hand, this concept follows from Young's inhibition model of hemispheric specialization. On the other hand, it speaks to Fischer's (1987) argument that periodic spurts in cross-zone synaptogenesis might spark punctuated bursts in skill growth. It also speaks to Damasio's (1989, 1994) concept of convergence zones in the brain, which are thought to help bind information from separated neural networks through codes that phase-lock their coactivation.

The current model is presented in detail in Tables 26.1–26.5. It describes a one-to-one correspondence between underlying central nervous system advances and the specific Neo-Piagetian stages-substages that have been proposed in the present model.

Note that the last five steps in the current 25-step developmental progression are seen to emerge from especially psychological and not macroneurological activation–inhibition coordination advances. However, findings that the brain continues its organization, pruning, and neuronal interconnective growth argues that a neuronal activation–inhibition coordination base underlies, in part, passage through adult developmental stages.

The recent work on dynamic coordinations and networks in the brain speaks to the issues that I have raised, but it is beyond the scope of the present work to describe in depth these fascinating advances in developmental neuroscience. Suffice it to say, there are consistent with the present argument that both the brain and behavior evidence increasing sophistication in activation-inhibition coordination and that mechanisms such as this could underlie developmental progression in both brain and behavior at both the macro and micro levels (Sporns, 2011; von der Malsburg, Phillips, & Singer, 2010).

**Table 26.1** Reflex levels in the development of left brain specialization

| Behavioral specialization (e.g., in right arm-hand) | Central specialization (and inhibition therein) |
|---|---|
| 1. Pairs of single reflexive behaviors (*reflex pairs*) not yet linked to activating mechanisms are evident, but do not manifest in fixed order (e.g., in proximal arm flexion and extension, in distal fingers open and flex; either example in reverse) | At first, reflex centers mature without stimulus sensitive activating mechanisms; nevertheless, they discharge, and this occurs even in pairs through lateral inhibition–activation interplay |
| 2. *Reflexive behavior hierarchies* manifest in two ways. First, they become subordinated to specific stimulus sensitivities in firing. Second, reflexive behavior pairs become fixed in sequence, but with second component only fortuitously on target (e.g., in proximal ipsilateral arm extension in tonic neck reflex, in distal finger opening to facilitate flexing on contact) | Fixed order established in reflex pairs by one-way inhibitory suppression of direction in their functional linkage. Also, full stimulus-provoked reflex arcs develop through control by inhibition–disinhibition timing |
| 3. Each component of reflex pair can become associated with simultaneously occurring movement, either reflexive or not, to assure better targeting of second component, thus creating primitive patterns. At this point, the primarily reflex related *primitive schemas* are being formed (e.g., in looking directed tonic neck reflex with subsequent proximal arm extension on appropriate side, in fingers open and move slightly before flexing to grip after noncentered contact) | Above process expands to include other components at second or both phases of movement. This may involve coupling with other reflexes and/or interdigitation with extrareflex neuronal centers primarily sensory-perceptual in nature |
| 4. Patterned, *schema* controlled, ballistic, preprogrammed behavior (i.e., sequential multiples of above) triggered, but not always directly to (on) target; in proximal activity (e.g., prereach agitation in front of target moves) and/or in distal activity (e.g., fingers serially extend and flex upon sheet contact on back of hand, with arm and hand agitation producing turning) | Level 3 units coordinated sequentially in time by inhibition–activation balancing |
| 5. Patterned behaviors above begin to differentiate with practice, as continual monitoring of movement and/or moving target render movement more smooth, flexible. *Independent schemas* no longer are dominated by reflexes (e.g., in proximal reaching adjustment to moving object, in distal fingers grasp target) | Movement becomes partly reflex-free as neuronal clusters incorporate via own inhibition–activation balancing extrareflex neuronal centers involved in control of spatiotemporal changes |

Adapted from Young (1990a)

The next tables present some unique features of the present model, as presented in Young (1990a). First, the left-hand columns indicate how the schemes and operations that Piaget had described in development from the first reflex substage in infancy to the postformal cognitive stage progress substage by substage in terms of these schemes-operations. Moreover, for each substage, I give examples involving motor behavior that are helpful in understanding the hypothesized development of activation–inhibition coordination and hemispheric specialization that are described in the right column

(continued)

**Table 26.1** (continued)

Other workers in the area of Neo-Piagetian development have explored the links between hemispheric specialization and steps in cognitive development, but this is the only one that has attempted a lifespan approach. Moreover, it examines functionality deriving from hemisphere specialization, and not just left–right differences in maturational cycles (see Table 9.7)

The work speculates that, as the hemispheres develop, there is an increase in the zone-areas that subserve the behaviors in question. One model of the developing brain is that there is an increasing cross-zone synchrony in firing, in a parallel, distributed process. However, there is localist tradition that still is quite important in neurology and neuropsychology, as witnessed by recent findings both at the level of the neuron and the brain (e.g., mirror neurons, Ramachandran & Altschuler, 2009; brain circuits, Imsel, 2010). The present work tries to find a balance between these two approaches; however, the particular steps presented need verification in this regard

In the first stage of reflexes, the table describes that by 1 month of age, the infant is no longer reflex-dominated. Neuronal circuitry developing in subcortical centers allows experience-adjusting schemes to develop. They exhibit some flexibility in behavior, and the types of reflex patterns described by Piagetians are quite different from those simpler varieties programmed by reflex arcs

**Table 26.2** Sensorimotor levels in the development of left brain specialization

| Behavioral specialization (e.g., in right arm-hand) | Central specialization (and inhibition therein) |
|---|---|
| 6. Through *schema coordination* parallel and (e.g., vision and appropriate movement), behavior patterns come under even more moment to moment control (e.g., in watching arm during proximal reach to target, in watching hand while distal fingers serially touch target) | By recruitment process similar to that in step 5, larger neuronal clusters form. They require intracluster inhibition–activation synchrony so that movement sequence is controlled for fine interference by perseverations, and intruding similar movements |
| 7. With *schema coordination hierarchies*, after behavior onset, goal can be established in context (primary releasing stimuli defined), and one schema in above schema coordination becomes primary; thus, there is directed target groping subserved by dominant-subordinate linkage of two schemas (e.g., in visually directed proximal reaching, in watching as distally manipulate target, in simple bimanual collaboration involving (right hand) reach then (left hand) grasp) | Neuronal cluster interdigitation goes one step beyond as pairs form a hierarchy with one subsumed to another by inhibition–activation regulation. The fine interference control described above also applies here |
| 8. Linked schemas above related more systematically, allowing *primitive representation of target*, permitting intentional end-focused goal from behavior onset (e.g., in proximal reach for hidden object, in two step movement to target, in distal exploratory manipulation either (a) alone or (b) in complex bimanual coordination, with complementary (left hand) stabilization) | Above process expands to permit larger zone-area mobilization. Neuronal cluster hierarchies are synchronized to permit inhibitory control of gross interference at outset and throughout unrelated neuronal clusters |

(continued)

**Table 26.2** (continued)

| Behavioral specialization (e.g., in right arm-hand) | Central specialization (and inhibition therein) |
|---|---|
| 9. Through multiplicative embedding of one simple intension or means in another, or in multiplicative combining of two means or ends, diagonal movement to target, in cooperative distal hand use in resolving an embedded hiding, in trial-and-error exploration of means-ends relationship, between distal manual activity and effects on objects | Widespread expansion into extra zone-area surround is a major step, ensuring that the gross interference control described above comes to include multiple surround neuronal clusters |
| 10. Organized sequences above being to differentiate into hierarchic branching of embedded, secondary sequential plans followed by return to primary one, which is the structure of a priori *symbolic plans* (e.g., in proximal hitting of rolled ball back to thrower, in resolution of an embedded hiding with a tool distally manipulated in the hand or in double embedded hiding resolution, in using distal hands to set apart one subset of a group and then another) | The range of interference control now extends cross zone-area, i.e., intrahemispherically to some extend, as the inhibition–activation balancing continues to expand |

Adapted from Young (1990a)
The infant makes great advances motorically in the first 2 years, and this is mirrored in an increasing in manual specialization and corresponding hemispheric specialization. From simple hand–eye coordinations in reaching and touching, to bimanual coordination in more complex activities, to following prior plans imagined for sequential actions toward specific ends, manual activity is elaborated and increasingly reflects the development of right-handedness dominance in daily practice. Schemas develop through the Piagetian series for the sensorimotor period, reflecting increasing coordinations, integrations, and presence of purposive activity

**Table 26.3** Perioperational levels in the development of left brain specialization

| Behavioral specialization (e.g., in right arm-hand) | Central specialization (and inhibition therein) |
|---|---|
| 11. *Symbolic plan coordination* found, as the child simultaneously holds in mind several symbol plans (e.g., in proximal hitting of rolled ball to side target, in using distal hands to simultaneously sort two subsets of a group of objects, in using memory to begin to learn to draw, write) | The process in level 10 radiates across the hemisphere, permitting cross zone-areas to being to form interlinked pairs |
| 12. The above pairs develop a dominant-subordinate *symbol plan hierarchization* (e.g., in proximal symbolic fantasy gesturing to help explicate a sentence, in speeded distal tapping interfered with or being subordinate to spared language in dual, time sharing tasks). This hierarchization also refers to the child placing own plan as dominant in relation to perception of those of parents, others (as in egocentric notions of good drawing, lettering) | Zone-areas in the same hemisphere form inhibition barriers between them to better control interference during their interrelating and simultaneous functioning |

(continued)

**Table 26.3** (continued)

| Behavioral specialization (e.g., in right arm-hand) | Central specialization (and inhibition therein) |
|---|---|
| 13–15. The above symbol plan hierarchies expand as they integrate other symbols into *symbol plan systems*. There is an increasing ability to hold things in mind while solving problems or even undue past learning about a problem, trying to use a primitive logic. In the next step, these systems are intercoordinated, inversed, alternated, ordered, etc. Such a structure allows a better logic, leading to rule-governed, skillful application (e.g., in art activity, writing, manual dexterity in music). Piaget's *concrete operations* develop in this context. Next, this process refines, as the child can use *logic in imagination* in restricted contexts | Interhemispheric communication-collaboration (controlled in left hemisphere) by commissural (corpus callosum) inhibition–activation coordination allows brain-wide mobilization. Several phases probably occur, involving intrahemispheric incorporation of emerging anterior areas into the process. The frontal regions, for example, are known for inhibition of action to allow for evaluation |

Adapted from Young (1990a)

For the perioperational stage of cognitive development, the table indicates that both at the level of manual development and corresponding inhibitory specializations that underlie them, there are broad-ranging advances. The child moves from behaviors indicative of symbol plan coordinations to advanced concrete operations and, motorically, drawing and writing reflect these advances. As for corresponding central specializations, wider within-hemisphere and cross-hemisphere coordinations are posited to grow, with inhibitory advances quite involved, e.g., in frontal lobe functions

**Table 26.4** Abstract levels in the development of left brain specialization

| Behavioral specialization (e.g., in right arm-hand) | Central specialization (and inhibition therein) |
|---|---|
| 16. A coordination of logic in imagination is found (e.g., in solving problems by allowing one variable at a time free to vary). This can lead to novel, *abstract, formal thought* in restricted contexts (e.g., genuine craft, interpretation in painting, music) | The process in level 15 expands to integration of major anterior (frontal) areas. Welsh and Pennington (1988) describe how these may emerge |
| 17–20. Abstract approaches explored. First, there is their pairwise comparison, or *abstract hierarchization* (with that of a mentor, between themselves, etc). Second, one may find *abstract systematization* of the approaches, leading to a better-desired outcome. Third, inhibition of major self-reinforcing dialectical *relativist abstraction* could lead to changing interapproach multiples, and thus superior creativity. Lastly, an empathic, *abstract universality* may prevail (e.g., in painting, music, theorizing) | Interhemispheric integration (controlled in the left hemisphere) occurs by optimal synchronization of inhibition–activation coordination. Several phases may occur, and in the last one the integration may include inhibition of major self-reinforcing systems |

Adapted from Young (1990a)

*Note*. Each level in these tables: (a) have described the Neo-Piagetian level on which it is based; (b) gives the cognitive control until seen to develop at the level (italicized); (c) provides examples in manual behavior consistent with the nature of the level; (d) suggests corresponding central advances that might underlie its development. Similar processes should be continuing in the ensuing adult years of collective intelligence

**Table 26.5** Postformal levels in the development of left brain specialization

| Behavioral specialization (e.g., in right arm-hand) | Central specialization (and inhibition therein) |
|---|---|
| 21. Pairs of *abstract integration superordinate structures* coordinate, juxtapose, etc. (e.g., in musical, architectural, sculptural, or other artistic planning and performance/composition, or theory/analysis related to them) | 21–25. To this point, I have emphasized macroprocesses in activation–inhibition coordination in the brain relating to increasing intra- and interzone/region integrations. However, throughout the process of hemispheric specialization and of brain growth, in general, microprocesses are taking place related to synaptogenesis, dendritic arborization, synaptic pruning, and sculpting. In a certain sense, circuitry formation and synaptic pruning/reorganization involve neuronal activation and inhibition coordination processes at the microlevel that complement the processes at the macrolevel. To arrive at any of the postformal stages in brain function and specializations, the macro- and microprocesses should be working in a complete, optimal balance |
| 22. Then, the postformal structure takes on a hierarchical relationship, where one component is primary or dominant in the relationship (*postformal hierarchization*) | |
| 23–25. In the next steps, the components systematize, multiply out throughout the full system, and achieve full integration (e.g., would a full musical symphonic composition and performance/orchestration qualify for this skill, or the graphic work in high-end mathematics, physics, or related science?) | |

This table is new to the model. I had not described the posformal stage for the series of tables. It allows me to speculate on the highest-order, cognitive-related manual skills. Moreover, it gives me the opportunity to discuss activation–inhibition coordination in terms of macro- and microprocesses (e.g., over brain regions, over neurons, respectively)

## Interim Summary

In the present work, activation–inhibition coordination is considered a dynamic integrating force in brain and behavior. It provides a common language to understand both manual specialization and hemispheric specialization. The skill might have evolved as a left hemisphere specialization to help animals avoid prey by synchronization of turning tendencies with the fleeing group. I have proposed a developmental model where an increasing left hemisphere specialization for activation–inhibition coordination contributes to cognitive advances in the proposed Neo-Piagetian sequence of 25 steps presented on the present work. This happens at both macro-, neurological and micro-, neuronal levels (e.g., over cerebral regions, over neurons, respectively).

In the section that follows, I discuss various models of the evolution of lateralization. This helps elaborate a phylogenetic basis for the current 25-step model of development. The works of MacNeilage and his colleagues and of Corballis are emphasized.

# Relations Between Ontogenesis and Phylogenesis

## *Evolution*

### Nonhuman Primate Evolution

MacNeilage, Studdert-Kennedy, and Lindblom (1987, 1988) hypothesized that early prosimians manifested a left hemisphere-controlled whole-body postural organization (e.g., hold to balance with right hand while performing a task with the left hand). The complementary specialization of the right hemisphere in early prosimians concerned a control of predation through left-hand, visually directed activities (e.g., reaching). Early higher primates evolved to locomote quadrupedally. Thus, the left hemisphere's specialization for whole-body postural control led it to become operative in bimanual, forceful foraging in the environment. This precipitated a role reversal in early higher primates relative to prosimian manual behavior, for the left hand now came to support right-hand manipulation instead of dominating for visually directed action. MacNeilage et al. admitted to possible paleomammalian precursor steps in the evolution of laterality, and have also suggested possible intermediate nonhuman primate steps involving early monkeys versus apes, in particular.

### Hominid Evolution

Corballis (1989, 1991, 1992) depicted a seven-step sequence in the evolution of human laterality and related behavior, while admitting that theorizing such as this is speculative due to a paucity of data. In the first step in the evolution of human laterality, early ape ancestors did not evidence more than some asymmetries in behavior and brain organization and language by manual gesture. The first hominids, *Australopithecus afarensis*, emerged about 4–8 million years ago, and showed upright posture, bipedalism, and freeing of the hands. Later australopithecines (gracile, africanus) were not much different. *Homo habilis* evolved as early as a little over 2 million years ago, and was characterized by a distinctly larger brain and a tool culture having manufacture and design specification. Toth (1985) determined that the flakes formed in tool manufacture and sharpening dating from this period suggest that the majority of the individuals in the species were right-handers. Tobias (1987) observed imprints in fossil skulls that indicate that these hominids possessed in the left hemisphere a larger speech production (Broca's) area as well as a probably larger speech reception (Wernicke's) area.

With the evolution of *Homo erectus* about 1.5 million years ago, tool culture came to involve biface hand axes. The next milestone about 300,000 years ago saw the appearance of Neandertal and other Archaic *Homo sapiens*. These relatively modern hominids were the first to possess a cranial size equivalent to contemporary humans. *Homo sapiens sapiens* evolved 150,000–200,000 years ago. They manifested (a) a vocal tract that permitted an extremely adaptive, rapid speech like our own (Lieberman, 1984) and (b) a flexibility and open-endedness (generativity) in tool blade manufacture and use. Finally, Cromagnon people appeared about 37,000 years ago, and exhibited an explosion in culture (e.g., in blade technology, cave art, body ornaments).

## Evolutionary Progression

By combining the two phylogenetic progressions just presented, one arrives at a sequence in primate and hominid evolution made up of up to 11 steps, after eliminating redundancies. The steps hypothesized to have taken place in evolution relate to the following levels: paleomammalian, early prosimian, ancestral monkey, ancestral ape, *Australopithecus afarensis*, *Homo habilis*, *Homo erectus*, Archaic *Homo sapiens*, *Homo sapiens sapiens*, Cromagnon people, and contemporary people.

The 25-step ontogenetic sequence presented in Tables 26.1–26.5 might help illustrate the phylogenetic emergence of our species. There may not be a one-to-one parallel in developmental stages and ancestral ones because of processes such as neoteny and acceleration (Gould, 1977), which function to alter or affect the former sequence in relation to the latter. [Neoteny concerns a retardation or delay in the appearance or full maturation of a developing behavior relative to the status predicted for it on the basis of prior evolution. Acceleration refers to the inverse of this process].

Nevertheless, comparison of developmental and evolutionary sequences can be instructive. In this regard, the best fit of the MacNeilage et al. and Corballis 11-step evolutionary sequence and the current 25-step developmental one would place the start of the former at the eighth level of the latter. This thesis is illustrated in the last columns of Tables 26.1–26.5. It also shows that the onset of the first four major stages in development that have been suggested (reflexive, sensorimotor, perioperational, abstract) seem to correspond to the evolution of key reptilian, paleomammalian, nonhominid primate, and hominid ancestors, respectively. This tight correspondence in the current theory between major transition points in ontogenetic and phylogenetic advances seems noteworthy. Also, note the symmetry in the pattern of the hypothesized evolutionary sequence, with eight evolutionary phases prior to those of the nonhuman primates, nine in these primates, and eight in contemporary people.

# Evolution of Mind

## *Toward the Theoretic Mind*

Donald (2008) reviewed his 1991 model of the evolution of the modern mind (Donald, 1991, 1993, 1995, 2001). He hypothesized that there are three major "stages" in the cultural-cognitive evolution of the hominid mind. The stages involve shifting (a) from the marginally symbolic (b) to the protosymbolic (c) to the fully symbolic mind. The corresponding age periods in the evolutionary course of these three evolutionary acquisitions, respectively, are about (a) 2–4 million years ago when the first hominid species appeared, (b) then about 400,000 years ago when the species *Homo sapiens* first appeared, and (c) then when the modern mind emerged in humans. Donald labeled the three stages as (a) mimetic, (b) mythic, and (c) theoretic. Before these three stages appeared, Donald indicated that the Miocene primates had developed an episodic-type mind. The episodic step involved complex event representation. The mimetic stage involved nonverbal action modeling and imitation. The mythic step involved advanced linguistic skills. Finally, the theoretic transition involved extensive use of symbols, formalisms, and external storage of memory.

## *Toward the Extended Mind*

Mithen (2007) reviewed his model of the evolution of the human mind presented in his books (Mithen, 1996, 2005). He described five steps in the evolution of the human mind, stretching from 2 million years ago to 50,000 years ago, and he also mentioned changes in the mind that had developed after the Ice Age, 10,000 years ago.

(a) In the first step, between 1.5 and 2 million years ago, an advance in brain size allowed our ancestors *Homo ergaster* to develop a theory of mind.
(b) Next, about 0.5 million years ago, a specialized intelligence evolved to allow for interaction with the social, natural, and technological milieux. For example, Acheulian technology developed, involving production of advanced hand axes that required specialized but isolated cognitive abilities (domain-specific, highly modular).
(c) In the next stage in the evolution of human psychology about 0.25 million years ago, the critical acquisition was an advanced holistic communication. This type of communication involved advanced vocal-gestural communicative abilities, or protolanguage. Mithen argued that the protolanguage allowed communication of "messages" rather than isolated words. In this middle and early late Pleistocene period, our ancestors became capable of "holistic, manipulative, multimodal, musical, and mimetic ('Hmmmm')" communication. Mithen speculated that the evolution of protolanguage in this time period was facilitated by a genetic mutation in the *FOXP2* gene (Enard et al., 2002). The gene appears to be related to skill in complex grammar (Bishop, 2002).

(d) In the fourth step of the evolution of the human mind, Mithen maintained that humans developed a cognitive fluidity, which concerns cross-modal thought. It appeared 100,000 years ago in association with *Homo sapiens*. The domain-specific mentality that had developed previously became more generalized and involved an intermodular integration. It permitted major cultural advances from about 50,000 years ago onwards.
(e) In the last step that Mithen described, beginning 50,000 years ago, modern humans developed an extended mind. We could extend beyond our brain into the material culture that today takes the form of computers, in particular, which provides "cognitive anchors." Disciplines could develop because of this extended mind, such as science and mathematics.
(f) Finally 10,000 years ago, with the end of the Ice Age, people began farming by using their intelligence. They developed intellectual skills, such as creating metaphors and analogies.

## *Towards the Postformal Mind*

The work of Donald and Mithen are complementary in their descriptions of the evolution of the human mind. Donald begins with his description of the episodic and mimetic stages in primate ancestors and in the earliest humans. Mithen continues with a six-step sequence between 2 million years ago and up to modern humans. Donald's mythic stage corresponds to Mithen's one of holistic communication about 300,000 years ago (in Neandertals). His theoretic stage corresponds to Mithen's description of the modern mind as extended. Mithen adds that the most recent developments took place with the end of the Ice Age.

Their combined models leave an eight-step sequence in the evolution of the modern mind. Moreover, the sequence corresponds to my own model that had been presented in Tables 26.6–26.10. However, my model has the advantage of relating the evolution of mind to equivalent steps in the development of the individual (although this is not a model of recapitulation, but of parallels in the two sequences).

In particular, the eight steps in the combined Donald–Mithen sequence in the evolution of mind corresponds to the first eight steps of the ten steps in my model that covers the perioperational stage and the abstract stage. It will be recalled that in each of these stages, I describe five substages.

Therefore, I would add that after the post-Ice Age acquisitions in the evolution of mind described by Mithen, two more steps in the evolution of the mind took place. First, the abstract systems that had developed beginning about 10,000 years ago entered a phase of multiplication, or spreading out. Most probably, this took place about 5,000 years ago with the establishment of small nonfarming communities. Next, the various abstract systems that had developed became more integrated into coherent abstract structures. This most probably took place within the last 3,000 years, as societies became more organized.

**Table 26.6** The reflex stage of cognitive development: control units, systems, origins

| Control unit in substage | Age range | Socioemotional system | Evolutionary origin |
|---|---|---|---|
| 1. Reflex-pair coordination | Earlier fetal life | Distance acts | Reptilian I |
| 2. Reflexive behavior hierarchization | Quite premature | Nursing acts | Reptilian II |
| 3. Primitive schema (systematization) | Somewhat premature | Outcome acts | Reptilian III |
| 4. Patterned schema (multiplication) | Full-term newborn | Caregiving acts | Reptilian IV |
| 5. Independent schema (integration) | 0–1 months | Emotional acts | Reptilian V |

Adapted from Young (1990b)

The next set of tables introduces two elements of the present model that expand it into the socioaffective realm and that indicate possible evolutionary origins. The tables were first published in Young (1990b). The first two columns repeat the structure of the control units in the 25 steps of the present model and their associated ages. The third column presents the hypothesized socioemotional systems that develop at each step. The fourth column presents the hypothesized evolutionary period in which their precursors seem to have emerged. For the socioemotional systems, they are presented as acts, preparing the way for their further description as based on dimensions with positive and negative poles. I indicate where Erikson's stages would fit in the sequence

The evolutionary sequence in hominid evolution is based on a literature review conducted for the 1990 work. Consultation of recent reviews does not lead to changes in the sequence (Gibbons, 2010; Green et al. 2006). There are additions, such as *H. floresiensis*, who had evolved after Neandertals, but not in direct lineage leading to present day humans. *H. heidelbergensis* appears to have evolved before Neandertals. The evolutionary tree now includes recent discoveries, such as *Ardipithecus ramidus*, who evolved about 4.4 million years ago, and *Ardipithecus kadabba*, who lived about 6 million years ago. These species and others that are being found are not considered to be part of the direct lineage leading to contemporary humans

**Table 26.7** The sensorimotor stage of cognitive development: control units, systems, origins

| Control unit in substage | Age range (months) | Socioemotional system | Evolutionary origin |
|---|---|---|---|
| 6. Schema coordination | 1–4 | Dyadic acts | Paleomammalian I |
| 7. Schema coordinate hierarchization | 4–8 | [a] | Paleomammalian II |
| 8. Primitive representation (systematization) | 8–12 | Sociability acts | Paleomammalian III |
| 9. Linear plans (multiplication) | 12–18 | [a] | Early prosimian |
| 10. Symbolic plans (integration) | 18–24 | Interactional acts | Early monkey |

Adapted from Young (1990b)

[a] Indicates levels (7, 9) where first two Eriksonian levels fit

**Table 26.8** The perioperational stage of cognitive development: control units, systems, origins

| Control unit in substage | Age range (years) | Socioemotional system | Evolutionary origin |
|---|---|---|---|
| 11. Symbolic plan coordination | 2–3½ | Superordinate acts | Early ape |
| 12. Symbolic plan hierarchization | 3½–5 | [a] | *Australopithecus afarensis* |
| 13. Symbolic plan systematization | 5–7 | Gender acts | *Homo habilis* |
| 14. Concrete operations (multiplication) | 7–9 | [a] | *Homo erectus* |
| 15. Logic in imagination (integration) | 9–11 | Role acts | Archaic *Homo sapiens* |

Adapted from Young (1990b)
[a] Indicates levels where third and fourth Eriksonian levels fit

**Table 26.9** The abstract stage of cognitive development: control units, systems, origins

| Control unit in substage | Age range (years) | Socioemotional system | Evolutionary origin |
|---|---|---|---|
| 16. Logic in imagination coordination | 11–13 | Conscious acts | *Homo sapiens* |
| 17. Abstract hierarchization | 13–16 | [a] | Cromagnon people |
| 18. Abstract systematization | 16–19 | Nurturing acts | Contemporary people |
| 19. Relativist abstraction | 19–22 | [a] | Contemporary people |
| 20. Abstract universality (integration) | 22–25 | Universal acts | Contemporary people |

Adapted from Young (1990b)
[a] Indicates levels where fifth and sixth Eriksonian levels fit

**Table 26.10** The collective intelligence stage of cognitive development: control units, systems, origins

| Control unit in substage | Age range (years) | Socioemotional system | Evolutionary origin |
|---|---|---|---|
| 21. Collective intelligence coordination | 25–28 | Metacollecting acts | Contemporary people |
| 22. Collective intelligence hierarchization | 28–39 | [a] | Contemporary people |
| 23. Collective intelligence systematization | 39–50 | Catalytic acts | Contemporary people |
| 24. Collective intelligence multiplication | 50–61 | [a] | Contemporary people |
| 25. Collective intelligence integration | 61 | Cathartic acts | Contemporary people |

Adapted from Young (1990b)
[a] Indicates levels where seventh and eighth Eriksonian levels fit

Finally, in my model I describe the adult as developing a postformal stage of collective intelligence. This would seem to be a very recent acquisition in the evolution of the human mind, and one limited in the percentage of people expressing it. Hopefully, it will be looked back upon one day as the start of a transforming evolution in the majority of adults in our species.

## Summary and Conclusions

The present model of Neo-Piagetian cognitive development involves 25 steps over the life span. Each cognitive substage that emerges is anchored in a unique executive or cognitive control unit that forges a range of interrelated but semi-independent acquisitions (e.g., conceptual, motoric, linguistic). In this chapter, I show how they might be related to steps in hemispheric specialization. Moreover, the steps might have evolutionary roots consistent with the evolution toward our species. This argument leads an integrated model of the concepts of the theoretic and extended mind that I call the postformal mind.

Activation–inhibition coordination processes seem to play a central role in development, from behavior to brain. In this chapter, I show that this dynamic might have been important in evolution, as well.

In the next two chapters, I examine another far-reaching concept that has been applied to behavior, the brain, and even nonliving systems, that of systems theory. I show that nonlinear dynamical system transition processes might be involved transitioning through developmental steps.

## References

Annett, M., & Kilshaw, D. (1984). Lateral preference and skill in dyslexics: Implications of the right shift theory. *Journal of Child Psychology and Psychiatry, and Allied Disciplines, 25*, 357–377.

Bishop, D. V. M. (2002). Putting language genes in perspective. *Trends in Genetics, 18*, 57–59.

Cantalupo, C., Pilcher, D., & Hopkins, W. D. (2003). Are planum temporale and sylvian fissure asymmetries directly related? A MRI study in great apes. *Neuropyschologia, 41*, 1975–1981.

Corballis, M. C. (1989). Laterality and human evolution. *Psychological Review, 96*, 492–505.

Corballis, M. C. (1991). *The lop-sided ape: Evolution of the generative mind*. New York: Oxford University Press.

Corballis, M. C. (1992). On the evolution of language and generativity. *Cognition, 44*, 197–226.

Corballis, M. C. (2010). Handedness and cerebral asymmetry: An evolutionary perspective. In K. Hugdahl & R. Westerhausen (Eds.), *The two halves of the brain: Information processing in the cerebral hemispheres* (pp. 65–88). Cambridge: MIT Press.

Crow, T. J. (2010). The origins of psychosis and the evolution of language: Cerebral asymmetry, sex chromosomes, and speciation. In K. Hugdahl & R. Westerhausen (Eds.), *The two halves of the brain: Information processing in the cerebral hemispheres* (pp. 621–661). Cambridge: MIT Press.

Crow, T. J., Crow, L. R., Done, D. J., & Leask, S. J. (1998). Relative hand skill predicts academic ability: Global deficits at the point of hemispheric indecision. *Neuropsychologia, 36*, 1275–1282.

Damasio, A. R. (1989). The brain binds entities and events by multiregion activation from convergence zones. *Neural Computation, 1*, 123–132.

Damasio, A. R. (1994). *Descartes' error: Emotion, reason, and the human brain*. New York: Avon.

Donald, M. (1991). *Origins of the modern mind: Three stages in the evolution of culture and cognition*. Cambridge: Harvard University Press.

Donald, M. (1993). Précis of origins of the modern mind with multiple reviews and author's response. *Behavior Brain Science, 16*, 737–791.

Donald, M. (1995). The neurobiology of human consciousness: An evolutionary approach. *Neuropsychologia, 33*, 1087–1102.

Donald, M. (2001). *A mind so rare: The evolution of human consciousness*. New York: Norton.

Donald, M. (2008). How culture and brain mechanisms interact in decision-making. In C. Engel & W. Singer (Eds.), *Better than conscious? Decision-making, the human mind, and implications for institutions* (pp. 191–225). Cambridge: MIT Press.

Enard, W., Przeworski, M., Fisher, S. E., Lai, C. S., Wiebe, V., Kitano, T., et al. (2002). Molecular evolution of FOXP2, a gene involved in speech and language. *Nature, 418*, 869–872.

Ferstl, E. C., Rinck, M., & von Cramon, D. Y. (2005). Emotional and temporal aspects of situation model processing during text comprehension: An event-related fMRI study. *Journal of Cognitive Neuroscience, 17*, 724–739.

Fischer, K. W. (1987). Relations between brain and cognitive development. *Child Development, 58*, 623–632.

Ghirlanda, S., & Vallortigara, G. (2004). The evolution of brain lateralization: A game-theoretical analysis of population structure. *Proceedings of the Royal Society of London B, 271*, 853–857.

Gibbons, A. (2010). How did ape-like creatures evolve into members of the human family? Research on fossil remains, including 4.4 million-year-old "Ardi," is leading to new insights into our origins. *Smithsonian*, 34–41.

Gould, S. J. (1977). *Ontogeny and phylogeny*. Cambridge: Belknap.

Green, R. E., Krause, J., Ptak, S. E., Briggs, A. W., Ronan, M. T., Simons, J. F., et al. (2006). Analysis of one million base pairs of Neanderthal DNA. *Nature, 444*, 330–336.

Hoenig, K., & Scheef, L. (2009). Neural correlates of semantic ambiguity during context verification. *NeuroImage, 45*, 1009–1019.

Hopkins, W. D. (2006). Comparative and familial analysis of handedness in great apes. *Psychological Bulletin, 132*, 538–559.

Hopkins, W. D., & Cantalupo, C. (2008). Theoretical speculations on the evolutionary origins of hemispheric specialization. *Current Directions in Psychological Science, 17*, 233–237.

Immordino-Yang, M. H. (2007). A tale of two cases: Lessons for education from the study of two boys living with half their brains. *Mind, Brain, and Education, 1*, 66–83.

Immordino-Yang, M. H. (2008). The smoke around mirror neurons: Goals as sociocultural and emotional organizers of perception and action in learning. *Mind, Brain, and Education, 2*, 67–73.

Imsel, T. R. (2010, April). Faulty circuits. *Scientific American, April.* Retrieved from http://www.scientificamerican.com/.

Joliot, M., Leroux, G., Dubal, S., Tzourio-Mazoyer, N., Houdé, O., Mazoyer, B., et al. (2009). Cognitive inhibition of number/length interference in a Piaget-like task: Evidence by combining ERP and MEG. *Clinical Neurophysiology, 120*, 1501–1513.

Kinsbourne, M. (2009). Development of cerebral lateralization in children. In C. R. Reynolds & E. Fletcher-Janzen (Eds.), *Handbook of clinical child neuropsychology* (3rd ed., pp. 47–66). New York: Springer Science + Business Media.

Lieberman, P. (1984). *The biology and evolution of language*. Cambridge: Harvard University Press.

Long, D. L., & Bayness, K. (2002). Discourse representation in the two cerebral hemispheres. *Journal of Cognitive Neuroscience, 14*, 228–242.

MacNeilage, P. F., Studdert-Kennedy, M. G., & Lindblom, B. (1987). Primate handedness reconsidered. *Behavioral and Brain Sciences, 10*, 247–263.

MacNeilage, P. F., Studdert-Kennedy, M. G., & Lindblom, B. (1988). Primate handedness: A foot in the door. *Behavioral and Brain Sciences, 11*, 737–746.

Mithen, S. (2007). Key changes in the evolution of human psychology. In S. W. Gangestad & J. A. Simpson (Eds.), *The evolution of mind: Fundamental questions and controversies* (pp. 256–266). New York: Guilford Press.

Mithen, S. J. (1996). *The prehistory of the mind: A search for the origin of art, science and religion*. London: Thames & Hudson/Orian.

Mithen, S. J. (2005). *The singing Neanderthals: The origin of music, language, mind and body*. London: Weidenfeld & Nicolson.

Peters, M., Reimers, S., & Manning, J. T. (2006). Hand preference for writing and associations with selected demographic and behavioral variables in 255,100 subjects: The BBC Internet study. *Brain and Cognition, 62*, 177–189.

Piaget, J. (1941/1952). *The child's conception of number*. New York: Basic Books. (Original in French, 1941).

Ramachandran, V. S., & Altschuler, E. L. (2009). The use of visual feedback, in particular mirror visual feedback, in restoring brain function. *Brain, 132*, 1693–1710.

Raz, S., Foster, M. S., Briggs, S. D., Shah, F., Baertchi, J. C., Lauterbach, M. D., et al. (1994). Lateralization of perinatal insult and cognitive asymmetry: Evidence from neuroimaging. *Neuropsychology, 8*, 160–170.

Sporns, O. (2011). *Networks of the brain*. Cambridge: MIT Press.

Stauder, J. E. A., Molenaar, P. C. M., & van der Molen, M. W. (1993). Scalp topography of event-related brain potentials and cognitive transition during childhood. *Child Development, 64*, 769–788.

Tobias, P. V. (1987). The brain of *Homo habilis*: A new level of organization in cerebral evolution. *Journal of Human Evolution, 16*, 741–761.

Toth, N. (1985). Archeological evidence for preferential right-handedness in the lower and middle pleistocene, and its possible implications. *Journal of Human Evolution, 14*, 607–614.

von der Malsburg, C., Phillips, W. A., & Singer, W. (2010). *Dynamic coordination in the brain: From neurons to mind*. Cambridge: MIT Press.

van der Mole, M. W., & Molenaar, P. C. (1994). Cognitive psychophysiology: A window to cognitive development and brain maturation. In G. Dawson & K. W. Fischer (Eds.), *Human behavior and the developing brain* (pp. 456–490). New York: Guilford.

Virtue, S., & Czarlinski, J. (2010). Hemispheric differences for enhancement and suppression mechanism during story comprehension. *Cognitive Neuroscience, 1*, 89–95.

Virtue, S., & van den Broek, P. (2005). Hemispheric processing of anaphoric inferences: The activation of multiple antecedents. *Brain and Language, 93*, 327–337.

Welsh, M., & Pennington, B. (1988). Assessing frontal lobe functioning in children: Views from developmental psychology. *Developmental Psychology, 4*, 199–230.

Young, G. (1990a). Early neuropsychological development: Lateralization of functions - hemispheric specialization. In C. A. Hauert (Ed.), *Developmental psychology: Cognitive, perceptuo-motor and neuropsychological perspectives* (pp. 113–181). Amsterdam: North Holland.

Young, G. (1990b). The development of hemispheric and manual specialization. In G. E. Hammond (Ed.), *Cerebral control of speech and limb movements* (pp. 79–139). Amsterdam: North Holland.

# Chapter 27
# Systems and Development

## Introduction

This chapter presents an introduction to nonlinear dynamical systems theory, chaos theory, related models, and their application in psychology (see Fig. 27.1). The next chapter explores in more detail the more advanced topics of attractors and complexity. In the chapter, I provide a model of transition processes in terms of attractors and complexity that seem to underpin the transitions in the present model of steps in development. For detailed presentation of nonlinear dynamical systems theory, see Abraham and Gilgen (1995), Boom (2004), Gleick (1987), Guastello, Koopmans, and Pincus (2009), Heath (2000), Howe and Lewis (2005), Lewis and Granic (2000), Masterpasqua and Perna (1997), Robertson and Combs (1995), Thelen and Smith (1994, 2006), Vallacher, Read, and Nowak (2002), and Ward (2002). For an introduction to complexity theory, see Johnson (2007) and Mitchell (2009). For a recent application of nonlinear dynamical systems to gender development, see Martin and Ruble (2010), and for a recent application of complex adaptive systems to pain, see Brown (2009).

## Development and Systems

### *Development*

Thelen and Smith (2006) explicated developmental modeling according to dynamic systems theory. "Dynamic systems" is a generic term referring to systems of elements changing over time. "Dynamical systems" is a more specific term, referring to a class of mathematical equations that depict system change. Thelen and Smith reviewed systems approaches that preceded nonlinear dynamical versions, including the work of Waddington (1957), Schneirla (1957), and Kuo (1970) on epigenesis. I note that the latter developmentalists had considered behavior as influenced by A- and W-processes in the organism, which are related to approach and withdrawal, and Thelen and Smith did not deal with this aspect of their work.

G. Young, *Development and Causality: Neo-Piagetian Perspectives*,
DOI 10.1007/978-1-4419-9422-6_27, © Springer Science+Business Media, LLC 2011

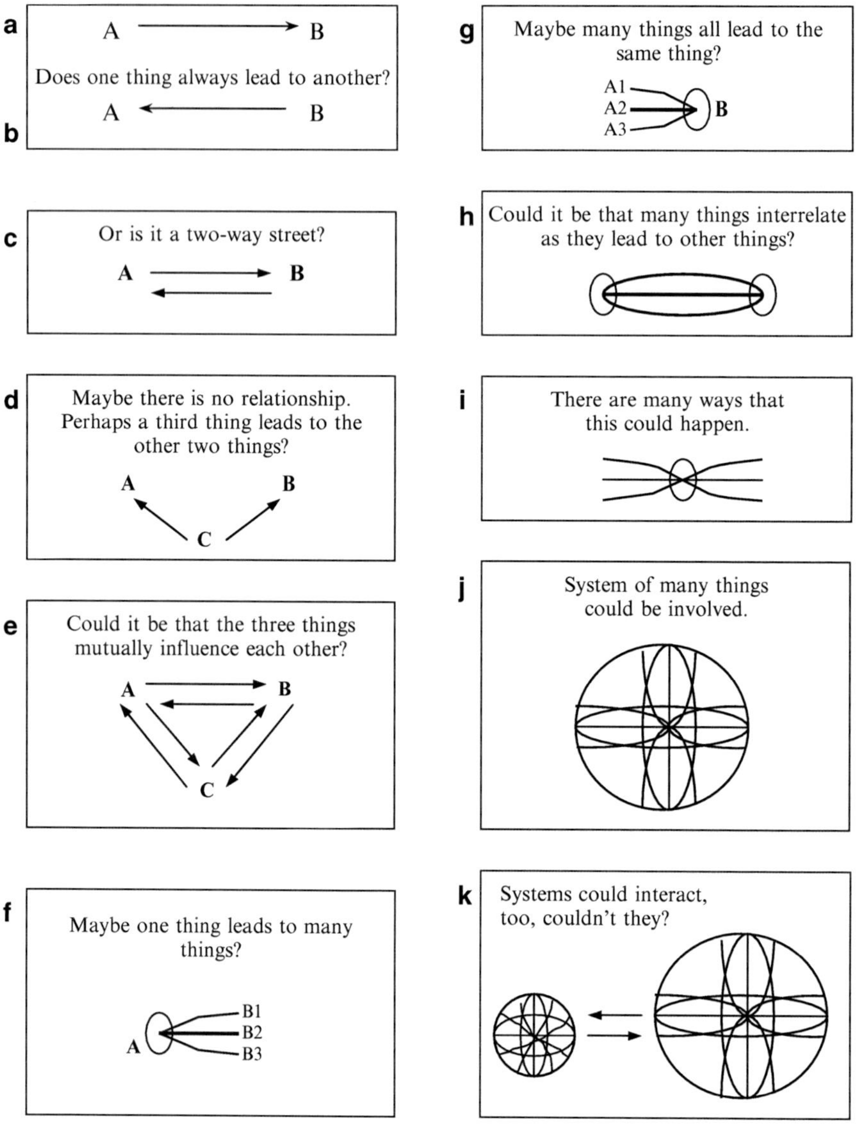


**Fig. 27.1** Systems and causality: simple answers hide complex issues. Things are never as simple as they seem, for everything is embedded in complex systems. Cause may appear to go from A to B, but usually it involves multiple factors and directions. Simple answers hide complex issues

In this regard, in the present work, I relate nonlinear dynamical systems theory to the process of activation–inhibition coordination, expanding the tradition of Schneirla and Kuo. Thelen and Smith (2006) described well the move in systems approaches from more general to nonlinear dynamical systems models involving attractors. In contrast to the present work, they do not discuss the related concept of complex adaptive systems.

An example of modern work related to epigenesis indicates that infant sensory capacities interact with maternal behavior to generate more advanced forms of vocalization. Vocal development is not driven exclusively by articulatory maturation, but involves multiple, interacting components. For example, Goldstein, King, and West (2003) showed that infants are reactive to caregivers responding to their sounds. In their study of 8- to 10-month-olds, infant babbling incorporated increased voicing and faster consonant–vowel transitions when mothers responded contingently to vocalizations of their infants. Another example concerns Camras's research on infant emotions, which I have presented in Chap. 22, a topic that I revisit at the end of the present chapter.

## *Systems*

Nature is "inhabited" by systemic patterns changing over time, and the changes are not "prespecified" but lie in the ongoing state of the system and its history in relation to its context. System changes are reiterative – each of its states is dependent on its prior state or reflects its momentum. Thelen and Smith (2006) provided the example of a mountain stream taking form and course according to local conditions encountered at the moment and, as well, according to the history of the stream's course up to the moment involved.

The pattern of change in a system's dynamic follows a course from complexity to simplicity to complexity. Systems elements cohere through self-organization into patterns that "live" in space and time. They represent compression of the degrees of freedom of the system's multiple, heterogeneous elements away from possibility of any form to actual form. At the same time, the system pattern is poised to dissolve and change in response to new conditions that are encountered, and the pattern over time becomes complex. The system is open to change because of the input of energy it receives so that it can organize locally increasingly complex and equilibrium-distant patterns, despite the general dissipation toward global equilibrium.

The system settles into a cooperative, coordinative mode of behavior limited by its reduced degrees of freedom. Its changes in state are governed by its macroscopic order parameter or collective variable (think of the qualitative transition from water to ice at zero centigrade). Even the most stable of systems are (a) "soft-assembled," or preferred but not inevitable, (b) temporary but not permanent, and (c) open to change in the right circumstances, or most severe perturbations, but not prespecified. Systems fluctuate around stable states, creating the conditions that allow new forms to coalesce. In stable system structure inhabiting a constant supporting context, for the most part, the fluctuations do not lead to change.

## *Change*

Change takes place when internal control parameters change enough or when the context changes enough. Note that a control parameter does not act to control the system in the classic sense of the word; rather, it reflects the parameter to which the system is sensitive. In nonlinear transitions of a system pattern, fluctuations are not damped down, and even minor noise can bring the system control parameter to the critical threshold involved, thereby leading to discontinuous change.

Moreover, different levels and time-scales of the system share similar characteristics. Microscopic change presages macroscopic ones and patterns at one level mirror or are self-similar to patterns nested at others (fractals, as with similarity in patterns of irregularities at the shore at the beach and in the grander map of coves).

Activity at any one level can influence any other, consistent with the adage that the whole is greater than the sum of the parts. Causality does not lie in any one location or level in the system, but in the inherent activity of its components coupling in multiple directions at multiple levels, with feedback, and over changing cascades in time. Coupling implies that all components of the system are continuously linked and mutually interactive, both within the individual and with the context.

## *Causality*

In Thelen and Smith's approach to developmental systems, product and process are one and the same. Prespecification does not exist so that, for present purposes, stage sequences are not prescribed in some sort of maturational program. If they are found, they are soft assembled through nonlinear dynamical processes at the individual level. If the pattern found in an individual resembles those in other individuals, this still does not mean that a simplified explanation in terms of universal programs related to biology, genetics, innateness, or heredity applies. Multicausality prevails; no single element, whether internal or external, has causal priority in the self-organization that governs system change over time. Moreover, it can be locally indeterminate and unpredictable, even if globally deterministic.

For Thelen and Smith (2006), development is best understood as a multiple, mutual, and continuous interaction of all levels of the systems involved. In terms of the different levels in a system, none have priority, just as none of its components or presumed causes express priority: "The system is dynamical all the way up and all the way down" (p. 307). A system reflects a nested process that unfolds over multiple timescales. Continuity refers to the seamless relationship between existing and prior states, and not to the possibility of dynamical qualitative changes, to which systems are prone to experience. Discontinuous stages can emerge, but "it makes no sense to ask what part of behavior comes from stages, mental structures, symbol systems, knowledge modules, or genes, because these constructs do not exist in timeless, disconnected form" (p. 307).

### *Comment*

Note that the approach in the present work is that stages are integral to the developmental project, and although they are soft-assembled at the individual level, the pattern of change involved is found quite universally because of its adaptive nature. Stages are trunks that guide systems in their individual developmental branching trajectories through the dynamic forces that create their emergence at the individual level. They do not govern developmental system change in a prespecified way, but their common emergence is predictable through knowledge of the whole, despite the individual construction involved. If stages are found universally, it is because the solutions to the adaptive dynamics that developing individuals confront leads to the form of their sequence for each individual separately, and therefore, as a by-product, they appear to represent a collectively governed program. Neo-Piagetian models help clarify this emerging stage growth process, while respecting the limitations and constraints in the process suggested by systems modeling.

## System Dynamics

### *Systems*

Horses pattern their limbs very differently when they switch from low speed to high speed. Instead of a jerky, asymmetric gait with the limbs of each girdle out of phase, the fluidity of symmetric gait manifests. Systems theory can readily help explicate this abrupt nonlinear, discontinuous, transition in form (Thelen, Kelso, & Fogel, 1987). A system can be defined as a set or network of related elements or component processes, together with their relationships, or linkages, that are liable to change over time. Note that the definition adds the possibility of no change in the system with time (because of homeostatic effects).

When collections are not functioning as systems, there elements might be independent and have an infinite range of ways of combining. By contrast, the elements of genuine systems are interrelated, interdependent, and interactive, producing patterned forms the whole of which is greater than the sum of the parts. In addition, elements of a system cannot be fully understood without reference to the whole.

Changing one element of a system, or adding or subtracting an element, risks changing the pattern in the whole. At the same time, the whole includes global, "top-down" influences that act to maintain stability in systems when they are perturbed by local, "bottom-up" influences. Given the sum of influences on them in relation to their internal stabilizing mechanisms, systems might exhibit tension, transition, or turbulent alternation between stability and instability, integration and disintegration, evolution and dissolution, and so on. However, even if a system enters a transitional turbulent phase, the new form that it might take could be quite stable and resistant to change, until the next round of tension manifests within its organization.

Dynamical systems are those that change over time and autonomously generate form and complexity. Dynamic variables are numbers that characterize the state of a system at a particular moment in time and so alter with time. Phase space functions map mathematically a system variable's dynamic over time. Dynamic schemes refer to the behavior of a system, and their graphical representation is called a response diagram. Bifurcation diagrams map responses that are nonlinear.

Dynamical systems constitute a variant of the general concept of a system. They differ from the general system description in their ability to autonomously generate form and complexity. If a dynamical system is nonlinear, its emergent form is discontinuous, abrupt, quite distinct from the preceding one, and so on. Even quite minor inputs can lead to disproportionate change in a system, as in the so-called "butterfly effect." When it operates with sensitivity to initial conditions, relatively minor inputs can lead to marked effects in a system trajectory or pathway of successive forms or states in the system.

Nonlinear dynamical systems are systems that continuously move toward equilibrium, and they transition naturally between equilibrium points in their environmental adaptation and self-organization. Conventional systems are static and have predetermined features, such as preconfigured thresholds of change in critical elements or variables. These are called control parameters. They result in preconfigured order in linear or conventional systems. However, nonlinear dynamical systems are continually evolving and adapting, with control and order changing and emerging out of interaction among the properties of the system and of the system with its context. Control in a system does not lie in inflexible, or prefigured, central command, but in flexible, contextual sensitivity (Thelen & Smith, 1994; Waldrop, 1992). Control parameters themselves are susceptible to change.

A system consists of a set of connected variables that interact and change over time. In a dynamical system, the system's present state characterizing its variables is influenced by the system's prior state. If the dynamical system is deterministic, its present state is completely dependent on the prior state. If it is linear, a combination of linear equations can specify all dependence. In a nonlinear dynamical system, linear equations cannot account adequately for its dependence. Stochastic systems have a random term added to their equations (Boom, 2004). (See the Appendix in Chap. 28 for the mathematical basis for nonlinear dynamical systems theory).

## Components

System components are defined by their function at a particular level of analysis. The system's elements do not exist in isolation of the system's pattern, nor do they exist at the level of organization of the system in which they are embedded. There is a mutuality, reciprocity, or relativity across layers of a system and the components of the layers, from the most basic layer of base elements to the most complex one, that is, their emergent global pattern. The elements of a system self-organize into the laminations of the system whole but, at the same time, the whole reciprocally exerts a conforming pressure on the system elements to behave according to the global pattern's influence. Depending on the perspective, the elements of a system show both homogeneity and heterogeneity, cooperativity and competition, heterarchy and hierarchy, basic forms and more complex ones, and presence in initial conditions or later emergence.

Even though the systemic whole encapsulates its elemental parts, the inverse corollary that the latter do not possess individuality beyond their system role might not obtain. Molecules of water may be interchangeable in a lake system, but family members are not in the human one. System parts dynamically contribute to the elaboration of the synergy in which they are embedded, might have characteristics independent of it, and might mark the system's chief attributes by their own. The whole and its parts are equally important. Most important for humans, individuals could develop emergent properties distinct from their component system(s). Emergent properties could further move individuals from the constraints on action, feeling, and thought of their prior systemic configurations and the whole system forces acting on them. Moreover, major system alterations could be instigated by an individual's emergent characteristics (unique abilities, motivation, liberty in action, leadership, etc.).

This possibility can arise because in human systems, components would also include internal maps, schemata, or representations that are flexible, plastic generalized representations not dependent on particular rules, programs, or effectors. While it may be true that patterns emerge out of local adaptations in time and context so that every moment represents unique system adjustments, and that globality (or stability) is neither built into systems nor causes local circumstances, this does not mean that there is no antecedent structure or "state maps" in systems. That is, dynamical systems theory might argue against prefigured fixities that instruct behavior (e.g., Thelen & Ulrich, 1991), but it does not deny the partial influence of past system dynamics created through experience. Moreover, these may be powerful filters that pull the system to their poles, although not in an irresistible fashion.

Although elements in a system can interrelate or combine with each other in many ways so that a system possesses many "degrees of freedom," a system's numerous degrees of freedom, or dynamic variables, become compressed in fewer dimensional "collective variables" (order parameters; the slaving principle; low-dimensional dynamics). These possess spatial and temporal order, i.e., they help characterize the states of the system. Because they mutually interact, in observing the dynamic changes in one, the nature and path of the others and of the whole can be deduced.

The environment provides some of the elements among a system's constituent parts. Moreover, systems are integrated into their milieux, being constantly sensitive to contextual conditions. In living systems, organism and surround can engage in cascading transactions. There is a constant exchange of information, input and output, energy absorption and deployment, etc.

## *Patterns*

System wholes are not loose, static agglomerations or consortiums. System elements coevolve in synergy. From an initial set of elemental units, collective or otherwise, a topological form or pattern not encoded by the set unfolds or falls out. A system's pattern dynamic is the rule describing the way it evolves with time. Dynamical systems are characterized by changing flows or maps of information over time.

Patterns emerge in the configuration of a system's elements by reverberation, fall-out, or soft-assemble dynamics. Systems inherently self-organize or self-modify in a spontaneous, context-adjusting way that produces more complex order. Patterns cannot be made, only facilitated. When the pace of resource (information, energy, and/or matter; e.g., task requirement) intake accelerates in a dynamic system, the output is nonlinear or not proportional to the level of input so that new patterns can emerge, and they could be qualitatively distinct and unpredictable from knowledge of the attributes of the contributing elements. A dynamical adjustment takes place when such perturbation is involved; however, systems might express change through "intrinsic" dynamic adaptation, or when there are no specific external perturbations.

Systems operate iteratively on the information that they generate and integrate. That is, through feedback mechanisms, dynamical systems can react to the effects produced by their own actions. Self-organization works through internal control, directive, and regulatory processes, including feedback and feed-forward, anticipatory processes. Thus, the system controls itself even if the immediate activation of the dynamics of change resides in the energy expansion into the system.

Over time, the constraining effect is evident – as lower-order, real-time, or moment-to-moment interactions lead to system reorganization, the system develops particular overall patterns that constrain it. Another way of describing this canalization is that, over time, macrotime processes, as opposed to microtime ones, compress the system, and it loses degrees of freedom. This resembles the bottom-up/top-down type of reciprocal interactions in systems discussed previously. In any system, habitual modes created in system landscapes function like rivulets of water running downhill. The impressions etch deeper, and, therefore, one finds more of a predictable course in streams or pathways. When cascades of real-time microchanges take place, for example, through reciprocal, recursive, and interconnected element interactions, the effect of each successive outcome of the cascade process is to limit the range of change possible at the macropattern level. Ultimately, the system experiences loss of flexibility and of possibility and, therefore, increased rigidity.

The system functions autonomously within the constraints on its inherent degrees of freedom in relation to its resources and the context. It arrives at an embodied, enactive pattern in a flexible manner without the imposition of prefigured progenitor pattern generators (Thelen & Smith, 1994). Indeed, systems can act autonomously to discover in an opportunistic manner appropriate solutions to contextual demands through varying their intrinsic dynamics in relation to the particular function to be performed (Thelen et al., 1993). In short, with self-organization, there can be patterns in a system's organization, constraints on its structure, change in its order, and even functional end points to which the system is dynamically oriented (but not predestined toward).

Change takes place in system patterns by component disassembly, reassembly, and tuning (Goldfield, 1995). Disassembly refers to the dissolution or breakdown of existing system component patterns so that they are amenable to repatterning. Assembly is an autoregulative process that establishes a (temporary) relationship among system components. The range of a system's new possible configurations is explored as the system adapts or entrains to its particular field.

Systems manifest different patterns of change. First, its elements may coalesce to produce a relatively minor property not contained in any one of them. There may be new coordinations, couplings, etc. Second, the state of the system itself might transform in a self-organizing way into a different state. Instead of local, gradual increments, there is more radical, qualitative alteration.

System ensembles reflect both a transition from simplicity to complexity and its inverse. On the one hand, an unorganized mass of elements coalesces to produce increased order. On the other hand, the resulting cohesion is organizationally structured or refined in morphology.

## *Living Systems*

Living systems are amenable to change, emergence, or repatterning because of their quasi-stability, a characteristic that permits adaptation to ongoing contextual conditions. They tend toward stability; however, their internal dynamics are not fixed but are intermittent so that they dynamically visit the region near preferred fixed points in their possible configurational landscape, and they do not live directly on it, thereby escaping its rigid capture. Each visit or particular experience on part of the landscape of possible system patterns in living systems biases the system to remain in the region visited, but that region only serves as a body with a gravitational pull, so that it can be countered by other forces in the orbits around it. Thus, variability is the major constant of living systems, and this characteristic is what allows for their evolution. In fact, it allows for the (extremely) novel forms that can help them survive (extremely) novel changes in environment.

Living systems, in particular, are self-organizing in that they incorporate external energy so that an "escapement" away from "disorder" is made possible (Kugler, Shaw, Vicente, & Kinsella-Shaw, 1991). System components can cooperate to create increasing complex patterns in living systems because they utilize energy in particular ways to maintain that complexity, and they incorporate continuously energy from the environment to counter the undermining effects of energy dissipation. For example, there are growth spurts apparent in developmental time, which are products of living systems' movement toward higher forms of order.

In summary, in a living system such as an individual organism, system parts relate in co-constructed negotiation or multimodal modulation to arrive at context-sensitive, real-time adaptive patterns or optimal field solutions. Each is a soft-molded, coordinative structure involving preferred, loose coalitions of elements that can be assembled, dissembled, and then reassembled in different configurations, depending on the organism's initial conditions, the relevant system components involved, and contextual factors. Thus, in a living system, organism, task, and context act together contingently to funnel cooperative assemblies, and this process excludes specific, predetermined instructions in genes or the environment. An important degree of system control derives from immediate contextual, "bottom-up" influences at the periphery of organism–environment contact, and not only from "top-down" central forces (Camras, 1992).

## *Causality and Prediction*

Predictions about systems can be made at both the specific and global level. The former refers to predictions about particular future patterns or immediate reactions that can be inferred either from the ongoing system dynamic or from knowledge of particular perturbations on that dynamic. The latter are more probabilistic, stochastic, and general. They concern especially longer and/or larger changes, or patterns of change over changing patterns. In both cases, the predictions are meant to reflect the determined nature of systems.

Whatever its stage of evolution, the pattern of element interplay in a system might not be linear but circular in its effect. Elements spiral in recursive feedback loops as they interact so that the original form of participant units and any source of causation are lost or recast in an emergent process. Causality cannot be assigned uniquely to any one component or group of components within or surrounding the system (e.g., some code, icon, schema, program, central plan, clock). Each system component simultaneously is both cause and effect. There is no single cause or entry point to understanding the cycle. Each element is equally salient in driving the system through its role in the totality, for they are heterarchically arranged rather than hierarchically structured in terms of executive process. Rules of organization governing pattern induction cannot be inferred from or linearly reduced to changes in component system units.

Given that a system's current patterned structure is a context-sensitive response by its elemental ensembles, causes and consequences are interlocked. In this sense, systems are both *multicausal and noncausal*. They are multicausal in that each system component is equipotential (not privileged) in constraining its form. They are noncausal in that control is distributed in executive ignorance or without address throughout the system. Indeed, external stimulation of a system might not affect it because of its internal conservative dynamics, or change might occur disproportionately to the quantitative aspects of any perturbations, or change might be effected in a system through its internal dynamics rather than through external perturbation.

Predictions from the current pattern of a system to a future one could be limited in accuracy because of this uncertainty about determinant and effect (although, theoretically, with their specification, prediction becomes infallible at the global level). Also, the system might function to exponentially and recursively amplify minor uncertainties, instabilities, or changes, rendering long-term prediction at the specific rather than global level all but impossible. Finally, adaptive internal configurations might be preferred or stable, but they are not prefigured, hardwired, or predetermined, because they are always online responses to ongoing system component distributions or totalities in their receptive context. Thus, they could end up fully novel, emergent, spontaneous, nonlinear, or unique compared to prior system configurations.

In short, systems canalize toward possibilities that their current organization contain, but the nature of their online contextual adaptation limits the predictions that can be made about the system at other than the global level. The implication here is that the behavior of any one system element might be determined but becomes impossible to predict because, at best, only the global form or pattern of changes in a system are predictable.

## *States*

Self-organization activity produces the states of a system, which are sometimes called phases or phase spaces. States might reflect patterns that had been configured previously out of the array of elements constituting a system. Or they might be new patterns that emerge because they are the most adaptive in context, given the ongoing adaptive efforts of the system. Nevertheless, the ensemble of constituent elements and the typical contexts that states inhabit constrain systems. Moreover, they have self-preserving, self-correcting, or self-righting, autoequilibrating internal forces that tend to conserve their existing state patterns or momentary states. Therefore, a system often has a limited number of possible states, so that when impinged upon by powerful external forces, or perhaps even when there are miniscule impacts when the system is poised for change, such as with the so-called butterfly effect, the system might jump abruptly from one state to another. Normally, a system resists change in response to perturbations, especially if these are minor, thus preserving its stability, and yet it will spring abruptly into another state when the pressures can no longer be resisted. For example, the states of water and ice alternate at the critical temperature threshold of zero centigrade, but do not do so immediately when the threshold is attained.

A state is the essential information about a system. A system state space is a geometric representation of all possible states of a system according to its key (collective) parameters. The occupiable regions of a state space (its manifold) might be curved rather than flat or straight, and in this sense it is not cartesian. Vectors indicate the degree and direction in change in the next instant of time of the current point in space that the system occupies. Each point might have multiple vectors, and vector collections are called vector fields. A trajectory is the path of a succession of states and their vectors. Trajectory maps are called phase portraits.

The system's current steady state is the particular ordered relationship or compressed configuration among its elements or patterns. Steady or collective states possess relatively constant, particular, ordered temporal and spatial properties. As mentioned, these relations among elements that define steady states are preferred but not fixed in that they are not prefigured by individual elements or external factors, but are responsive adjustments in the dynamic adjustments of the elements in their field. Steady states are contained within boundaries that help hold together and protect constituents and their patterns, regulating information exchange with the surround. Steady states could stabilize at "far-from" static equilibrium conditions, reducing the system's degrees of freedom. All biological systems are characterized by stable "far-from-equilibrium" conditions.

The steady states of systems can take several forms. Monostable or local stability regimes involve one steady state. In a bistable regime, each of the states usually is stable dynamically but can be marginally unstable in structural terms so that states can oscillate with or visit one another in spontaneous fluctuation under the same boundary conditions (Wolff, 1991).

Also, states can split, producing multiple substates or multistability. For example, in families there is a spousal (sub)state or subsystem, a parenting subsystem (parents plus others, e.g., grandparents, stepparents), and a sibling subsystem. (Sub) states are separated by boundaries with different degrees of permeability, stability, and change. Both within and across boundary lines, transactions are governed by (explicit and implicit) rules and programs. In general, substates interact either positively (reciprocal feedback, bootstrapping, etc.) or negatively (damping, competition, etc.). Changes in one substate might effect changes in others, but buffering could also take place, depending on the substates' degree of coordination. Thus, substates manifest a changing relationship when there are evolving constraints so that their coherence may shift from stability, perhaps having a gradual evolution, to instability and dissolution.

## *Resource Flow*

The patterned whole through which a system operates is regulated in its commerce with the milieu by rules of resource (e.g., information, energy) flow. The protective boundary enclosing the system permits resource exchange with the milieu, and any new incoming resource is evaluated as to whether it confirms or disconfirms existing structure or other system attributes. Feedback takes place when incoming resources are looped back so that part of the system's output later becomes its own input, thus modifying subsequent incoming resources (Chandler & Boutilier, 1992). Resources that register in a system can have either positive or negative feedback effects. Positive feedback acts to amplify the direction of an effect on a system suggested by an incoming resource; there is matched escalation, with mutual facilitation and initial and subsequent effect (as in reciprocal feedback, bootstrapping; van Geert, 1991). By contrast, negative feedback functions as a controlling device. When a resource is processed by the system, negative feedback loops act to constrain associated effects (e.g., correction, damping, inversion, competition).

There are two opposing views about the permeability of the boundaries enclosing systems. Maturana (Maturana & Varela, 1987) posited that systems are organizationally (not energetically) closed. That is, they are self-organizing ("autopoetic"), autonomous, and closed to external resources; information is merely something that interacts with systems. The dynamic, flexible nature of the structure of a system determines which events in its medium it can interact with and the way this can be achieved. External forces do not possess a corollary effect on the system. The relationship between such a "structurally determined" entity and its medium can be called "structurally coupled."

Prigogine and Stengers (1984) offer the more traditional perspective on information flow in systems. In physical systems, there is an inevitable movement toward disorder, or away from the entropic equilibrium of a stable closed system. Physical systems are governed by entropy, which concerns movement to a state of maximal disorganization, inability to do work, and zero information. However, living systems are dissipative of or export entropy, for they are in a relatively constant movement toward increasing complexity through their energy and matter absorption and exchange and through their organizational work. They possess "negentropy" (negative entropy), or far-from-equilibrium conditions, maximal order, organizational adaptability, and flexibility. That is, they are not only open to information, or a continuous flow of energy and matter both into and out of the system, but also stable, self-organizing, and self-protective. This latter position is consistent with the present work.

## *Energy*

Systems are considered "open" when they permit energy to enter and potentially galvanize change. Normally, systems exist in equilibrium with the contextual energy about them and in the inflow and outflow of that energy. They transform incoming energy into increasing self-organized patterns, and manage its dissipation and disordering potential. Although for humans, there are many examples related to the inflow and outflow of energy, per se, according to many adherents of nonlinear dynamical of systems theory, often, at the psychological level, the equivalent of energy flow as the driving force behind self-organizational system dynamics concerns information flow rather than energy flow. That is, in psychology, often information replaces energy as system energizer.

Humans are complex systems existing far from equilibrium. As they self-organize, they incorporate incoming energy into complex states far from the equilibrium and system complexity that might otherwise be expected. However, humans need continual energy entering their open system to maintain their complex self-organization. Humans draw in the energy, use it in system workings, lose some, and exchange some, in a dissipative process that needs renewal. For example, locomotion in the toddler is an energetic activity that needs energetic fuel to continue in the short term and to improve in the long term. As new states emerge or coalesce from the confluence of system interactions, they need continual energy to maintain stability, avoid regression or loss of transitional gains, and increase system order.

In these senses, living systems are energy sinks. They continually extract information (and energy), store it, maintain it, and order it. This leads to exchange with the environment and self-repair and restoration. In other words, systems try to increase the energy flow available for use, in an autocatalytic feedback process. Living systems cannot be defined independently of their energy surround. They exist in context. Thus, change in living systems might derive from either internal or external (energetic) system dynamics.

In general, biological systems evolve because of energy dynamics (Goerner, 1995). Energy seeks maximum flow within a system, and the more structured the flow within a system's internal architecture, the more rapid the flow becomes. If energy builds up in a system, a pressure or force to flow will increase. However, it is countered by the stabilizing resistances (inertia, barriers, etc.) of the system. This confrontation produces increased cycles of energetic flow within the current form of the system. However, the speed of any type of energy flow is constrained by the nature of the form that it takes. If energy flow pressure exceeds internal resistance to form changes within the system, a crisis point is reached. Consequently, a new system configuration that reinstates maximal energy fluidity within the confines of efficient organizational design evolves within the system network. That is, the system autocreates more complex interwoven structure to maximize energetic mobility. In this process, the information contained in the initial conditions alters to the point that new information is created.

Note that according to Valsiner (1991), in living systems, flow does not only proceed from outside to inside. Feed-forward mechanisms are important in purposive systems such as human ones. Intention, will, desire, and related functions are forward-oriented focuses of selection before consequences take place. They not only feed information into the environment but also select and modify it. Expectations feed forward to enable systems to find "desired" results (Michel, 1991).

## *Hierarchies*

The component elements of a system are equally complex. They form hierarchies where core or top-level units are more prominent than peripheral or lower-order ones. The system functions at multiple, parallel, interacting levels, yet none are more privileged in understanding its dynamic. An important feature of systems is that simpler systems could nest within more complex systems. Systems function at several hierarchically arranged strata, which interact mutually or reciprocally. Moreover, there might be subsystems involved. When a system changes its pattern, configuration, or state, all the levels and subsystems in the system are affected. Moreover such change happens simultaneously, not linearly or sequentially, because systems function as wholes and change as wholes. Because system patterns are determined in a multicausal, synergistic way, any reductionist explanation of causality would mask the transactional integration across their layers. Interlevel relations or reciprocal interactions between elements of different layers help drive system organization.

Core superordinate levels of hierarchies within systems might influence lower levels (which does not deny that there are effects from lower to higher levels, as well). Systems possess higher-order influences that act on lower levels to produce system reorganization. That is, there might be supervenient top-down effects, downward causation, reflective circularity, or emergent interactionism (Sperry, 1991) in system organization. Lower levels are embedded in the larger envelope of the whole system, which has its own "irreducible higher-level, forms." Thus, for example, the mind is not dualistic and immaterial, but is monistically mentalist or emergent through interaction. The top-down influence of higher levels in a system's hierarchical structure permits it to surpass passive drift. The feed-forward discussed previously is found. In short, higher-order pattern is created emergently out of system element organization, and then comes to influence that organization.

This being said, primary changes in systems also occur at lower levels, through interactions of elements. These interactions include coupling or cooperativity across the elements. In systems, lower-order interactions are termed bottom-up. Top-down processes are influenced the by bottom-up ones even as they are influenced by them (Granic & Patterson, 2006).

In hierarchical structuration, a superordinate level incorporates only some significant characteristics of subordinate ones. Thus, for example, in the developmental process, subordinate levels might manifest continuity in development, only gradually shifting, whereas superordinate ones might exhibit discontinuous, step-like progression.

However, systems theory today would conclude that despite a system's different subsystems, layers, and hierarchical structure, there is no one executive node running the others, or a machine within the machine. Output is a function of the contribution of all system elements, even if some might be differentially weighted in importance.

## *Stability*

Existing system states tend to stability. They seek plateaus or limited locations in their state space, or small regions restricting their boundary conditions (minima in connectionism), and not steep slopes of change. System stability is a function of contextual stability, in part, because systems dynamically soft-assemble patterns in context. Even if far from equilibrium, systems have homeostatic properties that act conservatively to maintain current patterns in a process of self-stabilization. Equilibrium is attained through a balancing of system parts so that they couple or reciprocally select, moderate to, or adjust to each other. System coherence damps or compresses its components' noise and degrees of freedom. Once a state is established, even if far from equilibrium, the system uses corrective (negative) feedback loops to preserve that set point, reducing system variability. The system's thermostat is regulated to resist change in the equilibrium state by altering internal conditions to adjust for modification in external ones. Actions that deviate from the equilibrium state induce "error-activated processes," prompting homeostasis. Another self-stabilizing mechanism, important in development, involves systems gravitating around a trajectory instead of one set point (e.g., catch-up in premature in physical maturation). Similarly, homeostasis necessarily does not concern one fixed equilibrium point, for it may involve complex rhythms over time.

Stability of a (sub)system can be maintained by coupling it with another one which can serve as a buffer. The system with greater degrees of freedom or variety in coupling can maintain, control, limit, reduce, and counteract (or even destroy) variety in the new amalgamated system unit and the environment in which it functions. In this way, for example, caregivers normally increase their infants' chance of survival.

To conclude, systems can exist in varying states of stability. It they are superstable, eventually they return to equilibrium no matter what the degree of perturbation. If system equilibrium is stable to begin with, even quite strong perturbations will not affect them significantly. However, if systems exist in unstable equilibrium, even relatively minor external perturbations might induce dramatic change in system behavior.

## *Iteration and Feedback*

Williams and Arrigo (2002) indicated that nonlinear dynamical systems have a propensity to behave as a feedback loop, in recursively and repetitively self-reinforcing interactions. A system can express either negative or positive feedback (Granic & Patterson, 2006). In the latter, system element interactions amplify certain variations, leading to system change. In the former, change is damped through preservation of existing element linkages, and minimization of new variation, thereby perpetuating stability. In positive feedback, cascades of change might develop as each new variation feeds into the system, facilitating its restructuring. The system heads toward increasing overall reorganization, to the point of creating instability and novel overall structure.

## *Change*

Systems tend toward preferred solutions in their configurational arrangements, not hard or prefigured ones. All systems possess some disorder or entropy that can be magnified. In the course of interacting with the surround, systems receive either positive, confirming information or negative, disconfirming information. The latter, or any destabilizing, dissipative element (e.g., novel, constant environmental stimulus), could trigger disequilibrium, symmetry breaking, or energy flow from one system part to another, creating regions of nucleation where fluctuations predominate. Systems in transition or far from equilibrium are more responsive to or attentive to variable input and minor perturbation. They test constantly their boundaries. They explore readily novel patterns or alternate regions in their state space. Minor disruptive perturbations might be amplified, leading to increasing deviation of the tonic equilibrium state, which then is consolidated in reorganized equilibrium. Morphogenesis, adaptive self-reorganization, or transformation of the system could result, despite attempted resistance. Even minute differences in initial conditions could lead to quite diverging system paths, for systems could be exquisitely sensitive to initial conditions.

## *Perturbations*

Typically, state-shift jumps, often called phase transitions, or bifurcations, occur in response to some perturbation, or trigger. Perturbations act on complete system organization over system elements, rather than on isolated parts of a system. Perturbations influence systems when they move critical variables beyond thresholds of change, although the thresholds might vary with context. The trigger can be tiny, as in the butterfly effect, if it sufficiently approaches parameters of change.

A new state could end up independent of its parent one, a nonlinear, discontinuous, qualitative, disjunctive leap, bifurcation, or shift in structure, without having a stable intermediate between it and the parent structure. The bifurcation is irreversible, for given a system pattern's contextual and historical origins, it can only change in new directions and not back to its old form, although it could end up resembling that form if reconfiguration dynamics dictate it as a solution to field vectors.

## *Self-Organization*

System dynamics constitute natural organizational processes with efficient, graceful, flexible, and adaptive characteristics. They possess self-organizational properties, both within and across levels. That is, systems reorganize without preprogrammed patterns of organization. New forms or system states assemble out of the matrix of ongoing system interactions, without external or internal instruction. The presence of preprogrammed patterns would prove inefficient for systems, because systems need flexibility for optimal functional adaptation to all possible contextual configurations in which they might become embedded.

Therefore, prefiguring all the necessary programs within such systems before the systems deploy would require too many such fixed patterns. Systems function most flexibly when they can self-organize online in context.

## *Emergence*

The capacity for self-organization in systems is essential for their optimal adaptation and emergence. Self-organization allows the spontaneous emergence of coherent patterns and order in a system from its nonlinear interactions of component parts, within the contexts in which it must adapt. When a whole develops a property not predictable from the sum of the parts, the new feature is an emergent property. Therefore, emergence is the self-organization of patterns having new properties not predictable uniquely from the local interactions of the system elements from which it arises. For example, mixing hydrogen and oxygen gases at room temperature will produce liquidity (water), an emergent property not predictable from the properties of the parts.

Schore (2000) underscored that nonlinear dynamical systems use energy to facilitate the development of emergent forms through self-organization. When systems are open to energy flow and energy use, they "incorporate" the energy into themselves, facilitating movement away from equilibrium. Energy input helps move a system toward conditions far from equilibrium, where discontinuous change, even to minor perturbations, becomes possible. Given the right conditions in a system, slow or minor change in a variable could lead to abrupt emergence of new discontinuous patterns within the system.

## *Dynamical Approach to Emotional Development*

### Introduction

Witherington and Crichton (2007) described the dynamic system approach to the study of emotional development. It emphasizes how emotions emerge in a self-organized manner in ongoing contexts and how their multiple components or subsystems coalesce in emotional expression. None of the components are considered primary and the emotional expression as a whole is considered multiply determined. There is no inherent control system through a set of instructions in the organism directing emotional expression because, instead, it is context-sensitive and specific.

Some proponents of the dynamic system perspective maintain that the functional approach is inappropriately causal, because in it, functions serve as antecedent conditions, dictating the generation of emotional expression. According to Witherington and Crichton, the Aristotelian explanation of causation can help in this matter. In this regard, the functional approach focuses on formal and final causes of explanation, whereas the dynamic system approach addresses efficient and material causes. That is, the functional approach emphasizes what is common across actions and contexts, whereas the dynamic systems approach adds how specific emotional expressions emerge in specific contexts. Overton (2006) presented a framework that allows an integrated view of these approaches, termed *relational developmental metatheory*. It can help specify the multiple levels of analysis and explanation of emotions, both in terms of specific contexts and organizational universals.

## Metatheory

Witherington (2007) explored the dynamic systems approach as a general metatheory for development psychology. For Witherington, at the mathematical level, a dynamic system reflects the operation of a recursive, iterative process, where the system state at time $t$ (system state $t$) is transformed at time $t+1$ into a differ state $(t+1)$, which serves as state $t$ for the subsequent step in the state's evolution, in a feedback process. [Witherington does not specify the difference between linear and nonlinear dynamical systems, but his approach is consistent with the latter view].

Witherington indicated there are two different camps within the approach, concerning whether higher-order forms emerge and influence the process of development, thereby complementing how lower-order, moment-to-moment microinteractions produce behavioral outcome. The first view is contextualist and emphasizes that in development everything can be explained by the moment-to-moment interactions in particular situations and their bottom-up influences on the system of behavior (Thelen & Smith, 2006), whereas the second view also considers higher-order form as emergent, adding top-down influences to the explanation of development (van Geert & Steenbeck, 2005). In the contextualist version of dynamic systems theory, moment-to-moment actions and changes of the ongoing system dynamic in specific contexts are critical to understanding systems. In the second version of dynamic systems theory, although real-time analysis of system behavior is important, it is also relevant to decipher higher-order, formal, abstracted, macroscopic variables. This approach is labeled the organismic-contextualist dynamic systems approach. Despite the relevance of this level in understanding systems for the organismic-contextualist position, it still emphasizes that real time, action in context holds primacy and serves to characterize the higher-order level.

Witherington maintained that the two versions of dynamic systems theory differ fundamentally in their worldviews about causation and explanation of behavior. In the contextualist approach, systems behave online in context and there are no higher-order forms that help explain behavior in terms of Aristotle's formal and final causes. For the contextualist perspective of systems theory, the perception that there is a sequential flow in development at the macroscopic level is immaterial in understanding the causal origins of behavior. System self-organization takes place exclusively in a bottom-up fashion, that is, in real-time assembly in context, or in material and efficient terms. Development is accrual of online, here-and-now actions in context. The form adopted by a system among its constituent components derive from the contextual ground, and higher-order patterns are either superficial global order without causal status, merely epiphenomenona, or even illusory. As for the more integrative, organismic-contextualist dynamic systems view of the development, it is more top-down and understands higher-order form as emergent and irreducible to bottom-up processes, thereby constituting another level of explanation of behavior and development. Clearly, the present work favors the latter view.

According to Witherington, it is possible to have a combined view of dynamic systems and of development, in which systems constitute reflections of both bottom-up and top-down causal processes, in a circular or interlevel causality. That is, in a combined dynamic systems model, causality is understood as involving all four Aristotelian causal mechanisms. The crux of emergence of higher-order forms in systems lies in circular or interlevel causality, as explained below.

## System Properties

For Witherington, and consistent with the present chapter, dynamic systems have been applied to a variety of living and nonliving phenomena. The mathematical modeling of systems lend themselves to graphic representation on the axes relevant to the particular system at issue, with the axes helping to map system state changes over time in the state space formed by the intersection of the axes. Trajectories are established that connect successive points as they change in the state space of the system. The trajectories are called velocity vectors and their movement in the state space field graphs patterns reflecting their direction and rate of change. The state change patterns reflect underlying differential and difference mathematical equations. When their solutions are stable, they can be depicted graphically as areas of a system state space toward which its trajectories converge. The system can reflect dramatic reconfigurations in patterning, depending on values of key parameters in its governing equations. When these control parameters reach bifurcation points, nonlinear and complex patterns emerge. Pattern configuration in a system is not reducible either to the components of the system or to its control parameters or to its axes used to describe the movement of the system in state space.

Witherington explained that self-organization in a system refers to emergence of new patterns in the system because of the manner of interaction among its components. For example, as basic elements of a system interact, new patterns are formed that have different and more complex properties than those of the components. The original components do not have inherent instructions or preconfigured designs for formation of the resultant patterns that emerge from the interaction. New patterns constitute new relations among system components that are more than isomorphic redescriptions of the atomistic, isolated components of the system. The new patterns emerge spontaneously out of the components matrix. Increasing order is created in the face of the natural tendency toward increasing disorder (that is, increasing entropy), assuming the system at issue is open to energy exchange with the environment, and thereby incorporating free energy that thermodynamically counters within the system the irreversible increasing entropy and movement toward disorder.

Lewis also has contributed pertinent ideas. Circular causality in systems refers to the vertical, reciprocal, hierarchical, nested, and hetarchical interactions across the different lower-order and higher-order levels of a system (Lewis, 2000a, 2000b). There are also horizontal, part–part interactions or couplings of system components within levels. The higher-level parts do not exist in and of themselves divorced from the lower-level ones, because the latter determine or even generate the control parameters that govern the higher-order ones. The collective action of the lower-order individual parts cooperatively determines the nature of the control parameters at upper levels, which, in turn act downward to constrain or "enslave" the lower-order parts (Haken, 1996). Stable synergies emerge as wholes that go beyond the component parts, and might not even change format if any of the individual parts change. At the same time, the parts interact amongst themselves to create forces toward emergence. Causality in the system lies in the meeting of lower and higher levels of the system and their mutual framing, organizing, or regulating influences. There are both part-whole and whole-part dynamics in systems; macrodevelopment cannot be reduced to a collection of microdevelopments, and the general and specific can coexist in one amalgamated system.

## Summary

The present chapter provides a tutorial on the basics of systems theory, including nonlinear dynamical ones. It has included developmental applications, such as in epigenesis and in the development of emotions. It prepares the way for the next chapter on the topics of attractors and complexity. Together, these two chapters provide a basis for understanding better causality, transition processes, or the how and why of development. A major issue in the field is whether nonlinear dynamical systems modeling is conducive to stage modeling. I adopt the point of view that the two approaches are not incompatible, and indeed, in the next chapter I describe a model of transitioning from attractors to complex adaptive system processes that appears to undergird the changes described by the present model of Neo-Piagetian cognitive development. Inevitably, some of the concepts given in an introductory way in this chapter are taken up again at a more complex level in the next.

## References

Abraham, F. D., & Gilgen, A. R. (Eds.). (1995). *Chaos theory in psychology*. Westport: Greenwood.

Boom, J. (2004). Commentary on: Piaget's stages: The unfinished symphony of cognitive development. *New Ideas in Psychology, 22*, 239–247.

Brown, C. A. (2009). Mazes, conflict, and paradox: Tools for understanding chronic pain. *Pain Practice, 9*, 235–243.

Camras, L. A. (1992). Expressive development and basic emotions. *Cognition and Emotion, 6*, 269–283.
Chandler, M. J., & Boutilier, R. G. (1992). The development of dynamic system reasoning. *Human Development, 35*, 121–137.
Gleick, J. (1987). *Chaos: Making a new science*. New York: Penguin.
Goerner, S. J. (1995). Chaos and deep ecology. In F. D. Abraham & A. R. Gilgen (Eds.), *Chaos theory in psychology* (pp. 3–18). Westport: Greenwood.
Goldfield, E. C. (1995). *Emergent forms: Origins and early development of human action and perception*. New York: Oxford University Press.
Goldstein, M. H., King, A. P., & West, M. J. (2003). Social interaction shapes babbling: Testing parallels between birdsong and speech. *Proceedings of the National Academy of Sciences, 100*, 8030–8035.
Granic, I., & Patterson, G. R. (2006). Toward a comprehensive model of antisocial development: A dynamic systems approach. *Psychological Review, 113*, 101–131.
Guastello, S. J., Koopmans, M., & Pincus, D. (Eds.). (2009). *Chaos and complexity in psychology: The theory of nonlinear dynamical systems*. New York: Cambridge University Press.
Haken, H. (1996). *Principles of brain functioning: A synergetic approach to brain activity, behavior and cognition*. New York: Springer.
Heath, R. A. (2000). *Nonlinear dynamics: Techniques and applications in psychology*. Mahwah: Erlbaum.
Howe, M. L., & Lewis, M. D. (2005). The importance of dynamic systems approaches for understanding development. *Developmental Review, 25*, 247–251.
Johnson, N. F. (2007). *Simply complexity: A clear guide to complexity theory*. New York: Oxford University Press.
Kugler, P. N., Shaw, R. E., Vicente, K. J., & Kinsella-Shaw, J. (1991). The role of attractors in the self-organization of intentional systems. In R. R. Hoffman & D. S. Palermo (Eds.), *Cognition and the symbolic processes: Applied and ecological perspectives* (pp. 387–431). Hillsdale: Erlbaum.
Kuo, Z.-Y. (1970). The need for coordinated efforts in developmental studies. In L. R. Aronson, E. Tobach, D. S. Lehrman, & J. S. Rosenblatt (Eds.), *Development and evolution of behavior: Essays in memory of T. C. Schneirla* (pp. 181–193). San Francisco: Freeman.
Lewis, M. D. (2000a). The promise of dynamic systems approaches for an integrated account of human development. *Child Development, 71*, 36–43.
Lewis, M. D. (2000b). Emotional self-organization at three time scales. In M. D. Lewis & I. Granic (Eds.), *Emotion, development, and self-organization: Dynamic systems approaches to emotional development* (pp. 37–69). Cambridge: Cambridge University Press.
Lewis, M. D., & Granic, I. (2000). Introduction: A new approach to the study of emotional development. In M. D. Lewis & I. Granic (Eds.), *Emotion, development, and self-organization: Dynamic systems approaches to emotional development* (pp. 1–12). Cambridge: Cambridge University Press.
Martin, C. L., & Ruble, D. N. (2010). Patterns of gender development. *Psychology, 71*, 353–381.
Masterpasqua, F., & Perna, P. (Eds.). (1997). *The psychological meaning of chaos: Translating theory into practice*. Washington: American Psychological Association.
Maturana, H. R., & Varela, F. J. (1987). *The tree of knowledge*. Boston: New Science.
Michel, G. F. (1991). Development of infant manual skills: Motor programs, schemata, or dynamic systems? In J. Fagard & P. H. Wolff (Eds.), *The development of timing control and temporal organization in coordinated action: Invariant relative timing, rhythms and coordination* (pp. 175–200). Amsterdam: North Holland.
Mitchell, M. (2009). *Complexity: A guided tour*. New York: Oxford University Press.
Overton, W. F. (2006). Developmental psychology: Philosophy, concepts, methodology. In W. Damon & R. M. Lerner (Eds.), *Handbook of child psychology: Vol. 1. Theoretical models of human development* (6th ed., pp. 18–80). Hoboken: Wiley.
Prigogine, I., & Stengers, I. (1984). *Order out of chaos: Man's new dialogue with nature*. New York: Bantam.

Robertson, R., & Combs, A. (Eds.). (1995). *Chaos theory in psychology and the life sciences*. Mahwah: Erlbaum.

Schneirla, T. C. (1957). The concept of development in comparative psychology. In D. B. Harris (Ed.), *The concept of development: An issue in the study of human behavior* (pp. 78–108). Minneapolis: University of Minnesota Press.

Schore, A. N. (2000). The self-organization of the right brain and the neurobiology of emotional development. In M. D. Lewis & I. Granic (Eds.), *Emotion, development, and self-organization: Dynamic systems approaches to emotional development* (pp. 155–185). Cambridge: Cambridge University Press.

Sperry, R. W. (1991). In defense of mentalism and emergent interaction. *Journal of Mind and Behavior, 12*, 221–248.

Thelen, E., Corbetta, D., Kamm, K., Spencer, J. P., Schneider, K., & Zernicke, R. F. (1993). The transition to reaching: Mapping intention and intrinsic dynamics. *Child Development, 64*, 1058–1098.

Thelen, E., Kelso, J. A. S., & Fogel, A. (1987). Self-organizing systems and infant motor development. *Developmental Review, 7*, 39–65.

Thelen, E., & Smith, L. B. (1994). *A dynamic systems approach to the development of cognition and action*. Cambridge: MIT Press.

Thelen, E., & Smith, L. B. (2006). Dynamic systems theories. In W. Damon & R. M. Lerner (Eds.), *Handbook of child psychology: Vol. 1. Theoretical models of human development* (6th ed., pp. 258–312). Hoboken: Wiley.

Thelen, E., & Ulrich, B. D. (1991). Hidden skills: A dynamical systems analysis of treadmill stepping during the first year. *Monographs of the Society for Research in Child Development, 56* (1, Serial No. 223).

Vallacher, R. R., Read, S. J., & Nowak, A. (2002). The dynamical perspective in personality and social psychology. *Personality and Social Psychology Review, 6*, 264–273.

Valsiner, J. (1991). Construction of the mental: From the 'cognitive revolution' to the study of development. *Theory and Psychology, 1*, 477–494.

van Geert, P. (1991). A dynamic systems model of cognitive and language grown. *Psychological Review, 98*, 3–53.

van Geert, P., & Steenbeck, H. (2005). Explaining after by before: Basic aspects of a dynamic systems approach to the study of development. *Developmental Review, 25*, 408–442.

Waddington, C. H. (1957). *The strategy of the genes*. London: Allen & Unwin.

Waldrop, M. M. (1992). *Complexity: The emerging science at the edge of order and chaos*. New York: Touchstone.

Ward, L. M. (2002). *Dynamical cognitive science*. Cambridge: MIT Press.

Williams, C., & Arrigo, B. (2002). *Law, psychology, and justice: Chaos theory and the new (dis) order*. Albany: State University of New York Press.

Witherington, D. C. (2007). The dynamic systems approach as metatheory for developmental psychology. *Human Development, 50*, 127–153.

Witherington, D. C., & Crichton, J. A. (2007). Framework for understanding emotions and their development: Functionalist and dynamic systems approaches. *Emotion, 7*, 628–637.

Wolff, P. H. (1991). Endogenous motor rhythms in young infants. In J. Fagard & P. H. Wolff (Eds.), *The development of timing control and temporal organization in coordinated action: Invariant relative timing, rhythms and coordination* (pp. 119–133). Amsterdam: North Holland.

# Chapter 28
# Attractors, Complexity

## Introduction

This chapter stands as the one most directly concerned with the approach of the present work to causality, determinants of behavior, and transition mechanisms underlying the present Neo-Piagetian model. I describe attractors and complexity to prepare description of a five-step transitional process in systems gravitating to increased adaptiveness. More traditional approaches to the origins of behavior concentrate on genetics, environment, or their interaction, and this approach has become quite refined through the concept of epigenesis, explained in depth in the two chapters following this one. However, a nonlinear dynamical systems theory is a transdisciplinary approach, and it carries the study of causality beyond living systems to systems, in general. In this sense, the five-step transitional model that I developed in terms of attractors and complexity could underwrite generic change processes beyond human development. In this regard, my study of the how and why in the process of development might help explain wider change processes.

## Attractors

### *Introduction*

When system dynamics that describe the movement of a system in its multiple state spaces repeatedly end at the same place in the system's trajectories, the system can be described as characterized by attractors. Attractors gravitate to attractor basins in its state space. As a metaphor, consider a child rolling a ball into a ditch and watching the ball then go up and down the sides until it stops moving. The image of the trajectory of the ball rolling down the sides of the ditch could represent the repeated differing trajectories of a system's path as it moves in its basin and eventually settles into an attractor state. In the present example, the attractor basin consists of no movement at the end of the ditch at its bottom. At this point, the movement has zero velocity, and the system comes to equilibrium through its lack of motion.

G. Young, *Development and Causality: Neo-Piagetian Perspectives*,
DOI 10.1007/978-1-4419-9422-6_28, © Springer Science+Business Media, LLC 2011

A basin can be described as converging on, settling into, having an affinity for, being sucked into, or visiting an attractor state. Convergent attractor forces in the basin of an attractor guide trajectories toward the attractor, whereas divergent ones increasingly separate them. In an intact attractor, the former forces are stronger than the latter, and this is especially true for more important central states in the attractor compared to more peripheral ones. Similarly, in a system with multiple attractors, each attractor exerts a contributing force on the system, and their configurational layout determines the system's dynamic.

Some attractors are repellors, which reject such visits rather than accepting them. In this regard, the ditch metaphor depicts them as inverted, with the ball at the top ready to roll down at the slightest shove from the nonpreferred cusp region.

A concrete example of the regular attractor involves activated receptor neurons during nerve cell assembly formation functioning as basins for attractors in perception (Freeman, 1995). Also, in the infant, the alternation of stepping movements functions as an attractor state because it is stable even when a treadmill moves one foot faster than the other (Thelen & Ulrich, 1991).

Attractors govern a system when the system almost always gravitates over time to certain fixed values, or to an oscillation among several values, irrespective of its initial value and later perturbations. Mathematical models can represent the movement of a system in state space. This movement refers to the manner in which the data generated by the system's movement can be graphed in time. Attractors, then, are mathematical structures that describe certain classes of motion of objects in space. Mathematically, an attractor exists within a phase space or vector field that has a neighborhood in which every point stays nearby and approaches the attractor as time goes to infinity, except under certain conditions. The graph of a system's trajectories in the neighborhoods or basins of one or more of its attractors is called its phase portrait.

Metaphorically, an attractor is like a magnet or center of gravity in mathematical space. An attractor pulls the system toward it from many different layouts in its state space, even when it is perturbed. Therefore, an attractor constitutes a stable pattern in system behavior. Communicated in another way, an attractor represents a point in phase space in which the system settles down, and ceases to change, at least momentarily. When a system settles into an attractor, with its stable properties, the system has entered a stable state.

Living systems are typically multistable, having several coexisting attractors (Granic & Patterson, 2006). For example, as young infants develop their leg movement skills, the data suggest that they function from an initial attractor state of repetitions of spring-like, alternating flexions and extensions (Thelen & Smith, 1994). However, in this example, the system is "soft-assembled," or prone to instability, as other elements in the motor system are acquired in development. Soft-assembled systems allow exploration of more complex attractors, and in this case, that would correspond to walking. This example suggests that rigid attractor system stability is not adaptive in the long term and that soft assembly in attractor formation is adaptive.

Attractors are always stable, at least in the short term, reaching equilibrium. However, inherent in any system pattern or organization are the seeds of renewed, more complex self-reorganization, as additional energy, information, acquisitions, or contextual demands influence the system. In general, attractors assemble out of the elements in a system as adaptive configurations, yet contain attributes that lend themselves to potential evolution to different configurations that are further adaptive to the system. Moreover, in the process of reaching equilibrium, the system might cycle between different poles, with both adaptive.

## *Latent Attractors*

Vallacher, Coleman, Nowak, and Bui-Wrzosinska (2010) modeled human group conflict in terms of dynamical systems and attractors. They indicated that dynamic modeling has been applied to living and nonliving systems, such as slime molds and galaxies, respectively. At the psychological level, attractors represent a restricted range of commonly experienced action tendencies and mental states. Thoughts and feelings coalesce around common meanings and develop higher-order global states, such as beliefs or social judgments, which resist alteration to new input. The attractor could be represented both mathematically and metaphorically.

Figure 28.1 represents a dynamical system with two attractors corresponding to opposite pulls in action tendency or mental state. The bottom of the well represents its "local energy minimum." The width of the well indicates the basin of attraction, or the range of states that are part of the attractor structure. The broader the well, the more the attractor represented could resist perturbation. The broader the well, the more it could assimilate or absorb a broad range of states, including

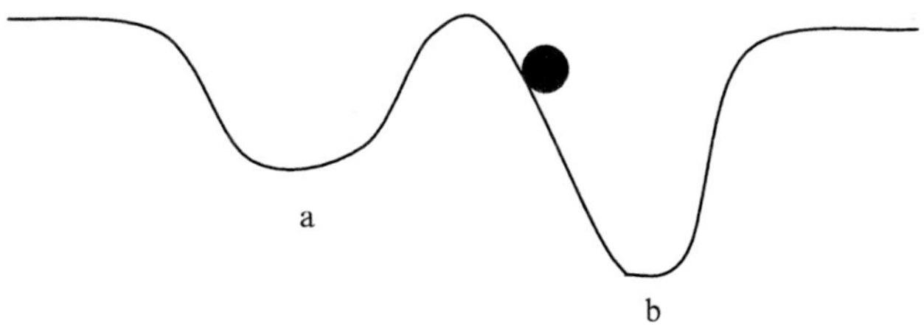


**Fig. 28.1** A dynamical system with two attractors corresponding to constructive relations (**a**) and destructive relations (**b**). The figure illustrates how behavior can tip into a positive or a negative pattern, depending on the pull of the attractors involved. In the figure, two attractors are illustrated, and their depth indicates the difficulty to get out of them while their width indicates the ease to fall into them. In the present case, the ball indicates the behavior falling into the negative attractor, which is the one that is more difficult to get out of. Reprinted with the permission of American Psychological Association. Vallacher, R. R., Coleman, P. T., Nowak, A., & Bui-Wrzosinska, L. (2010). Copyright © 2010. [Figure 1, Page. 266]

information, ideas, and events that appear inconsistent with its extant structure, without the pressure to lapse into disequilibrium and accommodate its structure. Also, the deeper the well, the better the attractor represented can resist changes to its ongoing state. The stronger the attractor, the better it resists perturbations even to strong influences, thereby resisting being dislodged, and so maintaining its equilibrium.

Inconsistencies act on the attractor, and when it is not broad enough or deep enough, it can be perturbed enough to gravitate into or transform into a new attractor structure or toward one (a latent attractor). When a threshold of change is reached, the jump to the new qualitative state is sudden, and the new state is qualitatively different than the preexisting one.

Hysteresis refers to when two states are comparable in strength and pull on action tendencies and mental states. Given the comparability of the states, whichever will be the dominant attractor alternates. Therefore, any incorporated information, events, or other influences can have diametrically opposite effects, depending on which of the attractors currently is dominant. Or a system could have multiple attractors within its confines that govern its dynamics and they could coexist rather than conflict.

Vallacher et al. pointed out the inevitability of change in systems that gravitate to new attractor states – latent attractors might be an inevitable consequence of a system having developed a "manifest" attractor. As attractors function, they might ignore, downplay, discount, or suppress some field elements while bolstering others. However, these background elements might self-organize to construct a latent attractor that could become suddenly manifest in a nonlinear way when conditions promote it to threshold degree. The new attractor could develop latently in a gradual, long-term, and imperceptible way but appear in a punctuated, discontinuous, abrupt way.

Control parameters represent the variables along which thresholds of discontinuous change are placed. When these are traversed, the change could lead to changes other than transforming into a new attractor. The variable might change only a small amount, but it might be sufficient to induce system change. The system could bifurcate into multiple attractors in its attractor landscape, and they might have different structures than the original.

## *Attractor Types*

There are different kinds of attractor states that have significance for biological systems. Point or fixed attractors, for the most part, draw the system to a single state of convergence. They fluctuate about stable periods, resist alternation, and return spontaneously from most changed courses after marginal perturbation. The system gravitates to a steady state or a constant value after perturbation, as when a pendulum returns to its resting point after perturbation.

Limit-cycle or periodic attractors are characterized by stable cycles of periodicity across alternative substates. The system gravitates periodically between two different locations in its state space, as in the movement of a pendulum.

Another type of attractor integrates two oscillatory ones, taking a torus or donut shape in trajectory pattern; think of a loosened pendulum that moves forward and back as well as to the sides. Torus attractors help explain the integration of two (motor) rhythms of different base frequency into a superordinate rhythm with a novel frequency related to the constituent ones in a "wrap-around" fashion.

"Strange" attractors function within a particular region of state space but produce random, nonredundant, locally nondeterministic trajectories within it; thus, they are bounded and globally determined but eventually pierce arbitrarily every small region in the attractor space. State movement within a strange attractor is labeled "chaotic," and these attractors often are called chaotic (discussed in the next section). It is well known that one class of attractors is called chaotic or strange, but so-called chaotic attractors are not chaotic in the common meaning of the term. Rather, from a global perspective, they are ordered structures. Mathematically, they are ordered data pattern generators in state space.

The stability of the preferred attractor in a system, its propensity to stay in one particular state and resist phase resetting, is determined by several factors. The more it is honed by continued coordinations or reentrant mappings of its components, the tighter its network (Thelen & Smith, 1994). System stability is influenced by its local relaxation time, or the duration needed to resist and return to the initial state after a small perturbation. In addition, the global stability of a system is regulated by its global equilibration time and the speed at which its governing controlling parameter is changing (see below). Also, noise sources from subsystems act to push the system away from preferred attractor states. Finally, the nature of the pattern of changes (variability, decay, etc.) in key components over time is important.

Attractors might contribute to system evolution through their competition when there is more than one in a system as it self-organizes. This competition only can occur in systems open to energy flow. That is, when energy thermodynamically "pumps" a system to a high-energy grade level, it can play a critical escapement role, permitting the budding of additional attractors. In living biological systems, such accrual of energy from the surround is a constant function. In behavioral systems, information can serve as the activator in attractor generation (Kugler, Shaw, Vicente, & Kinsella-Shaw, 1991). When there are two or more attractors in a system, their gradient fields interact in ways dependent on the attractors' unique layout. These attractors might compete within a system when the active portions of their gradient fields overlap. The interface boundary separating the attractor fields, where trajectories both converge and depart, is called a saddle point (A separatrix trajectory separates neighboring attractors, tending to neither.). The saddle point can relate the fields by creating a nonlinear higher-order attractor that simultaneously satisfies the constraints of subsumed gradient fields. At the same time, the latter fields would be annihilated.

## *Chaotic Change*

In system transformation, change can be either regulated or chaotic. Both are deterministic, but in the former case, resultant "solutions" follow expected or "laminar" flow patterns derived from the system's initial conditions and fixed properties, whereas in the latter case, turbulent, wild, sudden bursts interrupt regulated predictability (Gottman, 1991).

Thus, chaotic attractors are combinations of disorder and order. They exhibit deterministic, constrained randomness, or unpredictability, at the specific level, despite complete general determinism in the system. That is, at any one moment, it is impossible to predict over a long range the chaotic system's particular form, in contrast to its global realization or general pattern. Statements about the system can be made only about stochastic processes or hypothetical states encompassing more probable paths or trajectories.

However, the difficulty in arriving at certain predictability for aspects of a chaotic system does not mean that it is fully random. Accurate predictions of a chaotic system's global dynamic trajectory in its state phase space can be made. Each of its state patterns is predicted at a global level by prior state patterns, even if the status of each element in the state pattern is not, and even if long-term prediction is difficult if not impossible. Only the lack of knowledge of prior and existent state patterns makes global prediction difficult. Certain prechange patterns in a system's behavior might help predict that chaotic change is likely, and it might even be possible to predict which style of chaotic pattern could emerge. Thus, in this sense, even if the state pattern is irregular when it is undergoing change, it will be globally determined.

Although this "stretching" process is expected when large changes are involved in regulated systems, they also occur with small changes in chaotic ones, through an extreme sensitivity to initial conditions fostered by deviation-amplifying mechanisms. Minute perturbations are magnified logarithmically, producing macroscopic change in state space. Nearby trajectories diverge exponentially, leading to unpredictability, for no connection can be found between initial conditions and future outcome for any one system component.

In conclusion, the chaotic system's pattern is not entirely random or featureless, but has definite shape. There is order, or global determinism inherent in chaotic systems. This has moved Kauffman (1993) to term them antichaotic.

Similarly, Abraham (1995) argues that chaotic systems are not unpredictable systems. Their sensitivity to initial conditions guarantees that their trajectories will diverge and explore the many regions of its state space. However, conditional probability statements can be made even if it cannot be said exactly where and when a particular trajectory will be, for any trajectory is limited to its attractor's vector field. Moreover, all are equivalent in that each eventually visits every region of their attractor, giving the same clues about the vector field. In this sense, in chaotic organization there is *insensitivity* and not only sensitivity to initial conditions. Nevertheless, stochastic processes (random fluctuation of system components, noise, system elements that are variable by nature, etc.) ensure local unpredictability in chaotic systems.

## *Bifurcation*

Bifurcation points mark system pathway splits or transformations (Guastello, 1995). They are "critical junctions of instability" within a system's operating space, deriving from a system's quantitative movement from instability through a crisis point in a shift toward stability, where the system emerges with new forms different from the original. Bifurcation points are governed at crisis or threshold points by critical values in control parameters, which are variables that, when at bifurcation points, influence system behavior toward splitting. Attractors might diverge noticeably after splitting, or the resultant attractors, more simply, might alter form.

Control parameters could change due to system behavior, and as with any element of a system, they are responsive components to the configuration of the whole and its subsystems and levels. Nevertheless, there are limits in this regard.

Bifurcations might mark instabilities in system dynamics, but they are part of the process of system reconfiguration toward increasing adaptation. After a critical point is reached in a system dynamic, and transformation occurs, the system regains stability, albeit in different ways from the stable state beforehand. In another way of looking at it, because living systems generally take in energy, information, and so on, relative to what is given out, bifurcations and resultant multiattractor configurations help living systems reduce the ever increasing energetic and informational entropy in the system to manageable proportions. Through attractor splitting, each of the smaller resultant topologies has lower entropy. In attractor formation, system splitting could accelerate exponentially, in a bifurcation cascade, or a runaway process of "period doubling," before stability is reattained (Williams & Arrigo, 2002).

## *Fractals*

Fractals represent an interesting serial or multiple bifurcation patterning across different levels of a system. In fractals, structural similarity or equivalent shape is evident across multiple levels of magnification or scale of a system. There is self-similarity in pattern of geometric form over different strata of the system, yet they vary immensely in mathematical scale.

Mathematical scale differs across levels in fractals in terms of fractional equivalents or dimensional complexity, but the patterns are similar across the levels. As an example of a fractal, with self-similarity at different levels, from the microscopic to the macroscopic, think of the branching of a tree at its trunk, the branching of a tree limb at its joints, and the branching of leaves in its veins. Williams and Arrigo (2002) pointed out that fractals represent iterations that build not on themselves but "off of" themselves. As a system branches within, to smaller regions, only to repeat its basic pattern, it has more room for growth, complexity, stability, and adaptation. Because the iteration can be endless, there is unlimited local freedom in system dynamics despite a limiting global order, when the iterative pattern is repeated at increasingly lower levels.

# Complexity

## *Introduction*

There appear to be two major approaches to complexity theory, with the work of Holland on agents representing one (e.g., Holland, 1998). In the second approach, which I describe in the present work, complex adaptive systems are described (e.g., Kauffman, 1993). According to this approach, complexity theory emphasizes the way systems inherently self-organize toward more complex structures. Nonetheless, each new complex structure manifests simplicity in its order relative to the organization of the structures from which they derive. In certain conditions, systems could tend toward disorder. However, their natural tendency is to avert this region of state organization and to gravitate to more systematized complex regimes.

An unstable state is susceptible to major cascades, avalanches, or catastrophes, unless ordered, antichaotic, or canalizing ensembles characterize it. Minor fluctuations or perturbations cannot wildly amplify a system if the system is immersed with highly connected, frozen cores of locked, meshed elements. If the system is buttressed by interlinked scaffolds of constancy that "percolate" across it, its isolated islands of change will absorb most transformational impacts without repercussion for the majority fixed cores. Change manifests when a system is disordered, that is, when it does not inherently deamplify perturbations, or when it becomes governed by destabilizing attributes and rules.

Systems poised at the transition or boundary between disorder and order have moved to a position that might serve as powerful foci of dynamical, major change (e.g., in evolution or development). In fact, systems might seek out this dynamic region between constancy and randomness because it facilitates adaptations of increasing complexity. For example, with respect to natural selection, evolution might operate by adaptively "pulling" complex systems to this boundary region of order and disorder. "Selection achieves complex systems capable of adaptation" (Kauffman, 1993, p. 173). In general, systems might gravitate to this intermediate position in state space because it maximizes adaptability through the optimal, flexible system responses it permits to repeated perturbations (maximum computational ability, fitness, evolvability, and emergence [toward complexity]). In other words, as long as energy is added to systems, they possess an inherent affinity for the balance between subcritical orderliness and supercritical chaos, that is, for self-organized criticality.

In short, for Kauffman, systems live on "the edge of chaos" (chaos in the sense of disorder). This optimizes flexibility and rich exploratory component coordinative reassembly or couplings of multiple, similar, nonrigid attractors. This facilitates appropriate, efficient, accurate, and fit adaptation to novel contexts (Thelen & Smith, 1994). Thus, through its aperiodic organization, chaos can be seen as "a deliberately disordered state from which order springs" (Freeman, 1995, p. 28). In other words, systems might live on "the edge of chaos" (or at the edge of order-disorder), because systems living on cusps of possible change increase the probability of undergoing change to increased complexity, which is normally beneficial. Chaotic attractors provide the system the ground for advance in system organization in terms of complexity, especially when they compete with organization that is less complex, such as found in cyclical attractors.

Living systems are characterized by the presence of multiattractor assemblies (Granic & Patterson, 2006). Complex multiattractor assemblies can be considered a special case of complexity organization, as the integrated system accommodating them takes on its own adaptive quality. In this sense, integrated complex systems are referred to as complex adaptive systems. In the present conceptualization, I reserve this term exclusively to the processes involved in the formation of integrated, multiple attractor assemblies, avoiding its use when referring to complexly organized systems, in general. Perhaps, we need to distinguish between different degrees of complexity of complex adaptive systems (see below).

To conclude, systems gravitate to regions in their state space where movement toward increasing order and complexity is facilitated. However, there can also be movement toward instability and disorder. In terms of system organization, not all system change toward increased complexity is psychologically adaptive; for example, there are many examples of degenerating system organization in the case of human behavior despite an increase in order in organization, *qua* organization. That is, behavioral systems might become increasingly complex from the point of view of system organization, *qua* organization, stabilizing at a self-organized higher-order level but, from the point of view of psychological adaptation, they might be entrenching in maladaptive disorder.

## *Steps in the Evolution of Complexity*

In effect, complexity theory describes a two-phase process of complex system formation. First, systems tend to hover on the edge of order and disorder, or on the cusp of change, because remaining in stability might lead to a loss of flexibility. Second, on this cusp, when contextual factors are optimal, the system is in the optimal position in its state space to self-organize toward more complex forms. This happens through local rather than global processes of contextual adaptation; that is, system change is facilitated on the cusp of change by bottom-up rather than top-down processes. Nevertheless, top-down, holistic, self-organizational processes do play a role. The process typically described in adaptive change toward increasing complexity is this two-phase one. However, it is possible that the phases in a system's evolution toward increasing complexity involve processes more complex than a dual state-space transition. As systems evolve into multiple attractor assemblies, or complex adaptive systems, in long-term time frames, different orders of complexity in underlying processes might be involved. In this regard, I proceed to describe a five-step transition to integrated complex adaptive systems.

Systems might manifest evolving and dissolving attractor patterns over time (Thelen & Smith, 1994, 2006), a concept that appears related to Abraham's (1995) "dynamic schemes," or changing system behavior. Another way of describing dynamic schemes is in terms of logistic maps (Guastello & Liebovitch, 2009; see Fig. 28.2). Movement through system state space is dynamical. Before a system can gravitate to a region between order and disorder, it might have already produced ordered and/or chaotic attractor formations, and these, in turn, might have passed through less organized system configurations, such as cyclical attractors. In this respect, system change at any given moment builds on preceding system change patterns.

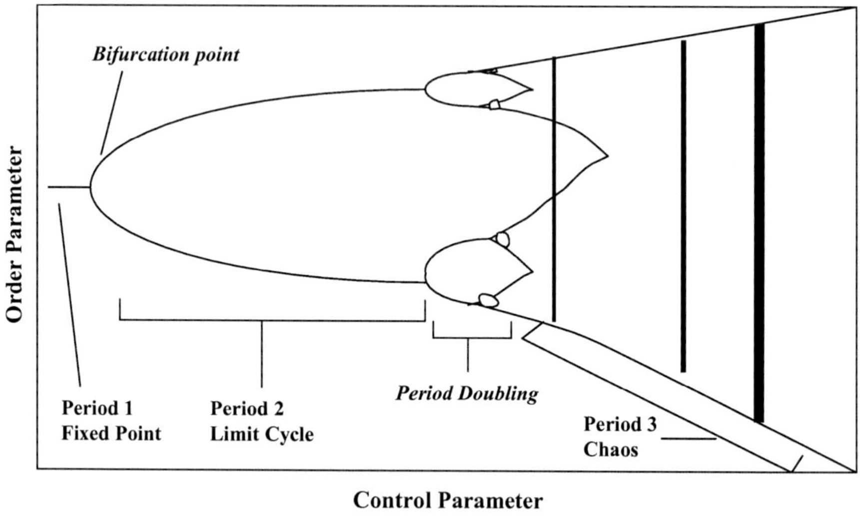


**Fig. 28.2** Bifurcation diagram for the logistic map
Logistic map showing various dynamics as the control parameter involved increases in value (see Fig. 28.1)
*Control parameters* are essentially independent variables. Order parameters are dependent measures. There might be more than one order parameter in some complex dynamical systems. Order parameters within a system might be completely independent of each other, or they might interact with each other as they evolve over time
The *logistic map* (Fig. 28.2) was studied extensively by May (1976). It represents the transition from a fixed point attractor to a limit cycle attractor, and from a limit cycle into chaos, as represented by equation:

$$Y_2 = BY_1(1 - Y_1), \quad 0 < Y_1 < 1, \tag{28.1}$$

where $Y$ is the order parameter, and $B$ is the control parameter
In the region of Fig. 28.2 labeled as Period 1, the system is globally stable, resembling a fixed point attractor. The bifurcation point marks the transition from Period 1 to Period 2, in which the attractor transforms to a limit cycle (Hopf bifurcation) as $B$ increases in value
Toward the end of Period 2, where $B$ has increased further in value, the bifurcation pattern bifurcates again, dividing the system into four smaller regions. Here, one finds cycles within cycles. This is the phenomenon of *period doubling*. As $B$ becomes even larger, the system bifurcates again, so that there are oscillations within oscillations within oscillations
After one more set of bifurcation, the system then enters Period 3, which is full-scale chaos once more. The behavior of $Y$ bears little resemblance to the relative order found in Periods 1 or 2. Windows of relative order striate the chaotic region. They contain ordered trajectories that create a path, with additional bifurcations, from one chaotic period to another
The logistic map can be expanded to reflect a dynamic that has the option of going into period doubling, such as the cubic variant in Eq. 28.2:

$$Y_2 = BY(1 - Y_1)(1 - Y_1). \tag{28.2}$$

Abraham, Abraham, and Shaw (1990) graphed mood and self-image in relation to a grief-inducing event according to transitions in psychological dependency. In this work, the state space sequences governing the system varied with the level of dependency as a control parameter. The attractor types that best characterized the bifurcation trajectory of the system moved from point attractors to cyclic ones to chaotic ones, a pattern that is consistent with the present model. Had other variables been added to the system, it is conceivable that more complex attractor assemblies could have developed as the system evolved and it could have been characterized as complex adaptive systems, and then "superordinate complex adaptive systems" (see Table 28.1 and Fig. 28.3).

In complexity theory, dynamic schemes are usually progressive, are self-organized, and tend to move toward increased system complexity. The transition of attractors at the edge of chaos, and from there to complex adaptive systems, suggests a powerful model of change processes in system behavior, involving multiple steps. Such change can originate from several earlier, less complex configurations

**Table 28.1** Five-step model of stages of change, with underlying nonlinear dynamical system transition mechanisms

| Product | | Process |
|---|---|---|
| Stages of development (Neo-Piagetian; Young, 1997) | Generic stages of change | Nonlinear dynamical system transitions |
| Reflexive | Coordination | Cyclical attractor |
| Sensorimotor | Hierarchization | Chaotic attractor |
| Perioperational | Systematization | Inhabiting cusp between order and disorder |
| Abstract | Multiplication | Complex adaptive system processes |
| Collective intelligence | Integration | Superordinate complex adaptive system processes |

*Note*. The sequences and their parallels are explained in the text
Adapted from Young and Chapman (2007), with last point in last column added
The present model posits that there are five major stages in development. Also, for each one there appears to be an underlying nonlinear dynamical force involved. In the table, I speculate that the five developmental stages reflect a generic model of stages of change. Also, the dynamical evolution described should undergird the processes of change involved when sequencing of stages such as the one in the table are found, whether in the living or nonliving realms

**Fig. 28.2** (continued) The logistic map function generalizes to an exponential function:

$$Y_2 = BY_1 \exp(Ay_1 t). \tag{28.3}$$

Reprinted with the permission of Cambridge University Press. Guastello, S.J., & Liebovitch, L.S. (2009). Copyright © 2009 Cambridge University Press. [Figure 1.3, Page. 15]

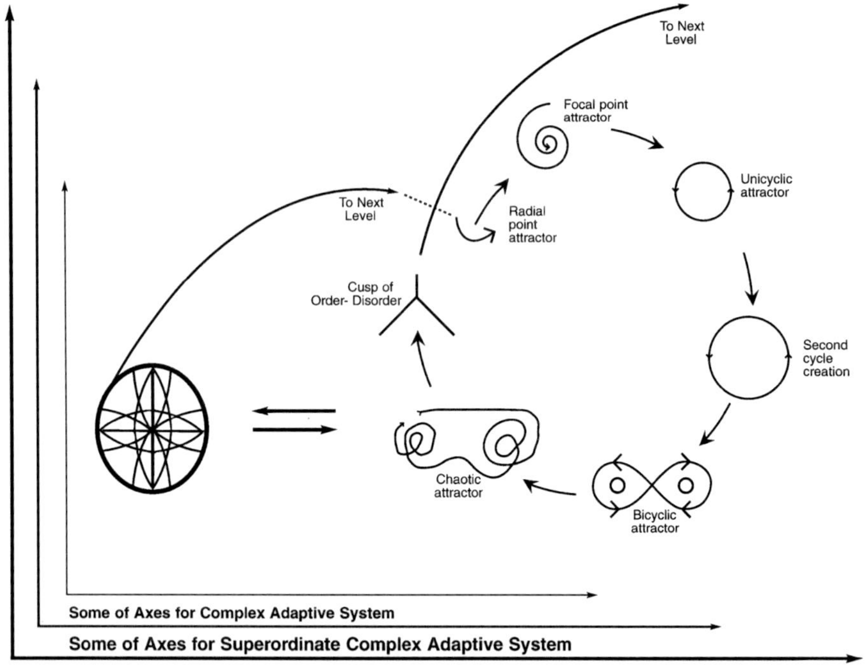


**Fig. 28.3** Nonlinear dynamical system transition mechanisms: from attractors to superordinate complex adaptive systems. The figure illustrates a five-step process model of change in terms of nonlinear dynamical system theory (cyclic attractors, chaotic attractors, gravitating to the cusp of change, complex adaptive systems processes, and superordinate complex adaptive systems processes). It indicates that there are cyclic recursions of these processes that can take place in systems. Also, it indicates the states of the systems that could precede this sequence, such as gravitating from point-type attractors to unicyclic ones. Complex adaptive systems are represented by an extra axis at the bottom of the graph, and superordinate ones by another. Systems are multiply constituted and multiply embedded, and when they are nonlinear, dynamical ones, especially as they reach the latter phases, their complexity is fluidly organized for maximum adaptivity

in the system's behavior, such as the presence of cyclical attractors, or even less complex attractors. They can even gravitate to system configurations that are more complex than complex adaptive systems, such as superordinate complex adaptive systems.

The pattern of system change evident in typical progress toward complex adaptive systems suggests the following five-stage model. With adequate energy input and use, systems might inherently self-organize to traverse through the processes of (a) cyclic attractors, (b) chaotic attractors, (c) gravitating to the region between order and disorder, or the cusp of change, (d) complex adaptive systems, and (e) superordinate complex adaptive systems.

There are many possible dynamic schemes; however, this suggested five-step model might self-organize especially under optimal conditions, facilitating increasing system complexity and adaptability. Similar models could involve the insertion of a torus attractor before the chaotic one, and/or dual/multiple, but not yet integrated, attractors after it.

Note that in terms of the concept of fractals, there might be iterative repetitions of evolution of complexity at different levels of a system, within nested systems, or within different subsystems, so that multiple repetitions of complexity formation processes could be taking place within an overall system. In this regard, the five-step nonlinear dynamical systems transition sequence that has been described could apply equally to changes over stages in development and changes over substages in development.

## *Controlling Parameters*

State shifts or reorganizations in a system are affected by change in controlling parameters (control parameters, control variables, rate-limited factors). These are quantitative, scalar variables that produce qualitative shifts in the collective behavior of a system beyond specified sensitive thresholds. Thus, when these special element(s) in a system are sufficiently modified, they fall beyond a particular value, producing reverberation throughout the system. System modifications are no longer minor, parametric, continuous, or linear. Past the critical point of the controlling parameter (e.g., growth of the parameter begins, value x is attained), existing instabilities in relations or energy distributions are amplified. System element relations and couplings fluctuate in transition, behaving like continual perturbations or noise in the system dynamic. This acts to produce greater disequilibrium, instability of existing patterns, resistance to return to equilibrium, enhanced behavioral variability, domination by the consequent system fluctuations, exploration of new cooperative patterns, selection of the most functionally adaptive pattern(s) to the new context, and ultimately, perturbation of the system's extant coherent mode or regime and a reorganized equilibrium in a new state (A concept similar to controlling parameters concerns transition criteria in stage-wise development according to catastrophe theory [e.g., sudden spurts, response variability, second-order transitions; called catastrophe flags; van der Maas & Molenaar, 1992]. Hysteresis refers to the temporal pattern of stable state followed by bifurcated change in a system undergoing gradual control parameter change.).

This does not mean that systems are controlled totally by an external agent, the controlling parameter. Rather, any one controlling parameter is internal to the system, and is influenced by the confluence of all its elements. Controlling parameters do not contain prescribed commands or formulas of change even if they are essential pathways to it. That is, systems are self-organized and tend toward the stability they set for themselves. The critical value of a system's key controlling parameter depends on a particular state of the system. "The system has control over itself" (Abraham et al., 1990; pp. 1–2). Finally, controlling parameters at one level of system organization must be consistent with those of another in any one system (e.g., brain and behavior).

Controlling parameter thresholds that lead to bifurcations of nonlinear change are called bifurcation points. Bifurcations may be subtle, catastrophic, or explosive. The first type involves a shift in attractor type, the second involves attractor annihilation or creation, and the third involves a sudden increase in attractor size (called implosive when the change concerns size reduction).

## *Development*

Thelen (1995; Thelen & Smith, 1994, 2006) showed that, in treadmill stepping, newborns maintain regularly alternating stepping (or manifest a stable behavioral attractor). This happens even when their feet are placed on treadmills of different speeds (or their behavioral attractor is perturbed). It happened in their subjects even though other motor skills of the leg were in the process of disappearing or were yet to be developed (or their behavioral attractor was not the product of a general maturational phenomenon). Thus, motor behavior appeared to be a contextually sensitive expression or performance of a multidimensional nature.

According to Thelen, subsystems pass through their own developmental trajectories, and these, in turn, coalesce to produce emergent solutions to pragmatic tasks. Moreover, skills become more differentiated, and they change in relative stability as they progress along the ontogenetic landscape. Similarly, in cognitive development theories that are based on biological, stage, or internal constraints without considering structural activities in problem-solving environments must be incomplete. There are no top-down rules, only bottom-up dynamic self-organizing adjustments.

Other developmentalists who have explored chaos theory have tackled the issue of stages in development. van Geert (1991) and Howe and Rabinowitz (1991) arrive at diametrically opposite conclusions about stages in development as seen from the perspective of attractors. The former maintained that formulas derived from chaos theory can model stage sequences in development and can be differentiated to generate both the cognitive Piagetian (incorporative, progressive) and socioemotional Eriksonian (recurrent, cyclical theme) variety of stage theory. The latter argued that stages might seem to emerge in the course of development, but what really unfolds in development are contiguous sequences generated by attractors.

Evidently, my bias is toward the former perspective. The concept of controlling parameters regulating state shifts could help explain general sequencing in development and the interrelations across domains evident in such sequencing. Controlling parameters, such as cognitive conflict, are those likely to be involved in major cognitive stage transitions.

## *Chaos and Complexity*

Guastello and Liebovitch (2009) provided an introduction to nonlinear dynamical theory and complexity science in terms of their mathematical underpinnings.

In addition, they described recent developments in the field, such as synergetics (Haken, 1984) and synchronization (Strogatz, 2003). For example, synergetics concerns the study of interacting subsystems in nonlinear dynamics. Subsystems in nonlinear dynamics might take the form of driver–slave relationships in the process of supervenience. In synchronization, separate entities that are oscillating independently, such as the flashing patterns found in fireflies, become synchronized in rate and timing. Guastello and Liebovitch (2009) described other developments in the field, such as catastrophe theory (Thom, 1975), which includes the cusp catastrophe response surface. In it, the stable and unstable states are plotted, and the critical regions in their transitioning at a cusp point are indicated. The reader is referred to this comprehensive summary of nonlinear dynamical theory, especially for clear explanation of critical concepts with accompanying mathematical equations.

## *Circular Causality and Emergence*

### Emergence

Jost, Bertschinger, and Olbrich (2009) examined systems from an epistemological perspective and came up with a plausible account of how system coupling and related processes facilitate emergence. They explained that systems could evolve to higher scales. They could contain regularities that are not accessible to lower levels, nor are they embedded in the individual elements of the system. In emergence, the regularities at a higher scale have no equivalent at lower scales, nor can they be inferred from lower scales. This being said, elements at the lower scale are not carried forward into the organization at the higher scale; rather, they are averaged out. Given the generality of what emerges compared to its constituent elements, the elements at a lower scale could be altered without altering the emergent regularity at the higher scale.

Jost et al. (2009) examined the question of degrees of freedom in the higher-order scales. At higher-order scales, systems achieve a degree of buffering against perturbations at lower scales. However, at first they reduce in their degrees of freedom. At a higher scale, systems are governed by central variables that reduce the number of variables and degrees of freedom that can influence it. Other variables become "enslaved" to the central ones, which "dominate and determine" the system. This means that variables are "discarded" in the system, especially when it moves from microscopic, faster time scales to macroscopic, slower ones.

The paradox is that in emergence, systems gain capabilities at higher scales. That is, they gain degrees of freedom, and not only lose them. This happens in two steps. First, at higher scales, the system elements become coupled, coordinated, or synchronized. In this first step, the system loses degrees of freedom. The coordination between the components "freezes" the system, and new regularities are obtained.

In the second step, the system "transfers" to a higher scale. We can depict each component of the dynamical structure as an attractor basin, and as they coalesce, they achieve a "collective momentum." This process enables them to shift to a new attractor dynamic, thereby gaining access to qualitatively different regions in the system's "fitness landscape." This enables the system to explore the regions in its state space that are in more inaccessible regions. In these new regions of its state space, the dynamical structure of the system could evolve into new forms by successive bifurcations. The new states of the system could then exist independently, having their own characteristics relative to the states from which they emerged.

The resultant dynamical structures "gain access" to capacities that surpass the capacities of the individual elements. Therefore, the component elements in the new dynamic structure created at the higher scale obtain increased degrees of freedom because, through their "mutual coordination," they come to "specialize" for different specific tasks. They achieve a "division of labor" as "agents" in the system. In short, the argument made by Jost et al. (2009) appears to be that systems form emerging structures with increased degrees of freedom through the coupling and related synchronizations of components that allow component specializations in a division of labor.

## Circular Causality

As seen in the last chapter, Lewis (2005) proposed a similar concept of "circular causality," which involves bidirectional influences across different levels of a system. In this perspective, however, higher-order forms could help induce lower-order couplings in system elements. In turn, lower-order couplings could influence higher-order forms. The top-down forms constrain or enslave, and the system loses degrees of freedom. The bottom-up influences are intimately related to the top-down ones.

## Circular Emergence

I suggest that a combined concept of "circular emergence" would accommodate the two concepts presented in this section. On the one hand, different levels of a system are reciprocally coordinated. The coordination in a system is vertical as well as horizontal, or over different levels of the system and not just over system elements in any one level. As coordinations synchronize either way (vertically or horizontally), emergence of higher-order capacities takes place in terms of new forms, subsystems, levels, etc. In this process, the system loses degrees of freedom. However, if a level that evolves in a system to a new organization still has room for further organization, especially through coordination that leads to division of labor or application, it gains complexity and degrees of freedom that permit better adaptation or fitness to context. Moreover, because different levels of systems interrelate, top-down influences, involving a newly organized level with an emergent division of labor inherent in its new organization, can help lower-order, enslaved levels to arrive themselves at increasingly organized structure and new divisions of labor, in a process that is akin to bootstrapping. That is, the present concept of circular emergence can help explain how multiple levels within a system percolate with horizontal and vertical reorganizations throughout its structure via dynamic processes.

The concept of circular emergence in systems might help explain how complex adaptive systems and superordinate complex adaptive systems obtain a self-organizational coherence as they gravitate to new system state spaces, integrating multiple attractors within and over multiple levels and dimensions. Causality system emergence seems not only circular but also simultaneously reciprocal, horizontal, vertical, bottom up, and top down. Only through this level of process complexity can the product complexity in systems keep emerging at high levels.

Despite the possible value of the present concept of circular emergence, it needs to be kept in mind that an underpinning dynamic that I have proposed to explain evolution of system dynamics relates to activation–inhibition coordination. The positive and negative feedback controls in system monitoring and change can only be stretched so far as system equilibrium approaches far-from-equilibrium conditions. To the degree possible, activation and inhibition coordination processes should serve to damp the explorations of a system in its state space so that it can tend toward remaining stable. However, beyond threshold points, ones that might even involve minor perturbations if the system has been stretched too far, activation–inhibition coordination processes also can help serve recreation of stability at higher levels of integration.

## Summary and Discussion

This completes presentation of nonlinear dynamical systems theory and its application to development. I present several models that can help explain development, including a five-step nonlinear dynamical transition process that terminates with superordinate complex adaptive systems and the concept of circular emergence that explains how systems could evolve to increased complexity.

It would seem that a systems view, with its emphasis on the whole, would be a far cry from the study of genetics and behavioral development, with its emphasis on genes and DNA. However, the study of causality itself forms a whole, and genetics is one component in the overall process. Yet, at the same time, genetics increasingly is lending itself to a genetic–environmental interaction through the concept of epigenesis so that it is also a systemic science.

## Appendix

Nonlinear dynamical systems, at the mathematical level, consist of a set of coupled differential equations. Differential equations describe changes over time in the values of a system. For example, if a variable's value at time $t+1$ is 10 greater than at $t$, linear growth is taking place in the system. However, growth is nonlinear when a quadratic (squared), or higher-order term, is involved, for example, variable $x$ at time $t_1 = x$ at $t$ multiplied by the constant $r$ ($1-x$ at $t$), which gives the formula $x_{(t+1)} = rx_t - rx_t^2$. The behavior of the system defined by this equation depends on whether $r$ can vary and on the initial condition of $x$, or $x_0$. For this equation, when $r$ is between 0 and 2, all $x$ values converge over time. However, when $r$ is around 2.7, the system's behavior becomes "totally" unpredictable for very small changes in the initial value, so that the final values of $x$ over time vary "wildly and irregularly" (Boom, 2004, p. 81). Even slight perturbations of the system could lead to radical state shifts, so that we can describe the system as becoming "chaotic" (The so-called "butterfly" effect, related to sensitivity to initial conditions in far-from-equilibrium system states, is consistent with this description of chaos by Boom.).

## References

Abraham, F. D. (1995). Introduction to dynamics: A basic language; a basic metamodeling strategy. In F. D. Abraham & A. R. Gilgen (Eds.), *Chaos theory in psychology* (pp. 31–49). Westport: Greenwood.

Abraham, F. D., Abraham, R. H., & Shaw, C. D. (1990). *A visual introduction to dynamical systems theory for psychology*. Santa Cruz: Aerial.

Boom, J. (2004). Commentary on: Piaget's stages: The unfinished symphony of cognitive development. *New Ideas in Psychology, 22*, 239–247.

Freeman, W. J. (1995). The kiss of chaos and the Sleeping Beauty of psychology. In F. D. Abraham & A. R. Gilgen (Eds.), *Chaos theory in psychology* (pp. 19–29). Westport: Greenwood.

Gottman, J. M. (1991). Chaos and regulated change in families: A metaphor for the study of transitions. In P. A. Cowan & M. Hetherington (Eds.), *Family transitions* (pp. 247–272). Hillsdale: Erlbaum.

Granic, I., & Patterson, G. R. (2006). Toward a comprehensive model of antisocial development: A dynamic systems approach. *Psychological Review, 113*, 101–131.

Guastello, S. J. (1995). *Chaos, catastrophe, and human affairs: Nonlinear dynamics in work, organizations, and social evolution*. Mahwah: Erlbaum.

Guastello, S. J., & Liebovitch, L. S. (2009). Introduction to nonlinear dynamics and complexity. In S. J. Guastello, M. Koopmans, & D. Pincus (Eds.), *Chaos and complexity in psychology: The theory of nonlinear dynamical systems* (pp. 1–40). New York: Cambridge University Press.

Haken, H. (1984). *The science of structure: Synergetics*. New York: Van Nostrand Reinhold.

Holland, J. H. (1998). *Emergence: From chaos to order*. New York: Basic Books.

Howe, M. L., & Rabinowitz, F. M. (1991). Development: Sequences, structure, chaos. In P. van Geert & L. P. Mos (Eds.), *Annals of theoretical psychology* (Vol. 7, pp. 65–71). New York: Plenum.

Jost, J., Bertschinger, N., & Olbrich, E. (2009). Emergence. *New Ideas in Psychology, 28*, 265–273.

Kauffman, S. (1993). *The origins of order: Self-organization and selection in evolution*. New York: Oxford University Press.

Kugler, P. N., Shaw, R. E., Vicente, K. J., & Kinsella-Shaw, J. (1991). The role of attractors in the self-organization of intentional systems. In R. R. Hoffman & D. S. Palermo (Eds.), *Cognition and the symbolic processes: Applied and ecological perspectives* (pp. 387–431). Hillsdale: Erlbaum.

Lewis, M. D. (2005). Self-organizing individual differences in brain development. *Developmental Review, 25*, 252–277.

May, R. M. (1976). Simple mathematical models with very complex dynamics. *Nature, 261*, 459–467.

Strogatz, S. (2003). *Sync: The emerging science of spontaneous order*. New York: Hyperion.

Thelen, E. (1995). Motor development: A new synthesis. *American Psychologist, 50*, 79–95.

Thelen, E., & Smith, L. B. (1994). *A dynamic systems approach to the development of cognition and action*. Cambridge: MIT Press.

Thelen, E., & Smith, L. B. (2006). Dynamic systems theories. In W. Damon & R. M. Lerner (Eds.), *Handbook of child psychology: Vol. 1. Theoretical models of human development* (6th ed., pp. 258–312). Hoboken: Wiley.

Thelen, E., & Ulrich, B. D. (1991). Hidden skills: A dynamical systems analysis of treadmill stepping during the first year. *Monographs of the Society for Research in Child Development, 56* (1, Serial No. 223).

Thom, R. (1975). *Structural stability and morphegenesis*. New York: Benjamin-Addison-Wesley.

Vallacher, R. R., Coleman, P. T., Nowak, A., & Bui-Wrzosinska, L. (2010). Rethinking intractable conflict: The perspective of dynamical systems. *American Psychologist, 65*, 262–278.

van der Maas, H. L., & Molenaar, P. C. (1992). Stagewise cognitive development: An application of catastrophe theory. *Psychological Review, 99*, 395–417.

van Geert, P. (1991). A dynamic systems model of cognitive and language grown. *Psychological Review, 98*, 3–53.

Williams, C., & Arrigo, B. (2002). *Law, psychology, and justice: Chaos theory and the new (dis) order*. Albany: State University of New York Press.

Young, G. (1997). *Adult development, therapy, and culture: A postmodern synthesis*. New York: Plenum.

Young, G., & Chapman, C. R. (2007). Pain, affect, nonlinear dynamical systems, and chronic pain: Bringing order to disorder. In G. Young, A. W. Kane, & K. Nicholson, *Causality of psychological injury: Presenting evidence in court* (pp. 197–241). New York: Springer Science + Business Media.

# Chapter 29
# Causes and Determinants of Behavior

## Introduction

The present chapter deals with a variety of topics related to causality. In the last four chapters, I focused on brain processes, especially related to hemispheric specialization, and on systems theory. In this chapter and the next, I examine epigenesis. Before beginning, I touch on the question of causality, in general. It has a storied history, and Aristotle proposed a classic model of four causes. The model is still referred to, and the study of causality is still important in philosophy (Beebee, Hitchcock, & Menzies, 2009). Tinbergen (1963) proposed a powerful model of causation also involving four types. It includes developmental processes, and is quite applicable to the present work. In contrast, the Aristotelian model has led to differing applications in psychology, and until there is a standard understanding of its pertinence, it is best to use more contemporary models. The present work adopts a biopsychosocial and relational metaframe in understanding behavior, and these types of models can integrate Tinbergen's four questions and expand upon them. As for even more general models, I refer to the four forces in physics and draw parallels with different levels of coherence in sociality, in particular.

The next part of the chapter deals with evolution. The current synthesis has added multiple understandings to Darwin's original concepts and the manner in which they had been expanded in the modern synthesis. Jablonka and Lamb (2010) have contrasted well the modern and contemporary approaches, and they emphasize the concept of epigenesis. The study of epigenesis in psychology had been undertaken without much work from a genetic perspective, but that is changing, especially in terms of the concept of gene × environment interaction (Rutter, 2007) and probabilistic epigenesis (Gottlieb, 2007), and the more recent, related one of neuroconstructivism (Westermann et al., 2007). More recent work in the area is even more genetic, and after reviewing the former approach, I introduced the second one. The area is fascinating, and the manner in which environmental effects can alter gene expression by silencing them (Champagne & Mashoodh, 2009), and then have the genetic changes passed on to the next generation by nonsexual means is described at length. I review the work of Meaney (2010), who provides an excellent introduction to the area. For developmental psychology, the work of Caspi and colleagues, in particular, is considered "groundbreaking."

G. Young, *Development and Causality: Neo-Piagetian Perspectives*,
DOI 10.1007/978-1-4419-9422-6_29, 

# Four Causes, Four Questions, and, Four Forces

## *Aristotle*

*Development*. According to Witherington and Crichton (2007), for Aristotle, there are four types of explanation and they work in parallel. They are material, efficient, formal, and final causes (see Table 29.1).

Material cause relates to questions such as, "What is this made of?" Material causes concern the compositional substance or substrate underlying a phenomenon. Examples include neurological structures underlying behavior.

An efficient cause concerns the producer of material products and their constituent material. Efficient causes concern conditions that precede a phenomenon, whether internal to the organism or external to it. Typically, in contemporary understandings of causality, efficient causes are emphasized. Examples include

**Table 29.1** Causes/questions and answers

| Wh- | Aristotle (four causes) | Tinbergen (four questions) | Contemporary |
|---|---|---|---|
| Why | Final | Adaptation (to Niche) | Adaptation (function) |
| What | Material | Proximate (causation) | Proximate (physiology; whole organism; biology) |
| When | | Evolution (phylogeny) | Evolution (epigenesis) |
| Where | | Development | Development (lifespan) |
| How | Efficient | Environment (immediate) | Environment (sociocultural, historico-political context) |
| Which | Formal | | Dynamical<br>Biopsychosocial<br>Person × environment<br>Diathesis-stress |

The table provides a concise look at some major ways questions are posed about causation or causality in behavior. The left-hand column indicates the traditional widely-used wh- questions. A classic manner of examining causation lies in Aristotle's four causes (Broadie, 2009), and these are still used actively today. In biology, Tinbergen (1963) distinguished between different proximate and ultimate causes, and they are understood to include environmental effects. In the right-hand column, I indicate that contemporary approaches are including the whole organism, and elaborating contextual mechanisms and systems

The biopsychosocial approach is widespread, and it takes the form of the diathesis-stress model in psychopathology. In the end, we are functional adaptive products of an interaction of our biological influences (e.g., genetic, physiological, neuronal, evolutionary), our personal/psychological (including our developmental) influences (e.g., individual differences in curiosity, personality, coping), and our familial, sociocultural, and politico-historical contexts. The causality of our behavior does not only reside in either our biology or our environment, but also in their interaction and in ourselves explaining behavior by means of muscle activity, neurological processes, specific stimuli, environment events, or general sociocultural factors.

Formal cause concerns statements such as, "What is this?" Formal causes concern creation of an ongoing, moment-to-moment organization, form, or pattern from particular details of a phenomenon such that the abstracted pattern serves as another level of explanation. In terms of behavior, examples include personality structures or cognitive schemes.

Final causes concern the purpose of use of the products. They involve the end, purpose, goal, or reason behind a phenomenon. Examples include stages of development, or directional patterns in behavior over time.

*Psychopathology*. Álvarez (2009) indicated that for psychopathology formal cause refers to the proximate, internal cause. Efficient cause refers to the distant antecedent or risk factor. Material cause refers to the object of experience of the subject. Final cause refers to the evolutionary pressures underlying the psychiatric condition.

Álvarez (2009) presented a revised model of Aristotle's four causes. For Álvarez, material cause is the organism, the formal cause is a representational model, the efficient cause is an agent, including self as agent, and the final cause is the teleological or reinforcement contingencies producing the outcome.

*Comment*. The developmental and psychopathological approaches to application of Aristotle's four causes to psychology are not uniformly the same. For example, for final causes, development considers stages but psychopathology considers evolution. Efficient causes typically are associated with causation in psychology, but the role of stages in development and evolution need to be placed in any model that considers itself adequate. Note that in the developmental model, material cause refers to neurological structure and efficient cause refers to neurological processes. This distinction is consistent with the present work, which emphasizes content, product, or what in development compared to mechanism, process, or how-why in development. Tinbergen's causal model includes all these various factors, and is reviewed next.

## *Tinbergen*

Tinbergen (1963) had a different conception of the four categories of questions and explanations involved in Aristotle's four types of causes. He argued that they concerned adaptation, evolution, development, and proximate causes, such as physiology. The first two concern population dynamics and the second two concern individual level dynamics. The first two allow for genetic expression, which in turn leads to the developmental and proximate mechanisms leading to behavior. Tinbergen related his four questions to Aristotle's four causes, e.g., adaptation to final cause and proximate cause to material cause.

## Conclusion

However, I find Tinbergen's parallels wanting. Instead of putting square pegs in round wholes, it is best to treat Aristotle's four causes as a breakthrough historical model rather than an active contemporary one. Indeed, in Beebee et al.'s (2009) handbook of causation in philosophy, Aristotle is given scant attention outside of the historical chapter that includes his work (Broadie, 2009). Moreover, in Young and Shore (2007), we cited Flew and Priest (2002), who understood that to apply the term cause to all four terms from Aristotle's list is "unfortunate."

In physics, the field is seeking a unified model that integrates the four known forces. In Table 29.2, I use the work in physics as a model for elaborating the social forces, in particular, which cohere individuals and groups (see Table 29.2). Psychologists should continue to seek the causal glue in our individual-social relational cohesion. The biopsychosocial model and similar models are helpful in this

**Table 29.2** A unified theory of forces

| Common level | Physics | Psychology |
|---|---|---|
| Coordination | Atomic particles | Intrasubjective |
| Hierarchization | Molecules | Interobjective |
| Systematization | Larger aggregates (in each body) | Family |
| Multiplication | Celestial bodies | Group |
| Integration | Universe | Universal |

*Note*. Levels based on Young's developmental model of cyclic recursion of substages in development over stages, seen as fractals, and viewed as a generic model of change across living and nonliving systems

In Table 29.2 on unified forces, I query to what degree the five-stage model can be applied at the level of atomic and molecular cohesion

A force is an agency or influence that is exerted or brought to bear on an object, free body, or situation or one that influences the relationship among objects, bodies, or situations. In physics, this refers to the fundamental forces or interactions (strong, weak, electromagnetic, gravitation). These forces are explained according to mathematical models. Physics is seeking a unified force, as part of a theory of everything. Strong and weak interactive forces concern nuclear forces, whereas electromagnetic and gravitational forces concern forces that govern larger scale interactions

The forces described in physics can serve as an analogy for the forces that govern human behavior. One can describe equivalent forces acting on the child and adult. They are socially binding ones, for the most part, but also refer to internal cohesive mechanisms so that we present in an integrated manner

(a) Within the person, there are intrapsychic or intrasubjective forces that are cohered into a unified self-presentation in normal circumstances
(b) As we relate to each other and other objective parts of our context, we widen the degree forces acting on us, and they are especially social. Infants gradually become aware and attach to their family members, and the family normally forms a cohesive unit

(continued)

**Table 29.2** (continued)

| |
|---|
| (c) Next, the growing child partakes in larger group activities of which he/she becomes aware, whether in playgroups, at school, or in other institutional or community settings |
| (d) Finally, we learn to participate in larger societal and cultural activities, and this grows to encompass concerns about our country, the environment, our planet, and so on |
| In terms of these forces, it could be argued that there are parallel levels that are at work in both the physics and psychology realms |
| (a) In the first level, the common model indicates that internal parts of entities are cohering due to strong internally directed forces that coordinate them |
| (b) Next, it appears that the parts become hierarchized in their internal to external relations. At the psychological level, this would refer to relating socially in dyadic exchanges; for example, the baby is subordinate to the caregiver, but the caregiver provides the scaffold to have the infant become more independent, or having a sense of control, too |
| (c) In the next level, the interactive forces refer to more systemic groupings. In physics, electromagnetic forces refer to cross-body interactions that act across larger body groupings, whereas for psychology, the forces unite family members |
| (d) In the next level, the forces spread in their effects, and for physics free bodies interact multiply through gravity, whereas for psychology, families and other social units form larger groupings and |
| (e) Finally, at the integrated level, the universe is understood as the outcome of a combined unified force, still to be identified, whereas in psychology, part of the forces acting on us, indeed, which, derive from us, is a deep sense of community and bond with all that is around us |
| In short, no matter where we look, we could find a common evolution in or series of forces relating to systems, whether in the nonliving or living realms. Systems form and cohere and forces generate the different degrees of system cohesions and unifications. Physics could inform psychology in understanding the forces acting in it by way of the precise work on its fundamental interactive forces and its search for a unifying one. However, perhaps psychology can inform physics in this topic by pointing out the commonalities in forces at the physical and living and even human levels. Just as with the world of physics, the human universe is a garden of wonderful forces and particles or entities that come together in ways that illustrate how energies and matter bind |

regard, but they should be married with other general approaches, such as systems theory and evolutionary theory, and they should be studied from the perspective of molecular genetics and epigenetics as much as by general work on gene-environment interactions.

## Evolution

Pigliucci and Müller (2010) described how the modern Darwinian synthesis of evolution has been expanded into what they referred to as an extended evolutionary synthesis (see Fig. 29.1). The main principles in the Darwinian model of evolution involve variation, inheritance, and natural selection. The modern synthesis builds upon the field of genetics, in particular.

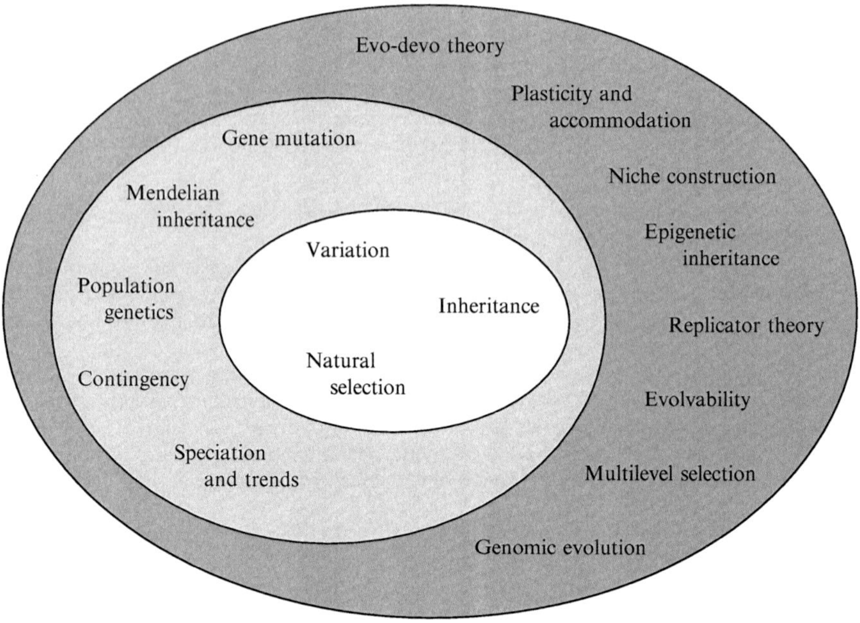


**Fig. 29.1** Schematic representation of key concepts of Darwinism, the modern synthesis, and the extended synthesis. The scheme is meant to depict the broad steps in the continuous expansion of evolutionary theory, not to enumerate all concepts belonging to each of these steps. Darwinism is represented in the inner field, the modern synthesis in the middle field and the extended synthesis in the outer field. Reprinted with the permission of The MIT Press. Pigliucci, M., & Müller, G. B. (2010). © 2010 Massachusetts Institute of Technology, by permission of The MIT Press

More recently, the extended synthesis has been formulated and includes epigenetic inheritance, multilevel selection, evolutionary developmental biology (evo-devo), and so on. According to the authors, the extended model overcomes several difficulties presented by the standard model. These difficulties are gradualism, externalism, gene-centrism. For example, evolution can be modeled by nonlinear complex dynamical models that indicate nongradual change, such as found in the paleo-ontological record. Also, the concept of externalism is consistent with the importance of development in evolutionary biology. This approach considers the internal generative properties of evolving phenotypes. Finally, gene-centrism has been replaced by a multicausal approach to evolution, including consideration of environment and genetic-epigenetic networking that is passed on to and elaborated upon in subsequent generations.

Jablonka and Lamb (2010) have described well the differences between the modern synthesis in evolution and the extended synthesis. I present the contrast in terms of major points of disagreement or nuance (see Table 29.3). A critical feature relates to epigenesis. This is discussed further below.

**Table 29.3** The modern synthesis vs. the extended synthesis in evolutionary thought

| Issue | Modern synthesis | Extended synthesis |
|---|---|---|
| 1. | Heredity via through transmission of germ-line genes. Hereditary variations derive from differences in DNA-base sequences. *There are no inherited variations that cannot be expressed in terms of inherited genetic differences* | Heredity involves more than DNA. There are heritable variations that are independent of variations in DNA sequence, and they possess a degree of autonomy from variations in DNA. Non-DNA variations could constitute an additional substrate for evolutionary change, and they could also guide genetic evolution (Jablonka & Lamb, 1995, 2005; Jablonka & Raz, 2009) |
| 2. | Hereditary variations are consequences of: (1) many random, sexually-generated combinations of preexisting alleles, and (2) mutations or new variations resulting from accidental changes in DNA. *Hereditary variations are not affected by the developmental history of the organism. There is no "soft inheritance"* | Soft inheritance exists (the inheritance of developmentally-induced and regulated variations), and could be important. It involves both non-DNA variations and developmentally-induced variations in DNA sequence (Jablonka & Lamb, 2005, 2008) |
| 3. | Heritable variations usually have small effects on the phenotype, and most often evolution takes places gradually. By natural selection of individual organisms having phenotypes making them slightly more adapted to their niche than are conspecifics in the population, some alleles increase in frequency. *Mutation pressure is not an important factor in the evolutionary process. Most often, macroevolution is continuous with microevolution, and it does not require any additional processes* | The rate at which heritable variations appears could be higher in stressful conditions, and the spectrum of variations might be different, involving amplification, transposition, and massive, heritable gene activation and inactivation (e.g., Cullis, 2005; Levy & Feldman, 2004). Changes such as these can lead to saltational evolution (Jablonka & Lamb, 2008; Lamm & Jablonka, 2008). Furthermore, variations in the expression and organization of a common small core of genes found in all phyla of animals could have dramatic phenotypic effects (Carroll, 2005). Macroevolution might reflect changes in this core gene set, in addition to the operation of stress-induced mechanisms that could result in systemic mutations and genome repatterning |
| 4. | The ultimate unit of selection is the gene. Although genes interact and the interactions are often nonlinear, it is the fitness effects of single genes functioning additively by natural selection that drive evolution. *The genetic-developmental network of the individual organism and the phenotype it generates are not heritable and cannot be a unit of evolution* | Rather than the gene, the focus of selection is the network of developmental interactions. A gene's expression, as well as the scope of its effects, often depends in part on the regulatory structure of the developmental network in which it is integrated (West-Eberhard, 2003; Wilkins, 2002). Developmental networks often are modular and stable during phenotypic evolution |

(continued)

**Table 29.3** (continued)

| Issue | Modern synthesis | Extended synthesis |
|---|---|---|
| 5. | Innovations are the result of gene mutations that, when beneficial, accumulate over time and lead to a qualitative new form. *Generic, physical-chemical properties have no role in morphological and physiological innovations, except to specify boundaries of possible forms* | Generic and evolved mechanisms that generate phenotypic plasticity have had important roles in evolution, initiating relevant transformations (Forgács & Newman, 2005; Kirschner & Gerhart, 2005; Newman & Müller, 2006) |
| 6. | The targets of selection are individual organisms, which are bounded entities. Even though conspecifics in groups interact and might coevolve, group selection and community selection happen rarely. Species selection might exist, but is of little significance. *The community only rarely is the target of selection, and species selection cannot explain the main patterns of macroevolutions* | Group selection, involving cooperating group members, is common (Wilson, 2009). It might be necessary to consider *communities* as targets of selection (Zilber-Rosenberg & Rosenberg, 2008). Patterns of macroevolutionary change often are the outcome of selection at the species level and above (Jablonski, 2005) |
| 7. | Evolution takes place through modifications from a common ancestor, and is based on vertical descent. *Horizontal transfer of genes or information is of little significance, and does not alter the basic branching structure of phylogenies. The main pattern of evolutionary progression is treelike and not weblike* | The "Tree of Life" pattern of divergence, does not explain the full range of similarities and differences between taxa. Sharing whole genomes (through hybridization, symbiosis, and parasitism) and partial exchange of genomes (through various types of horizontal gene transfer) lead to weblike patterns of relations in divergence (Arnold, 2006; Goldenfeld & Woese, 2007) |

Adapted from The MIT Press with permission. Pigliucci, M., & Müller, G. B. (2010). 

# Genes × Environment

## *Introduction*

The topic of epigenesis takes two forms in the developmental literature. (a) The first pertains to the view that causality in development involves neither genetic prespecifications nor an empirical blank slate on which experience writes the content and direction, but an interaction of the two influences. Moreover, the interaction is quite subtle, even involving early experiences generated by spontaneous firings of neurons. In this view, there is some prespecification that is in balance with learning and experience. However, there are no innate modules, no matter how few, because how would innate modules be built in the first place? The reductionism to find the initial innate reality would be an infinite regress.

(b) The second approach to epigenesis is quite specific to the genetic mechanisms involved, including DNA methylation. It seeks vulnerabilities and resiliencies conferred by specific variants or alleles of genes and how early adversity or support activates more positive or negative outcomes, depending on the nature of the experience received.

## *Probabilistic Epigenesis*

Gottlieb (1971) conceived development as a manifold having multiple, intercoordinated levels. Gottlieb (2007) expounded his model of probabilistic epigenesis (see Fig. 29.2). He maintained that phenotypic traits should be understood in their developmental context. The framework of probabilistic epigenesis for understanding developing behavior emphasizes the reciprocal relations among genetic activity, neural activity, behavior, and environment. Probabilistic epigenesis is a metatheoretical model and reflects the ubiquity of gene-environment interaction in the expression of phenotypic traits. Epigenetics refers to the control of gene expression by the different levels of the environment encountered by the embryo and its parts. The concept of probabilistic epigenesis is consistent with the concept of epigenetics. Probabilistic epigenesis contrasts with the construct of predetermined epigenesis. The latter is unidirectional concept that genetic activity gives rise to structures that start functioning as they mature without bidirectional influences.

Gottlieb (2007) specified that part of the environmental influences that impact behavior, structure, and genes include physical, social, and cultural aspects. He noted that he uses the label of "probabilistic" because there is no perfect deterministic coordination that takes place at all levels in the model, for example, from function to structure. Gottlieb (2007) further discussed the concept of reaction range and gene-environment coaction. He concluded that there is a, "primary inseparability or interconnectedness of genes and environment."

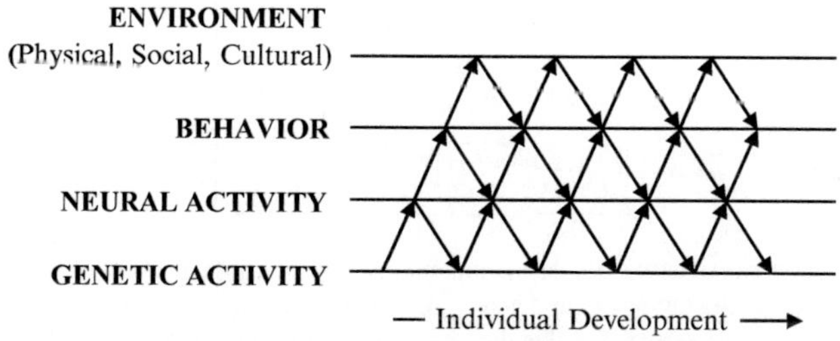


**Fig. 29.2** Bidirectional influences in probabilistic epigenesis in behavioral development. Metatheoretical model of probabilistic epigenesis: completely bidirectional influences over four levels of analysis (genetic activity, neural activity, behavior, physical, social, cultural aspects of environment). Reprinted with the permission of John Wiley & Sons, Inc. Gottlieb, G. (2007). Copyright © 2007 and Wiley-Blackwell. [Figure 1, Page. 2]

## *Neuroconstructivism*

Westermann et al. (2007) presented their development model of neuroconstructivism (see Fig. 29.3). It helps explain the construction of representations in the developing brain and how brain development is influenced by experience, constraints, and reciprocity across broad neural and cognitive levels. Their framework is consistent with the model of probabilistic epigenesis.

Neuroconstructivism is a model that consists of a nested hierarchy of interactions with the environment at the levels of neuronal, neural, cerebral, and related structures, as well as bodily structures and cognitive representations and processes. This takes place even at the cellular level in a process that the authors labeled "encellment." For example, even in early fetal development the development of cells is influenced by molecular interactions with neighboring cells (Jessell & Sanes, 2000).

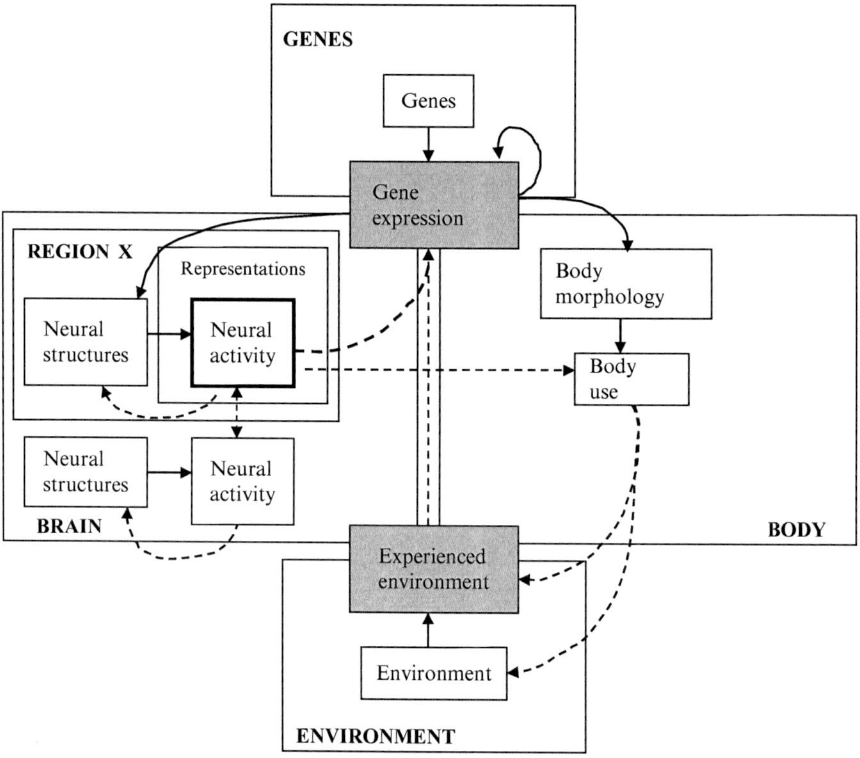


**Fig. 29.3** Neuroconstructivism: a developmental model. The multiple interacting constraints shaping the construction of representations (neural activation patterns) in a specific cortical region (X). Region X here is not a primary sensory area so that the effects of environmental changes are mediated through other cortical regions. Representations can effect their own progressive change through multiple loops involving genes, other brain areas, the body, and the environment. (*Solid lines* indicate a constraining relationship and *dashed lines* indicate the induction of change.) Reprinted with the permission of John Wiley & Sons, Inc. Westermann, G., Mareschal, D., Johnson, M. H., Sirois, S., Spratling, M. W., & Thomas, M. S. C. (2007). Copyright © 2007 and Wiley-Blackwell. [Figure 4, Page. 80]

In "embrainment," the authors referred to the interconnectivity of particular brain regions that are codeveloping with other brain regions. For example, brain regions are not modular but are context-sensitive and constrained by interactions, feedback, and so on, with other brain regions.

As for "embodiment," Westermann et al. indicated that mind exists within a body and the body functions as a filter for information received from the physical and social environment. The body also serves to manipulate the environment and to generate new sensory input and experience. The child is proactive in exploring the environment and even selects experiences involved in learning.

About "ensocialment," the particular environment of the child highly constrains development. For example, early stress, such as in child abuse, can greatly affect behavioral and neural development. Westermann et al. maintained that the various experiential effects and constraints are highly interactive and can even influence gene expression.

To conclude, the authors stated that cognitive development could be understood as emerging from experience-dependent effects on neural-related structures that are involved in mental representation. Neural development is multiply determined even down to the cellular level and includes a role for the external environment. Therefore, cognitive development could be mapped as a trajectory involving multiple impacts on neural structures and representations. Finally, neuroconstructivism lends itself to the study of abnormal as well as normal development.

## *Gene-Environment Correlation*

Rutter (2007) specified that there are four major types of gene-environment interdependence: epigenesis; variations in heritability depending on the environment; gene-environment correlations; and gene-environment interactions. Before elaborating on the terms, he explained what genes do. He reminded that the concept of a single gene to single outcome is too simplistic and that genes work through a multistep causal chain. I discuss the last three types of gene-environment interdependence in this section.

About heritability, research has established that it can account for only about half of the variation in the population for a trait. One interpretation of these results is that the gene × environment interaction could reflect a model of stress-diathesis. Other models that Rutter (2007) mentioned included the bioecological model and the environmental constraints/opportunities model. He explained that the particular mediating mechanisms involved "remain frustratingly unclear."

Next, Rutter (2007) addressed gene-environmental correlations, which concern genetic influences on individual variations and exposure to particular types of environments. Passive gene-environment correlation refers to the effects of parental genes on parenting behaviors involved in development (Plomin, DeFries, & Loehlin, 1977). For example, there is a positive correlation between passing on "risky" genes and giving the child a "risky" environment.

Another type of gene-environment correlation is termed active. It refers to the effects of the genes in the child on child behaviors involved in the child's selection of the environment.

A third type of gene-environment correlation is called evocative. It refers to the effects of the child's genes on child behavior that serves to influence interpersonal interactions and, therefore, how other people react to the child.

Rutter (2007) stated that all the types of gene-environment interactions are operative in development. The traditional notion is that gene and environment effects are strictly additive and noninteractive. However, gene-environment interaction research has shown that it influences conditions such as anxiety, depressive disorders, and even schizophrenia.

## *Other Models*

This section briefly presents two schematics related to the multiple biological, psychological, and social factors involved in development and how they interact over time. I add another schematic on the stress process (see Figs. 29.4–29.6).

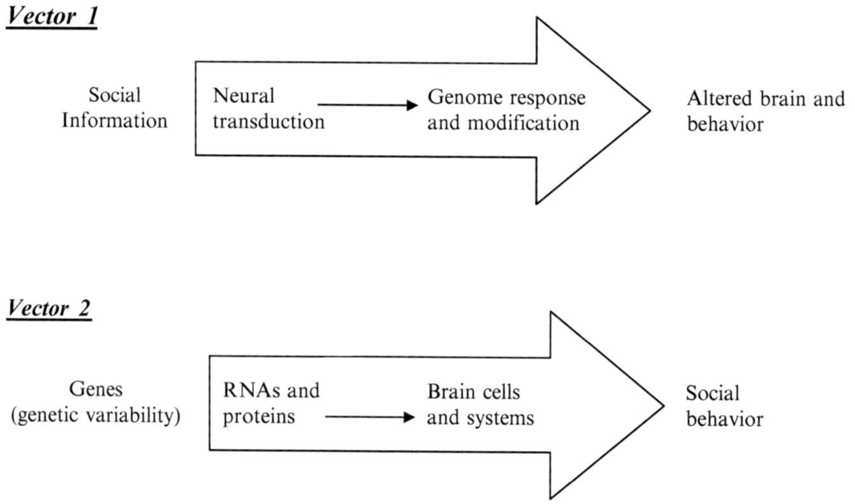


**Fig. 29.4** From social information to brain and behavior and genes to social behavior. Vector 1. From social information to changes in brain function and behavior. Social information is perceived by sensory systems and transduced into responses in the brain. Social information leads to developmental influences often mediated by parental care, as well as acute changes in gene expression that cause diverse effects (e.g., changes in metabolic states, synaptic connections, and transcriptional networks). Social information also can cause epigenetic modifications in the genome. Variation in both environment (Ve) and genotype (Vg) influences how social information is received and transduced and how these factors themselves interact (Ve × Vg). Vector 2. From genes to social behavior. Genes influence the social behavior of an individual through their effects on brain development and physiology. This linkage is sensitive to both genetic (Vg) and environmental (Ve) variation and to their interactions (Vg × Ve). Reprinted with the permission of AAAS. From Robinson, G. E., Fernald, R. D., & Clayton, D. F. (2008). [Figure 2, Page. 898; Figure 3, Page. 899]

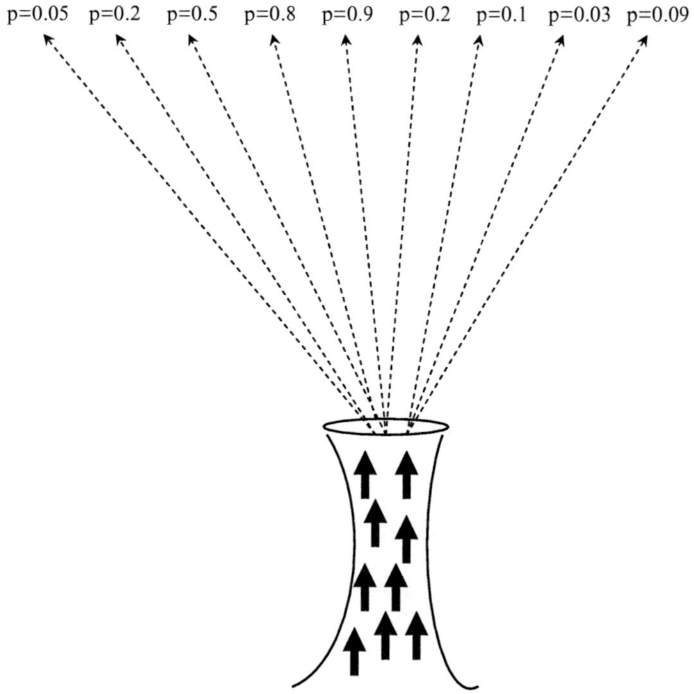


**Fig. 29.5** Counterfactual and probabilistic causes in the emergence of complex behavioral phenotypes. Counterfactual and probabilistic causes: These causes are distinguished from necessary and sufficient causes that result in certain, predetermined outcomes (e.g., in the case of traits under a single, Mendelian genetic mechanism). Counterfactual and probabilistic causes introduce and influence but do not determine outcomes. This type of causation is typically associated with traits whose inheritance is governed by mechanisms other than those captured by Mendel, that is, complex behavioral traits. The impact of genetic forces (shown in *solid arrows*) is "funneled" by environment (or any combination of forces acting interactively!) to result in different probabilistic outcomes (shown in *dotted arrows*); variation in environment (i.e., different type of funneling) leads to an array of possible probabilistic outcomes. Reprinted with the permission of John Wiley & Sons, Inc. Grigorenko, E. L. (2007). Copyright © 2007 and International Mind, Brain, and Education Society's. [Figure 2(b), Page. 197]

# Epigenesis

## *Introduction*

Meaney (2010) has provided a comprehensive summary of this fast-growing and important field (also see Champagne, 2010 for a lifespan perspective). He indicated that epigenetics concerns the functional modification to DNA that does not alter nucleotide sequence. There is structural modification to chromatin either in terms of histones or DNA itself that affects gene expression. The functional byproduct of epigenetic marks involves change in DNA transcription. The classic epigenetic change relates to DNA methylation, which involves adding a methyl

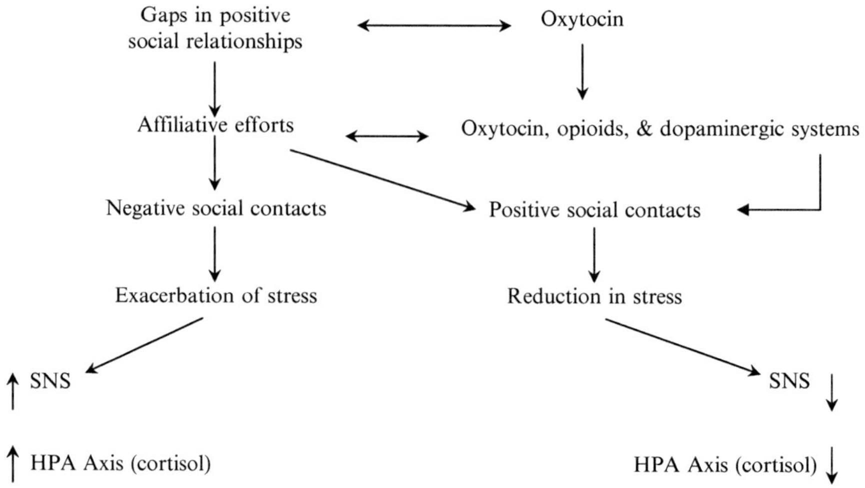


**Fig. 29.6** A model of affiliative responses to stress. Elevations in plasma oxytocin accompany gaps in positive social relationships and are believed to prompt affiliative efforts aimed at restoring positive social contacts; engagement of opioid and dopaminergic systems coupled with oxytocin may lead to a reduction in stress responses, including those of the sympathetic nervous systems (SNS) and the hypothalamic-pituitary-adrenocortical (HPA) axis. However, negative social contacts exacerbate stress, leading to an increase in these same biological stress responses. Reprinted with the permission of SAGE Publications. Taylor, S. E. (2006). Copyright © 2006 by Association for Psychological Science. [Figure 1, Page. 274]

group to cytosines in DNA. DNA methylation is associated with silencing gene transcription. Meaney indicated that we now understand that environmental signals can "actively remodel epigenetic marks that regulate gene expression," which constitutes a "rather radical change" in knowledge about the "environmental regulation of gene expression" (p. 57). Social events early in life are "imprinted" upon the genome, through the biological pathways that they activate, thereby "programming" it and gene expression in the adult.

Meaney (2010) indicated that environmental conditions early in life are capable of structurally altering DNA, leading to effects on phenotypic expression over the life of the individual. These early influences include maternal care received perinatally. DNA is being shown to be plastic due to environmentally driven factors. Genes and the environment are interdependent in the regulation of the genotype. It makes no sense to artificially separate genes and environment as main effects that do not interact.

Genes do not prescribe complex behaviors, such as intelligence. Rather, they code for molecules (RNAs, ribonucleic acids), and not directly for behavior. There are multiple and complex interceding steps at the level of cellular processes that lie between the sequences in DNA and the behavioral functionality associated with the gene product. Moreover, the association is but a correlation that does not imply direct causality. Only detailed study at the molecular level in concert with study of outcome can narrow down the understanding of causation in genetic study.

Moreover, the function of genes can be understood only in relation to their cellular environment. The latter is dynamic, changing constantly.

The studies of Meaney and colleagues with rats have indicated that adversity or decreased quality of parental investment behavior acts to increase defensive responses in offspring (emotional, autonomic, and endocrine responses to stress), which could compromise health in the long term. Maternal behavior early in life appears to program stable changes in gene expression that affect behavioral and neuro-endocrine response to stress in offspring even in the adult period.

However, these epigenetic effects on offspring due to early adversity or deprivation of parental care could be advantageous in an evolutionary sense. First, epigenetic effects work quickly, and learning processes would not be as effective for what the former accomplish. Second, epigenetic effects are reversible, unlike genomic changes. Therefore, when there were early difficulties in the environment of ancestral species (e.g., lack of nutrients, agents of infection) and their offspring, they were best served by having defensive responses, even at the risk of having stress reactions and health issue after the critical reproductive period. Flexible mechanisms that had heightened these defensive reactions were selected evolutionarily for their fitness advantages. Moreover, intergenerational transmission in the mechanism involved was selected, as well, because succeeding generations usually inhabit the same niche with its resource difficulties, so that it was evolutionarily economical for the mechanism involved to be passed on, but only as long as the niche remained the same.

Meaney concluded that the research on epigenetics indicates that there is neither an ideal phenotype nor an ideal style of parental care. The ultimate effect on gene transcription appears to be an emergent property of epigenesis acting on the genome. "The dynamic genome" is a concept replacing the notion that DNA represents a passive repository of nucleotide sequences in the "genetic code." In the postgenomic era, the genome needs to be considered as functional and interactive with the environment.

It is beyond the scope of the chapter to incorporate into my own review that follows in this chapter and the next the literature review conducted by Meaney (2010) on gene-environment interactions. However, I do provide a brief survey. The *5-HTTP* promoter region polymorphism (for those who carry at least one copy of the s allele) is associated with depression and anxiety, in particular, and leads to increased activation of the amygdala in processing fearful or angry facial expressions (Canli & Lesch, 2007; Pezawas et al., 2005; respectively). The *5-HTTP* polymorphism could have its effect by altering *5-HT* activity during early neural development, e.g., for the mouse, by muting the *5-HT1A* receptor gene in the first 3 weeks of life. Monkeys that bear the s compared to the l allele of the *5-HTTP* promoter polymorphism express reduced *5-HT* activity, increased impulsivity, etc., but this is especially true for monkeys reared in peer groups instead of their mothers (Suomi, 2006). The *DRD4* polymorphism has been found to interact with quality of parenting in determining the degree of internalizing and externalizing behavior in children (Propper, Willoughby, Halpern, Carbone, & Cox, 2007). McGowan et al. (2009) found an increased methylation of the exon 1F promoter in samples of the hippocampus taken from suicide victims, but only if there also had been child maltreatment earlier in the life of the victims. Overall, the results of many studies continually lead to the conclusion that variations in the quality of early parental care in humans can modify the epigenetic status of particular sites of the genome.

## Mechanisms in Epigenesis

Champagne and Mashoodh (2009) explained the contextual determinants of gene function, or what genes do. Genes are particular sequences of DNA. A gene consists of a sequence of DNA involving the four nucleotides G (guanine), C (cytosine), T (thymine), A (adenine), and they are preceded by a promoter region of DNA. The promoter region is responsive to factors that influence reading or transcription of the DNA. Enzymes read the DNA by binding to the promoter region of the gene, thereby activating them. DNA is activated by RNA polymerase, which produces messenger RNA (mRNA) in the process of transcription.

Champagne and Mashoodh (2009) explained that mRNA transcripts are copies of DNA sequences that can be translated further into proteins. It is the biochemical environment surrounding the DNA that contains critical factors allowing the DNA to be read. Epigenetic influences might determine the expression of DNA without actually altering the sequence of DNA (epigenetic means "in addition to genetic"). For example, DNA methylation is an epigenetic mechanism that alters gene activity. In DNA methylation, a methyl chemical group adds to specific sites within the gene sequence, modifying the DNA. Usually, DNA methylation functions to silence the gene involved by attaching to the promoter region, thereby blocking enzymes that transcribe DNA and so reducing the accessibility of DNA and decreasing gene activity. (Note that in epigenesis, normal "activation" processes are "blocked," a process that reminds of the present concept of activation–inhibition coordination).

The authors go on to explain how low-quality maternal care can affect the genes of offspring through epigenesis. In rodents, low-quality maternal care can alter genetic expression and the stress response. When there is a prolonged stress response, the hippocampus is affected. It is involved in learning and memory. Low levels of glucocorticoid receptors (GR) within the hippocampus lead to prolonged responses to stress. When DNA methylation within the regulatory region of the GR gene is analyzed, it has been shown that low levels of maternal care are associated with increased levels of DNA methylation, which functions to silence epigenetically the gene involved (Weaver et al., 2004).

Oberlander et al. (2008) conducted a human study with interesting results about DNA methylation of the GR gene promoter region. They extracted fetal blood cord and analyzed for methylation of the human glucocorticoid receptor gene (*NR3C1*). They examined the cortisol stress response of infants at 3 years of age. They showed a relationship with prenatal blood work results and maternal depression and anxiety during the third trimester, in relation to the stress response at 3 years of age. Specifically, they found that prenatal maternal depression and anxiety can lead to increased levels of DNA methylation of the GR gene promoter region, which had consequences for the 3-year stress response.

## *Epigenesis in Rodents*

About epigenesis, Meaney and his colleagues studied rats exposed to different nurturing environments (Cameron et al., 2005; Champagne et al., 2004; Meaney & Szyf, 2005; Weaver et al., 2004). These researchers noted that lactating mother rats varied in their licking and grooming, as well as arch-back nursing, of their neonatal offspring. Also, they noted that the offspring varied, in turn, in their behavior and responses to stress.

Jablonka and Lamb (2010) further described the research of Meaney and his colleagues. They noted that pups that received a lot of licking and grooming from their mothers were more stress-resistant. Moreover, when the daughter pups had offspring themselves, they exhibited the same high-rate of these maternal behaviors. In contrast, female pups of rat mothers who had been given less maternal care became more fearful and easily stressed. Moreover, as adults, these females treated their own pups in the same way that they had been treated as pups. Therefore, the research showed that the maternal behaviors were passed on, but in different ways, depending on the history of care received.

Meaney and colleagues found that changes over generations in behavior related to the hypothalamic-pituitary adrenal (HPA axis) (Weaver et al., 2004). When reared by more caring mothers, pups expressed increases of the glucocorticoid receptor gene in the hippocampus. Jablonka and Lamb (2010) stated that this is correlated with the changes in DNA methylation and histone acetylation in the gene's promoter region. For Jablonka and Lamb (2010), the results reflect an epigenetic effect.

By using a cross-fostering design, the researchers showed that the type of rearing received mediated an intergenerational influence on the offspring. Moreover, DNA methylation effects on a specific glucocorticoid receptor gene promoter region in the hippocampus mediated the results. The receptor effect in the hippocampus related to cortisol functioning, which is implicated in the stress response. These receptors function as a brake on the HPA axis stress response.

Meaney and colleagues next investigated whether the epigenetic effect was irreversible or whether it could be altered later in life. They used the drug trichostatin-A, which did reverse to some extent the methylation effect, altering the endocrine response to stress. The results show that the intergenerational effect was not simply due to DNA methylation.

Jablonka and Lamb (2010) also described the similar research of Curley, Champagne, Bateson, and Keverne (2008). They found that mouse mothers with a particular mutant gene provided low-quality maternal care to their offspring, which led them to be fearful and explore less. As these offspring reached adulthood themselves and had their own offspring, they provided them low quality maternal care; in turn, these offspring expressed greater fear and decreased exploration. Jablonka and Lamb (2010) noted that this happened even though these offspring did not carry the mutant gene.

## Gene-Environment Interactions and the Development of Risk

### *G×E Interactions*

Kim-Cohen and Gold (2009) reviewed literature on gene-environment interactions and mechanisms that promote resilience and development. They cited the "groundbreaking" research of Caspi and Moffitt (2006) and their colleagues on gene-environment interactions. In this G×E interaction, individuals exposed to risk who have the "protective" version (or allele) of the relevant gene express greatly reduced levels of psychopathology compared to individuals having the "vulnerable" allele of the gene.

### *Psychological Disorders and Life Stress*

Caspi et al. (2002) found a strong genetic-environment effect in their study of childhood maltreatment and antisocial-related disorders. Caspi and colleagues were the first to find that the association between childhood maltreatment and the development of later antisocial behavior was moderated by a particular functional polymorphism in the promoter (or regulatory) region of the gene encoding the enzyme monoamine oxidase A (*MAOA*). It is a neurotransmitter-metabolizing enzyme located in the X chromosome. The gene encodes the *MAOA* enzyme, which metabolizes various neurotransmitters, including norepinephrine, dopamine, and serotonin. Its effect is to render them inactive.

Caspi et al. found that maltreated children with low levels of *MAOA* expression due to their genotype developed higher levels of antisocial behavior later in adolescence and in adulthood compared to children who had been maltreated but who had the high activity version of the *MAOA* gene. In particular, the genetic variation concerned short and long (s and l) versions or alleles of the gene. Most children having the short form of the *MAOA* polymorphism who had been reared with severe maltreatment, as opposed to no or probable maltreatment, expressed some form of aggression on the measures used. In particular, the researchers found that the low-level gene variant is associated with conduct disorder, violent offenses, disposition towards violence, and antisocial personality disorder, but only if the participants in the study had been maltreated as children. In contrast, those participants having the long form of the genotype for *MAOA* activity expressed much less psychopathology-related behavior, even when they were exposed to severe maltreatment as a child.

As for the specific numerical results, the rate of conduct disorder outcomes with the adverse effect of maltreatment was 0.23 among youth with low *MAOA* activity and being in a nonmaltreatment group, compared to the rate of 0.81 for the maltreatment group. In contrast, for youth with high *MAOA* activity, the corresponding rates were 0.22 and 0.41, respectively.

Caspi et al. (2003) reported that the presence of the short allele of *5-HTT* was associated with more symptoms of depression and suicidality when stressful life events or child maltreatment had been experienced, relative to individuals with similar experience but with the long allele only of the gene. Caspi et al. (2005) found that an early heavy use of the drug cannabis predisposed individuals to develop schizophrenia-related disorders, but only if they possessed the val/val allelic variation of the catechol-o-methyl transferase (*COMT*) genotype.

In Caspi's studies the genes involved did not affect mental health outcome in individuals who were not exposed to risk. These finding have been replicated by independent studies and by meta-analysis (Kim-Cohen et al., 2006; Taylor & Kim-Cohen, 2007; Uher & McGuffin, 2007). However, Caspi and colleagues results are not always replicated. Brown and Harris (2008) noted that failures to replicate the Caspi et al. findings had measured life stress only in the months preceding the onset of depressive symptoms. In contrast, those studies that have replicated the Caspi et al. findings measured life stress events in the 5 years preceding the onset of depressive episodes.

## *Additional Research*

Cicchetti, Rogosch, and Sturge-Apple (2007) studied maltreatment and the *5-HTT* genotype. Since they had a large sample, they could investigate features of maltreatment in relation to G×E effects. In the prediction of depressive symptoms, overall maltreatment status did not interact with the *5-HTT* of genotype. However, levels of depressive symptoms were elevated among children who had the low-activity *MAOA* allele and who had experienced certain maltreatment subtypes. Also in their study, for adolescents who had two copies of the short allele of *5-HTT*, the experience of sexual abuse had a greater effect on the expression of internalizing symptoms than the experience of physical abuse alone or the experience of neglect. The authors noted that the sexual abuse group was defined in terms of a broad category of types of abuse. Therefore, they argued that experiencing multiple types of maltreatment is a risk factor that can trigger psychopathology by a genetically-mediated process.

## Summary

As I surveyed the literature on epigenesis, I was struck by the findings that the molecular activity involved in regulating genes includes suppression, silencing, or inhibition. It would appear that even at the molecular level in the functioning of DNA processes, mechanisms akin to activation–inhibition coordination are involved. This is consistent with the present work that argues that activation–inhibition coordination is a ubiquitous function across brain and behavior – and now we can add – and across their molecular underpinnings. As genes are silenced in epigenesis, processes akin to activation–inhibition coordination seem to be at play.

This chapter and the next describe the causal process of epigenesis from a genetic and psychological point of view. They complete the concentrated discussion of the causes, determinants, and origins of behavior. After the next chapter, I explore the final topics of the present work, and they do include some work on the topic of causality. The next chapter expands the work on epigenesis, and includes the work of Belsky and Pluess (2009a, 2009b) on genetic underpinnings to susceptibility and resilience. There are other topics in the next chapter, as well, including social genomics.

My only concern about this type of research is that the emphasis on gene-environment interactions takes precedence in understanding the whole person in development. The risk is a return to a passive model of development, where environmental risks are translated into psychological risks, even if apparently advantageous in the niches involved, without any role given to the person herself or himself in the developmental process. As development unfolds, one finds a role not only for nature and nurture but also their interaction. In addition, in concert with nature, nurture, and their interaction, human development is influenced by, if not led by, the active nobleness of the self and our individualized characteristics.

## References

Álvarez, M. P. (2009). The four causes of behavior: Aristotle and Skinner. *International Journal of Psychology and Psychological Therapy, 9*, 45–57.

Arnold, M. L. (2006). *Evolution through genetic exchange*. New York: Oxford University Press.

Beebee, H., Hitchcock, C., & Menzies, P. (2009). *The Oxford handbook of causation*. New York: Oxford University Press.

Belsky, J., & Pluess, M. (2009a). The nature (and nurture?) of plasticity in early human development. *Perspectives on Psychological Science, 4*, 345–351.

Belsky, J., & Pluess, M. (2009b). Beyond diathesis stress: Differential susceptibility to environmental influences. *Psychological Bulletin, 135*, 885–908.

Broadie, S. (2009). The ancient Greeks. In H. Beebee, C. Hitchcock, & P. Menzies (Eds.), *The Oxford handbook of causation* (pp. 21–39). New York: Oxford University Press.

Brown, G. W., & Harris, T. O. (2008). Depression and the serotonin transporter *5-HTTLPR* polymorphism: A review and a hypothesis concerning gene-environment interaction. *Journal of Affective Disorder, 111*, 1–12.

Cameron, N. M., Champagne, F. A., Parent, C., Fish, E. W., Ozaki-Kuroda, K., & Meaney, M. J. (2005). The programming of individual differences in defensive responses and reproductive

strategies in the rat through variations in maternal care. *Neuroscience and Biobehavioral Reviews, 29*, 843–865.
Canli, T., & Lesch, K.-P. (2007). Long story short: The serotonin transporter in emotion regulation and social cognition. *Nature Neuroscience, 10*, 1103–1109.
Carroll, S. B. (2005). *Endless forms most beautiful: The new science of Evo Devo and the making of the animal kingdom*. New York: Norton.
Caspi, A., McClay, J., Moffitt, T. E., Mill, J., Martin, J., Craig, I. W., et al. (2002). Role of genotype in the cycle of violence in maltreated children. *Science, 297*, 851–854.
Caspi, A., & Moffitt, T. E. (2006). Gene-environment interactions in psychiatry: Joining forces with neuroscience. *Nature Reviews Neuroscience, 7*, 583–590.
Caspi, A., Moffitt, T. E., Cannon, M., McClay, J., Murray, R., Harrington, H., et al. (2005). Moderation of the effect of adolescent-onset cannabis use on adult psychosis by a functional polymorphism in the *COMT* gene: Longitudinal evidence of a gene×environment interaction. *Biological Psychiatry, 57*, 1117–1127.
Caspi, A., Sugden, K., Moffitt, T. E., Taylor, A., Craig, I. W., Harrington, H., et al. (2003). Influence of life stress on depression: Moderation by a polymorphism in the *5-HTT* gene. *Science, 301*, 386–389.
Champagne, F. A. (2010). Early adversity and developmental outcomes: Interaction between genetics, epigenetics, and social experiences across the life span. *Perspectives on Psychological Science, 5*, 564–574.
Champagne, F. A., Chretien, P., Stevenson, C. W., Zhang, T. Y., Gratton, A., & Meaney, M. J. (2004). Variations in nucleus accumbens dopamine associated with individual differences in maternal behavior in the rat. *The Journal of Neuroscience, 24*, 4113–4123.
Champagne, F. A., & Mashoodh, R. (2009). Genes in context: Gene-environment interplay and the origins of individual differences in behavior. *Current Directions in Psychological Science, 18*, 127–131.
Cicchetti, D., Rogosch, F. A., & Sturge-Apple, M. L. (2007). Interactions of child maltreatment and serotonin transporter and monoamine oxidase A polymorphisms: Depressive symptomatology among adolescents from low socioeconomic status backgrounds. *Development and Psychopathology, 19*, 1161–1180.
Cullis, C. A. (2005). Mechanisms and control of rapid genomic changes in flax. *Annals of Botany, 95*, 201–206.
Curley J. P., Champagne F. A., Bateson P. P., Keverne E. B. (2008). Transgenerational effects of impaired maternal care on behavior of offspring and grandoffspring. *Animal Behavior, 75*, 1551–1561.
Flew, A., & Priest, S. (Eds.). (2002). *A dictionary of philosophy*. London: Pan.
Forgács, G., & Newman, S. A. (2005). *Biological physics of the developing embryo*. Cambridge: Cambridge University Press.
Goldenfeld, N., & Woese, C. (2007). Biology's next revolution. *Nature, 445*, 369.
Gottlieb, G. (1971). Ontogenesis of sensory function in birds and mammals. In E. Tobach, L. R. Aronson, & E. Shaw (Eds.), *The biopsychology of development* (pp. 67–128). New York: Academic Press.
Gottlieb, G. (2007). Probabilistic epigenesis. *Developmental Science, 10*, 1–11.
Grigorenko, E. L. (2007). Understanding the etiology of complex traits: Symbiotic relationships between psychology and genetics. *Mind, Brain, and Education, 1*, 193–199.
Jablonka, E., & Lamb, M. J. (1995). *Epigenetic inheritance and evolution: The Lamarckian dimension*. Oxford: Oxford University Press.
Jablonka, E., & Lamb, M. J. (2005). *Evolution in four dimensions: Genetic, epigenetic, behavioral, and symbolic variation in the history of life*. Cambridge: MIT Press.
Jablonka, E., & Lamb, M. J. (2008). The epigenome in evolution: Beyond the modern synthesis. *VOGis Herald, 12*, 242–254.
Jablonka, E., & Lamb, M. J. (2010). Transgenerational epigenetic inheritance. In M. Pigliucci & G. B. Müller (Eds.), *Evolution: The extended synthesis* (pp. 137–174). London: MIT Press.

Jablonka, E., & Raz, G. (2009). Transgenerational epigenetic inheritance: Prevalence, mechanisms, and implications for the study of heredity and evolution. *Quarterly Review of Biology, 84*, 131–176.

Jablonski, D. (2005). Mass extinctions and macroevolution. *Paleobiology, 31*, 192–210.

Jessell, T. M., & Sanes, J. R. (2000). The induction and patterning of the nervous system. In E. R. Kandel, J. H. Schwartz, & T. M. Jessell (Eds.), *Principles of neural science* (4th ed., pp. 1019–1040). New York: McGraw-Hill.

Kim-Cohen, J., Caspi, A., Taylor, A., Williams, B., Newcombe, R., Craig, I. W., et al. (2006). MAOA, maltreatment, and gene-environment interaction predicting children's mental health: New evidence and a meta-analysis. *Molecular Psychiatry, 11*, 903–913.

Kim-Cohen, J., & Gold, A. L. (2009). Measured gene-environment interactions and mechanisms promoting resilient development. *Current Directions in Psychological Science, 18*, 138–142.

Kirschner, M. W., & Gerhart, J. C. (2005). *The plausibility of life: Resolving Darwin's dilemma*. New Haven: Yale University Press.

Lamm, E., & Jablonka, E. (2008). The nurture of nature: Hereditary plasticity in evolution. *Philosophical Psychology, 21*, 305–319.

Levy, A. A., & Feldman, M. (2004). Genetic and epigenetic reprogramming of the wheat genome upon allopolyploidization. *Biological Journal of the Linnean Society of London, 82*, 607–613.

Mareschal, D., Johnson, M. H., Sirois, S., Spratling, M. W., Thomas, M. S. C., & Westmann, G. (2007). *Neuroconstructivism: Vol. 1. How the brain constructs cognition*. New York: Oxford University Press.

McGowan, P. O., Sasaki, A., Dymov, S., LaBoonté, B., Turecki, G., Szyf, M., et al. (2009). Epigenetic regulation of the glucocorticoid receptor in human brain associates with childhood abuse. *Nature Neuroscience, 12*, 342–348.

Meaney, M. J. (2010). Epigenetic and the biological definition of gene × environment interactions. *Child Development, 81*, 41–79.

Meaney, M. J., & Szyf, M. (2005). Maternal effects as a model for environmentally-dependent chromatin plasticity. *Trends in Neuroscience, 28*, 456–463.

Newman, S. A., & Müller, G. B. (2006). Genes and form: Inherency in the evolution of developmental mechanisms. In E. Neumann-Held & C. Rehmann-Sutter (Eds.), *Genes in development: Re-reading the molecular paradigm* (pp. 38–73). Durham: Duke University Press.

Oberlander, T. F., Weinberg, J., Papsdorf, M., Grunau, R., Misri, S., & Devlin, A. M. (2008). Prenatal exposure to maternal depression, neonatal methylation of human glucocorticoid receptor gene (*NR3C1*) and infant cortisol stress responses. *Epigenetics, 3*, 97–106.

Pezawas, L., Meyer-Lindenberg, A., Drabant, E. M., Verchinski, B. A., Munoz, K. E., Kolachana, B. S., et al. (2005). *5-HTTLPR* polymorphism impacts human cingulate-amygdala interactions: A genetic susceptibility mechanism for depression. *Nature Neuroscience, 8*, 828–834.

Pigliucci, M., & Müller, G. B. (Eds.). (2010). *Evolution: The extended synthesis*. London: MIT Press.

Plomin, R., DeFries, J. C., & Loehlin, J. C. (1977). Genotype-environment interaction and correlation in the analysis of human behavior. *Psychological Bulletin, 84*, 309–322.

Propper, C., Willoughby, M., Halpern, C. T., Carbone, M. A., & Cox, M. (2007). Parenting quality, DRD4, and the prediction of externalizing and internalizing behaviors in early childhood. *Developmental Psychobiology, 49*, 619–632.

Robinson, G. E., Fernald, R. D., & Clayton, D. F. (2008). Genes and social behavior. *Science, 322*, 896–900.

Rutter, M. (2007). Gene-environment interdependence. *Developmental Science, 10*, 12–18.

Suomi, S. J. (2006). Risk, resilience, and gene × environment interactions in rhesus monkeys. *Annals of the New York Academy of Sciences, 1094*, 83–104.

Taylor, A., & Kim-Cohen, J. (2007). Meta-analysis of gene-environment interactions in developmental psychopathology. *Development & Psychopathology, 19*, 1029–1037.

Taylor, S. E. (2006). Tend and befriend: Biobehavioral bases of affiliation under stress. *Current Directions in Psychological Science, 15*, 273–277.

Tinbergen, N. (1963). On aims and methods in ethology. *Zeitschrift für Tierpsychologie, 20*, 410–433.

Uher, R., & McGuffin, P. (2007). The moderation by the serotonin transporter gene of environmental adversity in the aetiology of mental illness: Review and methodological analysis. *Molecular Psychiatry, 13*, 131–146.

Weaver, I. C. G., Cervoni, N., Campagne, F. A., D'Alessio, A. C., Sharma, S., Seckl, J. R., et al. (2004). Epigenetic programming by maternal behavior. *Nature Neuroscience, 7*, 847–854.

West-Eberhard, M. J. (2003). *Developmental plasticity and evolution*. New York: Oxford University Press.

Westermann, G., Mareschal, D., Johnson, M. H., Sirois, S., Spratling, M. W., & Thomas, M. S. C. (2007). Neuroconstructivism. *Developmental Science, 10*, 75–83.

Wilkins, A. S. (2002). *The evolution of developmental pathways*. Sunderland: Sinauer.

Wilson, D. S. (2009). Convergent cultural evolution and multilevel selection: Reply to comments on Janet Landa's "The bioeconomics of homogenous middleman groups as adaptive units: Theory and empirical evidence viewed from a group selection framework". *Journal of Bioeconomics, 11*, 185–190.

Witherington, D. C., & Crichton, J. A. (2007). Framework for understanding emotions and their development: Functionalist and dynamic systems approaches. *Emotion, 7*, 628–637.

Young, G., & Shore, R. (2007). Dictionary of terms related to causality, causation, law, and psychology. In G. Young, A. W. Kane, & K. Nicholson, *Causality of psychological injury: Presenting evidence in court* (pp. 87–135). New York: Springer Science+Business Media.

Zilber-Rosenberg, I., & Rosenberg, E. (2008). Role of microorganisms in the evolution of animals and plants: The hologenome theory of evolution. *FEMS Microbiology Reviews, 32*, 723–735.

# Chapter 30
# Gene–Environment Interactions: Other Topics

## Introduction

The research being undertaken in the area of epigenesis is remarkable and is revolutionizing our understanding of psychology and its biological influences. This chapter highlights the differential susceptibility-resilience hypothesis of certain polymorphisms, depending on the degree of environmental support received. Genetic-environment interaction (G x E) research is indicating the complexities involved, and supports the notion of complex interactions involving G X El X E2. The research also indicates exogenous factors involved in the interactions. There are also gene-gene interactions and generalist genes to consider, as well as multi-gene X multi-environment modeling (G X G X E X E interactions). The developmental pathways that are being described to understand how these nuanced interactions unfold are neither nativist nor empiricist; they deny even a few basic, congenital modules at work in early core knowledge and domains. Neural networks become canalized through experience-dependent processes, and Hebbian learning takes place; neurons develop interconnections through repetitions or enhancements in firing of patterns. The brain is considered generalist. Mirror neurons capable of rapid learning are being found, and might be at work in mirror therapy. We are learning in social genomics that social-environmental influences (e.g., perceived loneliness) can affect the immune system response, and even survival, indicating that modern study of genetics needs to be "environmentally conscious."

## Interaction of Genes and Environment in Early Plasticity and Susceptibility

Belsky and Pluess (2009a, 2009b) questioned the typical diathesis-stress model of psychopathology by arguing that not only do certain genes confer disadvantages in terms of susceptibility to adversity but also they could confer benefits when there are supportive and enriching experiences. The common assumption is that certain genotypes and temperaments carry vulnerability to the adverse effects of negative experiences. However, evidence indicates that susceptibility genes function more like

G. Young, *Development and Causality: Neo-Piagetian Perspectives*,
DOI 10.1007/978-1-4419-9422-6_30, 

plasticity genes, promoting malleability in light of either positive or negative environmental factors. For example, the research on gene–environment interactions in the case of the development of antisocial behavior not only showed how certain genes conferred risk in combination with maltreatment but also showed that the genes involved conferred resilience if maltreatment was not present. In the following sections, I analyze in more depth the approach taken by Belsky and Pluess.

## *DRD4*

Recent research documents that careful measurements of genes and environments provide compelling evidence of positive rearing effects on susceptible children and not only negative rearing effects on them. For example, Bakermans-Kranenburg and van IJzendoorn (2006) studied the relationship between parental insensitivity and externalizing problems, as moderated by the presence of the 7-repeat allele of the *DRD4* gene. It codes for a type of dopamine receptor involved in attention, motivation, and reward mechanisms. Variants in *DRD4* differ in the amount of 48-base-pair tandem repeats in exon III, which ranges from 2 to 1. The 7-repeat allele has been linked to less efficiency in dopamine reception. Bakermans-Kranenburg and van IJzendoorn (2006) studied infants. They found that the 7-repeat allele moderated the association between parental insensitivity and externalizing difficulties in the children. Specifically, children with the allele who experienced insensitive mothering exhibited more externalizing behavior compared to children without the allele. The result was found independent of the degree of maternal sensitivity for the latter group. By contrast, children with the allele in question who were raised by sensitive mothers displayed the lowest levels of externalized problem behavior.

## *MAOA*

Belsky and Pluess (2009b) pointed out that even the groundbreaking research of Caspi et al. (2002) is consistent with their hypothesis that particular alleles could heighten vulnerability to a wide range of environments; that is, supportive and risky environments promote positive and negative child outcomes, respectively. Caspi et al. (2002) had examined the functional polymorphism in the promoter of the monoamine oxidase A (*MAOA*) gene.

Caspi et al.'s (2002) research showed that maltreatment effects on children are moderated by their genotype. In their study of young men, those having the allele associated with low *MAOA* activity ended up the most prone to violence, but only if they had experienced child maltreatment. Child maltreatment had little effect on those individuals having the high-*MAOA*-activity allele. In addition to these results, to their credit, Belsky and Pluess (2009b) noticed that participants in the Caspi et al. study who were most susceptible to adverse effects of childhood maltreatment and who simultaneously were not exposed to childhood maltreatment obtained the lowest scores on their measures of antisocial behavior.

Kim-Cohen et al. (2006) studied 7-year-old boys having the low-*MAOA*-activity allele. They were rated by their mothers and teachers as experiencing more mental health outcome difficulties, i.e., attention-deficit hyperactivity disorder, but only if they had been victims of childhood abuse. In contrast, if the boys had not been exposed to abuse, they had fewer problems than boys with the high-*MAOA*-activity genotype.

Foley et al. (2004) studied twin boys from 8 to 17 years of age. They found that the adolescents having the low-*MAOA*-activity allele had an increased probability of receiving the diagnosis of conduct disorder, but only if they had experienced higher levels of childhood adversity (parental neglect, exposure to interparental conflict, inconsistent parental discipline). In addition, they were less likely to be diagnosed if they had been exposed to lower levels of childhood adversity.

Other researchers also have found similar results in support of Belsky and Pluess (Ducci et al., 2008; Frazzetto et al., 2007; Nilsson et al., 2006; Widom & Brzustowicz, 2006). Taylor and Kim-Cohen (2007) reported a meta-analysis of seven studies investigating the *MAOA*–maltreatment interactions and found the effect to be robust.

## *5-HTTLPR*

The studies of the *5-HTTLPR* gene has provided further evidence in support of the particular genetic-environmental interaction model of differential susceptibility developed by Belsky and Pluess (2009a, 2009b). The serotonin-transporter-linked polymorphic region of the gene (*5-HTTLPR*) is a degenerate repeat polymorphic region in the gene SLC6A4. Most research focuses on two variants, the one having at least one short allele (s/s, s/l) and those that are homozygous for the long allele (l/l). The short allele is associated with lesser expression of the serotonin transporter molecule. This molecule is involved in the reuptake of serotonin from the synapse. It has been related to depression.

In their groundbreaking research, Caspi et al. (2003) found that *5-HTTLPR* moderates effects of stressful life events in early adulthood on depressive/suicidality outcomes. Young adults with two short alleles were the most negatively affected and those with homozygous long alleles experienced less or absent effects. Belsky and Pluess (2009b) noted that those individuals having the s/s allele obtained the lowest scores for negative outcomes if they had not experienced stressful life events.

In support of this research, Taylor et al. (2006) found that young adults having the s/s variant expressed more depressive symptoms compared to young adults without this variant, but only when they had been exposed to early adversity in childrearing or a high level of recent stressors. By contrast, individuals with this variant expressed the fewest depressive symptoms if they had experienced a supportive early child-rearing history or recent positive as opposed to negative experiences.

Other researchers also have found similar results about depression in support of Belsky and Pluess (Brummett et al., 2008; Eley et al., 2004; Wilhelm et al., 2006; Zalsman et al., 2006). Belsky and Pluess (2009b) described a similar research for *5-HTTLPR* and anxiety.

## *Conclusion*

Belsky and Pluess (2009b) described other genes having the same pattern of results, including HTR2A (e.g., Jokela, Lehtimaki, & Keltikangas-Jarviene, 2007a, 2007b), THP1 (Jokela, Raikkonen, Lehtimaki, Rontu, & Keltikangas-Jarvinen, 2007), DRD2 (Mills-Koonce et al., 2007), and cumulative effects of different gene variants (Belsky, Pluess, Comings, & MacMurray, 2009, cited in Belsky & Pluess, 2009b).

Belsky and Pluess (2009b) concluded that some individuals seem more susceptible to the adverse effects of nonsupportive environmental contexts and the beneficial effects of supportive ones. Some of the environmental factors involved include parenting, child-care quality, life events, rural vs. urban residence, and even birth season. Some of the outcomes involved include disorganized infant attachment, externalizing problems, antisocial behavior, depression, and health conditions. Moderating variables in this body of research include temperament, other phenotypic characteristics, and genotypic ones. Their new model stands in contrast with the classic diathesis-stress one.

Dodge (2009) proposed that the mechanisms for aggression involve three interrelated systems – neural, autonomic arousal, and information processing. Individual differences in the vulnerability of the brain also include factors such as environmental threat. This leads to a full model of genetic and environmental effects that includes gene by early interaction effects (G×E1) and gene by early environment by proximal environmental stimulus effects (G×E1×E2) (see Fig. 30.1).

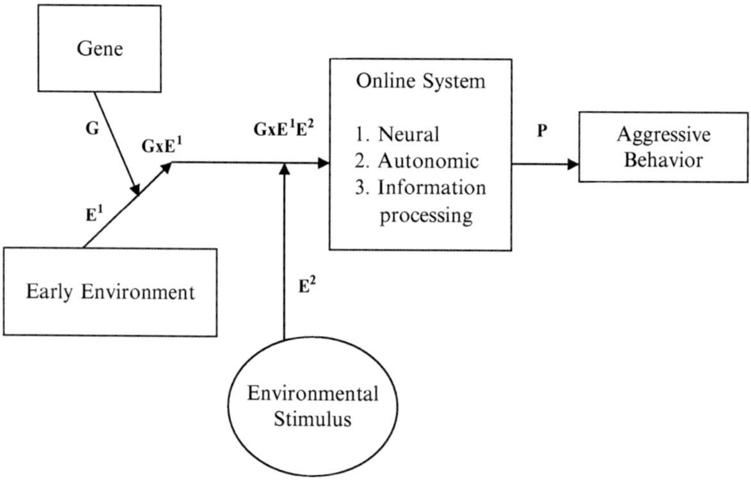


**Fig. 30.1** Model of the mechanisms through which gene–environment interaction affects aggressive behavior. In behavior genetics, models now include whether genetic vulnerabilities are activated by environmental stressors. Cognitive, emotional, and neurochemical brain processes function as mediating mechanisms through which the environment induces psychopathology. Reprinted with the permission of SAGE Publications. Dodge, K. A. (2009). Copyright © 2009 by Association for Psychological Science. [Figure 1, Page. 411]

## Links Between Genes, Behavior, Brain, and the Environment

### *Frontal Lobe Left-Right Asymmetry, Temperament, and the DRD4 Gene*

With colleagues, Fox has extended his work on frontal asymmetry by linking it to genetic underpinnings (Schmidt, Fox, Perez-Edgar, & Hamer, 2009). They found that resting frontal region brain electroencephalogram could help predict child temperament, but only in an interactive manner and not as a straight main effect. They referred to this result as reflecting gene–*endo*environment interaction. In particular, they found that the effect of the dopamine D4 receptor (*DRD4*) gene, which has long and short alleles, moderated the statistical relationship between 9-month resting frontal region electroencephalographic asymmetry (left vs. right EEG) and 48-month temperament. Children in the study were more soothable at 48-months of age if they had exhibited left-side frontal region EEG asymmetry at 9 months of age and also possessed the *DRD4* long allele. By contrast, those children with 9-month right frontal region EEG asymmetry had greater difficulties in focused and sustained attention at 48 months of age, but only if they also had the *DRD4* long allele. As a further sign of the interaction effects in the results for those children who did not have the *DRD4* long allele, their resting frontal region EEG asymmetry did not influence their 48-month temperament. The authors indicated that the results illustrate the presence of a gene–environment interaction involving endogenous factors in comparison to the typical studies on gene–environment interactions involving exogenous environmental factors.

Other studies on the *DRD4* gene have indicated interaction effects with the exogenous environment. For example, Sheese, Voelker, Rothbart, and Posner (2007) reported that those children having the *DRD4* long allele, and who receive lower-quality parenting, had indications of higher levels of sensation seeking. Similarly, Bakermans-Kranenburg and van IJzendoorn (2006) found that the presence of the long *DRD4* allele was associated with more externalizing behavior when the children had experienced insensitive caregiving.

That the long allele of the *DRD4* gene can moderate relationships between frontal EEG asymmetry and behavior in children is consistent with the literature on humans and animals for the effects of the long *DRD4* allele on approach-related behavior, positive affect, and stimulus responsivity. The gene is involved in the regulation of dopamine. In addition, the research of Fox, Henderson, Rubin, Calkins, and Schmidt (2001) illustrated that left resting frontal region EEG asymmetry is related to positive affect and "easy" temperament, whereas for the right side, it is associated with negative affect and "negative reactive" temperament.

The results in Schmidt et al. (2009) are consistent with the argument that the *DRD4* long allele functions as a susceptibility allele (Bakermans-Kranenburg, van IJzendoorn, Pijlman, Mesman, & Juffer, 2008). Belsky, Bakermans-Kranenburg, and van IJzendoorn (2007) maintained that a gene could be expressed in different directions depending on the environmental context. In this regard, for the particular results of Schmidt et al. (2009), the authors maintained that the *DRD4* long allele serves as a protective moderator if the endoenvironmental context consists of the left-frontal region EEG asymmetry. By contrast, this particular genotype constitutes an extra risk factor, rather than a protective factor, when the frontal asymmetry is toward the right. They concluded that complex gene–gene interactions might be at play, as well.

### *Maternal Social Support, Temperament, and the 5-HTTLPR Gene*

Fox, Hane, and Pine (2007) examined exogenous environment–genotype interactions for child temperament and maternal social support. The *5-HTTLPR* gene is involved in serotonin transport. Children who expressed a persistent, fearful temperament at age 7 and possessed the short allele of *5-HTTLPR* were found to have mothers who reported having low social support. The authors argued that the presence of an interaction of the short *5-HTTLPR* allele and a caregiver environment in which psychological threat is highlighted predisposes children to develop a persistently fearful temperament. Children develop an attentional bias toward threat, which exacerbates and maintains their anxious behavior, leading to changes in relevant affect-related neurocircuitry. By contrast, in their study, children with different alleles were protected from developing extreme inhibition in their behavior, even in cases where their mothers reported having experienced low social support. As for the particular neurocircuitry that is affected by the interactive presence of the *5-HTTLPR* genotype and low maternal social support, the authors included the ventral prefrontal cortex and the amygdala (see Fig. 30.2).

The results of Fox et al. (2007) are consistent with those of Caspi et al. (2003), who found that individuals homozygous for the short allele compared to those homozygous for the long allele of the *5-HTTLPR* gene, and who were exposed to five or more stressful events in their lives, were more likely to develop a major depressive episode. Similarly, Kaufman et al. (2004) found that children having the short *5-HTTLPR* allele, who had experienced a history of abuse by caregivers who were simultaneously under high stress loads, were at a greater risk to experience depression.

## Developmental Pathways

Spencer et al. (2009) presented a developmental systems view of development involving epigenesis (Gottlieb, 1991, 2007). Development takes the form of cascades of interaction over multiple causal levels, including genes and environment. The authors rejected nativist views of preordained primitives, endowments, cores,

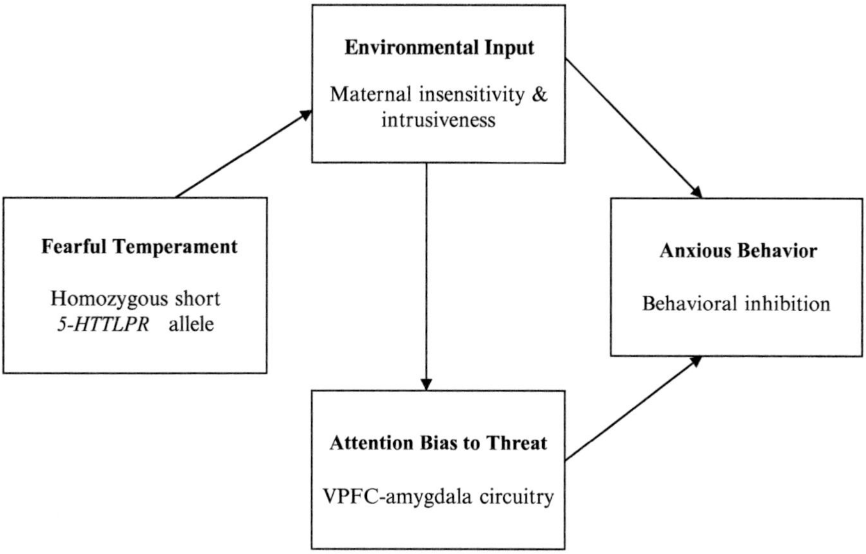


**Fig. 30.2** Plasticity for affective neurocircuitry model. A child's genetically disposed fearful temperament (due to homozygosity for the short allele of the serotonin transporter, *5-HTTLPR*, gene) elicits and is elicited by caregiver behavior (maternal insensitivity and intrusiveness) to shape attention bias to threat and the underlying neural circuitry (in the ventral prefrontal cortex, vPFC, and amygdala) supporting this bias. Exaggerated attention bias contributes to the emergence and maintenance of anxious behaviors. Reprinted with the permission of SAGE Publications. Fox, N. A., Hane, A. A., & Pine, D. S. (2007). Copyright © 2007 by Association for Psychological Science. [Figure 1, Page. 4]

and essences that are innate, fixed, or rigidly constrained. In addition, they disputed middle-ground perspectives between nativism and empiricism that there are only a few core primitives and they serve as foundations for acquisition of flexible skill and knowledge (Spelke & Kinzler, 2007). Spencer et al. argued that even predispositions still must develop and might need to do so by way of nonspecific factors beyond the boundaries of typical postnatal experience, e.g., as happens with self-stimulation in early imprinting. In another example, locomotor experience is needed to prime aspects of core spatial cognition. Based on these findings, the authors maintained that early acquisitions in perception, action, cognition, and emotion codevelop.

Karmiloff-Smith (2009) added that even the middle-ground position between nativism and empiricism should be firmly rejected; that is, there are no core primitives, innately specified core knowledge systems, or domain-specific mechanisms, even if they are reduced to a few by a middle ground position. Moreover, the proposed mechanisms of their elaboration, which involves statistical learning and associative learning, are insufficient to explain by themselves later developmental acquisitions, such as brain development and domain specificity. Karmiloff-Smith presented an alternative middle ground position. She argued that in initial stimulus processing, many cortical regions try to process many incoming inputs. Networks develop specializations in processing particular input types. Some areas reduce in activity of certain inputs and others activate more as fine-tuning in localization and specialization proceeds.

The process of specialization is augmented by tiny differences over regions of the brain that channel certain regions toward the processing of particular inputs, and continued repetitions of activation of these regions compared to others create a feedback effect that increasingly ingrains and constrains the networks involved. These regional differences that potentiate specialization include the following: neurons, neurotransmitters, myelination, lamination, proportion of gray to white matter, and so on. Regions win out in competition for specializations or domain-specific processing capacities.

Spencer et al. (2009) added that in their epigenetic perspective, genes and culture interact, interlevel interactions could be cascading, nonlinear, and nonobvious, no one level in a system is in control, levels exist in nested interactions, new patterns can emerge, and system dynamics change over time. The authors provided an excellent example illustrating these principles, involving the development of visual ocular dominance retinal-neuronal columns in the brain (e.g., thalamus). Spontaneous firings in the retina and the lateral geniculate nucleus function to provide the cellular competition needed to initiate downstream the cascading effects leading to the development of the dominance. In the following section, I describe the work of Del Giudice, Manera, and Keysers (2009), who proposed how initial experiences can interact with prespecified neurons in circuits related to the development of mirror neurons.

## Mirror Neurons

### *Hebbian Learning*

Del Giudice et al. (2009) proposed that mirror neurons develop partly through a process of Hebbian learning at the synaptic level (Hebb, 1942, 1949). Hebb was a pioneer in explaining how neurons develop interconnections through repetitions or enhancements in firing of patterns of the interconnections, which he had referred to as cell assemblies. Mirror neurons develop early because the organization of the nervous system is genetically preprogrammed to canalize their development through the effects of facilitating experience. In particular, the infant's perceptual-motor system is optimized in this direction. For example, as infants observe or even hear their own actions, they are priming Hebbian learning. They show synchronized theta EEG in mirror cortical areas as they watch themselves grasping. The neurons involved in grasping that are enhanced in connectivity by long-term potentiation at the synaptic level include ones in the circuit of the temporal, parietal, and premotor cortical regions (see Fig. 30.3).

For example, data that fit the concept of a prepotent learning related to grasping include the following. Reid, Belsky, and Johnson (2005) found that infants who

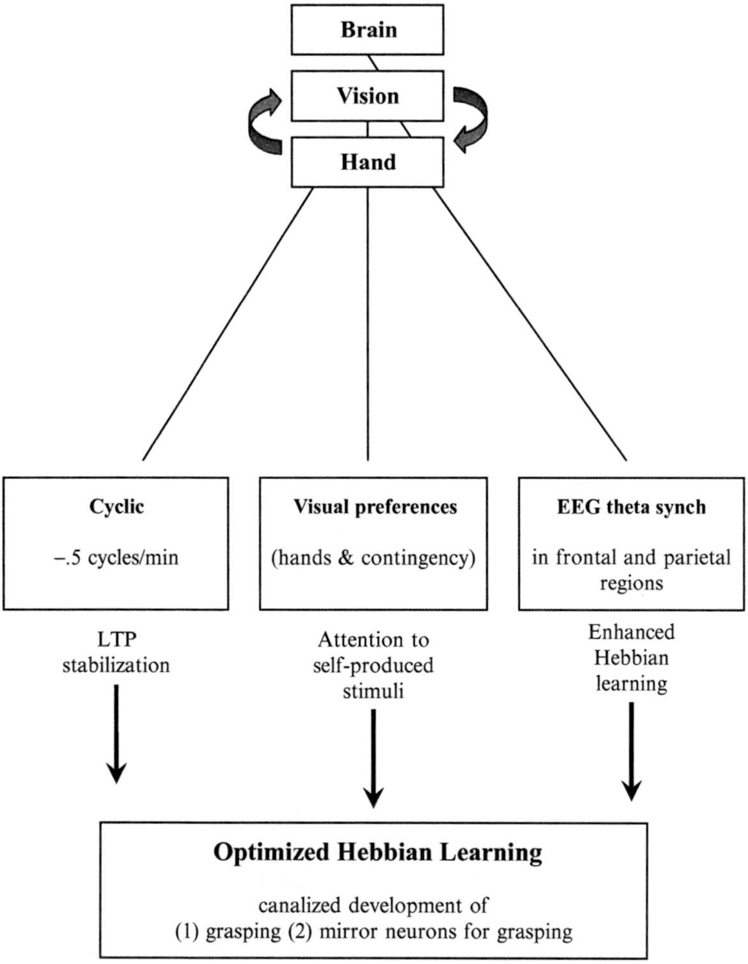


**Fig. 30.3** The development of mirror neurons for grasping. Infants' motor and perceptual characteristics lead to canalized Hebbian learning via observation of self-produced actions. Visual preference for hands, together with a preference for perfect action–perception contingency, directs infants' attention toward salient stimuli. Cyclic patterns of spontaneous movement provide optimal timing for stabilizing long-term potentiation (LTP) at the synaptic level; EEG synchronization at theta frequency (linked to attention) further enhances Hebbian learning, probably by coordinating neuronal firing in the proper time window. Adapted from John Wiley & Sons with permission. Del Giudice, M., Manera, V., & Keysers, C. (2009). Copyright © 2009 and Wiley-Blackwell. [Figure 2, Page. 353]

grasped better also discriminated better videos of anatomically possible and impossible grasping actions. Sommerville, Woodward, and Needham (2005) found that 3-month-olds trained in grasping perceived actions as having goals more often than did control infants.

Del Giudice et al. (2009) went on to suggest the presence of mirror neurons for emotions involving the premotor cortex and the insula. Because adults produce similar facial expressions in response to those of the infant, the infant receives the visual input needed to match the motor output produced in the expressions, facilitating Hebbian learning. Social cognition could depend on the experiential canalization of prewired motor and facial mirror neurons via Hebbian learning processes.

## Therapy

*Mirror therapy for limb dysfunction.* Mirror therapy has been used for cases of phantom limb pain and for hemiparesis (Chan et al., 2007; Ramachandran & Altschuler, 2009). For example, an oblong mirror is positioned beside the intact leg so that the amputee sees together side by side the good leg and a virtual leg via the mirrored image. The legs are viewed in a normal position, for example, extended on the bed. Then, the patient is asked to move the good leg, and the patient witnesses both the latter and the parallel virtual leg move in synchrony. The patient perceives the movements as coming from an intact leg, even if it is virtual.

Ramachandran and Altschuler (2009) posited that neurological conditions do not necessarily constitute irreversible brain damage to specialized modules. Rather, they might involve induction of short-term functional shifts that are reversible. Therefore, simpler therapies, such as in mirror visual feedback, could help restore limb function. The remapping technique works because the cortex is plastic and remapping is possible. Mirror therapy might work in functional limb restoration by stimulating mirror neurons and thereby providing the visual input needed to revive damaged motor neurons. The mirror neurons involved in this process would be residual surviving but dormant inactive ones. Moreover, their dormancy might be a form of learned paralysis, and mirror therapy might facilitate reuse of the unnecessarily inactive limb and spared regions in the damaged areas. Another way of understanding brain remapping involves Melzack's (Melzack & Katz, 2006) neuromatrix model of pain (Young & Chapman, 2007).

*Facial mirror therapy.* I had applied this technique to one of my patients with hemifacial droop due to a traumatic brain injury (Young, 2010). He had been in a catastrophic motor vehicle accident and sustained severe brain damage, a facial smash, and multiple other injuries, including blindness in one eye and deafness in one ear. I positioned two 18×24 in. mirrors without frames together on the desk, long side down, about 10° apart in the front and touching at the back end. This is wide enough to put into the opening one's face. I had him look into the opening, and he was asked to position his face at the midline on the edge of the left mirror. This resulted in a facial image in the double mirror of a face image consisting of his two right sides, in a chimeric facial figure. He perceived not only the right side but also the left side of his face as moving and not in pain, in contrast to its actual state. This had the added benefit of addressing the immobility in the left half of his face due to the strokes that took place after the accident. In the present case, the corporal maps of the face that might be altered to some extent through the exercises recommended would be addressing both its pain and immobility components. As far as I know, this is the first time that mirror therapy has been used to treat facial immobility due to stroke.

Immordino-Yang (2008) pointed out that working with mirror neurons in therapy through mirroring is not a passive process. For example, internalizations of another's actions take place in a culturally moderated and dynamic interaction across minds of self and other. In this regard, Immordino-Yang (2008) indicated that when involving mirroring in therapy and in education we need to consider the "smoke around the mirrors," that is, sociocultural and emotional factors.

*Comment*. The work on mirror neurons and mirroring is important and reflects that the brain is an active organizer and accommodates to injuries. Moreover, education and therapy can help in this regard. In addition, the socioemotional and cultural contexts should not be ignored. In this sense, the work in the area of mirror neurons and mirroring is a microcosm of the major themes in the study of behavior and development. I have qualified both behavior and brain as expressions of activation–inhibition dynamics throughout the present work. In this regard, mirror therapy and mirroring might help alter disequilibrium to the inhibition and activation balance induced by trauma to the brain. Also, it might also help in education and other non-neurological interventions by remapping activation–inhibition dynamics that have been upset in disordered or dysfunctional behavior.

## Other Topics

### *Epigenesis and the BDNF Gene*

Roth, Lubin, Funk, and Sweatt (2009) investigated epigenetic influences on the brain-derived neurotrophic factor (*BDNF*) gene in the study of early-life adversity in rats. The *BDNF* gene is the *BDNF* gene and is a mediator of neural plasticity in the prefrontal cortex and the hippocampus. The researchers exposed infant rats in their first postnatal week to stressed caretakers who expressed abusive behavior. The authors assessed throughout the life span of the pups patterns of DNA methylation and gene expression. In order to examine cross-generational influences, they assessed DNA methylation patterns in the offspring of the infant rats, as well. These infants were not exposed to stressed caretakers. As for the results, the first generation of infant rats that had been exposed to early maltreatment expressed persistent changes in DNA methylation of the *BDNF* gene, and these led to altered *BDNF* gene expression in the prefrontal cortex of the rats when they became adults. Moreover, the offspring of these female infant rats, who had not been exposed to early maltreatment, nevertheless, were observed to have altered *BDNF* DNA methylation. The authors concluded that epigenetic changes could contribute to cross-generational patterns of early maltreatment, with genetic consequences passed on from one generation to the next. They added that not only positive early environments but also manipulation by DNA demethylases or histone deacetylase inhibitors could prove helpful therapeutic strategies in dealing with early-life stress.

## *Epistasis*

Kim-Cohen and Gold (2009) reviewed research indicating gene–gene (G × G) interactions, or epistasis, in G × E research. For example, Kaufman et al. (2006) found that a polymorphism in the *BDNF* gene moderated the interaction of *5-HTT* and childhood maltreatment predicting depression. Also, Cicchetti, Rogosch, and Sturge-Apple (2007) found that adolescents who had been sexually abused and who had one or two copies of the *5-HTT* short allele as well as the high activity version of the *MAOA* gene ended up having significantly reduced levels of internalizing symptoms.

## *Environment*

G × E effects also seem to be moderated by nongenetic variables. Kaufman et al. (2006) found that maltreated children who were at risk genetically were protected from developing depression if they had a supportive adult relationship. This argues for a *multigene–multienvironment model* of vulnerability and resilience (G × G × E × E).

## *Brain*

Research is specifying the neural mechanisms underlying the genetics of risk and resilience. Imaging genomic studies are demonstrating that the low-activity *MAOA* allele and the *5-HTT* short allele help predict heightened responses of the amygdala to presentation of fearful or angry faces (Buckholtz & Meyer-Lindenberg, 2008; Hariri et al., 2005, respectively).

## *Intervention*

Bakermans-Kranenberg, van IJzendorn, Pijlman, Mesman, and Juffer (2008) showed that an intervention to increase sensitive responding in parents was more successful in reducing behavior problems in children having the version of a dopamine receptor gene (i.e., *DRD4* 7-repeat allele) found to be associated with increased risk for hyperactivity, impulsivity, and inattention.

Caspi et al. (2007) found that the benefits of breastfeeding in infancy in boosting IQ scores was evident only in children who have a specific allele of a gene involved in the metabolism of fatty acids, which have been taken to support optimal cognitive development.

## *Atypical Epigenesis*

Karmiloff-Smith (2007) examined atypical epigenesis. She argued that it might involve a lack of specialization and localization of brain function as development proceeds, even if resulting behavior appears normal or proficient. The developing brain starts out highly interconnected across regions, which allows the environment to play a crucial role in genetic expression and in phenotypic characteristics, including cognition (Meaney & Szyf, 2005). As described in a prior section of this chapter, she had indicated that the brain becomes progressively localized, restricted, specialized, and modularized, with little that is strictly predetermined, prespecified, or permanently fixed. The brain is initially "domain relevant" and not domain specific. That is, it has certain neuronal and neurochemical properties that make it more probable that it will be channeled toward processing certain kinds of inputs, in particular regions, and there is no innate modularization. The domain-relevant circuits compete with less specified circuits in the processing of incoming inputs and eventually "win out," becoming more domain-specific and modularized, e.g., by synaptic pruning. Karmiloff-Smith continued that because the early brain begins with domain-relevant predispositions that become domain-specific, they are open to environmental impacts and subtle impairments. In this regard, Karmiloff-Smith cited her research on William's Syndrome, in which the participants did not develop the typical right-hemisphere processing of the face, even though they displayed adequate facial processing.

## *Attention Genes*

Posner, Rothbart, and Sheese (2007) described their work on attention genes. They found a significant association between executive attention and two genes, dopamine receptor *DRD4* and *MAOA* (Fossella et al., 2002). Parasuraman, Greenwood, Kumar, and Fossella (2005) examined performance differences in visual-search attention orienting tasks and a gene involved in the neuromodulator acetylcholine (modulated by different alleles of a cholinergic gene, the alpha 4 subunit of the neural nicotine cholinergic receptor, *CHRNA4*). Ongoing research implicated a role for a particular form of a genetic polymorphism in the 3′ untranslated region of the dopamine transporter gene, *DATI*, in the attention performance of children. The results showed greater efficiency in conflict scores on the attention network test (ANT) for children with the pure long allele. Posner et al. (2007) also described research showing the influence of environment (training studies) on developing attentional networks.

Sheese et al. (2007) examined the quality of parenting in relation to sensation seeking in children. Children without the presence of the seven repeat allele of the D4DR gene were not influenced by quality of parenting with respect to their sensation seeking. However, children having the allele exhibited sensation seeking at higher than normal levels, but only if they had parenting of lower quality.

Sheese, Voelker, Posner, and Rothbart (2009) studied longitudinally children at 6–7 months of age and 8–20 months of age. They examined emotional and self-regulatory components of early temperament, as well parental rating of orienting. Their most important finding was that different genes moderated emotional reactivity and its regulation. Genetic variation in catechol-O-methyl-transfer (*COMT*) was related to the expression of positive affect at 6–7 months. Genetic variation in *SNAP25* was related to negative affect in both time periods. For 18–20-month-olds, genetic variation in *CH4NA4* was related to effortful control. In addition, they mentioned that different genes supported a positive and negative affect in infancy, and that both positive affect and negative affect are related to orienting.

Canli et al. (2005) suggested that the short allele of the *5-HTT* gene is related to neuromechanisms influencing areas involved in executive attention. Meyer-Lindenberg et al. (2006) found that alleles of the *MAOA* gene are related to activation of the ventral and dorsal regions of the anterior cingulate, which are related to the control of emotions and cognition, respectively. Posner et al. concluded that attention-related genes might affect the heritability of pathology.

## Attachment

Gervai et al. (2007) studied the interaction between disruptive maternal affective communication and *DRD4* gene polymorphism in relation to disorganized infant detachment. They found higher rates of disorganized attachment in the infants when the 7-repeat *DRD4* allele was absent. In terms of similar findings for the adult, Caspers et al. (2009) found an association between unresolved attachment due to traumatic loss in adults and the serotonin transporter promoter polymorphism (short allele of *5-HTTLPR*). They assessed adult attachment using the Adult Attachment Interview, and the results related, in particular, to speech related to loss, but not to overall coherence on the measure. They concluded that the incorporation of specific genetic markers into models that predict psychosocial outcomes could help understand gene–environment interaction.

## Social Genomics

Cole (2009) has described the field of social genomics, in which the social world can influence which genes are transcribed within the nuclei of cells. Genes and social behavior exist in a two-way relationship of influence and control. Different socioenvironmental conditions can influence gene functioning so that genes are subject to social regulation. These social processes influence gene expression by activating central nervous system processes that, in turn, influence hormone and neurotransmitter activity. Factors in the peripheral nervous system and endocrine system can influence cell receptors to activate transcription factors that bind to DNA segments in gene promoters, thereby initiating or repressing gene expression.

Cole (2009) noted that the person's objective perception of socioenvironmental conditions is a critical factor, rather than, for example, the actual number of social contacts in determining a sense of social isolation. Cole et al. (2007) studied social regulation in adults (who felt different degrees of social connectedness over 4 years) in relation to gene expression in their leukocytes, which are white blood cells. They found over 200 genes (related to the adults' acceleration or steering of their immune response) that showed different levels of expression in those adults who felt loneliness and distance from others. That socioenvironmental influences can affect the immune system response, and even survival, indicates that modern study of genetics needs to be "environmentally conscious."

## *Generalist Genes*

Plomin, Kovas, and Haworth (2007) described generalist genes. These are the same set of genes that are largely responsible for genetic influences across domains. For example, there are genes that are associated with no fewer than two particular learning abilities or disabilities. The authors noted that, "most genes are expressed throughout the brain, not just in one specific region." For example, *COMT* and *BDNF* are genes that are expressed in the cortex cerebellum, caudate nucleus, amygdala, corpus callosum, dorsal root ganglia, and spinal cord. The authors added that the effects of pleiotropy (each gene affects multiple traits) are amplified by polygenicity (each trait is affected by multiple genes). Therefore, any particular gene generally has only a small effect on behavior. The authors concluded that pleiotropy and polygenicity "make it likely that generalist genes result in 'generalist brains.'"

## *Generalist Stress*

The importance of early stresses on later development is being elucidated, including for the prenatal period (Coe & Lubach, 2008; Feldman & Eidelman, 2009; Geva & Feldman, 2008; see Fig. 30.4).

It is beyond the scope of the present work to describe in depth this research on fetal programming and stress, but it is related to the concept of epigenesis. This type of research needs to integrate the concept of allostatic load (McEwen, 2009, 2010). Ellison (2010) argued that epigenetic modification of gene expression affecting the HPA axis might be involved in "fetal programming" of the fetal origins of reduced energetic availability and effects on subsequent disease.

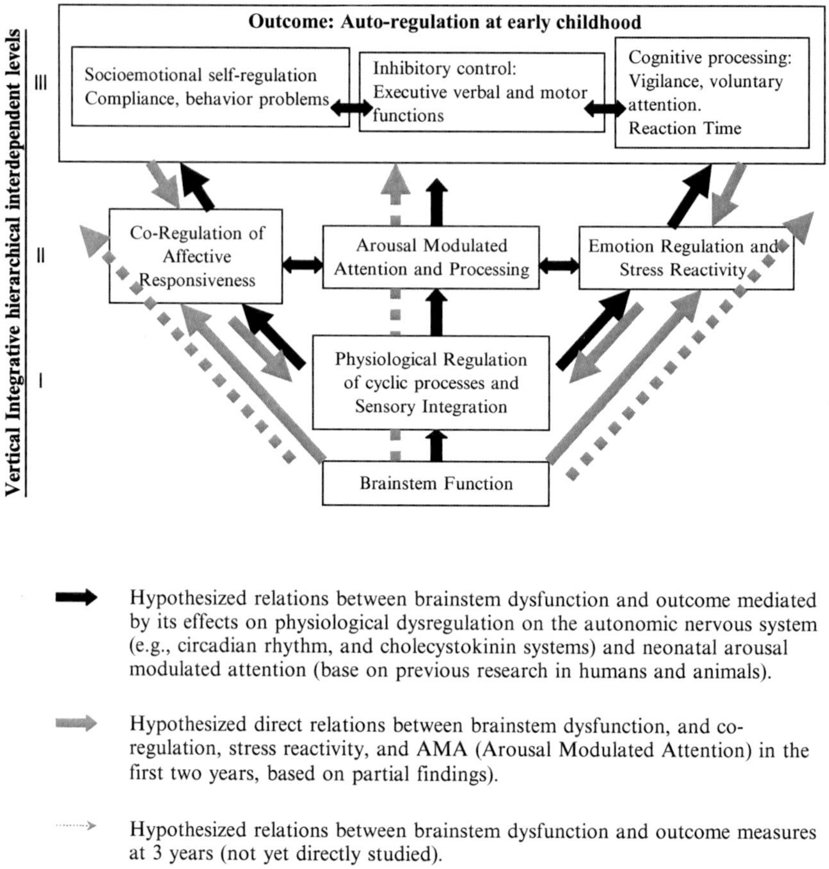


**Fig. 30.4** Neurobiological model: brainstem, emotions, development. A schematic representation of the neurobiological model for the effects of early brainstem functioning on the development of behavior and emotion regulation in infants. Reprinted with the permission of John Wiley & Sons, Inc. Geva, R., & Feldman, R. (2008). Copyright © 2008 and Association for Child and Adolescent Mental Health. [Figure 1, Page. 1033]

## Summary and Comments on Recent Literature

### *Epigenetics*

*Introduction.* Dick (2011) described Gene X Environment interactions a the statistical level as involving situations in which the effects of genes depend on the environment, or the effect of the environment depend on genotype, or both. Epigenetics concerns modifications to the genome that do not involve changes in any nucleotide sequence in DNA. However, genetic and environmental factors are not necessarily independent factors that can be separated to examine main effects, despite traditional statistical practice. For example, in active gene-environment correlation, an individual might act on the environment in ways consistent with the influence of the underlying genotype. Instead of trying to parse out the separate effects of gene and environment on the influence of behavior and seek which of the two is more critical, it is more productive to examine their effects in combination and to try to understand their influence on "pathways to risk."

Caspi, McClay, Moffitt, Mill, Martin, Craig, Taylor, and Poulton (2002) had examined the functional polymorphism related to the promoter region of the monoamine oxidase A (*MAOA*) gene. In particular, they reported a functional polymorphism in the gene that encodes *MAOA*, which is a neurotransmitter-metabolizing enzyme. The functional polymorphism moderated the effects of maltreatment. Specifically, male adolescents who carried the allele that conferred high levels of *MAOA* expression were less likely to develop antisocial behavioral problems had they been exposed to childhood maltreatment.

Belsky and Pluess (2009a, b) noticed that participants in the Caspi et al. (2002) study who were most susceptible to adverse effects of childhood maltreatment and who simultaneously were not exposed to childhood maltreatment obtained the lowest scores on their measures of anti-social behavior. Belsky and Pluess (2009a, b) posited that particular alleles could heighten vulnerability to a wide range of environments. In particular, supportive and risky environments promote positive and negative child outcomes, respectively. Their concept resembles that of Ellis and Boyce (2008) on biological sensitivity to context.

Caspi, Sugden, Moffitt, Taylor, Craig, Harrington, McClay, Mill, Martin, Braithwaite, and Poulton (2003) presented similar results for the influence of the serotonin transporter gene, *5-HTT*, for which carrying the short allele relative to being homozygous for long one was found to lead to a greater influence of stressful life events on depression (its symptoms and diagnosis, as well as suicidality).

Caspi, Hariri, Holmes, Uher, and Moffit (2010) indicated that there are at least four kinds of evidence for the involvement of the *5-HTT* gene in stress sensitivity. A recent meta-analysis supports the reliability of the research, finding strong evidence that *5-HTTLPR* moderates the relationship between stress and depression (Karg, Shedden, Burmeister, & Sen, 2011). Two prior meta-analyses were not supportive (Munafò, Durrant, Lewis, & Flint, 2009; Risch, Herrell, Lehner, Liang, Eaves, Hoh, Griem, Kovacs, Ott, & Merikangas, 2009). However, when research that examines specific stressors, and that does not use brief self-report measures is analyzed, the results generally support the Caspi et al. (2003) findings. Moreover, work in the area is expanding to link the polymorphism to broad range of stress-reactive behavioral phenotypes, including posttraumatic stress disorder and poor self-regulation of negative affect.

*Reaction range*. Dick (2011) indicated that the most appropriate manner in representing gene-environment interactions is in a cross-over graph rather than a fan-shaped graph. The fan-shaped interaction reflects the traditional diathesis-stress framework involving the concept of "vulnerability" genes, whereas the cross-over interaction framework shifts to a differential susceptibility model of genes ("plasticity *genes*"), as per Belsky and Pluess.

In epigenetics, unlike the case for gene silencing in cell specialization, chromosome X inactivation, and genomic imprinting, the DNA methylation involved does not occur only early in development and it is not stable. Rather, epigenetic modifications can continue to occur throughout development, and they are reversible and more dynamic or flexible. Therefore, I suggest that perhaps a good way of representing epigenesis is to indicate that it affects the reaction range of gene expression. It affects certain genotypes that support a range of behavioral phenotypes in response to supportive and non-supportive environmental conditions.

Similarly, Uher (2011) maintained that distal epigenetic effects in time (earlier) might alter genetic scripts with long lasting stamps, and then other maintaining environmental effects could serve to perpetuate the onsets that had been caused, with more proximal effects in adolescence providing the trigger for mental illness. However, later pharmacological or psychotherapeutic treatment could counterbalance the adverse effects that had been promoted in earlier phases in development.

Figure 30.5 presents one manner of representing the concept of epigenetics in a general fashion. The figure illustrates that in the traditional concept of reaction range, the possible phenotypic expressions related to a gene or gene complex might initially be associated with a relatively narrow range of variation possible in environments encountered (Rathunde & Czikszentmihalyi, 2006). As development proceeds in either supportive or adverse environments, phenotypic expression in development, respectively, could become either increasingly more or less adaptive in the range. That is, when there are epigenetic effects, the reaction range is expanded in adaptability in either direction, and more resilient and not only more problematic behavior can be found with time.

*Genomic imprinting*. Gregg (2010) explained that maternal and paternal genes appear to have differential and preferential effects on the development of the cortex and hypothalamus, respectively. He noted that maternally and paternally inherited chromosomes differ in their functional impact because of heritable epigenetic marks, called genomic imprints. These parent-specific programs of gene expression for the central nervous system reveal complex ways parents influence brain development and behavior in offspring. The nature of gene-environment interactions in development seems to involve parent epigenetic interactions, as well – clearly the research in this fast emerging area will continue to uncover astonishing findings. In terms of the major focus of the book on stages in development, their unfolding causally must represent a complex mix of which the study of epigenetics might reveal complex genetic-environmental interactions. As Gregg (2010) noted, parents influence brain development and behavior to the point that they can set us on our life course. I would add to this conclusion that we also have a role in our development; for example, our cortex submits to or is controlled by our personal developmental processes as much as to genetic and environmental ones.

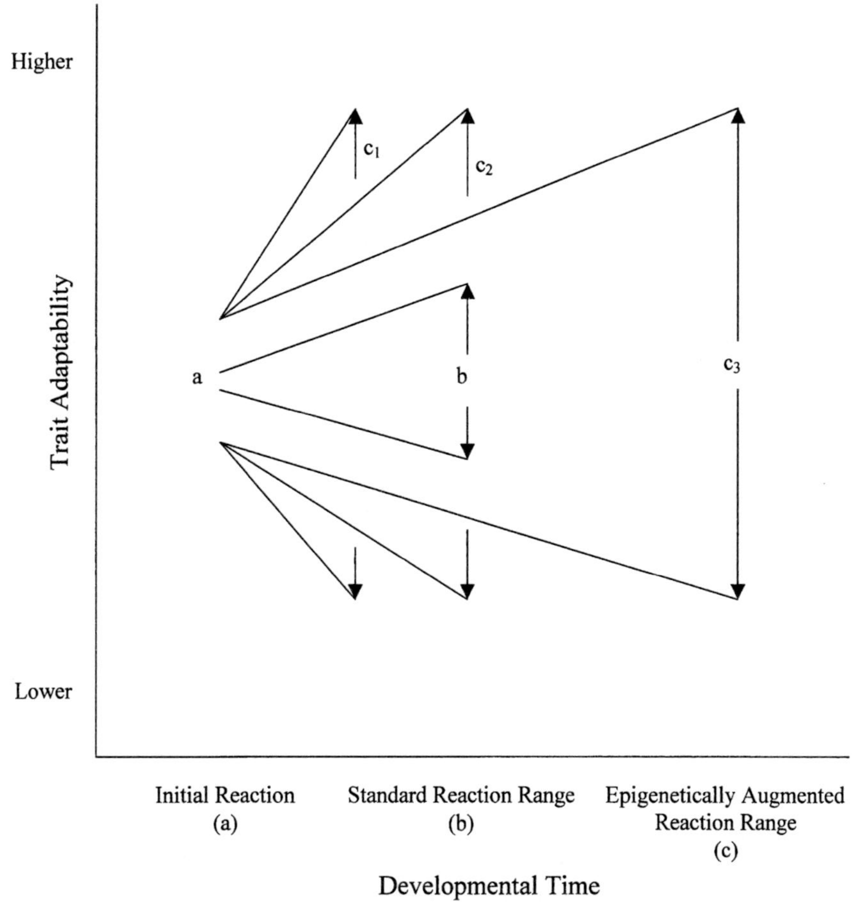


**Fig. 30.5** *Environmental Action Leads to Increased Reaction Range in Gene Expression for Certain Alleles.* In epigenetics, the outcome is not necessarily negative in cases of susceptible alleles affecting behavioral adaptation. Belsky and Pluess (2009 a, b) have posited that when genes are silenced in promoter regions involved in behavioral reactivity, the outcome could involve more resilience, and not only more behavioral difficulties, when the environment is supportive rather than adverse (differential susceptibility). The figure presents a model indicating how epigenetic effects can have either more negative or positive behaviorally adaptive outcomes, depending on individual and environmental differences. Moreover, the effects might be transmitted over generations, creating a dynamic trajectory of increased or decreased adaptation in individual lines

*Conclusion.* Boyce (2011) presented an elegant model of the interaction of biology and context on childhood morbidities. He referred to "symphonic causation" in bio-contextual interplay, and described five types of gene-environment interactions – potentiation, protection, sensitization, specification, and facilitation. Symphonic causation refers to a coming together or joining of elements that produces in their confluence new elements that cannot be derived from any one element alone. The model is akin to the nonlinear dynamical systems one.

## Causality

This chapter concludes presentation of the topic of causality in development, which is a major theme of the book and reflects its title. The study of causality in psychology has been very limited. The classic issue in science concerning causality relates to the distinction between correlation and causation. Philosophers, psychologists, and other scientists are beginning to expand this work (e.g., Beebee, Hitchcock, & Menzies, 2009; Gopnik & Schultz, 2008; Illari, Russo, & Williamson, 2011a, b; Markus, 2011; Pearl, 2009, 2011; Russo, 2009; Sloman, 2005), but they have been more concerned with immediate causal processes and learning, as represented by causal graphics and their mathematical underpinnings, and they have ignored other approaches, such as answering to Tinbergen's (1963) four questions about causation, which cover longer term causal processes and mechanisms, including evolution and development. In the present work, I have concentrated on the former question, but there is room for integrating them, for example, through the approach of nonlinear dynamic systems theory. In this approach to causation, systems are reworked constantly, even if in equilibrium, because of perturbations. Therefore, ensembles in systems can self-organize through both bottom-up and top-down processes, even to the point of emergence of new components and states in the system (see Chapters 27 and 28). This approach to causality speaks to both immediate short-term state re-organization and long-term restructurings.

## Evolution

*Introduction.* With respect to biological evolution, the present work has been informed by the life history approach (see Chapter 23). Each developmental stage and its prominent acquisitions have been selected for their concurrent contribution to survival (permitting eventual reproduction). They are not pre-adaptations that serve, in a teleological fashion, later adaptations, but they are primed to function in the equivalent of the niche in which they evolved.

*Eusociality.* Nowak, Tarnita, and Wilson (2010) presented a shift in interpretation of the evolution of eusociality, which occurs when some individuals of a species reduce their own reproductive potential over their lifetime in order to raise the offspring of others. In the social insects, this is evidenced in the sterile worker castes helping raise offspring of the queen and creating a colony, which has been described as a "superorganism." The traditional explanation of eusociality refers to kin selection, which is based on the concept of inclusive fitness. Nowak et al. argued that standard natural selection theory is sufficient to explain the evolution of eusociality, and that it is a genuine "gene-centered" approach, unlike the one of inclusive fitness.

In Novak et al.'s model, eusociality evolved in five steps. (a) First, groups formed in freely mixing populations. They built and occupied defensible nests because of "individual-level" selection. Relatedness is seen as a consequence rather than a cause of eusociality. (b) In the second phase, the groups more tightly formed. Spring-loaded pre-adaptations helped this happen. That is, adaptations that had served adaptation in other ways, by having spread through adaptive radiation into other niches, took on new functions by virtue of their fit to the niches involved for the new functions. In particular, in the present case, certain pre-adaptations facilitated the formation of tight groups; individuals could already behave eusocially when conditions had brought them together. (c) Next, actual eusocial alleles originated, either by mutation or recombination. Individuals functioned well as a cooperative eusocial colony and dispersal behavior was silenced. (d) Most likely, the fourth phase involved evolution of ecologically adaptive behaviors related to the nest, such as fierce defense against predators, parasites, and rival colonies. These are emergent traits arising out of the interaction of group members, and as with the other steps, they had been shaped through "natural selection by environmental forces." (e) Finally, in the fifth phase, the more advanced eusocial species evolved very specialized, elaborate social systems. In contrast to the other steps, this one involved multilevel selection, which includes group selection as well as natural selection. It served to help drive changes in the colony behavior to more elaborate extremes.

*Comment*. The research by Nowak et al. (2010) is consistent with several ways that causality is treated in the present work. First, I have described a five-stage sequence in lifespan cognitive development and related it to individual-level or natural selection, in particular (see Chapter 32). The advantages that the stages bring work in an adaptive sense by conferring increasing adaptedness at the individual level rather than at the group level. If other selection processes are involved in underpinning the stages, such as kin selection and inclusive fitness, they work by increasing individual-level gene co-option. Moreover, group selection seems to be involved for the last phase, as well, but perhaps in concert with natural selection in a complex, integrated process.

As for the five steps in the evolution of eusociality that had been described by Novak et al., there might be some basis for the common finding in our work of five phases in the growth of a system, despite my stage sequence concerning human development within the time frame of human lifetimes and their sequence concerning evolution over millions of years. In Chapter 31, I present a nonlinear dynamical systems model of the growth in systems, whether developmental, evolutionary or other, in which five steps might be the most economical, graceful, and good in fit. In the model, the steps are referred to as coordination, hierarchization, systematization, multiplication, and integration, which happen to be the names of the substages in the present developmental model, illustrative of the fractal nature of patterns over different levels of the developmental model being proposed.

The five steps described for the evolution of eusociality by Nowak et al. fit this pattern, as well. For example, first, there seems to have been social coordination in nest behavior, fitting the description that I would give it; then individuals seemed to have evolved to hierarchize their behavior to the group, as per the scheme in my model. Next, the behavior became systematized through eusocial alleles, consistent with the label that I use for the third period in my model. In the last evolutionary phases, the behavior seems to have become multiplied (the label for my the fourth step in my model), as in fierce defense of the nest. This step was followed by the evolution more elaborate and extreme eusocial behavior, which fits the integrative label that I would ascribe to this phase according to my model.

## *Free Will*

*Introduction.* A major dimension in causality of behavior concerns whether it is considered tied deterministically to the past and present and is the product of contextual forces, or whether it is considered free in choice and action. Another critical dimension is whether it is considered the product of deliberative and conscious processes, or whether it reflects the influences of past and present circumstances that can leave no room for forces that are genuinely conscious and volitional. The two issues are quite related, and help define the issue of free will in behavior.

*Evolution.* Free will can never be proven outright, but on average people believe they have it, which affects their behavior (Baumeister, 2008). Baumeister maintained that we have evolved a form of action-control involving self-control and rational choice, which corresponds to popular notions of free will. Therefore, free will involves: personal responsibility, conscious deliberation, abstract rules and principles in guiding behavior, autonomous initiative, and resisting urges.

Baumeister, Crescioni, and Alquist (2011) elaborated that free will evolved to meet the demands of "enlightened self-interest" in cultural context. This view is consistent with the present one that behavior evolved through steps of increasing gene co-option through individual-level natural selection, as described above. They added that four forms of behavior evolved sequentially to increase the capacity to behave as if we had free will. First, initiative evolved to actively guide motivation and behavior, which moved into an evolutionary period in which nascent ability for self-control emerged (overriding a response or impulse in order to act in a different manner). Rational choice followed (arriving at an intelligent choice by logical reasoning of the best course of action), which culminated in planful behavior (mentally working out and then executing an organized, optimal sequence of executed actions aimed at a desired result). The present work adopts a quite similar perspective on the steps in changes in free will, but instead of proceeding evolutionarily, it organizes a model of the development of free will around the present model of five stages in development (see Chapter 35).

In terms of consciousness, Baumeister (2010) related it to planning and simulating possibility. He uses the metaphor of making an inner movie that the brain constructs for itself. It helps in deciding what actions are performed. Consciousness is linked to free will, because only conscious though can conceptualize multiple options from which to choose. As with the capacities that permit the perception that one has free will in thought and action, consciousness evolved in steps and humans express the most advanced form. In Chapter 35, I show how consciousness seems to develop according to the present model of stages in development.

*Development*. Carlson (2010) also developed a model of the development of consciousness, based on the work of Zelazo (2004; Zelazo, Carlson, & Kesek, 2008). In the first year of life, consciousness is present, but minimal. Then, more deliberate action develops. Increases in reflection lead to more complex systems. Conscious control then develops, in which action is formulated based on explicit rule systems. Carlson and Zelazo (2008) adopted the Zelazo model to describe the manner in which levels of consciousness evolve with symbolic thought over four levels in the first 5 years of life. The infant in the first 7 months of life moves from being stimulus-bound to decoupling symbols up, to 18 months of age (thinking about representations in the absence of stimuli). In the next two phases, genuine symbols develop to guide behavior (treating symbols as symbols, e.g., full-blown pretend play develops) and, by five years of age, there is a better quality of symbol-referent relations (reflection on the quality of the symbol-referent relationship). Once more, I refer to my developmental model as a structure on which the Zelazo-Carlson model of consciousness could be elaborated to fit a more general developmental framework.

## *Causality Map or Landscape*

Causality is everywhere, yet it is nowhere, or just coming out of the shadows in the study of behavior. That is, it is studied prevalently in psychology, and even in introductory courses the dictum that correlation does not mean causation is mentioned early on. However, it fell victim to the philosophical mood of acausalism, and only in this century is it gaining momentum as a mainstream topic. The book by Illari, Russo, and Williamson (2011a) on causality in the sciences will help. However, the approach taken in this philosophical book does not consider the approach to causality taken in the present work – there is mention neither of epigenetics, for example, nor of Tinbergen's (1963) approach to four causal questions.

That the question of causality in the sciences is just gaining traction is illustrated by the author's "manifesto" of why one should study causality in the sciences (Illari, Russo, & Williamson, 2011b). Their book, in general, appears to emphasize mechanisms underlying behavior as an important topic in the field (Illari & Williamson, 2011; Psillos, 2011). However, mechanisms in behavior include a broad range of factors, such as those underlying evolution and development as well as physiology and the brain. I second the call for a manifesto on causality in the study of behavior, but we need to expand the manifesto to study causality in all its manifestations, such as those emphasized in the present work and not in theirs. By understanding the landscape or map of causality studies in psychology and the sciences, in general, the disparate and disjointed nature of the topic in the field might gain some semblance of movement toward coherence (Young & Baumeister, in preparation). As emphasized in the present work, nonlinear dynamical systems theory might provide a unifying frame for the study of causality (also see Kuhlmann, 2011).

## References


Bakermans-Kranenburg, M. J., & van IJzendoorn, M. H. (2006). Gene-environment interaction of the dopamine D4 receptor (DRD4) and observed maternal insensitivity predicting externalizing behavior in preschooler. *Development Psychobiology, 48*, 406–409.

Bakermans-Kranenburg, M. J., van IJzendoorn, M. H., Pijlman, F. T. A., Mesman, J., & Juffer, F. (2008). Experimental evidence for differential susceptibility: Dopamine D4 receptor polymorphism (DRD4 VNTR) moderate intervention effects on toddlers' externalizing behavior in a randomized controlled trail. *Developmental Psychology, 44*, 293–300.

Baumeister, R. F. (2008). Free will in scientific psychology. *Perspectives on Psychological Science, 3*, 14–19.

Baumeister, R. F. (2010). Understanding free will and consciousness on the basis of current research findings in psychology. In R. F. Baumeister, A. R. Mele, & K. D. Vohs (Eds.), *Free will and consciousness: How might they work?* (pp. 24–42). New York: Oxford University Press.

Baumeister, R. F., Crescioni, A. W., & Alquist, J. L. (2011). Free will as advanced action control for human social life and culture. *Neuroethics, 4*, 1–11.

Beebee, H., Hitchcock, C., & Menzies, P. (2009). *The Oxford handbook of causation*. New York: Oxford University Press.

Belsky, J., Bakermans-Kranenburg, M. J., & van IJzendoorn, M. H. (2007). For better and for worse: Differential susceptibility to environmental influences. *Current Directions in Psychological Science, 16*, 300–304.

Belsky, J., & Pluess, M. (2009a). The nature (and nurture?) of plasticity in early human development. *Perspectives on Psychological Science, 4*, 345–351.

Belsky, J., & Pluess, M. (2009b). Beyond diathesis stress: Differential susceptibility to environmental influences. *Psychological Bulletin, 135*, 885–908.

Belsky, J., Pluess, M., Comings, D. E., & MacMurray, J. P. (2009). *Plasticity genes X childhood divorce exposure predicts relationship instability in adulthood.* Unpublished manuscript.

Boyce, W. T. (2011). Biology and context: Symphonic causation and the distribution of childhood morbidities. In D. P. Keating (Ed.), *Nature and nurture in early child development* (pp. 114–144). Cambridge: Cambridge University Press.

Brummett, B. H., Boyle, S. H., Siegler, I. C., Kuhn, C. M., Ashley-Koch, A., Jonassaint, C. R., et al. (2008). Effects of environmental stress and gender on associations among symptoms of depression and the serotonin transporter gene linked polymorphic region (5-HTTLR). *Behavior Genetics, 38*, 34–43.

Buckholtz, J. W., & Meyer-Lindenberg, A. (2008). MAOA and the neurogenetic architecture of human aggression. *Trends in Neuroscience, 31*, 120–139.

Canli, T., Omura, K., Hass, B. W., Fallgatter, A., Todd, R., Constable, R. T., et al. (2005). Beyond affect: A role for genetic variation of the serotonin transporter in neural activation during a cognitive attention task. *Proceedings of the National Academy of Sciences, 102*, 12224–12229.

Caspers, K. M., Paradiso, S., Yucuis, R., Troutman, B., & Arndt, S. (2009). Association between the serotonin transporter promoter polymorphism (5-HTTLPR) and adult unresolved attachment. *Developmental Psychology, 45*, 64–76.

Caspi, A., Hariri, A. R., Holmes, A., Uher, R., & Moffitt, T. E. (2010). Genetic sensitivity to the envirormient: The case of the serotonin transporter gene and its implications for studying complex diseases and traits. *American Journal of Psychiatry, 167*, 509–527.

Caspi, A., McClay, J., Moffitt, T. E., Mill, J., Martin, J., Craig, I. W., et al. (2002). Role of genotype in the cycle of violence in maltreated children. *Science, 297*, 851–854.

Caspi, A., Sugden, K., Moffitt, T. E., Taylor, A., Craig, I. W., Harrington, H., et al. (2003). Influence of life stress on depression: Moderation by a polymorphism in the 5-HTT gene. *Science, 301*, 386–389.

Caspi, A., Williams, B., Kim-Cohen, J., Craig, I. W., Milne, B. J., Poulton, R., et al. (2007). Moderation of breastfeeding effects on the IQ by genetic variation in fatty acid metabolism. *Proceedings of the National Academy of Science of the USA, 104*, 18860–18865.

Carlson, S. M. (2010). Development of conscious control and imagination. In R. F. Baumeister, A. R. Mele, & K. D. Vohs (Eds.), *Free will and consciousness: How might they work?* (pp. 135–152). New York: Oxford University Press.

Carlson, S. M., & Zelazo, P. D. (2008). Symbolic thought. In M. M. Haith & J. B. Benson (Eds.), *Encyclopedia of infant and early childhood development* (Vol. 3, pp. 288–297). London: Elsevier.

Chan, B. L., Witt, R., Charrow, A. P., Magee, A., Howard, R., Pasquina, P. F., et al. (2007). Mirror therapy for phantom limb pain. *New England Journal of Medicine, 357*, 2206–2207.

Cicchetti, D., Rogosch, F. A., & Sturge-Apple, M. L. (2007). Interactions of child maltreatment and serotonin transporter and monoamine oxidase A polymorphisms: Depressive symptomatology among adolescents from low socioeconomic status backgrounds. *Development and Psychopathology, 19*, 1161–1180.

Coe, C. L., & Lubach, G. R. (2008). Fetal programming: Prenatal origins of health and illness. *Current Directions in Psychological Science, 17*, 36–41.

Cole, S. W. (2009). Social regulation of human gene expression. *Current Directions in Psychological Science, 18*, 132–137.

Cole, S. W., Hawkley, L. C., Arevalo, J. M., Sung, C. Y., Rose, R. M., & Cacioppo, J. T. (2007). Social regulation of gene expression in human leukocytes. *Genomic Biology, 8*, R189.

Del Giudice, M., Manera, V., & Keysers, C. (2009). Programmed to learn? The ontogeny of mirror neurons. *Developmental Science, 12*, 350–363.

Dick, D. M. (2011). Gene-environment interaction in psychological traits and disorders. *Annual Review of Clinical Psychology, 7*, 383–409.

Dodge, K. A. (2009). Mechanisms of gene-environmental interaction effects in the development of conduct disorder. *Perspectives on Psychological Science, 4*, 408–414.

Ducci, F., Encoh, M. A., Hodgkinson, C., Xu, K., Catena, M., Robin, R. W., et al. (2008). Interaction between a functional MAOA locus and childhood sexual abuse predicts alcoholism and antisocial personality disorder in adult women. *Molecular Psychiatry, 13*, 334–347.

Eley, T. C., Sugden, K., Corsico, A., Gregory, A. M., Sham, P., McGuffin, P., et al. (2004). Gene-environment interaction analysis of serotonin system markers with adolescent depression. *Molecular Psychiatry, 9*, 908–915.

Ellis, B. J., & Boyce, W. T. (2008). Biological sensitivity to context. *Current Directions in Psychological Science, 17*, 183–187.

Ellison, P. T. (2010). Fetal programming and fetal psychology. *Infant and Child Development, 19*, 6–21.

Feldman, R., & Eidelman, A. I. (2009). Biological and environmental initial conditions shape the trajectories of cognitive and social-emotional development across the first years of life. *Developmental Science, 12*, 194–200.

Foley, D. L., Eaves, L. J., Wormley, B., Silberg, J. L., Maes, H. H., Kuhn, J., et al. (2004). Childhood adversity, monoamine oxidase a genotype, and risk for conduct disorder. *Archives of General Psychiatry, 61*, 738–744.

Fossella, J., Sommer, T., Fan, J., Wu, Y., Swanson, J. M., Pfaff, D. W., et al. (2002). Assessing the molecular genetics of attention networks. *BMC Neuroscience, 3*, 14.

Fox, N. A., Hane, A. A., & Pine, D. S. (2007). Plasticity for affective neurocircuitry: How the environment affects gene expression. *Current Directions in Psychological Science, 16*, 1–5.

Fox, N. A., Henderson, H. A., Rubin, K. H., Calkins, S. D., & Schmidt, L. A. (2001). Continuity and discontinuity of inhibition and exuberance: Psychophysiological and behavioral influences across the first four years of life. *Child Development, 72*, 1–21.

Frazzetto, G., Di Lorenzo, G., Carola, V., Proietti, L., Sokolowska, E., Siracusano, A., et al. (2007). Early trauma and increased risk for physical aggression during adulthood: The moderating role of for physical aggression during adulthood: The moderating role of MAOA genotype. *PLoS One, 2*, e486.

Gervai, J., Novak, A., Lakatos, K., Toth, I., Danis, I., Ronai, Z., et al. (2007). Infant genotype may moderate sensitivity to maternal affective communications: Attachment disorganization, quality of care, and the DRD4 polymorphism. *Social Neuroscience, 2*, 307–319.

Geva, R., & Feldman, R. (2008). A neurobiological model for the effects of early brainstem functioning on the development of behavior and emotion regulation in infants: Implications for prenatal and perinatal risk. *Journal of Child Psychology and Psychiatry, 49*, 1031–1041.

Gopnik, A., & Schulz, L. (2008). *Causal learning: Psychology, philosophy, and computation.* New York: Oxford University Press.

Gottlieb, G. (1991). Experiential canalization of behavioral development: Theory. *Developmental Psychology, 27*, 4–13.

Gottlieb, G. (2007). Probabilistic epigenesis. *Developmental Science, 10*, 1–11.

Gregg, C. (2010). Parental control over the brain. *Science, 330*, 770–771.

Hariri, A. R., Drabant, E. M., Munoz, K. E., Kolachana, B. S., Mattay, V. S., Egan, M. F., et al. (2005). A susceptibility gene for affective disorders and the response of the human amygdale. *Archives of General Psychiatry, 62*, 146–152.

Hebb, D. O. (1942). The effect of early and late brain injury upon test scores and the nature of normal adult intelligence. *Proceedings of the American Philosophical Society, 85*, 275–292.

Hebb, D. O. (1949). *The organization of behavior.* New York: Wiley.

Illari, P. M., Russo, F., & Williamson, J. (Eds.) (2011a). *Causality in the Sciences*. New York: Oxford University Press.

Illari, P. M., Russo, F., & Williamson, J. (2011b). Why look at causality in the sciences? A manifesto. In P. M. Illari, F. Russo, & J. Williamson (Eds.), *Causality in the sciences* (pp. 3–22). New York: Oxford University Press.

Illari, P. M., & Williamson, J. (2011). Mechanisms are real and local. In P. M. Illari, F. Russo, & J. Williamson (Eds.), *Causality in the sciences* (pp. 818–844). New York: Oxford University Press.

Immordino-Yang, M. H. (2008). The smoke around mirror neurons: Goals as sociocultural and emotional organizers of perception and action in learning. *Mind, Brain, and Education, 2*, 67–73.

Jokela, M., Lehtimaki, T., & Keltikangas-Jarviene, L. (2007a). The influence of urban/rural residency on depressive symptoms is moderated by the serotonin receptor 2A gene. *American Journal of Medical Genetics. Part B: Neuropsychiatric Genetics, 144*, 918–922.

Jokela, M., Lehtimaki, T., & Keltikangas-Jarviene, L. (2007b). The serotonin receptor 2A gene moderates the influence of parental socioeconomic status on adulthood harm avoidance. *Behavior Genetics, 37*, 567–574.

Jokela, M., Raikkonen, K., Lehtimatki, T., Rontu, R., & Keltikangas-Jarvinen, L. (2007). Tryptophan hydroxylase 1 gene (TPH1) moderates the influence of social support on depressive symptoms in adults. *Journal of Affective Disorders, 100*, 191–197.

Karg, K., Shedden, K., Burmeister, M., & Sen, S. (2011). The serotonin transporter promoter variant (*5-HTTLPR*), stress, and depressionmta-analysis revisited: Evidence of genetic moderation. *Archives of General Psychiatry* [doi:10.1001/archgenpsychiatry.2010.189].

Karmiloff-Smith, A. (2007). Atypical epigenesis. *Developmental Science, 10*, 84–88.

Karmiloff-Smith, A. (2009). Preaching to the converted? From constructivism to neuroconstructivism. *Child Development Perspectives, 3*, 99–102.

Kaufman, J., Yang, B. Z., Douglas-Palumberi, H., Grasso, D., Lipschitz, D., Houshyar, S., et al. (2006). Brain-derived neurotrophic factor-f-HTTLPR gene interactions and environmental modifiers of depression in children. *Biological Psychiatry, 59*, 673–680.

Kaufman, J., Yang, B. Z., Douglas-Palumberi, H., Houshyar, S., Lipschitz, D., Krystal, J. H., et al. (2004). Social supports and serotonin transporter gene moderate depression in maltreated children. *Proceedings of the National Academy of Sciences, 101*, 17316–17321.

Kim-Cohen, J., Caspi, A., Taylor, A., Williams, B., Newcombe, R., Craig, I. W., et al. (2006). MAOA, maltreatment, and gene-environment interaction predicting children's mental health: New evidence and a meta-analysis. *Molecular Psychiatry, 11*, 903–913.

Kim-Cohen, J., & Gold, A. L. (2009). Measured gene-environment interactions and mechanisms promoting resilient development. *Current Directions in Psychological Science, 18*, 138–142.

Kuhlmann, M. (2011). Mechanisms in dynamically complex systems. In P. M. Illari, F. Russo, & J. Williamson (Eds.), *Causality in the sciences* (pp. 880–906). New York: Oxford University Press.

Markus, K. A. (2011). Real causes and ideal manipulations: Pearl's theory of causal inference from the point of view of psychological research methods. In P. M. Illari, F. Russo, & J. Williamson (Eds.), *Causality in the sciences* (pp. 240–269). New York: Oxford University Press.

McEwen, B. S. (2009). Stress and neuronal plasticity. In G. Fink (Ed.), *Stress science: Neuroendocrinology* (pp. 455–458). London: Elsevier.

McEwen, B. S. (2010). Stress: Homeostasis, rheostasis, allostasis and allostatic load. In G. Fink (Ed.), *Stress science: Neuroendocrinology* (pp. 10–14). London: Elsevier.

Meaney, M. J., & Szyf, M. (2005). Maternal effects as a model for environmentally-dependent chromatin plasticity. *Trends in Neuroscience, 28*, 456–463.

Melzack, R., & Katz, J. (2006). Pain in the 21st century: The neuromatrix and beyond. In G. Young, A. W. Kane, & K. Nicholson (Eds.), *Psychological knowledge in court: PTSD, Pain, and TBI* (pp. 129–148). New York: Springer Science+Business Media.

Meyer-Lindenberg, A., Buckholtz, J. W., Kolachana, B., Hariri, A. R., Pezawas, L., Blasi, G., et al. (2006). Neural mechanisms of genetic risk for impulsivity and violence in humans. *Proceedings of the National Academy of Sciences, 103*, 6269–6274.

Mills-Koonce, W. R., Propper, C. B., Gariepy, J. L., Blair, C., Garrett-Peters, P., & Cox, M. J. (2007). Bidirectional genetic and environmental influences on mother and child behavior: The family system as the unit of analyses. *Development and Psychopathology, 19*, 1073–1087.

Munafò, M. R., Durrant, C, Lewis, G., & Flint, J. (2009). Gene x environment interactions at the serotonin transporter locus. *Biological Psychiatry, 65*, 211–219.

Nilsson, K. W., Sjöberg, R. L., Damberg, M., Leppert, J., Öhrvik, J., Alm, P. O., et al. (2006). Role of monoamine oxidase A genotype and psychosocial factors in male adolescent criminal activity. *Biological Psychiatry, 59*, 121–127.

Nowak, M. A., Tamita, C. E., & Wilson, E. O. (2010). The evolution of eusociality. *Nature, 466*, 1057–1062.

Parasuraman, R., Greenwood, P. M., Kumar, R., & Fossella, J. (2005). Beyond heritability-neurotransmitter genes differentially modulate visuospatial attention and working memory. *Psychological Science, 16*, 200–207.

Pearl, J. (2009). *Causality: Models, reasoning, and inference* (2nd ed.). New York: Cambridge University Press.

Pearl, J. (2011). The structural theory of causation. In P. M. Illari, F. Russo, & J. Williamson (Eds.), *Causality in the sciences* (pp. 697–727). New York: Oxford University Press.

Plomin, R., Kovas, Y., & Haworth, C. M. A. (2007). Generalist *genes*: Genetic links between brain, mind, and education. *Mind, Brain, and Education, 1*, 11–19.

Posner, M. I., Rothbart, M. K., & Sheese, B. E. (2007). Attention genes. *Developmental Science, 10*, 24–29.

Psillos, S. (2011). The idea of mechanism. In P. M. Illari, F. Russo, & J. Williamson (Eds.), *Causality in the sciences* (pp. 771–788). New York: Oxford University Press.

Ramachandran, V. S., & Altschuler, E. L. (2009). The use of visual feedback, in particular mirror visual feedback, in restoring brain function. *Brain, 132*, 1693–1710.

Rathunde, K., & Csikszentmihalyi, M. (2006). The developing person: An experiential perspective. In W. Damon & R. M. Lerner (Eds.), Handbook of child psychology: Vol. 1. Theoretical models of human development (6th ed.) (pp. 465–515). New York: Wiley.

Reid, V., Belsky, J., & Johnson, M. H. (2005). Infant perception of human action: Toward a developmental cognitive neuroscience of individual differences. *Cognition, Brain, Behavior, 9*, 35–52.

Risch, N., Herrell, R., Lehner, T., Liang, K-Y., Eaves, L., Hoh, J., Griem, A., Kovacs, M., Ott, J., & Merikangas, K. R. (2009). Interaction between the serotonin transporter gene (*5-HTTLPR*), stressful life events, and risk of depression: A meta-analysis. *JAMA, 301*, 2462–2471.

Roth, T. L., Lubin, F. D., Funk, A. J., & Sweatt, J. D. (2009). Lasting epigenetic influence of early-life adversity of the BDNF gene. *Biology Psychiatry, 65*, 760–769.

Russo, F. (2009). *Causality and causal modeling in the social sciences: Measuring variations.* New York: Springer Science + Business Media.

Schmidt, L. A., Fox, N. A., Perez-Edgar, K., & Hamer, D. H. (2009). Linking gene, brain, and behavior: DRD4, frontal asymmetry, and temperament. *Psychological Science, 20*, 831–837.

Sheese, B. E., Voelker, P., Posner, M. I., & Rothbart, M. K. (2009). Genetic variation influences on the early development of reactive emotions and their regulation by attention. *Cognitive Neuropsychiatry, 14*, 332–355.

Sheese, B. E., Voelker, P. M., Rothbart, M. K., & Posner, M. I. (2007). Parenting quality interacts with genetic variation in dopamine receptor D4 to influence temperament in early childhood. *Development and Psychopathology, 19*, 1039–1046.

Sloman, S. (2005). *Causal models: How people think about the world and its alternatives*. New York: Oxford University Press.

Sommerville, J. A., Woodward, A. L., & Needham, A. (2005). Action experience alters 3-month-old infants' perception of others' actions. *Cognition, 96*, B1–B11.

Spelke, E. S., & Kinzler, K. D. (2007). Core knowledge. *Developmental Science, 10*, 89–96.

Spencer, J. P., Blumberg, M. S., McMurray, B., Robinson, S. R., Samuelson, L. K., & Tomblin, J. B. (2009). Short arms and talking eggs: Why we should no longer abide the nativist-empiricist debate. *Child Development Perspectives, 3*, 79–87.

Spencer, J. P., Samuelson, L. K., Blumberg, M. S., McMurray, B., Robinson, S. R., & Tomblin, J. B. (2009). Seeing the world through a third eye: Developmental systems theory looks beyond the nativist-empiricist debate. *Child Development Perspectives, 12*, 103–105.

Taylor, A., & Kim-Cohen, J. (2007). Meta-analysis of gene-environment interactions in developmental psychopathology. *Development & Psychopathology, 19*, 1029–1037.

Taylor, S. E., Way, B. M., Welch, W. T., Hilmert, C. J., Lehman, B. J., & Eisenberger, N. I. (2006). Early family environment, current adversity, the serotonin transporter promoter polymorphism, and depressive symptomatology. *Biological Psychiatry, 60*, 671–676.

Tinbergen, N. (1963). On aims and methods in ethology. *Zeitschrift für Tierpsychologie, 20*, 410–433.

Uher, R. (2011). Genes, environment, and personalized treatment for depression. In K. A. Dodge & M. Rutter (Eds.), *Gene-environment interactions in developmental psychopathology* (pp. 140–158). New York: Guilford Press.

Widom, C. S., & Brzustowicz, L. M. (2006). MAOA and the "cycle of violence": Childhood abuse and neglect, MAOA genotype, and risk for violent and antisocial behavior. *Biological Psychiatry, 60*, 684–689.

Wilhelm, K., Mitchell, P. B., Niven, H., Finch, A., Wedgwood, L., Scimone, A., et al. (2006). Life events, first depression onset and the serotonin transporter gene. *British Journal of Psychiatry, 188*, 210–215.

Young, G., & Baumeister, R. (In preparation). *Causality science and behavior: Interdisciplinary perspectives*. New York: Springer Science + Business Media.

Young, G. (2010). Causes in the construction of causal law: A psycho-ecological model. *International Journal of Law and Psychiatry, 33*, 73–83.

Young, G., & Chapman, C. R. (2007). Pain, affect, nonlinear dynamical systems, and chronic pain: Bringing order to disorder. In G. Young, A. W. Kane, & K. Nicholson, *Causality of psychological injury: Presenting evidence in court* (pp. 197–241). New York: Springer Science+Business Media.

Zalsman, G., Huang, Y. Y., Oquendo, M. A., Burke, A. K., Hu, X. Z., Brent, D. A., et al. (2006). Association of a triallelic serotonin transporter gene promoter region (5-HTTLPR) polymorphism with stressful life events and severity of depression. *American Journal Psychiatry, 163*, 1588–1593.

Zelazo, P. D. (2004). The development of conscious control in childhood. *Trends in Cognitive Sciences, 8*, 12–17.

Zelazo, P. D., Carlson, S. M., & Kesek, A. (2008). The development of executive function in childhood. In C. Nelson & M. Luciana (Eds.), *Handbook of developmental cognitive neuroscience* (2nd ed., pp. 553–574). Cambridge: MIT Press.

# Chapter 31
# Stages and Change in Development and Other Systems

## Introduction

The present chapter examines models of change in human development, in other areas of psychology, in fields outside of psychology, and even in nonliving systems. The goal is to show that the present stage and substage model is grounded in change mechanisms that cut across other areas of study involving changes in organization or output. For many areas of study, I have found a common five-step sequence, and the chapter presents a generic model of stages of change that can work across disciplines.

The key sequences in the present model that are involved in this one concern its sequence of cyclically recurring substages and its sequence of underlying nonlinear dynamical transition processes. The five-step substage sequence involves coordination, hierarchization, systematization, multiplication, and integration. The five-step transition process involves cyclic attractors, chaotic attractors, gravitating to the cusp of change, complex adaptive systems processes, and superordinate complex adaptive systems processes (see Chap. 28).

In this model, as a system evolves, at first, it starts to coordinate new acquisitions; then, its coupled acquisitions develop a dominant–subordinate relationship, with one being primary in the hierarchization. Next, the two acquisitions organize into a single coherent structure as it systematizes. In the fourth step, the new structure radiates throughout the system, multiplying its new-found skill or structure into multiple domains. Last, in the step of integration, the system is characterized in full by its new attributes, rules, or dynamic, which have impregnated all its constituent elements and their organization. Once a system reaches the stage of integration, it is ready for the next stage of coordination with other systems, in a process of cyclic recursion. These other systems could be parallel systems within the whole structure in which the system is embedded, so that there are, in effect, subsystems internal to it that involved. Or, the system could capture, attract, or otherwise coordinate systems extraneous to it.

Change processes have been described at multiple levels in psychology both at the individual and group levels. In this regard, there might be common underlying steps and processes in changes that take place at the psychological level. Moreover,

G. Young, *Development and Causality: Neo-Piagetian Perspectives*,
DOI 10.1007/978-1-4419-9422-6_31, 

similar change dynamics might take place at many other levels, including in societal institutions and disciplines of study. In this chapter, I apply the present model to change within disciplines of study, especially developmental psychology and also the new area of psychological injury and law. The chapter concludes that the dynamical step model in the present work is consistent with broader change mechanisms.

## Caveats

Before presenting the arguments in depth about the generic product-process change model being described, it is important to underline certain caveats about stage theories.

(a) First, not all developmental phenomena or areas marked by growth or change must pass through stages. This obtains because the elements of the systems involved and the pressures on their organization need to be propitious toward establishing stages.
(b) Second, even if stages appear applicable to a particular system, there is no reason that the changes must emerge in a particular sequence and in the same way for all exemplars of the system in question.
(c) Third, even if a stage in a particular systemic organization manifests in all exemplars of the system as it evolves, the system could be characterized by abundant individual differences in the specific manifestation of the system, depending on the system's particular context and pressures. Taken together, these different provisos about the growth of stages in a system indicate that the best way of understanding stage models is that, when the stages appear universal and uniform, there is still much room for individual variation in their expression. In this regard, any one stage in a system that is subject to stage change functions as a lattice for elaboration of major individual and group variations deriving from the environmental and system pressures acting on it.
(d) Fourth, even if a particular model of change that is based on universal and uniform stages appears to apply to a particular area, and even with considering that it can be constructed to accommodate individual differences, this does not mean that there must be an inherent internal program that guides the development and expression of the system through its stages. Systems might evolve in universal and uniform ways over stages not because the stages take forms or patterns that are inevitable as the system changes, or because of the presence of an interior preformulated control mechanism in the system that governs the change in an automatic way. Rather, systems might develop universal and uniform change patterns over stages because the sequence of stages involved is the most graceful, economical, and dynamic one that could emerge in context.

Systems adopt the best-fit structure in each moment of their evolution according to the constituent elements present, their past history and the forces acting on their components. This online adaptation ensures that any system adapts with optimal adjustment, search for equilibrium, and environmental accommodations to the pressures under which it is placed. If similarities in adjustment, pattern, and sequence of stages are found across systems as they evolve over stages, it is because of the simplicity afforded by the deep commonalities in the changing complexity. The steps that I describe in my own generic change model (Young, 1997, 2008; Young & Chapman, 2006, 2007) have been presented in a simple and logically consistent way. They unfold in the particular sequence presented not because systems have to do it this way, but because this is the best-fitting way that systems can adjust in order to have optimal economical and effective adaptation in context.

(e) Fifth, stages build on each other. They incorporate the elements comprising the prior stages and accommodate to their extant structure, while add incoming information or energy, as the case may be. They preserve parsimoniously and conservatively the adaptive function of prior stages while developing new properties and structure as their new pattern emerges.

(f) Sixth, stages have an underlying structure (product) and an underlying dynamic (process) but, in the end, it is difficult to separate these two components of stages in system evolution. Nevertheless, in the following, for heuristic reasons, often I deal separately with them.

## Generic Change

### *Introduction*

I have found evidence that many living and nonliving systems change according to five steps. Consider the following:

(a) Human development takes place at both macro and micro levels. When examined for patterns across levels, similarities can be found that suggest fractal processes at work (e.g., Young, 1997, the present work).

(b) Therapy involves stages of change (e.g., Prochaska, Wright, & Velicer, 2008). The stages in therapy that have been described are consistent with the developmental stages in my model (Young, 2008; Young & Chapman, 2006, 2007).

(c) Even regressive changes, such as found in the development of chronic pain, might follow patterns of change similar to the patterns in more progressive contexts, such as in therapy. The stages that appear evident in chronic pain are consistent with the present model (e.g., Young & Chapman).

(d) Researchers in the area of management/leadership/expertise have described stage models of change (e.g., Lichtenstein & Plowman, 2009; Sharpless & Barber, 2009). These are consistent with the present stage model (see Table 31.2 and Fig. 31.1).

(e) Economic theorists and political theorists have described stage changes in societal economies and political organizations that are similar to the present model (e.g., Rostow, 1990).

(f) The evolution of scholarly disciplines has been described in terms of general change processes (e.g., Piaget & Garcia, 1989). Careful examination of this work reveals that the stages involved are consistent with the present model.
(g) Going one step further, several researchers have formulated change models involving stages for more general living and nonliving contexts (Sabelli, 2005; Salthe, 2007). These are consistent with the present model.

## *Five Steps in Change*

Table 31.1 presents various five-step stage models from other areas of psychology and from other disciplines. Some of these models purport to be generic change models that can help explain a broad array of natural phenomena. Many of these models were developed out of awareness of each other. The commonalities evidenced in these independent conceptions of five steps in the change mechanisms that govern their particular areas of study, despite involving disparate systems, are striking.

(a) In this regard, many of the areas include a beginning stage with some form of coordination (e.g., old, new) as predicted by the present five-step model (e.g., reversing, denial).
(b) Then, in these different areas, often one finds an equivalent to the predicted stage of hierarchization that seems to appear (e.g., local order, global disorder).
(c) Next, the systematization predicted in the present model seems to offer some explanatory power (e.g., competence, arrival).
(d) In the fourth step of the present model, I describe that a multiplication or propagation of a new system structure in the whole system can take place. The multiplication that is predicted is evident (drive to maturity, expansion).
(e) Finally, the fifth stage in these various models presented in the table, which is a resume of stage models in different areas, often resembles a stage of integration (high, matured). This type of stage is the last one in the five-step sequence of the present model.

## *Comment*

The reader might find it striking that in the domains covered in this section there seems to be change processes that are described in terms of five steps, phases, transitions, or stages. However, one could argue that this happens merely because of coincidence. Or, one could postulate that there are many examples where stage and related models do not apply. Even if a stage or related model does apply to diverse phenomena, one could argue there is no reason to expect that the structure each time should involve five steps, phases, transitions, or stages. Nevertheless, these common patterns in the diverse models of steps and related outcomes in change are consistent with the present model. In addition, I had hypothesized the presence of a fractalization process in development, and suggest that sublevels of the substages should show the same five-step recursive pattern.

**Table 31.1** Five stages in system growth in various models of living and nonliving systems

| Topic | References | Stages |
|---|---|---|
| Expertise | Sharpless and Barber (2009) | Novice. Advanced beginner. Competence. Proficiency. Expertise |
| Leadership | Boyatzis (2008) | Seeing desired future. How acts with others. Developing learning agenda. Experimenting with new habitats. Others helping us |
| Business | Zadek (2004) | Denial/defensive. Compliance. Managerial: Managing responsibility. Strategic: Responsible business strategies. Toward civil action |
| Economics | Rostow (1990) | Traditional society. Preconditions for take-off. Take-off. Drive to maturity. High mass consumption |
| Disciplines | Piaget and Garcia (1989) | Intra-object. Inter-object. Trans-object (Expanded to five stages in the text) |
| Politics | Paxton (1998) | New way. Rooting. Arrival in power. Exercise of power. Dual power |
| Nonliving/systems/ Big Bang | Salthe (2007) | Global microscopic disorder. Local orders, global disorders. Global order. Accelerated expansion. Global symmetry |
| Bios/generic processes | Sabelli (2005) | Flux (continually reversing). Action processes (directed change). Information (co-creation). Structuration (transient stability, expanding). Organization (creating) |
| Complex systems | Chen and Fang (2008) | Initial. Differentiation. Evolution. Formation. Matured |

That so many diverse domains in living and nonliving systems reflect a five-step generic change process is more than coincidence. Systems that conform to nonlinear dynamical principles should evolve in the sequence indicated, or similar ones, because the sequence represents the most economical, graceful, efficient, dynamical, and continual restructuring of systems that is possible, everything else being equal

As systems evolve, they seek far-from-equilibrium conditions that maximize the possibility of change toward increasing adaptivity. They gravitate to regions in their state space that are on the cusp of change. There is no teleological purpose or built-in mechanism that they must increase in complexity. However, in reorganizing more adaptively at each new step in its evolution, everything else being equal, they gain better flexibility for adaptation, freeing resources for the task and increasing the possibility of getting and incorporating resources for the task. As new resources are freed or obtained, the degrees of freedom in adaptation can lead to entropic disorder in the system as it is overwhelmed, or it can lead to intrinsic dynamical adjustment toward better management and channeling of the excess

For these reasons, the generic model of change that I have proposed seems to be evident in multiple arenas of study. Although it takes different forms in the models, the meta-form and the constancy of the pattern stand out. That political systems and other group structures, as well as nonliving systems as large as the universe share the pattern found at the individual human level, in the present Neo-Piagetian stage model, could be considered exceptional

In this regard, in terms of the cognitive side of development, the work of Piaget and the Neo-Piagetians has prepared the way for discerning patterns in behavior that reflect more universal patterns in nature. Similarly, in terms of the socioaffective side of development, the work of Erikson and the Neo-Eriksonians, Bowlby and the attachment theorists, and Darwin and the emotional theorists have prepared the way for the development of models in the present work that allow for one-to-one parallels in cognitive/socioaffective correspondences over the lifespan, and thus reflections of universal patterns in nature

Moreover, in Young (1997), I had presented the work of Salthe (1993), who described a pattern of five stages in various evolutions, both living and nonliving. I indicated how Salthe's description of a general pattern of change according to a five-step model is consistent with the present model. I remind that I had indicated that the change model of Prochaska, Norcross, and DiClemente (1994; Maddox, 1995), which consists of five stages, is consistent with the present model. Finally, in more recent work, as mentioned, I have indicated (Young, 2008; Young & Chapman, 2006, 2007) that regressive changes that might take place, such as in the development of chronic pain as opposed to the progressive therapeutic changes that Prochaska et al. underscore, also could pass through the same five stages. For another example of five steps in the changes of a system, see Chap. 30 for presentation of the five steps in the evolution of eusociality (Nowak, Tarnita, & Wilson, 2010).

## Complexity Theory in Human Organization

### *Model*

Lichtenstein and Plowman (2009) addressed the development of leadership and management according to complex systems theory. They found successive organizational levels in its emergence that are consistent with the present five-step model (see Table 31.2 and Fig. 31.1). The sequence involves (a) a disequilibrium state, (b) amplifying actions, (c) recombination/self-organization, (d) stabilizing feedback, and (e) leading to a new emergent order in leadership. In the following, I show how the description of the authors of their five-step series in the growth of leadership is consistent with my own five-step model.

*Coordination.* The first organizational level in the evolution of leadership in systems in Lichtenstein and Plowman (2009) involves disrupting existing patterns, yet working with the uncertainty that results. The system exists outside the norm, implying the presence of simultaneously functioning normative and non-normative organizational patterns.

Lichtenstein and Plowman's description of a disequilibrium step that precedes system evolution is consistent with the present model. In my model, I emphasize that system growth begins with a coordination of two new acquisitions derived from the prior state of the system or an opposition between the prior system and the movements toward a new one.

*Hierarchization.* The second level in the sequence of organizational growth in the Lichtenstein and Plowman model involves encouraging novelty and experiments supporting collective action. The system is moving toward a new order.

According to the present model, the dual states in the first step in the change process of a system come to adopt a hierarchical relationship in the second one, with one dominant over the other, as the new structure solidifies its presence. Similarly, the Lichtenstein and Plowman model describes novelty seeking and experimentation toward collective action, implying that the new order in the system is taking hold.

**Table 31.2** Condition/sequence in leadership

| Condition/sequence | Definition |
|---|---|
| Disequilibrium state | Creating and maintaining a disequilibrium state of organizing is a central component of emergence theories. Findings from these three studies confirm that emergence is initiated by activities/events occurring "outside the norm" for each context (McKelvey, 2004a, 2004b) that push the system into a highly dynamic state (Anderson, 1999; Prigogine & Stengers, 1984). Sustaining this disequilibrium state for an extended period of time seems to be a requisite aspect of emergent order creation (Meyer, Gaba, & Colwell, 2005) |
| Amplifying actions | Complexity science shows that when systems are in a disequilibrium state, small actions and events – fluctuations in the system – can be amplified through positive feedback and a cycle of self-reinforcement (Anderson, 1999). This process of "deviation amplification" (Maryuyama, 1963) creates a dynamic whereby the emergence of one action/event in the system increases the likelihood that other similar events will emerge (Krugman, 1996). Dynamic systems sciences have been able to map these deviation loops for many years, with important results. In the dissipative structures model, these amplifications (which already are moving toward a new "attractor," Goldstein, 2007) grow to a critical point, a threshold (Anderson, 1999) |
| Recombination/ "self-organization" | At the other side of the threshold, a new "level of order" in the system comes into being (Anderson, 1999; Lichtenstein, 2007; Lichtenstein, Dooley, & Lumpkin, 2006). In one measure, this is created through a recombination of resources – a reaggregation of some kind that increases the capacity of the overall system to operate. Emergence is thus the outcome of the system – the creation of a new entity with qualities that are not reflected in the interactions of each agent within the system. Recombination thus "expands the pie" in a real way for all the agents in the ecology |
| Stabilizing feedback | Finally new emergent order, if it is creating value, will stabilize itself in short order, finding parameters that best increase its overall sustainability in the ecology. Stabilizing feedback anchors the change by slowing the nonlinear process that lead to the amplification of emergence in the first place (Sastry, 1997). In so doing these role-based actions help institutionalize the change throughout the system (Chiles, Meyer, & Hench, 2004), by slowly increasing the legitimacy of the new entity |

Adapted from Elsevier with permission. Reprinted from The Leadership Quarterly, Volume 20(4), Lichtenstein, B., & Plowman, D. A. (2009). Copyright 2009, with permission from Elsevier. [Table 2, Page. 620]

This table indicates diverse areas of study in which five stages in growth appear to have been found, supporting the generic model of change being proposed. Lichtenstein's work (Lichtenstein & Plowman, 2009) is quite compatible with the present model (see Table 31.2 and Fig. 31.1). On the one hand, he has found five stages in the emergence of leadership. On the other hand, he views their development in terms of nonlinear system dynamics

*Systematization.* The third step in the Lichtenstein and Plowman (2009) model of organizational change involves making sense and giving sense as a new organization restructures. The system develops a new order that improves the efficacy of the system.

This description of the third step in the five-step model of organizational change in Lichtenstein and Plowman is consistent with the present model. In particular, in

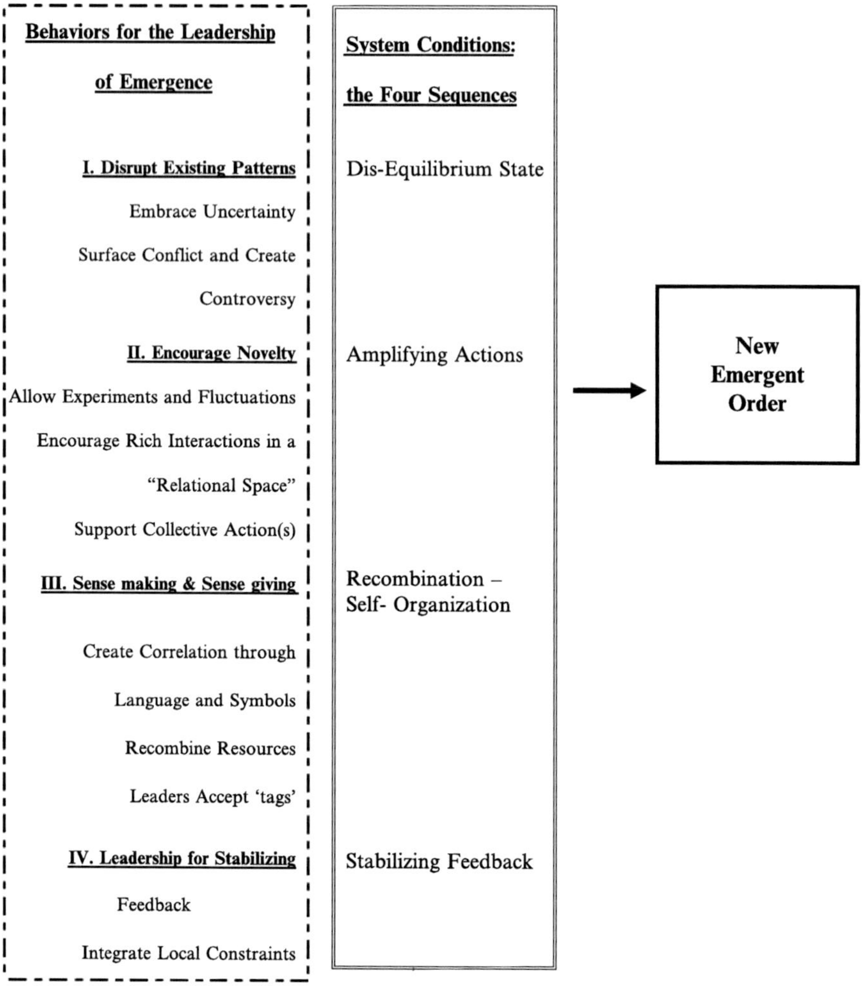


**Fig. 31.1** Behaviors that co-generate the conditions for new emergent order in leadership. The figure illustrates a model in the development of leadership that involves five steps. Moreover, it is couched in the language of nonlinear dynamical systems theory. In these two ways, it is consistent with the present model that a five-step stage model of change that had been developed to understand human cognitive development could represent a generic sequence with wide-ranging applicability, for example, to groups rather than just individuals, and to nonliving systems as they evolve. Adapted from Elsevier with permission. Reprinted from The Leadership Quarterly, Volume 20(4), Lichtenstein, B., & Plowman, D. A. (2009). Copyright 2009, with permission from Elsevier. [Figure 1, Page. 621]

the third step in the present model, I describe that a new system is created within the ongoing structure involved.

*Multiplication.* The fourth level in Lichtenstein and Plowman involves refining and constraining the new leadership in emergence. The system institutionalizes changes throughout, but at a slow level.

According to the present model, the fourth step in generic change concerns the multiplication throughout the ongoing structure of the new system that had developed in the prior stage. In this sense, the two models are entirely consistent.

*Integration.* The fifth level in Lichtenstein and Plowman's model of leadership growth involves the presence of a new leadership structure that facilitates a dramatic increase in organizational capacity. The system is primed for organizational expansion.

In the present change model, this fifth step is referred to as one involving an integration process. The entire system takes on the new characteristics of the new system that had developed and spread throughout the structure. The new structure is primed for the next step of coordinating with similar structures that might develop, repeating the cycle of growth initiated in the first phase of the generic change process.

### *Comment*

The Lichtenstein and Plowman (2009) model of organizational change in leadership is quite consistent with the present model even though they have different origins and targets. The other five-step sequences that have been presented in Table 31.2 do not map so clearly with the present model, but all use a five-step sequence like it.

## History of Major Schools of Thought in Developmental Psychology

### *Introduction*

In the next part of the chapter, I apply the present model of stages in development to the evolution of the major schools of thought in the history of developmental psychology. Piaget and Garcia (1989) had applied their cognitive developmental stage model to the history of mathematics. To my knowledge, the present analysis constitutes the first time that the history of the major schools of thought in the discipline of developmental psychology has been investigated for its steps from the perspective of cognitive steps. For pertinent information about the contemporary major schools of thought in the discipline, the reader should consult Cairns and Cairns (2006) and Damon and Lerner (2006).

Disciplines undergo paradigm shifts when conditions enable new perspectives to arise and these perspectives stimulate inquiry in the disciplines (Kuhn, 1965). In developmental psychology, the history of the field has been marked by debates on the importance of nature and nurture in development, or the role of biology and environment in development. Historically, the two elements were considered separately and, unlike in contemporary developmental theory, there was little notion of an interaction between the two as development unfolded.

Theory in the area of child psychology began to emerge about 100 years ago with the psychodynamic views of Freud, in which the child was considered the passive recipient of biological impulses (id) and environmental proscriptions (incorporated into the superego). The child did develop an unconscious, as well. In all these ways, the child was not active in her or his development, as multiple forces buffeted the child in one way or another. Freud added that personality structure consisted of a third element – the ego.

The concept of the ego represented a major breakthrough theoretically because it allowed for some influence of the child on her or his own development. Freud was a psychiatrist who functioned from the perspective of the medical model, and his understanding of energetics was conditioned by the physics of his time, so that in his concept of the id, it was considered a repository of a coursing libidinal or sexual energy that became invested in successive body zones, from the oral to the anal to the genital. This energy and the efforts needed to control and direct it to adaptive ends, and to suppress its excesses, was a focal task of the developing person for Freud. For our purposes, it illustrates that he considered the ego in service of these goals and not as a thriving, independent source of personal actualization and maturity, as we do today. Nevertheless, by proposing an ego in development, Freud launched a nascent model of the self, the importance of which was emphasized by James (1890). However, looking back, we are the ones who see it this way; in the Freudian model, the ego was considered a subservient psychological instrument to the whims of the id, as it tried to circumvent the constraints of the superego.

This very first major theory applicable to human development, the Freudian model, stands as one that not only gave us a concept of stages in development that is still current to some degree (and gave us the concept of the unconscious, that is still vastly important in understanding the person), but also as the theory that described the major causal factors that are still used in efforts to understand development. We find in Freud a juxtaposition of opposing contributory elements still current today – the biological (id), the environmental (superego), and the personal (ego). Contemporary work still is trying to understand how these three sources of influence interact in development.

## *Stages*

### Precoordination

One could posit that, in terms of the evolution of the discipline of psychology, or the study of human development over the last 100 years, from the perspective of the present generic model of five stages in system growth (coordination, hierarchization, systematization, multiplication, integration), the Freudian psychodynamic model represented a precoordination phase that led to later phases more directly indicative of the model. The major elements involved as influences on the developing human were first elucidated together by Freud (the biological, environmental, and personal). This prepared the way for their separation in individual theories that deal with them, and for the ensuing efforts to try to integrate them into coherent models. In addition, the work of Freud was not strictly psychological, given its psychodynamic origin. Therefore, developmental psychology emerged as a separate discipline after the Freudian model was formulated, which constitutes another reason to term the Freudian model as a precoordination one.

## Coordination

The first genuine phase in the evolution of developmental psychology took place in the period before WWII in the last century (e.g., the school of behaviorism). This initiatory phase can be construed as the phase of separation, differentiation, and juxtaposition in the study of the three major influences on the components in development as adduced by Freud in his own way – the biological, the environmental, and the personal. Therefore, in terms of the present generic model of system growth, the first stage in the emergence of developmental psychology fits the first step of the model, which has been characterized as one of coordination. This holds true because the various theories that emerged about the influences on development in this era considered the influence that they touted as the most important if not the exclusive one. Three major theories emerged in this period – behaviorism, ethology, and Piaget's stage model.

Behaviorism cast its stone against the inherent mentalism of the Freudian model, arguing that behavior can be understood uniquely through the environmental and learning contingencies impinging on and reinforcing the child, for example, through classical conditioning. The mind, if it exists at all, is part of a black box that is not important in understanding development. To summarize, behaviorism led to a better understanding of the role of the environment in development, one of the three influences on development inherent in Freud's expansive model.

Ethology is another school of thought that developed around this time. Its roots were in biology, but even then it informed developmental psychology. It focused on the biological bases of behavior by developing more refined models related to imprinting and instincts. In imprinting, the young of altricial birds, such a ducklings, will follow the parental figure in a critical period that lasts only hours shortly after birth. Normally, this is adaptive for survival and future reproduction because the typical object followed is the conspecific biological parent.

Piaget developed his model of cognitive development in this epoch. He focused on the developing child's contribution to her or his own behavior, through natural activity, active construction of cognitive schemas, and so forth. For Piaget, the child was not a passive recipient of environmental influences. The approach was constructivist, and the child could learn more from cognitive conflicts internal to contrasting schemes as they were applied to problems or through peer problem-solving, rather than by expert instruction from teachers or parents.

This completes the survey of the major schools of thought considered to have emerged in the coordination phase in the development of child psychology. In review, I note that the major influences that Freud had presented in his model on the developing person were each elaborated in more refined models, but they focused especially on one or the other of the influences, without attempting more integrative models where the influences were on more of an equal footing.

## Hierarchization

The post-WWII (and late prewar period) period witnessed differentiation of the major developmental models, but they still prioritized one of the three major elements in the triad of influences discussed in development as the most important one. In terms of the present generic model of system growth through steps, this period in the discipline's history fits the second stage of hierarchization in the model because of the differentiation in the prioritizations involved. In all cases, the developmental models of that time considered themselves primary, and the type of influence on development that each promulgated as central to development was considered either exclusive or subordinate to the others.

For example, later behavioral models added the learning mechanism of operant conditioning. Instead of classical conditioning, which elaborates by association stimuli that could instigate responses, operant conditioning elaborated the responses that could be elicited by stimuli through the reinforcement histories to which emitted behavior could be subjected.

Ethology added explanations of behavior that emphasized fixed action patterns and innate releasing mechanisms. It still was rooted in energy models of its time, but these were not libidinal, at least; for example, it examined the buildup of energy related to innate releasing mechanisms of the fixed action patterns that it described.

Piagetians explored the role of environmental effects through décalages, training studies, and simplified tasks, beginning the process of determining earlier ages for the appearance of certain skills relative to Piaget's formulation. Piaget had maintained that maturation was more critical than environmental aliments in moving stages forward in their development, but Piagetians who followed him were more open to different approaches that could ascertain an earlier acquisition of stages relative to Piaget's original model (e.g., Bruner, 1966).

Freudian models explored further the role of the nonlibidinal sources in development (Jung, Adler) and examined further the ego in development.

## Systematization

In the next stage in the development of the discipline of developmental psychology, the discipline found its voice and developed models unique to it. It would appear that in the next phase in the development of the discipline, in the 1960s to 1970s, the predominant theories undertook cross-fertilization and incorporated more than one central focus as influences on behavior. They emerged with novel theoretical approaches distinct from the precursor theories described, and the new theories merited their own labels.

This stage in the evolution of the child psychology fits the present model's emphasis that the third generic step in growth concerns systematization. For example, the school of ethology influenced the development of attachment theory, in which biological mechanisms related to seeking and maintaining proximity and contact were considered to interact with the quality of care giving received, leading to the development already in the first year of life of either secure or insecure attachments (as explained in this book).

Social learning theory added observational learning to the behavioral mechanisms in learning, and introduced motivation and attentional mechanisms in learning, as well, given that imitation can take place only after appropriate observation of the model (Bandura, 1986, 1989; Bandura, Caprara, Barbaranelli, Gerbino, & Pastorelli, 2003). This turn helped in bringing mentalism back into behaviorism, to a certain degree.

Erikson differentiated Freudian theory in several ways that gave more of a role to the person as he or she developed. His innovations included rendering the stages involved more psychosocial than psychosexual in origin, and he framed them in terms of challenges, issues, crises, or dangers that the individual must confront as the individual enters a stage. By expanding the stages from the original five stages in the Freudian model to eight in his model in order to cover the lifespan, and by emphasizing the mutuality with the environment as the developing person traversed the challenges inherent in each stage, Erikson offered psychology a model that placed importance on the all major influences on development as discussed in the present work. Erikson simultaneously considered in his model: the person, the ego; the environment and the mutuality with it; and the underlying biology, through the psychosexual stages with their libidinal influences (still part of the model even if displaced as primary in importance).

Neo-Piagetians also differentiated the stages in Piaget's theory, adding a postformal period, in particular, and positing cyclic recursions in substages. They emphasized environmental supports to facilitate passage through the various stages (as per the reviews in the present work).

## Multiplication

In addition to those theories that differentiated from the original ones that had developed in the field at the outset, new paradigms in the field of developmental psychology emerged in the 1970s and 1980s. Also, the major models in child psychology were not only multiplying but also increasing in the areas to which they were applied and the issues with which they dealt. Therefore, this phase in the history of the discipline can be conceived of as the phase of multiplication, to use the language of the present generic model of steps in change. Four new schools of thought in developmental psychology can be considered to have emerged in this time frame.

In the information-processing model of development, the computer provides the analogy and guide to how development is conceived. In this model of development, one finds input, output, their processing, and memory, in particular, with hardware and software considerations. The input into the child's cognitive architecture is processed by internal memory mechanisms, but the output is conditioned by mental factors, such as motivation and attention. As with the details needed to program computers, psychologists in this tradition engaged in detailed task analysis (Siegler, Deloache, & Eisenberg, 2010).

The sociocultural model built on the work of Vygotsky, whose ideas had been isolated from the West, delaying its impact. He published in the 1930s, but became prominent in the West well after WWII. (See Young, 1997, for a comprehensive account of his theory and more contemporary adaptations and additions.) According to the Vygotskian tradition, the child is influenced by the environment via experts functioning as guides or scaffolds in the zone of proximal development. At the same time, wider sociocultural and historico-political influences add to the influence of the environment, as they entrain the child, family, and expert to their messages through the tools of language and other internalizing procedures. However, for Vygotskians, the child is not simply a passive receptacle of the messages received or entrained, because learning takes place at two levels. First, the material provided by the environment is learned as instructed by the experts in the zone, but after this the child alters the learned material in order to have it fit her or his extant cognitive models and structures. Development obtains through this form-fitting of internalized material and existing cognitive architecture. The child is heavily involved in the process, although the expert (and mediational tools) is considered crucial.

Another school that emerged in this time frame was based on the concept of systems. In systems theory, families are considered as wholes, and the whole system of the family and its members is considered greater than the sum of its parts. According to this school, children are best understood within the context of family dynamics, and they cannot be isolated in therapy if it is to succeed. Children should not be scape-goated, for when the family has a presenting problem, the dynamics involved usually suggest that the solution lies in remedying family-wide issues (as explained in this book).

Another theory that developed in this time period is similar to the systems and sociocultural models, and is called the ecological model (Bronfenbrenner & Morris, 2006). In this model, the child is conceived of as an organism with initial characteristics that interact with an environment that can be differentiated into multiple components. In the model, a circular diagram represents the different levels of the environment as it acts on the child. It is constructed to have concentric layers, from more proximal influences, such as family, to more distal ones, such as media and cultural influences. These levels can influence each other, leading to indirect effects on the child (e.g., a parent loses a job, affecting how the family treats the child).

As the major developmental theories emerged and differentiated, thereby influencing each other and becoming more integrative, they were applied to an increasing range of developmental phenomena. To give several examples sufficient for present purposes, the Vygotskian model was applied to education systems, based on concepts such as guided participation and appropriation (see Young, 1997). The systems model became quite influential and evolved from an amalgam of general ideas to a tight theoretical model. In its nonlinear dynamical form, for example, Thelen and Smith applied systems theory to motor development, examined language development from its lens (Smith & Thelen, 1993). Computer models were used to study expert achievements in children, such as in chess. Ecological models were extended to children in applied and underprivileged contexts, such as the rehabilitative context.

## Integration

Subsequent models in the field of developmental psychology have been trying to differentiate further and integrate these diverse theories that had developed in prior stages of the discipline (the presentation of which in depth is beyond the scope of the present work, except for the case of some Neo-Piagetian and related models). Contemporary models are making progress in this regard, seeking overarching paradigmatic understanding of development (e.g., the developmental biopsychosocial model, diathesis-stress models of developmental psychopathology, current systems models). Moreover, developmental psychology is becoming increasingly interdisciplinary, borrowing from and integrating both biological and cultural scholarship (e.g., behavior genetics, cultural and minority studies, respectively).

Nevertheless, a valid integrative theory in human development needs to consider simultaneously the multiple theories that have emerged in the last century since the discipline emerged. For example, no major contemporary theory has successfully integrated Piagetian and Eriksonian concepts of stages in human development over the lifespan. These stages concern cognitive and socioemotional or affective acquisitions, respectively, but it is conceivable that they could be integrated into a common framework where the artificial distinction between these two central aspects of development is coordinated. Furthermore, once a common Piagetian-Eriksonian stage framework is constructed (and that has been the goal of the present work), it would be easier to envisage how the lattice of stages in the model would relate to other developmental acquisitions highlighted in other contemporary theories, such as in attachment theory, or how other developmental acquisitions, such as different temperaments and the emergence of primary emotions, which are not generally related to stage theories, fit into the combined model.

Another factor to consider is that contemporary developmental psychology exhibits a great gulf between stage and nonstage theories. Stage theories are in the minority, and often dismissed. This illustrates the need to address the present lack of a synthesis in the field along these lines, and accommodate the great divide between stage theories and nonstage theories. There are pertinent examples that indicate that gulfs in the field can be accommodated. For example, social learning theory has evolved independent of stage conceptions, but it is broadening from its behavioral and anti-mentalistic roots to consider concepts such as the sense of self-efficacy. Another indication of model integration in development should consider having sociocultural and ecological theories becoming grounded in stage theories to the point that families, societies, communities, political entities, and cultures can be understood in terms of stage models.

### Comment

In terms of the present generic model of steps in growth, I conclude that the tour of past and contemporary theories in the area of developmental psychology had been illuminating. Also, it points to the validity of the present model, because it has fit into its structure the trends that have been evident in the discipline of developmental psychology as it evolved. However, until there are overarching models in the discipline of developmental psychology that both respect the theories that have been fundamental in the evolution of the discipline and that also integrate them and their continuing innovations in a comprehensive framework, it can be conjectured that the field of developmental psychology is just beginning the integrative phase of its growth.

Later in the chapter, I indicate how a relatively new area of psychology, that of psychological injury and law, is emerging from the systematization stage into the multiplicative one. In the next part of the chapter, I examine some details of the present 25-step model of lifespan development.

## Closer Look at the Generic Step Model

### *Development*

I have proposed a stage-substage model with labels for the stages based on Piaget's work and labels for the substages based on the Neo-Piagetians. Moreover, I have suggested that in development a process of fractalization could characterize stage-substage relations. This implies that the five stages of the present model should be self-similar to the five substages of the present mode. Moreover, in this chapter I have suggested a generic change process applicable across living and nonliving systems. Therefore, given these considerations, I need to show how the Piagetian labels for the stages in the present model are consistent with the labels for the substages.

*Reflexive.* In this regard, the reflexive period posited by the present model to begin human development is consistent with the coordination stage of the generic model being presented. This argument applies because the newborn and premature express behavioral patterns to stimuli, such as looking, sucking, and grasping, that are not automatic, single-movement expressions, but are adaptive sequences aimed at eliciting targets and are coordinated with their elicitation.

*Sensorimotor.* As for the sensorimotor stage of the present model, its characteristics are consistent with a hierarchization process, in which motor activity is subordinated to the adaptive dynamics afforded by the sensory array deriving from participation in the environmental context. Moreover, it is the stage of development of the primary emotions, intersubjectivity, attachment, and autonomy, so that the infant is developing a self, but one subordinated to caregivers.

*Perioperational.* The stage of perioperations in the present model includes the Piagetian preoperational and concrete operational periods, and it especially involves representations. These developmental acquisitions allow the child to act on the environment with plans, to communicate with it by symbolic means, and to solve problems deriving from it with a certain, grounded logic. In this stage, the child is manifesting a new phase in growth that stands as a hallmark of a qualitatively distinct and advanced, self-contained systemic acquisitions in underlying cognitive schemes, so that the stage is consistent with the term of systematization, as used in the generic model being proposed.

*Abstract.* The abstract stage of cognitive development allows the adolescent and adult to engage in and solve advanced problems, including algebra, physics, and other sciences. Piaget has described the stage in terms of group theory. With the systematization of logical thinking in the prior stage of concrete operations, the movement in cognitive development in this stage proceeds to a superior level. Abstract thought can be applied not only to the full panoply of problems in a student's disciplinary study but also to the range of everyday social and intellectual challenges, and so on. In this regard, the label of multiplication, which is the one applicable to this cognitive stage in terms of the present generic model of change, fits it quite well. The young person expands personal, intellectual, and social horizons, although not quite to an integrated level.

*Collective intelligence.* In the next stage of collective intelligence, the adult builds superordinate abstract structures aimed not only at solving complex problems but also at constructing disciplinary and cross-disciplinary understanding and integration. These acquisitions are consistent with the fifth stage of the generic model of growth presented, which is labeled integration. As conceived in the present work, collective intelligence is not an esoteric acquisition limited to the genius few. Rather, it consists of integrations of abstract idea with abstract idea, self with other, as in brainstorming, and cognition and emotions. Therefore, it applies to daily life when we are called to think in more than minimal abstract terms, such as in writing good work manuals in a group.

## Pain and Therapy

Not all system changes that involve gravitation toward increased complexity are adaptive in the sense of reflecting increased psychological integration. I have shown how pain can be considered to pass through five stages equivalent to those of the present model as it becomes chronic and entrenched. Moreover, its origins might include developmental phenomena linked to the present five-stage model (Young, 2008; Young & Chapman, 2006, 2007; see Tables 31.3 and 31.4).

**Table 31.3** Parallel five-step models of stages of change in therapy and in chronic pain

| Stages of change in therapy | Stages of change in chronic pain |
|---|---|
| Contemplation | Coordination |
| Preparation | Hierarchization |
| Action | Systematization |
| Maintenance | Multiplication |
| Resolution | Integration |

*Note*. The stage model of therapy is presented in Prochaska et al. (1994) and Maddox (1995) Adapted from Young (2008)

The next two tables are more directly applied. They derive from my work with psychological injury (pain, posttraumatic stress disorder, traumatic brain injury) (Young, Kane, & Nicholson, 2006, 2007). In the first of the two tables, the steps that patients might go through as they develop chronic pain are provided. The five steps in this model are consistent with the five developmental stages of the present model (e.g., Young, 2008). The model is a generic one that is applicable to any system undergoing change, and the change can be progressive or regressive

The other table lists the types of threats to validity in assessing pain and related conditions, and how they might reflect developmental origins in their turn. In general, clinicians working in this area adhere to the biopsychosocial model. In Fig. 35.2, I show how these factors interact in the development of pain. In this area, one also needs to consider forensic factors, as per Fig. 35.3, which presents a combined biopsychosocial-forensic model. In Tables 35.3–35.5, I show how factors related to the three components of the biopsychosocial model interact in development of somatization

(a) For pain patients in therapy, the model suggests that, first, they show a readiness for change by coordinating their understanding of their present condition with an understanding of how much they can improve
(b) Then, the patients hierarchically organize as primary a will to effect change
(c) Next, they engage in deliberate action in order to change, such as participating more effectively in psychotherapy, so that a systematized application is evident in their behavior
(d) Next, they expand their motivated attitude and newly acquired habits into other aspects of their life
(e) Finally, in the last stage of integration, they attain an increasingly healthier lifestyle freer of pain

However, pain patients can sink increasingly toward a chronic state, and this process could be modeled by the same five stages of the present model

(a) In the coordination stage of chronic pain development, the negative effects of acute pain are coordinated with the patient's ongoing lifestyle
(b) In the hierarchization stage that develops next, their chronic pain becomes pervasive, and is the primary organizer relative to their prior lifestyle
(c) In the next stage, the patients develop a persistent chronic pain lifestyle, in that it systematizes.
(d) Next, chronic pain patients have the pain lifestyle gradually spread throughout all aspects of their lives
(e) Finally, for these patients, the pain has become deeply entrenched, resistant to treatment, and characterizes their personal identity

Depending on the direction taken, pain patients can gravitate to set points in which pain predominates or in which participation in therapy can help

(a) Young (1997) showed the parallel between the Prochaska et al. stage model of change and the present model of stages in change. Specifically, in terms of their stage of contemplating change, the individual can be considered to be *coordinating* the phases involving present condition and future possibility.
(b) In their next step of preparing/deciding/determining in transitions in therapy, the individual can be considered to be *hierarchically* organizing commitment and planning as primary in working toward goals.

**Table 31.4** Threats to validity of diagnosis of psychological injury: developmental origins

| Developmental level | Symptoms magnified/ intrapersonal conflict | Personality dimension and potential impairment |
|---|---|---|
| Physical | Illness behavior | Extraversion/agency |
| | Fear of pain | Action impairments |
| Emotional | Dependency | Stability/neuroticism |
| | Cry for help | Social impairments |
| Cognitive | Catastrophizing | Conscientiousness/constraint |
| | Call for attention | Cognitive impairments |
| Consciousness | Not taking responsibility | Agreeableness/affiliation |
| | Blaming anyone/anything | Neuroticism/relational impairments |
| Spiritual | Withdrawal | Openness/intellectual curiosity |
| | Isolation | Existential impairments |

Adapted from Young, G. (2008) [Table 2, Page. 250]

The table shows how psychological symptoms elicited by past or present stresses manifest themselves according to the five steps in development described in the present model. When underlying intrapersonal conflicts and tensions are left unresolved or in disarray, whether they are internally generated, externally generated, or a product of both, they might serve as a psychological base on which stresses can act. In all such cases, psychological symptoms could develop; or, if they are already present, they can be magnified. When the challenges, crises, dangers, issues, or problems associated with any new developmental level prove too difficult to deal with or negotiate, an individual might become focused on difficulties related to the particular level, thereby leading to the expression of psychological distress related to the negative pole involved in the level. Often, because of the earlier origins of these types of psychological difficulties, in addition to their long-term standing and inability or major difficulty in dealing with them, they are not openly acknowledged and are even repressed by unconscious processes. However, despite this latter process, they might displace, leak out, or otherwise manifest and disrupt ongoing psychological adaptation and integration

Given that in the present model I describe five stages in development, I suggest that there are five major types of negativity of over-focus or displaced psychological distress that one can experience (see Young, 1997; Young & Chapman, 2007). As mentioned, because this maladaptive process has developmental roots, typically, it is deeply ingrained. It forms the basis of symptom exacerbatory processes, leading to symptom exaggeration taking place unconsciously, out of awareness at the intrapersonal level, or deeply within the person's psyche. Not only might repressed-displacement cascades happen due to a history of developmental stresses, they might also happen when ongoing stresses are strong enough to bring out previously controlled developmental vulnerabilities or issues

Based on the present model, the table shows that the specific forms of unconscious, or intrapersonal, conflicts that might be expressed proceed from the physical to the emotional to the cognitive levels. Also, the model indicates that there should be three cognitive steps in the latter, thereby yielding a five-step sequence

(a) When an individual expresses psychological distress associated with an underlying unresolved intrapersonal tension related to the first stage of development, that of the neonatal (reflexive) period, the likely result is that magnification of physical symptoms occurs. The individual becomes physically over-focused, and, for example, might experience overreactions to pain, such as fearing it and engaging in illness behavior, which results in physical deconditioning. These factors could serve to increase somatization, sensitization, vicious circles in pain experience, and so on

(b) In the next level of intrapersonal conflict related to developmental crises and distress, which is associated with the infant period of sensorimotor intelligence, the magnified symptoms are likely emotional in nature, which is consistent with the infant's emotional nature. For example, the individual expresses a cry for help, and feels overwhelmed. The individual might become quite dependent

(continued)

**Table 31.4** (continued)

(c) In the third level, in parallel with the developing cognitive skills of the child, the intrapersonal conflict takes the form of cognitive dissonances, as in the case of a call for attention for one's plight. At its extreme, the cognitive style involves catastrophizing, or thinking the worst

(d) Next, in the fourth developmental stage of intrapersonal conflict and psychological symptom over-focusing, the individual experiences issues with identity, such as happens with teenagers. Behaviors are adopted that lead to avoidance of or rejection of responsibility, and this includes the blaming of everybody else for one's plight. One finds a superficial presentation of clear reasoning, but analysis reveals that it evidences unconscious, interfering components

(e) Finally, in the last developmental stage, the issues that manifest when there are intrapsychic conflicts are more existential ones. The individual feels overwhelmed by an unjust world, expresses spiritual doubt, and so on. The response of individuals is to withdraw socially, express isolation behavior, or retreat from action

Note that unconscious conflicts are not limited to one type or the other, but come in various combinations, depending on developmental history and circumstance. Nevertheless, one type might predominate. However, when predominant relative to other conflicts, the earlier problems reflect greater difficulties and, more likely, are more deeply ingrained and more difficult to accommodate

(c) In their stage of deliberate action, *systematization* can be considered to characterize organization, given that deliberate action implies a systemic plan out into action.
(d) Next, their maintenance phase reflects the spreading out or propagation of gains that have been made into wider regions of the system, similar to what I would call *multiplication*.
(e) Finally, their step of problem resolution indicates that the system is in dynamic *integration*, as the present model would predict.

It is noteworthy that Prochaska et al. referred to their model as trans-theoretical in nature (Prochaska et al., 2008). This reflects their belief that change processes are common to the workings of any therapeutic approach. In the same manner, the present model is a generic model of stages of change that can be applied across multiple fields of study and domains of application.

## *Psychological Injury and Law*

To show its generality, I apply the five-step generic model of change (coordination, hierarchization, systematization, multiplication, integration) to the discipline of forensic psychology, in general, and to one of its areas in which I am heavily involved, psychological injury and law, in particular.

In terms of the generic model of stages of change, it appears that in the first step of the development of the field of forensic psychology, the fields of law and psychology began to coordinate. However, it took time for psychology to find its voice, because the law conceived of psychology as subordinate to its goals, and psychologists generally internalized this status (hierarchization). Once forensic psychology found its feet, and developed as a somewhat separate entity (systematization), it could begin to spread its wings (multiplication). It tackled multiple areas with increasing methodological rigor and theoretical sophistication.

One of these areas concerned the area of psychological injury and law. In the years 2006–2010, the area established its own society (ASAPIL, Association for Scientific Advancement of Psychological Injury and Law, www.asapil.org; its own journal, *Psychological Injury and Law*, springer.com; and held its first annual meeting, in Toronto, Ontario in August, 2009). As the society and journal mature, the area of psychological injury and law will become an integrated one. It is developing theoretical models that distinguish it as a field, and it is developing tests that can help in its assessments (e.g., the FBS; Ben-Porath, Greve, Bianchini, & Kaufmann, 2009). At the same time, an adversarial divide animates the area (e.g., tort vs. defense experts in evidence presented to court). This is illustrated by the heated debate on the validity of the FBS instrument just mentioned (Butcher, Gass, Cumella, Kally, & Williams, 2008), and the ongoing debate in the journal PIL between the two mentioned sets of authors. The field will reflect better integration in its practice when the science in the field advances sufficiently to mediate the contentious issues that characterize it. The field is still in the multiplication phase in terms of the present model, seeking integrations to help it evolve.

## Summary and Conclusions

To summarize, the developmental model presented in this work elaborates a lifespan, five stage × five substage model of Neo-Piagetian development (Young, 1997). This is the only Neo-Piagetian theory that describes substages that cover the lifespan within a stage framework. Further, I show that there are equivalent five-step change models outside of child psychology, and even outside of psychology and the study of living systems. As far as is known, other models do not have the same range of parallels.

## References

Anderson, P. (1999). Complexity theory and organization science. *Organization Science, 10*, 216–232.

Bandura, A. (1986). *Social foundations of thought and action: A social cognitive theory*. Englewood Cliffs: Prentice-Hall.

Bandura, A. (1989). Human agency in social cognitive theory. *American Psychologist, 44*, 1175–1184.

Bandura, A., Caprara, G. V., Barbaranelli, C., Gerbino, M., & Pastorelli, C. (2003). Role of affective self-regulatory efficacy in diverse spheres of psychosocial functioning. *Child Development, 74*, 769–782.

Ben-Porath, Y. S., Greve, K. W., Bianchini, K. J., & Kaufmann, P. M. (2009). The MMPI-2 symptom validity scale (FBS) is an empirically-validated measure of over-reporting in personal injury litigants and claimants: Reply to Butcher et al. (2008). *Psychological Injury and Law, 2*, 62–85.

Boyatzis, R. E. (2008). Leadership development from a complexity perspective. *Consulting Psychology Journal: Practice and Research, 60*, 298–313.

Bronfenbrenner, U., & Morris, P. A. (2006). The bioecological model of human development. In W. Damon & R. M. Lerner (Eds.), *Handbook of child psychology: Vol. 1. Theoretical models of human development* (6th ed., pp. 793–828). Hoboken: Wiley.

Bruner, J. (1966). *Toward a theory of instruction*. Cambridge: Harvard University Press.

Butcher, J. N., Gass, C. S., Cumella, E., Kally, Z., & Williams, C. L. (2008). Potential for bias in MMPI-2 assessments using the fake bad scale (FBS). *Psychological Injury and Law, 1*, 191–209.

Cairns, R. B., & Cairns, B. D. (2006). The making of developmental psychology. In W. Damon & R. M. Lerner (Eds.), *Handbook of child psychology: Vol. 1. Theoretical models of human development* (pp. 89–165). New York: Wiley.

Chen, Y., & Fang, M. Q. (2008). A five-stage model for the evolvement of complex system, apocalypse and prospect from research on emergence. *Xitong Gongcheng Lilun Yu Shijian/System Engineering Theory and Practice, 28*, 40–44.

Chiles, T., Meyer, A., & Hench, T. (2004). Organizational emergence: The origin and transformation of Branson, Missouri's musical theaters. *Organization Science, 15*, 499–519.

Damon, W., & Lerner, R. M. (2006). *Handbook of child psychology: Vol. 1. Theoretical models of human development.*. New York: Wiley.

Goldstein, J. (2007). A new model for emergence and its leadership implications. In J. Hazy, J. Goldstein, & B. Lichtenstein (Eds.), *Complex systems leadership theory* (pp. 61–92). Boston: ISCE Press.

James, W. (1890). *The principles of psychology* (Vols. 1 and 2). New York: Holt.

Krugman, P. (1996). *The self-organizing economy*. Cambridge: Bradford Books.

Kuhn, T. S. (1965). *The structure of scientific revolutions*. Chicago: Chicago University Press.

Lichtenstein, B. (2007). A matrix of complexity for leadership. In J. Hazy, J. Goldstein, & B. Lichtenstein (Eds.), *Complex systems leadership theory* (pp. 285–304). Boston: ISCE Press.

Lichtenstein, B., Dooley, K., & Lumpkin, T. (2006). Measuring emergence in dynamics of new venture creation. *Journal of Business Venturing, 21*, 153–175.

Lichtenstein, B., & Plowman, D. A. (2009). The leadership of emergence: A complex systems leadership theory of emergence at successive organizational levels. *The Leadership Quarterly, 20*, 617–630.

Maddox, J. E. (1995). Yes, people can change, but can psychotherapists? *Contemporary Psychology, 40*, 1047–1048.

Maryuyama, M. (1963). The second cybernetics: Deviation-amplifying, mutual causal processes. *American Scientist, 51*, 164–179.

McKelvey, B. (2004a). Toward a complexity science of entrepreneurship. *Journal of Business Venturing, 19*, 313–342.

McKelvey, B. (2004b). Toward a 0th law of thermodynamics: Order-creation complexity dynamics from physics & biology to bieconomics. *Journal of Bioeconomics, 6*, 65–96.

Meyer, A. D., Gaba, V., & Colwell, K. A. (2005). Organizing far from equilibrium: Nonlinear change in organizational fields. *Organization Science, 16*, 456–473.

Nowak, M. A., Tarnita, C. E., & Wilson, E. O. (2010). The evolution of eusociality, *Nature, 466*, 1057–1062.

Paxton, R. O. (1998). The five stages of fascism. *The Journal of Modern History, 70*, 1–23.

Piaget, J., & Garcia, R. (1989). *Psychogenesis and the history of science*. New York: Columbia University Press.

Prigogine, I., & Stengers, I. (1984). *Order out of chaos: Man's new dialogue with nature*. New York: Bantam.

Prochaska, J. O., Norcross, J. C., & DiClemente, C. C. (1994). *Changing for good: The revolutionary program that explains the six stages of change and teaches you how to free yourself from bad habits*. New York: Morrow.

Prochaska, J. O., Wright, J. A., & Velicer, W. F. (2008). Evaluating theories of health behavior change: A hierarchy of criteria applied to the transtheoretical model. *Applied Psychology: An International Review, 57*, 561–588.

Rostow, W. W. (1990). *The stages of economic growth: A non-communist manifesto*. New York: Cambridge University Press.

Sabelli, H. (2005). *Bios: A study of creation*. Singapore: World Scientific.

Salthe, S. N. (1993). *Development and evolution: Complexity and change in biology*. Cambridge: MIT Press.

Salthe, S. N. (2007). The natural philosophy of work. *Entropy, 9*, 83–99.

Sastry, A. (1997). Problems and paradoxes in a model of punctuated organizational change. *Administrative Science Quarterly, 42*, 237–275.

Sharpless, B. A., & Barber, J. P. (2009). A conceptual and empirical review of the meaning, measurement, development, and teaching of intervention competence in clinical psychology. *Clinical Psychology Review, 29*, 47–56.

Siegler, R. S., Deloache, J., & Eisenberg, N. (2010). *How children develop* (3rd ed.). New York: Worth.

Smith, L. B., & Thelen, E. (1993). *A dynamic systems approach to development: Applications*. Cambridge: The MIT Press/Bradford Books.

Young, G. (1997). *Adult development, therapy, and culture: A postmodern synthesis*. New York: Plenum.

Young, G. (2008). Psychological injury: Systems, change processes, development. *Psychological Injury and Law, 1*, 243–254.

Young, G., & Chapman, C. R. (2006). Chronic pain and affect as a nonlinear dynamical system. In G. Young, A. W. Kane, & K. Nicholson (Eds.), *Psychological knowledge in court: PTSD, pain, and TBI* (pp. 181–192). New York: Springer Science+Business Media.

Young, G., & Chapman, C. R. (2007). Pain, affect, nonlinear dynamical systems, and chronic pain: Bringing order to disorder. In G. Young, A. W. Kane, & K. Nicholson, *Causality of psychological injury: Presenting evidence in court* (pp. 197–241). New York: Springer Science+Business Media.

Young, G., Kane, A. W., & Nicholson, K. (Eds.). (2006). *Psychological knowledge in court: PTSD, pain, and TBI*. New York: Springer Science+Business Media.

Young, G., Kane, A. W., & Nicholson, K. (2007). *Causality of psychological injury: Presenting evidence in court*. New York: Springer Science+Business Media.

Zadek, S. (2004). The path to corporate responsibility. *Harvard Business Review, 82*, 125–132.

# Chapter 32
# Collective Intelligence and Multilevel Selection

## Introduction

Multilevel selection concerns the evolutionary influence of group relative to individual adaptive pressures. It is being applied increasingly to human behavior, from development to economic dynamics. In the present chapter, I expand multilevel selection to five levels – (a) natural selection or individual fitness, (b) kin selection, (c) Group-for-Individual selection, (d) reciprocal altruism or selection, and (e) group (Individual-for-Group) selection. I speculate that the five levels of multilevel selection could have worked in concert to have helped evolve the five proposed Neo-Piagetian stages in human cognitive development – (a) reflexive, (b) sensorimotor, (c) perioperational (representational; preoperational and concrete operational), (d) abstract (formal), and (e) collective intelligence (postformal). The latter adult stage includes cognitive activities such as brainstorming at work, illustrating the adaptive advantages of behavioral products of group selection processes in human evolution.

Darwinian natural selection, or individual-level fitness, has been supplemented by other proposed evolutionary mechanisms in evolutionary biology. Group selection involves adaptations on a larger scale that are not adaptive or fit locally or relatively within a group. That is, they have not been differentially selected by natural selection or individual fitness pressures but by the group selection level (Wilson, 2009). Wilson added that empirically, in evolutionary study, there needs to be appropriate fitness comparisons, for example, of how competition among groups can lead to the most adaptive or fit group in terms of expressing the adaptation under study. Group selection can enable better survival and reproduction even to the point of marking the species under investigation. Wilson concluded that, "[H]uman social systems arise by a complicated mix of guided mechanisms (that themselves require an evolutionary explanation) and ongoing raw variation and selection" (p. 189).

Group selection had been denigrated in biology but has been regaining its rightful place and is considered an important and widespread evolutionary pressure underlying behavior even in the early evolution of life. However, it is just beginning to be applied with effectiveness to human behavior and human evolution.

G. Young, *Development and Causality: Neo-Piagetian Perspectives*,
DOI 10.1007/978-1-4419-9422-6_32, © Springer Science+Business Media, LLC 2011

# Evolution

## *Multilevel Selection and Psychological Acquisitions*

In this section, I review some basic concepts in evolutionary psychology, group selection, and their applications to psychology. This section is more like an introduction for psychologists, introducing the topic and some recent research, rather than a broad or in-depth survey for biologists.

Wilson, Van Vugt, and O'Gorman (2008) have applied multilevel selection to various psychological acquisitions and evolutionary transitions. The concept of group selection constitutes a process of higher-level selection in multilevel selection theory. Selection pressures are still at work in groups, but the unit is considered the group rather than the individual. For example, if a total population is characterized with groups of varying altruistic tendencies, everything else being equal, the most altruistic groups will contribute more to the total gene pool. In this example, there is between-group selection rather than within-group selection; however, it is rare that between-group selection is sufficiently strong enough to counteract within-group selection. That is, in effective group selection, the conditions need to be exactly right in terms of group dynamics, containment of possible defectors taking advantage of the adaptation through naturally selected "selfish" adaptations (Dawkins, 1976), etc.

When higher-level group selection becomes the more powerful evolutionary force, Wilson et al. (2008) argued that major evolutionary transition are facilitated and can take place so that in essence the group functions as a new, higher-level organism. The corollary of this argument is that the members of the group function like organs of a "superorganism." Nevertheless, individuals still compete within groups that function like superorganisms, due to within-group natural selection processes. However, between-group selection and the consequent social organization selected dominate.

Wilson et al. (2008) provided another example related to "group cognition," which is based on social interactions. Each individual's particular contributions in "group cognition" are limited relative to the outcome produced by the group. Cognitive cooperation helps the group solve problems that exceed the problem-solving capacity of any one individual. Wilson et al. also argued that humans have evolved social mechanisms for allowing group thinking to proceed even if leaders are involved.

In this regard, Goldstone, Roberts, and Gureckis (2008) have described how individuals organize themselves spontaneously into groups that develop emergent characteristics that members of the group might not have intended and do not necessarily comprehend, or even perceive. Innovations diffuse through the group, and the mechanisms involved are found to balance exploration and exploitation. Using computer-generated representations to study propagation of innovations in network groups, the authors found that collaborative and shared solutions within a group improved cognitive-related efficiency.

## *Multilevel Selection and Evolution*

### Group Selection

*Model.* D. S. Wilson and E. O. Wilson (2007) have provided a detailed explanation of multilevel selection theory. Group selection is defined in terms of the evolution of traits based on the differential survival and reproduction of groups having the traits. They argued that group selection has evolved as a concept and it should not be equated with extreme self-sacrifice to the benefit of the group and to the detriment of the individual with the group-selected trait. Rather, it would seem that group selection would have led to traits that favor social coordinating mechanisms beneficial to the group, yet they still would possess potential benefit to the individual members of the group. In their example, if there is a child burning in a house, it does not mean that a nonrelative will always rush in to save the child and endanger his or her life. Instead, group selection would have evolved social coordinating mechanisms and behaviors, such as organizing a fire department, paying for it, passing legislation on fire safety, enforcing the legislation, and so on. Group advantageous traits will favor group survival and reproduction, but not necessarily function disadvantageously for individuals within the group.

*Comment.* The example provided indicates that group selection could lead to traits in the individuals comprising a group that increase, on average, the survival and reproduction of each of its members. The example involves the socials coordination measure of fire safety. Another example that I consider important for this chapter is education for children. Group selection could have favored organizing an educational/instructive/teaching system, finding the resources to support it, passing legislation on teacher education, curriculum, etc., enforcing the legislation, and so on. This group advantageous trait would favor group survival and reproduction, and would function advantageously for individuals within the group, as well.

### Kin Selection and Reciprocity

There are other explanations of group-oriented traits in individuals that have been proposed. Critics of the concept have argued that proposed evolutionary mechanisms other than group selection could explain the apparent group-focus of certain behaviors that on the surface appear to be the outcome of group fitness selection mechanisms. For example, behaviors that are socially oriented, such as altruism, can be understood as a form of self-interest because, even if they do not help individuals to survive and produce, most often, they help relatives of the organisms exhibiting the traits to survive and reproduce. This type of thinking has led to the model of the evolutionary mechanism of kin selection (Hamilton, 1964). Although the unit of selection is not the individual, it still concerns the individual by way of the shared genes with kin.

Another way that other-oriented behaviors could be understood as products of selection that is individually oriented rather than group-oriented has been through the concept of reciprocity (Trivers, 1971). For example, in reciprocal altruism or selection, individuals express altruistic behavior to nonkin in the expectation of a comparable benefit. On the surface, it seems that there is a lack of self-interest underlying the reciprocal behavior, but careful examination reveals that the trait still serves the individual and still can be redescribed as explained by individual advantage. These types of explanation of individual-oriented traits have led Dawkins (1976) to refer to evolution in terms of the "selfish" gene. Other labels for kin selection involve inclusive fitness, and for reciprocal altruism or selection together, the label of evolutionary game theory has been used.

## Comment

Wilson and Wilson (2007) specified that these different models of evolution that do not involve groups (kin selection, reciprocal altruism) come in variations, complicating their application and interpretation. Moreover, the models can be translated or redescribed from one to the other and are not really antithetical to the model of group selection or the multilevel model of selection. Where a given trait evolves in a population, in order to determine the selection levels involved, a nested series of relative fitness comparisons needs to be undertaken. These include comparisons between genes within individuals, between individuals within groups, between groups within a population of groups, and so on. One needs to evaluate to what degree have the multiple selection processes led to traits that have been separately targeted for selection at each of the selection levels involved.

To illustrate the complexity of the evolutionary process and the central role that group selection has had from the earliest beginnings of life, Wilson and Wilson argued that even for cells and single-celled organisms, as well as individual organisms, the evolutionary steps that took place reflect group selection pressures and accommodations. Moreover, for the evolution of eusociality in social insects and other species, the unit of selection appears to be the colony or group, and explanations of this evolution in terms of kin selection are not sufficient to explain the data.

In the case of human evolution, our ancestors evolved the capacity to monitor others so that individuals could not dominate the group, in what has been called a "guarded egalitarianism." Humans have a "groupish" nature, and it is aided by "cultural group selection," wherein "cultural mutations" can propagate quickly in a group and provide a competitive advantage in between-group competition (or, as they write, "altruistic groups beat selfish groups" (p. 345). Also see Richerson & Boyd, 2005). This culturally driven process of group selection does not deny the presence of within-group individual selection, according to the multilevel selection model.

Social reciprocity, by definition, requires sophisticated cognitive skills, such as keeping tabs of favors granted to others, reminding oneself of expectations, developing a theory of mind and understanding of the thinking of the other, and having the capacity to deter cheating (van den Bergh & Gowdy, 2009). In this regard, it has been argued that the evolution of cognitive capacities that can facilitate these cognitive tasks has allowed the emergence of these advanced cooperative and social functions in human evolution. However, Wilson and Wilson (2007) have suggested that the social skills underlying the reciprocal behavior have evolved, first, in order to allow the necessary trust in social partnership to take place for the group processes to proceed. Therefore, they argued that there is a balance between levels of selection.

Finally, Wilson and Wilson maintained that it is important to examine all the component vectors of the final vector that underlie the average effects in population evolution of behavior. What are the targets of selection at each biological level? Also, where group selection seems to apply as opposed to individual selection, this does not deny that the final vector at play does not include individually selected components to the vector, at least in the environmental and social contexts in which evolution had taken place. The authors appear to be arguing that evolutionary processes are multimodal and work in concert in the evolution of complex cognitive and social systems.

## Human Applications

### *Multilevel Selection and Bioeconomic Organization*

*Landa.* Landa (2008, 2009) and van den Bergh and Gowdy (2009) have spearheaded recent application of multilevel selection to human bioeconomic organization. Landa (2008, 2009) interpreted her case example of homogeneous middlemen groups in Chinese trader's choice of trading partners as compatible with multilevel selection. In appropriating the roles of middlemen, more cooperative middleman groups better compete compared to less cooperative ones. They function as adaptive units that, although not considered superorganisms, conduct their work based on mutual trust and exchanges.

*Van den Bergh and Gowdy.* Van den Bergh and Gowdy (2009) examined the role of group dynamics in economics. They argued that economic theories are focused on the individual and that the theories reflect upward causation when explaining economic activity. However, the authors argued that both group processes and downward causation are equally important for understanding economic behavior, organizations, and institutions. The authors listed eight mechanisms of group selection, including population structure/dynamics and group coherence. They contrasted cultural group selection, which according to them is nongenetic and can happen quickly, and evolutionary group selection, and go on to discuss gene–culture coevolution. They distinguished between kin, reciprocal, and cultural group selection in the following way: "kin selection is relevant to family groups, reciprocity to medium sized groups where everyone knows each other, and cultural group selection comes into play in larger groups" (p. 17).

The authors concluded with recommendations fitting cultural group selection for economic activity, for example, about the selection of organizational routines, the selection of institutions and organizational structures, and rationality and markets. It should be noted that the traditional manner of approaching cultural selection in the evolutionary approach is to exclude sociocultural activities that are more loosely organized, develop quickly, and are transient, given the likely absence of particular evolutionary pressures on target behaviors.

*Comment.* Two implications derive from the work on human group behavior in the economic context from an evolutionary point of view. Together, these points present to the model described in this chapter on gene co-opting.

(a) It is noted that the social cooperatives described in the work of Landa on middlemen do offer their members collective and therefore individual advantage. This fits the present argument that where one finds the workings of group selection in evolution, it might not exclude simultaneous individual adaptive advantage.
(b) As for the work of Van den Bergh and Gowdy, it is noted that the different evolutionary mechanisms appear to have an increasing range of target numbers from the individual to the group, with kin selection and reciprocity oriented to smaller numbers than the group. This fits the present argument that different selection pressures might apply successively in evolution in a way to include increasingly others in the network of social processes.

Together, the two points to notice implicate a model of evolution of sociality in which humans increasingly co-opt others in the service of individual survival and reproductive advantage by way of new social skills that have evolved (and develop). These successively emerging skills in development have been selected by successively applied, different evolutionary pressures, which range from individual to group selection.

## Evolutionary Dynamic Model of Cooperation

*Model.* Nowak (2006) presented a mathematical model of how groups cohere, and it included group selection. New levels of organization emerge through cooperation, from genomes and cells to social organisms and human societies. In cooperation, replicators that normally act selfishly place themselves at risk for sacrificing a portion if not all of their reproductive potential for purposes of helping other members of the group. Cooperation is not promoted by strict natural or individual-level selection, unless other evolutionary mechanisms are in place. Nowak presented five mechanisms that can accomplish the task. These include kin selection, direct reciprocity, indirect reciprocity, network reciprocity, and group selection. For each mechanism, the model identifies a specific rule that conditions whether cooperation can evolve from natural selection.

Cooperators pay a cost (presumably energetic, survival-related, and ultimately reproductive) through the benefits offered others. However, a member of a group that defects from the group activity experiences no cost because benefits are not dealt out. In typical circumstances, natural selection favors defectors. However, Hamilton (1964) argued that natural selection could function to promote the evolution cooperation when genetic relatives are the focus of the altruistic actor. In this kin selection or inclusive fitness, the phenotypic behavior extends to genetically related phenotypes and, despite the altruistic self-sacrifice, it can be considered the product of "selfish *genes*" (Dawkins, 1976).

In order to explain cooperation among nonrelatives, Trivers (1971) proposed the mechanism of direct reciprocity or reciprocal altruism. In this mechanism, it pays to cooperate because bestowing a benefit to another member of the group could lead later to a return favor or act of cooperation. Nowak explained the mechanism in terms of game theory, for example, that there is a "win-stay, lose-shift" strategy instead of a tit-for-tat strategy, with its retaliation against defectors. In this evolutionary mechanism, by definition, the advantages gained or given reproductively do not concern kin, but the individual phenotype and its selfish *genes*.

For Nowak, indirect reciprocity can help explain why humans help strangers, behave altruistically without the possibility of direct reciprocity, or donate to charities when there is no immediate benefit to self or kin. The behaviors establish a good "reputation" and this leads to "rewards" by others. They require "substantial" cognitive capacities, for example, to monitor the complexities of dynamic group activities and also the reputations of group members. The unstated foundation is that altruistic actions are promoted evolutionarily through individual or selfish mechanisms rather than kin fitness.

In Nowak's model, in network reciprocity, cooperators can dominate defectors, or become evolutionarily stable, by forming network clusters, where the members help each other. In terms of dynamic models and benefit to cost ratios, the basin of attraction is at least one half toward cooperators. This model reminds of Landa's work on Chinese middlemen.

In group selection, a group of cooperators are more adaptive than a group of defectors, as explained above in presenting the multilevel selection model. Group selection, like the other rules for the evolution of cooperation presented by Nowak, can be described by a characteristic 2×2 payoff matrix (see Nowak's Table 1, p. 1562). For cooperation to take place effectively, defectors must be punished or retaliated against for transgressions or free loading. Nevertheless, along with natural selection and genetic mutation, Nowak considered "natural cooperation" as a fundamental principle of evolution. Presumably, for this concept of natural cooperation, he is referring to the coordinated effect of the multiple rules in evolution that govern the selection of cooperative behavior and protection against defectors.

*Comment.* In addition to its mathematical basis, Nowak's model is noteworthy for including natural selection, kin selection, reciprocal altruism, and group selection into one evolutionary model. In addition, it includes network reciprocity. The model underscores the individual genetic fitness deriving from kin selection and reciprocal altruism (direct reciprocity), as well as in network reciprocity, but does not do the same for group selection. Nevertheless, as has been mentioned above, group selection can indeed be redescribed to include individual reproductive advantages despite the self-sacrifice involved.

## Cultural Evolutionary Theory

*Model.* Mesoudi (2009) examined the relationship between cultural evolution and evolutionary mechanisms, such as group selection. He viewed the variations, competitions, and inheritance evident in human culture from the lens of cultural evolutionary theory and Darwinian processes. Microevolutionary cultural processes, such as mechanisms behind conformity, are responsible for particular patterns in social and cultural change. Culture is defined in terms of information acquired via social transmission modes, such as teaching and imitation.

According to Mesoudi, the research in the field of social psychology indicate that humans exhibit a "powerful" tendency to help group members, and the evolutionary mechanisms of kin selection and reciprocal altruism are incapable of explaining the cooperation. The cultural group selection model attempts to explain the behavior through the survival and reproductive advantage in recent human evolutionary history that is accorded by "strong" prosocial norms that encourage cooperation in the context of between-group competition (Richerson & Boyd, 2005). In the model, groups that cohere through cultural group selection are considered less vulnerable than groups that might have evolved through nongroup selection mechanisms. This obtains because cultural processes, such as conformity and punishment of norm violators, control potential free riders in the existing group and serve to integrate new immigrants, curtailing that they could act as free riders.

Mesoudi (2009) explained further that classic evolutionary theory dismisses any role for cultural evolution in understanding group behavior, and that in the standard view standard evolutionary concepts, such as in natural selection and reciprocal altruism, can explain cooperation. In this regard, cooperation and in-group favoritism are postulated to have evolved when our hominid ancestors lived in small groups where most members, if not all, were genetic relatives so that the evolution of a general helping disposition was adaptive.

However, Richerson and Boyd's (2005) review of both the paleontological and ethnographic data indicated that such ancestral groups were too large, for example, for this explanation to have any validity. They concluded that cultural group selection could be part of the evolutionary process that has led to rapid evolutionary changes in social norms.

A second objection to the concept of cultural evolution is that, unlike the case for genetics, culture does not parse itself into discrete units of transmission (units termed "memes," after Dawkins, 1982). However, even if ideas and beliefs could be fuzzy without definitive boundaries, they still can be passed on through cultural transmission in nonparticulate form and, moreover, at any rate, the brain does not store discrete replicators in this area.

Finally, for Mesoudi (2009), the theory of gene–culture coevolution (dual inheritance theory) examines how cultures and genes interact in human evolution (e.g., a cultural innovation leads to niche construction and can lead the spread of genetic adaptations underlying the cultural innovation (see Weber and Depew, 2003, on a related concept, the Baldwin effect)). Cultural variation has evolved through this coconstructing evolutionary mechanism, and it is not simply the product of different cultural pressures acting on standard genetically-underpinned universal programs that vary in different environments.

*Comment.* Kurzban and Aktipis (2007) pointed out that individual and group selection could have interacting contributions to the evolution of behavior. For example, with respect to cognition, in the environment of evolutionary adaptiveness (EEA) in which hominids evolved, greater benefits relative to costs for certain adaptations could have been evident both at the individual and group levels. As mentioned, the behavior of donating to charities appears to be derived from reputational gains that enhance individual survival and reproduction, despite its apparent group target. This line of argumentation is consistent with the present one that multiple selection processes can work in concert and that their products can be expressed together. Moreover, the combined modeling could produce behavior that maintains individual selective advantages despite their group nature.

Finally, Mesoudi (2009) aptly pointed out that gene–culture coevolution (dual inheritance theory) could be involved in selecting group behavior as much as separate individual and group processes. Moreover, the model implies that there are behaviors that would not evolve without the interaction of the two forces. Moreover, the output of their interaction could be powerful in action because of their dual basis, and the cultural component could have them spiral rapidly to increasing efficacy and range, beyond what could happen by individual or group selection alone

In the following, I present a model where multiple selection pressures can be seen to co-exist in the present model of cognitive development, consistent with the concept presented by Kurzban and Aktipis. In addition, it does not deny a role for cultural-genetic coevolution.

## Evolution of Multilevel Selection

### *Introduction*

At present, the multilevel selection model examines the three levels of gene, individual, and group and considers that the kin and reciprocal models as alternative models that can be readily translated or understood in terms of the others. However,

I present a model that accommodates all these five types of evolutionary pressures into one comprehensive, multimodal model, so it consists of five levels and not three levels.

I show that the present model of five stages in cognitive development can be seen as evolutionary products of these five types of evolutionary pressures, in a one-to-one fashion. Moreover, the parenting behaviors that can optimize development at each of the stages can be understood as products of the five evolutionary mechanisms. In another way of understanding my application of the model, I am applying the concept of component vectors to the sequential evolution of human parental adaptations and their parallel manifestation in offspring cognitive development.

Moreover, not only does the present version of multiple-level selection theory consist of more levels than previously described but also it is posited that they work in concert in selecting traits so that it is difficult to isolate one type of evolutionary pressure on one type of target behavior. Behavior forms integrated systems, which, in order to foster adaptive adjustment in context and environment, need to work together in equilibrium. Selection pressures might seem to be aimed at a particular component of the system, but in altering even one component of a system, the change can act to affect the whole, depending on the type of and degree of stability in the typical equilibrium expressed by the system. Conversely, the whole can dictate the any one isolated change that would otherwise appear beneficial in fitness does not lead to increased survival and reproduction. Therefore, in order to understand the functional dynamics of a behavioral system acting in context and adaptively online, we need to examine its multiple components together and the multiple selection pressures that have been brought to bear on it.

In addition, we need to examine the nature of behavioral system equilibrium, and how the differing components in the system coordinate or otherwise adjust to the tension that might arise from their differential survival and reproductive strategies, given the differing types of evolutionary pressures that have contributed to their evolution. For example, do behavioral targets that have been selected for individual adaptation outside of its effects on the group always remain in conflict with those that have been selected for their group adaptive advantages?

In a second conceptual innovation, which has appeared in the literature, as well, I emphasize the concept that group selection could have individual adaptive advantages. By definition, if an adaptation helps a group to survive better and to reproduce better in intergroup competition, on average, all group members must profit in the evolutionary fitness race. That is, a good strategy in evolutionary terms is to invest in group behavior, such as contributing to the educational system, even though one's offspring are greatly outnumbered by the many genetically unrelated children who profit from it.

(The reader needs to keep in mind that the present chapter examines evolutionary pressures that underlie adaptive behavior at the macro level and does not minimize that they translate into micro processes at the physiological level that govern behavior, or that the environment is heavily involved in phenotypic expression).

## *Cognitive Applications*

### Children

By creating group social structures, opportunities are provided to protect and promote the survival of constituent individuals' offspring, such as in the example provided of establishing an effective fire-prevention and fire-fighting system. More pertinent to the present case, for children, groups or societies that better establish through group action more effective educational systems or other learning opportunities, on average, are creating cultural adaptations that help individual children optimize their cognitive and social development and, therefore, their future survival and reproductive advantage.

This implies that offspring of individuals who are acting according to group-selected traits to foster group social and cultural structures that help the group better compete with other groups, in their turn, need to have concomitant traits that have been selected that allow them to profit optimally from the group-formulated structures. In short, offspring who possess the genetic underpinnings that have been selected to take advantage of group-created structures meant to optimize their development, such as at school in the human case, will develop, survive, and reproduce more effectively. That is, a complement to the notion that groups have evolved traits that help them survive and reproduce is the notion that members of the group have evolved traits that permit them to take advantage of group traits aimed at their survival and reproduction (and in a way that does not take advantage of the group, or in ways that can be monitored by the group if they try to).

In terms of offspring of group members, this is especially important, and in their case, we find an asymmetry in the group traits that have evolved and those behaviors that have been selected to take advantage of those traits. That is, in the human case, for example, children are too young to contribute to group functioning in an adaptive way for the group, yet profit handsomely from its largesse. Normally, it can be argued that, everything else being equal, to allow the group to function coherently, there is a balance in (a) group adaptations that surpass the behavioral tendencies deriving from selection pressures at the individual level, and (b) individual adaptations oriented to survival and reproduction without consideration of group dynamics. However, in the immature or developmental stage, asymmetry obtains in the manner indicated. This is especially important for the behaviors that have evolved to allow them to profit from the educational opportunities offered to them. (These opportunities could be informal as well as formal).

### Adults

The notion that behavioral systems are products of an integrated biological evolutionary vector the components of which should be examined for their concordance with target behaviors of the system points to the value of group thinking or problem solving as an important feedback mechanism to keep the group functioning effectively in its between-group competitions. Psychologically, groups exhibit a constant tension between individualistic and collective tendencies, and those groups that are more adaptive manage better the tension (van den Bergh & Gowdy, 2009).

Group thinking processes might provide the resources to manage better this tension, helping to avoid the conflicts that can arise within groups. Indeed, if properly cultivated and honed, this important cognitive evolutionary adaptation could also help groups avoid the tension between traits that have evolved due to individual selection and due to group selection, in general. That is, group evolutionary advances should include traits aimed at assuring that the competitive advantage of the group can continue indefinitely without sacrificing the survival and reproductive advantage of individuals who contribute to group functioning. By using the skill of thinking collectively in group thought processes, individuals might realize that they could profit from the products of the process, either in the immediate or long term, with respect to resources that facilitate survival and reproduction or in terms of actual survival and reproduction. For example, brainstorming might be a group activity, but it builds on the individual cognitive and creative processes of its members and their ability to integrate their ideas and those of others in the emerging group cognitive structure. Moreover, these group cognitive products could improve the ongoing adaptation of the group and, therefore, ultimately the fitness of its members.

## Comment

As defined, group selection can take place in very specific circumstances where the evolutionary advantages for the group in between-group competition outweigh the disadvantages. Moreover, the group has the social and cognitive capacity to monitor and punish defectors, keeping in line the competing tendency of group members to manifest naturally selected, individually advantageous behavior at the expense of the group. Nevertheless, group selection should not be construed as inimical to concurrent natural or individual selection in that it could involve traits having individually advantageous outcomes.

For example, cultural selection is a coevolutionary process where cultural variants lead to increased survival and reproduction, and underlying genetic underpinnings to the behaviors involved get selected (Richerson & Boyd, 2005). In this regard, evolutionary pressures that bring group fitness advantages seem to drive cultural selection, and it therefore can be considered more selfless than selfish, in Dawkinsian terms. Nevertheless, it still could work together with selection pressures that optimize individual fitness, as in this concept of gene–culture coevolution.

Note that Young (1997) gave distinct labels to the evolutionary selection pressures of group selection and the complementary one of adapting to the product of group selection. The labels given were Individual-for-Group selection and Group-for-Individual selection, respectively.

In this regard, these two evolutionary mechanisms indicate a dual model of group selection. This revised model of group selection involves coordinated

Group-for-Individual and Individual-for-Group selection. They appear to work in concert in the evolution of behavior, especially at the social level. By their very nature, as I conceive them, these selection pressures are aimed advancing individual survival and reproductive benefits as much as group ones. As adults, we express behaviors in groups that optimize survival and reproduction of ourselves and of our offspring. As children, members of our species express behaviors that optimally take advantage of the group efforts aimed at them. In both cases, I hypothesize that the behaviors are underwritten or have been selected for both their group and individual fitness advantages.

About Group-for-Individual selection, the group acts to structure organizational, institutional, and other tools that can foster group evolutionary adaptive advantage, such as constructing school and other educational settings. However, the offspring of the group members, or their kin, can profit from the societal constructions, and so the behavior appears governed by natural selection evolutionary pressures as much as group ones.

About Individual-for-Group selection, it especially concerns the selection of group behavior oriented to possible if not probable individual evolutionary or naturally selected advantage, such as would obtain with helping in construction of societal educational institutions for offspring or with helping in brainstorming at work. In the latter, those who do not cooperate with the group face individual consequences for survival and for reproduction. Defection would serve to reduce the quality of the collective product, thereby reducing the survival and reproductive benefit of defectors or noncooperators. Moreover, the group possesses the monitoring capacity to assure adequate participation by members so that defectors could be excluded next time around, receive poor work evaluations, etc. The argument being made is that, in Individual-for-Group selection, group behavior is facilitated that allows individuals to profit at the level of fitness from the collective effort made. This applies especially well to the cooperativity needed at work. Similarly, I posit that natural selection has favored behaviors that allow children to adapt to and take advantage of group-structured organizations and institutions, such as schools and other learning environments. This feeds into their future efforts to contribute in their turn to Group-for-Individual selected group behavior that increases the fitness of their offspring as well as the group.

## Young's Stage Model of Cognitive Development and Multilevel Selection

### *Review*

To review, in Young (1997) I proposed a Neo-Piagetian model of cognitive development consisting of five stages having five cyclically recurring substages. Piaget had developed a stage model of cognitive development that included four stages: sensorimotor, preoperational, concrete operational, and formal or abstract stages.

The Neo-Piagetian model developed in Young (1990a, 1990b, 1997, 2008) builds on the Piagetian model by splitting off the first substage of the sensorimotor period in his model, calling it a separate stage, combining the next two stages into a stage called perioperational (when Piaget referred to them together, he used the term representational), and adding a separate adult stage after his last one of formal or abstract thought, which emerges in adolescence. It is noteworthy, given the present discussion of group selection and group thinking processes, that I called this fifth stage of cognitive development in adulthood the stage of collective intelligence. Others have developed models of postformal thought (e.g., Labouvie-Vief, 1992; Richards & Commons, 1990), but they have not emphasized the group aspect to the thought.

I have argued that collective intelligence characterizes advanced adult thought, and its attributes suggest that it had been selected in part through group selection processes. At the same time, group selection is part of a multilevel model of selection. In Young (1997), I expanded the multilevel model of selection to include five levels: individual selection, kin selection, Group-for-Individual selection, reciprocal altruism or selection, and Individual-for-Group selection.

## Steps

In the present multilevel selection model, the five types constituting it are posited to have worked in concert in the evolution of the five cognitive stages in human development as described in the present model. In the following, I show how this might have worked in terms of the evolution of the parenting behavior that is associated optimally with each of the five stages of the present model.

In Young (1997), I emphasized how different behavioral strategies involving parental behavior have evolved in correspondence with each of the five cognitive stages. According to my work in Young (1997), they have been selected to promote optimal cognitive development at each stage, for example, their characteristics are in line with the five underlying evolutionary pressures comprising the model, although natural selection is not excluded from any of them.

*Reflexive.* In this regard, for the reflexive level, parenting is especially physical-based, consistent with the characteristics of the newborn at this stage and its needs for physical survival.

*Sensorimotor.* Shortly thereafter, at the sensorimotor level, parenting comes to include emotional nurturing and promotes attachment, consistent with the characteristics and needs of the baby in the first years. I relate this parental behavior to kin selection as much as anything else, because the behaviors in the parent are oriented to creating both family ties and kin cooperativity as the siblings in the family age (e.g., family play, imitation, learning, affection, support, and even care by older siblings of younger ones).

*Perioperational.* In the next stage of cognitive development, in which the child is thinking representationally, the parent acts to promote optimal development by contributing to the child's learning and education. This could refer to setting up informal play groups, facilitating imitation by modeling, informal instruction, arranging expert tutoring, creating institutional learning experiences, contributing to the learning by helping in homework, contributing to or supporting society policies and programs that educate teachers, construct curricula, etc.

In general, humans have been selected to function in groups that create social structures, such as schooling, which serve optimally the groups' offspring. These prestructured learning loci enhance the development of intellectual and knowledge-based skills. Parents participate in these learning environments by way of behaviors that have been selected via group selection as well as other pressures, where cooperativity leads to benefits for the children of the group, including one's own (as per Individual-for-Group selection and natural selection). The children embed easily in the educational structures created for them via behaviors consonant with the Group-for-Individual educational and learning structures that have been selected by complementary selection pressures.

*Abstract.* For the teenage years, in which offspring are expressing abstract thought, parents strive to promote positive peer interactions and habits, social and economic connections, alliance- and pact-promoting skills, and the like, allowing access to resources that help promote survival and reproduction. I relate this stage to the evolutionary pressure of reciprocal altruism (and natural selection), because parents foster social relations with nonkin that appear mutually beneficial.

*Collective Intelligence.* For the young person, parents remain involved and act to bring out the collective intelligence that they had already developed themselves. Collective intelligence concerns the development of superordinate abstract structures, and moreover, the process in their creation often is social. The individual integrates not only abstract ideas but also affective components into them, and the ideas of others. Brainstorming provides the classic example of how individuals both contribute to and profit from the collective thought that emerges beyond the contributions of any one individual in the group. In Young (1997), I referred to symbiotic sharing of ideas that allows not only contribution to the common good but also finding personal advantage and possibly adding to reproductive success. The university environment illustrates how students are developing this skill, and how instructors possess them in their disciplines and educate the critical thought needed to facilitate its acquisition. In the end, the collective intelligence that develops in the adult facilitates wider community integration and humanitarian thought, as well as allowing for replenishment of resources needed for survival and reproduction.

In Young (1997), I concluded that the effects of group selection on parenting should be visible at all levels in parenting. I wrote:

> In one sense a parent who has a collective-oriented psychology will manifest the appropriate behaviors necessary to promote the same attitude in their offspring right from the early years of the offspring. The collective-oriented intelligence and behavior that has been described ... including those that are related to parenting, represent the extension of the last-described Individual-for-Group level of selection (p. 275).

In the present modification to this approach, I highlight that natural selection appears the constant evolutionary pressure, with group processes involved, as well, as per the gene co-opting model that follows. Other pressures can be redescribed in its terms, except in cases of between-group behavior selected by group selection.

## Gene Co-opting

### *Introduction*

In the following section, I speculate that for each of the five stages in the cognitive developmental model proposed, a different evolutionary pressure had led to its adaptive traits. I associate the five developmental stages of (a) reflexive, (b) sensorimotor, (c) perioperational, (d) abstract, and (e) collective intelligence to the "evolutionary strategies" of (a) individual fitness or classic Darwinian natural selection, (b) kin selection, (c) Group-for-Individual selection, (d) reciprocal altruism or selection, and (e) Individual-for-Group selection pressures, respectively. The four latter pressures are considered more complex than natural selection and concern (a) inclusive fitness, (b) participating in prestructured activity by the group for its individuals, (c) mutually beneficial processes, and (d) participating communally to set up Group-for-Individual level activity, respectively. In this section, I introduce the concept of gene co-opting.

### *Qualifications*

There are some qualifications and cautions to the proposed model of the evolution of cognitive stages that should be addressed.

(a) First, it is not suggesting that patterns in evolution are necessarily recapitulated in development, or anything to that effect. There are adaptive advantages to the evolution of the behaviors described, and they are still functionally useful to the species in the present. This fits the concept of life history models of evolution, as presented in Chap. 23.
(b) Second, I am not specifying that group selection can explain all cultural activities, rendering them merely products of biological processes. Simply, I am proposing some possible influences on some group activities, with most cultural activities being environmentally driven. (For a refined account of different types of multilevel selection or group selection models (MLS1 and MLS2), and how they might apply to evolution, see Okasha, 2006).
(c) Third, I am not proposing a developmental sequence that is based solely on one corresponding evolutionary pressure at each stage, or that, for any one stage, only evolutionary influences can explain the behaviors. Simply, for the predominant behaviors in a stage, the proposed corresponding evolutionary pressure

is a factor to consider. This does not deny that multiple evolutionary pressures can be influencing behavior at any one age period, and other multiple nonevolutionary pressures (read environmental influences), as well.

(d) Fourth, in terms of influence on developmental stage, the pressures should be working cumulatively so that in the second stage there are two pressures that seem to be at play, in the third, there are three, and so on. A similar cumulative process takes place in the ontogenetic development of stages in cognitive development – earlier ones are incorporated and contribute to the efficacy of later ones.

(e) Fifth, although the model suggests evolutionary underpinnings to stages in cognitive development, these stages are not considered uniquely adaptationist. I am not suggesting that every level of cognitive and corresponding social organization is the product of some form of evolutionary pressure. This being said, it might be interesting to the reader to consider that the implication of the model is that even for the Neo-Eriksonian stages in development that it posits to develop in parallel to the cognitive substages, there might be evolutionary underpinnings of the type described. Despite this possibility, the model is limited to behaviors related to cognitive development and ignores domains such as cooperation that have received much more attention in the field.

(f) Sixth, although I emphasize evolutionary advantage stemming from increasing capacity for resource acquisition, management, etc., I acknowledge that this is not the sole means by which an evolutionary pressure can bring adaptive advantage, nor can adaptivity in an evolutionary sense be confined to these terms; fitness, broadly speaking, always is what confers adaptivity.

(g) Seventh, in what follows, I address the evolutionary value of the behavior of the developing individual, and not of parents. (I had dealt with this aspect in the prior section).

(h) Eighth, I am not trying to supplant leading models of evolution in the literature; other models of evolution and multilevel selection are better differentiated and in tune with contemporary biological thought compared to the present one, but the latter might offer insight into the limited task undertaken.

(i) Ninth, I am aware of the difficulties related to the concept of group selection in terms of free-riders, intergroup migration, within-group vs. between-group variation, third party punishment, and the difference between genetic and cultural group selection, but do not deal much with these in the present work.

(j) Tenth, I am aware that the gene is not the only biological unit of selection in evolution, especially considering the renewal of the concept of group selection. The present work is not especially about the validity of group selection, and the limitations of the concept, but how it might apply to the cognitive developmental context.

## *Model*

As mentioned, the five levels of the multilevel selection evolutionary model concern: (a) individual selection, (b) kin selection, (c) Group-for-Individual selection, (d) reciprocal altruism selection and (e) Individual-for-Group selection. The increasing scope of genes they serve to co-opt concern (a) the individual, (b) then kin, (c) then some nonkin, (d) then some group members beyond kin, and (e) then all group members, whether kin or nonkin.

The present five-step model of multilevel selection involves successive levels where each acts to increase the range of genes in others and their associated behaviors available in the service of the survival and reproduction, or fitness, of the individuals being influenced with them. That is, in the present five-step model, the range of genes co-opted in others, through their phenotypes, into helping the individual survive and reproduce, or prepare to do so, increasingly includes genes removed from the immediate organism as we move up the hierarchy from natural to group selection. There is an increasing distance of genetic relatedness involved in the target gene pools to which the successive levels of the system is addressed.

These five evolutionary pressures act to promote behavioral adaptations reflective of an increasing scope of co-opted genes. Individuals have their chances of survival and reproduction increased when they can call upon the resources of not only themselves, but also of, kin, then some nonkin, then some group members, and then all group members, whether kin or nonkin.

The target stages or behaviors need to be seen as products of multiple selection pressures acting in concert (see Table 32.1), with each new stage adding a new evolutionary pressure to the ones already applicable to the prior stages. The cognitive stages develop toward increasing complexity, and toward increasing the net of social and institutional interactions in which individuals can engage to increase their resource network, access, acquisition management, and replenishment, thereby facilitating better survival and reproduction, or fitness.

**Table 32.1** Evolutionary pressures in multilevel selection proposed to have facilitated the evolution of five Neo-Piagetian stages

| | Underlying evolutionary selection pressure | | | | |
|---|---|---|---|---|---|
| Neo-Piagetian stage | Individual fitness | Kin selection | Group for Individual | Reciprocal altruism | Individual for Group |
| Reflex | x | | | | |
| Sensorimotor | xx | xx | | | |
| Perioperational | xxx | xxx | xxx | | |
| Abstract, formal | xxxx | xxxx | xxxx | xxxx | |
| Collective intelligence | xxxxx | xxxxx | xxxxx | xxxxx | xxxxx |

*Note*. In the present multilevel selection model, the five types are posited to work in concert in the evolution of five cognitive stages in human development

This table presents a speculative model that casts a wider nomological net in which the present work is embedded. It argues that the five stages of development described in the present work might have different evolutionary pressures associated with them, at least to some degree. Further work is needed to clarify the model, for example, related to (a) the role of group selection in it, (b) the multilevels in selection it proposes, and (c) the concept of increasing co-option of resources to help in survival and reproduction afforded by the successive pressures and stages. The speculation should not be used to detract that there are evolutionary bases to each of the stages in the model that need to be clarified (also see Fig. 32.1). Partly adapted from Young, G. (1997) [Table 12.3, Page. 273]

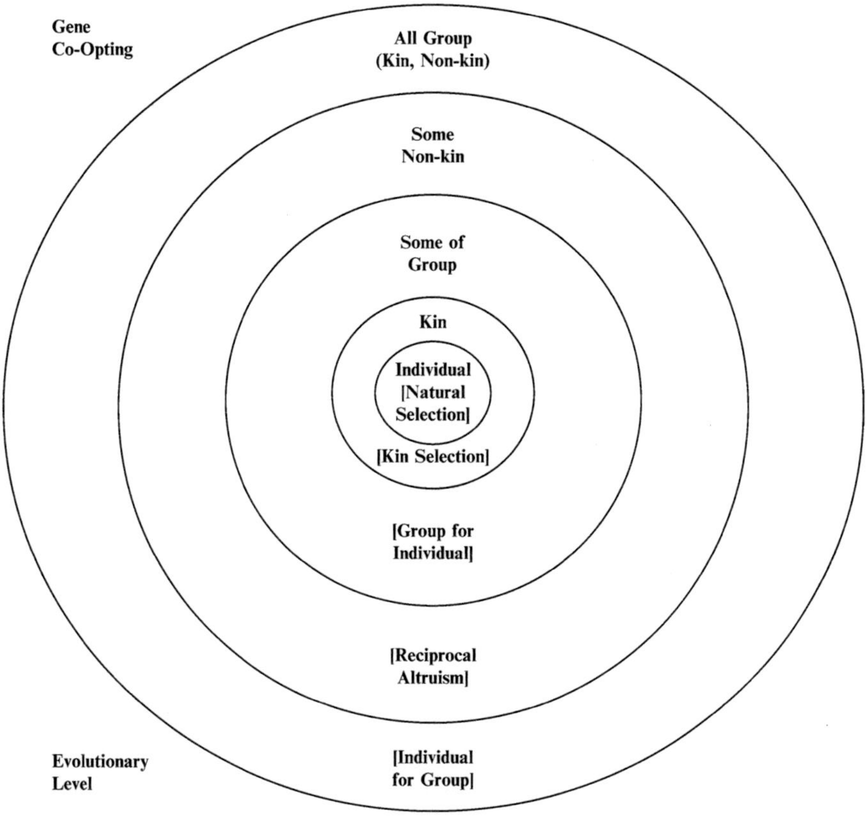


**Fig. 32.1** Degree of gene co-opting fostered by different levels of multilevel selection. Multilevel selection has been expanded to five levels. When they act in concert due to adaptational pressures in the evolution of differentiation of a behavioral system, such as for the present case of cognitive stages, which are seen to develop in five stages, they serve to increase the range of genes co-opted into promoting survival and reproduction. In this regard, the five levels of the multilevel selection evolutionary model concern (a) individual selection, (b) kin selection, (c) Group-for-Individual selection, (d) reciprocal altruism selection, and (e) Individual-for-Group selection. The increasing scope of genes they serve to co-opt concern (a) the individual, (b) then kin, (c) then some nonkin, (d) then some group members, and (e) then all group members, whether kin or nonkin. Adapted from Young, G. (1997). [Table 11.1, Page. 253]

Moreover, the evolution in the five levels described is the most economical, graceful one possible. As one level solidifies its evolutionary foothold, the next one is just one step ahead in terms of genetic relatedness in the sense described and it comes to bear its evolutionary pressure on the system. Given the increasing expansion of the genetic resource pool that each new level of the model of genetic co-option allows, it denotes that the comprehensive multilevel selection model being proposed itself is beneficial and reflects *the evolution of evolution* as it applies to the behavioral adaptations being addressed.

Multilevel selection includes five levels according to the present model. When they bring pressure in concert on a behavioral system, such as for the present case of five cognitive stages, they act to increase the range of genes co-opted into promoting survival and reproduction. That is, the present model illustrates that for the five cognitive stages proposed, we can find evolutionary traces ranging from natural to group selection. Specifically, the first stage should be shown to involve the first level, but the second the next two in concert, the third the next three, and so on. In the following section, I examine the specific cognitive stages involved in terms of their evolution according to the revised multilevel selection model.

## *Steps*

*Natural selection.* For the manner in which individual-level selection influences the expression of cognitive stage acquisitions, the behaviors of the stage facilitated (reflexive) appear directly aimed at resource accrual (surviving the first days, sucking nourishment, etc.). In this regard, they seem to have evolved due to natural selection and are based on the evolutionary competition among individuals whose phenotypic expressions had included underpinning genotypes involving reflexive cognition. This does not deny that parents provide the opportunities for the reflexive behaviors needed to sustain life, nor that behavior at this age involves more than this set of behaviors.

*Kin selection.* In kin selection and its associated cognitive level of sensorimotor intelligence, which begins in the first month, an increased resource networking is facilitated through recruitment of parental or other kin care. Children at this age engage in sensorimotor behavior that facilitates family caregiving and kin cooperativity. For example, there are family play, imitation, learning, affection, etc., that take place with siblings. Of course, natural selection processes are involved, as well.

*Group-for-Individual selection.* In the next level in the present model of multilevel selection, group selection is involved, but only in that members of the group (children) have developed behaviors that allow them to take advantage of group-selected traits. In this sense, the range of genetic resources to which the individual has access for survival and reproductive needs expands to members of the group, whether kin or nonkin, who are acting to create social and institutional structures that facilitate obtaining the survival and reproductive advantages.

The cognitive level promoted by the level of Group-for-Individual behavior concerns Piagetian representational structures, which allow for symbolic thought, language use, and so on, through preoperations and concrete operations. The latter, in particular, permit logical thought to be expressed in the physical contexts that the child encounters, such as in the particular school subjects to which school-age children are exposed.

Note that in the case of children profiting from learning and educational structures, one cannot speak of immediate reproductive advantages. However, the social and cognitive skills developed in the teaching and learning that takes place in educational and instructional settings, as well as the interpeer social interactions and links promoted, serve these goals in the long term. That is, the resource networking involved in children attending school and otherwise profiting from learning opportunities created by the group might not be readily apparent because the information and knowledge base acquired in the educational learning situations, as well as the social connections, might reveal their adaptive advantages only later in development.

*Reciprocity*. Next, reciprocal altruism or selection, as much as anything else, acts to increase the scope of gene pools aiding individual's survival and reproduction by capturing nonkin. In this sense, the formal abstract thought promoted encourages expanded peer and social interaction, mutually beneficial social exchanges, alliances and pacts, the tracking of resource donation and receipt, the monitoring of cooperation and free loading, and so on. This helps enhance resource networking access, acquisition, management, and replenishment, all necessary for survival, reproduction, adaptedness, and fitness.

*Individual-for-Group selection*. Finally, classical group selection, or Individual-for-Group selection, through the collective intelligence that it facilitates and the social and work groupings that it promotes, acts to increase the array of actors contributing to an individual's fitness, whether kin or nonkin. This acts to increase the extent of resource networking and accrual available to the individual for survival and reproduction. Also, the behavior allows the group to increase its resource access, acquisition, management, and replenishment (think of brainstorming at work), profiting all individuals in the group who are creating the collective product, and others who are indirectly involved (e.g., the profitability of the whole company increases). Granted, the behavior expressed by the individual may be self-sacrificial, but this need not be the case. Moreover, even if it is, the activity is oriented to increasing group competitiveness, so functions to ensure survival and reproduction of all its members, on the average, whether self or other, or whether kin or nonkin. Other examples for this type of collective intelligence refer to creation of informal and formal educational and learning opportunities.

*Summary*. To summarize, in humans, the first cognitive developmental stage of reflexes appears to be the outcome of straightforward natural selection at the individual level; these behaviors seem essential for survival and reproduction at the individual level. Sensorimotor intelligence is partly a product of kin selection because the infant profits in its survival and reproduction by the family links needed, by the behavior of family members co-opted in her or his care, etc. With perioperational or representational thought, the child can partake in group-created and group-governed education and learning regimens; the impact of Group-for-Individual evolutionary selection pressure and the child's adaptive response to the activity it promotes seems partly involved. With abstract thought, the teenager can create complex links with peers, including nonkin; this behavior appears partly a product of reciprocal altruism or selection. With collective intelligence, such as in brainstorming, the group outcome in the cognitive activity helps the group arrive at an adaptive and even competitive outcome. At this stage, the multilevel selection level of Individual-for-Group selection seems to partly apply.

*Comment.* In the current model of reproduction strategies as applied to parenting, the language of the substages (coordination to integration) of the present model can help. Thus, the first level of individual fitness permits a basic *coordination* between parents and offspring, but not much more. Second, kin selection allows a hierarchical arrangement between secure-base parents and attached offspring and, to a certain extent, across offspring. Next, at the Group-for-Individual level, which involved local community, larger *systems* in which offspring are implicated are allowed. Then, with reciprocally altruistic behavior, the range of social networks involved could be more widespread or *multiplied.* Last, group selection brings with it the potential for increasingly *integrated* behavior.

## Related Topics

### *Co-Memes and Co-Genes*

*Co-memes.* In Young (1997), I developed the concept of co-memes, which can help clarify the cultural products of cultural-group selection coevolutionary processes. They refer to collective emotional-cognitive repository structures of relational meaning. This recognizes that cognitive structures do not stand in isolation of emotional concomitants and that they are co-constructed in participatory interaction. When they develop as distinct and transmittable social constructions that characterize groups and pass on to the next generation, they have gene-like properties and so are best called co-memes instead of the typical use of memes in these contexts.

Briefly, then, co-memes refer to the smallest culturally derived units of information transmission over generations, and these are considered as codeveloped in cultural context. Granted, the concept of memes has been criticized, but others defend the notion (Mesoudi, 2009). In terms of the present model of collective intelligence in the adult period and how brainstorming can help construct more refined collective products in group-thinking processes, the concept of co-memes fits quite well. In the end, various higher-order abstract thought superordinate structures, as defined in the present model of collective intelligence, could take the form of co-memes.

*Co-genes.* Similarly, one could argue that genes are environmentally sensitive biological units of replication, and analogously should be called *co-genes*. Genes may reside on individual loci on chromosomes, but they are expressed in environments that support them, bring out alternative alleles, where applicable, and are subject to epigenetic influences (Jablonka & Lamb, 2005), etc.

Table 32.2 examines gene–culture co-evolution, and continues with the present theme of regarding the terms involved as interactive products of coaction by designating the evolutionary component of the term as coevolution. In complex social behavior, when examining the evolutionary and social

**Table 32.2** Co-genes and co-memes in gene–culture coevolution

| | Intergenerational unit transmission mechanisms | | |
|---|---|---|---|
| Level | Standard units | Coevolutionary units | Some other types |
| Biological | Genes | Co-genes | Epigenetic |
| Social | Memes | Co-memes | Cultural |

The concept of co-memes is explained in Young (1997). The concept of co-genes is new. Briefly, co-memes refer to the smallest culturally derived units of information transmission over generations, and these are considered as codeveloped in cultural context. Similarly, genes might reside on individual loci on chromosomes, but they are expressed in environments that support or suppress them, bring out alternative alleles, where applicable, etc. In this regard, analogous to the concept of co-memes, genes could be labeled co-genes. Consistent with the concept, in Chap. 30, gene–gene interactions are described. However, the present concept implicates more than internally driven gene–gene interactions because it also refers to the epigenetic process in which the environment could influence an individual's genes, e.g., through genomes underlying the phenotypes of others socially interacting with individuals and their genes (e.g., in care giving)

roots of the cognitive architecture and information involved, there should be signs of products of both *co-genes* and co-memes. Exactly how to disambiguate the two while showing how they interact to create a whole represents a formidable empirical and analytical task. However, conceptually, the base appears under construction.

## Social Selection and Society

*Social selection.* Moreover, there are other selection pressures to consider. For example, Flinn and Alexander (2007) described the evolutionary process of social selection, wherein evolutionary advances are made on the basis of selection pressures deriving from social interaction. Sexual selection (think of male peacock tails) is one type of social selection. Flinn and Alexander posited that social selection has elicited a runaway, fast-advancing sociality in humans and the underlying brain mechanisms that support them. A within-species arms race developed involving direct and indirect reciprocity.

*Society.* Tomasello (2009) described the multiple reasons why we cooperate and remarked that humans are the only species that create societal institutions. He examined our evolutionary and developmental roots, by studying chimpanzees and infants. More comparative work along these lines will help differentiate and integrate the various evolutionary pressures described in the literature into a cohesive model. For example, it would be interesting to examine our nonhuman primate relatives and determine to what degree their cognitive development approximates the earliest stages in ours and to what extent the corollary parenting or caregiving received at each stage approximates ours. Also, at each stage, how do we distinguish ourselves societally?

## *Dynamic Darwinism and Coevolutionary Cofractalization*

Kauffman (1993) has argued that species self-organize on a fitness landscape, optimizing the process of filling ecological niches by balancing as a system on the cusp and disorder. In this perspective, natural selection is not needed to explain species radiation. In the present work, I have created a five-step nonlinear dynamical transition process involving the movement from attractors to complex adaptive fitness processes, as described by Kauffman (1993; see Chap. 28).

It could be argued that even the five-step sequence derived from my revised model of multilevel selection theory, which I have applied to the evolution of the five stages of the present cognitive model, could have evolved to have sequential effects in the way described because of an underlying nonlinear dynamic transition process involving the five successive steps that I have described. In this sense, wider system factors could underwrite the evolution of all five of the pressures seen to work in the evolution of the human behaviors being discussed.

That is, as argued in Chap. 28, no matter what their content domain, systems might share in the five-step sequence because it represents the most economical, graceful, or less turbulent, resisting pathway in autoequilibration. In the system pattern wars, it might win the local battles because of *dynamic Darwinism*, a term that I coined in Young (1997). As Stewart (1995) has argued, evolutionary mechanisms evolve themselves. However, if diverse systems cooperate in a wider collectivity, dynamic Darwinism might be an insufficient metaphor. In this regard, I propose that evolution might be best considered a process of dynamic *coevolutionary cofractalization.*

## Summary and Conclusions

A manner of validating the present Neo-Piagetian stage model is to indicate its nomological network and extent of applications. For example, in this chapter I describe a revised model of multilevel selection theory and I apply it to the present stage model. In this regard, the reflexive stage is considered a product of natural (individual-level) selection in ancestral reptiles; the sensorimotor stage is viewed as an ancestral mammalian acquisition that evolved through kin selection; the perioperational stage is considered to have evolved in ancestral apes through Individual-for-Group pressure in evolution; the abstract stage is thought to have evolved in our forebear *Homo sapiens sapiens* by reciprocal altruism, and the stage of collective intelligence appears to partly reflect a recently evolved human quality, most likely through Group-for-Individual selection.

Nowak, Tarnita, and Wilson (2010) have described a model of the evolution of eusociality that is quite consistent with the present model. In eusociality, individuals in a species might reduce their lifetime reproductive output to help raise the offspring of conspecifics. The predominant model that is used to explain the evolution of eusocial behavior is kin selection. The authors argued that standard natural selection theory provides a more parsimonious theoretical fit and fits better the empirical data on eusociality. The authors started out by indicating that eusociality is seemingly a selfless behavior so that natural selection, traditionally conceived as a process to maximize survival and reproductive success, did not provide a proper model of eusociality, leading to the development of the concept of kin selection. However, inclusive fitness is the defining feature of kin selection, and examples among social insects were found in which eusociality is expressed, but the inclusive fitness does not apply. Other examples led the authors to conclude that the inclusive fitness as a model is an abstract enterprise and an unnecessary detour separated from the burgeoning empirical research in the field.

Nowak, Tarnita, and Wilson concluded that the genetic relatedness in eusocial insects is the consequence and not the cause of the behavior. The causative agent underlying the behavior appears to be the individual-level adaptive advantage provided by defensible nest construction within reach of an accessible food supply that accompanies the behavior. The authors proposed a plausible model of steps in the evolution of eusociality based on spring-loaded preadaptations that need no recourse to inclusive fitness to explain it. At the genetic level, the evidence suggests that the queen and her sterile working caste have the same genes that prescribe the caste and associated division of labor. Therefore, the view a colony constitutes a superorganism is supported, and a "gene-centered" approach to the evolution of eusociality makes most sense. In addition, multilevel selection forces shape the evolution of the colony life cycle and social structures.

The Nowak et al. model of natural selection forces that have underwritten the evolution of eusociality is consistent with the present model that multilevel selection comprises natural selection, kin selection, and group selection, but with a gene-coopting process that relates the various levels of the model. Types of selection other than natural selection play a role in the evolution of social behavior, or seem to do so, but the degree to which natural selection can explain their action needs to be considered and other types redescribed.

## References


Dawkins, R. (1976). *The selfish gene*. New York: Oxford University Press.

Dawkins, R. (1982). *The extended phenotype: The gene as the unit of selection*. San Francisco: Freeman.

Flinn, M., & Alexander, R. (2007). Runaway social selection in human evolution. In S. W. Gangstad & J. A. Simpson (Eds.), *The evolution of mind: Fundamental questions and controversies* (pp. 249–255). New York: Guilford Press.

Goldstone, R. L., Roberts, M. E., & Gureckis, T. M. (2008). Emergent processes in group behavior. *Current Directions in Psychological Science, 17*, 10–15.

Hamilton, W. D. (1964). The genetical evolution of social behavior I and II. *Journal of Theoretical Biology, 7*, 1–52.

Jablonka, E., & Lamb, M. J. (2005). *Evolution in four dimensions: Genetic, epigenetic, behavioral, and symbolic variation in the history of life*. Cambridge: MIT Press.

Kauffman, S. (1993). *The origins of order: Self-organization and selection in evolution*. New York: Oxford University Press.

Kurzban, R., & Aktipis, C. A. (2007). On detecting the footprints of multilevel selection in humans. In S. W. Gangstad & J. A. Simpson (Eds.), *The evolution of mind: Fundamental questions and controversies* (pp. 226–232). New York: Guilford Press.

Labouvie-Vief, G. (1992). A neo-Piagetian perspective on adult cognitive development. In R. J. Sternberg & C. A. Berg (Eds.), *Intellectual development* (pp. 197–228). Cambridge: Cambridge University Press.

Landa, J. T. (2008). The bioeconomics of homogenous middleman groups as adaptive units. *Journal of Bioeconomics, 10*, 259–278.

Landa, J. T. (2009). Homogenous middleman groups as superorganisms, endogenous ethnic groups, and trust networks: Reply to comments on Janet Landa's target article, 'The bioeconomics of homogenous middleman groups as adaptive units'. *Journal of Bioeconomics, 10*, 259–278.

Mesoudi, A. (2009). How cultural evolutionary theory can inform social psychology and vice versa. *Psychological Review, 116*, 929–952.

Nowak, M. A. (2006). Five rules for the evolution of cooperation. *Science, 314*, 1560–1563.

Nowak, M. A., Tarnita, C. E., & Wilson, E. O. (2010). The evolution of eusociality. *Nature, 466*, 1057–1062.

Okasha, S. (2006). *Evolution and the levels of selection*. Oxford: Clarendon.

Richards, F. A., & Commons, M. L. (1990). Postformal cognitive-developmental theory and research: A review of its current status. In C. N. Alexander & E. J. Langer (Eds.), *Higher stages of human development: Perspectives on adult growth* (pp. 139–160). New York: Oxford University Press.

Richerson, P. J., & Boyd, R. (2005). *Not by genes alone: How culture transformed human evolution*. Chicago: University of Chicago Press.

Stewart, J. E. (1995). Metaevolution. *Journal of Social and Evolutionary Systems, 18*, 113–147.

Tomasello, M. (2009). *Why we cooperate*. Cambridge: MIT Press.

Trivers, R. L. (1971). The evolution of reciprocal altruism. *Quarterly Review of Biology, 46*, 35–57.

Van den Bergh, J. C. J. M., & Gowdy, J. M. (2009). A group selection perspective on economic behavior, institutions, and organizations. *Journal of Economic Behavior & Organization, 72*, 1–20.

Weber, B. H., & Depew, D. J. (2003). *Evolution and learning: The Baldwin effect reconsidered*. Cambridge: MIT Press.

Wilson, D. S. (2009). Convergent cultural evolution and multilevel selection: Reply to comments on Janet Landa's 'The bioeconomics of homogenous middleman groups as adaptive units: Theory and empirical evidence viewed from a group selection framework'. *Journal of Bioeconomics, 11*, 185–190.

Wilson, D. S., Van Vugt, M., & O'Gorman, R. (2008). Multilevel selection theory and major evolutionary transitions: Implications for psychological science. *Current Directions in Psychological Science, 17*, 6–9.

Wilson, D. S., & Wilson, E. O. (2007). Rethinking the theoretical foundation of sociobiology. *The Quarterly Review of Biology, 82*, 327–348.

Young, G. (1990a). Early neuropsychological development: Lateralization of functions - hemispheric specialization. In C. A. Hauert (Ed.), *Developmental psychology: Cognitive, perceptuo-motor and neuropsychological perspectives* (pp. 113–181). Amsterdam: North Holland.

Young, G. (1990b). The development of hemispheric and manual specialization. In G. E. Hammond (Ed.), *Cerebral control of speech and limb movements* (pp. 79–139)). Amsterdam: North Holland.

Young, G. (1997). *Adult development, therapy, and culture: A postmodern synthesis*. New York: Plenum.

Young, G. (2008). Causality and causation in law, medicine, psychiatry, and psychology: Progression or regression? *Psychological Injury and Law, 1*, 161–181.

# Chapter 33
# Narrative Discourse Coding: Cohesion in Children's Narratives

## Introduction

Both Case and colleagues and Fischer and colleagues have studied narrative development in relation to their Neo-Piagetian stage models. This chapter and the next provide detailed coding schemes of cohesion and coherence that could help better understand the relationship between cognitive and narrative development. Halliday and Hasan (1976) have formulated a comprehensive model of cohesion from a functional linguistic perspective. However, research on cohesion use in children that investigates multiple aspects of their model is rare. In this chapter, I explain their model and how it has been used, and I describe a comprehensive coding scheme that organizes it into a usable system with children.

## Narrative Development in Children

### *Narrative and Cognition*

McKeough and Griffiths (2010) reviewed the literature on narrative development. With the advent of cognitive studies in psychology, the study of narrative began in earnest. Stein and Glenn (1979) developed a seminal schema to evaluate story structure. In the 1980s, research established that stories provided insight into children's developing cognitive skills (in their integration of syntax, semantics, etc.; e.g., Peterson & McCabe, 1983). Narrative was understood as having an interpretive function. Actions lead to consequences, and children learn that intentions in protagonists are involved (Bruner, 1986). Research flourished on multiple aspects in narrative development. For example, there was research on sociocultural aspects (Leichman, Wang, & Pillemer, 2003), moral development (Tappan & Packer, 1991); memory (Fivush & Haden, 2003), self-knowledge (Neisser & Fivush, 1994), gender roles (Nicolopoulou, 1997), literacy (Yussen & Ozcan, 1996), language (Nelson, 2000), processing capacity (Pratt, Boyes, Robins, & Manchester, 1989), clinical psychology (Schaefer, 2004), and education (McKeough, Davis, Forgeron, Marini, & Fung, 2005).

G. Young, *Development and Causality: Neo-Piagetian Perspectives*,
DOI 10.1007/978-1-4419-9422-6_33, © Springer Science+Business Media, LLC 2011

## *Narrative and Cohesion–Coherence*

Hickmann (2003) provided an extensive literature review about cohesion and coherence in discourse and narrative development. For example, she presented research on story structure and what makes them well formed. The story grammar of Stein and Glenn (1979) is classic. She cited the "pioneering" research of Applebee (1978). He showed that between 2 and 5 years of age, children's narrative production develops from using heaps and sequences, to primitive narratives and unfocused chains, to focused chains and well-formed narratives. The study of story grammar concerns the coherence of stories. Cohesion concerns the use of linguistic devices to regulate information across utterances. Hickmann (2003) maintained that study in the area should not confound these two critical aspects of narrative development. She called for more research to differentiate and relate coherence and cohesion in narrative development.

As for her own research, Hickmann (2003) studied discourse organization in children's narrative using a storytelling game. She used two picture sequences for each of the 200 monolingual children participants. The children were between 4 and 10 years of age, and they spoke English, German, French, or Mandarin Chinese. After preparing her database, Hickmann differentiated referring expressions used in the corpi into classes of nominals and pronominals. She analyzed how the various referential and related devices were used in the elicited narratives. For example, she analyzed reference maintenance and also forms of referring expressions. She analyzed for the relative impact of both structural and functional determinants in narrative. It is beyond the scope of the present work to present her results. She concluded that it is important to relate from a cross-cultural perspective sentence and discourse determinants of narrative acquisition. She added that young children's speech becomes increasingly comprehensible as they learn to recontextualize it ("Children learn to use language in its *own* context," Hickmann, p. 106).

## *Comment*

Hickmann (2003) based herself, in part, on the work of Halliday and Hasan (1976). They developed a comprehensive model of cohesion. For example, she described their various types of cohesion categories and the linguistic functions of the categories. Linguistic devices such as these are necessary to regulate the flow of information from one utterance to the next. She described two general principles governing language use in narratives. First, cohesive devices serve to mark information status, especially with respect to presupposition. With respect to information status, for example, speakers need to indicate whether denoted information is relatively new or a given, especially if there is a lack of relevant nonlinguistic context. It makes a great difference when speakers share the understanding of what listeners know (or do not know) about a particular referent. Second, linguistic devices help ground information. For example, what is the main information of focus and what is the secondary focus?

Despite the inclusiveness and power of Halliday and Hasan's (1976) system of categorizing cohesive devices and ties, Hickmann (2003) used sparingly the specific organization of Halliday and Hasan's coding scheme. In fact, this appears to be a general trend in the field. On the one hand, particular studies have research foci that might not require such an elaborate system. On the other hand, the system developed by Halliday and Hasan (1976) is so elaborate that it is unwieldy and would require enormous amounts of time, energy, and research funds to implement it fully in a study.

I conducted a survey of recent work on cohesion and children's narrative and found little directly involving Halliday and Hasan (1976), especially in a comprehensive manner. This collection of empirical work does contribute to the field, but means should be found to apply in more detail the work of Halliday and Hasan toward understanding children's functional use of language in discourse, text, storytelling, and narrative. In this regard, with the help of colleagues (chapter coauthors Lélia Young, Line Duceppe) on adapting the system for use in French as well as English, I have developed a comprehensive coding scheme of the cohesive ties proposed by Halliday and Hasan, and have modified it with improved elements. Hopefully, it can help in future empirical research.

For recent research on the development of cohesion in the narratives of children, the reader should consult the following articles: Arfé and Perondi (2008); Davis and Coelho (2004); Lorusso et al. (2007); and Serratrice (2006). As for recent research on the development of coherence in the narratives of children, the reader should examine the following studies: Case and McKeough (1989); Diehl, Bennetto, and Young (2006); Hay and Moran (2005); Hemphill, Uccelli, Winner, Chang, and Bellinger (2002); Nicolopoulou (2008); Symons, Peterson, Slaughter, Roche, and Doyle (2005); Trionfi and Reese (2009); and Westerveld, Gillon, and Moran (2008). Cain (2003) examined measures of both cohesion and coherence in children's fictional narratives. However, in her study, cohesion referred to interclausal connections, and she did not use Halliday and Hasan's (1976) system. It should be noted that the scoring system developed in the present work for cohesion includes both interclausal and across-sentence cohesive ties.

## Discourse and Narratives

### *Introduction*

As children tell stories, their utterances should be analyzed for different levels of discourse function. Within each utterance, one should analyze (a) verbal (syntactic) variables and (b) simultaneous nonverbal behavior of the speaker. Between utterances, it is especially important to examine types of (c) coherence and (d) cohesion. Toward this end, I have constructed scales relating to these latter areas of discourse analysis, in particular. Since the time they were constructed, there have been numerous publications on cohesion and coherence, but the area still could profit from the research that I have undertaken. Moreover, much of the literature cited to support the scales that I developed is classic, and the publications are still cited today. Furthermore, with respect to the topic of the present work, Neo-Piagetians have examined the relationship between cognitive level and story complexity. However, they have not undertaken the refined linguistic analysis suggested here. Finally, the measures might have a broader applicability because the use of scales in the area could simplify complex data sets, and lead to multivariate analyses that could complement the typical analysis of the language samples gathered.

For syntactic complexity in utterances, I created a scale that combines the work of Goldberg (1976) and Paul (1981). In terms of the goal of determining how syntax subserves textual integrity, their view of syntactic complexity in terms of degree of qualification or modification of an utterance can permit an accurate assessment of its content richness and linkage. I realize that there are other ways of treating syntactic complexity of utterances. For example, one can ask if utterances are passive in construction rather than active, or whether they conform to higher levels of more theoretical systems. However, a change from the active to passive voice in and of itself may add nothing to the topic, per se, even though it may reflect a relatively advanced linguistic skill. In contrast, the type of utterance qualifications addressed here can help topic communication in the following ways. They can help (a) compact information, (b) enrich descriptive density, (c) indicate principal vs. secondary characters, events, points of interest, etc., (d) hierarchize interrelated text elements, (e) indicate conjunctions with prior utterances, and (f) generally weave intratext relations.

Discourse analysis is coming to permeate many aspects of developmental psychology and psycholinguistics. The most impressive research uses a variety of procedures, comparing them and showing their complementarity in helping to understand developing discourse (e.g., Dorval & Eckerman, 1984; Frederiksen, Frederiksen, & Bracewell, 1985; McTear, 1985). However, I have not tried to integrate all available discourse analysis devices into one procedure. Essentially, I have ignored two large classes of discourse methods. First, research concerning pragmatic discourse functions has described a vast array of ways interactors *use* language as they work toward goals. This research is generally more microanalytic than the level that at which the scales are aimed. Second, alternate means of judging textual coherence have been developed. They concern story grammars and related concepts (e.g. Peterson & McCabe, 1983), given–new or theme–rheme analyses of neighboring utterances (e.g., Navet, Nespoulos, Lecours, 1984), and conceptual frames and semantic propositions (Frederiksen et al., 1985). This research is usually more macroanalytic than the levels indicated by the scales (although much fine analysis might be needed to arrive at the measures concerned). However, the textual coherence scale is partly based on story grammars and neighboring utterances relations.

All the measures that I constructed consist of scales with items ranging from low to high, or negative to positive. In particular, the order of the items was rationally derived for each scale, based on the literature (e.g., +2, 0, −9). For each of the measures there is a range of 21 points (e.g., +10 to −10). In general, the scales are really a juxtaposition of two subscales, one positive and one negative, which can be treated independently, if necessary. These ordinal scales permit more powerful statistical analyses of the data than the traditional measures of separate nominal categories. Moreover, the latter categories can be obtained, if needed, by treating each scale point or even their different subexamples as separate nominal categories. This being said, further empirical work is needed to establish the reliability of the scale orderings, to complement their rational construction.

In developing the scales, I analyzed a corpi of stories told by French-speaking young children (details available upon request). In segmenting the speakers' utterances into meaning units, I avoided the strategy of seeking out the minimum or smallest idea units (Chafe, 1980) or propositions (Frederiksen, 1986). Nor did I go to the other extreme and divide utterances into long chains where there were series of additive conjunctions ("and"). Rather, I adopted a more standard approach of defining utterances in terms of sentence-like syntactic structures used to communicate units of meaning (Roy, 1981). However, when clauses seemed to run on into each other without clear pause or intonation separation markers, as can happen in oral discourse, the clauses were separated according to their apparent syntactic boundaries unless they were clearly linked in a causal way (e.g., "He fell, he died"). Also, utterances were divided according to intonation cues, where warranted (Brinton & Fujiki, 1984). Finally, minor utterances, such as backchannels and interjections, were not discarded. With this approach, I generally arrived at moderate sized utterances, which is easier to analyze for relationships between adjacent utterances. It is at this level that the contents of utterances are woven into texts.

## *Cohesion*

### Halliday and Hasan

The nature of textual integrity was studied prior to Halliday and Hasan (1976), but they were the workers who induced an exponential increase in its investigation through their concept of cohesion. They defined cohesion as follows: "Cohesion occurs when the *interpretation* of some element in the discourse is dependent on that of another. The one *presupposes* the other, in the sense that it cannot be effectively decoded except by recourse to it. When this happens, a relation of cohesion is set up, and the two elements, the presupposing and the presupposed, are thereby at least potentially integrated into a text" (p. 4). Although cohesion may refer to interutterance relations, Halliday and Hasan emphasize intrautterance cohesion. In the present system, both are scored, but more weight is given to the latter.

Halliday and Hasan described five classes of cohesion. In the following section, they are enumerated.

(a) *Conjunction.* Conjunction coordinates clauses (utterances, sentences), permitting them to express a logical relationship. It refers to "specification of the way sentence meaning (i.e., content) that has gone before is to cohere with the content of the sentence to follow" (Liles, 1985a, p. 132). For example, the word "but" can conjoin neighboring clauses and can indicate an adversative relationship.
(b) *Substitution.* In substitution, an element such as a clausal unit is replaced by a shortened form. For example, the child replies, "I think so," to an appropriate question.
(c) *Ellipsis.* In ellipsis, substitution is by zero "in sentences, clauses, etc., whose structure is such as to presuppose some preceding item" (Dillinger, Bracewell, & Fine, 1983, p. 17). For example, the element "coming" is presumed in the verbal component of the child's felicitous answer "Yes, I am..."
(d) *Reference.* Reference involves a semantic relation between an item and information elsewhere in the text needed for its full understanding. "The information to be retrieved is the identity of the thing or class of things being referred to in the preceding or following text (i.e., anaphora or cataphora as opposed to exophora)" (Liles, 1985a, p. 132), Pronominal reference is very common in children *(Mary* came. *She's* nice).
(e) *Lexical Cohesion.* Finally, there is *lexical cohesion*, which is the most elusive category because it concerns the relationship between words in context. By relationship, Halliday and Hasan seem to be referring to the structural link between words as much as or even more than the semantic link, unlike the case for reference, where the latter is underscored. The lexical items might be identical or closely related and they might or might not have the same reference point. "Lexical cohesion is achieved by selection of vocabulary and is composed of general nouns that specify person, animate nonhuman, object, inanimate concrete mass, inanimate abstract, action, place, and fact. Lexical items that cohere are not necessarily coreferential, inclusive, or residing in the same environment" (Liles, 1985a, p. 133). For example, an item could be reiterated several times or it could be referred to using a synonym. Thus, lexical cohesion can involve reference, but such cases are not classified as reference, per se, because to some extent there are structural relations between the words.

## Stories: Research

*Introduction.* Investigation of the development of cohesive skills in the story (text) production of children has proceeded along a variety of paths. A primary emphasis has been placed on determining age effects, situational (genre) effects, and/or their interaction. A text is an oral or written passage that attempts to present a meaningful integrated "whole." Any text consists of subunits structured at various levels. For example, there is attempted (a) thematic continuity, (b) consistency of characterization, locale, etc., and (c) appropriate voice (e.g., narrative stance, or introductory comments such as "Once upon a time..."). In the following section, I review six studies about storytelling in children that helped formulate the present coding system (Haslett, 1983; Klecan-Aker & Lopez, 1985; Martin, 1983; Pappas, 1985; Pellegrini, 1986; Pellegrini, Galda, & Rubin, 1984).

*Martin* (1983). Martin examined types of conjunction and reference in 6–11-year-olds in the narratives that they produced by verbalizing a picture story, retelling this story, and retelling a fable. The results for certain conjunction and reference subtypes showed that the youngest children had the most difficulty. Moreover, this occurred for the first and third tasks, in particular. Finally, different conjunction and reference subtypes in these two tasks underlined the children's problems. For example, (a) the younger children treated the first task as a picture-describing one, therefore using more explicit presumed information and out-of-text reference (exophora). In general, they used less reference in the text (anaphora) and less bridging (see Table 33.1 for definition). (b) Also, the younger children made fewer changes in their conjunction use for what is expected in fables (in task 3). Thus, they used more temporals, such as "after," and less comparatives, such as "like" etc.

**Table 33.1** Definition of reference subcategories

| Subcategory | Definition |
|---|---|
| Personal pronoun | – "Personal pronouns, possessive determiners, and possessive pronouns that represent a single system of 'person', referring to the identity of relevant persons, objects, and events (e.g., 'he,' 'mine,' 'it,' and 'one.')" (Liles, 1985a, p. 132, punctuation, italics modified in quotes)<br>– They reference by replacing or assuming the exact identity of the antecedent item referred to<br>– "Code first person personal pronouns ('I,' 'you,' 'we,' and 'us') which are within quotes and refer to the speaker of the quote if he has been named in the text. For example: "Mary isn't home. Her note says, 'I will be home at six'" (Liles, 1982, in Weinland, 1984, p. 202)<br>– Third person personals are the most common (e.g., 'he,' 'her,' 'it,' and 'one' as generalized human)<br>– "I" and "you" as first and second person speech roles are not scored here, but in cohesive presumption<br>– A "dummy 'it' (e.g., 'It's a nice day') is not coded" (Dillinger, Bracewell, & Fine, 1983, p. 12)<br>– Cataphoric examples (e.g., 'I can't believe, it. I ate the whole thing') are coded |
| Relative pronoun | – A type of pronominal reference generally limited to within utterance cohesive ties<br>– They "are coded only when they are nonrestrictive" (Dillinger et al., 1983, p. 11). For example: "Old King Cole, *who* was a merry old soul," "Such nonrestrictive pronouns usually occur with a proper noun and often are marked off by punctuation or pauses in oral transcripts" (p. 11). An example of a restricted "who" follows: "The man who calls me blackguard twice condemns himself" |
| Demonstrative | – A form of verbal pointing using determiners "identifying the referent by location in place or item (e.g., 'this,' 'that,' 'then')" (Liles, 1985a, p. 132)<br>– Not coded if the specific referent is exophoric outside the text) |

(continued)

**Table 33.1** (continued)

| Subcategory | Definition |
|---|---|
| Definitive article | – Verbal pointing with the word "the"<br>– Not coded "if 'a' or 'some' can be substituted without producing a crucial change in the meaning of the text" (Weinland, 1984, p. 203). For example: "The newspaper was on a chair" |
| Comparative | – Two items are compared by certain adverbs or adjectives, in particular. The comparison may be "in terms of likeness and unlikeness, without respect to any particular property: two things may be the same, similar, or different… [or] in respect of quantity or quality" (Halliday & Hasan, 1976, pp. 6–7)<br>– "When both a demonstrative and a comparative reference are used (e.g., 'the other') code only as… comparative" (Liles, 1985a, p. 132)<br>– "'Another,' 'more' coded… though ellipsis is also involved" (Dillinger et al., 1983, p. 12)<br>– "'So,' 'such,' 'as': These are not always comparatives, but are sometimes intensifiers ('I'm so happy'). In which case they are not coded" p. 12) |
| Bridging | – The referent replacing the antecedent is implicitly linked to it, requiring inference for discovery. "A noun phrase requiring bridging usually contains a definite article or pronominal adjective. The information needed for interpretation of the noun phrase is *implicit* rather than explicit, although the referent is accessible usually as a word or phrase that implies the semantic content of the noun phrase" (Dillinger et al., 1983, p. 9). Thus, camping trip and diverse camping trip items, such as a sleeping bag, are linked by bridging, whereas the category camping trip items and its constituents are linked by superordinate-subordinate classification |

*Klecan-Aker and Lopez* (1985). Klecan-Aker and Lopez investigated first- and third graders who had to explain a common film that they had seen. References were analyzed for their ambiguity-appropriateness. Conjunctions were classified as either conjoining or subordinating (not a traditional approach, as per Halliday and Hasan). Grade differences were not apparent until the greater frequency of utterances (T-units) in third graders was controlled. At this point, the older children were shown to use proportionately fewer ambiguous reference ties.

*Pappas* (1985). Pappas studied first graders in three contexts: storytelling, story retelling, and assisted story writing. Only a general sum score across cohesion categories was used. The children employed more cohesive devices in the second compared to the third situation (other comparisons were nonsignificant). Moreover, cohesive harmony, an index of textual coherence built on cohesive tie information, also was highest in this situation.

*Pellegrini* (1986). Younger children (4- and 5-year-olds) were observed in play contexts (dramatic; housekeeping; constructive blocks) in same age–sex dyads. In terms of cohesion in the children's conversations, pronominal, comparative, and demonstrative reference were examined, as were in-text endophoric and out-of-text exophoric reference. Although older children used more explicit language, in general, there were no age differences with respect to the cohesion measures. Situation affected exophoric reference, for the constructive center elicited more out-of-text situational connections. There were no other situational differences.

*Pellegrini et al.* (1984). These workers looked at children in grades 1, 3, and 5 in four situations that varied according to demand (persuade someone, tell story) and mode (oral, written). There were complex main and interaction effects. For example, a sum score of reference, ellipsis, and substitution increased from grade 1 to grade 3, but not from grade 3 to 5. However, this behavior was especially manifested in the oral mode in grade 1, the written mode in grade 3, and equally across mode in grade 5. Also, first graders used less causal (e.g., but, if) conjunctions, especially in the persuasive written task. Finally, first graders used more exophora. In general, the results showed that competence in the production of cohesive text increased between the first and third grades, in particular.

*Haslett* (1983). Haslett investigated reference use in the oral and written stories of 6- and 7-year-old boys and girls. She obtained some straightforward main but complex interaction effects that I now try to simplify, especially in terms of how they relate to the oral mode. The primary results concerned both personal reference and demonstratives. Personal reference gave a more cohesive, explicit, chained text than demonstratives; for example, a series of sentences beginning with "she." The 6-year-olds used more demonstratives (e.g., this, there) and the 7-year-olds more personals (e.g., she, theirs). The boys especially accounted for the former result because they often used the definitive article "the" (scored as a demonstrative) as a reference tie. The latter result was qualified by the finding that 6-year-old girls also used more personals in the oral mode. In general, the 7-year-old boys used more reference. Clearly, then, the older children and the girls seemed more verbally advanced than their homologues. A result that seems somewhat in contrast to this one was that especially in the oral mode, the younger children used more textual anaphoric (backward) and cataphoric (forward) reference, whereas the older ones used more out-of-text (exophoric) reference. In the oral mode, personals were used most and comparatives (e.g., other, same) least, with the difference between usage at ages 6 and 7 largest for personals and smallest for comparatives. Personals and demonstratives bore a relation opposite to this one in the writing mode, in which comparatives were not used at all. The oral mode seemed to elicit more advanced cohesion indices.

*Summary*. The results across these studies emphasized age and situational differences in the cohesion used in the oral texts of children. First, children as young as 4 years of age (Pellegrini, 1986) used cohesive devices in their text production. Also, age effects were usually found, and they generally indicated increasing use of more in-text reference, more advanced cohesion classes, more advanced subcategories (e.g., personal reference, causal conjunction), and more appropriate use of categories. These trends were greatly affected by situation, with the oral mode, in particular, being conducive to cohesion use in the age range examined. However, some results need replication (e.g., Haslett's data on sex differences).

## Other Research

*Liles* (1985a, 1985b). Liles determined whether cohesion is used in the same way and with the same adequacy or accuracy in 7–10-year-old language-disordered children and matched controls ($N=20$). The subjects viewed a film and then described it to listeners who either saw the film, as well, or who did not. The children were also asked questions, especially to evaluate the children's grasp of story grammar or relationships between characters, their plans, events, and so on (Stein & Glenn, 1979). Stories were analyzed for all five cohesion classes and some subcategories of reference (although ellipsis, substitution, and comparative reference were all rare). The results did not vary with age, because the sample size was small for the large age range used, but the results did vary with listener condition, child language level, and story grammar knowledge, in particular. (a) There were more ties of personal reference and conjunction, and ties were more complete in adequacy when the listener had not seen the film. (b) The control children used more personal reference, whereas the language-disordered ones used more demonstrative reference, lexical cohesion, and ties that were in error or incomplete in adequacy. (c) Finally, the worse the language-disordered children understood story grammar as determined by the questions, the less they used demonstrative reference.

The first result about situation differences is a consistent one, given that more frequent and less ambiguous cohesive devices would be needed if the listener had not shared in viewing the film. Personal reference, in particular, is indicative of a more explicit, integrated, or chained storytelling skill in this age range. The second result about child group differences also is consistent, given this relative quality of personal vs. demonstrative reference and complete vs. incomplete and error ties. The language-disordered children can be differentiated from controls by examining skill of cohesion use in oral story production. However, many of the results in the study showed no difference between the groups. Indeed, the disordered children used more lexical cohesion than the control children. The third result about story grammar and cohesion is not clear according to Liles because it applies only to one group for one measure, and some subjects with excellent story grammar comprehension were poor in cohesion adequacy.

Consequently, Liles (1985b) further explored the relationship between story grammar comprehension and cohesion in her language-disordered subjects. She divided this sample of children by using a median split on their answers to the story grammar comprehension questions. Then, she analyzed the cohesion categories and adequacy levels of the three groups of children obtained: (a) controls; (b) language-disordered, good story grammar comprehension; and (c) language disordered, poor comprehension. Only the latter group differed from the controls in terms of the cohesion category variables listed in result "b" above (personal reference, demonstrative reference, lexical). Good story grammar "comprehenders" used cohesion like controls. By contrast, both disordered groups differed from the controls in terms of the cohesion adequacy variables listed in result "b" above (incompletes, errors). Good story grammar comprehenders used cohesion just as inadequately as poor story grammar comprehenders, despite their normal distribution of cohesion categories used.

The cohesive adequacy measure might be tapping a semantic organizational competence independent of the cohesive categories themselves.

*Comment.* Personal reference seemed a more refined category than demonstrative reference, in that Liles (1985a, 1985b) found that the former was associated with normal language, in contrast to the latter, which was associated with language disorder in conjunction with poor story grammar comprehension. Lexical cohesion is more difficult to categorize because it was associated with increasing literacy in Pettegrew (1981), but with language disorder in conjunction with poor story comprehension in Liles (1985a, 1985b). Poor cohesion use (inadequacy in Liles) also helped to discriminate the groups under investigation.

Cohesion does vary with more than just age and situation, because various cognitive and related factors are important. It can differ not only according to the type of child as determined by various cognitive-related criteria (literate or not, language disordered or not) but also according to the situation's cognitive workload (Freedle & Fine, 1983) and according to the child's cognitive style (Pratt & MacKenzie-Keating, 1985). Similar results about cohesion differences across different groups of children have been found in other studies. For example, Fine's study (1985a, 1985b) revealed differences in several cohesion categories in a variety of oral tasks in 10-year-old reading disabled and control children.

## Cohesion in Discourse: Toward a Coding Scheme

### *Preamble*

Before the subcategories of cohesion are introduced, a discussion is required of what is meant by "adequacy" and related concepts about cohesion. The quality of cohesion is referred to in several ways. For example, Halliday and Hasan (1976) deal with the *complexity* of the various cohesion categories (e.g., pp. 277–8). The literature review just presented emphasized the *cohesiveness* of the various cohesion categories. For example, personal reference compared to demonstrative reference was considered more explicit, conducive to chaining, etc. The widespread concept of *distance* between the antecedent or consequent tied item to the cohesive marker is also related here, for a link that is several utterances apart, for example, must be more powerful than one that is closer. A similar concept is the one of cohesive chaining, best expressed in Hasan's (1980) concept of cohesive *harmony* (described in Pappas, 1985). Martin introduced the concept of cohesive "*adequacy*" or *errors* (1977–1978; 1983; Rochester & Martin, 1979). Finally, there is the widespread concept of *exophora*, concerning out-of-text reference. Also, Rochester and Martin (1979), in particular, point to the need for a coherent system of in-text presumption.

About these concepts, I have incorporated them in the coding system in the following way. (a) The concept of complexity was incorporated directly into the coding of the subcategories of cohesion, in that for each cohesive category the subcategories were ordered from simplest to most complex. In constructing the series involved, I followed Halliday and Hasan (1976) for lexical cohesion and Liles (1985a; p. 131), in particular, for conjunction. However, I did not just depend on Halliday and Hasan, as I tried to develop an across-category approach based on presumed order of acquisition in development, syntactic complexity, semantic demands, and so on. (b) I discarded the concept of cohesiveness because for some cohesion categories, the least complex subcategory seemed the most cohesive, whereas the opposite relation or no relation seemed to hold for others.

I combined the concepts of (c) distance and (d) adequacy into a scale of cohesion quality. The positive portion was based on a distance measure, whereas the negative segment dealt with inadequacy-errors. (e) I judged that the construct of chaining cohesive harmony was too complex for application. Its ultimate purpose is to index textual coherence, but I developed a simpler coding scheme for this need.

Finally, I developed a separate scale for the measure of in-text and out-of-text (f) presumption and (g) exophora because previous research has not emphasized that such items generally are cohesive for text as text. However, in general, many presumptions of this type are cohesive, especially in the shared oral context of conversations, (re)telling stories to a listener or listeners, etc. For example, the use of the first person speech role, an exophoric situational reference, or mention of a commonly known cultural phenomenon, might provide a cohesive connection that should be recognized.

## *Subcategories*

*Introduction.* Tables 33.1 and 33.2 provide definitions and a series of examples for each subcategory of each class of cohesion. The subcategories are ordered according to their complexity (1–6). Some of the subcategories have been slightly altered compared to Halliday and Hasan's (1976) original categories to permit this ordering, whereas others are the result of splitting or grouping Halliday and Hasan's original categories.

There have been various attempts to modify the analysis of the cohesion categories, subcategories, and their examples since Halliday and Hasan's (1976) work first appeared. On the one hand, almost everyone has ignored certain variables such as the "functions" of cohesion as defined by Halliday and Hasan and the separation of their first-order subcategories into second-order subcategories. On the other hand, Halliday and Hasan admit that their classification system is somewhat arbitrary. For example, certain aspects of lexical cohesion, such as repetition, resemble pronominal reference. Ellipsis and substitution are quite similar to reference in certain ways. Thus, some have tried to redefine or modify certain categories (e.g., see Martin, 1983, on conjunction; Martin, 1977–1978; Rochester & Martin, 1979, on reference; Rentel & King, 1983, for a review concerning lexical cohesion). Also, others have tried to restructure the subcategories by creating different classifications of them (e.g., Fine 1985a, 1985b; McCutchen & Perfetti, 1982).

**Table 33.2** Reference complexity levels, subcategories, and examples

| Level | Category | Primary example | Secondary |
|---|---|---|---|
| 1 | Personal pronoun | Mary was invited, and she went.<br>The dogs ran. Then, *they* barked | He, him, his, hers, it, its, them, their, theirs |
| 2 | Relative pronoun | The girl *who* was invited came<br>She wore the dress *that* was red | Whose, which, whom |
| 3 | Demonstrative | She went to the party and found it *there*<br>Which dresses do you want? *These* are the ones | This, that, those, here |
| 4 | Definitive article | There was a party. At *the* party it happened<br>Students should have freedom, but *the* students should respect it | – |
| 5 | Comparative | There were two parties. The *second* party was the best<br>The *second* party was OK. John's was *less* fun | Last, first, more, fewer, other, same, so, similar, different, worse |
| 6 | Bridging | School is fun. But *math* is hard<br>The camping trip was set. The *sleeping* bags were ready | – |

I have been conservative about these efforts to alter the basic paradigm of Halliday and Hasan, but I did borrow some of the revisions, as shall be shown.

*Reference.* Halliday and Hasan (1976) described three major types of reference: demonstrative, pronominal, and comparative. I have split the first two of these types and added Rochester and Martin's (1979) concept of bridging (see Tables 33.1 and 33.2). With respect to pronominal reference, Halliday and Hasan (1976) did not include the relative pronouns as cohesive devices. However, others have done so (e.g., Dillinger et al., 1983). This category inevitably must almost always refer to within-utterance ties, which probably accounts for Halliday and Hasan's (1976) reluctance to include it in this category. As for demonstratives, the separation of the definite article subcategory from the demonstrative one seemed acceptable because it functions differently from demonstratives. Bridging could just have easily be placed in the category of lexical cohesion and not in the reference category, as in Fine (1985a, 1985b), given the fluidity between these two categories. However, I followed Rochester and Martin's (1979) original classification of this subcategory and kept it as a reference tie.

The order of complexity of the subcategories presented in the table is based on Halliday and Hasan's (1976) order of presentation of pronominal, demonstrative, and comparative reference. However, when I split the first two of these categories, the more complex of each new subcategory pair was placed in the more advanced position relative to the other. Bridging was considered the most complex subcategory, given the level of inference needed in its use.

*Lexical cohesion.* This category was the most difficult to deal with for Halliday and Hasan (1976), and they and others have modified its conception since its initial presentation (see Patry & Menard, 1985; Rentel & King, 1983). Just how many lexical cohesion subcategories are important and how they should be spliced or grouped seems to change from page to page in parts of Halliday and Hasan. However, Halliday and Hasan, themselves (pp. 278–9), have given the logical key to help disentangle the matter. They emphasized the first four of the subcategories outlined in Tables 33.3 and 33.4. By considering personal reference, as well, these subcategories were seen to form a five-point "continuum" of "reiteration" of lexical items.

I have slightly changed one of the subcategories; subordination seems little different from superordination in this context, so they are considered together as one subcategory. As for the remaining lexical cohesion subcategories often mentioned by Halliday and Hasan and others, but not included in their 5-point reiteration continuum, "root word" relations seem more complex than "general word" ones, whereas various hierarchized relations other than super(sub)ordination seem the most complex to master. The hierarchization subcategory is a convenient catchall

**Table 33.3** Definition of lexical cohesion subcategories

| Category | Definition |
|---|---|
| Repetition | – Exact reproduction of a lexical item so that the second occurrence of the item refers back to the first<br>– Exact reproductions need not be lexical repetitions. The surface form may be the same, but not the usage. The word is "recycled" in a different way (see hierarchization)<br>– Items like articles, auxiliaries, prepositions, con junctions, etc., are not coded |
| (Near) synonym | – "A word having a textual antecedent with the same or almost the same meaning. It must also be the same part of speech although not necessarily the same tense, voice, etc. a lexical synonym can refer to either words or phrases, and is influenced by the intent of the writer-speaker" (Dillinger et al., 1983, p. 27) |
| Superordinate-subordinate | – Words that have hyponomous textual links. They are related as a general class inclusion term and a specific example of the general class |
| General word | – "A superordinate item which operates anaphorically as a kind of synonym, and is almost always accompanied by 'the'" (Dillinger et al., 1983, p. 29) |
| Root word | – The rephrasing of a word into one of its root forms. Includes "singular and plural forms of nouns, differing tenses of verbs e.g., 'go,' 'went,' 'gone'), and comparative forms of adjectives (e.g., 'good,' 'better,' 'best')… Need not to be the same parts of speech, provided that they have related meanings, and share lexical roots" (Dillinger et al., 1983, p. 26)<br>– "Not to be coded as lexical roots are articles, auxiliaries, prepositions, conjunctions, any forms of the verb 'to be,' and most pronouns. Exceptions would be general pronouns such as 'somebody,' 'anything,' etc. Lexical pairs when one item is a proper noun and the other is a common noun are not always coded" (p. 26) |
| Hierarchization | – Semantic bonds with organized meaning relations. The words form textual links by being related through opposition, part–whole relationships, comembership in the same class, recycling by reiteration with change of function, equivalence in context, metaphor, etc. Superordinate and subordinate relations are coded apart (see above) |

**Table 33.4** Lexical cohesion, complexity levels, subcategories, and examples

| Level | Category | Primary example | Secondary |
|---|---|---|---|
| 1 | Repetition | Mary was invited and *Mary* went<br>The party was fun, but the *party* ended<br>A boy's climbing. The *boy's* falling<br>She climbed the stairs and *climbed* the ladder | – |
| 2 | (Near) synonym | I want a cookie. Do you want a *biscuits*?<br>I started the ascent of the mountain. The *climb* was easy | – |
| 3 | Superordinate-subordinate | She climbed the chair. The *task* was hard<br>I like meat. Do you like *hamburger*? | – |
| 4 | General word | Bring the food. Leave the *other stuff*<br>Here comes John. *The kid* is nice<br>The pen fell. The stupid *thing* broke | Man, woman, child, boy, girl, person, people, creature, object, place |
| 5 | Root word | Go to the party. I *went* yesterday<br>If you want it, wish. *Wishing* helps. | – |
| 6 | Hierarchization | These are the same. Those are *different*<br>Flowers are nice, especially their *petals*<br>She eats apples, not *pears*<br>She is a queen. Is a *queen* nice?<br>The girl is a good *artist*<br>The drawing is like a *dream* | Antonym, part-whole relation, comembership, recycling, equivalence, metaphor |

for various examples of complex lexical relations cited in Patry and Menard (1985) and Rentel and King (1983).

*Substitution–ellipsis.* I used these subcategories just as they were presented in Halliday and Hasan (1976) and summarized in Dillinger et al. (1983) (see Tables 33.5 and 33.6).

Note that examples that are readily assigned to substitution, ellipsis, reference, and lexical cohesion, depending on context (structure of the discourse and its sentences), can also be assigned to different cohesive markers. In such cases, one should be conservative and assign the lowest complexity score possible (e.g., reference 2, not lexical cohesion 4). When the same complexity level is encountered in such multiple classification cases, I use the following hierarchy: reference, substitution–ellipsis, and lexical cohesion. In general, the latter category requires the most inference compared to the others, whereas reference is usually quite straightforward.

*Conjunction.* For this category, I employed all but one of Halliday and Hasan's (1976) six subcategories; I excluded conjunction by intonation (see Tables 33.7 and 33.8). The latter subcategory essentially concerns prosodic cues parallel to the verbal

**Table 33.5** Definition of substitution and ellipsis subcategories

| Subcategory | Definition |
|---|---|
| | *Substitution* |
| Nominal | – A noun is replaced by the words 'one,' 'ones,' and 'same,' in particular, depending on the context |
| | – "The use of the substitute always involves some modifying element that is therefore defining, e.g., 'this one,' 'another one,' 'the biggest one, the one that got away, etc." (Dillinger et al., 1983, p. 16) |
| | – "Other non-S uses of one include: personal pronoun, cardinal number, indefinite article, and 'pro-noun' (e.g., 'such a one')" (p. 16) |
| Verbal | – A verb is replaced by the words 'do,' 'do so,' 'do it,' 'done,' 'didn't,' and similar variants, depending on the context |
| | – "Other non-S uses of do include: lexical verb ('I have something to do'), general verb ('They did another song' 'It does no harm,' 'They'll do your taxes for you'), 'pro-verb,' i.e., unspecified or unidentified actions ('What are you doing?'), verbal operator auxiliary: 'Does she sing?,' 'She doesn't swim')" (p. 16) |
| Clausal | – An entire clause is replaced by the words "so" or "not" |
| | – "Other non-S uses of so include: adverb… meaning 'true,' … conjunction meaning 'consequently,' … reference meaning 'like this'" (p. 16) |
| | *Ellipsis* |
| Nominal | – Zero substitution of a noun |
| | – "Dangling prepositions (e.g.,: 'He jumped in') are not coded" (p. 17) |
| Verbal | – Zero substitution of a verb |
| Clausal | – Zero substitution of an entire clause |

**Table 33.6** Substitution and ellipsis complexity levels, subcategories, and examples

| Level | Category | Primary example | Secondary |
|---|---|---|---|
| *Substitution* | | | |
| 1 | Nominal | Do you like this party? No, I like the other *one* | Ones |
| | | Did you eat this kind? No, the *same* as yours. | |
| | | Mary is mean to her? Was she *so* to him? | |
| 2 | Verbal | Are you inviting her? I can't *do it* now | Do, didn't, do so, be |
| | | He drew a dog. He could *have done* a cat | |
| | | He'll do *so*, too | |
| 3 | Clausal | Is she coming? I hope *so* | – |
| | | Is she invited? I hope *not* | |
| *Ellipsis* | | | |
| 4 | Nominal | There are three parties, and she's going to two … | – |
| | | She went and she's going to another … | |
| 5 | Verbal | Is the party still on? Yes, it is … | – |
| | | Are you coming? No, I'm not … | |
| 6 | Clausal | She went. Did you? … | – |
| | | She's coming. Are you? … | |

**Table 33.7** Definition of conjunction subcategories

| Category | Definition |
|---|---|
| Additive | – Conjoins [clauses, utterances] "which describe events that have occurred simultaneously … or … indicate [s] sequential information without intervening events or time lapse" (Weinland, 1984, p. 205). The latter refers to a juxtaposition of units related solely by their sequential order, as in "He turned the corner *and* he saw a skunk"<br>– "Meanings that cohere simply by denoting added information … and de-emphasis after thought" (Liles, 1985a, p. 132). When a series of the same additives are used to conjoin utterances, only the first one in the series is coded. Children have the habit of using "and" between utterances that would otherwise be independent ("pis" in French Quebecois), and should not be credited for conjunctive chaining in such cases |
| Comparative | – A type of additive conjunction involving contrast or similarity |
| Temporal | – The conjoined units express ordered events in time or "a relation that specifies time" (Liles, 1985a, p. 133). There is more than just a juxtaposition of units conjoined by the word "and" ("pis"), as conjunctions such as "then", "after that", and "previously," are used |
| Causative-conditional | – One of the conjoined units is considered the direct result, reason, purpose, or outcome of the other, or is considered a possible result, reason, purpose, or outcome if the other becomes a reality<br>– "Be wary of 'false ifs' (e.g., 'Do you know if …'). These can usually be replaced with 'whether' and are … not coded" (Dillinger et al., 1983, p. 19)<br>– "When two or more conjunctions (e.g., 'and then' or 'and so then') are conjoined … code only one of the conjunctions as a cohesive item. Select the item that is the most complex according to the [indicated] hierarchy" (Liles, 1985a, p. 132) |
| Adversative | – "The basic meaning of adversative relation is 'contrary to expectation'" (Halliday & Hasan, 1976, p. 250) |
| Continuative | – Items serving a backward linking function, or as a simple transition link between units. They can be prosodically simplified in the sense of being "unaccented and with reduced vowel values" (Halliday & Hasan, 1976, p. 268). "Their meaning as conjunctive items is (partly) derivable from their meaning as (other) forms". For example, "now" can serve to begin a new stage in communication, which it does not typically do, as in "Are you ready? Now when I tell you…" Similarly, "well" can serve to begin a response in dialogue<br>– There are other such pairs. For example, "of course" and "anyway" can be used to prepare the way for a (slightly) adversative opinion |

stream, not ones separate from it. Moreover, prosody is involved in the continuation subcategory. I split Halliday and Hasan's additive subcategory by separating comparatives from it, following Martin (1983). Comparative conjunctions of contrast and similarity seem more advanced than other additive exemplars. Note that one should exclude series of utterances conjoined by "and," because these often occur more by habit than design in the age range of concern. The causative category was expanded to include conditional "ifs," which are not considered in Halliday and

**Table 33.8** Conjunction complexity levels, subcategories, and examples

| Level | Category | Primary examples | Secondary |
|---|---|---|---|
| 1 | Additive | She didn't go there. *Nor* here<br>She came to the party *and* played...<br>...*And* she had a good time | And, also, or, and... to, and...not, nor, neither, further, besides, for instance, I mean, that is, incidentally |
| 2 | Comparative | She liked the party. By *contrast*, she didn't like him<br>She liked the party. *Similarly*, she... | Whereas, conversely, like, as |
| 3 | Temporal | I invited her, and *then* she came<br>She left after the party | Next, before that, meanwhile, finally, later, again |
| 4 | Causative-conditional | I like her, so I invited her<br>I would like her *if* she came | Therefore, because, thus, then, consequently, for, otherwise |
| 5 | Adversative | I usually like her, but not at the party<br>*Instead* of coming, go | Yet, though, however, despite, only |
| 6 | Continuative | Come, *Of course*, you don't have to<br>Not at the party? *Well*, maybe later | Surely, now, after all, anyway |

Hasan (1976) but are integral to Dillinger et al. (1983) and Martin (1983). Finally, the order assigned for most of the subcategories reflected Liles' (1985a) hierarchy (p. 132). However, I reversed the positions of causatives and adversatives in her approach, following Bloom et al. (1980) and Ervin-Tripp (1978, cited in McTear, 1985), who described the normative order of development of connectives in younger children (also see Braunwald, 1985). I placed continuatives, which Liles did not consider, at the most complex pole, because of their lexical and possible prosodic sophistication.

*Cohesion by presumption.* In the present scheme, the category of presumption without textual verbal referents is based on various exophoric categories (Halliday & Hasan, 1976) and reference retrieval categories (Rochester & Martin, 1979; Martin, 1977–1978, 1983), in particular. However, they have been somewhat modified for the present scaling needs. The simplest discourse presumptions without prior verbal antecedents concern the speaker's surround or self (1 and 2), whereas the more complex ones concern others (3 and 4) and extrasituational factors (5 and 6) (see Tables 33.9 and 33.10). Exophoric situational reference (1) is quite widespread even early in childhood, while use of the first person speech role (2) and presumption of knowledge of personal factors (3) often occurs. The listener(s) (4), or other(s) outside the discourse situation (5), become more salient with age. Extra situational reference often occurs. It can take several forms, because (5) more specific, limited, non culture-wide places or events could be mentioned (e.g., a shared favorite restaurant) or (6) commonly known places or events could be mentioned. The latter implies a general cultural reference, in particular (both homophoric using the definite article, such as in "the border," and unique naming, such as "Snoopy;" Rochester & Martin, 1979). When used appropriately, such presumption without

**Table 33.9** Definition of subcategories of cohesion by presumption

| Category | Definition |
|---|---|
| Situation | – Reference to part of the physical context. A traditional example of exophora |
| Self | – Statements in the first person, narratives<br>– Statements in which the speaker talks about himself using his name<br>– Generally concerns an interjected comment about the private life of the speaker<br>– Excludes quotes which are treated as cohesive reference, as in "She said, 'I...'" |
| Audience | – Statements in the second person, narratives, except for quotes as in the "self" category<br>– Statements in which the speaker talks to the listener using their name |
| Other(s) | – Other(s) outside of the speaker and audience are mentioned |
| Extrasituational (limited) | – Reference beyond the immediate physical context, but to a shared, specific idea, place, or event that is not culture wide (e.g., to local park, mayor of small city, lecture) |
| Extrasituational (general) | – Reference beyond the immediate physical context. Usually concerns the culture of the speaker (and audience) |

**Table 33.10** Cohesion by presumption: complexity levels, subcategories, and examples

| Level | Primary example | Secondary |
|---|---|---|
| 1. Situation | Give me *that* toy. [pointed to]<br>Stop *banging* | Exophora |
| 2. Self | She likes to go to parties. *I* do, too<br>It's for *me*<br>That reminds me of *when I saw the elephants*<br>*Mommy* will do that for you | Mine |
| 3. Audience | Do it *yourself*<br>*John*, come here please | You |
| 4. Other(s) | Is that *yours*? [in a general sense ]<br>*John* is a good kid. [mutual friend]<br>*Mummy's* coming<br>To build a house, *you* [in general sense] do the following | One (Exophora) |
| 5. Extrasituational (limited) | That *program* yesterday was great<br>Let's go *le Fedo* to eat; its great! | Exophora |
| 6. Extrasituational | *Mickey Mouse* is great<br>The cow jumped over the *moon* | Unique, homophoric |

prior verbal antecedents can be quite cohesive of text (and dialogue). It is only when they are obscurely, ambiguously, or wrongly employed that confusion is shown. This leads us to the next section of the measurement of the quality of cohesion.

In general, the categories of cohesion differ very little in English and French. The major difference is that certain nouns have two genders in French, unlike English, which gives a new example of root words. For the rest, plus ça change, plus c'est la même chose.

## *Cohesion Quality*

### Introduction

Table 33.11 outlines a measurement scale of cohesive quality. It is comprised of 15 points, with positive ones concerning distance between marked tie item and antecedent, in particular, and with negative ones concerning nature of adequacy of tie use or error in tie use. This 15-point scale could be added to the 6-point ones on complexity in cohesive ties to provide a 21-point total range of values for scoring any one cohesive tie.

Halliday and Hasan (1976) did emphasize *distance* between tied item and referent, as have many others, but we have built upon this previous work to include not only distance between sentences or utterances but also, in particular, whether the sentences or utterances are within the same (sub)topic. Halliday and Hasan (1976) also considered *problems* in cohesion use through their concept of *exophoric* reference, in particular. However, exophora is limited to out-of-text reference and it need not be disruptive, as the discussion of the topic of cohesion by presumption had implied. Thus, I have constructed a comprehensive 7-point system of cohesion adequacy errors based on the work of those who have at least several categories of problems in cohesion (Martin, 1977–1978, 1983; Liles, 1982, 1985a, 1985b; Pratt & MacKenzie-Keating, 1985).

Martin and Rochester (Martin, 1977–1978; 1983; Rochester & Martin, 1979) were the first to devise a separate category reflecting inadequate cohesion. They described "additioning," for which a nominal phrase is (a) treated as already given

**Table 33.11** Measurement scale of cohesive quality

| Value | Category |
|---|---|
| Positive (Distance) | |
| +7 | Forward cataphora |
| +6 | Far – across topics |
| +5 | Far – across subtopics |
| +4 | Far – within (sub) topic |
| +3 | Between utterances |
| +2 | Between clauses |
| +1 | Within clause |
| 0 | Presumed |
| Negative (Inadequacy-error) | |
| −1 | Chained to inadequate tie |
| −2 | Unnecessary reintroduction |
| −3 | Interruption induced inadequacy |
| −4 | Obscure tie |
| −5 | Multiple tie |
| −6 | No discernable tie |
| −7 | Wrong (error) tie |

and has no discernable referent or (b) has multiple referents. The examples that they provide are: "A donkey was crossing the *other* river:" and "A commuter and a skier are on a lift and he looks very cold;" respectively. Pratt and MacKenzie-Keating (1985) added to this system by separating the two kinds of additioning and by including (a) "bad bridging," where an implied connection is obscure, and (b) mistaken reintroduction of a referent previously given. As for Liles (1982; 1985a, 1985b), she underscored errors comprised of referents (a) that lead the reader to wrong information in the text, or (b) that guide the reader to ambiguous information (equivalent to the category of multiple reference). She also described incomplete ties, where information that has been referred to is not provided in the text (like the category of no discernable referent). Finally, Liles introduced the type of inadequate cohesion "incomplete- or error-tie." In this subcategory, the marker tie item has an adequate referent, but that original referent itself is inadequate as a tie. In my opinion, this type of error is not as significant as any of the others. This leads to the presentation of how the various subcategories of inadequate cohesion are ordered in the present scale.

### Negative

The first four subcategories of inadequate cohesion concern overt confusing errors. Liles' category of wrong error tie appears the worst (−7), in that the listener/reader is guided to wrong information. A marker with no discernable referent (−6; Rochester & Martin, Pratt & MacKenzie-Keating, Liles) is almost as confusing. When multiple ties (−5; Rochester & Martin, Liles, Pratt & MacKenzie-Keating) are found, part of the information referred to is correct, but unfortunately more than this information is referenced. In obscure tying (−4; Pratt & MacKenzie-Keating), one referent is indicated, but not in a fully clear way. In the remaining three categories of inadequate cohesion, the quality of the tie ultimately proves overtly adequate, but some doubt is still evident. In interruption induced inadequacy (−3), one of the subcategories −4 to −7 can be assigned to the original statement, but the problem arises because the speaker has either prematurely terminated the utterance or has it interrupted. The score of −2 refers to Pratt and MacKenzie-Keating's concept of unnecessary reintroduction. Finally, −1 refers to Liles' idea of an adequate tie chained to an inadequate one (−4 to −7).

### Positive

As for the positive side of the scale, the assumption is that the greater the distance of the tie from its referent, the better is the cohesion quality. When a presumption without textual reference occurs, the distance is 0. Values +1 to +3 describe a simple progression from a tie within the same clause (+1), to a tie between clauses of the same utterance (+2), to a tie between neighboring utterances (+3). This latter value is limited to utterances on the same topic (or subtopic, if the topic consists of several of these). Scale points +4 to +6 describe another progression. Here, ties are across nonadjacent utterances, which vary in their relationship in terms of topic. In +4, the utterances are within the same topic (or subtopic, if the topic consists of several of these). In +5, the utterances are in different subtopics. A score of +5 is assigned even for the case of neighboring utterances where the first is the terminal one of one subtopic and the second is the initial one of another subtopic. If the narrative structure does not include subtopics, this score cannot be assigned. The value +6 is defined the same way as +5, except that the utterances are in completely different topics. Finally, we come to the most complex cohesion quality subcategory – cataphora. In this subcategory, the referent is given *after* the marked item, not before, the latter being the usual case especially with children. It was implicitly understood that all of the six previous scale points were defined in terms of backward referencing, or anaphora. With forward cataphoric referencing, a score of +7 is assigned no matter what the distance, given the relatively rare manifestation of this cohesive device. Note that the distance between a cohesive item and its link is calculated only where there is no inadequate tie or error (negative score).

In a perfectly designed system, each of the 15 scale points of cohesion quality should be applicable to each subcategory of cohesion. In general, this should prove true, especially for cohesive reference, lexis, substitution, and ellipsis. However, for the most part, the conjunction subcategories, in practice, will concern neighboring clauses and utterances and will rarely be cataphoric (e.g., "If you go, I will…"). Also, for conjunction, the values of – 2, −6, and perhaps −4 seem unnatural, although far-fetched examples are always possible to construct. In terms of the definition of cohesion by presumption, this cohesion category can be scored only as zero or negative. Moreover, it is hard to imagine when a coder can determine with certainty that scale values −5 to −7 apply to the self and the personal subcategories, but again concocted examples are always possible.

## Summary and Conclusions

The next chapter examines the present coding schemes for coherence and for syntactic complexity, in particular. When combined with the cohesion system described in this chapter, they form an integrated system of functional linguistics that could be used in narrative development in children, and its relationship to cognitive development, for example, as described by the present Neo-Piagetian model.

## References

Applebee, A. (1978). *The child's concept of story: Ages two to seventeen*. Chicago: University of Chicago Press.

Arfé, B., & Perondi, I. (2008). Deaf and hearing students' referential strategies in writing: What referential cohesion tells us about deaf students' literacy development. *First Language, 28*, 355–374.

Bloom, W., Lahey, M., Hood, L., Lifter, K., & Fiess, K. (1980). Complex sentences: Acquisition of syntactic connectives and the semantic relations they encode. *Journal of Child Language, 7*, 235–261.

Braunwald, S. (1985). The development of connectives. *Journal of Pragmatics, 9*, 513–525.

Brinton, B., & Fujiki, M. (1984). Development of topic manipulation skills in discourse. *Journal of Speech and Hearing Research, 27*, 350–358.

Bruner, J. (1986). *Actual minds, possible worlds*. Cambridge, MA: Harvard University Press.

Cain, K. (2003). Text comprehension and its relation to coherence and cohesion in children's fictional narratives. *British Journal of Developmental Psychology, 21*, 335–351.

Case, R., & McKeough, A. (1989). Schooling and the development of central conceptual knowledge structure: An example from the domain of children's narrative. *International Journal of Educational Research, 13*, 835–855.

Chafe, W. (1980). The deployment of consciousness in the production of a narrative. In W. Chafe (Ed.), *The pear stories* (pp. 9–50). Norwood: Ablex.

Davis, G. A., & Coelho, C. A. (2004). Referential cohesion and logical coherence of narration after closed head injury. *Brain and Language, 89*, 508–523.

Diehl, J. J., Bennetto, L., & Young, E. C. (2006). Story recall and narrative coherence of high-functioning children with autism spectrum disorders. *Journal of Abnormal Child Psychology, 34*, 87–102.

Dillinger, M., Bracewell, R., & Fine, J. (1983). *Cohesion as a guide to discourse processes* (Discourse Processing Lab Rep. No. 2). Montreal: McGill University, Department of Educational Psychology.

Dorval, B., & Eckerman, C. (1984). Developmental trends in the quality of conversation achieved by small groups of acquainted peers. *Monographs of the Society for Research in Child Development, 49*, (2, Serial No. 206).

Ervin-Tripp, S. (1978). Some features of early child-adult dialogues. *Language in Society, 7*, 257–273.

Fine, J. (1985a). Cohesion as an index of social-cognitive factors: Oral language of the reading disabled. *Discourse Processes, 8*, 91–112.

Fine, J. (1985b). What do surface markers mean? Towards a triangulation of social, cognitive and linguistic factors. In J. Benson & W. Greaves (Eds.), *Systemic perspectives on discourse* (Selected applied papers from the 9th international systemic workshop, Vol. 2, pp. 102–115). Norwood: Ablex.

Fivush, R., & Haden, C. A. (2003). *Autobiographical memory and the construction of a narrative self: Developmental and cultural perspectives*. Mahwah: Erlbaum.

Frederiksen, C. (1986). Cognitive models and discourse analysis. In C. Cooper & S. Greenbaum (Eds.), *Studying writing: Linguistic approaches* (pp. 227–267). Beverly Hills: Sage.

Frederiksen, C., Frederiksen, J., & Bracewell, R. (1985). Discourse analysis of children's text production. In A. Matsuhashi (Ed.), *Writing in real time* (pp. 254–290). New York: Longmans.

Freedle, R., & Fine, J. (1983). An interactional approach to the development of discourse. In R. Freedle & J. Fine (Eds.), *Developmental issues in discourse* (Vol. 10, pp. 143–168). Norwood, NJ: Ablex.

Goldberg, G. (1976). Conduite du discours enfantin et complexite syntaxique [Child discourse and syntactic complexity]. *La Linguistique, 12*, 3–34.

Halliday, M. A. K., & Hasan, R. (1976). *Cohesion in english*. New York: Longman.

Hasan, R. (1980). The texture of a text. In M. Halliday & R. Hasan (Eds.), *Text and context: Aspects of language in a sociosemiotic perspective (Sophia Linguistica Working Papers in Linguistics No. 6)* (pp. 43–59). Tokyo: Sophia University, Linguistic Institute for International Communication.

Haslett, B. (1983). Children's strategies for maintaining cohesion in their written and oral stories. *Communication Education, 32*, 91–105.

Hay, E., & Moran, C. (2005). Discourse formulation in children with closed head injury. *American Journal of Speech-Language Pathology, 14*, 324–336.

Hemphill, L., Uccelli, P., Winner, K., Chang, C., & Bellinger, D. (2002). Narrative discourse in young children with histories of early corrective heart surgery. *Journal of Speech, Language, and Hearing Research, 45*, 318–331.

Hickmann, M. (2003). *Children's discourse: Person, space and time across languages*. New York: Cambridge University Press.

Klecan-Aker, J., & Lopez, B. (1985). A comparison of T-units and cohesive ties used by first and third grade children. *Language and Speech, 28*, 307–315.

Leichman, M. D., Wang, Q., & Pillemer, D. B. (2003). Cultural variations in interdependence and autobiographical memory: Lessons from Korea, China, India, and the United States. In R. Fivush & C. A. Haden (Eds.), *Autobiographical memory and the construction of a narrative self: Developmental and cultural perspectives* (pp. 73–97). Mahwah: Erlbaum.

Liles, B. (1982). *Procedure for the analysis of cohesion in spoken narratives*. Unpublished manuscript, University of Connecticut, Department of Communication Science.

Liles, B. (1985a). Cohesion in the narratives of normal and language-disordered children. *Journal of Speech and Hearing Research, 28*, 123–133.

Liles, B. (1985b). Production and comprehension of narrative discourse in normal and language disordered children. *Journal of Communication Disorders, 18*, 409–427.

Lorusso, M. L., Galli, R., Libera, L., Gagliardi, C., Borgatti, R., & Hollebrrandse, B. (2007). Indicators of theory of mind in narrative production: A comparison between individuals with genetic syndromes and typically developing children. *Clinical Linguistics & Phonetics, 21*, 37–53.

Martin, J. (1977–1978). Learning how to tell: Semantic systems and structures in children's narrative. *Dissertation Abstracts International* 38, 533A. (University Microfilms No. 78–70, 018).

Martin, J. (1983). The development of register. In J. Fine & R. Freedle (Eds.), *Development issues in discourse* (pp. 1–39). Norwood: Ablex.

McCutchen, D., & Perfetti, C. (1982). Coherence and connectedness in the development of discourse production. *Text, 2*, 113–139.

McKeough, A., Davis, L., Forgeron, N., Marini, A., & Fung, T. (2005). Improving story complexity and cohesion: A developmental approach to teaching story composition. *Narrative Inquiry, 15*, 96–125.

McKeough, A., & Griffiths, S. (2010). Adolescent narrative thought: Developmental and neurological evidence in support of a central social structures. In M. Ferrari & L. Vuletic (Eds.), *Developmental relations among mind, brain and education* (pp. 213–230). New York: Springer Science+Business Media.

McTear, M. (1985). *Children's conversation*. New York: Blackwell.

Navet, M., Nespoulos, J. L., & Lecours, A. (1984). Approches psycholinguistiques du discours du psychotique [Psycholinguistic approaches to discourse in psychotics]. *Actes du Congrès de la Federation Nationale des Orthophonistes, 7-8-9-10*, 411–439.

Neisser, U., & Fivush, R. (Eds.). (1994). *The remembering self: Construction and accuracy in the self narrative*. Cambridge: Cambridge University Press.

Nelson, K. (2000). The developmental psychology of language and thought. In M. Bennett (Ed.), *Developmental psychology: Achievements and prospects* (pp. 185–204). East Sussex: Psychology Press.

Nicolopoulou, A. (1997). Children and narratives: Toward an interpretive and sociocultural approach. In M. Bamberg (Ed.), *Narrative development: Six approaches* (pp. 179–216). Hillsdale: Erlbaum.

Nicolopoulou, A. (2008). The elementary forms of narrative coherence in young children's storytelling. *Narrative Inquiry, 18*, 299–325.

Pappas, C. (1985). The cohesive harmony and cohesive density of children's oral and written stories. In J. Benson & W. Greaves (Eds.), *Systemic perspectives on discourse* (Selected theorical papers from the 9th international systemic workshop, Vol. 1, pp. 169–186). Norwood: Ablex.

Patry, R., & Menard, N. (1985). *Specificite du lexique dans l'analyse de la cohesion: Problematique et perspective d'applications* [Lexical specificity in the analysis of cohesion: Issues and applied perspectives]. Paper presented at the XVIIe Colloquium of the Association de Linguistique Appliquée, Montreal.

Paul, R. (1981). Analyzing complex sentence development. In J. Miller (Ed.) *Assessing communicative behavior: Vol. 1. Assessing language production in children: Experimental procedures* (pp. 37–38, 40, 67–71). Baltimore: University Park Press.

Pellegrini, A. (1986). Play centers and the production of imaginative language. *Discourse Processes, 9*, 115–125.

Pellegrini, A., Galda, L., & Rubin, D. (1984). Context in text: The development of oral and written language in two genres. *Child Development, 55*, 1549–1555.

Peterson, C., & McCabe, A. (1983). *Developmental psycholinguistics: Three ways of looking at a child's narrative*. New York: Plenum.

Pettegrew, B. (1981). Text formation: A comparative study of literate and pre-literate first grade children. *Dissertation Abstracts International, 42,* 635 A. (University Microfilms No. 8115149).

Pratt, M. W., Boyes, C., Robins, S., & Manchester, J. (1989). Telling tales: Working memory and the narrative cohesion of story retellings. *Developmental Psychology, 25*, 628–635.

Pratt, M., & Mackenzie-Keating, S. (1985). Organizing stories; Effects of development and task difficulty on referential cohesion in narrative. *Developmental Psychology, 2*, 350–356.

Rentel, V., & King, M. (1983). *A longitudinal study of coherence in children's written narratives* (Tech. Rep. No. 143). Columbus: The Ohio State University, Research Foundation.

Rochester, S., & Martin, J. (1979). *Crazy talk: A study of the discourse of schizophrenic speakers*. New York: Plenum.

Roy, A. (1981). Identifying and counting utterances. *Semiotica, 377*, 15–25.

Schaefer, R. (2004). Narrating, attending, and empathizing. *Literature and Medicine, 23*, 241–251.

Serratrice, L. (2006). Referential cohesion in the narratives of bilingual English-Italian children and monolingual peers. *Journal of Pragmatics, 39*, 1058–1087.

Stein, N. L., & Glenn, C. G. (1979). An analysis of story comprehension in elementary school children. In R. O. Freedle (Ed.), *New directions in discourse processing* (New directions in discourse processes, Vol. 2, pp. 53–120). Norwood: Ablex.

Symons, D. K., Peterson, C. C., Slaughter, V., Roche, J., & Doyle, E. (2005). Theory of mind and mental state discourse during book reading and story-telling tasks. *British Journal of Developmental Psychology, 23*, 81–102.

Tappan, M., & Packer, M. (Eds.). (1991). Narrative and storytelling: Implications for understanding moral development. *New directions for child development, 54*. San Franciso: Jossey-Bass.

Trionfi, G., & Reese, E. (2009). A good story: Children with imaginary companions create richer narratives. *Child Development, 80*, 1301–1313.

Weinland, M. (1984). An investigation into the relationship between the use of cohesive ties in oral retellings and a comprehension process score for good and poor fifth grade readers. *Dissertation Abstracts International, 45,* 1087A. (University Microfilms No. DA8416078).

Westerveld, M. F., Gillon, G. T., & Moran, C. (2008). A longitudinal investigation of oral narrative skills in children with mixed reading disability. *International Journal of Speech-Language Pathology, 10*, 132–145.

Yussen, S. R., & Ozcan, N. M. (1996). The development of knowledge about narratives. *Issues in Education, 2*, 1–68.

# Chapter 34
# Narrative Discourse Coding: Syntactic Complexity-Errors and Coherence

## Introduction

This chapter is the second of two on a narrative coding scheme on cohesion and coherence for children. In this chapter, I deal with syntactic complexity and coherence, in particular. This chapter provides examples in French more than in the last chapter.

## Syntactic Complexity

In this section, I treat the complexity and error portions of the scale of syntactic complexity-errors. The complexity side of the scale (−3 to +10) is organized around the work of Goldberg (1976) and Paul (1981).

## Two Prior Schemes

*Goldberg* (1976). Goldberg analyzed children's oral discourse from diverse perspectives and began with the syntactic complexity of utterances. I used her approach to this issue as a point of departure because it is amenable to the development of an ordinal scale of syntactic complexity congruent with the present theoretical stance. Goldberg elaborated a system based on Loban's "weighted index of subordination" in utterances (unreferenced citation). This is a three-point scale assigning scores principally depending on whether subordinate clauses are primary or secondary and having a verbal "construction" (e.g., infinitive) or not. Goldberg refined Loban's scale, devising her own system of syntactic complexity of utterances. In reviewing her system, it becomes evident that complexity is defined especially in terms of all manners of qualification and modifiers, such as the use of nominal propositions, infinitive expansions, etc., and not just in terms of dependent, relative, subordinate, or embedded clauses. Although Goldberg's categories were hierarchically organized from simpler to complex, she did not try to arrange them

G. Young, *Development and Causality: Neo-Piagetian Perspectives*,
DOI 10.1007/978-1-4419-9422-6_34, 

into an ordinal scale, as Loban had. I now examine the 10-point scale of syntactic complexity derived from Goldberg (1976).

(i) *SVO utterance* (Goldberg's category of "enonce simple- sans circonstants... facultatif(s)"). The subject–verb–object (SVO) structure of the sentence is not qualified except in the sense that the object of the sentence qualifies the rest (e.g., "They have a sister"). To Goldberg's examples, I add others that are qualified by one adverb or adjective (e.g., "I'm quickly going there"; "I have a big brother"). Even some simple verbal constructions can be classified here according to Goldberg (futur proche: "Je vais partir").

(ii) *Simple utterance with adverbs/adjectives.* I separated utterances with multiple different adverbs or adjectives from the first category because the degree of modification seems quite complex compared to that in category (i). Items can involve qualification of any component of the SVO structure (e.g., "I have a big bad teddy bear"; "I'm going to leave very quickly"; "The hungry bear ate the sweat honey").

(iii) *Simple utterance with proposition.* For the most part, Goldberg's complex utterance number "I" concerns propositions, or optional expansions without predicates. There are two major kinds, nominal and verbal, as illustrated in the sentence, "The boy on the bike fell on the ground." Her example is: "*Je* suis partie dimanche dernier avec ma soeur."

(iv) *Utterance with automatic infinitive.* Goldberg's complex utterance II consists of automatic and autonomous infinitive expansions, which she considers quite distinct in complexity. The first ones constitute this scale point and are characterized by their fixed, obligatory (stereotypic?) status (e.g., "I must leave," "He wants to leave," "Il faut partir," "Je veux partir"). Goldberg included in this category infinitives preceded by prepositions conveying obligation (e.g., "He decided to go"; "Il est necessaire de partir") because these are often followed in a obligatory fashion by an infinitive.

(v) *Utterance with autonomous infinitive.* Here, the infinitives are not fixed, can vary, and do not concern obligation (e.g., "I went to make him happy"; "J'y suis allé pour lui faire plaisir").

(vii) *Utterance with automatic subordinate clause.* Goldberg's complex utterance III consists of several subcategories of subordinate clauses of different complexity. In French, an utterance with an automatic subordinate clause especially refers to subordination using certain modal words followed by the word "que" ("that"). Examples include, "It is necessary that ('il faut que') we leave, Je trouve que c'est bien." In this type of structure, a principal proposition is expressed as an auxiliary to a predicate of declaration, obligation, etc.

(vi, viii) *Conjoined utterances.* Conjunction of utterances through (vi) simple coordinations (e.g., "and," "but," "parce que," "pis" [a Québecois expression meaning "puis"]) or (viii) more complex subordinate conjunctions ("subordinats circonstancielles," such as "although," "since," "puisque," "ou"). Note that we treat the French "parce que" ("because") as a coordinate conjunction, although Goldberg mentioned that in some contexts it could be considered subordinate.

Her difficulty in operationalizing the distinction that is involved led me to this conservative decision (following traditional grammar). Goldberg noted that conjoined utterances sometimes are evident only in context; intonation suggests juxtaposition of neighboring clauses, although syntax might not (e.g., "He was tickled; he laughed"). One should follow this suggestion only when a clear causal semantic link is evident. Goldberg suggested that simple coordinated utterances are not really examples of complex utterance III, but could involve the category complex utterance II (see her p. 10), which is why for the present scale I placed it between levels v (an example of level II) and vii (an example of level III).

(ix) *Utterance with nonembedded clause.* The simpler type of dependent clause (e.g., "She's *wearing* a dress *which* is dirty"; sentences with "qui," "ce qui").

(x) *Utterance with embedded clause.* A most refined level of language where the clause concerned qualifies an antecedent within another clause (e.g., "The dress that she is wearing is dirty").

*Paul* (1981). Paul (in Miller, 1981) constructed a lengthy list of embedded utterance categories. In each utterance category, a clause, defined as a dependent constituent sentence-like segment that contains a main verb, is subordinated within a main matrix sentence (see Table 34.1). Sentences with single concatenives are not

**Table 34.1** Paul's (1981) categories of complex embedded sentences

| Category | Definition | Examples |
|---|---|---|
| 1. Let's, let me | Automatic clause introducers<br>Complex in form not structure | Let's get in<br>Let me see<br>Let's go |
| 2. Infinitive clause, simple | Simple infinitive clause marked by "to" with subject equivalent to or same as that of main sentence<br>Clause subject usually deleted | I have to leave<br>He wants to eat<br>They like to go |
| 3. Full propositional clause | Complete surface sentence containing full propositional complement<br>Usually headed by verbs like "think, guess, wish, wonder, know, hope, show, remember, pretend, forget, say, mean, and tell." Clause may begin with "that" | I think we have a lot<br>Pretend you said it<br>I know that you said it |
| 4. Simple wh-clause | Clause begins with a wh-word such as "when, what, why, where, how, if, and like." Infinitive marker "to" absent | |
| 5. Infinitive clause, different subject | Subject of an infinitive clause is different from that of main sentence<br>Clause subject usually appears | This is for you to do<br>You want me to go there?<br>I like Daddy to wear ties |
| 6. Relative clause | Modifiers a noun. Can begin with "what, which, who, and that" | Look at the man I drew?<br>Take the pen that I won?<br>That's the dog that did it |
| 7. Gerund clause | Sentence contains verb ending in "-ing" as part of noun clause<br>Gerund adjectives excluded. | See him walking around?<br>I washed by rubbing<br>I have running shoes [no] |

(continued)

**Table 34.1** (continued)

| Category | Definition | Examples |
|---|---|---|
| 8. Infinitive clause, unmarked | Infinitive clause not headed by "to"<br>Usually begun by "make, help, let, and watch" | You help me do this<br>I'll let you begin<br>She made him talk |
| 9. Infinitive clause, wh- | Marked by both a wh-word and "to" | Show me what to get<br>Do I know when to go?<br>Tell me how to leave |
| 10. Double embedding | An embedded clause contained in another embedded clause. One of the clauses may include a concatenive. | Do you think you know how this works?<br>I know we gotta pour it<br>I wanna let it go |

considered embedded utterances (e.g., "I wanna go"). Also, according to Paul, the first category of the ten listed is not a "truly complex" embedded sentence (e.g., "Let's go"). Using this list of embedded sentences, Paul analyzed the transcripts of 59 children between 2.5 and 7 years of age who were involved in 15-min free-play sessions with their mothers. The children were divided into five groups according to their MLU (mean length utterance; 3–3.5 to 5+). The developmental order of emergence of the categories was determined by calculating for each category the first MLU group to reach the criterion of at least one use by over 50% of the subjects in the group.

One to several categories emerged in each of the first four MLU groupings, helping to specify a partial developmental progression for the categories. However, the categories did not emerge one after another in the order indicated in the table where Paul presented and defined the categories. In particular, the last category of double embedding emerged fifth. Furthermore, according to Paul's method, there is no way of distinguishing the developmental differences of categories that emerged in the same MLU stage. However, it is likely that the order in which the categories are presented in the table within each MLU level where there is more than one category reflects their order of acquisition. If this is true, two more possible problems emerge; the ninth category might emerge before the eight and the second before the first. The latter inversion is not serious because the first category is not considered a true complex embedded sentence. The former inversion also is not serious, in the case of Francophones, in that the eighth category does not apply to the French language. However, this issue should be clarified before the scale is applied to English transcripts.

A final comment about Paul's scale of sentence complexity is that it does not directly deal with conjoined sentences (they are treated independently of embedded sentences). As has been shown by Goldberg (1976), this juxtaposition does not always apply.

Aram, Ekelman, and Whitaker (1986) applied Paul's (1981) complex sentence classification system to their study of spontaneous language samples of unilaterally lesioned children and matched controls. They maintained that the order of category presentation in Paul (1981) reflects a "simple to complex" progression. However, I have shown that this is not entirely true, especially for double embeddings, which may not be the most complex level despite its placement at the end of the list. Moreover, the same difficulty in classifying is evident for let me/let's constructions, which have been placed at the beginning of the list even though they are not considered truly embedded. In general, the results of Aram et al. were consistent with expectations: early left-hemisphere lesions led to deficits in the more complex category types, whereas early right-hemisphere lesions had almost no effect on complex utterance use. The control groups used all categories except, paradoxically, double embeddings (in the left-hemisphere matched group). According to these results, Paul had been correct in classifying this category as the most complex, although the results belie this conclusion. Given the consistent ambiguities about this category, prudence should be used in any scaling attempt until more research is performed.

## *Combining the Two Prior Schemes*

The two scales of syntactic complexity that have been presented are quite complementary. What one misses the other describes. I combined them into a 14-point scale, the first 10 (+1 to +10) of which treat truly complex utterances as defined by Paul (embedded, conjoined). The remaining four categories deal with simpler utterances, and thus are classified as neutral or negative for present purposes. Note that the 14-point Goldberg–Paul sequence covers the first 14 points of the two scales given in the two tables (Tables 34.2 and 34.3).

Table 34.2 summarizes how the present system combines the work of Goldberg and Paul. Of the 14 scale points, 5 are combined or parallel Goldberg and Paul categories, 5 are from Goldberg alone (4 directly from Goldberg, 1 we added, (ii) and 4 are from Paul alone. Note that in using the scale, self-repaired utterances should be not be penalized for their initial errors.

**Table 34.2** Scale of syntactic complexity-errors: positive

| | Category | Goldberg (1976) equivalent | Paul (1981) equivalent |
|---|---|---|---|
| +10 | Complex embedding | x | X |
| +9 | Infinitive clause, wh- or unmarked | | IX, VIII |
| +8 | Gerund clause | | VII |
| +7 | Nonembedded relative clause | ix | VI |
| +6 | Utterance conjoined by subordinate conjunction | viii | |
| +5 | Infinitive clause, different | v | V |
| +4 | Wh- clause, simple (questions) | | IV |
| +3 | Utterance conjoined by coordinate conjunction | vi | |
| +2 | Propositional clause, automatic | vii | III |
| +1 | Infinitive clause, automatic | iv | II |
| 0 | Simple utterance with proposition | iii | |

*Note*. Categories +5 and +2 switched for French

**Table 34.3** Scale of syntactic complexity-errors: negative

| | Category | Goldberg (1976) equivalent | Paul (1981) equivalent |
|---|---|---|---|
| −1 | Simple utterance with adverbs/adjectives | ii | |
| −2 | SVO utterance | i | |
| −3 | Simple utterance without qualifier | | I |
| −4 | Laconic, partial utterance | | |
| −5 | Utterance with minor error | | |
| −6 | Utterance with confusing error | | |
| −7 | Utterance with missing functional group | | |
| −8 | Telegraphic utterance | | |
| −9 | Utterance with syntactic error | | |
| −10 | Utterance with semantic anomaly | | |

(−3) *Simple utterance without qualifier.* When complete, this sentence is the simplest type possible (subject–verb, S–V structure), and it is not qualified by multiple adjectives or adverbs, an adjectival, nominal, or verbal proposition, infinitive expansions, embedded clauses, etc. Examples include "I have" and "I'm going." Paul's category of Let's/let's see (I) and also concatenives should be scored at this scale point because even though multiple verbs seem present in the surface form, they are really conjoined, easily learned automatisms. There are no comparable examples in French. This scale point should be assigned not only for the kinds of utterances mentioned but also when a more complex utterance has been produced in a nonspontaneous way (e.g., imitation, folk saying, stereotypic cultural automatism).

The scale from this point up to point +10 has been formulated to apply to well-formed utterances, in particular. Nevertheless, this criterion does not mean that one should automatically exclude from scoring utterances that are well formed at this point, aside from ellipses. In the same vein, one should not automatically exclude partial or incomplete utterances appropriate to the context and whose meaning is clear in the context. This refers to backchannels appropriate in context, incomplete sentences as answers to questions, collaboratively produced utterances, vocatives, interjections, greetings, sounds produced to function as words, etc. Nevertheless, these types of partial utterances will usually be too complex according to our criteria to be scored as 0 or more. That is, these types of utterances will usually be problematic enough so that they should be scored as negative (−1 to −4 at best).

(−2 to 0) *Intermediate.* Scale points i to iii derived from Goldberg find no real parallel with Paul, for Paul does not treat categories that are like Goldberg's truly complex utterances.

(+1) *Infinitive clause, automatic.* Here, Goldberg and Paul seem to be describing very similar phenomena with their categories: Utterance with automatic infinitive, iv (Goldberg) and Infinitive clause, simple, II (Paul). In both cases, there is a forced automaticity of paired verbs (e.g., "Je dois partir," "He has to leave," respectively). The major difference between Goldberg and Paul's categories is that Paul not only includes Goldberg's examples, which especially concern varieties of obligation, but also she includes more general examples where subjects differ between main and infinitive clause without recourse to words of obligation. Note that sentences such as, "I am going to go," "Je vais partir" (Goldberg's example of "Future proche"), etc., would not be scored here but in category −2 according to Goldberg. In this type of example, there are forced verb pairings but only because the verb is being expanded.

(+2) *Propositional clause, automatic.* Goldberg and Paul seem to describe the same category in Automatic subordinate clause, vii, and Full propositional clause, III, respectively. Both categories concern subordinate clauses having a type of marker verb that fixes noninfinitive clauses supplying most of the information of the sentence. For Goldberg, these are French "modaux" (modals, e.g., "Il faut que..."), fixed or automatic in function. Paul gives comparable examples with "I think..." "I say...," etc. Note that for Paul, the list of fixing marker verbs is much more general than Goldberg would permit. The first major problem in applying the scale to French occurs at this point because the category currently under discussion and category +5 are switched in position in Goldberg's scale. Vive la différence.

(+4) *Wh-clause, simple (questions).* Direct from Paul (Simple wh-clause, IV) in English. However, this category does not apply in French (infinitives are not marked by separate words equivalent to "to" susceptible to exclusion, e.g., "to eat" = "manger"), although another one comparable to it does. There are many interrogative constructions in French that are difficult to transform into one equivalent declarative form, or that cannot be placed on the scale that is being described, and often these involve wh-words, which are at the heart of Paul's category IV. Moreover, these interrogative structures seem more complex than coordinated utterances (+3) but less complex than French automatic subordinate clauses (+5). Some examples follow: "C'est quoi que tu veux?" "C'est quand que tu vas venir?" "Est-ce que tu m'aime?"

(+5) *Infinitive clause, different.* This represents the second of the categories where Goldberg and Paul contribute equally. Each of them seems to be saying that infinitive clauses with subjects different from that of the matrix sentence are autonomous in structure (utterance with autonomous infinitive, v; Infinitive clause, different subject, V, respectively). However, in French, Paul's examples do not really apply, although the concept does apply. We remind that, as discussed, the complexity categories +2 and +5 are inverted in French and English. Note that an utterance with embedded speech (e.g., "He said: 'I... '") is scored like other utterances, except that I treat it as if the word "that" has been elided (e.g., "He said that he..."). Generally, this would lead me to score such utterances at this level of +5 (automatic subordinate), or higher (e.g., +10, embedded clause). However, if the utterance contains syntax errors, it is scored as negative.

(+3, +6) *Intermediate.* Paul treats conjoined sentences separately from embedded ones, but Goldberg treats these sentence types together, and thus helps to find the optimal placement of conjoined utterances (vi = +3, viii = +6) among the various categories of embedded sentences. It will be recalled that coordinated sentences were considered more complex than Autonomous infinitives, v (now +2), which justifies the score of +3 in the combined scale. Moreover, it seems less complex than both the English and French versions of Paul's category IV, which is based on wh-clauses, in particular.

(+7) *Nonembedded relative clause.* Here, Goldberg and Paul again use different labels for the same linguistic event (categories ix and VI, respectively).

(+8) *Intermediate.* Straight from Paul (VII).

(+9) *Infinitive clause, wh- or unmarked.* The prior discussion about the uncertainty of the order of complexity of categories VIII and IX described by Paul dictates that they should be combined. Moreover, because of the same problem encountered in category +3 – French infinitives are not marked by a word equivalent to "to" susceptible to exclusion – only examples from IX will be found in French. Note that many of the translations into French of the examples of Paul's category IV fit into category IX.

(+10) *Complex embedding.* Paul's category, Double embedding, X, was shown to be an ambiguous category difficult to place on that author's scale by itself. It's similarity to Goldberg's Embedded clause, x, suggests that one can group these two more complex types of embedding into one category.

Note that it is possible that an utterance appears syntactically ambiguous or semantically anomalous at the verbal level, but when analyzed in its nonverbal context, no problem is evident. That is, paralinguistic variables (e.g., prosody, communicative gestures, situational referencing) clarify the verbal lacunae. In such cases, the speaker should be given the benefit of the doubt and scored as if there were no problem.

## *Syntactic Problems*

The prior comment shows that boundary between acceptable and nonacceptable syntax is not always clear, especially in oral discourse and interchange, and especially when children are involved. However, limits must be placed on our tolerance. The speaker should be penalized for incomplete utterances that are evidently syntactically incomplete or do not make any sense in context. This leads to the present scale of degree of syntactic error, which is based on the work of Navet, Nespoulous, and Lecours (1984), who analyzed the written discourse of psychotic adolescents from a variety of psycholinguistic avenues. Points −4 to −9 of the present scale are borrowed directly from Navet et al. and deal with various evident syntactic errors. Point −10 concerns semantic confusion, as described in Navet et al., a choice that will be justified later on. Note that they did not suggest an order of error severity for their categories, although it turns out that the order I created more or less follows their order of presentation of the categories. Also note that I split their category "b" into two separate categories (−5, −6) and drop their category "d" because it is not an error for children, unlike for psychotics.

(−4) *Laconic, partial utterance.* Not only is the utterance incomplete but also it seems either too stilted, idiomatic, opaque, stereotypic, or automatic. A laconic utterance is fully comprehendable in context, unlike an uncompleted utterance. For example, the child says "because" or "parce que" instead of giving a requested full explanation.

(−5) *Utterance with minor error.* Refers to omission or substitution of minor element(s) of object, subject, verb, etc., which do not greatly compromise the syntax and the semantics of the sentence. The category also refers to phonological ambiguity, which does not compromise utterance syntax and semantics.

(−6) *Utterance with confusing error.* An omission or substitution that compromises the syntax and semantics of the utterance, unlike in −5 (e.g., a child dressing says, "I put my foot on the pants").

(−7) *Utterance with missing functional group.* Omission of functional word group, such as subject, verb, object ("I to park"; "t'allé au parc").

(−8) *Telegraphic utterance.* The whole utterance seems to be reduced to a style emphasizing barest essentials. There are missing words in several parts of sentence, but the omissions do not compromise the utterance's message.

(−9) *Utterance with syntactic error.* Refers to inversion of word groups that overtly compromise syntax (e.g., "Jean ont saute et Jim"; "The bear there went").

(−10) *Utterance with semantic anomaly.* Despite apparently adequate syntax, the utterance manifests no internal logical consistency. Navet et al. (1984) described three types. (a) Combinatorial: one component of the utterance does not satisfy the requirements imposed elsewhere in the utterance (e.g., "The invaders will be kind with me."). (b) Logical: often concerns contradiction, improper cause-effect relations, or chronology (e.g., "He was a stranger because one of his parents was over 100 years old."). (c) Referential: the utterance's contents differ from the expected (e.g., "The fox wiped his bum…"). Note that in a child's story, such semantic anomalies are often found, as the child invents humorous or creative fantasies. In such cases, the child should not be penalized. I envisage no difficulty in considering such semantic anomalies as part of one scale emphasizing syntactic complexity and errors because often the latter add to or detract from the semantic message.

Appropriate intonation or reference to the specific situation, as in communicative pointing, can complement the verbal stream with information, such as clarification of ambiguities in meaning, thematic emphasis, and topic continuity and reintroduction (Michaels & Collins, 1984). Also, filled and unfilled pauses, or repetitions when strategically placed prior to or during sentence production, might involve these clarification-emphatic functions or might indicate planning to the listener (MacWhinney & Osser, 1977). Finally, the oral mode better permits spontaneous repairs and corrections, which add to the feeling that the child is trying to plan and trying to cope toward text unity (Evans, 1985). By contrast, inappropriate prosody, gestures, or excessive pauses might give the impression of poorer or slipping clarity, unity, or planning. Similarly, botched repairs, excessive repetitions, and so on, might give an impression opposite to that of textual integrity (e.g., Nicolas, Obler, Albert, & Helm-Estabrooks, 1985).

## Coherence

### *Introduction*

I have formulated a novel 21-point scale of textual coherence based on some common concepts in discourse analysis. I defined coherence in a broad sense as a logical and/or structural continuity in the emergent (perhaps collectively produced) discourse of (a) speaker(s). Primarily, it concerns a topical integrity communicated through the linked sequential verbal utterances of one particular speaker. However, when not controlled, the listener's comments and the linkage between the speaker and listener must also be considered. In this regard, concepts such as turnabout are important; a turnabout concerns how a speaker can retrospectively comment on the partner's prior turn and at the same time set up a prospective continuity (e.g., McTear, 1985; Torrance & Olson, 1984).

The positive and negative sides of the scale have different sources of inspiration. At the heart of positive side of the scale, I have tried to show a complementarity between the topic manipulation concept, which essentially concerns between-utterance relations, and more global approaches of across-utterance judgments of story integrity. Various measures of topic manipulation (maintenance, and its shifting; e.g., Brinton & Fujiki, 1984; Dorval & Eckerman, 1984) are used to show how topics cohere in conversations involving children. Thus, the lower positive scale points often directly reflect categories found in Brinton and Fujiki (1984) and Dorval and Eckerman (1984). The higher more advanced positive scale points of the scale are derived from the levels of Botvin and Sutton-Smith's (1977) scheme for globally judging the complexity of children's stories. I describe these pertinent articles in detail to prepare the presentation of the scale.

### *Research*

*Brinton and Fujiki* (1984). These researchers investigated topic structure in the spontaneous 15-min conversations of 5- and 9-year-olds and adults. Although there were evident individual differences, developmental trends showed an increased in topic maintenance and shading (akin to topic association; see below), in particular. Brinton and Fujiki (1984) performed a type of topic "content analysis." Observers assigned a descriptive label each time that they felt a new topic was introduced in the discourse (e.g., "trip to France"). Various indices for each utterance helped arrive at this judgment: "propositional content, grammatical form, physical context, social context, and the linguistic context (… surrounding utterances), referential cues… cohesive devices." The topic heading rarely was overtly stated, could occur at several levels (e.g., topic, subtopic), and could sometimes be found only after several consecutive utterances were considered together. In summary, following Keenan and Scheiffelin (1976), coders determined what they thought was being "talked about," what was the "central concern," or what was the "focus of attention." Once topic boundaries were determined, each utterance was qualified as to whether it was maintained, shaded, changed, etc.

Many of the categories that I borrowed from Brinton and Fujiki (1984) were also found in Dorval and Eckerman (1984). They looked at conversations in acquainted peers ranging in age from 7 years to adult.

*Botvin and Sutton-Smith* (1977). These authors analyzed the complexity of the spontaneous told stories of 3–12-year-old children. Following Propp (1968), each primary plot was analyzed into its units of action (e.g., a lack or insufficient state, its liquidation; villainy, its nullification). Then, the organization of the distilled structure was assigned one of seven levels of complexity hypothetically arranged in an ordered sequence of development. The results showed that, in general, story complexity increased with chronological age.

Kemper (1984) compared several global story complexity measures, including Botvin and Sutton-Smith's and another based on Propp (Maranda & Maranda, 1971). Kemper asserted that for the age of 5 years and onward the Botvin and Sutton-Smith method showed the most reliable appropriate age changes. Inspection of her figures showed that the method is even applicable to younger ages. The present use of the Botvin and Sutton-Smith procedure has been greatly modified. I do not assign one global score like they do. Rather, each utterance is assigned its own score, just like in the topic maintenance procedures.

*Michaels and Collins* (1984). It is important to emphasize that textual coherence may be derived from more than logical, sequential, verbal structure. That is, textual coherence might also lie in either (a) structured, nonsequential, verbal linkages, or (b) nonverbal sequential linkages. These categories refer to associated, parallel storytelling styles in the former case and prosodic, associated emphases in the latter case (Michaels & Collins, 1984). Negative coherence should especially be based on prematurely cutoff story interruptions, asides, irrelevant, incoherent connections, etc. This type of data is often discarded in storytelling studies, but such a procedure is misguided. Note that in direct discourse there can be utterances that could seem negative in coherence, especially if an argument or disagreement is the topic under development. However, these utterances should be considered positive.

## *Positive Text Coherence*

Before I present the specific scale points, the idea of self- and other-linked utterances is introduced. Each utterance can be linked to a previous utterance of the self or the other. For example, if one of the topic maintenance categories is assigned, a coder should indicate whether the narrative continuity refers to a link with an utterance of the speaker or the listener. Or if there is a turnabout, the coder should indicate whether the speaker is making a retrospective link with something the speaker or the other said, and whether the prospective suggestion is toward the other or the self.

Before beginning, I introduce the concept of turnabout, in detail, even though it is not the initial point of the scale, because it is especially important to clarify what is meant by self and by other linkages with respect to this concept.

(+6) *Turnabout.* The concept of turnabout is applicable especially to dyadic exchange (McTear, 1985; Torrance & Olson, 1984). However, the types of retrospective and prospective links that this concept entails can be readily applied to the speaker's own continuous discourse. A typical turnabout sees the speaker prospectively request an acknowledgement from the listener after having given information retrospectively in response to a request by the listener. A speaker might make a prospective link in her/his own discourse in several analogous ways. For example, use of a rhetorical question is one such device. Similarly, a new topic might be abruptly introduced with a qualification that it shall soon be discussed or elaborated. As for retrospective links in a speaker's discourse, these refer to typical topic maintenance categories. Thus, a turn that is both retrospective and prospective with respect to the speakers' own discourse is complex and might not occur frequently in young children, but it should manifest more frequently as conversational abilities mature.

Some hypothetical examples of the four possible types of turnabouts are offered:

I. Other retrospective – other prospective;
"Are you going? (speaker 1)
No I'm not, and are you?" (2)

II. Other retrospective – self prospective;
"Are you going? (1)
Yes, I am and I can think of a reason why; because I want to… (etc.)" (2)

III. Self retrospective – other prospective;
"'Are you going?,' she asked. (1)
She wasn't sure, so what do you think that she should say?" (1)

IV. Self retrospective – self prospective;
"'Are you going?' she asked. (1)
Her answer was clear, and why not, for victory was hers." (1)

These examples should make clear why I consider the turnabout a most powerful coherent connecting device in conversational discourse. At its optimal, it aligns speaker and listener in intertwined communicative exchanges within a common meaning framework, or it chains the speaker's utterances in a Janus-like vise via narrative devices that can help to captivate the listener, or it does both.

Note that a turnabout structure should not always be scored as +6. If the utterance simultaneously involves a higher-order scale point, that scale point should be assigned. In the same vein, if the simultaneous scale point is lower but positive, the turnabout structure takes precedence and a score of +6 should be assigned. Finally, if a turnabout structure involves an utterance that can be scored on the negative portion of the scale of textual coherence, the negative weighting must be attributed.

**Table 34.4** Scale of textual coherence

| | Positive | | Negative |
|---|---|---|---|
| +10 | Secondary subplot | −1 | Heap association |
| +9 | Successive subplot | −2 | Shade association |
| +8 | Single subplot | −3 | Nonverbal association |
| +7 | Topic return | −4 | Topic search |
| +6 | Turnabout | −5 | Interjected private speech |
| +5 | New subtopic | −6 | Aside comment |
| +4 | Topic refinement | −7 | Topic cutoff |
| +3 | Topic addition | −8 | Cutoff imposition |
| +2 | Topic matching | −9 | Inadequate coherence |
| +1 | Utterance imitation | −10 | Incoherence |
| 0 | Topic find | | |

I proceed discuss the more standard topic maintaining and shifting categories. Self or other linking becomes quite straightforward in all the remaining positive scale points. It simply refers to whether an utterance involving a type of topic maintenance or shifting refers to previous utterance(s) by the speaker or the listener. Thus, I do not repetitively elaborate upon this concept with the introduction of each scale value.

(+10 to +8) *Subplotting.* Scale points +10 to +8 (see Table 34.4) deal with subplots, which can be defined as self-contained units within a story or conversation that are hierarchically embedded in that story or conversation (i.e., presented before termination or resolution of the higher-order unit to which it is subordinated). Botvin and Sutton-Smith (1977) assigned one global score for the whole story, whereas in the present system the first utterance of the subplot is assigned the score of +8, +9, or +10, and the remaining utterances of the subplot are scored according to their relationship to this first utterance by using any of the other 18 points of the scale. Subplotting represents the most advanced type of topic maintenance. In this, we find a correspondence with the previously described scale of syntactic complexity, in which utterances with embedded clauses are assigned the highest score.

Level 10 concerns a subplot within a subplot (secondary subplotting). Note that at one point Botvin and Sutton-Smith (1977) speak of a "subordination of plots within plots" when describing their level 7, but everything else about its presentation suggests that this level does not consider at all such secondary subplotting.

The eighth and ninth scale points of single and successive subplotting somewhat resemble Botvin and Sutton-Smith's levels 6 and 7, respectively. Level 9 subplotting would introduce another subplot after termination of a first one, whereas level 10 subplotting would involve a secondary subplot embedded in the first before its termination. Note that the first subplot of a series should be given the score of +8, while the remaining one(s) receive(s) a score of +9.

(+7) *Topic return.* A topic introduced beforehand and not immediately part of the prior neighboring utterance is reintroduced. Generally, this refers to a later elaboration of a topic terminated beforehand in a way that did not exclude such elaboration.

There are *intervening* utterances between the apparent end of the topic the first (last) time it was introduced and its reintroduction. This scale point could also refer to the return to the major plot after termination of a subplot. Or, it could occur when a seemingly abandoned episode is reintroduced later on in the discourse. In these examples, there is no hint of the *hierarchical* coherence that is evident in the prior three levels and thus they are scored lower than these levels. However, the points lower than this one on the positive side of the scale level involve only proximal linear coherence across neighboring utterances. Thus, this seventh level is scored higher than these lower ones. Note that this level, in particular, might be hard to distinguish from some of the negative scale points unless a global impression of the text is obtained before actual coding begins. Nevertheless this scale point should not be assigned when the speaker returns to a topic after a moment of confusion in coherence, an interruption, etc. Usually, the regular topic maintenance categories (e.g., +2, +3) should be assigned in such cases (see below). Brinton and Fujiki provided the following example of a topic return.

"You can have one of mine if you let me have one of your chips. (1)
OK. (2)
OK, here's yours. (1)
I got a rattlesnake. (2) [a change]
Well, I got a cobra snake. (1)
And I got a snake. (2)
Dragon tongue. (1)
I took another long chip." (2) [return]

Next, I discuss the scale points involving proximal linear coherence between neighboring utterances. The turnabout, scale point +6, previously defined, is placed atop all other proximal coherence categories because it is comprised of both backward and forward elements, as has been shown.

(+5) *New subtopic.* An utterance serves as the beginning of a new episode in a story or conversation after at least one episode related to it has already been introduced. This does not refer to initiation of the first developed topic after a false start, but it can refer to any developed subtopic after a (sub)topic has been introduced, partly developed, and then aborted. However, usually it is a fully developed unit that successively follows another fully developed (sub)topic that has been normally terminated. In this sense, a subtopic is self-contained, like a subplot, but it is not embedded in another larger unit, unlike a subplot. This scale point corresponds to Botvin and Sutton-Smith's (1977) levels 5 and 4, where there is a concatenation of primitive episodes with (5) or without (4) internal expansion.

Because a subtopic can safely be removed from discourse without affecting its coherence, it cannot be scored as high as a level 6 turnabout. Nevertheless, it is advanced compared to what follows, since the remaining scale points below do not deal with relations between larger units such as subplots or subtopics. Rather, these five scale points involve internal expansion of these larger units. That is, all concern relations between neighboring utterances that are "judged to share at least one semantic element" (Dorval & Eckerman, 1984, p. 20).

(+4) *Topic refinement.* An utterance is classified as a refinement when it more than just adds basic information to the first utterance of a story or discourse or to an already begun (sub)plot, (sub)topic, episode, etc. The utterance adds an interesting twist, an unexpected development, a creative element, etc. In short, the storytelling skill of the speaker is judged in this point. After all, the present scale concerns coherence and a skillfully woven story inevitably coheres better. Note that Dorval and Eckerman (1984) described an interesting category that could be scored at this scale point. Perspective-related turns concern talk about people, not facts or personal experiences (p. 23).

(+3) *Topic addition.* Brinton and Fujiki (1984) stated that in this kind of topic maintenance, the topic of the utterance incorporates the topic of the preceding utterance and adds requested additional information (p. 352). Their examples follow in the last two utterances listed:

"I'm thinking of quitting work to give myself a little more time. (1)
Well, see I have. (2)
I figure once we're in school we'll just have to quit. (2)
A lot of people don't." (1)

Dorval and Eckerman (1984) have a similar category called factually related turns, "which contribute new information with respect to the topic-related particulars of the directly preceding turn…; the topic is embodied in the directly preceding turn" (p. 20). Their examples include the following: (a) elaborations of a topic, either by positively answering a question or negatively adding information, or giving a directive, (b) evaluations of another's topic, and (c) related questions. In the following exchange, one finds examples of all three kinds of topic additions.

"Bet that was funny. (1)
It was *cool*, Bud! (2) [evaluation]
You live there? (1) [question]
Yeah, I live just down the street." (2) [elaboration]

Topic addition somewhat corresponds to levels 2 and 3 of Botvin and Sutton-Smith's (1977) system, where plot units are chained into simple narratives of minimal (2) or more elaborate (3) lengths. They give the following example: "An astronaut went into space. He was attacked by a monster. The astronaut got in his spaceship and flew away" (p. 379).

(+2) *Topic matching.* This scale point represents a quite primitive type of coherent sequencing. There is a limited elaboration without much qualification, for the most part; however, continuity is maintained, although with a difficult sluggishness. There is no or little change in the topic from one utterance to the next, as in the last three utterances of the following sequence.

"Oh, over to French. (1)
To France, yeah. (2)
Well, maybe. (1)
To France, yep." (1) (Brinton & Fujiki, 1984, p. 352).

Dorval and Eckerman (1984) have a somewhat similar category of "minimally related turns," where "there is no additional relationship other than sharing the same local topic; ... one... turn is not related to the particular of a preceding... turn" (pp. 21–22). Note that the example that they gave on p. 21 fits this category very well ("Yesterday it-it was – hot! (1). It sure was. (2)), but most of those on p. 22 seem like additions. Dorval and Eckerman added that minimally related turns might be 'agreements, disagreements, expletives, questions, answers, story continuations, listings, directives, etc.'" (p. 21).

(+1) *Utterance imitation*. There is unsolicited (almost) word for word reproduction. Coherence is maintained, but barely so, compared to other categories. Younger children speaking with their parents often use such imitation, and it can be quite cohesive for them.

(0) *Topic find*. This category does not refer to subplot initiation, topic reintroduction, etc., which have been discussed previously, nor does it concern premature topic cutoff terminations, which are presented below. Rather, it is assigned in any one of the following six circumstances. (a) One participant tries to shape the discourse of the other with very specific suggestions about grammar or topic development, which are directly incorporated (e.g., "Why don't you ..."). Both members of this type of exchange would be scored as topic finding. (b) The participants talk about finding a topic or establish who is to continue. (c) Confusion is introduced, as one participant (e.g., parent, teacher) interrupts or intervenes, or one participant tries to cut off another. Only the confused party should be assigned the topic find scale score of 0. Note that this scale score should be assigned even when a new subplot or subtopic is introduced. The participant inducing the confusion should get a score of −5 to −10, as per below. (d) One participant tries to subtly guide the other. This can especially occur when an adult and a child are involved, and not only during shared symmetric situations but also during asymmetric child monologs in which the adult is the listener. For example, the mother asks a question meant to prompt and guide or promote and teach. Her behavior is a well-timed intervention that does not make a specific recommendation. Her behavior would be scored as 0 because it is a help to topic finding. The child's response would be scored anywhere along the 21-point scale, depending on its quality level. (e) The first utterance of any story, conversation, narrative, etc. is assigned the score 0, reflecting the fact that a topic is being introduced. This category does not concern the first utterance of a subplot or subtopic, if present, which already has been discussed. (f) Finally, assign the neutral score 0 when the child ends a narrative with the marker, "The end."

## *Negative Text Coherence*

The positive portion of the scale of textual coherence is concerned with various types and degrees of logical linear sequencing between utterances. The negative portion begins by considering three categories of associative linking between utterances.

The discourse is still coherent, but less so because the sequencing is not a strictly verbal, logical one. Then, five categories of interruptions are discussed. In the first three, continuity is sacrificed for reasons that are not destructive. Rather, indecision, distraction, carelessness, etc. seem to be the source. In the next two categories, there is willful cutoff induction. Instead of refined topic continuation, in effect, there is course topic termination. In the last two categories of the negative portion of the scale of text coherence, there is an evident attempt at continuity, but it is unsuccessful due to the apparent incompetence of the speaker. The result is inadequate or incoherent discourse.

(−1) *Heap association.* The utterance adds to the topic only because it is temporally congruent with other utterances. The utterances seem to be related only by "associative concatenation" (Botvin & Sutton-Smith, 1977; level I). Items "leapfrog" from event to event (Garnett, 1986). There is a lack of structural unity, as in the following example: "The little duck went swimming. Then the crab came. A lobster came. And a popsicle was playing by itself" (Botvin & Sutton-Smith, p. 379). Note that the third utterance seems more indicative of topic matching (+2). The use of the word "heap" in the title of this category is consistent with Applebee (1978), who described a similar story style.

(−2) *Shade association.* Michaels and Collins (1984) especially emphasized this story style, where utterance sequences are not logically related in a linear fashion, but reflect parallel jumps in topic. The associations are not free, skipping, random, and unmotivated, but are "implicitly linked to a topical event or theme" (p. 224). Dorval and Eckerman (1984) call this category "tangential."

Brinton and Fujiki (1984) tried to operationalize the scoring of this category. They described it as a "subtle topical shift… tangentially related to the preceding topic" (p. 353). Brinton and Fujiki's (1984) two criteria were that "the topic focus was not strictly maintained" and that "some aspect of the propositional content of an utterance was derived from the preceding utterance." That is, "the speaker included some aspect of the preceding utterance, but shifted the subject matter or question of immediate concern." An example they used is quite representative for children.

"This is a neat bracelet. (1)
My aunt gave it to me for my birthday. (1)
My aunt had a baby." (2)

Michaels and Collins (1984) do not denigrate this style compared to the more linear one because it seems to occur more in some cultures or groups (cf. Wanska & Bedrosian, 1985) compared to others. Nevertheless, I place this category on the negative portion of the story coherence scale because by definition the scale treats linear story coherence. Moreover, I do have a safety valve on the positive scale (+4), concerning topic refinement, which can include creative use of shade-like structuring.

(−3) *Nonverbal association.* Michaels and Collins (1984) show that the associative style often is accompanied by prosodic cueing to indicate topic continuity, thematic focus, return to topic, utterance interconnection, and so on. In the "topic associating style," they found that, "prosodically, rhythm and high holding pitches, rather than sharp rising and falling pitch contours, were used to organize information thematically" (p. 224). For example, a child speaks about a person introduced previously and "uses vowel elongation and a high rise-fall contour on 'man,' which serves as a cue that he is talking about old information" (p. 236). It is conceivable that topic continuity is indicated nonverbally by other than prosodic means. Appropriate gesturing, such as pointing at an object, might readily indicate topic reintroduction in certain circumstances, for example. Also, the child will often link apparently out-of-context utterances to ongoing play with objects.

I now present coherence interruption categories. The first few concern more indecisive, careless, or less overtly interfering interruptions, while the last ones seem more premeditated and interfering.

(−4) *Topic search.* An utterance reflects a quest of an appropriate topic. An utterance begins a new topic, but it is immediately abandoned as the topic is aborted. This does not refer to premature topic shifts after adequate topic development, a category that I deal with later, nor does it refer to elaboration of the difficulty of finding a topic, which is scored as topic finding (0), as discussed.

(−5) *Interjected private speech.* The speaker or listener might absentmindedly switch from an ongoing topic to a personal matter that she/he reflects upon without any communicative intent.

(−6) *Aside comment.* In this category, the topic switch to a personal matter is directly communicated to the other.

(−7) *Topic cutoff.* The speaker or listener interferes with or prematurely terminates a topic before its normal termination point has become apparent. There is no shared "common elements of meaning" between the utterances, although "one could invent a relation" (Dorval & Eckerman, 1984, p. 20). This is the classic category of topic change or shift. It does not refer to situations where the cutoff is deliberately induced or imposed by the other; rather, the decision appears spontaneous. The mood of the cutoff performer is not negative in any way. (Cutoff impositions are dealt with just below at a more negative position on the scale.) Nor does topic cutoff refer to topic change after subplot introduction or completion of a previous topic. These categories have already been discussed in the positive points of the scale. Nor does cutoff induction refer to subtle guided manipulation by one participant to influence the topic choice or development of the other. Such topic shaping is dealt with like any conversational exchange. Nor does it refer to an utterance of the other that manifests confusion due to this interference. Provision has been made to score such utterances in the neutral score category. The following example is quite illustrative of topic cutoff (Brinton & Fujiki, 1984, pp. 352–353).

"I'm saying the doctoral students scare me. (1)
Oh. (2)
Cause they're just so… (1)

Thats' cause they kind of have ideas. (2)
Some of 'em." (2)
I've got to go and do some Christmas shopping. (1)

In the example, the listener responds with topic change behavior. Of course, the speaker could have uttered this cutoff behavior, showing that speakers can be credited for it, as well.

(−8) *Cutoff imposition.* Cutoff induction takes place in a forceful dominant way with no or little room for debate on the question. The mood of the cutoff performer can be curt, abrupt, rejecting, aggressive, etc. Note that *nonresponse* to a question demanding a response can also be scored in this category.

These latter two categories of cutoff behavior are not considered as negative as the following two involving lack of coherence in topic continuity. Cutoff behavior might lead to topic termination, but at least it is coherent in itself. By contrast, an attempt at coherent topic continuity that is clearly unsuccessful is the ultimate failure in terms of the organizing principal of the present scale.

(−9) *Inadequate coherence.* An utterance that seems ambiguous in context, bearing an uncertain relationship with the utterance preceding it, is considered to demonstrate inadequate textual coherence. The utterance might be one that seems out of place in the topic development of a speaker, or it may be an *inadequate response* to a question. Utterances that are semantically incoherent in themselves might of necessity be scored in either this category or the next one.

(−10) *Incoherence.* An utterance bears an incoherent relationship with a preceding one when it is illogical in context. In general, it is part of a topic or story (episode) but with no rational reason for being included, or it is an *irrelevant response* to a question.

## Nonverbal Level

### *Introduction*

For purposes of elaborating a comprehensive discourse process coding system, I developed material related to nonverbal/pragmatic aspects of discourse, narrative, and storytelling in children. One level of nonverbal behavior concerns behavior parallel to but distinct from the language output, a behavior that often serves goals different than the ones evident in the output. This level is found only in discourse where there is a receiver of the communication. That is, in discourse often there is verbal output and a parallel nonverbal level of behavior that concerns emotional and face-to-face dyadic signals (e.g., smiles, looking) distinct from the language process.

**Table 34.5** Categories and definitions of complementary (nonverbal) behavior

| Category | Definition |
|---|---|
| Pause | An internal of more than 0.5 s of nonverbalization occurring in the verbal stream. It can occur between words or sentences. It can be silent or filled with hesitation sounds, such as "ah, er, um" and words like "well" and "you know," when they are not used to convey a particular meaning (MacWhinney & Osser, 1977) |
| Repetition | Reduplication without change or with almost no change of a word or words for no grammatical reason |
| Self-repair | "Interruption of an utterance unit followed by ... reformulation of part or all of the utterance preceding the stopping point" (Evans, 1985, p. 367) ... "The correction of one or more words through substitution, deletion, or addition ..." (MacWhinney & Osser, 1977, p. 981). The repair is spontaneous or prompted only by a general verbal or nonverbal interrogative (e.g., "What"; "Eh?") |
| Prosodic emphasis | Part(s) of the utterance highlighted by a shift in the normal intonation pattern |
| Gestural communication | Symbolic or nonsymbolic activities of any part of the body used to complement, supplement, or replace a word or words, or a sound or sounds in an utterance (e.g., pretend play action, point in context) |

calming is not optimal, a whine is muted, or an utterance change is not fully smooth. At the higher level of intensity, it could be that a look lasts for many seconds, a pout is very marked, bodily agitation is extreme, a laugh is dynamically lively, or an utterance change is terribly botched by an excessively long pause.

Another nonverbal level important to communication concerns paralinguistic and related signals (e.g., vocal intonation, communicative gestures, pauses in speech) intrinsic to rather than distinct from language output. In such behavior, messages in coordination with the corpus of utterances are provided in secondary channels *complementary* to the primary verbal one. These behaviors are expressed even if there is no receiver in a dyadic exchange, as in storytelling to a mirror. Table 34.5 provides examples and definitions, including of pauses, repetitions, self-repairs, prosodic emphasis, and gestural communication.

## Summary and Conclusions

This is the last chapter of the book before the concluding one. It completes the review of linguistic function and narrative in children in the present work. With the prior chapter, it points toward how the present Neo-Piagetian model can be investigated for language correspondences through a comprehensive coding scheme. The coding scheme should be useful in the study of language, in general, in children, because it is based on scales and could supplement research that generally proceeds without scales.

## References

Applebee, A. (1978). *The child's concept of story: Ages two to seventeen*. Chicago: University of Chicago Press.

Aram, D., Ekelman, B., & Whitaker, H. (1986). Spoken syntax in children with acquired unilateral hemisphere lesions. *Brain and Language, 27*, 75–100.

Botvin, G., & Sutton-Smith, B. (1977). The development of structural complexity in children's fantasy narratives. *Developmental Psychology, 13*, 377–388.

Brinton, B., & Fujiki, M. (1984). Development of topic manipulation skills in discourse. *Journal of Speech and Hearing Research, 27*, 350–358.

Dorval, B., & Eckerman, C. (1984). Developmental trends in the quality of conversation achieved by small groups of acquainted peers. *Monographs of the Society for Research in Child Development, 49*(2, Serial No. 206).

Evans, M. (1985). Self-initiated speech repairs: A reflection of communicative monitoring in young children. *Developmental Psychology, 21*, 365–371.

Garnett, K. (1986). Telling tales: Narratives and learning-disabled children. *Topics in Learning Disorders, 6*, 44–56.

Goldberg, G. (1976). Conduite du discours enfantin et complexite syntaxique [Child discourse and syntactic complexity]. *La Linguistique, 12*, 3–34.

Keenan, E., & Schieffelin, B. (1976). Topic as a discourse notion: A study of topic in the conversation of children and adults. In C. Li (Ed.), *Subject and topic: A new typology of language* (pp. 337–384). New York: Academic Press.

Kemper, S. (1984). The development of narrative skills: Explanation and entertainments. In S. Kuczaj II (Ed.), *Discourse development* (pp. 99–124). New York: Springer.

MacWhinney, B., & Osser, H. (1977). Verbal planning functions in children's speech. *Child Development, 48*, 978–985.

Maranda, E., & Maranda, K. (1971). Structural models in folklore and transformational essays. In E. Kongas-Maranda & P. Maranda (Eds.), *Towards the investigation of narrative combinatorics: Introduction* (pp. 11–15). The Hague: Mouton.

McTear, M. (1985). *Children's conversation*. New York: Basil Blackwell.

Michaels, S., & Collins, J. (1984). Oral discourse styles: Classroom interaction and the acquisition of literacy. In D. Tannen (Ed.), *Coherence in spoken and written discourse* (pp. 219–244). Norwood: Ablex.

Miller, J. (1981). *Assessing communicative behavior: Vol. 1. Assessing language production in children: Experimental procedures*. Baltimore: University Park Press.

Navet, M., Nespoulos, J. L., & Lecours, A. (1984). Approches psycholinguistiques du discours du psychotique [Psycholinguistic approaches to discourse in psychotics]. *Actes du Congrès de la Federation Nationale des Orthophonistes, 7-8-9-10*, 411–439.

Nicolas, M., Obler, L., Albert, M., & Helm-Estabrooks, N. (1985). Empty speech in Alzheimer's disease and fluent aphasia. *Journal of Speech and Hearing Research, 28*, 405–410.

Paul, R. (1981). Analyzing complex sentence development. In J. Miller (Ed.), *Assessing communicative behavior: Vol. 1. Assessing language production in children: Experimental procedures* (pp. 37–38, 40, 67–71). Baltimore: University Park Press.

Propp, V. (1968). *The morphology of the folktale*. Austin: University of Texas Press. (Original work published 1928)

Torrance, N., & Olson, D. (1984). Oral language competence and the acquisition of literacy. In A. Pellegrini & T. Yawkey (Eds.), *The development of oral and written language in social contexts* (pp. 167–181). Norwood: Ablex.

Wanska, S., & Bedrosian, J. (1985). Conversational structure and topic performance in mother-child interaction. *Journal of Speech and Hearing Research, 28*, 579–584.